Rick Steves' ®

SPAIN

2012

Spain

Atlantic Ocean

Cabo Ortegal

RIAS ALTAS

Ferrol
A Coruña
San Martín
Ribadeo
Canero
La Espina
Avilés
Gijón
COSTA VERDE

Cabo Finisterre
Santiago de Compostela
Lugo
Oviedo
Cangas
ALTAMIRA CAVES
PICOS DE EUROPA
Comi

GALICIA
ASTURIAS
Piedrafita
AP66
FUENTE DÉ
Potes

Pontevedra
Redondela
O Cebreiro
Ponferrada
Las Medulas
León
CANTABRI

Vigo
Guilarei
Ourense
EL BIERZO
Astorga
Aguilar

Valença
Viana do Castelo
S. Maria
Becilla
Palencia
Lerm

A3
Braga
Bragança
Benavente
S P

DOURO VALLEY
Mirandela
Zamora
Valladolid

Porto
Amarante
Vila Real
Pinhaõ
Medina del Camp
CASTILE-LEÓ

Vila Nova de Gaia
Douro
Peso da Régua
Pocinho

Aveiro
Viseu
Salamanca
Peñaranda
Sego

A1
Mondego
Guarda
Vilar
Ciudad Rodrigo
Ávila
AP6
VALLEY OF THE FALLEN
LA C

Figueira da Foz
Coimbra
Piedranita
EL ESCORIAL
Madrid

Batalha
PORTUGAL
Plasencia
Talavera de la Reina

Nazaré
Castelo Branco
Tajo
Toledo

Fátima
Alcobaça
Valencia de Alcántara
A5
Almoncid
CASTI

Óbidos
Entroncamento
Santarém
Cáceres
Trujillo
La Nava
Consuegra

Cabo da Roca
Sintra
Tajo
Portalegre
Zorita
Puerto Lapice

Estoril
Lisbon
A1
Elvas
Badajoz
Mérida
Don Benito

Cascais
A6
Setúbal
Évora
La Albuera
Ciudad Real
Tom

ALENTEJO
EXTREMADURA
Llerena
Alcarecejos
Puertollano

A2
Beja
AVE High-Speed Rail
Linares

Vila do Bispo
Funcheira
Jabugo
MEDINA AZAHARA
Córdoba
Jaén

Sagres
ALGARVE
Loulé
Ayamonte
ITÁLICA
A49
Carmona
A44

Lagos
Tunes
A22
Vila Real
Lepe
Huelva
Sevilla
Écija
Granada

Salema
Albufeira
Faro
Cacela Velha
Tavira
Guadalquivir
Utrera
WHITE HILL TOWNS
Bobadilla
ALHAMBR

Atlantic Ocean
AP4
Sanlúcar
Jerez
Arcos
Zahara
Grazalema
Antequera
SIERRA NEVADA
Frigiliana
NERJA C

Rota
Medina-Sidonia
Benaojan
Ronda
PILETA CAVE
Málaga
Torremolinos
Motri

Cádiz
San Pedro
Marbella
Fuengirola
Nerja
Salobre

Vejer
AP7
COSTA DEL SOL

COSTA DE LA LUZ
Algeciras
La Línea
GIBRALTAR (UK)

Tarifa
Strait of Gibraltar

Tangier
CEUTA (Spain)

MOROCCO
Tétouan

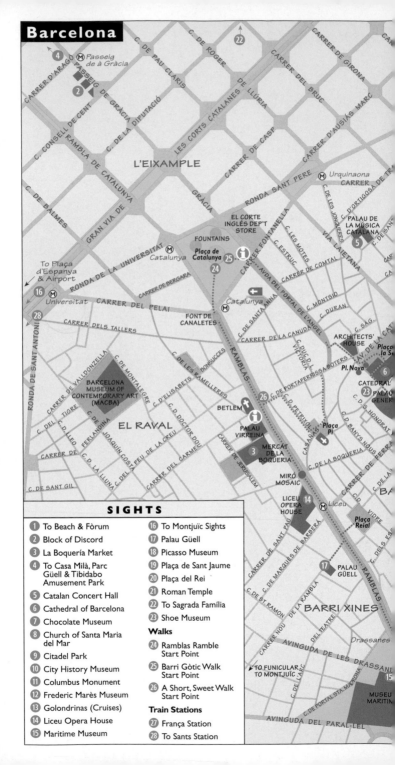

Barcelona

C. DE ROGER

C. DE PAU CLARIS

4 Ⓜ Passeig
de à Gràcia

22

CARRER DE GIRONA

CARRER DEL BRUC

CARRER D'ARAGÓ

PASSEIG

2

DE

DE

LLÚRIA

CARRER DE CENT

RAMBLA DE CATALUNYA

C. DE LA DIPUTACIÓ

CONSELL DE

LES CORTS CATALANES

CARRER DE CASP

CARRER D'AUSIAS MARC

L'EIXAMPLE

GRÀCIA

CARRER D'ORTIGOSA DE TR

C. DE BALMES

GRAN VIA DE

RONDA SANT PERE

Ⓜ Urquinaona
CARRER

C. DE LES JONQUERES

PALAU DE
LA MÚSICA
CATALANA

VIA LAIETANA

C. DE SAN

5

To Plaça
d'Espanya
& Airport

16 Ⓜ
Universitat

RONDA DE LA UNIVERSITAT

EL CORTE
INGLÉS DEP'T
STORE

FOUNTAINS

Plaça de
Catalunya 25 ℹ

24

Ⓜ
Catalunya

CARRER FONTANELLA

C. ESTRUC

C. LES MOTES

AVDA DEL PORTAL DE L'ANGEL

CARRER DE COMTAL

C. MONTSIO

C. DURAN

CARRER DE BERGARA

CARRER DEL PELAI

FONT DE
CANALETES

CARRER DELS TALLERS

28

RONDA DE SANT ANTONI

CARRER DE VALLDONZELLA

C. DE MONTALEGRE

BARCELONA
MUSEUM OF
CONTEMPORARY
ART
(MACBA)

C. DE LES RAMELLERES

C. DE LES

BONÉUCES

RAMBLAS

C. DE SANTA ANNA

CARRER DE LA CANUDA

C. PUIG

VICTÒRIA

ARCHITECTS'
HOUSE

Plaça
la S

Pl. Nova

6

CATEDRAL

C. DE PORTAFERRISSA

BOTERS

C. DE S. HONORAT

23 PALAU
GENER

C. D'ELISABETS

C. DEL TIGRE

C. DE JOINA

C. DEL LLEO

FERLANDINA

JOAQUIN COSTA

PEU DE LA CREU

EL RAVAL

CARRER DE

C. D. LA LLUNA

C. DEL CARME

CARRER DEL CARME

CARRER DE JERUSALEM

BETLEM ✝

26

C. PETRIXOL

C. DE BANYS NOUS

C. DE LA

C. D. S. DOMINGO

Plaça
Pi

BA

PALAU
VIRREINA

3

MERCÁT
DE LA
BOQUERÍA

ℹ

CASANAS

C. DE LA BOQUERIA

C. DE SANT GIL

MIRÓ
MOSAIC

LICEU
OPERA
HOUSE

14 Ⓜ Liceu

Plaça
Reial

17 PALAU
GÜELL

RAMBLAS

CARRER DE SANT PAU

CARRER DE MARQUÈS DE BARBERA

CARRER NOU DE LA RAMBLA

C. DE ST. RAMON

BARRI XINES

DEL TEATRE

Drassanes

AVINGUDA DE LES DRASSANE

TO FUNICULAR
TO MONTJUÏC

C. DE

MUSEU
MARITIM

AVINGUDA DEL PARAL-LEL

C. DE PORTAL STA. MADRONA

15

SIGHTS

1 To Beach & Fòrum
2 Block of Discord
3 La Boquería Market
4 To Casa Milà, Parc
Güell & Tibidabo
Amusement Park
5 Catalan Concert Hall
6 Cathedral of Barcelona
7 Chocolate Museum
8 Church of Santa Maria
del Mar
9 Citadel Park
10 City History Museum
11 Columbus Monument
12 Frederic Marès Museum
13 Golondrinas (Cruises)
14 Liceu Opera House
15 Maritime Museum

16 To Montjuïc Sights
17 Palau Güell
18 Picasso Museum
19 Plaça de Sant Jaume
20 Plaça del Rei
21 Roman Temple
22 To Sagrada Família
23 Shoe Museum

Walks

24 Ramblas Ramble
Start Point
25 Barri Gòtic Walk
Start Point
26 A Short, Sweet Walk
Start Point

Train Stations

27 França Station
28 To Sants Station

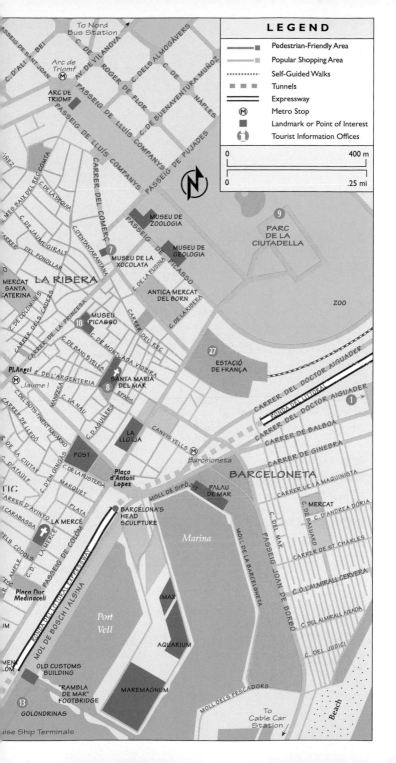

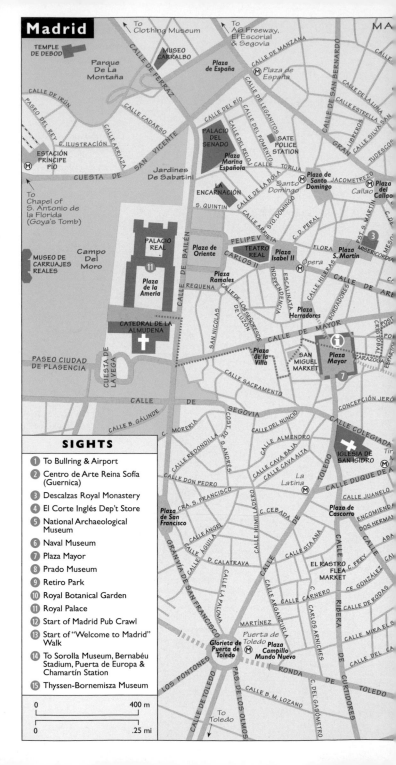

Madrid

TEMPLE DE DEBOD

Parque De La Montaña

MUSEO CARRALBO

CALLE DE FERRAZ

Plaza de España

To Clothing Museum

To A6 Freeway, El Escorial & Segovia

CALLE DE MANZANA

CALLE DE SAN BERNARDO

CALLE DE LA LUNA

CALLE ESTRELLA SAN

GRAN VÍA

CALLE SILVA SAN

LIBREROS

TUDESCO

CALLE DE IRÚN

PASEO DEL REY

C. ILUSTRACIÓN

CALLE DE SAN VICENTE

CALLE ARRIAZA

CALLE CADARSO

CALLE DEL RÍO

CALLE DEL FOMENTO

CALLE DE LEGANITOS

CALLE TORIJA

SATE POLICE STATION

Plaza de Santo Domingo

JACOMETREZO

Plaza del Callao

ESTACIÓN PRÍNCIPE PÍO

CUESTA DE SAN VICENTE

Jardines De Sabatini

PALACIO DEL SENADO

Plaza Marina Española

CALLE

Santo Domingo

CALLE DE LA BOLA

CALLE STO DOMINGO

PST. S. MARTÍN

To Chapel of S. Antonio de la Florida (Goya's Tomb)

LA ENCARNACIÓN

S. QUINTIN

FELIPE V

C. D. PERAL

FLORA

MISERICORDIA

3

MUSEO DE CARRUAJES REALES

Campo Del Moro

PALACIO REAL

11

Plaza de la Ameria

CALLE DE BAILÉN

Plaza de Oriente

TEATRO REAL

CARLOS II

Plaza Isabel II

Opera

Plaza S. Martín

CALLE ARRIETA

CALLE DE ARE

CALLE HILERAS

Plaza Ramales

CALLE REQUENA

CALLE DE LOS SENORES DE LUZON

INDEPENDENCIA

ESCALINATA

Plaza Herradores

BORDADORES

CRISTOBAL

POST

CATEDRAL DE LA ALMUDENA

SAN NICOLAS

CALLE DE MAYOR

i

Plaza de la Villa

SAN MIGUEL MARKET

Plaza Mayor

7

ZARAZOGA

ESPART

PASEO CIUDAD DE PLASENCIA

CUESTA DE LA VEGA

CALLE SACRAMENTO

CONCEPCIÓN JERÓ

CALLE

DE

SEGOVIA

CALLE B. GÁLINDE

C. MORERÍA

CALLE DEL NUNCIO

CALLE COLEGIADA

Tir

SIGHTS

1 To Bullring & Airport

2 Centro de Arte Reina Sofía (Guernica)

3 Descalzas Royal Monastery

4 El Corte Inglés Dep't Store

5 National Archaeological Museum

6 Naval Museum

7 Plaza Mayor

8 Prado Museum

9 Retiro Park

10 Royal Botanical Garden

11 Royal Palace

12 Start of Madrid Pub Crawl

13 Start of "Welcome to Madrid" Walk

14 To Sorolla Museum, Bernabéu Stadium, Puerta de Europa & Chamartín Station

15 Thyssen-Bornemisza Museum

CALLE REDONDILLA

COST. DE S. ANDRÉS

CALLE ALMENDRO

CALLE CAVA BAJA

CALLE CAVA ALTA

IGLESIA DE SAN ISIDRO

CALLE DON PEDRO

La Latina

CALLE TOLEDO

CALLE DUQUE DE A

CALLE JUANELO

Plaza de San Francisco

CRA. S. FRANCISCO

C. CEBADA DE

Plaza de Cascorro

ENCOMIEND/

DOS HERMAN

GRAN VÍA DE SAN FRANCISCO

CALLE ÁNGEL

CALLE AGUILA

D. CALATRAVA

CALLE STA ANA

EL RASTRO FLEA MARKET

C. FREY

CE. GONZÁLEZ

CALLE DE RODAS

CAI

CALLE LA PALOMA

CALLE CARNERO

RIBERA

ABA

CALLE MIRA EL

MARTÍNEZ

Puerta de Toledo

CARLOS ARNICHES

CALLE ARGANZUELA

DE

CALLE DEL CAI

0   400 m

0   .25 mi

Glorieta de Puerta de Toledo

Plaza de Campillo Mundo Nuevo

LOS PONTONES

PAS. DE TOLEDO

RONDA

DE

CUKTIDORES

To Toledo

CALLE DE TOLEDO

CALLE B. M. LOZANO

C. DEL GASOMETRO

To Los Olmos

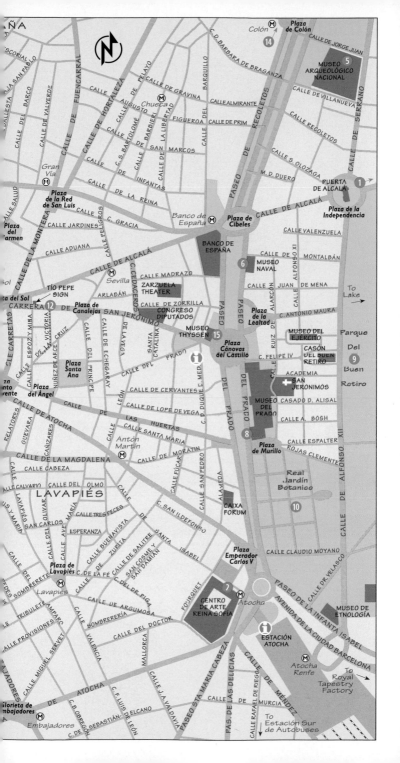

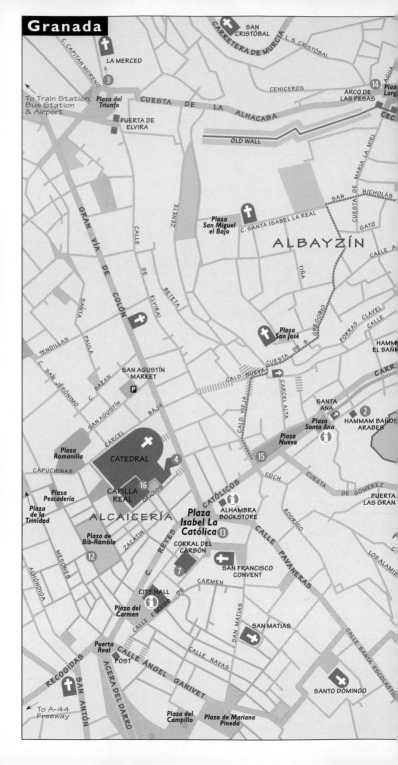

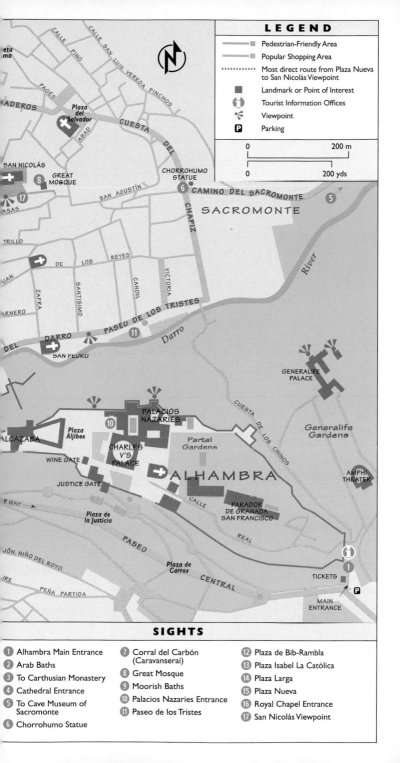

LEGEND

- Pedestrian-Friendly Area
- Popular Shopping Area
- Most direct route from Plaza Nueva to San Nicolás Viewpoint
- Landmark or Point of Interest
- Tourist Information Offices
- Viewpoint
- Parking

0 ——— 200 m
0 ——— 200 yds

SIGHTS

1. Alhambra Main Entrance
2. Arab Baths
3. To Carthusian Monastery
4. Cathedral Entrance
5. To Cave Museum of Sacromonte
6. Chorrohumo Statue
7. Corral del Carbón (Caravanserai)
8. Great Mosque
9. Moorish Baths
10. Palacios Nazaries Entrance
11. Paseo de los Tristes
12. Plaza de Bib-Rambla
13. Plaza Isabel La Católica
14. Plaza Larga
15. Plaza Nueva
16. Royal Chapel Entrance
17. San Nicolás Viewpoint

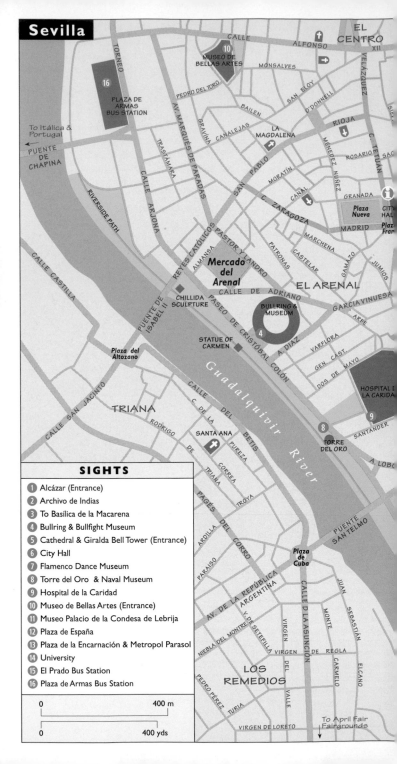

Sevilla

EL CENTRO

CALLE ALFONSO XII

MUSEO DE BELLAS ARTES

MONSALVES

VELAZQUEZ

TORNEO

PEDRO DEL TORO

SAN ELOY

O'DONNELL

RIOJA

PLAZA DE ARMAS BUS STATION

AV. MARQUÉS DE PARADAS

GRAVINA

CANALEJAS

BAILEN

LA MAGDALENA

MENENDEZ NÚÑEZ

ROSARIO

C. TETUÁN

SAG

To Itálica & Portugal

PUENTE DE CHAPINA

TRASTÁMARA

CALLE ARJONA

SAN PABLO

MORATÍN

CANAL

GRANADA

Plaza Nueva

CITY HALL

RIVERSIDE PATH

C. ZARAGOZA

MADRID

Plaza Fran

MARCHENA

CALLE CASTILLA

REYES CATÓLICOS

PASTOR Y LANDRO

ALMANSA

Mercado del Arenal

PATRONAS

CASTELAR

GAMAZO

JUMIOS

PUENTE DE ISABEL II

CHILLIDA SCULPTURE

PASEO DE CRISTÓBAL COLÓN

CALLE DE ADRIANO

EL ARENAL

GARCIA VINUESA

BULLRING & MUSEUM

ARFE

STATUE OF CARMEN

4

A. DIAZ

VARFLORA

Plaza del Altozano

GEN. CAST.

DOS DE MAYO

HOSPITAL DE LA CARIDAD

TRIANA

Plaza San Jacinto

C. DE LA

Guadalquivir River

CALLE DEL

8

9

SANTANDER

RODRIGO

SANTA ANA

PUREZA

CORREA

TORRE DEL ORO

A. LOBO

BETIS

DE

PAGÉS DEL CORRO

TRIANA

TROYA

ARDILLA

PARAISO

PUENTE SAN TELMO

Plaza de Cuba

AV. DE LA REPÚBLICA ARGENTINA

V. DE SETEFILLA

VIRGEN

CALLE D. LA ASUNCIÓN

JUAN

SEBASTIÁN

NIEBLA DEL MONTE

VIRGEN DEL

DE REGLA

MONTE

CARMELO

ELCANO

PEDRO PÉREZ

LOS REMEDIOS

VALLE

TURIA

VIRGEN DE LORETO

To April Fair Fairgrounds

SIGHTS

1. Alcázar (Entrance)
2. Archivo de Indias
3. To Basílica de la Macarena
4. Bullring & Bullfight Museum
5. Cathedral & Giralda Bell Tower (Entrance)
6. City Hall
7. Flamenco Dance Museum
8. Torre del Oro & Naval Museum
9. Hospital de la Caridad
10. Museo de Bellas Artes (Entrance)
11. Museo Palacio de la Condesa de Lebrija
12. Plaza de España
13. Plaza de la Encarnación & Metropol Parasol
14. University
15. El Prado Bus Station
16. Plaza de Armas Bus Station

| 0 | | 400 m |
| 0 | | 400 yds |

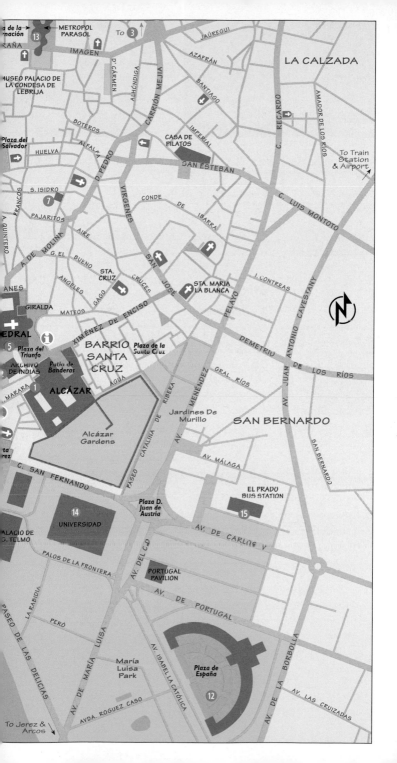

CONTENTS

Spain

España

Like a grandpa bouncing a baby on his knee, Spain is a mix of old and new, modern and traditional. For the tourist, Spain means bullfights, massive cathedrals, world-class art, Muslim palaces, vibrant folk life, whitewashed villages, and bright sunshine. Yes, you'll find those things...but the country's special charm lies in its people and their unique lifestyle. Spain has a richness of history, of culture, and of people that has little to do with GDP stats. From the stirring *sardana* dance in Barcelona to the sizzling rat-a-tat-tat of flamenco in Sevilla, this country creates its own beat amid the heat.

Spain's diverse landscape and diverse history (a blend of Roman, Muslim, and Christian) have forged a country with a wide variety of regions, languages, and customs. If you fly over Spain you'll see that much of the country's center is a parched, red-orange desert. But Spain's topography resembles a giant upside-down bowl, with the high, flat, dry central plateau and a coastal lip. The north is mountainous and rainy; the south is hilly and hot. Ringing it all is 2,000 miles of coastline.

Spain's geography makes it less a centralized nation than a collection of distinct regions. In the central plain sits the urban island of Madrid, a region unto itself. Just south is Toledo,

a medieval showpiece and melting-pot city with Christian, Muslim, and Jewish roots. Farther south is Andalucía, a region formerly ruled by Muslims, now home to sleepy, sun-baked *pueblos blancos* (whitewashed hill towns). Spain's south coast, the Costa del Sol, is a palm-tree jungle of beach resorts, casinos, time-share condos, discos, and sunburned Brits on holiday. Along the Mediterranean coast (to the east), Spain has an almost Italian vibe, and Barcelona and Catalunya keep one eye cocked toward trends sailing in from the rest of Europe. Tourism is huge here. With 47 million inhabitants, Spain entertains 50 million visitors annually.

To the north is the Basque Country, which combines sparkling beaches, cutting-edge architecture, and proudly feisty locals. From here gregarious modern-day pilgrims follow the Camino de Santiago westward across the parched north of Spain into mellow and lush Galicia, where moss-covered churches and tree-strewn rolling hillsides beckon. Beyond its contiguous lands, Spain clings to the last of its far-flung holdings: a few Mediterranean islands (including Menorca, Mallorca, and Ibiza), Ceuta in Morocco, and the distant Canary Islands.

"Castilian"—what we call "Spanish"—is spoken throughout the country. But Catalans (around Barcelona) speak their own Romance language, Catalan. The Galicians speak Galego. And in the far north the Basques keep alive the ancient tongue of Euskara. A fringe group of separatist Basques (with their notorious and unpopular terrorist wing, ETA) has lobbied hard and sometimes violently for self-rule. But every region in Spain has its own dialect, customs, and (often half-hearted) separatist movement. Each region also hosts local festivals, whether parading Virgin Mary statues through the streets, running in front of a pack of furious bulls, or pelting each other with tomatoes. People think of themselves first and foremost as Basques, Catalans, Andalusians, Galicians, Leonese, and so on...and only second as Spaniards.

Spain is in Europe, but not *of* Europe—it has a unique identity and history, thanks largely to the Pyrenees Mountains that physically isolate it from the rest of the Continent. For

more than 700 years (711-1492), Spain's dominant culture was Muslim, not Christian. And after a brief Golden Age financed by New World gold (1500-1600), Spain retreated into three centuries of isolation (1600-1900). Spain's seclusion contributed to the creation of unusual customs—bullfights, flamenco dancing, and a national obsession with ham. Even as other countries opened up to one another in the 20th century, the fascist dictator Francisco Franco virtually sealed off Spain from the rest of Europe's democracies. But since Franco's death in 1975, Spaniards have almost swung to the opposite extreme, becoming wide open to new trends and technologies. (For more on Spanish history, see the Spain: Past & Present chapter.)

Spain Almanac

Official Name: It's officially the Reino de España (Kingdom of Spain), but locals just call it España.

Population: 47 million. Most speak the official national language of Castilian, but about 17 percent speak Catalan, 7 percent Galego, and 2 percent Euskara (the Basque language). The country is 94 percent Roman Catholic.

Latitude and Longitude: 40°N and 4°W (similar latitude to New York City).

Area: 195,000 square miles (about 18 percent bigger than California). This includes the Canary and Balearic Islands, and small enclaves in Morocco. Spain's long-standing claim to Gibraltar remains a nagging dispute with Britain.

Geography: The interior of Spain is a high, flat plateau (the Meseta Central), with hot, dry summers and harsh winters. Surrounding the plateau are mountains (including the Pyrenees in the north) and 2,000 miles of coastline.

Agua Agua Everywhere: A leader in hydropower and irrigation, Spain, for its size, has more man-made lakes from dams (about 1,400) than any other country. Still, the average Spaniard uses one-third less energy than the average American. Spain's 1,800 rivers are mostly small, less than 50 miles long. The 600-mile Tajo River (a.k.a. Tagus in English, or Tejo in Portuguese) runs westward from Toledo through Portugal to the Atlantic. The Guadalquivir irrigates Andalucía and makes Sevilla an oceangoing port city.

Biggest Cities: Madrid (3.3 million; at more than 2,000 feet in altitude, it's Europe's highest capital), Barcelona (1.6 million),

Valencia (810,000), and Sevilla (704,000). Spaniards are urban dwellers—only one in five lives outside a metropolitan area.

Economy: The Gross Domestic Product is $1.4 trillion; the GDP per capita is about $30,000. Major moneymakers include tourism, clothes, shoes, olives, wine, oranges, machine parts, and ships. Recently it had a 21 percent unemployment rate—nearly 10 million Spaniards were out of work.

Government: Guided symbolically by King Juan Carlos I, Spain is a parliamentary monarchy. The prime minister is chosen by election. Some of the 600-plus legislators (in two houses) are elected directly, some by regional parliaments. The country has 17 regional autonomous governments (e.g., Andalucía, Catalunya, Castile–La Mancha, Madrid), which in time will have full responsibility for health care, social programs, and education.

Flag: Spain's flag has three horizontal bands of red, yellow, and red. To the left of center is the coat of arms—a shield with a crown, framed by the Pillars of Hercules that symbolically flank the Straits of Gibraltar.

Soccer: The two perennial powerhouses in La Liga (The League) are Real Madrid and FC Barcelona. In 2010, the Spanish national team won the World Cup, sparking a nationwide fiesta.

The Average José: The average Spaniard is 40 years old, will live to age 79, and resides in a home with one car and one TV. More than half of Spaniards use the Internet, and 1 in 10 owns a cat. The average Spaniard has 1 mobile phone, 1.3 kids, and sleeps 40 minutes less every night than the typical European.

Spaniards are proud and stoic. They can be hard to get to know—but once you've made that connection, you've

got a friend for life. The Spanish people have long had a reputation as thrifty, straightforward, and un- pretentious. Traditionally, their lives revolved around the Catholic Church and the family. Young adults tended to live at home until they got married—even into their late twenties. Spaniards prided themselves on their non- materialistic values, owning just one car and one TV, and living in small urban apartments instead of giant suburban houses. The notorious "machismo" culture of domineering men ruled.

But Spain's old ways have changed very quickly in the de- cades since Franco. Although the vast majority of Spaniards are still nominally Catholic, the country is at the forefront of liberal reforms in abortion and gay marriage. Spain's extreme religiosity has been replaced by an extreme secularism. The old hierarchy of aristocrats, peasants, priests, and old ladies in black has become democratic and hang-loose. The allure of consumerism and status symbols has enticed many Spanish people to save (or borrow) for high-fashion clothes, second cars, and summer chalets, though the economic downturn has pushed materialistic dreams further out of reach. Still, throughout its recent economic boom and bust, Spain has re- mained affordable for visitors.

Even as the country plunges into the 21st century, some things never change. Daily lives focus on friends and family, as they always have. Many people (especially in rural areas) still follow the siesta schedule, which emphasizes a big midday meal with the family. Spaniards tend to have a small, quick breakfast, grab a late-morning sandwich to tide them over, then gather with friends and family for the siesta. From around 1:00 to 4:00 p.m., many businesses close as people go home to eat lunch,

socialize, and maybe grab a quick nap. The siesta is not so much a time to sleep as it is an opportunity for everyone to shut down their harried public life, and enjoy good food and the comfort of loved ones.

In the cool of the evening, Spain comes back to life. Whole families pour out of their apartments to stroll through the streets and greet their neighbors—a custom called the paseo. Even the biggest city feels like a rural village. People stop at bars for a drink or to watch a big soccer match on TV. They might order a bite to eat, enjoying appetizers called tapas. Around 10:00 p.m. in the heat of summer, it's finally time for a light dinner. Afterward, even families with young children might continue their paseo or attend a concert. Spaniards are notorious night owls. Many clubs and restaurants don't even

open until after midnight. Dance clubs routinely stay open until the sun rises, and young people stumble out bleary-eyed and head for work. The antidote for late nights? The next day's siesta.

Spanish food is hearty and unrefined. Remember that Spain is not Mexico—you won't find tacos, Tabasco, or tequila. (Even things that sound Mexican can be very different—for example, a *tortilla* is an omelet.) Major meals feature meat (such as roast suckling pig) or seafood. Popular regional foods are gazpacho (cold tomato soup) and paella (seafood and meat cooked with saffron-flavored rice). Spaniards snack between meals on tapas. Most bars offer a variety of these appetizers served hot or cold. A few small plates of olives, chorizo (sausage), grilled shrimp, Russian salad, or deep-fried nuggets can add up to a multicourse meal.

The most treasured delicacy in Spain is *jamón*—cured ham that is sliced thin and served cold. Bars proudly hang pigs' legs on their walls as part of the decor. Like connoisseurs of fine wine, Spaniards debate the merits of different breeds of pigs, what part of the pig they're eating, what the pig has eaten, and the quality of curing.

Drinking is part of the Spanish meal, and part of the social ritual. Spain produces large quantities of wine, especially their spicy red Rioja, made from the *tempranillo* grape. (For more on Spanish drinks, see page 32.)

For a country its size, Spain has produced an astonishing number of talented artists with distinctive styles—from El Greco's mystical religiosity to the sober realism of Diego

Velázquez. (Madrid's Prado Museum is a veritable showcase of European Renaissance art, bought with the spoils from the New World.) Francisco Goya painted the Golden Age in decline. In the 20th century, Pablo Picasso shattered the art world, then pasted it back together by inventing Cubism. Later, he painted *Guernica,* an epic snapshot of Spain's horrific Civil

War. It's one of the most powerful antiwar paintings ever created (now displayed in Madrid). Salvador Dalí created surreal juxtapositions of old and new, while his fellow Catalan Joan Miró picked up the Surrealist baton and ran with it. Spain carries on this rich tradition today, with a thriving contemporary arts scene.

In music, Spain continues its long tradition of great guitarists—classical, flamenco, and Gipsy Kings–style "new flamenco." In dance, you'll find the fiery flamenco (from Andalucía) and the stately do-si-do of the *sardana* (from Catalunya). Contemporary film includes works by director Pedro Almodóvar, who explores changing family and social roles as Spain moves from its conservative past to its wide-open future. And there's one contemporary Spaniard whose works will be known and appreciated for generations to come: Santiago Calatrava, an architect who designs buildings and bridges for the 21st century.

Whereas you can see some European countries by just passing through, Spain is a destination. Learn its history and accept it on its own terms. Gain (or just fake) an appreciation for cured ham, dry sherry, and bull's-tail stew, and the Spaniards will love you for it. If you go, go all the way. Immerse yourself in Spain.

INTRODUCTION

This book breaks Spain into its top destinations and will help you make the most of your trip—it offers a balanced, comfortable mix of exciting cities and cozy towns, topped off with an exotic dollop of Morocco. It covers the predictable biggies and stirs in a healthy dose of "Back Door" intimacy. Along with seeing a bullfight, the Prado, and flamenco, you'll greet pilgrims at Santiago de Compostela, visit a bull bar in Madrid, and buy cookies from cloistered nuns in a sun-parched Andalusian town. I've been selective, including only the most exciting sights and experiences. Rather than listing Spain's countless Costa del Sol beach resorts, I recommend my favorite: Nerja.

You'll get all the specifics and opinions necessary to wring the maximum value out of your limited time and money. If you plan a month or less in Spain, and you have a normal appetite for information, this book is all you need. If you're a travel-info fiend (like me), you'll find that this book sorts through all the superlatives and provides a handy rack upon which to hang your supplemental information.

Experiencing Spain's culture, people, and natural wonders economically and hassle-free has been my goal for nearly four decades of traveling, tour-guiding, and writing. With this book I pass on to you the lessons I've learned, updated for 2012.

The best of Spain is, of course, only my opinion. But after spending half of my adult life researching and tour-guiding in Europe, I've developed a sixth sense for what travelers enjoy.

Top Destinations in Spain

CANTABRIA

BASQUE COUNTRY

NEAR BARCELONA

SANTIAGO

CAMINO DE SANTIAGO

BARCELONA

SALAMANCA

N.W. OF MADRID

TOLEDO   MADRID

SEVILLA

CÓRDOBA

GRANADA

WHITE HILL TOWNS

SOUTH COAST

TANGIER

MOROCCO

DCH

About This Book

Rick Steves' Spain 2012 is a tour guide in your pocket. This book is organized by destinations.

Each destination is a mini-vacation on its own, filled with exciting sights, strollable neighborhoods, affordable places to stay, and memorable places to eat. In the following chapters, you'll find these sections:

Planning Your Time suggests a schedule for how to best use your limited time.

Orientation includes specifics on public transportation, helpful hints, local tour options, easy-to-read maps, and tourist information.

Sights describes the top attractions and includes their cost and hours.

Self-Guided Walks takes you through interesting neighborhoods, with a personal tour guide in hand.

Sleeping describes my favorite hotels, from good-value deals to cushy splurges.

Eating serves up a range of options, from inexpensive eateries to fancier restaurants.

Connections outlines your options for traveling to destina-

Key to This Book

Updates

This book is updated every year—but once you pin down Spain, it wiggles. For the latest, visit www.ricksteves.com /update, and for a valuable list of reports and experiences— good and bad—from fellow travelers, check www.ricksteves .com/feedback.

Abbreviations and Times

I use the following symbols and abbreviations in this book:
Sights are rated:

▲▲▲	**Don't miss**
▲▲	**Try hard to see**
▲	**Worthwhile if you can make it**
No rating	**Worth knowing about**

Tourist information offices are abbreviated as **TI,** and bathrooms are **WCs**. To categorize accommodations, I use a **Sleep Code** (described on page 22).

Like Europe, this book uses the **24-hour clock.** It's the same as ours through 12:00 noon, then keeps going: 13:00, 14:00, and so on. For anything over 12, subtract 12 and add p.m. (14:00 is 2:00 p.m.).

When giving **opening times,** I include both peak-season and off-season hours if they differ. So, if a museum is listed as "May-Oct daily 9:00-16:00," it should be open from 9 a.m. until 4 p.m. from the first day of May until the last day of October (but expect exceptions).

For **transit** or **tour departures,** I first list the frequency, then the duration. So, a train connection listed as "2/hour, 1.5 hours" departs twice each hour, and the journey lasts an hour and a half.

---

tions by plane, train, and bus. I've included route tips for drivers in car-friendly regions.

The **Spain: Past & Present** chapter gives you a quick overview of Spanish history, art, and architecture, and the tradition of bullfighting.

The **appendix** is a traveler's tool kit, with telephone tips, useful phone numbers, transportation basics (on trains, buses, car rentals and driving, and flights), recommended books and films, a festival list, a climate chart, a handy packing checklist, a hotel reservation form, and Spanish survival phrases and pronunciation guide.

Browse through this book, choose your favorite destinations, and link them up. Then have a *maravilloso* trip! Traveling like a temporary local, you'll get the absolute most out of every mile, minute, and dollar. As you visit places I know and love, I'm happy you'll be meeting my favorite Spanish people.

INTRODUCTION

Planning

This section will help you get started on planning your trip—with advice on trip costs, when to go, and what you should know before you take off.

Travel Smart

Your trip to Spain is like a complex play: It's easier to follow and better appreciated on second viewing. While no one does the same trip twice to gain that advantage, reading this book in its entirety before your trip accomplishes much the same thing.

Design an itinerary that enables you to visit sights at the best possible times. Note holidays and specifics on sights, such as days they are closed. If you'll be using public transportation or renting a car, read "Transportation" in the appendix. A smart trip is a puzzle—a fun, doable, and worthwhile challenge.

Be sure to mix intense and relaxed periods in your itinerary. To maximize rootedness, minimize one-night stands. It's worth a long drive after dinner to be settled into a town for two nights. Every trip—and every traveler—needs slack time (laundry, picnics, people-watching, and so on). Pace yourself. Assume you will return.

Reread this book as you travel, and visit local TIs. Upon arrival in a new town, lay the groundwork for a smooth departure; write down (or print out from an online source) the schedule for the train or bus that you'll take when you depart. Drivers can study the best route to their next destination.

Get online at Internet cafés or your hotel, and buy a phone card or carry a mobile phone: You can find tourist information, learn the latest on sights (special events, English tour schedule, etc.), book tickets and tours, make reservations, reconfirm hotels, research transportation connections, and keep in touch with your loved ones.

Enjoy the friendliness of the Spanish people. Connect with the culture. Set up your own quest for the best main square, paella, cloister, tapas bar, or whatever. Ask questions—most locals are eager to point you in their idea of the right direction. Slow down and be open to unexpected experiences. Keep a notepad in your pocket for organizing your thoughts. Wear your money belt, learn the currency, and figure out how to estimate prices in dollars. Those who expect to travel smart, do.

Trip Costs

Five components make up your trip costs: airfare, surface transportation, room and board, sightseeing and entertainment, and shopping and miscellany.

Airfare: A basic round-trip flight from the US to Barcelona or Madrid can cost $800-1,600 (including taxes and fuel charges), depending on where you fly from and when (cheaper in winter). Smaller budget airlines may provide bargain service from several European capitals to many cities in Spain. If your trip covers a wide area, consider saving time and money by flying into one city and out of another—for instance, into Barcelona and out of Santiago de Compostela.

Surface Transportation: For a three-week whirlwind trip of all my recommended destinations, allow $550 per person for second-class trains and buses ($750 for first-class trains). For a three-week car rental, tolls, gas, and insurance, allow $900 per person (based on two people sharing). Leasing is worth considering for trips of two and a half weeks or more. Car rental or leases are cheapest if arranged from the US. Train passes are normally available only outside Europe. You may save money by simply buying tickets as you go. (For more on public transportation and car rental, see "Transportation" in the appendix.)

Room and Board: You can thrive in Spain in 2012 on $90 a day per person for room and board (more in big cities). This allows $10 for lunch, $20 for dinner, and $60 for lodging (based on two people splitting the cost of a $120 double room that includes breakfast). Students and tightwads can enjoy Spain for as little as $60 a day ($30 for a bed, $30 for meals and snacks).

Sightseeing and Entertainment: In big cities, figure about $8-15 per major sight (Madrid's Prado, Barcelona's Picasso Museum, Granada's Alhambra), $5 for minor ones (climbing church towers), and about $35-50 for splurge experiences (flamenco, bullfights). An overall average of $20 a day works for most people. Don't skimp here. After all, this category is the driving force behind your trip—you came to sightsee, enjoy, and experience Spain.

Shopping and Miscellany: Figure roughly $2 per coffee, beer, ice-cream cone, and postcard. Shopping can vary in cost from nearly nothing to a small fortune. Good budget travelers find that this category has little to do with assembling a trip full of lifelong and wonderful memories.

Sightseeing Priorities

Depending on the length of your trip, and taking geographic proximity into account, here are my recommended priorities:

3 days: Madrid and Toledo

6 days, add:	Barcelona
10 days, add:	Sevilla, Granada
13 days, add:	Nerja, Ronda, Tangier (Morocco)
15 days, add:	Salamanca, Segovia
17 days, add:	Santiago de Compostela
21 days, add:	Basque Region (San Sebastián and Bilbao)
25 days, add:	Camino de Santiago (by car)

This includes nearly everything on the map on page 9.

When to Go

Spring and fall offer the best combination of good weather, light crowds, long days, and plenty of tourist and cultural activities.

July and August are the most crowded and expensive in the coastal areas, and less crowded but uncomfortably hot and dusty in the interior. Air-conditioning is essential. During these steamy months, lunch breaks can be long, especially in Andalucía.

Off-season, roughly November through March, expect shorter hours, more lunchtime breaks, and fewer activities. Confirm your sightseeing plans locally, especially when traveling off-season.

Though it can be brutally hot in the summer, winters can be bitter cold, and spring and fall can be surprisingly crisp. For weather specifics, see the climate chart on page 850.

Know Before You Go

Your trip is more likely to go smoothly if you plan ahead. Check this list of things to arrange while you're still at home.

You need a **passport**—but no visa or shots—to travel in Spain. You may be denied entry into certain European countries if your passport is due to expire within three to six months of your ticketed date of return. Get it renewed if you'll be cutting it close. It can take up to six weeks to get or renew a passport (for more on passports, see www.travel.state.gov). Pack a photocopy of your passport in your luggage in case the original is lost or stolen.

Book **rooms in advance** if you'll be traveling during any major **holidays** (see page 846).

Consider **making reservations for Granada's Alhambra** before leaving home. Although you can reserve tickets upon arrival in Spain (ideally before you reach Granada), tickets can be obtained up to three months in advance, and it's really worth booking just as soon as you are confident of your dates (you'll need to know your credit-card's PIN code to pick up your tickets; for more information, see page 510). You'll also need reservations if you want to visit the Salvador Dalí House near Cadaqués (see page 137).

Call your **debit- and credit-card companies** to let them know the countries you'll be visiting, to ask about fees, and more (see page 14).

Do your homework if you want to buy **travel insurance.** Compare the cost of the insurance to the likelihood of your using it and your potential loss if something goes wrong. For more tips, see www.ricksteves.com/insurance.

If you're bringing a mobile device, you can download free information from **Rick Steves Audio Europe,** featuring hours of travel interviews and other audio content about Spain (via www.ricksteves.com/audioeurope, iTunes, or the Rick Steves Audio Europe free smartphone app; for details, see page 841).

If you're planning on **renting a car** in Spain, you'll need your US driver's license. An International Driving Permit is required (see page 836).

If you're taking an **overnight train,** especially to international destinations, and you need a sleeping berth *(litera)*—and you must leave on a certain day—consider booking it in advance through a US agent (such as www.raileurope.com), even though it may cost more than buying it in Spain. All high-speed trains in Spain require a seat reservation, but it's usually possible to make arrangements in Spain just a few days ahead unless it's a holiday weekend. (For more on train travel, see the appendix.)

Because **airline carry-on restrictions** are always changing, visit the Transportation Security Administration's website (www.tsa.gov/travelers) for an up-to-date list of what you can bring on the plane with you, and what you have to check.

Practicalities

Emergency and Medical Help: In **Spain,** dial 091 for police help and 112 in any emergency (medical or otherwise). In **Morocco,** dial 19 for police.

If you get sick, do as the Spanish do and go to a pharmacist for advice. Or ask at your hotel for help; the desk staff knows where to find the nearest medical and emergency services.

Theft or Loss: To replace a passport, you'll need to go in person to a US embassy (see page 826). If your credit and debit cards disappear, cancel and replace them (see "Damage Control for Lost Cards" on page 15). File a police report, either on the spot or within a day; it's required to submit an insurance claim for lost or stolen railpasses or travel gear, and it can help with replacing your passport or credit and debit cards. For more information, see www.ricksteves.com/help.

Thieves target tourists throughout Spain, especially in Barcelona, Madrid, Granada, and Sevilla. While hotel rooms are generally safe, thieves break into cars, snatch purses, and pick pockets. Thieves zipping by on motorbikes grab handbags from pedestrians or even from cars in traffic (by reaching through open

Whirlwind Three-Week Trip of Spain

Day	Plan	Sleep in
1	Arrive in Barcelona	Barcelona
2	Barcelona	Barcelona
3	Barcelona, evening train to Madrid	Madrid
4	Madrid	Madrid
5	Day trip to El Escorial	Madrid
6	Madrid, late afternoon to Toledo	Toledo
7	Toledo, evening train to Sevilla	Sevilla
8	Sevilla	Sevilla
9	Arcos	Arcos
10	Tarifa	Tarifa
11	Day trip to Morocco	Tarifa
12	Gibraltar, on to Nerja	Nerja
13	Beach day in Nerja, evening to Granada	Granada
14	Granada	Granada
15	Travel day to Segovia	Segovia
16	Segovia, evening to Salamanca	Salamanca
17	Salamanca	Salamanca
18	Travel to Santiago	Santiago
19	Santiago	Santiago
20	Travel to San Sebastián	San Sebastián
21	San Sebastián, side-trip to Bilbao	San Sebastián

This itinerary is designed for public transportation, but can be done by car with a few variations. Spain's long distances make it worth considering the option of flying for at least a portion of the trip. If you rent a car, it's best for the White Hill Towns (Arcos, Rhonda, and more, in southern Spain), Camino de Santiago (east–west route in northern Spain), and Cantabria (chunk of north-central coast with beaches, mountains, and prehistoric cave replica), where sparse public transportation limits the efficiency of your sightseeing. To mix car and train transportation, consider getting a Spain Rail & Drive pass.

If you're a fan of Salvador Dalí's art, or if you want to make a pilgrimage to the holy site of Montserrat, allot an extra day in Barcelona for side-trips. If you want more Moorish sights, stay another day in Sevilla to make a quick trip to Córdoba (45 minutes on AVE high-speed train). If you're not interested in day-tripping to Tangier, Morocco, you could skip Tarifa and go to Ronda instead. To allow time to explore Gibraltar, add an extra day between Tarifa (or Ronda) and Nerja. If you're exploring the Camino de Santiago by car, consider reversing the above itiner-

ary to start in San Sebastián, and figure on adding several days to a week to your trip.

The suggested itinerary assumes you'll fly into Barcelona and out of San Sebastián. If you're returning to Barcelona or Madrid from San Sebastián, it's roughly a six-hour train ride or a one-hour flight. Or you can take the new TGV train from Figueres (north of Barcelona) to Paris (5.5 hours).

Shorter Itineraries: You can end the three-week route several days early by returning to Madrid from Salamanca and saving northern Spain for another trip. The north is less rewarding per mile and day.

Here's a two-week alternative, which could include a few car days in southern Spain near the end of your trip: Start in Barcelona (stay two days); train to Madrid (stay five days total, with two days in Madrid and three for side-trips to Toledo, El Escorial, and Segovia or Ávila); train to Granada (two days); bus to Nerja (one day, could rent car here); both Ronda and Arcos for drivers, or just Ronda by train (two days); to Sevilla (drop off car, two days); and then train to Madrid and fly home.

Spain at a Glance

These attractions are listed (as in this book) roughly from north to south.

▲▲▲**Barcelona** The Catalan capital, with famous Ramblas people zone, atmospheric Gothic old town, and works by native sons Antoni Gaudí, Pablo Picasso, and Joan Miró.

▲**Near Barcelona** Top stops in Catalunya, including Salvador Dalí sights (Figueres and Cadaqués), pilgrimage to a rugged mountain retreat (Montserrat), and beach resort (Sitges).

▲**Basque Country** Feisty would-be breakaway region, anchored by the culinary capital of San Sebastián and the iconic modern Guggenheim Museum in Bilbao, with other attractions scattered through the countryside and across the border into France.

▲**The Camino de Santiago** Centuries-old pilgrimage route running across the top of Spain from France to Santiago, with stops at big cities (Pamplona, Burgos, León) and charming villages (Puente de la Reina, O Cebreiro)...and plenty of pilgrim bonding.

▲**Santiago de Compostela** Moss-covered pilgrim capital, and the top town in green Galicia.

Cantabria The rustic northern coast of Spain, featuring world-class prehistoric art (Altamira Caves) and high-mountain scenery (Picos de Europa).

▲**Salamanca** Spain's quintessential university town, with the country's finest main square.

▲▲▲**Madrid** The lively Spanish capital, boasting top-notch art treasures (Prado's collection, Picasso's *Guernica*), an unsurpassed

car windows at stoplights). A fight or commotion is created to enable pickpockets to work unnoticed. Be on guard, use a money belt, and treat any disturbance around you as a smoke screen for theft. Don't believe any "police officers" looking for counterfeit bills. Drivers should read the tips on page 839. When traveling by train, keep your luggage in sight and get a *litera* (berth in an attendant-monitored sleeping car) for safety on overnight trips.

Time Zones: Spain, like most of continental Europe, is generally six/nine hours ahead of the East/West Coasts of the US. The exceptions are the beginning and end of Daylight Saving Time: Europe "springs forward" the last Sunday in March (two

tapas scene, and urban Spain at its best.

▲**Northwest of Madrid** Sights ranging from El Escorial (imposing Inquisition palace of Spanish royalty) and the Valley of the Fallen (a stern, underground Franco-era monument to Spain's Civil War; under restoration but may reopen in 2012) to the pleasant towns of Segovia (with a towering Roman aqueduct) and Ávila (encircled by a medieval wall).

▲▲**Toledo** Hill-capping former capital, with a colorfully complex history, a magnificent cathedral, and works by hometown boy El Greco.

▲▲▲**Granada** Grand Moorish capital, home to the magnificent Alhambra palace and still-pungent North African culture.

▲▲▲**Sevilla** Soulful, flamenco-flavored cultural capital of southern Spain.

▲**Córdoba** Home to Spain's top surviving Moorish mosque, the Mezquita.

▲**Andalucía's White Hill Towns** Classic heartland of southern Spain, famous for its windswept landscape and idyllic towns, including Arcos de la Frontera, Ronda, and Grazalema.

Spain's South Coast "Costa del Sol" beach-resort zone, featuring a few charming towns (Nerja, Tarifa, and British-flavored Gibraltar) tucked between the concrete and traffic jams.

▲▲**Tangier, Morocco** Newly revitalized gateway to Africa, and an easy day trip from the Costa del Sol.

weeks after most of the US), and "falls back" the last Sunday in October (one week before the US). Moroccan time is an hour earlier than Spain's, but can run up to two hours earlier with Daylight Saving Time (see page 771). For a handy online time converter, try www.timeanddate.com/worldclock.

Business Hours: For visitors, Spain is a land of strange and frustrating schedules. Many businesses respect the afternoon siesta. When it's 100 degrees in the shade, you'll understand why.

The biggest museums stay open all day. Smaller ones often close for a siesta. Shops are generally open from 9:00 to 13:00 and from 16:00 to 20:00, longer in touristy places. Small shops are often open on Saturday only in the morning, and are closed all day Sunday. Banking hours are generally Monday through Friday from 9:00 to 14:00.

Saturdays are virtually weekdays, with earlier closing hours. Sundays have similar pros and cons as they do for travelers in the US: Special events and weekly markets pop up, sightseeing attractions are generally open, and there's no rush hour, but shops and banks are closed and public transportation options are fewer. Rowdy evenings are rare on Sundays.

Watt's Up? Europe's electrical system is 220 volts, instead of North America's 110 volts. Most newer electronics (such as laptops, battery chargers, and hair dryers) convert automatically, so you won't need a converter plug, but you will need an adapter plug with two round prongs, sold inexpensively at travel stores in the US. Avoid bringing older appliances that don't automatically convert voltage; instead, buy a cheap replacement in Europe.

Discounts: Discounts are not listed in this book. However, many sights offer discounts for youths (up to age 18), students (with proper identification cards, www.isic.org), families, seniors (loosely defined as retirees or those willing to call themselves seniors), and groups of 10 or more. Always ask. Some discounts are available only for EU citizens.

News: Americans keep in touch via the *International Herald Tribune* (published almost daily throughout Europe and online at www.iht.com). Another informative site is http://news.bbc.co.uk. Every Tuesday the European editions of *Time* and *Newsweek* hit the stands with articles of particular interest to travelers in Europe. Sports addicts can get their daily fix online or from *USA Today*. Many hotels have CNN and BBC News television channels.

Money

This section offers advice on how to pay for purchases on your trip (including getting cash from ATMs and paying with plastic), dealing with lost or stolen cards, VAT (sales tax) refunds, and tipping.

What to Bring

Bring both a credit card and a debit card. You'll use the debit card at cash machines (ATMs) to withdraw cash for most purchases, and the credit card to pay for larger items. Some travelers carry a third card, in case one gets demagnetized or eaten by a temperamental machine.

As an emergency backup, bring several hundred dollars in hard cash in easy-to-exchange $20 bills. Avoid using currency exchange booths (lousy rates and/or outrageous fees); if you have

---

Exchange Rate

1 euro (€) = about $1.40

To convert prices in euros to dollars, add about 40 percent: €28 = about $25, €50 = about $70. (Check www.oanda.com for the latest exchange rates.) Just like the dollar, one euro is broken down into 100 cents. You'll find coins ranging from €0.01 to €2, and bills ranging from €5 to €500.

Gibraltar uses pounds (£) but also takes euros; you'll get a better exchange rate using pounds (£1 = about $1.60).

For Morocco, I list prices in dirhams (the official currency; 8 dirhams = about $1), although euros and dollars are usually accepted. I abbreviate dirhams as "dh" in this book, but the official abbreviation is MAD, to differentiate the currency from dirhams used by other countries.

---

foreign currency to exchange, take it to a bank. Don't use traveler's checks—they're not worth the fees or long waits at slow banks.

Cash

Cash is just as desirable in Europe as it is at home. Small European businesses (hotels, restaurants, shops, etc.) prefer that you pay your bills with cash. Some vendors will charge you extra for using a credit card, and some won't take credit cards at all. Cash is the best—and sometimes only—way to pay for bus fares, taxis, and local guides.

Throughout Europe, ATMs (called a *cajero automático* in Spain) are the standard way for travelers to get cash. Most ATMs in Spain are located outside a bank. Try to use the ATM when the branch is open; if your card is munched by a machine, you can immediately go inside for help.

To withdraw money from an ATM, you'll need a debit card (ideally with a Visa or MasterCard logo for maximum usability), plus a PIN code. Know your PIN code in numbers; there are only numbers—no letters—on European keypads. For security, it's best to shield the keypad when entering your PIN at an ATM. Although you can use a credit card for ATM transactions, it's generally more expensive because it's considered a cash advance rather than a withdrawal.

When using an ATM, try to withdraw large sums of money to reduce the number of per-transaction bank fees you'll pay. If the machine refuses your request, try again and select a smaller amount (some cash machines limit the amount you can withdraw—don't take it personally). If that doesn't work, try a different machine. It's easier to pay for purchases with smaller bills; if the ATM gives you

INTRODUCTION

big bills, try to break them at a bank or larger store.

To keep your cash safe, use a money belt—a pouch with a strap that you buckle around your waist like a belt and wear under your clothes. Pickpockets target tourists. A money belt provides peace of mind, allowing you to carry lots of cash safely. Don't waste time every few days tracking down a cash machine—withdraw a week's worth of money, stuff it in your money belt, and travel!

Credit and Debit Cards

For purchases, Visa and MasterCard are more commonly accepted than American Express. Just like at home, credit or debit cards work easily at larger hotels, restaurants, and shops.

I typically use my debit card to withdraw cash to pay for most purchases. I use my credit card only in a few specific situations: to book hotel reservations by phone, to make major purchases (such as car rentals, plane tickets, and long hotel stays), and to pay for things near the end of my trip (to avoid another visit to the ATM). While you could use a debit card to make most large purchases, using a credit card offers a greater degree of fraud protection (because debit cards draw funds directly from your account).

Ask Your Credit- or Debit-Card Company: Before your trip, contact the company that issued your debit or credit cards.

• Confirm that your card will work overseas, and alert them that you'll be using it in Europe; otherwise, they may deny transactions if they perceive unusual spending patterns.

• Ask for the specifics on transaction **fees.** When you use your credit or debit card—either for purchases or ATM withdrawals—you'll often be charged additional "international transaction" fees of up to 3 percent (1 percent is normal) plus $5 per transaction. If your card's fees are too high, consider getting a card just for your trip: Capital One (credit cards only, www.capitalone.com) and most credit unions have low-to-no international transaction fees.

• If you plan to take out cash from ATMs, confirm your daily **withdrawal limit** (€300 is usually the maximum). Some travelers prefer a high limit that allows them to take out more cash at each ATM stop, while others prefer to set a lower limit in case their card is stolen.

• Ask for your credit card's **PIN** in case you encounter Europe's "chip-and-PIN" system; since the card company is unlikely to reveal your PIN over the phone, allow time for it to be mailed.

Chip and PIN: If your card is declined for a purchase in Europe, it may be because of chip and PIN, which requires cardholders to punch in a PIN instead of signing a receipt. While chip and PIN is not yet common in Spain, much of Europe, including Great Britain, Ireland, France, Belgium, the Netherlands, and Scandinavia, is adopting it. Some merchants rely on it exclusively. If, when you're using your card, you're prompted to enter your PIN but don't know it, ask if the cashier can swipe your card and print a receipt for you to sign instead; if not, just pay cash. You're most likely to encounter chip and PIN at automated payment machines, such as those at train and subway stations, toll roads, parking garages, luggage lockers, bike-rental kiosks, and self-serve pumps at gas stations. If a machine won't take your card, look for a cashier nearby who can make your card work, or see if one of the machines takes cash.

You can avoid potential hassles by getting your own chip-and-PIN card just for your trip, but so far your options are limited. Chase is offering a Visa credit card with a chip called J. P. Morgan Select, but it comes with a hefty annual fee and requires a stellar credit rating. Travelex has a chip-and-PIN cash card called "Cash Passport" that's preloaded with euros or British pounds and sold at many airports; it comes with exorbitant exchange rates and only works at places that accept MasterCard. While handy, these cards are probably not worth it unless you're staying for several weeks in a country that's converted to chip-and-PIN cards, and you're willing to pay for the convenience.

Dynamic Currency Conversion: If merchants offer to convert your purchase price into dollars (called dynamic currency conversion, or DCC), refuse this "service." You'll pay even more in fees for the expensive convenience of seeing your charge in dollars.

Damage Control for Lost Cards

If you lose your credit, debit, or ATM card, you can stop people from using your card by reporting the loss immediately to the respective global customer-assistance centers. Call these 24-hour US numbers collect: Visa (410/581-9994, toll-free number in Spain is 900-991-124); MasterCard (636/722-7111); and American Express (623/492-8427).

At a minimum, you'll need to know the name of the financial institution that issued the card, along with the type of card (classic, platinum, or whatever). Providing the following information will allow for a quicker cancellation of your missing card: full card number, whether you are the primary or secondary cardholder, the cardholder's name exactly as printed on the card, billing address, home phone number, circumstances of the loss or theft, and identification verification (your birth date, your mother's maiden name, or your Social Security number—memorize this, don't carry a copy). If you are the secondary cardholder, you'll also need to provide the primary cardholder's identification-verification details. You can generally receive a temporary card within two or three business days in Europe (see www.ricksteves.com/help for more).

If you promptly report your card lost or stolen, you typically won't be responsible for any unauthorized transactions on your account, although many banks charge a liability fee of $50.

Tipping

Tipping in Spain isn't as automatic and generous as it is in the US, but for special service, tips are appreciated, if not expected. As in the US, the proper amount depends on your resources, tipping philosophy, and the circumstances, but some general guidelines apply.

Restaurants: If you order a meal at a counter—as you often will when sampling tapas at a bar—there's no need to tip. At restaurants with table service, most Spaniards tip nothing or next to nothing; a service charge is generally included in the bill *(servicio incluido)*. If you like to tip for good service, give up to 5 percent extra. If service is not included *(servicio no incluido)*, you could tip up to 10 percent. At most places, you can leave the tip on the table. But if you're eating at an outdoor café, hand the tip to your server to avoid having it swiped by a passerby. Also, it's best to tip in cash even if you pay with your credit card. Otherwise the tip may never reach your server.

Taxis: To tip the cabbie, round up. Spanish people rarely give tips in taxis, unless it's to round up to the next full euro (if the fare is €4.85, they'll give €5). If the cabbie hauls your bags and zips you to the airport to help you catch your flight, you might want to toss in a little more. But if you feel like you're being driven in circles or otherwise ripped off, skip the tip.

Special Services: Tour guides at public sights sometimes hold out their hands for tips after they give their spiel. If I've already paid for the tour, I don't tip extra, unless the guide has really impressed me. If you let a hotel porter carry your luggage, it's polite to give a euro for each bag (another reason to pack light). If you tip the maid, you can leave a euro per overnight at the end of your stay.

In general, if someone in the service industry does a super job for you, a small tip (a euro or two) is appropriate...but not required.

When in doubt, ask. If you're not sure whether (or how much) to tip for a service, ask your hotelier or the tourist information office; they'll fill you in on how it's done on their turf.

Getting a VAT Refund

Wrapped into the purchase price of your Spanish souvenirs is a Value-Added Tax (VAT) of 18 percent (in Spain, it's called IVA— *Impuesto sobre el Valor Añadido*). You're entitled to get most of that tax back if you purchase more than €90.15 (about $126) worth of goods at a store that participates in the VAT-refund scheme. Typically, you must ring up the minimum at a single retailer— you can't add up your purchases from various shops to reach the required amount.

Getting your refund is usually straightforward and, if you buy a substantial amount of souvenirs, well worth the hassle. If you're lucky, the merchant will subtract the tax when you make your purchase. (This is more likely to occur if the store ships the goods to your home.) Otherwise, you'll need to:

Get the paperwork. Have the merchant completely fill out the necessary refund document. You'll have to present your passport at the store. Be sure to retain your original sales receipt.

Get your stamp at the border or airport. Process your VAT document at your last stop in the EU (for instance, at the airport) with the customs agent who deals with VAT refunds. Before checking in for your flight, find the local customs office, and be prepared to stand in line. Keep your purchases in your carry-on for viewing, but if they're too large or dangerous (such as knives) to carry on, have your purchases easily accessible in the bag you're about to check, ready to show the customs agent. You're not supposed to use your purchased goods before you leave. If you show up at customs wearing your new flamenco outfit, officials might look the other way—or deny you a refund.

Collect your refund. You'll need to return your stamped document to the retailer or its representative. Many merchants work with services, such as Global Blue (www.global-blue.com) or Premier Tax Free (www.premiertaxfree.com), which have offices at major airports, ports, or border crossings (after check-in and security, probably strategically located near a duty-free shop). These services, which extract a 4 percent fee, can refund your money immediately in cash or credit your card (within two billing cycles). If the retailer handles VAT refunds directly, it's up to you to contact the merchant for your refund. You can mail the documents from home or, more quickly, from your point of departure (using a stamped, addressed envelope you've prepared or one that's been provided by the merchant). You'll then have to wait—it can take months.

Customs for American Shoppers

You are allowed to take home $800 worth of items per person duty-free, once every 30 days. You can also bring in duty-free a liter of alcohol. As for food, you can take home many processed and pack-aged foods: vacuum-packed cheeses, dried herbs, jams, chocolate, oil, vinegar, and honey. However, fresh fruits and vegetables and most meats are not allowed. Any liquid-containing foods must be packed in checked luggage, a potential recipe for disaster. To check customs rules and duty rates, visit www.cbp.gov.

Sightseeing

Sightseeing can be hard work. Use these tips to make your visits to Spain's finest sights meaningful, fun, efficient, and painless.

Plan Ahead

Set up an itinerary that allows you to fit in all your must-see sights. For a one-stop look at opening hours, see the "At a Glance" side-bars for major cities: Barcelona, Madrid, Toledo, Granada, and Sevilla. Most sights keep stable hours, but you can easily confirm the latest by checking with the TI or visiting museum websites.

Don't put off visiting a must-see sight—you never know when a place will close unexpectedly for a holiday, a strike, or restora-tion. On holidays (see list on page 846), expect reduced hours or closures. Many museums have shorter hours off-season, and in summer some sights may stay open late.

When possible, visit the major sights in the morning (when your energy is best) and save other activities for the afternoon. Hit the highlights first, then go back to other things if you have the stamina and time.

Avoid crowds if you can. This book offers tips on the best times to see specific sights. In general, try visiting popular sights very early, at lunch, or very late. Evening visits are usually peaceful with fewer crowds.

Several cities offer sightseeing passes that are worthwhile val-ues for serious sightseers; do the math to see if they'll save you money.

Study up. To get the most out of the sight descriptions in this book, read them before you visit.

At Sights

Here's what you can typically expect:

Some important sights use metal detectors or conduct bag searches that will slow your entry. Most museums require you to check daypacks and coats. They'll be kept safely. If you have some-thing you can't bear to part with, stash it in a pocket or purse. To avoid checking a small backpack, carry it under your arm like a purse as you enter. From a guard's point of view, a backpack is generally a problem whereas a purse is not.

At churches—which generally offer interesting art (usually free) and a cool, welcome seat—a modest dress code (no bare shoulders or shorts) is encouraged.

Flash photography is often banned, but taking photos without a flash is usually allowed. Look for signs or ask. Flashes damage oil paintings and distract others in the room. Even without a flash, a handheld camera will take a decent picture (or you can buy postcards or posters at the museum bookstore). If photos are permitted, video cameras are generally OK, too.

Museums may have special exhibits in addition to their permanent collection. Some exhibits are included in the entry price, while others come at an extra cost (which you may have to pay even if you don't want to see the exhibit).

Expect changes—artwork can be on tour, on loan, out sick, or shifted at the whim of the curator. To adapt, pick up any available free floor plans as you enter, and ask the museum staff if you can't find a particular item. Say the title or artist's name, or point to the photograph in this book, and ask, "¿*Dónde está?*" (dohn-day ay-stah; meaning, "Where is?").

Many sights rent audioguides, which generally offer dry-but-useful recorded descriptions in English (about €3-4). If you bring along your own pair of headphones and a Y-jack, you can sometimes share one audioguide with your travel partner and save money.

Guided tours in English (usually about €6 and widely ranging in quality) are most likely to be offered during peak season. Some sights also run short films featuring their highlights and history. These are generally well worth your time. I make it standard operating procedure to ask when I arrive at a sight if there is a film in English.

Important sights may have an on-site café or cafeteria—usually a good place to rest and have a snack or light meal. The WCs at sights are free and generally clean; it's smart to carry tissues in case a WC runs out of TP.

Many sights sell postcards and guidebooks that highlight their attractions. Before you leave, scan the postcards and thumb through the biggest guidebook (or skim its index) to be sure you haven't overlooked something that you'd like to see.

Most sights stop admitting people 30-60 minutes before closing time, and some rooms close early (often about 45 minutes before the actual closing time). Guards usher people out, so don't save the best for last.

Every sight or museum offers more than what is covered in this book. Use the information in this book as an introduction—not the final word.

Sleeping

INTRODUCTION

I favor hotels and restaurants that are handy to your sightseeing activities. Rather than list hotels scattered throughout a city, I describe two or three favorite neighborhoods and recommend the best accommodations values in each, from $30 bunk beds to fancy-for-my-book $300 doubles with all the comforts.

A major feature of this book is its extensive listing of good-value rooms. I like places that are clean, central, relatively quiet at night, reasonably priced, friendly, small enough to have a hands-on owner and stable staff, run with a respect for Spanish traditions, and not listed in other guidebooks. (In Spain, for me, six out of these eight criteria means it's a keeper.) I'm more impressed by a handy location and a fun-loving philosophy than flat-screen TVs and shoeshine machines.

Rates and Deals

I've described my recommended accommodations using a Sleep Code (see the sidebar). Prices listed are for one-night stays in peak season, and assume you're booking directly (not through a TI or online hotel-booking engine). Using an online booking service costs the hotel about 20 percent and logically closes the door on special deals. Book direct.

Given the economic downturn, hoteliers are willing and eager to make a deal. I'd suggest emailing several hotels to ask for their best price. Comparison-shop and make your choice.

In general, prices can soften if you do any of the following: offer to pay cash, stay at least three nights, or mention this book. You can also try asking for a cheaper room or a discount, or offer to skip breakfast.

As you look over the listings, you'll notice that some accommodations promise special prices to my readers who book direct (without using a room-finding service or hotel-booking website, which take a commission). To get these rates, you must mention this book when you reserve, and then show the book upon arrival. Some readers with ebooks have reported difficulty getting a Rick Steves discount. If this happens to you, please show this to the hotelier: Rick Steves discounts apply to readers with ebooks as well as printed books.

For tips on making reservations, see page 24.

Travel Review Websites: TripAdvisor (www.tripadvisor.com) and similar review websites are popular tools for finding hotels, but have drawbacks. To write a review, people need only an email address—making it easy to hide their true identity. If a hotel is well reviewed in a guidebook or two, and also gets good ratings on

TripAdvisor, it's probably a safe bet—but I wouldn't stay at a hotel based solely on a TripAdvisor recommendation.

Types of Accommodations

Hotels

Spain offers some of the best accommodations values in Western Europe. Most places are government-regulated, with posted prices. Don't judge hotels by their bleak and dirty entryways. Landlords, stuck with rent control, often stand firmly in the way of hardworking hoteliers who'd like to brighten up their buildings.

Rooms with private bathrooms are often bigger and renovated; cheaper rooms without bathrooms often will be dingier and/or on the top floor. All rooms have sinks with hot and cold water, and any room without a bathroom has access to one in the corridor.

Spain has recently instituted stringent restrictions on smoking in public places. Smoking is not permitted in common areas, but hotels can designate 10 percent of their rooms for smokers.

Hotels are officially prohibited from using central heat before November 1 and after April 1 (unless it's unusually cold); prepare for cool evenings if you travel in spring and fall. Summer can be extremely hot. Consider air-conditioning, fans, and noise (since you'll want your window open), and don't be shy about asking for ice at the fancier hotels. Many rooms come with mini-refrigerators (if it's noisy at night, unplug it). Conveniently, expensive business-class hotels in big, nonresort cities often drop their prices in July and August, just when the air-conditioned comfort they offer is most important.

Be aware that some hotels have centrally controlled air-conditioning—the manager chooses the temperature (with an eye on his bottom line). In some hotel rooms, air-conditioning units are mounted high on the wall. These come with control sticks (like a TV remote, sometimes require a deposit) that generally have similar symbols: fan icon (toggle through wind power); louver icon (choose steady air flow or waves); snowflake and sunshine icons (heat or cold); clock ("O" setting: run x hours before turning off; "I" setting: wait x hours to start); and the temperature control (20 degrees Celsius is comfortable).

If you're arriving on an early flight or an overnight train, your room probably won't be ready first thing in the morning. You should be able to safely check your bag at the hotel and dive right into sightseeing.

Street noise in Spain is high (Spaniards are notorious night owls), and walls and doors tend to be very thin—earplugs are a necessity. Always ask to see your room first. If you suspect night noise will be a problem, request a quiet *(silencioso)* room in the back

Sleep Code

(€1 = about $1.40)

Price Rankings

To help you sort easily through these listings, I've divided the accommodations into three categories based on the price for a standard double room with bath during high season:

$$$	Higher Priced
$$	Moderately Priced
$	Lower Priced

I always rate hostels as $, whether or not they have double rooms, because they have the cheapest beds in town. Prices can change without notice; verify the hotel's current rates online or by email. For other updates, see www.ricksteves.com/update.

Abbreviations

To pack maximum information into minimum space, I use the following code to describe accommodations in this book. Prices listed are per room, not per person. When a price range is given for a type of room (such as double rooms listed for €100-150), it means the price fluctuates with the season, size of room, or length of stay; expect to pay the upper end for peak-season stays, especially in resort areas. In Spain, high season *(temporada alta)* is from July to September; shoulder season *(tempo-*

---

or on an upper floor *(piso alto)*. In most cases, view rooms *(con vista)* come with street noise. You'll often sleep better and for less money in a room without a view.

Hoteliers can be a great help and source of advice. Most know their city well, and can assist you with everything from public transit and airport connections to finding a good restaurant, the nearest launderette, or an Internet café. But even at the best places, mechanical breakdowns occur: Air-conditioning malfunctions, sinks leak, hot water turns cold, and toilets gurgle and smell. Report your concerns clearly and calmly at the front desk. For more complicated problems, don't expect instant results. Any legitimate place is legally required to have a complaint book *(libro de reclamaciones)*. A request for this book will generally prompt the hotelier to solve your problem to keep you from writing a complaint.

To guard against theft in your room, keep valuables out of sight. Some rooms come with a safe, and other hotels have safes at the front desk. Use them if you're concerned.

Checkout can pose problems if surprise charges pop up on your bill. If you settle up your bill the night before you leave, you'll have time to discuss and address any points of contention (before 19:00, when the night shift usually arrives).

rada media) is roughly April through June and October; and low season (*temporada baja*) runs from November through March. The prices and seasons are posted at or near the hotel desk. Some hotels include the 8 percent IVA tax in the room price; others tack it onto your bill. Many hotels charge extra for breakfast; check the individual hotel listings for details.

S = Single room (or price for one person in a double).

D = Double or twin. "Double beds" are often two twins sheeted together and are big enough for nonromantic couples.

T = Triple (generally a double bed with a single).

Q = Quad (usually two double beds; adding an extra child's bed to a T is usually cheaper).

b = Private bathroom with toilet and shower or tub.

s = Private shower or tub only (the toilet is down the hall).

According to this code, a couple staying at a "Db-€140" hotel would pay a total of €140 (about $196) for a double room with a private bathroom. Unless otherwise noted, hotel staff speak basic English and credit cards are accepted.

If I mention "Internet access" in a listing, there's a public terminal in the lobby for guests to use. If I use the terms "Wi-Fi" or "cable Internet," you can access the Internet in your room, but only if you have your own laptop or other Wi-Fi device.

Above all, keep a positive attitude. Remember, you're on vacation. If your hotel is a disappointment, spend more time out enjoying the city you came to see.

Historic Inns: Spain has luxurious government-sponsored, historic inns called *paradores*. These are often renovated castles, palaces, or monasteries, many with great views and stately atmospheres. While full of Old World character, they are usually run in a sterile, bureaucratic way and are generally pricier than hotels (doubles $100-240, for details, bonus packages, and family deals, see www.parador.es). If you're not eligible for any deals, you'll get a better value by sleeping in what I call (and list in this book as) "poor man's *paradores*"—elegant, normal places that offer double the warmth and Old World intimacy for half the price.

Budget Hotels: *Hostales* and *pensiones* are easy to find, inexpensive, and, when chosen properly, a fun part of the Spanish cultural experience. These places are often family-owned, and may or may not have amenities like private bathrooms and air-conditioning. Don't confuse a *hostal* with a hostel—a Spanish *hostal* is an inexpensive hotel, not a hostel with bunks in dorms.

Hotels Beyond this Book: If you're traveling beyond my recommended destinations, you'll find accommodations where you

Making Reservations

Given the quality of the accommodations I've found for this book, I'd recommend that you reserve your rooms in advance, particularly if you'll be traveling during peak season. Book several weeks ahead, or as soon as you've pinned down your travel dates. Note that some national holidays jam things up and merit your making reservations far in advance (see "Holidays and Festivals" on page 846).

Phoning: To call Spain from the US or Canada, dial 011-34 and then the local number. (The 011 is our international access code, and 34 is Spain's country code.) If you're calling Spain from another European country, dial 00-34-local number. (The 00 is Europe's international access code.) To make calls within Spain, simply dial the nine-digit number (area codes are not used in Spain). For more tips on calling, see page 820.

Requesting a Reservation: To make a reservation, contact hotels directly by email, phone, or fax. Email is the clearest and most economical way to make a reservation. Or you can go straight to the hotel website; many have secure online reservation forms and can instantly inform you of availability and any special deals. But be sure you use the hotel's official site and not a booking agency's site—otherwise you may pay higher rates than you should. Most recommended hotels are accustomed to guests who speak only English.

The hotelier wants to know these key pieces of information (also included in the sample request form in the appendix):
- number and type of rooms
- number of nights
- date of arrival
- date of departure
- any special needs (for example, bathroom in the room or down the hall, twin beds vs. double bed, air-conditioning, quiet, view, ground floor)

When you request a room, use the European style for writing dates: day/month/year. For example, for a two-night stay in July, I would request "1 double room for 2 nights, arrive 16/07/12, depart 18/07/12." Consider carefully how long you'll stay; don't just assume you can tack on extra days once you arrive. Make sure you mention any discounts—for Rick Steves readers or otherwise—when you make the reservation.

need them. Any town with tourists has a TI that books rooms or can give you a list and point you in the right direction. In the absence of a TI, ask people on the street or in restaurants for help.

Private Homes, *Casas Rurales,* and Hostels

Rooms in Private Homes: Especially in touristy areas, residents often open up a spare room to make a little money on the side.

Confirming a Reservation: If the hotel's response tells you its room availability and rates, it's not a confirmation. You must tell them that you want that room at the given rate. Most hoteliers will request your credit-card number to hold the room. While you can email your credit-card information (I do), it's safer to share that confidential info via phone call, fax, split between two emails, or via a secure online reservation form (if the hotel has one on its website).

Canceling a Reservation: If you must cancel your reservation, it's courteous to do so with as much advance notice as possible. Simply make a quick phone call or send an email. Family-run hotels lose money if they turn away customers while holding a room for someone who doesn't show up. Understandably, many hoteliers bill no-shows for one night.

Cancellation policies can be strict: For example, you might lose a deposit if you cancel within two weeks of your reserved stay, or you might be billed for the entire visit if you leave early. Internet deals may require prepayment, with no refunds for cancellations. Ask about cancellation policies before you book.

If canceling via email, request confirmation that your cancellation was received to avoid being accidentally billed.

Reconfirming Your Reservation: Always call to reconfirm your room reservation a few days in advance from the road. (Don't have a TI call for you; they may take a commission.) Smaller hotels and B&Bs appreciate knowing your estimated time of arrival. If you'll be arriving late (after 17:00), alert your hotelier. On the small chance that a hotel loses track of your reservation, bring along a hard copy of their emailed or faxed confirmation.

Reserving Rooms as You Travel: You can make reservations as you travel, calling hotels a few days to a week before your arrival. If everything's full, don't despair. Call a day or two in advance and fill in a cancellation. If you'd rather travel without any reservations at all, you'll have greater success snaring rooms if you arrive at your destination early in the day. When you anticipate crowds (weekends are worst), call hotels at about 9:00 or 10:00 on the day you plan to arrive, when the hotel clerk knows who'll be checking out and just which rooms will be available. If you encounter a language barrier, ask the fluent receptionist at your current hotel to call for you.

These rooms are usually as private as hotel rooms, often with separate entries. Especially in resort towns, the rooms might be in small apartment-type buildings. Ask for a *cama, habitación,* or *casa particular.* They're cheap ($15-30 per bed without breakfast) and usually a good experience.

Casas Rurales: Located mainly in rural areas throughout Spain, these accommodations can be furnished rooms, whole farmhouses, villas, or sprawling ranches. Some are simple, but others are luxurious, and they are mostly used by Spaniards, so you'll really be going local. Many are in the countryside, so you will need a car. For more information and reservations, try www.ecoturismorural.com or www.micasarural.com.

Hostels: Spain has plenty of youth hostels, but considering the great bargains on other accommodations, I don't think they're worth the trouble and usually don't cover them in this book. But if you're on a starvation budget or just prefer hosteling, information is available at www.hihostels.com, www.hostelz.com, and www.hostelseurope.com.

Eating

Spanish cuisine is hearty and served in big, inexpensive portions. You can eat well in restaurants for about €15—or even more cheaply if you graze on tapas in bars.

The Spanish eating schedule—lunch from 13:00 to 16:00, dinner after 21:00—frustrates many visitors. Most Spaniards eat one major meal of the day—lunch *(comida)*—around 14:00, when stores close, schools let out, and people gather with their friends and family for the siesta. Because most Spaniards work until 19:30, supper *(cena)* is usually served at about 21:00 or 22:00. And, since few people want a heavy meal that late, many Spaniards build a light dinner out of appetizer portions called tapas.

Don't buck this system. Generally, no self-respecting *casa de comidas* ("house of eating"—when you see this label, you can bet it's a good, traditional eatery) serves meals at American hours. If you're looking for the "nontouristy restaurant," remember that a popular spot is often filled with tourists at 20:00; then at 22:00 the scene is entirely different—and more authentic.

Not only are mealtimes different—the portions are, too. It's unusual to find a restaurant with "starters" and "main dishes." Instead, most restaurants (like bars) serve their dishes in portions called *raciones*, or the smaller half- *(media-) raciones*. (The smaller tapas, and even tinier *pinchos*, are more commonly served at bars than at sit-down restaurants; for details, see later.) Enjoy this as an opportunity to explore the regional cuisine. Ordering half-*raciones* may cost a bit more per ounce, but you'll broaden your tasting experience. Two people can fill up on four *media-raciones*.

The Spanish diet—heavy on ham, deep-fried foods (usually fried in olive oil), more ham, weird seafood, and ham again—can be brutal on Americans more accustomed to salads, fruit, and grains. A few perfectly good vegetarian and lighter options exist, but you'll have to seek them out. The secret to getting your veggies at restaurants is to order two courses, because the first course generally has a green option. Resist the cheese-and-ham appetizers and instead choose first-course menu items such as creamed vegetable soup, *parrillada de verduras* (sautéed vegetables), or *ensalada mixta*. (Spaniards rarely eat only a salad, so salads tend to be small and simple—just iceberg lettuce, tomatoes, and maybe olives and tuna.) Main courses such as meats or fish are usually served with only a garnish, not a side of vegetables. Fruit isn't normally served for breakfast or as a snack—it's a dessert. After-meal dessert menus usually have a fruit option.

Survival Tips: To get by in Spain, either adapt yourself to the Spanish schedule and cuisine, or scramble to get edible food in between. Have an early light lunch at a bar. Many Spaniards have a *bocadillo* (sandwich) at about 11:00 to bridge the gap between their coffee-and-roll breakfast and lunch at 14:00 (hence the popularity of fast-food sandwich chains such as Pans & Company). Besides *bocadillos,* bars often have slices of *tortilla española* (potato omelet) and fresh-squeezed orange juice.

Then, either have your main meal at a restaurant at 15:00, followed by a light tapas snack for dinner later; or reverse it, having a tapas meal in the afternoon, followed by a late restaurant dinner. Either way, tapas in bars are the key (see sidebar on page 30).

Breakfast

Hotel breakfasts are generally handy, optional, and pricey (about €6). Start your day instead with a Spanish flair at a corner bar or at a colorful café near the town market hall (and pay just €2-3). Ask for the *desayunos* (breakfast special, usually only available until noon), which can include coffee, a roll (or sandwich), and juice for one price—much cheaper than ordering them separately. In Andalucía, get your morning protein with the *mollete con jamón y aceite,* a soft roll of bread with Spanish ham and finger-licking good olive oil (sometimes comes with cheese, too). If you like a Danish and coffee in American greasy-spoon joints, you must try the Spanish equivalent: greasy cigar-shaped fritters called *churros* (or the thicker *porras*) that you dip in warm chocolate pudding or your *café con leche.*

Here are some key words for breakfast:

café solo	shot of espresso
café con leche	espresso with hot milk
cortado	espresso with a little milk
té	tea
zumo de fruta	fruit juice

zumo de naranja (natural)	orange juice (freshly squeezed)
pan (de molde or *de barra)*	bread (cheap white bread or sliced baguette)
tortilla española	potato omelet (inexpensive dish cooked fresh each morning, served in slices)
sandwich (tostado)	white bread (toasted)
bocadillo	baguette sandwich
...con jamón/queso/mixto	...with ham/cheese/both
...mixto con huevo	...with ham and cheese topped by an over-easy egg
croissant a la plancha	grilled croissant slathered with butter
tostada con aceite (y tomate)	a standard breakfast—toasted bread with oil (sometimes comes with tomato)

Restaurants

When restaurant hunting, choose a spot filled with locals, not the place with the big neon signs boasting, "We Speak English and Accept Credit Cards." Venturing even a block or two off the main drag leads to higher-quality food for less than half the price of the tourist-oriented places. Locals eat better at lower-rent locales.

Don't expect "My name is Carlos and I'll be your waiter tonight" cheery service. Service is often *serio*—it's not friendly or unfriendly...just white-shirt-and-bow-tie proficient.

Although not fancy, Spanish cuisine comes with an endless variety of regional specialties. Two famous Spanish dishes are paella and gazpacho. Paella features saffron-flavored rice as a background for whatever the chef wants to mix in— seafood, sausage, chicken, peppers, and so on. While paella is heavy for your evening meal, jump (like everyone else in the bar) at the opportunity to snare a small plate of paella when it appears hot out of the kitchen in a tapas bar. Avoid the paella shown in pretty pictures on a separate menu—it's from the microwave. Gazpacho, an Andalusian specialty, is a chilled soup of tomatoes, bread chunks,  and spices—refreshing on a hot day and commonly available in the summer (sometimes served in a glass). Spanish cooks love garlic and olive oil—many dishes are soaked in both. The cheapest meal is simply a *bocadillo de jamón* (sandwich of ham on French bread), sold virtually everywhere.

For a budget meal in a restaurant, try a *plato combinado* (combination plate), which usually includes portions of one or two main dishes, a vegetable, and bread for a reasonable price; or the *menú del día* (menu of the day, also known as *menú turístico*), a substantial three- to four-course meal that usually comes with a carafe of house wine.

Sometimes the distinction between a bar and a restaurant blurs. Formal restaurants have a standard à la carte menu. Most eateries have a bar with some tables in the back or outside. And though tourists are often hot on tapas, these places are likely to serve *raciones* rather than tapas or restaurant entrées. Typically, couples or small groups order a few *raciones* and share the plates family-style. This can be very economical if you don't over-order.

Whether you go to a restaurant or bar, you won't be bothered by indoor smoke. Smoking has been banned in closed public spaces.

Tapas Bars

You can eat well any time of day in tapas bars. Tapas are small portions, like appetizers, of seafood, salads, meat filled pastries, deep-fried tasties, and on and on—normally displayed under glass at the bar.

Tapas typically cost about €1.50-2. Most bars push larger portions called *raciones* (dinner plate–sized) rather than smaller tapas (saucer-sized). Ask for the smaller tapas portions or a *media-ración* (listed as ½ *ración* on a menu), though some bars simply don't serve anything smaller than a *ración*. There are happy exceptions: Small free tapas may be included with your drink in a few cities, including León, Santiago de Compostela, Salamanca, Granada, and Nerja.

Eating and drinking at a bar is usually cheapest if you sit or stand at the counter *(barra)*. You may pay a little more to eat sitting at a table *(mesa)* and still more for an outdoor table *(terraza)*. Locate the price list (often posted in fine type on a wall somewhere) to know the menu options and price tiers. (It's bad form to order food at the bar, then take it to a table. If you're standing and a table opens up, it's OK to move as long as you signal to the waiter; anything else you order will be charged at the higher *mesa* price.) In the right place, a quiet snack and drink on a terrace on the town square is well worth the extra charge. But the cheapest seats sometimes get the best show. Sit at the bar and study your bartender—he's an artist.

Ordering Tapas

You can often just point to what you want on the menu, say *por favor*, and get your food, but these words will help you learn the options and fine-tune your request.

Tapas Terms

pincho	bite-size portion
pinchito	tiny *pincho*
tapas	snack-size portions
ración	full portion
media-ración	half portion
frito	fried
...a la plancha	grilled on a flat-top griddle
...a la parrilla	barbecued
¿Cuánto cuesta una tapa?	How much per tapa?

Sandwich Words

bocadillo	baguette sandwich, cheap and basic, a tapa on bread
canapé	tiny open-faced sandwich
pulguitas	small closed baguette sandwich
montadito	small bun (or baguette slice) with the tapa "mounted" on top
flautas	sandwich made with flute-thin baguette
pepito, pulga	yet two more words for a little sandwich

Typical Tapas

aceitunas	olives
almendras	almonds
atún	tuna
bacalao	cod
banderilla	small skewer of spicy, pickled veggies—eat all at once for the real punch (it's named after the spear matadors use to spike the bull)
bombas	fried meat and potatoes ball
boquerones (en vinagre)	fresh anchovies marinated in olive oil, vinegar, and garlic
calamares fritos	fried squid rings
caracoles	snails (May-Sept)
cazón en adobo	salty, marinated dogfish
champiñones	mushrooms
croquetas de...	breaded and fried béchamel (made of flour and milk), usually with chunks of *jamón* (ham)
empanadillas	pastries stuffed with meat or seafood

ensalada rusa	potato salad with lots of mayo, peas, and carrots
espinacas (con garbanzos)	spinach (with garbanzo beans)
gambas (a la plancha, al ajillo)	shrimp (grilled, with garlic)
gazpacho	cold soup, made with tomato, bread, garlic, and olive oil
guiso	stew
mejillones	mussels
paella	rice dish with saffron, seafood, meat, and/or chicken
pan	bread
patatas bravas	fried chunks of potato with spicy tomato sauce
pescaditos fritos	assortment of fried little fish
picos	little breadsticks
pimiento (relleno)	peppers (stuffed)
pisto	mixed sautéed vegetables
pulpo	octopus
queso	cheese
queso manchego	sheep-milk cheese
rabas	squid tentacles
rabo de toro	bull's-tail stew (fatty and oh so tender)
revuelto de...	scrambled eggs with...
...setas	...wild mushrooms
tabla serrana	hearty plate of mountain meat and cheese
tortilla española	potato omelet
tortilla de jamón/queso	potato omelet with ham/cheese
variado fritos	typical Andalusian mix of various fried fish

Cured Meats (*Charcutería*)

jamón serrano	cured ham
jamón ibérico	best cured ham, from acorn-fed pigs
salchichón	sausage
chorizo	spicy sausage
lomo	pork tenderloin

Typical Desserts

flan de huevo	crème caramel
arroz con leche	rice pudding
helados (variados)	ice cream (various flavors)
fruta de la estación	fruit in season
queso	cheese

Be assertive or you'll never be served. *Por favor* (please) grabs the guy's attention. Don't worry about paying until you're ready to leave (he's keeping track of your tab). To get the bill ask: "*¿La cuenta?*" (or *la dolorosa*—meaning literally "the painful"—always draws a confused laugh).

Bars come with a formidable language barrier, and the bartender isn't there to help you sort through your options—he wants to take your order, period. Hang back and observe before ordering. Read the posted or printed menu (occasionally in English, but often not). A small working vocabulary is essential for tapas proficiency (see sidebar on page 30) and will help you eat better, too.

Chasing down a particular bar for tapas nearly defeats the purpose and spirit of tapas—they are impromptu. Just drop in at any lively place. I look for the noisy spots with piles of napkins and food debris on the floor (go local and toss your trash, too), lots of customers, and the TV blaring. Popular television-viewing includes bullfights and soccer games, American sitcoms, and Spanish interpretations of soaps and silly game shows (you'll see Vanna Blanco). Although tapas are served all day, the real action begins late—21:00 at the earliest. But for beginners, an earlier start is easier and comes with less commotion.

Get a fun, inexpensive sampler plate. Ask for *una tabla de canapés variados* to get a plate of various little open-faced sandwiches. Or ask for a *surtido de* (an assortment of...) *charcutería* (a mixed plate of meat) or *queso* (cheese). *Un surtido de jamón y queso* means a plate of different hams and cheeses. Order bread and two glasses of red wine on the right square, and you've got a romantic (and €10) dinner for two.

Spanish Drinks

Spain is one of the world's leading producers of grapes, and that means lots of excellent wine: both red *(tinto)* and white *(blanco)*.
Major wine regions include Valdepeñas and Penedès (Cabernet-style wines from near Barcelona); Rioja (spicy, lighter reds from the *tempranillo* grape, from the high plains of northern Spain); and Ribera del Duero (northwest of Madrid). For a basic glass of red wine, you can order *un tinto*. But for quality wine, ask for *un crianza* (old), *un reserva* (older), or *un gran reserva* (oldest). In fact, the single most important tip for good, economical wine drinking is to ask for *un crianza*—for little or no extra money, you'll get a quality, aged wine.

How Was Your Trip?

Were your travels fun, smooth, and meaningful? If you'd like to share your tips, concerns, and discoveries, please fill out the survey at www.ricksteves.com/feedback. I value your feedback. Thanks in advance—it helps a lot.

Sherry, a fortified wine from the Jerez region, is a shock to the taste buds if you're expecting a sweet dessert drink. It ranges from dry *(fino)* to sweet *(dulce)*—Spaniards drink the *fino* and export the *dulce. Cava* is Spain's answer to champagne. Sangria (a punch of red wine mixed with fruit slices) is refreshing and popular with tourists.

Most places just have the standard local beer—a light lager—on tap. The brand is determined by regional pride, rather than quality. (For instance, Cruzcampo—which is very light so that hot, thirsty drinkers can consume more—is big in the south, whereas San Miguel is big in the north.) Nonalcoholic beer is quite popular and often on tap. If you say *"sin,"* which means "without," it's assumed you want a nonalcoholic beer (common and often on tap). While *sin* comes with less than 1 percent alcohol, you can get totally alcohol-free brew by asking for "zero point zero" (0.0). To get a small draft beer, ask for a *caña.* If you'd prefer a grape juice alternative to wine, ask for *mosto* (it comes in red or white).

Spain's bars often serve fresh-squeezed orange juice *(zumo de naranja natural).* For something completely different, try *horchata de chufas,* a sweet, milky beverage extracted from *chufa* tubers (a.k.a. earth almonds). If ordering mineral water in a restaurant, request a *botella grande de agua* (big bottle). They push the more profitable small bottles.

Here are some words to help you quench your thirst:

agua con/sin gas	water with/without bubbles
un vasito de agua or *un vaso de agua del grifo*	glass of tap water (The waiter may counter with "A bottle?" hoping to sell you something. Be strong and insist on tap water and you'll get it.)
una jarra de agua	pitcher of tap water
refresco	soft drink (common brands are Coca-Cola; Fanta—limón or naranja; and Schweppes—limón or tónica)
mosto	nonalcoholic grape juice served wherever wine is served

INTRODUCTION

un tinto/blanco	small glass of house red/white wine (generally table wine)
un crianza	a glass of aged, quality wine
chato	small glass of house wine
tinto de verano	lighter sangria (more popular with Spaniards than sangria)
vermú	vermouth
mucho cuerpo	full-bodied
afrutado	fruity
seco	dry
dulce	sweet
cerveza	beer
caña	small glass of draft beer
sin	nonalcoholic beer
doble, tubo	tall glass of beer
¡Salud!	Cheers!

Traveling as a Temporary Local

We travel all the way to Spain to enjoy differences—to become temporary locals. You'll experience frustrations. Certain truths that we find "God-given" or "self-evident," such as cold beer, ice in drinks, bottomless cups of coffee, hot showers, and bigger being better, are suddenly not so true. One of the benefits of travel is the eye-opening realization that there are logical, civil, and even better alternatives. A willingness to go local ensures that you'll enjoy a full dose of Spanish hospitality.

Europeans generally like Americans. But if there is a negative aspect to the image the Spanish have of Americans, it's that we are big, loud, aggressive, impolite, rich, and a bit naive.

While Spaniards look bemusedly at some of our Yankee excesses—and worriedly at others—they nearly always afford us individual travelers all the warmth we deserve.

Judging from all the happy feedback I receive from travelers who have used this book, it's safe to assume you'll enjoy a great, affordable vacation—with the finesse of an independent, experienced traveler.

Thanks, and *buen viaje!*

Back Door Travel Philosophy
From *Rick Steves' Europe Through the Back Door*

Travel is intensified living—maximum thrills per minute and one of the last great sources of legal adventure. Travel is freedom. It's recess, and we need it.

Experiencing the real Europe requires catching it by surprise, going casual..."Through the Back Door."

Affording travel is a matter of priorities. (Make do with the old car.) You can eat and sleep—simply, safely, and enjoyably—anywhere in Europe for $120 a day plus transportation costs (allow more for bigger cities). In many ways, spending more money only builds a thicker wall between you and what you traveled so far to see. Europe is a cultural carnival, and time after time, you'll find that its best acts are free and the best seats are the cheap ones.

A tight budget forces you to travel close to the ground, meeting and communicating with the people. Never sacrifice sleep, nutrition, safety, or cleanliness to save money. Simply enjoy the local-style alternatives to expensive hotels and restaurants.

Connecting with people carbonates your experience. Extroverts have more fun. If your trip is low on magic moments, kick yourself and make things happen. If you don't enjoy a place, maybe you don't know enough about it. Seek the truth. Recognize tourist traps. Give a culture the benefit of your open mind. See things as different, but not better or worse. Any culture has plenty to share.

Of course, travel, like the world, is a series of hills and valleys. Be fanatically positive and militantly optimistic. If something's not to your liking, change your liking.

Travel can make you a happier American, as well as a citizen of the world. Our Earth is home to nearly seven billion equally precious people. It's humbling to travel and find that other people don't have the "American Dream"—they have their own dreams. Europeans like us, but with all due respect, they wouldn't trade passports.

Thoughtful travel engages us with the world. In tough economic times, it reminds us what is truly important. By broadening perspectives, travel teaches new ways to measure quality of life.

Globetrotting destroys ethnocentricity, helping us understand and appreciate other cultures. Rather than fear the diversity on this planet, celebrate it. Among your most prized souvenirs will be the strands of different cultures you choose to knit into your own character. The world is a cultural yarn shop, and Back Door travelers are weaving the ultimate tapestry. Join in!

BARCELONA

Barcelona is Spain's second city, and the vibrant capital of the proud and distinct region of Catalunya. Catalan flags wave side by side with the Spanish flag, and both languages—Spanish and Catalan—are spoken almost equally on the streets. The lively, local culture is on an unstoppable roll in Spain's most cosmopolitan and European corner.

Barcelona bubbles with life in its narrow Barri Gòtic alleys, along the pedestrian boulevard called the Ramblas, and throughout the chic, grid-planned new part of town, called Eixample. Its Old City is made for seeing on foot, full of winding lanes that emerge into secluded squares dotted with palm trees and ringed with cafés. The waterfront bristles with new life, overlooked by the park-like setting of Montjuïc. Everywhere you go, you'll find the city's architecture to be colorful, playful, and unique. Rows of symmetrical ironwork balconies are punctuated with fanciful details: bay windows, turrets, painted tiles, hanging lanterns, and carved reliefs.

Barcelona is full of history. You'll see Roman ruins, a medieval cathedral, and traces of Columbus and the sea trade. By the year 1900, the city was a cradle of Modernism, and teenage Picasso was on the verge of reinventing painting. His legacy is today's Picasso Museum, one of the world's best. Antoni Gaudí and fellow Modernist architects remade the city's skyline with curvy, playful fantasy buildings, culminating in Gaudí's over-the-top Sagrada Família, a church still under construction. Barcelona's 20th-century heritage is on display in museums dedicated to hometown boys Joan Miró and Antoni Tapies. And in 1992, Barcelona hosted the Summer Olympics, an event that energized the city and left a legacy of sights.

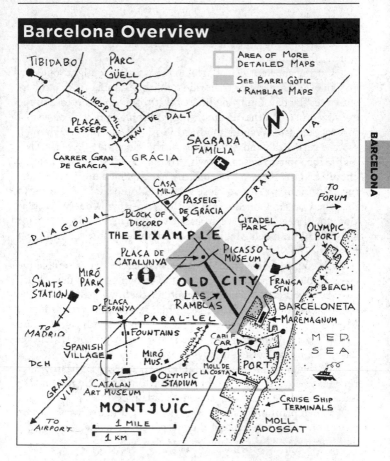

Barcelona Overview

TIBIDABO
PARC GÜELL

AREA OF MORE DETAILED MAPS

SEE BARRI GÒTIC + RAMBLAS MAPS

AV. HOSP. MIL.
PLAÇA LESSEPS
DE DALT
TRAV.
SAGRADA FAMÍLIA
CARRER GRAN DE GRÀCIA
GRÀCIA
CASA MILÀ
PASSEIG DE GRÀCIA
BLOCK OF DISCORD
THE EIXAMPLE
DIAGONAL
GRAN
VIA
TO FORUM
CITADEL PARK
OLYMPIC PORT
PLAÇA DE CATALUNYA
PICASSO MUSEUM
OLD CITY
FRANÇA STN.
BEACH
MIRÓ PARK
SANTS STATION
PLAÇA D'ESPANYA
LAS RAMBLAS
BARCELONETA
MAREMAGNUM
TO MADRID
PARAL-LEL
FOUNTAINS
FUNICULAR
CABLE CAR
M E D. S E A
SPANISH VILLAGE
DCH
MIRÓ MUS.
MOLL DE LA COSTA
PORT
CATALAN ART MUSEUM
OLYMPIC STADIUM
GRAN VIA
MONTJUÏC
CRUISE SHIP TERMINALS
MOLL ADOSSAT
TO AIRPORT
1 MILE
1 KM

BARCELONA

But it's today's Barcelona that has the most charm. They still join hands and dance the everyone's-welcome *sardana* in front of the cathedral. Neighborhood festivals crowd the events calendar. The cafés are filled by day, and people crowd the streets at night, pausing to fortify themselves with seafood and a drink at a tapas bar. If you're in the mood to surrender to a city's charms, let it be in Barcelona.

Planning Your Time

Located in the far northeast corner of Spain, Barcelona makes a good first or last stop for your trip. With the fast AVE train, Barcelona is three hours away from Madrid. Or you could sandwich Barcelona between flights. From the US, it's as easy to fly into Barcelona as it is to land in Madrid, Lisbon, or Paris. Those who plan on renting a car at some point during their trip can start here first, fly or train to Madrid, and sightsee Madrid and Toledo, all before picking up their car—cleverly saving on several days' worth of rental fees.

On the shortest visit, Barcelona is worth one night, one day, and an evening flight or train ride out. The Ramblas is two different streets by day and by night. Stroll it from top to bottom in the evening and again the next morning, grabbing breakfast on a stool in a market café. Wander the Barri Gòtic (BAH-ree GOH-teek), see the cathedral, and have lunch in the Eixample (eye-SHAM-plah). The top two sights in town, Antoni Gaudí's Sagrada Família church and the Picasso Museum, are usually open until 20:00 during the summer (Picasso closed Mon). Note that if you want to tour the Catalan Concert Hall, with its oh-wow Modernista interior, you'll need to reserve at least two days in advance (see page 84). The illuminated Magic Fountains on Montjuïc make a good finale for your day.

Of course, Barcelona in a day is insane. To better sample the city's ample charm, spread your visit over two or three days. With two days, you could divide and conquer the town geographically: one day for the Barri Gòtic (Ramblas, cathedral area, Picasso Museum); and another for the Eixample and Gaudí sights (Casa Milà, Sagrada Família, Parc Güell). Do Montjuïc on whichever day you're not exhausted (if any).

With more time, several tempting day trips await nearby—see the Near Barcelona chapter for tips on Montserrat, Sitges, and the Salvador Dalí sights at Figueres and Cadaqués.

When planning your time, be aware that many top sights are closed on Monday—making them especially crowded on Tuesday and Sunday.

Orientation to Barcelona

Like Los Angeles, Barcelona is a basically flat city that sprawls out under the sun between the sea and the mountains. It's huge (1.6 million people, with about 5 million people in greater Barcelona), but travelers need only focus on four areas: the Old City, the harbor/Barceloneta, the Eixample, and Montjuïc.

A large square, **Plaça de Catalunya,** sits at the center of Barcelona, dividing the older and newer parts of town. Sloping downhill from the Plaça de Catalunya is the Old

City, with the boulevard called the Ramblas running down to the harbor. Above Plaça de Catalunya is the modern residential area called the Eixample. The Montjuïc hill overlooks the harbor. Outside the Old City, Barcelona's sights are widely scattered, but with a map and a willingness to figure out the sleek Metro system (or a few euros for taxis), all is manageable.

Here are more details per neighborhood:

The **Old City** is where you'll probably spend most of your time. This is the compact soul of Barcelona—your strolling, shopping, and people-watching nucleus. It's a labyrinth of narrow streets that once were confined by the medieval walls. The lively pedestrian drag called the **Ramblas**—one of Europe's great people-watching streets—runs through the heart of the Old City from Plaça de Catalunya down to the harbor. The Old City is divided into thirds by the Ramblas and another major thoroughfare, Via Laietana. To the west of the Ramblas is the **Raval,** enlivened by its university and modern-art museum. The Raval is of least interest to tourists (and, in fact, some parts of it are quite seedy and should be avoided). Far better is the **Barri Gòtic** (Gothic Quarter), between the Ramblas and Via Laietana, with the cathedral as its navel. To the east of Via Laietana is the trendy **Ribera** district (a.k.a. "El Born"), centered on the Picasso Museum and the Church of Santa Maria del Mar.

The **harborfront** has been energized since the 1992 Olympics. A pedestrian bridge links the Ramblas with the modern Maremagnum shopping/aquarium complex. On the peninsula across the harbor is **Barceloneta,** a traditional fishing neighborhood that's home to some good seafood restaurants and a string of sandy beaches. Beyond Barceloneta, a man-made beach, several miles long, leads east to the commercial and convention district called the **Fòrum.**

North of the Old City, beyond the bustling hub of Plaça de Catalunya, is the elegant **Eixample** district—its grid plan is softened by cut-off corners. Much of Barcelona's Modernista architecture is found here. To the north is the **Gràcia** district and, beyond that, Antoni Gaudí's **Parc Güell.**

The large hill overlooking the city to the southwest is **Montjuïc,** home to a variety of attractions, including some excellent museums (Catalan Art, Joan Miró) and the Olympic Stadium.

Apart from your geographical orientation, you'll need to orient yourself linguistically to a language distinct from Spanish. Although Spanish ("Castilian"/*castellano*) is widely spoken, the native tongue in this region is Catalan—nearly as different from Spanish as Italian (see the sidebar on page 50).

Tourist Information

Barcelona's TI has several branches. The main one is at **Plaça de Catalunya** (daily 9:00-21:00, under the main square near recommended hotels—look for red sign, tel. 932-853-832). Other convenient branches include at the top of the **Ramblas** (daily 9:00-21:00, at #115); **Plaça de Sant Jaume,** just south of the cathedral (Mon-Fri 8:30-20:00, Sat 9:00-19:00, Sun 10:00-14:00); **Plaça d'Espanya** (daily July-Sept 10:00-20:00, Oct-June 10:00-16:00); the **airport** (daily 9:00-21:00, offices in both sections A and B of terminal 2); **Sants train station** (Mon-Fri 8:00-20:00, Sat-Sun 8:00-14:00, near track 6); **Nord bus station** (daily July-Sept 9:00-21:00, Oct-June 9:00-15:00); and more. Throughout the summer, young red-jacketed tourist-info helpers appear in the most touristy parts of town. The central information number for all TIs is 932-853-834 (www.barcelonaturisme.cat).

At any TI, pick up the free city map (although the free Corte Inglés map provided by most hotels is better), the small Metro map, and the free quarterly *See Barcelona* guide (practical information on museum hours, restaurants, transportation, history, festivals, and so on). The monthly *Barcelona Metropolitan* magazine and quarterly *What's On Barcelona* (both free and in English) have timely and substantial coverage of topics and events. The TI is a handy place to buy tickets for the Tourist Bus (described later, under "Getting Around Barcelona"). Some TIs (at Plaça de Catalunya, Plaça de Sant Jaume, and the airport) also provide a room-booking service.

The main TI, at Plaça de Catalunya, offers guided walks (described later, under "Tours in Barcelona"). Its Modernisme desk gives out a handy route map showing all the Modernista buildings and offers a sightseeing discount package (€12 for a great guidebook and 20 percent discounts to many Modernisme sites—worthwhile if going beyond my big three; for €18 you'll also get a guidebook to Modernista bars and restaurants).

The **all-Catalunya TI** works fine for the entire region, and even Madrid (Mon-Sat 10:00-19:00, Sun 10:00-14:00, on Plaça de Joan Carlos I, at the intersection of Diagonal and Passeig de Gràcia, Passeig de Gràcia 107, tel. 932-388-091).

Articket Card: This ticket includes admission to seven art museums and their temporary exhibits, including the recommended Picasso Museum, Casa Milà, Catalan Art Museum, and Fundació Joan Miró (€22, valid for six months, sold at TIs and participating museums, www.articketbcn.org). If you're planning to go to three or more of the museums, this time-saver pays for itself. To skip the ticket-buying line at a museum, show your Articket Card (to the ticket-taker, at the info desk, or at the group entrance), and you'll get your entrance ticket pronto.

Barcelona Card: This card covers public transportation

(buses, Metro, Montjuïc funicular, and *golondrina* harbor tour) and includes free admission to minor sights and discounts on major sights (€27.50/2 days, €33.50/3 days, €38/4 days, €45/5 days, sold at TIs and El Corte Inglés department store).

Arrival in Barcelona
By Train

Virtually all trains end up at Barcelona's Sants train station (described below). But be aware that many trains also pass through other stations en route, such as **França Station** (between the Ribera and Barceloneta neighborhoods), or the downtown **Passeig de Gràcia** or **Plaça de Catalunya** stations (which are also Metro stops—and very close to most of my recommended hotels). Figure out which stations your train stops at, and get off at the one most convenient to your hotel. (AVE trains from Madrid go only to Sants Station.)

Sants Station is vast and sprawling, but manageable. In the large lobby area under the upper tracks, you'll find a TI; ATMs; a world of handy shops and eateries; and a classy, quiet Sala Euromed lounge for travelers with first-class reservations (TV, free drinks, study tables, and coffee bar). Sants is the only Barcelona station with luggage storage (small bag-€3/day, big bag-€4.50/day, requires security check, daily 5:30-23:00, follow signs to *consigna*, at far end of hallway from tracks 13-14).

There's also a long wall of ticket windows. Figure out which is right for you before you wait in line (all are labeled in English). Generally, windows 1-10 (on the left) are for local trains, such as to Sitges; windows 11-21 handle advance tickets for long-distance trains; the information windows are 23-26—go here first if you're not sure which window you want; windows 27-31 sell tickets for long-distance trains leaving today. The two information booths by windows 1 and 21 can help you find the right line and can provide some train schedules. If you know what you want, there are also automated train-ticket vending machines for mid-distance trains *(media distancia)*, just beyond window 1. If you made online reservations in advance and have a confirmation code for long-distance trains, you can print your tickets at the purple ATM-like machines, but you can't buy tickets from them.

To get into downtown Barcelona from Sants Station, simply follow signs for the Metro. The L3 (green) line zips you directly to a number of useful points in town, including all of my recommended hotels. Alternatively, local trains leave from track 8 for Plaça de Catalunya (catch *cercanías* lines C1, C3, C4, or C7). Purchase tickets for the trains or Metro (€1.45) at touch-screen machines near the tracks (where you can also buy the cost-saving T10 Card, explained on page 45).

If departing from the downtown **Passeig de Gràcia Station,** where three Metro lines converge with the rail line, you might find the underground tunnels confusing. You can't access the RENFE Station directly from some of the entrances. Use the northern entrances to this station (rather than the southern "Consell de Cent" entrance, which is closest to Plaça de Catalunya).

By Plane

Barcelona's **El Prat de Llobregat Airport,** eight miles southwest of town, has two large terminals: 1 and 2. Terminal 2 is divided into sections A, B, and C. Terminal 1 and the bigger sections of terminal 2 (A and B) each have a post office, a pharmacy, a left-luggage office, plenty of good cafeterias in the gate areas, and ATMs (avoid the gimmicky machines before the baggage carousels; instead, use the bank-affiliated ATMs at the far-left end of the arrivals hall as you face the street). Airport info tel. 913-211-000, www.aena.es.

You have two options for getting downtown cheaply and quickly: The **Aerobus** (#A1 and #A2, corresponding with terminals 1 and 2) stops immediately outside the arrivals lobby of both terminals (and in each section of terminal 2). In about 30 minutes, it takes you to downtown, where it makes several stops, including Plaça d'Espanya and Plaça de Catalunya—near many of my recommended hotels (departs every 6 minutes, from airport 6:00-1:00 in the morning, from downtown 5:30-24:15, €5.30 one-way, €9.15 round-trip, buy ticket from machine or from driver, tel. 934-156-020). The line to board the bus can be very long, but—thanks to the high frequency of buses—it moves fast.

The second option from terminal 2 is the RENFE *cercanías* **train,** which involves more walking. Head down the long orange-roofed overpass between sections A and B to reach the station (2/hour at about :08 and :38 past the hour, 20 minutes to Sants Station, 25 minutes to Passeig de Gràcia Station—near Plaça de Catalunya and many recommended hotels, 30 minutes to França Station; €3 or covered by T10 Card, which you can purchase at automated machines at the airport train station). Long-term plans call for the RENFE *cercanías* train and eventually the AVE to be extended to terminal 1, and for the Metro's L9 (orange) line to be extended to both terminals 1 and 2. Stay tuned.

A **taxi** between the airport and downtown costs about €30—about €25 on the meter plus a €3.10 airport supplement and fee of €1 per bag. For good service, add an additional 10 percent tip (or €33 total).

Some budget airlines, including Ryanair, use **Girona–Costa Brava Airport,** located 60 miles north of Barcelona near Girona. Sagalés buses link to Barcelona (departures timed to meet flights, 1.25 hours, €12, tel. 935-931-300 or 902-361-550, www.sagales .com). You can also go to Girona on a Sagalés bus (hourly, 25 minutes, €3) or a taxi (€25), then catch a train to Barcelona (at least hourly, 1.25 hours, €15-20). A taxi between the Girona airport and Barcelona costs at least €120. Airport info tel. 972-186-600.

By Car

Barcelona's parking fees are outrageously expensive (the lot behind La Boquería market charges upward of €25/day). You won't need a car in Barcelona, because the taxis and public transportation are so good.

By Cruise Ship

Cruise ships arrive in Barcelona at seven different terminals, spread among three different ports (all just southwest of the Old City, beneath Montjuïc).

Most American cruise lines put in at **Moll Adossat/Muelle Adosado,** a long two miles from the bottom of the Ramblas. This port has four modern, airport-like terminals (lettered A through D); most have a café and shops; some have Internet access and other services). Another terminal, **Moll de la Costa,** is tucked just beneath Montjuïc. The **World Trade Center,** just off the southern end of the Ramblas, has two terminals: Terminal N (north) and Terminal S (south).

From any of the cruise terminals, it's easy to reach the Ramblas.

Taxis meet each arriving ship and are waiting as you exit any of the terminal buildings. The short trip into town (i.e., to the bottom of the Ramblas) runs about €10. During high season, a ride into town can take longer and cost €10 more. For a one-way journey to other parts of town, expect to pay these fares: to the Picasso Museum or Plaça de Catalunya—€15; to the Sagrada Família—€20; and to the airport—€35-40.

Getting to the sights via **public transportation** requires heading to the Columbus Monument at the bottom of the Ramblas. From Moll Adossat/Muelle Adosado take the shuttle bus (*lanzadera*, #T3, a.k.a. Portbús, departs from parking lot in front of terminal—follow *Public Bus* signs, €3 round-trip, €2 one-way, buses leave every 20-30 minutes, timed to cruise ship arrival, tel. 932-986-000). The shuttle drops you right at the Columbus Monument; pay careful attention to where they drop you off if you want to catch the return bus later.

If you arrive at Moll de la Costa, you're not allowed to walk through the port area. You'll ride a free, private shuttle bus to the World Trade Center. From the World Trade Center, you can easily walk into town: Head straight up the wide pier for about five minutes, bear right along the waterfront (walking alongside the long sandstone building), and you'll pop out at the Columbus Monument. From there you can connect—by foot, Metro, or bus—to wherever you're going in town (see "Getting Around Barcelona," later).

Barcelona attracts more than one million cruise passengers every year. If your trip includes cruising beyond Barcelona, consider my new guidebook, *Rick Steves' Mediterranean Cruise Ports*.

Helpful Hints

Theft Alert: You're more likely to be pickpocketed here—especially on the Ramblas—than about anywhere else in Europe. Most of the crime is nonviolent, but muggings do occur. Leave valuables in your hotel and wear a money belt.

Street scams are easy to avoid if you recognize them. Most common is the too-friendly local who tries to engage you in conversation by asking for the time, talking sports, asking whether you speak English, and so on. Beware of thieves posing as lost tourists who ask for your help. A typical street gambling scam is the pea-and-carrot game, a variation on the shell game. The people winning are all ringers, and you can be sure that you'll lose if you play. Also beware of groups of women aggressively selling carnations, people offering to clean off a stain from your shirt, and people picking things up in front of you on escalators. If you stop for any commotion or show on the Ramblas, put your hands in your pockets before someone else does. Assume any scuffle is simply a distraction by a team of thieves. Crooks are inventive, so keep your guard up. Don't be intimidated...just be smart.

Some areas feel seedy and can be unsafe after dark; I'd avoid the southern part of the Barri Gòtic (basically the two or three blocks directly south and east of Plaça Reial—though the strip near the Carrer de la Mercè tapas bars is better), and I wouldn't venture too deep into the Raval (just west of the Ramblas). One block can separate a comfy tourist zone from the junkies and prostitutes.

US Consulate: It's at Passeig Reina Elisenda 23 (passport services Mon-Fri 9:00-13:00, closed Sat-Sun, tel. 932-802-227, after-hours emergency tel. 915-872-200).

Emergency Phone Numbers: General emergencies—112, police—092, ambulance—061 or 112.

Sight Reservations: To avoid standing in long lines, call or go online to book ahead for the Picasso Museum (see page 78), Sagrada Família (see page 93), Casa Batlló (see page 91), and Casa Milà (see page 88). An Articket Card (described earlier) allows you to skip the lines at the Picasso Museum and Casa Milà, but not at Sagrada Família or Casa Batlló. To tour the Catalan Concert Hall, you'll need to reserve at least two days in advance (see page 84).

Internet Access: Navega Web has hundreds of computers for accessing the Internet and burning pictures onto a disk. It's conveniently located across from La Boquería market, downstairs in the bright Centre Comercial New Park (daily 10:00-24:00, Ramblas 88-94, tel. 933-179-193).

Pharmacy: A 24-hour pharmacy is near La Boquería market at #98 on the Ramblas.

Laundry: Several self-service launderettes are located around the Old City. **Wash 'n Dry** is on the edge of the tourist zone, near a seedy neighborhood just down the street past the Palau Güell (self-service: wash-€5/load, dry-€2/load, daily 7:00-22:00; full-service: €15/load, daily 9:00-14:00 & 16:00-22:00; Carrer Nou de la Rambla 19, tel. 934-121-953).

Bike Rental: Biking is a joy in Citadel Park, the Eixample, and along the beach (suggested route described on page 86)—but it's stressful in the city center, where pedestrians and cars rule. There are plenty of bike-rental places around Citadel Park and La Ribera's Church of Santa Maria del Mar. The handy **Un Cotxe Menys** ("One Car Less"), near the Church of Santa Maria del Mar (50 yards behind the flame memorial), rents bikes and gives out maps and suggested biking routes (€5/hour, €10/4 hours, €18/24 hours, daily 10:00-19:00, leave €150 or photo ID for deposit, Esparteria 3, tel. 932-682-105, www .bicicletabarcelona.com); they also lead bike tours (see "Tours in Barcelona," later).

To rent a bike on the Barceloneta beach, consider **Biciclot** (€6/hour, €13/3 hours, €18/24 hours; summer Mon-Thu 10:00-15:00 & 16:00-20:00, Fri-Sun 10:00-15:00 & 16:00-21:00; off-season Sat-Sun only; on the sand 300 yards from Olympic Village towers at Passeig Maritime 33, tel. 932-219-778). Closer to downtown, **Barcelona Rent-A-Bike** is three blocks downhill from Plaça de Catalunya (€6/2 hours, €10/4 hours, €15/24 hours, daily 9:00-20:00, inside the courtyard at Carrer dels Tallers 45, tel. 933-171-970).

Getting Around Barcelona

By Metro: Barcelona's Metro, among Europe's best, connects just about every place you'll visit. Rides cost €1.45. The T10 Card is a great deal—€8.25 gives you 10 rides (cutting the per-ride cost

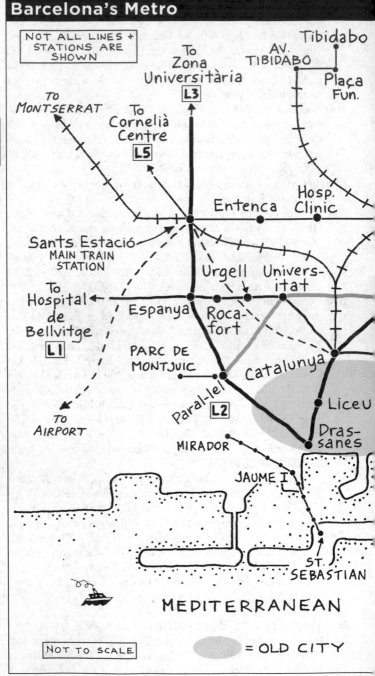

Barcelona's Metro

NOT ALL LINES +
STATIONS ARE
SHOWN

To Zona Universitària **L3**

To Cornelià Centre **L5**

To MONTSERRAT

To Hospital de Bellvitge **L1**

Sants Estació
MAIN TRAIN STATION

Espanya

To AIRPORT

PARC DE MONTJUIC

Urgell

Roca-fort

Universi-tat

Entenca

Hosp. Clinic

Av. TIBIDABO

Tibidabo

Plaça Fun.

Paral-lel **L2**

Catalunya

Liceu

Dras-sanes

MIRADOR

JAUME I

ST. SEBASTIAN

MEDITERRANEAN

NOT TO SCALE

= OLD CITY

BARCELONA

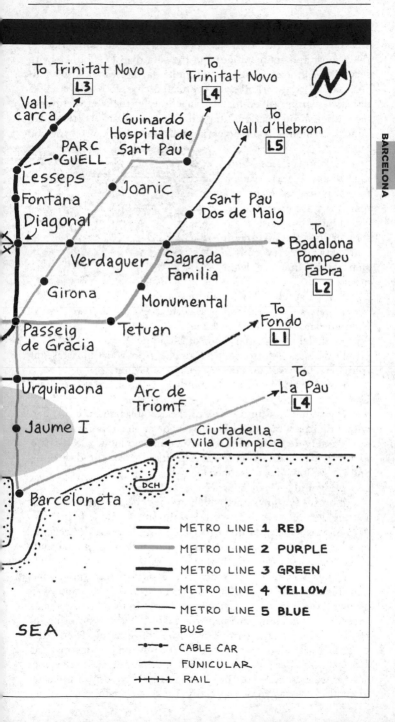

nearly in half), and the card is shareable. It's good on all Metro and local bus lines as well as the RENFE train lines (including rides to the airport and train station) and the suburban FGC lines (with service to Montserrat). Full- and multi-day passes are also available (€6.20/1 day, €11.50/2 days, €16.50/3 days, €21/4 days, €25/5 days, www.tmb.cat). Automated machines at the Metro entrance have English instructions and sell all types of tickets (these can be temperamental about accepting bills, so try to have change on hand).

Pick up the free Metro map (at any TI) and study it to get familiar with the system. There are several color-coded lines, but most useful for tourists is the **L3 (green)** line. Handy city-center stops on this line include (in order):

Sants Estació—Main train station

Espanya—Plaça d'Espanya, with access to the lower part of Montjuïc and trains to Montserrat

Paral-lel—Funicular to top of Montjuïc

Drassanes—Bottom of the Ramblas, near Maritime Museum, Maremagnum mall, and the cable car up to Montjuïc

Liceu—Middle of the Ramblas, near the heart of the Barri Gòtic and cathedral

Plaça de Catalunya—Top of the Ramblas and main square with TI, airport bus, and lots of transportation connections

Passeig de Gràcia—Classy Eixample street at the Block of Discord; also connection to L2 (purple) line to Sagrada Família and L4 (yellow) line (described below)

Diagonal—Gaudí's Casa Milà

The **L4 (yellow)** line, which crosses the L3 (green) line at Passeig de Gràcia, is also useful. Helpful stops include **Joanic** (bus #116 to Parc Güell), **Jaume I** (between the Barri Gòtic/cathedral and La Ribera/Picasso Museum), and **Barceloneta** (at the south end of the Ribera, near the harbor action).

When you enter the Metro, first look for your line number and color, then follow signs to take that line in the direction you're going. The names of the end stops are used to indicate directions. Insert your ticket into the turnstile (with the arrow pointing in), then reclaim it. On board, most trains have handy Metro-line diagrams with dots that light up next to upcoming destinations. Because the lines cross one another multiple times, there can be several ways to make any one journey. (It's a good idea to keep a general map with you—especially if you're transferring.) Watch your valuables. If I were a pickpocket, I'd set up shop along the made-for-tourists L3 (green) line.

By Public Bus: Given the excellent Metro service, it's unlikely you'll take a local bus (also €1.45 or covered by T10 Card, insert ticket in machine behind driver), although I've noted places where the bus makes sense. In particular, bus #50 is good for a tour of Gràcia and Montjuïc (see page 53).

By Tourist Bus: The handy hop-on, hop-off Tourist Bus (Bus Turístic) offers three multi-stop circuits in colorful double-decker

buses that go topless in sunny weather. The two-hour blue route covers north Barcelona (most Gaudí sights); the two-hour red route covers south Barcelona (Barri Gòtic, Montjuïc); and the shorter, 40-minute green route covers the beaches and Fòrum. All have headphone commentary (44 stops, daily 9:00-22:00 in summer, 9:00-21:00 in winter, buses run every 5-25 minutes, most frequent in summer, no green route Oct-March). Ask for a brochure (includes city map) at the

TI or at a pick-up point. One-day (€23) and two-day (€30) tickets, which you can buy on the bus or at the TI, offer 10-20 percent discounts on the city's major sights and walking tours, which will likely save you about the equivalent of half the cost of the Tourist Bus. From Plaça de Catalunya, the blue northern route leaves from El Corte Inglés; the red southern route leaves from the west—Ramblas—side of the square (www.barcelonabusturistic.cat).

By Taxi: Barcelona is one of Europe's best taxi towns. Taxis are plentiful (there are more than 10,000) and honest (whether they like it or not—the light on top shows which tariff they're charging). They're also reasonable (€2 drop charge, €1/kilometer, these *"Tarif 2"* rates are in effect 7:00-21:00, pay higher *"Tarif 1"* rates off-hours, luggage-€1/piece, other fees posted in window). Save time by hopping a cab (figure €10 from Ramblas to Sants Station).

Tours in Barcelona

Walking Tours—The TI at Plaça de Sant Jaume offers great guided walks through the **Barri Gòtic** in English only (€13, daily at 10:00, 2 hours, groups limited to 35, buy your ticket 15 minutes early at the TI desk—not from the guide, in summer call ahead to reserve, tel. 932-853-832, www.barcelonaturisme.cat). A local guide will explain the medieval story of the city as you walk from Plaça de Sant Jaume through the cathedral neighborhood.

The TI at Plaça de Catalunya offers a **Picasso** walk, taking

"You're not in Spain, You're in Catalunya!"

This is a popular nationalistic refrain you might see on T-shirts or stickers around town. Catalunya is *not* the land of bullfight-ing and flamenco that many visi-tors envision when they think of Spain (best to wait until you're in Madrid or Sevilla for those).

The region of Catalunya—with Barcelona as its capital—has its own language, history, and culture, and the people have a proud, independent spirit. Historically, Catalunya ("Cataluña" in Spanish, some-times spelled "Catalonia" in English) has often been at odds with the central Spanish government in Madrid. The Catalan language and culture were discouraged or even outlawed at various times in Spanish history, as Catalunya often chose the wrong side in wars and rebellions against the kings in Madrid. In the Spanish Civil War (1936-1939), Catalunya was one of the last pockets of democratic resistance against the military coup of the fascist dictator Francisco Franco, who punished the region with four decades of repression. During that time, the Catalan flag was banned—but locals vented their national spirit by flying their football team's flag instead.

Three of Barcelona's monuments are reminders of royal and Franco-era suppression. Citadel Park (Parc de la Ciutadella) was originally a much-despised military citadel, constructed in the 18th century to keep locals in line. The Castle of Montjuïc, built for similar reasons, has been the site of numerous political exe-cutions, including hundreds during the Franco era. The Sacred Heart Church atop Tibidabo, completed under Franco, was meant to atone for the sins of Barcelonans during the Spanish Civil War—the main sin being opposition to Franco. Although rivalry between Barcelona and Madrid has calmed down in recent times, it rages any time the two cities' football clubs meet.

you through the streets of his youth and early career and finish-ing in the Picasso Museum (€19.50, includes museum admission; Tue, Thu, and Sat at 16:00; 2 hours plus museum visit). There are also **gourmet** walks (€19.50, Fri and Sat at 10:00, 2 hours) and **Modernisme** walks (€13, Fri and Sat June-Sept at 18:00, Oct-May at 15:00, 2 hours). These tours depart from the TI at Plaça de Catalunya.

Guided Bus Tours—The Barcelona Guide Bureau offers several sightseeing tours leaving from Plaça de Catalunya. Departure times can vary—confirm locally. The **Gaudí** tour visits the facades of

To see real Catalan culture, look for the *sardana* dance (described on page 76) or an exhibition of *castellers*. These teams of human-castle builders come together for festivals throughout the year to build towers of flesh that can reach more than 50 feet high, topped off by the bravest member of the team—a child! The Gràcia festival in August and the Mercè festival in September are good times to catch the *castellers*.

The Catalan language is irrevocably tied to the history and spirit of the people here. Since the end of the Franco era in the mid-1970s, the language has made a huge resurgence. Now most school-age children learn Catalan first and Spanish second. While all Barcelonans still speak Spanish (and the basic survival words are the same), nearly all understand Catalan, three-quarters speak Catalan, and half can write it.

Here are the essential Catalan phrases:

English	Catalan	Pronounced
Hello	*Hola*	OH-lah
Please	*Si us plau*	see oos plow
Thank you	*Gracies*	GRAH-see-es
Goodbye	*Adéu*	ah-DAY-oo
Exit	*Sortida*	sor-TEE-dah
Long live Catalunya!	*¡Visca Catalunya!*	BEE-skah kah-tah-LOON-yah

Most place names in this chapter are listed in Catalan. Here's a pronunciation guide:

Plaça de Catalunya	PLAS-sah duh kah-tah-LOON-yah
Eixample	eye-SHAM plah
Passeig de Gràcia	PAH-sage duh grass-EE-ah
Catedral	KAH-tah-dral
Barri Gòtic	BAH-ree GOH-teek
Montjuïc	MOHN-jew-eek

Casa Batlló and Casa Milà, as well as Parc Güell and the Sagrada Família (€45, includes Sagrada Família admission, daily at 9:00, also mid-April-Oct Mon-Sat at 15:15, 3 hours). Other tours offered year-round include the **Montjuïc** tour (€33, includes Spanish Village admission, daily at 12:00, 3 hours); the **All Barcelona Highlights** tour (€60, includes Sagrada Família and Spanish Village admissions, daily at 9:00, 6 hours); and the **Montserrat** tour (€40, Mon-Sat at 15:00, 4 hours), which offers a convenient way to get to this mountaintop monastery if you don't want to deal with public transportation (see Near Barcelona chapter). During

Barcelona at a Glance

▲▲▲**Ramblas** Barcelona's colorful, gritty, tourist-filled pedestrian thoroughfare. **Hours:** Always open. See page 54.

▲▲▲**Picasso Museum** Extensive collection offering insight into the brilliant Spanish artist's early years. **Hours:** Tue-Sun 10:00-20:00, closed Mon. See page 78.

▲▲▲**Sagrada Família** Gaudí's remarkable, unfinished cathedral. **Hours:** Daily April-Sept 9:00-20:00, Oct-March 9:00-18:00. See page 93.

▲▲**City History Museum** One-stop trip through town history, from Roman times to today. **Hours:** Tue-Sat April-Oct 10:00-19:00, Nov-March 10:00-17:00, Sun 10:00-20:00, closed Mon. See page 77.

▲▲**Catalan Concert Hall** Best Modernista interior in Barcelona. **Hours:** 50-minute English tours daily every hour 10:00-15:00, plus frequent concerts. See page 84.

▲▲**Casa Milà** Barcelona's quintessential Modernista building, the famous melting-ice-cream Gaudí creation. **Hours:** Daily March-Oct 9:00-20:00, Nov-Feb 9:00-18:30. See page 88.

▲▲**Catalan Art Museum** World-class collection of this region's art, including a substantial Romanesque collection. **Hours:** Tue-Sat 10:00-19:00, Sun 10:00-14:30, closed Mon. See page 106.

▲**Maritime Museum** Housed in an impressive medieval shipyard, it's a sailor's delight. **Hours:** Most exhibits closed for renovation, others daily 10:00-20:00. See page 69.

▲**Columbus Monument** Elevator ride to the best easy view in town. **Hours:** Daily May-Oct 9:00-20:30, Nov-April 10:00-18:30. See page 71.

the high season, there's also the **Gaudí Plus** tour, which combines the Gaudí tour with some "off-the-beaten-path masterpieces" (€52, mid-April-Oct Mon-Sat at 9:00, 4 hours). You can get detailed information and book tickets at a TI, on their website, or simply by showing up at their departure point on Plaça de Catalunya in front of the Hard Rock Café—look for the guides holding orange umbrellas. Buying tickets online can save you a few euros—usually about 10 percent. You can also buy tickets at many hotels for no

▲**Cathedral of Barcelona** Colossal Gothic cathedral ringed by distinctive chapels. **Hours:** Mon-Fri 8:00-12:45 & 17:15-19:30, Sat 8:00-12:45 & 17:15-20:00, Sun 8:00-13:45 & 17:15-20:00. See page 72.

▲*Sardana* **Dances** Patriotic dance in which proud Catalans join hands in a circle. **Hours:** Every Sun at 12:00, usually also Sat at 18:00, no dances in Aug. See page 76.

▲**Church of Santa Maria del Mar** Catalan Gothic church in La Ribera, built by wealthy medieval shippers. **Hours:** Daily 9:00-13:30 & 16:30-20:00. See page 84.

▲**Barcelona's Beach** Fun-filled, man-made stretch of sand reaching from the harbor to the Fòrum. **Hours:** Always open. See page 86.

▲**Block of Discord** Noisy block of competing Modernista facades by Gaudí and his rivals. **Hours:** Always viewable. See page 90.

▲**Palau Güell** Exquisitely curvy Gaudí interior and fantasy rooftop. **Hours:** Tue-Sun April-Sept 10:00-20:00, Oct-March 10:00-17:30, closed Mon. See page 92.

▲**Parc Güell** Colorful park at the center of an unfinished Gaudí-designed housing project. **Hours:** Daily 10:00-20:00. See page 101.

▲**Fundació Joan Miró** World's best collection of works by Catalan modern artist Joan Miró. **Hours:** Tue-Sat July-Sept 10:00-20:00, Oct-June 10:00-19:00, Thu until 21:30, Sun 10:00-14:30, closed Mon. See page 104.

▲**Magic Fountains** Lively fountains near Plaça d'Espanya. **Hours:** Almost always May-Sept Thu-Sun 21:00-23:30, no shows Mon-Wed; Oct-April Fri-Sat 19:00-21:00, no shows Sun-Thu. See page 107.

extra charge (tel. 933-152-261, www.barcelonaguidebureau.com). **Bus #50 Self-Guided Tour**—Taking bus #50 (€1.45 or use T10 card) gives you an inexpensive, 45-minute tour through Gràcia and Montjuïc. You can catch bus #50 at the Sagrada Família along Carrer de Mallorca (around the right from the church's ticket entrance). Grab a seat on the right side of the bus. You'll wind through Gràcia's streets down to the Gran Via de les Corts Catalanes, crossing the Passeig de Gràcia (a block away from Plaça de Catalunya). Enjoy the long blocks of Gràcia until you reach Plaça d'Espanya, where on the right you'll see Barcelona's bullring (which is being turned into a mall). You'll go through the two towers of Plaça d'Espanya, with the Catalan Art Museum on the hill in front of you. Then you'll loop through the hills of Montjuïc, passing the Spanish Village, the site of the '92 Olympics (with the communications tower and stadium), the Fundació Joan Miró, and the funicular and cable car up to the Castle of Montjuïc. The end of the line is about a block away from the funicular. From here you can walk back to the Joan Miró or Catalan Art museums; or continue in the direction of the bus route down the hill to a different cable car, which takes you to the Barceloneta area.

Bike Tours—Several companies run bike tours around Barcelona. **Un Cotxe Menys** ("One Car Less") organizes three-hour English-only bike tours daily at 11:00 (April-mid-Sept also Fri-Mon at 16:30). Your guide leads you from sight to sight, mostly on bike paths and through parks, with a stop-and-go commentary (€22 includes bike rental and drink, no reservations needed, see bike-rental listing earlier, under "Helpful Hints").

Local Guides—The Barcelona Guide Bureau is a co-op with about 20 local guides who give personalized four-hour tours (weekdays-€216, per-person price drops as group gets bigger; weekends and holidays-€256, no price break with size of group); **Joana Wilhelm** and **Carles Picazo** are excellent (Via Laietana 54, tel. 932-682-422 or 933-107-778, www.bgb.es). **Jose Soler** is a great and fun-to-be-with local guide who enjoys tailoring a walk through his hometown to your interests (€195/half-day per group, mobile 615-059-326, www.pepitotours.com, info@pepitotours.com).

Self-Guided Walks

These walks through the atmospheric Old City introduce you to places you may want to explore further. They're easy to follow, pass by some major sights, and provide background to this complex metropolis. The first begins at Barcelona's main square and leads you down the city's main drag: the Ramblas. The second walk guides you into the heart of the Barri Gòtic, the neighborhood around Barcelona's impressive cathedral.

▲▲▲The Ramblas Ramble: From Plaça de Catalunya to the Waterfront

For over a century, this walk down Barcelona's main boulevard has drawn locals and visitors alike. While its former elegance has been tackified somewhat by tourist shops and fast-food joints, this is still the best place to see the city in action. Walk the Ramblas at least once to get the lay of the land, then venture farther afield.

The Ramblas Ramble

Legend:
- Ramblas
- Ramblas Walk
- Ⓜ Metro Station
- Ⓑ Bus Stop

RONDA

TO BLOCK OF DISCORD + CASA MILÀ

PLAÇA DE CATALUNYA

EL CORTE INGLÉS DEP'T. STORE

BERGARA

FNAC

FGC TRAIN INFO

START

Ⓑ BUS TO AIRPORT (+ TAXIS)

Ⓜ Catalunya

PORTAL DE L'ANGEL

BARCELONA

BONSUCCES

SANTA ANNA

CLOCK

XUCLA

PINTOR

FORT.

ROMAN NECRO-POLIS

CANUDA

CAFÉ GRANJA VIADER

CARME

PORTAFERRISSA

CULTURAL INFO PALAU DE LA VIRREINA

ARCS

PL. NOVA

PALLA

TO CATHEDRAL

LA BOQUERÍA MARKET

Ⓜ Liceu

CIGARS

EROTIC

DEL PI

U. CARD.

PL. PI

MIRO MOSAIC

NOUS

BANYS

S. MARIA DEL PI

Liceu Ⓜ

DRAGON

SANT PAU

BOQUERIA

CAFÉ DE OPERA

TO PLAÇA S. JAUME

LICEU OPERA HOUSE

CARRER FERRAN

D'AVINYO

NOU RAMBLA

PLAÇA REIAL

200 YARDS

PALAU GÜELL

HERB. FERRAN

PL. ORWELL

200 METERS

L'ARC TEATRE

ESCUDELLERS

CODOLS

SKY-SCRAPER

PROST. MARKS

NOU SAN FRAN

MARITIME MUSEUM

Ⓜ Drassanes

MUSEU DE CERA

PL. MED.

CLAVE

PASSEIG DE COLÓM

COLUMBUS MONUMENT

FINISH

MOLL DE BOSCH

SHUTTLE BUS FOR MOLL ADOSSAT

HARBOR

GOLONDRINAS CRUISES

RAMBLA DE MAR

TO MAREMAGNUM

Points of interest:
1. Plaça de Catalunya
2. Fountain of Canaletes
3. Rambla of the Little Birds
4. Betlem Church
5. Rambla of Flowers
6. La Boqueria
7. Liceu—Heart of the Ramblas
8. Plaça Reial
9. The Raval Neighborhood
10. Columbus Monument & Waterfront

EL RAVAL

It's a one-hour, downhill stroll, with an easy way to get back by Metro.

This pedestrian-only Champs-Elysées takes you from rich (at the top) to rough (at the port). You'll raft the river of Barcelonese

life past a grand opera house, elegant cafés, flower stands, retread prostitutes, brazen pickpockets, power-dressing con men, artists, street mimes, an outdoor bird market, great shopping, and people looking to charge more for a shoeshine than what you paid for the shoes.

The word "Ramblas" is plural, and the street is actually a succession of five separately named segments. But street signs and addresses treat it as a single long street—"La Rambla," singular. *Rambla* means "stream" in Arabic, and it used to be a drainage ditch along the medieval wall of the Barri Gòtic (Gothic Quarter). Today that "stream" has become a river of humanity.

• *Start your ramble at the top of the Ramblas, where it connects with Plaça de Catalunya.*

❶ **Plaça de Catalunya:** Dotted with fountains, statues, and pigeons, and ringed by grand Art Deco buildings, this plaza is

Barcelona's center. It's the hub for the Metro, bus, airport shuttle, and Tourist Bus. It's where Barcelona congregates to watch soccer matches on the big screen, to demonstrate, to celebrate, and to enjoy outdoor concerts and festivals. It's the center of the

world for seven million Catalan people.

Geographically, the 12-acre square links old Barcelona (the narrow streets to the south) with the new (the broad boulevards to the north). Four great thoroughfares radiate from here. The Ramblas is the popular pedestrian promenade. Passeig de Gràcia has fashionable shops and cafés (and noisy traffic). Rambla de Catalunya is equally fashionable but cozier and more pedestrian-friendly. Avinguda Portal de l'Angel (shopper-friendly and traffic-free) leads to the Barri Gòtic.

Historically, Plaça de Catalunya links the modern city with its past. In the 1850s, when Barcelona tore down its medieval walls to expand the city, this square on the edge of the walls was one of the first places to be developed.

Overlooking the square, the huge **El Corte Inglés** department store offers everything from bonsai trees to a travel agency, haircuts, and cheap souvenirs—get the complete list by picking up an English directory at their info desk. There's a supermarket in the basement and a ninth-floor view café (Mon-Sat 10:00-22:00, closed Sun). Across the square is **FNAC,** a French department store popular for electronics, music, and books. It also sells tickets for major concerts and events (Mon-Sat 10:00-22:00, closed Sun).

In case you're wondering, the odd, inverted-staircase statue in the square honors a former president of Catalunya. It was designed by the sculptor Josep María Subirachs, whose work you'll see at the Sagrada Família (see page 93). The venerable Café Zürich, at the corner of the square near the Ramblas, is a popular downtown rendezvous spot for locals. Homesick Americans might prefer the nearby Hard Rock Café.

• *Start heading down the Ramblas, and pause 20 yards down at the ornate lamppost with a fountain as its base (near #129).*

❷ **Fountain of Canaletes:** This black-and-gold drinking fountain has been a local favorite for over a century. When Barcelona tore down its medieval wall and transformed the Ramblas from a drainage ditch into an elegant promenade, this fountain was one of its early attractions. Legend says that a drink from the fountain ensures that you'll return to Barcelona one day.

It's still a popular let's-meet-at-the fountain rendezvous spot and a gathering place for celebrations and demonstrations. Fans of the Barcelona soccer team rally here before a big match—some touch their hand to their lips, then "kiss" the fountain with their hand for good luck.

Continue downhill. All along the Ramblas, you'll see newspaper stands (open 24 hours, selling phone cards). Among their souvenirs, you'll see soccer paraphernalia, especially the scarlet-and-blue of FC Barcelona (known as "Barça"). You'll also pass ONCE booths. All over town, these sell lottery tickets that support Spain's organization of the blind, a powerful advocate for the needs of people with disabilities.

Got some change? As you wander downhill, drop coins into the cans of the human statues (the money often kicks them into entertaining gear). If you take a photo, it's considered good etiquette to drop in a coin. Warning: Wherever people stop to gawk, pickpockets are at work.

• *Walk 100 yards downhill to #115 and the...*

❸ **Rambla of the Little Birds:** Traditionally, kids bring their parents here to buy pets, especially on Sundays. Apartment-dwellers find birds, turtles, fish, hamsters, and rabbits easier to handle than dogs and cats. If you're walking by at night, you'll hear the sad sounds of little tweety birds locked up in their collapsed kiosks.

The Academy of Science's clock (at #115) marks official Barcelona time—synchronize. The Carrefour Express supermarket has cheap groceries (at #113, Mon-Sat 10:00-22:00, closed Sun, shorter checkout lines in back of store).

At #122 (the big, modern Citadines Hotel), a 100-yard detour through the passageway leads to a recently discovered **Roman necropolis.** Here you can look down and imagine the tomb-lined road leading into the Roman city of Barcino 2,000 years ago.

• *Backtrack to the Ramblas and continue down another 100 yards. At Carrer del Carme (at #105), look over your right shoulder at the main entrance to the...*

❹ **Betlem Church:** This 17th-century church is Baroque; check out its sloping roofline, ball-topped pinnacles, corkscrew

columns, and scrolls above the entrance. Baroque is unusual in Barcelona; the city's heyday was during the medieval period. After 1500, the city's importance dropped when New World discoveries shifted lucra-tive trade to ports on the Atlantic. The church is dedicated to Bethlehem, and for centuries locals have flocked here at Christmastime to see Nativity scenes.

For a sweet treat, head down the narrow lane behind the church (going uphill parallel to the Ramblas about 30 yards) to the recommended **Café Granja Viader,** which has specialized in baked and dairy delights since 1870. (For more sugary treats nearby, follow "A Short, Sweet Walk" on page 127.)

• *Continue down the boulevard, through the stretch called the...*

❺ **Rambla of Flowers:** This colorful block, lined with flower stands, is the "Rambla" of the Flowers. Check out the balconies of the buildings. Elegant ironwork is found all over the city. Generally speaking, buildings with balconies adorned with plants and flowers are living spaces; balconies with air-

conditioners generally indicate offices. The plane trees that line the Ramblas (called sycamores in America) are known for their peeling bark and hardiness in urban settings.

• *Continue to the Metro stop marked by the red* M. *At #91 (on the right) you'll find the arcaded entrance to...*

❻ **La Boquería:** This lively produce market is an explosion of chicken legs, bags of live snails, stiff fish, delicious oranges, odd

odors, and sleeping dogs (Mon-Sat 8:00-20:00, best mornings after 9:00, closed Sun). Since as far back as 1200, Barcelonans have bought their animal parts here. Originally located by the walled city's entrance (as many medieval markets were), it expanded into the colonnaded courtyard of a

now-gone monastery before being topped with a colorful arcade in 1850. Wander around—as local architect Antoni Gaudí used to—and gain inspiration.

The Graus Conserves shop (straight in, near the back) sells 25 kinds of olives. Full legs of ham abound. Of the many varieties of *jamón serrano*, the best are *Paleta Ibérica de Bellota*, costing about €140 each (see "Sampling *Serrano* Ham," on page 348). Beware: *Huevos del toro* are bull testicles—surprisingly inexpensive...and oh so good.

Drop by a café for an *espresso con leche* or breakfast *tortilla española* (potato omelet). Try the recommended **Pinotxo Bar**—it's just inside the market, under the sign—and snap a photo of Juan. Animated Juan and his family are always busy feeding shoppers. Getting Juan to crack a huge smile and a thumbs-up for your camera makes a great shot...and he loves it. The stools nearby are a fine perch for enjoying both your coffee and the people-watching. The market and lanes nearby are busy with tempting little eateries (see page 118).

Across the boulevard at #96, the **Museum of Erotica** is your standard European sex museum (€9, daily 10:00-20:00).

To the left, at #100, **Gimeno** sells cigars. Step inside and appreciate the dying art of cigar boxes. Go ahead, do something forbidden in America but perfectly legal here...buy a Cuban (little singles for €1). Tobacco shops sell stamps and phone cards, plus bongs and marijuana gear—the Spanish approach to pot is very casual.

• *Continue down the Ramblas, glancing to the left through a modern archway for a glimpse of the medieval church tower of Santa Maria del Pi. It's clear that, as you walk the Ramblas, you're skirting along the west boundary of the old Barri Gòtic neighborhood. After 100 yards, you reach the Liceu Metro station, marking the...*

❼ Liceu—Heart of the Ramblas: At the Liceu Metro station, the Ramblas widens a bit into a small, lively square (Plaça de la Boquería). Liceu marks the midpoint of the Ramblas, halfway between Plaça de Catalunya and the waterfront.

Underfoot in the center of the Ramblas, find the much-trod-upon red-yellow-and-blue **mosaic** by homegrown abstract artist Joan Miró. The mosaic's black arrows represent anchors, a reminder of the city's attachment to the sea. Miró's childlike designs are found all over the city, from murals to mobiles to the La Caixa bank logo.

The surrounding buildings have playful ornamentation typical of the city. The Chinese dragon holding a lantern (at #82) decorates a former umbrella shop still adorned with umbrellas. Hungry? The recommended **Taverna Basca Irati** tapas bar is a block up Carrer del Cardenal Casenas.

A few steps down is the **Liceu Opera House,** which hosts world-class opera, dance, and theater. Opposite the opera house is Café de l'Opera (#74), an elegant stop for a beverage. This bustling café, with Modernista decor and a historic atmosphere, boasts that it's been open since 1929, even during the Spanish Civil War.

• *To cut this walk short, you could catch the Metro back to Plaça de Catalunya. Otherwise, continue down the Ramblas another 30 yards. The wide, straight street that crosses the Ramblas at this point (Carrer de Ferran) leads to Plaça de San Jaume, the government center.*

Continue down the Ramblas another 50 yards (to #46), and turn left down an arcaded lane (Correr de Colom) to a square filled with palm trees.

❽ Plaça Reial: Dotted with palm trees, surrounded by an arcade, and ringed by yellow buildings with white Neoclassical trim, this elegant square has a colonial ambience. It comes complete with old-fashioned taverns, modern bars with patio seating, and a Sunday coin-and-stamp market (10:00-14:00). Completing the picture are Gaudí's first public works (the two colorful helmeted lampposts) and characters who don't need the palm trees to be shady. **Herbolari Ferran** is a fine and aromatic shop of herbs, with fun souvenirs such as top-quality saffron, or *safra* (Mon-Fri 9:30-14:00 & 16:30-20:00, closed Sat-Sun, downstairs at Plaça Reial 18—to the right  as you enter the square). The small streets stretching toward the water from the square are intriguing, but less safe.

Back on the other side of the Ramblas, a half-block detour to Carrer Nou de la Rambla 3-5 brings you to the **Palau Güell,** designed by Antoni Gaudí (1886-90). Even from the outside, you get a sense of this innovative apartment, the first of Gaudí's Modernist buildings. The two parabolic-arch doorways and elaborate wrought-iron work signal his emerging nonrectangular style. Recently renovated, the Palau Güell offers an informative look at a Gaudí interior (for cost and hours, see page 92). Pablo Picasso had a studio at #10 (though there's nothing to see there today).

• *Continue downhill on the Ramblas.*

❾ **The Raval Neighborhood (Barri Xines):** The neighborhood on the right-hand side of this stretch of the Ramblas is El Raval. Its nickname was Barri Xines—the world's only Chinatown with nothing even remotely Chinese in or near it. Named for the prejudiced notion that Chinese immigrants go hand-in-hand with poverty, prostitution, and drug dealing, the neighborhood's actual inhabitants were poor Spanish, North African, and Roma (Gypsy) people. At night, the Barri Xines was frequented by prostitutes, many of them transvestites, who catered to sailors wandering up from the port. Today, it's becoming gentrified, but it's still a pretty rough neighborhood. Prostitution is nothing new here. Check out the thresholds at #22 and #24 (along the left side of the Ramblas) with holes worn in long ago by the heels of anxious ladies.

Take note of the Drassanes Metro stop (near the Museo de Cera, or wax museum), which can take you back to Plaça de Catalunya when this walk is over. The skyscraper to the right of the Ramblas is the Edificio Colón. When it was built in 1970, the 28-story structure was Barcelona's first high-rise. Near the skyscraper is the Maritime Museum, housed in what were the city's giant medieval shipyards (see page 69).

• *Up ahead is the...*

❿ **Columbus Monument and Waterfront:** The 200-foot column marks the spot where Christopher Columbus debarked after

returning from America (see page 71 for more).

Continue ahead to the waterfront. Barcelona is one of Europe's top-10 ports, though this stretch of the harbor is a pleasant marina with sailboats.

Stand here and survey some of your sightseeing options: At your feet are the *golondrinas* harbor cruise boats (page 71). Across the harbor (though not really visible from here) is the spit of land called Barceloneta, home to some nice restaurants and sandy beaches (see page 120). To the right of the harbor rises the majestic, 570-foot bluff of Montjuïc, a park-like setting dotted with a number of sights and museums (see page 102).

The pedestrian bridge jutting into the harbor is a modern extension of the Ramblas called La Rambla del Mar ("Rambla of the Sea"). This popular wooden bridge—with waves like the sea—leads to Maremagnum, a shopping mall with a cinema, a huge aquarium, restaurants, and piles of people. Late at night, it's a rollicking youth hangout.

• *Your ramble is over. The easiest way home is to backtrack to the Drassanes Metro stop or catch buses #14 or #59 to Plaça de Catalunya.*

▲▲The Barri Gòtic:
From Plaça de Catalunya to the Cathedral

Barcelona's Barri Gòtic, or Gothic Quarter, is a bustling world of shops, bars, and nightlife packed into narrow, winding lanes and undiscovered courtyards. This is Barcelona's birthplace—where the ancient Romans built a city, where medieval Christians built their cathedral, and where Barcelonans lived within a ring of protective walls until the 1850s, when the city expanded.

Today, it's Barcelona's most historic, atmospheric, characteristic, and colorful neighborhood. Concentrate on the area around the cathedral (since the section near the port is somewhat dull and seedy). The Barri Gòtic is a tangled-yet-inviting grab bag of grand squares, schoolyards, Art Nouveau storefronts, baby flea markets (on Thu, closed Aug), musty junk shops, classy antiques shops (on Carrer de la Palla), street musicians strumming Catalan folk songs, and balconies with domestic jungles behind wrought-iron bars. Go on a cultural scavenger hunt. Write a poem. Take artsy pictures. This self-guided walk gives you a structure, covering the main sights and offering a historical overview before you get lost.

• *Start on Barcelona's bustling main square, **Plaça de Catalunya** (described on page 56). From the southeast corner (near El Corte Inglés), head downhill along the broad pedestrian boulevard called…*

❶ **Avinguda Portal de l'Angel:** For much of Barcelona's history, this was one of the main boulevards leading into town. A medieval wall enclosed the city, and there was an entrance here—the "Gate of the Angel" that gives the street its name. An angel statue atop the gate kept the city safe from plagues, and bid voyagers safe journey as they left the security of the city. Imagine the fascinating scene here at the Gate of the Angel, where Barcelona stopped and the wilds began.

Today's street is pretty globalized and sanitized, full of international chain stores. Pause at Carrer de Santa Anna to admire the Art Nouveau awning at (another) El Corte Inglés store.

• *A half-block detour down Carrer de Santa Anna (at #32) leads to a pleasant, flower-fragrant courtyard with the…*

❷ **Eglesia de Santa Anna:** This 12th-century gem was one of those *extra muro* churches, with its marker cross still standing

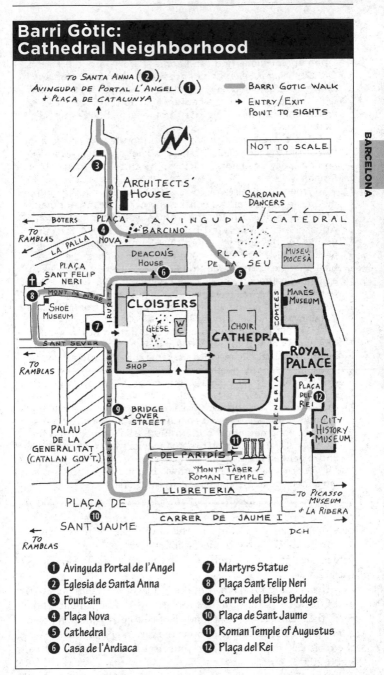

Barri Gòtic: Cathedral Neighborhood

TO SANTA ANNA (2),
AVINGUDA DE PORTAL L'ANGEL (1)
+ PLAÇA DE CATALUNYA

━━━ BARRI GOTIC WALK

→ ENTRY/EXIT
POINT TO SIGHTS

NOT TO SCALE

BARCELONA

ARCHITECTS' HOUSE

SARDANA DANCERS

BOTERS · PLAÇA · AVINGUDA CATEDRAL

TO RAMBLAS

LA PALLA

+ "BARCINO"

NOVA

PLAÇA SANT FELIP NERI

DEACON'S HOUSE

PLAÇA DE LA SEU

MUSEU DIOCESÀ

MONT DE BISBE

SHOE MUSEUM

CLOISTERS

GEESE WC

CHOIR

CATHEDRAL

MARÈS MUSEUM

COMTES

ROYAL PALACE

SANT SEVER

TO RAMBLAS

SHOP

PLAÇA DEL REI

FRENERIA

CITY HISTORY MUSEUM

BRIDGE OVER STREET

PALAU DE LA GENERALITAT (CATALAN GOV'T.)

CARRER DEL BISBE

C. DEL PARIDÍS

"MONT" TÀBER ROMAN TEMPLE

LLIBRETERIA

TO PICASSO MUSEUM + LA RIBERA

PLAÇA DE SANT JAUME

CARRER DE JAUME I

DCH

TO RAMBLAS

1. Avinguda Portal de l'Angel
2. Eglesia de Santa Anna
3. Fountain
4. Plaça Nova
5. Cathedral
6. Casa de l'Ardiaca
7. Martyrs Statue
8. Plaça Sant Felip Neri
9. Carrer del Bisbe Bridge
10. Plaça de Sant Jaume
11. Roman Temple of Augustus
12. Plaça del Rei

Mapping Barcelona's History

Open up your map and read some history into it. Find the Old City (*Ciutat Vella*), the dense neighborhood of higgledy-piggledy streets between Plaça de Catalunya and the water, with the cathedral at the center. Around that stretches the waffle-shaped grid of modern boulevards built as the city expanded.

The city grew with its history. Find the original Roman town from the time of Christ. It's the knot of streets clustered around today's cathedral, enclosed by an oval-shaped ring of Roman walls.

When Rome fell (around A.D. 500), the Christian Visigoths made the cathedral the center of town, and the populace remained huddled inside the Roman walls. During the Dark Ages, the city was ruled briefly by Moors (714-801) and Franks (ninth century). When the Counts of Barcelona unified Catalunya (10th century), the city began expanding. They built churches outside the Roman walls (or *extra muro*), each a magnet gathering a small community. By 1250, they needed to build a larger wall to contain these new settlers. This medieval wall is the arc on your map that stretches from Plaça de Catalunya to the sea, embracing the whole Old Town.

By 1850, the growing city was bursting at the seams. The outer wall was torn down and replaced by a series of circular boulevards (named Rondas, meaning "to go around"). The city expanded northward in a regimented grid of modern boulevards. The small-street neighborhoods in this urban waffle show where a little town was consumed by the growing city. The popular Passeig de Gràcia was literally the "Road to Gràcia"—once a separate town, now a characteristic Barcelona neighborhood. In 1992, Barcelona hosted the Summer Olympics, which greatly accelerated modernization and expanded the city still more.

Today, the population sprawls beyond city maps, creating a metropolitan area of some five million people.

outside. As part of a convent, the church has a fine cloister, an arcaded walkway around a leafy courtyard (viewable through the gate to the left of the church). Climb the modern stairs for views of the bell tower.

If the church is open, you'll see a bare Romanesque interior and Greek-cross floor plan, topped with an octagonal wooden roof. The recumbent-knight tomb is of Miguel de Boera, renowned admiral of Charles V. The door at the far end of the nave leads to the cloister (church hours vary but usually daily 9:00-13:00 and 18:00-20:00).

• *Continue down Avinguda Portal de l'Angel until you run into a building at a fork in the road, with a...*

❸ Fountain: The fountain's blue-and-yellow tilework depicts ladies carrying jugs of water. In the 17th century, this was the last watering stop for horses before leaving town. As recently as 1940, one in nine Barcelonans got their water from fountains like this. It's still used today.

• *Take the left fork, passing by the Royal Art Circle Museum (temporary exhibits). Enter the large square called the...*

❹ Plaça Nova: Two bold **Roman towers** flank the main street. These once guarded the entrance gate of the ancient Roman

city of Barcino. The big stones that make up the base of the (reconstructed) towers are actually Roman. At the base, find the **modern bronze letters** spelling out "BARCINO." The city's name may have come from Barca, one of Hannibal's generals, who is said to have passed through during Hannibal's roundabout invasion of Italy. At Barcino's peak, the **Roman wall** (see the section stretching to the left of the towers) was 25 feet high and a mile around, with 74 towers. It enclosed an area of 30 acres—population 4,000.

One of the towers has a section of **Roman aqueduct** (a modern reconstruction). These bridges of stone carried fresh water from the distant hillsides into the walled city. Here the water supply split into two channels, one to feed Roman industry, the other for the general populace. The Roman aqueducts would be the best water system Barcelona would have until the 20th century.

Opposite the towers is the modern College of Architects building with a **frieze designed by Picasso** (1960). In Picasso's distinctive childlike style, it shows branch-waving kings and children celebrating a local festival. Picasso spent his formative years (1895-1904, ages 14-23) in the Barri Gòtic. He had a studio a block east of here (where the big Caixa Catalunya building stands today). He drank with fellow bohemians at the "Four Cats," two blocks north (where a touristy incarnation stands today), and frequented brothels a few blocks south of here on Carrer d'Avinyo ("Avignon"), which inspired his seminal Cubist painting *Les Demoiselles d'Avignon*. Picasso's Barri Gòtic was a hotbed of trend-setting art, propelling Picasso forward just before he moved to Paris and remade modern art.

• *Now head to the left and take in the mighty façade of the...*

❺ Cathedral of Barcelona (Catedral de Barcelona): This location has been the center of Christian worship since the fourth century, and this particular building dates (mainly) from the 14th century. The façade is a virtual catalog of Gothic motifs: a pointed arch over the entrance, robed statues, tracery in windows, gargoyles, and bell towers with winged angels. The style is French Flamboyant (meaning "flame-like"), and the roofline sports the prickly spires meant to give the impressions of a church flickering with spiritual fires. The facade is typically Gothic...but not medieval. It's a Neo-Gothic work from the 19th century. The area in front of the cathedral is where they dance the *sardana* (see page 76).

The cathedral's interior—with its vast size, peaceful cloister, and many ornate chapels—is worth a visit. For a self-guided tour, see "Cathedral of Barcelona" on page 72.

• *The Frederic Mares Museum (see page 78 for details) is just to the left of the cathedral. But for now, return to the Roman towers. Pass between the towers up Carrer del Bisbe, and take an immediate left, to the staircase entrance of the...*

❻ **Casa de l'Ardiaca *(Archivo):*** It's free to enter this mansion, which was once the archdeacon's house and today functions as the city archives. The elaborately carved doorway is Renaissance. To the right of the doorway is a carved mail slot by 19th-century Modernist architect Lluís Domènech i Muntaner. Enter into a small courtyard with a fountain. Notice how the century-old palm tree seems to be held captive by urban man. Next, step inside the lobby of the city archives. You can't tour the archives, but there are often temporary exhibits in the lobby. At the left end of the lobby, step through the archway and look down into the stairwell—this is the back side of the ancient Roman wall. Back in the courtyard, head up to the balcony for views of the cathedral steeple and gargoyles.

• *Return to Carrer del Bisbe and turn left. After a few steps you reach a small square with a bronze statue ensemble.*

❼ **Martyrs Statue:** Five Barcelona patriots calmly receive their last rites before being garroted (strangled) for resisting Napoleon's 1809 invasion of Spain. They'd been outraged by French atrocities in Madrid (depicted in Goya's "Third of May" painting in the Prado Museum—see page 391). The plaque marking their mortal remains says these martyrs to independence gave their lives *"por Dios, por la Patria, y por el Rey"*—for God, country, and king.

The plaza offers interesting views of the cathedral's towers. The doorway here is the (not-always-open) "back door" entrance to the cathedral (at the cloister), letting you avoid the long lines at the cathedral's main entrance.

• *Exit the square down tiny Carrer de Montjuïc del Bisbe. This leads to the cute...*

❽ **Plaça Sant Felip Neri:** This square serves as the playground of an elementary school and is often bursting with youthful energy. The Church of Sant Felip Neri, which Gaudí attended, is still pocked with bomb damage from the Civil War. As a stronghold of democratic, anti-Franco forces, Barcelona saw a lot of fighting. The

shrapnel that damaged this church was meant for the nearby Catalan government building (Palau de la Generalitat, described below).

Study the carved reliefs on nearby buildings, paid for by the guilds that powered the local economy. It's clear that the building on the far right must have housed the shoemakers. In fact, just next door is the fun little Shoe Museum (described on page 77).

• *Exit the square down Carrer de Saint Felip Neri, turn left, and return to the square with the Martyrs Statue. Then turn right, walking along Carrer del Bisbe. Up ahead is the...*

❾ **Carrer del Bisbe Bridge:** This Bridge-of-Sighs-like structure connects the Catalan government building on the right with the Catalan president's residence (ceremonial, not actual). Though the bridge looks medieval, it was constructed in the 1920s by Joan Rubió, who also did the carved ornamentation on the buildings.

It's a photographer's delight. Check out the jutting angels on the bridge, the basket-carrying maidens on the president's house, the gargoyle-like faces on the government building. Zoom in even closer. Find monsters, skulls, goddesses, old men with beards, climbing vines, and coats of arms—a Gothic museum in stone.

• *Continue along Carrer del Bisbe to...*

❿ **Plaça de Sant Jaume** (jow-mah): This stately central square of the Barri Gòtic, once the Roman forum, has been the seat of city government for 2,000 years. Today the two top governmental buildings in Catalunya face each other.

For more than six centuries, the **Palau de la Generalitat** has housed the autonomous government of Catalunya. It always flies the Catalan flag (red and yellow stripes) next to the obligatory Spanish one. Above the doorway is Catalunya's patron saint— St. Jordi (George), slaying the dragon. From these balconies, the nation's leaders (and soccer heroes) greet the people on momentous days. The square is often the site of demonstrations, from a single aggrieved citizen with a megaphone to riotous thousands.

The **Barcelona City Hall** (Casa de la Ciutat) sports a statue of "Jaume el Conqueridor," for whom this plaza is named (free, open Sun 10:00-13:30). King Jaume I (1208-1276, also called "the Just") is credited with freeing Barcelona from French control, granting self-government, and setting it on a course to become a major city. He was the driving force behind construction of the Royal Palace (which we'll see shortly).

Locals treasure the independence these two government buildings represent. In the 20th century, Barcelona opposed the dictator Francisco Franco (who ruled from 1939 to 1975) and Franco retaliated. He abolished the regional government and (effectively) outlawed the Catalunyan language and customs. Two years after Franco's death, joyous citizens packed this square to celebrate the return of self-rule.

Look left and right down the main streets branching off the square. Carrer de Ferran (which leads to the Ramblas) is classic Barcelona—lined with ironwork streetlamps and balconies draped with plants.

In ancient Roman days, Plaça de Sant Jaume was the town's forum or central square, located at the intersection of the two main streets—the *decumanus* (Carrer del Bisbe) and the *cardus* (Carrer de la Llibreteria). The forum's biggest building was a massive temple of Augustus, which we'll see next.

• *Facing the Generalitat, exit the square to the right, heading uphill on tiny Carrer del Paradís. Follow this street as it turns right. When it swings left, pause at #10, the entrance to the...*

⓫ **Roman Temple of Augustus:** You're standing at the summit of Mont Tàber. A plaque on the wall says it all: "Mont Tàber, 16.9 meters"—elevation 55 feet. The Barri Gòtic's highest spot is also marked with a millstone inlaid in the pavement at the doorstep of #10. It was here, atop this lofty summit, that the ancient Romans founded the town of Barcino around 15 B.C. They built a *castrum* (fort) on the hilltop, protecting the harbor.

Step inside for a peek at the imposing Roman temple (Temple Roma d'August). These four huge columns, from around A.D. 1, are as old as Barcelona itself. They were part of the ancient town's biggest structure, a temple dedicated to the Emperor Augustus, worshipped as a god. These Corinthian columns (with deep fluting and topped with leafy capitals) were the back corner of a 120-foot-long temple that extended from here to the Fòrum (free, good English info; April-Sept Tue-Sun 10:00-20:00; Oct-March Tue-Sat 10:00-14:00 & 16:00-19:00, Sun 10:00-20:00; closed Mon year-round).

• *Continue down Carrer del Paridís one block. When you bump into the back end of the cathedral, take a right, and go downhill a block (down Baixada de Santa Clara) until it emerges into a square called...*

⓬ **Plaça del Rei:** The buildings that enclose this square once housed Spain's kings and queens. The central section (topped by a six-story addition) was the core of the Royal Palace. It has a vast hall on the ground floor that served as the throne room and reception room. From the 13th to the 15th centuries, the Royal Palace housed Catalunya's counts as well as resident Spanish kings. In

1493, a triumphant Christopher Columbus, accompanied by six New World natives (whom he called "Indians") and several pure-gold statues, entered the Royal Palace. King Ferdinand and Queen Isabel rose to welcome him home, and honored him with the title "Admiral of the Oceans."

To the right is the palace's church, the Chapel of Saint Agatha. It sits atop the foundations of the Roman wall.

To the left is the Viceroy's Palace (for the ruler's right-hand man), which also served as the archives of the Kingdom of Aragon. After Catalunya became part of Spain in the 15th century, the Royal Palace became a small regional residence, and the Viceroy's Palace became the headquarters of the local Inquisition. Today the Viceroy's Palace is once again home to the archives. Step inside the courtyard. It has an impressive Renaissance courtyard, a staircase with coffered wood ceilings, and a temporary exhibit space. Among the archive's treasures (though it's rarely on display) is the 1491 Santa Fe Capitulations, a contract between Columbus and the monarchs about his upcoming voyage.

Ironically, Columbus and the Kingdom of Aragon played a role in Barcelona's decline as an independent kingdom. When Ferdinand of Aragon married Isabel of Castile, Catalunya got swallowed up in greater Spain. Columbus' discovery of new trade routes made Barcelona's port less important, and soon the royals moved elsewhere.

The City History Museum's entrance is at the near end of Plaça del Rei. This museum (see details on page 77) is the only way to see the interior of the Royal Palace and Chapel of Saint Agatha. It's a fine way to retrace all the history we've seen on this walk—from modern to medieval to the Roman foundations of Barcino.

• *Your tour is over. It's easy to get your bearings by backtracking to either Plaça de Sant Jaume or the cathedral. The Jaume I Metro stop is two blocks away (head downhill and turn left). Or simply wander and enjoy Barcelona at its Gothic best.*

Sights in Barcelona

Barcelona's Old City

I've divided Barcelona's Old City sights into three neighborhoods: near the harbor, at the bottom of the Ramblas; the cathedral and nearby (Barri Gòtic); and the Picasso Museum and nearby (La Ribera).

On the Harborfront, at the Bottom of the Ramblas

▲**Maritime Museum (Museu Marítim)**—Barcelona's medieval shipyard, the best preserved in the entire Mediterranean, has an

BARCELONA

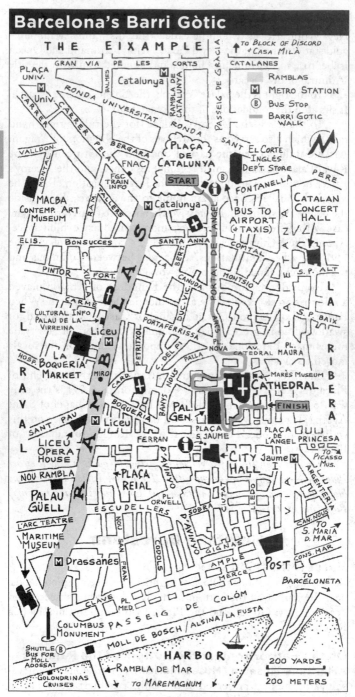

Barcelona's Barri Gòtic

impressive collection covering the salty history of ships and navigation from the 13th to the 20th centuries. Riveting for nautical types, and interesting for anyone, its modern and beautifully presented exhibits will put you in a seafaring mood. The museum is undergoing a major renovation, closing off large sections one at a time through 2013, so what you see will depend on when you visit. The museum's cavernous halls evoke the 14th-century days when Catalunya was a naval and shipbuilding power, cranking out 30 huge galleys a winter. As in the US today, military and commercial ventures mixed and mingled as Catalunya built its trading empire. The excellent included audioguide tells the story and explains the various seafaring vessels displayed—including an impressively huge and richly decorated royal galley. Your ticket also includes entrance to the Santa Eulàlia, an early 20th-century sailing vessel docked just a short walk from the Columbus Monument.

Cost and Hours: €2.50, prices may change as more exhibits reopen, museum—open daily 10:00-20:00, last entry 30 minutes before closing; Santa Eulàlia—generally open Mon-Sat 12:00-17:30, Sun 10:00-17:30, but hours vary with seasons; breezy courtyard café, Avinguda de la Drassanes, Metro: Drassanes, tel. 933-429-920, www.mmb.cat.

▲**Columbus Monument (Monument a Colóm)**—Marking the point where the Ramblas hits the harbor, this 200-foot-tall monument was built for an 1888 exposition. The tight four-person elevator takes you to the glassed-in observation area at the top for congested but sweeping views. There is also a small TI inside. It was here in Barcelona that Ferdinand and Isabel welcomed Columbus home after his first trip to America. It's ironic that Barcelona would so honor the man whose discoveries ultimately led to its downfall as a great trading power.

Cost and Hours: €4, daily May-Oct 9:00-20:30, Nov-April 10:00-18:30.

Golondrinas **Cruises**—At the harbor near the foot of the Columbus Monument, tourist boats called *golondrinas* offer two different unguided trips. The shorter version goes around the harbor in 35 minutes (€6.80, daily on the hour 11:30-19:00, every 30 minutes mid-June-mid-Sept, may not run Nov-April—call ahead, tel. 934-423-106). The longer 1.5-hour trip goes up the coast to the Fòrum complex and back (€14, can disembark at Fòrum in summer only, about 7/day, daily 11:30-19:30, shorter hours in winter).

▲Cathedral of Barcelona

This has been Barcelona's holiest spot for 2,000 years. The Romans built their Temple of Jupiter here. In A.D. 343, the pagan temple was replaced with a Christian cathedral. That building was supplanted by a Romanesque-style church (11th century). The current Gothic structure was built in the 14th century (1298-1450), during the glory days of the Catalan nation. The facade was humble, so in the 19th century the proud local bourgeoisie redid it in a more ornate, Neo-Gothic style. Construction was capped in 1913 with the central spire, 230 feet tall.

The church is worth visiting for its vast nave, rich chapels, tomb of St. Eulàlia, and the oasis-like setting of the cloister. Other sights inside (sometimes requiring separate admission charges) are the elaborately carved choir, the elevator up to the view terrace, and the altarpiece museum.

Cost: Until 14:00, the cathedral is free to enter, but you must pay to visit several sights inside: the choir (€2.50), terrace (€2.50), and museum (€2). The cathedral is closed in the afternoon; starting at 17:15, you pay €6 to enter, which also covers admission to the three special sights (tel. 933-151-554, www.catedralbcn.org). The dress code is strictly enforced; don't wear tank tops, shorts, or skirts above the knee.

Hours: Cathedral—Mon-Fri 8:00-12:45 & 17:15-19:30, Sat 8:00-12:45 & 17:15-20:00, Sun 8:00-13:45 & 17:15-20:00; choir—Mon-Sat 9:00-12:45 & 17:15-19:00, Sun 9:00-12:45; terrace—Mon-Sat 9:00-12:30 & 17:15-18:00, closed Sun; museum—daily 10:00-12:30 & 17:15-19:00.

Avoiding Lines: Mornings are most crowded. You can sometimes avoid lines at the main entrance by entering through the cloister (around the right side of the church, on Carrer del Bisbe—see page 73), although this entrance isn't always open. The elevator to the view terrace often has lines, which you can't avoid.

WCs: Tiny, semi-private WC in the center of the cloister.

Getting There: The huge can't-miss-it cathedral is in the center of the Barri Gòtic, on Plaça de la Seu, Metro: Jaume I. For an interesting way to reach the cathedral from Plaça de Catalunya, and some commentary on the surrounding neighborhood, see my self-guided walk of the Barri Gòtic, described earlier.

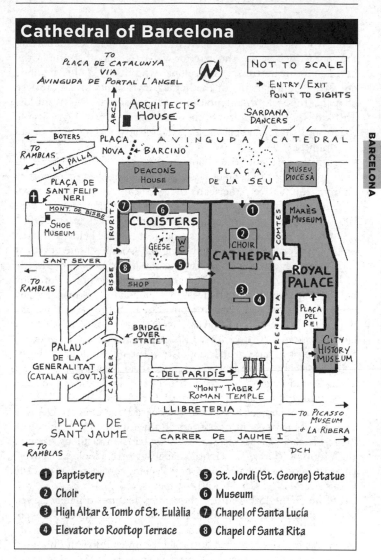

Cathedral of Barcelona

TO PLAÇA DE CATALUNYA VIA AVINGUDA DE PORTAL L'ANGEL

ARCHITECTS' HOUSE

SARDANA DANCERS

NOT TO SCALE

→ ENTRY/EXIT POINT TO SIGHTS

BOTERS

TO RAMBLAS

LA PALLA

PLAÇA NOVA "BARCINO"

AVINGUDA CATEDRAL

DEACON'S HOUSE

PLAÇA DE LA SEU

MUSEU DIOCESÀ

PLAÇA DE SANT FELIP NERI

SHOE MUSEUM

MONT. DE BISBE

CLOISTERS

GEESE   WC

CHOIR   CATEDRAL

MARÈS MUSEUM

ROYAL PALACE

SANT SEVER

TO RAMBLAS

SHOP

PLAÇA DEL REI

BRIDGE OVER STREET

PALAU DE LA GENERALITAT (CATALAN GOV'T.)

CITY HISTORY MUSEUM

C. DEL PARIDÍS

"MONT" TÀBER ROMAN TEMPLE

LLIBRETERIA

TO PICASSO MUSEUM & LA RIBERA

PLAÇA DE SANT JAUME

CARRER DE JAUME I

TO RAMBLAS

DCH

1 Baptistery

2 Choir

3 High Altar & Tomb of St. Eulàlia

4 Elevator to Rooftop Terrace

5 St. Jordi (St. George) Statue

6 Museum

7 Chapel of Santa Lucía

8 Chapel of Santa Rita

BARCELONA

⊘ Self-Guided Tour: The spacious church is 300 feet long and 130 feet wide. Tall pillars made of stone blocks support the crisscross vaults. Each round keystone where the arches cross features a different saint. Typical of many Spanish churches, there's a choir—an enclosed area of wooden seats in the middle of the nave. The Gothic church also has fine stained glass, ironwork chandeliers, a 16th-century organ (left transept), tombstones in the pavement, and an "ambulatory" floor plan, allowing worshippers to amble around to the chapel of their choice.

Side Chapels: The nave is ringed with 28 chapels. Besides being worship spaces, these serve as interior buttresses supporting the roof (which is why the exterior walls are smooth, without the normal Gothic buttresses). Barcelona—the city of 32 official public holidays—honors many of the homegrown saints found in these chapels. The rich ornamentation was sponsored by local guilds. Think of it: The church was the community's most high-profile space, and these chapels were a kind of advertising to illiterate worshippers.

On the left side, the chapel at the back of the nave has an old baptism font that once stood in the original fourth-century church. The Native Americans that Columbus brought to town were supposedly baptized here. The first chapel along the left wall is dedicated to St. Severus, the bishop here way back in A.D. 290.

On the right side, the first chapel features the beloved "Christ of Lepanto" crucifix. They say the angular wooden figure of Christ leaned to dodge a cannonball during the history-changing Battle of Lepanto (1571). The second chapel has a statue of St. Anthony holding the Baby Jesus. His feast day (January 17) is one of many celebrated in the city with an appearance by the *gegantes* (giant puppets), a street fair, horse races, and a blessing of pets. The third chapel honors a 20th-century bishop who survived an assassination attempt in the cathedral cloister. The golden fourth chapel is for St. Roch, whose feast day is celebrated joyously in the Barri Gòtic in mid-August. The fifth chapel has a black-and-white sideways statue of St. Ramon (Raymond) of Penyafort (1190-1275), the Dominican Bishop of Barcelona who heard Pope Gregory IX's sins and is the patron saint of lawyers. Ramon figures into the city's biggest festival, La Mercè, since Ramon had a miraculous vision of the Virgin of Mercy. The eighth chapel is worth a look for its over-the-top golden altarpiece of Bishop Pacian, considered one of the Church fathers (c. A.D. 310-391).

Choir: The 15th-century choir *(coro)* features ornately carved stalls. During the standing parts of the Mass, the chairs were folded up, but VIPs still had those little wooden ledges to lean on. Each was creatively carved and—since you couldn't sit on sacred things—the artists were free to enjoy some secular and naughty fun here. In 1519, the stalls were painted with the coats of arms of Europe's nobility. They gathered here as members of the Knights of the Golden Fleece to honor Charles V, King of Spain, who was making his first trip to the country he ruled. Find Charles' two-headed eagle, with the dangling lamb of the Golden Fleece. Next to Charles is the emblem (red and blue shield with lions and fleur-de-lys) of another invited guest, Henry VIII of England—who was a no-show. Check out the detail work on the impressive wood-carved pulpit near the altar, supported by flying angels.

High Altar: Look behind the altar (beneath the crucifix) to find the archbishop's chair, or cathedra. As a cathedral, this church is the archbishop's seat—hence its Catalan nickname of *La Seu*. To the left of the altar is the organ and the elevator up to the terrace. To the right of the altar, the wall is decorated with Barcelona's yellow-and-red coat of arms. The two wooden coffins on the wall are of two powerful Counts of Barcelona (Ramon Berenguer I and his wife, Almodis) whose marriage united Barcelona with the kingdom of Aragon. This power couple ordered construction of the 11th-century Romanesque cathedral that preceded this structure.

Tomb of Eulàlia: Descend the steps beneath the altar, into the crypt, to see the marble-and-alabaster sarcophagus (1327-1339) with the remains of St. Eulàlia. The cathedral is dedicated to this saint.

Thirteen-year-old Eulàlia, daughter of a prominent Barcelona family, was martyred by the Romans for her faith in A.D. 304. Murky legends say she was subjected to 13 tortures: First she was stripped naked and had her head shaved, though a miraculous snowfall hid her nakedness. Then she was rolled down the street in a barrel full of sharp objects. When nothing would kill her, she was crucified on an X-shaped cross—a symbol you'll find carved into pews and seen throughout the church.

The relief on the coffin's side tells her story in three episodes: she preaches Christianity to the pagan Roman ruler; he orders her to die (while she pleads for mercy); and she's crucified on the X-shaped cross. As one of Barcelona's patron saints, Eulàlia is honored with a weeklong festival (with *gegantes*—giant puppets, fireworks, and human towers) in mid-February.

Terrace: The elevator to the left of the altar takes you up to the rooftop terrace for a view.

Cloisters: Exit out the right transept and into the circa-1450 cloister—the arcaded walkway surrounding a lush courtyard.

Ahhhh. It's a tropical atmosphere of palm, orange, and magnolia trees; a fish pond; trickling fountains; and squawking geese. From within the cloisters, look back at the arch, an impressive mix of Romanesque (from the earlier church) and Gothic. One fountain has a tiny statue of St. Jordi slaying the dragon. Jordi (George) is one of the patron saints of Catalunya and by far the most popular boy's name here. During the Corpus Christi festival (June), kids come here to watch a hollow egg dance atop the fountain's spray.

As you wander the cloisters, check out the coats of arms as well

Sardana Dances

Patriotic *sardana* dances are held at the cathedral (every Sun at 12:00, usually also Sat at 18:00, none in Aug). Locals of all ages seem to spontane- ously appear. For some it's a highly symbolic, politically charged action representing Catalan unity—but for most it's just a fun chance to kick up their heels. Participants gather in circles after putting their things in the center— symbolic of community and sharing (and the ever-present risk of theft). All are wel- come, even tourists cursed with two left feet.

Holding hands, dancers raise their arms—slow-motion, *Zorba the Greek*–style—as they hop and sway gracefully to the music. The band *(cobla)* consists of a long flute, tenor and soprano oboes, strange-looking brass instruments, and a tiny bongo-like drum *(tambori)*. The rest of Spain mocks this lazy circle dance, but considering what it takes for a culture to sur- vive within another culture's country, it is a stirring display of local pride and patriotism. The event lasts between one and two hours.

as the tombs in the pavement. These were rich merchants who paid good money to be buried as close to the altar as possible. Notice the symbols of their trades: scissors, shoes, bakers, and so on.

The resident geese have been here for at least 500 years. There are always 13, in memory of Eulàlia's 13 years and 13 torments. Other legends say they're white as a symbol of her virginity, or perhaps the geese are descendants of long-ago geese in the ancient Roman temple. Before modern security systems, they acted as alarms. Any commotion would get them honking, alerting the monk in charge. Faithful to tradition, they honk to this very day.

In one corner of the cloister is the dark, barrel-vaulted Chapel of Santa Lucía, a small 13th-century remnant of the earlier Romanesque cathedral. People hoping for good eyesight (Santa Lucía's specialty) leave candles outside. Farther along the cloister, the Chapel of Santa Rita (patron saint of impossible causes) usu- ally has the most candles.

Museum (Museu Capitular): The little museum has the 6-foot-tall 14th-century Great Monstrance, a ceremonial display case for the communion wafer. Made of gold and studded with jewels, it's really three separate parts: a church-like central section, topped with a crown canopy, standing on a golden chair. This huge monstrance with its wafer is paraded through the streets during the Corpus Christi festival. Nearby is a gold-plated silver statue of St. Eulàlia, carrying the X-shaped cross she was crucified on. There's also an 11th-century baptismal font from the Romanesque church.

The next room, the Sala Capitular, has several altarpieces, including a *pietá* by Bartolomé Bermejo (1490). An anguished Mary cradles a twisted Christ against a bleak, stormy landscape. It's unique in Spanish art for its Italianesque, Renaissance 3-D. Rather than your basic gold backdrop, this has a strong foreground (the mourners), middle distance (the cross), and background (the city and distant hills). The kneeling donors who paid for the painting are photorealistic, complete with reading glasses and five-o-clock shadows.

In the Barri Gòtic, near the Cathedral

For an interesting route from Plaça de Catalunya to the cathedral neighborhood, see my self-guided walk of the Barri Gòtic (page 62). And if you're in town on a weekend, don't miss the *sardana* dances (see sidebar).

Shoe Museum (Museu del Calçat)—Shoe-lovers enjoy this small museum of footwear in glass display cases, watched over by an earnest attendant. You'll see shoes from the 1700s to today: fancy ladies' boots, Tibetan moccasins, big clown shoes, and shoes of minor celebrities such as the president of Catalunya. The huge shoes at the entry are designed to fit the foot of the Columbus Monument at the bottom of the Ramblas.

Cost and Hours: €2.50, Tue-Sun 11:00-14:00, closed Mon, one block beyond outside door of cathedral cloister, behind Plaça de G. Bachs on Plaça Sant Felip Neri, Metro: Jaume I, see page 66 for directions, tel. 933-014-533.

▲▲City History Museum (Museu d'Història de la Ciutat)— Walk through the history of the city with the help of an included audioguide. First watch the nine-minute introductory video in the small theater (playing alternately in Catalan, Spanish, and English)—it's worth viewing in any language. Then take an elevator down 65 feet (and 2,000 years—see the date spin back while you descend) to stroll the streets of Roman Barcelona. You'll see sewers, models of domestic life, and bits of an early-Christian church. Finally, an exhibit in the 11th-century count's palace shows you Barcelona through the Middle Ages.

Cost and Hours: €7, free all day first Sun of month and other Sun from 15:00 in summer, no audioguide during free times; Tue-Sat April-Oct 10:00-19:00, Nov-March 10:00-17:00; Sun

10:00-20:00, closed Mon, last entry 30 minutes before closing; Plaça del Rei, enter on Vageur street, Metro: Jaume I, tel. 932-562-122.

Frederic Marès Museum (Museu Frederic Marès)—This museum has an eclectic collection of local artist (and packrat) Frederic Marès, and sprawls around a peaceful courtyard through several old Barri Gòtic buildings. The biggest part of the collection is sculpture, hailing from ancient times to the early 20th century. But even more interesting is Marès' vast collection of items he found representative of everyday life in the 19th century—rooms upon rooms of fans, stamps, pipes, and other bric-a-brac, all lovingly displayed. There are also several sculptures by Frederic Marès himself, and temporary exhibits. The delightfully tranquil courtyard café offers a nice break, even when the museum is closed.

Cost and Hours: €4.20, free Sun from 15:00; open Tue-Sat 10:00-19:00, Sun 11:00-20:00, closed Mon; Plaça de Sant Iu 5-6, Metro: Jaume I, tel. 932-563-500, www.museumares.bcn.cat.

▲▲▲Picasso Museum (Museu Picasso)

This is the best collection in the country of the work of Spaniard Pablo Picasso (1881-1973), and—since he spent his formative years (age 14-23) in Barcelona—it's the best collection of his early works anywhere. By seeing his youthful, realistic art, you can more fully appreciate the artist's genius and better understand his later, more challenging art. The collection is scattered through several connected Gothic palaces, six blocks

from the cathedral in the Ribera district (for more on this area, see page 82).

Cost and Hours: €10, free all day first Sun of month and other Sun from 15:00; open Tue-Sun 10:00-20:00, closed Mon, last entry 30 minutes before closing; Montcada 15-23, ticket office at #21, Metro: Jaume I, tel. 932-563-000, www.museupicasso.bcn.cat.

Crowd-Beating Tips: There's almost always a line, sometimes with waits of more than an hour. Mornings until 13:00 and all day Tuesday are busiest. If you have an Articket Card (see page 40), skip the line by going to the "Meeting Point" entrance. You can also skip the line by buying your ticket online at www.museupicasso.bcn.cat (no additional booking fee). Stuck in line without a ticket? Figure that about 25 people are admitted every 10 minutes.

Services: The ground floor has a required bag check, as well as a handy array of other services (bookshop, WC, and cafeteria).

Cuisine Art: The museum itself has a good **café** (€8 sandwiches and salads). Across the street, the **Dhub Café** hides in a pleasant courtyard next door to the Textile Museum (Montcada 12-14, tel. 932-954-657). And just down the street is a neighborhood favorite for tapas, the recommended **El Xampanyet** (closed Mon).

Background: Picasso's personal secretary amassed a huge collection of his work and bequeathed it to the city. Picasso, happy to have a museum showing off his work in the city of his youth, added to the collection throughout his life. (Sadly, since Picasso vowed never to set foot in a fascist, Franco-ruled Spain, and died two years before Franco, the artist never saw the museum.)

❍ Self-Guided Tour: Though the rooms are sometimes rearranged, the collection (291 paintings) is always presented chronologically. With the help of thoughtful English descriptions for each stage (and guards who don't let you stray), it's easy to follow the evolution of Picasso's work. You'll see his art pass through these stages:

Boy Wonder, Age 10-14: Pablo's earliest art is realistic and serious. A budding genius emerges at age 12, as Pablo moves to Barcelona and gets serious about art. Even this young, his portraits of grizzled peasants show great psychological insight and flawless technique. You'll see portraits of Pablo's first teacher, his father *(El Padre del Artista)*. Displays show his art-school work. Every time Pablo starts breaking rules, he's sent back to the standard classic style. The assignment: Sketch nude models to capture human anatomy accurately. Early self-portraits (1896, 1897) show the self-awareness of a blossoming intellect (and a kid who must have been a handful in junior high school). When Pablo is 13, his father quits painting to nurture his young prodigy.

Adolescence, Developing Talent: During a short trip to Málaga, Picasso dabbles in Impressionism (otherwise unknown in Spain at the time). As a 15-year-old, Pablo dutifully enters art-school competitions. His first big work—while forced to show a religious subject *(Primera Comunión,* or *First Communion)*—is more an excuse to paint his family. Notice his sister Lola's exquisitely painted veil. This piece was heavily influenced by local painters.

Look closely at the portrait of his mother *(Retrato de la Madre del Artista)*. Pablo, age 15, is working on the fine details and gradients of white in her blouse and the expression in her cameo-like face. Notice the signature. Spaniards keep both parents' surnames, with the father's first, followed by the mother's:

Pablo Ruiz Picasso. Pablo is closer to his mom than his dad, and eventually he keeps just her name.

Early Success: *Ciencia y Caridad (Science and Charity),* which won second prize at a fine-arts exhibition, got Picasso the chance to study in Madrid. Now Picasso conveys real feeling. The doctor (Pablo's father) represents science. The nun represents charity and religion. From her hopeless face and lifeless hand, it seems that Picasso believes nothing will save this woman from death. Pablo painted a little perspective trick: Walk back

and forth across the room to see the bed stretch and shrink. Three small studies for this painting show how this was an exploratory work. The frontier: light.

Picasso travels to Madrid for further study. Finding the stuffy fine-arts school in Madrid stifling, Pablo hangs out in the Prado Museum and learns by copying the masters. Notice his nearly perfect copy of Philip IV by Diego Velázquez. Having absorbed the wisdom of the ages, in 1898 Pablo visits Horta de San Juan, a rural Catalan village, and finds his artistic independence. Poor and without a love in his life, he returns to Barcelona.

Barcelona Freedom, 1900: Art Nouveau is all the rage. Upsetting his dad, Pablo quits art school and falls in with the avant-garde crowd. These bohemians congregate daily at Els Quatre Gats ("The Four Cats," slang for "a few crazy people"—a popular restaurant to this day). Further establishing his artistic freedom, he paints portraits—no longer of his family... but of his new friends. Still a teenager, Pablo puts on his first one-man show.

Paris, 1900-1901: Nineteen-year-old Picasso arrives in Paris, a city bursting with life, light, and love. Dropping the paternal surname Ruiz, Pablo establishes his commercial brand name: "Picasso." Here the explorer Picasso goes bohemian and befriends poets, prostitutes, and artists. He paints Impressionist landscapes like Claude Monet, cancan dancers like Toulouse-

Lautrec, still lifes like Paul Cézanne, and bright-colored Fauvist works like Henri Matisse. (*La Espera*—with her bold outline and strong gaze—pops out from the Impressionistic background.) It is Cézanne's technique of "building" a figure with "cubes" of paint that will inspire Picasso to invent Cubism—soon.

Blue Period, 1901-1904: The bleak Paris weather, the suicide of his best friend, and his own poverty lead Picasso to his "Blue Period." He cranks out stacks of blue art just to stay housed and fed. With blue backgrounds (the coldest color) and depressing subjects, this period was revolutionary in art history. Now the artist is painting not what he sees but what he feels. The touching portrait of a mother and child, *Desamparados* (*Despair*, 1903), captures the period well. Painting misfits and street people, Picasso, like Velázquez and Toulouse-Lautrec,

sees "the beauty in ugliness." Back home in Barcelona, Picasso paints his hometown at night from rooftops *(Azoteas de Barcelona)*. The paintings still blue, here we see proto-Cubism...five years before the first real Cubist painting.

Rose Period, 1904-1907: The woman in pink *(Retrato de la Señora Canals)*, painted with classic "Spanish melancholy," finally lifts Picasso out of his funk, moving him out of the blue and into a happier "Rose Period" (of which this museum has only the one painting).

Cubism, 1907-1920: Pablo's invention in Paris of the shocking Cubist style is well-known—at least I hope so, since this museum has no true Cubist paintings. In the age of the camera, the Cubist gives just the basics (a man with a bowl of fruit) and lets you finish it. (In the museum you'll see some so-called "Synthetic Cubist" paintings—a later variation that flattens the various angles, as opposed to the purer, original "Analytical Cubist" paintings, in which you can simultaneously see several 3-D facets of the subject.)

Eclectic, 1920-1950: Picasso is a painter of many styles. In *Mujer con Mantilla*, we see a little Post-Impressionistic Pointillism in a portrait that looks like a classical statue. After a trip to Rome, he paints beefy women, inspired by the three-dimensional sturdiness of ancient statues. To Spaniards, the expressionist horse symbolizes the innocent victim. In bullfights, the horse—clad with blinders and pummeled by the bull—has nothing to do with the fight. To Picasso, the horse symbolizes the feminine, and the bull, the masculine. Picasso mixes all these styles and symbols—

including this image of the horse—in his masterpiece *Guernica* (in Madrid's Centro de Arte Reina Sofía—see page 396) to show the horror and chaos of modern war.

Picasso and Velázquez, 1957: A video introduces you to Velázquez's *Las Meninas* (the original is displayed in Madrid's

Prado Museum—see page 387). Picasso, who had great respect for Velázquez, painted more than 50 interpretations of this piece that many consider the greatest painting by anyone, ever. These two Spanish geniuses were artistic equals. Picasso seems to enjoy a relationship with Velázquez. Like artistic soul mates, they spar and tease. He deconstructs Velázquez, and then injects playful uses of light, color, and perspective to horse around with the earlier masterpiece. In the big black-and-white canvas, the king and queen (reflected in the mirror in the back of the room) are hardly seen, while the self-portrait of the painter towers above everyone. The two women of the court on the right look like they're in a tomb—but they're wearing party shoes. See the fun Picasso had playing paddleball with Velázquez's masterpiece—filtering Velázquez's realism through the kaleidoscope of Cubism.

The French Riviera: The Spaniard spends the last decades of his life living simply in the south of France. Picasso said many times that "Paintings are like windows open to the world." We see his sunny Riviera world: With simple black outlines and Crayola colors, Picasso paints sun-splashed nature, peaceful doves, and the joys of the beach. He dabbles in the timeless art of ceramics, shaping bowls and vases into playful animals decorated with simple, childlike designs. He now has little kids of his own and hangs out with childlike artists like Marc Chagall.

Picasso died with brush in hand, still growing. To the end, Picasso continued exploring and loving life through his art. As a child, he was taught to paint as an adult. Now, as an old man, he paints like a child.

In La Ribera, near the Picasso Museum

There's more to the Ribera neighborhood than just the Picasso Museum. While the nearby waterfront Barceloneta district was for the working-class sailors, La Ribera housed the wealthier shippers and merchants. Its streets are lined with their grand mansions—which, like the much-appreciated Church of Santa Maria del Mar, were built with shipping wealth.

La Ribera (also known as "El Born") is separated from the

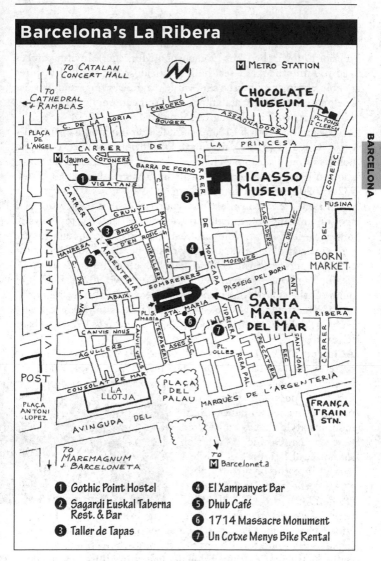

Barcelona's La Ribera

TO CATALAN CONCERT HALL

M METRO STATION

TO CATHEDRAL & RAMBLAS

CHOCOLATE MUSEUM

PL. PONS I CLERCH

CARDERS

BOUGER

C. DE LA BORIA

ASSAONADORS

PLAÇA DE L'ANGEL

CARRER DE LA PRINCESA

COTONERS

M Jaume I

BARRA DE FERRO

PICASSO MUSEUM

VIGATANS

CARRER DE

FLASSADERS

C. DEL REC

FUSINA

COMERC

CARRER DE MONTCADA

GRUNYI

BROSOL

D'EN ROSIC

D'EN VELLS

MIRALLERS

MANRESA

L'ARGENTERIA

DE LA NAU

BORN MARKET

ABAIX

SOMBRERERS

MOSQUES

PASSEIG DEL BORN

ANT.

SANTA MARIA DEL MAR

RIBERA

PL. S. MARIA STA. MARIA

VIDRIERA

CANVIS NOUS

CANVIS VELLS

L'ESPARTERIA

ESPASERIA

ASES

PESCATERIA

SANT JOAN

REC

CARRER

AGULLERS

PL. OLLES

RERA PAL.

POST

CONSOLAT DE MAR

PLAÇA DEL PALAU

MARQUÈS DE L'ARGENTERIA

FRANÇA TRAIN STN.

PLAÇA ANTONI LOPEZ

LA LLOTJA

AVINGUDA DEL

TO MAREMAGNUM & BARCELONETA

TO M Barceloneta

1 Gothic Point Hostel

2 Sagardi Euskal Taberna Rest. & Bar

3 Taller de Tapas

4 El Xampanyet Bar

5 Dhub Café

6 1714 Massacre Monument

7 Un Cotxe Menys Bike Rental

Barri Gòtic by Via Laietana, a four-lane highway built through the Old City in the early 1900s to alleviate growing traffic problems. From the Plaça de l'Angel (Metro: Jaume I), cross this busy street to enter an up-and-coming zone of lively and creative restaurants and nightlife. The Carrer de l'Argenteria ("Goldsmiths Street"— streets in La Ribera are named after the workshops that used to occupy them) runs diagonally from the Plaça de l'Angel straight down to the Church of Santa Maria del Mar. The Catalan Concert Hall is to the north.

▲▲**Catalan Concert Hall (Palau de la Música Catalana)**— This concert hall, finished in 1908, features my favorite Modernista interior in town (by Lluís Domènech i Muntaner). Inviting arches lead you into the 2,138-seat hall. A kaleidoscopic skylight features a choir singing around the sun, while playful carvings and mosaics celebrate music and Catalan culture. You can only get in by tour, which starts with a relaxing 12-minute video.

Cost and Hours: €12, 50-minute tours in English run daily every hour 10:00-15:00, may have longer hours on weekends and holidays, tour times may change based on performance schedule, about 6 blocks northeast of cathedral, Metro: Urquinaona, tel. 932-957-200, www.palaumusica.org.

The Catch: You must buy your ticket in advance to get a spot on an English guided tour (tickets available up to 7 days in advance—ideally buy yours at least 2 days before, though they're sometimes available the same day or day before). You can buy the ticket in person at the concert hall box office (open daily 9:30-15:30); by phone with your credit card (toll tel. 902-485-475); or online at the concert hall website (€1 fee, www.palaumusica.org).

Concerts: It might be easier to get tickets for a concert (300 per year, tickets for some performances as cheap as €7, see website for details).

▲**Church of Santa Maria del Mar**—This church is the proud centerpiece of La Ribera. "Del Mar" means "of the sea," and that's where the money came from. The proud shippers built this church in only 55 years, so it has a harmonious style that is considered pure Catalan Gothic. As you step in, notice the figures of workers carved into the big front doors. During the Spanish Civil War (1936-1939), the Church sided  with the conservative forces of Franco against the people. In retaliation, the working class took their anger out on this church, burning all of its wood furnishings and decor (carbon still blackens the ceiling). Today it's stripped down—naked in all its Gothic glory. The tree-like columns inspired Gaudí (their influence on the columns inside his Sagrada Família church is obvious). Sixteenth-century sailors left models of their ships at the foot of the altar for Mary's protection. Even today there remains a classic old Catalan ship at Mary's feet. As within Barcelona's cathedral, here you can see the characteristic Catalan Gothic buttresses flying inward, defining the chapels that ring the nave.

Cost and Hours: Free entry, daily 9:00-13:30 & 16:30-20:00, Plaça Santa Maria, Metro: Jaume I, tel. 933-102-390.

Nearby: Exit the church from the side, and you arrive at a square with a modern **monument** to a 300-year-old massacre that's still part of the Catalan consciousness. On September 11, 1714, the Bourbon king ruling from Madrid massacred Catalan patriots, who were buried in a mass grave on this square. From that day on, the king outlawed Catalan culture and its institutions (no speaking the language, no folk dances, no university, and so on). The eternal flame burns atop this monument, and 9/11 is still a sobering anniversary for the Catalans.

To the Picasso Museum: From behind the church, the Carrer de Montcada leads two blocks to the Picasso Museum (described earlier). The street's mansions—built by rich shippers centuries ago—now house galleries, shops, and even museums. The Picasso Museum itself consists of five such mansions laced together.

Passeig del Born—Just behind the church, this long square was formerly a jousting square (as its shape indicates). This is the neighborhood center and a popular springboard for exploring tapas bars, fun restaurants, and nightspots in the narrow streets all around. Wandering around here at night, you'll find piles of inviting and intriguing little restaurants (I've listed my favorites on page 123). Enjoy a glass of wine on the square facing the church, or consider renting a bike here for a pedal down the beach promenade to the Fòrum (described on next page).

Chocolate Museum (Museu de la Xocolata)—This museum, only a couple of blocks from the Picasso Museum (and near Citadel Park—see next), is a delight for chocolate-lovers. Operated by the local confectioners' guild, it tells the story of chocolate from Aztecs to Europeans via the port of Barcelona, where it was first unloaded and processed. But the history lesson is just an excuse to show off a series of remarkably ornate candy sculptures. These works of edible art—which change every year but often include such Spanish themes as Don Quixote or bullfighting—begin as store-window displays for Easter or Christmas. Once the holiday passes, the confectioners bring the sculptures here to be enjoyed.

Cost and Hours: €4.30, Mon-Sat 10:00-19:00, Sun 10:00-15:00, Carrer Comerç 36, Metro: Jaume I, tel. 932-687-878, www.museuxocolata.com.

Near the Waterfront, East of the Old City and Harbor

Citadel Park (Parc de la Ciutadella)—In 1888 Barcelona's biggest, greenest park, originally the site of a much-hated military citadel, was transformed for a World's Fair (Universal Exhibition). The stately Triumphal Arch at the top of the park, celebrating the removal of the citadel, was built as the main entrance. Inside you'll find wide pathways, plenty of trees and grass, a zoo, and museums of geology and zoology. Barcelona, one of Europe's most densely populated cities, suffers from a lack of real green space. This park is a haven, and is especially enjoyable on weekends, when it teems with happy families. Enjoy the ornamental fountain that the young Antoni Gaudí helped design, and consider a jaunt in a rental rowboat on the lake in the center of the park. Check out the tropical Umbracle greenhouse and the Hivernacle winter garden, which has a pleasant café-bar (daily 8:00-20:00, Metro: Arc de Triomf, east of França train station).

▲**Barcelona's Beach, from Barceloneta to the Fòrum**— Barcelona has created a summer tourist beach trade by building a huge stretch of beaches east from the town center. Before the 1992 Olympics, this area was an industrial wasteland nicknamed the "Catalan Manchester." Not anymore. The industrial zone was demolished and dumped into the sea, while sand was dredged out of the sea bed to make the pristine  beaches locals enjoy today. The scene is great for sunbathing and for an evening paseo before dinner. It's like a resort island—complete with lounge chairs, volleyball, showers, bars, WCs, and bike paths.

Bike the Beach: For a break from the city, rent a bike (in La Ribera or Citadel Park—for details, see page 45) and take the following little ride: Explore Barcelona's "Central Park"—Citadel Park—filled with families enjoying a day out (described above). Then roll through Barceloneta. This artificial peninsula was once the home of working-class sailors and shippers. From the Barceloneta beach, head west to the Olympic Village, where the former apartments for 13,000 visiting athletes now house permanent residents. The village's symbol, Frank Gehry's striking "fish," shines brightly in the sun. A bustling night scene keeps this stretch of harborfront busy until the wee hours. From here you'll come to a series of man-made crescent-shaped beaches, each with trendy bars and cafés. If you're careless or curious (down by Platja de la Mar Bella), you might find yourself pedaling through people working on an all-over tan. In the distance you see the huge solar panel marking the site of the Fòrum shopping and convention center.

The Fòrum—The original 1860 vision for Barcelona's enlargement continued the boulevard called Diagonal right to the sea. Developers finally realized this goal nearly a century and a half later, with the opening of the Fòrum. Go here for a taste of today's Barcelona: nothing Gothic, nothing quaint, just big and modern—a mall and a convention center. In 2004 Barcelona hosted the "Forum of the Cultures," an attempt to create a world's fair that recognized not states, but peoples. Roma (Gypsies), Basques, Māoris, Native Americans, and Catalans all assembled here in a global celebration of cultural diversity, multiculturalism, peace, and sustainability.

The Fòrum also tries to be an inspiration for environmental engineering. Waste is burned to create heat. The giant solar panel creates perfectly clean and sustainable energy. The bash for this planet's "nations without states" was a moderate success, with follow-ups in Mexico in 2007 and Chile in 2010. Local government officials hoped the event—like other "expos"—would goose development...and it did. Barcelona now has a modern part of town.

You can get out to the Fòrum by bike, bus, or taxi via the long and impressive beach. Or the Metro zips you there in just a few minutes from the center (Fòrum Station). Once there, browse around the modern shopping zone.

The Eixample: Modernisme and Antoni Gaudí

Wide sidewalks, hardy shade trees, chic shops, and plenty of Art Nouveau fun make the Eixample a refreshing break from the Old City. For the best Eixample example, ramble Rambla de Catalunya (unrelated to the more famous Ramblas) and pass through Passeig de Gràcia (Metro for Block of Discord: Passeig de Gràcia, or Metro for Casa Milà: Diagonal).

The 19th century was a boom time for Barcelona. By 1850 the city was busting out of its medieval walls. A new town was planned to follow a grid-like layout. The intersection of three major thoroughfares—Gran Via, Diagonal, and Meridiana—would shift the city's focus uptown. But uptown Barcelona is a unique variation on the common grid-plan city: Barcelona snipped off the building corners to create light and spacious eight-sided squares at every intersection.

The Eixample, or "Expansion," was a progressive plan in which everything was made accessible to everyone. Each 20-block-square district would have its own hospital and large park, each 10-block-square area would have its own market and general services, and each five-block-square grid would house its own schools and daycare centers. The hollow space found inside each "block" of apartments would form a neighborhood park.

Although much of that vision never quite panned out, the Eixample was an urban success. Rich and artsy big shots bought plots along the grid. The richest landowners built as close to the center as possible. For this reason, the best buildings are near the Passeig de Gràcia. While adhering to the height, width, and depth limitations, they built as they pleased—often in the trendy new Modernista style.

For many visitors, Modernista architecture is Barcelona's main

Modernisme

The Renaixensa (Catalan cultural revival) gave birth to Modernisme (Catalan Art Nouveau) at the end of the 19th century. Barcelona is its capital, and the Eixample neighborhood shimmers with the colorful, leafy, flowing, blooming shapes of Modernisme in doorways, entrances, facades, and ceilings. Meaning "a taste for what is modern"—things like streetcars, electric lights, and big-wheeled bicycles—  this free-flowing organic style lasted from 1888 to 1906. Its aim was to create objects that were both practical and decorative. Breaking with tradition, artists experimented with glass, tile, iron, and brick. The structure was fully modern, using rebar and concrete, but the decoration was a clip-art collage of nature images, exotic Moorish or Chinese themes, and fanciful Gothic crosses and knights to celebrate Catalunya's medieval glory days. It's Barcelona's unique contribution to the Europe-wide Art Nouveau movement. Modernisme was a way of life as Barcelona burst into the 20th century.

Antoni Gaudí (1852-1926), Barcelona's most famous Modernista artist, was descended from four generations of metalworkers, a lineage of which he was quite proud. He incorporated ironwork into his architecture and came up with novel approaches to architectural structure and space.

Two more Modernista architects famous for their unique style are Lluís Domènech i Muntaner and Josep Puig i Cadafalch. You'll see their work on the Block of Discord.

---

draw. (The TI even has a special desk set aside just for Modernisme-seekers.) And one name tops them all: **Antoni Gaudí** (1852-1926). Barcelona is an architectural scrapbook of Gaudí's galloping gables and organic curves. A devoted Catalan and Catholic, he immersed himself in each project, often living on-site. At various times, he called Parc Güell, Casa Milà, and the Sagrada Família home.

First I've covered the main Gaudí attractions close to the Old City. The Sagrada Família and Parc Güell are farther afield, but worth the trip. And since many visitors do those two sights together, I've included tips on how to connect them.

Gaudí Sights near the Old City

▲▲**Casa Milà (La Pedrera)**—This Gaudí exterior laughs down on the crowds filling Passeig de Gràcia. Casa Milà, also called La

Modernista Sights

ⓑ Bus Stop   Ⓜ Metro Station

BARCELONA

- Ronda de Dalt
- Torre de Bellesguard
- Parc Güell
- Gaudí House + Museum
- #24, #92 + Tourist Bus
- Finca Güell
- Finca Miralles
- Col·legi de las Teresianes
- Lesseps
- #116 ⓑ
- Terrace + Front Entrance
- Girona
- Diagonal
- Casa Vicens
- ⓑ #116
- Trav. Dalt
- Sants Train Stn.
- Trav. Gracia
- Fontana
- Hospital de la Santa Creu i Sant Pau (by Muntaner)
- **Block of Discord**
  - Casa Batlló—by Gaudí
  - Casa Amatller by Cadafalch
  - Casa Lleó Morera by Muntaner
  - Fundació Antoni Tàpies by Muntaner
- **Casa Milà**
- ⓑ #92
- Av. Gaudí
- Diagonal
- Passeig
- Provença
- ⓘ ⓑ #19 + #30
- Passeig de Gràcia
- **Sagrada Família**
- Gran Via
- Plaça d'Espanya
- Paral·lel
- Plaça de Catalunya + ⓑ #24
- Casa Calvet
- **Catalan Concert Hall** (by Muntaner)
- Montjuïc
- Ramblas
- Liceu
- Barri Gòtic
- Olympic Port + "Fish" (by Gehry)
- **Palau Güell**
- Drass.
- França Train Stn.
- **Not to Scale**
- Harbor
- DCH

Pedrera ("The Quarry"), has a much-photographed roller coaster of melting-ice-cream eaves. This is Barcelona's quintessential

Modernista building and was Gaudí's last major work (1906-1910) before dedicating his final years to the Sagrada Família.

You'll visit three sections of Casa Milà: the apartment, the attic, and the rooftop. It's best to reserve ahead—sometimes there's a 1.5-hour wait to get in.

Cost and Hours: €14, good audioguide-€4, daily March-Oct 9:00-20:00, Nov-Feb 9:00-18:30, last entry 30 minutes before closing, Passeig de Gràcia 92, Metro: Diagonal, info toll tel.

902-400-973, advance tickets toll tel. 902-101-212, www.lapedrera educacio.org.

Visiting the Casa Milà: Enter and head upstairs to the apartment. If it's near closing time, continue up to see the attic and rooftop first, to make sure you have enough time to enjoy Gaudí's works and the views.

The typical fourth-floor **apartment** is decorated as it might have been when the building was first occupied by middle-class urbanites (a seven-minute video explains Barcelona society at the time). Notice Gaudí's clever use of the atrium to maximize daylight in all of the apartments.

The **attic** houses a sprawling multimedia exhibit tracing the history of the architect's career with models, photos, and videos of his work. It's all displayed under distinctive parabola-shaped arches. While evocative of Gaudí's style in themselves, the arches are formed this way partly to support the multilevel roof above. This area was also used for ventilation, helping to keep things cool in summer and warm in winter. Tenants had storage spaces and did their laundry up here.

From the attic, a stairway leads to the fanciful, undulating, jaw-dropping **rooftop,** where 30 chimneys play volleyball with the clouds.

Back at the **ground level** of Casa Milà, poke into the dreamily painted original entrance courtyard. The first floor hosts free art exhibits.

Concerts: On summer weekends, Casa Milà has an evening rooftop concert series, "La Pedrera by Night," featuring live jazz. In addition to the music, it gives you the chance to see the rooftop illuminated (€25, mid-June-Aug Fri-Sat 20:30-23:00, advance tickets toll tel. 902-101-212, http://obrasocial.caixacatalunya.com).

Eating: Try the recommended **La Bodegueta,** a long block away (daily lunch special).

▲**Block of Discord**—Several colorful Modernista facades compete for your attention along this single stretch of Passeig de Gràcia. All were built by well-known architects at the end of the 19th century. Because the mansions look as though they are trying to outdo each other in creative twists, locals nicknamed the noisy block the "Block of Discord."

It's on Passeig de Gràcia between Consell de Cent and Aragó streets. It's three blocks north of Plaça de Catalunya (and four blocks south of Casa Milà), right by the Passeig de Gràcia Metro stop.

Visit Casa Milà or Casa Batlló?

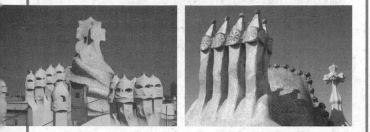

These two Antoni Gaudí houses offer similar, up-close looks at Modernista architecture. Casa Batlló's rooftop (above right) is smaller, all on one level, and less impressive than the expansive rooftop at Casa Milà (above left). But the unfurnished Casa Batlló is less of a museum and better allows the architecture to speak for itself. If you're choosing one, Casa Milà is cheaper and has the superior rooftop, but Gaudí fans will find both worthwhile.

Casa Batlló (#43): First and most famous is the green-blue ceramic-speckled facade of Casa Batlló, designed by Antoni Gaudí.

It has tibia-like pillars and shell-like balconies, inspired by the time-tested natural forms that Gaudí knew made the best structural supports. The tiled roof has a soft-ice-cream-cone turret topped with a cross. The humpback roofline suggests a cresting dragon's back. Gaudí based the work on the popular legend of St. Jordi (George) slaying the dragon. By the way, if you're tempted to snap photos from the middle of the street, be careful—Gaudí died after being struck by a streetcar.

You can tour the interior. You'll see the main floor (with a funky mushroom-shaped fireplace nook), the blue-and-white-ceramic-slathered atrium, the attic (more parabolic arches), and the rooftop, all with the help of the good audioguide. Because preservation of the place is privately funded, the entrance fee is steep—but the interior is even more fanciful and over-the-top than Casa Milà's. There's barely a straight line in the house (€18.15, includes audioguide, daily 9:00-20:00, may close early for special events—closings posted in advance at entrance, tel. 932-160-306, www .casabatllo.cat). Avoid lines (especially in the morning) by calling

932-853-832 or buying online at http://bcnshop.barcelonaturisme .com.

Casa Amatller (#41): Next door is Josep Puig i Cadafalch's creative mix, combining three of Spain's historical traditions. There are Moorish-style pentagram-and-vine designs; Gothic-style tracery, gargoyles, and bay windows; and the step-gable roof from Spain's Habsburg connection to the Low Countries. Look through the bay window to see the corkscrew column inside. Pop inside for more peeks at the elaborate entrance hall.

Casa Lleó Morera (#35): A few doors to the left, the corner building offers another paella-like mix of styles. The lower floors have classical columns and a Greek-temple-like bay window. Farther up are Gothic balconies of rosettes and tracery, while the upper part has faux Moorish stucco work. The whole thing is ornamented with fantastic griffins, angels, and fish. Unfortunately, the wonderful interior is closed to the public. The architect, Lluís Domènech i Muntaner, also designed the Catalan Concert Hall (you'll notice similarities).

More Discord: While these three buildings were done by famous, ground-breaking architects, the whole block is a jumble of delightful architectural whimsy. Reliefs, coats of arms, ironwork, gables, and bay windows adorn otherwise ordinary buildings.

A half-block from Casa Batlló is the **Fundacio Antoni Tapies,** a museum dedicated to Tapies, a 20th-century abstract artist from Barcelona. The Muntaner-designed building sums up the Modernist credo: constructed of modern brick, iron, and glass; decorated with playful motifs; and spacious, functional, and full of light inside. Inside, you can see Tapies' distinct mud-caked canvases (there's a new array every few months). Tapies (b. 1923) lays the canvas on the floor; covers it with wet varnish; sprinkles in dust, dirt, and paint; then draws simple designs in the still-wet goop. He tries to capture the primitive power of cavemen tracing the first art in mud with a stick (€7 includes audioguide, Tue-Sun 10:00-20:00, closed Mon, tel. 934-870-315, www.fundacio tapies.org).

The recommended **La Rita** restaurant, just around the corner from the Block of Discord on Carrer Aragó, serves a fine three-course lunch for a great price (Mon-Fri from 13:00).

▲**Palau Güell**—Just as the Picasso Museum reveals a young genius on the verge of a breakthrough, this early Gaudí building (completed in 1890) shows the architect taking his first tentative steps toward what would become his trademark curvy style. The parabolic-arch doorways, viewable from the outside, are the first clue that this is not a typical townhouse. The Neo-Gothic cellar was used as a stable—notice the big carriage doors in the back and the rings on some of the posts used to tie up the horses. But the most dramatic space is its rooftop; Gaudí slathered the 20 chimneys with bits of stained glass, ceramic tile, and marble. Despite the fanciful roof (visible from the street if you crane your neck), I'd skip the Palau Güell if you plan to see the more interesting Casa Milà (€10, Tue-Sun April-Sept 10:00-20:00, Oct-March 10:00-17:00, closed Mon, a half-block off the Ramblas at Carrer Nou de la Rambla 3-5, Metro: Liceu or Drassanes, tel. 934-725-775, www.palauguell.cat).

▲▲▲Sagrada Família (Holy Family Church)

There's something powerful about a community of committed people with a vision, working on a church that won't be finished in their lifetime—as was standard in the Gothic age.

Antoni Gaudí's most famous and persistent work is this unfinished, super-sized church. Gaudí labored on the Sagrada Família for 43 years, from 1883 until his death in 1926. Since then, construction has moved forward in fits and starts. Even today, the half-finished church is not expected to be completed for years. But over 30 years of visits, I've seen considerable progress. It's a testament to the generations of architects, sculptors, stonecutters, fundraisers, and donors who've been caught up in the audacity of Gaudí's astonishing vision.

Cost and Hours: €12.50 (cash only), daily April-Sept 9:00-20:00, Oct-March 9:00-18:00, tel. 932-073-031, www.sagradafamilia.cat.

Getting There: The Sagrada Família Metro stop puts you right on the doorstep: Exit toward Plaça de la Sagrada Família. The entrance for individuals (not groups) is on the west side of the church.

Crowd-Beating Tips: Waits in the ticket line can be up to 45 minutes at peak times. It's most crowded in the morning, and less crowded 14:00-15:00 and after 18:30.

Advance Tickets: To skip the ticket-buying line, you can reserve an entry time and buy tickets (with a €1.30 booking fee) from ATMs at many La Caixa bank branches throughout the city—including the branch just to the left of the Passion Facade. If tickets are available, you can buy them for the same day, even for immediate entry. However, not every La Caixa ATM sells tickets (use their larger ServiCaixa machines), and the instructions may be in Spanish (though English-only users can figure it out). Start the transaction by selecting "Event Tickets/Entrada Espectáculos"

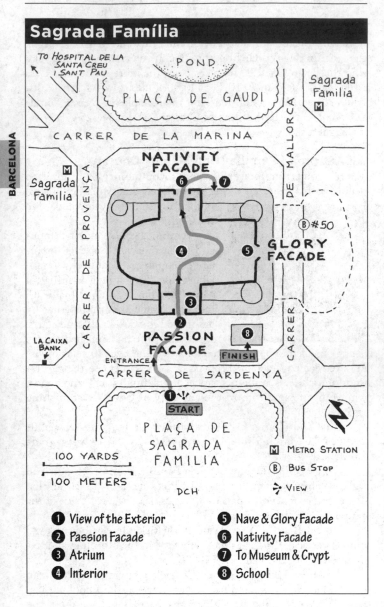

Sagrada Família

To Hospital de la Santa Creu i Sant Pau

POND

PLAÇA DE GAUDÍ

CARRER DE LA MARINA

BARCELONA

Sagrada Família Ⓜ

Sagrada Família Ⓜ

CARRER DE PROVENÇA

CARRER DE MALLORCA

NATIVITY FACADE

❻

❼

GLORY FACADE

Ⓑ #50

❹

❺

❸

❷

La Caixa Bank

PASSION FACADE

ENTRANCE

❽

FINISH

CARRER DE SARDENYA

CARRER

❶

START

PLAÇA DE SAGRADA FAMÍLIA

100 YARDS

100 METERS

DCH

Ⓜ Metro Station

Ⓑ Bus Stop

⤜ View

❶ View of the Exterior
❷ Passion Facade
❸ Atrium
❹ Interior

❺ Nave & Glory Facade
❻ Nativity Facade
❼ To Museum & Crypt
❽ School

at the top of the screen. You can also reserve tickets and an entry time online at www.servicaixa.com—you'll pick your tickets up at the ServiCaixa machine outside the Passion Facade (instructions may be in Spanish). With your La Caixa–bought ticket in hand, you'll enter through an immediate-entry gate at the Passion Facade.

Tours: The 45-minute English tours (€4) run June-Oct daily at 11:00, 12:00, and 13:00; Nov-May Mon-Fri at 11:00 and 13:00, Sat-Sun at 11:00, 12:00, and 13:00. Or rent the good 70-minute audioguide (€4).

Elevators: Two different elevators (€2.50 each, pay at main ticket office) take you partway up the towers for a great view of the city and a gargoyle's-eye perspective of the loopy church. The Passion Facade elevator takes you 215 feet up, where you can climb higher if you want; then an elevator takes you back down. The Nativity Facade elevator is similar, but you can also cross the dizzying bridge between the towers—and you must walk all the way down. If you plan to climb higher, expect the spiral stairs to be tight, hot, and congested. Lines can be up to two hours long. For the shortest lines, arrive right when the church opens and go directly to the elevators. The Nativity Facade elevator generally has a shorter line.

❷ Self-Guided Tour: Start at the ticket entrance (at the Passion Facade) on the western side of the church. The view is best from the park across the street.

❶ View of the Exterior: Stand and imagine how grand this church will be when completed. The four 330-foot spires topped with crosses are just a fraction of this mega-church. When finished, the church will have 18 spires. Four will stand at each of the three entrances. Rising above those will be four taller towers, dedicated to the four Evangelists. A tower dedicated to Mary will rise still higher—400 feet. And in the very center of the complex will stand the grand 560-foot Jesus tower, topped with a cross that will shine like a spiritual lighthouse, visible even from out at sea.

The Passion Facade that tourists enter today is only a side entrance to the church. The grand main entrance will be around to the right. That means that the nine-story apartment building will eventually have to be torn down to accommodate it. The three facades—Passion, Nativity, and Glory—will chronicle Christ's life from birth to death to resurrection.

When Gaudí died in 1926, only one spire (on the Nativity Facade) had been completed. The rest of the church has been inspired by Gaudí's vision but designed and executed by others. This artistic freedom was amplified in 1936, when Civil War shelling burned many of Gaudí's blueprints. Gaudí knew he wouldn't live to complete the church and recognized that later architects and artists would rely on their own muses for inspiration. It's a long-range vision. If there's any building on earth I'd like to see, it's the Sagrada Família...finished.

• *Pass through the ticket entrance into the complex, approaching closer to the...*

four spires were designed by Gaudí and completed (quite faithfully) in 1976. But the lower part was only inspired by Gaudí's designs. The stark sculptures were interpreted freely (and controversially) by Josep María Subirachs (b. 1927), who completed the work in 2005.

Subirachs tells the story of Christ's torture and execution. The various scenes—Last Supper, betrayal, whipping, and so on—zigzag up from bottom to top, culminating in Christ's crucifixion over the doorway. The style is severe and unadorned, quite different from Gaudí's signature playfulness. But the bone-like archways are very much in the Gaudí style. And Gaudí had made it clear that this facade should be grim and terrifying.

The facade is full of symbolism: there's a stylized Alpha-and-Omega over the door. Jesus, hanging on the cross, has hair made of an open book, symbolizing the word of God. To the left of the door, there's a grid of numbers, always adding up to 33—Jesus' age at the time of his death. The distinct face of the man below and just left of Christ is a memorial to Gaudí. Now look high above: The two-ton figure suspended between the towers is the soul of Jesus, ascending to heaven.

• *Enter the church. As you pass through the ❸ Atrium, look down at the fine porphyry floor (with scenes of Jesus' entry into Jerusalem) and look right to see one of the elevators up to the towers. For now, continue into the...*

❹ **Interior:** Walk through a forest of 56 massive columns to the center of the church. Part of Gaudí's religious vision was a love for nature. He said, "Nothing is invented; it's written in nature." Like the trunks of trees, these columns blossom with life, complete with branches, leaves, and knot-like capitals. Little windows let light filter in like the canopy of

A Dream Made Real

For 130 years, Barcelona has labored to bring Antoni Gaudí's vision to reality. Local craftsmen often cap off their careers by spending a couple of years on this exciting construction site. The present architect has been at it since 1985. The work is funded exclusively by private donations and entry fees, which is another reason its completion has taken so long. Your admission helps pay for the ongoing construction.

Like Gothic churches of medieval times, the design has evolved over the decades. At heart, it's Gothic, a style much admired by Gaudí. He added his own Art Nouveau/Modernisme touches, guided by nature and engineering innovations. Today the site bristles with cranking cranes, rusty forests of rebar, and scaffolding. Sagrada Família offers a fun look at a living, growing bigger-than-life building.

Sagrada Família Timeline

1882 The church is begun.

1883 Gaudí is hired.

1893 He begins the Nativity Facade.

1925 The first bell tower is completed.

1926 Gaudí dies with the project about 20 percent complete.

1936-39 The Spanish Civil War halts all work.

1950s Building resumes in earnest with the start of the Passion Facade.

1976 The four Passion spires are completed, bringing to eight the total that have been completed.

1980s Computer technology is introduced, greatly accelerating the pace of construction.

2000 The nave roof is completed.

2005 Passion statues are completed.

2010 Crossing vaults are finished (enclosing the roof), and the church is dedicated as a basilica.

2026? Tentative plans are that the church will be finished in time for the 100th anniversary of Gaudí's death. Make a date to attend the dedication ceremonies with your kids...to teach them a lesson in delayed gratification.

a rain forest, giving both privacy and an intimate connection with God.

The columns are a variety of colors—brown clay, gray granite, dark-gray basalt. The taller columns are 72 feet tall—the shorter ones are exactly half that.

At the center of the church, find the four red porphyry columns. These support a ceiling vault that's 200 feet high. Eventually, these columns will support the central steeple, the 560-foot Jesus tower with the shining cross. The steeple will be further supported by four underground support pylons, each consisting of 8,000 tons of cement. It will be the tallest church steeple in the world.

• *Stroll (to the right) down the nave, to what will eventually be the main entrance.*

❺ The Nave and Glory Facade: The church floor-plan is in the shape of a Latin cross, 300 feet long and 200 feet wide. Ultimately, the church will encompass 48,000 square feet, accommodating 8,000 worshippers. The U-shaped choir, suspended above the nave, can seat 1,000. The singers will eventually be backed by four organs (there's one now).

The nave's roof is 150 feet high. The crisscross arches of the ceiling (the vaults) show off Gaudí's distinctive engineering. You'll see both parabolas (u-shaped) and hyperbolas (flatter, elliptical shapes). Gaudí's starting point was the Gothic pointed arch used in medieval churches. But he tweaked it after meticulous study of which arches are best at bearing weight.

The church's roof and flooring were only completed in 2010—just in time for Pope Benedict XVI to arrive and consecrate the church. Sagrada Família is a Catholic church and is used regularly for services. Future construction is focused on a few major tasks. They need to stabilize the existing nave, which has been rattled by vibrations from Metro and AVE train lines passing underground. They're also replacing the temporary clear windows with stained glass. Gaudí envisioned a semi-dark church for a contemplative mood.

The largest remaining construction project is the third, biggest entry—the Glory Facade. When completed, the Glory Facade will have a grand staircase leading up to the doors. Four towers will rise up. The facade's sculpture will represent how the soul passes through death, faces the Last Judgment, avoids the pitfalls of Hell, and finds its way to eternal glory with God. Gaudí purposely left the facade's design open for later architects—stay tuned. Above the Glory doorway (inside the church) stands Subirachs' statue of one of Barcelona's patron saints, St. Jordi (George of dragon-slaying fame).

• *Backtrack up the nave and exit out the right transept. Once outside, back up as far as you can to take in the...*

❻ **Nativity Facade:** The four spires decorated with Gaudí's unmistakable cake-in-the-rain sculpture mark this facade as part of his original design. It's the only part of the church essentially finished in his lifetime.

The theme is Christ's birth. A statue above the doorway shows Mary, Joseph, and Baby Jesus in the manger, while curious cows peek in. It's the Holy Family—or "Sagrada Família"—for whom this church is dedicated. Flanking the doorway are the three Magi and adoring shepherds. Other statues show Jesus as a young carpenter and angels playing musical instruments. Higher up on the facade, in the arched niche, God crowns Mary triumphantly.

The facade is all about birth and new life, from the dove-covered Tree of Life on top to the turtles at the base of the columns flanking the entrance. It's as playful as the Passion Facade is grim. Gaudí's plans were for this facade to be painted. Cleverly, this attractive facade was built and finished first to attract financial support for the project.

The four spires are dedicated to Apostles, and they bear the word "Sanctus," or holy. Their colorful ceramic caps symbolize the miters (formal hats) of bishops. Mixing Gothic-style symbolism, images from nature, and Modernista asymmetry, the Nativity Facade is the best example of Gaudí's original vision, and it established the template for future architects.

To the left of the facade is one section of the cloister. Whereas most medieval churches have their cloisters (or arcaded walkways) inside the church, surrounding a courtyard, the Sagrada Família's cloister will wrap around the building, more than 400 yards long.

• *Notice the second elevator up to the towers. But for now, head down the ramp to the left of the facade, which leads to the...*

❼ **Museum:** Housed in what will someday be the church's crypt, the museum displays Gaudí's original models and drawings, and chronicles the progress of construction over the last 130 years.

Wander among the plaster models used for the church's construction, including a model of the nave so big you walk beneath it. You'll notice that the models don't always match the finished product—these are ideas, not blueprints set in stone. The Passion Facade model shows Gaudí's original vision, with which Subirachs tinkered (very freely). The models make clear that the church's design is a fusion of nature, architecture, and religion. The columns seem light, with branches springing forth and capitals that look like palm trees.

The most intriguing display is the hanging "Funicular Model." It illustrates how Gaudí used gravity to calculate the arches that support the church. Wires dangle like suspended chains, forming perfect hyperbolic arches. Attached to these are bags, representing the weight the arches must support. Flip these arches over, and they can bear the heavy weight of the roof. The mirror above the model shows how the right-side-up church is derived from this.

Nearby, you'll find some original Gaudí architectural sketches in a dimly lit room, and a worthwhile 20-minute movie (generally shown in English at :50 past each hour). You can peek into a busy workshop still used for making the same kind of plaster models Gaudí used to envision the final product in 3-D.

You'll see photos of Gaudí himself. Look for the replicas of the pulpit and confessional that Gaudí, the micro-manager, designed for his church. Photos and a timeline illustrate how construction work has progressed from Gaudí's day to now.

❽ School and Rest of Visit: Outside the Passion Facade stands a small building—a school Gaudí erected for the children of the workers building the church. Along with temporary exhibits, you'll see a classroom and a replica of Gaudí's desk as it was the day he died.

Gaudí is buried in the crypt beneath the apse. Gaudí lived on the site for more than a decade, and is buried in a Neo-Gothic 19th-century crypt (which is where the church began). His tomb is viewable for free from the small church around the corner from the main ticket entrance (during Mass—Mon-Sat 8:30-10:00 & 18:30-21:00, longer hours on Sun). There's a move afoot to make Gaudí a saint. Perhaps someday his tomb will be a place of pilgrimage. Gaudí—a faithful Catholic whose medieval-style mysticism belied his Modernista architecture career—was certainly driven to greatness by his passion for God. When undertaking a lengthy project, he said, "My client"—meaning God—"is in no hurry."

Scenic Connection to Parc Güell: If your next stop is Parc Güell (described next), and you don't want to spring for a taxi, try this route: With the Nativity Facade at your back, walk to the near-left corner of the park across the street. Then cross the street to reach the diagonal Avinguda Gaudí (between the Repsol gas station and the KFC). From here you'll follow the funky lampposts four blocks gradually uphill (about 10 minutes) along Avinguda Gaudí, a pleasantly shaded, café-lined pedestrian street. When you reach the striking Modernista-style Hospital de la Santa Creu i Sant Pau (designed by Lluís Domènech i Muntaner), cross the street and go up one block (left) on St. Antonio Maria Claret street to catch bus #92, which will take you to the side entrance of Parc Güell.

From the Sagrada Família, you could also get to Parc Güell by taking the Metro to the Joanic stop, then hop on bus #116 (described under "Getting There" for Parc Güell), but that involves two changes...and less scenery.

More Bus Connections: From the Sagrada Família, bus #19 makes an easy 15-minute journey to the Old City (stops near the cathedral and La Ribera district); bus #50 goes from the Sagrada

Família to the corner of Gran Via de les Corts Catalanes and Passeig de Gràcia, and to Montjuïc, skipping the funicular but taking you past all the sights (see "Getting to Montjuïc" on page 103).

▲Parc Güell

Gaudí fans enjoy the artist's magic in this colorful park. Gaudí intended this 30-acre garden to be a 60-residence housing project—a kind of gated community. As a high-income housing development, it flopped; but as a park, it's a delight, offering another peek into Gaudí's eccentric genius. Notice the mosaic medallions that say "park" in English, reminding folks that this is modeled on an English garden.

Cost and Hours: Free, daily 10:00-20:00, tel. 932-130-488.

Getting There: From Plaça de Catalunya, the blue Tourist Bus or bus #24 will leave you at the park's side entrance, or an €8 taxi will drop you off at the main entrance. From elsewhere in the city, do a Metro-plus-bus combination: Go by Metro to the Joanic stop and look for the Carrer de l'Escorial exit. Walk up Carrer de l'Escorial to the bus stop in front of #20. Take bus #116 directly to the park's main entrance; you'll see gingerbread-gate houses and a grand stairway. To get back to the city center after your visit, catch bus #116 going in the same direction; get off at Plaça de Lesseps and take the Metro from there.

◯ Self-Guided Tour: This tour assumes you're arriving at the front/main entrance (by taxi or bus #116). If you instead arrive at the side entrance, walk straight ahead through the gate to find the terrace with colorful mosaic benches, then walk down to the stairway and front entrance.

As you wander the park, imagine living here a century ago—if this gated community had succeeded and was filled with Barcelona's wealthy.

Front Entrance: Entering the park, you walk by Gaudí's wrought-iron gas lamps (1900-1914). His dad was a blacksmith, and he always enjoyed this medium. Two gate houses made of gingerbread flank the entrance. One houses a good bookshop; the other is home to the skippable Center for Interpretation of Parc Güell (Centre d'Interpretació), which shows Gaudí's building methods plus maps, photos, and models of the park (€2.30, daily 11:00-15:00, tel. 933-190-222). The Gaudí House and Museum, described later, is better.

Stairway and Columns: Climb the grand stairway, past the famous ceramic dragon fountain. At the top, dip into the "Hall of 100 Columns," designed to house a produce market for the neighborhood's 60 mansions. The fun columns—each different, made from concrete and rebar, topped with colorful ceramic, and studded with broken bottles and bric-a-brac—add to the market's vitality.

As you continue up (on the left-hand staircase), look left, down the playful "pathway of columns" that supports a long arcade. Gaudí drew his inspiration from nature, and this arcade is like a surfer's perfect tube.

Terrace: Once up top, sit on a colorful bench—designed to fit your body ergonomically—and enjoy one of Barcelona's best views. Look for the Sagrada Família church in the distance. Gaudí was an engineer as well. He designed a water-catchment system by which rain hitting this plaza would flow into and through the columns from the market below, and power the park's fountains.

When considering the failure of Parc Güell as a community development, also consider that it was an idea a hundred years ahead of its time. Back then, high-society ladies didn't want to live so far from the cultural action. Today, the surrounding neighborhoods are some of the wealthiest in town, and a gated community here would be a big hit.

Gaudí House and Museum: This pink house with a steeple, standing in the middle of the park (near the side entrance), was actually Gaudí's home for 20 years, until his father died. His humble artifacts are mostly gone, but the house is now a museum with some quirky Gaudí furniture and a chance to wander through a model home used to sell the others. Though small, it offers a good taste of what could have been (€5.50, daily April-Sept 10:00-20:00, Oct-March 10:00-18:00).

Montjuïc

Montjuïc ("Mount of the Jews"), overlooking Barcelona's hazy port, has always been a show-off. Ages ago it had an impressive fortress. In 1929 it hosted an international fair, from which most of today's sights originated. And in 1992 the Summer Olympics directed the world's attention to this pincushion of attractions once again.

I've listed these sights by altitude, from highest to lowest; if you're visiting all of them, do them in this order so that most of

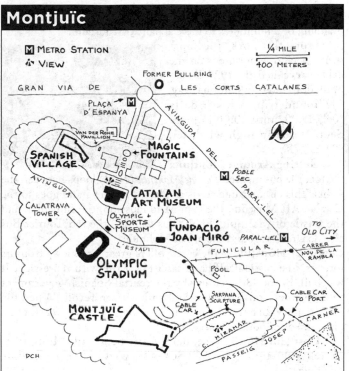

Montjuïc

M METRO STATION

⁂ VIEW

¼ MILE

400 METERS

FORMER BULLRING

GRAN VIA DE · · LES CORTS CATALANES

PLAÇA D'ESPANYA

AVINGUDA DEL

VAN DER ROHE PAVILLION

SPANISH VILLAGE

MAGIC FOUNTAINS

AVINGUDA

POBLE SEC

PARAL-LEL

CATALAN ART MUSEUM

CALATRAVA TOWER

OLYMPIC SPORTS MUSEUM

FUNDACIÓ JOAN MIRÓ

PARAL-LEL M

TO OLD CITY

L'ESTADI

FUNICULAR

CARRER NOU DE LA RAMBLA

OLYMPIC STADIUM

POOL

MONTJUÏC CASTLE

CABLE CAR

SARDANA SCULPTURE

CABLE CAR TO PORT

MIRAMAR

CARNER

PCH

PASSEIG JOSEP

BARCELONA

your walking is downhill (for selective sightseers, the Fundació Joan Miró and Catalan Art Museum are the most worthwhile). Note that if you want to visit only the Catalan Art Museum, you can just take the Metro to Plaça d'Espanya and ride the escalators up (with some stair-climbing as well) to the museum.

Getting to Montjuïc: You have several options. The simplest is to take a **taxi** directly to your destination (about €7 from downtown).

Buses from various points in the city take you up to Montjuïc, including bus #50 (from the corner of Gran Via and Passeig de Gràcia, or from the Sagrada Família), bus #55 (from Plaça de Catalunya, next to Caja de Madrid building), and the red Tourist Bus.

A **funicular** takes visitors from the Paral-lel Metro stop up to Montjuïc (covered by a Metro ticket, every 10 minutes, 9:00-22:00). To reach the funicular, take the **Metro** to the Paral-lel stop, then follow signs for *Parc Montjuïc* and the little funicular icon—you can enter the funicular directly without using another ticket (number of minutes until next departure posted at start of entry tunnel). From the top of the funicular, turn left and walk two minutes to the Joan Miró museum, six minutes to the Olympic Stadium, or ten minutes to the Catalan Art Museum.

From the port, the most scenic way to Montjuïc is on the **cable car,** called the 1929 Transbordador Aereo (€9.50 one-way, €13 round-trip, 3/hour, daily 10:45-19:00, until 20:00 in June-Sept, closed in high wind, tel. 932-252-718).

Getting Around Montjuïc: Up top, the bus marked *Parc de Montjuïc* (#PM) loops between the sights. This circular line starts at Plaça d'Espanya and goes to the Catalan Art Museum, the Joan Miró museum, the funicular, and the Castle of Montjuïc. Public bus #50 and the red Tourist Bus also do circuits around the top of Montjuïc.

Castle of Montjuïc—The castle offers great city views from its fortress. The castle itself has a fascist past rife with repression. It was built in the 18th century by the central Spanish government to keep an eye on Barcelona and stifle citizen revolt. When the 20th-century dictator Franco was in power, the castle was the site of hundreds of political executions.

Cost and Hours: Free, daily April-Sept 9:00-21:00, Oct-March 9:00-19:00, tel. 932-564-445, www.bcn.cat/castellde montjuic.

Getting There: To spare yourself the hike up to the castle, and to catch some great views of the city, take the **cable car** from just above the upper station of the Montjuïc funicular (€6.50 one-way, €9.30 round-trip, June-Sept daily 10:00-21:00, until 19:00 March-May and Oct, until 18:00 Nov-Feb).

▲**Fundació Joan Miró**—Showcasing the talents of yet another Catalan artist, this museum has the best collection of Joan Miró

art anywhere. You'll also see works by other Modern artists (such as *Mercury Fountain* by American sculptor Alexander Calder). If you don't like abstract art, you'll leave here scratching your head. But those who love this place are not faking it...they understand the genius of Miró and the fun of abstract art.

As you wander, consider this: Miró believed that everything in the cosmos is linked—colors, sky, stars, love, time, music, dogs, men, women, dirt, and the void. He mixed childlike symbols of these things creatively, as a poet uses words. It's as liberating for the visual artist to be abstract as it is for the poet: Both can use metaphors rather than being confined to concrete explanations. Miró would listen to music and paint. It's interactive, free interpretation. He said, "For me, simplicity is freedom."

Here are some tips to help you enjoy and appreciate Miró's art: First meditate on it, then read the title (for example, *The Smile of a Tear*), then meditate on it again. Repeat the process until you have an epiphany. There's no correct answer—it's pure poetry. Devotees of Miró say they fly with him and don't even need drugs. You're definitely much less likely to need drugs if you take advantage of the wonderful audioguide, well worth the €4 extra charge.

Cost and Hours: €9; Tue-Sat July-Sept 10:00-20:00, Oct-June 10:00-19:00, Thu until 21:30; Sun 10:00-14:30, closed Mon, 200 yards from top of funicular, Parc de Montjuïc, tel. 934-439-470, www .bcn.fjmiro.es. The museum has a cafeteria, a café, and a bookshop.

Olympic and Sports Museum (Museu Olímpic i de l'Esport)—This museum, opened in 2007, rides the coattails of the stadium across the street (see next listing). You'll twist down a timeline-ramp that traces the history of the Olympic Games, interspersed with random exhibits about various sports. Downstairs you'll find exhibits designed to test your athleticism, a play-by-play rehash of the '92 Barcelona Olympiad, a commemoration of Spaniard Juan Antonio Samaranch (the influential president of the IOC for two decades), a sports media exhibit, and a schmaltzy movie collage. High-tech but hokey, the museum is worth the time and money only for those nostalgic for the '92 Games.

Cost and Hours: €4.50; Tue-Sat April-Sept 10:00-20:00, Oct-March 10:00-18:00; Sun 10:00-14:30, closed Mon, Avinguda de l'Estadi 60, tel. 932-925-379, www.fundaciobarcelona olimpica.es.

Olympic Stadium (Estadi Olímpic)—For two weeks in the summer of 1992, the world turned its attention to this stadium (between the Catalan Art Museum and the Fundació Joan Miró at Passeig Olímpic 17). Redesigned from an earlier 1929 version, the stadium was updated, expanded, and officially named for Catalan patriot Lluís Companys i Jover.

The XXV Olympiad kicked off here on July 25, when an archer dramatically lit the Olympic torch—which still stands high at the end of the stadium overlooking the city skyline—with a flaming arrow. Over the next two weeks, Barcelona played host to the thrill of victory (most memorably at the hands of Michael Jordan, Magic Johnson, Larry Bird, and the rest of the US basketball "Dream Team") and the agony of defeat (i.e., the nightmares of the Dream Team's opponents).

Hovering over the stadium is the futuristic Montjuïc Communications Tower, designed by Santiago Calatrava and used to transmit Olympic highlights and lowlights around the world. Aside from the memories of the medals, Olympic Stadium offers little to see today.

Spanish Village (Poble Espanyol)—This tacky five-acre model village uses fake traditional architecture from all over Spain as a shell to contain gift shops. Craftspeople do their clichéd thing only in the morning (not worth your time or €8.90, www.poble -espanyol.com). After hours, it's a popular local nightspot.

▲▲Catalan Art Museum (Museu Nacional d'Art de Catalunya)—The big vision for this wonderful museum is to showcase Catalan art from the 10th century through about 1930. Often called "the Prado of Romanesque art" (and "MNAC" for short), it holds Europe's best collection of Romanesque frescoes.

Cost and Hours: €8.50, ticket valid for two days within one month, free first Sun of month; audioguide-€3.10; open Tue-Sat 10:00-19:00, Sun 10:00-14:30, closed Mon, last entry 30 minutes before closing; in massive National Palace building above Magic Fountains, near Plaça d'Espanya—take escalators up; tel. 936-220-376, www.mnac.es.

❍ Self-Guided Tour: As you enter, pick up a map (helpful for such a big and confusing building). The left wing is Romanesque, and the right wing is Gothic, exquisite Renaissance, and Baroque. Upstairs is more Baroque, plus modern art, photography, coins, and more.

The MNAC's rare, world-class collection of **Romanesque** art came mostly from remote Catalan village churches in the Pyrenees (saved from unscrupulous art dealers, including many Americans). The Romanesque wing features frescoes, painted wooden altar fronts, and ornate statuary. This classic Romanesque art—with flat 2-D scenes, each saint holding his symbol, and Jesus (easy to identify by the cross in his halo)—is impressively displayed on replicas of the original church ceilings and apses.

Across the way, in the **Gothic** wing, fresco murals give way to vivid 14th-century wood-panel paintings of Bible stories. A roomful of paintings (Room 34) by the Catalan master Jaume Huguet (1412-1492) deserves a look, particularly his altarpiece of one of Barcelona's patron saints, Jordi.

For a break, glide under the huge dome (which once housed an ice-skating rink) over to the air-conditioned cafeteria. This was the prime ceremony room and dance hall for the 1929 International Exposition. Then, from the big ballroom, ride the glass elevator upstairs, where the **Modern** section takes you on a delightful walk from the late 1800s to about 1930. It's kind of a Catalan Musée d'Orsay, offering a big chronological clockwise circle covering Spain's Golden Age (Zurbarán, heavy religious scenes, Spanish royals with their endearing underbites), Symbolism and Modernisme (furniture complements the empty spaces you likely saw in Gaudí's buildings), Impressionists, *fin de siècle* fun, and Art Deco.

Upstairs you'll also find photography, seductive sofas, and the chic Oleum restaurant, with vast city views (and €27 fixed-price lunches).

▲**Magic Fountains (Font Màgica)**—Music, colored lights, and huge amounts of water make an artistic and coordinated splash on summer nights at Plaça d'Espanya (20-minute shows start on the half-hour; almost always May-Sept Thu-Sun 21:00-23:30, no shows Mon-Wed; Oct-April Fri-Sat 19:00-21:00, no shows Sun-Thu; from the Espanya Metro stop, walk toward the towering National Palace).

Away from the Center

Tibidabo—Tibidabo comes from the Latin for "to thee I shall give," the words the devil used when he was tempting Christ. It's still an enticing offer: At the top of Barcelona's highest peak, you're offered the city's oldest fun-fair (€25.20, erratic hours, tel. 932-117-942, www.tibidabo.cat), the Neo-Gothic Sacred Heart Church, and—if the weather and air quality are good—an almost limitless view of the city and the Mediterranean.

Getting there is part of the fun: Start by taking the Metro from the Plaça de Catalunya Station (under Café Zürich) to the Tibidabo stop. (The blue Tourist Bus stops here, too.) Then take Barcelona's only remaining tram—the Tramvía Blau—from Plaça John F. Kennedy to Plaça Dr. Andreu (€4.50 round-trip, 2-4/hour). From there, take the funicular to the top (€4, fare is reimbursable with paid admission, toll tel. 906-427-017). A special "Tibibus" runs from Plaça de Catalunya to the park every day at 10:30 (€2.80, reimbursable with paid admission).

Camp Nou Stadium—The home turf of FC Barcelona is a mecca for soccer fans. A tour takes you into the press room, by the box seats, through the trophy room, and past the warm-up bench, ending in a ground-level view of the field and, of course, a big shop to buy all your official "Barça" gear.

Tours: €18/person, Mon-Sat 10:00-17:30, mid-April-mid-Dec until 19:00, Sun 10:00-13:30, shortened hours on game days, Metro: Maria Cristina or Collblanc, toll tel. 902-189-900, www .fcbarcelona.cat.

Nightlife in Barcelona

Refer to the *See Barcelona* guide (free from TI) and ask about the latest at a TI. Major sights open until 20:00 include the Picasso Museum (closed Mon), Gaudí's Palau Güell (closed Mon), Sagrada Família (daily, until 18:00 Oct-March), Casa Milà (daily, until 18:30 Nov-Feb), and Parc Güell (daily). On Thursday, Montjuïc's Joan Miró museum stays open until 21:30 (otherwise open July-Sept Tue-Sat until 20:00).

Many lesser sights also stay open at least until 20:00, such as La Boquería market (Mon-Sat), Columbus Monument (May-Oct daily), Church of Santa Maria del Mar (daily), Casa Batlló (daily), Parc Güell's Gaudí House and Museum (April-Sept daily), Castle of Montjuïc (April-Se pt daily), and Citadel Park (daily). The Magic Fountains on Plaça d'Espanya make a splash on weekend evenings (Fri-Sat, plus Thu and Sun in summer). The Tourist Bus runs until 22:00 every day in summer.

Music and Entertainment: The weekly *Guía del Ocio,* sold at newsstands for €1 (or free in some hotel lobbies), is a Spanish-language entertainment listing (with guidelines for English-speakers inside the back cover; www.guiadelocio.com). The monthly *Barcelona Metropolitan* magazine and quarterly *What's On Barcelona* are also helpful (free from the TI). For music, consider a performance at Casa Milà ("La Pedrera by Night" summer concert series, see page 90), the Liceu Opera House (page 60), or the Catalan Concert Hall (page 84). There are many nightspots around Plaça Reial (such as the popular Jamboree, Plaça Reial 17, Metro: Liceu, tel. 933-191-789).

Palau de la Virreina, an arts-and-culture TI, offers information on Barcelona cultural events—music, opera, and theater (daily 10:00-20:00, Ramblas 99, see map on page 55).

Festivals: Barcelona celebrates more festivals, markets, and street fairs than your average city. They dance the *sardana,* build human pyramids, parade colorful *gegantes* (giant puppets), and have fireworks displays called *correfoc.* For a list of some of the major events, see www.spain.info.

Sleeping in Barcelona

Book ahead. Barcelona is Spain's most expensive city. Still, it has reasonably priced rooms. Cheap places are more crowded in summer; fancier business-class hotels fill up in winter and offer discounts on weekends and in summer. When considering relative hotel values, in summer and on weekends you can often get modern comfort in business-class hotels for about the same price (€100) as you'll pay for ramshackle charm (and only a few minutes' walk from the Old City action). Some TI branches (including those at Plaça de Catalunya, Plaça de Sant Jaume, and the airport) offer a room-finding service, though it's cheaper to go direct. A few hotels offer free breakfasts to those who book direct with this guidebook.

While many of my recommendations are on pedestrian streets, night noise can be a problem (especially in cheap places, which have single-pane windows). For a quiet night, ask for "*tranquilo*" rather than "*con vista*."

Business-Class Comfort near Plaça de Catalunya

These hotels have sliding-glass doors leading to plush reception areas, air-conditioning, and perfectly sterile modern bedrooms. Most are on big streets within two blocks of Barcelona's exuberant central square. As business-class hotels, they have hard-to-pin-down prices that fluctuate wildly. I've listed the average

---

Sleep Code

(€1 = about $1.40, country code: 34)
S = Single, **D** = Double/Twin, **T** = Triple, **Q** = Quad, **b** = bathroom, **s** = shower only. Unless otherwise noted, credit cards are accepted, English is spoken, and prices listed generally include the 7-8 percent tax. Hotel breakfasts can range from free to simple €6 spreads to €21 buffets.

To help you easily sort through these listings, I've divided the accommodations into three categories, based on the price for a standard double room with bath (during high season):

$$\$ **Higher Priced**—Most rooms €150 or more.
$\$ **Moderately Priced**—Most rooms between €100-150.
$ **Lower Priced**—Most rooms €100 or less.

Prices can change without notice; verify the hotel's current rates online or by email. For other updates, see www.ricksteves.com/update.

rate you'll pay. But in summer and on weekends, supply often far exceeds the demand, and many of these places cut prices to around €100—always ask for a deal.

$$$ Hotel Catalonia Duques de Bergara has four stars, an elegant old entryway, splashy public spaces, slick marble and hardwood floors, 150 comfortable but simple rooms, and a garden courtyard with a pool a world away from the big-city noise (Db-€200 but can drop to as low as €100, extra bed-€35, breakfast-€16, air-con, elevator, free Internet access and Wi-Fi, a half-block off Plaça de Catalunya at Carrer de Bergara 11, tel. 933-015-151, fax 933-173-442, www.hoteles-catalonia.com, duques@hoteles-catalonia.es).

$$$ Nouvel Hotel, in an elegant, Victorian-style building on a handy pedestrian street, is less business-oriented and offers more character than the others listed here. It boasts royal lounges and 78 comfy rooms (Sb-€110, Db-€192, includes breakfast; manager Roberto promises a 10 percent discount on these prices with this book in 2012—you must reserve direct by email, not their website; extra bed-€35, deposit for TV remote-€20, air-con, elevator, pay Wi-Fi, Carrer de Santa Anna 20, tel. 933-018-274, fax 933-018-370, www.hotelnouvel.com, info@hotelnouvel.com).

$$ Hotel Reding, on a quiet street a five-minute walk west of the Ramblas and Plaça de Catalunya action, is a slick and sleek place renting 44 mod rooms at a good price (Db-€120—this rate includes breakfast with this book in 2012 but only if you book direct, prices go up during trade fairs, extra bed-€38, breakfast-€14, online deals don't include breakfast, air-con, elevator, free Internet access and Wi-Fi, near Metro: Universitat, Gravina 5-7, tel. 934-121-097, fax 932-683-482, www.hotelreding.com, recepcion@hotelreding.com).

$$ Hotel Denit is a small hotel with contemporary decor on a pedestrian street two blocks off the Plaça de Catalunya (Sb-€99, Db-€119, superior Db-€139, includes breakfast when you book direct—otherwise pay €6, air-con, elevator, free Wi-Fi, Metro: Plaça de Catalunya, Estruc 24-26, tel. 935-454-001, fax 935-454-001, www.denit.com, info@denit.com).

$$ Hotel Inglaterra, on the other side of Plaça de Catalunya, is owned by the same people as Hotel Denit and has a similar style for a tad more (Sb-€119-149, Db-€129-159, higher rates are for bigger and exterior rooms, pay Internet and Wi-Fi, Metro: Plaça de Catalunya, Pelai 14, tel. 935-051-100, www.hotel-inglaterra.com, recepcion@hotel-inglaterra.com).

$$ Hotel Duc de la Victoria, with 156 rooms, is professional yet friendly, buried in the Barri Gòtic just three blocks off the Ramblas (Db-€140, rates fluctuate with demand, bigger "superior" rooms on a corner with windows on 2 sides-€25 extra, breakfast-€15, air-con, elevator, Internet access, free Wi-Fi in lobby—30-minute limit, Duc 15, tel. 932-703-410, fax 934-127-747, www.nh-hotels.com, nhducdelavictoria@nh-hotels.com).

$$ Hotel Lleó (YEH-oh) is well-run, with 89 big, bright, and comfortable rooms; a great breakfast room; and a generous lounge (Db-€130 but flexes way up with demand, can be cheaper in summer, extra bed-about €30, breakfast-€13, air-con, elevator, small rooftop pool, free Internet access and Wi-Fi, 2 blocks west of Plaça de Catalunya at Carrer de Pelai 22, tel. 933-181-312, fax 934-122-657, www.hotel-lleo.com, info@hotel-lleo.com).

$$ Hotel Atlantis is solid, with 50 big, homey-yet-mod rooms and great prices for the location (Sb-€92, Db-€108, Tb-€125, check for deals on website, breakfast-€9, air-con, elevator, free Internet access and Wi-Fi, older windows let in a bit more street noise than other hotels in this category—request a room with double-paned windows or a quieter room in back, Carrer de Pelai 20, tel. 933-189-012, fax 934-120-914, www.hotelatlantis-bcn.com, inf@hotelatlantis-bcn.com).

Hotels with "Personality" on or near the Ramblas

These recommended places are generally family-run, with ad-lib furnishings, more character, and lower prices. Only the Jardí offers a quaint square buried in the Barri Gòtic ambience—but you're definitely paying for the location.

$ Hostería Grau is homey, family-run, and almost alpine. Its 25 cheery, garden-pastel rooms are a few blocks off the Ramblas in the colorful university district. The first two floors have seven-foot-high ceilings, then things get tall again (S-€35, D-€65, Db-€90, extra bed-€15; 2-bedroom family suites: Db-€95, Tb-€130, Qb-€160; slippery prices jump during fairs and big events, prices include breakfast, 5 percent discount off these rates when you book direct and show this book in 2012, air-con, elevator, free Internet access and Wi-Fi, 200 yards up Carrer dels Tallers from the Ramblas at Ramelleres 27, tel. 933-018-135, fax 933-176-825, www.hostalgrau.com, reservas@hostalgrau.com, Monica). Before booking, confirm the hotel's strict cancellation policy—generally if canceling a room less than 48 hours in advance (or a suite less than five days in advance), you'll pay for the first night.

$ Hostal el Jardí offers 40 clean, remodeled rooms on a breezy square in the Barri Gòtic. Many of the tight, plain, comfy rooms come with petite balconies (for an extra charge) and enjoy an almost Parisian ambience. It's a good deal only if you value the cute square location. Book well in advance, as this family-run place has an avid following (small basic interior Db-€75, nicer interior Db-€90, outer Db with balcony or twin with window-€95, large

BARCELONA

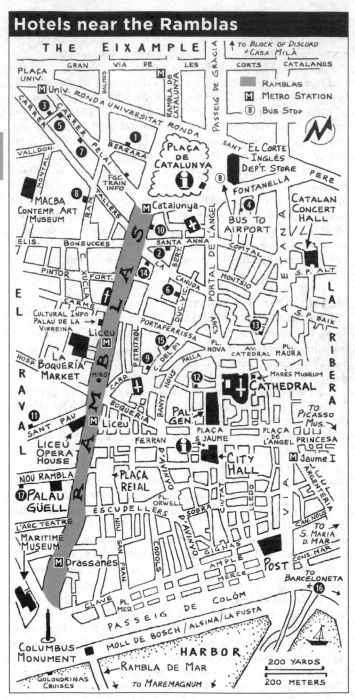

Hotels near the Ramblas

THE EIXAMPLE

GRAN VIA DE LES

PLAÇA UNIV.

M Univ. RONDA UNIVERSITAT RONDA

3 BERGARA

5

7

BALMES
CARRER PELAI
CARRER
VALLDON.
MONTAL.
TALLERS

RAMBLA DE CATALUNYA

PLAÇA DE CATALUNYA
i

PASSEIG DE GRÀCIA

CORTS CATALANES

↑ TO BLOCK OF DISCORD + CASA MILÀ

Ramblas
M Metro Station
B Bus Stop

M

SANT
El Corte Inglés Dep't. Store

B
FONTANELLA

4
BUS TO AIRPORT

PERE

Catalan Concert Hall

FGC TRAIN INFO

8
MACBA CONTEMP. ART MUSEUM

RAM.

M Catalunya

10

ELIS.
BONSUCCES
SANTA ANNA
2
BERT.
LA

S.P. ALT

COMTAL
MONTSIO

PORTAL DE L'ANGEL

LA RIBERA

PINTOR
XUCLA
FORT.

CARME

14

6
CANUDA
DUC. VIC.

PORTAFERRISSA

EL

CULTURAL INFO PALAU DE LA VIRREINA →
Liceu
M

MIRO

LA BOQUERÍA MARKET

PETRITXOL

15
9
C. DEL PI
BANYS NOUS
PALLA

ARCS

PL. NOVA
AV. CATEDRAL MAURA

PL.

13

S.P. BAIX

MARÈS MUSEUM

12
CATHEDRAL

RAVAL

HOSP.

11
SANT PAU

CARD.
BOQUERIA

M Liceu

BANYS NOUS

PAL. GEN.

PLAÇA S. JAUME

PLAÇA DE L'ANGEL

TO PICASSO MUS. →

PRINCESA

L

LICEU OPERA HOUSE

FERRAN
D'AVINYO

i
CITY HALL

M Jaume I

ARGENTERIA

NOU RAMBLA

PLAÇA REIAL

PL. ORWELL
CIUTAT
LLEDO

CAN. NOUS

TO S. MARIA D. MAR →

17 PALAU GÜELL

ESCUDELLERS
SOBRA.
D'AVINYO

L'ARC TEATRE

MARITIME MUSEUM

NOU SAN FRAN.
COTLS.

GIGNAS
AMPLE

CONS. MAR

POST

TO BARCELONETA

M Drassanes

CLAVE
PL. MED.
MERCE

16

PASSEIG DE COLÓM

COLUMBUS MONUMENT

MOLL DE BOSCH / ALSINA / LA FUSTA

HARBOR

RAMBLA DE MAR

200 YARDS
200 METERS

GOLONDRINAS CRUISES

to MAREMAGNUM ↓

Hotels Key

1. Hotel Catalonia Duques de Bergara
2. Nouvel Hotel
3. Hotel Reding
4. Hotel Denit
5. Hotel Inglaterra
6. Hotel Duc de la Victoria
7. Hotels Lleó & Atlantis
8. Hostería Grau & Barcelona Rent-A-Bike
9. Hostal el Jardí
10. Hotel Continental Barcelona
11. Hostal Opera
12. Hotel Neri
13. Hotel Regencia Colón
14. Hostal Campi
15. Hostal Maldá
16. To Sea Point Hostel
17. Launderette

outer Db with balcony or square-view terrace-€110, extra bed-€12, breakfast-€6, air-con, elevator, some stairs, free Wi-Fi in lobby, halfway between Ramblas and cathedral at Plaça Sant Josep Oriol 1, tel. 933-015-900, fax 933-425-733, www.eljardi-barcelona.com, reservations@eljardi-barcelona.com).

$ **Hotel Continental Barcelona,** in a building overlooking the top of the Ramblas, offers classic, tiny-view balcony opportunities if you don't mind the noise. Its comfortable rooms come with double-thick mattresses, wildly clashing carpets and wallpaper, and perhaps one too many clever ideas (they're laden with microwaves, fridges, a "command center" of light switches, and Tupperware drawers). Choose between your own little Ramblas-view balcony (where you can eat your breakfast) or a quieter back room (Sb-€90, Db-€100, twin Db-€110, Db with Ramblas balcony-€120, extra bed-€40, 5 percent discount on these rates with this book in 2012, prices include breakfast, air-con, elevator, free Internet access and Wi-Fi, Ramblas 138, tel. 933-012-570, fax 933-027-360, www.hotelcontinental.com, barcelona@hotelcontinental .com). J. M.'s (José María's) free breakfast and all-day snack-and-drink bar are a plus.

$ **Hostal Opera,** with 70 stark rooms 20 yards off the Ramblas, is clean, institutional, and modern. The street can feel seedy at night, but it's safe, and the hotel is very secure (Sb-€43-60, Db-€63-90, no breakfast, air-con only in summer, elevator, pay Internet access, free Wi-Fi in lobby, Carrer Sant Pau 20, tel. 933-188-201, www.operaramblas.com, info@operaramblas.com).

Deep in the Barri Gòtic

$$$ **Hotel Neri** is chic, posh, and sophisticated, with 22 rooms spliced into the ancient stones of the Barri Gòtic, overlooking an overlooked square (Plaça Sant Felip Neri) a block from the cathedral. It has big plasma-screen TVs, pricey modern art on

the bedroom walls, and dressed-up people in its gourmet restaurant (Db-€300, suites-€365-450, generally cheaper on weekdays, breakfast-€21, air-con, elevator, free Wi-Fi, rooftop tanning deck, St. Sever 5, tel. 933-040-655, fax 933-040-337, www.hotelneri .com, info@hotelneri.com).

$$ Hotel Regencia Colón, one block in front of the cathedral square, offers 50 solid, well-priced rooms in a handy location (Db-€110, more on weekends, breakfast-€12, air-con, elevator, Carrer Sagristans 13-17, tel. 933-189-858, fax 933-172-822, www .hotelregenciacolon.com, info@hotelregenciacolon.com).

Humble, Cheaper Places Buried in the Old City

$ Hostal Campi is big, subdued, and ramshackle, but offers simple class. This easygoing old-school spot rents 24 rooms a few doors off the top of the Ramblas (S-€33, D-€56, Db-€65, T-€75, Tb-€85, no breakfast, lots of stairs with no elevator, pay Internet access, free Wi-Fi in some rooms, Canuda 4, tel. & fax 933-013-545, www.hostalcampi.com, reservas@hostalcampi.com, friendly Margarita and Nando).

$ Hostal Maldá rents the best cheap beds I've found in the old center. With 25 rooms above a small shopping mall near the cathedral, it's a time-warp—quiet and actually charming. It generally remains full through the summer, but it's worth a shot (S-€15, D-€30, T-€45, cash only, free Wi-Fi, lots of stairs with no elevator, 100 yards up Carrer del Pi from delightful Plaça Sant Josep Oriol, Carrer del Pi 5, tel. 933-173-002, www.hostalmalda.com). Good-natured Aurora doesn't speak English, but Delfi, who works only half the year, does.

Hostels in the Center of Town

Barcelona has a wonderful chain of well-run and centrally located hostels (www.equity-point.com), providing €21-29 dorm beds in 4- to 14-bed coed rooms with €2 sheets and towels, free Internet access, Wi-Fi, breakfast, lockers (B.Y.O. lock, or buy one there), and plenty of opportunities to meet other backpackers. They're open 24 hours but aren't party hostels, so they enforce quiet after 23:00. There are three locations to choose from: Eixample, Barri Gòtic, or near the beach.

$ Centric Point Hostel is a huge place renting 430 cheap beds at what must be the best address in Barcelona (bar, kitchen, Passeig de Gràcia 33, see map on page 116, tel. 932-151-796, fax 932-461-552, www.centricpointhostel.com).

$ Gothic Point Hostel rents 150 beds a block from the Picasso Museum (roof terrace, Carrer Vigatans 5, see map on page 83, tel. 932-687-808, www.gothicpoint.com).

$ Sea Point Hostel has 70 beds on the beach nearby (Plaça del Mar 4, tel. 932-247-075, www.seapointhostel.com).

In the Eixample

For an uptown, boulevard-like neighborhood, sleep in the Eixample, a 10-minute walk from the Ramblas action (see map on page 116).

$$ Hotel Granvía, filling a palatial 1870s mansion, offers Botticelli and chandeliers in the public areas; a sprawling, peaceful sun patio; and 54 spacious, comfy rooms. Its salon is plush and royal, making the hotel an excellent value for romantics. To reduce street noise, ask for a quiet interior room or a room overlooking the courtyard in the back of the building (Sb-€60-114, Db-€76-162, Tb-€103-200, can be cheaper in slow times, best available rates promised with this book in 2012 when you reserve direct and mention my name, prices include breakfast, air-con, elevator, free Internet access and Wi-Fi, Gran Via de les Corts Catalanes 642, tel. 933-181-900, fax 933-189-997, www.hotel granvia.com, hgranvia@nnhotels.com, Asun works the morning shift).

$$ Hotel Continental Palacete, with 19 rooms, fills a 100-year-old chandeliered mansion. With flowery wallpaper and ornately gilded stucco, it's gaudy in the city of Gaudí, but it's also friendly, clean, quiet, and well-located. Most of the rooms have been recently updated, there's an outdoor terrace, and guests have unlimited access to the "cruise-inspired" fruit, veggie, and drink buffet—worth factoring into your comparison-shopping (Sb-€103, Db-€138, €35-45 more for bigger and brighter view rooms, extra bed-€55, 5 percent discount with this book in 2012, prices include breakfast, air-con, free Internet access and Wi-Fi, 2 blocks north of Plaça de Catalunya at corner of Carrer Diputació, Rambla de Catalunya 30, tel. 934-457-657, fax 934-450-050, www.hotel continental.com, palacete@hotelcontinental.com).

$ Hostal Residencia Neutral, with a central Eixample address and 28 very basic rooms, is a family-run time warp and a fine value (tiny S-€38, Ds-€65, Db-€70, Ts-€80, Tb-€85, Qb-€89, can be €5 more in high season, €6 continental breakfast in pleasant breakfast room, request a back room to avoid street noise, thin walls, fans, elevator, free Internet access and Wi-Fi, elegantly located 2 blocks north of Gran Via at Rambla de Catalunya 42, tel. 934-876-390, fax 934-876-848, www.hostalneutral.es, info @hostalneutral.es, Julia and Anna).

$ Hotel Ginebra is minimal, clean, and quiet considering its central location. The Herrera family rents 12 rooms in a dated apartment building overlooking the main square (Db-€75-80, extra bed-€15, air-con, elevator, free Wi-Fi, Rambla de Catalunya

BARCELONA

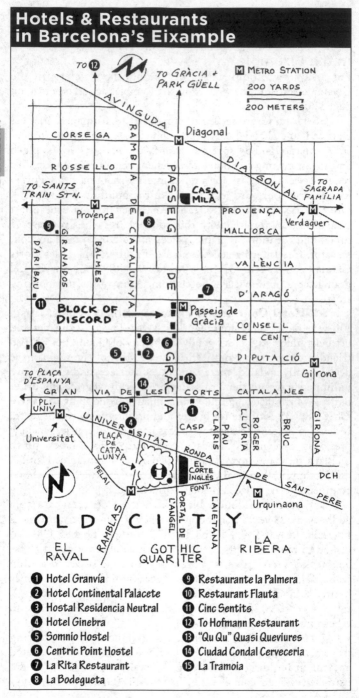

Hotels & Restaurants in Barcelona's Eixample

1. Hotel Granvía
2. Hotel Continental Palacete
3. Hostal Residencia Neutral
4. Hotel Ginebra
5. Somnio Hostel
6. Centric Point Hostel
7. La Rita Restaurant
8. La Bodegueta
9. Restaurante la Palmera
10. Restaurant Flauta
11. Cinc Sentits
12. To Hofmann Restaurant
13. "Qu Qu" Quasi Queviures
14. Ciudad Condal Cerveceria
15. La Tramoia

1/3, third floor, tel. 933-171-063, www.hotelginebra.net, info@hotel ginebra.net, Juan speaks English).

$ Somnio Hostel, an innovative newer place run by a pair of American expats, has both dorm beds and private rooms (dorm bed-€26, S-€44, D-€78, Db-€87; prices include sheets, towels, and lockers; air-con, elevator, free Internet access and Wi-Fi, Carrer de la Diputació 251, second floor, tel. 932-725-308, www.somnio hostels.com, info@somniohostels.com).

Apartments in Barceloneta

$$ 1001 Nights Barcelona, run by American Frederick and his Spanish wife, rents 40 renovated apartments with kitchens near the beach in the lively Barceloneta neighborhood, the former fishermen's quarter that's become increasingly gentrified (2 people-€100 April-Oct, €80 Nov-March; first child to age 10 years old pays, second kid free; prices vary with size—see photos and videos on website, €40 cleaning fee, 3-night minimum stay, 10 percent less for 7-night stay, 20 percent deposit required to reserve online, pay balance in cash when you arrive, no breakfast, Frederick or an associate will meet you to check in—arrange when you reserve, mobile 620-585-594, www.1001nights.es, info@1001nights.es). They also have 12 units in the somewhat seedy Barri Gòtic near Las Ramblas.

Eating in Barcelona

Barcelona, the capital of Catalan cuisine—featuring seafood—offers a tremendous variety of colorful eateries, ranging from basic

and filling to chic and trendy. Because of their common struggles, Catalans seem to have an affinity for Basque culture, so you'll find a lot of Basque tapas places here, too. (For more on Basque food, see page 155.) Most of my listings are lively spots with a busy tapas scene at the bar, along with restaurant tables for *raciones*. A regional specialty is *pa amb tomaquet* (pah ahm too-MAH-kaht), bread topped with a mix of crushed tomato and olive oil.

I've listed mostly practical, characteristic, colorful, and affordable restaurants. My recommendations are grouped by neighborhood—along the Ramblas; in Barceloneta; in the Barri Gòtic; in the Ribera neighborhood (best for foodies); and in the Eixample—followed by some budget options scattered throughout the city.

Note that many restaurants close in August (or July), when the owners take a vacation.

Restaurants generally serve lunch from 13:00 to 16:00 and dinner from 20:00 until very late (Spaniards don't start dinner until about 21:00). It's deadly to your Barcelona experience to eat too early—if a place feels touristy, come back later and it may be a thriving local favorite. For an afternoon sweet treat, I've suggested "A Short, Sweet Walk" (see page 127).

Along the Ramblas

Within a few steps of the Ramblas you'll find handy lunch places, an inviting market hall, and a slew of vegetarian options.

Lunching Simply yet Memorably near the Ramblas

Although these places are enjoyable for a lunch break during your Ramblas sightseeing, many are also open for dinner. For locations, see the map on page 122.

Taverna Basca Irati serves 40 kinds of hot and cold Basque *pintxos* for €1.80 each. These are small open-faced sandwiches—like sushi on bread. Muscle in through the hungry local crowd, get an empty plate from the waiter, and then help yourself. Every few minutes, waiters prance proudly by with a platter of new, still-warm munchies. Grab one as they pass by...it's addictive. You pay on the honor system: You're charged by the number of toothpicks left on your plate when you're done. Wash it down with €2-3 glasses of Rioja (full-bodied red wine), Txakolí (sprightly Basque white wine) or *sidra* (apple wine) poured from on high to add oxygen and bring out the flavor (daily 11:00-24:00, a block off the Ramblas, behind arcade at Carrer Cardenal Casanyes 15, Metro: Liceu, tel. 933-023-084).

Restaurant Elisabets is a happy little neighborhood eatery packed with antique radios; it's popular with locals for its €11 "home-cooked" three-course lunch special. Stop by for lunch, survey what those around you are enjoying, and order what looks best (Mon-Sat 7:30-23:00, closed Sun and Aug, lunch special served 13:00-16:00, otherwise only €3 tapas—not full meals except for Friday night's fixed-price dinner, 2 blocks west of Ramblas on far corner of Plaça Bonsucces at Carrer Elisabets 2, tel. 933-175-826, run by Pilar).

Café Granja Viader is a quaint time capsule, family-run since 1870. They boast about being the first dairy business to bottle and distribute milk in Spain. This feminine-feeling place—specializing in baked and dairy delights, toasted sandwiches, and light meals—is ideal for a traditional breakfast. Or indulge your sweet tooth: Try a glass of *orxata* (or *horchata*—*chufa*-nut milk, summer only), *llet mallorquina* (Majorca-style milk with cinnamon, lemon, and sugar), *crema catalana* (crème brûlée, their specialty), or *suis* ("Swiss"—hot chocolate with a snowcap of whipped cream). *Mel y mató* is fresh cheese with honey...very Catalan (Tue-Sat 9:00-13:30 & 17:00-20:30, Mon 17:00-20:30 only, closed Sun, a block off the Ramblas behind El Carme church at Xucla 4, tel. 933-183-486).

Picnics: Shoestring tourists buy groceries at **El Corte Inglés** (Mon-Sat 10:00-22:00, closed Sun, supermarket in basement, Plaça de Catalunya) and **Carrefour Market** (Mon-Sat 10:00-22:00, closed Sun, Ramblas 113).

In and near La Boquería Market

Try eating at La Boquería market at least once (#91 on the Ramblas). Like all farmers' markets in Europe, this place is ringed by colorful, good-value eateries.

Lots of stalls sell fun take-away food—especially fruit salads and fresh-squeezed fruit juices. There are several good bars around the market busy with shoppers munching at the counter (breakfast, tapas all day, coffee). The market, and most of the eateries listed here (unless noted), are open Monday through Saturday from 8:00 until 20:00 (though things get very quiet after about 16:00) and are closed on Sunday.

Pinotxo Bar is just to the right as you enter the market. It's a great spot for coffee, breakfast (spinach *tortillas,* or whatever's cooking with toast), or tapas. Fun-loving Juan and his family are La Boquería fixtures. Grab a stool across the way to sip your drink with people-watching views. Have a Chucho?

Kiosko Universal is popular for its great prices on wonderful fish dishes. As you enter the market from the Ramblas, it's all the way to the left in the first alley. If you see people waiting, ask who's last in line *("¿El último?").* You'll eat immersed in the spirit of the market (€14 fixed-price lunches with different fresh-fish options 12:00-16:00, always packed but better before 12:30, tel. 933-178-286).

Restaurant la Gardunya, at the back of the market, offers tasty meat and seafood meals made with fresh ingredients bought directly from the market (€13 fixed-price lunch includes wine and bread, €16 three-course dinner specials don't include wine, €10-20 à la carte dishes, Mon-Sat 13:00-16:00 & 20:00-24:00, closed Sun, mod seating indoors or outside watching the market action, Carrer Jerusalem 18, tel. 933-024-323).

Vegetarian Eateries near Plaça de Catalunya and the Ramblas

Biocenter, a Catalan soup-and-salad restaurant popular with local vegetarians, takes its cooking very seriously and feels a bit more like a real restaurant than most (€7-10 weekday lunch specials include soup or salad and plate of the day, €15 dinner specials, Mon-Sat 13:00-23:00, Sun 13:00-16:00, 2 blocks off the Ramblas at Pintor Fortuny 25, Metro: Plaça de Catalunya, tel. 933-014-583).

Juicy Jones is a tutti-frutti vegan/vegetarian eatery with colorful graffiti decor, a hip veggie menu (served downstairs), groovy laid-back staff, and a stunning array of fresh-squeezed juices served at the bar. Pop in for a quick €3 "juice of the day." For lunch you can get the Indian-inspired €6 *thali* plate, the €6.25 plate of the day, or an €8.50 meal including one of the two plates plus soup or salad and dessert (daily 13:00-23:30, also tapas and salads, Carrer Cardenal Casanyes 7, tel. 933-024-330). There's another location on the other side of the Ramblas (Carrer Hospital 74).

In Barceloneta

La Mar Salada is a traditional seafood restaurant with a slight modern twist, located on the strip leading to the Barceloneta beach. Their à la carte menu includes seafood-and-rice dishes, fresh fish, and homemade deserts. A nice meal will run you about €30-35 per person (€15 fixed-price weekday meal, Wed-Mon 13:00-16:00 & 20:00-23:00, Sat-Sun 13:00-23:00, closed Tue, indoor and outdoor seating, Passeig Joan de Borbó 59, tel. 932-212-127).

In the Barri Gòtic

These eateries populate Barcelona's atmospheric Gothic Quarter, near the cathedral. Choose between a sit-down meal at a restaurant or a string of tapas bars.

Restaurants in the Barri Gòtic

Café de l'Academia is a delightful place on a pretty square tucked away in the heart of the Barri Gòtic—but patronized mainly by the neighbors. They serve "honest cuisine" from the market with Catalan roots. The candlelit, air-conditioned interior is rustic yet elegant, with soft jazz, flowers, and modern art. And if you want to eat outdoors on a convivial, mellow square...this is the place. Reserve for Friday nights (€10-13 first courses, €12-16 second courses, fixed-price lunch for €10 at the bar or €14 at a table, Mon-Fri 13:30-16:00 & 20:30-23:30, closed Sat-Sun, near the City Hall square, off Carrer de Jaume I up Carrer Dagueria at Carrer Lledo 1, tel. 933-198-253).

Popular Chain Restaurants: Barcelona enjoys a chain of several bright, modern restaurants. These five are a hit for their modern, artfully presented Spanish and Mediterranean cuisine, crisp ambience, and unbeatable prices. Because of their three-course €10 lunches and €16-20 dinners (both with wine), all are crowded with locals and in-the-know tourists (all open daily 13:00-15:45 & 20:30-23:30, unless otherwise noted). My favorite of the bunch is **La Crema Canela,** which feels cozier than the others and is the only one that takes reservations (opens at 20:00 for dinner, 30 yards north of Plaça Reial at Passatge de Madoz 6, tel. 933-182-744). The rest are notorious for long lines at the door—arrive 30 minutes before opening, or be prepared to wait. Like La Crema Canela, the next two are also within a block of the Plaça Reial: **La Fonda** (opens at 19:30 for dinner, Carrer dels Escudellers 10, very close to a seedy stretch of street—approach it from the Ramblas rather than from Plaça Reial, tel. 933-017-515) and **Les Quinze Nits** (on Plaça Reial at #6—you'll see the line, tel. 933-173-075). The fourth place, **La Dolça Herminia,** is near the Catalan Concert Hall (2 blocks toward Ramblas from Catalan Concert Hall at Carrer de les Magdalenes 27, tel. 933-170-676). The fifth restaurant in the chain, **La Rita,** is described later, under "Restaurants in the Eixample."

Tapas on Carrer de la Mercè in the Barri Gòtic

Barcelona boasts great *tascas*—colorful local tapas bars. Get small plates (for maximum sampling) by asking for "tapas," not the big-

ger "*raciones*." Glasses of *vino tinto* go for about €1. And though trendy uptown restaurants are safer, better-lit, and come with English menus and less grease, these places will stain your journal. The neighborhood's dark, the regulars are rough-edged, and you'll get a glimpse of a crusty Barcelona from before the affluence hit. Nowadays some new, mod restaurants are popping up in this area, but don't be seduced—you came here for something different. Try *pimientos de padrón*—Russian roulette with peppers that are lightly fried in oil and salted...only a few are jalapeño-spicy. At the cider bars, it's traditional to order *queso de cabrales* (a traditional, very moldy bleu cheese) and spicy chorizo (sausage), ideally prepared *al diablo* ("devil-style")—soaked in wine, then flambéed at your table. Several places serve *leche de pantera* (panther milk)—liquor mixed with milk.

From the bottom of the Ramblas (near the Columbus Monument), hike east along Carrer Clave. Then follow the small street that runs along the right side of the church (Carrer de la Mercè), stopping at the *tascas* that look fun. For a montage of

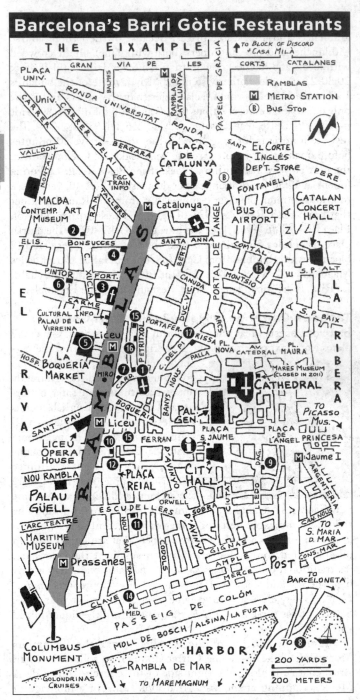

Barcelona's Barri Gòtic Restaurants

Restaurants Key

1. Taverna Basca Irati
2. Restaurant Elisabets
3. Café Granja Viader
4. Supermarket
5. La Boquería Market Eateries
6. Biocenter Veggie Rest.
7. Juicy Jones
8. To La Mar Salada
9. Café de l'Academia
10. La Crema Canela
11. La Fonda
12. Les Quinze Nits
13. La Dolça Herminia
14. Carrer de la Mercè Tapas Bars
15. Casa Colomina
16. Granja La Pallaresa
17. Fargas Chocolate Shop

BARCELONA

edible memories, wander Carrer de la Mercè west to east and consider these spots, stopping wherever looks most inviting. I've listed ye olde dives, but there are many trendy places here as well. Most of these places close down around 23:00.

La Pulpería (at #16) has a bit less character than the others, but eases you into the scene with fried fish, octopus, and *patatas bravas*, all with Galician Ribeiro wine. Farther down at the corner (#28), **La Plata** keeps things wonderfully simple, serving extremely cheap plates of sardines (€1.70), little salads (€1.50), and small glasses of keg wine (less than €1). **Tasca el Corral** (#17) serves mountain favorites from northern Spain by the half-*ración* (see their list), such as *queso de cabrales* and chorizo *al diablo* with *sidra* (hard cider sold by the bottle-€5.50). **Sidrería Tasca La Socarrena** (#21) offers hard cider from Asturias in €6.50 bottles with *queso de cabrales* and chorizo. At the end of Carrer de la Mercè, **Cervecería Vendimia** slings tasty clams and mussels (hearty *raciones* for €4-6 a plate—they don't do smaller portions, so order sparingly). Sit at the bar and point to what looks good. Their *pulpo* (octopus) is more expensive and is the house specialty. Carrer Ample and Carrer Gignas, the streets parallel to Carrer de la Mercè inland, have more refined bar-hopping possibilities.

In the Ribera District, near the Picasso Museum

La Ribera, the hottest neighborhood in town, sparkles with eclectic and trendy as well as subdued and classy little restaurants hidden in the small lanes surrounding the Church of Santa Maria del Mar. While I've listed a few well-established tapas bars that are great for light meals, to really dine, simply wander around for 15 minutes and pick the place that tickles your gastronomic fancy. I think those who say they know what's best in this area are kidding themselves—it's changing too fast and the choices are too personal. One thing's for sure: There are a lot of talented and hard-working restaurateurs with plenty to offer. Consider starting your evening off with a glass of fine wine at one of the *enotecas* on the square facing the Church of Santa Maria del Mar. Sit back and admire the pure Catalan Gothic architecture. My first three listings are all on the main drag, Carrer de l'Argenteria. For locations, see the map on page 83.

Sagardi offers a wonderful array of Basque goodies—tempting *pinchos* and *montaditos* at €1.80 each—along its huge bar. Ask for a plate and graze (just take whatever looks good). You can sit on the square with your plunder for 20 percent extra. Wash it down with Txakolí, a Basque white wine poured from the spout of a huge wooden barrel into a glass as you watch. When you're done, they'll count your toothpicks to tally your bill (daily 12:00-24:00, Carrer de l'Argenteria 62-64, tel. 933-199-993).

Sagardi Euskal Taberna, hiding behind the thriving Sagardi tapas bar (described above), is a mod, rustic, and minimalist woody restaurant committed to serving Basque T-bone steaks and grilled specialties with only the best ingredients. Crisp, friendly service and a big open kitchen with sizzling grills contribute to the ambience. Reservations are smart (€10-20 first courses, €20-30 second courses, plan on €45 for dinner, daily 13:00-16:00 & 20:00-24:00, Carrer de l'Argenteria 62, tel. 933-199-993).

Taller de Tapas ("Tapas Workshop") is an upscale, trendier tapas bar and restaurant that dishes up well-presented, sophisticated morsels and light meals in a medieval-stone-yet-mod setting. Pay 10 percent more to sit on the square. Elegant, but a bit stuffy, it's favored by local office workers who aren't into the Old World Gothic stuff. Four plates will fill a hungry diner for about €20 (daily 8:30-24:00, Carrer de l'Argenteria 51, tel. 932-688-559).

El Xampanyet, a colorful family-run bar with a fun-loving staff (Juan Carlos, his mom, and the man who may be his father), specializes in tapas and anchovies. Don't be put off by the seafood from a tin: Catalans like it this way. A *sortido* (assorted plate) of *carne* (meat) or *pescado* (fish) with *pa amb tomaquet* (bread with crushed-tomato spread) makes for a fun meal. It's filled with tourists during the sightseeing day, but this is a local favorite after dark. The scene is great but—especially during busy times—it's tough without Spanish skills. When I asked about the price, Juan Carlos said, "Who cares? The ATM is just across the street." Plan on spending €20 for a meal with wine (same price at bar or table, Tue-Sat 12:00-15:30 & 19:00-23:00, Sun 12:00-16:00 only, closed Mon, a half-block beyond the Picasso Museum at Montcada 22, tel. 933-197-003).

In the Eixample

The people-packed boulevards of the Eixample (Passeig de Gràcia and Rambla de Catalunya) are lined with appetizing eateries featuring breezy outdoor seating. Choose between a real restaurant or an upscale tapas bar. For locations, see the map on page 116.

Restaurants in the Eixample

La Rita is a fresh and dressy little restaurant serving Catalan cuisine near the Block of Discord. Their lunches (three courses with wine for €10, Mon-Fri 13:00-15:45) and dinners (€10 plates, Sun-Thu 20:00-23:30, Fri-Sat from 21:00) are a great value. Like most of its sister restaurants—described under "Dining in the Barri Gòtic," earlier—it takes no reservations and its prices attract long lines, so arrive just before the doors open...or wait (a block from Metro: Passeig de Gràcia, near corner of Carrer de Pau Claris and Carrer Aragó at Aragó 279, tel. 934-872-376).

La Bodegueta is an atmospheric below-street-level bodega serving hearty wines, homemade vermouth, *anchoas* (anchovies), tapas, and *flautas*—sandwiches made with flute-thin baguettes. Its daily €12 lunch special of three courses with wine is served 13:00-16:00. A long block from Gaudí's Casa Milà, this makes a fine sightseeing break (Mon-Sat 8:00-24:00, Sun 19:00-24:00, at intersection with Provença, Rambla de Catalunya 100, Metro: Provença, tel. 932-154-894).

Restaurante la Palmera serves a mix of Catalan, Mediterranean, and French cuisine in an elegant room with bottle-lined walls. This place offers great food, service, and value—for me, a very special meal in Barcelona. They have three zones: the classic main room, a more forgettable adjacent room, and a few outdoor tables. I like the classic room. Reservations are smart (€12-16 plates, creative €17 six-plate *degustation* lunch, Tue-Sat 13:00-15:45 & 20:30-23:15, closed Sun-Mon, Enric Granados 57, at the corner with Mallorca, tel. 934-532-338).

Restaurant Flauta fills two floors with enthusiastic eaters (I prefer the ground floor). It's fresh and modern, with a fun, no-stress menu featuring €5 small plates, creative €4 *flauta* sandwiches, and a €12.50 three-course lunch deal including a drink. Good €2.30 wines by the glass are listed on the blackboard. This is a place to order high on the menu for a satisfying, moderately priced meal (Mon-Sat 13:00-24:00, closed Sun, fun-loving and helpful staff recommends the fried vegetables, no reservations, just off Via Diputació at d'Aribau 23, tel. 933-237-038).

Cinc Sentits ("Five Senses"), with only about 30 seats, is my gourmet recommendation. It's a chic, minimalist, smoke-free, but slightly snooty place where all the attention goes to the fine service and elegantly presented dishes. It's run by Catalans who lived in Canada (so there's absolutely no language barrier) and serve avant-garde cuisine inspired by Catalan traditions and ingredients. Their €49 and €69 *degustation menus* are unforgettable extravaganzas. Reservations are required (Tue-Sat 13:30-15:00 & 20:30-23:00, closed Sun-Mon, near Carrer d'Aragó at d'Aribau 58, tel. 933-239-490).

A Bit Farther Out: **Hofmann** is a renowned cooking school with an excellent if pricey restaurant serving modern Mediterranean market cuisine. Dress up and dine in intimate rooms papered with photos of famous patrons. The four-course €40 lunches are made up of just what the students are working on that day—so there's no choice (watch the students as they cook). Dinners can easily cost twice as much (à la carte). Save room (and euros) for the incredible desserts. Reserve long in advance, because locals love this place (Mon-Fri 13:30-15:15 & 21:00-23:15, closed Sat-Sun and Aug, 4 blocks northwest of Casa Milà at La Granada del Penedès 14-16, tel. 932-187-165, www.hofmann-bcn.com).

Tapas Bars in the Eixample

Many trendy and touristic tapas bars in the Eixample offer a cheery welcome and slam out the appetizers. These three are my favorites.

Quasi Queviures ("Qu Qu" for short) serves upscale tapas, sandwiches, or the whole nine yards—classic food served fast from a fun menu with modern decor and a high-energy sports-bar ambience. It's bright, clean, and not too crowded. Walk through their enticing kitchen to get to the tables in back. Committed to developing a loyal following, they claim, "We fertilize our local customers with daily specialties" (€2-5 tapas, €5 dinner salads, €8 plates, prices 17 percent higher on the terrace, daily 8:00-24:00, between Gran Via and Via Diputació at Passeig de Gràcia 24, tel. 933-174-512).

Ciudad Condal Cerveceria brags that it serves the best *montaditos* (€2-3 little open-faced sandwiches) and beers in Barcelona. It's an Eixample favorite, with an elegant bar and tables plus good seating out on the Rambla de Catalunya for all that people-watching action. It's classier than Qu Qu and packed after 21:00, when you'll likely need to put your name on a list and wait. While it has no restaurant-type menu, the list of tapas and *montaditos* is easy, fun, and comes with a great variety (including daily specials).

This place is a cut above your normal tapas bar, but with reasonable prices (most tapas around €4-10, daily until 24:00, facing the intersection of Gran Via and Rambla de Catalunya at Rambla de Catalunya 18, tel. 933-181-997).

La Tramoia, at the opposite corner from Ciudad Condal Cerveceria, serves piles of *montaditos* and tapas at its ground-floor bar and at nice tables inside and out. If Ciudad Condal Cerveceria is jammed, you're more likely to find a seat here. The brasserie-style restaurant upstairs bustles with happy local eaters enjoying grilled meats (€8-20 plates), but I'd stay downstairs for the €4-10 tapas (open daily, also facing the intersection of Gran Via and Rambla de Catalunya at Rambla de Catalunya 15, tel. 934-123-634).

Budget Options Around Town

Bright, clean, and inexpensive sandwich shops proudly hold the cultural line against the fast-food invasion hamburgerizing the rest of Europe. Catalan sandwiches are made to order with crunchy French bread. Rather than butter, locals prefer *tomaquet* (a spread of crushed tomatoes). You'll see two big local chains (Pans & Company and Bocatta) everywhere, but these serve mass-produced McBaguettes ordered from a multilingual menu. I've

had better luck with hole-in-the-wall sandwich shops—virtually as numerous as the chains—where you can see exactly what you're getting. Kebab places are another good, super-cheap standby.

A Short, Sweet Walk

Let me propose this three-stop dessert (or, since these places close well before the traditional Barcelona dinnertime, a late-afternoon snack). You'll try a refreshing glass of *orxata*, munch some *churros con chocolate*, and visit a fine *xocolateria*, all within a three-minute walk of one another in the Barri Gòtic just off the Ramblas. Start at the corner of Carrer Portaferrissa midway down the Ramblas. For the best atmosphere, begin your walk at about 18:00 (note that the last place is closed on Sun). For locations, see the map on page 122.

Turrón at **Casa Colomina:** Walk down Carrer Portaferrissa to #8 (on the right). Casa Colomina, founded in 1908, specializes in homemade *turróns*—a variation of nougat made with almond, honey, and sugar, brought to Spain by the Moors 1,200 years ago. Three different kinds are sold in €8-12 slabs: *blando, duro,* and *yema*—soft, hard, and yolk (€2 smaller chunks also available). In the summer, the shop also sells ice cream and the refreshing *orxata* (or *horchata*—a drink made from the *chufa* nut). Order a glass and ask to see and eat a *chufa* nut (a.k.a. earth almond or tiger nut; Mon-Sat 10:00-20:30, Sun 12:30-20:30, tel. 933-122-511).

Churros con Chocolate at Granja La Pallaresa: Continue down Carrer Portaferrissa, taking a right at Carrer Petritxol to this fun-loving *xocolateria*. Older, elegant ladies gather here for the Spanish equivalent of tea time—dipping their greasy *churros* into pudding-thick cups of hot chocolate (€4.25 for five *churros con chocolate*, Mon-Fri 9:00-13:00 & 16:00-21:00, Sat-Sun 9:00-13:00 & 17:00-21:00, Carrer Petritxol 11, tel. 933-022-036).

Homemade Chocolate at Fargas: For your last stop, head for the ornate Fargas chocolate shop. Continue down Carrer Petritxol to the square, hook left through the two-part square, and then left up Carrer del Pi—it's on the corner of Portaferrissa and Carrer del Pi. Since the 19th century, gentlemen with walking canes have dropped by here for their chocolate fix. Founded in 1827, this is one of the oldest and most traditional chocolate shops in Barcelona. If they're not too busy, ask to see the old chocolate mill *("¿Puedo ver el molino?")* to the right of the counter. They sell even tiny quantities (one little morsel) by the weight, so don't be shy. A delicious chunk of the crumbly semi-sweet house specialty costs €0.45 (tray by the mill). The tempting bonbons in the window cost about €1 each (Mon-Fri 9:30-13:30 & 16:00-20:00, Sat 10:00-14:00 & 16:00-20:00, closed Sun, tel. 933-020-342).

Barcelona Connections

By Train

Unless otherwise noted, all of these trains depart from the Sants Station; however, some trains also stop at other stations more convenient to the downtown tourist zone: França Station, Passeig de Gràcia, or Plaça de Catalunya. Figure out if your train stops at these stations (and board there) to save yourself the trip to Sants.

The **AVE train to Madrid** has shaved hours off that journey, making it faster than flying (when you consider that you're zipping from downtown to downtown). The train departs almost hourly. The nonstop train is a little more expensive (€140, 2.5-3 hours) than the slightly slower train that makes a few stops and adds about a half-hour (€120, 3.5 hours). Regular reserved AVE tickets can be prepurchased at www.renfe.com and picked up at the station. If you have a railpass, you'll pay only a reservation fee of €25 for first class, which includes a meal (€15 second class, buy at any train station in Spain). Passholders can't reserve online through RENFE but can make the reservation at www.raileurope.com for delivery before leaving the US ($17 in second class, $40 in first class).

From Barcelona by Train to: Sitges (4/hour, 30-35 minutes, €3), **Montserrat** (departs from Plaça d'Espanya, hourly, 1.5 hours, €17 round-trip, includes cable car or rack train to monastery—see details on page 144), **Figueres** (hourly, 2 hours, €30 round-trip), **Sevilla** (3/day—two fast, 5.5 hours, €145; one slow, 12 hours, €62), **Granada** (1/day Wed, Fri, and Sun only, 11.5 hours, €61; also 1 night train/day, 12 hours, €63), **Salamanca** (8/day, 6-7.5 hours, change in Madrid from Atocha Station to Chamartín Station via Metro; 1 direct/day, 11.25 hours), **San Sebastián** (2/day, 5.5 hours, €62), **Málaga** (3/day—two fast, 5.5 hours, €145; one slow, 13.5 hours, €66), **Lisbon** (no direct trains, head to Madrid and then catch night train to Lisbon, 17 hours, about €100), **Nice** (1/ day via Montpelier, about €100; cheaper connections possible with multiple changes including Cerbère), **Avignon** (5/day, fewer on weekends, 6-9 hours, about €40, or about €65 for change in Montpellier), **Paris** (2/day, 7.5 hours, change in Figueres, more connections possible with multiple changes; 1 night train/day, 13.5 hours, about €200, or €50 with railpass, reservation mandatory). Train info: toll tel. 902-320-320, www.renfe.com.

By Bus

Destinations include **Madrid** (nearly hourly, 8 hours, €29—a fraction of the AVE train price, departs from Nord bus station at Metro: Arc de Triomf, bus info toll tel. 902-260-606, Alsa bus company toll tel. 902-422-242), **Salamanca** (4/day, 11 hours, Alsa buses), and **Cadaqués** (2/day, 2.75 hours, €23). Sarfa buses serve all the **coastal resorts** (tel. toll 902-302-025, www.sarfa.com). For bus schedules, see www.barcelonanord.com.

By Plane

Check the reasonable flights from Barcelona to Sevilla or Madrid. Vueling is Iberia's most popular discount airline (e.g., Barcelona–Madrid flights as low as €40 if booked in advance, toll tel. 902-333-933, www.vueling.com). Iberia (toll tel. 902-400-500, www.iberia.com) and Air Europa (toll tel. 902-401-501 or 932-983-907, www.aireuropa.com) offer €80 flights to Madrid. Also, for flights to other parts of Europe, consider British Airways (toll tel. 902-111-333, www.britishairways.com), easyJet (toll tel. 902-299-992, www.easyjet.com), and Ryanair (www.ryanair.com).

Most flights use Barcelona's **El Prat de Llobregat Airport** (tel. 913-211-000). Its two terminals serve both domestic and international flights and are linked by shuttle buses. Air France, Air Europa, American, British, Continental, Delta, Iberia, Lufthansa, Spanair, US Airways, Vueling, and others use the newer terminal 1.

EasyJet and minor airlines use terminal 2. Ryanair uses a smaller airstrip 60 miles away, called **Girona–Costa Brava Airport** (tel. 972-186-600). Information on both airports can be found on the official Spanish airport website, www.aena.es.

For details on getting between either airport and downtown Barcelona, see "Arrival in Barcelona—By Plane" on page 42.

BARCELONA

NEAR BARCELONA

Figueres • Cadaqués • Sitges • Montserrat

Four fine sights are day-trip temptations from Barcelona. Fans of Surrealism can combine a fantasy in Dalí-land by stopping at the Dalí Theater-Museum in Figueres (about two hours from Barcelona) and spending a day or two in the classy but sleepy port-town getaway of Cadaqués (pictured above, an hour from Figueres; note that the Salvador Dalí House in Cadaqués requires reservations to visit). For the consummate day at the beach, head 45 minutes south to the charming and free-spirited resort town of Sitges. Pilgrims with hiking boots head an hour into the mountains for the most sacred spot in Catalunya: Montserrat.

Figueres

The town of Figueres (feeg-YEHR-ehs)—conveniently connected by train to Barcelona—is of sightseeing interest only for its Salvador Dalí Theater-Museum. In fact, the entire town seems Dalí-dominated.

Getting to Figueres

Figueres is an easy day trip from Barcelona, or a handy stopover en route to France. It's cheap and convenient to take a regional train to Figueres Station—they depart from Barcelona's Sants Station or from the RENFE Station at Metro: Passeig de Gràcia (hourly, 2 hours, €30 round-trip). High-speed trains between Barcelona and France stop instead at the recently opened Figueres-Vilafant Station, on the other side of town. But even if you're visiting

Near Barcelona

Figueres on your way to Paris, it's best to take the slower, regional train to Figueres Station in the morning, visit the museum, then go back to the same station to catch the night train to Paris. For bus connections to Cadaqués, see page 136.

Arrival in Figueres: From Figueres Station, simply follow *Museu Dalí* signs (and the crowds) for the 15-minute walk to the museum.

Sights in Figueres

▲▲▲Dalí Theater-Museum (Teatre-Museu Dalí)

This is *the* essential Dalí sight—and, if you like Dalí, one of Europe's most enjoyable museums, period. Inaugurated in 1974, the museum is a work of art in itself. Ever the entertainer and promoter, Dalí personally conceptualized, designed, decorated, and painted it to showcase his life's

work. The museum fills a former theater and is the artist's mausoleum (his tomb is in the crypt below center stage). It's also a kind
of mausoleum to Dalí's creative spirit.

Dalí had his first public art showing at age 14 here in this
building when it was a theater, and he was baptized in the church
just across the street. The place was sentimental to him. After the
theater was destroyed in the Spanish Civil War, Dalí struck a deal
with the mayor: Dalí would rebuild the theater as a museum to
his works, Figueres would be put on the sightseeing map...and the
money's been flowing in ever since.

Even the building's exterior—painted pink, studded with
golden loaves of bread, and topped with monumental eggs and a
geodesic dome—exudes Dalí's outrageous public persona.

Cost and Hours: €12; July-Sept daily 9:00-20:00; Oct and
March-June Tue-Sun 9:30-18:00, closed Mon; Nov-Feb Tue-Sun
10:30-18:00, closed Mon; last entry 45 minutes before closing, tel.
972-677-500, www.salvador-dali.org. No flash photography. The
free bag check has your belongings waiting for you at the exit.

Coin-Op Tip: Much of Dalí's art is movable and coin-
operated—bring a few €0.20 and €1 coins.

Visiting the Museum: The museum has two parts: the
theater-mausoleum and the "Dalí's Jewels" exhibit in an adjacent
building. There's no logical order for a visit (that would be un-
Surrealistic), and the museum can be mobbed at times. Naturally,
there's no audioguide. Dalí said there are two kinds of visitors:
those who don't need a description, and those who aren't worth a
description.

❍ Self-Guided Tour: At the risk of offending Dalí, I've written this loose commentary to attach some meaning to your visit.

Stepping through or around the courtyard, go into the **theater** (with its audience of statues) and face the stage—and Dalí's
unmarked crypt. You know how you can never get a cab when it's
raining? Pop a coin into Dalí's personal 1941 Cadillac, and it rains
inside the car. Look above, atop the tire tower: That's the boat Dalí
enjoyed with his soul mate, Gala—his emotional life preserver,
who kept him from going overboard. When she died, so did he
(for his last seven years). Blue tears made of condoms drip below
the boat.

Up on the **stage,** squint at the big digital Abraham Lincoln,
and president #16 comes into focus. Approach the painting to find
that Abe's facial cheeks are Gala's butt cheeks. Under the painting, a door leads to the **Treasures Room,** with the greatest collection of original Dalí oil paintings in the museum. (Many of
the artworks on the walls are prints.) You'll see Cubist visions of
Cadaqués and dreamy portraits of Gala. Crutches—a recurring
Dalí theme—represent Gala, who kept him supported whenever a

Salvador Dalí
(1904-1989)

When Salvador Dalí was asked, "Are you on drugs?" he replied, "I am the drug...take me."

Labeled by various critics as sick, greedy, paranoid, arrogant, and a clown, Dalí produced some of the most thought-provoking and trail-blazing art of the 20th century. His erotic, violent, disjointed imagery continues to disturb and intrigue today.

Born in Figueres to a well-off family, Dalí showed talent early. He was expelled from Madrid's prestigious art school—twice—but formed longtime friendships with playwright Federico García Lorca and filmmaker Luis Buñuel.

After a breakthrough art exhibit in Barcelona in 1925, Dalí moved to Paris. He hobnobbed with fellow Spaniards Pablo Picasso and Joan Miró, along with a group of artists exploring Sigmund Freud's theory that we all have a hidden part of our mind, the unconscious "id," that surfaces when we dream. Dalí became the best-known spokesman for this group of Surrealists, channeling his id to create photorealistic dream images (melting watches, burning giraffes) set in bizarre dreamscapes.

His life changed forever in 1929, when he met an older, married Russian woman named Gala who would become his wife, muse, model, manager, and emotional compass. Dalí's popular-

meltdown threatened.

The famous **Homage to Mae West room** is a tribute to the sultry seductress. Dalí loved her attitude. Saying things like, "Why marry and make one man unhappy, when you can stay single and make so many so happy?" Mae West was to conventional morality what Dalí was to conventional art. Climb to the vantage point where the sofa lips, fireplace nostrils, painting eyes, and drapery hair come together to make the face of Mae West.

Dalí's art can be playful, but also disturbing. He was passionate about the dark side of things, but with Gala for balance,

ity spread to the US, where he (and Gala) weathered the WWII years.

In his prime, Dalí's work became less Surrealist and more classical, influenced by past masters of painted realism (Velázquez, Raphael, Ingres) and by his own study of history, science, and religion. He produced large-scale paintings of historical events (e.g., Columbus discovering America, the Last Supper) that were collages of realistic scenes floating in a surrealistic landscape, peppered with thought-provoking symbols.

Dalí—an extremely capable technician—mastered many media, including film. *An Andalusian Dog* (*Un Chien Andalou*, 1929, with Luis Buñuel) was a cutting-edge montage of disturbing, eyeball-slicing images. He designed Alfred Hitchcock's big-eye backdrop for the dream sequence of *Spellbound* (1945). He made jewels for the rich and clothes for Coco Chanel, wrote a novel and an autobiography, and pioneered what would come to be called "installations." He also helped develop "performance art" by showing up at an opening in a diver's suit or by playing the role he projected to the media—a super-confident, waxed-mustached artistic genius.

In later years Dalí's over-the-top public image contrasted with his ever-growing illness, depression, and isolation. He endured the scandal of a dealer overselling "limited editions" of his work. When Gala died in 1982, Dalí retreated to his hometown, living his last days in the Torre Galatea of the Theater-Museum complex, where he died of heart failure.

Dalí's legacy as an artist includes his self-marketing persona, his exceptional ability to draw, his provocative pairing of symbols, and his sheer creative drive.

NEAR BARCELONA

he managed never to go off the deep end. Unlike Pablo Casals (the Catalan cellist) and Pablo Picasso (another local artist), Dalí didn't go into exile under Franco's dictatorship. Pragmatically, he accepted both Franco and the Church, and was supported by the dictator. Apart from the occasional *sardana* dance (see sidebar on page 76), you won't find a hint of politics in Dalí's art.

Wander around. You can spend hours here, wondering, is it real or not real? Am I crazy, or is it you? Beethoven is painted with squid ink applied by a shoe on a stormy night. Jesus is made with candle smoke and an eraser. It's fun to see the Dalí-ization of art classics. Dalí, like so many modern artists, was inspired by the masters—especially Velázquez.

The former theater's **smoking lounge** is a highlight, displaying portraits of Gala and Dalí (with a big eye, big ear, and a dark side) bookending a Roman candle of creativity. The fascinating ceiling painting shows the feet of Gala and Dalí as they bridge earth and the heavens. Dalí's drawers are wide open and empty, indicating that he gave everything to his art.

Leaving the theater, keep your ticket and pop into the adjacent **"Dalí's Jewels"** exhibit. It shows sketches and paintings of jewelry Dalí designed, and the actual pieces jewelers made from those surreal visions: a mouth full of pearly whites, a golden finger corset, a fountain of diamonds, and the breathing heart. Explore the ambiguous perception worked into the big painting titled *Apotheosis of the Dollar.*

Cadaqués

Since the late 1800s, Cadaqués (kah-dah-KEHS) has served as a haven for intellectuals and artists alike. The fishing village's craggy coastline, sun-drenched colors, and laid-back lifestyle inspired Fauvists such as Henri Matisse and Surrealists such as René Magritte, Marcel Duchamp, and Federico García Lorca. Even Picasso, drawn to this enchanting coastal haunt, painted some of his Cubist works here.

Salvador Dalí, raised in nearby Figueres, brought international fame to this sleepy Catalan port in the 1920s. As a kid Dalí spent summers here in the family cabin, where he was inspired by the rocky landscape that would later be the backdrop for many Surrealist canvases. In 1929 he met his future wife, Gala, in Cadaqués. Together they converted a fisherman's home in nearby Port Lligat into their semi-permanent residence, dividing their time between New York, Paris, and Cadaqués. And it was here that Dalí did his best work.

In spite of its fame, Cadaqués is mellow and feels off the beaten path. If you want a peaceful beach-town escape near Barcelona, this is a good place. From the moment you descend into the town, taking in whitewashed buildings and deep blue waters, you'll be struck by the port's tranquility and beauty. Join the locals playing chess or cards at the cavernous Casino Coffee House (harborfront, with games and Internet access). Have a glass of *vino tinto* or *cremat* (a traditional rum-and-coffee drink served flambé-style) at one of the seaside cafés. Savor the lapping waves, brilliant sun, and gentle breeze. And, for sightseeing, the reason to come to Cadaqués is the Salvador Dalí House, a 20-minute walk from the town center at Port Lligat.

Getting to Cadaqués
Reaching Cadaqués is very tough without a car. There are no trains and only a few buses a day.

By Car: It's a twisty drive from Figueres (figure 45-60 minutes). In Cadaqués, drivers should park in the big lot just above the city—don't try to park near the harborfront. To reach the Salvador Dalí House, follow signs near Cadaqués to Port Lligat (easy parking).

By Bus: Sarfa buses serve Cadaqués from **Figueres** (3/day, 1 hour, €6) and from **Barcelona** (2/day, more in July-Aug, 2.75 hours, €23). Bus info: Barcelona toll tel. 902-302-025, Cadaqués tel. 972-258-713, Figueres tel. 972-674-298, www.sarfa.com.

Tourist Information

The TI is at Carrer Cotxe 2 (July-Sept Mon-Sat 9:00-21:00, Sun 10:00-13:00, shorter hours off-season plus closed for lunch, tel. 972-258-315, www.visitcadaques.org).

Sights near Cadaqués

In Port Lligat

▲▲▲Salvador Dalí House (Casa Museu Salvador Dalí)— Once Dalí's home, this house gives fans a chance to explore his

labyrinthine compound. This is the best artist's house I've toured in Europe. It shows how a home can really reflect the creative spirit of an artistic genius and his muse. The ambience, both inside and out, is perfect for a Surrealist hanging out with his creative playmate. The bay is ringed by sleepy islands. Fishing boats are jumbled on the beach. After the fishermen painted their boats, Dalí asked them to clean their brushes on his door—creating an abstract work of art he adored (which you'll see as you line up to get your ticket).

The interior is left almost precisely as it was in 1982, when Gala died and Dalí moved out. See Dalí's studio (the clever easel cranks up and down to allow the artist to paint while seated, as he did eight hours a day); the bohemian-yet-divine living room (complete with a mirror to reflect the sunrise onto their bed each morning); the phallic-shaped swimming pool, which was the scene of orgiastic parties; and the painter's study (with his favorite mustaches all lined up). Like Dalí's art, his home is offbeat, provocative, and fun.

Cost and Hours: €11; mid-June-mid-Sept daily 9:30-21:00; mid-Feb-mid-June and mid-Sept-early Jan Tue-Sun 10:30-18:00, closed Mon; closed early Jan-mid-Feb. Last tour departs 50 minutes before closing. No bags of any kind are allowed in the house;

the baggage check is free.

Reservations: You must reserve in advance—call, use the website, or send email with specifics on the day and time you want to visit (tel. 972-251-015, www.salvador-dali.org, pllgrups @fundaciodali.org). In summer, book a week in advance. You must arrive 30 minutes early to pick up your ticket, or they'll sell it.

Touring the House: Only 8-10 people are allowed in (no large groups) every 10 minutes. Once inside, there are five sections, each with a guard who gives you a brief explanation in English, and then turns you loose for a few minutes. The entire visit takes 50 minutes. Before your tour, enjoy the 15-minute video that plays in the waiting lounge (with walls covered in Dalí media coverage) just across the lane from the house.

Getting There: Parking is free nearby. There are no buses or taxis. The house is a 20-minute, one-mile walk over the hill from Cadaqués to Port Lligat. (The path, which cuts across the isthmus, is much shorter than the road.)

Sleeping in Cadaqués

$$ Hotel Llané Petit, with 37 spacious rooms (half with view balconies), is a small resort-like hotel with its own little beach, a 10-minute walk south of the town center (Db-€124 mid-July-Aug, €92 in shoulder season, €59 in winter, €35 more for seaview rooms, air-con, elevator, Dr. Bartomeus 37, tel. 972-251-020, fax 972-258-778, www.llanepetit.com, info@llanepetit.com). Reserve direct with this book to get a free €12 breakfast (not valid on weekends and mid-July-Aug).

Sleep Code

(€1 = about $1.40, country code: 34)

S = Single, **D** = Double/Twin, **T** = Triple, **Q** = Quad, **b** = bathroom, **s** = shower only. Unless otherwise noted, credit cards are accepted and English is spoken.

To help you easily sort through these listings, I've divided the accommodations into two categories, based on the price for a standard double room with bath (during high season):

  $$ Higher Priced—Most rooms €85 or more.
  $ Lower Priced—Most rooms less than €85.

Prices can change without notice; verify the hotel's current rates online or by email. For other updates, see www .ricksteves.com/update.

$ Hotel Nou Estrelles is a big concrete exercise in efficient, economic comfort. Facing the bus stop a few blocks in from the waterfront, this family-run hotel offers 15 rooms at a great value (Db-€85 in high season, €60-74 in shoulder season, €55 in winter, extra bed-€10, breakfast-€7, air-con, elevator, Carrer Sant Vicens, tel. 972-259-100, www.hotelnouestrelles.com, reservas@hotelnou estrelles.com, Emma).

$ Hostal Marina is a cheap, low-energy place, with 27 rooms and a great location a block from the harborfront main square (high season: D-€55, Db-€80; low season: D-€40, Db-€50; balcony rooms-€10 extra, no breakfast, no elevator, no English, Riera 3, tel. 972-159-091).

Eating in Cadaqués

There are plenty of eateries along the beach. A lane called Carrer Miguel Rosset (across from Hotel La Residencia) also has several places worth considering. At **Casa Anita** you'll sit with others around a big table and enjoy house specialties such as *calamares a la plancha* (grilled squid) and homemade *helado* (ice cream). Finish your meal with a glass of sweet Muscatel (closed Mon, Calle Miquel Rosset 16, tel. 972-258-471, Juan and family).

Sitges

Sitges (SEE-juhz) is one of Catalunya's most popular resort towns. Because the town beautifully mingles sea and light, it's long been an artists' colony. Here you can still feel the soul of the Modernistas...in the architecture, the museums, the salty sea breeze, and the relaxed rhythm of life.

Today's Sitges is a world-renowned vacation destination among the gay community. Despite its jet-set status, the Old Town has managed to retain its charm. With a much slower pulse than Barcelona, Sitges is an enjoyable break from the big city.

If you visit during one of Sitges' two big **festivals** (St. Bartholomew on Aug 24 and St. Tecla on Sept 23), you may see teams of *castellers* competing to build human pyramids.

NEAR BARCELONA

Getting to Sitges

Southbound trains depart Barcelona from Sants Station (take *cercanías* train on the dark green line number 2 toward Sant Vincenç de Calders, 4/hour, 30-35 minutes, €3 each way). Closer to Barcelona's city center, you can catch this same train at the Passeig de Gràcia RENFE Station.

Orientation to Sitges

Tourist Information

The **main TI** is a couple of blocks northwest of the train station (mid-June–mid-Sept Mon-Sat 9:00-20:00, closed Sun; mid-Sept–mid-June Mon-Fri 9:00-14:00 & 16:00-18:30, closed Sat-Sun; Sínia Morera 1). Convenient branch kiosks are in front of the **train station** (mid-June–mid-Sept daily 9:00-13:00 & 17:00-21:00, closed off-season) and down at the start of the **beach promenade** (mid-June–mid-Sept Mon-Sat 10:00-14:00 & 16:00-20:00, Sun 10:00-14:00; mid-Sept–mid-June daily 10:00-14:00 plus Fri-Sat 16:00-19:00). Sitges' TIs share the same phone number (toll tel. 902-103-428) and website (www.sitgestur.com). At any TI, pick up the good map (with info on sights on the back) and brochures for any museums that interest you. The TI can also help you find a room.

Arrival in Sitges

From the train station, exit straight ahead (past a TI kiosk—open in summer) and walk down Carrer Francesc Gumà. When it dead-ends, continue right onto Carrer de Jesús, which takes you to the town's tiny main square, Plaça del Cap de la Villa. (Keep an eye out for directional signs.) From here turn right down Carrer Major ("Main Street"), which leads you past the old market hall (now an art gallery) and the town hall, to a beautiful terrace next to the main church. Poke into the Old Town or take the grand staircase down to the beach promenade.

Sights in Sitges

Sitges basically has two attractions: Its tight-and-tiny Old Town (with a few good museums) and its long, luxurious beaches.

Old Town—Take time to explore the Old Town's narrow streets. They're crammed with cafés, boutiques, and all the resort staples.

The focal point, on the waterfront, is the 17th-century Baroque-style **Sant Bartomeu i Santa Tecla Church.** The terrace in front of the church will help you get the lay of the land.

As an art town, Sitges has seen its share of creative people—some of whom have left their mark in the form of appealing muse-

ums. Walking along the water behind the church, you'll find two of the town's three museums, which unfortunately will likely be closed for the next couple of years. When open, the **Museu Maricel** displays the eclectic artwork of a local collector, including some Modernista works, pieces by local Sitges artists, and a collection of maritime-themed works. The **Museu Cau Ferrat** bills itself as a "temple of art," as collected by local intellectual Santiago Rusiñol. In addition to paintings and drawings, there's ironwork, glass, and ceramics. Also on this square, you'll see **Palau Maricel**—a sumptuous old mansion that's sometimes open to the public for concerts in the summer (ask at TI). The third museum, which will remain open during the closure of the first two, is the **Museu Romàntic.** Offering a look at 19th-century bourgeois lifestyles in an elegant mansion, the museum is a few blocks up (one block west of main square: Head out of the square on the main pedestrian street, then take the first right turn, to Sant Gaudenci 1). Inside, amidst gilded hallways, you'll find a collection of more than 400 dolls (€3.50; July-Sept Tue-Sat 9:30-14:00 & 16:00-19:00, Sun 10:00-15:00, closed Mon; Oct-June Tue-Sat 9:30-14:00 & 15:30-18:30, Sun 10:00-15:00, closed Mon, tel. 938-942-969).

Beaches—Nine beaches, separated by breakwaters, extend about a mile southward from town. Stroll down the seaside promenade, which stretches from the town to the end of the beaches. Anyone can enjoy the sun, sea, and sand; or you can rent a beach chair to relax like a pro. The crowds thin out about halfway down, and the last three beaches are more intimate and cove-like. Along the way, restaurants and *chiringuitos* (beachfront bars) serve tapas, paella, and drinks.

If you walk all the way to the end, you can continue inland to enjoy the nicely landscaped **Terramar Gardens** (Jardins de Terramar; free, daily mid-June-mid-Sept 10:30-20:30, mid-Sept-mid-June 9:00-19:00).

Sleeping in Sitges

Because it's an in-demand resort town, hotel values are not much better here than in Barcelona (especially in summer). But if you prefer a swanky beach town to a big city, consider these options. Note that this is a party town, so expect some noise after hours (request a quiet room). I've listed peak-season prices (roughly mid-July-mid-Sept); these drop substantially off-season. The first one is on the beach, whereas the other two are old villas with colorful tile

NEAR BARCELONA

floors a few blocks into town.

$$ Hotel Celimar, with 26 small but modern rooms, occupies a classic Modernista building facing the beach (Db-€150, €20 extra for sea view, average price off-season-€90, check website for latest prices, air-con, elevator, free Wi-Fi, Paseo de la Ribera 20, tel. 938-110-170, fax 938-110-403, www.hotelcelimar.com, info @hotelcelimar.com).

$$ Hotel Romàntic is family-run, old-fashioned-elegant, and quirky. Its 78 rooms (including some in the annex, Hotel de la Renaixença) are nothing special, but the whole place feels classic and classy—especially the plush lounge and bar (S-€75, Sb-€89, D-€105, Db-€123, €10 extra for balcony, includes breakfast, no air-con or elevator, free Wi-Fi, Sant Isidre 33, tel. 938-948-375, fax 938-114-129, www.hotelromantic.com, romantic@hotelromantic.com).

$$ El Xalet (as in "Chalet") is of a similar vintage, with a little less style and lower prices. They have 11 rooms in the main hotel and another 12 in their annex, Hotel Noucentista, up the street—both in fine old Modernista buildings (Db-€100, €25 extra for suite, includes breakfast, air-con, free Wi-Fi, Carrer Illa de Cuba 35, tel. 938-110-070, fax 938-945-579, www.elxalet.com, info@elxalet.com).

Montserrat

Montserrat—the "serrated mountain"—rockets dramatically up from the valley floor northwest of Barcelona. With its unique rock formations, a dramatic mountaintop monastery (also called Montserrat), and spiritual connection with the Catalan people and their struggles, it's a popular day trip. This has been Catalunya's most important pilgrimage site for a thousand years. Hymns explain how the mountain was carved by  little angels with golden saws. Geologists blame nature at work.

Once upon a time, there was no mountain. A river flowed here, laying down silt that hardened into sedimentary layers of hard rock. Ten million years ago, the continents shifted, and the land around the rock massif sank, exposing this series of peaks that reach upward to 4,000 feet. Over time, erosion pocked the face with caves and cut vertical grooves near the top, creating the famous serrated look.

The monastery is nestled in the jagged peaks at 2,400 feet, but it seems higher because of the way the rocky massif rises out of nowhere. The air is certainly fresher than in Barcelona. In a quick day trip, you can view the mountain from its base, ride a funicular up to the top of the world, tour the basilica and museum, touch a Black Virgin's orb, hike down to a sacred cave, and listen to Gregorian chants by the world's oldest boys' choir.

Montserrat's monastery is Benedictine, and its 30 monks carry on its spiritual tradition. Since 1025 the slogan *"ora et labora"* ("prayer and work") has pretty much summed up life for a monk here.

The Benedictines welcome visitors—both pilgrims and tourists—and offer this travel tip: Please remember that the most important part of your Montserrat visit is not enjoying the architecture, but rather discovering the religious, cultural, historical, social, and environmental values that together symbolically express the life of the Catalan people.

Getting to Montserrat

Barcelona is connected to the valley below Montserrat by a convenient train; from there a cable car or rack railway (your choice) takes you up to the mountaintop. Both options are similar in cost and take about the same amount of time (hourly trains, 1.5 hours each way from downtown Barcelona to the monastery). For ticket options, see the sidebar. Driving or taking the bus round out your options.

Train Plus Cable Car or Rack Railway

By Train: Trains leave hourly from Barcelona's Plaça d'Espanya to Montserrat. Take the Metro to Espanya, then follow signs showing a picture of a train to the FGC (Ferrocarrils de la Generalitat de Catalunya) underground station. Once there, look for train line R5 (direction: Manresa, departures at :36 past each hour).

You'll ride about an hour on the train. As you reach the base of the mountain, you have two options: Get out at Montserrat-Aeri for the cable car, or continue another few minutes to the next stop—Monistrol de Montserrat (or simply "Monistrol de M.")—for the rack railway. (You'll have to make this decision when you buy your ticket in Barcelona—see "Tickets to Montserrat" sidebar.)

Cable Car or Rack Train? For the sake of scenery and fun, I enjoy the little German-built cable car more than the rack railway. Departures are more frequent (4/hour rather than hourly on the railway), but because the cable car is small, you might have to wait for a while to get on. If you are afraid of heights, take the rack train. Paying the extra €5 to ride both isn't worthwhile.

By Cable Car, at the Montserrat-Aeri Stop: Departing the

Tickets to Montserrat

Various combo-tickets cover your journey to Montserrat, as well as some of the sights you'll visit there. All begin with the train from Barcelona's Plaça d'Espanya, and include either the cable car or rack railway—you'll have to specify one or the other when you buy the ticket (same price for either option). You can't go one way and come back the other, unless you pay extra (about €5) for the leg that's not included in your ticket.

The basic option is to buy a **train ticket** to Montserrat (€16 round-trip, includes the cable car or rack railway to monastery, Eurailpass not valid, tel. 932-051-515, www.fgc.es). Note that if you buy this ticket in Barcelona, then decide at Montserrat that you want to use the funiculars to go higher up the mountain or to the Sacred Cave, you can buy an €8.35 ticket covering both funiculars at the TI or at either funicular.

If you plan to do some sightseeing once at Montserrat, it makes sense to spend a little more on one of two combo-tickets from the train company: The €23.10 **Trans Montserrat** ticket includes your round-trip Metro ride in Barcelona to and from the train station, the train trip, the cable car or rack railway, unlimited trips on the two funiculars at Montserrat, and entry to the disappointing audiovisual presentation. The €38.45 **Tot Montserrat** ticket includes all of this, plus the good Museum of Montserrat and a self-service lunch (served daily 12:00-16:00, Easter-Sept in the big building on the way to the parking lot, off-season in the cafeteria near the TI). Both tickets are well-explained in the Barcelona TI's online shop (http://bcnshop.barcelonaturisme.com; look for them under the "Near Barcelona" tab).

If you plan to do it all, you'll save at least €5 with either of these combo-tickets. But during the off-season, ask the TI if one of the funiculars or the cable car is closed for maintenance; if so, the combo-ticket may not be worth it.

You can buy any of these tickets from the automated machines at Barcelona's Plaça d'Espanya Station (tourist officials are standing by in the morning to help you figure it out). To use your included round-trip Metro ride to get *to* the station, buy the ticket in advance at the Plaça de Catalunya TI in Barcelona, or at the uncrowded FGC La Molina office next to Plaça de Catalunya (Mon-Fri 10:00-14:00 & 16:30-20:30, Sat 10:00-14:00, closed Sun, see map on page 55 for location, Pelai 17-39 Triangle, tel. 933-664-553).

train, follow signs to the cable-car station (€6 one-way, €9 round-trip, covered by your train or combo-ticket, 4/hour, 5-minute trip, daily March-Oct 9:40-14:00 & 14:35-19:00, Nov-Feb 10:10-14:00 & 14:35-17:45—note the lunch break). Because the cable car is smaller than the train, don't linger or you might have to wait for the next car. On the way back down, cable cars depart from the monastery every 15 minutes; make sure to give yourself enough time to catch the Barcelona-bound trains leaving at :48 past the hour.

By Rack Railway (Cremallera), at the Monistrol de Montserrat Stop: From this stop you can catch the Cremallera rack railway up to the monastery (€5.30 one-way, €8.45 round-trip, cheaper off-season, covered by your train or combo-ticket, hourly, 20-minute trip, www.cremalleradmontserrat.com). On the return trip, this train departs the monastery at :15 past the hour (:22 past the hour on winter weekdays), allowing you to catch the Barcelona-bound train leaving Monistrol de Montserrat at :44 past the hour. The last convenient connection back to Barcelona leaves the monastery at 18:15 (or 20:15 in July-Aug). Confirm the schedule when you arrive, as specific times tend to change year to year. Note that there is one intermediate stop on this line (Monistrol-Vila, at a large parking garage), but—going in either direction—you want to stay on until the end of the line.

By Car or Bus

By Car: Once drivers get out of Barcelona (Road #82, then C-55), it's a short 30-minute drive to the base of the mountain, then a 10-minute series of switchbacks to the actual site (where you can find parking for €5/day). It may be easier to park your car down below and ride the cable car up.

By Bus: One bus per day connects downtown Barcelona directly to the monastery at Montserrat (departs from Viriat Street near Barcelona's Sants Station daily at 9:15, returns from the monastery to Barcelona at 18:00 June-Sept or at 17:00 Oct-May, €5 each way, one-hour trip depending on traffic). You can also take a four-hour bus tour offered by the Barcelona Guide Bureau (€40, leaves Mon-Sat at 15:00 from Plaça Catalunya; see page 50). However, since the other options are scenic, fun, and relatively easy, the only reason to take a bus is to avoid transfers.

Orientation to Montserrat

When you arrive at the base of the mountain, look up the rock face to find the cable-car line, the monastery near the top, and the tiny building midway up (marking the Sacred Cave).

However you make your way up to the Montserrat monastery, it's easy to get oriented once you arrive at the top. Everything is within a few minutes' walk of your entry point. All of the transit options—including the rack railway and cable car—converge at the big train station. Above those are both funicular stations: one up to the ridgetop, the other down to the Sacred Cave trail. Across the street is the TI, and above that (either straight up the stairs, or up the ramp around the left side) is the main square. To the right of the station, a long road leads along the cliff to the parking lot; a humble farmers' market along here sells *mel y mató*, a characteristic Catalan cheese with honey.

Crowd-Beating Tips: Arrive early or late, as tour groups mob the place midday. Crowds are less likely on weekdays and worst on Sundays.

Tourist Information

The square below the basilica houses a helpful TI, right across from the rack railway station (daily from 9:00, closes just after last train heads down—roughly 18:15, or 20:15 in July-Aug, tel. 938-777-701, www.montserratvisita.com). Pick up the free map and get your questions answered. A good audioguide, available only at the TI, describes the general site and basilica (€6 includes book; €12 includes entrance to museum, bland audiovisual presentation, and book). If you're a hiker, buy a hiking brochure here. Trails offer spectacular views (on clear days) to the Mediterranean and even (on clearer days) to the Pyrenees.

The audiovisual center (upstairs from the TI) provides some cultural and historical perspective—and an entrance to their big gift shop. The lame interactive exhibition—nowhere near as exciting as the mountains and basilica outside—includes computer touch-screens and a short 20-minute video in English. Learn about the mountain's history, and get a glimpse into the daily lives of the monastery's resident monks (€2, covered by Trans Montserrat and Tot Montserrat combo-tickets, same hours as TI).

Self-Guided Spin Tour

From the monastery's main square, Plaça de Santa Maria, face the main facade and take this spin tour, moving from right to left: Like a good pilgrim, face Mary, the centerpiece of the facade. Below her to the left is St. Benedict, the sixth-century monk who established the rules that came to govern Montserrat's monastery. St. George,

The History of Montserrat

The first hermit monks built huts at Montserrat around A.D. 900. By 1025, a monastery was founded. The Montserrat Escolania, or Choir School, soon followed, and is considered to be the oldest music school in Europe (they still perform—see "Choir Concert" on page 150).

Legend has it that in medieval times, some shepherd children saw lights and heard songs coming from the mountain. They traced the sounds to a cave (now called the Sacred Cave, or Santa Cova), where they found the Black Virgin statue (La Moreneta), making the monastery a pilgrim magnet.

In 1811 Napoleon's invading French troops destroyed Montserrat's buildings, though the Black Virgin, hidden away by monks, survived. Then, in the 1830s, the Spanish royalty—tired of dealing with pesky religious orders—dissolved the monasteries and convents.

But in the 1850s, the monks returned as part of Catalunya's (and Europe's) renewed Romantic appreciation for all things medieval and nationalistic. (Montserrat's revival coincided with other traditions born out of rejuvenated Catalan pride: the much-loved Football Club Barcelona; Barcelona's Palace of Catalan Music; and even the birth of local sparkling wine, *cava*.) Montserrat's basilica and monastery were reconstructed and became, once more, the strongly beating spiritual and cultural heart of the Catalan people.

Then came Francisco Franco, the dictatorial leader who wanted a monolithic Spain. To him Montserrat represented Catalan rebelliousness. During Franco's long rule, from 1939 to 1973, the *sardana* dance was still illegally performed here (but with a different name), and literature was published in the outlawed Catalan language. In 1970, 300 intellectuals demonstrating for more respect for human rights in Spain were locked up in the monastery for several days by Franco's police.

But now Franco is history. The 1990s brought another phase of rebuilding (after a forest fire and rain damage), and the Montserrat community is thriving once again, unafraid to display its pride for the Catalan people, culture, and faith.

the symbol of Catalunya, is on the right (amid victims of Spain's Civil War).

Five arches line the base of the church. The one on the far right leads pilgrims to the high point of any visit, the Black Virgin (a.k.a. La Moreneta). The center arch leads into the basilica, and the arch second from left directs you to a small votive chapel filled with articles representing prayer requests or thanks.

Left of the basilica, the delicate arches mark the old monks' cloister. Beneath that are four trees planted by the monks, hoping to harvest only their symbolism (palm = martyrdom, cypress = eternal life, olive = peace, and laurel = victory). Next to the trees are a public library and a peaceful reading room. The big archway is the private entrance to the monastery. Then comes the modern hotel and, below that, the modern, white museum. Other buildings provide cells for pilgrims. The Sant Joan funicular lifts hikers up to the trailhead (you can see the tiny building at the top). From there you can take a number of fine hikes (described later). Another funicular station descends to the Sacred Cave. And, finally, five arches separate statues of founders of the great religious orders. Step over to the arches for a commanding view (on a clear day) of the Llobregat River, meandering all the way to the Mediterranean.

Sights in Montserrat

Basilica—Although there's been a church here since the 11th century, the present structure was built in the 1850s, and the facade only dates from 1968. The decor is Neo-Romanesque, so popular with the Romantic artists of the late 19th century. The basilica itself is ringed with interesting chapels, but the focus is on the Black Virgin sitting high above the main altar.

Montserrat's top attraction is **La Moreneta,** the small wood statue of the Black Virgin, discovered in the Sacred Cave in the 12th century. Legend says she was carved by St. Luke (the Gospel writer and supposed artist), brought to Spain by St. Peter, hidden away in the cave during the Moorish invasions, and miraculously discovered by shepherd children. (Carbon dating says she's 800 years old.) While George is the patron saint of Catalunya, La Moreneta is its patroness, having been crowned as such by the pope in 1881. "Moreneta" is usually translated as "black" in English, but the Spanish name actually means "tanned." The statue was originally lighter, but darkened over the centuries from candle smoke, humidity, and the natural aging of its original varnish. Pilgrims shuffle down a long, ornate passage leading alongside the church for their few moments alone with the virgin (free, daily 8:00-10:30 & 12:00-18:30, plus 19:30-20:15 in summer, www.aba diamontserrat.net). The church itself has longer hours and daily services (Mass at 11:00, vespers at 18:45).

Join the line of pilgrims (along the right side of the church). Though Mary is behind a protective glass case, the royal orb she cradles in her hands is exposed. Pilgrims touch Mary's orb with one hand and hold their other hand up to show that they accept Jesus. Newlyweds in particular seek Mary's blessing.

Immediately after La Moreneta, turn right into the delightful Neo-Romanesque prayer chapel, where worshippers sit behind the Virgin and continue to pray. The ceiling, painted in the Modernista style in 1898 by Joan Llimona, shows Jesus and Mary high in heaven. The trail connecting Catalunya with heaven seems to lead through these serrated mountains. The figures depicted lower are people symbolizing Catalan history and culture.

You'll leave by walking along the Ave Maria Path (along the outside of the church), which thoughtfully integrates nature and the basilica. Thousands of colorful votive candles are all busy helping the devout with their prayers. Before you leave the inner courtyard and head out into the main square, pop in to the humble little room with the many votive offerings. This is where people leave personal belongings (wedding dresses, baby's baptism outfits, wax replicas of body parts in need of healing, and so on) as part of a prayer request or as a thanks for divine intercession.

Museum of Montserrat—The bright, shiny, and cool collection of paintings and artifacts was mostly donated by devout Catalan Catholics. While it's nothing really earth-shaking, you'll enjoy an air-conditioned wander past lots of antiquities and fine artwork. Head upstairs first to see some lesser-known works by the likes of Picasso, El Greco, Caravaggio, Monet, Renoir, Pissarro, Degas, John Singer Sargent, and some local Modernista artists. One gallery shows how artists have depicted the Black Virgin of Montserrat over the centuries in many different styles. There's even a small Egyptian section, with a sarcophagus and mummy. Down on the main floor, you'll see ecclesiastical gear, a good icon collection, and more paintings, including—at the very end—a Dalí painting, some Picasso sketches and prints, and a Miró (€6.50, covered by Tot Montserrat combo-ticket; July-Aug daily 10:00-18:45; Sept-June Mon-Fri 10:00-17:45, Sat-Sun 10:00-18:45; tel. 938-777-745).

Sant Joan Funicular and Hikes—This funicular climbs 820 feet above the monastery in five minutes (€4.65 one-way, €7.40 round-trip, covered by Trans Montserrat and Tot Montserrat combo-tickets, goes every 20 minutes, more often with demand). At the top of the funicular, you are at the starting point of a 20-minute walk that takes you to the Sant Joan Chapel (follow sign for *Ermita de St. Joan*). Other hikes also begin

at the trailhead by the funicular (get details from TI before you ascend; basic map with suggested hikes posted by upper funicular station). For a quick and easy chance to get out into nature, simply ride up and follow the most popular hike, a 45-minute mostly downhill loop through mountain scenery back to the monastery. To take this route, go left from the funicular station; the trail—marked *Monestir de Montserrat*—will first go up to a rocky crest before heading downhill.

Sacred Cave (Santa Cova)—The Moreneta was originally discovered in the Sacred Cave (or Sacred Grotto), a 40-minute hike down from the monastery (then another 50 minutes back up). The path (c. 1900) was designed by devoted and patriotic Modernista architects, including Gaudí and Josep Puig i Cadafalch. It's lined with Modernista statues depicting scenes from the life of Christ. While the original Black Virgin statue is now in the basilica, a replica sits in the cave. A three-minute funicular ride cuts 20 minutes off the hike (€1.90 one-way, €3 round-trip, covered by Trans Montserrat and Tot Montserrat combo-tickets, goes every 20 minutes, more often with demand).

If you're here late in the afternoon, check the schedule before you head into the Sacred Cave to make sure you don't miss the final ride back down the mountain. Missing the last funicular could mean catching a train back to Barcelona later than you had planned.

Choir Concert—Montserrat's Escolania, or Choir School, has been training voices for centuries. Fifty young boys, who live and study in the monastery itself, make up the choir, which performs daily except Saturday (Mon-Fri at 13:00, Sun-Thu at 18:45, and Sun also at 12:00, choir on vacation late June-late Aug). The boys sing for only 10 minutes, the basilica is jam-packed, and it's likely you'll see almost nothing. Also note that if you attend the evening performance, you'll miss the last train or cable-car ride down the mountain.

Sleeping in Montserrat

An overnight here gets you monastic peace and a total break from the modern crowds. There are ample rustic cells for pilgrim visitors, but tourists might prefer this place:

$$ Hotel Abat Cisneros, a three-star hotel with 82 rooms and all the comforts, is low-key and appropriate for a sanctuary (Sb-€43-66, Db-€74-115, price depends on season, includes breakfast, half- and full-board available, elevator, pay Internet access, free Wi-Fi, tel. 938-777-701, fax 938-777-724, www.abadiamontserrat.cat, reserves@larsa-montserrat.cat).

THE CAMINO DE SANTIAGO

St. Jean-Pied-de-Port • Pamplona • Burgos • León • O Cebreiro • Lugo

The Camino de Santiago—the "Way of St. James"—is Europe's ultimate pilgrimage route. Since the Middle Ages, humble pilgrims have trod hundreds of miles across the north of Spain to pay homage to the remains of St. James in his namesake city, Santiago de Compostela. After several lonely centuries, the route has been rediscovered, and more and more pilgrims are traveling—by foot, bike, and horse—along this ancient pathway.

While dedicating a month of your life to walk the Camino is admirable, you might not have that kind of time. But with a car (or public transportation), any traveler can use the Camino as a sightseeing spine—a string of worthwhile cities, towns, and countryside sights—and an opportunity to periodically "play pilgrim."

There were many ancient pilgrimage routes across Europe to Santiago de Compostela, but the most popular one across Spain—and the route described here—has always been the so-called "French Road" (Camino Francés), which covers nearly 500 miles across northern Spain from the French border to Santiago.

The route begins in the French foothills of the Pyrenees, in the Basque village of St. Jean-Pied-de-Port. Twist up and over rugged Roncesvalles Pass into Spain, and on to Pamplona—the delightful, Basque-flavored capital of Navarre, famous for its Running of the Bulls. From here head west through the fertile hills of Navarre to the vineyards of La Rioja, then across the endless wheat fields and rough, arid plains of northern Castile to Burgos and León, with their beautiful dueling Gothic cathedrals—one a riot of architectural styles, the other gracefully simple but packed with stained glass.

As the path crosses into Galicia near the time-passed stony

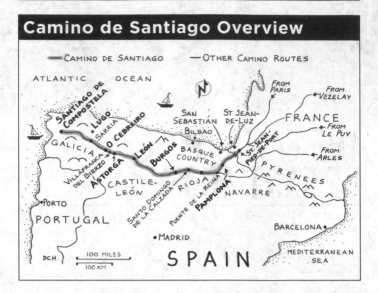

Camino de Santiago Overview

mountain village of O Cebreiro, the terrain changes, becoming lush and green. This last leg of the journey, in Galicia, is the most popular: Pilgrims pass simple farms, stone churches, moss-covered homes with slate roofs, apple orchards, flocks of sheep, dense forests of oak, sweet chestnut, and eucalyptus...and plenty of other pilgrims. Just before Santiago, the ancient walled Roman city of Lugo is a worthwhile detour for car travelers.

Whether undertaken for spiritual edification or sightseeing pleasure, the Camino de Santiago ties together some of Spain's most appealing landscape, history, architecture, and people.

Getting Around the Camino de Santiago

By Car: This chapter is geared for car pilgrims who want to trace the Camino and linger at the highlights. Italicized directions marked by a bullet point are designed for drivers (with specific route tips, road numbers, and directional signs). To supplement these instructions, it's essential to get a good road map (most TIs can give you a free map covering just their province, or you can buy a better one by Michelin or Mapa Total for about €6). Driving the full Camino nonstop would take about 12 hours. Assuming you're taking the most direct (expressway/*autovía*) route, figure these estimated times for specific legs of the Camino by car (these times don't take into account stops or detours, such as the La Rioja Wine Loop):

- St. Jean-Pied-de-Port to Pamplona—1.5 hours
- Pamplona to Burgos—3.5 hours
- Burgos to León—2 hours

- León to Astorga—1 hour
- Astorga to O Cebreiro—1.5 hours
- O Cebreiro to Lugo—1 hour
- Lugo to Santiago—1.5 hours

Many freeways are marked *Autovía Camino de Santiago* to keep you on track. But be warned that *Camino de Santiago* directional signs in small towns can be misleading, since they're sometimes intended for foot pilgrims, not drivers. Navigate by town names and road numbers instead.

By Public Transportation: Most of the Camino route can be done by bus and/or train. However, it can be difficult, or even impossible, to reach some of the out-of-the-way stops between the big cities (such as O Cebreiro), and there's no good, direct link from St. Jean-Pied-de-Port to Pamplona. Where feasible, I've listed train and bus connections for each of the main stops. Trains cover all the major cities, and Alsa buses also link the main stops. See the special "Xacobeo" section on the Alsa bus website (www .alsa.es) for routes delivering pilgrims to all the possible starting points for the Camino.

The Old-Fashioned Way: If you're walking or biking the entire Camino, don't rely exclusively on my coverage in this chapter (which describes the major towns and cities, but ignores so much more). Equip yourself with a good day-by-day guidebook with details on each leg, and get good advice about what to pack. For starters, see the sidebar "Walking the Way," on page 268.

CAMINO DE SANTIAGO

Planning Your Time

Drivers begin in Basque Country (San Sebastián in Spain or St. Jean-de-Luz in France), where you can pick up your rental car. If you're in a hurry or don't plan to visit France, you can skip St. Jean-Pied-de-Port and connect easily to Pamplona from Spain's Basque Country.

Day 1: Drive through the French Basque villages (see previous chapter) to St. Jean-Pied-de-Port, then over Roncesvalles Pass to Pamplona. Sleep in Pamplona.

Day 2: Explore Pamplona, then drive westward to Burgos (stopping en route at Puente de la Reina, and detouring for the La Rioja Wine Loop if you have time and a healthy interest in wine). Sleep in Burgos.

Day 3: Sightsee Burgos this morning, then drive to León and dip into the cathedral there. Sleep in León—or, if you're tired of

La Historia del Camino

The first person to undertake the Camino de Santiago was... Santiago himself. After the death of Christ, the apostles scattered to the corners of the earth to spread the Word of God. Supposedly, St. James went on a missionary trip from the Holy Land all the way to the northwest corner of Spain, which, at that point, really was the end of the world. (For more on St. James, see the sidebar on page 301.)

According to legend, St. James' remains were discovered in 813 in the town that would soon bear his name. This put Santiago de Compostela on the map, as one of three places—along with Rome and Jerusalem—where remains of apostles are known to be buried. In 951 Godescalco, the Bishop of Le Puy in France, walked to Santiago de Compostela to pay homage to the relics. As other pilgrims followed his example, the Camino de Santiago informally emerged. Then, in the 12th century, Pope Callistus II decreed that any person who walked to Santiago in a Holy Year, confessed their sins, and took communion at the cathedral would be forgiven. This opportunity for a cheap indulgence made the Camino de Santiago one of the most important pilgrimages in the world.

It's probably no coincidence that St. James' remains were "discovered" and promoted just as the Reconquista was in full swing. The pope's decree helped to consolidate the Christians' hold over lands retaken from the Moors. Pilgrims were ideal candidates to repopulate and defend northern Spain. Many of those who made the journey to Santiago stuck around somewhere along the route (often because of privileges granted them by local rulers who needed help rebuilding). It became a self-sustaining little circle: Pilgrims came along the Camino, saw great sights, and decided to stay...to build even greater sights for the next pilgrims to enjoy.

The Christian monarchy designated an old Roman commercial road from France across northern Iberia as the "official" route, and soon churches, monasteries, hostels, hospitals, blacksmiths, and other pilgrims' services began to pop up. Religious-military orders such as the Knights of Santiago and the Knights Templar protected the route from bandits and fought alongside Christian armies against the Moorish resurgence, allowing the evolving Catholic state to gather strength in the safe haven created by the Camino.

In the Middle Ages, pilgrims came to Santiago from all over Europe—mostly from France, but also from Portugal, Italy, Britain, the Netherlands, Germany, Scandinavia, and Eastern Europe. Many prominent figures embarked on the journey, including St. Francis of Assisi, Dutch painter Jan van Eyck, and the Wife of Bath in Chaucer's *Canterbury Tales*.

This steady flow of pilgrims from around Europe resulted in a rich exchange of knowledge, art, and architecture. Even today you'll find magnificent cathedrals along the Camino in cities such as Burgos and León, which incorporated and improved on the latest in cathedral design from France at that time.

By 1130 the trek was so popular that it prompted a French monk named Aimery Picaud to pen (likely with the help of some ghost-writers) a chronicle of his journey, including tips on where to eat, where to stay, the best way to get from place to place, and how to pack light and use a money belt. This *Codex Calixtinus* (Latin for "Camino Through the Back Door") was the world's first guidebook—the great-great-granddaddy of the one you're holding right now.

In the age of Columbus, the Renaissance, and the Reformation, interest in the Camino dropped way off. When the Moors were finally defeated in 1492, the significance of Reconquista icon St. James fell by the wayside. The discovery of the New World in the same year led both the Church and the monarchy to turn their attention across the Atlantic, and the pilgrimage began to wane. That was followed by a century of religious wars pitting Catholics against Protestants, which also distracted potential pilgrims. Feeling threatened by the pirate Francis Drake (not considered "sir" in Spain), the church hid the remains of St. James so thoroughly that they were actually lost for generations. Meanwhile, the rise of humanism during the Renaissance diminished the mystique of the pilgrimage. For the next centuries, and as recently as a few decades ago, only a few hardy souls still followed the route.

Then, in the late 1960s, a handful of parish priests along the Camino began working to recover the route, establishing associations of "friends of the Camino" that would eventually agree on a path and mark it. In 1982, and again in 1989, Pope John Paul II visited Santiago de Compostela, reminding the world of the town's historic significance. In 1987 the European Union designated the Camino as Europe's first Cultural Itinerary. And after the success of the 1992 Expo in Sevilla, the Galician government decided to pour funds into reviving the tradition for the Holy Year in 1993. They made Santiago a high-profile destination and shelled out big pesetas for concerts by stars including the Rolling Stones, Bruce Springsteen, and Julio Iglesias (whose father was born in Galicia).

The plan worked, and now—aided by European Union funding—the route has enjoyed a huge renaissance of interest, with 100,000 pilgrims each year trekking to Santiago. Shirley MacLaine has made the journey (her book *The Camino: A Journey of the Spirit* is popular among pilgrims). Pope Benedict XVI, who visited Santiago in November 2010, said he came "as a pilgrim." And even Hollywood has joined the trek with the 2010 movie *The Way,* starring Martin Sheen as a grieving father making his way along the Camino after his estranged son dies during an attempt at the pilgrimage. Cyclists and horse riders are now joining hikers on the journey, and these days it's "in" to follow the seashells to Santiago.

Best Stages for a Short Walk

The Camino de Santiago is divided into stages of about 12-15 miles apiece (approximately one day's walk). Even if you're doing most of the Camino by car, consider taking an extra day or two to walk one of these recommended stages (to get back to your car, catch a bus—TIs have schedules—or, where buses aren't an option, take a taxi). These stages are scattered throughout the Camino, and are listed from east to west.

Roncesvalles to Zubiri (21.5 km/13.5 miles)—This is the first stage in Spain, after the arduous trek over the Pyrenees. It's mostly (though not entirely) downhill, through rolling hills and meadows, amidst sheep and charming villages.

Puente de la Reina to Estella (19 km/12 miles)—Here the Camino becomes a bit more level and arid. This leg begins in an appealing pilgrim town, then passes through gentle farm fields and along a three-and-a-half-mile stretch of Roman road (from Cirauqui to Lorca).

Pieros to Villafranca del Bierzo (7.5 km/5 miles)—For this stretch, the Camino ascends through the hilly El Bierzo region, en route to Galicia. The last bit of this leg takes you through vineyards and vegetable patches into Villafranca, entering town at the Romanesque church of Santiago.

Ambasmestas to O Cebreiro (13.2 km/8.2 miles)—If you're not intimidated by a steep uphill hike, this leg is a gorgeous introduction to Galicia—culminating at the perfect little hilltop village.

Sarria to Portomarin (21.5 km/13.5 miles)—Because it's about 100 kilometers (62 miles) from Santiago (the minimum to qualify for a *compostela* certificate), Sarria is a popular starting point for short-haul pilgrims. From here you can make it to Santiago in less than a week. The terrain: pretty Galicia.

big cities, continue an hour farther to sleep in Astorga.

Day 4: Continue westward to Galicia, stopping at O Cebreiro and Lugo before arriving at Santiago de Compostela.

Orientation to the Camino

The term "Camino de Santiago," as mentioned earlier, actually refers to many different routes across Europe. All (like this chapter) travel from east to west. For our description of the popular "French Road" (Camino Francés), we'll begin in the French Basque town of St. Jean-Pied-de-Port, cross over the Pyrenees at Roncesvalles, then pass through three northern Spanish cities

(Pamplona, Burgos, León), before climbing into green Galicia, ending at Santiago de Compostela.

Tourist Information: Pilgrims will find no shortage of helpful resources along the way. In addition to TIs in each town (listed in this chapter), you'll also find "Pilgrim Friend" associations and other offices (often attached to an *albergue* or *refugio*) that offer kind advice to the weary traveler.

Holy Year: The Compostela Holy Year *(Año Xacobeo)* occurs when the Feast of St. James (July 25) falls on a Sunday (next in 2021); during a Holy Year, traffic on the trails doubles, and the pilgrim atmosphere is even more festive.

Tours: Iberian Adventures runs guided and self-guided walking tours in English for individuals and small groups along the Camino de Santiago and in the La Rioja wine region. Company owner Jeremy Dack highlights each area's natural environment, history, culture, cuisine, and wine, and emphasizes environmental awareness and respect for local customs (mobile 620-939-116, www.iberianadventures.com, info@iberianadventures.com). Jeremy also leads hiking tours of Spain's major mountain ranges.

St. Jean-Pied-de-Port

Just five miles from the Spanish border, the walled town of St. Jean-Pied-de-Port (san zhahn-pee-ay-duh-por) is the most popular village in all the French Basque countryside (you may also see it labeled as Donibane Garazi, its Basque name). Traditionally, St. Jean-Pied-de-Port has been the final stopover in France for Santiago-bound pilgrims, who gather here to cross the Pyrenees together and continue their march through Spain. The scallop shell of "St. Jacques" (French for "James") is

etched on walls throughout the town.

Visitors to this town are equal parts pilgrims and French tourists. Gift shops sell a strange combination of pilgrim gear (such as quick-drying shirts and shorts) and Basque souvenirs. This place is packed in the summer (so come early or late).

Orientation to St. Jean-Pied-de-Port

Tourist Information

The TI, on the main road along the outside of the walled Old Town, can give you a town map (hours vary, generally July-Aug Mon-Sat 9:00-19:00, Sun 10:00-12:00; Sept-June Mon-Sat 9:00-12:00 & 14:00-18:00, Sun 10:00-12:00; maybe less in winter; tel. 08 10 75 36 71). For Camino information, you'll do better at the Pilgrim Friends Office (described below). Ask the TI about weekly *pelota vasca* games (usually Mon at 16:00 or 17:00 at Trinquet court on place du Trinquet).

Arrival in St. Jean-Pied-de-Port

Parking is ample and well-signed from the main road. If arriving by **train,** exit the station to the left, then follow the busy road at the traffic circle toward the city wall.

Sights in St. Jean-Pied-de-Port

There's little in the way of sightseeing here, other than pilgrim-spotting. But St. Jean-Pied-de-Port feels like the perfect "Welcome to the Camino" springboard for the upcoming journey. Many modern pilgrims begin their Camino in this traditional spot because of its easy train connection to Bayonne, and because—as its name implies ("St. John at the Foot of the Pass")—it offers a very challenging but rewarding first leg: up, over, and into Spain.

Cross the old bridge over the Nive River (the same one that winds up in Bayonne) to the **Notre-Dame Gate,** which was once a drawbridge. Then head up the main walking drag, **rue de la Citadelle.** With its rosy-pink buildings and ancient dates above its doorways, this lane simply feels old. Notice lots of signs for *chambres* (rooms) and *refuges*—humble, hostel-like pilgrim bunkhouses.

Partway up, on the left at #39, look for the **Pilgrim Friends Office** (Les Amis du Chemin de Saint-Jacques, daily 7:30-12:00 & 13:30-20:00 & 21:15-22:00, tel. 05 59 37 05 09). This is where pilgrims check in before their long journey to Santiago; more than 35,000 pilgrims started out here in 2010 (compared with just 4,000 about a decade ago). For €2 a pilgrim can buy the official credential *(credenciel)* that she'll get stamped at each stop between here and Santiago to prove she walked the whole way and earn her *compostela* certificate. Pilgrims also receive a warm welcome, lots of advice, and help finding a

CAMINO DE SANTIAGO

bunk (the well-traveled staff swears that no pilgrim ever goes without a bed in St. Jean-Pied-de-Port).

A few more steps up, on the left, you'll pass the skippable €3 Bishop's Prison (Prison des Evêques, sometimes closed in winter). Continue on up to the **citadel,** dating from the mid-17th century—when this was a highly strategic location, keeping an eye on the easiest road over the Pyrenees between Spain and France. Although not open to the public (as it houses a school), the grounds around this stout fortress offer sweeping views over the French Basque countryside.

Sleeping in St. Jean-Pied-de-Port

Lots of humble pilgrim dwellings line the main drag, rue de la Citadelle. If you're looking for a bit more comfort, consider these options.

$$ Hotel Ramuntcho** is the only real hotel option in the Old Town, located partway up rue de la Citadelle. Its 16 rooms above a restaurant are straightforward but modern (Sb-€56-64, Db-€79-85, breakfast-€9, free Wi-Fi, 1 rue de France, tel. 05 59 37 03 91, fax 05 59 37 35 17, http://perso.wanadoo.fr/hotel.ramuntcho, hotel.ramuntcho@wanadoo.fr).

$$ Itzalpea, a café and tea house, rents five rooms along the main road just outside the Old Town (Sb-€55-58, Db-€65-80 depending on size, includes breakfast, closed Sat off-season,

Camino de Santiago: Eastern Half

air-con, 5 place du Trinquet, tel. 05 59 37 03 66, fax 05 59 37 33 18, www.maisondhotes-itzalpea.com, itzalpea@wanadoo.fr).

$ Chambres Chez l'Habitant has five old-fashioned, pilgrim-perfect rooms along the main drag. Welcoming Maria and Jean Pierre speak limited English, but their daughter can help translate (€20-25 per person in D, Db, Q, or Qb, includes breakfast, 15 rue de la Citadelle, tel. 05 59 37 05 83).

Eating in St. Jean-Pied-de-Port

Tourists, pilgrims, and locals alike find plenty of places to eat along rue de la Citadelle and also off rue du Trinquet, the main drag into town. Consider **Café Navarre** (1 place Juan de Huarte, tel. 05 59 37

01 67) or **Cafe Ttipia** (2 place Charles Floquet, tel. 05 59 37 11 96).

Picnics: If you're lucky enough to land here on a Monday morning, shop at the weekly market. Farmers, cheesemakers, and winemakers bring their products in from the countryside.

St. Jean-Pied-de-Port Connections

A scenic train conveniently links St. Jean-Pied-de-Port to **Bayonne** (€9, 3/day, 6/day in summer, 1.5 hours), and from there to **St. Jean-de-Luz** (about 30 minutes beyond Bayonne, www.sncf.fr). It's about a 1.25-hour drive from St. Jean-de-Luz. Unfortunately, there are no buses from St. Jean-Pied-de-Port to **Pamplona;** to connect the cities by public transport, you'll have to go back to Bayonne, then to San Sebastián, then catch a bus or train to Pamplona from there.

Between St. Jean-Pied-de-Port and Pamplona

The first stretch of the Camino, crossing the Pyrenees from France into Spain, is among the most dramatic. There's little in the way of civilization, but it's a memorable start for the journey.

• *From St. Jean-Pied-de-Port, follow road signs to* Arnéguy *on road D-933. (But be warned that the road signs for the Camino de Santiago take a much more roundabout high-mountain, one-lane road instead of the direct road to the border.)*

Crossing the Pyrenees: Roncesvalles (Roncevaux / Orreaga)

As you go over the stone bridge in the village of **Arnéguy,** you're also passing from France to Spain. For centuries this bridge was the site of a delicate dance between nervous smugglers and customs police. Today you'll barely notice you've crossed a border.

The road meanders through a valley before twisting up to the pass called **Puerto de Ibañeta** (also known as the Roncesvalles Pass). This scrubby high-mountain pass is one of the Basque Country's most historic spots. The most accessible gateway through the Pyrenees between France and Spain, this pass has been the site of several epic battles. According to a popular medieval legend, Charlemagne's nephew Roland was killed fighting here. Vengeful Basque tribes, seeking retribution for Charlemagne's sacking of Pamplona, followed the army as it began its return to France—and felled the mighty Roland along this very road. Several centuries later, Napoleon used the same road to invade Spain.

Coming down from the pass, you reach **Roncesvalles/ Orreaga** ("Valley of Pines"), which gave this area its name. This jumble of buildings surrounding a monastery is sort of a pilgrim depot, where travelers can pause to catch their collective breath after clearing the first arduous leg of the Camino. The big building on the right is a simple *refugio,* filled with bunk beds. In the afternoon you might see  pilgrims washing their clothes at the spigots in front, then hanging them to dry amidst the cows and knobby trees out back. The big church (on the left) has a tourable cloister and museum (€4 for both, cloister only-€1, audioguide-€1.20, guided tours but no fixed times or guarantee in English). As you leave town, you pass the first sign for Santiago de Compostela...790 kilometers (490 miles) straight ahead.

From here to Pamplona, the Camino passes through some pretty rolling hills and meadows, and several appealing villages. The first after Roncesvalles, called **Auritz/Burguete,** was supposedly Hemingway's favorite place to fish for trout when he needed to recover from a Pamplona bender.

• *Around that next bend is the first big city on the Camino: Pamplona.*

Pamplona

Proud Pamplona, with stout old walls standing guard in the Pyrenees foothills, is the capital of the province of Navarre ("Navarra" in Spanish). At its peak in the Middle Ages, Navarre was a grand kingdom that controlled parts of today's Spain and France. (The current king of Spain, Juan Carlos, is a descendant of the French line of Navarre royalty.) After the French and Spanish parts split, Pamplona remained the capital of Spanish Navarre.

Today Pamplona—called "Iruña" in the Basque language—feels at once affluent (with the sleek new infrastructure of a town on the rise), claustrophobic (with its warren of narrow lanes), and fascinating (with its odd traditions, rich history, and ties to Hemingway). Culturally, the city is a lively hodgepodge of Basque and *Navarro*. Locals like to distinguish between *Vascos* (people of Basque citizenship—not them) and *Vascones* (people who identify culturally as Basques—as do many *Navarros*). Pamplona is also an important seat for a controversial wing of the Catholic Church, Opus Dei, founded in Spain in 1928 by the Catholic priest Josemaría Escrivá. He established the private Pamplona-based University of Navarra, and Opus Dei also runs a hospital and several schools in the city.

Of course, Pamplona is best known as the host of one of Spain's (and Europe's) most famous festivals: the Running of the Bulls (held in conjunction with the Fiesta de San Fermín, July 6-14). For latecomers, San Fermín Txikito ("Little San Fermín") offers a less touristy alternative in late September. But there's more to this town than bulls—and, in fact, visiting at other times is preferable to the crowds and 24/7 party atmosphere that seize Pamplona during the festival. Contrary to the chaotic or even backward image that its famous festival might suggest, you'll find Pamplona welcoming, sane, and enjoyable.

Orientation to Pamplona

Pamplona has about 200,000 people. Most everything of interest is in the tight, twisting lanes of the Old Town (Casco Antiguo), centered on the main square, Plaza del Castillo. The newer Ensanche ("Expansion") neighborhood just to the south—with a sensible grid plan—holds several good hotels and the bus station.

Tourist Information

Pamplona's well-organized TI is located near the Running of the Bulls Monument. Pick up the handy map/guide and get your questions answered (likely Mon-Sat 10:00-14:00 & 16:00-19:00, Sun 10:00-14:00, Avenida Roncesvalles 4, tel. 848-420-420, www .turismonavarra.es). The TI sells colorful posters of San Fermín festivities from the 1900s for €0.60.

Local Guide: Francisco Glaría is a top-notch guide—and simply a delight to be with—who enjoys leading visitors through Pamplona (€140/half-day up to 4 hours, tel. 948-383-755, mobile 629-661-604, www.novotur.com, novotur@novotur.com).

No Bull—There's Another Fiesta: The last weekend in September, Pamplona celebrates **San Fermín Txikito** ("Little San Fermín"), a bull-free and practically tourist-free festival centered around the church of San Fermín de Aldapa (located behind the Mercado Santo Domingo on Calle Aldapa). Used only for Mass the rest of the year (and housing little of interest except a small statue of the saint), each fall this church opens its doors to become the heart of a celebration involving concerts, brass-band and food competitions, and parades of giant mannequins throughout the city.

Arrival in Pamplona

You can store bags at the bus station, but not at the train station.

By Bus: The sleek, user-friendly bus station is underground along the western edge of the Ensanche area, about a 10-minute walk from the Old Town sightseeing zone. On arrival, go up the escalator, cross the street, turn left, and walk a half-block, where you can turn right down the busy Conde Oliveto street. Along this street you're near several of my recommended accommodations— or you can walk two blocks to the big traffic circle called Plaza Príncipe de Viana. From here, turn left up Avenida de San Ignacio to reach the Old Town.

By Train: The RENFE Station is farther from the center, across the river to the northwest. It's easiest to hop on public bus #9 (€1.10, every 12-20 minutes), which drops you at the big Plaza Príncipe de Viana traffic circle south of the Old Town (described above)—look for a square with a fountain in the center.

By Car: Everything is well-marked: Simply follow the bull's-eyes to the center of town, where individual hotels are clearly sign-posted. There's also handy parking right at Plaza del Castillo.

By Plane: The Pamplona Airport is located about four miles outside the city (tel. 902-404-704, www.aena.es). Bus #21 connects the airport to downtown (hourly, €1).

Self-Guided Walk

The Walking of the Tourists

Even if you're not in town for the famous San Fermín festival, you can still get a good flavor of the town by following in the foot- and hoof-steps of its participants. This walk takes you through the town center along the same route of the famous Running of the Bulls.

• *Begin by the river, at the...*

Bull Corral: During the San Fermín festival, the bulls are released from here at 8:00 each morning. They first run up Cuesta de Santo Domingo; signs labeled *El Encierro* mark their route. Follow them.

A few blocks ahead on the left, the **Museum of Navarre** (Museo de Navarra) has four floors of artifacts and paintings celebrating the art of Navarre, from prehistoric to modern. Art is displayed chronologically, with prehistoric tools and pottery and Roman mosaics on the first floor, Gothic and Renaissance artifacts on the second floor, Baroque and 19th- and 20th-century works (including Goya's painting *Retrato de Marques de San Adrian*) on the third floor, and 20th- and 21st-century paintings by local artists on the top floor. The ground floor hosts rotating exhibitions, often of modern art. Spacious and well-arranged, the museum can be toured within an hour—consider circling back here after our walk (€2, free on Sat afternoons and all day Sun, open Tue-Sat 10:00-14:00 & 17:00-19:00, Sun 11:00-14:00, closed Mon, Santo Domingo 47, tel. 848-426-492, www.cfnavarra.es/cultura /museo). Formerly a 16th-century hospital, the building retains its Plateresque facade. Check out the adjoining church (on the right as you enter), with its impressive golden Baroque-Rococo altarpiece depicting the Annunciation.

Continue along Cuesta de Santo Domingo. Embedded in the wall on your right, look for the small shrine containing an image of San Fermín. Farther up on your left is the food market of Santo Domingo, a handy spot to buy picnic supplies, including fine local cheeses (Mon-Sat 8:00-14:00, closed Sun).

• *Ahead in the square is the...*

City Hall (Ayuntamiento): When Pamplona was just starting out, many Camino pilgrims who had been "just passing through"

Pamplona

━━━ RUNNING OF THE BULLS ROUTE

P PARKING

⁊ VIEW

1. Gran Hotel La Perla
2. Palacio Guendulain
3. Hostal Navarra
4. Hotel Europa
5. Hotel Yoldi
6. Hotel Castillo de Javier
7. Pensión Arrieta
8. Bar Cervecería La Estafeta & Bodegon Sarria
9. Gaucho Bar
10. Café Roch
11. La Mandarra de la Ramos & San Nicolás Eateries
12. Café Iruña
13. San Ignacio Restaurante
14. Ultramarinos Beatriz Shop
15. Kukuxumusu T-Shirt Shop
16. Hemingway Bust
17. Navarre Govt. Building
18. Museum of the Running of the Bulls

200 YARDS

200 METERS

CALLE B. TIRAPU

CALLE RIO ARGA

LA RUNA PARK

BULL CORRAL

ARGA

S. DOMINGO

SANTO

ROCHAPEA BRIDGE

MUSEUM OF NAVARRE

CURTIDORES

PASEO RONDA

DESCALZOS

JARAUTA

HILARION

TO TRAIN STN. & SAN SEB.

PUBLIC SHOWER

ESCLAVA

RECOLETAS

CALLE

AVENIDA

SAN. FRAN.

SAN LORENZO

TACO-NERA PARK

BOSQUECILLO

TACONERA

NUEVA

NAVAS

TOLOSA DE

PADRE

CHINCHILLA

AVENIDA

DEL

CITADEL

DCH

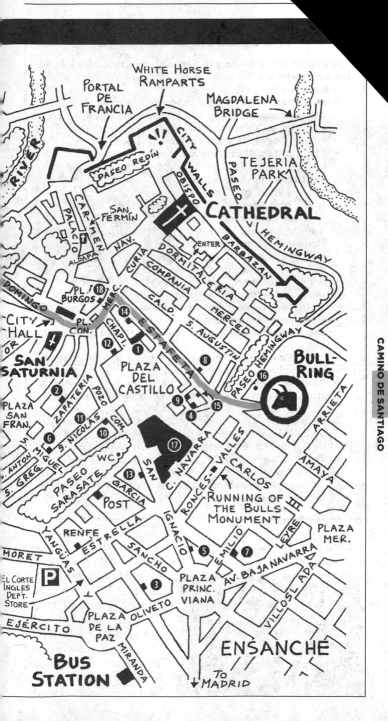

CAMINO DE SANTIAGO

Symbols of Santiago

...eading to Santiago de Compostela—and ...rife with symbolism. Here are a few of the ...along the way.

... Camino's namesake is also its single biggest symbol. St. James can be depicted three ways: as a pilgrim, as an apostle, and as a Crusader (slaughtering Moors). For more, see the sidebar on page 301.

- **The Scallop Shell (Vieira):** Figuratively, the various routes from Europe to Santiago come together like the lines of a scallop shell. And literally, scallops are abundant on the Galician coast. Though medieval pilgrims only carried shells with them on the return home—to prove they'd been here, and to  scoop water from wells—today's pilgrims also carry them on the way *to* Santiago. The yellow sideways shell that looks like a starburst marks the route for bikers.

- **The Gourd:** Gourds were used by pilgrims to drink water and wine.

- **The Yellow Arrow:** These arrows direct pilgrims at every intersection from France to Santiago.

- **The Red Cross:** This long, skinny cross with curly ends at the top and sides, and ending in a sword blade at the bottom, represents the Knights of Santiago. This 12th-century Christian military order had a dual mission: to battle Muslim invaders while providing hospice and protection to pilgrims along the Camino de Santiago.

- **The Tomb and Star:** St. James' tomb (usually depicted as a simple coffin or box), and the stars that led to its discovery, appear throughout the city of Santiago, either together or separately.

decided to stick around. They helped to build the city you're enjoying today, but tended to cling to their own regional groups, which

squabbled periodically. So in 1423, the King of Navarre (Charles III) tore down the internal walls and built a City Hall here to unite the community. This version (late Baroque, from the 18th century) is highly symbolic: Hercules demonstrates the city's strength, while the horn-blower trumpets Pamplona's greatness.

The festival of San Fermín begins and ends on the balcony of this building (with the flags). Look in the direction you just came (also the route of the bulls), and find the line of metal squares in the pavement—used to secure barricades for the run. There are four rows, creating two barriers on each side. The inner space is for press and emergency medical care; spectators line up along the outer barrier. This first stretch is uphill, allowing the bulls to use their strong hind legs to pick up serious momentum.

• *Follow the route of the bulls two blocks down Mercaderes street (next to Alexander Jewelry). Turn right onto...*

La Estafeta Street: At this turn, the bulls—who are now going downhill—begin to lose their balance, often sliding into the barricade. At the **Museum of the Running of the Bulls** (El Museo del Encierro), you can learn all about this unique Pamplona tradition, get your picture taken with an actual (stuffed) bull, and view a simulation of the event (€8, Mon-Fri 11:00-14:00 & 16:00-20:00, Sat-Sun 11:00-20:00, last entry 30 minutes before closing, between Plaza del Ayuntamiento and Calle Estafeta at Calle Mercaderes 17, www.sanferminencierro.com). Note that if you want to side-trip to the cathedral—described later, under "Sights in Pamplona"—it's dead ahead, three blocks up the skinny lane called "Curia" from this corner.

Once the bulls regain their footing, they charge up the middle of La Estafeta. Notice how narrow this street is: No room for barricades... no escape for *mozos*.

On days that the bulls aren't running, La Estafeta is one of the most appealing streets in Pamplona. It's home to some of the best tapas bars in town (see "Eating in Pamplona," later). Because the Old Town was walled right up until 1923, space in here was at a premium—making houses tall and streets narrow.

Partway down the first block on the right, look for the hole-in-the-wall **Ultramarinos Beatriz** shop (at #22)—most locals just call it "Beatriz"—makers of the best treats in Pamplona (Mon-Fri 9:00-14:00 & 16:30-20:00, Sat 9:00-14:00, closed Sun, tel. 948-220-618). Anything with chocolate is good, but the mini-croissants are sensational. They come in three types: *garrotes de chocolate,* filled with milk chocolate; *cabello de angel,* filled with sweet pumpkin fibers; and *manzana,* or apple (€3 for a box of six, also sold by weight). So simple...but oh so good.

Halfway down the street, notice the alley on the right leading to the main square (we'll circle back to the square later). Farther down, near the very end of La Estafeta (on the right, at #76), look for the shop called **Kukuxumusu**—Euskara (Basque) for "the kiss of a flea." These whimsical, locally designed cartoon T-shirts are a

The Running of the Bulls: Fiesta de San Fermín

"A San Fermín pedimos, por ser nuestro patrón, nos guíe en el encierro, dándonos su bendición."
"We ask San Fermín, because he is our Patron, to guide us through the Running of the Bulls, giving us his blessing."
—Song sung before the run

For nine days each July, a million visitors pack into Pamplona to watch a gang of reckless, sangria-fueled adventurers thrust themselves into the path of an oncoming herd of furious bulls. Locals call it *El Encierro* (literally, "the enclosing"—as in, taking the beasts to be enclosed in the bullring)...but everyone else knows it as the "Running of the Bulls."

The festival begins at City Hall at noon on July 6, with various events filling the next nine days and nights. Originally celebrated as the feast of San Fermín—who is still honored by a religious procession through town on July 7—it has since evolved into a full slate of live music, fireworks, general revelry, and an excuse for debauchery. After dark the town erupts into a rollicking party scene. To beat the heat, participants chug refreshing sangria or *kalimotxo* (*calimocho* in Spanish)—half red wine, half cola. The town can't accommodate the crowds, so some visitors day-trip in from elsewhere (such as San Sebastián), and many young tourists simply pass out in city parks overnight (public showers are on Calle Hilarión Eslava in the Old Town).

The Running of the Bulls takes place each morning of the

festival and is broadcast nationwide on live TV. The bulls' photos appear in the local paper beforehand, allowing runners to size up their opponents. If you're here to watch, stake your claim at a vantage point along the outer barrier by 6:30 or 7:00 in the morning. Don't try to stand along the inner barrier—reserved for press and medical personnel—or you'll be evicted when the action begins.

Before the run starts, runners sing a song to San Fermín (see lyrics above) three times to ask for divine guidance. Soon the bulls will be released from their pen near Cuesta de Santo Domingo. From here they'll stampede a half-mile through the town center...with thrill-seekers called *mozos* (and female *mozas*) running in front of the herd, trying to avoid a hoof or horn in the rear end.

Mozos traditionally wear white with strips of red tied around their necks and waists, and carry a newspaper to cover the bull's eyes when they're ready to jump out of the way. Two legends explain the red-and-white uniform: One says it's to honor San Fermín, a saint (white) who was martyred (red); the other says that the runners dress like butchers, who began this tradition. (The bulls are color-blind, so they don't care.)

At 8:00, six bulls are set loose. The beginning of the run is marked by two firecrackers—one for the first bull to leave the pen, and another for the last bull. The animals charge down the street, while the *mozos* try to run in front of them for as long as possible before diving out of the way. The bulls are kept on course by fencing off side-streets (with openings just big enough for *mozos* to escape). Shop windows and doors are boarded up.

A bull becomes most dangerous when separated from the herd. For this reason, a few steer—who are calmer, slower, have bigger horns, and wear a bell—are released with the bulls, and a few more trot behind them to absorb angry stragglers and clear the streets. (There's no greater embarrassment in this *machismo* culture than to think you've run with a bull...only to realize later that you actually ran with a steer.)

The bulls' destination: the bullring...where they'll be ceremonially slaughtered as the day's entertainment. (For more on bull-fighting, see page 814.)

If you're considering running with the bulls, it's essential to equip yourself with specific safety information not contained in this book. Locals suggest a few guidelines: First, understand that these are very dangerous animals, and running with them is entirely at your own risk. Be as sober as possible, and wear good shoes to protect your feet from broken glass and from being stepped on by bulls and people. (Runners wearing sandals might be ejected by police.) You're not allowed to carry a backpack, as its motion could distract the bulls. If you fall, never stand up—it's better to be trampled by six bulls than to be gored by one. Ideally, try to get an experienced *mozo* to guide you on your first run.

Cruel as this all seems to the bulls—who scramble for footing on the uneven cobblestones as they rush toward their doom in the bullring—the human participants don't come away unscathed. Each year, dozens of people are gored, trampled, or otherwise injured. Over the last century, 15 runners have been killed at the event. But far more people have died from over-consumption of alcohol.

The festival ends at midnight on July 14, when the townspeople congregate in front of the City Hall, light candles, and sing their sad song, *"Pobre de Mí"*: "Poor me, the Fiesta de San Fermín has ended."

local favorite. The giant digital clock outside the shop counts down to the next Running of the Bulls.

• *La Estafeta eventually leads you right to Pamplona's...*

Bullring: At the end of the run, the bulls charge down the ramp and through the red door. The bullring is used only nine days each summer (during the festival). The original arena from 1923 was expanded in the 1960s (see the extension at the top), doubling its capacity and halving its architectural charm. Bullfights start at 18:00, and tickets are expensive. But the price plummets if you buy tickets from scalpers after the first or second bull. The audience at most bullfights is silent, but Pamplona's spectators are notorious for their raucous behavior. They're known to intentionally spill things on tourists just to get a reaction...if you respond with a laugh and a positive attitude, they'll respect you and you'll have the time of your life.

Look for the big bust of **Ernest Hemingway,** celebrated by Pamplona as if he were a native son. Hemingway came here for the first time during the 1923 Running of the Bulls. Inspired by the spectacle and the gore, he later wrote about the event in his bullfighting classic *The Sun Also Rises.* He said that he enjoyed seeing two wild animals running together: one on two legs, and the other on four. This literary giant put Pamplona and its humble, obscure bullfighting festival on the world map; visitors come from far and wide even today, searching for adventure in Hemingway's Pamplona. He came to his last Running of the Bulls in 1959 and reportedly regretted the attention his writing had brought to what had been a simple local festival. But the people of Pamplona appreciate "Papa" as one of their own. At the beginning of the annual festival, young people tie a red neckerchief around this statue so Hemingway can be properly outfitted for the occasion.

• *Walk 20 yards along the right side of the bullring, then cross the busy street and walk a block into the pedestrian zone to the life-size...*

Running of the Bulls Monument (Monumento al Encierro): This statue (from 2007, pictured on page 244) shows six bulls, two steer, and ten runners in action. Find the self-portrait of the sculptor (bald, lying down, and about to be gored). The statue has quickly become a local favorite, but is not without controversy: There are 10 *mozos* but no *mozas*—where are the female runners?

• *From here you can turn right and walk two blocks up the street to the main square...*

Plaza del Castillo: While not as grand as Spain's top squares, there's something particularly cozy and livable about Pamplona's. It's dominated by the Navarre government building (sort of like a state capitol). Several Hemingway sights surround this square. The recommended Hotel Perla in the corner was his favorite place to stay. It recently underwent a head-to-toe five-star renovation,

but Hemingway's room was kept exactly as he liked it, right down to the furniture he used while writing...and two balconies overlooking the bull action on Estafeta street. He also was known to frequent Bar Txoko at the top of the square (as well as pretty much every other bar in town) and the venerable Café Iruña at the bottom of the square. The recommended Café Iruña actually has a separate "Hemingway Corner" room, with a life-size statue of "Papa" to pose with.

• *You've survived the run. Now enjoy the rest of Pamplona's sights.*

Sights in Pamplona

▲Cathedral (Catedral)

The Camino de Santiago is lined with great cathedrals, but—frankly—Pamplona's is an also-ran. Still, the cathedral does have some unique sights and a museum that are worth a visit.

Cost and Hours: €4, mid-March-mid-Nov Mon-Sat 10:00-19:00, closed Sun; mid-Nov-mid-March Mon-Sat 10:00-17:00, closed Sun; tel. 948-212-594.

❂ **Self-Guided Tour:** The cathedral—a Gothic core wrapped in a Neoclassical shell—is a bit drab from the outside. But the inside is more appealing. Head up the street to the right, follow signs for *entrada a museo,* buy your ticket, go inside, and turn right into the **museum.** The highlight here is the fascinating collection of old Mary sculptures from local village churches. Since they're displayed chronologically, you can actually watch artistic styles evolve. The earliest ones, from the 12th century, show a very stiff, uncaring Mary—she's not touching, or even looking at, the Baby Jesus, who's perched stiffly on her lap like a ventriloquist's dummy. But as women gained more power in the 13th century, we see Mary loosen up and morph into a good mother—smiling, playfully holding the orb (representing perfection), and finally (gasp!) touching her baby with her hands. In the 14th century Mary boldly stands up and even cradles Jesus. And by the 17th century she's looking like a real mother.

The museum is displayed in the former refectory (dining hall) of the monks. Find the small, attached room where you can peer up inside the five gigantic chimneys. Exiting the museum, notice the fountain at the corner of the cloister—used to wash up at mealtime.

Continue around the cloister and find the side entrance into the cathedral. Above the door, see the depiction of the Dormition (eternal sleep, rather than death) of Mary...with Jesus up above, returning the favor of her evolving maternity by cradling her soul like a baby as she's welcomed into heaven.

The cathedral interior is Gothic. In the **choir**, look for the statue nicknamed "Mary of the Adopted Child." The Baby Jesus was stolen from this statue in the 16th century and replaced with a different version...which looks nothing like his mother. (The mother, dating from the 13th century, is the only treasure surviving from the previous church that stood on this spot.)

The prominent **tomb** dominating the middle of the nave holds Charles III (the king of Navarre who united the disparate groups of Pamplona) and his wife. The blue fleur-de-lis pattern is a reminder that the kings of Navarre once controlled a large swath of France. Notice that Charles' face is realistic, indicating that it was sculpted while he was still alive, whereas his wife's face is idealized—done after she died. Around the base of the tomb, monks from various orders mourn the couple's death.

In the back-left corner chapel, find the Renaissance **crucifix**—shockingly realistic for a no-name artist of the time (compare it with the more typical one in the next chapel over). The accuracy of Christ's musculature leads some to speculate that the artist had a model. (When you drive a nail through a foot, toes splay as you see here...but rarely see on other crucifixes of the time.) It's said that if the dangling lock of hair touches Jesus' chest, the world will end.

Corner of the White Horse Ramparts View: Leaving the cathedral, circle the church, passing the front facade again, around to the tree-lined square. Continue to the small viewpoint overlooking the ramparts. This is your best chance to see part of Pamplona's imposing **city walls**—designed to defend against potential invaders from the Pyrenees, still 80 percent intact, and now an inviting parkland. Belly up to the overlook, with views across the city's suburban sprawl. Beyond those hills on the horizon to the left are San Sebastián and the Bay of Biscay. Camino pilgrims enter town through the gate below and on the left. This area is popular with people who are in town for the Running of the Bulls but didn't make hotel reservations. Sadly, it's not unusual for people to fall asleep on top of the wall...then roll off to their deaths.

Other Churches

As a prominent town on a pilgrim route, Pamplona has its share of other interesting churches. These two are worth a quick visit. They're both on the Camino trail through town; to reach them, simply head west along Calle Mayor from the City Hall Square (where the self-guided walk began).

Church of San Saturnino—The most important pilgrim church in Pamplona, this is an architectural combination: 15th-century Gothic, with 18th-century Baroque in front. Duck inside (free, daily 9:15-12:30 & 18:00-20:00): This is where pilgrims can get their credential stamped (someone's usually on duty in the pews). At the end across from where you enter, you'll see an altar with the Holy Virgin of the Camino. As you continue your journey, you'll notice that most churches along the Camino are dedicated to Mary. According to legend, when St. James himself came on a missionary trip through northern Spain, he suffered a crisis of faith around Zaragoza (not far from here). But, inspired by the Virgin, he managed to complete his journey to Galicia. Pilgrims following in his footsteps find similar inspiration from Mary today.

Church of San Lorenzo—San Fermín is a big name in town, and you will find him in a giant side-chapel of this church, over-

looking the ring road at the edge of the Old Town (free, Mon-Fri 8:15-12:00 & 18:30-20:00, Sat-Sun 8:15-12:00 & 18:00-20:00). Enter the church and turn right down the transept to find the statue of **San Fermín,** dressed in red and wearing a gold miter (tall hat). Pamplona was founded by the Roman Emperor Pompey (hence the name) in the first century B.C. Later, a Roman general here became the first in the empire to allow Christians to worship openly. The general's son—Fermín— even preached the word himself...until he was martyred. Fermín has been the patron saint here ever since. Just below the statue's Adam's apple, squint to see a reliquary holding Fermín's actual finger. The statue—gussied up in an even more over-the-top miter and staff—is paraded around on Fermín's feast day, July 7, which was the origin of today's bull festival. This chapel is the most popular place in town for weddings.

Sleeping in Pamplona

(€1 = about $1.40, country code: 34)
Because Pamplona is a business-oriented town, prices go up during the week; on weekends (Fri-Sun), you can usually score a discount. When I've listed a range, you can assume the high prices are for weekdays (Mon-Thu). All prices go way, way up for the San Fermín festival, when you must book as far in advance as possible.

$$$ Gran Hotel La Perla is the town's undisputed top splurge. Hemingway's favorite hotel, sitting right on the main square, has recently undergone a top-to-bottom five-star renovation. Its 44 rooms offer luxury at Pamplona's best address (standard Db-€260, bigger and fancier rooms-€300-520, rates can drop dramatically—check for deals online, breakfast-€20, air-con, elevator, Internet access and Wi-Fi, restaurant, Plaza del Castillo 1, tel. 948-223-000, fax 948-222-324, www.granhotellaperla.com, informacion@granhotellaperla.com). Well-heeled lit-lovers can drop €520 for a night in the Hemingway room, still furnished as it was when "Papa" stayed there (with a brand-new bathroom grafted on the front).

$$$ At Palacio Guendulain, pander to your inner aristocrat at a recently opened hotel owned by the Count of Guendulain. Currently living in Madrid, he had his mansion in Pamplona converted into a luxurious 25-room hotel decorated with family crests, antiques, and Spanish Old Masters. A collection of carriages in the courtyard, ultra-modern bathrooms, and a gym under construction over the family chapel create a curious juxtaposition of old and new (Db *"clasica"*-€150-175, Db *"deluxe"*-€180-205, Db suite-€250-280, extra bed-€50, rates can drop off-season, breakfast-€15, air-con, elevator, Internet access and Wi-Fi, restaurant also open to non-guests, Zapateria 53, tel. 948-225-522, fax 948-225-532, www.palacioguendulain.com).

$$ Hostal Navarra is the best value in Pamplona, with 15 modern, well-maintained, clean rooms. Near the bus station, but an easy walk from the Old Town, it's well-run by Miguel, who speaks English (Sb-€45, Db-€60, includes tax, breakfast-€7, free Wi-Fi, reception closes at 19:00—notify if you will be arriving later, Calle Tudela 9, tel. 948-225-164, fax 948-223-426, www.hostalnavarra.com, info@hostalnavarra.com).

$$ Hotel Europa, a few blocks off the square, offers 21 rooms with reasonable prices for its high class and ideal location (Sb-€69-78, Db-€75-92, breakfast-€9.50, air-con, elevator, free Wi-Fi, Calle Espoz y Mina 11, tel. 948-221-800, fax 948-229-235, www.hoteleuropapamplona.com, europa@hreuropa.com). The ground-floor restaurant is a well-regarded splurge.

$$ Hotel Yoldi is a comfortable business-style hotel in a 19th-century building. Well-located just off Plaza del Príncipe de Viana, its 50 modern rooms are handy for travelers arriving by bus from the train station (Sb-€60-70, Db-€76-90, elevator, Wi-Fi, café, Avenida de San Ignacio 11, tel. 948-224-800, fax 948-212-045, www.hotelyoldi.com, yoldi@hotelyoldi.com).

$$ Hotel Castillo de Javier, right on the bustling San Nicolás bar street (request a quieter back room), rents 19 simple, new-feeling rooms (Sb-€45, Db-€63, includes tax, breakfast-€4.30, air-con, elevator, free Wi-Fi, Calle San Nicolás 50-52, tel. 948-203-040, fax 948-203-041, www.hotelcastillodejavier.com, info@hotel castillodejavier.com). This is a step up from the several cheap *hostales* that line the same street.

$ Pensión Arrieta is an old-fashioned budget option renting 12 basic rooms in two buildings in the new part of town. Carmen and Maximo don't speak English, but their daughter Maika does (D-€45, Db-€55, a few euros more July-Sept, Calle de Emilio Arrieta 27, tel. 948-228-459, www.pensionarrieta.net, pension arrieta@pensionarrieta.net).

Eating in Pamplona

All of these eateries are within a couple minutes' walk of one another, and the tapas bars make a wonderful little pub crawl.

Tapas Crawl

Tapas on Calle de la Estafeta: The best concentration of trendy tapas bars is on and near the skinny drag called La Estafeta. My favorites here are **Bar Cervecería La Estafeta** (try the *gulas*—baby eels—stuffed in a red pepper, daily, at #54, tel. 639-948-545) and **Bodegon Sarria** (great bull photos, English menu, dining room to enjoy Navarre dishes, at #52, tel. 948-227-713).

Gaucho Bar is a proud little prizewinning place serving gourmet tapas cooked to order for €2.50-3 each. You could sit down and enjoy three tapas, and have an excellent meal (daily, just a few steps off the main square at Calle Espoz y Mina 7, tel. 948-225-073, no English).

Café Roch is a time-warp with a line of delightful tapas (€1.60 each). Their most popular are the stuffed pepper and the fried Roquefort (find the *tabacco* at #35 on Plaza del Castillo—it's a block away at Calle de las Comedias 6, tel. 948-222-390).

Tapas on Calle San Nicolás: The narrow and slightly seedy Calle San Nicolás has more than its share of hole-in-the-wall tapas joints, with an older, more traditional clientele, and greasier, more straightforward tapas. **La Mandarra de la Ramos** ("Ramos' Apron"), at #9, is a pork-lover's paradise, where cured legs dangle enticingly over your head. Ham it up with a couple of *tostadas de jamón*, best washed down with a glass of the local *vino tinto* (daily, just around the corner from Café Roch, tel. 948-212-654).

Restaurants

Café Iruña, which clings to its venerable past and its connection to Hemingway (who loved the place), serves up drinks out on the main square and food in the delightful old 1888 interior. While the food is mediocre, the ambience is great. Find the little "Hemingway's Corner" (El Rincón de Hemingway) side-eatery in back, where the bearded one is still hanging out at the bar. Enjoy black-and-white photos of Ernesto, young and old, in Pamplona (€13.50 fixed-price meal for lunch and dinner, pricier €22 Sat dinner deal, open daily, Plaza del Castillo 44, tel. 948-222-064).

San Ignacio Restaurante is a good choice for a real restaurant, with a classy upstairs dining room serving local fare (€10-15 starters, €12-20 main dishes, fixed-price meal-€15 on weekdays or €40 on weekends, open daily for lunch 13:00-15:30, Thu-Sat also dinner from 21:00, facing the back of the Navarre government building at Avenida San Ignacio 4, tel. 948-221-874).

Pamplona Connections

Note that the bus station is closer to the Old Town than the train station, and most connections are faster by bus anyway.

From Pamplona by Bus to: Burgos (3/day, 2.5 hours), **San Sebastián** (8/day, 1 hour), **Bilbao** (6/day, 2 hours), **Madrid** (6/day, 5 hours), **Madrid Barajas Airport** (10/day, 5-7 hours; this bus may also serve other airports in the future—see www.alsa.es; buy ticket online or from the driver). For bus schedules, see www.autobuses denavarra.com, tel. 948-203-566.

By Train to: Burgos (1/day, 2 hours), **San Sebastián** (2/day, 2 hours), **León** (1/day, 4 hours), **Madrid** (4/day direct, 3 hours).

From Pamplona to Burgos

The stretch of the Camino between Pamplona and Burgos is particularly appealing, with several tempting stopovers. As you finish your descent from the rugged Pyrenees, you enter the flatter, more cultivated landscape that typifies the long middle stretch of the Camino (basically from here to Galicia). The two best stops along here are the small town of Puente de la Reina (with an iconic old bridge and fun pilgrim vibes) and a potential detour for wine-lovers through La Rioja wine country.

• *Begin by taking the A-12 expressway west from Pamplona (toward Logroño). Consider stopping in Puente de la Reina, as it's a very easy detour—the exit (Puente de la Reina norte) is well-marked from the expressway.*

Puente de la Reina / Gares

The Camino de Santiago's two French routes converge in this cozy sun-baked village, just one walking stage (about 12 miles) west of Pamplona. Named for a graceful 11th-century stone bridge at its center, the village retains a pilgrims' vibe (**TI** open Tue-Sat 10:00-13:00 & 16:00-19:00, Sun 11:00-14:00, closed Mon, Calle Mayor 105, tel. 948-341-301). All the sights here fall on a straight axis: church, main street, and bridge. Parking the car and wandering around here gives "car hikers" a whiff of Camino magic.

As you enter the town, watch (on the left) for the **Church of the Crucifixion** (Iglesia del Crucifijo), with a stork's nest on the steeple. The Knights Templar, who came to protect pilgrims from the Moors, likely founded this church in the 12th century. Inside you'll find a distinctive Y-shaped crucifix that shows a Christ who's dead, yet still in pain (by a German craftsman—a reminder of the rich influx of pan-European culture the Camino enjoyed). It was likely carried by German pilgrims all the way across Europe to this spot. Across the street is a pilgrims' *refugio,* offering bunks and credential stamps to Camino walkers.

The straight, wide Calle Mayor connects the church and *refugio* with the bridge. Classic Camino towns feature main drags like this one. They were born as a collection of services flanking the path. Pilgrims needed to eat, sleep, pray, and deal with health problems. The more stone a house showed off (rather than brick), the wealthier the owner. You'll see modern flooring being stripped away to reveal now-trendy river-pebble cobbles inside.

The main street leads directly to the most interesting sight in town (and its namesake), the **"Bridge of the Queen"** (which you'll

see on the right as you drive across the modern bridge near the end of town). With a graceful six-arch Romanesque design that peaks in the middle, the bridge represents life: You can't quite see where you're going until you get there. The extra holes were designed to let high water through, so that water pressure wouldn't push the stone construction over—clever 11th-century engineering. Pilgrims enjoy congregating on the riverbank under the arches of this bridge—a great place to stop and stretch your legs. Ponder this scene: the bridge, pilgrims, the flowing river, happy birdsong...it's timeless.

• *From here hop immediately back on the A-12 expressway (toward Estella) to speed along. As you pass by Estella/Lizarra (home to the imposing Romanesque Palace of the Kings of Navarre), you'll gradually*

La Rioja Wine Loop

Serious wine-lovers enjoy detouring off the Camino at Logroño to visit the wine village of Laguardia, tour some unique wineries, and sample Rioja wine.

For many lovers of Spanish wines, it just doesn't get better than Rioja (ree-OH-*h*ah, with a guttural *h*). Rioja wine is a D.O.C. product, meaning that by definition it can only be produced in La Rioja region. Protected from the elements by the Cantabrian Mountains to the north (which you'll see from Laguardia), vineyards have thrived in the valley of the Ebro River since Roman times. Rioja wines (which can be red, white, or rosé) grow in a variety of soil types dominated by red clay and limestone. The reds, made primarily from the *tempranillo* grape (Spain's "noble grape"), are medium- to full-bodied in the Bordeaux style and characterized by aging in oak barrels—infusing them with overtones of vanilla. With their balance of tannins and fruitiness, red Riojas go well with grilled meats and strong cheeses, such as an aged manchego. You'll see four types of Rioja wines, depending on how long they've been aged (from shortest to longest, and cheapest to most expensive): simply Rioja (or sometimes *cosecha*, "harvest"), Rioja Crianza, Rioja Reserva, and Rioja Gran Reserva.

Be warned that the Rioja region is not well set up for impromptu visitors. All wine-tasting experiences prefer reservations, and most require them. You can't just go tasting on the fly as you can elsewhere in Europe. If you're serious about your Rioja, set up here for a day or two, do some homework (www.laguardia-alava.com is helpful), and reserve at the wineries of your choice. Although Laguardia is connected by bus to Pamplona (via Logroño), most of the experience here lies in the countryside—workable only by car.

• *From Logroño follow A-124 northwest (toward Vitoria, through more and more scenic vineyards, with a picturesque mountain ridge as a backdrop) to Laguardia, and park just outside the town wall.*

Laguardia is the scenic center of La Rioja wine-tasting country. This walled town—literally "The Guard," for its position watching out for potential invaders coming in from the mountains—is perched on a promontory with fine views of the surrounding region. There's not much in the way of sightseeing, but poke around a bit. Under your feet are more than 200 wine cellars (*bodegas*) where Rioja quietly ages. Only two in town are open for visitors: **El Fabulista** (€6 for two tastes and a guided visit, €10 includes snacks, tel. 945-621-192, www.bodegael fabulista.com, Alonso) and **Carlos San Pedro** (€3.50 for one taste, tel. 605-033-043); for both, you can try just dropping in, but it's better to call ahead. Laguardia's **TI** can give you information on wine-tastings in town and nearby, but—once again—they'll warn you that most wineries require reservations (TI open Mon-Fri 10:00-14:00 & 16:00-19:00, Sat 10:00-14:00 & 17:00-19:00, Sun 10:45-14:00, Plaza San Juan, tel. 945-600-845, www.laguardia-alava.com).

The countryside around Laguardia is blanketed with vineyards. For those just passing through, three wine-related attractions are worth considering. All are within a few minutes' drive of Laguardia. Note that Ysios and Marqués de Riscal are architectural gems worth dropping by to see even if you couldn't care less about the wine.

Villa Lucía is a sort of wine museum about La Rioja's favorite product, as well as its traditional architecture. As with everything around here, it's wise to call ahead if you want to join a tour (various programs for €6-14, Tue-Sun 9:00-14:00 & 16:30-20:00, closed Mon, on the right as you reach the edge of town, tel. 945-600-032, www.villa-lucia.com).

Ysios is a modern winery with an undulating silver roof designed by the bold and prolific Spanish architect Santiago

Calatrava. Wine-lovers enjoy the tours of the cellar, in which countless casks age under the wavy ceiling (€5, includes one taste; Mon-Fri at 11:00, 13:00, and 16:00; Sat-Sun at 11:00 and 13:00; one hour, call first to ensure a space, tel. 945-600-640, www.bodegasysios.com). But even from the outside, it's a worthwhile photo op for anyone (just a three-minute drive behind Laguardia, toward the mountains—behind the town, look for Ysios signs; you'll see the building from far off).

• *From the Laguardia area, follow signs south to Elciego (on A-3210) to reach...*

Marqués de Riscal, in the village of Elciego, was one of the pioneer winemakers of the Rioja wine industry. Its new winery features a distinctive hotel designed by Frank Gehry (of Bilbao Guggenheim fame). The wine cellar is tourable (€10, includes two tastes, sometimes 1/day in English, closed Mon, call first, tel. 945-180-888, www.marquesderiscal.com). The hotel (Db-€400-1,000), with its colorful, wavy design, is striking in such an otherwise humble village.

• *Just to the northwest is the midsized town of Haro, offering even more tasting opportunities. But if you're ready to move along, you can head south from Elciego toward Cenicero. In Cenicero you can rejoin the AP-68 expressway, or continue down (following signs for Nájera) to highway N-120 to join the Camino road into Burgos.*

begin to notice that you're entering wine country—with scrubby vegetation, red soil, and hill towns dotting the landscape. Take exit 44, direction: Ayegui, and follow signs to Irache Monastery.

Even if you're on the expressway, it's worth another quick detour (again well-signed, just beyond Estella) to the fun...

Irache Monastery and Wine Fountain (Monasterio de Irache)

This monastery, immersed in vineyards, has a unique custom of offering free wine to pilgrims. From the parking lot near the monastery, walk down following signs for *fuente de vino* to find a faucet that dispenses free wine (daily 8:00-20:00; also one for water). The Spanish poem on the sign explains, "To drink without abusing, we invite you happily; but to be able to take it along, you must pay for the wine." In other words, pilgrims are allowed to drink as much wine as they like... provided they don't take any with them. (And though the wine is free, you'll likely end up buying a little glass from the machine, essentially paying €1 for a glass of bad wine.) Note the webcam—if you have your mobile phone on you, text friends to look for you at www .irache.com. Hi, Mom!

• *Continuing south, you can choose your route: To save time, zip on the A-12 expressway right to Logroño. But for a scenic and only slightly slower meander through some cute villages (El Busto, Sansol) and larger towns (Los Arcos and Viana), take the expressway only as far as Los Arcos, then follow N-111 from there. Either way, you'll end up at...*

Logroño and La Rioja

Just before the skippable big city of Logroño, you'll cross the Ebro River. Today, as in centuries past, this river marks the end of the Basque territory (and Navarre) and the beginning of the rest of Spain. With 150,000 residents, Logroño is the largest city of La Rioja. Renowned for its robust wines, the Rioja region has historically served as a buffer between the Basques and the powerful forces to the south and east (the Moors or the Castilian Spaniards).

• *Again, choose your route from here. If you have time and a healthy interest in wine (and vineyard scenery), detour off the Camino by heading north on A-124 to the village of Laguardia, rejoining the expressway (and the Camino) later. For this option, see the sidebar on the previous pages. Otherwise, stick with the expressway to Santo Domingo de la Calzada.*

Note that west of Logroño, the expressway does a big jog to the north

(AP-68, then AP-1). You'll save miles (though not necessarily time) and stick closer to the Camino if instead you take the N-120 highway from here to Burgos. Along the way is...

Santo Domingo de la Calzada

This Rioja town has a fine cathedral, oodles of historic buildings, tranquil squares, and all the trappings of a pilgrim zone (seashells

in the pavement, *refugios*, vending machines, and launderettes). You'll see images of a rooster and a hen everywhere in town, thanks to a colorful local legend: A chaste pilgrim refused to be seduced by the amorous daughter of an innkeeper. For revenge she hid a silver cup in his bed and accused him of theft. The judge, eager to hang the lad, proclaimed that the pilgrim was as dead as the roasted rooster and hen the judge was about to eat. The charred birds suddenly stood up and began to crow and cluck, saving the pilgrim from certain death.

• *Soon after Santo Domingo de la Calzada, you pass into the region of...*

Castile and León (Castilla y León)

Welcome to Spain's largest "state" (about the size of Indiana). If you've always wanted to see the famous plains of Spain...this is it. This vast, arid high-altitude Meseta Central ("Inner Plateau") stretches to hilly, rainy Galicia in the northwest and all the way past Madrid to the south coast. Those walking the entire Camino find this flat, dry stretch to be either the best part (getting away from it all with a pensive stroll) or the worst part (boring and potentially blistering-hot).

• *The next big city on the Camino is just around the bend: Burgos.*

Burgos

Burgos (BOOR-gohs) is a pedestrian-friendly city lined up along its pretty river. Apart from its epic history and urban bustle, Burgos has one major claim to touristic fame: its glorious Gothic-style cathedral, packed to the gills with centuries' worth of elaborate decorations.

Like so many towns in the north of Spain, the burg of Burgos was founded during the Reconquista to hold on to land that had been won back from the Moors. Its position on the Camino de Santiago, and the flourishing trade in wool (sent to the Low

Burgos

1. Hotel Silken Gran Teatro
2. Mesón del Cid
3. Hotel Centro Burgos Los Braseros
4. El Hotel Jacobeo
5. Pensión Peña
6. Calle Sombrerería Eateries
7. Casa Pancho
8. Casa Ojeda
9. Rincón de España
10. RENFE Train Tickets

(B) Bus Stop

CITY WALLS
CASTLE
CENTRO DE ARTE
CATHEDRAL
Arco de Fernan González
SANTA ÁGUEDA
PASEO DE LOS CUBOS
EMBAJA.
C. ED. MARTINEZ
PLAZA DE CASTILLA
BARRANTES
APARICIO Y RUIZ
LA ISLA
AV. PALENCIA
CALLE DE
C. DE LA ESTACIÓN
CALLE CARMEN
C. BARRIO
LA MERCED
C. CONCEPCIÓN
PL. S. MARIA
PLAZA DEL REY
ST. MARYS GATE
FERNAN
CABEST.
TO LAS HUELGAS MONASTERY & LEÓN

DCH

Countries to become Flemish tapestries), helped it to thrive. Beginning in 1230, it became the capital of the kingdom of Castile for half a millennium (having usurped the title from León). The town's favorite son is the great 11th-century Spanish hero El Cid (Spaniards say "el theeth"), who valiantly fought against the Moors. The 20th century saw the town decline, even as it briefly became the capital of Franco's forces dur-

ing the Civil War (1936-1939). Later the dictator industrialized Burgos to even out the playing field (Catalunya and the Basque Country—on the political and geographical fringes of Spain—had previously been the centers of industry).

Today's Burgos still feels workaday, but with a hint of ele-

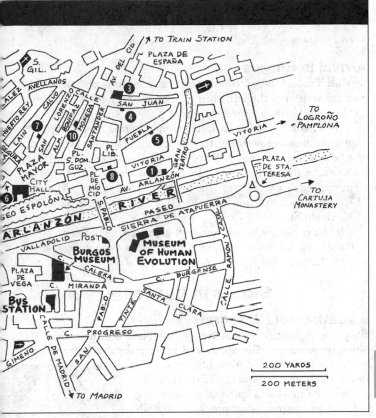

gance. The city constantly seems to be trying to improve itself—they're making a bold bid for the prestigious 2016 European City of Culture award, and have recently opened the Museum of Human Evolution. Wealthy, well-dressed locals fill Burgos' churches on weekends for weddings, christenings, and first communions. Stately plane trees line up along the riverside promenade. And watching over everything is that grand cathedral.

Orientation to Burgos

With about 175,000 inhabitants, Burgos is bisected by the Arlanzón River. The Old Town is centered on the huge cathedral. The city center is mostly pedestrianized and very manageable.

Tourist Information

Burgos' TI is on the square along the side of the cathedral (just across from the side entrance). Pick up the free map and information brochure (daily 10:00-14:00 & 16:30-19:30, July-Aug daily 10:00-20:00, Plaza del Rey San Fernando, tel. 947-288-874, www.aytoburgos.es).

Arrival in Burgos

By Bus: The bus station is just across the river from the cathedral. Exit the station to the left, then turn right at the busy street and cross the bridge (you'll see the spires).

By Train: Burgos' Rosa de Lima Station is a long 40-minute walk from town, and the bus service into town isn't much of a help to tourists (bus #25 to Plaza España, then a 15-minute walk to cathedral, 2/hour, no buses Sat-Sun). Unless you're poor or a pilgrim, catch a taxi for €7. The RENFE office at Calle Moneda 21 sells train tickets (Mon-Fri 9:30-13:30 & 16:30-19:30, Sat 9:30-13:30, closed Sun).

By Car: Burgos is easy and well-signed. Simply follow signs to the city center *(centro ciudad)*, then look for a pay garage when you see the cathedral spires.

Sights in Burgos

▲▲Cathedral (Catedral)

Burgos is rightfully famous for its showpiece Gothic cathedral. With its soaring, frilly spires and an interior that's been aug-

mented across the centuries, Burgos' cathedral is an impressive sight. Unfortunately, the church's cultural and spiritual significance is badly presented; what precious English information it provides is stilted and boring. Fortunately, you're holding a self-guided tour in your hands.

Cost and Hours: €5, or €2.50 for pilgrims; daily mid-March-Oct 9:30-19:30, Nov-mid-March 10:00-19:00, last entry one hour before closing, free lockers, tel. 947-204-712, www.catedraldeburgos.es. My self-guided tour covers the basics. The €3.50 audioguide offers little of interest.

❷ **Self-Guided Tour:** Begin by facing the **main facade** of the grand church, which was built over the course of a century. You can read the building's history into its architecture: It was started in the 13th century by French architects, who used a simple, graceful style similar to the famous Notre-Dame (mentally erase the tops of the spires and you'll see that famous Parisian cathedral). In the 14th century, German cathedral-builders took over, adding the flamboyant fringe to the tops of the towers (similar to the cathedral in Köln, Germany).

The entrance on this side is open only for worshippers, who have access to two chapels at the back of the cathedral (where hourly Mass takes place). Tourists head around the right side of the church to buy tickets and enter. As you walk there, you'll realize that this "front door" facade is only one small part of the vast complex—more spires and frills lie beyond.

Buy your ticket and enter through the side door. After you show your ticket, you'll turn left and do a clockwise spin around the church, stopping at many of the 18 **chapels.** These chapels were added over many centuries, in different styles, and were decorated in creative ways by a wide range of benefactors. (To aid with navigation for certain stops, I've listed the numbers that are posted for audioguide users.) The first few chapels are just a warm-up: the Chapel of St. John of Sahagún (#6) features a Baroque relic altar and some frescoes (unusual in this church), while the Chapel of the Presentation (#8) features a painting by an Italian Renaissance master, Il Piombo.

At the back of the church, the barriers separate the worship area from the tourist zone. But look high up, just to the right of the rose window, to see the church mascot: The **"Fly-Catcher" clock** (El Papamoscas), which rings out every quarter-hour. Above the clock is a whimsical statue of its German maker, whose mouth opens and closes when the bell rings at the top of each hour. (The tourists who congregate here and crane their necks to gape up at the show seem to be imitating the clockmaker.)

Continue to the next chapel, dedicated to **St. Anne** (Santa Ana, #12). Here you'll find a spectacular Gothic altar, showing the family tree of Jesus springing out of a reclining Jesse. (The sculptor included his self-portrait as one of the evangelists—find the bespectacled guy, the second from left in the bottom row.) Facing the altar is a Flemish tapestry and some original 15th-century vestments.

You've now circled back around to the transept. On your left are the sumptuous **Golden Stairs** (#13, designed by a Flemish Renaissance master who had studied under Michelangelo). On

the right you can enter the choir area. Step into the very center of the choir—also the very center of the cathedral—and place yourself directly under the sumptuous Plateresque-style dome, then look up and spin. Look back down again to see the **tomb of El Cid** (Rodericus Didaci Campidoctor) and his wife (#15). (El Cid's well-traveled remains were interred in Valencia, then in various points in Burgos, before being brought here in the early 20th century.)

Take a look at the **main altar,** with a fine statue of Mary slathered in silver. Also poke around the carved wooden **choir,** with a giant 16th-century songbook for Gregorian chants and two organs (used only for special occasions).

Directly behind the main altar, enter the cathedral's best chapel, the **Chapel of the High Constable** (#22). Because it has its

own altar, two side naves, and a choir and organ (in the back), it's been called "the cathedral within the cathedral." A high constable is a knight who won a crown in battle for his king or queen—the highest of VIPs in the Middle Ages. And yet, this chapel shows the influence not of a powerful man, but of a powerful woman. It was commissioned by the high constable's wife (who's entombed with him at the center of the chapel). She wanted the chapel decorations to demonstrate equality of the sexes (a bold statement in the late 15th century). Notice that most of the decorations on "his" side (left) are male-oriented, including the two brutes holding the coat of arms up above, and the figures on the side altar. But "her" decorations (right) are more feminine—damsels holding the coat of arms, and mostly women decorating the side altar. The yin and yang of the sexes is even suggested by the black-and-white flooring. Also notice a pair of grand paintings here (unrelated to the sexual politics): on "his" side a beautiful Flemish depiction of a woman in a red dress (likely from the school of Hans Memling); and on "her" side Mary Magdalene, by a favorite pupil of Leonardo da Vinci's (who probably put his own touches on the work as well).

Continuing around you'll enter the **cloister** (#24), walking past the beautifully carved main sacristy (#23). The tour route takes you counterclockwise around this cloister, to a few more chapels and museum exhibits: The Corpus Christi Chapel (#26) features stairs up to the library (closed to the public) and access to the chapter house (#27), where the monks would meet. The next chapel (Santa Catalina's Chapel, #28) displays a remarkable 10th-century Bible. In the same case is a copy of El Cid's pre-nup. (To protect his assets, he found a clever legal loophole to transfer ownership of all he had to his wife.) Around the top of this room are dozens of paintings depicting centuries' worth of bishops.

Continuing to the **Chapel of St. John the Baptist and St. James** (#29), you find the cathedral's museum collection, including ecclesiastical items (such as some exquisitely detailed crosses and chalices), an emotive statue of Christ being whipped, and an altar depicting St. James the Moor-Slayer (see page 301).

Finally you'll head downstairs to the **lower cloister** (#33). At the foot of the stairs is a schmaltzy portrait of El Cid and, beyond

that, a series of three chambers lead off to the right. In the first is a model of the original Romanesque church (with the current Gothic footprint around it for comparison), Romanesque capitals from cathedral columns, and a sarcophagus. The second chamber emphasizes the Gothic aspects of the cathedral and contains a large model of the entire cathedral complex. Farther down the cloister, Renaissance exhibits include a restored heraldic stained-glass window and a carved nativity scene. The third chamber on the right is a mini-cinema showing a 15-minute film documenting the history of the cathedral and its recent restorations (Spanish only, 2/hour).

Return to El Cid, and then continue around the cloister to see glass cases displaying several original statues and carvings retrieved during the restoration work (and replaced with copies). The patio often houses contemporary art exhibitions (open May-Sept only). Exit through the ticket office, which also contains the gift shop and the lockers. Go in peace.

Other Sights

On a short visit, the cathedral is the main sight. But if you have the time, a few other attractions might be worth a look.

Museum of Human Evolution (Museo de la Evolución Humana)—This museum was inspired by discoveries of Pleistocene-era remains in the nearby Atapuerca Mountains, about nine miles east of Burgos. The Atapuerca find constitutes one of the most important settlements of the first Europeans. Housed in a new glass building by the river, the museum displays the remains found at Atapuerca. Flanking the museum are a research center and a large conference center (€6, Tue-Fri 10:00-14:30 & 16:30-20:00, Sat-Sun 10:00-20:00, closed Mon, Paseo Sierra de Atapuerca, tel. 902-024-246, www.museoevolucionhumana.com).

Other Museums—On the hill behind the cathedral, **Centro de Arte** is a contemporary art museum with temporary exhibits (free, Tue-Sat 11:30-14:00 & 17:00-21:00, Sun 11:00-14:30, closed Mon, tel. 947-256-550). And just across the river, near the bus station, is the **Museo de Burgos,** which celebrates the cultural heritage of Burgos province. Its five floors of painting and sculpture and two floors of archaeological exhibits ring the gorgeous courtyard of a fine old 1540 convent. The somewhat-hard-to-appreciate museum features the sword of El Cid (€1.20; July-Sept Tue-Sat 10:00-14:00 & 17:00-20:00, Sun 10:00-14:00, closed Mon; Oct-June Tue-Sat 10:00-14:00 & 16:00-19:00, Sun 10:00-14:00, closed Mon; audioguide-€1, Calle Miranda 13, tel. 947-265-875).

Plaza Mayor and Promenade—Burgos' main square, a long block from the cathedral, is urban-feeling and strangely

uninviting, with long marble benches. The stone building with two clock towers is the town hall; if you walk under here you'll emerge at the city's delightful riverside promenade. Lined with knobby plane trees and outdoor cafés, it has an almost Provençal ambience. Going left along the promenade takes you to **Plaza del Mío Cid,** with an equestrian statue celebrating Burgos' favorite son, "My El Cid." Going right along the promenade leads you to the impressive **St. Mary's Gate,** one of six surviving entrances of this stout-walled city's original 12 gates (built in the 13th century, decorated in 16th-century Renaissance style). Look up at the gate, and in a deep, strong voice, declare: "Burgos." Passing through this gate takes you directly to the cathedral.

▲**Huelgas Monastery**—In addition to its grand cathedral, Burgos has a pair of impressive monasteries. The Cistercian monastery of Huelgas is the easiest to reach (though still a bit of a walk from the cathedral). Entrance is by one-hour tour only, and English tours are very rare (€5, free on Wed, open Tue-Sat 10:00-13:00 & 15:45-17:30, Sun 10:30-14:00, closed Mon, tours depart about every 20 minutes, try asking your guide for

some English info, tel. 947-201-630). Inside you'll see a "pantheon" of royal tombs, a Gothic cloister with Mudejar details, a chapter house with 13th-century stained glass, and a Romanesque cloister. The highlight is a statue of St. James with an arm that could be moved to symbolically "knight" the king by placing a sword on his shoulders (since only a "saint"—or statue of a saint—was worthy of knighting royalty). Finally you'll tour a museum of rare surviving clothes from common people (not just religious vestments) from the 13th and 14th centuries.

Getting There: It's about a 20-minute walk west of the city center, or you can take bus #5, #7, or #35 (catch the bus across the bridge from the cathedral).

Cartuja Monastery (Cartuja de Miraflores)—Since this is far-ther out of town, seeing both Huelgas and Miraflores is probably redundant unless you adore monasteries. However, the Cartuja Monastery is a nice destination for a pleasant three-mile walk. (Bring a picnic.) To get there, cross the river by Plaza del Mío Cid and turn left, following the river until you reach the monastery. Or take a taxi there (€6) and walk back (free entry, Mon-Fri 10:15-15:00 & 16:00-18:00, Sat-Sun 11:00-15:00 & 16:00-18:00).

Tourist Train—This little attraction runs both by day and by night (€4 for either tour, departs from in front of TI on Plaza del Rey, buy tickets from machine outside TI door, tel. 947-101-888). The shorter 45-minute day tour is only really worth taking if you want to get a good shot of the cathedral from the best viewpoint in town—the Mirador, up by the ruins of the castle (2/hour; July-Sept daily 11:00-21:00; Oct-March Mon-Fri 15:00-18:00, Sat-Sun 11:00-18:00). I prefer the one-hour night tour for an enjoyable view of Burgos after dark, when its monuments are illuminated (July-Sept only, departs at 22:00 and 23:00).

Near Burgos

Atapuerca—Nine miles out of Burgos sit the Sierra de Atapuerca Mountains, home to the site where archaeologists have discov-ered human remains dating back over a million years. Scholars are drooling over the find, which offers significant new insights into the lives of prehistoric humans—well-explained by the Museum of Human Evolution in Burgos (described earlier). To visit Atapuerca, travel by car or taxi from Burgos to the village of Ibeas de Juarros, where a shuttle bus will transfer you to the site (advance reserva-tions essential, get details at TI, tel. 902-024-246, www.atapuerca.org, reservas@museoevolucionhumana.com).

Santo Domingo de Silos—This unassuming village—about 40 miles (an hour's drive) south of Burgos—has a fine Benedictine monastery that's become a quirky footnote in popular music. The monastery's monks are famous for their melodic Gregorian chants, which were recorded and released as the hugely popular album *Chant* in 1994. (It went on to sell six million copies.) Although the monks don't perform concerts, some of their daily services—which are free and open to the public—include chanting. The lengthy vespers *(vísperas)* service is entirely chanted (daily at 19:00, 2.5 hours); there's also some chanting at the shorter Eucharist service (Mon-Fri at 9:00, Sat-Sun at 12:00). You can also tour the cloister and museum (€3.50, open to the public Tue-Sat 10:00-13:00 & 16:30-18:00, Sun 16:30-18:00 only, closed Mon). Call to confirm before making the trip (tel. 947-390-049, www.abadiadesilos.es).

Sleeping in Burgos

(€1 = about $1.40, country code: 34)

When I've listed a price range, it fluctuates with demand; the top rates are for summer (June-Sept).

$$$ Hotel Silken Gran Teatro is comfortable, modern, and well-located beside the river (connected by a footbridge to the Museum of Human Evolution complex). Room prices vary wildly depending on season and view—book well in advance for a good deal (Sb-€68-155, Db-€65-175, extra bed-€35, breakfast-€13, air-con, elevator, free Wi-Fi, café, restaurant, free gym, no public lounge, parking-€15, Avenida de Arlanzón 8, tel. 947-253-900, fax 947-253-901, www.hotelgranteatro.com, comercial.granteatro @hoteles-silken.com).

$$ Mesón del Cid enjoys Burgos' best location, gazing across a quiet square at the cathedral's front facade (full-frontal cathedral views are worth the extra €15). The 55 rooms in two buildings come with classy tile floors and old-fashioned furniture (Sb-€60-70, Db-€70-90, includes tax, breakfast-€11, air-con, elevator, free Internet access and Wi-Fi, Plaza de Santa María 8, tel. 947-208-715, fax 947-269-460, www.mesondelcid.es, mesondelcid@meson delcid.es).

$$ Hotel Centro Burgos Los Braseros, set back a little from the street, offers modern class for reasonable prices. Its lobby and 57 rooms are slick and stylish (Sb-€55, Db-€65, includes breakfast, air-con, elevator, request quiet room, free Wi-Fi, restaurant, café, Avenida del Cid 2, tel. 947-252-958, www.hotelcentroburgos.com, reservas@hotelcentroburgos.com).

$$ El Hotel Jacobeo is a cheaper option, with 14 modern rooms along a lively pedestrian street (Sb-€35-40, Db-€45-72, breakfast-€4.50, free Wi-Fi, all rooms face the back—so it's quiet, Calle de San Juan 24, tel. 947-260-102, fax 947-260-100, www .hoteljacobeo.com, hoteljacobeo@hoteljacobeo.com).

$ Pensión Peña is Burgos' best budget option. Lively Loli, who speaks no English, rents eight simple but bright and well-maintained rooms (sharing three bathrooms) on the second floor of an old apartment building with a new elevator. Loli takes no advance reservations, but you can call in the morning to see if she has a room (D-€30, La Puebla 18, tel. 947-206-323, mobile 639-067-089, loli.arauzo@hotmail.com).

Eating in Burgos

On Calle Sombrerería: Several good eateries are on this street. **Bar Gaona Jardin,** at #29, has a leafy interior and cooks up nice, hot tapas. **Estrella de Galicia,** with a modern, bright ambience, offers a preview of the cuisine you'll enjoy in Santiago—Galician food, wine, and beer (€11 meal offered weekdays, €5-7 *raciones*, €10-15 main dishes, daily, alongside church at Calle de la Paloma 35, tel. 947-276-902). Across the street, **Cervecería Morito** offers a more chaotic local ambience—one tight room with tables and a bar, or pay a little more to eat at the terrace across the road (€3-4 sandwiches, €5-7 *raciones*, handy photo menu, daily, Calle Sombrerería 27, tel. 947-267-555). At the end of the street, **Pecaditos** is a local favorite for its tasty tapas and bargain prices (€1 tapas, daily, Calle Sombrerería 3, tel. 947-267-633).

Elsewhere in Burgos: **Casa Pancho** is a long, inviting bar where hardworking José, Angel, and Begona churn out fresh-cooked tapas. Two or three tapas off of their *Carta de los Pinchos* can make a good meal (the menu's photos of dishes are described in English). Their specialty is *cojonuda* (quail egg, blood sausage, and green pepper on bread—all for €1). You're welcome to take a table for about 10 percent extra—still a great value. To sample a good Spanish wine with your tapas, try a glass of the strong local red, Ribera del Duero, or a white Albariño from Galicia—each about €2.50 (daily, Calle San Lorenzo 13, tel. 947-203-405). A couple more good tapas bars are within steps of here.

Casa Ojeda is a venerable institution that's a reliable choice for a real restaurant meal. Specializing in Burgos cuisine, they offer seating at the bar downstairs (tapas, €6 half-*raciones*, €13 combo-plate) or in the upstairs dining room (pricier meals served 21:00-24:00: €10 starters, €16-40 main dishes). Relax and enjoy the subdued, rapidly aging ambience (closed Sun, Calle Vitoria 5, tel. 947-209-052).

Rincón de España has a great location on Plaza del Rey, close to the cathedral. It's popular with locals for its regional dishes, including *cochinillo* (roast suckling pig) and *cordero* (roast lamb) cooked in a wood-fired oven. The restaurant's two indoor rooms often are full with wedding parties on weekends, and its outdoor terrace sports views of the cathedral spires. Brothers Javi and Fernando (who speaks English) are sommeliers and have a good local wine list. Try their traditional *leche frito* (fried milk) for dessert (€14.50 fixed-price meal available for lunch and dinner, €7.50-20 main dishes, daily 12:30-15:45 & 19:30-23:30, closed Mon-Tue afternoons in Oct-April, Calle Nuño Rastura 11, tel. 947-205-955, www.rincondeespana.com).

Burgos Connections

From Burgos by Bus to: Pamplona (3/day, 2.5 hours), **León** (4/day, 3 hours, Alsa), **Bilbao** (4/day, 2 hours, Continental), **Santiago de Compostela** (1/day, 8.5 hours, Alsa), **San Sebastián** (6/day,

Walking the Way

The Camino by car? Purists cringe at the thought—arguably, it contradicts the whole point of the Camino to do it in a rush. If you have a month of your life to devote to the trek, consider following the Camino the intended and traditional way.

As walking the Camino is in vogue, there's no shortage of good Camino guidebooks and maps. Try *Walking the Camino de Santiago* by Bethan Davies and Ben Cole, *A Pilgrim's Guide to the Camino de Santiago* by John Brierly, or *Buen Camino* by Jim and Eleanor Clem. For a more philosophical take, check out *Following the Milky Way* by Elyn Aviva and *On Pilgrimage* by Jennifer Lash. For a good website, see http://bit.ly/d1mjax.

Get a good book. Read and study it. Pack carefully. Solicit advice from people who've done it. Then enjoy the journey.

The procedure for walking the Camino has remained the same throughout history. The gear includes a cloak; a pointy, floppy hat; a walking stick; and a gourd (for drinking from wells). The route of the Camino is marked with yellow arrows or scallop shells at every intersection. (For more on the significance of these items, and others, see sidebar on page 242.)

Early in the journey, pilgrims buy their "credential" *(credencial)*—a sort of passport, which they get stamped and dated at churches and lodgings along the way. (They can also show it to stay at cheap *refugios* and to get a reduced pilgrim's rate at many museums and churches en route.) At the end, they present their stamped credential in Santiago and receive a special certificate called a *compostela*. Only those who meet the two principal criteria qualify: You must do the pilgrimage for "spiritual" reasons; and you must walk at least the last 100 kilometers (about 62 miles, roughly from Sarria) or ride your bike or horse the last 200 kilometers (124 miles) into Santiago.

Doing the entire French Road from the border to Santiago takes about four to six weeks on foot (averaging 12-15 miles per day, with an occasional rest day—32 days is a typical Camino). Bikers can do it in about two weeks. Many of the trails, originally dirt paths, are now being paved. The journey itself is a type of hut-hopping: At regular intervals along the route (about every 5-10 miles), pilgrims can get a bunk for the night at humble little hostels called *albergues* (ahl-BEHR-gehs), *refugios* (reh-FOO-hee-ohs), or *hospitales* (oh-spee-TAH-lehs). Some of these are run by the government (€5-10 per bunk, closer to €3 in Galicia, even if they're "free" a donation is requested; no reservations taken—first-come, first-served, with priority given to credential-holding pilgrims arriving on foot). Others are privately run (typically a bit more expensive—€10-20—and sometimes take reservations). A wide variety of other accommodations are available for those who prefer more comfort, ranging from simple *hostales* to grand hotels and *paradores* (I've listed my favorites in this chapter).

What began as a religious trek to atone for one's sins has evolved into a journey undertaken by anyone—spiritual or secular—who just wants some time to think. Although some pilgrims do the trip for "fun," those who take it seriously caution that it's one of the most wrenching things you can do. After a few weeks on the Camino, many pilgrims begin to develop a telltale limp...you'll notice it getting more pronounced as you move west. (There's a reason old pilgrim hostels are sometimes called "hospitals.")

But there are worse things than blisters and sore muscles. The Camino can take a psychological toll on pilgrims. Trudging step after step across endless plains toward an ever-receding horizon, you're forced to introspection. Religious or not, you can't help but come to terms with your regrets, demons, "sins," or anything else that's on your conscience.

This process of self-reflection is symbolized by picking up a small stone somewhere early on the Camino, then depositing it at the Iron Cross near the end of the trek—releasing yourself from whatever's been weighing you down. The absolution of sins that awaited medieval pilgrims isn't so different from the "find myself" motives of today's iPhone-toting tourists. Whether you're pardoned by the Church, or simply unburdened of what's been nagging you, it's liberating all the same.

On a lighter note, a wonderful pilgrim camaraderie percolates along the length of the Camino, as a United Nations of vagabonds—young and old—swap stories and tips. Driving, on foot, or on bike, you'll keep crossing paths with the same pilgrims again and again...the guy who checked in before you at the hotel last night is at the cathedral with you the next morning. Along the way, the standard greeting (like a Jacobean "Happy Travels") is *"Buen Camino!"*

No matter how you get to Santiago, you'll share in the jubilation pilgrims have felt through the ages when—four miles out of town—the spires of the cathedral come into view.

CAMINO DE SANTIAGO

3 hours), **Salamanca** (2/day, 3-4 hours, Alsa), **Madrid** (9/day, 3 hours, Continental). Keep in mind that Sunday connections are very sparse.

By Train to: Pamplona (1/day, 2 hours), **León** (2/day, 2 hours), **Bilbao** (4/day, 2.5-3 hours), **San Sebastián** (6/day, 3 hours), **Salamanca** (2-3/day, 2.5 hours), **Madrid** (6/day, 2.5-4.5 hours).

From Burgos to León

While there are some worthwhile stops between Burgos and León, this is a good place to put some serious miles under your belt: Follow signs for the A-231 expressway and zip between the cities in less than two hours. Sticking with the true Camino—a confusing spaghetti of roads without a single, straight highway to keep you on track—takes you through a poorer, very humble countryside with few sights. Some travelers enjoy dipping into towns along here such as **Castrojeriz, Frómista,** and **Carrión de los Condes,** but on a tight itinerary, your time is better spent in Burgos or our next stop, León.

León

With a delightfully compact Old Town (surrounded by ugly sprawl), León (lay-OWN) has an enjoyable small-town atmosphere. But most importantly, it has a pair of sights that serve as a textbook for medieval European art styles: Romanesque (the San Isidoro Monastery, with astonishingly well-preserved frescoes) and Gothic (the cathedral, with the best stained glass outside of France).

León means "lion" in Spanish—but in this case, the name derives from Rome's seventh legion, which was stationed here. Founded as a Roman camp at the confluence of two rivers in A.D. 68, León gradually grew prosperous because of the gold trade that passed through here (mined in the Las Médulas hillsides to the west). Later, as the Moors were pushed ever southward, the capital of the Reconquista moved from Ovideo to here in 910, and for three centuries León was the capital of a vast kingdom (until it was supplanted by Burgos). Today's León has relatively little industry, but is the capital of one of Spain's biggest provinces, making it an administrative and business center. It's also a major university town, with some 15,000 students who imbue it with an enjoyable vitality.

Orientation to León

The big city of León, with 140,000 people (200,000 in the metro area), sits along the Bernesga River. On a short visit tourists can ignore everything outside the rectangular Old Town, which is set a few blocks up from the river.

Tourist Information

León's TI is on the square facing the cathedral (July-mid-Sept daily 9:00-20:00; Oct-June Mon-Sat 9:00-14:00 & 16:00-19:00, Sun 9:30-17:00; Plaza de la Regla 2, tel. 987-237-082).

Local Guide: Blanca Lobete is an excellent, energetic teacher who shares León's architectural gems with travelers (3-hour tour-€91, mobile 669-276-335, guiaslegio@hotmail.com).

Arrival in León

By Train or Bus: The train and bus stations are along the river, about a 15-minute walk from the town center. To reach the Old Town from the stations, cross the big bridge and walk straight up Avenida Ordoño II. You'll hit the turreted Gaudí building, marking the start of the Old Town. From here the San Isidoro Museum is to the left, and the cathedral is straight ahead (up Calle Ancha).

By Car: Compared to the other cities in this chapter, León is not well-signed. Do your best to follow directions to the city center (*centro ciudad*); once there, you can park in a very convenient underground parking garage at Plaza Santo Domingo (€16/day), right at the start of the Old Town (and within a three-minute walk of all my recommended accommodations). Nearby Plaza Mayor also has a parking garage.

Sights in León

León's two most worthwhile sights complement each other perfectly: the remarkable Romanesque frescoes at San Isidoro, and the gorgeous stained glass of the cathedral. While you can do these in either order, to appreciate the architectural progression it makes sense to do San Isidoro first. (If you're rushed and have time for only one, make it the cathedral.)

▲▲San Isidoro Museum (Museo de San Isidoro)

San Isidoro is an 11th-century Romanesque church that's been gradually added on to over the centuries. The church itself is free and always open to worshippers, but the attached museum is the real attraction. Inside you'll see a library, a cloister, a chapter house, and a "pantheon" of royal tombs featuring some of the most

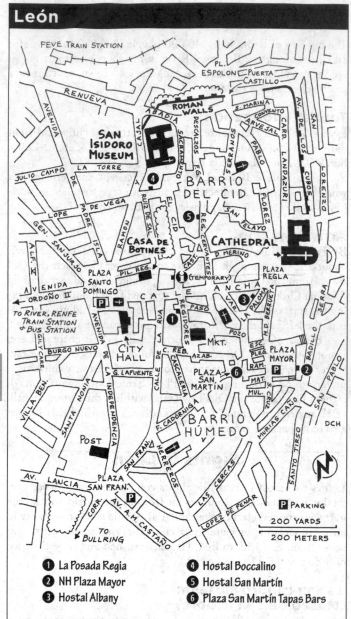

León

P Parking

200 YARDS
200 METERS

1. La Posada Regia
2. NH Plaza Mayor
3. Hostal Albany
4. Hostal Boccalino
5. Hostal San Martín
6. Plaza San Martín Tapas Bars

exquisite Romanesque frescoes in Spain.

Cost and Hours: €4; July-Aug Mon-Sat 9:00-20:00, Sun 9:00-14:00; Sept-June Mon-Sat 10:00-13:30 & 16:00-18:30, Sun 10:00-13:30; Plaza San Isidoro 4, tel. 987-876-161, www.sanisidoro deleon.net.

● **Self-Guided Tour:** Buy your ticket and go directly into the **Royal Pantheon** (Panteón Real). This area, now enclosed in the middle of the complex, was once the portico in front of the west door of the church. In 2002, historians discovered the tombs of several medieval kings and queens (which are now held in the stone tombs). But who's buried here pales in comparison to the beautiful, vivid frescoes on the vaulting above them. Created in the late 11th and early 12th centuries, these frescoes have never been repainted—they're incredibly well-preserved. While most Romanesque frescoes have been moved to museums, this is a rare opportunity to see some in situ (where they were originally intended).

Follow along as the frescos trace the life of Christ (counter-clockwise, starting on the wall in the front right corner). In the scene of the Annunciation you'll notice a sense of motion (Mary's billowing clothes) that's unusual for typically stiff and un lifelike Romanesque art. Above that, on the ceiling in the corner, an angel appears to shepherds dressed in traditional 11th-century Leonese clothing. There's even a Leonese mastiff dog, lapping at his master's milk (while he's distracted by the angel).

In the next ceiling section (closer to the entry), Roman soldiers carry out the gruesome slaughter of the innocents. Then it's time for the Last Supper (center of the ceiling). As you take in the bold colors, notice that only 11 of the Apostles have halos...all but Judas (under the table). At the corner, find the black rooster *(gallus)*, a symbol of Jesus, who harkened the dawn of a new day for God's people. But in the next section we see the rooster used as a different symbol—as Peter denies Christ three times before the cock crows. Also see Jesus' arrest, Simon helping Jesus carry the cross, and Pontius Pilate washing his hands of the whole business. Finally (on wall, left of main altar) we see Jesus nailed to the cross.

The final panel, in the middle of the room, is the most artistically and thematically impressive: Jesus returning triumphant to judge the living and the dead. He's depicted here as Pantocrator ("all-powerful"). Over his shoulders are the symbols for alpha and omega, and he's surrounded by the four evangelists, depicted—according to the prophecy of Ezekiel—as animals: angel, bull, eagle, and lion. The most interesting detail is the calendar running along the archway near Jesus' right hand. The 12 medallions—one for each month (labeled in Latin)—are symbolized by people's

CAMINO DE SANTIAGO

activities during that month. In January, the man closes one door (or year) while he opens the next. He proceeds to warm himself by the fire (February), prune (March), plant his crops (April), harvest (July), forage (September), slaughter the fattened pig (October), and bless his bread by the fire at Christmas (December). The message: Jesus is present for this entire cycle of life.

There's more to the museum. Continue into the **cloister,** where you'll find a small room with a giant 12th-century rooster weathervane that used to top the nearby tower (now replaced by a replica)—a symbol of the city.

You can also climb the tight spiral staircase (near where you came in) to the evocative old **library** (with a giant Mozarabic Bible from 960—you can page through a facsimile in the gift shop) and the **chapter house,** displaying a glittering assortment of Romanesque reliquary chests.

Our tour is over. But for a peek at a remaining section of León's **Roman walls,** turn right out of the museum, then head right down the street.

• *For the most interesting approach to the cathedral, walk south from the San Isidoro Museum (and the surviving chunk of wall) along the busy street called Ramón y Cajal. At the roundabout (Plaza Santo Domingo), turn left. You're at the start of...*

Calle Ancha and the Old Town

This "Wide Street," which cuts through the heart of the Old Town, was widened in the mid-19th century to create an appropriate pathway to the cathedral. It was lined with grand mansions of local wealthy people who wanted to live close to God. It's only been pedestrianized for the last decade, creating a much-enjoyed people zone.

At the start of Calle Ancha, the turreted medieval-looking building is the **Casa de Botines**—one of few works by Antoni Gaudí outside of Catalunya (another is the Bishop's Palace in Astorga, described later in this

chapter). Now the Casa de Botines is a bank and generally not open to visitors unless there's a special exhibition. Gaudí preferred to use local materials, such as the slate roof (typical in León province). The rough stone exterior is intended to hang on to falling snow to create an atmospheric effect. Over the door is St. George, the patron saint of Gaudí's native Catalunya. Notice the architect himself on the bench across the square, appreciating his work.

As you walk up Calle Ancha toward the cathedral, the neighborhood to the left is called **Barrio del Cid** (for a supposed former resident). The area to the right is known as the **Barrio Húmedo,** or "Wet Quarter," for all the bars that speckle its streets (see "Eating in León," later). Deep in the Barrio Húmedo is the appealing main square, or **Plaza Mayor,** overshadowed by the cathedral a few blocks down Calle Ancha.

▲▲Cathedral (Catedral)

León's 13th-century Gothic cathedral is filled with some of the finest stained glass in all of Europe.

Cost and Hours: Cathedral entrance is free, Mon-Sat 8:30-13:30 & 16:00-19:00 (until 20:00 June-Aug), Sun 8:30-13:30 & 17:00-19:00; cloister-€2, museum-€3; cloister and museum closed Sat afternoon Oct-May and all day Sun year-round. Audioguides are available Mon-Fri 10:00-12:45 & 16:15-18:45. There are guided night visits in English (April-Sept Sat-Sun 23:30-24:15); inquire at information office for daytime guided visit times. Purchase tickets and rent audioguides at the ticket office and bookstore on the right, near the entrance. Tel. 638-479-419, www.catedralde leon.org.

◑ Self-Guided Tour: Take a look at the **facade.** If you've just seen Burgos' cathedral, León's—while impressive—might seem  a letdown. Reserve judgment until you get inside. León's cathedral was actually built in response to the one in Burgos, to keep León on the map after Burgos wrested capital status from León in 1230. But, whereas Burgos' was built over two centuries, this cathedral took only about 50 years to complete. The focus was on creating a simple, purely Gothic cathedral to showcase its grand stained-glass windows. The three porticos (doorways with pointed arches) are textbook Gothic. Notice the gap between the two towers and the main facade, which allows even more light to reach those windows. This also gives the cathedral a feeling of lightness. The one exception to the pure-Gothic construction: Notice the tower on the right is a bit taller—it was capped in the 15th century with a frilly spire to keep up with what was going on in Burgos.

Now approach the **main door,** above which is a carving of the Last Judgment. Above Mary, St. Michael weighs souls to determine who is going to party with the musicians of heaven (left; his scale bar is missing) or burn with the cauldrons and demons of hell (right). If you look carefully you'll see that all of those kicking back in heaven are members of the clergy or royalty. This subtle message made the Camino de Santiago even more appealing to pilgrims: If you weren't a priest or an aristocrat, completing the Camino was your only ticket to eternal bliss.

Before entering, ponder the crucial role that **light** plays in this house of holy glass. Like all cathedrals, the main door faces the west, and the altar (at the far end) faces east—toward Jerusalem. But that also means that the sun rises behind the altar (where Jesus symbolically resides) and sets at the Last Judgment. This theme is continued again and again inside.

Speaking of which, go on in and let your eyes adjust to the light. Notice how the purely Gothic structure—extremely high, with columns and pointed arches to direct your gaze ever heavenward—really allows the stained glass to take center stage. Of all this glass (the second-most glass in any European cathedral, after Chartres in France), 70 percent is original, from the 13th to the 16th centuries.

Imagine how the light in here changes, like living inside a kaleidoscope, as the sun moves across the sky each day. Notice that the colors differ thematically in various parts of the cathedral. Above the main door, the rose window (dedicated, like the cathedral itself, to St. Mary, with 12 angels playing instruments around her) is the most colorful, as it receives the most light at the end of the day. Turning to face the front altar, notice that the glass on the left (north) side of the church, which gets less light, symbolizes darkness and obscurity—blue dominates this side. The glass on the right (south) side of the church, which is bathed in light much of the day, symbolizes brightness and has a greater variety of colors.

Now trace the layers of Gothic **cathedral construction** from the bottom up, as the building (like your eyes) stretches ever higher, closer to God. The lowest level is the stone foundation (with pointed archways embedded in the walls), symbolic of the mineral world. The first windows show flowers, trees, and animals—the natural world. At the top of each nature window are three medallions showing the human world: common people doing their thing—both vices and virtues.

Above this first row of **windows,** notice the stone gallery (used for window maintenance). It's very rare to have windows in this section of a cathedral (in this case, replicas of coats-of-arms of nobles who funded the cathedral's construction). The tall windows at the very top show biblical characters. On the left (north) side—the "darkness" side, before Christ—is the Old Testament; on the right (south) side—the "light" side, after Christ—is the New

Testament. The two sides meet at the rose window (above the main altar) of Jesus—who is illuminated by the rising sun each morning, enlightening the entire cathedral.

If you notice **scaffolding,** it's part of a painstaking restoration of the cathedral's windows. Each piece of glass is being carefully removed from its old iron frame and reset in a brass frame. You can climb up to see the work, and the window, up close—100,000 visitors have done so already (€2, entrance outside—around the left side as you face the main facade, tours every 30 minutes, Spanish only but English brochure provided, closed Sun-Mon).

Peek into the carved wooden **choir** at the center of the nave (closed to visitors). The curved wooden part over the top of the chair is a "sounding board" *(tornavóz)*, helping voices to carry. The giant glass door replaced a solid wooden one in the early 20th century—opening up the church even more to God's light.

Head for the **transept.** Unfortunately, this part of the cathedral almost didn't survive a well-intended but botched Baroque-era reconstruction. A heavy dome placed over the transept proved too heavy for the four graceful main pillars, causing a significant chunk of the church to collapse. The transept's blue (north) rose window, featuring Christ, survives from the 13th century, while the red (south) one, with Mary, is from the 19th century.

Circling back behind the altar, you'll find a chapel with the **"White Virgin"** on the right, the original 13th-century statue (whose face was painted white) from the front facade of the church. Note the differences between the 16th-century stained glass above the Virgin (with one large, multipaneled scene) and the 13th- and 14th-century glass in the flanking chapels (with one scene per panel—and even tinier bits of glass).

From the left transept you can enter the **cloister** and **museum** (see page 275 for cost and hours). The cloister offers a good view of the flying buttresses that made the stained glass structurally possible. By removing the weight from the walls and transferring it to these buttresses, medieval engineers could build higher and make larger and larger windows. In the **museum** are a series of rooms displaying some giant discarded Baroque elements (such as turret-tops) that were added to the facade in the 16th century, and later removed because they cluttered up the architectural harmony.

Sleeping in León

(€1 = about $1.40, country code: 34)
All of these listings are inside the Old Town. If there's a range, you can assume that the high end is for summer. Hotels often make last-minute or off-season deals.

Camino de Santiago: Western Half

$$$ La Posada Regia is a smart little hotel with 36 rooms in two buildings just off the main walking street. The old-fashioned, pleasant decor is a combination of wood beams and patches of stone (Sb-€60-70, Db-€97-139, includes breakfast, Regidores 9-11, tel. 987-213-173, fax 987-213-031, www.regialeon.com, posada @regialeon.com).

$$$ NH Plaza Mayor is the Old Town splurge, with 51 rooms right on Plaza Mayor (some with views for no extra charge—request one). Part of a classy chain, this place offers modern four-star comfort at reasonable prices (Sb-€80-100, Db-€90-120, breakfast-€14, air-con, elevator, 30 minutes free Wi-Fi, Plaza Mayor 15, tel. 987-344-357, fax 987-215-596, www.nh-hotels.com,

nhplazamayor@nh-hotels.com).

$$ Hostal Albany offers 19 very mod rooms at a good price, just a few steps off the main walking street and cathedral square (Sb-€40-51, Db-€57-68, includes tax, breakfast-€3.50, air-con, elevator, free Wi-Fi, Calle La Paloma 13, tel. 987-264-600, www.albanyleon.net, info@albanyleon.net).

$$ Hostal Boccalino, spacious and practical, rents 35 good rooms at a good price on a stately square facing the monastery (Sb-€40-50, Db-€60-70, Tb-€90, elevator, free Wi-Fi and drinks from cooler, Plaza de San Isidoro 9, tel. 987-220-017, www.hostalboccalino.com, boccalino_3@hotmail.com). They also have 10 comparable rooms above their restaurant in a nearby building (similar prices, same reception, no elevator).

$ Hostal San Martín is a good budget option. Popular with pilgrims, it has 12 rooms overlooking a small square in the Old Town (S-€23, Sb-€31, Db-€43, Tb-€55, includes tax, request quiet room in back, no elevator, free Wi-Fi, cozy lounge; Plaza Torres de Omaña 1—located up the stairs on the right as you enter, second floor; tel. 987-875-187, fax 987-875-249, www.sanmartinhostales .com, sanmartinhostal@hotmail.com).

Eating in León

León is one of few Spanish cities whose bars still honor the old tradition of giving a free (if modest) tapa to anyone buying a drink. Your best bet for finding eats in León is to stroll the **Barrio Húmedo** area, south of Calle Ancha. This zone is packed with restaurants and bars offering good food and ambience.

Plaza San Martín Pub Crawl: In the "Wet Quarter," locals head for Plaza San Martín to eat and drink. Survey the many little bars on or near the square, noting how locals know each bar's specialty and generally stick to that dish when ordering. Consider these joints: **La Bicha** is a dirty little hole-in-the-wall where Paco works hard maintaining his reputation for making León's best *morcilla* (made of tripe—like haggis without the skin) and for being a colorful local character. He'll fry up a plateful and serve it with some buttered toast and a nice *crianza* wine (plate big enough for four, €6). **El Llar** is famous for its potatoes (free with a drink). Of the two sauces, I'd get the cheese (tapas in bar, restaurant upstairs serves €5-10 starters and €12-15 main dishes). **Bar Rebote** serves six different croquettes—one free with each drink. If you're still hungry, head down Calle Mulhacín to find **La Competencia.** Fight your way in for free pizza slices (downstairs) and potatoes with ham (upstairs). **Mesón el Tizón** fills one tight room with a bar in front and seating in back—order hot *raciones* from its chalkboard menu (Calle de las Carnicerías 1).

León Connections

From León by Bus to: Astorga (hourly, 50 minutes), **Burgos** (4/day, 3 hours), **Santiago de Compostela** (5/day, 7 hours), **Madrid** (10/day, 4 hours). Note that all buses are run by Alsa.

    By Train to: Burgos (2/day, 2 hours), **San Sebastián** (1/day, 5 hours), **Pamplona** (1/day, 4 hours), **Santiago de Compostela** (1-2/day, 6 hours), **Madrid** (9/day, 4.5 hours).

From León to Galicia

This is arguably the most diverse stretch of the Camino. It begins in the flatness of the Meseta Central around León. Then, around Astorga, the landscape gradually becomes more varied and lush, as the Camino approaches the mountainous El Bierzo region (the northwest fringe of Castile and León). Before you know it, you're in the very Celtic-feeling terrain of Galicia.

• *Begin by making your way west, to Astorga. You can stay on the N-120 highway, or pay a €4 toll to zip there more quickly on the AP-71 expressway.*

Astorga

Astorga (ah-STOR-gah) sits at the intersection of two ancient roads: the Camino and a north–south trade route from Sevilla to the north coast. When León was a humble Roman camp, "Asturica" was the provincial capital. But today the fortunes are reversed, as welcoming, laid-back, sleepy Astorga (with about 15,000 people)—just big enough to have some interesting sight-seeing and good hotels and restaurants—is a nice small-town alternative to the big city of León. The main attraction here is the memorable Bishop's Palace by Antoni Gaudí.

Tourist Information: Astorga's TI shares a square with the Bishop's Palace and cathedral (daily in summer 10:00-13:30 & 16:00-19:00, until 18:30 and closed Sun-Mon off-season, Plaza Eduardo de Castro 5, tel. 987-618-222).

Arrival in Astorga: The **bus** station is just outside the Old Town, behind the Bishop's Palace. **Drivers** follow signs for *centro ciudad* and *centro urbano*, drive through the middle of town, and park in front of the TI and cathedral (to park in a blue-painted spot, prepay at the meter and put the ticket on your dashboard).

Sights: The striking **Bishop's Palace** (Palacio Episcopal), rated ▲, is a fanciful Gothic-style castle. It's one of the few buildings that Catalan architect Antonio Gaudí built outside his native land. Inside you'll see Gaudí's genius in the bishop's fine rooms,

decorated with frescoed tapestries. The palace hosts a museum that describes the Camino and the history of Astorga, and provides a safe place for some of the region's fine medieval church art. You'll see a 17th-century statue of Pilgrim James, a few historical Camino documents, ecclesiastical gear, and a gallery of contemporary Spanish art from the

CAMINO DE SANTIAGO

surrounding region. Not as good as it should be, with little posted information (and none in English), the museum is worthwhile mostly for a chance to see a very medieval Gaudí interior (€2.50, €4 combo-ticket with cathedral museum—see below; late-March–late-Sept Tue-Sat 10:00-14:00 & 16:00-20:00, Sun 10:00-14:00, closed Mon; off-season Tue-Sat 11:00-14:00 & 16:00-18:00, Sun 11:00-14:00, closed Mon; tel. 987-616-882).

Next to (and upstaged by) the palace is Astorga's light-filled Gothic **cathedral,** with a marvelously carved choir. It's free to enter in the morning (9:00-11:00), but after 11:00 you can get in only by paying for the attached museum, which shows off a treasury collection of paintings, altarpieces, and vestments (€2.50, €4 combo-ticket with Bishop's Palace, daily April-Sept 10:00-14:00 & 16:00-20:00, Oct-March 11:00-14:00 & 16:00-18:00). Rounding out Astorga's attractions are a chocolate museum and a Roman museum.

Sleeping in Astorga: If you prefer to sleep in a small town, Astorga is a good alternative to the big city of León (though values here are no better than in the city).

$$ Hotel Gaudí has 35 woody rooms over a restaurant across from the cathedral; some have views of the Bishop's Palace (Sb-€52-55, Db-€72-78, breakfast-€9, air-con in most rooms, elevator, free Wi-Fi, Plaza Eduardo de Castro 6, tel. 987-615-654, fax 987-615-040, www.gaudihotel.es, reservas@gaudihotel.es).

$$ Astur Hotel Plaza, which feels more business-class, has 37 rooms right on the main square. Choose between a room overlooking the square—with a clock tower that clangs every 15 minutes—or a quieter back room (Sb-€50-63, Db-€69-105, breakfast-€8, air-con, Wi-Fi, Plaza de España 2-3, tel. 987-618-900, fax 987-618-949, www.asturplaza.com, asturplaza@asturplaza.com).

Eating in Astorga: Restaurante Las Termas, a couple of blocks from the cathedral right along the Camino, is well-regarded for its food—especially the traditional stew, *cocido maragato* (€10-16 main dishes, open for lunch only—13:00-16:00, closed Mon, Calle Santiago 1, tel. 987-602-212). **Hotel Gaudí,** listed earlier, has an atmospheric bar with tapas and *raciones*, and a restaurant with €13-16 fixed-price meals and €10-20 main dishes (open daily).

Connections: Astorga is well-connected by bus to **León** (hourly, 50 minutes), **Ponferrada** (hourly, 1 hour), **Villafranca del Bierzo** (4/day, 2 hours), and **Lugo** (5/day, 3 hours).

• *After Astorga you can either zip up to Galicia on the A-6 expressway (toward Ponferrada), or stick with the Camino a bit farther south on much slower regional roads (LE-142). These two routes converge again at the small city of Ponferrada. Soon after, A-6 climbs up into the hills and to the town of Villafranca del Bierzo (described later).*

If you're sticking with the Camino, you'll be near the...

Iron Cross (Cruz de Ferro)

Near the top of Mount Irago is an iron cross atop a tall wooden pole, set in a huge pile of stones built up over the years by pilgrims unloading their "sins" brought from home (or picked up en route). It's a major landmark for Camino pilgrims, but difficult to reach for drivers (figure an hour's hike off the main road). From the cross it's a 30-minute walk to the nearly ruined stone village of Foncebadón.

Villafranca del Bierzo

Villafranca is the capital of the westernmost part of León, El Bierzo, which is trying to build a good reputation for its wine

and culinary specialties. Dubbed "Little Compostela" for its array of historical buildings, this town is set in an attractive hilly terrain strewn with grapevines, cherry trees, and vegetable patches. Though hardly thrilling, Villafranca del Bierzo is worth a quick stop for its pilgrim ambience (TI open daily 10:00 14:00 & 16:00-20:00, tel. 987-540-028, www.villafrancadelbierzo.org).

Church of St. James' Gate of Forgiveness—To play pilgrim, hike from the main square up to the town's stout 14th-century castle (not open to the public). Then follow signs to the Romanesque 12th-century Church of St. James (Santiago). The church has a "gate of forgiveness" (*puerta de pardon*, on the side facing the town). Thanks to a 16th-century papal ruling, if a pilgrim had come this far, fell ill, and couldn't continue over the rugged terrain to Santiago, he or she was pardoned anyway. (Handy loophole.)

Villafranca *Albergue*—Next to the church is a funky pilgrims' dorm with oodles of pilgrims bonding. It was built on the site of a medieval clinic that cared for those who needed to take advantage of the *puerta de pardon* (at the time, the clinic here was the only source of medical aid for 300 miles). Today this 80-bed volunteer-run *albergue* provides €5 bunks to 10,000 pilgrims a year. If you'd like to learn about the system (or buy a scallop shell), stop in. They welcome curious non-pilgrims, albeit with the motto "The tourist demands, the pilgrim thanks."

Sleeping and Eating: $ Hotel La Puerta del Perdón is just the place for fancy pilgrims or anyone needing a comfortable and economical place to sleep and eat in Villafranca. It's got seven rooms and is warmly run by Herminio. Their fine little restaurant is open to the public for lunch, but only to hotel guests for dinner (Db-€55-70, includes breakfast, facing the castle on the uphill side a block below the Church of St. James at Plaza de Prim 4,

tel. 987-540-614, www.lapuertadelperdon.com, info@lapuertadel perdon.com).
• *Just after Villafranca del Bierzo on the A-6 expressway, you cross into the final region on the Camino: Galicia.*

Galicia

In its final stretch, the Camino leaves the broad expanse of the Meseta Central and climbs steeply into Galicia (gah-LEE-thee-ah). Green and hilly, Galicia shatters visitors' preconceptions about Spain. There's something vaguely Irish about Galicia—and it's not just the mossy stonework and green, rolling hills. The region actually shares a strain of Celtic heritage with its cousins across the Cantabrian Sea. People here are friendly, and if you listen hard enough, you might just hear the sound of bagpipes.
• *Shortly after entering Galicia, take the freeway exit for Pedrafita do Cebreiro. From Pedrafita, a well-maintained mountain road (LU-633) twists its way up to the classic Galician pilgrim village of O Cebreiro.*

O Cebreiro

An impossibly quaint hobbit hamlet perched on a ridge high above nothing, O Cebreiro (oh theh-BRAY-roh) whispers, "Welcome to Galicia." This rustic village evokes an uncomplicated, almost prehistoric past, when people lived very close to nature, in stone igloos with thatched roofs. With sweeping views across the verdant but harsh Galician landscape, O Cebreiro is constantly pummeled by some of the fiercest weather in  Spain. And it's all within a five-minute drive of the freeway.

Wander around. Enjoy the remoteness. O Cebreiro smells like wood fires, manure, and pilgrim B.O. Get a snack or drink at a bar, or browse through a gift shop. A few townspeople (who jabber at each other in Galego—see page 291—and cock their heads quizzically when asked about newfangled inventions like email) share the town with weary pilgrims on an adrenaline high after finally reaching Galicia. The local dogs, who've known each other their whole lives, still bark at each other territorially from across the street, completely ignoring the backpackers who regularly trudge through town.

Sights in O Cebreiro

▲**Pallozas**—From Celtic times 1,500 years ago, right up until the 1960s, the villagers of O Cebreiro lived in humble round stone

huts with peaked thatched roofs, called *pallozas*. One of the nine surviving *pallozas* has been turned into a loosely run museum, where an attendant is paid by the government to welcome visitors and answer questions (free, Wed-Sun 11:00-14:00 & 15:00-18:00, closed Mon-Tue; if a door of a round hut is open, poke inside). Here visitors can learn about the lifestyle of the people who lived in *pallozas* until not so long ago. Entering a *palloza* you'll find the only "private" room in the house, belonging to the parents. Beyond that is a living area around a humble fire. (Notice there's no chimney—smoke lets itself out through the thatch.) Ponder the ancient furniture. Surrounding the fire are clever benches (which were also used, by the kids, as very hard beds) with pull-down counters so they could double as a table at mealtime. The big beam with the chain could be swung over the fire for cooking. Looking up, you'll see the remains of a wooden ceiling that prevented sparks from igniting the thatch. The giant black-metal spirals suspended from the ceiling were used to smoke chorizo (sausage)—very efficient. Attached to this living area is a miniature "barn." Animals lived on the lower level, while people slept on the upper level (which has been removed, but you can still see on the wall where the floor was once supported)—kept warm by all that livestock body heat. About a dozen people (and their animals) lived in one small hut. But thanks to the ideal insulation provided by the thatch, and the warmth from the fire and animals, it was toasty even through the difficult winter.

▲**Royal St. Mary's Church (Santa María la Real)**—All roads lead to the village church. Founded in the year 836—not long after the remains of St. James were found in Santiago—this

pre-Romanesque building is supposedly the oldest church on the entire French Road of the Camino. The interior is surprisingly spacious, but very simple (free, daily 9:00-21:00). Notice the sunken floor: The building is actually embedded

CAMINO DE SANTIAGO

into the ground for added protection against winter storms. The desk inside stamps pilgrims' credentials and sells votive candles. (I don't think there's anything wrong with giving your guidebook an O Cebreiro stamp—I did.) The baptistery, in a tiny side room near the entrance, is separate from the main part of the church, as dictated by ancient tradition. It has a giant and very rough font used for immersion baptisms. In the chapel to the right of the main altar is a much-revered 12th-century golden chalice and reliquary, which holds items relating to a popular local miracle: A peasant from a nearby village braved a fierce winter snowstorm to come to this church for the Eucharist. The priest scoffed at his devotion, only to find that the host and wine had physically turned into the body and blood of Christ, staining the linens beneath them, which are now in the silver box.

Sleeping and Eating in O Cebreiro

(€1 = about $1.40, country code: 34)
The only businesses in town are a half-dozen very humble pub-restaurants, which feed pilgrims and other visitors hearty Galician cuisine in a smoky atmosphere. You'll see signs offering a stick-to-your-ribs €9 "pilgrim menu." Many of these places also rent a few rooms upstairs. Be warned that these rooms are very rustic, English can be tricky, and reservations are only by phone. Try **$$ Hospedería San Giraldo de Aurillac** (Db-€60, 17 rooms in 3 buildings, tel. 982-367-182); **$ Casa Carolo** (D-€35, Db-€48, tel. 982-367-168); or **$ Mesón Antón** (D/Db-€45, tel. 982-151-336). The *albergue,* which is open only to pilgrims, is perched on a hill at the edge of town and charges €3 per bed.

O Cebreiro Connections

By Car
From O Cebreiro you've got another route decision to make.

To stick with the Camino, you'll continue on LU-633, along twisty roads, toward Santiago. Along the way you'll pass through some interesting larger towns: **Sarria,** which is just over 100 kilometers (62 miles) from Santiago, is a popular place to begin a truncated pilgrimage (since you need to walk at least that far to earn your *compostela* certificate). **Portomarín** is a relatively new town, built only after the River Miño was flooded to create a reservoir in the 1950s. The stout and blocky late-Romanesque Church of San Juan was moved to a new site, stone by stone—and if you look closely enough you can see how the stones were numbered to keep track of where they fit.

I prefer the faster expressway route (backtrack to A-6, which you'll take north, following signs for A Coruña), which offers the opportunity to dip into the appealing walled city of Lugo.

Lugo

While not technically on the French Road of the Camino de Santiago, the midsized city of Lugo (pop. 90,000) warrants a detour  for car travelers. Boasting what are arguably the best-preserved Roman walls in Spain—a mile and a third long, completely encircling the town, draped with moss, and receding into the misty horizon—Lugo offers an ideal place for an evocative stroll. Lugo feels like a poor man's Santiago, with a patina of poverty and atmospherically crumbling buildings. Evocative chimneys thrust up through rickety old slate roofs. And yet there's something proud and welcoming about the town. Aside from the walls, Lugo has a cathedral and gregarious Galician charm, making it a fine place to spend some time.

Orientation to Lugo

Tourist Information
The TI is a few steps up a pedestrian street off the main square, Plaza Maior—look for the yellow signs (July-Aug daily 10:00-14:00 & 16:00-20:00, Sept-June until 19:00 and closed Sun, Rua Miño 10-12, tel. 982-231-361).

Arrival in Lugo
The **bus** station is just outside the town walls; once inside the Old Town, the main square and TI are a block away. The **train** station is two blocks east of the town walls. **Drivers** follow signs to *centro ciudad* and *centro urbano*. Once you enter the town walls, parking garages are signed.

Sights in Lugo

The town's **Roman walls** *(murallas Romanas)* are free and always open, providing a kind of circular park where locals and visitors can stroll at rooftop level. You can access the walls at various points around town (you'll find stairs near most of the gates where traffic enters the Old Town), and it takes about 45 minutes to walk the entire way around. With less time the most interesting stretch is along the west side of town: Walk up the ramp behind the cathedral and turn right, watching behind you for tingly views of the walls and cathedral spires.

Lugo's **cathedral** is vast, dark, and dusty, with a glittering silver altarpiece (free, daily 8:00-20:30, €2 to enter cloister). While it's a lovely cathedral, it pales in comparison to Santiago's.

Lugo also has a provincial museum and a Roman museum.

Sleeping in Lugo

(€1 = about $1.40, country code: 34)

Sleeping in Lugo is worth considering to break the long journey to Santiago from Cantabria or León. Budget *hostales* cluster just southeast of the town walls (near the bus station). The following two hotels are the only ones inside the Old Town. They may be willing to deal—ask for their best price.

$$$ Pazo Orban e Sangro is the town splurge, renting 12 rooms with hardwood floors, flat-screen TVs, and luxurious furnishings. It's just inside the town walls near the cathedral (Db-€80-120, includes breakfast, air-con, elevator, Wi-Fi, Travesía do Miño, tel. 982-240-217, fax 982-245-645, www.pazodeorban.es, info@pazodeorban.es).

$$ Hotel Méndez Núñez, right in the heart of the Old Town, has a classy old lobby, a medieval-feeling lounge, and 70 rooms with worn furniture but new bathrooms (Sb-€50-60, Db-€60-100, breakfast-€6, air-con, elevator, free Internet access and Wi-Fi, Calle Reina 1, tel. 982-230-711, fax 982-229-738, www.hotelmendez nunez.com, hotel@hotelmendeznunez.com).

Lugo Connections

Lugo is connected by bus to **Santiago de Compostela** (7/day, 2 hours, run by Empresa Freire), **Astorga** (5/day, 3 hours, run by Alsa), and **León** (2/day, 4 hours, run by Alsa).

• *After Lugo, the end is in sight. You have one final route decision to make: The fastest way (about 1.5 hours to Santiago) is to stick with the A-6 expressway north to A Coruña, then pay €5 to take the AP-9 toll-way back south to Santiago. But if you'd like to rejoin the Camino for the last stretch—following in the footsteps (or tire treads) of a millennium of pilgrims—follow signs from Lugo toward Ourense (on N-540/N-640, about 20-30 minutes longer than expressway option). In Guntín, split off on N-547 and head for Santiago de Compostela.*

However you arrive, see the next chapter and enjoy one of Europe's great pilgrim cities.

Buen Camino!

SANTIAGO DE COMPOSTELA

The best destination in the northwestern province of Galicia, Santiago de Compostela might well be the most magical city in Spain. This place has long had a powerful and mysterious draw on travelers—as more than a thousand years' worth of pilgrims have trod the desolate trail across the north of Spain just to peer up at the facade of its glorious cathedral.

But there's more to this city than pilgrims and the remains of St. James. Contrary to what you've heard, the rain in Spain does *not* fall mainly on the plain—it falls in Galicia. This "Atlantic Northwest" of Spain is like the Pacific Northwest of the United States, with hilly, lush terrain that enjoys far more precipitation than the interior, plus dramatic coastal scenery, delicious seafood, fine local wines, and an easygoing ambience. The Spanish interior might be arid, but the northwest requires rain gear. Even the tourists here have a grungy vibe: Packs of happy hippie pilgrims seek to find themselves while hiking the ancient Camino de Santiago from France (described in the previous chapter).

You'll see few signs of the country's financial problems in Santiago—many locals hold stable jobs in the public sector while others work to serve the constant flow of tourists. As a pilgrim mecca, the city's accommodations, eateries, and sights are geared toward low-budget travelers. Santiago's top sight—the cathedral—is free to enter, along with many of its other attractions.

Santiago has a generally festive atmosphere, as travelers from every corner of the globe celebrate the end of a long journey. It's a sturdy city that, in its day, was one of Europe's most important religious centers, built of granite and later turned mossy green by the notorious weather.

Planning Your Time

Santiago's biggest downside is its location: Except by air, it's a very long trip from any other notable stop in Spain. But if you decide to visit, you—like a millennium's worth of pilgrims before you—will find it's worth the trek. You can get a good feel for Santiago in a day, but a second day relaxing on the squares makes the long trip here more worthwhile.

The city has one real sight: the cathedral, with its fine museum and the surrounding squares. The rest of your visit is for munching seafood, pilgrim-watching, and browsing the stony streets. The highlight of a visit just may be hanging out on the cathedral square at about 10:00 to welcome pilgrims completing their long journey.

Orientation to Santiago

Santiago is built on hilly terrain, with lots of ups and downs. The tourist's Santiago is small: You can walk across the historic center, or Zona Monumental, in about 15 minutes. There you'll find the city's centerpiece—the awe-inspiring cathedral—as well as several other churches, a maze of pretty squares, a smattering of small museums, a bustling restaurant scene, and all of my recommended hotels.

The historic center is circled by a busy street that marks the former location of the town wall (easy to see on a map). Outside of that is the commercial city center, which is a modern, urban district called Céntrico. A 10-minute walk through Céntrico takes you to the train station.

Tourist Information

On Rúa do Vilar in the town center there are two separate information offices: one for the region and pilgrims, and the other for visitors to the city.

The city TI is at Rúa do Vilar 63 (daily June-Sept 9:00-21:00, Oct-May 9:00-14:00 & 16:00-19:00, tel. 981-555-129, www.santiagoturismo.com). It runs walking tours and rents MP3-player audioguides (see "Tours in Santiago," later). Ask the TI what's going on when you're in town, and grab a free copy of the monthly *Culturall*.

The office for the region of Galicia and for pilgrims shares a location at Rúa do Vilar 30 (Mon-Fri 10:00-20:00, Sat 11:00-14:00 & 17:00-19:00, Sun 11:00-14:00, tel. 981-584-081, www.turgalicia.es).

Arrival in Santiago de Compostela

Note that there's luggage storage at the bus station, but not at the train station.

The Galego Language

Like Catalunya and the Basque Country, Galicia has its own distinctive language. Galego (called *gallego* in Spanish, and sometimes called "Galician" in English) is a cross between Spanish and Portuguese. Historically, Galego was closer to Portuguese. But Queen Isabel imported the Spanish language to the region in the 15th century, and ever since, the language has gradually come to sound more and more like Spanish. In an attempt at national unity, dictator Francisco Franco banned Galego in the mid-20th century (along with Catalan and the Basque language, Euskara). During these trying times, Galicians spoke Spanish in public—and Galego at home. Since the end of the Franco era, Galego is a proud part of this region's cultural heritage. Street signs and sight names are posted in Galego, and I've followed suit in this chapter.

If you don't speak Spanish, you'll hardly notice a difference. Most apparent is the change in articles: *el* and *la* become o and a—so the big Galician city La Coruña is known as "A Coruña" around here. You'll also see a lot more *x*'s, which are pronounced "sh" (such as "Xacobeo," shah-koh-BAY-oh, the local word for St. James' pilgrimage route). The Spanish greeting *buenos días* becomes *bos días* in Galego. The familiar *plaza* becomes *praza*. And if you want to impress a local, say *graciñas* (grah-THEEN-yahs)—a super-polite thank you.

By Train: Santiago's train station is on the southern edge of the modern Céntrico district. You'll find ATMs, a cafeteria, car-rental offices, and a helpful train information office. To reach the center of town, leave the station and walk up the grand granite staircase, jog right, cross the busy Avenida de Lugo, and walk uphill for 10 minutes on Rúa do Hórreo to Praza de Galicia, a few steps from the historical center. A taxi from the station to your hotel will cost you about €5.

By Bus: From the bus station, northeast of the cathedral, it's about a 15-minute, mostly uphill walk to the center. Exit the station straight ahead (on Rúa de Ánxel Casal) and go to the roundabout called Praza da Paz. Turn left here onto Rúa da Pastoriza, which will bring you into town. To avoid the uphill hike, I'd rather hop on local bus #5 (€1) and take it to the Praza de Galicia.

By Plane: Santiago's small airport (airport code: SCQ) is about six miles from the city center. A bus connects the airport to the bus station, then to Rúa do Doutor Teixeiro (stop is at #24), a long block beyond Praza de Galicia at the south end of the historical center (€3, catch bus at exit by car rentals, runs at least hourly between 7:00 and 21:30, 35 minutes, may have to place big bags underneath the bus, www.empresafreire.com). A taxi into town costs €20.

By Car: There are only two freeway off-ramps to the city. The north exit #67 is best for the airport and the old center.

Helpful Hints

Closed Days: Many museums (except church-related ones) are closed on Monday. The colorful produce market is closed on Sunday, slow on Monday, and busiest on Thursday and Saturday mornings.

Church Hours: The cathedral and other major churches in Santiago are open 9:00-21:00 without a siesta, while minor ones have limited visiting hours. Special Masses for pilgrims are held daily at noon in the cathedral. The big Masses on Sunday are at 10:00 and noon.

Festivals: Late July is the main party time in Santiago, when the city hosts a world music festival and impromptu concerts all over town, along with fireworks on July 24 and 31. During this time, the royal family (or their representative) attends Mass in Santiago, staying at the parador in a suite overlooking the square (see listing on page 310). Crowds and prices increase in Holy Years (when the Feast of St. James—July 25—falls on a Sunday, next in 2021). The second-most important musical event in town—with several days of free concerts—occurs around Ascension (May 17 in 2012). In late May, an international film festival called *Curtocircuito* offers showings at various venues throughout the city (tel. 948-542-303, www.curtocircuito.org).

Internet Access: You'll see signs for places around the historic center. The handiest and best-equipped is **Cyber Nova 50** (Mon-Fri 9:00-24:00, Sat-Sun 10:00-24:00; faxing, phones, printing, and other services; Rúa Nova 50, tel. 981-564-133). Many cafés in town offer free Wi-Fi to customers with wireless devices (look for window signs).

Laundry: You'll find a self-service *lavandería* called **Axiña** a 15-minute walk from the historic center (€6/load self-service, €7 for full service, Mon-Fri 8:30-13:00 & 16:00-20:30, Sat 8:30-13:30, closed Sun, Rúa de Ramón Cabanillas 1, tel. 981-591-323).

Shopping: Jet, the black gemstone (called *azabache* in Spanish) similar to onyx, is believed to keep away evil spirits—and to bring in tourist euros. Along with jet, the silver trade has long been important in Santiago...and continues to be a popular item for tourists. Although the Galicians are a superstitious people and have beliefs about good and bad witches, the made-in-Taiwan witches you see in souvenir shops around the city are a recent innovation. Maybe the best souvenir is a simple seashell, like the ones pilgrims carry with them along the Camino.

Best Views: There are beautiful views back toward the cathedral from the Alameda park. From the cathedral, follow Rúa do Franco to the end. Swing right into the park and continue up Paseo de Santa Susana to the viewpoint *(mirador)* along Paseo da Ferradura. There is another excellent view from the very top of the park (clearly marked on TI maps).

Tours in Santiago

The TI offers a two-hour English-language **walking tour** that covers the cathedral and the surrounding plazas (€10, April-Oct Tue and Sun at 13:00, get details at the city TI). Ask about the TI's other tours, including gastronomy tours, nighttime tours, and more. Or you can rent an **MP3-player audioguide** at the city TI, and follow the suggested three-hour route (€12/24-hour rental). Either tour is better than taking the silly **tourist train,** which only does a circuit around the outskirts of the old city (€5, 45 minutes, meet in front of the cathedral in Praza do Obradoiro).

It's easy to visit the cathedral and nearby sights on your own with the information in this book, but if you have the extra cash, you could hire a **local guide** (for 3.5 hours: €90 Mon-Fri, €100 Sat-Sun). Patricia Furelos (mobile 630 781 795, patriciaguia@latin mail.com) and Manuel Ruzo (mobile 639-888-064, manuel@art naturagalicia.com) are equally good, or contact the Association of Professional Guides of Galicia (tel. 981-569-890, fax 981-553-329, guiasgalicia@ctv.es).

Sights in Santiago

▲▲The Cathedral

Santiago's cathedral isn't the biggest in Spain, nor is it the most impressive. Yet it's certainly the most mystical, exerting a spiritual magnetism that attracts people from all walks of life and from all corners of the globe. (To more fully appreciate the pilgrim experience, read the first part of the previous Camino de Santiago chapter before visiting the cathedral.)

Exploring one of the most important churches in Christendom, you'll do some time travel, putting yourself in the well-worn shoes of the millions of pilgrims who have trekked many miles to this

Santiago de Compostela

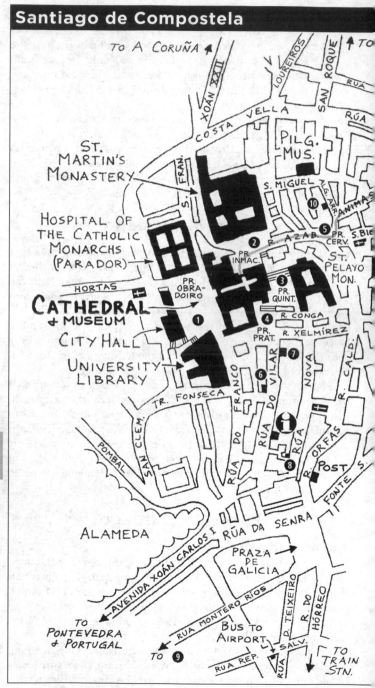

TO A CORUÑA

XOÁN XXII

LOUREIROS

SAN ROQUE

RÚA

RÚA

COSTA VELLA

S. FRAN.

PILG. MUS.

ST. MARTIN'S MONASTERY

S. MIGUEL

ALG. ARR.

ANIMAS

10

HOSPITAL OF THE CATHOLIC MONARCHS (PARADOR)

2

R. AZAB.

5

PR. CERV.

S. BIE

PR. INMAC.

ST. PELAYO MON.

HORTAS

PR. OBRA- DOIRO

3

PR. QUINT.

CATHEDRAL + MUSEUM

1

4

R. CONGA

CITY HALL

PR. PRAT.

R. XELMÍREZ

7

R. CALD.

UNIVERSITY LIBRARY

6

RÚA DO VILAR

NOVA

TR. FONSECA

RÚA DO FRANCO

i

RÚA

R. ORFAS

POMBAL

SAN CLEM.

8

Post

FONTE S.

RÚA

ALAMEDA

RÚA DA SENRA

PRAZA DE GALICIA

AVENIDA XOÁN CARLOS I

RÚA MONTERO RIOS

BUS TO AIRPORT

RÚA P. TEIXEIRO

R. DO HÓRREO

RÚA SALV.

TO PONTEVEDRA + PORTUGAL

TO 9

RÚA REP.

TO TRAIN STN.

SANTIAGO DE COMPOSTELA

BUS STATION

GALICIAN CONTEMPORARY
ART MUSEUM

MUSEUM OF THE
GALICIAN
PEOPLE

RAMÓN

DAS RODAS

CASAS

SAN PEDROA

→ TO
AIRPORT,
CITY OF CULTURE OF GALICIA (2013),
ARZUA, LEÓN & PARIS

PORTA DO
CAMIÑO

DA CERCA

TO

PR. ABASTOS

MARKET

VIRXE

RÚA DA

UNIV.

TROMPAS

PONT.

1 Praza do Obradoiro
2 Praza da Inmaculada
3 Praza Quintana
4 Praza das Praterías
5 Praza de Cervantes
6 Regional & Pilgrim Info Center
7 Office for Pilgrims
8 Internet Café
9 To Launderette
10 Folk Music Clubhouse

SANTIAGO DE COMPOSTELA

——— CAMINO DE SANTIAGO

100 YARDS
100 METERS

DCH

powerful place.

Cost and Hours: Free, daily 9:00-21:00; if a service is going on, the front entrance is usually closed—enter around either side about a hundred yards to the left or the right; www.catedralde santiago.es.

Backpacks: If you're not allowed to bring backpacks into the church, you'll find free baggage storage next to the Office for Pilgrims on Rúa do Vilar (see map).

❷ **Self-Guided Tour:** Begin facing the cathedral's main facade, in the big square called...

Praza do Obradoiro

Find the pavement stone with the scallop shell right in the middle of this square. For more than a thousand years this spot has

been where millions of tired pilgrims have taken a deep breath and thought to themselves: "I made it!" To maximize your chance of seeing pilgrims, be here at about 10:00—the last stop on the Camino de Santiago is two miles away, and pilgrims try to get to the cathedral in time for the 12:00 Mass. It's great fun to chat with pilgrims who've just completed their journey. They seem to be very centered and content with the experience, and tuned in to the important things in life...like taking time to talk with others. You'll likely see pilgrims who met along the way, arrive separately and then leave together, having reunited at the grand finale. Every time I visit, I find myself taking photos for people and agreeing to email copies to them. Even if you're shy, it's a fun and easy way to meet pilgrims by offering to capture their personal triumphs.

• *Before heading into the cathedral, take a spin around the square (start facing the cathedral).*

To your left is the **Hospital of the Catholic Monarchs** (Hostal dos Reis Católicos). Isabel and Ferdinand came to Santiago in 1501 to give thanks for successfully forcing the Moors out of Granada. When they arrived they found many sick pilgrims at the square. (Numerous pilgrims came to Santiago to ask for help in overcoming an illness, and the long walk here often only made their condition worse.) Isabel and Ferdinand decided to build this hospital

SANTIAGO DE COMPOSTELA

to give pilgrims a place to recover on arrival (you'll see their coats of arms flanking the intricately carved entryway). It was free and remained a working hospital until 1952—many locals were born there—when it was converted into a fancy parador and restaurant (see "Sleeping in Santiago" and "Eating in Santiago," later). The modern white windows set against the old granite facade might seem jarring—but this contrast is very common in Galicia, maximizing the

brightness that accompanies any sunny spells in this notoriously rainy region.

Another 90 degrees to the left is the Neoclassical **City Hall** (Concello). Notice the equestrian statue up top. That's St. James, riding in from heaven to help the Spaniards defeat the Moors. All over town, Santiago's namesake and symbol—a Christian evangelist on a horse, killing Muslims with his sword—is out doing his bloody thing. See any police on the square? There's a reason for their presence. In its medieval day, Santiago's cathedral was one of the top three pilgrimage sites in the Christian world (after Jerusalem and Rome). It remains important today, and with St. James taking such joy in butchering Muslims, it is considered a high-profile target for Islamic fundamentalists.

Completing the square (90 more degrees to the left) is the original **University** building (its rectory faces the square, the tower behind with the flags marks the original building, which is now the library). Santiago has Spain's third-oldest university, with more than 30,000 students (medicine and law are especially popular).

You'll likely see Spanish school groups on the square, fieldtripping from all over the country. Teachers love to use this spot for an architecture lesson, since it features four different architectural styles (starting with the cathedral and spinning left): 18th-century Baroque; 16th-century Plateresque; 18th-century Neoclassical; and medieval Romanesque (the door of the rectory).

• Now take a look at the...

Cathedral Facade

Twelve hundred years ago a monk followed a field of stars (probably the Milky Way) to the little Galician village of San Fiz de Solovio and discovered what appeared to be the long-lost tomb of St. James. On July 25, 813, the local bishop declared that St. James' remains had been found. They set to building a church here and named the place Santiago (St. James) de Compostela (*campo de estrellas,* or "field of stars," for the celestial bodies that guided the monk).

Originally a simple chapel, the cathedral you see today has gradually been added on to over the last 12 centuries. By the 11th century, the church was overwhelmed by the crowds. Construction of a larger cathedral began in 1075, and the work took 150 years. (The granite workers who built it set up shop on this very square— still called Praza do Obradoiro, literally, "Workers' Square.") Much of the design is attributed to a palace artist named Maestro Mateo, whom you'll meet a little later.

The exterior of the cathedral you see today is *not* the one that medieval pilgrims saw (though the interior is much the same). In the mid-18th century, Santiago's bishop—all fired up from a trip to Baroque-slathered Rome and wanting to improve the original, now-deteriorating facade—decided to spruce up the building with a new Baroque exterior. He also replaced the simple stonework in the interior with gaudy gold.

Study the facade. Atop the middle steeple is St. James (dressed like the pilgrim he was). Beneath him is his tomb, marked

by a star—one of the many symbols you'll see all over the place (to decipher the symbols, see sidebar on page 242). On either side of the tomb are Theodorus and Athanasius, James' disciples who brought his body to Santiago. On the side pillars are, to the left, James' father, Zebedee; and to the right, his mother, Salomé.

Don't you wish you had a miniature replica of this beautiful facade to carry around with you? Actually, you probably do. Check your pocket for a copper-colored euro coin worth €0.01, €0.02, or €0.05. There it is! Of all the churches in Spain, they chose this one as their representative in euro-land. It's even more important when you consider the significance of the images depicted on Spain's other euro coinage: a portrait of the author of *Don Quixote,* Miguel de Cervantes, Spain's greatest contributor to world literature; and the current king, Juan Carlos I. Sevilla and Toledo may have bigger cathedrals, but Santiago has the symbolism to propel its church into this powerful triumvirate.

The cathedral also houses a museum with three parts; as you face this facade, the door to the main museum is to the right, the entry to the crypt is dead ahead (under the staircase), and the door on the left leads to an empty palace and the cathedral rooftop (see Gelmírez Palace listing, later).

• *Now, head up the stairs and enter the cathedral. Once inside go to the rear of the nave and look up at the...*

Portico of Glory

The portico is currently being restored in stages (until 2013). If everything is covered with scaffolding when you visit, be sure to watch the free video that shows the portico in all its glory. The video runs in the crypt (go outside and downstairs to crypt, then make free reservation for viewing time); after a live intro, usually in Spanish, the video is presented in several languages.

Whether you view the portico in its place or in the video, imagine taking a step back in time. Remember, it used to be the main facade of the cathedral, sculpted in about 1180 by Maestro Mateo. Pretend you're a medieval pilgrim, and you've just walked 500 miles from the Frankish lands to reach this cathedral. You're here to request the help of St. James in recovering from an illness or to give thanks for a success. Maybe you've come to honor the wish of a dying relative or to be forgiven for your sins. Whatever the reason, you came here on foot.

You can't read, but you can tell from the carved images that this magnificent door represents the Glory of God. Old Testament prophets on the left announce Christ's coming. New Testament apostles on the right spread his message. Jesus reigns directly above, approachable to the humble Christian pilgrim via St. James with his staff.

Theologically, pilgrims are coming not for St. James, but to get to Christ via St. James. Look for Jesus, front and center, surrounded by Matthew, Mark, Luke, and John. Beside them are angels carrying tools for the Crucifixion—the cross, the crown of thorns, the spear, and a jug of vinegar. Arching above them are 24 musicians playing celestial music—each one with a different medieval instrument. Below St. James is a column with the Tree of Jesse—showing the genealogy of Jesus with Mary near the top and, above her, the Holy Trinity: Father, Son, and a dove representing the Holy Spirit.

As a pilgrim, you would walk to the column in the middle of the entryway (now ringed by a railing to keep crowds from gathering here). Squint down the nave to the end, and you'll see the stone statue of St. James that marks his tomb. Trembling with excitement at the culmination of your long journey, you'd place your hand into the well-worn finger holes on the column (see five grooves at about chest level) and bow your head, giving thanks to St. James for having granted you safe passage. Then you'd go around to the other side of the post and, at knee level, see Maestro Mateo, who carved this fine facade. What a smart guy! People used to kneel and tap their heads against his three times to help improve their intelligence (a ritual among university scholars here)—until a metal barrier was erected. (Student grades have dropped recently.) Such a high-profile self-portrait of an artist in the 12th century was unprecedented. In Santiago he was something like the Leonardo of his day.

• *Now wander down the...*

Nave

Look up, noticing the barrel vault and the heavy, dark Romanesque design of the church. (The original freestanding church had about 80 glorious alabaster windows. They are now mostly bricked up due to a complex of buildings built around the church.) Up near the top, notice the gallery. This is where sweaty, smelly pilgrims slept.

• *Continue up the nave until you reach the high altar, where you'll see a thick rope hanging from a pulley system high in the dome, which is sometimes attached to the...*

Botafumeiro

This huge silver-plated incense burner (120 pounds and about the size of a small child) is suspended from the ceiling during spe-

cial Masses, occurring about 13 times a year (ask at TI if one is scheduled during your visit, or check www.catedraldesantiago.es), or when a pilgrim pays about €300 to see it in action. During Holy Years, it swings nearly daily at the end of each pilgrims' Mass at 12:00. Supposedly the custom of swinging this giant incense dispenser began in order to counteract the stench of the pilgrims. After communion, eight men (called *tiraboleiros*) pull on the rope, and this huge contraption swings in a wide arc up and down the transept, spewing sweet-smelling smoke. If you're here to see it, the most impressive view is sitting or standing on either side of the main altar. From this position, the *botafumeiro* seems to whiz directly over your head. When not in use, the *botafumeiro* and a replica are kept on display in the cathedral library (see "Cathedral Museum," later).

• *Stand in the center of the nave, in front of the...*

Altar

The big gold altar has all three representations of St. James in one place (see sidebar on page 304): Up top, on a white horse, is James

SANTIAGO DE COMPOSTELA

St. James

Santiago is Spanish for "St. James." James and his brother John, sons of Zebedee and Salomé, were well-off fishermen on the Sea of Galilee. One fateful day, a charismatic visionary came and said to them, "Come with me, and I will make you fishers of men." They threw down their nets and became apostles.

Along with Peter, James and John were supposedly Jesus' favorites—he called them the "sons of thunder." After Jesus' death, the apostles spread out and brought his message to other lands. St. James spent a decade as a missionary bringing Christianity to the farthest reaches of the known world—which, back then, was northwest Spain. The legend goes that as soon as he returned home to the Holy Land, in A.D. 44, James was beheaded by Herod Agrippa. Before his body and head could be thrown to the lions—as was the custom in those days—they were rescued by two of his disciples, Theodorus and Athanasius.

These two brought his body back to Spain in a small boat and entombed it in the hills of Galicia—hiding it carefully so it would not be found by the Roman authorities. There it lay hidden for almost eight centuries. In 813, a monk—supposedly directed by the stars—discovered the tomb, and the local bishop proudly exclaimed that St. James was in Galicia. Santiago de Compostela was born.

But is this the *real* story? Historians figure the "discovery" of the remains of St. James in Spain provided a necessary way to rally Europe against the Moors, who had invaded Spain and were threatening to continue into Europe. The "marketing" of St. James was further bolstered by his miraculous appearance, on horseback and wielding a sword, to fight for the Christian army in the pivotal battle of Clavijo during the Reconquista. With St. James *Matamoros* ("the Moor-Slayer") in Iberia, all of Europe was inspired to rise up and push the Muslims back into Africa...which they finally did in 1492. James eventually became Spain's patron saint, and for centuries Spanish armies rode into battle with the cry, *"Santiago y cierra España!"* ("St. James and strike for Spain!").

Sure, the whole thing was likely a propaganda hoax to get a local populace to support a war. But yesterday's and today's pilgrims may not care whether the body of St. James actually lies in this church. The pilgrimage to Santiago is a spiritual quest powered through the ages by faith.

the *Matamoros*—Moor-Slayer; below that (just under the canopy) is pilgrim James; and below that is the original stone Apostle James by Maestro Mateo—still pointing down to his tomb after all these centuries.

The dome over the altar was added in the 16th century to bring some light into this dark Romanesque church.

On the columns up and down the nave and transept, notice the symbols carved into the granite. These are the markings of the masons who made the columns—to keep track of how many they'd be paid for.

• *Following the pilgrims' route, go down the ambulatory on the left side of the altar—passing where the* botafumeiro *rope is moored to the pillar—and walk down the little stairway (see the green light, on your right) to the level of the earlier, 10th-century church and the...*

Tomb of St. James

There he is, in the little silver chest, marked by a star—Santiago. Pilgrims kneel in front of the tomb and make their request or say their thanks.

• *Continue through the little passage, up the stairs, turn left, and wander around the ambulatory, noticing the various chapels (built by noblemen who wanted to be buried close to St. James). At the very back of the church (behind the altar) is the greenish...*

Holy Door

This special door is open only during Holy Years, when pilgrims use it to access the tomb and statue of the apostle. The current door, sculpted by a local artist for the 2004 Holy Year, shows six scenes from the life of St. James: the conversion moment when Jesus invited those Galilean fishermen to become "fishers of men"; Jesus with the 12 apostles (James is identified by his scallop shell); James doing his "fishing" in Spain; his return to Jerusalem in A.D. 44 to be beheaded; the ship taking his body back to Spain; and the discovery of James' body by a local monk in 813. At the bottom, the little snail is the symbol of the pilgrim...slow and steady, with everything on its back.

Hug St. James

There's one more pilgrim ritual to complete. Find the little door near the exit from the tomb (perhaps with a line of pilgrims—10 yards away, by another green light, closed 13:30-16:00 and after 20:00). Climb the stairs under the huge babies, find Maestro

Mateo's stone statue of St. James—gilded and caked with precious gems. Embrace him from behind and enjoy a saint's-eye view of the cathedral...under the vigilant eye of a cathedral watchman, there to ensure you're not overcome by the unholy temptation to pry loose a jewel.

• *Congratulations, pilgrim! You have completed the Camino de Santiago. Now go in peace.*

Other Sights at the Cathedral

The Cathedral Museum (enter through door on the right, as you face main facade) and crypt (under the main staircase in front) share one ticket; the Gelmírez Palace (door on the left) and roof-top are covered by a separate ticket.

▲▲**Cathedral Museum (Museo da Catedral) and Crypt**— The cathedral's museum shows off some interesting pieces from the fine treasury collection and artifacts from the cathedral's history.

Cost and Hours: €5, or €3 for pilgrims; June-Sept Mon-Sat 10:00-14:00 & 16:00-20:00, Sun 10:00-14:00; Oct-May Mon-Sat 10:00-13:30 & 16:00-18:30, Sun 10:00-13:30; last entry 50 minutes before closing, tel. 981-569-327, www.catedraldesantiago.es.

❍ **Self-Guided Tour:** The museum is laid out chronologically from bottom to top. There's virtually no English inside, so pick up the included English guide booklet as you enter. The museum is being renovated through part of 2012; exhibits may move and some rooms may be closed.

Ground Floor: Here you'll find the remaining pieces of Maestro Mateo's original stone choir (stone seats for priests; these seats filled the center of the nave in the 12th century), pieced together as part of a new replica. Nearby, look for a miniature model of the choir. Notice the expressive faces Mateo carved into the granite. Working in the Romanesque style, he was well ahead of his time artistically. Consider the cultural value of a place in Europe where people from all corners came together, shared, and then dispersed.

In some ways, the concept of Europe as a civilization was being born when Santiago was in its 12th-century heyday. You'll also see fragments of Roman settlements, dating from before the tomb of St. James was discovered here.

First Floor: The two statues of a pregnant Mary illustrate a theme that's unusual in most of Europe, but common in Galicia. The coin collection shows off examples of money that pilgrims brought with them from all over Europe (see the displayed map).

The Three Santiagos

You'll see three different depictions of St. James in the cathedral and throughout the city:

1. Apostle James: James dressed in typical apostle robes, often indiscernible from the other apostles (sometimes with a pilgrim's stick or shell).

2. Pilgrim James: James wearing some or all of the traditional garb of the Camino de Santiago pilgrim: brown cloak, floppy hat, walking stick, shell, gourd, and sandals. Among pilgrims, he's the one carrying a book.

3. Crusader James, the Moor-Slayer: Centuries after his death, the Spaniards called on St. James for aid in various battles against the Moors. According to legend, St. James appeared from the heavens on a white horse and massacred Muslim foes. Locals don't particularly care for this depiction—especially these days, when the rising tide of Islamic fundamentalists could justifiably find it provocative.

The dirham coin in the center case is dated 387; since Muhammad became a prophet in 612, this coin dates from the year 999 on the Christian calendar. The map on the wall illustrates the various pilgrimage routes. The original route was along the coast. Today's route (parallel but farther south) was established after that area was taken from the Muslims to help consolidate Christian control. To answer the common question, "Why the shell?" notice how trails from all across Europe converge, eventually coming together (like the lines on the scallop shell) at Santiago.

Cloister: Enter the cloister on the second floor. The tombs lining its floor hold the remains of priests from the cathedral. In the courtyard you'll see a fountain (which once stood in front of the cathedral and was used by pilgrims to cleanse themselves) and the original church bells (replaced with new models in 1989). As you walk left (clockwise) around the cloister, the second door leads to the Royal Chapel, with a beautiful-smelling cedar altar that houses dozens and dozens of relics. The centerpiece (eye level) holds the remains (likely the skull) of St. James the Lesser (the *other* Apostle James). Look up to find St. James riding heroically out of the woodwork to rally all of Europe to reconquer the Iberian Peninsula. This altarpiece was restored after a fire around 1900.

• Cross the hall to the...

Treasury: Look for the wood altar, carved in England (c. 1420), depicting the tale of St. James—including his beheading, and his body being taken back to Galicia. The fancy solid-gold monstrance is used for carrying the communion host around the cathedral on Corpus Christi (the wafer sits in the little round window in the middle). Pilgrims hugged this jeweled, silver cape of St. James for 300 years until it was finally replaced in 2004 by the one above the altar, which pilgrims hug today.

• *Return to the cloister and back through the door you entered to the...*

Library: This is where they store old books, a funky rack for reading those huge tomes ("turn pages" by spinning the rack), and the *botafumeiro* (gigantic incense burner). There's always a replica here offering a close-up look. The next room shows how tapestries could warm a stone palace. Notice the painted ceilings. To prove that they're carved out of granite, one patch is left unpainted to expose the stone.

• *Pass back through the library and go up one more floor. If the doors are open, enjoy views from a fine balcony overlooking Praza do Obradoiro. You'll then walk through several rooms of restored tapestries.*

Third Floor: The first room is from designs by Rubens. The two middle rooms show idealistic 18th-century peasant life—wives helping their men to be less moronic (but there's still a man peeing in the corner). Don't miss the intimate 18th-century Madonna and Child statue in the glass case. The nursing *Virgen de la Leche* looks out at us as she feeds her son. The last room has a tapestry, based on a design by Goya, with exacting details of life around 1790.

Crypt: After visiting the museum, drop into the crypt (same ticket, under main stairs into cathedral) and see some serious medieval engineering. Since the church was built on a too-small hill, the crypt was made to support the part of the nave that hung over the hillside. The Romanesque vaulting and carved decoration is more Maestro Mateo mastery. Look at the medieval musical instruments—models of the impressively realistic ones featured in Mateo's heavenly Portico of Glory.

Gelmírez Palace (Pazo de Xelmírez)—Though the rooms of this now empty medieval home (the traditional residence of the archbishop) are stark and stony, the attraction here is the opportunity to walk on the rooftop of the cathedral. The experience offers little more than a fine view and a chance to burn your clothes at the cross—a once-common practice for pilgrims. You can visit the palace and rooftop only with a one-hour tour, which is usually in Spanish; try dropping by or calling ahead to see if an English tour is scheduled, and to reserve a spot (€10, or €8 if you bought a ticket to the Cathedral Museum, tours depart hourly 10:00-14:00 & 16:00-20:00, tel. 981-552-985, www.catedraldesantiago.es).

Cathedral Squares

There is a square on each side of the cathedral. You've already visited Praza do Obradoiro, in the front. Here are the other three, working clockwise (to reach the first one, go up the passage—which street musicians appreciate for its acoustics—to the left as you're facing the main cathedral facade).

Praza da Inmaculada—This was the way most medieval pilgrims using the French Road actually approached the cathedral. Across the square is **St. Martin's Monastery** (Mosteiro de San Martiño Pinario), one of two monasteries that sprang up around the church to care for pilgrims. Today it houses a museum of ecclesiastical artifacts and special exhibits.

Walk to the corner of the square with the arcade, and go to the post with the sign for *Rúa da Acibechería* (next to the garbage can, under the streetlight). If you look to the roof of the cathedral, between the big dome and the tall tower, you can make out a small green cross. This is where the clothes of medieval pilgrims were burned when they finally arrived at Santiago. This ritual was created for hygienic reasons in an age of frightful diseases...and filthy pilgrims.

• *Continue along the arcade and around the corner, and you'll enter...*

Praza Quintana—The door of the cathedral facing this square is the Holy Door, only opened during Holy Years. There's St. James, flanked by the disciples who brought his body back to Galicia. Below them are more Biblical characters, perhaps the 12 apostles and 12 prophets. Tip: Old Testament prophets hold scrolls. New Testament apostles hold books.

Across the square from the cathedral stands the imposing **St. Pelayo Monastery** (Mosteiro San Paio). The windows of its cells (now used by Benedictine sisters—notice the bars and privacy screens) face the cathedral. The church at the north end of this monastery is worth a peek. It has a frilly Baroque altar and a statue with a typical Galician theme: a pregnant Mary (to the left as you face main altar). The nuns sing at the evening vespers following the 19:30 Mass (Mon-Fri; 30 minutes earlier Sat-Sun). Just off this sanctuary is the entrance to the monastery's **Sacred Art Museum** (Museo de Arte Sacra), with a small but interesting collection (€1.50, Mon-Sat 10:30-13:30 & 16:00-19:00, closed Sun). The nuns of St. Pelayo make Galicia's famous *tarta de Santiago*—almond cake with a cross of Santiago in powdered sugar dusted on top. To buy one, exit the church to the right, head up the stairs, and walk around behind the monastery to find the entrance on Rúa de San Paio de Antealtares. Once inside, go to the small window on the left (generally open Mon-Sat 9:00-14:00 & 15:00-19:00; they only sell entire cakes—a big one for €10.50 and a very big one for €18).

• *Continue around to the...*

Praza das Praterías—This "Silversmiths' Square" is where Santiago's silver workers used to have their shops (and some still do). Overlooking the square is a tall **tower.** Imagine the fortified cathedral complex before the decorative Baroque frills were added; it looked more like a hulking fortress for fending off invading enemies from Normans to Moors to English pirates.

The **fountain** features a woman sitting on St. James' tomb, holding aloft a star—a typical city symbol. The mansion facing the cathedral is actually a collection of buildings with a thin-yet-effective Galician Baroque facade built to give the square architectural harmony. Its centerpiece even copies the fountain's star.

Beyond the fountain, a few steps down Rúa do Vilar (on the left), is the **Office for Pilgrims.** This is where pilgrims stop to pick up their *compostela,* the certificate that documents their successful *camino.* (The adjacent gift shop displays a copy of one in its window.) While tourists aren't really welcome in here, you can pop your head into the hallway, where there's often a pile of hiking sticks abandoned by happy pilgrims who've finished their trek. Upstairs is a RENFE train ticket information desk (does not sell tickets).

More Sights

▲▲Market (Praza de Abastos)—This wonderful market, housed in Old World stone buildings, offers a good opportunity to

do some serious people-watching (Mon-Sat 8:00-14:00, closed Sun). It's busiest and best on Thursday and Saturday, when villagers from the countryside come to sell things. (Monday's the least interesting day, since the fishermen don't go out on Sunday.)

The market was built in the 1920s (to consolidate Santiago's many small markets) in a style perfectly compatible with the medieval wonder that surrounds it. Today it offers an opportunity to get up close and personal with some still-twitching seafood. Keep an eye out for the specialties you'll want to try later—octopus, shrimp, crabs, lobsters, and expensive-as-gold *percebes* (barnacles; see sidebar on page 317). You'll also see the local *chorizo* (spicy sausage). *Grelos* are a local type of turnip greens with a thick stalk and long, narrow leaves—grown only here, and often used in the *caldo galego* soup. The little green *pimientos de padrón* (in season June-Oct) look like jalapeños, but lack the kick...sometimes.

In the cheese cases you'll see what look like huge yellow Hershey's Kisses...or breasts—in fact, this cheese is called *tetilla* ("small breast" in Galego). According to local legend, artists at the cathedral sculpted a very curvaceous woman and the locals loved it. The bishop made them redo the statue with less sexy lines, so the locals got even by making their cheese look like breasts. Through the centuries since, Santiago has been full of tasty reminders of a woman's physical beauty.

▲**Museum of Pilgrimages (Museo das Peregrinacións)**—This museum examines various aspects of the pilgrimage phenomenon. You'll see a map of pilgrimage sites around the world, and then learn more about the pilgrimage that brings people to Santiago. There are models of earlier versions of the cathedral, explanations of the differing depictions of St. James throughout history (apostle, pilgrim, and Crusader), and coverage of the various routes to Santiago and stories of some prominent pilgrims. This well-presented place lends historical context to all of those backpackers you see in the streets. Although exhibits are not described in English, the thorough info sheets available throughout the museum are well worth reading. The museum will move closer to the cathedral, possibly in 2012; call ahead or check at TI before you visit (free, €2.40 after move, Tue-Fri 10:00-20:00, Sat 10:30-13:30 & 17:00-20:00, Sun 10:30-13:30, closed Mon, at Rúa de San Miguel 4 but will move to Praza das Praterías, tel. 981-581-558, www.mdperegrinacions.com).

Museum of the Galician People (Museo do Pobo Galego)—This museum gives insights into rural Galician life. As you tour this collection, remember that if you side-trip a few miles into the countryside, you'll find traditional lifestyles thriving even today. Beautifully displayed around an 18th-century cloister, the museum springs from a unique triple staircase, which provided privacy to various hierarchies of the monks who lived here, depending  on which stairway you climbed. The collection shows off boatbuilding and fishing techniques, farming implements and simple horse-drawn carts, tools of trade and handicrafts (including carpentry, pottery, looms, and baskets), traditional costumes, and a collection of musical instruments, with an emphasis on the bagpipes *(gaitas)*. If the farm tools seem old-fashioned, there's a reason: Old inheritance laws mean that plots are increasingly smaller, so modern farming machinery is impractical—keeping traditional equipment alive. There's virtually no English, except for a helpful €1.50 guidebook (€3, Tue-Sat 10:00-14:00 & 16:00-20:00, Sun 11:00-14:00, closed Mon, at northeast edge of historical center in monastery of San Domingos de Bonaval, just beyond Porta do Camiño, tel. 981-583-620, www.museodopobo.es). Behind the museum is a plush and peaceful park—once crowded with tombstones.

Next door, in the striking modern building, is the **Galician Contemporary Art Museum** (Centro Galego de Arte Contemporánea), with continually rotating exhibits—mostly by local artists (free, Tue-Sun 11:00-20:00, closed Mon, tel. 981-546-619).

City of Culture of Galicia (Cidade da Cultura de Galicia)—This super-modern cultural complex, built on a hillside near Santiago de Compostela, was intended to put Santiago on the map as a 21st-century city (similar to Bilbao's Guggenheim). Instead, its costs have exceeded its expectations. Inaugurated in 2011 as the Archives and Library of Galicia, it offers exhibits and tours (free, daily 8:30-14:30 & 16:00-20:00, tours at 12:30 and 18:30, tel. 881-997-565, www.cidadedacultura.org).

Entertainment in Santiago

Street Music—You'll likely hear bagpipes *(gaitas)* being played in the streets of Santiago. Nobody knows for certain how this unlikely instrument caught on in Galicia, but supposedly the tradition has been passed down since the Celts lived here. (Bagpipes seem to be unique to Celts like the Scottish and Irish, but nearly all ethnic groups have had bagpipes in their past. If anything, the Celts just endured their sound more willingly.) Some singers use bagpipes, too, including Milladoiro (a group popular with middle-aged Galicians) and Carlos Nuñez (trendy with younger people). Caped university students, called *tunas,* can be seen singing traditional songs (without bagpipes) around town every night during the summer.

Galician Folk-Music Concerts—Whereas summertime is lively with folk-music concerts (ask for details at the TI), the rest of the year is not. One good bet is to drop by a practice session of the troupe called Cantigas e Agarimos (meets Wed and Fri at 21:30 for an hour, maybe at Rúa da Algalia de Arriba 11 or possibly playing at a nearby location—confirm schedule at TI, tel. 981-581-257). Since 1921 this group has shared the traditional Galician culture with visitors in performances throughout the year.

Sleeping in Santiago

To cater to all those pilgrims, Santiago has a glut of cheap, basic accommodations. There aren't many affordable big hotels in town for tour groups, so they tend to stay along the Rías Baixas (fjord-like estuaries) about an hour to the south, where beds are cheap. That means many of Santiago's visitors are day-trippers, arriving at about 10:30 and leaving in the afternoon. After dark it's just you, the locals, the pilgrims, and St. James. High season is roughly Easter through September; most places charge more during this time. The trickiest dates to book are Easter Sunday weekend and the Feast of St. James (July 24-25), so if you plan to be in town around these times, reserve your rooms well ahead. When I list a range of prices, it represents low season to high season. Any single prices listed are an average (midseason). The *hostales* speak enough English to make a reservation by phone (though sometimes not much more).

$$$ Altaïr Hotel, owned by the Liñares family (see Costa Vella listing, later), is located in a renovated three-story residence. Its 11 spacious rooms and mod decor can best be described as "rustic minimalist." Exposed stone walls and open beams mixed with a sleek design provide a unique yet surprisingly affordable experience (Sb-€70-85, Db-€90-115, superior Db-€110-140, extra bed-€20-25, tasty breakfast free with this book in 2012, free Wi-Fi, affordable laundry service for guests, Rúa dos Loureiros 12, tel. & fax 981-554-712, www.altairhotel.net, info@altairhotel.net).

$$$ Hostal dos Reis Católicos (Hospital of the Catholic Monarchs) was founded by the Catholic Monarchs at the beginning of the 16th century to care for pilgrims arriving from the Camino. It was converted into an upscale parador in 1952 and inaugurated by Franco (when royal family members are in town, they stay in his former suite overlooking the square). This grand building has 137 rooms surrounding a series of four courtyards packed with Santiago history. It has the best address in Santiago... and prices to match (standard Db-€280 includes tax and great breakfast, check website or call for deals, parking-€18, Praza do Obradoiro 1, tel. 981-582-200, fax 981-563-094, www.paradores-spain.com/spain/pscompostela.html, santiago@parador.es). Ask Enrique, who has worked here for 40 years, to print out the history of the parador in English.

Still remembering its roots, the parador follows Ferdinand and Isabel's edict to watch over pilgrims by offering three free meals to the first 10 who arrive each day (usually around 8:00). Pilgrims dine in a special room next to the staff quarters. They were originally allowed to eat in the main dining room, but guests started complaining about the stink. At first, special cloaks were

Sleep Code

(€1 = about $1.40, country code: 34)
S = Single, **D** = Double/Twin, **T** = Triple, **Q** = Quad, **b** = bathroom,
s = shower only. Unless otherwise noted, credit cards are
accepted, English is spoken, and breakfast generally costs
extra.

To help you easily sort through these listings, I've divided
the accommodations into three categories, based on the price
for a standard double room with bath:

$$$ Higher Priced—Most rooms €95 or more.
  $$ Moderately Priced—Most rooms between €50-95.
    $ Lower Priced—Most rooms €50 or less.

Prices can change without notice; verify the hotel's
current rates online or by email. For other updates, see www
.ricksteves.com/update.

given to pilgrims to try to mask the odor, but after that failed, they
were moved to their own eating quarters.

$$$ Hotel Virxe da Cerca is on the edge of the historical
center, across the busy street from the market. Its standard rooms
are in a modern building, but some of its "superior" and all of its
"special" historic rooms—with classy old stone and hardwoods—
are in a restored 18th-century Jesuit residence. While the mod-
ern rooms feel particularly impersonal, all 42 rooms surround a
lush garden oasis (standard Db €75 130, superior Db-€10 extra,
bigger "special" Db-€20 extra, breakfast-€10, beautiful glassed-
in breakfast room overlooks garden, elevator, free Internet access
and Wi-Fi, Rúa da Virxe da Cerca 27, tel. 981-569-350, fax 981-
586-925, www.pousadasdecompostela.com, vdacerca@pousadasde
compostela.com).

$$ Hotel Residencia Costa Vella is my favorite spot in
Santiago, with 14 comfortable rooms combining classic charm and
modern comforts. The glassed-in breakfast room and lounge terrace
overlook a peaceful garden, with lovely views of a nearby church
and monastery and into the countryside beyond. They deserve a feature in *Better Stones and Tiles* magazine (Sb-€55, standard Db-€75,
Db with balcony-€90, breakfast-€6, free Wi-Fi, affordable laundry
service for guests, parking-€9/day, Rúa da Porta da Pena 17, tel.
981-569-530, fax 981-569-531, www.costavella.com, hotelcostavella
@costavella.com, friendly José, Roberto, and wonderful staff).

$$ Hotel Airas Nunes, Hotel San Clemente, and **Hotel
Pombal** are affiliated with Hotel Virxe da Cerca. They're uni-
formly good, stress-free, and professional-feeling, all located in

Santiago Hotels & Restaurants

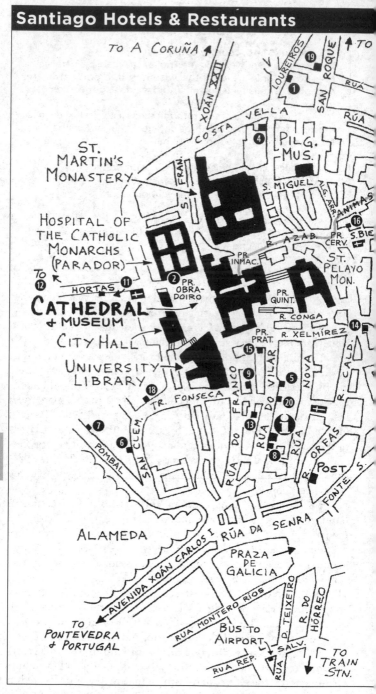

SANTIAGO DE COMPOSTELA

TO A CORUÑA

TO

XOÁN XXII

COSTA VELLA

S. FRAN.

ST. MARTIN'S MONASTERY

HOSPITAL OF THE CATHOLIC MONARCHS (PARADOR)

TO 12

HORTAS

CATHEDRAL + MUSEUM

CITY HALL

UNIVERSITY LIBRARY

PR. OBRA-DOIRO

PR. INMAC.

PR. PRAT.

TR. FONSECA

SAN CLEM.

POMBAL

ALAMEDA

AVENIDA XOÁN CARLOS I

RÚA DO FRANCO

RÚA MONTERO RÍOS

RÚA DA SENRA

PRAZA DE GALICIA

BUS TO AIRPORT

RÚA REP.

RÚA SALV.

R. DO TEIXEIRO

R. DO HÓRREO

TO TRAIN STN.

TO PONTEVEDRA & PORTUGAL

LOUREIROS

SAN ROQUE

RUA

RÚA

PILG. MUS.

S. MIGUEL

ALG. ARR.

ANIMAS

PR. CERV.

S. BIE.

ST. PELAYO MON.

R. AZAB.

PR. QUINT.

R. CONGA

R. XELMÍREZ

NOVA

R. CALD.

RÚA DO VILAR

RÚA

R. ORFAS

POST

FONTE S.

BUS STATION

GALICIAN CONTEMPORARY ART MUSEUM

MUSEUM OF THE GALICIAN PEOPLE

RAMÓN

DAS RODAS

CASAS

SAN PEDROA

PORTA DO CAMIÑO

DA CERCA

ITO

PR. ABASTOS

MARKET

UNIV.

RÚA DA VIRXE

TROMPAS

ANT.

17
10
3

TO AIRPORT, CITY OF CULTURE OF GALICIA (2013), ARZUA, LEÓN & PARIS

① Altaïr Hotel

② Hostal dos Reis Católicos, Dos Reis & Enxebre Rest.

③ Hotel Virxe da Cerca

④ Hotel Residencia Costa Vella, Pensión Girasol & Café Costa Vella

⑤ Hotel Airas Nunes

⑥ Hotel San Clemente

⑦ Hotel Pombal

⑧ Hostal Suso

⑨ Hospedaje Ramos

⑩ Hostal Residencia Giadás

⑪ Casa Marcelo Restaurante

⑫ To El Mercadito Restaurante

⑬ O Gato Negro

⑭ A Curtidoría Restaurante

⑮ O Beiro Vinoteca

⑯ Restaurante Casa Manolo

⑰ O Dezaseis Restaurante

⑱ Cotolay Bar Restaurante

⑲ La Bodeguilla de San Roque

⑳ Café Casino

CAMINO DE SANTIAGO

100 YARDS

100 METERS

SANTIAGO DE COMPOSTELA

DCH

restored old buildings with classy touches. All three hotels charge €6 for breakfast and €20 for extra beds, and share the same contact info (tel. 981-569-350, www.pousadasdecompostela.com, info@pousadasdecompostela.com). Hotel Airas Nunes is deep in the old center a few blocks in front of the cathedral (10 rooms, Db-€70-96, Rúa do Vilar 17, reception tel. 981-554-706). Hotel San Clemente is just outside the historical center (Db-€70-95, Rúa de San Clemente 28, reception tel. 981-569-260). Hotel Pombal is a slight step up from the other two in terms of quality and price. Situated in Alameda Park, many of its rooms offer great views of the cathedral (Db-€80-95, €10 more for views, Rúa do Pombal 12, reception tel. 981-569-350).

$ **Hostal Suso,** run by the four Quintela brothers, is a great value, offering 10 inexpensive, new-feeling rooms around an airy atrium over a fun little bar, which rustles up a good €4 *tortilla de gambas* (shrimp omelet). The place is located in the heart of Santiago, nearly next door to the TI (Sb-€20, Db-€40-49, breakfast-€3-5, Rúa do Vilar 65, tel. 981-586-611, www.hostalsuso.com, hostalsuso@gmail.com, reservations only by phone).

$ **Hospedaje Ramos** rents 10 big, tasteful, clean rooms right in the center. It has lots of stairs, which is a blessing since they take you farther away from the night noise (Sb-€26, Db-€39, includes tax, no credit cards, no breakfast, Rúa da Raiña 18, tel. 981-581-859, Louisa speaks a few words of English).

$ **Hostal Residencia Giadás,** tucked away just beyond the market, faces a tidy little square as if it owns it. The eight rooms, some with slanted floors, are simple but charming (Sb-€35, Db-€55, Tb-€74, elevator, next to Porta do Camiño at Praza do Matadoiro 2, tel. & fax 981-587-071, lolagiadas@gmail.com, Giadás family).

$ **Pensión Girasol** rents 12 decent rooms above a cheery cafeteria for a good price in a great neighborhood (S-€25, Sb-€40, D-€45, Db-€55, Porta da Pena 4, tel. 981-566-287, www.hgirasol.com, girasol@hgirasol.com).

Eating in Santiago

Strolling through the streets of Santiago is like visiting a well-stocked aquarium: Windows proudly display every form of edible sealife, including giant toothy fish, scallops and clams of every shape and size, monstrous shrimp, and—most importantly—octopus. The fertile fjords of the Galician coast are just 20 miles away, and the region's

many fishing villages keep the capital city swimming in seafood. As the seafood is so fresh, the focus here is on purity rather than sauces. The seafood is served simple—generally just steamed or grilled, and seasoned only with a little olive oil, onions, peppers, and paprika.

Tasting octopus *(pulpo)* is obligatory in Galicia; it's most often prepared *a la gallega* (also called *pulpo a feira*): After the octopus is beaten to tenderize it, then boiled in a copper pot, its tentacles are snipped into bite-size pieces with scissors. It's topped with virgin olive oil, coarse sea salt, and a mixture of sweet and spicy paprika, then served on a round wooden plate. Eat it with toothpicks, never a fork. It's usually accompanied by large hunks of country bread to sop up the olive oil, and washed down by local red *mencia* or white *ribeiro* wine, often served in little saucer-like ceramic cups *(cunca)*.

Not a fan of seafood? You can slurp the *caldo galego,* a traditional broth that originally came from the leftover stock used to prepare an elaborate Sunday feast (cabbage or *grelos,* potatoes, and so on—not too exciting, but providing comfort on a rainy day). Starting in July, look for *pimientos de padrón*—miniature green peppers sautéed in olive oil with a heavy dose of rock salt.

Restaurants generally serve lunch from 13:00 to 16:00 and dinner from 20:00 until very late (Spaniards don't start dinner until about 21:00). It's frustrating to try to eat before the locals do. If you find a restaurant serving before 13:00 or 21:00, you'll be all alone with a few sorry-looking tourists. Early-bird eaters should know that ordering a drink at any bar will generally get you a free tapa—Santiago is one of the few places in Spain that still honors this tradition.

For a quick meal on the go, grab a traditional meat pie, or *empanada,* which comes *de carne* (with pork), *de bonito* or *de atún* (tuna), *de bacalao* (salted cod), *de zamburiñas* (tiny scallops), *de berberechos* (cockles)—and these days, even *de pulpo* (octopus).

And for dessert: Locals enjoy *queixo con mel* (cheese with honey) at the end of a meal. In the tourist zones, bakeries push samples of *tarta de Santiago,* the local almond cake. Historically, the cake was cooked by sisters in Santiago's convents.

Gourmet Dining, Modern Cuisine

Casa Marcelo, Santiago's elite gourmet option, earned a Michelin star for its international cuisine. If you want to dine elegantly and have the money, this dressy 11-table restaurant is the place. For €60 (plus wine) you get a fixed-price meal featuring the chef's seasonal specials. The kitchen is in plain view, so you'll get caught up in the excitement of cooking (open for dinner Tue-Sat, also open for lunch on Sat, closed Sun-Mon, reservations required—usually days in advance, down the steep lane below the cathedral, at Rúa das Hortas 1, tel. 981-558-580).

El Mercadito Restaurante is a classy yet trendy eight-table establishment with a following among locals. It seems that Chef Gonzalo Rei is going for a Michelin star with his well-presented and creative contemporary cuisine. He serves only an eight-course, €48 tasting menu (open daily 13:45-15:45, Wed-Sat 21:30-23:30, closed Sun-Tue evenings, hike below the cathedral, past Casa Marcelo to Rúa das Galeras 18, tel. 981-574-239).

Restaurant Row in the Old Center: Rúa do Franco

Since hungry pilgrims first filled the city in the Middle Ages, Rúa do Franco (named not for the dictator but for the first French pilgrims) has been lined with eateries and bars. Today this street, which leads away from the cathedral, remains lively with foreign visitors—both tourists and pilgrims. There are plenty of seafood places, a few time-warp dives, and several lively bars with little €1.50 *montaditos* (sandwiches) for the grabbing. I'd stroll it once to see what appeals, and then go back to eat. **O Gato Negro,** a no-frills seafood tapas bar stuck in the past and filled with loyal locals, is worth seeking out. It's one of the last places to serve *ribeiro* wine in a ceramic cup (Tue-Sat 12:30-15:00 & 19:00-late, Sun 12:30-15:00, closed Mon, near Rúa do Franco at Rúa da Raiña—look for black cat sign outside).

Memorable Eating in the Old Center

A Curtidoría Restaurante ("The Tannery") is a modern, spacious, and romantic place in the old town, rare for its open feeling. While the food is nothing exceptional, the setting is enjoyable and it's a solid value (€13 lunch special menu, paella and fish, €15-22 per plate, Rúa da Conga 2, tel. 981-554-342).

O Beiro Vinoteca, designed to show off the fine wines of Galicia and Spain, serves by the glass from a huge menu and complements its wine with simple, appropriate *raciones*. Run by Pepe Beiro, it's much classier than your average tapas bar. The tasting action is on the ground floor while the tables for dining are upstairs. If you drop in for just a glass of wine, you'll get a free tapa (closed Sun and sometimes Mon, half a block from cathedral at Rúa da Raiña 3, tel. 981-581-370).

Hostal dos Reis Católicos, the fancy old hospital sharing the square with the cathedral, has two fine restaurants downstairs. The main restaurant, **Dos Reis,** fills a former stable with a dramatic stone vault. It offers international dishes—often with live piano and nearly dead guests. A typical parador restaurant, it comes with stiff tuxedoed service, white tablecloths, and not a hint of fun (daily, tel. 981-582-200). Surprisingly, a few steps away is a

Percebes = Barnacles

Local barnacles, called *percebes,* are a delicacy. Since they grow only on rocks that see a lot of dangerous waves, it takes specialists—a team of two gatherers—to harvest them; one with a rope tied to his waist, the other spotting him from above. Because of the danger, barnacles are really expensive. You'll see them stacked in the windows of seafood bars that charge about €7 per 100 grams ($40 a pound). Check the price carefully and confirm it clearly. There are variations that can cost many times that already expensive figure. Two beers and a small 100-gram plate to split make a wonderful snack. Just twist, rip, and bite—it's a bit like munching the necks off of butter clams. I ask for toasted bread on the side.

For the freshest *percebes* at half the price—and twice the experience—buy them from any fisherwoman at the market. Let Ramon or Maria at Churro-Mania boil them for you right there in their market café. They'll boil up any seafood you buy in the market (it takes just a few minutes; minimum portion a half-kilo or about one pound), charging €3 per person for table service, plus 10 percent of your market bill; you must bring the receipt for whatever they're cooking up for you (Mon-Sat 11:00-17:00, closed Sun, aisle 5 in the market, tel. 981-577-633, mobile 616-911-228). They'll also prepare you a nice chop or piece of steak.

wonderful alternative—**Enxebre** has a livelier easygoing-tavern vibe, good traditional Galician food, and reasonable prices (€5-14 dishes, daily, tel. 981-050-527).

Restaurante Casa Manolo serves only one thing: a €9 fixed-price meal consisting of two generous courses, water, bread, and a packaged dessert. It's popular with students on a tight budget who want a classy meal out. This smart little family-run eatery combines sleek contemporary design, decent Galician and Spanish food, and excellent prices. The service is rushed (a good thing if you're in a hurry), but the value is unbeatable (arrive when they open or plan on waiting; Mon-Sat lunch 13:00-16:00, dinner 20:00-23:30, Sun lunch only, at the bottom of Praza de Cervantes, tel. 981-582-950).

Budget Values Away from the Tourist Center

O Dezaseis ("The Sixteen") is every local's favorite (and mine, too). As soon as you walk down into its sprawling, high-energy vaulted dining room, you know this is the best place in town. In-the-know

SANTIAGO DE COMPOSTELA

locals are dining under stone walls, heavy beams, and modern art while enjoying friendly service. You can choose from meat and fish plates (€12-14), but simply ordering one *ración* per person (€4-11) and splitting their hearty mixed salad for some veggies make a fine and inexpensive meal. They do octopus just right here and have nice wines at good prices (Mon-Sat 14:00-16:00 & 20:30-midnight, closed Sun, reservations smart, Rúa de San Pedro 16, tel. 981-564-880).

Cotolay Bar Restaurante and two adjacent bar-restaurants are a hit with locals for drinks with free tapas. They are good budget bets for a meal of *raciones* without the tourists (€5-15 *raciones*, Mon-Sat 11:00-late, closed Sun, Rúa de San Clemente, tel. 981-573-014).

La Bodeguilla de San Roque offers a good selection of *raciones* and wines in a relaxed neighborhood atmosphere. If the upstairs restaurant is full, have a drink at the bar to pass the time (€5-8 *raciones*, Rúa da San Roque 13, tel. 981-564-379).

Cafés

Café Costa Vella, in the breakfast room and garden of the highly recommended Hotel Residencia Costa Vella, is a little Eden tucked just beyond the tourist zone. The café welcomes non-guests for coffee and a relaxing break in a poetic time-warp garden with leafy views (great €3.50 toasted sandwiches, plus a wide array of drinks, daily 8:00-23:00, Rúa da Porta da Pena 17, tel. 981-569-530).

Café Casino, a former private club, is a tired taste of turn-of-the-20th-century elegance with occasional live piano music. Local tour guides recommend this café to their timid British groups, who wouldn't touch an octopus with a 10-foot pole. While they have sandwiches and salads, I would just consider this an elegant coffee or tea stop (Rúa do Vilar 35).

Santiago Connections

From Santiago de Compostela by Train to: Madrid (2/day, 7.25-9.5 hours, overnight train departs at 22:33, arrives in Madrid Chamartín at 8:00), **Salamanca** (take train to Zamora—2/day, 5 hours—then transfer to hourly bus for 1-hour ride to Salamanca), **León** (1-2/day direct, 6 hours), **Bilbao** (1/day direct, 11 hours), **San Sebastián** (1/day direct, 11 hours), **Santander** (1/day, 13 hours, transfer in Palencia), **Lugo** (3/day, 3-4 hours, requires transfer in A Coruña—bus is better), **Porto,** Portugal (1/day via Vigo, departs at 16:20, 3.25 hours). Train info: toll tel. 902-320-320, www.renfe.com.

By Bus to: Lugo (7/day, 2 hours), **Madrid** (5/day, 8 hours, includes night bus 21:30-6:30, arrives at Estación Sur), **Salamanca**

(2/day, 1 with a transfer in Vigo, 7 hours), **Astorga** (5/day, 5 hours), **León** (5/day, 7 hours), **Burgos** (2/day, includes 1 night bus, 7-9 hours), **Bilbao** (3/day, 2 continue to **San Sebastián,** includes 2 night buses, 9.5-12 hours to Bilbao, 1.5 hours more to San Sebastián), **Porto,** Portugal (2/day, 4 hours). Bus info: tel. 981-542-416. All long-distance destinations are served by the Alsa bus company (toll tel. 902-422-242, www.alsa.es).

CANTABRIA

Santillana del Mar • Altamira Caves •
Comillas • Picos de Europa

If you're connecting the Basque Country and Galicia (Santiago de Compostela) along the coast, you'll go through the provinces of Cantabria and Asturias. Both are interesting, but Cantabria (kahn-TAH-bree-ah) has a few villages and sights that are especially worth a visit. The quaint town of Santillana del Mar makes a fine home base for visiting the prehistoric Altamira Caves. Comillas is a pleasant beach town.

The dramatic peaks of the Picos de Europa and their rolling foothills define this region, giving it a more rugged feel than the "Northern Riviera" ambience of the Basque region. A drive through the Cantabrian countryside is rewarded with endless glimpses of charming stone homes. Though it's largely undiscovered by Americans, Cantabria is heavily touristed by Europeans in July and August, when it can get very crowded.

Planning Your Time

Cantabria doesn't rank high on the list of sightseeing priorities in Spain. Don't go out of your way to get here. However, if you're passing through, there are some charming diversions along the way. A night or two in this region breaks up the long drive from Bilbao to Santiago (figure over seven hours straight through).

Assuming you're coming from San Sebastián, this is a good plan:

Day 1: Leave San Sebastián early for the Guggenheim in Bilbao (trip takes about an hour by expressway, longer along the coast). After seeing the museum, continue on to explore (and sleep in) Santillana del Mar or Comillas. If you arrive early enough,

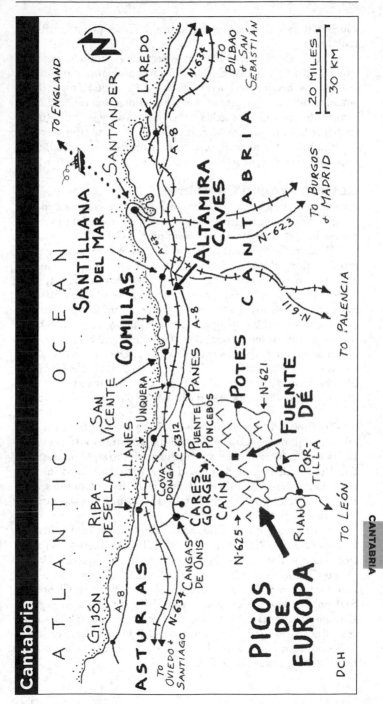

you might have time to see the Altamira Caves (near Santillana) tonight.

Day 2: Troglodytes will want to visit the Altamira Caves right when it opens (9:30, closed Mon). Hikers and high-mountain fans will make a beeline for Fuente Dé in the Picos de Europa. If you get an early start on either of these attractions, you can still make it to Santiago de Compostela by the end of a very long day (figure six hours from this region to Santiago). It's saner to sleep a second night in this area, in which case it's possible (though rushed) to do both the caves and the mountains on Day 2.

Getting Around Cantabria

This region is best by car; public transportation is complicated, and the payoffs are not so great. Unless you have a special interest in prehistoric art, non-drivers will want to skip Cantabria.

By Car: Drivers enjoy Cantabria. The A-8 expressway runs roughly along the coast from San Sebastián to Gijón, where it becomes an express two-lane highway the rest of the way to A Coruña in Galicia. To reach Santillana del Mar and Comillas, follow signs to *A-67* (a jog off the expressway toward Santander), then take the exit for CA-131 (signed for *Santillana del Mar*). This highway takes you through Santillana, Comillas, and San Vicente de la Barquera. After San Vicente, CA-131 intersects with N-621 in the town of Unquera; this leads south through La Hermida Gorge into the Picos de Europa (follow signs for *Potes*). If you want to go directly to the Picos, there's an exit for N-621 directly off the A-8 expressway.

By Bus: Without a car, you'll rely on the bus from the port city of Santander—Cantabria's capital and transportation hub. Buses run from Santander to Santillana del Mar, Comillas, and San Vicente de la Barquera (5-7/day each way, about 35 minutes from Santander to Santillana, then 15 minutes to Comillas, then 15 more minutes to San Vicente, tel. 942-720-822, www.transporte decantabria.es).

A different bus goes from Santander to Potes in the Picos de Europa (2-3/day, 2.25 hours, tel. 942-880-611). There's also a bus from León to Potes, but only in summer (1/day, 3 hours).

By Train: Santander, the region's public transportation hub, is connected by train with **Madrid** (3/day, 4.5-5 hours, Chamartín Station), **Bilbao** (3/day, 3 hours on FEVE), and **Santiago de Compostela** (1/day, 13 hours, transfer in Palencia). A scenic train line called the FEVE runs from Bilbao to Santander and to Ovideo, but it's not particularly helpful for visiting the destinations in this chapter (www.feve.es).

Santillana del Mar

Every guidebook imparts the same two tidbits about Santillana del Mar: One is that it's known as the "town of three lies," as it's neither holy *(santi)*, nor flat *(llana)*, nor on the ocean *(del Mar)*. The other is that the existentialist philosopher Jean-Paul Sartre once called it the "prettiest village in Spain."

The town is worth the fuss. Santillana is a proud little stone village, with charming time-warp qualities that have (barely) survived the stampede of multinational tour groups here to visit the nearby Altamira Caves. Despite it all, the town is what Spaniards would call *preciosa*.

Santillana is three cobbled streets and a collection of squares, climbing up over mild hills from where the village meets the main road. While Santillana has several sights that cater to the tourist throngs (including a much-promoted zoo), the only sight that makes a visit worthwhile—aside from the town itself—is the cave paintings of Altamira in the nearby countryside.

Tourist Information: The modern TI is right at the entrance to the town (daily July-mid-Sept 9:00-21:00, off-season 9:30-13:30 & 16:00-19:00, Jesús Otero 20, tel. 942-818-251). Only residents (and guests of hotels that offer parking) are allowed to drive in the center—leave your car in the big lot by the TI (pay in-season, free off season).

Sleeping in Santillana

Santillana makes a good home base for visiting the region and the caves. My listings are right in town; the first three places are on Santillana's main square, Plaza Ramón Pelayo. The fourth is farther up, just around the corner (to the right) from the big Collegiate Church.

$$$ *Paradores:* Two swanky, arrogant *paradores* hold court on the main square—**Parador de Santillana** (Sb-€148, Db-€156-188 depending on amenities, look for deals online, breakfast-€18, Plaza Ramón Pelayo 11, tel. 942-818-000, fax 942-818-391, www.parador.es, santillana@parador.es) and **Parador de Santillana Gil Blas** (Sb-€140, Db-€180-280 depending on amenities, breakfast-€17, same address, tel. 942-028-028, fax 942-818-391, www.parador.es, santillanagb@parador.es).

CANTABRIA

Sleep Code

(€1 = about $1.40, country code: 34)

S = Single, **D** = Double/Twin, **T** = Triple, **Q** = Quad, **b** = bathroom, **s** = shower only. Unless otherwise noted, English is spoken, credit cards are accepted, and tax is not included. Prices vary with season (highest July-Aug and Holy Week). I've listed shoulder- and peak-season rates.

To help you sort easily through these listings, I've divided the accommodations into three categories based on the price for a standard double room with bath:

$$$ Higher Priced—Most rooms €110 or more.
 $$ Moderately Priced—Most rooms between €70-110.
  $ Lower Priced—Most rooms €70 or less.

Prices can change without notice; verify the hotel's current rates online or by email. For other updates, see www.ricksteves.com/update.

$$ Hotel Altamira offers 32 well-priced rooms in an atmospheric 16th-century palace on the main square (Sb-€52-60, standard Db-€74-86, big Db with sitting room a worthwhile splurge at €84-102, 20 percent more in Aug and Holy Week, cheaper Nov-March, extra bed-€22, breakfast-€8.50, Calle Cantón 1, tel. 942-818-025, fax 942-840-136, www.hotelaltamira.com, info@hotelaltamira.com).

$ Hospedaje Octavio is a fine budget option with 11 comfortable wood-beamed rooms (Db-€30-40 depending on season, cheaper for bathroom on the hall, Plaza Las Arenas 4, tel. & fax 942-818-199, pensioncasaoctavio@gmail.com, Octavio and Milagros don't speak English, but their sons do).

Altamira Caves

Not far from Santillana del Mar, the Altamira Caves (worth ▲) contain some of the best examples of prehistoric art anywhere. In 1879 the young daughter of a local archaeologist discovered several 14,000-year-old paintings in a limestone cave. By the 1960s and 1970s, it became a tremendously popular tourist destination. All of the visitors got to be too much for the delicate paintings, and the cave was closed in 1979. A replica cave and museum opened in 2001 near the original site, allowing visitors to experience these pieces of prehistoric artwork in something approximating their original setting. The Spanish cultural ministry hopes to someday reopen the original cave on a restricted basis, but those plans are on hold for the time being. Although you can't visit the original cave, prehistoric-art fans will still find Altamira worth the trip.

Note that if all you're really interested in is the art itself, replicas of the paintings are at Madrid's National Archaeological Museum; however, they won't be on display until after a museum renovation wraps up sometime in 2012.

Getting to the Altamira Caves

The caves are on a ridge in the countryside a little over a mile southwest of Santillana del Mar. There's no public transportation to the site. To get from Santillana del Mar to the caves, it's either a 30-minute walk or a cheap taxi ride (mobile 608-483-441). Bolder travelers hitch a bus ride with a friendly tour group.

Orientation to the Altamira Caves

Cost and Hours: €3, free Sat from 14:30 and Sun; open May-Oct Tue-Sat 9:30-20:00, can be open even later some nights in summer, Sun 9:30-15:00; Nov-April Tue-Sat 9:30-18:00, Sun 9:30-15:00; closed Mon year-round; last tour departs 30 minutes before closing; tel. 942-818-815, http://museodealtamira .mcu.es.

Visiting the Caves: Your visit has two parts: First, there's a fine museum with good English descriptions, featuring models and reproductions of the cave dwellers who made these drawings (and their clothes, tools, and remains). Videos and illuminated pictures help bring these people to life. The second part is either a 30-minute guided tour of the highly detailed replica cave, or a visit on your own. Unfortunately, English-speakers get no respect at Altamira: Posted information in English is measly, and tours in English are rare. If your guide speaks English, ask if he or she will translate the highlights for you. Otherwise, follow along with my self-guided tour.

Reservations: Only 240 people are allowed to enter the replica cave each hour (20 people/tour, tours leave every 5 minutes— or when enough people gather, never more than a 30-minute wait). This means that in the busy summer season, spaces fill up fast. In July and August and on free Sundays, they recommend getting to the museum when it opens (9:30) to claim your tour appointment.

During the busy season, it's best to make an advance reservation for the replica cave (no extra charge) through the bank Santander Centro Hispano—drop by a branch, or, even easier, call them (tel. 902-242-424, wait through recording and ask for English speaker). If you *comprende Español,* you can make a reservation (for Tue-Sat) online at https://secure .santander.com/ventaentradas/Altamira. Request a specific date and time (one-hour window) for your visit. Take your ticket or your confirmation number to the information counter at the caves, where you can schedule a guided tour. Having the ticket in advance doesn't guarantee you'll have a slot on the guided tour of the replica cave; however, it does guarantee at least the museum and a visit to the cave on your own.

Self-Guided Tour

You'll begin the tour by watching a four-minute film about the various inhabitants of the cave, the discovery of the paintings in 1879, and the era of over-visitation. Then you'll enter the first part of the replica cave, where you're on your own for English information. The English descriptions that the guide eagerly points out are marginally helpful, but here's the gist:

In the Cave

The painstaking replica in the *Neocueva* ("Neo-cave") was achieved with special computers so that the cave art can still be enjoyed without endangering the actual paintings. The Neo-cave also simulates the original cave's temperature, sounds, and humidity.

About 14,000 years ago, hunters, gatherers, and fishermen lived in these caves. They huddled around a fire, protected from the elements. They liked the location because of its proximity to the ocean and a river.

Excavation Site

This area displays tools used by modern scientists to dig up relics from various periods. We're talking about the Upper Paleolithic era—the time of Cro-Magnon cave people, with big hands and high foreheads. The Upper Paleolithic is divided into three periods, and this cave was inhabited, on two separate occasions, during two of those periods: the Solutrean (about 18,500 years ago) and the Magdalenian (14,000 years ago). You'll see that there are three layers to the excavation: On the bottom are artifacts from Solutrean cavemen (hunting tools and chips of flint); above that is mostly clay, with the remains of a cave bear you'll see in a few minutes; and the top layer holds hearths and tools from the Magdalenian period.

As you continue on to the next stop, you'll pass the bones of a cave bear that once lived in Altamira. Look for his paw prints nearby.

Artists' Workshop

See the tools used by the prehistoric artists, as well as a video showing how the paintings were created. The most dramatic paintings—all the red buffaloes—were made with reddish ochre dissolved in water, outlined in black charcoal. Marrow-burning stone lamps provided light. Many of the images were engraved into the surface of the cave (using flint) before being painted. The reproductions in the Neo-cave were done using the same techniques.

Art!

Finally we reach the paintings themselves. This part of the cave has various names, including the "Great Hall," the "Polychrome Room," or even "the Sistine Chapel of Prehistoric Art." The ledge with the lights shows the floor level of the original cave. This didn't give the cavemen much room to paint, making their creations even more remarkable. Among the fauna depicted in this room are 16 bison, a couple of running boars, some horses, and a giant deer—plus a few handprints and several mysterious symbols.

Unfortunately, the posted English information ends here. These are some of the things to look for:

Bumps and Cracks: The artists incorporated the ceiling's many topographical features into their creations (see the bison with the large, swollen back, or the one with the big head).

Overlap: Some paintings actually overlap onto each other. These were painted during two different eras. (The most impressive batch—including all those bison—is thought to be by the same artist.)

Detail: While a few paintings are incomplete, others are finished. Check out the bison with the highly detailed hooves and beard.

The "Old Horse": The horse with its back against the wall is probably among the oldest in the cave.

The "Great Deer": The biggest painting of all (over seven feet across) is the deer with the little black bison under his chin. Notice it's not quite in proportion; due to the tight quarters, the artist couldn't take a step back to survey his work.

Symbols: The strange, hieroglyphic-like symbols scattered around the cave, called tectiforms, are difficult to interpret. Scientists have found very similar symbols in caves that were far apart and wondered if they were some sort of primitive written language (for example, an outline of a horse with a particular symbol might explain how to set traps for hunting).

Behavior: The artists captured not only the form, but also the behavior of the animals they depicted. Notice the lowing bison; the curled-up bison; the bison turning its head; and the running boars (with the extra legs).

What's amazing about these paintings is simply that they were made by Cro-Magnon cave people. And yet the artists had an incredible grasp of delicate composition, depicting these animals with such true-to-life simplicity. Some of them are mere outlines, a couple of curvy lines—masterful abstraction that could make Picasso jealous.

So why did they make these paintings? Nobody knows for sure. General agreement is that it wasn't simply for decoration and that the paintings must have served some religious or shamanistic purpose.

Final Cave

The most impressive paintings were discovered in a single room (whose replica you just visited). However, beyond that room, the cave extended another several hundred feet, though that area was not reproduced. As you leave the replica cave, you'll see a few more replicas—mostly carvings—that came from other parts of the original cave. Most of them are those mysterious symbols, but at the very end you'll also see three masks carved into the rock.

And with that, your cave visit is over. Yabba dabba doo!

Comillas

Just 15 minutes beyond Santillana del Mar, perched on a hill overlooking the Atlantic, you'll find quirky Comillas. Comillas presides over a sandy beach, but feels more like a hill town, with twisty lanes clambering up away from the sea. Comillas is not as undeniably charming as Santillana—it would do well to go traffic-free, as its neighbor has—but it makes for a fine home base if you prefer beach access and a more lived-in feel to touristy quaintness.

Most notably, Comillas also enjoys a surprising abundance of striking Modernista architecture. Three buildings line up along a ridge at the west end of town (just beyond the town center and parking lot, over the big park). Antoni Gaudí, Barcelona's favorite son, designed a villa here called El Capricho—now a recommended restaurant (closed Mon in winter). Next door is the pointy spire of a 17th-century church, and at the end of the row is the Palace of Sobrellano, by Gaudí's mentor Joan Martorell, which hints at early Barcelona-style Modernisme. Peering back at these

CANTABRIA

buildings from a parallel ridge is the huge Pontifical University building, decorated by yet another early-20th-century Catalan architect, Lluís Domènech i Muntaner. These Modernista master-pieces are compliments of Don Antonio López y López, who left Spain to find fortune in America. He returned to Barcelona (where he acquired a taste for Gaudí and company) and eventually became the Marquis of Comillas.

The beachside road below is lined with tacky tourist hotels, but the town center, up on the hill, is much more pleasant—with an odd jumble of squares surrounding the big Parochial Church.

Tourist Information: The westernmost square, Plaza Joaquín de Piélagos, is where you'll find the TI (unpredictable hours, posted as July-Aug daily 9:00-21:00; Sept-June Mon-Sat 10:30-13:30 & 16:30-19:30, Sun 10:30-13:30, but often closed; Calle Aldea 6, tel. 942-720-768).

Near Comillas

As you continue west from Comillas, the road becomes bumpy and follows the coast, soon crossing a wide bay over a long, dramatic bridge to **San Vicente de la Barquera.** This salty seaside resort overlooks a boat-filled harbor, with glimpses of the dramatic Picos de Europa in the distance.

Sleeping in Comillas

($1 = about €1.40, country code: 34)

Both of these listings are in the town center, south of the big Parochial Church, near the long, skinny restaurant-lined Plaza de Primo de Rivera (also known as "El Corro"). The first hotel is the big red building a block off the south end of the square; the other is a few blocks above the square, on the uphill street with the blue-trimmed railing.

$$ Hotel Marina de Campíos offers 20 modern, colorful rooms, each named for a different opera (standard Db-€75-110, "junior" Db-€95-130, "senior" Db-€125-150, higher prices are for mid-July-Aug, includes breakfast and tax, closed on weekdays mid-Sept-April and completely closed mid-Dec-mid-Jan, elevator, Calle General Piélagos 14, tel. 942-722-754, fax 942-722-749, www .marinadecampios.com, reservas@marinadecampios.com).

$ Pasaje San Jorge, with 11 basic but comfortable rooms in a hundred-year-old house, hovers just over the town center (Db-€62-65, or €75 July-Aug and Holy Week, cheaper off-season, includes breakfast and tax, Calle Carlos Díaz de la Campa 16, tel. & fax 942-720-915, www.pasajesanjorge.com, pasajesanjorge@pasajesan jorge.com).

Eating in Comillas

El Capricho is a surprising piece of Antoni Gaudí architecture hiding on a ridge above Comillas' center. The sunflower-dappled exterior alludes to Gaudí's plan for the building: His "sunflower design" attempted to maximize exposure to light by arranging rooms so that they would get sun during the part of the day that they were most used. Today the building is an exclusive-feeling restaurant serving traditional Spanish cuisine. Look around the back for the sculpture of the architect admiring his work. Don't even try to get inside if you're not eating here. Reservations are smart, especially in season (€20-30 entrées, Mon-Sat 13:00-16:00 & 21:00-23:30, Sun 13:00-16:00 only; shorter hours in winter—lunch ends at 15:30 and dinner at 23:00, also closed Mon; tel. 942-720-365). There are two roads to this hard-to-find restaurant; both are at the west end of town, and both are sometimes closed. Ask a local for directions.

Picos de Europa

The Picos de Europa—comprising one of Spain's most popular national parks—are a relatively small stretch of cut-glass mountain peaks (the steepest in Spain, some taller than 8,500 feet) just 15 miles inland from the ocean. These dramatic mountains are home to goats, brown bears, eagles, vultures, wall-creepers (rare birds), and happy hikers. Outdoorsy types could spend days exploring this dramatic patch of Spain, which is packed with visitors in the summer. We'll focus on the two most important excursions: taking the Fuente Dé funicular up to a mountaintop, and hiking the yawning chasm of the Cares Gorge.

Orientation to the Picos de Europa

The Picos de Europa are a patch of mountains covering an area of about 25 miles by 25 miles. They're located where three of Spain's regions converge: Cantabria, Asturias, and León. (Frustratingly, each region's tourist office pretends that the parts of the park in the other regions don't exist—so it's very hard to get information, say, about Asturias' Cares Gorge in Potes, Cantabria.) In addition to three regions, the park contains three different limestone massifs, or large masses of rock, separated by rivers.

As you venture into the Picos de Europa, pick up a good map; the green 1:80,000-scale map that you'll see is handy, featuring roads, trails, and topographical features. Serious hikers will want a guidebook (I like the Sunflower guide, published by a British company—www.sunflowerbooks.co.uk). These resources, along with a wide variety of other maps and books, are available locally.

I'll focus on the Cantabrian part of the Picos, which contains the region's most accessible and enjoyable bits: the scenic drive through La Hermida Gorge, the charming mountain town of Potes, and the sky-high views from the top of the Fuente Dé cable car. This part of the Picos is doable as a long day trip from Santillana del Mar or Comillas (but is easier if you stay in Potes). The next best activity (in León and Asturias, not Cantabria) is the Cares Gorge hike—deeper in the park and requiring another full day.

Planning Your Time

If you're really serious about tackling the region, and want to do both Fuente Dé and the Cares Gorge, this is the most sensible plan:

Day 1: Drive from Comillas/Santillana del Mar to Potes and do the Fuente Dé cable car and hike (sleep in Potes).

Day 2: Day-trip to the Cares Gorge hike via Caín (sleep in Potes).

Day 3: Move on to your next destination.

Getting Around the Picos de Europa

The Picos de Europa are best with a car. If you don't have wheels, skip it, because bus connections are sparse, time-consuming, and frustrating (see "Getting Around Cantabria" on page 322).

The A-8 expressway squeezes between the Picos and the north coast of Spain; roads branch into and around the Picos, but beware: Many of them traverse high-mountain passes—often on bad roads—and can take longer to drive through than you expect. *Puerto* means "pass" (slow going) and *desfiladero* means "gorge" (quicker but often still twisty).

Assuming you're most interested in Potes and Fuente Dé, you'll focus on the east part of the park, approaching from the A-8 expressway (or from Santillana del Mar and Comillas). You'll go through Unquera and catch N-621 into the park (follow signs for

Potes). Wind your way through La Hermida Gorge (Desfiladero de la Hermida) en route to Potes.

The Cares Gorge can be approached from either the south (the village of Caín, deep in the mountains beyond Potes) or the north (Puente Poncebos, with easier access).

Sights in the Picos de Europa

I've arranged these sights as you'll come to them if you approach from the northeast (that is, from the expressway, Santillana del Mar, or Comillas).

Potes—This quaint mountain village, at the intersection of four valleys, is the hub of Cantabria's Picos de Europa tourist facilities. It's got an impressive old convent and a picturesque stone bridge spanning the Río Deva. It's a good place to buy maps and books. Check in at the **TI** with any travel questions (unpredictable hours, but generally July-Sept daily 10:00-14:00 & 16:00-19:00; less off-season—often closed Sun and Mon afternoons and all day Tue; Plaza de las Serna, tel. 942-730-787).

Sleeping in Potes: **$ Casa Cayo** has 17 cozy rooms and a fine restaurant that overlooks the river (Sb-€40, Db-€50, Tb-€65, tax included but breakfast extra, closed Christmas-Feb, Calle Cántabra 6, tel. 942-730-150, fax 942-730-119, www.casacayo.com, informacion@casacayo.com).

▲▲Fuente Dé Cable Car (Teleférico Fuente Dé)—Perhaps the single most thrilling activity in Picos de Europa is to take the cable car at Fuente Dé. The longest single-span cable car in Europe zips you up 2,600 feet in just four ear-popping minutes (but in summer you may have to wait more than two hours to take it). Once at the top (altitude 6,000 feet) you're rewarded with a breathtaking panorama of the Picos de Europa. The huge, pointy  Matterhorn-like peak on your right is Peña Remoña (7,350 feet). The cable-car station on top has WCs, a cafeteria (commanding views, miserable food), and a gift shop (limited hiking guides—equip yourself before you ascend).

Once you're up there, those with enough time and strong knees should consider hiking back down. From the cable-car station at the top, follow the yellow-and-white signs to *Espinama*, always bearing to the right. You'll hike gradually uphill (gain about 300 feet), then down (3,500 feet) the back side of the mountain, with totally different views than the cable-car ride up: green, rolling hills instead of sharp, white peaks. Once in Espinama, you'll continue down along the main road back to the parking lot at the base of the cable car (signs to *Fuente Dé*). Figure about four hours total (nine miles) at a brisk pace from the top back to the bottom. Note that the trails are covered by snow into April and sometimes even May; ask at the ranger station near Potes about conditions before you hike (see "Information," below).

Cost and Hours: €15.50 round-trip, €9.20 one-way (if you're hiking down), every 30 minutes (or with demand), in summer Mon-Fri 10:00-18:00, Sat-Sun 9:00-20:00, in winter daily 10:00-18:00, closed Jan unless weather is unseasonably good. When it's busy, there are constant departures. Note that this is a very popular destination in summer, and you may have to wait in long lines both to ascend and to descend (up to 2.5 hours in early Aug, 1 hour in late July; quieter in June, early July, and Sept—if you're concerned, call ahead to find out how long the wait is before you make the 14-mile drive from Potes).

Information: Cable car tel. 942-736-610. The Picos de Europa National Park runs a helpful information kiosk in the parking lot during peak season (July-Aug), with handouts and advice on hikes (including the one described above). Even better, stop at the bigger National Park office on the way to Fuente Dé from Potes; about a mile after you leave Potes, look on the right for the green *Picos de Europa* signs (daily in summer 9:00-20:00, in winter 9:00-18:00, tel. 942-730-555).

Getting There: By car, the road dead-ends at Fuente Dé (to return to Potes, you'll have to backtrack). If you're relying on public transportation, you can take the bus from Potes to Fuente Dé (2/day)—but it runs only in summer.

▲**Cares Gorge (Garganta del Cares)**—This impressive gorge hike—surrounded on both sides by sheer cliff walls, with a long-distance drop running parallel to (and sometimes under) the trail—is ideal for hardy hikers. The trail was built in the 1940s to maintain the hydroelectric canal that runs through the mountains, but today it has become a very popular summer-hiking destination. The trail follows the Río Cares seven miles between the towns of Caín (in the south) and Camarmeña (near Puente Poncebos, in the north). Along the way you'll cross harrowing bridges and take trails burrowed into the rock face. Because it's deeper in the mountains and requires a good six hours (13 miles round-trip, with some ups and downs), it's best left to those who are really up for a hike and not simply passing through the Picos. Visitors who just want a glimpse will hike only partway in before heading back.

Getting There: To reach Caín from Potes, you'll drive on rough, twisty roads (N-621) over the stunning Puerto de San Gloria pass (5,250 feet, watched over by a sweet bronze deer), into

CANTABRIA

a green, moss-covered gorge. Just past the village of Portilla de la Reina, turn right (following signs for *Santa Marina de Valdeón*) to reach Caín. Note that this is a very long day trip from Potes, and almost brutal if home-basing in Comillas or Santillana del Mar.

The approach to the gorge from the north (Puente Poncebos) is easier, but won't take you near Potes and Fuente Dé. You can reach Puente Poncebos via AS-114 to Las Arenas, then follow the Cares River on AS-264 to Puente Poncebos.

SALAMANCA

This sunny sandstone city boasts Spain's grandest plaza, its oldest university, and a fascinating history, all swaddled in a strolling, college-town ambience. Salamanca—a youthful and untouristy Toledo—is a series of monuments and clusters of cloisters. The many students help keep prices down. Take a paseo with the local crowd down Calle de Rúa Mayor and through Plaza Mayor. The young people congregate until late in the night, chanting and cheering, talking and singing. When I asked a local woman why young men all alone on Plaza Mayor suddenly break into song, she said, "Doesn't it happen where you live?"

Planning Your Time

Salamanca, with its art, university, and atmospheric Plaza Mayor, is

worth a day and a night, but it is stuck out in the boonies. It's feasible as a side-trip from Madrid (it's 2.5 hours one-way from Madrid by car, bus, or train), even with a stop in Ávila on the way. If you're bound for Santiago de Compostela or Portugal, Salamanca is a natural stop.

Orientation to Salamanca

Tourist Information

The main TI is on **Plaza Mayor** (summer: Mon-Fri 9:00-14:00 & 16:30-20:00, Sat 10:00-20:00, Sun 10:00-14:00; winter: Mon-Sat until 18:30, Sun until 14:00; Plaza Mayor 19, tel. 923-218-342). Pick up the free map, city brochure, and current list of museum hours.

Another TI at **Casa de Las Conchas** on Calle de Rúa Mayor serves the region and province, as well as the city (July-mid-Sept daily 9:00-20:00; mid-Sept-June Mon-Sat 9:30-14:00 & 16:00-19:00, Sun 9:30-17:00; tel. 923-268-571). Summertime-only TIs spring up at the train and bus stations.

The TI website (www.salamanca.es) is a good source of practical information, including a printable city-center map *(Plano de la ciudad)*, a downloadable city guide, and directions on how to arrive from various points in Spain. Both TIs rent decent MP3 audioguides of the city (€12/24 hours, €50 deposit, includes map). Other than that, unfortunately, Salamanca offers relatively little in the way of organized tourism for the English-speaking visitor.

Arrival in Salamanca

From either Salamanca's train or bus station to Plaza Mayor, it's a 25-minute walk, an easy bus ride (€1, pay driver), or a €7 taxi trip. The train station has no lockers; day-trippers can store bags at the bus station *(consignas;* €2, at bay level facing main building on your left).

By Train: Salamanca has two train stations: the main train station and (a bit closer to the town center) Salamanca Alamedilla Station. To walk from the main train station into the center, exit left and walk down to the ring road, cross it at Plaza de España, then angle slightly left up Calle Azafranal. Alternatively, from the main station you can take bus #1, which lets you off at Plaza del Mercado (the market), next to Plaza Mayor. Some trains continue on to Salamanca Alamedilla Station, which is closer to town: Walk down Avenida Alamedilla past a park to Plaza de España, then to Calle Azafranal. Note that you cannot depart from or buy tickets at Salamanca Alamedilla Station.

By Bus: To walk into the center, exit right and walk down Avenida Filiberto Villalobos; take a left on the ring road and the first right on Ramón y Cajal, head through Plaza de las Augustinas, and continue on Calle Prior to reach Plaza Mayor. Or take bus #4 (exit station right, catch bus on same side of the street as the station) to the city center; the closest stop is on Gran Vía, about two blocks east of Plaza Mayor (ask the driver or a fellow passenger, "*¿Para Plaza Mayor?*").

Salamanca

1 NH Puerta de la Catedral
2 Le Petit Hotel
3 Rest. La Fonda Casa de Comidas del Arcediano
4 Carrefour Market
5 To Calle Van Dyck Eateries
6 To Salamanca Alamedilla Train Station

By Car: Drivers will find a handy underground parking lot at Plaza Santa Eulalia (€12.10/day, open 24 hours daily). Two other convenient lots are Parking Plaza del Campillo and Parking Lemans (€14/day). You can also try one of the hotels with valet parking for comparable fees.

Helpful Hints

Book Ahead for September: During this month, Salamanca's Feria, patron saint celebration, and bullfighting events fill up

SALAMANCA

hotels and increase room prices.

Internet Access: Navega Internet Center has several computers and a call center; it also sells phone cards (Mon-Sat 11:00-24:00, Sun 16:00-23:00, between Plaza del Mercado and Gran Vía at Obispo Jarrín 14, tel. 923-215-447).

Travel Agency: Viajes Salamanca books flights, trains, and some buses, including buses to Coimbra, Portugal (Plaza Mayor 24, tel. 923-211-414).

Local Guide: Ines Criado Velasco, a good English-speaking guide, is happy to tailor a town walk to your interests (€80/2 hours—a special rate for readers of this book in 2012, €95/3-5 hours, €150/day for groups of 1-30, mobile 609-557-528, ines-scriado@yahoo.es).

Tourist Tram: The small tram you might see waiting at the New Cathedral does 20-minute loops through town with Spanish narration (€4, daily 10:00-14:00 & 16:00-20:00, departs every 30 minutes from cathedral, mobile 649-625-703).

Sights in Salamanca

▲▲**Plaza Mayor**—Built from 1729 to 1755, this ultimate Spanish plaza is a good place to nurse a cup of coffee (try the venerable Art

Nouveau–style Café Novelty) and watch the world go by.

The town hall, with the clock, grandly overlooks the square. The Arco del Toro (built into the eastern wall) leads to the covered market. While most European squares honor a king or saint, this golden-toned square—ringed by famous Castilians—is for all the people. The square niches above the colonnade surrounding the plaza depict writers (Miguel de Cervantes), heroes and conquistadors (Christopher Columbus and Hernán Cortés), as well as numerous kings and dictators (Francisco Franco).

Plaza Mayor has long been Salamanca's community living room. The most important place in town, it seems to be continually hosting some kind of party. Imagine the excitement of the days (until 1893) when bullfights were held in the square. Now old-timers gather here each day, remembering an earlier time when the girls would promenade clockwise around the colonnade while the boys cruised counterclockwise, looking for the perfect *queso* (cheese), as they'd call a cute dish. Perhaps the best time of all for people-watching is Sunday after Mass (13:00-15:00), when the grandmothers gather here in their Sunday best.

▲▲**Cathedrals, Old and New**—These cool-on-a-hot-day cathedrals share buttresses, and both are richly ornamented. The Old

Cathedral is 12th-century Romanesque while the "New" Cathedral, built from 1513 to 1733, is a spacious, towering mix of Gothic, Renaissance, and Baroque.

Cost and Hours: New Cathedral—free, daily April-Sept 9:00-20:00, sometimes closed 14:00-16:00, Oct-March 9:00-13:00 & 16:00-18:00; Old Cathedral—€4.75, free entry if you attend Mass (though you'll still have to pay to enter the cloister), daily April-Sept 10:00-19:30, sometimes closed 13:30-16:00, Oct-March 10:00-12:30 & 16:00-17:30; tower—€3.75

but free Tue 10:00-12:00, open daily 10:00-20:00, Jan-Feb until 18:00, last entry 45 minutes before closing. Tel. 923-217-476, www.catedralsalamanca.org.

❷ Self-Guided Tour: To get to the old, you have to walk through the new.

New Cathedral: Before entering the New Cathedral, check out its ornate front door (west portal on Rúa Mayor). The **facade** is decorated Plateresque, with masonry so intricate it looks like silverwork *(plata)*. It's Spain's version of Flamboyant Gothic. At the side door (around the corner to the left as you face the main entrance), look for the astronaut added by a capricious restorer in 1993. This caused an outrage in town, but now locals shrug their shoulders and say, "He's the person closest to God." I'll give you a chance to find him on your own. Otherwise, look at the end of this listing for help.

Inside, fancy stone trim is everywhere, and the dome decoration is particularly wonderful. Occasionally the music is live, not recorded. The *coro,* or choir, blocks up half of the church (normal for Spanish Gothic), but its wood carving is sumptuous; look up to see the recently restored, elaborate organ.

• *Head into the Old Cathedral (the entrance is near the rear of the New Cathedral). A free English leaflet is available.*

Old Cathedral: Sit in a front pew to study the altarpiece's 53 scenes from the lives of Mary and Jesus (by the Italian Florentino, 1445) surrounding a precious 12th-century statue of the Virgin of the Valley. High above, notice the dramatic Last Judgment fresco of Jesus sending condemned souls into the literal jaws of hell.

Enter the **cloister** (off the right transept) and explore the chapels, notable for their unusual tombs, ornate altarpieces, and ceilings with leering faces. If you speak Spanish, press the button on the wall at the entrance of each chapel to hear a description. In the Capilla de Santa Barbara (second on the left as you enter), you can sit like students did for their tests. During these final exams, a stern circle of professors formed around the student at the tomb of the Salamanca bishop, who founded the University of Salamanca around 1230. (The university originated with a group of teacher-priests who met in this room.)

As you continue through the cloister, you'll see the chapter-house *(salas capitulares)*, contained in three rooms on your left, with a gallery of 15th-century Castilian paintings. Next is the Capilla de Santa Catalina, with two rows of spooky saint statues and two original gargoyles from the cathedral, in the form of a seahorse and a frog. The Capilla de Anaya, farthest from the cloister entrance, has a gorgeously carved 16th-century alabaster tomb (with the dog and lion at its foot making peace—or negotiating who gets to eat the worried-looking rabbit) and a wooden 16th-century Mudejar organ. (Mudejar is the Romanesque-Islamic Moorish design style made in Spain after the Christian conquest.)

Tower: For a fantastic view of the upper floors and terraces of both cathedrals, and a look at the inside passages with small exhibits about the cathedrals' history and architecture, visit the tower (marked *Jerónimos*). It was sealed after Lisbon's 1755 earthquake to create structural support and reopened in 2002. You may be able to reach the tower from inside the Old Cathedral (this entrance is open sporadically); if not, exit the cathedral to the left to find a separate entrance around the corner.

Finally, go find that astronaut: He's just a little guy, about the size of a Ken-does-Mars doll, entwined in the stone trim to the left of the door, roughly 10 feet up. If you like that, check out the dragon (an arm's length below). Historians debate whether he's eating an ice-cream cone or singing karaoke.

▲▲**University**—The University of Salamanca, the oldest in Spain (est. 1230), was one of Europe's leading centers of learning for 400 years. Columbus came here for travel tips. Today, though no longer so prestigious, it's laden with history and popular with Americans, who enjoy its excellent summer program. The old lecture halls around the cloister, where many of Spain's Golden Age heroes studied, are open to the public.

Cost and Hours: Lecture halls—€4, free Mon mornings, open Mon-Fri 9:30-13:30 & 16:00-19:30, Sat until 19:00, Sun 10:00-13:30, last entry 30 minutes before closing; museum—free, Tue-Sat 9:30-13:30 & 16:00-18:30, Sun 10:00-14:00, closed Mon, no photos allowed. Enter university from Calle Libreros, tel. 923-294-400, ext. 1150.

● **Self-Guided Tour:** The ornately decorated grand **entrance** of the university is a great example of Spain's Plateresque style. During your visit, the university may be restoring and cleaning the facade. But even if the entryway is covered by scaffolding, you'll probably see a tarp with a printed image of the original covering the work. The people studying the facade aren't art fans. They're trying to find a tiny frog on a skull that students looked to for good luck.

But forget the frog. Follow the **facade**'s symbolic meaning. It was made in three sections by Charles V. The bottom celebrates the Catholic Monarchs. Ferdinand and Isabel saw that the university had no buildings befitting its prestige, and they granted the money for this building. The Greek script says something like, "From the monarchs, this university. From the university, this tribute as a thanks."

The immodest middle section celebrates the grandson of Ferdinand and Isabel, Charles V. He appears with his queen, as well as the Habsburg double-headed eagle and the complex coat of arms of the mighty Habsburg Empire. Since this is a Renaissance structure, it features Greek and Roman figures in the shells. And, as a statement of educational independence from medieval Church control, the top shows the pope flanked by Hercules and Venus.

• *Pay the admission fee to enter the university's old lecture halls. Pick up a free English-language leaflet, and follow it by going left (clockwise) around the courtyard.*

In the **Hall of Fray Luis de León,** the narrow wooden-beam tables and benches—whittled down by centuries of studious doodling—are originals. Professors spoke from the Church-threatening *cátedra* (pulpit). It was here that freethinking brother Luis de León returned, after the Inquisition jailed and tortured him for five years; he had challenged the Church's control of the word of God by translating part of the Bible into Castilian. He started his first post-imprisonment lecture with, "As we were saying..." Such courageous men of truth believed the forces of the Inquisition were not even worth acknowledging.

The altarpiece in the **chapel** on the opposite side of the courtyard depicts professors swearing to Mary's virginity. (How did they know?) Climb upstairs for a peek into the oldest **library** in Spain. Outside the library, look into the courtyard at the American sequoia, brought here 150 years ago and standing all alone. Notice also the big nests in the bell tower. Storks stop here from February through August on their annual journey from Morocco to northern Europe. There are hundreds of these stork nests in Salamanca.

As you leave the university, you'll see the statue of Fray Luis de León. Behind him, to your left, is the entrance to a peaceful courtyard. Within the courtyard is the **Museum of the University,** notable for Gallego's fanciful 15th-century *Sky of Salamanca.*

Can't forget about the frog? It's on the right pillar of the facade, nearly halfway up, on the leftmost of three skulls.

▲Art Nouveau Museum (Museo Art Nouveau y Art Deco)— Located in the Casa Lis, this museum—with its beautifully displayed collection of stained glass, vases, furniture, jewelry, cancan statuettes, and toy dolls—is a refreshing change of pace. Nowhere else in Spain will you enjoy an Art Nouveau collection in a building from the same era. Find the stunning sculptures of Josephine Baker and Carmen Miranda, along with lots of pieces by René Lalique. The museum is a donation of a private collection. The English brochure contains a translation of the Spanish text posted in each room of the collection. After your visit, sit with a reasonably priced coffee and contemplate the stained-glass facade from the interior of the museum's beautiful Art Nouveau café.

Cost and Hours: €4; April-mid-Oct Tue-Fri 11:00-14:00 & 17:00-21:00, Sat-Sun 11:00-21:00; mid-Oct-March Tue-Fri 11:00-14:00 & 16:00-19:00, Sat-Sun 11:00-20:00; closed Mon year-round; strictly no photos—required camera check at ticket counter, between the cathedrals and the river at Calle Expolio 14—the name of this street was recently changed from "Calle Gibraltar," tel. 923-121-425, www.museocasalis.org.

Church of San Esteban—Dedicated to St. Stephen (Esteban) the martyr, this complex contains a recently restored cloister, tombs, museum, sacristy, and church.

Cost and Hours: €3, Mon-Sat 10:00-14:00 & 16:00-20:00, until 19:00 in winter, Sun 10:00-14:00, museum closed Sun-Tue, last entry 45 minutes before closing, tel. 923-215-000.

◑ Self-Guided Tour: The visitors' entrance is to the right of the church entrance, which is closed except during services.

Before you enter, notice the Plateresque **facade** and its bas-relief of the stoning of St. Stephen. The crucifixion above is by Italian Renaissance artist Benvenuto Cellini. As you enter the building, look at the large poster explaining the facade's many characters.

After buying your ticket, walk around the cloister to the opposite corner, where signs indicate ways to the church *(iglesia),* sacristy *(sacristía),* choir *(coro),* and museum *(museo).* Head to the church first. Once inside, follow the free English pamphlet.

The nave is overwhelmed by a 100-foot, 4,000-piece wood **altarpiece** by José Benito Churriguera (1665-1725) that replaced the original Gothic one in 1693. You'll see St. Dominic on the left, St. Francis on the right, and a grand monstrance holding the Communion wafers in the middle, all below a painting of

St. Stephen being stoned. This is a textbook example of the intricately detailed Churrigueresque style that influenced many South American mission buildings. Quietly ponder the dusty, gold-plated cottage cheese, as tourists shake their heads and say "too much" in their mother tongue.

Upstairs, step into the balcony **choir loft** for a fine overview of the nave. The staircase itself is architecturally unique, built without any interior support; the staircase is still standing, but you'll notice that when you walk, you definitely lean inward. The big spinnable book holder in the middle of the room held giant music books—large enough for all to chant from in an age when there weren't enough books for everyone.

The **museum** next door has temperature-controlled glass cases that preserve illustrated 14th- to 16th-century Bibles and choir books. Notice also how the curved ivory Filipino saints all look like they're carved out of an elephant's tusk. And don't miss the fascinating "chocolate box reliquaries" on the wall from 1580. Survey whose bones are collected between all the inlaid ivory and precious woods.

Convento de las Dueñas—Located next door to the Church of San Esteban, the much simpler *convento* is a joy. It consists of a double-decker cloister with a small museum of religious art. Check out the stone meanies exuberantly decorating the capitals on the cloister's upper deck. No English information is displayed, but an English booklet is available for €1.50. The nuns sell sweets daily except Sunday (€4.50 for a small box of their specialty, *amarguillos*—almonds, egg whites, and sugar; no assortments possible even though their display box raises hopes).

Cost and Hours: €2, variable hours but generally Mon-Sat in summer 10:30-12:45 & 16:30-19:30, in winter 11:00-12:45 & 16:30-17:30, closed Sun year-round.

Roman Bridge—Historians enjoy the low-slung Roman Bridge (Puente Romano), much of it original, spanning the Río Tormes. The *ibérico* (ancient pre-Roman) faceless bull blindly guards the entrance to the bridge; you'll find this symbol of Salamanca on every city coat of arms in town.

▲**Tuna Music**—Traditionally, Salamanca's poorer students earned money to fund their education by singing in the streets. This 15th- to 18th-century tradition survives today, as musical groups of students (representing the various faculties)—dressed in the traditional black capes and leggings—sing and strum mandolins and guitars. They serenade the public in the bars on and around Plaza Mayor. The name *tuna*, which has nothing to do with fish, refers to a vagabond student lifestyle and later was applied to the music these students sing. They're out only on summer weeknights (singing for tips from 22:00 until after midnight), because they make more serious money performing for weddings on weekends.

Sleeping in Salamanca

Salamanca, a student town, has plenty of good eating and sleeping values. Most of my listings are on or within a three-minute walk of Plaza Mayor (NH Puerta de la Catedral and Le Petit Hotel are a little farther—for locations, see map on page 337). Directions are given from Plaza Mayor, assuming you are facing the building with the clock (e.g., 3 o'clock is 90 degrees to your right as you face the clock). The city is noisy on the weekends, so if you're a light sleeper, ask for an interior room.

$$$ NH Puerta de la Catedral is a fancy business-class hotel on a quiet pedestrian street around the corner from the cathedral entrance. It's worth the extra euros for a room with a great view of the cathedral (Db-€90, extra bed-€45, €20 more for view/terrace rooms, higher rates on weekends and holidays, breakfast-€14.50, air-con, elevator, free Wi-Fi in lobby, parking-€17/day, Plaza de Juan XXII 5, tel. 923-280-829, fax 923-265-992, www.nh-hotels.com, nhpuertadelacatedral@nh-hotels.com).

$$$ Hotel Torre del Clavero has little character, but its 26 rooms are clean and contemporary. It's conveniently located

Sleep Code

(€1 = about $1.40, country code: 34)
S = Single, **D** = Double/Twin, **T** = Triple, **Q** = Quad, **b** = bathroom, **s** = shower only. Unless otherwise noted, credit cards are accepted, English is spoken, and the IVA hotel tax and breakfast are not included.

To help you easily sort through these listings, I've divided the accommodations into three categories, based on the price for a standard double room with bath during high season:

$$$ Higher Priced—Most rooms €70 or more.
  $$ Moderately Priced—Most rooms between €45-70.
    $ Lower Priced—Most rooms €45 or less.

Prices can change without notice; verify the hotel's current rates online or by email. For other updates, see www.ricksteves.com/update.

SALAMANCA

Central Salamanca

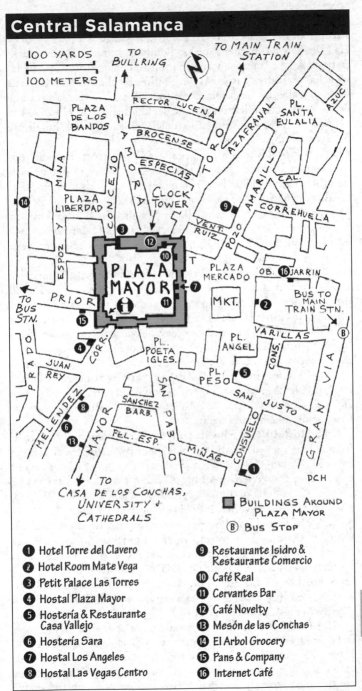

100 YARDS
100 METERS

TO BULLRING
TO MAIN TRAIN STATION

PLAZA DE LOS BANDOS

RECTOR LUCENA

BROCENSE

ESPECIAS

PL. SANTA EULALIA

AZUC

AZAFRANAL

AMARILLO

CAL.

CLOCK TOWER

CORREHUELA

PLAZA LIBERTAD

MINA

ESPOZ Y MINA

VENT. RUIZ

PLAZA MAYOR

PLAZA MERCADO

MKT.

OB. JARRIN

BUS TO MAIN TRAIN STN.

PRIOR

TO BUS STN.

PL. POETA IGLES.

PL. ANGEL

PL. PESO

VARILLAS

CONS.

GRAN VIA

JUAN REY

CORR.

SANCHEZ BARB.

SAN PABLO

SAN JUSTO

PRADO

MELENDEZ

MAYOR

FEL. ESP.

MIÑAG.

CONSUELO

DCH

TO CASA DE LOS CONCHAS, UNIVERSITY & CATHEDRALS

BUILDINGS AROUND PLAZA MAYOR
Ⓑ BUS STOP

❶ Hotel Torre del Clavero
❷ Hotel Room Mate Vega
❸ Petit Palace Las Torres
❹ Hostal Plaza Mayor
❺ Hostería & Restaurante Casa Vallejo
❻ Hostería Sara
❼ Hostal Los Angeles
❽ Hostal Las Vegas Centro

❾ Restaurante Isidro & Restaurante Comercio
❿ Café Real
⓫ Cervantes Bar
⓬ Café Novelty
⓭ Mesón de las Conchas
⓮ El Arbol Grocery
⓯ Pans & Company
⓰ Internet Café

between Plaza Mayor and the Church of San Esteban, across the street from the Clavero tower. Its private garage is a plus for drivers (Db-€50-84, higher rates on holidays, extra bed-€25, breakfast-€3.50, free Internet access, parking-€11/day; from Casa de las Conchas on Calle de Rúa Mayor, go three blocks south on Calle de Jesús to Calle del Consuelo 21, or from Gran Vía turn onto Calle de las Varillas then left onto Calle del Consuelo; tel. 923-280-410, fax 923-217-708, www.hoteltorredelclavero.com, info@hoteltorre delclavero.com).

$$$ Hotel Room Mate Vega, across the street from the covered market, has wannabe-hip business-class rooms in a good location (Sb-€65, Db-€80, Tb-€110, more on weekends and holidays, breakfast-€6, air-con, elevator, free Internet access and Wi-Fi, parking-€9/day; 2 blocks off Plaza Mayor, across from covered market, exit Plaza Mayor at 3 o'clock, Plaza del Mercado 16; tel. 923-272-250, fax 923-270-932, www.room-matehotels.com, vega @room-matehotels.com).

$$$ Petit Palace Las Torres is a chain hotel with 53 modern, spacious rooms (several with see-through bathroom doors) and all the amenities. It's nothing special...except that it's located right on Plaza Mayor (Sb-€60-150, Db-€60-170, Tb-€90-220, lower prices are for non-view rooms and weekdays, higher prices are for Plaza Mayor views and weekends, 30 percent more during religious festival in Sept, breakfast-€9, air-con, elevator, free Internet access and Wi-Fi, a few free loaner bikes, pay parking at nearby Lemans lot, exit Plaza Mayor at 11 o'clock to find hotel entry just off square at Calle Concejo 4, tel. 923-212-100, fax 923-212-101, www.ht hotels.com, tor@hthotels.com).

$$ Hostal Plaza Mayor, with 19 nicely decorated but small rooms, has a good location a block southwest of Plaza Mayor (Sb-€30-36, Db-€50-60, Tb-€75-90, air-con, most rooms served by elevator, free Wi-Fi, parking-€12/day, exit Plaza Mayor at 7 o'clock, Plaza del Corrillo 20, tel. 923-262-020, fax 923-217-548, www.hostalplazamayor.es, info@hostalplazamayor.es).

$$ Hostería Casa Vallejo is a welcoming, family-run place, with 12 rustic and renovated rooms a block away from Plaza Mayor. The attached, recommended tapas bar/restaurant serves up tasty deals (Sb-€30-38, Db-€45-80, 3rd or 4th person-€12 each, breakfast-€3, air-con, elevator, San Juan de la Cruz 3, tel. 923-280-421, fax 923-213-112, www.hosteriacasavallejo.com, info @hosteriacasavallejo.com, Amparo).

$$ Le Petit Hotel, while away from the characteristic core, faces a peaceful park and a church, two blocks east of Gran Vía. It rents 23 spotless and homey yet modern rooms. The rooms with views of the church are brightest, and the fourth-floor rooms are the most recently updated—request *vista de iglesia* and *cuarta* *planta* (Sb-€36, Db-€49, Tb-€59, Qb-€69, breakfast-€4, cash only, air-con, elevator, desk staffed but phone not answered after 22:30, about six blocks east of Plaza Mayor at Ronda Sancti Spiritus 39; exit Plaza Mayor at 3 o'clock and continue east, turn left on Gran Vía, right on Sancti Spiritus at Banco Simeon, and left after the church; tel. & fax 923-600-773, www.lepetithotel.net, reserve by simply calling and leaving your name and time of arrival no more than 15 days in advance, Hortensia doesn't speak English).

$$ Hostería Sara offers tidy rooms with simple decor and handy kitchenettes. Ask for the upper floors for quieter rooms with double-paned windows (Sb-€48-53, Db-€53-58, Tb-€70-78; higher rates are for rooms with kitchenettes that have a fridge, two burners, and a sink; rates drop about €10 off-season, air-con, elevator, free Wi-Fi; 2 blocks off Plaza Mayor, exit the square at about 7 o'clock, toward cathedral at Meléndez 11; tel. 923-281-140, fax 923-281-142, www.hostalsara.org, info@hostalsara.org).

$ Hostal Los Angeles rents 15 simple but cared-for rooms, four of which overlook the square. Stand on the balcony and inhale the essence of Spain. View rooms are popular and more expensive—when you reserve, request *"Con vista, por favor"* (S-€15-30, Sb-€25-40, D-€30-38, Db-€35-55, T-€65, Tb-€75, Q-€85, rates drop on weekdays and off-season, includes tax, breakfast on plaza-€5, Plaza Mayor 10, about 3 o'clock, tel. & fax 923-218-166, www.pensionlosangeles.com, info@pensionlosangeles.com, Orlando).

$ Hostal Las Vegas Centro is clean, bright, quiet, and cheap, with 17 cozy rooms (Sb-€24, Db-€36-45, Tb-€50-60, Qb-€70-80, higher rates are for weekends, first night charged when you reserve, 48-hour notice required for refund; 2 blocks off Plaza Mayor, exit the square at about 7 o'clock, toward cathedral at Meléndez 13, first floor; tel. & fax 923-218-749, www.lasvegascentro.net, reservas @lasvegascentro.es).

Eating in Salamanca

Local specialties include *serrano* ham, which is in just about everything (see sidebar, next page), roast suckling pig (called *tostón* around here), and *sopa de ajo*, the local garlic soup. *Patatas meneadas* (potatoes with Spanish paprika and bacon) is a simple but tasty local tapa. If you always wanted seconds at Communion, buy a bag of the local specialty called *obleas*—flat wafers similar to giant Communion hosts.

Plenty of good, inexpensive restaurants are located between Plaza Mayor and Gran Vía, and as you leave Plaza Mayor toward Calle de Rúa Mayor. You'll also find lots of tapas places along and around Calle de Rúa Mayor, but they are often overrun with students. Restaurants generally serve lunch from 13:30 to 16:00 and

Sampling *Serrano* Ham

Jamón serrano is cured in the *sierras* (mountains) of Spain. Though there are many variations of this cured ham from different regions of Spain, Spanish people have a special appreciation for *jamón ibérico,* made with the back legs of black pigs fed mainly on acorns. Originating in Spain, these black pigs are fatter and happier (slaughtered much later than regular pigs). Spaniards treasure memories of Grandpa thinly carving a *jamón,* supported in a *jamonero* (ham-holder), during Christmas, just as we savor the turkey-carving at Thanksgiving. To sample this delicacy without the high price tag you'll find in bars and restaurants, go to the local market, ask for 100 grams (*cien gramos de jamón ibérico extra;* about €70/kilo, so your portion will run about €7), and enjoy it as a picnic with red wine and bread.

dinner from about 20:30 until very late (remember, Spaniards don't start dinner until about 21:00). Tapas bars and cafés may be open all day, though they serve simpler food off hours.

Drinks ordered at a bar usually come with a free *pincho,* a taste of one of the larger portions of tapas. Sometimes you can even choose between several options. For the price of three drinks, you can make a light meal of *pinchos* while standing or sitting at the bar. Try the recommended Cervantes Bar or one of the places outside the old town.

Sit-Down Meals

Restaurante Casa Vallejo is known for its grilled meats, traditional dishes, and good wine. You'll spend about €35-40 for a satisfying meal (Tue-Sat 13:30-16:00 & 20:30-23:00, Sun 13:30-16:00, closed Mon, restaurant is inside the recommended Hostería Casa Vallejo at San Juan de la Cruz 3, tel. 923-280-421).

La Fonda Casa de Comidas del Arcediano is a dark, woody place with solid, traditional cuisine that caters to longtime residents. You'll happily spend about €30 for dinner (daily 13:30-16:00 & 21:00-24:00, reserve on weekends, 15 yards down the arcade from corner of Gran Vía and Cuesta de Sancti Spiritus at La Reja 2—see map on page 337, tel. 923-215-712).

Restaurante Isidro is a thriving Salamancan (and guidebook) favorite—a straightforward, hardworking eatery where Alberto offers a good assortment of fish and specialty meat dishes with quick and friendly service. Alberto also runs **Restaurante Comercio,** next door, where similar-quality food is served in a more contemporary setting (€11 fixed-price meal, €25 à la carte dinners, big portions, good roasts, Tue-Sat 13:00-16:00 & 20:00-24:00, Sun 13:00-16:00, closed Mon, Pozo Amarillo 19, about a block north of covered market near Plaza Mayor, tel. 923-262-848).

Casual Eateries on Plaza Mayor and Rúa Mayor

Here you can enjoy a meal sitting on the finest square in Spain and savor some of Europe's best people-watching. The bars, with little tables spilling onto the square, serve *raciones* and €2 glasses of wine. A *ración de la casa* (house specialty of hams, sausages, and cheese), a *ración* of *patatas bravas* (chunks of potatoes with a slightly spicy tomato sauce), and two glasses of wine make up a nice dinner for two for about €25—one of the best eating values in all of Europe. For dessert, stroll with an ice-cream cone from Café Novelty.

Café Real serves tapas-style bar snacks (daily 8:00-24:00, tel. 923-210-556).

Cervantes Bar is more of a restaurant, with a wide selection of meals, €10 salads, and sandwiches. They also have an indoor section with tables that overlook Plaza Mayor from one floor up; it's a popular student hangout. Don't forget to ask for your *pincho*, a snack that comes with your drink, if you're standing at the bar (daily 10:00-24:00, tel. 923-217-213).

Café Novelty is Plaza Mayor's Art Nouveau café. It dates from 1905—and has some customers who look like they've been there since it opened. It's filled with character and literary memories. The metal sculpture depicts a famous local writer, Torrente Ballester. Their ice cream sweetens a stroll around the plaza (daily 8:00-24:00, tel. 923-214-956).

Mesón de las Conchas, on the main pedestrian drag to the cathedral, attracts a mix of locals and tourists. They offer tapas and meals—but, as is common here, they bump up tapa prices for outdoor seating (daily, bar 8:00-24:00, restaurant 12:30-16:00 & 20:00-24:00, Calle de Rúa Mayor 16, tel. 923-212-167).

Picnic Food

The covered *mercado* (market) on Plaza Mercado has fresh fruits and veggies (Mon-Sat 8:00-14:30, closed Sun, on east side of Plaza Mayor).

Supermarkets: A small El Arbol grocery, two blocks west of Plaza Mayor at Iscar Peyra 13, has just the basics (Mon-Sat 9:30-21:30, closed Sun). For variety, the big Carrefour Market supermarket is your best bet, but it's a six-block walk north of Plaza

Mayor on Calle del Toro (Mon-Sat 9:30-21:30, closed Sun, across from Plaza San Juan de Sahagún and its church).

Sandwiches: The **Pans & Company** sandwich chain is always fast and affordable, with a branch on Calle Prior across from Burger King (daily 10:30-24:00).

Off the Beaten Path

Locals and students head just a bit outside the old town to hit the tapa/*pincho* scene along a main artery called Calle Van Dyck. It's about a 20-minute walk or a short taxi ride from the edge of the old town, but it's worth the effort as there are several cheap and tasty options. You'll spend, on average, €2.50 for a *caña* (small beer), which comes with a small tapa. To get there on foot, go to the end of Calle del Toro, cross the main drag (Avenida de Mirat), and go up Calle Maria Auxiliadora; after crossing the wide Avenida de Portugal, take the third left onto Calle Van Dyck.

Start at the neighborhood classic, which has been around for more than 40 years—**Cafe Bar Chinitas** at #18—where Victorio, Manoli, and their son Javi serve up a delicious selection of 45 tapas (closed Mon, also closed Sun June-July and all of Aug, tel. 923-229-471). Or try the Galician seafood eatery **Casa Chicho,** farther down the street at #34 (closed Sun night and all day Mon-Tue, tel. 923-123-775). There are many other options on the streets around Van Dyck; try **Bahía de Salamanca** for Andalusian-style seafood, especially the *fritura variada* (fried fish mix) or the *boquerones rellenos* (stuffed anchovies; closed Wed, Avenida de Portugal 76).

Salamanca Connections

From Salamanca by Train to: Madrid (7/day, 2.5 hours, Chamartín Station), **Ávila** (6/day, 1 hour), **Barcelona** (8/day, 6-7.5 hours, change in Madrid from Chamartín Station to Atocha Station via Metro; 1 direct/day, 11.25 hours), **Santiago** (first take hourly bus for 1-hour ride to Zamora, then transfer to train—2/day, 5 hours to Santiago), **Burgos** (2-3/day, 2.5 hours), **Lisbon,** Portugal (1/day, 7 hours, departs Salamanca Station at about 4:30 in the morning, no kidding; catch a taxi to the train station, ask your hotel to arrange taxi in advance). Train info: toll tel. 902-320-320, www.renfe.com.

By Bus to: Madrid (hourly express, 2.5 hours, arrives at Madrid's Estación Sur de Autobuses, €22 one-way, www.avanzabus.com), **Segovia** (2-4/day, 3 hours; transfer in Labajos, could make a brief stop in Ávila en route, Auto-Res or La Sepulvedana buses, consider reserving a seat for the Salamanca–Labajos leg in advance), **Ávila** (Mon-Fri 4/day, Sat-Sun 2/day, 1.5 hours, Auto-Res buses), **Ciudad Rodrigo** (nearly hourly, 1 hour, El Pilar buses),

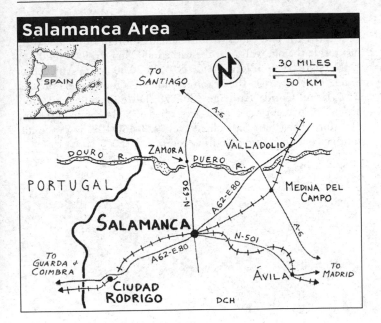

Salamanca Area

Santiago (2/day, 1 with a transfer in Vigo, 7 hours), **Barcelona** (4/day, 11 hours, Alsa buses), **Burgos** (2/day, 3-4 hours, Alsa buses), **Coimbra**, Portugal (1/day, departs at 12:30, 5 hours, one-way-€34, round-trip-€58; same bus continues to **Lisbon** in 8.25 hours, one-way-€44, round-trip-€76; Alsa buses, tel. 902-422-242, www.alsa .es). Bus info: tel. 923-236-717 or 902-020-052 (Auto-Res).

Ciudad Rodrigo

Ciudad Rodrigo is worth a visit only if you're driving from Salamanca to Coimbra, Portugal (although buses connect Salamanca and Ciudad Rodrigo with surprising efficiency in about an hour).

This rough-and-tumble old town of 16,000 people caps a hill overlooking the Río Agueda. Spend an hour wandering among the Renaissance mansions that line its streets and exploring its cathedral and Plaza Mayor. Have lunch or a snack at **El Sanatorio** (Plaza Mayor 14, tel. 923-460-024). The tapas are cheap, the crowd is local, and the walls are a Ciudad Rodrigo scrapbook, including some bullfighting that makes the Three Stooges look demure.

Ciudad Rodrigo's cathedral—pockmarked with scars from Napoleonic cannon balls—has some entertaining carvings in the choir and some pretty racy work in its cloisters. Who says, "When you've seen one Gothic church, you've seen 'em all"?

The **TI** is two blocks from Ciudad Rodrigo's Plaza Mayor, just inside the old wall near the cathedral (Mon-Fri 9:00-14:00 & 17:00-19:00, Sat-Sun 10:00-14:00 & 17:00-20:00, Plaza Ameyuelas 5, tel. 923-460-561). They can recommend a good hotel, such as **$$$ Hotel Conde Rodrigo** (Sb-€78, Db-€90, rates can drop almost 50 percent off-season, extra bed-€18, 34 rooms, air-con, elevator, Plaza San Salvador 9, tel. 923-461-408, www.conde rodrigo.com, info@conderodrigo.com).

MADRID

Today's Madrid is upbeat and vibrant. You'll feel it. Even the living-statue street performers have a twinkle in their eyes.

Madrid is the hub of Spain. This modern capital—Europe's highest, at more than 2,000 feet—has a population of 3.2 million, with about 6 million living in greater Madrid. Like its people, the city is relatively young. In 1561, when Spain ruled the world's most powerful empire, King Philip II decided to move his capital from Toledo to Madrid. One hundred years ago, Madrid had only 400,000 people—so the majority of today's city is modern sprawl surrounding an intact, easy-to-navigate historic core.

Madrid is working hard to make itself more livable—and more fun to visit. To support its bids to host the Olympics and World Cup, the city has undertaken some massive urban-improvement projects. New squares, pedestrian streets, beltway tunnels, parks, and Metro stations are popping up everywhere. You'll see how the investment is turning ramshackle zones into trendy ones. The macro-Metro station in Puerta del Sol, with a modern glass fish for a main entrance, accommodates a super-efficient commuter line that connects the city's two train stations and the main square. Newly installed posts are keeping cars off sidewalks, streets are safer after dark, and old buildings are being restored.

Tourists are the real winners. Dive headlong into the grandeur and intimate charm of Madrid. The lavish Royal Palace, with its gilded rooms and frescoed ceilings, rivals Versailles. The Prado has Europe's top collection of paintings. The city's huge Retiro Park invites you to take a shady siesta and hopscotch through a

MADRID

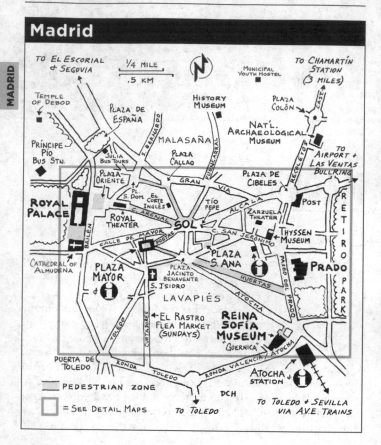

mosaic of lovers, families, skateboarders, pets walking their masters, and expert bench-sitters. Save time for Madrid's elegant shops and people-friendly pedestrian zones. On Sundays, cheer for the bull at a bullfight or bargain like mad at a mega-size flea market. Lively Madrid has enough street-singing, bar-hopping, and people-watching vitality to give any visitor a boost of youth.

Planning Your Time

Madrid is worth two days and three nights on even the fastest trip. Divide your time among the city's top three attractions: the Royal Palace (worth a half-day), the Prado Museum (also worth a half-day), and the bar-hopping contemporary scene. On a Sunday, consider allotting extra time for the flea market (year-round) and/or a bullfight (some Sundays March–mid-Oct; generally daily during San Isidro festival—mid-May–mid-June).

Here's how I'd spend my time:

Day 1: Take a brisk 20-minute good-morning-Madrid walk

from Puerta del Sol to the Prado (from Puerta del Sol, walk three blocks south to Plaza de Jacinto Benavente, left to Plaza del Ángel, then take the pedestrianized Calle de las Huertas). Spend the rest of the morning at the Prado, then take an afternoon siesta in Retiro Park, or tackle modern art at the Centro de Arte Reina Sofía (Picasso's *Guernica*) and/or the Thyssen-Bornemisza Museum. Ride bus #27 from the Prado out through Madrid's modern section for a dose of the non-touristy, no-nonsense big city. End your day with a tapas dinner around Plaza Santa Ana.

Day 2: Follow my "Welcome to Madrid" self-guided walk, tour the Royal Palace, and have lunch at Café de Oriente or near Plaza Mayor. Your afternoon is free for other sights, shopping, or a side-trip to the palace at El Escorial (closed Mon; see next chapter). Be out at the magic hour—before sunset—when beautifully lit people fill Madrid.

Note that many top sights are closed on Monday, including the Prado, Thyssen-Bornemisza Museum, and El Escorial; sights remaining open on Monday include the Royal Palace (open daily) and Centro de Arte Reina Sofía (closed Tue). For good day-trip possibilities from Madrid, see the next two chapters (Northwest of Madrid and Toledo).

Orientation to Madrid

Puerta del Sol marks the center of Madrid. No major sight is more than a 20-minute walk or a €5 taxi ride from this central square. Get out your map and frame off Madrid's historic core: To the west of Puerta del Sol is the Royal Palace. To the east, you'll find the Prado Museum, along with the Thyssen-Bornemisza and Reina Sofía museums. North of Puerta del Sol is Gran Vía, a broad east-west boulevard bubbling with shops and cinemas. Between Gran Vía and Puerta del Sol is a lively pedestrian shopping zone. And southwest of Puerta del Sol is Plaza Mayor, the center of a 17th-century, slow-down-and-smell-the-cobbles district.

This entire historic core around Puerta del Sol—Gran Vía, Plaza Mayor, the Prado, and the Royal Palace—is easily covered on foot. A wonderful chain of pedestrian streets crosses the city east to west, from the Prado to Plaza Mayor (along Calle de las Huertas) and from Puerta del Sol to the Royal Palace (on Calle del Arenal). Between Puerta del Sol and Atocha train station (to the southeast) stretches the colorful, up-and-coming, multiethnic Lavapiés district.

Tourist Information

Madrid's many TIs share a phone number (tel. 915-881-636) and website (www.esmadrid.com).

The best and most central TI is on **Plaza Mayor** (daily 9:30-20:30, air-con, limited free Internet access). They offer several €4 English guided walks each day (described later, under "Tours in Madrid") and a free downloadable self-guided art walk. They also provide a foreign tourist assistance program (called SATE) to aid travelers who've run into trouble.

Madrid's other TIs have the same hours (daily 9:30-20:30), unless otherwise noted: near the **Prado Museum** (Duque de Medinaceli 2, behind Palace Hotel); **Chamartín train station** (near track 20); **Atocha train station** (in AVE side); and **airport** (Terminals 2 and 4, daily 9:00-20:00). Small info kiosks are in **Plaza de Callao** and in **Plaza de Cibeles.**

At any TI, pick up a map, the handy *Traveler's Tips* booklet, and the *Es Madrid* English-language monthly, and confirm your sightseeing plans. The TI's free, well-designed *Public Transport* map includes a detailed map of the center. Get this and use it. TIs have the latest on bullfights and zarzuela (light Spanish opera).

Sightseeing Pass: Very energetic travelers can save a little money and some valuable sightseeing time by buying the **Madrid Card.** It covers nearly 40 sights (including the Royal Palace, the Prado, Thyssen-Bornemisza, and Reina Sofía) and lets you skip lines—a definite plus in high season, especially at the palace and the Prado. Additionally, the pass covers the palace at El Escorial (outside of Madrid—see next chapter), the Bernabéu Stadium tour, and all of the Discover Madrid tours, and it's good for discounts on flamenco tickets (20 percent at Las Carboneras, 10 percent at Las Tablas—see page 407). The three-day card is the best bargain (€52; other options include €32/24 hours and €42/48 hours, online discounts available, www.madridcard.com). You can pay extra to add the hop-on, hop-off bus tour (saves a maximum of €2) or public transport (only worthwhile if you ride multiple times a day).

Entertainment Guides: For arts and culture listings, the TI's printed material is not very good. Pick up the Spanish-language weekly entertainment guide *Guía del Ocio* (€1, sold at newsstands) or check their complete website: www.guiadelocio.com. It lists daily live music *("Conciertos"),* museums (under *"Arte"*—with the latest times and special exhibits), restaurants (an exhaustive listing), TV schedules, and movies ("V.O." means original version, *"V.O. en inglés sub"* means a movie is played in English with Spanish subtitles rather than dubbed).

Helpful Website: While not officially part of the TI, www .madridman.com is run with passion by American Scott Martin and offers tips on sightseeing, hotels, restaurants, and more.

Arrival in Madrid

For more information on arriving at or departing from Madrid's airport, train stations, and bus stations, see "Madrid Connections," at the end of this chapter.

By Train

Madrid's two train stations, Chamartín and Atocha, are both on Metro lines with easy access to downtown Madrid. Chamartín handles most international trains and the AVE (AH-vay) train to and from Segovia. Atocha generally covers southern Spain, as well as the AVE trains to and from Barcelona, Córdoba, Sevilla, and Toledo. For details on both stations, see page 427.

Traveling Between Chamartín and Atocha Stations: You can take the Metro (line 1, 30-40 minutes, €1; see "Getting Around Madrid" on page 361), but the *cercanías* trains are faster (6/hour, 13 minutes, Atocha-Sol-Chamartín lines C3 and C4 are the most convenient, €1.35, free with railpass or any train ticket to Madrid—show it at ticket window in the middle of the turnstiles, depart from Atocha's track 2 and generally Chamartín's track 1, 3, 8, or 9—but check the *Salidas Inmediatas* board to be sure).

By Bus

Madrid has several bus stations, each one handy to a Metro station: Príncipe Pío (for Segovia, Metro: Príncipe Pío); Estación Sur de Autobuses (for Ávila and Granada, Metro: Méndez Álvaro); Plaza Elíptica (for Toledo, Metro: Plaza Elíptica); Estación Intercambiador de Moncloa (for El Escorial, Metro: Moncloa); and Intercambiador de Avenida de América (for Pamplona and Burgos, Metro: Avenida de América). If you take a taxi from the station to your hotel, you'll pay an extra €3 supplement. For bus connections, see page 430.

By Plane

Both international and domestic flights arrive at Madrid's Barajas Airport. Options for getting into town include public bus, Metro, taxi, and minibus shuttle. For details, see page 431.

Helpful Hints

Theft Alert: Be wary of pickpockets—anywhere, anytime. Areas of particular risk are Puerta del Sol (the central square), El Rastro (the flea market), Gran Vía (the paseo zone: Plaza del Callao to Plaza de España), the Ópera Metro station (or anywhere on the Metro), bus #27, the airport, and any crowded streets. Be alert to the people around you: Someone wearing a heavy jacket in the summer is likely a pickpocket. Lately, Romanian teenagers dress like American teens and work the

Greater Madrid

N

1 MILE

1 KM

CHAMARTÍN
TRAIN STATION

Chamartín

PLAZA DE
CASTILLA

BERNABÉU
STADIUM

Santiago
Bernabéu

M-30 FREEWAY

MURILLO

CASTELLANO

BRAVO

TO EL ESCORIAL
& SEGOVIA

A-6

FERNANDEZ

J. COSTA

AMÉRICA

TO BARAJAS
AIRPORT
Barcelona &

A-2

CLOTHING
MUSEUM

ARCO
VICTORIA

MUSEUM OF THE
AMERICAS

Moncloa

SAN
ANTONIO

PRINCESA

SAN BERNARDO

SOROLLA
MUSEUM

Iglesia

RECOLETOS

Ventas

VENTAS
BULLRING

CASA
DE
CAMPO

Norte

PLAZA
ESPAÑA

GRAN

VÍA

Sol

MALA-
SAÑA

PLAZA
COLÓN

ALCALÁ

PRÍNCIPE
PÍO
TRAIN & BUS
STATIONS

MANZANARES

Royal
PALACE

SOL

PLAZA
MAYOR

Atocha
RENFE

Prado

RETIRO
PARK

MEDITERRANEO

A-3

CALLE
TOLEDO

CABEZA

ATOCHA
TRAIN STN.

Méndez
Álvaro

MÉNDEZ ÁLVARO

ROYAL
TAPESTRY
FACTORY

Menéndez
Pelayo

DCH

TO ⑤ & TOLEDO VIA N-401

TO TOLEDO & SEVILLA
VIA A.V.E. TRAINS

① Estación Sur de Autobuses

② Principe Pío Station
(Sepulvedana Buses)

③ Intercambiador de Moncloa

④ To Intercambiador de Avenida
de América

⑤ To Plaza Elíptica Station

☐ = HISTORIC CITY CENTER
SEE DETAIL MAPS

M METRO STATION - NOT ALL SHOWN

→ BUS #27 SELF-GUIDED TOUR

MADRID

areas around the three big art museums; being under 18, they can't be arrested by the police. Assume a fight or any commotion is a scam to distract people about to become victims of a pickpocket. Wear your money belt. The small streets north of Gran Vía are particularly dangerous, even before nightfall. Muggings occur, but are rare. For help, see the next listing.

Tourist Emergency Aid: SATE is an assistance service for tourists who might need, for any reason, to visit a police station or lodge a complaint. Help ranges from canceling stolen credit cards to assistance in reporting a crime (central police station, daily 9:00-24:00, near Plaza de Santo Domingo at Calle Leganitos 19). The Plaza Mayor TI also serves as a SATE branch of sorts and is an easy place to start if you run into trouble. They can help you get to the police station and will even act as an interpreter if you have trouble communicating with the police. Or you can call in your report to the SATE line (24-hour tel. 902-102 112, English spoken once you get connected to a person), then go to the police station (where they'll likely speak only Spanish) to sign your statement.

You may see a police station in the Sol Metro station; this office handles only Metro theft.

Prostitution: Diverse by European standards, Madrid is spilling over with immigrants from South America, North Africa, and Eastern Europe. Many young women come here, fall on hard times, and end up on the streets. While it's illegal to make money from someone else selling sex (i.e., pimping), prostitutes over 18 can solicit legally (€30, FYI). Calle de la Montera (leading from Puerta del Sol to Plaza Red de San Luis) is lined with what looks like a bunch of high-school girls skipping out of school for a cigarette break. Again, don't stray north of Gran Vía around Calle de la Luna and Plaza Santa María Soledad—while the streets may look inviting... this area is a meat-eating flower.

Embassies: The US Embassy is at Calle Serrano 75 (tel. 915-872-200); the Canadian Embassy is at Paseo de la Castellana 259D (tel. 913-828-400).

One-Stop Shopping: The dominant department store is **El Corte Inglés,** which takes up several huge buildings in the commercial pedestrian zone just off Puerta del Sol (Mon-Sat 10:00-22:00, Sun 11:00-21:00, navigate with the help of the info desk near the door of the main building—the tallest building with the biggest sign, Preciados 3, tel. 913-798-000). They give out good, free Madrid maps. In the main building, you'll find two handy travel agencies (see listing later), a post office, a modern cafeteria (seventh floor), and a supermarket with a fancy "Club del Gourmet" section in the basement. Across the street is its Librería branch—a huge bookstore. The second building fronting Puerta del Sol contains six floors of music, computers, home electronics, and SIM cards for mobile phones, with a box office on the top floor selling tickets to whatever's on in town. Locals figure you'll find anything you need at El Corte Inglés. Salespeople wear flag pins indicating which languages they can speak.

Free Sights: The Prado is free Tue-Sat 18:00-20:00 and Sun 17:00-20:00, while the Reina Sofía museum is free weekdays 19:00-21:00 (except Tue, when it's closed), Sat afternoon after 14:30, and all day Sun. These Madrid sights are always free: CaixaForum, Naval Museum, Chapel of San Antonio de la Florida, Bullfighting Museum, Caja Madrid, and the Temple de Debod.

Internet Access: There are plenty of centrally located places to check your email. Any *locutorio* call center should have a few computers and is generally the cheapest Internet option in the neighborhood. Near Plaza Santa Ana, **La Bolsa de Minutos** has plenty of terminals, offers a disc-burning service, and is a productive place to kill time if you're waiting for the tapas-crawl action to heat up (daily 9:30-24:00, Calle Espoz y Mina 17—see map on page 420, tel. 915-322-622).

Phone Cards: You can buy cheap international phone cards at some newsstands, at Internet cafés, or at the easy-to-find *locutorio* call centers (generally uncomfortable places to sit and make calls). When choosing a phone card, remember that toll-free numbers start with 900, whereas 901 and 902 numbers can be expensive. Ask your hotel if they charge for the 900 number before making calls.

Bookstores: For books in English, try **FNAC Callao** (Calle Preciados 28, tel. 915-956-100), **Casa del Libro** (English on ground floor, Gran Vía 29, tel. 915-212-219), and **El Corte Inglés** (guidebooks and some fiction, in its Librería branch kitty-corner from main store, fronting Puerta del Sol—see "One-Stop Shopping," earlier).

Laundry: Self-service launderettes are hard to find in Madrid. Ask your hotelier if they have laundry service. Or try **Higiensec,** which offers self-service laundry (€5/load to wash, a few euros more to dry) as well as drop-off laundry service and dry cleaning (Mon-Fri 9:00-14:00 & 16:00-20:00, Sat 9:00-17:00, closed Sun, between Calle del Arenal and Calle Mayor at Plaza de Herradores 8—see map on page 410, tel. 915-428-492).

Travel Agencies: The grand department store **El Corte Inglés** has two travel agencies (air and rail tickets, but not reserva-

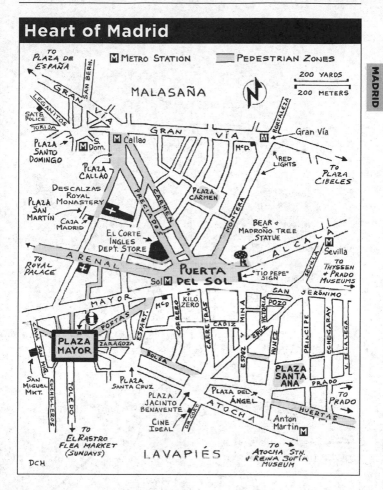

Heart of Madrid

M METRO STATION   PEDESTRIAN ZONES

200 YARDS
200 METERS

TO PLAZA DE ESPAÑA

MALASAÑA

GRAN VIA

SAN BERN.

LEGANITOS

SATE POLICE

TORIJA

GRAN VIA

Gran Vía

Callao

Mcᴰ.

HORTALEZA

PLAZA SANTO DOMINGO

S. Dom.

PLAZA CALLAO

RED LIGHTS

TO PLAZA CIBELES

Descalzas Royal Monastery

PLAZA SAN MARTIN

Caja Madrid

El Corte Ingles Dept. Store

PRECIADOS

CARMEN

PLAZA CARMEN

MONTERA

BEAR & MADROÑO TREE STATUE

ALCALA

Sevilla

TO ROYAL PALACE

ARENAL

Sol

PUERTA DEL SOL

"TIO PEPE" SIGN

SEVILLA

TO THYSSEN & PRADO MUSEUMS

MAYOR

MAYOR

Mcᴰ

KILO. ZERO

CORREOS

CARRETAS

MINA

CADIZ

VICTORIA

POZO

SAN JERONIMO

PRINCIPE

ECHEGARAY

V. DE LA VEGA

CAVA SAN MIG.

POSTAS

ESPART.

ZARAGOZA

PLAZA MAYOR

BOLSA

ESPOZ

CRUZ

NUÑEZ

PLAZA SANTA ANA

PRADO

TO PRADO

SAN MIGUEL MKT.

CUCHILLEROS

TOLEDO

PLAZA SANTA CRUZ

PLAZA JACINTO BENAVENTE

CINE IDEAL

LA CRUZ

PLAZA DEL ÁNGEL

ATOCHA

HUERTAS

Anton Martin

TO EL RASTRO FLEA MARKET (SUNDAYS)

LAVAPIÉS

TO ATOCHA STN. & REINA SOFÍA MUSEUM

DCH

tions for railpass-holders, €2 fee, on first and seventh floors, for hours and contact info see "One-Stop Shopping," earlier).

Getting Around Madrid

If you want to use Madrid's excellent public transit, pick up and

study the fine *Public Transport* map/flier (available at TIs or at Metro info booths in most stations—near the entrance turnstiles).

By Metro: The city's broad streets can be hot and exhausting. A subway trip of even a stop or two saves time and energy.

MADRID

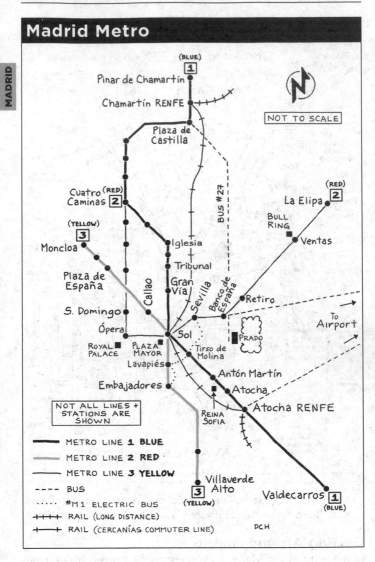

Madrid Metro

Madrid's Metro is simple, speedy, and cheap. It costs €1 for a ride within zone A, which covers most of the city, but not trains out to the airport. The 10-ride Metrobus ticket can be shared by several travelers and works on both the Metro and buses (€9.30—or €0.93 per ride). Buy tickets in the Metro (from easy-to-use machines or ticket booths), at newspaper stands, or at tobacco shops. Insert your ticket in the turnstile, then retrieve it and pass through. The Metro stops running at 1:30 in the morning and resumes operation at 6:00. At all times, be alert to thieves, who thrive in crowded stations.

Pick up a free Metro map—the simplified map on the opposite page can get you started. The lines are color-coded and numbered; use the end-of-the-line station names to choose your direction of travel. Once in the Metro station, signs direct you to the train line and direction (e.g., Linea 1, *Valdecarros*). To transfer, follow signs in the station leading to connecting lines. Once you reach your final stop, look for the green *salida* signs pointing to the exits. Use the helpful neighborhood maps to choose the right *salida*, and save yourself lots of walking. Metro info: www.metromadrid.es or www.ctm-madrid.es.

By Bus: City buses, though not as easy as the Metro, can be useful (€1 tickets sold on bus, €9.30 for a 10-ride Metrobus ticket, bus maps at TI or info booth on Puerta del Sol, poster-size maps usually posted at bus stops, buses run 6:00-24:00, much less frequent *Buho* buses run all night).

By Taxi: Madrid's 15,000 taxis are reasonably priced and easy to hail. Foursomes travel as cheaply by taxi as by Metro. For example, a ride from the Royal Palace to the Prado costs about €6. After the €2.10 drop charge, the per-kilometer rate depends on the time: *Tarifa 1* (€1/kilometer) is charged Mon-Fri 6:00-22:00; *Tarifa 2* (€1.17/kilometer) is valid after 22:00 and on Saturdays, Sundays, and holidays. If your cabbie uses anything other than *Tarifa 1* on weekdays (shown as an isolated "1" on the meter), you're being cheated. Rates can be higher if you go outside of Madrid. Other legitimate charges include the €5.50 supplement for the airport, the €3 supplement for leaving any train or bus station, and €18.50 per hour for waiting. Make sure the meter is turned on as soon as you get into the cab so the driver can't tack anything onto the official rate. If the driver starts adding up "extras," look for the sticker detailing all legitimate surcharges (which should be on the passenger window).

Tours in Madrid

Discover Madrid—The Plaza Mayor TI organizes a daily schedule of cheap, interesting guided walks. Tours last about 1.5 hours, are in English only, cost €4, and depart daily from the Plaza Mayor TI. Check their detailed booklet or online for specifics and departure times, which change frequently (www.esmadrid.com /descubremadrid_en). Groups can be very small, so you almost feel like you have a private guide. Buy your ticket at the TI, over the phone at 902-221-424, or online at www.entradas.com (search for "Descubre Madrid"). Tours can fill up in high season, so booking at least a few hours in advance is a good idea.

"Bus Turístico Madrid" Hop-On, Hop-Off Tours—Two different hop-on, hop-off circuits cover the city: historic and modern.

Madrid at a Glance

▲▲▲**Royal Palace** Spain's sumptuous, lavishly furnished national palace. **Hours:** April-Sept Mon-Sat 9:00-19:00, Sun 9:00-16:00; Oct-March Mon-Sat 10:00-18:00, Sun 10:00-16:00. See page 375.

▲▲▲**Prado Museum** One of the world's great museums, loaded with masterpieces by Diego Velázquez, Francisco de Goya, El Greco, Hieronymus Bosch, Albrecht Dürer, and more. **Hours:** Tue-Sun 9:00-20:00, closed Mon. See page 381.

▲▲▲**Centro de Arte Reina Sofía** Modern-art museum featuring Picasso's epic masterpiece *Guernica*. **Hours:** Mon and Wed-Sat 10:00-21:00, Sun 10:00-14:30, closed Tue. See page 394.

▲▲**Puerta del Sol** Madrid's lively central square. **Hours:** Always bustling. See page 367.

▲▲**Thyssen-Bornemisza Museum** A great complement to the Prado, with lesser-known yet still impressive works and an especially good Impressionist collection. **Hours:** Tue-Sun 10:00-19:00, closed Mon. See page 393.

▲▲**Bullfight** Spain's controversial pastime. **Hours:** Scattered Sundays and holidays March-mid-Oct, plus almost daily mid-May-mid-June. See page 403.

▲▲**Flamenco** Captivating music and dance performances, at various venues throughout the city. **Hours:** Shows every night, some places closed on Sun. See page 406.

▲**Plaza Mayor** Historic cobbled square. **Hours:** Always open. See page 371.

▲**Retiro Park** Festive green escape from the city, with rental

Buy a ticket from the driver (€17.50/1 day, €22/2 days), and you can hop from sight to sight and route to route as you like, listening to a recorded English commentary along the way. Each route has about 15 stops and takes about 1.5 hours, with buses departing every 10 or 20 minutes. The two routes intersect at the south side of Puerta del Sol and in front of Starbucks across from the Prado (daily 9:30-24:00 in summer, 10:00-19:00 in winter, tel. 917-791-888, www.emtmadrid.es).

Letango Tours—Carlos Galvin, a Spaniard who speaks flawless English (and led tours for my groups for more than a decade), and

rowboats and great people-watching. **Hours:** Closes at dusk. See page 398.

▲**Royal Botanical Garden** A relaxing museum of plants, with specimens from around the world. **Hours:** Daily 10:00-21:00, until 18:00 in winter. See page 399.

▲**Naval Museum** Seafaring history of a country famous for its Armada. **Hours:** Tue-Sun 10:00-18:00, closed Mon and Aug. See page 399.

▲**Museum of the Americas** Pre-Colombian and colonial artifacts from the New World. **Hours:** May-Oct Tue-Sat 9:30-20:30, Nov-April until 18:30, Sun 10:00-15:00, closed Mon. See page 400.

▲**National Archaeological Museum** Traces the history of Iberia through artifacts. Under major renovation, with only 300 pieces of its collection on display until 2012. **Hours:** Tue-Sat 9:30-20:00, Sun 9:30-15:00, closed Mon. See page 400.

▲**Clothing Museum** A clothes look at the 18th-21st centuries. **Hours:** Tue-Sat 9:30-19:00, Sun 10:00-15:00, closed Mon. See page 401.

▲**Chapel of San Antonio de la Florida** Church with Goya's tomb, plus frescoes by the artist. **Hours:** Tue-Fri 9:30-20:00, Sat-Sun 10:00-14:00, closed Mon. See page 401.

▲**El Rastro** Europe's biggest flea market, filled with bargains and pickpockets. **Hours:** Sun 9:00-15:00, best before 11:00. See page 405.

▲**Zarzuela** Madrid's delightful light opera. **Hours:** Evenings. See page 406.

his wife from Seattle, Jennifer, run city tours and more. Carlos mixes a market walk in the historic center with a culinary-and-tapas introduction to get close to the Madrileños, their culture, and their food. His walk gives a good four-hour orientation to the fascinating and tasty culture of Madrid (€225/group, up to 5 people, more affordable group tours available for solo travelers and families, includes *churros* and chocolate, also comes with brief consultation about your trip). Carlos also offers customized tours (whether city, regional, or country-wide), and he can help book apartments, hotels, airport transfers, and bullfight and soccer tickets all around

Spain (tel. 913-694-752, mobile 661-752-458, www.letangospain tours.com, tours@letango.com).

Local Guides—Frederico, Cristina, and their team are licensed guides who lead city walks through the pedestrian streets of the historic core of Madrid. They offer all-ages tours of the big sights, including the Royal Palace and the Prado, Reina Sofía, and Thyssen-Bornemisza museums, as well as a tapas tour (€195/ group for 4-hour tour, this rate is for Rick Steves readers; does not include entry fees, transportation, or tapas; shorter and longer tours also available: €155/2 hours, €235/6 hours). If you're look- ing to get outside of Madrid, consider their guided excursions to surrounding towns, available on either public or private transit (inquire about rates; all tours are private and family-friendly; tel. and fax 913-102-974, mobile 649-936-222, www.spainfred.com, spainfred@gmail.com).

Inés Muñiz Martin is a good, licensed guide. It's impossible to get more local than Inés, who's a third-generation Madrileña (what Spaniards call a *gata*). She has led my tour groups in the city for years. She also guides in surrounding areas, such as El Escorial and Toledo (€107-178 for 2-5 hours, 25 percent more on weekends and holidays, these discounted rates are for Rick Steves readers, prices do not include transportation or entry fees, mobile 629-147- 370, www.immguidedtours.com, info@immguidedtours.com).

Susana Jarabo, with a master's in art history, is another excellent independent guide (mobile 667-027-722, susanjarabo @yahoo.es).

Hernán Amaya Satt directs a group of licensed guides who take individuals around Madrid, including its museums, on 18 per- sonalized tours (rates vary according to tour and number of people, 20 percent discount off official rates for Rick Steves readers, family rates, mobile 680-450-231, www.madridmuseumtours.com, info @madridmuseumtours.com).

Stephen Drake-Jones, a British expat, leads walks of his- toric old Madrid almost daily. A historian with a passion for the Duke of Wellington (the general who stopped Napoleon), Stephen founded Madrid's Wellington Society and has been its chair- man for over 30 years. For €50, you become a member and get a three-hour tour with three stops for drinks and tapas (€10 more for fine wines, morning or afternoon). Eccentric Stephen sorts out Madrid's Habsburg and Bourbon history. He likes his wine— if that's a problem, skip the tour. He also does day trips in the countryside (from €275 per couple) and a four-hour wine-tasting tour that lets you sample regional cheese and ham (€85 per person; mobile 609-143-203, www.wellsoc.org, chairman@wellsoc.org).

Big-Bus City Sightseeing Tours—Julià Travel leads standard guided bus tours departing from Plaza de España 7 (office open

Mon-Fri 8:00-19:00, Sat-Sun 8:00-15:00, tel. 915-599-605). Their city offerings include a three-hour Madrid tour with a live guide in two or three languages (€22, one stop for a drink at Hard Rock Café, one shopping stop, no museum visits, daily at 9:45 and 15:00, no reservation required—just show up 15 minutes before departure). Julià Travel also runs tours to destinations near Madrid, such as El Escorial (€55, 5 hours, Tue-Sun at 8:45, none Mon). Three trips include Toledo: one of the city itself (€43/5 hours, daily at 8:45 and 15:00, or €58/8 hours, daily at 9:45); one of Madrid and Toledo together (€56, half-day in Toledo plus panoramic 3-hour Madrid tour, daily at 9:00); and a tour of El Escorial and Toledo (€90, full day, Tue-Sun at 9:00, none Mon). Note that just the eight-hour Toledo-only tour includes the cathedral, while the half-day Toledo and combo-tours skip this town's one must-see sight... but not the long shopping stops, because the shops give kickbacks to the guides. See their website for other tours and services (www.juliatravel.com/en).

Self-Guided Walk

Welcome to Madrid:
From Puerta del Sol to the Royal Palace

Connect the sights with the following commentary. Allow an hour for this half-mile walk. Begin at Madrid's central square, Puerta del Sol (Metro: Sol).

• *Head to the middle of the square, by the equestrian statue of King Charles III, and survey the scene.*

▲▲Puerta del Sol

The bustling Puerta del Sol is named for a long-gone medieval gate with the sun carved onto it. It's a hub for the Metro, *cercanías*

trains, political demonstrations, and pickpockets. In recent years it has undergone a facelift to become a mostly pedestrianized, wide-open, cement-filled space without benches or trees (making it hot as the *sol* in summer).

The venerable *Tío Pepe* **sign,** advertising a famous sherry for more than 100 years, was Madrid's first billboard, and today it's the only such ad allowed on the square.

Because of his enlightened urban policies, **King Charles III** (who ruled until 1788) is affectionately called "the best mayor of Madrid." He decorated the city squares with beautiful fountains, got those meddlesome Jesuits out of city government, established

MADRID

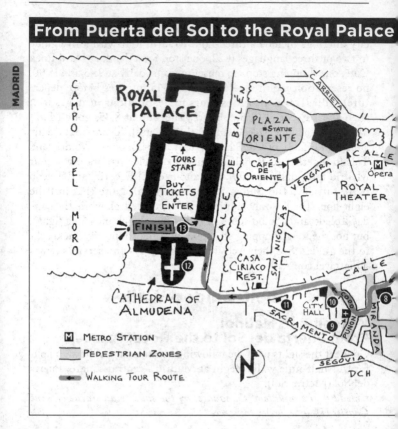

From Puerta del Sol to the Royal Palace

the public school system, mandated underground sewers, made the Retiro a public park rather than a royal retreat, and generally cleaned up Madrid.

Turn left and take a short walk away from the king. Just beyond the Metro entrances you'll see a **statue of a bear** pawing a tree—a symbol of Madrid. Bears used to live in the royal hunting grounds outside Madrid. And the *madroño* trees produce a berry that makes the traditional *madroño* liqueur.

Walk back toward the king, past the glass-fish entrance to the *cercanías* trains and Metro. Look left to a red-and-white building with a bell tower. This was Madrid's first post office, founded by Charles III in the 1760s. Today it's the **county governor's office** (Residencia de la Comunidad de Madrid), though it's notorious for having been dictator Francisco Franco's police headquarters. An amazing number of those detained and interrogated by the Franco police tried to "escape" by jumping out its windows to their deaths. Notice the hats of the civil guardsmen at the entry. It's said the hats have square backs, cleverly designed so that the men can lean

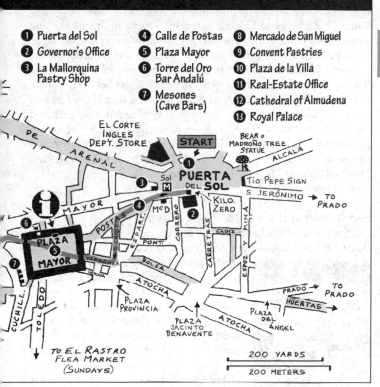

1. Puerta del Sol
2. Governor's Office
3. La Mallorquina Pastry Shop
4. Calle de Postas
5. Plaza Mayor
6. Torre del Oro Bar Andalú
7. Mesones (Cave Bars)
8. Mercado de San Miguel
9. Convent Pastries
10. Plaza de la Villa
11. Real-Estate Office
12. Cathedral of Almudena
13. Royal Palace

against the wall while enjoying a cigarette.

Appreciate the **harmonious architecture** of the buildings that circle the square—yellow-cream, four stories, balconies of iron, shuttered windows, and balustrades along the rooflines (with TV antennas on top).

Crowds fill the square on New Year's Eve as the rest of Madrid watches the action on TV. As Spain's "Big Ben" atop the governor's office chimes 12 times, Madrileños eat one grape for each ring to bring good luck through each of the next 12 months.

• *Cross the square, walking to the governor's office.*

Look at the curb directly in front of the entrance to the governor's office. The marker is **"kilometer zero,"** the very center of Spain (with its six main highways indicated).

Near the building's entrance are **two plaques** tied to important dates, expressing thanks from the regional government to its citizens for assisting in times of dire need. To the left of the entrance, a plaque on the wall honors those who helped during the terrorist bombings of March 11, 2004 (we have our 9/11, and Spain commemorates its 4/11). A similar plaque on the right marks the spot where the war against Napoleon started in 1808. Napoleon wanted his brother to be king of Spain. Trying to finagle this, he brought nearly the entire Spanish royal family to France for negotiations. An anxious crowd gathered outside this building awaiting word of the fate of their royals. This was just after the French Revolution, and there was a general nervousness between France and Spain. When the people of Madrid heard that Napoleon had appointed his own brother as the new king of Spain, they gathered angrily in the streets. The French guard simply massacred the mob. Painter Francisco de Goya, who worked just up the street, observed the event and captured the tragedy in his paintings *Second of May, 1808* and *Third of May, 1808,* now in the Prado.

• *Now head...*

From Puerta del Sol to Plaza Mayor

On the corner of Calle Mayor and Puerta del Sol (downhill end of Puerta del Sol, across from McDonald's) is the busy *confitería* **La**

Mallorquina (daily 9:00-21:00, closed mid-July-Aug; with the awning bragging *fundida in 1,894*). Go inside for a tempting peek at racks with goodies hot out of the oven. Enjoy observing the churning energy at the bar lined with Madrileños popping in for a fast coffee and a sweet treat. The shop is famous for its cream-filled *Napolitana* pastry (€1.20). Or sample Madrid's answer to doughnuts, *rosquillas* (*tontas* means "silly"—plain, and *listas* means "all dressed up and ready to go"—with icing, about €0.50 each). The room upstairs is more genteel.

From inside the shop, look back toward the entrance and notice the tile above the door with the 18th-century view of Puerta del Sol. Compare this with today's view out the door. This was before the square was widened, when a church stood where the *Tío Pepe* sign is today. The French used this church to detain Spanish patriots awaiting execution.

• *Head west on busy Calle Mayor, just past McDonald's, and veer left up the pedestrian alley called **Calle de Postas**.*

The street sign shows the post coach heading for that famous first post office. Medieval street signs included pictures so the illiterate (and monolingual tourists) could "read" them. Fifty yards up the street, at Calle San Cristóbal, is Pans & Company, a popular Catalan sandwich chain offering lots of healthy choices. While Spaniards consider American fast food unhealthy—both culturally and physically—they love it. (The McDonald's and Burger Kings in Spain are thriving.)

• *From here, turn left and hike up Calle San Cristóbal.*

Within two blocks you'll pass the local feminist bookshop (Librería Mujeres) and reach a small square. At the square, notice the big brick 17th-century Ministry of Foreign Affairs building (with the pointed spire)—originally a jail for aristocratic prisoners, since even the black sheep of fine families were given special treatment.

• *Turn right, and walk down Calle de Zaragoza under the arcade into...*

▲Plaza Mayor

This square, built in 1619, is a vast, cobbled, traffic-free chunk of 17th-century Spain. Each side of the square is uniform, as if a

grand palace were turned inside-out. The equestrian statue (wearing a ruffled collar) is of Philip III, who ordered the square's construction. Before the statue stood here, this site served as the city's 17th-century theater/multimedia center. Upon this stage, much Spanish history has

been played out: bullfights, fires, royal pageantry, and events of the gruesome Inquisition. Reliefs serving as seatbacks under the lampposts tell the story. During the Inquisition, many were tried here—suspected heretics, Protestants, Jews, tour guides without a local license, and Muslims whose "conversion" to Christianity was dubious. The guilty were paraded around the square before their executions, wearing billboards listing their many sins (bleachers were built for bigger audiences, while the wealthy rented balconies). Some were slowly strangled as they held a crucifix, hearing the reassuring words of a priest as this life was squeezed out of them with a garrote. Others were burned.

The square is painted a democratic shade of burgundy—the result of a citywide vote. Since Franco's death in 1975, there's been

a passion for voting here. Three different colors were painted as samples on the walls of this square, and the city voted for its favorite.

A stamp-and-coin market bustles here on Sundays from 10:00 to 14:00; on any given day it's a colorful and affordable place to enjoy a cup of coffee. (Skip the overpriced food.) Throughout Spain, lesser *plazas mayores* provide peaceful pools in the white-water river of Spanish life. The TI (daily 9:30-20:30, wonderfully air-conditioned and with free but limited Internet access) is under the building on the north side of the square. The TI is also a meeting point for cheap daily walking tours—consider dropping by to reserve a spot (see "Tours in Madrid," earlier).

• *For some interesting, if gruesome, bullfighting lore, drop by the...*

La Torre del Oro Bar Andalú

This bar is a good place to finish off your Plaza Mayor visit (north side of the square at #26, a few doors to the left of the TI). Step inside, stand at the bar, and order a drink. The bar has *Andalú* (Andalusian) ambience and an entertaining staff. Warning: They push expensive tapas on tourists. But buying a beer is safe and painless—just order a *caña* (small beer, shouldn't cost more than €2.50). The price list posted outside the door makes your costs perfectly clear ("*barra*" indicates the price at the bar; "*terraza*" is the price at an outdoor table).

The interior of the Torre del Oro bar is a temple to bullfighting, festooned with gory decor. Notice the breathtaking action captured in the many photographs. Look under the stuffed head of Barbero the bull. At eye level you'll see a *puntilla,* the knife used to put a bull out of his misery at the arena. This was the knife used to kill Barbero. The plaque explains: weight, birth date, owner, date of death, which matador killed him, and the location. Just to the left of Barbero, there's a photo of longtime dictator Franco with the famous bullfighter Manuel Benítez Pérez—better known as El Cordobés, the Elvis of bullfighters and a working-class hero. At the top of the stairs to the WC, find the photo of El Cordobés and Robert Kennedy—looking like brothers. At the end of the bar, in a glass case, is the "suit of lights" the great El Cordobés wore in an ill-fated 1967 fight, in which the bull gored him. El Cordobés survived; the bull didn't. Find the photo of Franco with El Cordobés at the far end, to the left of Segador the bull. Under the bull (to the left, over the counter) is a photo of El Cordobés' illegitimate son kissing a bull. Disowned by El Cordobés senior, yet still using his dad's famous name after a court battle, the junior El Cordobés is one of this generation's top fighters.

Consider taking a break at one of Torre del Oro's sidewalk tables (or at any café/bar terrace facing Madrid's grandest square). Cafetería Margerit (nearby) occupies the sunniest corner of the square and is a good place to enjoy a coffee with the view. The scene is easily worth the extra euro you'll pay for the drink.

• *Leave Plaza Mayor on Calle de Ciudad Rodrigo (at the northwest corner of the square) and begin walking...*

From Plaza Mayor to City Hall

As you stroll, you'll pass a series of solid turn-of-the-20th-century storefronts and sandwich joints, such as Casa Rúa, famous for their cheap *bocadillos de calamares*—fried squid rings on a roll.

From the archway, head toward the covered market hall. Before you reach it, look left down the street called Cava de San Miguel. If you like singing and sangria, come back after 22:00 and visit one of the *mesones* that line the street. These cave-like bars, stretching far back from the street, get packed with Madrileños out on tacky dates who—emboldened by sangria, the setting, and Spain—are prone to suddenly break out in song. It's a lowbrow, electric-keyboard, karaoke-type ambience, best on Friday and Saturday nights. The odd shape of these bars isn't a contrivance for the sake of atmosphere—Plaza Mayor was built on a slope, and these underground vaults are part of a structural system that braces the leveled plaza.

To wash down those *calamares* in a more refined setting, pop into the covered **Mercado de San Miguel** (ornate iron posts, on left) for a glass of wine (Mon-Wed and Sun 10:00-24:00, Thu-Sat 10:00-2:00 in the morning). This historic iron-and-glass structure, built in the early 1900s, has high-end food vendors. The market is frequented by tourists and locals alike looking for refreshment or gourmet picnic supplies.

• *From Plaza de San Miguel in front of the market, follow the pedestrian lane left and downhill. At the first corner, turn right and cross the small plaza to the modern brick church (straight ahead).*

At the convent **Church of Corpus Christi,** notice the proud coat of arms over the main entry. In 17th-century Spain, the most prestigious thing a noble family could do was build and maintain a convent. To harvest all the goodwill created in your community, you'd want your family's insignia right there for all to see.

In the alley across the plaza, a big brown door on the left (at #3 Calle del Codo) has a sign: *Venta de Dulces* (Sweets for Sale). To buy goodies from the cloistered nuns, buzz the *monjas* button, then wait patiently for the sister to respond over the intercom. Say "*dulces*" (DOOL-thays), and she'll let you in (Mon-Sat 9:30-13:00 & 16:00-18:30, closed Sun). When the lock buzzes, push open the door and follow the sign to the *torno,* the lazy Susan that lets the sisters sell their baked goods without being seen (smallest quantity: *medio*-kilo—around €8). Of the many choices listed, *galletas* (shortbread cookies) are the least expensive. Or try the *pastas de almendra* (almond cookies).

• *Follow Calle del Codo (where those in need of bits of armor shopped—see the street sign) uphill around the convent toward the Plaza de la Villa (pictured at top of next page). Before entering the square, notice (on your left, wood lined with metal, at the* Real Sociedad Económica *sign) what's considered the oldest door in town on Madrid's oldest building—inhabited since 1480. Now continue into the square, dominated by Madrid's...*

City Hall

Imagine how Philip II took this city by surprise when he decided to move the capital of Europe's largest empire—in the 17th century, it was even bigger than ancient Rome—from Toledo to humble Madrid. To better administer their empire, the Habsburgs went on a building spree. But because their empire was drained of its riches by prolonged religious wars, they built Madrid with cheap brick instead of elegant granite.

The statue in the garden is of Don Alvaro de Bazán—mastermind of the Christian victory over the Turkish Ottomans at the naval battle of Lepanto in 1571. This pivotal battle, fought off the coast of Greece, slowed the Ottoman threat to Christian Europe. This square was the heart of medieval Madrid, though little remains of the 14th-century town.

• *From here, busy Calle Mayor leads downhill to the Royal Palace.*

From City Hall to the Royal Palace

Two blocks down Calle Mayor (on the left), at #75, a **real-estate office** *(inmobiliaria)* advertises apartments for rent (*alquilar*, apartments or condos, priced by the month, are in the hundreds or low thousands of euros) and condos for sale (*venta*, with six-digit prices). To roughly convert square meters to square feet, multiply by 10. Notice how, for expensive items, Spaniards still think in terms of pesetas ("pts")—the Spanish currency before euros took over in 2002.

A few steps farther down, on a tiny square, a statue memorializes a 1906 bombing. The target was Spain's King Alfonso XIII and his bride, Victoria Eugenie (grandparents of today's King Juan Carlos I), as they paraded by on their wedding day. While the crowd was throwing flowers, an anarchist (what terrorists used to be called) threw a bouquet lashed to a bomb from a balcony of #84, which was a hotel at the time. He missed the royal newlyweds, but killed 23 people. Gory photos of the event hang inside the recommended Casa Ciriaco restaurant on the square (at #84, closed Wed and Aug; photos to the right of the entrance).

• *Continue down Calle Mayor one block to a busy street, Calle de Bailén.*

Across the busy street is Madrid's **Cathedral of Almudena** (built 1883-1993). It faces the Royal Palace, but you'll enter on the side from Calle de Bailén. Before entering (€1 donation requested), notice the central door featuring a relief of the cathedral's 1993 consecration with Pope John Paul II, King Juan Carlos, Queen Sofía, and Princess María Mercedes (the king's mom, in a wheelchair). While the exterior is a contemporary mix of styles, the interior is Neo-Gothic, with a refreshingly modern and colorful ceiling, glittering 5,000-pipe organ, and a grand 15th-century painted altarpiece—striking in the otherwise modern interior. The historic highlight is the 12th-century coffin (empty, painted leather on wood, in a chapel behind the altar) of Madrid's patron saint, Isidro. A humble farmer, the exceptionally devout Isidro was said to get angels to do the plowing for him while he prayed. Forty years after he died, this coffin was opened and his body was found miraculously preserved, which convinced the pope to canonize him as the patron saint of Madrid and of farmers, with May 15 as his feast day.

• *Facing the cathedral, turn right on Calle de Bailén and walk one block to the **Royal Palace**. Visit the palace now, using my self-guided tour (on page 376). When you're finished, you may want to...*

Return to Puerta del Sol

With your back to the palace, face the equestrian statue of Philip IV and (beyond the statue) the Neoclassical **Royal Theater** (Teatro Real, rebuilt in 1997). On your left, the once-impressive **Madrid Tower** skyscraper marks Plaza de España. Walk behind the Royal Theater (on the right, passing Café de Oriente—a favorite with theater-goers) to another square, where you'll find the Ópera Metro stop and the wonderfully pedestrianized Calle del Arenal, which leads back to Puerta del Sol.

Sights in Madrid

▲▲▲Royal Palace (Palacio Real)

This is Europe's third-greatest palace, after Versailles and Vienna's Schönbrunn. It has arguably the most sumptuous original interior, packed with tourists and royal antiques.

After a fortress burned down on this site in the 18th century, Philip V (1683-1746), the first Bourbon (French) king of Spain, commissioned this huge palace as a replacement. Though he ruled Spain for 45 years, Philip remained very French. (The grandson of Louis XIV, he was born in

Versailles and ordered his tapas in French.) He built this palace as his own Versailles (although his wife's Italian origin had a tremendous impact on the style). It's big—more than 2,000 rooms, with tons of luxurious tapestries, a king's ransom of chandeliers, priceless porcelain, and bronze decor covered in gold leaf. While these days the royal family lives in a mansion a few miles away, this place still functions as a royal palace, and is used for formal state receptions, royal weddings, and tourists' daydreams.

The lions you'll see throughout were symbols of power. The Bourbon kings considered previous Spanish royalty not up to European par, and this palace—along with their establishment of a Spanish porcelain works and tapestry works—was their effort to raise the bar.

Cost: €10 without a tour, €17 with a one-hour tour (explained below).

Hours: April-Sept Mon-Sat 9:00-19:00, Sun 9:00-16:00; Oct-March Mon-Sat 10:00-18:00, Sun 10:00-16:00; last entry one hour before closing. The palace can close for royal functions; call a day ahead to check (tel. 914-548-800).

Crowd-Beating Tips: The palace is most crowded on Wednesdays and Thursdays, when it's free for locals. To minimize the time you'll be in line, arrive early or go late any day except Wednesday or Thursday. Madrid Card-holders get to skip the line (enter around the right side, a block down, along Calle de Bailén).

Getting There: To get to the palace from Puerta del Sol, walk down the pedestrianized Calle del Arenal. Metro: Ópera.

Information: Tel. 914-548-800, www.patrimonionacional.es.

Services: Free lockers and a WC are just past the ticket booth. Upstairs you'll find a refreshing air-conditioned cafeteria (with salad bar) and a more serious bookstore.

Eating Nearby: For eateries in the neighborhood, see page 422.

Touring the Palace: A simple one-floor, 24-room one-way circuit is open to the public. You can wander on your own or join an English-language tour (check time of next tour and decide as you buy your ticket; the English-language tours depart sporadically, not worth a long wait). The tour guides, like the museum guidebook, demonstrate a passion for meaningless data. The €4 audioguides are much more interesting, and they complement what I describe below. If you enjoy sightseeing cheek-to-cheek, share the audioguide with your companion. The armory and the pharmacy (included in your ticket) are in the courtyard. Photography is not allowed.

◉ Self-Guided Tour: If you tour the palace on your own, here are a few details beyond what you'll find on the little English descriptions posted in each room.

The Palace Lobby: In the old days, horse-drawn carriages would drop you off here. Today, limos for gala events do the same thing. Look for a sign that divides the visitors waiting for a tour from those going in alone. The modern black bust in the corner is of the current, very popular constitutional monarch—King Juan Carlos I. He's a "people's king," credited with bringing democracy to Spain after 40-plus years under dictator Franco.

The Grand Stairs: Fancy carpets are rolled down (notice the little metal bar-holding hooks) for formal occasions. At the top of

the first landing, the blue-and-red coat of arms represents Juan Carlos. While Franco chose him to be his successor, J. C. knew Spain was ripe for democracy. Rather than become "Juan the Brief" (as some were nicknaming him), he turned real power over to the parliament. You'll see his (figure) head on the back of the Spanish €1 and €2 coins.

Continue up to the top of the stairs. Before entering the first room, look to the right of door to find a white marble bust of J. C.'s great-great-g-g-g-great-grandfather Philip V, who began the Bourbon dynasty in Spain in 1700 and had this palace built.

Guard Room: The palace guards used to hang out in this relatively simple room. Notice the clocks. Charles IV (r. 1788-1808), a great collector, amassed more than 700. The 150 clocks displayed in this palace are all in working order. Look up to see the first ceiling fresco in a series by the great Venetian painter Giambattista Tiepolo. Much of what you see in the palace dates from the 18th century. But the carpet in this room was made in 1991 (see the corner folded over). Though modern, it was woven the traditional way—by hand in Madrid's royal tapestry factory.

Hall of Columns: Originally a ballroom and dining room, today this space is used for formal ceremonies. (For example, this is where Spain formally joined the European Union in 1985—see plaque on far wall.) The tapestries (like most you'll see in the palace) are 17th-century Belgian, from designs by Raphael. The central theme in the ceiling fresco is Apollo driving the chariot of the sun, while Bacchus enjoys wine, women, and song with a convivial gang. This is a reminder that the mark of a good king is to drive the chariot of state as smartly as Apollo, while providing an environment where the people can enjoy life to the fullest.

Throne Room: Red velvet walls, lions, and frescoes of Spanish scenes symbolize the monarchy in this Rococo riot. The 12 mirrors, impressive in their day, each represent a different month. The chandeliers (silver and crystal from Venice's island of Murano) are the best in the house. And though the room is decorated in the 18th-century style, the throne dates only from 1977. In Spain, a new one is built for each king or queen (with a gilded portrait on the back). This is where the king's guests salute Juan Carlos before dinner. He receives them relatively informally...standing at floor level, rather than seated up on the throne. The coat of arms above the throne shows the complexity of the Bourbon empire across Europe—which, in the 18th century, included Tirol, Sicily, Burgundy, the Netherlands, and more.

The ceiling fresco (1764) is the last great work by Tiepolo, who died in Madrid in 1770. This painting celebrates the days of the vast Spanish empire—upon which the sun also never set. Find the Native American (hint: follow the rainbow to the macho red-caped conquistador who motions to someone he conquered).

The next several rooms were the living quarters of King Charles III (r. 1759-1788). After his lounge (with the round sofa in the center), you come to the...

Antechamber: The four paintings are of King Charles IV (looking a bit like a dim-witted George Washington) and his wife, María Luisa (who wore the pants in the palace)—all originals by Francisco de Goya. To meet the demand for his work, he made copies of these (which you'll see in the Prado). The clock—showing Cronus, god of time, in porcelain, bronze, and mahogany—sits on a music box. The gilded decor you see throughout the palace is bronze with gold leaf. Velázquez's famous painting, *Las Meninas* (which you'll marvel at in the Prado), originally hung in this room.

Gasparini Room: This was meant to be Charles III's bedroom, but it wasn't yet finished when he died. Instead, with its painted stucco ceiling and inlaid Spanish marble floor, it became the royal dressing room. It's a triumph of the Rococo style, with the taste for exotic motifs during that period clearly evident in the Asian figures sculpted into the corners of the ornate ceiling. In 1992, the embroidered silk wall-hangings were restored to their original splendor. Note the micro-mosaic table—a typical royal or aristocratic souvenir from any visit to Rome in the mid-1800s. For a divine monarch, dressing was a public affair. The court bigwigs would assemble here as the king, standing on a platform—notice the height of the mirrors—would pull on his leotards and toy with his wig.

In the next room, the silk wallpaper is from modern times ("*J.C.S.*" indicates King Juan Carlos and Queen Sofía).
• *Pass through the silk room to reach...*

Charles III Bedroom: This room is dedicated to Charles III, known as one of the enlightened monarchs, who died here in his bed in 1788. His grandson, Ferdinand VII, commissioned the fresco on the ceiling, showing thanks to God for the birth of the first male grandson (that would be Ferdy himself) to continue the dynasty. Decorated in Neoclassical style, the chandelier is in the shape of the fleur-de-lis (symbol of the Bourbon family) capped with a Spanish crown. The thick walls separating each room hide service corridors for servants, who scurried about mostly unseen.

Porcelain Room: The walls and ceiling of this incredible room are lined with porcelain panels decorated with garlanded vines and mythological figures. The entire ensemble was disassembled for safety during the Spanish Civil War. (Find the little screws in the greenery that hides the seams.)

The Neoclassical Yellow Room was a study for Charles III. Notice the chandelier, with properly cut crystal that shows all the colors of the rainbow.

Gala Dining Room: Up to 12 times a year, the king entertains as many as 144 guests at this bowling lane-size table, which can be extended to the length of the room. The parquet floor was the preferred dancing surface when balls were held in this fabulous room. Note the vases from China and the ceiling fresco depicting Christopher Columbus kneeling before Ferdinand and Isabel, presenting exotic souvenirs and his new, red-skinned friends. Imagine the lighting when the 15 chandeliers (and their 900 bulbs) are fired up.

Cinema Room: In the early 20th century, the royal family enjoyed "Sunday afternoons at the movies" here. Today, this room stores glass cases filled with coins and medals. The table was used as a staging area for the lavish bouquets of flowers and fruits that ended up in the dining room as centerpieces, effectively making it impossible for guests to talk across the table.

Silver Room: This collection of silver tableware dates from the 19th century. The older royal silver was melted down by Napoleon's brother to help fund wars of the Napoleonic Age. If you look carefully, you can see quirky royal necessities, including a baby's silver rattle.

China Rooms: Several collections of china from different kings (some actually from China, others from royal workshops in Europe such as Sèvres and Meissen) are displayed in this room. This room illustrates how any self-respecting European royal family had to have its own porcelain works (the porcelain technique itself was a royal secret).

• *Exit to the hallway and notice the interior courtyard you've been circling one room at a time. You can see how the royal family lived in the spacious middle floor while staff was upstairs, and the kitchens, garage, and storerooms were on the ground level. Between statues of the giants of Spanish royal history (Isabel and Ferdinand), you'll enter the...*

Royal Chapel: This chapel (likely still closed for restoration in 2012) is used for private concerts and funerals. The royal coffin sits here before making the sad trip to El Escorial to join the rest of Spain's past royalty (see next chapter).

Queen's Boudoir: This room was for the ladies.

Stradivarius Room: The current queen likes classical music. When you perform for her, do it with these precious 350-year-old violins. Of all the instruments Antonius Stradivarius made, only 300 survive. This is the only matching quartet set: two violins, a viola, and a cello.

Billiards and Smoking Rooms: The billiards room (with its English men's-club paneling) and the adjacent smoking room were for men only. The porcelain and silk of the smoking room imitates a Chinese opium den, which, in its day, was furnished only with pillows.

Queen's Tearoom: Small and intimate, the Neoclassical Wedgwood-like decoration stands out.

Fine Woods Room: Fine 18th- and 19th-century French inlaid-wood pieces decorate this room.

• *Exit the palace down the same grand stairway you climbed 24 rooms ago. Cross the big courtyard, heading to the far right corner to the...*

Armory: Here you'll find weapons belonging to many great Spanish historical figures. Circle the big room clockwise.

In the three glass cases on the left, you'll see the oldest pieces in the collection: the sword of El Cid (the 11th-century Castilian who valiantly fought the Moors); the shield of Boabdil (the last Moorish king, who surrendered Granada in 1492); and the armor and swords of Ferdinand (husband of Isabel, and Boabdil's contemporary).

The long wall on the left displays the armor of Charles V, the ruler of Spain at its peak of power, in the 16th century. At the far end, you'll meet Charles V on horseback. The mannequin of the king wears the same armor and assumes the same pose as in Titian's famous painting of him (in the Prado).

The opposite wall showcases the armor and weapons of Philip II, Charles' son, who watched Spain start its long slide downward. Philip, who impoverished Spain with his wars against the Protestants, anticipated that debt collectors would ransack his estate after his death and specifically protected his impressive collection of armor.

The tapestry above the armor warmed the walls of the otherwise stark palace that predated this one. Tapestries traveled ahead of royals to decorate their living space. They made many palaces "fit for a king" back when the only way to effectively govern was to be on the road a lot.

Downstairs is more armor, a mixed collection mostly from the

17th century. Before you leave, notice the life-saving breastplates dimpled with bullet dents (to right of exit door).

Climb the steps from the armory exit to the viewpoint. This vast palace backyard, today a city park, was the king's hunting ground.

Pharmacy: The royal pharmacy is opposite the armory, near the entry. Wander through six rooms stacked with jars and jugs of herbal cures, past exotic beakers, and under portraits of royal doctors. Good English descriptions explain 18th- and 19th-century medicine.

Leaving the Palace: The upstairs, above the exit, has an air-conditioned cafeteria and a bookstore, which has a good variety of books on Spanish history.

As you leave the palace, walk around the corner to the left, along the palace exterior, to the grand yet people-friendly **Plaza de Oriente** (with my recommended lunch spot, Café de Oriente; wonderful €15 lunch special, Mon-Fri 13:00-16:00 only). Throughout Europe, energetic governments are turning formerly car-congested wastelands into public spaces like this. Madrid's last mayor was nicknamed "The Mole" for all the digging he did. Where's all the traffic? Under your feet.

Madrid's Museum Neighborhood

Three great museums, all within a 10-minute walk of one another, cluster in east Madrid: El Prado (Europe's top collection of paintings), the Thyssen-Bornemisza (a baron's collection of European art, from the old masters to the moderns), and the Centro de Arte Reina Sofía (modern art, including Picasso's famous *Guernica*).

Combo-Ticket: If visiting all three museums, save a few euros by buying the **Paseo del Arte** combo-ticket (€17.60, available at any of the three museums, good for a year). Note that the Prado and Reina Sofía have free-admission evenings throughout the week (Prado: Tue-Sat 18:00-20:00, Sun 17:00-20:00; Reina Sofía: Mon and Wed-Fri 19:00-21:00, Sat after 14:30, and all day Sun). The Prado and Thyssen-Bornemisza are closed Monday, and the Reina Sofía is closed Tuesday.

▲▲▲Prado Museum (Museo Nacional del Prado)

With more than 3,000 canvases, including entire rooms of masterpieces by superstar painters, the Prado (PRAH-doh) is overwhelming. But if you use the free English floor plan (be sure to pick it up as you enter) and follow my self-guided tour, you'll be impressed. The Prado is *the* place to enjoy the great Spanish painter Francisco de Goya, and it's also the home of Diego Velázquez's *Las Meninas,* considered by many to be the world's finest painting, period. In addition to Spanish works, you'll find paintings by Italian and Flemish masters, including Hieronymus Bosch's fantastical *Garden of Earthly Delights* altarpiece.

Cost: €8 for permanent collection, additional (optional) charge for temporary exhibits, free Tue-Sat 18:00-20:00 and Sun 17:00-20:00, and free anytime to anyone under 18.

Hours: Tue-Sun 9:00-20:00, closed Mon, last entry 30 minutes before closing.

Crowd-Beating Tips: Lunchtime (14:00-16:00) and weekdays are generally less crowded. It's always packed on free evenings and on weekends; it's worth paying the entry price on other days to have your space. The ticket-buying lines at the Goya entrance can be long. Here are some alternatives:

1. Use the ticket machines at the Goya entrance (credit cards only).

2. Buy online (www.museodelprado.es, a bargain at €7, you must reserve an entrance time, same-day reservations are possible), or reserve by phone (tel. 902-107-077).

3. Buy a Paseo del Arte combo-ticket (see earlier) at the less-crowded Thyssen-Bornemisza or Reina Sofía museums.

4. Get a Madrid Card beforehand, which lets you skip the line (see page 356).

Getting There: It's at the Paseo del Prado. The nearest Metro stops are Banco de España (line 2) and Atocha (line 1), each a five-minute walk from the museum. It's a 15-minute walk from Puerta del Sol.

Getting In: There are several entrances—see the map on page 384. You must buy tickets at the Goya (north) entrance. (Even at free-entry times, you need to pick up a gratis ticket at the Goya ticket window.) Once you have your ticket, you can enter at either the Jerónimos or Velázquez entrances. The Murillo entrance is reserved for groups.

Information: Tel. 913-302-800, www.museodelprado.es.

Audioguide: The €3.50 audioguide is a helpful supplement to my self-guided tour. Given the ever-changing locations of paintings (making my tour tough to follow), the audioguide is a good investment, allowing you to wander and dial up commentary on 120 masterpieces. And, if you're on a tight budget, remember that two can listen cheek-to-cheek, sharing one device.

Cloakroom: Your bags will be scanned as you enter. Bags larger than roughly 16 by 16 inches must be checked (free). No drinks, food, backpacks, or large umbrellas are allowed inside.

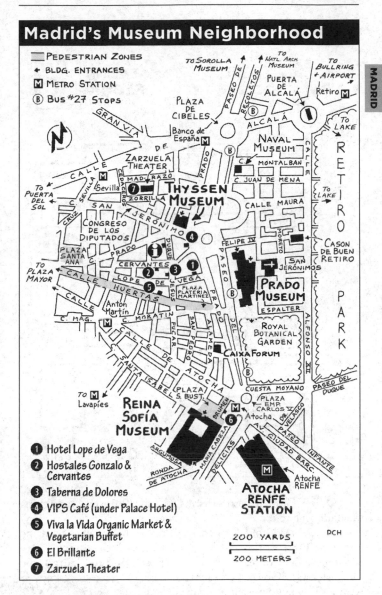

Madrid's Museum Neighborhood

PEDESTRIAN ZONES
BLDG. ENTRANCES
Ⓜ **METRO STATION**
Ⓑ **BUS #27 STOPS**

❶ Hotel Lope de Vega
❷ Hostales Gonzalo & Cervantes
❸ Taberna de Dolores
❹ VIPS Café (under Palace Hotel)
❺ Viva la Vida Organic Market & Vegetarian Buffet
❻ El Brillante
❼ Zarzuela Theater

200 YARDS
200 METERS

DCH

Services: The Jerónimos entrance has an information desk, bag check, audioguides, bookshop, WCs, and café. The self-service restaurant is open 9:00-18:00 (€15 *menu del dia,* €8 main dishes, €5 salads and sandwiches, hot dishes served only 12:15-16:00). The coffee-and-pastry bar stays open until 19:30.

Photography: Not allowed.

MADRID

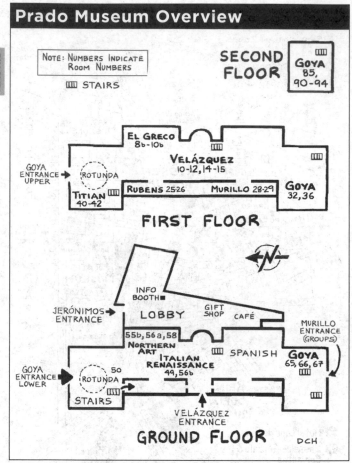

Prado Museum Overview

NOTE: NUMBERS INDICATE
ROOM NUMBERS

▥ STAIRS

SECOND FLOOR

GOYA
85,
90-94

EL GRECO
8b-10b

VELÁZQUEZ
10-12, 14-15

GOYA
ENTRANCE
UPPER

ROTUNDA

TITIAN
40-42

RUBENS 25-26

MURILLO 28-29

GOYA
32, 36

FIRST FLOOR

← N

INFO
BOOTH ■

JERÓNIMOS →
ENTRANCE

LOBBY

GIFT
SHOP

CAFÉ

MURILLO
ENTRANCE
(GROUPS)

55b, 56a, 58
NORTHERN
ART

SPANISH

GOYA
65, 66, 67

GOYA
ENTRANCE
LOWER

ROTUNDA

50

ITALIAN
RENAISSANCE
49, 56b

STAIRS

VELÁZQUEZ
ENTRANCE

GROUND FLOOR

DCH

❍ **Self-Guided Tour:** Thanks to Gene Openshaw for writing the following tour.

New World gold funded the Prado, the greatest painting museum in the world. You'll see world-class Italian Renaissance art (especially Titian), Northern art (Bosch, Rubens, Dürer), and Spanish art (El Greco, Velázquez, Goya). This huge museum is not laid out chronologically, so this tour will not be chronological. Instead, we'll hit the highlights with a minimum of walking. Make sure to have a map (free, available at entry). Paintings are moved around frequently—if you

can't find a particular one, ask a guard.

• *Once you have your ticket, go through the Jerónimos entrance. You're on the ground floor, or what the museum calls Level 0. Our tour starts in Room 49. To get there, head for the "Collection" in the Villabuena building. Follow signs to "Sala 49." Look for the following paintings in Room 49 and the adjoining rooms.*

Italian Renaissance: During its Golden Age (the 1500s), Spain may have been Europe's richest country, but Italy was still the most cultured. Spain's kings loved how Italian Renaissance artists captured a three-dimensional world on a two-dimensional canvas, bringing Bible scenes to life and celebrating real people and their emotions.

When still just a prince, Spain's Charles IV visited Rome and picked up **Raphael**'s *Portrait of a Cardinal* (c. 1510). Charles might have been drawn to the easy superiority with which the cardinal, a prince of the church, locks eyes with the viewer. As his contemporaries put it, Raphael could "paint people more real than they are."

Fra Angelico's *The Annunciation (La Anunciación*, c. 1426, in nearby Room 56b) is half medieval piety, half Renaissance real-

ism. In the crude Garden of Eden scene (on the left), a scrawny, sinful First Couple hovers unrealistically above the foliage, awaiting eviction. The angel's Annunciation to Mary (right side) is more Renaissance, both with its upbeat message (that Jesus will be born to redeem sinners like Adam and Eve) and in the budding photorealism, set beneath 3-D arches. (Still, aren't the receding bars of the porch's ceiling a bit off? Painting three dimensions wasn't that easy.)

In the tiny *Death of the Virgin* (*El Tránsito de la Virgen*, likely in Room 56b), **Andrea Mantegna** (c. 1431-1506) shows his mastery of Renaissance perspective. The apostles mourn in a crowded room, while the floor tiles recede into the distance, creating the subconscious effect of carrying Mary's soul out the window into the serene distance.

• *Find examples of Northern European art, including Dürer, in Room 55b.*

Northern Art: Albrecht Dürer's *Self-Portrait (Autorretrato),* from 1498, is possibly the first true self-portrait. The artist, age 26, is German, but he's all dolled up in a fancy Italian hat and permed hair. He'd recently returned from Italy and wanted to impress his countrymen with his sophistication. Dürer (1471-1528) wasn't simply vain. He'd grown accustomed, as an artist in Renaissance Italy, to being treated like a prince. Note Dürer's signature, the pyramid-shaped "A. D." (D inside the A), on the windowsill.

Dürer's 1507 *Adam and Eve* (two separate panels; recently restored, they should be back on view in 2012) are the first full-size nudes in Northern European art. Like Greek statues, they pose in their separate niches, with three-dimensional, anatomically correct bodies. This was a bold humanist proclamation that the body is good, man is good, and the things of the world are good.

• *Return to Room 49, and enter the adjoining Room 57b. Keep going until you find Room 58.*

The Descent from the Cross (El Descendimiento) is a masterpiece by Flemish painter **Roger van der Weyden** (c. 1399-1464). He reveals the psychological drama of this biblical event through the characters of real people in a contemporary (1435) scene. The Flemish were masters of detail, as you can see in the cloth, jewels, faces, and even tears. The creative composition suggests that, in losing her son, Mary suffered along with Jesus. As the Netherlands was then a part of the Spanish empire, this painting ended up in Madrid.

• *Continue to Room 56a.*

Hieronymus Bosch (c. 1450-1516), in his cryptic triptych *The Garden of Earthly Delights (El Jardín de las Delicias)*, relates the message that the pleasures of life are fleeting, and we'd better avoid them or we'll wind up in hell.

The large altarpiece has so many interesting small figures that it helps to "frame off" small sections to catch the details. In the

central panel, men on horseback ride round and round, searching for but never reaching the elusive Fountain of Youth. Others frolic in earth's "Garden," oblivious to where they came from (paradise, left panel) and where they may end up (hell, right panel). On the left, innocent Adam and Eve get married, with God himself performing the ceremony. The right panel is hell, a burning wasteland where genetic-mutant demons torture sinners. Everyone gets their just desserts, like the glutton who is eaten and re-eaten eternally. In the center, hell is literally frozen over. A creature with a broken eggshell body, tree-trunk legs, and a witch's cap stares out—it's the face of Bosch himself. Many other fascinating *El Boscos* are in this room.

Nearby, **Pieter Bruegel** the Elder's (c. 1525-1569) work chronicles the 16th century's violent Catholic-Protestant wars in *The Triumph of Death (El Triunfo de la Muerte)*. The painting is one big, chaotic battle, featuring skeletons attacking helpless mortals. Bruegel's message is simple and morbid: No one can escape death.

• *But you can escape this room. Continue through the next few rooms (55a and 55) until you emerge near the elevators. Go up to Level 1. Exiting the elevator, turn left into Room 11. This is one of several rooms with work by Velázquez—including* Las Meninas, *around the corner in the large, lozenge-shaped Room 12.*

Diego Velázquez (1599-1660): Velázquez (vel-LAHTH-keth) was the photojournalist of court painters, capturing the Spanish king and his court with a blend of formal portrait and candid snapshot.

Prince Balthazar Carlos on Horseback (El Príncipe Baltasar Carlos, a Caballo) is exactly the kind of portrait Velázquez was called on to produce. The prince prances like a Roman emperor—only this "emperor" is just a cute little five-year-old acting oh so serious. Get up close and notice that his remarkably detailed costume is nothing but a few messy splotches of pink and gold paint—the proto-Impressionism Velázquez helped pioneer.

The Surrender of Breda (La Rendición de Breda) is a piece of artistic journalism, chronicling Spain's victory over the Dutch. The defeated Dutchman starts to kneel, but the Spaniard stops him—no need to rub salt in the wound. Twenty-five lances silhouetted against the sky reinforce the optimistic calm-after-the-battle mood.

Velázquez's boss, King Philip IV, had an affair, got caught, and repented by commissioning the *Crucifixion (Cristo Crucificado)*. Christ hangs his head, humbly accepting his punishment, while Philip is left to stare at the slowly dripping blood, contemplating

how long Christ had to suffer to atone for Philip's sins.

Velázquez's *The Maids of Honor (Las Meninas)* is a peek at nannies caring for Princess Margarita and, at the same time, a behind-the-scenes look at Velázquez at work. One hot summer day in 1656, Velázquez (at left, with paintbrush and

Dalí moustache) stands at his easel and stares out at the people he's painting—the king and queen. They would have been standing about where we are, and we see only their reflection in the mirror at the back of the room. Their daughter (blonde hair, in center) watches her parents being painted, joined by her servants *(meninas)*, dwarves, and the family dog. At that very moment, a man happens to pass by the doorway at back and pauses to look in.

This frozen moment is lit by the window on the right, splitting the room into bright and shaded planes that recede into the distance. The main characters look right at us, making us part of the scene, seemingly able to walk around, behind, and among the characters.

If you stand in the center of the room, the 3-D effect is most striking. This is art come to life.

Now look around and see how Velázquez enjoyed capturing light—and capturing the moment. *The Drinkers (Los Borrachos)* is a cellphone snapshot in a blue-collar bar, with a couple of peasants mugging for a photo-op with a Greek god— Bacchus, the god of wine. This was an early work, before Velázquez got his court-painter gig. A personal homage to the hardworking farmers enjoying the fruit of their labor, it shows how Velázquez had a heart for real people and believed they deserved portraits, too.

• *From Room 12, exit into Room 27, part of a long gallery of paintings (Rooms 25-29). In the gallery, find works by Murillo (to the left) and Rubens (to the right).*

Bartolomeo Murillo (1618-1683): Bartolomeo Murillo's *Immaculate Conception (La Inmaculada "de El Escorial")* puts a human face on the abstract Catholic doctrine that Mary was conceived and born free of original sin. Floating in a cloud of Ivory Soap purity, this "immaculate" virgin radiates youth and wholesome goodness. (Murillo and his style are described on page 582.)

Peter Paul Rubens (1577-1640): A native of Flanders, Rubens painted Baroque-style art meant to play on the emotions, titillate the senses, and carry you away. *Diana and Her Nymphs Discovered by a Satyr (Diana y Sus Ninfas Sorprendidas por Sátiros)* ripples from left to right with a wave of figures, as the nymphs flee from the half-human sex predators. But Diana, queen of the hunt, turns to bravely face the satyrs with her spear. All of Rubens' trademarks

are here—sex, violence, action, emotion, bright colors, fleshy bodies—with the wind machine set on 10.

Rubens' *The Three Graces (Las Tres Gracias)* celebrates cellulite. The ample, glowing bodies intertwine as the women exchange meaningful glances. The Grace at left is Rubens' young second wife, Hélène Fourment, who shows up regularly in his paintings.

• *El Greco's works are nearby, in the adjoining Room 9b and beyond*

El Greco (1541-1614): El Greco was born in Greece (his name is Spanish for "The Greek"), trained in Venice, then settled in Toledo—60 miles from Madrid. His paintings are like Byzantine icons drenched in Venetian color and fused in the fires of Spanish mysticism. (For more on El Greco, see page 485 and visit Toledo.)

In *Christ Carrying the Cross (Cristo Abrazado a la Cruz)*, Jesus accepts his fate, trudging toward death with blood running down his neck. He hugs the cross and directs his gaze along the crossbar. His upturned eyes (sparkling with a streak of white paint) lock onto his next stop—heaven.

The Adoration of the Shepherds (La Adoración de los Pastores), originally painted for El Greco's own burial chapel in Toledo, has the artist's typical two-tiered composition—heaven above, earth below. The long, skinny shepherds are stretched unnaturally in between, flickering like flames toward heaven.

The Nobleman with His Hand on His Chest (El Caballero de la Mano al Pecho) is an elegant and somewhat arrogant man whose hand has the middle fingers touching—El Greco's trademark way of expressing elegance (or was it the 16th-century symbol for "Live long and prosper"?). The signature is on the right in faint Greek letters—"Doménikos Theotokópoulos," El Greco's real name.

• *Return to the main gallery and head to the right, exiting into the rotunda and turning left, into Room 42, one of several rooms with works by Titian.*

Titian (c. 1490-1576): Titian painted portraits of Spain's two Golden Age kings—both staunch Catholics—who amassed this racy collection. *Charles V on Horseback (El Emperador Carlos V en la Batalla de Mühlberg)* rears on his horse, raises his lance, and rides out to crush an army of Lutherans. Charles, having inherited many kingdoms and baronies through his family connections, was the world's most powerful man in the 1500s. (You can see the suit of armor depicted in the painting in the Royal Palace.)

Danae and the Shower of Gold (Danae Recibiendo la Lluvia de Oro), from Greek mythology, shows the princess opening her legs to receive Zeus, the lecherous king of the gods, who descends as a shower of gold. Danae is helpless with rapture, while her servant tries to catch the holy spurt with a towel.

In contrast, Charles V's son, *Philip II (Felipe II),* looks pale, suspicious, and lonely—a scholarly and complex figure. He built the austere, monastic palace at El Escorial, but also indulged himself with Titian's bevy of Renaissance Playmates—a sampling of which is here in the Prado.

• *Return to the main gallery, and walk the entire length—past Rubens, past Murillo. At the far end, enter the round Room 32, where you'll see royal portraits by Goya.*

Francisco de Goya (1746-1828): Follow this complex man through the stages of his life—from dutiful court painter, to political rebel and scandal-maker, to the disillusioned genius of his "black paintings."

The Family of Charles IV (La Familia de Carlos IV) is all decked out in their Sunday best for this group portrait. Goya himself stands to the far left, painting the court (a tribute to Velázquez in *Las Meninas*) and revealing the shallow people beneath the royal trappings. King Charles, with his ridiculous hairpiece and goofy smile, was a vacuous, henpecked husband. His

domineering queen upstages him, arrogantly stretching her swan-like neck. The other adults, with their bland faces, are bug-eyed with stupidity.

• *To the right, in Room 36, is Goya's most scandalous work.*

Rumors flew that Goya was fooling around with the vivacious Duchess of Alba, who may have been the model for two similar paintings, *Nude Maja (La Maja Desnuda)* and *Clothed Maja (La Maja Vestida).*

A *maja* was a trendy, working-class girl. Whether she's a duchess or a *maja*, Goya painted a naked lady. And that was enough to risk incurring the wrath of the Inquisition. The nude stretches in a Titian-esque pose to display her charms, the pale body highlighted by cool green sheets. According to a believable legend, the two paintings were displayed in a double frame, with the *Clothed Maja* sliding over the front to hide the *Nude Maja* from Inquisitive minds.

• *Find the nearby staircase and elevator, and head up to Level 2 for more Goya.*

Goya's Tapestry Cartoons: These rooms display Goya's designs on canvas (known as "cartoons") for tapestries for nobles'

palaces. The scenes make it clear that, while revolution was brewing in America and France, Spain's lords and ladies played—picnicking, dancing, flying kites, playing paddleball and Blind Man's Bluff, or just relaxing in the sun—as in the well-known *The Parasol (El Quitasol,* Room 85).

• *For more Goya, take the stairs or elevator down to Level 0. Find Room 66, which leads into Goya's final paintings, with a darker edge.*

Goya's *Third of May* and Black Painting: Goya became a political liberal, a champion of democracy. He was crushed

when France's hero of the Revolution, Napoleon, morphed into a tyrant and invaded Spain. In the *Second of May, 1808,* Madrid's citizens protest the occupation in Puerta del Sol, and the French send in their dreaded Egyptian mercenaries. They plow through the dense tangle of Madrileños, who have nowhere to run. The next day, the *Third of May, 1808,* the French rounded up ringleaders and executed them. The colorless firing squad—a faceless machine of death—mows them down, and they fall in bloody, tangled heaps. Goya throws a harsh prison-yard floodlight on the main victim, who spreads his arms Christ-like to ask, "Why?"

Politically, Goya was split—he was a Spaniard but he knew France was leading Europe into the modern age. His art, while political, has no Spanish or French flags. It's a universal comment on the horror of war. Many consider Goya the last classical and first modern painter...the first painter with a social conscience.

• *About face to the "black paintings" in Rooms 66 and 67.*

Depressed and deaf from syphilis, Goya retired to his small home and smeared its walls with his "black paintings"—dark in color and in mood. From this point until his death, Goya would paint his nightmares...literally. The style is considered Romantic—emphasizing emotion over beauty—but it foreshadows 20th-century Surrealism with its bizarre imagery, expressionistic and thick brushstrokes, and cynical outlook.

Stepping into these rooms, you are surrounded by art from Goya's dark period. These paintings are the actual murals from the walls of his house, transferred onto canvas. Imagine this in your living room. Goya painted what he felt with a radical technique unburdened by reality—a century before his time. And he painted without being paid for it. This room contains, I believe, the first rare art done without a commission.

Dark forces convened continually in Goya's dining room, where *The Witches' Sabbath (El Aquelarre)* hung. The witches, who look like skeletons, swirl in a frenzy around a dark, Satanic goat in monk's clothing who presides over the obscene rituals. The main witch exudes wild-eyed adoration and lust, while a noble lady (right of center) folds her hands primly in her lap ("I thought this was a Tupperware party!"). Or, perhaps it's a pep rally for her execution, maybe inspired by the excited frenzy that accompanied Plaza Mayor executions. Nobody knows for sure.

In the *Battle to the Death (Duelo a Garrotazos)*, two giants stand face to face, buried up to their knees, and flail at each other with clubs. It's a standoff between superpowers in the never-ending cycle of war—a vision of a tough time when people on the streets would kill for a piece of bread.

The Dog (El Perro) is, according to some, the hinge between classical art and modern art. The dog, so full of feeling and sadness, is being swallowed by quicksand...much as, to Goya, the modern age was overtaking a more classical era.

In *Saturn Devouring One of His Sons (Saturno)*, the king of the Roman gods—fearful that his progeny would overthrow him—eats one of his offspring. Saturn, also known as Cronus (Time), may symbolize how time devours us all. Either way, the painting brings new meaning to the term "child's portion."

• *The rest of the Prado is also tasty, but our tour is over. Hungry? Try the café in the Jerónimos entrance.*

▲▲Thyssen-Bornemisza Museum (Museo del Arte Thyssen-Bornemisza)

Locals call this stunning museum simply the Thyssen (TEE-sun). It displays the impressive collection that Baron Thyssen (a wealthy German married to a former Miss Spain) sold to Spain for $350 million. The museum offers a unique chance to enjoy the sweep of all art history—including a good sampling of the "isms" of the 20th century—in one collection. It's basically minor works by major artists and major works by minor artists. (Major works by major artists are in the Prado.) But art lovers appreciate how the good baron's art complements the Prado's collection by filling in where the Prado is weak—such as Impressionism, which is the Thyssen's forte.

Cost: €8 (up to €8 more for optional special exhibits), children under 12 free.

Hours: Tue-Sun 10:00-19:00, closed Mon, last entry 30 minutes before closing.

Getting There: It's kitty-corner from the Prado at Paseo del Prado 8 in Palacio de Villahermosa (Metro: Banco de España).

Information: Free baggage storage, €4 audioguide, café, shop, no photos, tel. 914-203-944, www.museothyssen.org.

Touring the Museum: After purchasing your ticket, continue down the wide main hall past larger-than-life paintings of King Juan Carlos and Queen Sofía, and then paintings of the baron (who died in 2002) and his art-collecting baroness, Carmen. At the info desk, pick up two museum maps (one for numbered rooms, another for lettered rooms). Each floor is divided into two separate areas: the permanent collection (blue-numbered rooms) and additions from the baroness since the 1980s (red-lettered rooms). Most visitors stick to the permanent collection.

Ascend to the top floor and work your way down, taking a delightful walk through art history. Visit the rooms on each floor in numerical order, from Primitive Italian (Room 1) to Surrealism and Pop Art (Room 48).

Temporary exhibits at the Thyssen often parallel those at the free **Caja Madrid** exhibit hall, across from the Descalzas Royal Monastery on Plaza San Martín, a short walk from Puerta del Sol (see page 400).

Leaving the Museum: If you're heading to the Reina Sofía and you're tired, hail a cab at the gate to zip straight there, or take bus #27, which stops in the square with the Neptune fountain, in front of the Starbucks (ride to the end of Paseo del Prado, get off at the McDonald's, and cross the street, going away from the Botanical Gardens, to Plaza Sánchez Bustillo and the museum).

▲▲▲Centro de Arte Reina Sofía

Home to Picasso's *Guernica,* the Reina Sofía is one of Europe's most enjoyable modern art museums. Its exceptional collection

of 20th-century art is housed in what was Madrid's first public hospital. The focus is on Spanish artists—Picasso, Dalí, Miró, Gris, and Tàpies—but you'll also find plenty of works by Kandinsky, Braque, and many other giants of modern art.

The current curator, who has a passion for cinema, has paired paintings with films from the same decade, which play continuously in nearby rooms. This provides a fascinating insight into the social context that inspired the art of Spain's tumultuous 20th century.

Cost: €6 (includes temporary exhibits); free on Mon and Wed-Fri after 19:00, Sat afternoon after 14:30, and all day Sun (free times on weekends are often crowded; even when admission is free, you need to pick up a ticket). Ask about free entry if you're under 18 or over 65.

Hours: Mon and Wed-Sat 10:00-21:00, Sun 10:00-14:30, closed Tue.

Getting There: It's a block from the Atocha Metro stop, on Plaza Sánchez Bustillo (at Calle de Santa Isabel 52). In the Metro station, follow signs for the Reina Sofía exit. Emerging from the Metro, walk straight ahead a half-block and look for an opening between the group of buildings. You'll see the tall, exterior glass elevators that flank the museum's main entrance.

Information: Free map, good information sheets, no tours in English, hardworking €4 audioguide; photos without flash OK, but no *Guernica* photos allowed; tel. 914-675-062, www.museo reinasofia.es.

Services: Bag storage is free. The *librería* just outside the Nouvel wing has a larger selection of Picasso and Surrealist reproductions than the main gift shop at the entrance. The museum's café (a long block around the left from the main entrance) is a standout for its tasty cuisine.

❷ Self-Guided Tour: The permanent collection is primarily on the second floor (art of 1900-1945) and fourth floor (1945-

1968), with a small selection in the adjoining Nouvel wing, Level 0 (1968-present). Temporary exhibits are on the first and third floors. While the collection is roughly chronological, it's displayed thematically. You'll find Picassos, for example, scattered throughout the museum.

• *Ride the fancy glass elevator to Level 2, and start in Room 206, with the museum's highlight...*

Picasso's *Guernica:* Pablo Picasso's epic painting shows the horror of modern war. While it's become a timeless classic representing all war, it was born in response to a specific conflict—the Spanish Civil War (1936-1939), which pitted the democratically elected government against the fascist general Francisco Franco (for more on the war, see the sidebar on the next page). Franco won and ended up ruling Spain with an iron fist for the next 37 years. During his reign, the anti-Franco painting was sent to New York City and displayed at the Museum of Modern Art. It was only after Franco's death, in 1975, that *Guernica* was allowed to return. After 44 years in exile, the painting finally came home on September 10, 1981, and now stands as Spain's national piece of art. For a complete description, read the sidebar.

• *After seeing* Guernica, *walk around the nearby rooms to view exhibits that put the painting in its social context.*

Other *Guernica* **Exhibits:** First find the **photos** showing the evolution of the painting, from Picasso's first conception to the final product. The photos were taken by Dora Maar, Picasso's mistress-du-jour (and whose portrait by Picasso hangs nearby). Notice how the defiant fist in early versions was eventually replaced by a terrified horse.

Two rooms contain **studies** Picasso did for *Guernica*. These studies are filled with motifs that turn up in the final canvas—iron-nail tears, weeping women, and screaming horses.

In the room directly opposite *Guernica*, the film *España 1936* has a fierce anti-Franco perspective. Produced by the Madrid government (Spain's "last red city") late in the war, it features images of Franco's infamous ally (Hitler), the Franco-fascist war machine, and brave peasants fighting back in heroic solidarity *(solidaridad)*.

A **model of the Spanish Pavilion** at the 1937 Paris Expo shows where *Guernica* was first displayed for the world to see (look inside to see Picasso's work). Picasso was preparing to paint something light and typically Spanish, such as flamenco and matadors, for the Expo. But the bombing of Guernica jolted him into the realization that "the real Spain" was a country torn by war. The pavilion was a vessel for propaganda against Franco. Nearby, you'll see posters and political cartoons that are pro-communist and anti-Franco.

A couple of rooms to the right of *Guernica*, another film, *Songs*

Guernica

Perhaps the single most impressive piece of art in Spain is Pablo Picasso's *Guernica*. The monumental canvas—one of Europe's must-see sights—is not only a piece of art but a piece of history, capturing the horror of modern war in a modern style.

History

Pablo Picasso (1881-1973), a Spaniard, was in Paris in 1937, preparing an exhibition of paintings for the city's world's fair. Meanwhile, a bloody Civil War was being fought in his own country. The legally elected democratic government was being challenged by traditionalist right-wing forces under Francisco Franco.

On April 26, 1937, Guernica—a proud Basque market town in northern Spain—was the target of the world's first saturation-bombing raid on civilians. Franco gave permission to his fascist ally, Hitler, to use the town as a guinea pig to try out Germany's new air force. The raid leveled the town, causing destruction that was unheard of at the time (though by 1944 it would be commonplace). For more on the town of Guernica and the bombing, see page 186.

News of the bombing reached Picasso in Paris. He scrapped earlier plans and immediately set to work sketching scenes of the destruction as he imagined it. In a matter of weeks he put these bomb-shattered shards together into a large mural (286 square feet). For the first time, the world could see the destructive force of the rising fascist movement—a prelude to World War II.

The Painting

The bombs are falling, shattering the quiet village. A woman looks up at the sky (far right), horses scream (center), and a man falls from a horse and dies, while a wounded woman drags herself through the streets. She tries to escape, but her leg is too thick, dragging her down, like trying to run from something in a nightmare. On the left, a bull—a symbol of Spain—ponders it all, watching over a mother and her dead baby...a modern *pietà*. A woman in the center sticks her head out to see what's going on. The whole scene is lit from above by the stark light of a bare bulb. Picasso's painting threw a light on the brutality of Hitler and Franco, and suddenly the whole world was watching.

Picasso's abstract, Cubist style reinforces the message. It's as if he'd picked up the shattered shards and pasted them onto a canvas. The black and white tones are as gritty as the black-and-white newspaper photos that reported the bombing. The drab colors create a depressing, almost nauseating mood.

Picasso chose images with universal symbolism, making the work a commentary on all wars. Picasso himself said that the central horse, with the spear in its back, symbolizes humanity succumbing to brute force. The fallen rider's arm is severed and his sword is broken, more symbols of defeat. The bull, normally a proud symbol of strength and independence, is impotent and frightened. Near the bull, the dove of peace can do nothing but cry.

Reaction

The bombing of Guernica—like the entire Spanish Civil War—was an exercise in brutality. As one side captured a town, it might systematically round up every man, old and young—including priests—line them up, and shoot them in revenge for atrocities by the other side.

Thousands of people attended the Paris fair, and *Guernica* caused an immediate sensation. They could see the horror of modern war technology, the vain struggle of the Spanish Republicans, and the cold indifference of the fascist war machine. After the Paris exhibition, *Guernica* was exiled to America until Franco's death. Picasso also vowed never to return to Spain while Franco ruled. (Franco outlived him.)

With each passing year, the canvas seemed more and more prophetic—honoring not just the hundreds or thousands who died in Guernica, but also the estimated 500,000 victims of Spain's bitter Civil War and the 55 million worldwide who perished in World War II. Picasso put a human face on what we now call "collateral damage."

After a War, uses pompous clips from Franco's own propaganda films to mock him. Made in 1971, the film couldn't be shown in Spain until after Franco's death.

• *After maxing out on* Guernica, *find Room 205 to locate the signature works of...*

   Salvador Dalí: In this room, you'll see Dalí's distinct, Surrealist, melting-object style. He places familiar items in a stark landscape, creating an eerie effect. Figures morph into faces and body parts. Background and foreground play mind games—is it an animal (seen one way) or a man's face? A waterfall or a pair of legs? *The Great Masturbator* is exhausting psychologically, depicting in its Surrealism a lonely, highly sexual genius, in love with his muse, Gala, while she is still married to a French poet.

   Dalí was another Spaniard who found refuge outside Spain during its turbulent years. Check out the propaganda movie produced by the Spanish Republic (pre-Franco) that shows the sad state of its people.

• *Head to Room 203.*

   Along with several early works by Dalí, you'll see the classic Surrealist film, *The Andalusian Dog* (c. 1930). It was directed by Luis Buñuel, who had help from friends Dalí and the poet Federico García Lorca. Both were members of "The Generation of '27," a group of nonconformist, creative Spanish bohemians who had a huge influence culturally and artistically on their era.

   The Rest of the Museum: Room 210 shows the birth of Cubism (with works by Picasso, Braque, Léger, and Gris)—a movement in which Spaniards were very much at the forefront.

   The permanent collection continues on the **fourth floor.** Room 419 is especially interesting, with works by Picasso and Miró. On this floor, you can watch films documenting Spain's slow recovery from its devastating Civil War. The physical and psychological damage of the war weighed on Spain for decades afterward.

   End your visit in the **Nouvel wing,** which has fewer big names, but demonstrates that Spanish art is still alive and well.

Near the Prado

▲**Retiro Park (Parque del Buen Retiro)**—Once the private domain of royalty, this majestic park has been a favorite of Madrid's commoners since Charles III decided to share it with his subjects in the late 18th century. Siesta in this 300-acre green-and-breezy escape from the city. At midday on Saturday and Sunday, the area around the lake becomes a street carnival, with jugglers, puppeteers, and lots of local color. These peaceful gardens offer great picnicking and people-watching (closes at dusk). From the Retiro Metro stop, walk to the big lake (El Estanque), where you can rent a rowboat. Past the lake, a grand boulevard of statues leads to the Prado.

▲**Royal Botanical Garden (Real Jardín Botánico)**—After your Prado visit, you can take a lush and fragrant break in this sculpted park. Wander among trees from around the world. The flier in English explains that this is actually more than a park—it's a museum of plants.

Cost and Hours: €2.50, daily 10:00-21:00, until 18:00 in winter, last entry 30 minutes before closing, entrance is opposite Prado's Murillo/south entry, Plaza de Murillo 2.

▲**Naval Museum (Museo Naval)**—This museum tells the story of Spain's navy, from the Armada to today, in a plush and fascinating-to-boat-lovers exhibit. Given Spain's importance in maritime history, there's quite a story to tell. Because this is a military facility, you'll need to show your passport to get in. A good English brochure is available.

Cost and Hours: Free, Tue-Sun 10:00-18:00, closed Mon and Aug, a block north of the Prado, across boulevard from Thyssen-Bornemisza Museum, Paseo del Prado 5, tel. 915-239-884.

CaixaForum—Across the street from the Prado and Royal Botanical Garden, this impressive exhibit hall has sleek architecture and an outdoor hanging garden—a bushy wall festooned with greens designed by a French landscape artist. The forum, funded by La Caixa Bank, features world-class art exhibits—generally 20th-century art, well-described in English and changing three times a year. Ride the elevator to the top, where you'll find a chic café with €12 lunch specials and sperm-like lamps swarming down from the ceiling; from here, explore your way down.

Cost and Hours: Free, daily 10:00-20:00, Paseo del Prado 36, tel. 913-307-300.

Elsewhere in Madrid

Descalzas Royal Monastery (Monasterio de las Descalzas Reales)—Madrid's most visit-worthy monastery was founded in the 16th century by Philip II's sister, Joan of Habsburg (known to Spaniards as Juana and to Austrians as Joanna). She's buried here. The monastery's chapels are decorated with fine art, Rubens-designed tapestries, and the heirlooms of the wealthy women who joined the order (the nuns were required to give a dowry). Because this is still a working Franciscan monastery, tourists can enter only when the nuns vacate the cloister, and the number of daily visitors is limited. The scheduled tours often sell out—come in the morning to buy your ticket, even if you want an afternoon tour.

Cost and Hours: €5, visits guided in Spanish or English depending on demand, Tue-Thu and Sat 10:30-13:30 & 16:00-18:30, Fri 10:30-13:30, Sun 11:00-14:30, closed Mon, last entry one hour before closing, Plaza de las Descalzas Reales 3, near the

Ópera Metro stop and just a short walk from Puerta del Sol, tel. 914-548-800.

Nearby: Across the street from the monastery, the free **Caja Madrid** exhibit hall showcases temporary exhibits that parallel those at the Thyssen-Bornemisza Museum (Tue-Sat 10:00-20:00, closed Mon and when there are no temporary exhibits, tel. 913-792-050, www.fundacioncajamadrid.es).

▲**Museum of the Americas (Museo de América)**—Thousands of pre-Colombian and colonial artworks and artifacts make up the bulk of this worthwhile museum. Covering the cultures of the Americas (North and South), its exhibits focus on language, religion, and art, and provide a new perspective on the cultures of our own hemisphere. Highlights include one of only four surviving Mayan codices (ancient books) and a section about the voyages of the Spanish explorers, with their fantastical imaginings of mythical creatures awaiting them in the New World.

Cost and Hours: €3, free on Sun, open Tue-Sat 9:30-20:30, Nov-April until 18:30, Sun 10:00-15:00, closed Mon, northwest of the city center at Avenida de los Reyes Católicos 6, Metro: Moncloa, tel. 915-492-641, http://museodeamerica.mcu.es.

Getting There: The museum is a 10-minute walk from the Moncloa Metro stop: Take the Calle de Isaac Peral exit, cross Plaza de Moncloa, and veer right to Calle de Fernández de los Ríos. Follow that street (toward the shiny Faro de Moncloa tower), and turn left on Avenida de los Reyes Católicos. Head around the base of the tower, which stands at the museum's entrance.

▲**National Archaeological Museum (Museo Arqueológico Nacional)**—This museum is under major renovation and scheduled to be finished sometime in 2012. Until then, only about 300 of its most noteworthy pieces will be on display. If you're here after all of its rooms have reopened, you'll follow a chronological walk through the story of Iberia. With a rich collection of artifacts, the walk shows off the wonders of each age: Celtic pre-Roman, Roman, a fine and rare Visigothic section, Moorish, Romanesque, and beyond. You may also find underwhelming replica artwork from northern Spain's Altamira Caves (big on bison), giving you a faded peek at the skill of the cave artists who created the originals 14,000 years ago. For more on the real Altamira Caves, see the Cantabria chapter.

Cost and Hours: Free, Tue-Sat 9:30-20:00, Sun 9:30-15:00, closed Mon, north of the Prado at Calle Serrano 13, Metro: Serrano or Colón, tel. 915-777-912, http://man.mcu.es.

Sorolla Museum (Museo Sorolla)—Painter Joaquín Sorolla (1863-1923) is known for his portraits, landscapes, and use of light. It's a relaxing experience to stroll through the rooms of his former house and studio, especially to see the lazy beach scenes of his hometown Valencia. The museum is best experienced when daylight streams through the house, which is how the artist intended for people to view his work. Take a break after your visit to reflect in the small garden in front of his house.

Cost and Hours: €3, free on Sun, open Tue-Sat 9:30-20:00, Sun 10:00-15:00, closed Mon, north of city center at General Martínez Campos 37, Metro: Iglesia, tel. 913-101-584, http://museosorolla.mcu.es.

History Museum (Museo de Historia)—This museum covers the history of Madrid in old paintings and models. The entrance features a fine Baroque door by architect Pedro de Ribera, with "St. James the Moor-Slayer" (see page 301). The museum has been closed for renovation but should be open by the time you visit—confirm with the TI before you make the trip (free, call for hours, Calle Fuencarral 78, Metro: Tribunal or Bilbao, tel. 917-011-863).

▲Clothing Museum (Museo del Traje)—This museum shows the history of clothing from the 18th century until today. In a cool and air-conditioned chronological sweep, the museum's one floor of exhibits includes regional ethnic costumes, a look at how bullfighting and the French influenced styles, accessories through the ages, and Spanish flappers. The only downside of this marvelous, modern museum is that it's a long way from anything else of interest.

Cost and Hours: €3, free Sat 14:30-19:00 and all day Sun, open Tue-Sat 9:30-19:00, Sun 10:00-15:00, closed Mon, last entry 30 minutes before closing, northwest of city center at Avenida de Juan Herrera 2; Metro: Moncloa and a longish walk, bus #46, or taxi; tel. 915-497-150.

▲Chapel of San Antonio de la Florida—In this simple little Neoclassical chapel from the 1790s, Francisco de Goya's tomb stares up at a splendid cupola filled with his own proto-Impressionist frescoes. He frescoed this using the same unique technique that he employed for his "black paintings." Use the mirrors to enjoy the drama and energy he infused into this marvelously restored masterpiece.

Cost and Hours: Free, Tue-Fri 9:30-20:00, Sat-Sun 10:00-14:00, closed Mon, Glorieta de San Antonio de la Florida; Metro: Príncipe Pío, then five-minute walk down Paseo de San Antonio de la Florida; tel. 915-420-722.

Royal Tapestry Factory (Real Fábrica de Tapices)—Have a look at traditional tapestry-making. You can actually order a tailor-made tapestry (starting at $10,000).

Cost and Hours: €3.50, by tour only, on the half-hour, Mon-Fri 10:00-14:00, closed Sat-Sun and Aug, last entry at 13:30, some English tours, south of Retiro Park at Calle Fuenterrabia 2, Metro: Menendez Pelayo, take Gutenberg exit, tel. 914-340-550.

Temple de Debod—In 1968, Egypt gave Spain its own ancient temple. It was a gift of the Egyptian government, which was grateful for the Spanish dictator Franco's help in rescuing monuments that had been threatened by the rising Nile waters above the Aswan Dam. Consequently, Madrid is the only place I can think of in Europe where you can actually wander through an intact original Egyptian temple—complete with fine carved reliefs from 200 B.C. Set in a romantic park that locals love for its great city views (especially at sunset), the temple—as well as its art—is well-described. The much-touted but uninspiring "grand Madrid view" only causes me to wonder why anyone would build a city here.

Cost and Hours: Free; April-Sept Tue-Fri 10:00-14:00 & 18:00-20:00, Sat-Sun 10:00-14:00, closed Mon; Oct-March Tue-Fri 9:45-13:45 & 16:15-18:15, Sat-Sun 10:00-14:00, closed Mon; in Parque de Montaña, north of the Royal Palace.

Experiences in Madrid

▲▲Self-Guided Bus Tour: Paseo de la Castellana—Tourists risk leaving Madrid without ever seeing the modern "Manhattan" side of town. But it's easy to do. From the Prado Museum, bus #27 makes the trip straight north along Paseo del Prado and then Paseo de la Castellana, through the no-nonsense skyscraper part of this city of more than three million. The line ends at the leaning towers of Puerta de Europa (Gate of Europe). This trip is simple and cheap (€1, buses run every 10 minutes, sit on the right if possible, beware of pickpockets). You just joyride for 30 minutes to the last stop (longer if it's rush hour), get out when everyone else does, ogle the skyscrapers, and catch the Metro for a 20-minute ride back to the city's center. At twilight, when fountains and facades are floodlit, the ride is particularly enjoyable.

Historic District: Bus #27 rumbles from Atocha Station past the Royal Botanical Garden (opposite McDonald's) and the Velázquez entrance to the Prado (if you're starting from here, catch the bus from the museum side to head north).

Look out for these landmarks: the Prado Museum (right); a square with a fountain of Neptune (left); an obelisk and war memorial to those who have died for Spain (right, with the stock market behind it); the Naval Museum (right); Plaza de Cibeles (with the fancy City Hall, the Bank of Spain, and other huge buildings); and then the National Library (right).

Modern District: The square with a statue of Columbus marks the end of the historic town and the beginning of the modern city. At this point the boulevard changes its name. It used to be named for Franco; now it's named for the people he no longer rules—*la Castellana* (Castilians). Next comes the American Embassy (hard to see behind its fortified wall, right) and Franco's ministries (left, typical fascist architecture, c. 1940s, some still used). Continuing up the boulevard, look left to see the Picasso Tower, resembling one of New York's former World Trade Center towers (both buildings were designed by the same architect), the huge Bernabéu soccer stadium (right, home of Real Madrid, Europe's most successful soccer team, described later), and the Ministry of Defense (left).

Your trip ends at Plaza de Castilla, where you can't miss the avant-garde Puerta de Europa, consisting of the twin "Torres Kios," office towers that lean at a 15-degree angle (one has the big green bear logo of the Bank of Madrid). In the distance, you can see four of the tallest buildings in Spain. The plaza sports a futuristic obelisk by contemporary Spanish architect Santiago Calatrava.

It's the end of the line for the bus—and for you. You can return directly to Puerta del Sol on the Metro, or cross the street and ride bus #27 along the same route back to the Prado or Atocha Station.

▲**Electric Minibus Joyride Through Lavapiés**—For a relaxing ride through the characteristic old center of Madrid, hop little electric minibus #M1 (€1, 5/hour, 20-minute trip, Mon-Sat 8:00-20:00, none on Sun). These are designed mostly for seniors who could use a lift (offer your seat if there's a senior standing). Catch the minibus at the Sevilla Metro stop and simply ride it to the end (Metro: Embajadores). Enjoy this gritty slice of workaday Madrid—both people and architecture—as you roll slowly through Plaza Santa Ana, down a bit of the pedestrianized Calle de las Huertas, past gentrified Plaza Tirso de Molina (its junkies now replaced by a family-friendly flower market), through Plaza de Lavapiés and a barrio of African and Bangladeshi immigrants, until you get to Embajadores. From there, you can catch the next #M1 minibus (which returns to the Sevilla Metro stop along a different route) or descend into the subway system.

▲▲**Bullfight**—Madrid's Plaza de Toros hosts Spain's top bullfights on some Sundays and holidays from March through mid-

October, and nearly every day during the San Isidro festival (mid-May through mid-June—often sold out long in advance). Fights start between 17:00 and 21:00 (early in spring and fall, late in summer). The bullring is at the Ventas Metro stop (a 25-minute Metro ride from Puerta del Sol, tel. 913-562-200, www.las-ventas.com). For info on the background and "art" of bullfighting, see page 814.

Getting Tickets: Bullfight tickets range from €5 to €150. There are no bad seats at Plaza de Toros; paying more gets you in the shade and/or closer to the gore. (The action often intentionally occurs in the shade to reward the expensive-ticket holders.) To be close to the bullring, choose areas 8, 9, or 10; for shade: 1, 2, 9, or 10; for shade/sun: 3 or 8; for the sun and cheapest seats: 4, 5, 6, or 7. Note these key words: *corrida*—a real fight with professionals; *novillada*—rookie matadors and younger bulls. Getting tickets through your hotel or a booking office is convenient, but they add 20 percent or more and don't sell the cheap seats. There are two booking offices; call both before you buy: at Plaza del Carmen 1 (Mon-Sat 9:30-13:00 & 16:30-19:00, Sun 9:30-14:00, tel. 915-319-131, or buy online at www.bullfightticketsmadrid.com; run by English-speaking José, who also sells soccer tickets) and at Calle Victoria 3 (Mon-Fri 10:00-14:00 & 17:00-19:00, Sat-Sun 10:00-13:00, tel. 915-211-213).

To save money, you can stand in the ticket line at the bullring. Except for important bullfights—or during the San Isidro festival—there are generally plenty of seats available. About a thousand tickets are held back to be sold in the five days leading up to a fight, including the day of the fight. Scalpers hang out before the popular fights at the Calle Victoria booking office. Beware: Those buying scalped tickets are breaking the law and can lose the ticket with no recourse.

For a dose of the experience, you can buy a cheap ticket and just stay to see a couple of bullfights. Each fight takes about 20 minutes, and the event consists of six bulls over two hours. Or, to keep your distance but get a sense of the ritual and gore, tour the bull bar on Plaza Mayor (described on page 417).

Bullfighting Museum (Museo Taurino): This museum, located at the back of the bullring, is not as good as the ones in Sevilla or Ronda (free, Tue-Fri 9:30-14:30, Sun 10:00-13:00, closed Sat and Mon and early on fight days, tel. 917-251-857).

"Football" and Bernabéu Stadium—Madrid, like most of Europe, is enthusiastic about soccer (which they call *fútbol*). The Real ("Royal") Madrid team plays to a spirited crowd Saturdays and Sundays from September through May (tickets from €50—sold at bullfight box offices listed earlier). One of the most popular sightseeing activities among European visitors to Madrid is touring the 80,000-seat stadium. The €16 unguided visit includes the box seats, dressing rooms, technical zone, playing field, trophy room, and a big panoramic stadium view (Mon-Sat 10:00-19:00, Sun 10:30-18:30, Metro: Santiago Bernabéu, tel. 913-984-300, www.realmadrid.com).

Shopping in Madrid

Shoppers focus on the colorful pedestrian area between Gran Vía and Puerta del Sol. The giant Spanish department store El Corte Inglés, a block off Puerta del Sol, is a handy place to pick up just about anything you need (Mon-Sat 10:00-22:00, Sun 11:00-21:00, see page 425).

El Rastro: Europe's biggest flea market, rated ▲, is a field day for shoppers, people-watchers, and pickpockets (Sundays

only, 9:00-15:00). It's best before 11:00, though bargain shoppers like to go around 14:00, when vendors are more willing to strike end-of-day deals. Thousands of stalls titillate more than a million browsers with mostly new junk. Locals have lamented the tackiness of El Rastro lately—on the main drag, you'll find cheap underwear and bootleg CDs, but no real treasures.

For an interesting market day (Sunday only), start at Plaza Mayor, where Europe's biggest stamp and coin market thrives. Enjoy this genteel delight as you watch old-timers paging lovingly through each other's albums, looking for win-win trades. When you're done, head south or take the Metro to Tirso de Molina. Walk downhill, wandering off on the side streets to browse antiques, old furniture, and garage-sale-style sellers who often simply throw everything out on a sheet. A typical Madrileño's Sunday could involve a meander through the Rastro streets with several stops for *cañas* (small beers) at the gritty bars along the way, then a walk to the Cava Baja area for more beer and tapas (see page 417). El Rastro offers a fascinating chance to see gangs of young thieves overwhelming and ripping off naive tourists with no police anywhere in sight. Seriously: Don't even bring a wallet. The pickpocket action is brutal, and tourists are targeted.

Fans: Casa de Diego sells *abanicos* (fans), *mantones* (typical Spanish shawls), *castañuelas* (castanets), *peinetas* (hair combs), and umbrellas. Even if you're not in the market, it's fun to watch the women flip open their final fan choices before buying (Mon-Sat 9:30-20:00, closed Sun, Puerta del Sol 12, tel. 915-226-643).

Classical Guitars: Guitar-lovers know that the world's finest classical guitars are made in Spain. Several of the top workshops, within an easy walk of Puerta del Sol, offer inviting little show-rooms with a peek at their craft and an opportunity to strum the final product. Consider the workshops of José Romero (Calle de Espoz y Mina 30, tel. 915-214-218) and José Ramirez (Calle de la Paz 8, tel. 915-314-229). Union Musical is a popular guitar shop off

Puerta del Sol (Carrera de San Jerónimo 26, tel. 914-293-877). If you're looking to buy, be prepared to spend €1,000.

Nightlife in Madrid

Those into clubbing may have to wait until after midnight for the most popular places to even open, much less start hopping. Spain has a reputation for partying very late and not stopping until offices open in the morning. (Spaniards, who are often awake into the wee hours of the morning, have a special word for this time of day: *la madrugada*.) If you're out early in the morning, it's actually hard to tell who is finishing their day and who's just starting it. Even if you're not a party animal after midnight, make a point to be out with the happy masses, luxuriating in the cool evening air between 22:00 and midnight. The scene is absolutely unforgettable.

▲▲▲**Paseo**—Just walking the streets of Madrid seems to be the way the Madrileños spend their evenings. Even past midnight on a hot summer night, entire families with little kids are strolling, enjoying tiny beers and tapas in a series of bars, licking ice cream, and greeting their neighbors. A good area to wander is along Gran Vía (from about Metro: Callao to Plaza de España). Or start at Puerta del Sol, and explore in the direction of Plaza Santa Ana. The pedestrianized Calle de las Huertas is also popular with strollers.

▲**Zarzuela**—For a delightful look at Spanish light opera that even English speakers can enjoy, try zarzuela. Guitar-strumming Napoleons in red capes; buxom women with masks, fans, and castanets; Spanish-speaking pharaohs; melodramatic spotlights; and aficionados clapping and singing along from the cheap seats, where the acoustics are best—this is zarzuela...the people's opera. Originating in Madrid, zarzuela is known for its satiric humor and surprisingly good music. You can buy tickets at Theater Zarzuela, which alternates between zarzuela, ballet, and opera throughout the year (€16-40, 50 percent off for Wed shows and anytime for those over 65, box office open 12:00-18:00 for advance tickets or until showtime for that day, near the Prado at Jovellanos 4—see map on page 383, Metro: Sevilla or Banco de España, tel. 915-245-400, http://teatrodelazarzuela.mcu.es; to purchase tickets online, go to the theater section of www.servicaixa.com). The TI's monthly guide has a special zarzuela section.

▲▲**Flamenco**—Although Sevilla is the capital of flamenco, Madrid has a few easy and affordable options. And on summer evenings, Madrid puts on live flamenco events in the Royal Palace gardens (ask TI for details).

Taberna Casa Patas attracts big-name flamenco artists. You'll quickly understand why this intimate venue (30 tables, 120 seats) is named "House of Feet." Since this is for locals as well as tour groups, the flamenco is contemporary and may be jazzier than your notion—it depends on who's performing (€32 includes cover and first drink, Mon-Thu at 22:30, Fri-Sat at 21:00 and 24:00, closed Sun, 1.25-1.5 hours, reservations smart, no flash cameras, Cañizares 10—see map on page 420, tel. 913-690-496, www.casapatas.com). Its restaurant is a logical spot for dinner before the show (€30 dinners, Mon-Sat from 20:00). Or, since it's three blocks south of the recommended Plaza Santa Ana tapas bars, this could be your pre- or post-tapas-crawl entertainment.

Las Carboneras, more downscale, is an easygoing, folksy little place a few steps from Plaza Mayor with a nightly hour-long flamenco show (€30 includes an entry and a drink, €58 gets you a table up front with dinner and unlimited cheap drinks if you reserve ahead, manager Enrique promises a €5/person discount if you book direct and show this book in 2012, Mon-Thu at 22:30 and often at 20:30, Fri-Sat at 20:30 and 23:00, closed Sun, reservations recommended, Plaza del Conde de Miranda 1—see map on page 415, tel. 915-428-677). Though Las Carboneras lacks the pretense of Casa Patas, Casa Patas has better-quality artists and a riveting seriousness. Considering that Las Carboneras raised its prices to essentially match Casa Patas, the "House of Feet" is the better value.

Las Tablas Flamenco offers a less expensive nightly show respecting the traditional art of flamenco. You'll sit in a plain room with a mix of tourists and Madrileños in a modern, nondescript office block just over the freeway from Plaza de España (€25 with drink, reasonable drink prices, Sun-Thu 22:00, Fri-Sat 20:00 & 22:00, 1.25-hour show, corner of Calle de Ferraz and Cuesta de San Vicente—see map on page 423, tel. 915-420-520, www.las tablasmadrid.com).

Regardless of what your hotel receptionist may want to sell you, other flamenco places—such as Arco de Cuchilleros (Calle de los Cuchilleros 7), Café de Chinitas (Calle Torija 7, just off Plaza Mayor), Corral de la Morería (Calle de Morería 17), and Torres Bermejas (off Gran Vía)—are filled with tourists and pushy waiters.

Mesones—These long, skinny, cave-like bars, famous for customers drinking and singing late into the night, line the lane called Cava de San Miguel, just west of Plaza Mayor (see map on page 415). If you were to toss lowbrow barflies, Spanish karaoke, electric keyboards, crass tourists, cheap sangria, and greasy calamari into a late-night blender and turn it on, this is what you'd get. It's generally lively only on Friday and Saturday.

Late-Night and Jazz Bars—If you're just picking up speed at midnight and looking for a place filled with old tiles and a Gen-X crowd, power into **Bar Viva Madrid** (daily 13:00-3:00 in the morning, downhill from Plaza Santa Ana on Calle Manuel Fernández y González—see map on page 420, tel. 914-293-640). The same street has other late-night bars filled with music. Or hike on over to **Chocolatería San Ginés** (described on page 426) for a dessert of *churros con chocolate*.

For live jazz, **Café Central** is the old town favorite. Since 1982 it's been known as the place where rising stars get their start (€14, 22:00 nightly, cheap drinks, great scene, Plaza del Ángel 10—see map on page 420, tel. 913-694-143, www.cafecentralmadrid.com).

Movies—During the dictatorial days of Franco, movies were always dubbed in Spanish, making them easier to censor. (One famously awkward example: Franco's censors were scandalized by a film depicting a man and a woman having an implied affair, so they edited the voiceover to make the characters brother and sister. But the onscreen chemistry was still sexually charged—so they wound up turning a questionable relationship into an incestuous one.) As a result, movies in Spain remain about the most often dubbed in Europe. To see a movie with its original soundtrack, look for "V.O." (meaning "original version"). Cine Ideal, with nine screens, is a good place for the latest films in V.O. (€8, €6.50 on Mon, assigned seats during most days and showings, good to get tickets early on weekends, 5-minute walk south of Puerta del Sol at Calle del Dr. Cortezo 6—see map on page 361, tel. 913-692-518 for info, www .yelmocines.es). For extensive listings, see the *Guía del Ocio* entertainment guide (described on page 356) or a local newspaper.

Sleeping in Madrid

Madrid has plenty of centrally located budget hotels and *pensiones*. Most of the accommodations I've listed are within a few minutes' walk of Puerta del Sol.

You should be able to find a sleepable double for €50, a good double for €90, and a modern, air-conditioned double with all the comforts for €120. Prices vary throughout the year at bigger hotels, but remain about the same for the smaller hotels and *hostales*. It's almost always easy to find a place. Anticipate full hotels only during May (the San Isidro festival, celebrating Madrid's patron saint with bullfights and zarzuelas—especially around his feast day on May 15) and September (when conventions can clog the city). During the hot months of July and August, prices can be soft—always ask for a discount.

With all of Madrid's street noise, I'd request the highest floor possible. Also, twin-bedded rooms are generally a bit larger than double-bedded rooms for the same price. Remember, you may find good deals by emailing several hotels (including business-class

---

Sleep Code

(€1 = about $1.40, country code: 34)
S = Single, **D** = Double/Twin, **T** = Triple, **Q** = Quad, **b** = bathroom, **s** = shower only. Unless otherwise noted, credit cards are accepted, English is spoken, and breakfast is *not* included.

To help you easily sort through these listings, I've divided the accommodations into three categories, based on the price for a standard double room with bath during high season:

$$$ **Higher Priced**—Most rooms €110 or more.

 $$ **Moderately Priced**—Most rooms between €70-110.

  $ **Lower Priced**—Most rooms €70 or less.

Prices can change without notice; verify the hotel's current rates online or by email. For other updates, see www.ricksteves.com/update.

---

hotels) to ask for their best price. And during slow times, drop-ins can often score a room in business-class hotels for just a few euros more than the budget hotels (which don't have prices that fluctuate as wildly with demand).

Smoking bans have changed the atmosphere in hotel reception areas and hallways, but things aren't completely smoke-free, as hotels are still allowed to designate up to 10 percent of their rooms for smokers.

Mid-Range and Fancier Places

These mostly business-class hotels are good values (especially Hotel Europa) for those willing to spend a little more. Their formal prices may be inflated, but most offer weekend and summer discounts when it's slow. Drivers pay about €24 a day in garages.

Between Puerta del Sol and Gran Vía

These hotels are located in and around the pedestrian zone north and west of Puerta del Sol. For most of these, use Metro: Sol (except Hotel Ópera—Metro: Ópera; and Hotel Preciados—Metro: Callao).

$$$ Hotel Liabeny rents 220 plush, spacious, business-class rooms offering all the comforts (Sb-€110, Db-€125, Tb-€182, 10 percent cheaper mid-July-Aug and Fri-Sat, prices vary widely according to demand, breakfast-€16, air-con, sauna, gym, off Plaza del Carmen at Salud 3, tel. 915-319-000, fax 915-327-421, www.liabeny.es, info@liabeny.es).

$$$ Hotel Preciados, a four-star business hotel, has 73 welcoming, sleek, and modern rooms as well as elegant lounges. It's

MADRID

Madrid's Center—
Hotels & Restaurants

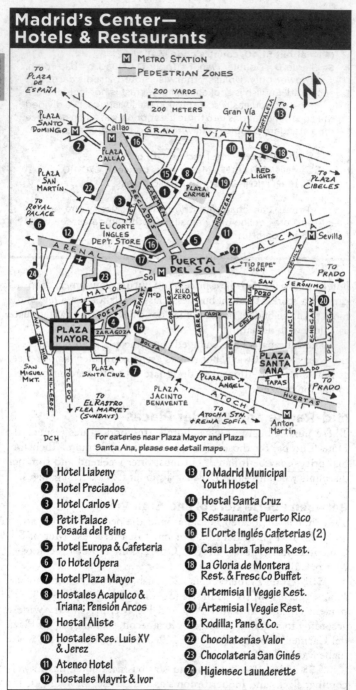

- **1** Hotel Liabeny
- **2** Hotel Preciados
- **3** Hotel Carlos V
- **4** Petit Palace
  Posada del Peine
- **5** Hotel Europa & Cafeteria
- **6** To Hotel Ópera
- **7** Hotel Plaza Mayor
- **8** Hostales Acapulco &
  Triana; Pensión Arcos
- **9** Hostal Aliste
- **10** Hostales Res. Luis XV
  & Jerez
- **11** Ateneo Hotel
- **12** Hostales Mayrit & Ivor

- **13** To Madrid Municipal
  Youth Hostel
- **14** Hostal Santa Cruz
- **15** Restaurante Puerto Rico
- **16** El Corte Inglés Cafeterias (2)
- **17** Casa Labra Taberna Rest.
- **18** La Gloria de Montera
  Rest. & Fresc Co Buffet
- **19** Artemisia II Veggie Rest.
- **20** Artemisia I Veggie Rest.
- **21** Rodilla; Pans & Co.
- **22** Chocolaterías Valor
- **23** Chocolatería San Ginés
- **24** Higiensec Launderette

well-located and reasonably priced for the luxury it provides (Db-€125-160, prices are often soft, checking Web specials in advance or dropping in will likely enable you to snag a room for around €100, breakfast-€15, Wi-Fi, parking-€18, just off Plaza de Santo Domingo at Calle Preciados 37, tel. 914-544-400, fax 914-544-401, www.preciadoshotel.com, preciadoshotel@preciadoshotel.com).

$$$ Hotel Carlos V is a Best Western with 67 sharp, high-ceilinged rooms, elegant breakfast, and a pleasant lounge (Sb-€80-105, standard Db-€100-173, Tb-€115-200, rates depend on demand and season, tax not included, breakfast-€9, air-con, non-smoking floors, elevator, Wi-Fi, Maestro Victoria 5, tel. 915-314-100, fax 915-313-761, www.hotelcarlosv.com, recepcion@hotelcarlosv.com).

$$ Hotel Europa, with sleek marble, red carpet runners along the halls, happy Muzak charm, and an attentive staff, is a tremendous value. It rents 102 squeaky-clean rooms, many with balconies overlooking the pedestrian zone or an inner courtyard. The hotel has an honest ethos and offers a straight price (Sb-€74, Db-€92, Db with view-€110, Tb-€130, Qb-€155, Quint/b-€175, tax not included, breakfast extra, air-con, elevator, free Internet access and Wi-Fi, Calle del Carmen 4, tel. 915-212-900, fax 915-214-696, www.hoteleuropa.net, info@hoteleuropa.net, run by Antonio and Fernando Garaban and their helpful and jovial staff, Javi and Jim). The recommended Europa cafeteria-restaurant next door is a lively and convivial scene—fun for breakfast.

$$ Hotel Ópera, a serious and contemporary hotel with 79 classy rooms, is located just off Plaza Isabel II, a four-block walk from Puerta del Sol toward the Royal Palace (Db-€85-110 but prices spike wildly with demand, includes breakfast, air-con, elevator, free Internet access, ask for a higher floor—there are nine—to avoid street noise, Cuesta de Santo Domingo 2, Metro: Ópera, tel. 915-412-800, fax 915-416-923, www.hotelopera.com, reservas@hotelopera.com). Hotel Ópera's cafeteria is deservedly popular. Consider their "singing dinners"—great operetta music with a delightful dinner—offered nightly at 22:00 (around €65, reservations smart, call 915-426-382 or reserve at hotel).

$$ Ateneo Hotel, just steps off Puerta del Sol, lacks public spaces and character, but its 38 rooms are close to business-class (Db-€75-90, occasionally less or more, 5 percent discount if you book direct with this year's book, air-con, elevator, Internet access and free Wi-Fi, Calle de la Montera 22, tel. 915-212-012, fax 915-233-136, www.hotel-ateneo.com, info@hotel-ateneo.com).

Near Plaza Mayor
Both of these are a block off Plaza Mayor.

$$$ Petit Palace Posada del Peine feels like part of a big, modern chain (which it is), but fills its well-located old building with fresh, efficient character. Behind the ornate and sparkling Old World facade is a comfortable and modern business-class hotel with 67 rooms (Db-€100-160 depending on demand, tax not included, breakfast-€15, air-con, free use of laptops and Internet access in all rooms, Calle Postas 17, tel. 915-238-151, fax 915-232-993, www.hthoteles.com, pos@hthoteles.com).

$$ Hotel Plaza Mayor, with 34 solidly outfitted rooms, is tastefully decorated and beautifully situated a block off Plaza Mayor (Sb-€70, Db-€85-90, superior Db-€110, Tb-€120, air-con, elevator, free Wi-Fi, Calle Atocha 2, tel. 913-600-606, fax 913-600-610, www.h-plazamayor.com, info@h-plazamayor.com). Director Leo offers a free breakfast to travelers who book direct (by email, phone, or fax, not through the website), pay the rates listed above, and show this book.

Near the Prado
$$$ Hotel Lope de Vega offers good business-class hotel value near the Prado. It is a "cultural-themed" hotel inspired by the 17th-century writer Lope de Vega. With 60 rooms, it feels cozy and friendly for a formal hotel (Sb-€105, Db-€115-135, Tb-€180, rates can vary based on demand, one child under 12 sleeps free, air-con, elevator, Internet access and Wi-Fi, parking-€25/day, Calle Lope de Vega 49—see map on page 383, tel. 913-600-011, fax 914-292-391, www.hotellopedevega.com, lopedevega@hotellopedevega.com).

Cheap Sleeps
Near Plaza del Carmen
These three are all in the same building at Calle de la Salud 13, north of Puerta del Sol. The building overlooks Plaza del Carmen—a little square with a sleepy, almost Parisian ambience.

$ Hostal Acapulco rents 16 bright rooms with air-conditioning and all the big hotel gear. The neighborhood is quiet enough that it's smart to request a room with a balcony (Sb-€49-54, Db-€59-64, Tb-€77-80, elevator, free Internet access and Wi-Fi, fourth floor, tel. 915-311-945, fax 915-322-329, www.hostalacapulco.com, hostal_acapulco@yahoo.es, Ana and Marco).

$ Hostal Triana, also a good deal, is bigger—with 40 rooms—and offers a little less charm for a little less money (Sb-€42, Db-€55, Tb-€75, includes taxes, rooms facing the square have air-con and cost €3 extra, other rooms have fans, elevator, free Wi-Fi, first floor, tel. 915-326-812, fax 915-229-729, www.hostaltriana.com, triana@hostaltriana.com, Victor González).

$ Pensión Arcos is tiny, granny-run, and old-fashioned—it's been in the Hernández family since 1936. You can reserve by phone (in Spanish), and you must pay in cash—but its five rooms are clean, quiet, and served by an elevator. You also have access to a tiny roof terrace and a nice little lounge. For cheap beds in a great locale, assuming you can communicate, this place is unbeatable (D-€36, Db-€40, fifth floor, air-con, closed Aug, tel. 915-324-994, Anuncia and Sabino).

Near Puerta del Sol

$ Hostal Santa Cruz, simple and well-located, has 16 rooms at a good price (Sb-€45, Db-€58, Tb-€85, air-con, elevator, Plaza de Santa Cruz 6, second floor, tel. 915-222-441, fax 915-237-088, www.hostalsantacruz.com, info@hostalsantacruz.com).

$ Hostal Mayrit and **Hostal Ivor** rent 28 rooms with thoughtful touches on pedestrianized Calle del Arenal (Sb-€50, Db-€65, air-con, elevator, near Metro: Ópera at Calle del Arenal 24, reception on third floor, tel. 915-480-403, www.hostalivor.com, reservas@hostalivor.com).

At the Top of Calle de la Montera

These places are a few minutes' walk from Puerta del Sol and a stone's throw from Gran Vía at the top of Calle de la Montera, which some dislike because of the young prostitutes who hang out here. They're legal, and the zone is otherwise safe and comfortable.

$ Hostal Aliste rents 11 decent rooms in a dreary-yet-secure building at a great price for readers of this book (Sb-€30, Db-€40, extra bed-€20, these prices for Rick Steves readers in 2012, air-con, elevator, Internet access and Wi-Fi, Caballero de Gracia 6, third floor, tel. 915-215-979, www.hostalaliste.net, info@hostal aliste.net, Rachael and Edward speak English).

$ Hostal Residencia Luis XV is a big, plain, well-run, and clean place offering a good value. It's on a quiet eighth floor (there's an elevator). It can be smoky, so ask for a non-smoking room. They also run the 36-room **Hostal Jerez**—similar in every way—on the sixth floor (Sb-€45, Db-€59, Tb-€75, includes tax, air-con, elevator, free Wi-Fi, Calle de la Montera 47, tel. 915-221-021, fax 915-221-350, www.hrluisxv.net, reservas@hrluisxv.net).

Near the Prado, at Cervantes 34

Two fine budget *hostales* are at Cervantes 34 (Metro: Antón Martín—but not handy to Metro; see map on page 383). Both are homey, with inviting lounge areas; neither serves breakfast.
$ Hostal Gonzalo has 15 spotless, comfortable rooms on the third floor and is well-run by friendly and helpful Javier. It's deservedly in all the guidebooks, so reserve in advance (Sb-€45, Db-€55, Tb-€70, air-con, elevator, Wi-Fi, tel. 914-292-714, fax 914-202-007, www.hostalgonzalo.com, hostal@hostalgonzalo.com).

Downstairs, the nearly as polished **$ Hostal Cervantes** also has 15 rooms (Sb-€50, Db-€60, Tb-€75, includes tax, cheaper when slow and for longer stays, some rooms with air-con, Internet access and Wi-Fi, tel. 914-298-365, fax 914-292-745, www.hostal-cervantes .com, correo@hostal-cervantes.com, Fabio).

Youth Hostel

$ Madrid Municipal Youth Hostel (Albergue Juvenil Madrid) is fairly new and decidedly big, with 132 beds. A Metro ride north of downtown, it has four to six beds per room with lockers, modern bathrooms, and lots of extras, such as a laundry room, billiards, and movies (dorm bed-about €25, co-ed rooms, includes breakfast, Internet access, 24-hour reception, Metro: Tribunal, then walk two minutes down Calle de Barceló to Calle de Mejia Lequerica 21, tel. 915-939-688, fax 915-939-684, www.ajmadrid.es, info @ajmadrid.es).

Apartment Rentals

$$ 1001 Nights Madrid, run by American Frederick and his Spanish wife, rents 15 roomy apartments with fully furnished kitchens in various locations throughout the heart of Madrid. Some are near Puerta del Sol, and others are within easy walking distance of the Prado and Reína Sofia (2 people-€80-120, 4 people-€100-180, larger apartments available, prices vary depending on season and size—see photos and videos on website, first child under 10 is full price but the second stays for free, 3-night minimum stay, 10 percent less for 7-night stay, €40 cleaning fee, 20 percent deposit required to reserve online, pay the balance in cash when you arrive, no breakfast, air-con, free Wi-Fi, mobile 620-585-594, www.1001nights.es, info@BCNflats.net).

Eating in Madrid

In Spain, only Barcelona rivals Madrid for taste-bud thrills. You have three dining choices: a memorable, atmospheric sit-down meal in a well-chosen restaurant; a forgettable, basic sit-down meal; or a meal of tapas at a bar or two...or four. Unless otherwise noted, these places start serving lunch at 13:00 or 13:30 and dinner around 20:30. At opening time, you'll often find the places nearly empty with a few forlorn early-bird tourists, and then thriving with locals after 14:00 and 22:00. Many restaurants close in August. Madrid has famously good tap water, and waiters willingly serve it free—just ask for *agua del grifo*. A ban on smoking in enclosed public places should clear the air in formerly notoriously smoky restaurants.

Eating near Plaza Mayor

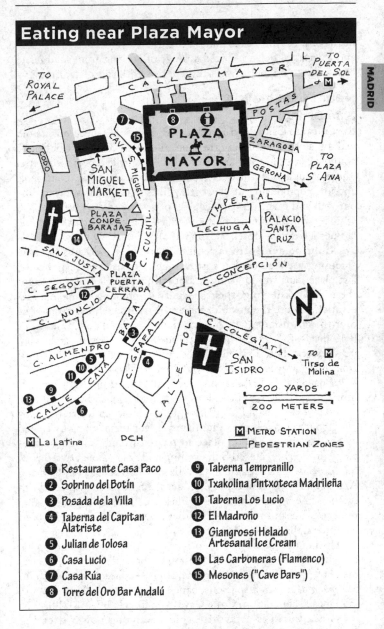

1. Restaurante Casa Paco
2. Sobrino del Botín
3. Posada de la Villa
4. Taberna del Capitan Alatriste
5. Julian de Tolosa
6. Casa Lucio
7. Casa Rúa
8. Torre del Oro Bar Andalú
9. Taberna Tempranillo
10. Txakolina Pintxoteca Madrileña
11. Taberna Los Lucio
12. El Madroño
13. Giangrossi Helado Artesanal Ice Cream
14. Las Carboneras (Flamenco)
15. Mesones ("Cave Bars")

I've grouped the recommended restaurants by neighborhood—near Plaza Mayor, Plaza Santa Ana, the Royal Palace, the Prado, and Puerta del Sol. I've listed a range of options, from splurges to cheap eats to fun pub crawls and churros with chocolate. Enjoy!

Near Plaza Mayor

Fine Dining

Restaurante Casa Paco is a Madrid tradition. Check out its old walls plastered with autographed photos of Spanish celebrities who have enjoyed their signature dish—ox grilled over a coal fire. Though popular with tourists, the place is authentic, confident, and uncompromising. It's a worthwhile splurge if you want to dine out well and carnivorously (€15-25 plates, ox sold by weight, 200 grams—which is almost half a pound—is a hearty steak, Plaza de la Puerta Cerrada 11, tel. 913-663-166).

Sobrino del Botín is a hit with many Americans because "Hemingway ate here." It's grotesquely touristy, pricey, and the last place Papa would go now...but still, people love it and go for the roast suckling pig, their specialty. If phoning to make a reservation, choose the upstairs for a still-traditional, but airier style over the downstairs, which has a dark, medieval-cellar ambience (€40 meals; €43 fixed-price meal includes wine, bread, gazpacho, pig, dessert; daily 13:00-16:00 & 20:00-24:00, a block downhill from Plaza Mayor at Cuchilleros 17, tel. 913-664-217).

Posada de la Villa serves Castilian cuisine in a 17th-century inn. This sprawling, multi-floor restaurant has open-beam ceilings, which give it a rustic flair. Peek into the big oven to see the baby pigs about to make some diner happy. If you're not going to Toledo or Sevilla, this is a good place to try roast lamb, the house specialty (€25 dishes, closed Sun evening and Aug, Calle Cava Baja 9, tel. 913-661-860). Posada de la Villa's twin, **Taberna del Capitan Alatriste,** is fresher and more modern, a half-block away, and run by the same owners. They serve classic cuisine with lots of game under open beams in a stylish medieval vault (€20-25 plates, closed Mon, Grafal 7, tel. 913-661-883).

Julian de Tolosa is chic, pricey, elegantly simple, and popular with natives who know good food. They offer a small, quality menu of Navarra's regional cuisine, from T-bone steak *(chuletón)* to red *tolosa* beans, in a spacious, sane setting with nothing touristy (€50 meals, closed Sun, Calle Cava Baja 18, tel. 913-658-210).

Casa Lucio is a favorite splurge among power-dressing Madrileños. The king and queen of Spain eat in this formal place, but it's accessible to commoners. This is a good restaurant for a special night out and a full-blown meal, but you pay extra for this place's fame (€50 for dinner, nightly from 21:00, closed Aug, Calle Cava Baja 35; unless you're the king or queen, reserve several days in advance—and don't even bother on weekends; tel. 913-653-252).

Eating Cheaply near Plaza Mayor

Madrileños enjoy a bite to eat on Plaza Mayor (without its high costs) by grabbing food to go from a nearby bar and just planting themselves somewhere on the square to eat (squid sandwiches are popular). But for many tourists, dinner at a sidewalk café right on Plaza Mayor is worth the premium price (consider Cervecería Pulpito, southwest corner of the square at #10).

Squid Sandwiches: Plaza Mayor is famous for its *bocadillos de calamares.* For a tasty €2.65 squid-ring sandwich, line up at **Casa Rúa** at Plaza Mayor's northwest corner, a few steps up Calle Ciudad Rodrigo (daily 11:00-23:00). Hanging up behind the bar is a photo-advertisement of Plaza Mayor from the 1950s, when the square contained a park.

Bullfighting Bar: **La Torre del Oro Bar Andalú** on Plaza Mayor has walls lined with grisly bullfight photos (read the gory description on page 814). This place is good for drinks, but you pay a premium for the tapas and food...the cost of munching amidst all that bullephenalia while enjoying their excellent Plaza Mayor outdoor seating (daily 8:00-15:00 & 18:00-24:00, closed in Jan).

Tapas on Calle Cava Baja

Just a few minutes' walk south of Plaza Mayor, Calle Cava Baja fills each evening with mostly young, professional Madrileños prowling for chic tapas and social fun. Come at night only and treat the entire street as a destination (make sure to study the tapas terms on page 30 before heading out). I've listed a few standards, but excellent new eateries are always opening up. For a good, authentic Madrid dinner experience, take time to survey the many options along this street and then choose your favorites. Remember, it's easier and touristy early, jammed with locals later. (If you want a formal dining experience on this street, try Posada de la Villa, Julian de Tolosa, or Casa Lucio—all recommended under "Fine Dining," earlier.) These tapas bars, listed in the order you'll reach them as you walk from Plaza Mayor up Calle Cava Baja, are worth special consideration:

El Madroño ("The Berry Tree," a symbol of Madrid) is more of a cowboy bar, a block to the right (with your back to Plaza Mayor) off the top of Calle Cava Baja. (Their other bar with the same name, located between Calle Cava Baja and Plaza Mayor, doesn't have the same ambience.) Preserving a bit of old Madrid, a tile copy of Velázquez's famous *Drinkers* grins from its facade. Inside, look above the stairs for photos of 1902 Madrid. Study the coats of arms of Madrid through the centuries as you try a *vermut* (vermouth) on tap and a €4 sandwich. Or ask to try the *licor de madroño;* a small glass *(chupito)* costs €2. Indoor seating is bright and colorful; the sidewalk tables come with great people-watching (which is why you pay more to eat the same food outside). Munch *raciones* at the bar or front tables to be in the fun scene, or have a quieter sit-down meal at the tables in the back (closed Mon, Plaza de la Puerta Cerrada 7, tel. 913-645-629).

Txakolina Pintxoteca Madrileña is a thriving bar serving Basque-style *pinchos* (tiny fancy sandwiches—*pintxo* in Basque) to a young crowd (€3/*pincho*, Calle Cava Baja 26, tel. 913-664-877).

Taberna Los Lucio is a jam-packed bar serving good tapas, salads, *huevos estrellados* (scrambled eggs with fried potatoes), and wine. If you'd like to make it a sit-down meal, head to the tables in the back. Their basement is much less atmospheric (Calle Cava Baja 30, tel. 913-662-984).

Taberna Tempranillo, ideal for hungry wine-lovers, offers fancy tapas and fine wine by the glass (see listing on the board). While there are a few tables, the bar is just right for hanging out. With a phrase book in hand or a spirit of adventure, use their fascinating menu to assemble your dream meal. It's packed and full of commotion—the crowds can be overwhelming. Arrive by 20:00 or plan to wait (closed Aug, Calle Cava Baja 38, tel. 913-641-532).

Ice Cream Finale: **Giangrossi Helado Artesanal,** a popular chain, serves Argentinean-style ice cream, considered to be some of Madrid's best. With a plush white leather lounge and lots of great flavors, this hipster ice cream shop offers a sweet way to finish your dining experience in this area (at the end of Calle Cava Baja at #40, 50 yards from La Latina Metro stop, tel. 902-444-130).

Near Plaza Santa Ana

These places surround Plaza Santa Ana, a few minutes' walk southeast of Puerta del Sol.

Fine Dining

El Caldero ("The Pot") is romantic and *the* place for paella and other rice dishes. A classy, in-the-know crowd appreciates its subdued elegance and crisp service. The house specialty is *arroz caldero* (a variation on paella). Served with panache from a cauldron hanging from a tripod, it serves two for €28. Most of the formal rice dishes come in pots for two—like the €30-per-couple paella (€36 with seafood; closed Sun-Mon, Calle de las Huertas 15, tel. 914-295-044). Wash down your meal with the house sangria.

The Madrid Pub-Crawl Dinner (for Beginners)

For maximum fun, people, and atmosphere, go mobile for dinner: Do the *tapeo*, a local tradition of going from one bar to the next,

munching, drinking, and socializing. While tiny €1.50-2 tapas plates are standard in Andalucía (and commonly served in Madrid's Calle Cava Baja area), these days most of Madrid's bars offer bigger plates for around €6. Called *raciones*, these are ideal for a small group to share. The real action begins late (around 21:00). But for beginners, an earlier start, with less commotion, can be easier. The litter on the floor is normal; that's where people traditionally toss their trash and shells (it's unsanitary to put it back on the bar). Don't worry about paying until you're ready to go. Then ask for *la cuenta* (the bill).

If done properly, a pub crawl can be a highlight of your trip. Before embarking upon this culinary adventure, study and use the tapas tips on page 30. Your ability to speak a little Spanish will get you a much better (and less expensive) experience.

Prowl the area between Puerta del Sol and Plaza Santa Ana. There's no ideal route, but the little streets between Puerta del Sol, San Jerónimo, and Plaza Santa Ana hold tasty surprises. Nearby, Calle de Jesús de Medinaceli is also lined with popular tapas bars. Here I've described a five-stop tapa crawl. These places are good, but don't be afraid to make some discoveries of your own. The more adventurous should read this crawl for ideas, and skip directly to the advanced zone (Lavapiés), described at the end of this section. For a more trendy pub crawl with designer tapas and finer wine, visit the bars on Calle Cava Baja (listed earlier).

• *From Puerta del Sol, walk east a block down Carrera de San Jerónimo to the corner of Calle Victoria.*

Museo del Jamón (Museum of Ham): This frenetic, cheap, stand-up bar (with famously rude service) is an assembly line of fast and simple *bocadillos* and *raciones*. It's tastefully decorated—unless you're a pig (or a vegetarian). Take advantage of the easy photo-illustrated menus that show various dishes and their prices. The best ham is the pricey *jamón ibérico*—from pigs who led stress-free lives in acorn-strewn valleys. Point clearly to what you want, and be very specific to avoid being served a pricier meal than you intended. For instance, if you're on a budget, don't let them sell you the *jamón ibérico*, which costs €14; a plate of low-end *jamón blanco*

MADRID

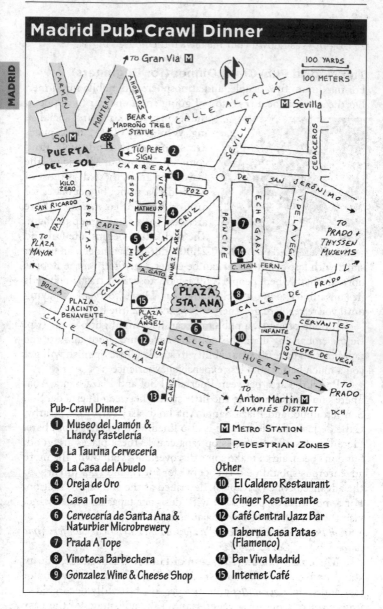

Madrid Pub-Crawl Dinner

Pub-Crawl Dinner

1. Museo del Jamón & Lhardy Pastelería
2. La Taurina Cervecería
3. La Casa del Abuelo
4. Oreja de Oro
5. Casa Toni
6. Cervecería de Santa Ana & Naturbier Microbrewery
7. Prada A Tope
8. Vinoteca Barbechera
9. Gonzalez Wine & Cheese Shop

Other

10. El Caldero Restaurant
11. Ginger Restaurante
12. Café Central Jazz Bar
13. Taberna Casa Patas (Flamenco)
14. Bar Viva Madrid
15. Internet Café

Ⓜ METRO STATION

▨ PEDESTRIAN ZONES

costs just €2.50. For a small sandwich, ask for a *chiquito* (€1.50, or €4 for *ibérico*; daily 9:00-24:00, sit-down restaurant upstairs, air-con).

• *Nearby are two options. Across the street is the touristy and over-priced bull bar,* **La Taurina.** *(I wouldn't eat here, but you're welcome to ponder the graphic photos that celebrate the gory art of bullfighting.) And next door take a detour from your pub crawl with something better for grandmothers:*

Lhardy Pastelería: Offering a genteel taste of Old World charm in this district of rowdy pubs, this place has been a fixture since 1839 for Madrileños wanting to duck in for a cup of soup or a light snack. Step right in, and pretend you're an aristocrat back between the wars. Serve yourself. You'll pay as you leave (on the honor system). Help yourself to the silver water dispenser (free), a line of elegant bottles (each a different Iberian fortified wine: sherry, port, and so on, €2.50/glass), a revolving case of meaty little pastries (€1 each), and a fancy soup dispenser (chicken broth con-sommé–€2.50, or €3 with a splash of sherry...local style—bottles in the corner, help yourself; Mon-Sat 9:30-15:00 & 17:00-21:30, Sun 10:00-15:00, Carrera de San Jerónimo 8).

• *Next, forage up Calle Victoria to the tiny...*

La Casa del Abuelo: This is where seafood-lovers savor siz-zling plates of tasty little *gambas* (shrimp) and *langostinos* (prawns),

with bread to sop up the delight-ful juices. As drinks are cheap and dishes are small and pricey, you might just want to share a *ración* or sample some wine. Try *gambas a la plancha* (grilled shrimp, €9.10) or *gambas al ajillo* (ah-HEE-yoh, shrimp version of escargot, cooked in oil and garlic, €8.90) and a €2.10 glass of sweet red house wine (daily 12:00-24:00, Calle Victoria 12).

• *Across the street is...*

Oreja de Oro: The "Golden Ear" is named for what it sells—sautéed pigs' ears (*oreja*, €5). While pig ears are a Madrid specialty, this place is Galician—they serve *pimientos de padrón* (sautéed miniature green peppers—quite possibly the tastiest plate of the entire crawl, €4.50) and the distinctive *ribeiro* (ree-BAY-roh) wine, served Galician-style, in characteristic little ceramic bowls to dis-guise its lack of clarity (closed Wed).

• *For a finale, continue uphill and around the corner to...*

Casa Toni: This memorable little spot is my favorite stop on this crawl. Run by Toni, it has a helpful English menu and sev-eral fun, classic dishes to try: *patatas bravas* (fried potatoes in a spicy sauce, €4), *berenjena* (deep-fried slices of eggplant, €5), *champiñones* (sautéed mushrooms, €5.50), and gazpacho—the cold tomato-and-garlic soup (€2.50) that is generally served only during the hot season, but available here year-round just for you (closed July, Calle Cruz 14).

More Options: If you're hungry for more, and want a trendy, up-to-date, pricier tapas experience, head for Plaza Santa Ana, with lively bars spilling out onto the square. Survey the entire scene. Consider **Cervecería de Santa Ana** (tasty tapas with two zones: rowdy, circa-1900 beer-hall and classier sit-down) or **Naturbier,** a local microbrewery. **Vinoteca Barbechera,** at the downhill end of the square, has an inviting menu of tapas and fine wines by the glass (indoor and outdoor seating).

Prada A Tope, just off Plaza Santa Ana, is where locals gather—either at the bar or at wooden tables in the back—for hearty, typical Spanish *raciones*. Quality ingredients, good wine, and friendly waiters make for a fine and fun meal (daily 12:00-16:00 & 20:00-24:00, Calle Principe 11, tel. 914-295-921).

Gonzalez, a venerable gourmet cheese and wine shop with a circa-1930s interior, offers a genteel opportunity to enjoy a plate of first-class cheese and a fine glass of wine with friendly service and a fun setting. Their €15 assortment of five Spanish cheeses—more than enough for two—is a cheese-lover's treat (€10 lunch buffet, nice wines by the glass, closed Sun night, three blocks past Plaza Santa Ana at Calle de León 12, tel. 914-295-618, Francisco).

Near the Royal Palace

Casa Ciriaco is popular with Madrileños who appreciate good traditional cooking—stews and partridge—with no affectation (€35 meals, €20 fixed-price lunch and dinner, closed Wed and Aug, Calle Mayor 84, tel. 915-480-620). It was from this building in 1906 that an anarchist bombed King Alfonso XIII and his bride on their wedding day; he missed them, but killed many others (for details, see page 374). Photos of the carnage are inside the front door.

La Bola Taberna, touristy but friendly and tastefully elegant, specializes in *cocido Madrileño*—Madrid stew. The stew consists of various meats, carrots, and garbanzo beans in earthen jugs. This is a winter dish, prepared here for the tourists. The stew is served as two courses: First you enjoy the broth as a soup, then you dig into the meat and veggies (€19 stew, about €35/person for full meal, closed Sun, cash only, midway between Royal Palace and Gran Vía at Calle Bola 5, tel. 915-476-930).

Café de Oriente serves a great three-course lunch special (€15, Mon-Fri, 13:00-16:00 only) in fin-de-siècle elegance immediately across the park from the Royal Palace. While its cafeteria area is reasonable, its restaurant is pricey (Plaza de Oriente 2, tel. 915-413-974).

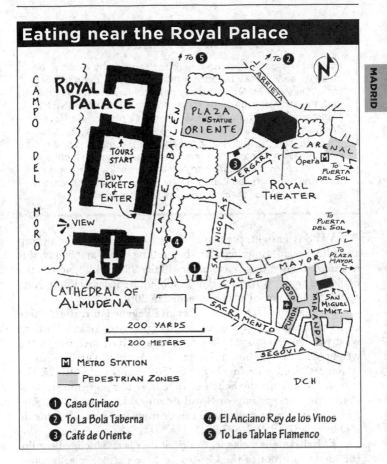

Eating near the Royal Palace

❶ Casa Ciriaco
❷ To La Bola Taberna
❸ Café de Oriente
❹ El Anciano Rey de los Vinos
❺ To Las Tablas Flamenco

El Anciano Rey de los Viños is a venerable, circa-1909 wine bar famous for its vermouth on tap. It's an expensive place to dine, but offers affordable tapas and drinks at its classic bar. A free small plate of tapas comes with each drink (closed Tue, across busy street from cathedral at Calle de Bailén 19, tel. 915-595-332).

Casual Dining near the Prado

Each of the three big art museums has a decent cafeteria. Or choose from these eateries. The first three are within blocks of the Prado, and the last is just steps from the Reina Sofía (for locations, see map on page 383).

Taberna de Dolores, a winning formula since 1908, is a commotion of locals enjoying €2.50 *canapés* (open-face sandwiches), tasty *raciones* of seafood, and *cañas* (small beers) at the bar or at a few tables in the back (all cold tapas, daily 11:00-24:00, Plaza de Jesús 4, tel. 914-292-243).

Breakfast in Madrid

Most hotels don't include breakfast (and many don't even serve it), so you may be out on the streets first thing looking for a place to eat. Non-touristy cafés only offer a hot drink and a pastry, with perhaps a potato omelet and sandwiches (toasted cheese, ham, or both). Touristy places will have a *desayuno* menu with various ham-and-eggs deals. Try *churros* once (see the listings for my favorite places); if you're not in the mood for heavy chocolate in the morning, go local and dip your *churros* in a *café con leche*. Starbucks, a temptation for many due to its familiarity, is often nearby. Get advice from your hotel staff for their favorite breakfast place.

VIPS is a bright, popular chain restaurant, handy for a cheap and filling salad. Engulfed in a shop selling books and candy, this is a high-energy, no-charm eatery (daily 9:00-24:00, across the boulevard from northern end of Prado, under Palace Hotel). Next door is Spain's first Starbucks, opened in 2001.

Viva la Vida Organic Market and Vegetarian Buffet, a tiny deli, offers a take-away buffet that delights vegetarians. Dish up what you like on a paper plate or in a paper box, then pay by the weight (€2.10/100 grams, a plateful is generally 300 grams—about 10 ounces, fixed-price lunch-€10 for 500 grams and a drink). Eat your meal on a nearby bench or hike over to the picnic-friendly Prado Museum grounds or Royal Botanical Garden (daily 11:00-24:00, a few blocks toward the center from the Prado at Calle de las Huertas 57, tel. 913-697-254).

El Brillante is a classic dive right on Plaza Sánchez Bustillo, the square in front of the Centro de Arte Reina Sofía. It offers pricey tapas and baguette sandwiches, but everyone comes for the fried squid sandwiches (evidenced by the older *señoras* with mouthfuls of *calamares*). Sit at the simple bar or at an outdoor table (long hours daily, two entrances—one on Plaza Sánchez Bustillo, the other at Plaza del Emperador Carlos V 8, tel. 915-392-806).

North of Puerta del Sol
Eating Cheaply
See the map on page 410 for locations.

Restaurante Puerto Rico fills a long, congested hall by serving good meals for great prices to smart Madrileños (€10 three-course fixed-price meal, closed Sun, Chinchilla 2, between Puerta del Sol and Gran Vía, tel. 915-219-834).

Hotel Europa Cafetería is a fun, high-energy scene with a mile-long bar, old-school waiters, great people-watching, local cuisine, and a fine €11 fixed-price lunch (daily 7:00-24:00, next to

Hotel Europa, 50 yards off Puerta del Sol at Calle del Carmen 4, tel. 915-212-900). The menu lists three price levels: bar (inexpensive), table (generally pricey), or terrace (sky-high but with good people-watching). Your best value is to stick to the lunch menu if you're sitting inside, or order off the plastic *barra* menu if you sit at the bar (the €3 ham-and-egg toast or the homemade *churros* make a nice breakfast).

El Corte Inglés' top-floor cafeterias (in both of its buildings) are fresh, modern, and popular, though not particularly cheap. One is just off Puerta del Sol at the intersection of Calle de Preciados and Calle de Tetuán, but the better one is near Plaza Callao. The lunch hour is busy, though it's worth the wait for its great views of Gran Vía and Plaza de España. Take a number for both the *terraza* and the cafeteria, and see which number comes up first (Mon-Sat 10:00-22:00, closed Sun even though rest of store is open).

Casa Labra Taberna Restaurante is famous as the birthplace of the Spanish Socialist Party in 1879…and as a spot for great cod. Packed with Madrileños, it manages to be both dainty and rustic. It's a wonderful scene with three distinct sections: the stand-up bar (cheapest, with two lines: one for munchies, the other for drinks), a peaceful little sit-down area in back (a little more expensive but still cheap; €6 salads), and a fancy restaurant (€20 fixed-price lunch). Their tasty little €1.25 *tajada de bacalao* cod dishes put them on the map. The waiters are fun to joke around with (daily 11:00-15:30 & 18:00-23:00, a block off Puerta del Sol at Calle Tetuán 12, tel. 915-310-081).

La Gloria de Montera Restaurante, a hip Spanish bistro with white tablecloths and a minimalist-library ambience, serves mediocre food at a cheap price and with fast, American-style table-turning—no long coffee klatches here (€8-12 fish and meat plates, daily, no reservations—arrive early or put your name on the list, a block from Gran Vía at Caballero de Gracia 10, tel. 915-234-407). **Ginger Restaurante,** a twin with the same menu and formula and a little more comfortable seating, is just off Plaza Santa Ana (on Calle de las Huertas at Plaza del Ángel 12—see map on page 420, tel. 913-691-059).

Fresc Co is the place for a cheap, modern, fast, and buffet-style meal. It's a chain with a winning plan: a long, appealing salad and buffet bar with one cheap price for all-you-can-eat, including dessert, a drink, and unlimited refills on everything (€9 lunch, €10 dinner, daily 12:30-24:00, air-con, Caballero de Gracia 8, tel. 915-216-052).

Vegetarian: **Artemisia II** is a hit with vegetarians who like good, healthy food without the typical hippie ambience that comes with most veggie places (great €12 three-course fixed-price lunch Mon-Fri only, open daily 13:30-16:00 & 21:00-24:00, 2 blocks north of Puerta del Sol at Tres Cruces 4, a few steps off Plaza del Carmen, tel. 915-218-721). **Artemisia I,** II's older sister, is located two blocks east of Plaza Santa Ana at Ventura de la Vega 4, off Carrera de San Jerónimo (same hours, tel. 914-295-092).

Fast Food and Picnics

For an easy, light, cheap meal, try **Rodilla**—a popular sandwich and salad chain with a shop on the northeast corner of Puerta del Sol at #13 (daily 9:30-23:00). **Pans & Company,** with shops throughout Madrid and Spain, offers healthy, tasty sandwiches and pre-packaged salads (daily 9:00-24:00, locations at Puerta del Sol, on Plaza Callao, at Gran Vía 30, and many more).

For a picnic, the department store **El Corte Inglés** has well-stocked meat and cheese counters downstairs (Mon-Sat 10:00-22:00, Sun 11:00-21:00).

Churros con Chocolate

Those not watching their cholesterol will want to try the deep-fried doughy treats called *churros* (or the thicker *porras*), best enjoyed by dipping them in pudding-like hot chocolate. Though many *chocolaterías* offer the dunkable fritters, *churros* are most delicious when consumed fresh out of the greasy cauldron at a place that actually fries them. Two of my favorites are near Puerta del Sol (see the map on page 410 for locations).

Chocolaterías Valor is a modern chain that does *churros* with pride and gusto. A few minutes' walk from nearly all my hotel recommendations, it's a fine place for breakfast. With a website like www.amigosdelchocolate.com, you know where their heart is (€4 *churros con chocolate,* daily 8:00-22:30, Fri-Sat until 24:00, a half-block below Plaza Callao and Gran Vía at Postigo de San Martín 7, tel. 915-229-288).

Chocolatería San Ginés is a classy institution, much beloved by Madrileños for its *churros con chocolate* (€4.30). Dunk your *churros* into the chocolate pudding, as locals have done here for more than 100 years. Though quiet before midnight, it's packed with the disco crowd in the wee hours; the popular dance club Joy Eslava is next door (open 21 hours a day—it's only closed 6:30-9:30; from Puerta del Sol, take Calle del Arenal 2 blocks west, turn left on bookstore-lined Pasadizo de San Ginés, and you'll see the café at #5; tel. 913-656-546).

Lavapiés District Tapas Crawl (for the Adventurous)

The neighborhood called Lavapiés is where the multiethnic tapestry of Madrid society enjoys pithy, cheap, seedy-yet-fun-loving life on the streets. Neighborhoods like this typically experience the same familiar evolution: Initially they're so cheap that only the immigrants, downtrodden, and counter-culture types live there. The diversity and color they bring attracts those with more money. Businesses erupt to cater to those bohemian/trendy tastes. Rents go up. Those who gave the area the colorful liveliness in the first place can no longer afford to live there. They move out...and here comes Starbucks. For now, Lavapiés is still edgy, yet comfortable enough for most.

This district has almost no tourists. (It's too scary.) Old ladies with their tired bodies and busy fans hang out on their tiny balconies as they have for 40 years, watching the scene. Shady types lurk on side streets (don't venture off the main drag, don't show your wallet or money, and don't linger on Plaza de Lavapiés).

For food, you'll find all the various kinds of tapas bars described earlier in "The Madrid Pub-Crawl Dinner," plus great Indian (almost all run by Bangladeshis) and Moroccan eateries. I've listed a couple of places that appealed to me...but explore your options. I'd recommend taking the entire walk once, then backtracking and eating at the place or places that appeal to you.

From the Antón Martín Metro stop (or Plaza Santa Ana), walk down Calle del Ave María (on its way to becoming Calle del Ave Allah) to Plaza de Lavapiés (where old ladies hang out with the swarthy drunks and a mosaic of cultures treat this square as a communal living room; the Lavapiés Metro station is here). Then head up Calle de Lavapiés to the recently remodeled square, Plaza Tirso de Molina (Metro stop). This square was once plagued by druggies. Now home to flower kiosks and a playground, it's homey and inviting. This is a good example of Madrid's vision for its public spaces.

On Calle Ave María: **Bar Melos** is a thriving dive jammed with a hungry and nubile crowd. It's famous for its giant patty melts called *zapatillas de lacón y queso* (because they're the size and shape of a *zapatilla* or slipper, €7, feeds at least two, Ave María 44). **Nuevo Café Barbieri,** one of a dying breed of mirrored cafés with a circa-1940 ambience, offers classical music in the afternoon and jazz in the evening (Calle del Ave María 45).

On Calle de Lavapiés: Consider the Indian place at #44, or drop into **Montes Wine Bar** (countless wines open and served by the glass, good tapas, crawl under the bar to get to the WC).

Madrid Connections

By Train

Madrid has two main train stations: Chamartín and Atocha. Both stations offer long-distance trains *(largo recorridos)* as well as smaller local trains *(regionales* and *cercanías)* to nearby destinations.

You can **buy tickets** at the stations, at travel agencies, or online. (For all the details, see the sidebar on page 830 in the appendix.) While travel agencies add a small fee, they can be a good place to buy tickets, especially during the high season or holidays, when the station's ticket counters have long lines. Convenient locations include the El Corte Inglés Travel Agency at Atocha (Mon-Fri 8:00-22:00, Sat-Sun 10:00-18:00, on ground floor of AVE side at the far end) and the El Corte Inglés department store at Puerta del Sol (see "Travel Agencies" on page 360).

Chamartín Station
The TI is opposite track 19. The impressively large information, tickets, and customer-service office is at track 11. You can relax in the Sala VIP Club if you have a first-class railpass and first-class seat or sleeper reservations (between tracks 13 and 14, cooler of free drinks). Luggage storage *(consignas)* is across the street, opposite track 17. The station's Metro stop is also called Chamartín (not "Pinar de Chamartín"). For train connections from here, see later.

Atocha Station
The station is split in two: an AVE side (mostly long-distance trains) and a *cercanías* side (mostly local trains to the suburbs or *cercanías* and the Metro for connecting into downtown). These two parts are connected by a corridor of shops. Each side of the station has separate schedules and customer-service offices. The TI, which is in the AVE side, offers tourist info, but no train info (Mon-Sat 8:00-20:00, Sun 9:00-14:00, tel. 915-284-630). To get to Atocha Station, use the "Atocha RENFE" Metro stop (not "Atocha").

Ticket Offices: The *cercanías* side has two offices—a small one for local trains and a big one for major trains (such as AVE). The AVE side has a pleasant, airy office that sells tickets for AVE and other long-distance trains (there are two lines: "Tickets in Advance" or "Selling Out Today"/"Departures Today"). A ticket counter will sometimes open up to sell tickets for trains departing soon—if you need to make a last-minute purchase, look for your destination and departure time, and get in line at that counter. If the line at one office is long, check the other offices. To secure your place in line, grab a number from a machine, usually located in the middle of the office by a sign with an image of a ticket.

AVE Side: Located in the towering old-station building, this half of the station boasts a lush, tropical garden filling its grand hall. It has the AVE trains, other fast trains

(Grandes Líneas), a pharmacy (daily 8:00-22:00, facing garden), and the wicker-elegant Samarkanda—both an affordable cafeteria (daily 13:00-20:00) and a pricey restaurant (daily from 21:00, tel. 915-309-746). Luggage storage *(consigna)* is below Samarkanda (daily 6:00-22:20). In the departure lounge on the upper floor, TV monitors announce track numbers. (A few trains, such as those for Toledo, Alicante, and Valencia, depart from the lower floor.) For information, try the *Información* counter (daily 6:30-22:30), next to Centro Servicios AVE (which handles only AVE changes and problems). The *Atención al Cliente* office deals with problems on Grandes Líneas (daily 6:30-23:30). Also on the AVE side is the Club AVE/Sala VIP, a lounge reserved solely for AVE business-class travelers and for first-class ticket-holders or Eurailers with a first-class reservation (upstairs, past the security check on right; free drinks, newspapers, showers, and info service).

Cercanías **Side:** This is where you'll find the local *cercanías* trains, *regionales* trains, some eastbound faster trains, and the "Atocha RENFE" Metro stop. The *Atención al Cliente* office in the *cercanías* section has information only on trains to destinations near Madrid. During busy times, some AVE trains will pull in on this side— clearly marked signs lead you to the Metro, taxi stand, or back to the AVE side.

Terrorism Memorial: The terrorist bombings of March 11, 2004, took place in Atocha and on local lines going into and out of the station. Security is understandably tight here. A moving memorial is in the *cercanías* part of the station near the Atocha RENFE Metro stop. Walk inside and under the cylinder to read the thousands of condolence messages in many languages (daily 11:00-14:00 & 17:00-19:00). Its 36-foot cylindrical glass memorial towers are visible from outside on the street.

AVE Trains

Spain's AVE bullet train opens up some good itinerary options. You can get from Madrid's Atocha Station to **Barcelona** in about three hours, with trains running almost hourly. The AVE train is generally faster (timed from downtown to downtown) and easier than flying, but not necessarily cheaper. Basic second-class tickets are €120 one-way for most departures and €140 for the fastest, peak-time departures. First-class tickets are €210. Advance purchase discounts (40-60 days ahead) are available through the national rail company (RENFE), but sell out quickly. Save by not traveling on holidays.

The AVE is also handy for visiting **Sevilla** (and, on the way, **Córdoba**). The basic Madrid-Sevilla second-class AVE fare is €85, depending upon departure time; first-class AVE costs €130 and comes with a meal. Consider this exciting day trip: 7:00-depart

Madrid, 8:45-12:40-in Córdoba, 13:30-20:45-in Sevilla, 23:15-back in Madrid.

Other AVE destinations include **Toledo** (€11), **Segovia** (€11), and **Valencia** (about €70). Prices vary with times and class. Eurailpass-holders get a big discount (e.g., Madrid to Sevilla is €10.35 second-class, but only at RENFE ticket windows—discount not available at ticket machines). Reserve each AVE segment ahead (tel. 902-320-320 for Atocha AVE info). For the latest, pick up the AVE brochure at the station, or check www.renfe.com.

Train Connections

Below I've listed both non-AVE and (where available) AVE trains, to help you compare your options.

From Madrid by Train to: Toledo (AVE or cheaper Avant: nearly hourly, 30 minutes, from Atocha), **El Escorial** (1-2/hour, but bus is better—see page 436), **Segovia** (AVE: 8/day, 35 minutes plus 20-minute shuttle bus into Segovia center, from Chamartín, take train going toward Valladolid; slower *cercanías* trains: 9/day, 2 hours, from both Chamartín and Atocha), **Ávila** (hourly until 21:30, 1.5 hours, more departures from Chamartín than Atocha), **Salamanca** (hourly, 2.5 hours, from Chamartín), **Valencia** (AVE: nearly hourly, 1.75 hours, from Atocha; in Valencia, AVE passengers arrive at Joaquín Sorolla station but can take free shuttle bus to the main Estación del Nord), **Santiago de Compostela** (2/day, 7-8.5 hours, includes night train, from Chamartín), **Barcelona** (AVE: almost hourly, 3 hours from Atocha; plus 1 night train from Chamartín, 9 hours), **San Sebastián** (2/day, 5-6 hours, from Chamartín), **Bilbao** (2/day, 5 hours, from Chamartín), **Pamplona** (4/day, 3 hours, from Atocha), **Burgos** (6/day, 2.5-4.5 hours, from Chamartín), **León** (9/day, 4.5 hours, from Chamartín), **Granada** (2/day, 4.5 hours, from Atocha), **Sevilla** (AVE: hourly, 2.5 hours, departures from 16:00-19:00 can sell out far in advance, from Atocha), **Córdoba** (AVE: 1-2/hour, 1.75 hours; Altaria trains: 4/day, 2 hours; all from Atocha), **Málaga** (AVE: 12/day, 2.5-3 hours, from Atocha), **Algeciras** (2/day, 5.25 hours, from Atocha), **Lisbon** (1/day departing at 22:25, 9 hours, overnight Hotel Train from Chamartín), **Paris** (1/day, may not run Tue-Wed off-season, 13 hours, direct overnight—a €185 Hotel Train, reserve more than 15 days in advance and hope there are seats left in the €89 *tarifa promo* deals, from Chamartín). General train info: toll tel. 902-320-320, for international journeys: tel. 902-243-402, www.renfe.com.

By Bus

Madrid has several major bus stations, connected by Metro. If you take a taxi from any bus station, you'll be charged a legitimate €3 supplement (not levied for trips to the station).

Plaza Elíptica Station: Buses to **Toledo** leave from here (2/ hour, 1-1.5 hours, €5 one-way, *directo* faster than *ruta*, Continental Auto bus company, tel. 915-272-961, Metro: Plaza Elíptica).

Estación Sur de Autobuses (South Bus Station): From here, you can catch buses to **Ávila** (8/day, 4/day on weekends, 1.5 hours, €13 round-trip), **Salamanca** (hourly express, 2.5 hours, €22 one-way, tel. 902-020-052, www.avanzabus.com), **León** (10/day, 4 hours, €25 one-way), **Santiago de Compostela** (5/day, 8 hours, includes 24:30-9:00 night bus), and **Granada** (nearly hourly, 5.25 hours, €17 one-way, tel. 915-272-961). The station sits squarely on top of Metro: Méndez Álvaro (has TI, tel. 914-684-200, www .estacionautobusesmadrid.com).

Príncipe Pío Station: Príncipe Pío is the old North train station, which has now morphed into a trendy mall and a bus hub for local lines including **Segovia** (2/hour departing on half-hour from platforms 6 or 7, 1.25-1.5 hours, runs from around 6:30-21:30, service starts later on Sun, €7 one-way, €12 round-trip). From Metro: Príncipe Pío, follow signs to *terminal de autobuses* or follow pictures of a bus. Buy a ticket from the Sepulvedana window (platform 4, tel. 915-598-955, www.lasepulvedana.es). Reservations are rarely necessary.

Intercambiador de Moncloa Station: This station, in the Moncloa Metro station, serves **El Escorial** (4/hour, 45-55 minutes; for details, see page 436). To reach the **Valley of the Fallen** (which may be closed during your visit), it's best to connect via El Escorial (see page 436 for details).

Intercambiador de Avenida de América Station: Located at the Avenida de América Metro, buses go to **Burgos** (9/day, 3 hours) and **Pamplona** (6/day, 5 hours, Alsa, tel. 915-272-961, www .movelia.es).

By Plane

Madrid's Barajas Airport

Ten miles east of downtown, Madrid's modern airport has four terminals. Terminals 1, 2, and 3 are connected by long indoor walkways (about an 8-minute walk apart) and serve airlines including Continental, Delta, Northwest, United, US Airways, Air Canada, and Spanair. The newer Terminal 4 serves airlines including Iberia, Vueling, British, and American, and also has a separate satellite terminal called T4S. To transfer between Terminals 1-3 and Terminal 4, you can take a 10-minute shuttle bus (free, leaves every 10 minutes from departures level), or take the Metro (stops at Terminals 2 and 4). Make sure to allow enough time if you need to travel between terminals (and then for the long walk within Terminal 4 to the gates). For more information about navigating this massive airport, go to www.aena.es.

International flights typically use Terminals 1 and 4. At the Terminal 1 arrivals area, you'll find a helpful English-speaking **TI** (marked *Oficina de Información Turística,* Mon-Sat 8:00-20:00, Sun 9:00-14:00, tel. 913-058-656), **ATMs,** a **flight info office** (marked simply *Information* in airport lobby, open daily 24 hours, tel. 902-353-570), a **post-office** window, a **pharmacy,** lots of **phones** (buy a phone card from the nearby machine), a few scattered **Internet** terminals (small fee), **eateries,** a **RENFE office** (where you can get train info and buy long-distance train tickets, daily 8:00-21:00, tel. 902-320-320), and on-the-spot **car-rental agencies.** The super-modern Terminal 4 offers essentially the same services. The **luggage storage** *(consigna)* is in Terminal 2, near the Metro exit. Some buses leave from the airport to far-flung destinations, such as Pamplona (see www.alsa.es; buy ticket online or from the driver).

Iberia, Spanair, and Air Europa are Spain's airlines, connecting a reasonable number of cities in Spain, as well as international destinations (ask for best rates at travel agencies). Vueling is the most popular discount airline in Iberia (e.g., Madrid-Barcelona flight as cheap as €30 if booked in advance, tel. 902-333-933, www.vueling.com).

Getting Between the Airport and Downtown

By Public Bus: The yellow **Exprés Aeropuerto** runs between the airport (all terminals) and Atocha train station (€2, pay driver in cash, departing from arrivals level every 15-20 minutes, ride takes about 40 minutes, runs 24 hours a day; from 23:30 to 6:00, the bus only goes to Plaza de Cibeles, not all the way to Atocha). From Atocha, you can take a taxi or the Metro to your hotel. The bus back to the airport leaves Atocha from near the taxi stand on the *cercanías* side (from 23:30-6:00, it departs downtown from Plaza de Cibeles).

Bus #200 (from Terminals 1, 2, and 3) and **bus #204** (from Terminal 4) are less handy than the express bus because they leave you farther from downtown (at the Metro stop at Avenida de América, northeast of the historical center—from here, you can ride the Metro or take a taxi to your hotel). These buses depart from the arrivals level about every 10 minutes and take about 20 minutes to reach Avenida de América (buy €1 ticket from driver; or get a shareable 10-ride Metrobus ticket at a tobacco shop, runs 6:00-24:00).

By Metro: Considering the ease of riding the Exprés Aeropuerto bus in from the airport, I'd rather bus than Metro. The subway involves two transfers to reach the city; it's not difficult, but usually involves climbing some stairs (€2; or add a €1 supplement to your 10-ride Metrobus ticket). The airport's futuristic "Aeropuerto T-1, T-2, T-3" Metro stop (notice the ATMs, subway info booth, and huge lighted map of Madrid) is in Terminal 2. Access the Metro at the check-in level; to reach the Metro from Terminal 1's arrivals level, stand with your back to the baggage claim, then go to your far right, up the stairs, and follow red-and-blue Metro diamond signs to the station (8-minute walk). The Terminal 4 stop is the end of the line. To get to Puerta del Sol, take line 8 for 12 minutes to Nuevos Ministerios, then continue on line 10 to Tribunal, then line 1 to Puerta del Sol (30 minutes more total); or exit at Nuevos Ministerios and take a €5 taxi or bus #150 straight to Puerta del Sol.

By Minibus Shuttle: The AeroCity shuttle bus provides door-to-door transport in a seven-seat minibus with up to three hotel stops en route. It's promoted by hotels, but if you want door-to-door service, simply taking a taxi generally offers a better value.

By Taxi: With cheap and easy alternatives available, there's not much reason to take a taxi unless you have lots of luggage or just want to go straight to your hotel. If you do take a taxi between the airport and downtown, allow about €30 during the day *(Tarifa 1)* or €35-40 at night and on Saturdays, Sundays, and holidays *(Tarifa 2)*. For Terminal 4, add about €10. Insist on the meter. The €5.50 airport supplement is legal. There is no charge for luggage. Plan on getting stalled in traffic.

By Car

Avoid driving in Madrid. If you're planning to rent a car, do it when you depart the city.

Renting a Car: It's cheapest to make car-rental arrangements before you leave home. In Madrid, consider **Europcar** (central reservations tel. 902-105-030, San Leonardo 8 office tel. 915-418-892, Chamartín Station tel. 913-231-721, airport tel. 913-937-235), **Hertz** (central reservations tel. 902-402-405, Plaza de España 18 tel. 915-425-805, Chamartín Station tel. 917-330-400, airport tel. 913-937-228), **Avis** (central reservations tel. 902-200-162, Gran Vía 60 tel. 915-484-204, airport tel. 913-937-223), and **National Atesa** (central reservations tel. 902-100-515). Ask about free delivery to your hotel. At the airport, most rental cars are returned at Terminal 1.

Route Tips for Drivers: To leave Madrid from Gran Vía, simply follow signs for *A-6* (direction *Villalba* or *A Coruña*) for Segovia, El Escorial, or the Valley of the Fallen (see next chapter for details).

NORTHWEST OF MADRID

*El Escorial • Valley of the Fallen •
Segovia • Ávila*

Before slipping out of Madrid, consider several fine side-trips northwest of Spain's capital city, all conveniently reached by car, bus, or train.

Spain's lavish, brutal, and complicated history is revealed throughout Old Castile. This region, where the Spanish language originated, is named for its many castles—battle scars from the long-fought Reconquista.

An hour from Madrid, tour the imposing and fascinating palace at El Escorial, headquarters of the Spanish Inquisition. Nearby, at the awe-inspiring Valley of the Fallen, pay tribute to the countless victims of Spain's bloody civil war. (This memorial has been closed for major restoration, but should reopen sometime in 2012—call before heading out: tel. 918-905-611.)

Segovia, with its remarkable Roman aqueduct (pictured at top of page) and romantic castle, is another worthwhile side-trip. At Ávila you can walk the perfectly preserved medieval walls.

Planning Your Time

You can see El Escorial (and if it reopens in time for your visit, the Valley of the Fallen) in less than a day, but don't go on a Monday, when both sights are closed. By car, see them en route to Segovia; by bus, make them a day trip from Madrid.

Northwest of Madrid

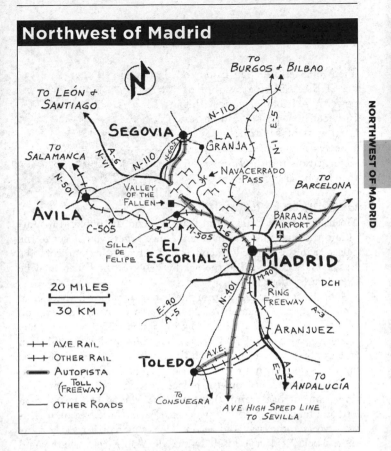

Segovia, worth a half-day of sightseeing, is easy to reach from Madrid. If you have time, spend the night—the city is a joy in the evenings. Ávila, while charming, merits only a quick stop (if you're driving and in the area) to marvel at its medieval walls and, perhaps, check out St. Teresa's finger (1.5 hours from Madrid, also a logical stop on the way to/from Salamanca by train).

In total, these sights are worth two days if you're in Spain for less than a month. If you're a history buff in Spain for just a week, squeeze in a quick side-trip from Madrid to El Escorial (and the Valley of the Fallen, if it's open).

El Escorial

The Monasterio de San Lorenzo de El Escorial is a symbol of power rather than elegance. This 16th-century palace, 30 miles northwest of Madrid, gives us a better feel for the Counter-Reformation and the Inquisition than any other building.

Getting to El Escorial

Most people visit El Escorial from Madrid. By public transportation, the bus is most convenient (since it gets you closer to the palace than the train). Remember that it makes sense to combine El Escorial with a visit to the nearby Valley of the Fallen (may be closed during your visit).

By Bus: Buses leave from the Intercambiador de Moncloa, which is in the basement of Madrid's Moncloa Metro station (4/hour, fewer on weekends, 45-55 minutes, €3.50 one-way, buy ticket from driver; in Madrid take bus #664 or slower #661 from Intercambiador's platform 11, Herranz Bus, tel. 918-969-028). The bus drops you downtown in San Lorenzo de El Escorial, a pleasant 10-minute stroll from the palace (see map): Exit the bus station from the back ramp that leads over the parked buses, turn left, and follow the cobbled pedestrian lane, Calle San Juan. This street veers to the right and becomes Calle Juan de Leyva. In a few short blocks, it dead-ends at Duque de Medinaceli, where you'll turn left and see the palace. Stairs lead past several decent eateries, through a delightful square, past the TI (Tue-Sat 10:00-14:00 & 15:00-18:00, Sun 10:00-14:00, closed Mon; tel. 918-905-313), and directly to the tourist entry of the immense palace/monastery.

By Train: Local trains (*cercanías* line C-8A) run once or twice an hour from Madrid's Atocha and Chamartín stations to El Escorial. From the station, walk 20 minutes uphill through Casita del Príncipe park, straight up from the station. Or you can take a shuttle bus from the station (2/hour, usually timed with arrival of trains, €1) or a taxi (€5) to the San Lorenzo de El Escorial town center and the palace.

By Car: It's quite simple. Taxi to your car-rental office in Madrid (or ask if they'll deliver the car to your hotel). Pick up the car by 8:30 and ask for directions to highway A-6. From Gran Vía in central Madrid, follow signs to *A-6* (direction *Villalba* or *A Coruña*). The freeway leads directly out of town. Stay on A-6 past

El Escorial Town

P PARKING
10-MINUTE WALK FROM BUS STATION TO PALACE

200 YARDS
200 METERS

DCH

❶ Entrance to Palace   ❸ Tavolata Reale Restaurant
❷ Mercado Público (Market)

the first El Escorial exit. At kilometer 37 you'll see the cross marking the Valley of the Fallen ahead on the left. Exit 47 takes you to both the Valley of the Fallen (after a half-mile, a granite gate on right marks Valle de los Caídos turnoff) and El Escorial (follow *San Lorenzo del Escorial* signs).

The nearby **Silla de Felipe** (Philip's Seat) is a rocky viewpoint where the king would come to admire his palace as it was being built. From El Escorial, follow directions to Ávila, then M-505 to Valdemorillo; look for a sign on your right after about a mile.

When you leave El Escorial for Madrid, Toledo, or Segovia, follow signs to *A-6 Guadarrama*. After about six miles you pass the Valley of the Fallen and hit the freeway.

Sights in El Escorial

▲▲▲Monasterio de San Lorenzo de El Escorial

Built at a time when Catholic Spain felt threatened by Protestant "heretics," the construction of this palace dominated the Spanish economy for a generation (1562-1584). Because of this bully in the national budget, Spain has almost nothing else to show from this most powerful period of her history.

Cost: €10; for €7 more, a guided 1.5-hour **tour** takes you through the complex and covers other buildings on the grounds, including the Palace of the Bourbons (Palacio de los Borbones), House of the Infants (Casita del Infante), and House of the Prince (Casita del Príncipe). Unfortunately, there are so few tours in English that it generally isn't worth waiting around for one. Ask when the next tour in English is scheduled, and if nothing's running soon, go on your own.

Hours: April-Sept Tue-Sun 10:00-19:00, Oct-March until 18:00, closed Mon year-round, last entry one hour before closing.

Information: To visit on your own, follow my self-guided tour, which covers the basics, or rent the €4 audioguide. You'll find scant captions in English within the palace. For more information, get the *Guide: Monastery of San Lorenzo El Real de El Escorial*, which follows the general route you'll take (€9, available at any of several shops in the palace). Tel. 918-905-904, www.patrimonio nacional.es.

⊙ Self-Guided Tour: The *monasterio* looks confusing at first, but the *visita* arrows and signs help guide you through one continuous path. This is the general order you'll follow.

• *Pass through the security scanner, buy your ticket, and then continue down the hall past the* consigna *baggage check (Sala 1) to the...*

Museum of Tapestries: This chamber is hung with 16th-century tapestries, including fascinating copies of Hieronymus Bosch's most famous and preachy paintings (which Philip II fancied). Don't miss El Greco's towering painting of the *Martyrdom of St. Maurice.* This was the artist's first commission after arriving in Spain from Venice. It was too subtle and complex for the king, so El Greco moved on to Toledo to find work.

• *Continue downstairs to the fascinating...*

Museum of Architecture (Museo de Arquitectura): It has long, parallel corridors of fine models of the palace and some of the actual machinery and tools used to construct it. Huge stone-pinching winches, fat ropes, and rusty mortar spades help convey the immensity of this 21-year project involving 1,500 workers. At the big model, you can see how the complex is shaped like a grill. San Lorenzo—St. Lawrence, a Christian Spaniard martyred by pagan Romans (A.D. 258)—was burned to death on a grill. Throughout

El Escorial—Ground Floor

the palace, you'll see this symbol associated with the saint. The grill's "handle" was the palace, or residence of the royal family. The monastery and school gathered around the huge basilica.

• Next linger in the...

Museum of Paintings: Consider the 15th- to 17th-century Flemish, Spanish, and Italian works. Contemplate Roger van der Weyden's *Calvary*, with mourning Mary and St. John at the feet of the crucified Christ. (It's interesting to compare it with van der Weyden's similar *Descent from the Cross*, which hangs in the Prado in Madrid.)

• Pass through the peaceful and empty Courtyard of the Fountainheads, and go upstairs to the...

Hall of Battles (Sala de Batallas): Its paintings celebrate Spain's great military victories—including the Battle of San Quentin over France (1557) on St. Lawrence's feast day, which inspired the construction of El Escorial. The sprawling series, painted in 1590, helped teach the new king all the elements of warfare. Stroll the length for a primer on army skills.

• Head downstairs, following signs to Palacio de los Austrias, then follow a corridor lined with various family trees (some scrawny, others lush and fecund). The hall leads into the...

History of El Escorial

The giant, gloomy building made of gray-black stone looks more like a prison than a palace. About 650 feet long and 500 feet wide, it has 2,600 windows, 1,200 doors, more than 100 miles of passages, and 1,600 overwhelmed tourists.

Four hundred years ago, the enigmatic, introverted, and extremely Catholic King Philip II (1527-1598) ruled his bulky empire and directed the Inquisition from here. To Philip, the building embodied the wonders of Catholic learning, spirituality, and arts. To 16th-century followers of Martin Luther, it epitomized the evil of closed-minded Catholicism. To architects, the building—built on the cusp between styles—exudes both Counter-Reformation grandeur and understated Renaissance simplicity. Today it's a time capsule of Spain's "Golden Age," packed with history, art, and Inquisition ghosts. (And at an elevation of nearly 3,500 feet, it can be friggin' cold.)

The building was conceived by Philip II to serve several purposes: as a grand mausoleum for Spain's royal family, starting with his father, Charles V (known as Carlos I in Spain); as a monastery to pray (a lot) for the royal souls; as a small palace to use as a Camp David of sorts for Spain's royalty; and as a school to embrace humanism in a way that promoted the Catholic faith.

Royal Living Quarters (the building's grill handle): Immediately inside the first door, find the small portrait of Philip II flanked by two large paintings of his daughters. The palace was like Philip: austere. Notice the simple floors, plain white walls, and bare-bones chandelier. This was the bedroom of one of his daughters. The sheet warmer beside her bed was often necessary during the winter. Bend down to see the view from her bed...of the high altar in the basilica next door. The entire complex of palace and monastery buildings was built around that altar.

In the next room, the **Guard's room,** notice the reclinable sedan chair that Philip II, thick with gout, was carried in (for seven days) on his last trip from Madrid to El Escorial. He wanted to be here when he died.

The **Audience Chamber** is now a portrait gallery filled with Habsburg royals painted by popular local artists. The portraits of unattractive people that line the walls provide an instructive peek at the consequences of mixing blue blood with more of the same blue blood (inbreeding among royals was a common problem throughout Europe in those days).

The Spanish emperor Charles V (1500-1558) is over the fireplace mantel. Charles, Philip II's dad, was the most powerful man in Europe, having inherited not only the Spanish crown, but also Germany, Austria, the Low Countries (Belgium and the Netherlands), and much of Italy. When he announced his abdication in 1555, his son Philip II inherited much of this territory... plus the responsibility of managing it. Philip's draining wars with France, Portugal, Holland, and England—including the disastrous defeat of Spain's navy, the Spanish Armada, by England's Queen Elizabeth I (1588)—knocked Spain from its peak of power and began centuries of decline.

The guy with the good-looking legs next to Charles was his illegitimate son, Don Juan de Austria—famous for his handsome looks, thanks to a little fresh blood. Other royal offspring weren't so lucky: When one king married his niece, the result was Charles II (1665-1700, opposite Charles V). His severe underbite (an inbred royal family trait) was the least of his problems. An epileptic before that disease was understood, poor "Charles the Mad" would be the last of the Spanish Habsburgs. He died without an heir in 1700, ushering in the continent-wide War of the Spanish Succession and the dismantling of Spain's empire.

In the **Walking Gallery,** the royals got their exercise privately, with no risk of darkening their high-class skins with a tan. Study the 16th-century maps along the walls. The slate strip on the floor is a sundial from 1755. It lined up with a (now plugged) hole in the wall so that at noon a tiny beam hit the middle of the three lines. Palace clocks were set by this. Where the ray crossed the strip indicated the date and sign of the zodiac.

As you enter the **King's Antechamber,** look back to study the fine inlaid-wood door (a gift from the German emperor that celebrates the exciting humanism of the age).

Philip II's bedroom is austere, like his daughter's. Look at the king's humble bed...barely queen-size. He too could view Mass at the basilica's high altar without leaving his bed. The red box next to his pillow holds the royal bedpan. But don't laugh—the king's looking down from the wall to your left. At age 71, Philip II, the gout-ridden king of a dying empire, died in this bed (1598).

• *From here his body was taken to our next stop, the...*

Royal Pantheon (Panteón Real): This is the gilded resting place of 26 kings and queens...four centuries' worth of Spanish monarchy. All the kings are included—but the only queens here are the ones who became mothers of kings.

A post-mortem filing system is at work in the Pantheon. From the entrance, kings are on the left, queens on the right. (The only exception is Isabel II, since she was a ruling queen and her husband was a consort.) The first and greatest, Charles V and his Queen Isabel, flank the altar on the top shelf. Her son, Philip II, rests below Charles and opposite (only) one of Philip's four wives, and so on. There is a waiting process, too. Before a royal corpse can rest in this room, it needs to decompose for several decades. The three empty niches are already booked. The bones of the current king Juan Carlos' grandmother, Victoria Eugenia (who died in 1964), are ready to be moved in, but the staff can't explain why they haven't been transferred yet. Juan Carlos' father, Don Juan (who died in 1993), is also on the waiting list...controversially. Technically, he was never crowned king of Spain—Franco took control of Spain before Don Juan could ascend to the throne, and he was passed over for the job when Franco reinstituted the monarchy. Juan Carlos' mother is the most recent guest in the rotting room. So where does that leave Juan Carlos and Sofía? This hotel is *todo completo*.

The next rooms are filled with the tombs of lesser royals: Each bears that person's name (in Latin), relationship to the king, and slogan or epitaph. From here, it's on to the wedding-cake **Pantheon of Royal Children** (Panteón de los Infantes), which holds the remains of various royal children who died before the age of seven (and their first Communion).

• *Head past the tiny gift shop and continue upstairs to the...*

Chapter Rooms (Salas Capitulares): These rooms (some of which may be under renovation) are where the monks met to do church business; they're also lined with big-name paintings by José Ribera, El Greco, Titian, and Velázquez. (More great paintings are in the monastery's Museum of Painting.) Continue to the final room to see some atypical Bosch paintings and the intricate, portable altar of Charles V.

• *Next find the...*

Cloister: The cloister glows with bright, restored paintings by Pellegrino Tibaldi. Off the cloister is the **Old Church** (Iglesia Vieja), which they used from 1571 to 1586, while finishing the basilica. During that time the bodies of several kings, including Charles V, were interred here. Among the many paintings, look for the powerful *Martyrdom of St. Lawrence* by Tiziano (Titian) above the main altar.

• *Follow the signs to the...*

Basilica: Find the flame-engulfed grill in the center of the altar wall that features San Lorenzo (the same St. Lawrence from the painting) meeting his famous death—and taking "turn the other cheek" to new extremes. Lorenzo was so cool, he reportedly told his Roman executioners, "You can turn me over now—I'm done on this side." With your back to the altar, go to the right corner for the artistic highlight of the basilica: Benvenuto Cellini's marble sculpture, *The Crucifixion*. Jesus' features are supposedly modeled after the Shroud of Turin. Cellini carved this from Carrara marble for his own tomb in 1562 (according to the letters under Christ's feet).

• *Last comes the immense...*

Library *(biblioteca):* It's clear that education was a priority for the Spanish royalty. Savor this room. The ceiling (by Tibaldi,

depicting various disciplines labeled in Latin, the lingua franca of the multinational Habsburg Empire) is a burst of color. At the far end of the room, the armillary sphere—an elaborate model of the solar system—looks like a giant gyroscope, revolving unmistakably around the Earth, with a misshapen, under-explored North America. As you leave, look back above the wooden door. The plaque warns *"Excomunión..."*—you'll be excommunicated if you take a book without checking it out properly. Who needs late fees when you hold the keys to hell?

Eating in El Escorial

The **Mercado Público,** a four-minute walk from the palace, is the place to shop for a picnic (Mon-Fri 9:30-13:30 & 17:00-20:00, Sat 9:30-14:00, closed Thu and Sat afternoons and all day Sun, Calle del Rey 9).

Tavolata Reale dishes out pizza and offers a change of pace from Spanish fare (Tue-Sat 12:00-17:00 & 20:00-24:00, Sun 12:00-17:00, closed Mon, inside a mini–shopping gallery off Plaza Jacinto Benavente at Plaza de las Ánimas 3, tel. 918-961-189).

Valley of the Fallen

Six miles from El Escorial, high in the Guadarrama Mountains, is the Valley of the Fallen (Valle de los Caídos). A 500-foot-tall granite cross marks this immense and powerful underground monument to the victims of Spain's 20th-century nightmare—its Civil War (1936-1939).

In April 2010 the site and funicular to the base of the cross closed for major renovation. It's slated to reopen sometime in 2012, and when it does, admission fees, hours, and services may change. If the site is closed during your visit, you may be able to see the basilica by attending a service (see "Mass," below).

Cost and Hours: Closed until 2012; when open likely €5, combo-ticket with El Escorial may be available, ask about audioguide; April-Sept Tue-Sun 10:00-19:00, Oct-March until 18:00, closed Mon, last entry one hour before closing, basilica closes 30 minutes before site closes; funicular—also closed until 2012; when running, about €1.50 one-way, €2.50 round-trip, pay fare at machine; April-Sept Tue-Sun 11:00-18:30, 3/hour; Oct-March Tue-Sun 11:00-16:30, 2/hour; closed Mon; last ticket sold 30 minutes before closing, tel. 918-905-611, www.patrimonio nacional.es.

Mass: During renovations, you can enter the basilica during Mass, but you can't sightsee or linger afterwards. One-hour services run Tue-Sat at 11:00 and Sun at 11:00, 13:00, and 17:00. During services, the entire front of the basilica (altar and tombs) is closed. Mass is usually accompanied by the resident boys' choir, the "White Voices" (Spain's answer to the Vienna Boys' Choir).

Getting There: Most visitors side-trip to the Valley of the Fallen from the nearby El Escorial. If you don't have your own wheels, the easiest way to get between these two sights is to negotiate a deal with a **taxi** (to take you from El Escorial to Valley of the Fallen, wait for you 30-60 minutes, and then bring you back to El Escorial, about €45 total). When the site reopens, ask about bus service between El Escorial and the Valley of the Fallen (likely 1/day Tue-Sun, 15 minutes, discounted bus fare may be available with site admission). Drivers can find tips under "Getting to El Escorial—By Car" on page 436.

⊙ Self-Guided Tour: Approaching by car or bus, you enter the sprawling park through a granite gate. The best views of the cross are from the bridge (but note that it's illegal for drivers to

The Spanish Civil War
(1936-1939)

Thirty-three months of warfare killed roughly 500,000 Spaniards. Unlike America's Civil War, which split the US north and south, Spain's war was between classes and ideologies, dividing every city and village, and many families. It was especially cruel, with atrocities and reprisals on both sides.

The war began as a military coup to overthrow the democratically elected Republic, a government that the army and other conservative powers considered too liberal and disorganized. The rebel forces, called the Nationalists (Nacionalistas), consisted of the army, monarchy, Catholic Church, big business, and rural estates, with aid from Germany, Italy, and Portugal. Trying to preserve the liberal government were the Republicans (Republicanos), also called Loyalists: the government, urban areas, secularists, small business, and labor unions, with aid from the United States (minimal help) and the "International Brigades" of communists, socialists, and labor organizers.

In the summer of 1936, the army rebelled and took control of its own garrisons, rejecting the Republic and pledging allegiance to Generalísimo Francisco Franco (1892-1975). These Nationalists launched a three-year military offensive to take Spain region by region, town by town. The government ("Republicans") cobbled together an army of volunteers, local militias, and international fighters. The war pitted conservative Catholic priests against socialist factory workers, rich businessmen against radical students, sunburned farmers loyal to the old king against upwardly mobile small businessmen. People suffered. You'll notice that many elderly Spaniards are very short—a product of growing up during these hungry and very difficult Civil War years.

Spain's Civil War attracted international attention. Adolf Hitler and Benito Mussolini sent troops and supplies to their fellow fascist Franco. It was Hitler's Luftwaffe that helped Franco bomb the town of Guernica (April of 1937), an event famously captured on canvas by Pablo Picasso (for more on the bombing, see sidebar on page 186; to read about the painting, see page 396). On the Republican side, hundreds of Americans (including Ernest Hemingway) steamed over to Spain, some to fight for democracy as part of the "Abraham Lincoln Brigade."

By 1938, only Barcelona and Madrid held out. But they were no match for Franco's army. On April 1, 1939, Madrid fell and the war ended, beginning 37 years of iron-fisted rule by Franco.

stop anywhere along this road). To the right, tiny chapels along the ridge mark the Stations of the Cross, where pilgrims stop on their hike to this memorial.

In 1940 prison workers dug 220,000 tons of granite out of the hill beneath the cross to form an underground basilica, then used the stones to erect the cross (built like a chimney, from the inside). Since it's built directly over the dome of the subterranean basilica, a seismologist keeps a careful eye on things.

The stairs that lead to the imposing monument are grouped in sets of tens, meant to symbolize the Ten Commandments (including "Thou shalt not kill"—hmm). The emotional *pietà* draped over the basilica's entrance is huge—you could sit in the palm of Christ's hand. The statue was sculpted by Juan de Ávalos, the same artist who created the dramatic figures of the four Evangelists at the base of the cross. It must have had a powerful impact on mothers who came here to remember their fallen sons.

Basilica: A solemn silence and a stony chill fill the basilica. At

300 yards long, it was built to be longer than St. Peter's...but the Vatican had the final say when it blessed only 262 of those yards. Many Spaniards pass under the huge, foreboding angels of fascism to visit the grave of General Franco—an unusual place of pilgrimage, to say the least.

After walking through the two long vestibules, stop at the iron gates of the actual basilica. The line of torch-like lamps adds to the shrine ambience. Franco's prisoners, the enemies of the right, dug this memorial out of solid rock from 1940 to 1950. (Though it looks like bare rock still shows on the ceiling, it's just a clever design.) The sides of the monument are lined with copies of 16th-century Brussels tapestries of the Apocalypse, and side chapels contain alabaster copies of Spain's most famous statues of the Virgin Mary.

Interred behind the high altar and side chapels (marked "RIP, 1936-1939, died for God and country") are the remains of the approximately 50,000 people, both Franco's Nationalists and the anti-Franco Republicans, who lost their lives in the war. Regrettably, the urns are not visible, so it is Franco who takes center stage. His grave, strewn with flowers, lies behind the high altar. In front of the altar is the grave of José Antonio Primo de Rivera (1903-1936), the founder of Spanish fascism, who was killed by Republicans during the Civil War. Between these fascists' graves, the statue of a crucified Christ is lashed to a timber Franco himself is said to have felled. The seeping stones seem to weep for the victims. Today, families of the buried Republicans remain upset that their kin are lying with Franco and his Nationalists.

As you leave, stare into the eyes of those angels with swords and two right wings and think about all the "heroes" who keep dying "for God and country," at the request of the latter. The expansive view from the monument's terrace includes the peaceful, forested valley and sometimes snow-streaked mountains.

Visiting the Cross: For an even better view of the area, consider taking a funicular trip (closed during renovation) to the base of the cross. The funicular ride includes a short commentary in English and there's a restaurant and public WC at the top. You can hike back down in 25 minutes. If you have a car, you can drive up past the monastery and hike from the start of the trail marked *Sendero a la Cruz.*

Sleeping and Eating: Near the parking lot and bus stop at Valley of the Fallen are a small snack bar and some picnic tables. Basic overnight lodging is available at the **$$$ Hospedería del Valle de los Caídos,** a 100-room monastery behind the cross (Sb €46, Db-€91, includes meals, tax, and a pass to enter and leave the park after hours, tel. 918-905-494, fax 918-961-542, no English spoken). A meditative night here is good mostly for monks.

Segovia

Fifty miles from Madrid, this town of 55,000 boasts a thrilling Roman aqueduct, a grand cathedral, and a historic castle. Since the city is more than 3,000 feet above sea level and just northwest of a mountain range, the city is exposed to cool northern breezes, and people come here from Madrid for a break from the summer heat.

Day-Tripping from Madrid: Considering the easy train and bus connections (35 minutes one-way by AVE train, 1.5 hours by bus), Segovia makes a fine day trip from Madrid. The disadvantages of this plan are that you spend the coolest hours of the day (early and late) en route, you miss the charming evening scene in Segovia, and you'll pay more for a hotel in Madrid than in Segovia. If you have time, spend the night. But even if you just stay the day, Segovia still offers a rewarding and convenient break from the big-city intensity of Madrid.

Orientation to Segovia

Segovia is a medieval "ship" ready for your inspection. Start at the stern—the aqueduct—and stroll up Calle de Cervantes and Calle Juan Bravo to the prickly Gothic masts of the cathedral. Explore the tangle of narrow streets around playful Plaza Mayor and then descend to the Alcázar at the bow.

Tourist Information

Segovia has four TIs. The TI on Plaza Mayor covers both Segovia and the surrounding region (at #10, daily July-mid-Sept 9:00-20:00, mid-Sept-June 9:00-14:00 & 16:00-19:00, tel. 921-460-334). The TI at Plaza del Azoguejo, at the base of the aqueduct, specializes in Segovia and has friendly staff, WCs, and a gift shop (daily 10:00-19:00, Sat until 20:00, see wooden model of Segovia, tel. 921-466-720, www.turismodesegovia.com). Smaller TIs are at the bus station (behind a window, daily 10:00-14:00 & 15:30-17:00, tel. 921-436-569) and at the AVE train station (Mon-Fri 9:00-17:00, Sat-Sun 10:30-18:30, tel. 921-447-262).

Arrival in Segovia

Unfortunately, neither of the train stations nor the bus station has luggage storage. If day-tripping from Madrid, check the return schedule when you arrive here (or get one at the Segovia TI).

By Bus: It's a 10-minute walk from the bus station to the town center: Exit left out of the station, continue straight across the street, and follow Avenida Fernández Ladreda, passing San Millán church on the left, then San Clemente church on the right, before coming to the aqueduct.

By Train: From the **AVE train station** (called Guiomar), ride bus #11 for 20 minutes to the base of the aqueduct. To reach the center from the less-convenient *cercanías* **train station,** you can catch bus #6 or #8, take a taxi, or walk 30 minutes (start at Paseo del Conde de Sepulvedana—which becomes Paseo Ezequiel González—then head to the bus station, then turn right and head down Avenida Fernández Ladreda to the aqueduct).

By Car: For driving directions and parking tips, see "Route Tips for Drivers" on page 460.

Helpful Hints

Shopping: If you buy handicrafts such as tablecloths from street vendors, make sure the item you want is the one you actually get; some unscrupulous vendors substitute inferior goods at the last minute. A flea market is held on Plaza Mayor on Thursdays (roughly 8:00-15:00).

Segovia

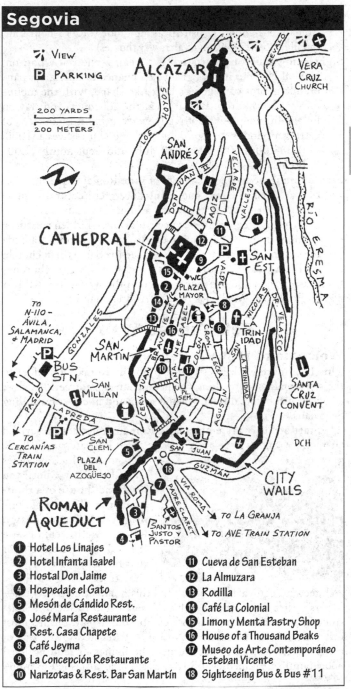

View

Parking

200 YARDS
200 METERS

ALCÁZAR

VERA CRUZ CHURCH

LOS HOYOS

SAN ANDRÉS

DON JUAN II

VELARDE

DAOIZ

VALLEJO

RÍO ERESMA

CATHEDRAL

❶

⓫

⓬

P

⑨

⑮

WC

❷

PLAZA MAYOR

VALDE.

SAN EST.

LA TRINIDAD

NICOLAS DE VELASCO

TO N-110 – ÁVILA, SALAMANCA, & MADRID

GONZALES

⑭

⑬

⑯

❽

⑩

⑰

SAN MARTIN

CERV. JUAN BRAVO

CANA. INF. ISABEL

COLON

CRON.

LECEA

AGUSTIN

SANTA CRUZ CONVENT

P

BUS STN.

SAN MILLÁN

PASEO

LA PREDA

SAN CLEM.

P

TO CERCANÍAS TRAIN STATION

PLAZA DEL AZOGUEJO

⑤

PL. SEM.

⑱

SAN JUAN

GUZMÁN

DCH

CITY WALLS

ROMAN AQUEDUCT

③

④

⑦

VÍA ROMA

PADRE CLARET

SANTOS JUSTO Y PASTOR

TO LA GRANJA

TO AVE TRAIN STATION

❶ Hotel Los Linajes
❷ Hotel Infanta Isabel
❸ Hostal Don Jaime
❹ Hospedaje el Gato
❺ Mesón de Cándido Rest.
❻ José María Restaurante
❼ Rest. Casa Chapete
❽ Café Jeyma
❾ La Concepción Restaurante
❿ Narizotas & Rest. Bar San Martín

⓫ Cueva de San Esteban
⓬ La Almuzara
⓭ Rodilla
⓮ Café La Colonial
⓯ Limon y Menta Pastry Shop
⓰ House of a Thousand Beaks
⓱ Museo de Arte Contemporáneo Esteban Vicente
⓲ Sightseeing Bus & Bus #11

Local Guide: Elvira Valderrama Rascon, a hardworking young woman, is a good English-speaking guide (€100/3-hour tour, mobile 636-227-949, elvisvalrras@yahoo.es).

Sightseeing Bus: Bus Turístico is a weak version of a hop-on, hop-off bus, but it does give you a chance to take great panoramic photos of Segovia's boat-like shape, with the mountains as a backdrop. Pick it up at the aqueduct, and stay on for the full loop—it's not really worth using it as a means of getting around town (€5.70, buy ticket on bus; leaves at 11:00, 12:00, 13:00, 16:00, and 17:00; July-mid-Sept hourly 11:00-23:00; tel. 902-330-080).

Free Churches: Segovia has plenty of little Romanesque churches that are free to enter, and many have architecturally interesting exteriors that are worth a look. On your way to the main sights, keep your eyes peeled for these hidden treasures: Coming from the bus station on Avenida Fernández Ladreda toward the center of town, you can see the San Millán church; on Plazas San Martín and San Esteban are two churches sharing their squares' names; and on the way to the Alcázar on Plaza de la Merced is the San Andrés church.

Self-Guided Walk

Welcome to Historic Segovia

This 15-minute walk goes uphill from the Roman aqueduct to the city's main square along the pedestrian-only street. It's most enjoyable just before dinner, when it's cool and filled with strolling Segovians.

Start at Segovia's emblematic Roman aqueduct (described later, under "Sights in Segovia"). Walk about 100 yards up Calle de

Cervantes, which becomes Calle Juan Bravo, until you reach the **"house of a thousand beaks."** This building's original Moorish design is still easy to see, despite the wall just past the door that blocks your view from the street. This wall, the architectural equivalent of a veil, hid this home's fine courtyard—Moors didn't flaunt their wealth. You can step inside to see art students at work and perhaps an exhibit on display, but it's most interesting from the exterior. Notice its truncated tower, one of many fortified towers that marked the homes of feuding local noble families. In medieval Spain, clashing loyalties led to mini–

civil wars. In the 15th century, as Ferdinand and Isabel centralized authority in Spain, nobles were required to lop their towers. You'll see the once-tall, now-stubby towers of 15th-century noble mansions all over Segovia. Another example of a similar once-fortified, now-softened house with a cropped tower is about 50 yards farther down the street, on the left, on tiny Plaza del Platero Oquendo.

Continue uphill until you come to the complicated **Plaza de San Martín,** a commotion of history surrounding a striking statue of Juan Bravo. When Charles V, a Habsburg who didn't even speak Spanish, took power, he imposed his rule over Castile. This threatened the local nobles, who, inspired and led by Juan Bravo, revolted in 1521. Although Juan Bravo lost the battle—and his head—he's still a symbol of Castilian pride. This statue was erected in 1921 on the 400th anniversary of his death.

In front of the Juan Bravo statue stands the bold and bulky **House of Siglo XV.** Its fortified *Isabelino* style was typical of 15th-century Segovian houses. Later, in a more peaceful age, the boldness of these houses was softened with the decorative stucco work—Arabic-style floral and geometrical patterns—that you see today (for example, in the big house across the street). The 14th-century Tower of Lozoya, behind the statue, is another example of the lopped off towers.

On the same square, the 12th-century Church of St. Martín is Segovian Romanesque in style (a mix of Christian Romanesque and Moorish styles).

If you continue up the street another 100 yards, you'll see the **Corpus Christi Convent** on the left. For a donation, you can pop in to see the Franciscan church, which was once a synagogue, which was once a mosque. While sweet and peaceful, with lots of art featuring St. Francis, the church is skippable.

Keep going until you reach Segovia's inviting **Plaza Mayor**—once the scene of executions, religious theater, and bullfights with spectators jamming the balconies. The bullfights ended in the 19th century. When Segovians complained, they were given a more gentle form of entertainment—bands in the music kiosk. Today the very best entertainment here is simply enjoying a light meal, snack, or drink in your choice of the many restaurants and cafés lining the square. The Renaissance church opposite the City Hall and behind the TI was built to replace the church where Isabel was proclaimed Queen of Castile in 1474. The symbol of Segovia is the aqueduct where you started—find it in the seals on the Theater Juan Bravo and atop the City Hall. Finally, treat yourself to the town's specialty pastry, *ponche segoviano* (marzipan cake), at the recommended Limón y Menta, the bakery on the corner where you entered Plaza Mayor.

Sights in Segovia

▲**Roman Aqueduct**—Segovia was a Roman military base and needed water. Emperor Trajan's engineers built a nine-mile aque-

duct to channel water from the Río Frío to the city, culminating at the Roman castle (which is the Alcázar today). The famous and exposed section of the 2,000-year-old *acueducto romano* is 2,500 feet long and 100 feet high, has 118 arches, was made from 20,000 granite blocks without any mor-

tar, and can still carry a stream of water. It actually functioned until the late 19th century. On Plaza del Azogüejo, a grand stair-way leads from the base of the aqueduct to the top—offering close-up looks at the imposing work.

▲**Cathedral**—Segovia's cathedral, built in Renaissance times

(1525-1768, the third on this site), was Spain's last major Gothic build-ing. Embellished to the hilt with pinnacles and flying buttresses, the exterior is a great example of the final, overripe stage of Gothic, called Flamboyant. Yet the Renaissance arrived before it was finished—as evidenced by the fact that the cathe-dral is crowned by a dome, not a spire.

Cost and Hours: €3, free on Sun 9:30-13:15 but cathedral access

only—no cloisters, open daily April-Oct 9:30-18:30, Nov-March 9:00-17:30, tel. 921-462-205.

➋ **Self-Guided Tour:** The spacious and elegantly simple inte-rior provides a delightful contrast to the frilly exterior. The **choir** features finely carved wooden stalls from the previous church (1400s). The *cátedra* (bishop's chair) is in the center rear of the choir.

The many side chapels are mostly 16th-century, and come with big locking gates—a reminder that they were the private sacred domain of the rich families and guilds who "owned" them. They could enjoy private Masses here with their names actually spoken in the blessings and a fine burial spot close to the altar.

Find the **Capilla La Concepción** (a chapel in the rear that looks like a mini–art gallery). Its many 17th-century paintings hang behind a mahogany wood gate imported from colonial

America. The painting, *Tree of Life*, by Ignacio Ries (left of the altar), shows hedonistic mortals dancing atop the Tree of Life.

As a skeletal Grim Reaper prepares to receive them into hell (by literally chopping down the tree...timberrrr), Jesus rings a bell imploring them to wake up before it's too late. The center statue is Mary of the Apocalypse (as described in Revelations, standing on a devil and half moon, which looks like bull's horns). Mary's pregnant and the devil licks his evil chops, waiting to devour the baby Messiah.

Opposite from where you entered, a fine door (which leads into the cloister) is crowned by a painted Flamboyant Gothic *pietà* in its tympanum (the statue of Jesus with a skirt, on the left, is a reminder of how prudishness from the past looks silly in the present).

The **cloisters** hold a nice little one-room museum containing French tapestries, paintings, and silver reliquaries. Outside in the courtyard, a glass case displays keys to the 17th-century private-chapel gates. The gilded chapter room is draped with precious Flemish tapestries. Notice the gilded wagon. The Holy Communion wafer is placed in the top of this temple-like cart and paraded through town each year during the Corpus Christi festival. From the cloister courtyard, you can see the Renaissance dome rising above the otherwise Gothic rooftop.

▲**Alcázar**—In the Middle Ages, this fortified palace was one of the favorite residences of the monarchs of Castile, a key fortress for controlling the region. The Alcázar grew through the ages, and its function changed many times: After its stint as a palace, it was a prison for 200 years, and then a Royal Artillery School. It burned in 1862. Since the fire, it's basically been a museum.

Cost and Hours: €4.50 for palace, €2 for tower, daily April-Sept 10:00-19:00, Oct-March 10:00-18:00 (tower closed third Tue of month). Buy your tickets at Real Laboratorio de Chimia, facing the palace on your left. At the entrance, pass your ticket through the turnstiles on the right for the palace, or the turnstiles on the left for the tower.

Information: 45-minute, €3 audioguide describes each room.

Pick up a free English leaflet. Tel. 921-460-759, www.alcazarde segovia.com.

➋ **Self-Guided Tour:** You'll enjoy a one-way route through 11 rooms, including a fine view terrace. Visit the tower afterward; its 152 steps up a tight spiral staircase reward you with the only 360-degree city view in town. What you see today in the Alcázar is rebuilt—a Disney-esque exaggeration of the original. Still, its fine Moorish decor and historic furnishings are fascinating. The sumptuous ceilings are accurately restored in Mudejar style, and the throne-room ceiling is the artistic highlight of the palace.

Look for a big mural of Queen Isabel the Catholic being proclaimed Queen of Castile and León in Segovia's main square in 1474. The **Hall of the Monarchs** is lined with the busts of the 52 rulers of Castile and León who presided during the long and ultimately successful Reconquista (711-1492): from Pelayo (the first), clockwise to Juana VII (the last). There were only seven queens during the period (the numbered ones). In this current age of Islamic extremists decapitating Christians, study the painting of St. James the Moor-Slayer—with Muslim heads literally rolling at his feet (poignantly...in the chapel). James is the patron saint of Spain. His name was the rallying cry in the centuries-long Christian crusade to push the Muslim Moors back into Africa.

Stepping onto the **terrace** (the site of the original Roman military camp, circa A.D. 100) with its vast views, marvel at the natural fortification provided by this promontory cut by the confluence of two rivers. The terrace is closed in the winter and sometimes on windy days. The Alcázar marks the end (and physical low point) of the gradual downhill course of the nine-mile-long Roman aqueduct. Can you find the mountain nicknamed *Mujer Muerta* ("dead woman")?

In the **armory** (just after the terrace), find the king's 16th-century ornately carved ivory crossbow, with the hunting scene shown in the adjacent painting. The final rooms are the Museum of Artillery, recalling the period (1764-1862) when this was the Royal Artillery School. It shows the evolution of explosive weaponry, with old photos and prints of the Alcázar.

Church of Santos Justo y Pastor—This simple yet stately old church has fascinating 12th- and 13th-century frescoes filled with Gothic symbolism, plus a stork's nest atop its tower. From the base of the aqueduct, it's a short climb uphill into the newer part of town. Kind old Rafael, the volunteer caretaker, probably won't let you risk climbing the dangerous, claustrophobic bell tower for a commanding Segovia view until they've finished cleaning the pigeon poop and renovating the tower, which may take a while, as they're having trouble gathering sufficient resources to finish the job.

Cost and Hours: Free, Tue-Sat 11:00-14:00 & 16:00-18:00; closed Sun-Mon and when the caretaker, Rafael, needs to run an errand; located a couple of blocks from Plaza del Azogüejo.

Museo de Arte Contemporáneo Esteban Vicente—A collection of local artist Esteban Vicente's abstract art is housed in two rooms of the remodeled remains of Henry IV's 1455 palace. Wilder than Rothko but more restrained than Pollock, Vicente's vibrant work influenced post-WWII American art. The temporary exhibits can be more interesting than the permanent collection.

Cost and Hours: €3, free on Thu, roughly Tue-Fri 11:00-14:00 & 16:00-19:00, Sat-Sun 11:00-20:00, closed Mon, tel. 921-426-010, www.museoestebanvicente.es.

Near Segovia

Vera Cruz Church—This 12-sided, 13th-century Romanesque church, built by the Knights Templar, once housed a piece of the "true cross." You can enjoy a postcard view of the city from the church, and more views follow as you continue around Segovia on the small road below the castle, labeled *ruta turística panorámica.*

Cost and Hours: €2, Tue-Sun 10:30-13:30 & 16:00-19:00, until 18:00 in winter, closed Mon and Nov; outside town beyond the castle, a 25-minute walk from main square; tel. 921-431-475.

▲**La Granja Palace**—This "little Versailles," six miles south of Segovia, is much smaller and happier than nearby El Escorial.

The palace and gardens were built by the homesick French-born King Philip V, grandson of Louis XIV. Today it's restored to its original 18th-century splendor, with its royal collection of tapestries, clocks, and crystal (actually made at the palace's royal crystal factory). Plumbers and gardeners imported from France and Italy made Philip a garden that rivaled Versailles'. The fanciful fountains feature mythological stories (explained in the palace audioguide).

The Bourbon Philip chose to be buried here rather than with his Habsburg predecessors at El Escorial. His tomb is in the adjacent church, included with your ticket.

Cost and Hours: €5 with Spanish-speaking guide, €4.50 without guide; April-Sept Tue-Sun 10:00-19:00; Oct-March Tue-Sat 10:00-14:30 & 15:00-18:00, Sun 10:00-15:00; closed Mon year-round, last entrance one hour before closing, tel. 921-470-019, www.patrimonionacional.es.

Getting There: Fourteen buses a day (fewer on weekends) make the 25-minute trip from Segovia (catch at the bus station) to San Ildefonso–La Granja. The park is free (daily 10:00-20:00, until 19:00 in winter).

Sleeping in Segovia

The best places are on or near the central Plaza Mayor. This is where the city action is—the best bars, most tourist-friendly and *típico* eateries, and the TI. During busy times—on weekends and in July and August—arrive early or call ahead.

In the Old Center, near Plaza Mayor

$$$ **Hotel Los Linajes** is ultra-classy, with rusticity mixed into its poured concrete. This poor man's parador is a few blocks beyond Plaza Mayor, with territorial views and modern, air-conditioned niceties (Sb-€90, Db-€125, Tb-€147, these are rack rates—prices much lower off-season and on some weekdays, breakfast-€11, elevator, parking-€14, Dr. Velasco 9, tel. 921-460-475, fax 921-460-479, www.loslinajes.com, hotelloslinajes@terra.es). From Plaza Mayor, take Escuderos downhill; at the five-way intersection, angle right on Dr. Velasco. Drivers, follow brown hotel signs from the aqueduct to its tight but handy garage.

$$$ **Hotel Infanta Isabel,** right on Plaza Mayor, is the ritziest hotel in the old town, with 38 elegant rooms, some with plaza views (Sb-€67-77, Db-€97-125 depending on room size, Sb and Db-€60 in winter, breakfast on the square-€9, elevator, valet parking-€12, tel. 921-461-300, fax 921-462-217, www.hotelinfanta isabel.com, admin@hotelinfantaisabel.com).

Sleep Code

(€1 = about $1.40, country code: 34)
S = Single, **D** = Double/Twin, **T** = Triple, **Q** = Quad, **b** = bathroom, **s** = shower only. Unless otherwise noted, you can assume credit cards are accepted and English is spoken. Breakfast is generally not included.

To help you easily sort through these listings, I've divided the accommodations into three categories, based on the price for a standard double room with bath during high season:

  $$$ **Higher Priced**—Most rooms €80 or more.
  $$ **Moderately Priced**—Most rooms between €40-80.
  $ **Lower Priced**—Most rooms €40 or less.

Prices can change without notice; verify the hotel's current rates online or by email. For other updates, see www.ricksteves.com/update.

Outside the Old Town, near the Aqueduct

$$ Hostal Don Jaime, opposite the Church of San Justo, is a friendly family-run place with 38 basic, worn, yet well-maintained rooms. Seven more rooms are in an annex across the street (S-€25, D-€32, Db-€50, Tb-€60, Qb-€70, show this book and get a free breakfast in 2012—otherwise €3.75, parking-€8, Ochoa Ondategui 8—from TI at Plaza del Azogüejo, cross under the aqueduct, go right, angle left, then snake uphill for 2 blocks, tel. & fax 921-444-787, hostaldonjaime@hotmail.com).

$ Hospedaje el Gato, a family-run place on a quiet nondescript square just outside the old town, has 10 modern, comfortable rooms (Sb-€25, Db-€40, Tb-€55, air-con, smoky bar serves breakfast and good tapas, parking-€10, uphill from Hostal Don Jaime and aqueduct at Plaza del Salvador 10, tel. 921-423-244, mobile 678-405-079, fax 921-438-047, hbarelgato@yahoo.es but prefer phone or fax reservations).

Eating in Segovia

Look for Segovia's culinary claim to fame, roast suckling pig (*cochinillo asado:* 21 days of mother's milk, into the oven, and

onto your plate—oh, Babe). It's worth a splurge here, or in Toledo or Salamanca.

For lighter fare, try *sopa castellana*—soup mixed with eggs, ham, garlic, and bread—or warm yourself up with the *judiones de La Granja,* a popular soup made with flat white beans from the region.

Ponche segoviano, a dessert made with an almond-and-honey *mazapán* base, is heavenly after an earthy dinner or with a coffee in the afternoon (at the recommended Limón y Menta).

Places to Eat Roast Suckling Pig

Mesón de Cándido, one of the top restaurants in Castile, is famous for its memorable dinners. Even though it's filled with tourists, it's a grand experience. Take time to wander around and survey the photos of celebs—from King Juan Carlos to Antonio Banderas and Melanie Griffith—who've suckled here. Try to get a table in a room with an aqueduct view (figure on spending €35-40, daily 13:00-16:30 & 20:00-23:00, Plaza del Azogüejo 5, air-con, under aqueduct, call for reservations or make them online, tel. 921-428-103, www.mesondecandido.es, candido@mesonde candido.es). Three gracious generations of the Cándido family still run the show.

José María is *the* place to pig out in the old town, a block off Plaza Mayor. And though it doesn't have the history or fanfare of Cándido, Segovians claim this high-energy place serves the best roast suckling pig in town. It thrives with a hungry mix of tourists and locals (€40 à la carte dinner, daily 13:00-16:00 & 20:30-23:30, air-con, Cronista Lecea 11, call for reservations or make them online, tel. 921-466-017, www.rtejosemaria.com, reservas@rtejose maria.com).

Restaurante Casa Chapete, a homey little place filled with smoke, happy diners, and not a tourist in sight, serves traditional lamb and pig dishes—but only for lunch (€18 three-course meals including wine, €30 quarter *cochinillos* for 2-3 people, €8 simple three-course fixed-price meals on weekdays, daily 12:30-16:00, 2 blocks beyond aqueduct, across from recommended Hostal Don Jaime at Calle Ochoa Ondategui 7, tel. 921-421-096).

Mostly Pig-Free Places in the Old Center

Plaza Mayor, the main square, provides a great backdrop for a light lunch, dinner, or drink. Prices at the cafés are generally reasonable, and many offer a good selection of tapas and *raciones*. Grab a table at the place of your choice and savor the scene. **Café Jeyma** has a fine setting and cathedral view. **La Concepción Restaurante** is also good (€35 meals, closer to the cathedral).

Narizotas serves more imaginative and non-Castilian alternatives to the gamey traditions. Dine outside on a delightful square or inside with modern art under medieval timbers. For a wonderful dining experience, try their chef's choice mystery samplers, either the "Right Hand" (€44, about 10 courses) or the "Left Hand" (€35, about six courses); both include wine, water, dessert, and coffee. They offer a less elaborate three-course €16 fixed-priced meal, and their à la carte menu is also a treat (daily 13:00-16:00 & 20:30-24:00, midway down Calle Juan Bravo at Plaza de Medina del Campo 1, tel. 921-462-679).

Restaurante Bar San Martín, a no-frills place popular with locals, has a lively tapas bar, great outdoor seating by a fountain on the same square as Narizotas (listed above), and a smoky restaurant in the back. I'd eat here only to enjoy the setting on the square (€10 three-course fixed-price meal on weekdays, €20 fixed-price *cochinillo* meal on Sat-Sun, tapas bar open Tue-Sun 9:00-24:00, restaurant open Tue-Sun 13:30-16:00 & 20:30-23:00, both closed Mon, Plaza de San Martín 3, tel. 921-462-466).

Cueva de San Esteban serves traditional home cooking with a stress-free photo menu at the door, and hearty, big-enough-to-split plates (daily 11:00-24:00, full meals 13:00-16:00, two blocks past Plaza Mayor on a quiet back street, Calle Valdelaguila 15, tel.

921-460-982).

La Almuzara is a garden of veggie and organic delights: whole-wheat pizzas, tofu, seitan, and even a few dishes with meat (€10 plates, Tue 20:00-24:00, Wed-Sun 13:00-16:00 & 20:00-24:00, closed Mon, between cathedral and Alcázar at Marques del Arco 3, tel. 921-460-622).

Rodilla, the popular chain, offers a tasty selection of sandwiches and salads (Mon-Fri 9:30-22:00, Sat-Sun 10:00-22:30, on Calle Juan Bravo, at intersection with Calle de la Herrería).

Breakfast: In the morning, I like to eat on Plaza Mayor (many choices) while enjoying the cool air and the people scene. Or, 100 yards down the main drag toward the aqueduct, **Café La Colonial** serves good breakfasts (with seating on a tiny square or inside, Plaza del Corpus).

Nightlife: Inexpensive bars and eateries line Calle de Infanta Isabel, just off Plaza Mayor. For nightlife, the bars on Plaza Mayor, Calle de Infanta Isabel, and Calle de Isabel la Católica are packed. There are a number of late-night dance clubs along the aqueduct.

Dessert: **Limón y Menta** offers a good, rich *ponche segoviano* (marzipan) cake by the slice for €3—or try the lighter honey-and-almond *crocantinos* (daily 9:30-21:30 but hours can vary, seating inside, Calle de Isabel la Católica 2, tel. 921-462-141).

Market: An outdoor produce market thrives on Plaza Mayor on Thursday (roughly 8:00-15:00). Nearby, a few stalls are open daily except Sunday on Calle del Cronista Ildefonso Rodríguez.

Segovia Connections

From Segovia to Madrid: You have three options: bus, fast train, or slow train. Even though the 35-minute AVE train takes less than half as long as the bus, you'll spend more time getting to the AVE stations in Segovia and Madrid than to the bus stations, so the total time spent in transit is about the same. *Cercanías* commuter trains also run to Madrid, but take two hours and don't save you much money.

Buses run from Segovia to Madrid's Príncipe Pío Metro station; many stop first at Madrid's Moncloa Metro station, where you can get off if convenient to your hotel (2/hour, departing on the half-hour, 1.25-1.5 hours, €7; Mon-Fri first departure at 6:00, Sat at 6:45, Sun at 8:30; last return at 21:30; tel. 915-598-955, www .lasepulvedana.es). Consider busing from Segovia to Ávila for a visit, then continuing to Salamanca by bus or train.

If you're riding the bus from Madrid to Segovia, about 30 minutes after leaving Madrid you'll see—breaking the horizon on the left—the dramatic concrete cross of the Valley of the Fallen. Its grand facade marks the entry to the mammoth underground memorial (described earlier in this chapter).

The **AVE train** goes between Segovia's Guiomar station and Madrid's Chamartín station (8/day, 35 minutes, €10). To get to Guiomar station, take city bus #11 from the base of the aqueduct (20 minutes, buses usually timed to match arrivals). You can also take the *cercanías* **commuter train** to Madrid, though this option is slower (9/day, 2 hours, €6, leaves from Segovia's inconvenient *cercanías* station, arrives in Madrid at both Chamartín and Atocha stations). To reach the sleepy, dead-end *cercanías* station, walk 20 minutes past the bus station along Paseo de Ezequiel González (which turns into Paseo del Conde de Sepulvedana); catch bus #6 (leaves from the bus station) or #8 (leaves from the aqueduct); or take a taxi. Train info: tel. 902-320-320.

From Segovia by Bus to: La Granja Palace (14/day, fewer on weekends, 25 minutes), **Ávila** (5/day weekdays, 2/day weekends, 1.25 hours), **Salamanca** (2-4/day, 3 hours, transfer in Labajos; it's smart to reserve a seat for the Labajos–Salamanca segment—call Madrid's La Sepulvedana office at tel. 915-598-955).

Route Tips for Drivers

From Madrid to Segovia: Leave Madrid on A-6. Exit 39 gets you to Segovia via a slow, winding route over the scenic mountain. Exit at 60 (after a long €3 toll tunnel) or get there quicker by staying on the toll road all the way to Segovia (add €2 weekdays or €3 on weekends). At the Segovia aqueduct, follow *casco histórico* signs to the old town (on the side where the aqueduct adjoins the crenellated fortress walls).

Parking in Segovia: Free parking is available in the Alcázar's lot, but you must move your car out by 19:00 (or by 18:00 Oct-March), when the gates close. Or try the lot northwest of the bus station by the statue of Cándido, along the street called Paseo de Ezequiel González. Outside the old city, there's an Acueducto Parking underground garage kitty-corner from the bus station. Although it can be a hard slog up the hill to the Alcázar on a hot day, it beats trying to maneuver uphill through tight bends. There's also the huge convenient Padre Claret garage near the aqueduct (€1.55/hour).

The city center has lots of parking spaces, but they're not free. If you want to park in the old town, be legal or risk an expensive ticket. Buy a ticket from the nearby machine to park in areas marked by blue stripes, and place the ticket on your dashboard (€1.50/hour, pay meter every 2 hours 9:00-14:00 & 16:30-20:00; free parking 20:00-9:00, Sat afternoon, and all day Sun).

Segovia to Salamanca (100 miles): Leave Segovia by driving around the town's circular road, which offers good views from below the Alcázar. Then follow signs for *Ávila* (road N-110). Notice the fine Segovia view from the three crosses at the crest of the first hill. The Salamanca road leads around the famous Ávila walls to the right. The best wall view is from the signposted Cuatro Postes, a mile northwest of town. Salamanca (N-501) is clearly marked, about an hour's drive away.

About 20 miles before Salamanca, you might want to stop at the huge bull on the left side of the road. There's a little dirt lane leading right up to it. As you get closer, it becomes more and more obvious it isn't alive. Bad boys climb it for a goofy photo. For a great photo op of Salamanca, complete with river reflection, stop at the edge of the city (at the light before the first bridge). The only safe parking in Salamanca is in a garage; try the underground lot at Plaza Santa Eulalia, Plaza del Campillo, or Lemans (closer to recommended Petit Palace Las Torres). See the Salamanca chapter for more information.

Ávila

Yet another popular side-trip from Madrid, Ávila is famous for its perfectly preserved medieval walls, as the birthplace of St. Teresa, and for its yummy *yema* treats. For more than 300 years, Ávila was on the battlefront between the Muslims and Christians, changing hands several times. Today perfectly peaceful Ávila has a charming old town. With several fine churches and monasteries, it makes for an enjoyable quick stop between Segovia and Salamanca (each about an hour away by car).

Orientation to Ávila

On a quick stop, everything in Ávila that matters is within a few blocks of the cathedral (actually part of the east end of the wall).

Tourist Information

The TI has good, free maps and information on walking tours (daily 9:30-14:00 & 16:00-19:00, no afternoon closure July-mid-Sept, on Calle San Segundo, just outside the wall gate near the cathedral, tel. 920-211-387). Another TI, with a friendlier staff, is located outside the wall, opposite the Basilica of San Vicente. They sell handy €1 mini-guidebooks in English, which provide details on the palaces and churches. If you want to see more than

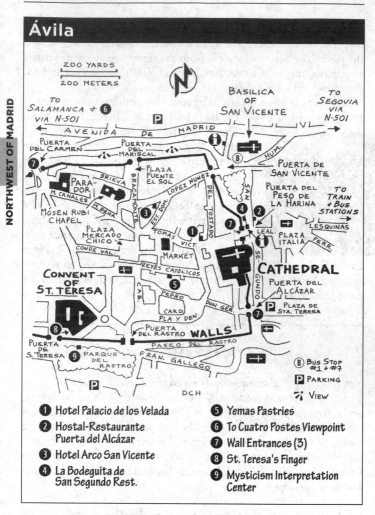

Ávila

Legend:
1. Hotel Palacio de los Velada
2. Hostal-Restaurante Puerta del Alcázar
3. Hotel Arco San Vicente
4. La Bodeguita de San Segundo Rest.
5. Yemas Pastries
6. To Cuatro Postes Viewpoint
7. Wall Entrances (3)
8. St. Teresa's Finger
9. Mysticism Interpretation Center

the highlights, consider the general *Descubre Ávila*, which outlines 10 walking-tour itineraries in the old town (daily April-Oct 9:00-20:00, Nov-March 9:00-17:30, public WCs).

Sightseeing Train: A clunky tourist train departs from outside the wall by Puerta de San Vicente, choo-choos into town, exits at the westernmost gate, heads out to the Cuatro Postes viewpoint, loops by the Monasterio de la Encarnación (where St. Teresa lived), and then shudders along back to the north wall. Check the *próxima salida* sign for departure times, which are usually twice an hour (€4 day, daily 9:00-18:00, narration in Spanish unless you specify English, mobile 629-222-218).

Arrival in Ávila

Approaching by bus, train, or car, you'll need to make your way through the nondescript modern part of town to find the walled old town.

By Bus or Train: From the cathedral and wall, the bus station is a 15-minute walk, while the train station is a 20-minute walk. City buses #4 and #1 run from the train station to the Basilica of San Vicente (to find the bus stop, exit the station, walk one block, and turn right at the first street). There are lockers at Ávila's bus station (use the newer-looking locks), but not at the train station.

By Car: Drivers can use the public parking east of Puerta del Alcázar, just south of the cathedral, or at Parking Dornier (€1.25/hour).

NORTHWEST OF MADRID

Sights in Ávila

▲**The Wall**—Built from around 1100 on even more ancient remains, Ávila's fortified wall is the oldest, most complete, and

best-preserved in Spain. It has four entrances, allowing visitors the chance to walk almost three-quarters of the wall: One entrance is just off Plaza de Santa Teresa (Puerta del Alcázar). The best one, which leads to a longer walk, starts from inside the TI on Calle San Segundo, by the gate closest to the cathedral (Puerta del Peso de la Harina) and takes you to the third and fourth gates: Puerta del Carmen and Puerta Puente Adaja (on the end farthest from the cathedral—look for the door marked *subida a la muralla*).

An interesting paseo scene takes place along the wall each night—make your way along the southern wall (Paseo del Rastro) to Plaza de Santa Teresa for spectacular vistas across the plains.

Cost and Hours: €4, Tue-Sun April-mid-Oct 10:00-20:00, mid-Oct-March 11:00-18:00, closed Mon except July-Aug, last entry 30 minutes before closing.

Viewing the Wall: The best views of the wall itself are actually from street level. If you're wandering the city and see arched gates leading out of the old center, pop out to the other side and take in the impressive wall from the ground. Drivers can see the especially impressive north side as they circle to the right from Puerta de San Vicente to catch the highway to Salamanca.

Viewing Ávila from Cuatro Postes—The best overall view of the walled town of Ávila is about a mile away on the Salamanca road (N-501), at a clearly marked turnout for the Cuatro Postes (four posts). You can reach the Cuatro Postes on the tourist train (described earlier), or catch city bus #7 (€1) at the stop in front of the Basilica of San Vicente—it goes through the old town, then out to the Cuatro Postes viewpoint, back to San Vicente, and on to the RENFE train station.

Cathedral—While it started as Romanesque, Ávila's cathedral, finished in the 16th century, is considered the first Gothic cathedral in Spain. Its position—with its granite apse actually part of the fortified wall—underlines the "medieval alliance between cross and sword." You can tour the cathedral, its sacristy, cloister, and museum—which includes an El Greco painting.

Cost and Hours: €4; Mon-Fri 10:00-18:00, Sat 10:00-19:00, Sun 12:00-17:30; off-season Mon-Sat 10:00-17:00, Sun 12:00-17:00—but hours often vary; Plaza de la Catedral.

Convent of St. Teresa—Built in the 17th century on the spot where the saint was born, this convent is a big hit with pilgrims (10-minute walk from cathedral). St. Teresa (1515-1582)—reforming nun, mystic, and writer—bought a house in Ávila and converted it into a convent with more stringent rules than the one she belonged to. She faced opposition in her hometown from rival nuns and those convinced her visions of heaven were the work of the devil. However, with her mentor and fellow mystic St. John of the Cross, she established convents of Discalced (shoeless) Carmelites throughout Spain, and her visions and writings led her to sainthood (she was canonized in 1622).

A lavishly gilded side chapel marks the actual place of her birth (left of main altar, door may be closed). A separate room of relics (outside, facing the church on your right, Sala de Reliquias) houses a shop that shows off Teresa's finger, complete with a fancy emerald ring, along with one of her sandals and the bones of St. John of the Cross. A museum dedicated to the saint is in the crypt at the side entrance and is worth a visit for devotees.

Cost and Hours: Convent—free, daily 9:30-13:30 & 15:30-19:30, until 19:00 in winter, no photos of finger allowed; museum—€2, April-Oct Tue-Sun 10:00-14:00 & 16:00-19:00, Nov-March Tue-Sun 10:00-13:30 & 15:30-17:30, closed Mon year-round, last entry 30 minutes before closing.

Mysticism Interpretation Center (Centro de Interpretación del Misticismo)—If St. Teresa were alive today, she'd love this place, which explores modern mysticism from a Catholic perspective. Pick up the English handout that explains the art and texts, then take the elevator down on a "journey to the inner realms of the Self."

Cost and Hours: €2, April-Oct Tue-Sun 10:00-13:30 & 16:00-19:00, until 18:30 Nov-March, closed Mon year-round, last entry 30 minutes before closing, tel. 920-212-154, www.avilamistica.es.

Yemas—These pastries, made by local nuns, are like soft-boiled egg yolks that have been cooled and sugared. They're sold all over town. The shop Las Delicias del Convento is actually a retail outlet for the cooks of the convent (€3.60 for a small box, Tue-Sat 10:30-14:00 & 17:00-20:00, Sun 10:30-18:00, closed Mon, hours and closed day vary by season, a block from TI at Calle de los Reyes Católicos 12, tel. 920-220-293).

Sleeping in Ávila

(€1 = about $1.40, country code: 34)

Ávila is cold in fall, winter, and early spring, so you'll likely need to turn up the heat in these hotels.

$$$ Hotel Palacio de los Velada is antique and classy and faces the cathedral. Located in a five-centuries-old palace, it has 145 elegant rooms surrounding a huge and inviting arcaded courtyard (Sb-€150, Db-€190, third person-€30 extra on weekends, lower rates Mon-Thu and for 2-night weekend stays, higher on holidays, rates fluctuate wildly—check website for latest, air-con, elevator, Plaza de la Catedral 10, tel. 920-255-100, fax 920-254-900, www.veladahoteles.com, reserves.avila@veladahoteles.com).

$$ Hostal Puerta del Alcázar has 27 basic yet spacious rooms right next to the Puerta del Peso de la Harina just outside the wall (Sb-€43, Db-€55, Tb-€77, Qb-€99, €10 less off-season, includes tax and breakfast, no air-con, San Segundo 38, tel. 920-211-074, fax 920-211-075, www.puertadelalcazar.com, info@puertadel alcazar.com). It's home to a recommended restaurant.

$$ Hotel Arco San Vicente has a friendly staff and a great location two blocks from the cathedral and one block from the Basilica of San Vicente, with its handy stop for buses to the train station or the Cuatro Postes viewpoint (Sb-€35/40, Db-€50/65, breakfast-€6, air-con, elevator, free Wi-Fi, limited parking-€10, Calle López Núñez 6, tel. 920-222-498, fax 920-229-532, www.arcosanvicente.com, info@arcosanvicente.com).

Eating in Ávila

Ávila specialties include *chuletón*, a thick steak, and *judías del Barco de Ávila*, big white beans often cooked in a meaty stew. Around Plaza del Mercado Chico, the main square of the old center, are several good spots to try the stew or to have a reasonable fixed-price meal (many of which include the *judías*).

La Bodeguita de San Segundo is good for a light lunch. Owned by a locally famous wine connoisseur, it serves fine wine by the glass with tapas such as smoked-cod salad and wild-mushroom scrambled eggs (daily 12:00-24:00, €2 bread charge, along the outside of wall near cathedral at San Segundo 19, tel. 920-257-309).

Hostal-Restaurante Puerta del Alcázar, filled with more locals than hotel guests, serves elaborate salads, fixed-price meals (for €13 and €21), and more. You can sit indoors or, even better, outdoors with cathedral views (Mon-Sat 13:30-16:00 & 21:00-23:30, Sun 13:30-16:00, San Segundo 38, tel. 920-211-074).

Picnics: The town's market house is a good spot to pick up fruit and water (Mon-Thu 9:00-14:00 & 17:00-20:00, Fri 9:00-20:00, Sat 9:00-14:00, closed Sun, between Plaza del Mercado Chico and the cathedral). On Friday mornings, there's a farmers' market on Plaza del Mercado Chico.

Café: For a pleasant break from sightseeing, pop in to the courtyard of the recommended **Hotel Palacio de los Velada** for a drink (€3 coffee and hot chocolate).

Ávila Connections

The bus terminal is closed on Sundays, but you can purchase tickets when boarding the bus.

From Ávila to: Segovia (5 buses/day weekdays, 2 on weekends, 1.25 hours), **Madrid** (1 train/hour until 21:55, 1.5 hours, more frequent connections with Chamartín Station than Atocha; 8 buses/day, 4 on weekends, 1.5 hours; Estación Sur de Autobuses in Madrid, tel. 914-684-200), **Salamanca** (6 trains/day, 1 hour; 4 buses/day, 2 on weekends, 1.5 hours). Train info: toll tel. 902-320-320, www.renfe.com. Bus info: tel. 902-222-282, www.lasepulvedana.es.

TOLEDO

An hour south of Madrid, Toledo teems with tourists, souvenirs, and great art by day, and delicious dinners, echoes of El Greco, and medieval magic by night. Incredibly well preserved and full of cultural wonder, the entire city has been declared a national monument.

Spain's former capital crowds 2,500 years of tangled history—Roman, Jewish, Visigothic, Moorish, and Christian—onto a high, rocky perch protected on three sides by the Tajo River. To keep the city's historic appearance intact, the Spanish government has forbidden any modern exteriors. The rich mix of Jewish, Moorish, and Christian heritages makes it one of Europe's artistic highlights.

Today, Toledo thrives as a provincial capital and a busy tourist attraction. The last decade has been an eventful one for Toledo. A high-speed AVE train connection has made Toledo a quick, 30-minute ride from Madrid. While locals worried that this link would turn their town into a bedroom community for wealthy Madrileños, the already high real-estate prices minimized the impact. A new convention center was just completed: the Palacio de Congresos Miradero (by Rafael Moneo, architect of the Los Angeles Cathedral and Kursaal Conference Center in San Sebastián). While the center itself is of little interest to tourists, its huge underground parking garage and escalator into town make arrival by car much more efficient. The long-term vision is to make the old city center essentially traffic-free (except for residents' cars, public transit, and service vehicles).

Toledo remains the historic, artistic, and spiritual center of Spain. Despite tremendous tourist crowds, Toledo sits enthroned on its history, much as it was when Europe's most powerful king,

Charles V, and its most famous resident artist, El Greco, called it home.

Planning Your Time

To properly see Toledo's sights—including its museums (great El Greco) and cathedral (best in Spain)—and to experience its medieval atmosphere (wonderful after dark), you'll need two nights and a day.

Get an early start and stay out late. If going by train, keep in mind that the early and late trains tend to sell out to commuters and day trippers. Plan carefully for lunchtime closures and take a rest break during Toledo's notorious midday heat in summer.

Orientation to Toledo

Toledo sits atop a circular hill, with the cathedral roughly dead-center. Lassoed into a tight tangle of streets by the sharp bend of

the Tajo River (called the "Tejo" in Portugal, where it hits the Atlantic at Lisbon), Toledo has Spain's most confusing medieval street plan. But it's a small town within its walls, with only 10,000 inhabitants (82,000 total live in greater Toledo, including its modern suburbs). The major sights are well-signposted, and most locals will politely point you in the right direction if you ask. (You are, after all, the town's bread and butter.)

The top sights stretch from the main square, Plaza de Zocodover (zoh-koh-doh-VEHR), southwest along Calle Comercio (a.k.a. Calle Ancha, "Wide Street") to the cathedral, and beyond that to Santo Tomé and more. The visitor's city lies basically along this small but central street, and most tourists never stray from this axis. Make a point to get lost. The town is compact. When it's time to return to someplace familiar, pull out the map or ask, "¿Para Plaza de Zocodover?" From the far end of town, handy bus #12 circles back to Plaza de Zocodover (see "Bus #12 Self-Guided Tour" on page 489).

Keep in mind that sights appear closer on maps than they really are, because local maps don't factor into account the slope of the hill. In Toledo, they say everything's uphill—it certainly feels that way.

Tourist Information

Toledo has four TIs. There's one at the **train station** (daily 9:00-17:00, tel. 925-239-121); one at **Bisagra Gate,** in a freestanding building in the park just outside the gate (Mon-Fri 9:00-18:00, Sat 9:00-19:00, Sun 9:00-15:00, longer hours in summer, tel. 925-220-843); another on **Plaza del Ayuntamiento** near the cathedral (daily 10:00-18:00, WC, tel. 925-254-030); and a fourth on **Plaza de Zocodover** in Casa del Mapa (daily 10:00-18:00). At any TI, you can pick up the town map, *Toledo Tourist and Cultural Guide,* monthly *Cultural Agenda,* and *Traveller's Gazette* (event listings). The TIs share a website: www.toledo-turismo.com.

Toledo's History

Perched strategically in the center of Iberia, for centuries Toledo was a Roman transportation hub with a thriving Jewish population. After Rome fell, the city became a Visigothic capital (A.D. 554). In 711 the Moors (Muslims) made it a regional center. In 1085 the city was reconquered by Christians, but many Moors remained in Toledo, tolerated and respected as scholars and craftsmen.

Whereas Jews were commonly persecuted elsewhere in Europe, Toledo's Jewish community—educated, wealthy, and cosmopolitan—thrived from the city's earliest times. Jews of Spanish origin are called Sephardic Jews. The American expression "Holy Toledo" likely originated from the Sephardic Jews who eventually immigrated to America. To them, Toledo was the holiest Jewish city in Europe...Holy Toledo!

During its medieval heyday (c. 1350), Toledo was a city of the humanities, where God was known by many names. In this haven of cultural diversity, people of different faiths lived together in harmony.

Toledo remained Spain's political capital until 1561, when Philip II moved to more-spacious Madrid. Historians fail to agree on the reason for the move; some say that Madrid was the logical place for a capital in the geographic center of newly formed *España*, while others say that Philip wanted to separate politics from religion. (Toledo remained Spain's religious capital.) Whatever the reason, when the king moved out, Toledo was mothballed, only to be rediscovered by 19th-century Romantic travelers. They wrote of it as a mystical place, which it remains today.

Arrival in Toledo

"Arriving" in Toledo means getting uphill to Plaza de Zocodover. As the bus and train stations are outside the town center and parking can be a challenge, this involves a hike, a taxi, or a city bus ride.

By Train: Toledo's early-20th-century train station is Neo-Moorish and a national monument itself for its architecture and art, which celebrate the three cultures that coexisted here.

Remember that early and late trains can sell out; reserve ahead. If you haven't yet bought a ticket for your departure from Toledo (even if it's for the next day), get it before you leave the Toledo station and choose a specific time rather than leave it open-ended. (If you prefer more flexibility, take the bus instead—see

"By Bus" below.)

From the train station to Plaza de Zocodover, it's a €4 **taxi** ride, a 20-minute hike (described below), or an easy ride on various buses. You can take **city bus** #5 or #6 (can also be marked #6.1 or #6.2); leaving the station, you'll see the bus stop 30 yards to the right (€1, pay on bus, confirm by asking, "¿*Para Plaza de Zocodover?*"). The **Tourist Bus** (described on page 473), which circles the city, also picks up outside the station, and stops briefly at the famous El Greco viewpoint before heading up to Plaza de Zocodover (€5; €8 for hop-on, hop-off version). Another option, the red **Centro Directo bus** (€2), is scheduled to meet arriving trains.

To **walk** into town, turn right leaving the station, cross the bridge with the mighty Alcázar (now the Army Museum) on your left, pass the bus station (on your right), go straight through the roundabout, continue uphill to Bisagra Gate, and head into the old town to Plaza de Zocodover.

By Bus: At the bus station, buses park downstairs. Luggage lockers and a small bus-information office—where you can buy locker tokens—are upstairs opposite the cafeteria. Before leaving the station, confirm your departure time (probably 2/hour to Madrid). Unlike the faster trains, buses don't tend to get booked up. You can put off buying a return ticket for the bus until just minutes before you leave Toledo. Specify you'd like a *directo* bus, because the *ruta* trip takes longer (1 hour versus 1.5 hours). However, if you miss the *directo* bus (or if it's sold out), the *ruta* option offers a peek of off-the-beaten-path Madrid suburbia; you'll arrive at the same time as taking the next *directo* bus. From the bus station, Plaza de Zocodover is a 15-minute hike, a €4 taxi ride, or a short bus ride (catch #5 or #12 downstairs; €1, pay on bus).

By Car: If you're arriving by car, you can enjoy a scenic big-picture orientation by following the *Ronda de Toledo* signs on a big circular drive around the city. You'll view the city from many angles along the Circunvalación road across the Tajo Gorge. Stop at a viewpoint or drive to Parador de Toledo, just south of town, for the view (from the balcony) that El Greco made famous in his portrait of Toledo. The best time for this trip is the magic hour before sunset, when the top viewpoints are busy with tired old folks and frisky young lovers.

The most convenient place to park is in the big Miradero Garage at the convention center (€16/day; drive through Bisagra Gate, go uphill half a mile, look for sign on the left directing you to *Plaza del Miradero*). There is also parking farther into town at the Alcázar Garage (opposite the Alcázar—€1.60/hour, €16.20/day).

A car is useless within Toledo's city walls, where the narrow,

Central Toledo

STREET WIDTH IS
EXAGGERATED
FOR CLARITY

200 YARDS
200 METERS

TO BULLRING
& MADRID

BISAGRA
GATE

BUS
STATION

CARD. TAV.

C. DE LA CARRERA

CITY
WALLS

TO
TRAIN
STATION

TO
RING ROAD
& PARADOR

ESCALATORS

SUBIDA LA GRANJA

MEZQUITA

CUESTA

CRISTO

ARABAL

CADENAS NUNEZ

ARMAS

MIRA-
DERO
ESCALATOR

SANTA
CRUZ
MUSEUM

CERVANTES

CALLE REAL

MERCED

ALJIBES

S. ILD.

S. LEO.

TEND.

VISI-
GOTHIC
MUSEUM

POST

LA PLATA

SILL

NAV. GABLO

CADENAR

COMERCIO

MARKET

SAN JUAN
DE LOS
REYES

DON.

S. ROMAN

NUNCIO

SANTO TOMÉ

ANGEL

ALFONSO XII

S. TOMÉ

TRINIDAD

ALCÁZAR
(ARMY MUSEUM)

SINAGOGA
DE
SANTA MARÍA
LA BLANCA

SALVADOR

S. JUAN DIOS

S. MORO

S. URSULA

ISABEL

CATHEDRAL

MUSEO
VICTORIO
MACHO

EL GRECO
MUSEUM

PARK

& CITY HALL
(AYUNTAMIENTO)

RIO TAJO

SINAGOGA DEL
TRÁNSITO

DCH

VIEW

P PARKING

B BUS
STOP

TOLEDO'S MAIN DRAG

① Plaza de Zocodover

② Mariano Zamorano
Knife Workshop

③ Mezquita del Cristo de la Luz (Mosque)

④ Visigothic Museum

⑤ Escalator to Miradero Garage

TOLEDO

twisting streets are no fun to navigate. Ideally, see the old town outside of car-rental time. Pick up or drop off your car on the outskirts of town; **Avis** is at the train station (Mon-Fri 9:30-13:30 & 16:30-19:30, Sat 9:30-13:30, closed Sun, handy early and late drop options, tel. 925-214-535).

By Escalator into Town: A series of escalators runs outdoors past Bisagra Gate, giving you a free ride up, up, up into town (until 22:00). You'll end up near San Ildefonso and far from Plaza de Zocodover, but it's fun for the novelty. The other escalator, stretching from the Miradero Garage up nearly to Plaza de Zocodover, is only helpful for people using the garage.

Helpful Hints

Internet Access: You'll find **Internet Locutorio** shops throughout Toledo (open long hours).

Local Guidebook: Consider the readable *Toledo: Its Art and Its History* (€5-6 big version, €4 small version, same text and photos in both, sold all over town). It explains all of the sights (which generally provide no on-site information) and gives you a photo to point at and say, *"¿Dónde está...?"*

Tours in Toledo

▲**Tourist Bus**—This bus is a great option for day-trippers. Meet the bus at the train station, ride along the river to the famous lookout point, where you can get off for a five-minute photo stop (or wait an hour for the next bus), then continue around the city and up to Plaza de Zocodover, where you can get off and visit Toledo. A hop-on, hop-off version allows you to stop at Bisagra Gate and the San Martín medieval bridge; at the end of the day, hop back on at Plaza de Zocodover to finish the loop back to the station (€5; €8 for hop-on, hop-off option; pay driver; first bus leaves train station at 9:50, then almost hourly until 18:00; March-Sept until 21:00, recorded English commentary on headphones, tel. 925-258-157).

Tourist Train—For a pleasant city overview, hop on the cheesy white Tren Imperial Tourist Tram. Crass as it feels, you get a 45-minute putt-putt through Toledo and around the Tajo River Gorge. It's a fine way for non-drivers to enjoy views of the city from across the Tajo Gorge (€4.40, buy ticket from convenience store at Calle de la Sillería 14, leaves Plaza de Zocodover daily on the hour from 11:00 into the evening, recorded English/Spanish commentary, tel. 925-220-300). There are no photo stops, but it goes slowly—for the best views of Toledo across the gorge, sit on the right side, not behind the driver.

Public Buses—For the cheapest tour, use public transportation. Take the "Bus #12 Self-Guided Tour" through town (see page 489). Or, for a "gorge-ous" loop trip, try bus #7.1, which leaves Plaza de Zocodover hourly (7:45-21:45) and offers the same classic view across the gorge as the tourist train; its route circles around to El Greco's famous viewpoint, where you can hop off and snap some photos, then wait at the same stop for the next bus to take you back.

Local Guides—Two good guides who enjoy sharing their hometown in English are **Juan José Espadas** (a.k.a. Juanjo, tel. 667-780-475, juanjo@guiadetoledo.es) and **Almudena Cencerrado** (tel. 610-765-067, almuzen@hotmail.com). For a three-hour tour, they each charge about €140 (€155 on weekends).

TOLEDO

TOLEDO

Toledo at a Glance

▲▲▲**Cathedral** One of Europe's best, with a marvelously vast interior and great art. **Hours:** Mon-Sat 10:00-18:30, Sun 14:00-18:30. See page 475.

▲▲**Santa Cruz Museum** Renaissance building housing wonderful artwork, including 15 El Grecos. **Hours:** Mon-Sat 10:00-18:30, Sun 10:00-14:00. See page 480.

▲**Santo Tomé** Simple chapel with El Greco's masterpiece, *The Burial of the Count of Orgaz.* **Hours:** Daily April-mid-Oct 10:00-18:45, mid-Oct-March 10:00-17:45. See page 484.

▲**Museo Victorio Macho** Collection of 20th-century Toledo sculptor's works, with expansive river-gorge view. **Hours:** Mon-Sat 10:00-19:00, Sun 10:00-15:00. See page 486.

▲**San Juan de los Reyes Monasterio** Church/monastery intended as final resting place of Isabel and Ferdinand. **Hours:** Daily 10:00-18:45, until 17:45 in winter. See page 487.

Army Museum Covers all things military—with the glaring exception of Spain's controversial Civil War—located in the imposing fortress, the Alcázar. **Hours:** June-Sept Tue-Sat 10:00-21:00, Sun 10:00-15:00, closed Mon; Oct-May Tue-Sat 10:00-19:00, Sun 10:00-15:00, closed Mon. See page 482.

Visigothic Museum Romanesque church housing the only Visigothic artifacts in town. **Hours:** Tue-Sat 10:00-14:00 & 16:00-18:30, Sun 10:00-14:00, closed Mon. See page 483.

El Greco Museum Small collection of paintings, including the *View and Plan of Toledo,* El Greco's panoramic map of the city. **Hours:** Tue-Sat 10:00-20:00, Sun 10:00-15:00, closed Mon. See page 485.

Sinagoga del Tránsito Museum of Toledo's Jewish past. **Hours:** Tue-Sat 9:30-20:00—until 18:00 in winter, Sun 10:00-15:00, closed Mon. See page 485.

Sinagoga de Santa María la Blanca Synagogue that harmoniously combines Toledo's three religious influences: Jewish, Christian, and Moorish. **Hours:** Daily April-Sept 10:00-18:45, Oct-March 10:00-17:45. See page 487.

Sights in Toledo

▲▲▲Cathedral

Holy Toledo! Spain's leading Catholic city has a magnificent cathedral. Shoehorned into the old center (on the spot where a mosque once stood), its exterior is hard to appreciate. But the interior is so lofty, rich, and vast that it'll have you wandering around like a Pez dispenser stuck open, whispering "Wow."

Cost and Hours: Cathedral tickets are sold in the shop opposite the church entrance on Calle Cardenal. €7, Mon-Sat 10:00-18:30, Sun 14:00-18:30, open earlier for prayer only, last entry 30 minutes before closing, audioguide-€3, no photos, tel. 925-222-241. A WC is in the ticket center.

TOLEDO

⊙ Self-Guided Tour: Wander among the pillars, thick and sturdy as a redwood forest. Sit under one and imagine a time when the lightbulbs were candles and the tourists were pilgrims—before the *No Photo* signs, when every window provided spiritual as well as physical light. The cathedral is primarily Gothic. But since it took more than 250 years to build (1226-1495)—with continuous embellishments after that (every archbishop wanted to leave his imprint)—it's a mix of styles, including Gothic, Renaissance, Baroque, and Neoclassical. Enjoy the elaborate wrought-iron work, lavish wood carvings, and window after colorful window of 500-year-old stained glass. Circling the interior are ornate chapels, purchased by the town's most noble families. The sacristy has a collection of paintings that would put any museum on the map.

This confusing collage of great Spanish art deserves a close look. Hire a private guide, discreetly freeload on a tour (they come by every few minutes during peak season), rent an audioguide, or follow this quick tour. Here's a framework for your visit:

High Altar: First, walk to the high altar to marvel through the iron grille at one of the most stunning altars in Spain. Real gold on wood, by Flemish, French, and local artists, it's one of the country's best pieces of Gothic art. Don't miss the finely worked gold-plated iron grille itself—considered to be the best from the 16th century in Spain. About-face to the...

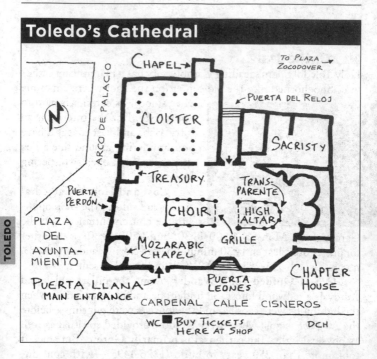

Toledo's Cathedral

(Map labels:)
CHAPEL
TO PLAZA ZOCODOVER
ARCO DE PALACIO
CLOISTER
PUERTA DEL RELOJ
SACRISTY
TREASURY
TRANS-PARENTE
PUERTA PERDÓN
CHOIR
HIGH ALTAR
PLAZA DEL AYUNTAMIENTO
MOZARABIC CHAPEL
GRILLE
CHAPTER HOUSE
PUERTA LLANA
MAIN ENTRANCE
PUERTA LEONES
CARDENAL CALLE CISNEROS
WC ■ BUY TICKETS HERE AT SHOP
DCH

TOLEDO

Choir: Facing the high altar, the choir is famous for its fine and richly symbolic carving. It all seems to lead to the archbishop's throne in the rear center. First, look carefully at the fine alabaster relief above the throne: It shows a seventh-century Visigothic miracle, when Mary came down to give the local bishop the holy robe, legitimizing Toledo as the spiritual capital (and therefore political capital) of Spain.

Because of its primacy in Iberia, Toledo was the first city in the crosshairs of the Reconquista Christian forces. They recaptured the city in 1085 (over 400 years before they retook Granada). The fall of Toledo marked the beginning of the end of the Muslim domination of Iberia. A local saying goes, "A carpet frays from the edges, but the carpet of Al-Andalus (Muslim Spain) frayed from the very center" (meaning Toledo).

The lower wooden stalls are decorated with scenes showing the steady one-city-at-a-time finale of the Christian Reconquista, when Muslims were slowly pushed back into Africa. Set in the last decade of the Reconquista, these images celebrate the retaking of the towns around Granada: Each idealized castle has the reconquered town's name on it, culminating in the final victory at Granada in 1492 (the reliefs flank the archbishop's throne). Although the castles are romanticized, the carvings of the clothing, armor, and weaponry are so detailed and accurate that historians have studied them to learn the evolution of weaponry.

The upper stalls feature Old Testament figures—an alabaster genealogy of the church—starting with Adam and Eve and working clockwise to Joseph and "S. M. Virgo Mater" (St. Mary the Virgin Mother). Notice how the statues on the Adam and Eve side are more lifelike; they were done by Alonso Berruguete, nicknamed "the Michelangelo of Spain" for his realistic figures. All this imagery is designed to remind viewers of the legitimacy of the bishop's claims to religious power. Check out the seat backs, made of carved walnut and featuring New Testament figures—with Peter (key) and Paul (sword)—alongside the archbishop himself.

And, as is typical of choir decoration, the carvings on the misericords (the tiny seats that allowed tired worshippers to lean while they "stand") represent various sins and feature the frisky, folksy, sexy, profane art of the day. Apparently, since you sat on it, it could never be sacred anyway.

Take a moment to absorb the marvelous complexity, harmony, and cohesiveness of the art around you. Look up. There are two fine pipe organs: one early 18th-century Baroque and the other late 18th-century Neoclassical. As you leave the choir, note the serene beauty of the 13th-century Madonna and child at the front (Virgin Blanca), thought to be a gift from the French king to Spain. Its naturalism and intimacy was proto-Renaissance—radical in its day.

The iron grille of the choir is notable for the dedication of the man who built it. Domingo de Céspedes, a Toledo ironworker, accepted the commission to build the grille for 6,000 ducats. The project, which took from 1541 to 1548, was far more costly than he anticipated. The medieval Church didn't accept cost overruns, so to finish it he sold everything he owned and went into debt. He died a poor—but honorable—man. (That's a charming story, but the artistic iron gate before the high altar—described earlier—is the true treasure.)

Chapter House (Sala Capitular): Face the altar, and go around it to your right to the chapter house. Under its lavish ceiling, this fresco celebrates the humanism of the Italian Renaissance. There's a Crucifixion, a *pietà*, and a Resurrection on the front wall; they face a fascinating Last Judgment, where the seven sins are actually spelled out in the gang going to hell: arrogance (the guy striking a pose), avarice (holding his bag of coins), lust (the easy woman with the lovely hair and fiery crotch), anger (shouting at lust), gluttony (the fat guy), envy, and laziness. Think about how instructive this was in 1600.

Below the fresco, a pictorial review of 1,900 years of Toledo archbishops circles the room. The upper row of portraits dates from the 16th century. Except for the last two, these were not painted from life (the same face seems to be recycled over and over). The lower portraits were added one at a time from 1515 on and are of more historic than artistic interest. Imagine sitting down to church business surrounded by all this tradition and theology.

The current cardinal—whose portrait will someday grace the next empty panel—is the top religious official in Spain. He's as conservative as Pope Benedict XVI on issues unpopular with Spain's young: divorce, abortion, and contraception. When he speaks, it makes news all over Spain.

As you leave, notice the iron-pumping cupids carved into the pear-tree panels lining the walls.

Transparente: The Transparente, behind the high altar, is a unique feature of the cathedral. In the 1700s, a hole was cut into the ceiling to let a sunbeam brighten Mass.  Melding this big hole with the Gothic church presented a challenge, and the result was a Baroque masterpiece. Gape up at this riot of angels doing flip-flops, babies breathing thin air, bottoms of feet, and gilded sunbursts. Step back to study the altar, which looks chaotic, but is actually structured thoughtfully: The good news of salvation springs from Baby Jesus, up past the archangels (including one in the middle who knows how to hold a big fish correctly) to the Last Supper high above, and beyond into the light-filled dome. I like it, as did (I guess) the two long-dead cardinals whose faded red hats hang from the edge of the hole. (A perk that only a cardinal enjoys is to choose a burial place in the cathedral, and hang his hat over that spot until the hat rots.)

Sacristy: The cathedral's sacristy is a mini-Prado, with 18 El Grecos and masterpieces by Francisco de Goya, Titian, Peter Paul Rubens, Diego Velázquez, Caravaggio, and Giovanni Bellini. First, notice the fine perspective work on the ceiling (fresco by Lucca Giordano from Naples, c. 1690). Then walk to the end of the room for the most important painting in the collection, El Greco's *The Spoliation* (a.k.a. *Christ Being Stripped of His Garments*).

Spain's original great painter was Greek, and this is his first masterpiece after arriving in Toledo. El Greco's painting from 1579 hangs exactly where he intended it to—in the room where priests prepared themselves for Mass. It shows Jesus surrounded by a sinister mob and suffering the humiliation of being stripped in public before his execution.

The scarlet robe is about to be yanked off, and the women (lower left) avert their eyes, turning to watch a carpenter at work (lower right) who bores the holes for nailing Jesus to the cross. While the carpenter bears down, Jesus—the other carpenter— looks up to heaven. The contrast between the motley crowd gambling for his clothes and Jesus' noble face underscores the quiet dignity with which he endures this ignoble treatment. Jesus' delicate white hand stands out from the flaming red tunic with an odd gesture that's common in El Greco's paintings. Some say this was the way Christians of the day swore they were true believers, not merely Christians-in-name-only, such as former Muslims or Jews who converted to survive.

On the right is a rare religious painting by Goya, the *Betrayal of Christ,* which shows Judas preparing to kiss Jesus, thus identifying him to the Roman soldiers. A small-but-lifelike 17th-century carving of St. Francis by Pedro de Mena is just to the right of the Goya. Before you leave the sacristy, enjoy the many other El Grecos located here.

The Cloister: The cloister, undergoing restoration, should reopen sometime in 2012. Take a peaceful detour to a funerary chapel located at the far side of the cloister from the entrance. The ceiling over the marble tomb of a bishop is a fresco by a student of Giotto (a 14th-century Italian Renaissance master).

Treasury: The *tesoro* is tiny, but radiant with riches. The highlight is the 10-foot-high, 430-pound monstrance—the tower designed to hold the Holy Communion wafer (the host) during the festival of Corpus Christi ("body of Christ") as it's paraded through the city. Built in 1517 by Enrique de Arfe, it's made of 5,000 individual pieces held together by 12,500 screws. There are diamonds, emeralds, rubies, and 400 pounds of gold-plated silver. The inner part (which is a century older) is 35 pounds of solid gold. Yeow. The base is a later addition from the Baroque period.

To the right of the monstrance is a beautiful red-coral cross given by the Philippines. To the right of the cross is a facsimile of a 700-year-old Bible hand-copied and beautifully illustrated by French monks; it was a gift from St. Louis, the 13th-century king of France. Imagine looking on these lavish illustrations with medieval eyes—an exquisite experience. (The precious and fragile lambskin original is preserved out of public view.) The finely painted small crucifix on the opposite side in the corner—by the great Gothic Florentine painter Fra Angelico—depicts Jesus alive on the back and dead on the front, and was a gift from Mussolini to Franco. Underneath, you'll find Franco's rather plain sword. Hmmm. Near the door, find the gift (humble amid all this splendor) from Toledo's sister city: Toledo, Ohio.

Before 10:00, the cathedral is open only for prayer (from north entrance). If you're here to worship at the 9:00 Mass (daily except Sunday), you can peek into the otherwise-locked **Mozarabic**

Chapel (Capilla Mozárabe). This Visigothic Mass (in Latin) is the oldest surviving Christian ritual in Western Europe. You're welcome to partake in this stirring example of peaceful coexistence of faiths. Toledo's proud Mozarabic community of 1,500 people traces its roots to Visigothic times.

Central Toledo

In addition to the cathedral, the city's historic core contains these sights:

Plaza de Zocodover—The main square is Toledo's center and your gateway to the old town. The word Zocodover derives from the Arabic for "livestock market."

Because Toledo is the state capital of Castile–La Mancha, the regional government adminis-

tration building overlooks Plaza de Zocodover. Look for the three flags: one for Europe, one for Spain, and one for Castile–La Mancha. And speaking of universal symbols—find the low-key McDonald's. A source of controversy, it was finally allowed... with only one small golden arch.

The square is a big local hangout and city hub. Once the scene of Inquisition executions and bullfights, today it's a lot more peaceful. Old people arrive in the morning, and young people come in the evening. The goofy white tourist train leaves from here, as well as the Tourist Bus, Centro Directo bus, and city buses #5 and #6, which lumber to the train station. Just uphill is the stop for bus #12, which travels around the old town to Santo Tomé (and works as a good self-guided tour—described on page 489) and for bus #7.1, which heads out to the panoramic viewpoint made famous by El Greco.

▲▲Santa Cruz Museum (Museo de Santa Cruz)—This stately

Renaissance building, which reopened in 2011 after years of renovation, features 15 El Grecos. Formerly an orphanage and hospital, the building was funded by money left by the humanist and diplomat Cardinal Mendoza when he died in 1495. The cardinal, confirmed as Chancellor of Castile by Queen Isabel, was so influential that he was called "the third king."

Cost and Hours: Free but may begin charging admission in 2012, Mon-Sat 10:00-18:30, Sun 10:00-14:00, may close on Mon in 2012; from Plaza de Zocodover, go through arch to Calle Miguel de Cervantes 3; tel. 925-221-036. A WC is in the far corner of the lower cloister.

Touring the Sight: Your visit has several parts—the cloister, rooms of tiles and ceramics (above the cloister), and the main building (with temporary exhibits on the ground floor and the permanent collection upstairs, including the El Grecos).

Look at the **building** itself. Its facade, cloister arches, and stairway leading to the upper cloister are fine examples of the Plateresque style. This ornate strain of Spanish Renaissance is named for the fancy work of silversmiths of the 16th century. During this time (c. 1500-1550), the royal court moved from Toledo to Madrid—when Madrid was a village, and Toledo was a world power. (You'll see no Plateresque work in Madrid.) Note the Renaissance-era mathematics, ideal proportions, round arches, square squares, and classic columns.

Have a stroll in the peaceful **cloister** (from the main entrance, go to the right). Above the cloister is a wonderful exhibit of **tiles and ceramics;** to reach it, head up the wide stairs to the upper cloister and take a right. This private collection, which the Carranza family has loaned to the museum for the last 20 years, dates from the end of the Reconquista (1492). Each piece is categorized by the Spanish region where it was made. In spite of the lack of English explanations, this may be the only place in Spain where you can compare regional differences in tile work and pottery.

The **permanent collection** is on the upper floor of the main building (exit the ceramics exhibit, go past the cloister stairs you initially came up, and at the far corner, head up the stairs to the museum).

The museum, like the footprint of the building it's in, has the shape of a Greek cross. As 1500 was a time of transition, the fine ceiling is an impressive mix of two styles: indigenous Moorish and trendier Italian Renaissance.

The museum's collection is eclectic. Entering the first arm of the cross, you'll see a selection of prehistoric pieces, some Roman items, and a marble well bearing an Arabic inscription. Note the grooves in the sides made by generations of Muslims pulling their buckets up by rope. This well was once located in the courtyard of an 11th-century mosque, which stood where the cathedral does today.

Continue left to the medieval section, where you'll find the lavish but faded *Astrolabe Tapestry* (c. 1480, Belgian). It shows a new view of the cosmos at the dawn of the Renaissance and the Age of Discovery: God (far left) oversees all, as Atlas (with the help of two women and a crank handle) spins the universe, containing the circular earth. The wisdom gang (far right) heralds the

Toledo's Muslim Legacy

You can see the Moorish influence in these sights:

- Mezquita del Cristo de la Luz, the last of the town's mosques
- Sinagoga del Tránsito's Mudejar plasterwork
- Sinagoga de Santa María la Blanca's mosque-like horseshoe arches and pinecone capitals
- Puerta del Sol (Gate of the Sun) and other surviving gates (with horseshoe arches) along the medieval wall
- The city's labyrinthine, medina-like streets

wonders of the coming era. Rather than a map of earth, this is a chart showing the cosmic order of things as the constellations spin around the stationary North Star (center).

Following the medieval collection are the Renaissance pieces, and finally the 15 El Greco paintings at the right arm of the building's cross. A highlight is the impressive *Assumption of Mary*, a spiritual poem on canvas. This altarpiece, finished one year before El Greco's death in 1614, is the culmination of his unique style, combining all of his techniques to express an otherworldly event.

Study the *Assumption* (which some believe is misnamed, and actually shows the Immaculate Conception—the plaque describing the work entitles it *Inmaculada Concepción*). Bound to earth, the city of Toledo sleeps, but a vision is taking place overhead. An angel in a billowing robe spreads his wings and flies up, supporting Mary, the mother of Christ. She floats up through warped space, to be serenaded by angels and wrapped in the radiant light of the Holy Spirit. Mary flickers and ripples, charged from within by her spiritual ecstasy, caught up in a vision that takes her breath away. No painter before or since has captured the supernatural world better than El Greco.

Army Museum (Museo del Ejército)—This new museum features endless rooms of Spanish military collections of armor, uniforms, cannons, guns, paintings, and models. Unfortunately Spain's Civil War is still too hot a topic to address here, even though an exhibit of the major 20th-century event would be fascinating and teach valuable lessons.

The museum is located in the Alcázar, the huge former imperial residence that dominates Toledo's skyline. Built on the site of Roman, Visigothic, and Moorish fortresses, the Alcázar became a kind of right-wing Alamo during Spain's Civil War, when Franco's Nationalists (and hundreds of hostages) were besieged for two months in 1936. Finally, after many fierce but futile Republican attacks that destroyed much of the Alcázar, Franco sent in an army that took Toledo. The place was rebuilt and glorified under Franco.

Cost and Hours: €5, free on Sun; June-Sept Tue-Sat 10:00-21:00, Sun 10:00-15:00, closed Mon; Oct-May Tue-Sat 10:00-19:00, Sun 10:00-15:00, closed Mon; last entry 30 minutes before closing, audioguide-€4, English descriptions, tel. 925-238-800, www.museo.ejercito.es.

Mezquita del Cristo de la Luz—Of Muslim Toledo's 10 mosques, this barren little building (dating from about 1000) is

the best survivor. Looking up, you'll notice the Moorish fascination with geometry—each dome is a unique design. The lovely keyhole arch faces Mecca. In 1187, after the Reconquista, the mosque was changed to a church, the Christian apse (with its crude Romanesque art) was added, and the former mosque got its current name. The fine garden with its fountains is a reminder of the Quranic image of heaven.

Cost and Hours: €2.30, daily 10:00-14:00 & 15:00-18:45, until 17:45 in winter, Cuesta de las Carmelitas Descalzas 10, tel. 925-254-191.

Visigothic Museum in the Church of San Roman (Museo Visigoda Iglesia de San Román)—This 13th-century Mudejar church (with its rare, strangely modernist 13th-century Romanesque frescoes) provides an exquisite space for a small but interesting collection of Visigothic artifacts. The Visigoths were the Christian barbarian tribe who ruled Spain between the fall of Rome and the rise of the Moors. The only thing Visigothic about the actual building are the few capitals topping its columns, recycled from a seventh-century Visigothic church. Though the elaborate crowns are copies (the originals are in Madrid), other glass cases show off metal and stone artifacts from the age when Toledo was the capital of the Visigoths. The items, while featuring almost no human figures, are rich in symbolism. Their portability fits that society's nomadic heritage. Archaeologists have found almost no Visigothic artifacts within Toledo's fortified hill location. They lived in humble settlements along the river—apparently needing no defense system...until the Moors swept through in 711, ending two centuries of Visigothic rule in Iberia.

Cost and Hours: Free, Tue-Sat 10:00-14:00 & 16:00-18:30, Sun 10:00-14:00, closed Mon, tel. 925-227-872. Unfortunately the museum thinks the entire world speaks Spanish: The only English explains the cost of admission.

Southwest Toledo

These sights cluster at the southwest end of town. For efficient sightseeing, visit them in this order, then zip back home on bus #12 (listed at the end of this section).

▲**Santo Tomé**—A simple chapel on the Plaza del Conde holds El Greco's most beloved painting. *The Burial of the Count of Orgaz* couples heaven and earth in a way only The Greek could. It feels so right to see a painting left in situ, where the artist placed it 400 years ago.

Take this slow. Stay a while—let it perform. The year is 1323. Count Don Gonzalo Ruiz has died. You're at his burial right here in this chapel. The good count was so holy, even saints Augustine and Stephen have come down from heaven to lower his body into the grave. (The painting's subtitle is "Such is the reward for those who serve God and his saints.")

More than 250 years later, in 1586, a local priest (depicted on the far right, reading the Bible) hired El Greco to make a painting of the burial to hang over the count's tomb. The funeral is attended by Toledo's most distinguished citizens. (El Greco used local nobles as models.) The painting is divided in two by a serene line of noble faces—heaven above and earth below. Above the faces, the count's soul, symbolized by a little baby, rises up through a mystical birth canal to be reborn in heaven, where he's greeted by Jesus, Mary, and all the saints. A spiritual wind blows through as colors change and shapes stretch. This is Counter-Reformation propaganda—notice Jesus pointing to St. Peter, the symbol of the pope in Rome, who controls the keys to the pearly gates. Each face is a detailed portrait. El Greco himself (eyeballing you, seventh figure in from the left) is the only one not involved in the burial. The boy in the foreground—pointing to the two saints as if to say, "One's from the first century, the other's from the fourth...it's a miracle!"—is El Greco's son. On the handkerchief in the boy's pocket is El Greco's signature, written in Greek.

Don Gonzalo Ruiz's actual granite tombstone is at your feet. The count's two wishes upon his death were to be buried here and for his village to make an annual charity donation to feed Toledo's poor. Finally, more than two centuries later, the people of Orgaz

El Greco
(1541-1614)

Born on Crete and trained in Venice, Doménikos Theotokópoulos (tongue-tied friends just called him "The Greek") came to Spain to get a job decorating El Escorial. He failed there, but succeeded in Toledo, where he spent the last 37 years of his life. He mixed all three regional influences into his palette. From his Greek homeland, he absorbed the solemn, abstract style of icons. In Italy, he learned the bold use of color, elongated figures, twisting poses, and dramatic style of the later Renaissance. These elements were then fused in the fires of fanatic Spanish-Catholic devotion.

Not bound by the realism so important to his fellow artists, El Greco painted dramatic visions of striking colors and figures—bodies unnatural and lengthened as though stretched between heaven and earth. He painted souls, not faces. His work is on display at nearly every sight in Toledo. Thoroughly modern in his disregard for realism, he didn't impress the austere Philip II. But his art still seems as fresh as contemporary art does today.

said, "Enough!" and stopped the payments. The last of the money was spent to pay El Greco for this painting.

Cost and Hours: €2.30, daily 10:00-18:45, until 17:45 mid-Oct-March, tel. 925-256-098. This sight almost always has a line, but try going early or late to avoid tour groups.

El Greco Museum (Museo del Greco)—This small museum, built near the site of El Greco's house, reopened in 2011 after years of renovation. Its small collection of paintings is now accompanied by interactive touch screens and several audiovisuals. The highlight is the *View and Plan of Toledo*, El Greco's panoramic map of the city where you can locate all the places in town you've visited. However, if you've been to the Santa Cruz Museum, cathedral, and Santo Tomé chapel, you probably don't need this small dose of El Greco.

Cost and Hours: €3, free Sat afternoon from 14:00 and all day Sun, Tue-Sat 10:00-20:00, Sun 10:00-15:00, closed Mon, next to Sinagoga del Tránsito on Calle Samuel Leví, tel. 925-223-665.

Sinagoga del Tránsito (Museo Sefardí)—Built in 1361, this is the best surviving slice of Toledo's Jewish past. Serving as Spain's national Jewish museum, it displays Jewish artifacts, including costumes, menorahs, and books. The synagogue's interior decor looks more Muslim than Jewish. After Christians reconquered the city in 1085, many Moorish workmen stayed on, beautifying the city with their unique style called Mudejar. The synagogue's intricate, geometrical carving in stucco features leaves, vines, and flowers; there are no human shapes, which are forbidden by the Torah—like the Quran—as being "graven images." In the frieze (running along the upper wall, just below the ceiling), the Arabic-looking script is actually Hebrew, quoting psalms (respected by all "people of the book"—Muslims, Jews, and Christians alike). The side-wall balcony is the traditional separate worship area for women. Scale models of the development of the Jewish quarter (on the ground floor) and video displays (upstairs) give a fuller picture of Jewish life in medieval Toledo.

This 14th-century synagogue was built at the peak of Toledo's enlightened tolerance—constructed for Jews with Christian approval by Muslim craftsmen. Nowhere else in the city does Toledo's three-culture legacy shine brighter than at this synagogue. But in 1391, just a few decades after it was built, the Church and the Spanish kings began a violent campaign to unite Spain as a Christian nation, forcing Jews and Muslims to convert or leave. In 1492 Ferdinand and Isabel exiled Spain's remaining Jews. It's estimated that in the 15th century, a third of Spain's Jews were killed, a third survived by converting to Christianity, and a third moved elsewhere.

Cost and Hours: €3, free Sat afternoon from 14:00 and all day Sun, open Tue-Sat 9:30-20:00—until 18:00 in winter, Sun 10:00-15:00, closed Mon, last entry 15 minutes before closing, audioguide-€3, near El Greco Museum on Calle de los Reyes Católicos, tel. 925-223-665.

▲**Museo Victorio Macho**—Overlooking the gorge and Tajo River, this small, attractive museum—once the home and workshop of the early-20th-century sculptor Victorio Macho—offers a delightful collection of his bold Art Deco–inspired work. Even if you skip the museum, enjoy the terrace view from its gate.

The house itself is an oasis of calm in the city. Your visit comes in four stages: ticket room with theater, courtyard with view, crypt, and museum.

The small theater in the ticket room shows a good nine-minute video about the history of Toledo (request the English-language version). Macho was Spain's first great modern sculptor. When his Republican politics made it dangerous for him to stay in Franco's Spain, he fled to Mexico and Peru, where he met his wife, Zoila. They later returned to Toledo, where they lived and worked until he died in 1966. Zoila eventually gave the house and Macho's art to the city.

Enjoy the peaceful and expansive view from the terrace. From here it's clear how the Tajo River served as a formidable moat protecting the city. Imagine trying to attack. The 14th-century bridge on the right, and the remains of a bridge on the left, connected the town with the region's *cigarrales*—mansions of wealthy families, whose orchards of figs and apricots dot the hillside even today.

The door marked *Crypta* leads to *My Brother Marcelo*—the touching tomb Macho made for his brother. Eventually he featured his entire family in his art.

A dozen steps above the terrace, you'll find a single room marked *Museo* filled with Macho's art. A *pietà* is carved expressively in granite. Self-portraits show the artist's genius. Exquisite pencil-on-paper studies illustrate how a sculptor must understand the body (in this case, Zoila's body). Other statues show the strength of the peoples' spirit as Republicans stood up to Franco's fascist forces, and Spain endured its 20th-century bloodbath. The highlight is *La Madre* (from 1935), Macho's life-size sculpture of his mother sitting in a chair. It illustrates the sadness and simple wisdom of Spanish mothers who witnessed so much suffering. Upon a granite backdrop, her white marble hands and face speak volumes.

Cost and Hours: €3, Mon-Sat 10:00-19:00, Sun 10:00-15:00, between the two *sinagogas* at Plaza de Victorio Macho 2, tel. 925-284-225.

Sinagoga de Santa María la Blanca—This synagogue-turned-church has Moorish horseshoe arches and wall carvings. It's a vivid reminder of the religious cultures that shared (and then didn't share) this city. While it looks  like a mosque, it never was one. Built as a Jewish synagogue by Muslim workers around 1200, it became a church in 1492 when Toledo's Jews were required to convert or leave—hence the mix-and-match name. After being used as horse stables by Napoleonic troops, it was further ruined in the 19th century. Today, it's an evocative space, beautiful in its simplicity.

Cost and Hours: €2.30, daily April-Sept 10:00-18:45, Oct-March 10:00-17:45, Calle de los Reyes Católicos 2, tel. 925-227-257.

▲San Juan de los Reyes Monasterio—"St. John of the Monarchs" is a grand Franciscan monastery, impressive church, and delightful cloistered courtyard. The style is late Gothic, contemporaneous with Portugal's Manueline (c. 1500) and Flamboyant Gothic elsewhere in Europe. It was the intended burial site of the

Catholic Monarchs, Isabel and Ferdinand. But after the Moors were expelled in 1492 from Granada, their royal bodies were planted there to show Spain's commitment to maintaining a Moor-free peninsula.

Cost and Hours: €2.30, daily 10:00-18:45, until 17:45 in winter, last entry 30 minutes before closing, San Juan de los Reyes 2, tel. 925-223-802.

Touring the Sight: The **facade** is famously festooned with 500-year-old chains. Moors used these to shackle Christians in Granada until 1492. It's said that the freed Christians brought these chains to the church, making them a symbol of their Catholic faith.

Even without the royal tombs that would have dominated the space, the glorious **chapel** gives you a sense of Spain when it was Europe's superpower. The monastery was built to celebrate the 1476 Battle of Toro, which made Isabel the queen of Castile. Since her husband, Ferdinand, was king of Aragon, this effectively created the Spain we know today. (You could say 1476 is to Spain what 1776 is to the US.) Now united, Spain was able to quickly finish the Reconquista, ridding Iberia of its Moors within the next decade and a half.

Sitting in the chapel, you're surrounded by propaganda proclaiming Spain's greatness. The coat of arms is repeated obsessively. The eagle with the halo disk represents St. John, protector of the royal family. The yoke and lions remind people of the power of the kingdoms yoked together under Ferdinand and Isabel. The coat of arms is complex because of Iberia's many kingdoms (e.g., a lion for Lyon, and a castle for Castile). Arrows represent the 10 or so kingdoms of Iberia—weak when single, yet mighty when bound together. This notion inspired fascists such as Franco and Mussolini (who used a similar image of sticks bound together for strength—called a *fascio*). All of this is carved in actual stone,

not made of stucco—rare in Toledo.

As you leave, look up over the door to see the Franciscan coat of arms—with the five wounds of the crucifixion (the stigmata—which St. Francis earned through his great faith) flanked by angels with dramatic wings.

Enjoy a walk around the **cloister.** Notice details of the fine carvings. Everything had meaning in the 15th century. In the corner (opposite the entry), just above eye level, find a monkey—an insulting symbol of Franciscans—on a toilet reading the Bible upside-down. Perhaps a stone carver snuck in a not-too-subtle comment on Franciscan pseudo-intellectualism, with their big libraries and small brains.

Napoleon's troops are mostly to blame for the destruction of the church, a result of Napoleon's view that monastic power in Europe was a menace. While Napoleon's biggest error was to invade Russia, his second dumbest move was to alienate the Catholic faithful by destroying monasteries such as this one. This strategic mistake eroded popular support from people who might have seen Napoleon as a welcome alternative to the tyranny of kings and the Church.

▲**Bus #12 Self-Guided Tour (A Sweat-Free Return Trip from Santo Tomé to Plaza de Zocodover)**—When you're finished with the sights at the Santo Tomé end of town, you can hike all the way back (not fun)—or simply catch bus #12 from Plaza del Conde in front of Santo Tomé (fun!). Santo Tomé is the end of the line, so buses wait to depart from here twice hourly (at :25 and :55, until 21:55, pay driver €1), heading to Plaza de Zocodover. Closer to the synagogues and monastery, you can also catch the same bus at Plaza del Barrio Nuevo. The bus offers tired sightseers a quick, interesting 15-minute look at the town walls. Here's what you'll see on your way from Santo Tomé:

Leaving Santo Tomé, you'll first ride through Toledo's Jewish section. On the right, you'll pass the El Greco Museum, Sinagoga del Tránsito, and Sinagoga de Santa María la Blanca, followed by—on your left—the ornate Flamboyant Gothic facade of San Juan de los Reyes Monasterio. After squeezing through the 16th-century city gate, the bus follows along the outside of the mighty 10th-century wall. (Toledo was never conquered by force...only by siege.)

Just past the big escalator (which brings people from parking lots up into the city), the wall gets fancier, as demonstrated by the little old Bisagra Gate. Soon after, you see the big new Bisagra Gate, the main entry into the old town. While the city walls date from the 10th century, this gate was built as an arch of triumph in the 16th century. The massive coat of arms of Emperor

Charles V, with the double eagle, reminded people that he ruled a unified Habsburg/Bourbon empire, and they were entering the capital of an empire that, in the 1500s, included most of Western Europe and much of America.

The TI is just outside the big gate, at the edge of a well-maintained and shaded park—a picnic-perfect spot and one of Toledo's few green areas. After a detour to the bus station basement to pick up people coming from Madrid, you swing back around Bisagra Gate. As you climb back into the old town, notice how the modern Palacio de Congresos Miradero convention center is incorporated into the more historic cityscape. After passing the fine Moorish (14th-century) Sun Gate, within moments you pull into the main square, Plaza de Zocodover. You can do this tour in reverse by riding bus #12 from Plaza de Zocodover to Plaza del Conde (departing at :25 and :55, same price and hours).

Shopping in Toledo

Toledo probably sells more souvenirs than any city in Spain. This is *the* place to buy medieval-looking swords, armor, maces, three-

legged stools, lethal-looking letter-openers, and other nouveau antiques. It's also Spain's damascene center, where, for centuries, craftspeople have inlaid black steel with gold, silver, and copper wire. Spain's top bullfighters wouldn't have their swords made anywhere else.

Knives: At the workshop of English-speaking **Mariano Zamorano,** you can see swords and knives being made. Judging by what's left of Mariano's hand, his knives are among the sharpest (Mon-Fri 10:00-14:00 & 16:00-19:00, Sat-Sun 10:00-14:00—although you may not see work done on weekends, 10 percent discount with this book, behind Ayuntamiento/City Hall at Calle Ciudad 19, tel. 925-222-634, www.marianozamorano.com).

Damascene: Shops selling the shiny inlaid plates and decorative wares are everywhere. The damascene is a real tourist racket, but it's fun to pop into a shop and see the intricate handwork in action.

Nun-Baked Sweet Treats: Convents all over town earn a little money by selling *Dulces Artesanos* (marzipan).

El Martes: Toledo's colorful outdoor market is a lively scene on Tuesdays at Paseo de Merchan, better known to locals as "La Vega" (9:00-14:00, outside Bisagra Gate near TI).

Sleeping in Toledo

Madrid day-trippers darken the sunlit cobbles, but few stay to see Toledo's medieval moonrise. Spend the night. Hotels often have a two-tiered price system, with prices 20 percent higher on Friday and Saturday. Spring and fall are high season; November through March and July and August are less busy. Similar to other places in Spain, Toledo's big and small hotels are making deals to confront the hard economic times. Fish around for deals and discounts.

Near Plaza de Zocodover

$$ Hotel Toledo Imperial sits efficiently above Plaza de Zocodover, and rents 29 business-class rooms that are a solid value (Db-€60 Sun-Thu, Db-€100 Fri-Sat, includes tax and breakfast, air-con, free Wi-Fi, Calle Horno de los Bizcochos 5, tel. 925-280-034, fax 925-280-205, www.hoteltoledoimperial.com, hotel@hoteltoledoimperial.com).

$$ Hotel Las Conchas, a three-star hotel with 33 rooms, gleams with marble. It's so sleek and slick it almost feels more like a hospital than a hotel (Sb-€55, Db-€85, Db with terrace-€100, includes tax, breakfast-€6, air-con, near the Alcázar at Juan Labrador 8, tel. 925-210-760, fax 925-224-271, www.lasconchas.com, lasconchas@ctv.es, Pablo and Yuki).

$ Hostal Centro rents 28 spacious rooms with sparse, well-worn furniture and a ramshackle feel. It's wonderfully central, with a third of its rooms overlooking the main square. Request a quiet room on the back side to minimize night noise (Sb-€35, Db-€50, Tb-€65, 10 percent discount with this book on weekdays, inviting

Near Plaza de Zocodover

1 Hotel Toledo Imperial
2 Hotel Las Conchas
3 Hostal Centro
4 Hostal Alcázar
5 Pensión Castilla
6 Restaurante Ludeña
7 El Trébol & La Tabernita Tapas Bars
8 Supermarket Coviran
9 Santo Tomé Mazapán Shop
10 Tourist Train
11 Convention Center & Escalator to Miradero Garage

* NOT TO SCALE-
PLAZA ZOCODOVER TO
MAGDALENA CHURCH IS A
3 MIN. WALK
STREET WIDTH IS
EXAGGERATED FOR CLARITY

Astroturf roof terrace with lounge chairs, 50 yards off Plaza de Zocodover—take the first right off Calle Comercio to Calle Nueva 13, tel. 925-257-091, fax 925-257-848, www.hostalcentro.com, hostalcentro@telefonica.net, warmly run by Asun and David).

$ Hostal Alcázar, with 12 simple and spacious rooms and no public spaces, is quiet, modern, and a good value (Sb-€30, Db-€45-50, bigger Db-€60, Tb-€65, Qb-€75-80, includes tax, no breakfast, air-con, elevator, Juan Labrador 10, tel. 925-222-620, fax 925-226-278, www.hostalalcazar.es, hostalalcazar@movistar .es, César).

$ Pensión Castilla, a tidy family-run cheapie with firm beds, is so humble you can imagine lashing your burro out front. It rents seven basic rooms with ceiling fans (S-€18, D-€30, Db-€35, cash only, no air-con, Calle Recoletos 6, tel. 925-256-318, Teresa doesn't speak English).

Near Bisagra Gate

$$$ Hacienda del Cardenal, a 17th-century cardinal's palace built into Toledo's wall, is quiet and elegant, with a cool garden, a less-than-helpful staff, and a stuffy restaurant. This poor man's parador, at the dusty old gate of Toledo, is closest to the station, but below all the old-town action (Sb-€80, Db-€135, 20 percent cheaper mid-Dec-mid-March, breakfast-€10, free Wi-Fi, enter through town wall 100 yards below Bisagra Gate, Paseo de Recaredo 24, tel. 925-224-900, fax 925-222-991, www.haciendadelcardenal.com, hotel @haciendadelcardenal.com).

$$ Hospedería de los Reyes has 15 colorful and thoughtfully appointed rooms in a new, attractive yellow building 100 yards downhill from Bisagra Gate, outside the wall. They also offer six apartments a block away, with kitchens and living rooms (Sb-€40-50, Db-€55-75, apartments-€70-90, hotel rooms include breakfast, air-con, free Wi-Fi, free street parking nearby, Calle Perala 37, tel. 925-283-667, fax 925-283-668, www.hospederiadelosreyes.com, hospederiadelosreyes@hospederiadelosreyes.com, Alicia).

$$ Hostal Puerta de Bisagra is in a sprawling old building that is fresh and modern inside. Located just across from Bisagra Gate, it's convenient for arrivals, but a long hike uphill to the action (hop on any bus). Its 33 comfortable rooms are rented at some of the best prices in town (Db-€70; off-season Db-€50 Sun-Thu, €60 Fri-Sat; breakfast-€5, air-con, free Wi-Fi, Calle del Potro 5, tel. & fax 925-285-277, www.puertabisagra.com, hostal@puertabisagra.com).

$ Hotel Sol, with 15 nicely decorated pastel rooms, is a good value. It's on a quiet, ugly side street between Bisagra Gate and Plaza de Zocodover (Sb-€44, Db-€59, Tb-€72, includes tax, 10 percent discount with this book, breakfast-€4, air-con, free Wi-Fi, private parking-€10/day; leave the busy main drag at Hotel Imperial and head 50 yards down the lane to Azacanes 8; tel. 925-213-650, fax 925-216-159, www.hotelyhostalsol.com, info@hotelyhostalsol .com, José Carlos). Their 11-room **$ Hostal Sol** annex across the street is just as comfortable, smoke-free, and a bit cheaper (Sb-€36, Db-€49, Tb-€59, Qb-€72, includes tax, 10 percent discount with this book, breakfast-€4, free Wi-Fi).

Deep in Toledo

$$ La Posada de Manolo rents 14 thoughtfully furnished rooms across from the downhill corner of the cathedral. Manolo Junior opened this fine *hostal* according to his father's vision: a comfortable place with each of its three floors themed differently—Moorish, Jewish, and Christian. They are deservedly listed in several US and European guidebooks, so they tend to fill up (Sb-€42, Db-€72, big Db-€84, includes buffet breakfast, 10 percent discount with this book when you reserve direct, air-con, no elevator, free Wi-Fi, two nice view terraces, Calle Sixto Ramón Parro 8, tel. 925-282-250, fax 925-282-251, www.laposadademanolo.com, toledo@laposadademanolo.com).

$$ Hotel Eurico, fresh and new, cleverly fits 23 sleek rooms into a medieval building buried deep in the old town. The staff is friendly, and the hotel offers a good value (Sb-€55-60, Db-€60-90, Tb-€70-120, breakfast-€8, air-con, Calle Santa Isabel 3, tel.

Toledo Hotels & Restaurants

200 YARDS

200 METERS

STREET WIDTH IS EXAGGERATED FOR CLARITY

TO MADRID & 7

TO 2

BUS STATION

BISAGRA GATE

CARD. TAV.

C. DE LA CARRERA

CITY WALLS

C. ARRABAL

CARACANES

CUESTA

TO TRAIN STATION & 8

TO

ESCALATORS

SUBIDA LA GRANSA

MERCED

ALFILERES

MEZQUITA

POST

LA PLATA

NUÑEZ

SILLERIA

ARMAS

MIRA-DERO ESCALATOR

SANTA CRUZ MUSEUM

CERVANTES

CALLE REAL

S. LEO.

S. ILD.

NAV.

CABIO

ALEX.

ROMAN

NUÑEZ

COMERCIO

PL. ZOC.

ALFÉRECE

SAN JUAN DE LOS REYES

DON.

VISI-GOTHIC MUSEUM

ALFONSO X

ALCÁZAR (ARMY MUSEUM)

SANTO TOMÉ

ANGEL

S. JUAN DIOS

STO. TOMÉ

TRINIDAD

SALV.

CATHEDRAL

SINAGOGA DE SANTA MARÍA LA BLANCA

MUSEO VICTORIO MACHO

PASEO TRANS.

PARK

T. MORO

URSULA

STA. ISABEL

CITY HALL (AYUNTAMIENTO)

RÍO TAJO

SINAGOGA DEL TRÁNSITO

PCH

EL GRECO MUSEUM

⚇ VIEW   Ⓟ PARKING

Ⓑ BUS STOP   ▨ TOLEDO'S MAIN DRAG

❶ Hacienda del Cardenal
❷ To Hospedería de los Reyes
❸ Hostal Puerta de Bisagra
❹ Hotel Sol
❺ La Posada de Manolo & Madre Tierra Restaurante Vegetariano
❻ Hotel Eurico & Hotel Santa Isabel
❼ To Hotel María Cristina & Hostal Madrid
❽ To Albergue Juvenil San Servando (Hostel)

❾ To Parador de Toledo
❿ Los Cuatro Tiempos Rest.
⓫ Casa Aurelio I
⓬ Casa Aurelio II & III (on Sinagoga) & Pizzeria Pastucci
⓭ Rest./Cafeteria Casón López de Toledo & La Abadia Tapas Restaurante
⓮ Adolfo Vinoteca
⓯ Restaurante-Mesón Palacios
⓰ Mercado Municipal (Market)

925-284-178, fax 925-254-017, www.hoteleurico.com, reservas @hoteleurico.com).

$ Hotel Santa Isabel, in a 15th-century building two blocks from the cathedral, has 41 clean, modern, and comfortable rooms and squeaky tile hallways (Sb-€35, small old Db-€45, big new Db-€55, Db with view-€60-70, extra bed-€10, includes tax, 5 percent discount with this book, breakfast-€5, air-con, elevator, free

Wi-Fi, scenic roof terrace, parking-€10/day, buried deep in old town—take a taxi instead of the bus, drivers enter from Calle Pozo Amargo, Calle Santa Isabel 24, tel. 925-253-120, fax 925-253-136, www.hotelsantaisabel.net, info@hotelsantaisabel.net).

Outside of Town, near the Bullring

These places are on a modern street next to the bullring (Plaza de Toros, bullfights only on holidays), just beyond Bisagra Gate. In this area, parking is free on the street. The bus station is a five-minute walk away, and city buses lumber by, all going directly to Plaza de Zocodover. There are many other similarly nondescript, comfy, and cheap places in this neighborhood.

$$$ Hotel María Cristina, a sprawling 74-room hotel, has all the comforts under a thin layer of prefab tradition. Rates vary greatly—ask them for any special pricing (Sb-€68, Db-€105, Tb-€148, suites-€140-170, tax not included, breakfast-€9, air-con, elevator, restaurant, parking-€12/day, Marqués de Mendigorría 1, tel. 925-213-202, fax 925-212-650, www.hotelmariacristina.com, informacion@hotelmariacristina.com).

$ Hostal Madrid has two locations on the same street with 29 rooms and a café next door (Sb-€28, Db-€40, Tb-€54, includes tax, air-con, parking-€8/day, Marqués de Mendigorría 7 and 14, reception at #7, tel. 925-221-114, fax 925-228-113, www.hostal-madrid.net, info@hostal-madrid.net).

Hostel

$ Albergue Juvenil San Servando youth hostel is lavish but fairly cheap, with 96 beds and small rooms for two or four people (€16/bed plus €12 obligatory *alberguista* membership, extra €3.50/day for the first six days of membership, swimming pool, views, cafeteria, good management, located in 10th-century Arab castle of San Servando, 10-minute walk from train station, 15-minute hike from town center, over Puente Viejo outside town, tel. 925-224-554, reservations tel. 925-221-676, alberguesclm@jccm.es, no English spoken).

Outside of Town with the Grand Toledo View

$$$ Parador de Toledo, with 79 rooms, is one of Spain's best-known inns. Its guests enjoy the same Toledo view that El Greco made famous from across the Tajo Gorge (Sb-€142, Db-€170, Db with view-€200, Tb-€230, Tb with view-€265, tax included, call or check online for deals, breakfast-€18, €34 fixed-price meals sans drinks in their fine restaurant overlooking Toledo, 2 windy miles from town at Cerro del Emperador—it may come up as Carretera de Cobisa on GPS systems, tel. 925-221-850, fax 925-225-166, www.parador.es, toledo@parador.es).

Eating in Toledo

Dining in Traditional Elegance

A day full of El Greco and the romance of Toledo after dark puts me in the mood for game and other traditional cuisine. Typical Toledo dishes include partridge *(perdiz)*, venison *(venado)*, wild boar *(jabalí)*, roast suckling pig *(cochinillo asado)*, or baby lamb *(cordero*—similarly roasted after a few weeks of mother's milk). After dinner, find a *mazapán* place (such as the Santo Tomé shops) for dessert. Restaurants generally serve lunch from 13:00 to 16:00 and dinner from 20:00 until very late (Spaniards don't start dinner until about 21:00).

Los Cuatro Tiempos Restaurante ("The Four Seasons") specializes in local game and roasts, proficiently served in a tasteful and elegant setting. They offer spacious dining with an extensive and inviting Spanish wine list. It's a good choice for a quiet, romantic dinner, and a good value for a midday meal (€16 weekday and €19 weekend three-course lunches, €30 à la carte dinners, Mon-Sat 13:00-16:00 & 20:30-23:00, Sun 13:00-16:00 only, at downhill corner of cathedral, Sixto Ramón Parro 5, tel. 925-223-782).

The venerable **Casa Aurelio** has three branches, each offering traditional cooking (game, roast suckling pig, traditional soup, €45 dinners) in a classy atmosphere more memorable than the meals (generally 13:00-16:30 & 20:00-23:30, air-con). None has outdoor seating, and all are within three blocks of the cathedral: The location at Sinagoga 1 is the newest and dressiest of the three with a wine cellar and a more modern presentation (closed Mon, tel. 925-221-392); Plaza del Ayuntamiento 4 is festive (closed Mon, tel. 925-227-716); and Sinagoga 6 is most *típico* (closed Wed, tel. 925-222-097).

Restaurante Casón López de Toledo, a fancy restaurant located upstairs in an old noble palace, specializes in Castilian food, particularly venison and partridge. As you tuck in your napkin, you'll feel like an 18th-century aristocrat (€25 fixed-price weekday lunch, €40 fixed-price dinner, €52 tasting *menu*, closed Sun night, reservations smart, near Plaza de Zocodover at Calle de la Sillería 3, tel. 925-254-774).

Cafeteria Casón López de Toledo is the ground-floor version of the restaurant with the same name (previous listing). While called a "cafeteria," it's actually a quality restaurant in its own right, without the pretense you find upstairs and with a simpler and much less expensive menu. This is where the locals dine, enjoying the fancy restaurant's kitchen at half the price (€12 plates, great €11 weekday lunch special, open daily, same address and phone as *restaurante*).

La Abadia Tapas Restaurante is a trendy scene, great for classy tapas and a young local crowd who want imaginative plates and quality ingredients. Their €14 "selection plate" feeds two. The front area is the bar scene. Beyond that is a labyrinth of isolated little dining rooms (daily, 20 yards downhill from Restaurante Casón López de Toledo at Plaza de San Nicolás 3, tel. 925-251-140).

Adolfo Vinoteca is the wine bar of the highly respected local chef Adolfo, who runs a famous gourmet restaurant nearby. His

hope is to introduce the younger generation to the culture of fine food and wine. The bar offers up a pricey but always top-notch list of gourmet plates (€7-15 each) and fine local wines (€2-6 per glass—don't economize here), as well as a €13 fixed-price selection of tapas and dessert (€19 on weekends). Adolfo's son, Javier, proved to me the importance of matching each plate with the right wine. I like to sit next to the kitchen to be near the creative action. If the Starship *Enterprise* had a Spanish wine-and-tapas bar on its holodeck, this would be it. Wine is sold to take home or drink there for €3-8 more than the shop price (daily 12:00-24:00, across from cathedral at Calle Nuncio Viejo 1, tel. 925-224-244).

Eating Simply

For locations, see the maps on pages 492 and 494.

Restaurante-Mesón Palacios is a simple, sticky diner, serving good regional food at reasonable prices to families and tourists. Their bean soup with partridge *(judías con perdiz)* and roast suckling lamb and pig are good. The kitchen's hours are unusually long for Spain (Mon-Sat 12:00-23:00, Sun 12:00-16:00, €19 complete dinner with local favorites, near Plaza de San Vicente at Alfonso X El Sabio 3, tel. 925-215-972, run by ladies' man Jesús).

Restaurante Ludeña is a classic eatery with a bar, a well-worn dining room in back, and four tables on a sunny courtyard. It's very central; locals duck in here to pretend there's no tourism in Toledo (Plaza de la Magdalena 13, tel. 925-223-384).

Madre Tierra Restaurante Vegetariano is Toledo's answer to a vegetarian's prayer. Bright, spacious, classy, air-conditioned, and tuned in to the healthy eater's needs, its appetizing dishes are based on both international and traditional Spanish cuisine (€7-12 plates, €12 fixed-price weekday meal, good tea selection, great veggie pizzas, closed Mon night and all day Tue, 20 yards below La Posada de Manolo just before reaching Plaza de San Justo at Bajada de le Tripería 2, tel. 925-223-571).

Pizzeria Pastucci, while nondescript, is a local favorite for pizza and pasta (big €14 pizza feeds two, closed Mon, near cathedral at Calle de la Sinagoga 10).

Tapas Just Off Plaza de Zocodover: Plaza de Zocodover is busy with eateries serving edible food at affordable prices, and its people-watching scene is great. But to eat better with locals, drop by **El Trébol**, tucked peacefully away just a short block off Plaza de Zocodover. Señor Ventura seems to be the mastermind behind every new trendy bar in town, and at El Trébol he offers a menu elegant in its simplicity, a crisp interior, and an inviting outdoor terrace. It's also good for coffee and toast if you've arrived on the early train or want to avoid a pricey hotel breakfast (daily 9:00-23:00, Calle de Santa Fe 1). The specialties are *pulgas* (fine little €2.50 sandwiches) and *bombas* (potato and meat with spicy sauce). **La Tabernita,** half a block away, is another good tapas bar (also a Ventura adventure) with more extensive and expensive tapas and a fun local scene. They serve a free tapa with each drink (Calle de Santa Fe 14).

Picnics: Picnics are best assembled at the city market, **Mercado Municipal,** on Plaza Mayor (on the Alcázar side of cathedral, with a supermarket inside open Mon-Sat 9:00-15:00 & 17:00-20:00 and stalls open mostly in the mornings until 14:00, closed Sun). **Supermarket Coviran,** on Plaza de la Magdalena, has groceries at good prices (daily 9:30-22:00, just below Plaza de Zocodover).

For a picnic with people-watching on an atmospheric square, consider Plaza de Zocodover or Plaza del Ayuntamiento.

And for Dessert: *Mazapán*

Toledo's famous almond-fruity-sweet *mazapán* is sold all over town. As you wander, keep a lookout for convents advertising their version, *Dulce Artesano*. The big *mazapán* producer is **Santo Tomé** (several outlets, including a handy one on Plaza de Zocodover, daily 9:00-22:00). Browse their tempting window displays. They sell *mazapán* goodies individually (two for about €1.50, *sin relleno*— without filling—is for purists, *de piñon* has pine nuts, *imperiales* is with almonds, others have fruit fillings). Boxes are good for gifts, but sampling is much cheaper when buying just a few pieces. Their *Toledana* is a nutty, crumbly, not-too-sweet cookie with a subtle thread of squash filling (€1.20 each).

For a sweet and romantic evening moment, pick up a few pastries and head down to the cathedral. Sit on the Plaza del Ayuntamiento's benches (or stretch out on the stone wall to the right of the TI). The fountain is on your right, Spain's best-looking City Hall is behind you, and there before you is her top cathedral—built back when Toledo was Spain's capital—shining brightly against the black night sky.

Toledo Connections

While the AVE bullet train makes the trip to Madrid in half the time, buses depart twice as frequently. Either way, Madrid and Toledo are very easily connected.

From Toledo to Madrid: By bus (2/hour, 1-1.5 hours, €5 one-way, *directo* is faster than *ruta*, bus drops you at Madrid's Plaza Elíptica Metro stop, Continental Auto bus company, tel. 925-223-641; you can almost always just drop in and buy a ticket minutes before departure), **by train** (AVE or Avant to Madrid's Atocha Station: nearly hourly, 30 minutes, €11, www.renfe.com), **by car** (40 miles, 1 hour; see "Route Tips for Drivers," next). Toledo bus info: tel. 925-215-850; train info: tel. 902-240-202.

From Toledo to Other Points: To get to Granada and elsewhere in Spain from Toledo, assume you'll have to transfer in Madrid. See "Madrid Connections" at the end of that chapter for information on reaching various destinations.

Route Tips for Drivers

Granada to Toledo (250 miles, 5 hours): The Granada–Toledo drive is long, hot, and boring. Start early to minimize the heat and make the best time you can. Follow signs for *Madrid/Jaén/N-323* into what some call "the Spanish Nebraska"—La Mancha (see next section). After Puerto Lapice, you'll see the Toledo exit.

Toledo to Madrid (40 miles, 1 hour): It's a speedy *autovía* north, past one last billboard to Madrid (on N-401). The highways converge into M-30, which encircles Madrid. Follow it to the left (*Nor* or *Oeste*) and take the Plaza de España exit to get back to Gran Vía. If you're airport-bound, keep heading into Madrid until you see the airplane symbol (N-II).

To drive to Atocha Station in Madrid, take the exit off M-30 for Plaza de Legazpi, then take Delicias (second on your right off the square). Parking for rental-car return is on the north side of the train station.

La Mancha

La Mancha, which is worth a visit if you're driving between Toledo and Granada, shows a side of Spain that you'll see nowhere else—vast and flat. Named for the Arabic word for "parched earth," it makes you feel small—lost in rough seas of olive-green polka dots. Random buildings look like houses and hotels hurled off some heavenly Monopoly board.

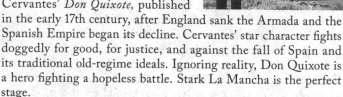

This is the setting of Miguel de Cervantes' *Don Quixote*, published in the early 17th century, after England sank the Armada and the Spanish Empire began its decline. Cervantes' star character fights doggedly for good, for justice, and against the fall of Spain and its traditional old-regime ideals. Ignoring reality, Don Quixote is a hero fighting a hopeless battle. Stark La Mancha is the perfect stage.

The epitome of *Don Quixote* country, the town of **Consuegra** (TI tel. 925-475-731, www.aytoconsuegra.es) must be the La Mancha Cervantes had in mind. Drive up to the ruined 12th-century castle and joust with a windmill. It's hot and buggy here, but the powerful view overlooking the village, with its sun-bleached light-red roofs, modern concrete reality, and harsh, windy silence, makes for a profound picnic (a one-hour drive south of Toledo). The castle belonged to the Knights of St. John (12th and 13th centuries) and is associated with their trip to Jerusalem during the Crusades. Originally built from the ruins of a nearby Roman circus, it has been newly restored (€4, includes windmill and archaeological museum in town). Sorry, the windmills are post-Cervantes, only 200 to 300 years old—but you can go inside the one that serves as the TI to see how it works (€1.50, included with €4 castle entry).

The next castle north (above Almonacid, 8 miles from Toledo) is free. Follow the ruined lane past the ruined church up to the ruined castle. The jovial locals hike up with kids and kites.

TOLEDO

GRANADA

For a time, Granada was the grandest city in Spain. But after the tumult that came with the change from Moorish to Christian rule, it lost its power and settled into a long slumber. Today, Granada seems to specialize in evocative history and good living. Settle down in the old center and explore monuments of the Moorish civilization and its conquest. Taste the treats of a North African–flavored culture that survives here today.

Compared to other Spanish cities its size, Granada is delightfully cosmopolitan—it's worked hard to accept a range of cultures, and you'll see far more ethnic restaurants here than elsewhere in Andalucía. Its large student population (70,000 students, including more than 10,000 from abroad) also lends it a youthful zest. The Grenadine people are serious about hospitality, and have earned a reputation among travelers for being particularly friendly and eager to help you enjoy their historic city.

Granada's magnificent Alhambra fortress was the last stronghold of the Moorish kingdom in Spain. The city's exotically tangled Moorish quarter, the Albayzín, invites exploration. From its viewpoints, romantics can enjoy the sunset and evening views of the grand, floodlit Alhambra.

An old Spanish saying goes, "Give him a coin, woman, for there is nothing worse in this life than to be blind in Granada." This city has much to see, yet it reveals itself in unpredictable ways; it takes a poet to sort through and assemble the jumbled shards of Granada. Peer through the intricate lattice of a Moorish window. Hear water burbling unseen among the labyrinthine hedges of the Generalife Gardens. Listen to a flute trilling deep in the swirl of alleys around the cathedral. Don't be blind in Granada—open all your senses.

Planning Your Time

Granada is worth two days and two nights, but you could conceivably hit its highlights in one very busy day. No matter what, reserve in advance for the Alhambra—at least several days, or, better, several weeks ahead (see sidebar on page 510).

If you only have one full day here, you could fit in the top sights by following this intense plan: In the morning, stroll the Pescadería market streets and follow my self-guided walk of the old town (or catch the 10:30 Cicerone walking tour), including a visit to the cathedral and its Royal Chapel. After a quick lunch, do the Alhambra in the afternoon (reservation essential). Hike the hippie lane into the Albayzín Moorish quarter (or catch minibus #31 or #32) to the San Nicolás viewpoint for the magic hour before sunset, then find the right place for a suitably late dinner (taxi home for safety if in the Albayzín late). This is an extremely ambitious one-day plan; if you can spread it over two days, you'll be able to slow down and smell the incense (or make the most of one and a half days—e.g., if you're arriving in the early afternoon, do the self-guided walk before dinner).

When you're ready to move on, consider heading to nearby Nerja, the Costa del Sol's best beach town (1.5 hours by car, 2-2.5 hours by bus). You can also get to White Hill Towns such as Ronda (2.5 hours by train). Sevilla is an easy 2.5-hour train ride away. The Madrid–Granada train service is slow (5 hours), but passes through beautiful countryside.

Orientation to Granada

Modern Granada sprawls (300,000 people), but its sights are all within a 20-minute walk of Plaza Nueva, where dogs wag their tails to the rhythm of modern hippies and street musicians. Most of my recommended hotels are within a few blocks of Plaza Nueva. Make this the hub of your Granada visit.

Plaza Nueva was a main square back when kings called Granada home. This historic center is in the Darro River Valley, which separates two hills (the river now flows under the square). On one hill is the great Moorish palace, the Alhambra, and on the other is the best-preserved Moorish quarter in Spain, the Albayzín. To the southwest are the cathedral,

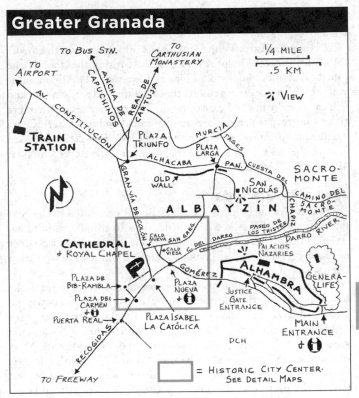

Greater Granada

Royal Chapel, and Alcaicería (Moorish market), where the city's two main drags—Gran Vía de Colón (often just called "Gran Vía" by locals) and Calle Reyes Católicos—lead away into the modern city.

Tourist Information

The main TI is tucked away just above Plaza Nueva on Santa Ana (Mon-Fri 9:00-19:30, Sat-Sun 9:30-15:00, above the church, tel. 958-575-202). Another TI is at the entrance of the Alhambra, inside the ticket office (mid-March-mid-Oct Mon-Fri 8:00-20:00, Sat 8:00-19:00, Sun 8:00-13:30, off-season closes at 18:00 on weekdays, tel. 958-544-002). Get a free city map and the *Pocket Guía* magazine in easy Spanish, and verify your Alhambra plans. To save yourself a trip to the train or bus stations, get schedule information here; both TIs post all departures on their walls. These TIs cover not only Granada, but also Andalucía (pick up good, free maps for wherever else you're going in the region). A municipal TI, which covers only Granada, is inside City Hall on Plaza del Carmen, a short walk from the cathedral; they also sell the Bono Turístico city pass described later (Mon-Sat 10:00-19:00, Sun 10:00-14:00, tel. 958-248-280).

Alhambra Info: While any TI has information on the town's top sight, the very helpful info desk just inside the door of the official Alhambra bookstore (Tienda Librería de la Alhambra) is your best resource, as it's run by the Alhambra administration and is located right in the heart of town. The counter sells Alhambra tickets for future dates (no same-day sales) and has a ServiCaixa machine for printing pre-booked tickets (daily 9:30-20:30, between Plaza Isabel La Católica and Plaza Nueva at Calle Reyes Católicos 40, tel. 958-227-846).

Arrival in Granada

By Train: Granada's modest train station is connected to the center by frequent buses, a €7 taxi ride, or a 30-minute walk down Avenida de la Constitución and Gran Vía. The train station does not have luggage storage. If your itinerary is set, reserve your train out upon arrival.

Taxis wait out front, and it's a three-minute walk to reach the bus stop: Exiting the train station, walk straight ahead down the tree-lined Avenida Andaluces. At the first major intersection, turn right onto Avenida de la Constitución, and within a block you'll see a series of bus stops with routes marked on the signposts. Most of these buses stop at the cathedral (Gran Vía 1), which is four stops from the train station and the nearest stop to Plaza Nueva. Check the easy-to-read routes for the "Gran Vía 1" stop (your options include buses #1, #3, #4, #5, #6, #7, #8, #9, and others). An electronic board shows how long the wait is for each bus. When you board, buy a €1.20 ticket from the driver. For Plaza Nueva and most of my recommended hotels, get off at the cathedral (ask, "¿Catedral?"—kah-tay-DRAHL); cross the busy Gran Vía and walk three short blocks to Plaza Nueva.

By Bus: Located on the city outskirts, Granada's bus station (*estación de autobuses*) has a good and cheap cafeteria, ATMs, luggage lockers (€3.50), coin-op Internet access, and a privately run tourist agency masquerading as a TI—all of these are downstairs, where you exit the buses. Upstairs is the main arrivals hall with ticket windows, automated ticket machines, and a helpful information counter in the main hall that hands out printed schedules for each route. All buses are operated by Alsa (tel. 902-422-242, www.alsa.es).

To get from the bus station to the city center, either take a 10-minute taxi ride (€8) or bus #3 or #33 (€1.20, pay driver). It's about a 20-minute bus ride; nearing the center, the bus goes up Gran Vía. For Plaza Nueva, get off at the "Gran Vía 1" stop near the cathedral (cathedral not visible from bus, ask, "¿Catedral?"—

kah-tay-DRAHL), a half-block before the grand square called Plaza Isabel La Católica. From here, it's a short three-block walk to Plaza Nueva and most of my recommended hotels.

By Car: Driving in Granada's historic center is restricted to buses, taxis, and (technically) tourists with hotel reservations. Signs are posted to this effect, and entrances are strictly controlled—but generally not by an officer. Hidden cameras snap a photo of your license plate as soon as you enter the restricted zone. Getting into the old center and finding your hotel or a parking garage is a major frustration because of these strict controls and the many one-way streets. Many hoteliers recommend simply not driving in the historic center. However, if you choose to drive, here's what to do: Contact your hotelier in advance with your license-plate number (usually a couple of days is enough), and they'll contact the police department to register your car, preventing a nasty surprise when you return your rental car. Be sure to ask your hotelier for detailed driving instructions into the historic center, then follow them exactly. Each hotel district has a strict route that their guests must follow; any deviations are caught by cameras and result in fines. Some hoteliers have deals with nearby garages and provide directions to those spots.

If, upon arrival in Granada, you're driving directly to the Alhambra, you can easily avoid the historic center (see "Getting There" on page 521).

By Plane: Granada's sleepy airport, which serves only a dozen or so planes a day, is about 10 miles west of the city center. To get between the airport and downtown, you can take a taxi (€25) or, much cheaper, the airport bus, timed to leave when flights arrive and depart (€3, 12/day, 40 minutes). If you're leaving from the town center, use the bus stop at Gran Vía del Colón, nearly across from the cathedral. Airport info: tel. 958-245-223 (press "9" for English).

Helpful Hints

Theft Alert: Roma (Gypsy) women, usually hanging out near the cathedral and Alcaicería, will accost you with sprigs of rosemary. The twig is free...and then they grab your hand and read your fortune for a tip. Coins are "bad luck," so the minimum payment they'll accept is €5. Don't make eye contact, don't accept a sprig, and say firmly but politely, *"No, gracias."* Though aggressive (especially in the morning), these Spanish Roma are harmless. Locals warn that Gypsies from Romania (who tend to have gold teeth) are more likely to be pickpockets. In general, be on guard for pickpockets, especially late at night in the Albayzín. Your biggest threat is being conned while enjoying drinks and music in Sacromonte.

City Pass: The **Bono Turístico** city pass covers the Alhambra, cathedral, Royal Chapel, Carthusian Monastery, and several trips on city buses, plus minor sights and discounts on others (€25/3 days, €30/5 days—this version also includes CitySightseeing bus, www.bonoturisticogranada.com). When you buy your pass, the vendor schedules a time for your Alhambra visit. Note that 300 Alhambra reservations each day are allotted to Bono Turístico buyers; if all 300 have already been claimed—which is very rare—it's possible that you won't get a time. Be sure that slots are available before you buy the pass.

Passes are sold at the TI in City Hall on Plaza del Carmen, at the Caja Granada Bank branch in Plaza Isabel La Católica, and at the "This is Granada" kiosk on Plaza Nueva. You can also buy a pass and book your Alhambra palace visit in advance online (http://caja.caja-granada.es; click "Inform. y Compra Bono Turístico"). Fancier hotels provide one free pass per room for stays of two or more nights; check with your hotel before buying a pass yourself.

The local TI is working on creating a **new combo-ticket** that will allow you to pick and choose which specific sights are included (for details, ask at the TI).

Festivals and Concerts: From late June to early July, the **International Festival of Music and Dance** offers classical music, ballet, flamenco, and zarzuela (light opera) nightly in the Alhambra at reasonable prices. The ticket office is located in the Corral del Carbón (open mid-April-Oct). Beginning in February, you can also book tickets online at www.granadafestival.org. This festival is one of the most respected and popular in Spain, and tickets for major performers typically sell out months in advance. During the festival, flamenco is free every night at midnight; ask the ticket office or TI for the venue.

From fall through spring, the **City of Granada Orchestra** offers popular concerts—mostly on weekends—that generally sell out quickly (€6-23, late Sept-mid-May only, Auditorio Manuel de Falla, ticket office in Corral del Carbón, Mon-Fri 12:00-14:00 & 17:00-19:00, Sat 12:00-14:00, closed Sun, tel. 958-221-144, www.orquestaciudadgranada.es).

Internet Access: Almost all Granada hotels have Wi-Fi for their guests, and some have computers for use as well. Many

Internet points are scattered throughout Granada, often part of *locutorios* (call centers).

Laundry: Tintorería-Lavandería Duquesa, a few blocks west of the cathedral area, offers a pricey service to wash, dry, and fold your clothes (€10/small load, same-day service possible if you bring it in the morning, no self-service, Mon-Fri 9:30-14:00 & 17:00-21:00, Sat 9:30-14:00, closed Sun, Duquesa 24, tel. 958-280-685).

Post Office: It's on Puerta Real (Mon-Fri 8:30-20:30, Sat 9:30-14:00, closed Sun, tel. 958-221-138).

Travel Agencies: All travel agencies book flights, and many also sell long-distance bus and train tickets. Mega-chain **El Corte Inglés** sells plane, train, and bus tickets (Mon-Sat 10:00-22:00, closed Sun, Acera del Darro, floor 2, tel. 958-282-612).

Getting Around Granada

With cheap taxis, frisky minibuses, good city buses, and nearly all points of interest an easy walk from Plaza Nueva, you'll get around Granada easily.

Tickets for minibuses and city buses cost €1.20 per ride (buy from driver). Credibus magnetic cards save you money if you'll be riding often—or, since they're shareable, if you're part of a group (€5/7 trips, €10/16 trips, plus €2 for each card issued). You can buy these from the driver as well. To get a €5 card, ask for *"un bono de cinco euros."* For a €10 card, request *"un bono de diez euros."* These are valid on minibuses and city buses (no fee for connecting bus if you transfer within 45 minutes).

By Minibus: Handy little made-for-tourists red minibuses, which cover the city center, depart every few minutes from Plaza Nueva and Plaza Isabel La Católica until late in the evening (about 22:00 or 23:00; some bus stops marked on map on page 520). Here are several handy minibus routes to look for:

Bus #32 is the best for a trip up to the Alhambra, connecting the Alhambra and Albayzín (from Plaza Isabel La Católica, the bus goes up to the Alhambra, returns to Plaza Isabel La Católica, then loops through Plaza Nueva on its way up to the Albayzín and back down Gran Vía del Colón).

Bus #31 does the Albayzín loop, departing from Plaza Nueva.

Bus #35 follows the same route as #31, but also makes a side-trip into Sacromonte. It runs less frequently (every 30-40 minutes).

By City Bus: These are handy if you're visiting the Carthusian Monastery (bus #8) or going to the bus station (#3 or #33) or train station (#3-#9).

Granada at a Glance

▲▲▲**The Alhambra** The last and greatest Moorish palace, highlighting the splendor of that civilization in the 13th and 14th centuries. Reservations are a must if you plan to visit during the day. **Hours:** The entire complex is open daily mid-March–mid-Oct 8:30–20:00, off-season 8:30–18:00. Palacios Nazaries and Generalife Gardens are open for nighttime visits mid-March–mid-Oct Tue-Sat 22:00–23:30, closed Sun–Mon; off-season Fri-Sat 20:00–21:30, closed Sun–Thu. See page 519.

▲▲**Royal Chapel** Lavish 16th-century Plateresque Gothic chapel with the tombs of Queen Isabel and King Ferdinand. **Hours:** March-Oct daily 10:15–13:30 & 16:00–19:30 except opens at 11:00 on Sun; in Nov-Feb daily 10:15–13:30 & 15:30–18:30 but opens at 11:00 on Sun. See page 536.

▲▲**San Nicolás Viewpoint** Breathtaking vista over the Alhambra and the Albayzín. **Hours:** Always open; best at sunset. See page 544.

▲**Cathedral** The second-largest cathedral in Spain, unusual for its bright Renaissance interior. **Hours:** April-Oct Mon-Sat 10:45–13:30 & 16:00–20:00, Sun 16:00–20:00; Nov-March until 19:00. See page 540.

▲**The Albayzín** Spain's best old Moorish quarter. **Hours:** Always open, but use caution after dark. See page 541.

▲**Cave Museum of Sacromonte** A center with caves and displays on Roma cave building, crafts, food, and music. **Hours:** April-Oct Tue-Sun 10:00–14:00 & 17:00–20:30, Nov-March Tue-Sun 10:00–14:00 & 16:00–19:00, closed Mon. See page 547.

Tours in Granada

Walking Tours—Cicerone, run by María and Rosa, offers informative 2.5-hour city tours. Their excellent guides describe the fitful and fascinating changes the city underwent as it morphed from a Moorish capital to a Christian one 500 years ago. While the tour doesn't enter any actual sights, it weaves together bits of the Moorish heritage that survive around the cathedral and the Albayzín. Tours start on Plaza de Bib-Rambla and finish on Plaza Nueva. Groups are small (may cancel if less than five show up, although you have the option of paying more for it to go); to help them gauge if there's enough interest, reservations are encouraged (though not required). Visits are generally only in English, but may

Alcaicería Tiny shopping lanes filled with tacky tourist shops. **Hours:** Always open, with shops open long hours. See page 514.

Corral del Carbón Granada's only surviving caravanserai (inn for traveling merchants), with impressive Moorish door. **Hours:** Always viewable. See page 512.

Paseo de los Tristes A prime strolling strip above the Darro River lined with eateries and peppered with Moorish history. **Hours:** Always open; best in the evenings. See page 517.

Hammam El Bañuelo 11th-century ruins of Moorish baths. **Hours:** Unreliably Tue-Sat 10:00-14:00, April-Sept opens at 9:00, closed Sun-Mon year-round. See page 518.

Great Mosque of Granada Islamic house of worship featuring a minaret with a live call to prayer, an information center for the Muslim perspective on Granada history, and a courtyard with commanding views. **Hours:** Daily 11:00-14:00 & 18:00-20:30. See page 545.

Hammam Baños Árabes Tranquil spot for soaks and massages in Arab baths. **Hours:** Daily 10:00-24:00. See page 541.

Zambra Dance Touristy flamenco-like dance performance in Sacromonte district. **Hours:** Shows generally daily at 22:00. See page 548.

Carthusian Monastery Lavish Baroque monastery on the outskirts of town. **Hours:** Daily April-Oct 10:00-13:00 & 16:00-20:00, Nov-March 10:00-13:00 & 15:00-18:00. See page 549.

GRANADA

be in both English and Spanish on slow days (€12, show this book to save €2, kids under 14 free, March-Oct Sun-Fri at 10:30, Nov-Feb Sun-Fri at 11:00, Sat tours are generally in Spanish only; to book a tour, visit the kiosk labeled *Meeting Point* on Plaza de Bib-Rambla—staffed by cheerful Alma, or call mobile 607-691-676, 670-541-669, or 600-412-051; www.ciceronegranada.com, reservas @ciceronegranada.com). They also offer tours of the Alhambra that include an entry time to Palacios Nazaries—handy if you have trouble getting a reservation on your own (€45-47, try to book at least 3-4 days ahead).

Local Guides—**Margarita Ortiz de Landazuri,** an English-speaking guide, is a charming and effective teacher (tel. 958-221-406, www.alhambratours.com, info@alhambratours.com).

Getting Tickets for the Alhambra's Palacios Nazaries

The Alhambra fortress's top sight is Palacios Nazaries, the Moorish palace. Sadly, many tourists never get to see it, because they didn't make reservations. Since only 300 visitors are allowed to enter per half-hour (in 50-person spurts every five minutes), it's critical to make a reservation as soon as you're ready to commit to a time (especially if you're visiting during Holy Week, on weekends, or on major holidays). During the off-season (July-Aug and winter), you might be able to walk right in—but it's not worth the risk. Getting a reservation is easy.

Get the **General Daytime Visit** ticket (described on page 519). Be careful not to accidentally buy a different type of ticket—this is the only one that lets you in Palacios Nazaries by day. It comes with a reservation to enter the palace at a certain time; for advice on timing your visit, see the sidebar on page 524.

Reserving in Advance: You can reserve up to three months in advance of your visit, in one of four ways: online, by phone, through your hotelier, and by buying a city pass. The first three ways come with a surcharge of about €1.30 (well worth it). If you order online or by phone, you'll still need to pick up a printed ticket once you're in Spain—it's not difficult, but make sure you bring both the same credit card that you used to book the reservation and its PIN code (every credit card has one; ask your bank if you don't know yours). If you run into trouble retrieving your ticket, your passport will come in handy—yet another reason to always keep it with you (tucked safely in a money belt).

Here are details on your reservation options:

• Order online at www.alhambra-tickets.es. This is easy and just takes a few minutes. On the first page, select "Buy Ticket" under the "General Daytime Visit" category. On the next page, select your date and time period—morning (De 8:30h a 14h) or afternoon (De 14h a 20h)—then the exact half-hour time window for entry into Palacios Nazaries (Agotado means "sold out"). Unless you're traveling with a child under 12 (Niños menos 12 a), ignore the "special offers" options and simply hit "Continue."

• Order by phone. Within Spain, dial 934-923-750 (or toll tel. 902-888-001; from the US, dial 011-34-934-923-750; phone answered Mon-Fri 8:00-21:00 Spanish time, not answered Sat-Sun; while you wait for an operator, a recording tells you the date of the next available tickets).

• When you book your room, ask if your hotelier can reserve Alhambra tickets; if so, request a time slot.

• Get a Bono Turístico pass, which covers the Alhambra (and most other sights—worthwhile for a two-day visit); book your Palacios Nazaries appointment when you buy it (see page 506).

Picking Up Tickets: If you bought your tickets online, you can print them anytime at one of Spain's many yellow ATM-like **ServiCaixa machines.** In downtown Granada, you'll find one inside the official Alhambra bookstore (between Plaza Isabel

La Católica and Plaza Nueva) and another at the La Caixa bank just a couple of blocks around the corner, across from the cathedral (at the corner of Gran Vía de Colón and Calle Carcel Baja). If your card isn't accepted by the machine, go to the downtown Alhambra bookstore's information desk, where they can print your tickets for you. Printing your tickets before arriving at the Alhambra saves time (see next) and walking (see "Justice Gate Shortcut Entrance," page 522).

If you arrive at the Alhambra without printed tickets, go to the main entrance about an hour before your Palacios Nazaries appointment, since the line to pick up tickets may require a wait of up to 20 minutes, and walking from the ticket office to the palace takes 15 minutes. Don't forget to bring the right credit card, its PIN number, and (to be safe) your passport. If you reserved your tickets online, follow *Bookings collection with credit card* signs (after passing the bookstore on your right and café on your left, you'll see a series of yellow ServiCaixa machines; English-speaking staff are usually on hand to help). Otherwise, wait in line to pick up your reserved tickets at the windows marked *Retirada de Reservas* (next to the much longer *Venta Directa* line).

If You're in Granada Without a Palace Reservation: You still have a number of options.

• Ask your hotel if they can book a reservation for you.

• Check www.alhambra-tickets.es, and cross your fingers.

• Drop by the downtown Alhambra bookstore at least a day ahead of your palace visit (they can't sell same-day tickets).

• Buy a Bono Turístico city pass, which comes with a reservation for the palace (same-day reservations may be available; for details, see "Helpful Hints," page 506).

• Wake up early and stand in line. The Alhambra admits about 7,700 visitors a day. While the vast majority of tickets are sold in advance, some same-day tickets are sold each day at the Alhambra ticket office (the number changes daily). The window labeled *Venta Directa*, for cash-only, same-day tickets, is where most early-risers line up. Smart visitors avoid the line by using the yellow ServiCaixa machines (beyond the bookstore and café), which issue same-day tickets (starting at the same time the ticket windows open). Go as early as you can. During the busy months, if you're in line by about 7:30, you'll likely get an entry time, probably for later that day. On a slow day, you'll get in right away. On an extremely busy day, however (such as over Easter weekend), lining up at 5:30 still doesn't guarantee you a ticket. A PA system and screens above the ticket-office door provide periodic updates on how many tickets are left for the day—which can help you judge whether it's worth waiting in line.

• Take a tour of the Alhambra (see "Tours," pages 508 and 522).

• See the Generalife Gardens and Alcazaba fort by day (these don't sell out), then return to visit Palacios Nazaries at night (see "The Alhambra by Moonlight" on page 525).

If Margarita is busy, her partner, Miguel Ángel, and her cousin, Patricia Ortiz de Landazuri Quero (patlandazuri@yahoo.es, tel. 619-053-972), are also very good. Guide rates are standard (€130/2.5 hours, €260/day).

Hop-On, Hop-Off Bus Tour—CitySightseeing operates a route with 11 stops around the city, including Gran Vía de Colón (in front of the cathedral), at the Alhambra, and at the Carthusian Monastery. However, the bus concentrates on far-flung areas that are far less interesting than the easy-to-walk city center (€18, 9:30-20:00 in summer, 9:30-18:00 in winter, tel. 958-535-028).

This is Granada Audio Tour—You can rent an MP3 player preloaded with four different walking-tour itineraries around the city, including the Alhambra. Two people get the system for up to three days for €15 (maybe longer off-season; rent from "This is Granada" kiosk on Plaza Nueva, includes map, tel. 958-210-239).

Olive Oil Tour—This company helps you explore Granada's countryside and taste some local olive oil. Choose between a three-hour tour that departs in the morning or afternoon (€38) or a six-hour tour that includes lunch (€55). Tours are in English, and a driver will pick you up at your hotel (tel. 958-559-643, mobile 651-147-504, www.oliveoiltour.com, reservas@oliveoiltour.com).

Self-Guided Walk

▲▲The Transition from Moorish to Christian

This short walk serves as an orientation to the old town, and covers all the essential sights beyond the Alhambra. Along the way, we'll see vivid evidence of the dramatic changes brought about by the Reconquista, the long and ultimately successful battle to retake Spain from the Moors and re-establish Christian rule.

• *Start at Corral del Carbón, near Plaza del Carmen.*

❶ **Corral del Carbón:** A caravanserai (of Silk Road fame) was a protected place for merchants to rest their camels, spend the night, get a bite to eat, and spin yarns. This, the only surviving caravanserai of Granada's original 14, was just a block away from the silk market (Alcaicería; the next stop on this walk). Stepping through the caravanserai's grand Moorish door, you find a square with 14th-century Moorish brick-

work surrounding a water fountain. This plain-yet-elegant structure evokes the times when traders would gather here with exotic goods and swap tales from across the Muslim world.

It's a common mistake to think of the Muslim Moors as

Granada's Old Town Walk

B Bus Stop w/ #s
#32 to Alhambra
#31 + #35 to Albayzín

P Parking

T Taxi Stand

→ Entry Point to Sights

100 YARDS
100 METERS

TO TRAIN & BUS STATIONS

ALBAYZÍN MOORISH QUARTER

GRAN VÍA

CALLE

MERCADO SAN AGUSTÍN

VAL.

CATHEDRAL + ROYAL CHAPEL

DE

TO TRAIN STN. + AIRPORT

CALD. NUEVA

S. GREGORIO

TO SAN NICOLÁS VIEWPOINT + PLAZA LARGA

CETTI.

ELVIRA

CALD. VIEJA

CARCEL ALTA

AIRE

TO SACRAMONTE

COLÓN

COSTA

PL. PESC.

OFICIOS

ALMIR.

ABE.

PAN.

DARRO

PLAZA DE BIB-RAMBLA

ZACATIN

LA MADRAZA

PLAZA NUEVA

PL. S. ANA

ARAB BATHS

REYES CATÓLICOS

PLAZA ISABEL LA CATÓLICA

#32

S. ANA

CUCH.

ANIMAS

CUESTA

GOMEREZ

START

PAVANERAS

TO ALHAMBRA

CALLE

NAVAS

PLAZA DEL CARMEN

CITY HALL

PUERTA REAL

Walk
❶ Corral del Carbón
❷ Alcaicería
❸ Plaza de Bib-Rambla
❹ Cathedral
❺ Royal Chapel Square
❻ Plaza Isabel La Católica

❼ Plaza Nueva
❽ To Paseo de los Tristes & Moorish Baths

Other
❾ Alhambra Bookstore, Info & Servi-Caixa Machine (Alhambra Tickets)
❿ ServiCaixa Machine
⓫ Bus from Train & Bus Stations
⓬ Bus to Train & Bus Stations; Airport

GRANADA

somehow not Spanish. They lived here for seven centuries and were really just as "indigenous" as the Romans, Goths, and Celts. While the Moors were Muslim, they were no more connected to Arabia than they were to France.

After the Reconquista, this space was used as a coal storage facility (hence "del Carbón"). These days it houses two offices where you can buy tickets for musical events.

• *From the caravanserai, exit straight ahead and walk down Puente del Carbón to the big street named Calle Reyes Católicos (for the*

"Catholic Monarchs" Ferdinand and Isabel, who finally conquered the Moors). The street covers a river that once ran openly here, with a series of bridges (like the "Coal Bridge," Puente del Carbón) lacing together the two parts of town. Continue one block farther to the yellow gate marked Alcaicería. *The pedestrian street you're crossing, Zacatín, was the main drag, which ran parallel to the river before it was covered. Today it's a favorite paseo destination, busy each evening with strollers. Pass through the Alcaicería gate and walk 20 yards into the old market to the first intersection.*

❷ Alcaicería: Originally a Moorish silk market with 200 shops, the Alcaicería (al-kai-thay-REE-ah) was filled with precious

salt, silver, spices, and silk. It had 10 armed gates and its own guards. Silk was huge in Moorish times, and silkworm-friendly mulberry trees flourished in the countryside. It was such an important product that the sultans controlled and guarded it by constructing this fine, fortified market. After the Reconquista, the Christians realized this market was good for business and didn't mess with it. Later, the more zealous Philip II had it shut down. A terrible fire in 1850 destroyed what was left. Today's Alcaicería was rebuilt in the late 1800s as a tourist souk (marketplace) to complement the romantic image of Granada popularized by the writings of Washington Irving.

Explore the mesh of tiny shopping lanes: overpriced trinkets, popcorn machines popping, men selling balloons, leather goods spread out on streets, kids playing soccer, barking dogs, dogged shoe-shine boys, and the whirring grind of bicycle-powered knife sharpeners. You'll invariably meet obnoxious and persistent Gypsy women pushing their sprigs on innocents in order to extort money. Be strong.

• Turn left down Ermita lane. After 50 yards, leave the market via another fortified gate and enter a big square. The Neptune fountain marks the center of the...

❸ Plaza de Bib-Rambla: This exuberant square, just two blocks behind the cathedral (from the fountain you can see its blocky spire peeking above the big orange building) was once the center of Moorish Granada. While Moorish rule of Spain lasted 700 years, the last couple of those centuries were a period of decline as Muslim culture split

under weak leadership and Christian forces grew more determined. The last remnants of the Moorish kingdom united and ruled from Granada. As Muslims fled south from reconquered lands, Granada was flooded with refugees. By 1400 Granada had 120,000 people—huge for medieval Europe. This was the main square, the focal point of market and festivals, but it was much smaller then than now, pushed in by the jam-packed city.

Under Christian rule, Moors and Jews were initially tolerated (as they were considered good for business), and this area became the Moorish ghetto. Then, with the Inquisition (under Philip II, c. 1550), ideology trumped pragmatism, and Jews and Muslims were evicted or forced to convert. The elegant square you see today was built, and built big. In-your-face Catholic processions started here. To assert Christian rule, all the trappings of Christian power were layered upon what had been the trappings of Moorish power. Between here and the cathedral were the Christian University (the big orange building) and the adjacent archbishop's palace.

Today Plaza de Bib-Rambla is good for coffee or a meal amid the color and fragrance of flower stalls and the burbling of its Neptune-topped fountain. It remains a multigenerational hangout, where it seems everyone is enjoying a peaceful retirement. A block away (Neptune would get there if he could just turn 180 degrees and walk 100 yards), the Pescadería square is a smaller, similarly lively version of Bib-Rambla.

• *Leave the square by walking toward the cathedral, heading down the lane between the big orange building and Bar Manolo. In a block you come to a small square fronting a very big church.*

❹ **Cathedral:** Wow, the cathedral facade just screams triumph. That's partly because its design is based on a triumphal arch,

built over a destroyed mosque. Five hundred yards away, there was once open space outside the city wall with good soil for a foundation. But the Christian conquerors said, "No way." Instead, they destroyed the mosque and built their cathedral right here on difficult, sandy soil. This was the place where the people of Granada traditionally worshipped—and now they would worship as Christians.

The church has a Gothic foundation and was built mostly in the Renaissance style. Hometown artist Alonso Cano finished it, at the king's request, in Baroque. Accentuating the power of the Roman Catholic Church, the emphasis here is on Mary rather than Christ. The facade declares *Ave Maria*. (This was Counter-Reformation time and the Church was threatened

GRANADA

by Protestant Christians. Mary was also more palatable to Muslim converts, as she is revered in the Quran.)

• *Walk around to the right, popping into the Baroque chapel if it's open. (The entrance to the cathedral itself is on the far side of the church; we'll pass it soon.) Then circle around the cathedral, keeping it to your left, until you reach the small square facing the Royal Chapel.*

❺ **Royal Chapel Square:** This square was once ringed by important Moorish buildings. A hammam (public bath), a madrassa (school), a caravanserai (Day's Inn), the silk market, and the leading mosque were all right here. With Christian rule, the madrassa (the faux-gray-stone building with the walls painted in 3-D Baroque style) became Granada's first City Hall. The royal coffins were moved from the Alhambra's parador to the oval Royal Chapel in 1521. (See the self-guided tour of the Royal Chapel on page 537.)

• *Continue up the cobbled, stepped lane to the big street, Gran Vía de Colón. With the arrival of cars and the modern age, the people of Granada wanted a Parisian-style boulevard. In the early 20th century they mercilessly cut through the old town and created Gran Vía and its French-style buildings—in the process destroying everything in its path, including many historic convents.*

From here you could enter the cathedral (the interior is described in the self-guided cathedral tour on page 540), catch minibus #32 to the Alhambra, or go left two blocks, cross the street, and walk up Calle Cárcel Baja into the Albayzín. But for now let's continue our orientation tour. Cross the busy street, turn right, and walk down Gran Vía to the big square ahead. Face the statue above the fountain from across the busy intersection.

❻ **Plaza Isabel La Católica:** Granada's two grand boulevards, Gran Vía and Calle Reyes Católicos, meet a block off Plaza Nueva at Plaza Isabel La Católica. Above the fountain, a beautiful statue shows Columbus unfurling a long contract with Isabel. It lists the terms of Columbus' *mcccclxxxxii* voyage: "For as much as you, Columbus, are going by our command to discover and subdue some Islands and Continents in the ocean...." The two reliefs show the big events in  Granada of 1492: Isabel and Ferdinand accepting Columbus' proposal and a stirring battle scene (which never happened) at the walls of the Alhambra.

Isabel was driven by her desire to spread Catholicism. Columbus was driven by his desire for money. As a reward for adding territory to Spain's Catholic empire, Isabel promised

Columbus the ranks of Admiral of the Oceans and Governor of the New World. To sweeten the pie, she tossed in one-eighth of all the riches he brought home. Isabel died thinking that Columbus had found India or China. Columbus died poor and disillusioned.

Calle Reyes Católicos leads from this square to the busy intersection with Puerta Real. From there, Acera del Darro takes you through modern Granada to the river via the huge El Corte Inglés department store and lots of modern commerce. This area erupts with locals out strolling each night. For the best Granada paseo, wander the streets here around 19:00.

• *Follow Calle Reyes Católicos a couple of blocks to the left where you'll find another square.*

❼ **Plaza Nueva:** Long a leading square in Granada, Plaza Nueva is dominated by the Palace of Justice (grand Baroque facade with green Andalusian flag). The fountain is capped by a stylized pomegranate—the symbol of the city, always open and fertile. The main action here is the comings and goings of the busy little shuttle buses serving the Alhambra and Albayzín. The local hippie community, nicknamed the *pies negros* (black feet) for obvious reasons, hangs out here and on Calle de Elvira. They squat—with their dogs and guitars—in abandoned caves above those the Gypsies occupy in Sacromonte. Many are the children of rich Spanish families from the north, hell-bent on disappointing their high-achieving parents.

• *Our tour continues with a stroll up Paseo de los Tristes. Leave Plaza Nueva opposite where you entered (via the street to the left of the church) and walk up the Darro River Valley. This is particularly enjoyable in the cool of the evening. If you're tired, note that minibuses #31 and #32 run from Plaza Nueva, up this lane, and then hook into and through the Albayzín quarter.*

❽ **Paseo de los Tristes:** This "Walk of the Sad Ones" was once the route of funeral processions to the cemetery at the edge

of town. Leaving Plaza Nueva, pass the Church of Santa Ana on your right. This was originally a mosque—the church tower replaced a minaret. Notice the ceramic brickwork. This is Mudejar art by Moorish craftsmen, whose techniques were later employed by Christians. Inside you'll see a fine Alhambra-style cedar ceiling.

Follow Carrera del Darro high above the River Darro, which flows along the base of the Alhambra (look down by the river for a glimpse of feral cats). Six miles upstream, part of the Darro is diverted to provide water for the Alhambra's many fountains—a remarkable feat of Moorish engineering that allowed the grand fortress complex to be resistant to siege.

After passing two small, picturesque bridges, you'll see the broken nub of a once-grand 11th-century bridge over the river, leading to the Alhambra. Notice two slits in the column: One held an iron portcullis to keep bad guys from entering the town via the river. The second held a solid door that was lowered to build up water, then released to flush out the riverbed and keep it clean.

• *Across from the remains of the bridge (and the stop for minibuses #31 and #35) is the brick facade of an evocative Moorish bath, the Hammam El Bañuelo.*

❾ Hammam El Bañuelo (Moorish Baths): In Moorish times, hammams were a big part of the community (working-class homes didn't have bathrooms). Baths were strictly segregated (as they are today) and functioned as more than a place to wash: Business was done here, and it was a social meeting point. In Christian times it was assumed that conspiracies brewed in these baths—therefore, only a few of them survive. This place gives you the chance to explore the stark but evocative ruins of an 11th-century Moorish public bath (free, unreliably Tue-Sat 10:00-14:30, April-Sept opens at 9:00, closed Sun-Mon year-round, borrow the English description at the door).

Entering the baths, you pass the house of the keeper and the foyer, then visit the cold room, the warm room (where services like massage were offered), and finally the hot or steam room. Beyond that, you can see the oven that generated the heat, which flowed under the hypocaust-style floor tiles (the ones closest to the oven were the hottest). The romantic little holes in the ceiling once had stained-glass louvers that attendants opened and closed with sticks to regulate the heat and steaminess. Whereas Romans soaked in their pools, Muslims just doused. Rather than being totally immersed, people scooped and splashed water over themselves. Imagine attendants stoking the fires under the metal boiler...while people in towels and wooden slippers (to protect their feet from the heated floors) enjoyed all the spa services you can imagine as beams of light slashed through the mist.

This was a great social mixer. As all were naked, class distinctions disappeared—elites learned the latest from commoners. Mothers found matches for their kids. A popular Muslim phrase sums up the attraction of the baths: "This is where anyone would spend their last coin."

• *Continuing straight ahead, on your right is the Church of San Pedro, the parish church of Sacromonte's Gypsy community (across from the Mudejar Art Museum). Within its rich interior is an ornate oxcart used to carry the host on the annual pilgrimage to Rocio, a town near the Portuguese border. Just past this, on your left, is Santa Catalina de Zafra, a convent of cloistered nuns (they worship behind a screen that divides the church's rich interior in half).*

This walk ends at Paseo de los Tristes—with its restaurant tables spilling out under the floodlit Alhambra. From here, the road arcs up into Sacromonte. If you've worked up a hunger, you can backtrack a few blocks to Calle de Gloria where the Convento de San Bernardo sells cookies and monastic wine. Look for the Venta de Dulces *sign; goods are sold from behind a lazy Susan.*

Sights in Granada

▲▲▲The Alhambra

This last and greatest Moorish palace is one of Europe's top sights. Attracting up to 8,000 visitors a day, it's the reason most tourists come to Granada. Nowhere else does the splendor of Moorish civilization shine so beautifully.

The last Moorish stronghold in Europe is, with all due respect, really a symbol of retreat. For centuries, Granada was merely a regional capital. Gradually the Christian Reconquista moved south, taking Córdoba (1237) and Sevilla (1248). The Nazarids, one of the many diverse ethnic groups of Spanish Muslims, held together the last Moorish kingdom, which they ruled from Granada until 1492. As you tour their grand palace, remember that while Europe slumbered through the Dark Ages, Moorish magnificence blossomed—ornate stucco, plaster "stalactites," colors galore, scalloped windows framing Granada views, exuberant gardens, and water, water everywhere. Water—so rare and precious in most of the Islamic world—was the purest symbol of life to the Moors. The Alhambra is decorated with water: standing still, cascading, masking secret conversations, and drip-dropping playfully.

Cost: Various tickets cover the sights of the Alhambra. The one you want is the €13 **"General Daytime Visit"** *(visita diurna general)* ticket, which covers the Alcazaba fort, Palacios Nazaries, and Generalife Gardens (all described in the sidebar on page 524). This ticket is the only one that allows you to see Palacios Nazaries during the day. Note that same-day tickets are virtually never available—reservations are essential. If you don't bother to make a reservation, you deserve the frustration of not seeing this great sight (for details, see sidebar on page 510).

The Alhambra

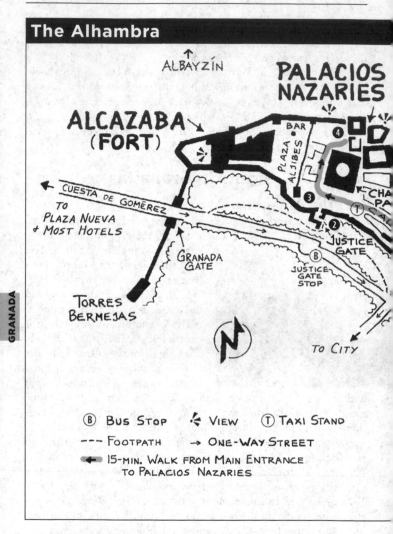

↑ ALBAYZÍN

PALACIOS NAZARIES

ALCAZABA (FORT)

BAR • PLAZA ALJIBES

④

③

②

CUESTA DE GOMEREZ

TO PLAZA NUEVA & MOST HOTELS

GRANADA GATE

Ⓣ

CHAPA

JUSTICE GATE

Ⓑ JUSTICE GATE STOP

TORRES BERMEJAS

Ⓝ

TO CITY

Ⓑ BUS STOP   ⬎ VIEW   Ⓣ TAXI STAND

--- FOOTPATH   → ONE-WAY STREET

◀ 15-MIN. WALK FROM MAIN ENTRANCE TO PALACIOS NAZARIES

GRANADA

Other, less-ideal tickets are available for people who've waited too long to get the General Daytime Visit ticket:

- Daytime ticket for just the Alcazaba and Generalife Gardens—€7
- Nighttime ticket for just Palacios Nazaries—€8
- Nighttime ticket for just the Generalife Gardens—€5
- "Circular Azul" ticket, which allows a nighttime visit of the Palacio Nazaries, then (the next morning) the Alcazaba and Generalife Gardens—€15

The Alhambra grounds are free to visit, as is Charles V's Palace (and the Alhambra Museum inside it).

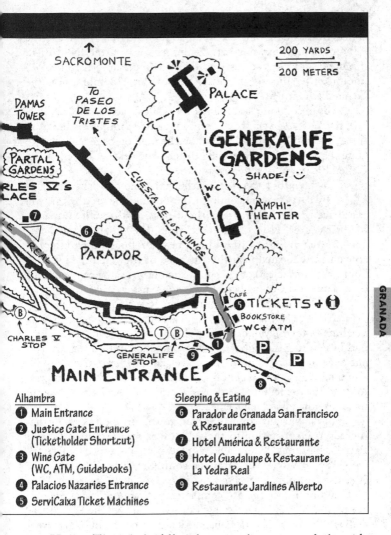

↑ SACROMONTE

200 YARDS
200 METERS

DAMAS TOWER

To PASEO DE LOS TRISTES

PARTAL GARDENS

PALACE

GENERALIFE GARDENS

SHADE! ☺

...RLES V's ...LACE

CUESTA DE LOS CHINOS

WC

AMPHI-THEATER

7

...E REAL

6

PARADOR

CAFÉ

⑤ TICKETS & ℹ

BOOKSTORE

WC & ATM

Ⓑ

CHARLES V STOP

Ⓣ Ⓑ

④ ①

P

GENERALIFE STOP

⑨

MAIN ENTRANCE ➤

P

P

⑧

Alhambra
① Main Entrance
② Justice Gate Entrance (Ticketholder Shortcut)
③ Wine Gate (WC, ATM, Guidebooks)
④ Palacios Nazaries Entrance
⑤ ServiCaixa Ticket Machines

Sleeping & Eating
⑥ Parador de Granada San Francisco & Restaurante
⑦ Hotel América & Restaurante
⑧ Hotel Guadalupe & Restaurante La Yedra Real
⑨ Restaurante Jardines Alberto

GRANADA

Hours: The whole Alhambra complex is open daily mid-March–mid-Oct 8:30–20:00, off-season 8:30–18:00 (ticket office opens at 8:00, last entry one hour before closing, toll tel. 902-441-221).

Palacios Nazaries and Generalife Gardens are also open most **evenings** (see "The Alhambra by Moonlight," page 525) mid-March–mid-Oct Tue-Sat 22:00–23:30 (ticket office open 21:30-22:30), closed Sun-Mon; and off-season Fri-Sat 20:00–21:30 (ticket office open 19:30-20:30), closed Sun-Thu.

Getting There: You have four options for getting to the Alhambra.

1. On foot: From Plaza Nueva, hike 30 minutes up the street called Cuesta de Gomérez. Keep going straight—you'll see the Alhambra high on your left. (Along the way, after about 10-15 minutes, look for the Justice Gate shortcut, described below.) The ticket pavilion is on the far side of the Alhambra, near the Generalife Gardens.

2. By bus: From Plaza Isabel La Católica, catch a red #32 minibus, marked *Alhambra* (€1.20, runs every 10-15 minutes). There are three Alhambra stops (all shown on the map on page 520): Justice Gate (best if you have a printed ticket—see next), Charles V, and Generalife (main ticket office and the gardens).

3. By taxi: It's a €5 ride from the taxi stand on Plaza Nueva.

4. By car: If you're coming from outside the city by car, you can drive to the Alhambra without passing through Granada's historic center. From the freeway, take the exit marked *Ronda Sur–Alhambra*. Signs will lead you to the Alhambra parking lot, conveniently located near the entrance of the Alhambra (€1.50/hour). When you leave, be careful to go out the same way you came in, avoiding the driving ban in Granada's historic center.

Justice Gate Shortcut Entrance: If you already have your printed ticket in hand (i.e., you picked it up from a ServiCaixa machine in town), you can take a shortcut to the core of the complex by entering through the Justice Gate, downhill from the main entrance (if you're walking, this saves about 15 minutes of uphill climbing; you can also get off the minibus here). But if you want to go to the Generalife Gardens first, or don't yet have a ticket in hand, use the upper, main entrance.

Tours: Various companies run tours for about €45-50 that include transportation to the Alhambra and a guided tour of Palacios Nazaries (for example, GranaVisión has a tour for €49, tel. 958-535-875, www.visitargranada.com; Cicerone, listed on page 508, also has tours for €45-57).

Audioguides: The €6 "complete" audioguide brings the palace to life, with 33 stops throughout the complex. The €4 "garden" audioguide covers just 15 stops, mostly outside the buildings (rent it at the entrance or at Charles V's Palace, leave €20 cash deposit or your ID—you'll need to return the audioguide where you picked it up). If you want to use headphones with these audioguides, you must bring your own. Audioguides are not available for night visits.

Guidebooks: Consider getting a guidebook in town and reading it the night before to understand the layout and history of this remarkable sight before entering. Official Alhambra bookstores (including the one in town, and those up at the grounds) push the €18 *Official Guide,* a well-produced scholarly tome loaded with history, photos, maps, and practical information—but it weighs a ton.

Unofficial bookstores sell other options. Of these, I enjoy the slick *Alhambra and Generalife in Focus,* which has vibrant color photos and a visually pleasing layout (€8); the thinner *The Alhambra and the Generalife* has less information and mostly photos (also €8).

Photography: Photos are permitted.

Eating: Within the Alhambra walls, your food options are somewhat limited. Choose between the restaurant at the **parador** (*cafetería*: €7-12 sandwiches, €12-20 light meals; restaurant—get a table on the terrace: €10-15 starters, €18-27 main dishes, €34 fixed-price meal); the courtyard of the **Hotel América** (with pricey €15-20 meals but affordable €6 sandwiches and a great peaceful ambience, Sun-Fri 12:30-16:30, closed Sat); a small **bar-café kiosk** in front of the Alcazaba fort (€3 basic sandwiches and other snacks); and **vending machines** (at the WC) next to the Wine Gate, near Charles V's Palace. You're welcome to bring in a **picnic** as long as you eat it in a public area.

For better-value (but touristy) options, head outside to the area around the parking lot and ticket booth at the top of the complex. **Restaurante La Yedra Real,** a short walk up from the gate, is pleasantly efficient and your best economical sit-down eatery (€3 sandwiches, €5-7 salads, €8-14 main dishes, Tue-Sun 9:30-17.00, closed Mon, easy photo menu, air-con, over the Alhambra parking lot at Paseo de la Sabica 28, tel. 958-229-145). **Restaurante Jardines Alberto,** closer to the main entrance and across from the breezy Restaurante La Mimbre, has a nice courtyard, offers a more formal menu, and feels a little more dignified (€5 sandwiches, €8-12 salads, €12-22 main dishes, €14 fixed-price lunch, daily 9:00-20:00).

Nearby: If you're going to the Albayzín afterward, catch minibus #32, which goes from the three Alhambra stops back through Plaza Isabel La Católica and then up into the Albayzín. Or, for a delightful "Back Door" escape, walk back into town along the Cuesta de los Chinos. (It starts near the ticket booth, by Restaurante La Mimbre and the minibus stop.) You'll walk on a desolate lane downhill along a stream, beneath the Alhambra ramparts, and past the sultan's cobbled horse lane leading up to Generalife Gardens. In 10 minutes you're back in town at Paseo de los Tristes. You can't get lost.

➲ Self-Guided Tour: I've listed these sights in the order you're likely to visit them. The first three sights cluster at the bottom/far end of the complex, while the Generalife Gardens are about a 15-minute walk away, at the top (main entrance). If you have a long time to wait for your Palacios Nazaries appointment, you could do the gardens first, then head down to the other three; otherwise it makes sense to start on the lower end of the hill.

Planning Your Time at the Alhambra

The Alhambra consists of four sights clustered together atop a hill:

▲▲▲**Palacios Nazaries**—Exquisite Moorish palace, the one must-see sight. To see it during the day, advance reservations are a must.

▲▲**Charles V's Palace**—Christian Renaissance palace plopped on top of the Alhambra after the Reconquista, with the fine Alhambra Museum (free entry).

▲**Generalife Gardens**—Fancy, manicured gardens with small summer palace.

Alcazaba—Empty old fort with tower and views.

When to Go

Daytime tickets for Palacios Nazaries come stamped with a 30-minute time slot. Time your visit around that appointment, as your reservation is only good if you enter the palace within that 30-minute window. (Once inside the palace, you can linger as long as you like.)

How best to see the rest of the Alhambra complex depends on whether your Palacios Nazaries reservation is for a time before or after 14:00. If your entry time for Palacios Nazaries is before 14:00, you can visit the other Alhambra sights (the Alcazaba, Generalife Gardens, and Charles V's Palace) anytime in the morning, see Palacios Nazaries at your appointed time, and leave the Alhambra by 14:00 (although you can get away with staying longer in the fort, gardens, or Palacios Nazaries, you won't be allowed to *enter* any of these sites after 14:00). If your ticket is stamped for 14:00 or later, you cannot enter the Alhambra sights any earlier than 14:00. For instance, if you have a reservation to visit Palacios Nazaries at 16:30, you can enter the Alhambra sights any time after 14:00 and see the fort and Generalife Gardens before Palacios Nazaries.

Because of the time restriction on afternoon visits, morning tickets sell out the quickest. But for most travelers, an afternoon is ample time to see the site—the light is perfect, and there are fewer tour groups.

If you're picking up your tickets at the main entrance (at the top end), or just want to start with the gardens, be aware that you're a 15-minute walk away from Palacios Nazaries at the other end. Be sure to arrive at the Alhambra with enough time to make it to the palace before your allotted half-hour entry time slot ends. The ticket-checkers at Palacios Nazaries are strict.

Your Route

To minimize walking, see Charles V's Palace and the Alcazaba fort before your visit to Palacios Nazaries. When you finish touring the palace, you'll leave through the Partal Gardens, a pleasant 15-to-20-minute walk from the Generalife Gardens. Depending on the time, you can visit the Generalife Gardens before or after seeing Palacios Nazaries. If you have any time to kill before your palace appointment,

do it luxuriously on the breezy view terrace of the parador bar (actually within the Alhambra walls; for other options see "Eating," page 523). Drinks, WCs, and guidebooks are available at the Wine Gate, near the entrance of Palacios Nazaries, but not inside the palace.

The Alhambra by Moonlight

If you prefer doing things after dark, you can avoid the reservation hassle. Late-night visits to the Alhambra are easy (separate

nighttime tickets are sold for Palacio Nazaries and the Generalife Gardens; see "Cost," page 519)—just buy your ticket upon arrival, as night-visit tickets hardly ever sell out. Keep in mind that two separate tickets (Alcazaba and Generalife Gardens by day, Palacios Nazaries by night) cost the same as the Circular Azul ticket, and offer more flexibility, as you're not locked into the Circular Azul's next-morning stipulation.

You can't see the Alcazaba fort or Charles V's Palace at night, but, hey, Palacios Nazaries provides 80 percent of the Alhambra's thrills anyway. Although a few small sections of both the palace and the gardens are closed at night, you'll see most of what the daytime visitors see. While some find the Alhambra disappointing at night, others find it even more magical (less crowded and beautifully lit); either way, it's better than not seeing it at all (for exact times see "Hours," page 521).

▲▲Charles V's Palace and the Alhambra Museum

It's only natural for a conquering king to build his own palace over his foe's palace, and that's exactly what the Christian king Charles V did. Palacios Nazaries wasn't good enough for Charles, so he built this new home, which was financed by a salt-in-the-wound tax on Granada's defeated Muslim population. With a unique circle-within-a-square design by Pedro Machuca, a pupil of Michelangelo, this is Spain's most impressive Renaissance building. Stand in the circular courtyard  surrounded by mottled marble columns, then climb the stairs. Perhaps Charles' palace was designed to have a dome, but it was never finished—his son, Philip II, abandoned it to build his own much more massive palace outside Madrid, El Escorial (the final and most austere example of Spanish Renaissance architecture). Even without the dome, acoustics are perfect in the center—stand in the middle and sing your best aria. The palace doubles as one of the venues for the popular International Festival of Music and Dance.

The **Alhambra Museum** (Museo de la Alhambra, on the ground floor of Charles V's Palace) shows off some of the Alhambra's best surviving Moorish art. While modest compared to the other Alhambra sights, the museum's artifacts—including tiles, pottery, pieces of fountains, and a beautiful carved-wood door—help humanize the Alhambra. Everything is well-described in English (free, Tue-Sun 8:30-14:30, closed Mon). The **Fine Arts Museum** (Museo de Bellas Artes, upstairs, also free) is of little interest to most.

If you have an early-morning reservation to Palacios Nazaries, you'll notice that other tourists with reservations line up immediately for that sight. While they're in line, you can take a few minutes to pop into Charles V's Palace, and have it all to yourself.

• *From the front of Charles V's palace (as you face the Alcazaba fort), the entrance to Palacios Nazaries is to the right (look for the line snaking along the outside edge of the garden), while the Alcazaba is across a moat straight ahead (to get there, bear left through the keyhole-shaped Wine Gate—described in the sidebar on page 535—then hook right and walk up to the open area in front of the fort).*

Alcazaba

This fort—the original "red castle" ("Alhambra")—is the oldest and most ruined part of the complex, offering exercise and fine city views. What you see is from the mid-13th century, but

there was probably a fort here in Roman times. Once upon a time, this tower defended a medina (town) of 2,000 Muslims living within the Alhambra walls. It's a huge, sprawling complex—wind your way through passages and courtyards, over uneven terrain, to reach the biggest tower at the tip of the complex. Then climb stairs steeply up to the very top. From there (looking north), find Plaza Nueva and the San Nicolás viewpoint (in the Albayzín). To the south are the Sierra Nevada Mountains. Is anybody skiing today? Notice the tower's four flags: the blue of the European Union, the green and white of Andalucía, the red and yellow of Spain, and the red and green of Granada.

Speaking of flags, imagine that day in 1492 when the Christian cross and the flags of Aragon and Castile were raised on this tower, and the fleeing Moorish king Boabdil (Abu Abdullah, in Arabic) looked back and wept. His mom chewed him out, saying, "You weep like a woman for what you couldn't defend like a man." With this defeat, more than seven centuries of Muslim rule in Spain came to an end. Much later, Napoleon stationed his troops at the Alhambra, contributing substantially to its ruin when he left.

• *If you're going from the Alcazaba to Palacios Nazaries, you'll have to backtrack through the Wine Gate, then look for the people lined up along the gardens in front of Charles V's Palace.*

▲▲▲Palacios Nazaries

During the 30-minute entry time slot stamped on your ticket, enter the jewel of the Alhambra: the Moorish royal palace. Once you're in, you can relax—you're no longer under any time constraints. You'll walk through three basic sections: royal offices, ceremonial rooms, and private quarters. Built mostly in the 14th century, this palace offers your best possible look at the refined, elegant Moorish civilization of Al-Andalus (the Arabic word for the Iberian Peninsula).

You'll visit rooms decorated from top to bottom with carved wood ceilings, stucco "stalactites," ceramic tiles, molded-plaster walls, and filigree windows. Open-air courtyards feature fountains with bubbling water, which give the palace a desert-oasis feel. A garden enlivened by lush vegetation and peaceful pools is the

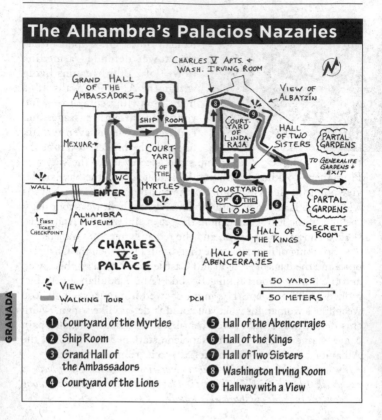

The Alhambra's Palacios Nazaries

1. Courtyard of the Myrtles
2. Ship Room
3. Grand Hall of the Ambassadors
4. Courtyard of the Lions
5. Hall of the Abencerrajes
6. Hall of the Kings
7. Hall of Two Sisters
8. Washington Irving Room
9. Hallway with a View

Quran's symbol of heaven. The palace is well-preserved, but the trick to fully appreciating it is to imagine it furnished and filled with Moorish life...sultans with hookah pipes lounging on pillows upon Persian carpets, heavy curtains on the windows, and ivory-studded wooden furniture. The whole place was painted with bright colors, many suggested by the Quran—red (blood), blue (heaven), green (oasis), and gold (wealth). Throughout the palace, walls, ceilings, vases, carpets, and tiles were covered with decorative patterns, mostly poems and verses of praise from the Quran written in calligraphy. Much of what is known about the Alhambra is known simply from reading the inscriptions that decorate its walls.

As you wander, keep the palace themes in mind: water, a near absence of figural images (forbidden by the Quran), "stalactite" ceilings—and few signs telling you where you are. As tempting as it might be to touch the stucco, don't—it is very susceptible to the oils from your hand. Use the map above to locate the essential stops listed below.

• *Begin by walking through a few administrative rooms (the* mexuar) *with a stunning Mecca-oriented prayer room (the* oratorio, *with a niche on the right facing Mecca) and a small courtyard with a round fountain, until you hit the big rectangular courtyard with a fish pond lined by a myrtle-bush hedge.*

❶ Courtyard of the Myrtles

Moors loved their patios—with a garden and water, under the sky. In accordance with medieval Moorish mores, women rarely

went out, so they stayed in touch with nature in courtyards like the Courtyard of the Myrtles (Patio de los Arrayanes)—named for the two fragrant myrtle hedges that added to the courtyard's charm. Notice the wooden screens (erected by jealous husbands) that allowed the cloistered women to look out without being clearly seen. The upstairs was likely for winter use, and the cooler ground level was probably used in summer.

If the Courtyard of the Lions and the Hall of the Kings (described later) are still being renovated—likely through early 2012—you may see, at the right end of this courtyard, a temporary exhibit displaying those newly restored lion statues, with videos about the archaeologists' work.

• *Head left from the entry through gigantic wooden doors into the long narrow antechamber to the throne room, called the...*

❷ Ship Room

It's understandable that many think the Ship Room (Sala de la Barca) is named for the upside-down-hull shape of its fine cedar ceiling. But the name is actually derived from the Arab word *haraka*, meaning "divine blessing and luck" (which was corrupted to *barca*, the Spanish word for "ship" or "boat"). As you passed through this room, blessings and luck are exactly what you'd need—because in the next room, you'd be face-to-face with the sultan.

• *Oh, it's your turn. Enter the ornate throne room.*

❸ Grand Hall of the Ambassadors

The palace's largest room, the Gran Salón de los Embajadores (also known as the Salón de Comares), functioned as the throne room. It was here that the sultan, seated on a throne opposite the entrance, received foreign emissaries. Ogle the room—a perfect cube—from top to bottom. The star-studded, domed wooden ceiling (made from 8,017 inlaid pieces like a giant jigsaw puzzle) suggests the complexity of Allah's infinite universe. Wooden "stalactites" form

Islamic Art

Rather than making paintings and statues, Islamic artists expressed themselves with beautiful but functional objects. Ceramics (most of them blue and white, or green and white), carpets, glazed tile panels, stucco-work ceilings, and glass tableware are covered with complex patterns. The intricate interweaving, repetition, and unending lines suggest the complex, infinite nature of God, known to Muslims as Allah.

You'll see only a few pictures of humans or animals, since Islamic doctrine is wary of any "graven images" or idols forbidden by God. However, secular art by Muslims for their homes and palaces was not bound by this restriction; you'll get an occasional glimpse of realistic art featuring men and women enjoying a garden paradise, a symbol of the Muslim heaven.

Look for floral patterns (twining vines, flowers, and arabesques) and geometric designs (stars and diamonds). The most common pattern is calligraphy—elaborate lettering of an inscription in Arabic, the language of the Quran. A quote from the Quran on a vase or lamp combines the power of the message with the beauty of the calligraphy.

the cornice, running around the entire base of the ceiling. The stucco walls, even without their original paint and gilding, are still glorious, decorated with ornamental flowers made by pressing a mold into the wet plaster. The filigree windows once held stained glass and had heavy drapes to block out the heat. Some precious 16th-century tiles survive in the center of the floor.

A visitor here would have stepped from the glaring Courtyard of the Myrtles into this dim, cool, incense-filled world, to meet the silhouetted sultan. Imagine the alcoves functioning busily as work stations, and the light at sunrise or sunset, rich and warm, filling the room.

Let your eyes trace the finely carved Arabic script. Muslims avoided making images of living creatures—that was God's work.

But they could carve decorative religious messages. One phrase—"only Allah is victorious"—is repeated 9,000 times throughout the palace. Find the character for "Allah"—it looks like a cursive W with a nose on its left side. The swoopy toboggan blades underneath are a kind of artistic punctuation used to set off one phrase.

In 1492, two historic events likely took place in this room. Culminating a 700-year-long battle, the Reconquista was completed here as the last Moorish king, Boabdil, signed the terms of his surrender before eventually leaving for Africa.

And it was here that Columbus made one of his final pitches to Isabel and Ferdinand to finance a sea voyage to the Orient. Imagine the scene: The king, the queen, and the greatest minds from the University of Salamanca gathered here while Columbus produced maps and pie charts to make his case that he could sail west to reach the East. Ferdinand and the professors laughed and called Columbus mad—not because they thought the world was flat (most educated people knew otherwise), but because they thought Columbus had underestimated the size of the globe, and thus the length and cost of the journey.

But Isabel said, "*Sí, señor.*" Columbus fell to his knees (promising to pack light, wear a money belt, and use the most current guidebook available).

Opposite the Ship Room entrance, photographers pause for a picture-perfect view of the tower reflected in the Courtyard of the Myrtles pool. This was the original palace entrance (before Charles V's Palace was built).

• *Continue deeper into the palace, to a courtyard where, 600 years ago, only the royal family and their servants could enter. It's the much-photographed...*

❹ Courtyard of the Lions

The Patio de los Leones features a fountain that's usually ringed with 12 lions; however, they've been missing for the past several years as they undergo restoration (they should be back in place by early 2012).

Why did the fountain have 12 lions? Since the fountain was a gift from a Jewish leader celebrating good relations with the sultan (Granada had a big Jewish community), the lions probably represent the 12 tribes of Israel. During Moorish times, the fountain functioned as a clock, with a different lion spouting water each hour. (Conquering Christians disassembled the fountain to see how it worked, and it's never worked since.) From the center, four streams went out—figuratively to the corners of the earth and literally to various apartments of the royal family. Notice how the court, with its 124 columns, resembles the cloister of a Catholic monastery. The craftsmanship is first-class. For example, the lead fittings between the pre-cut sections of the columns allow things to flex during an earthquake, preventing destruction during shakes.

Six hundred years ago, the Muslim Moors could read the Quranic poetry that ornaments this court, and they could understand the symbolism of this lush, enclosed garden, considered the embodiment of paradise or truth. ("How beautiful is this garden / where the flowers of Earth rival the stars of Heaven. / What can compare with this alabaster fountain, gushing crystal-clear water? / Nothing except the fullest moon, pouring light from an unclouded sky.") Imagine—they appreciated this part of the palace even more than we do today.

• *On the right, off the courtyard, is a square room called the...*

❺ Hall of the Abencerrajes

This was the sultan's living room, with an exquisite ceiling based on the eight-sided Muslim star. The room has a sad history. The father

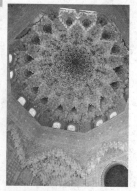

of Boabdil took a new wife and wanted to disinherit the children of his first marriage—one of whom was Boabdil. In order to deny power to Boabdil and his siblings, the sultan killed nearly all of the pre-Boabdil Abencerraje family members. He thought this would pave the way for the son of his new wife to be the next sultan. He stacked 36 Abencerraje heads in the pool, under the sumptuous honeycombed stucco ceiling in this hall, called the Sala de los Abencerrajes. But his scheme failed, and

Boabdil ultimately assumed the throne. Bloody power struggles like this were the norm here in the Alhambra.

• *At the end of the court opposite where you entered is the . . .*

❻ Hall of the Kings

Notice the ceilings of the three chambers branching off this gallery, the Sala de los Reyes. Breaking from the tradition of imageless art, paintings on the goat-leather ceiling depict scenes of the sultan and his family. The center room's group portrait shows the first 10 of the Alhambra's 22 sultans. The scene is a fantasy, since these people lived over a span of many generations. The two end rooms display scenes of princely pastimes, such as hunting and shooting skeet. In a palace otherwise devoid of figures, these offer a rare look at royal life in the palace.

• *As you exit, you'll pass doors leading right and left to a 14th-century WC plumbed by running water and stairs up to the harem. Next is the...*

❼ Hall of Two Sisters

The Sala de Dos Hermanas—nicknamed for the giant twin slabs of white marble on the floor flanking the fountain—has another oh-wow stucco ceiling lit from below by clerestory windows. The room features geometric patterns and stylized Arabic script quoting verses from the Quran. If the inlaid color tiles look "Escher-esque," you've got it backward: Escher is Alhambra-esque. M. C. Escher was inspired by these very patterns on his visit. Study the patterns—they remind us of the Moorish expertise in math. The sitting room (farthest from the entry) has low windows, because Moorish people sat on the floor. Some rare stained glass survives in the ceiling. From here the sultana enjoyed a grand view of the medieval city (before the 16th-century wing was added that blocks the view today).

• *That's about it for the palace. From here, wander past the domed roofs of the old baths down a hallway to a pair of rooms decorated with a mahogany ceiling. Marked with a large plaque is the...*

❽ Washington Irving Room

Washington Irving wrote *Tales of the Alhambra* in this room. While living in Spain in 1829, Irving stayed in the Alhambra. It was a romantic time, when the palace was home to Gypsies and donkeys. His "tales" kindled interest in the Alhambra, causing it to become recognized as a national treasure. A plaque on the wall thanks Irving, who later served as the US ambassador to Spain (1842-1846). Here's a quote from Irving's *The Alhambra by Moonlight:* "On such heavenly nights I would sit for hours at my window inhaling the sweetness of the garden, and musing on the checkered fortunes of those whose history was dimly shadowed out in the elegant memorials around."

• *As you leave, stop at the open-air...*

❾ Hallway with a View

Here you'll enjoy the best-in-the-palace view of the labyrinthine Albayzín—the old Moorish town on the opposite hillside. Find the famous San Nicolás viewpoint (below where the white San Nicolás church tower breaks the horizon). Creeping into the mountains on the right are the Gypsy neighborhoods of Sacromonte. Still circling old Granada is the Moorish wall (built in the 1400s to protect the city's population, swollen by Muslim refugees driven

GRANADA

south by the Reconquista). For more
on Albayzín sights, see page 541.

The Patio de Lindaraja (with
its maze-like hedge pattern garden)
marks the end of the palace visit.
Before exiting, you can detour right
into the adjacent "Secrets Room"—
stark brick rooms of the former bath
with fun acoustics. Whisper into a
corner, and your friend—with an
ear to the wall—can hear you in the
opposite corner. Try talking in the exact center.

• *Leaving the palace, you enter the Partal Gardens (El Partal), where
you can enjoy the reflecting pond of the Partal Palace. Climb a few
stairs, continue through the gardens, and follow signs directing you left
to the Generalife Gardens or right to the Alcazaba (and the rest of the
Alhambra grounds). If you're interested in poking around the Alhambra
grounds, exit and do it now before entering the Generalife (because
you can't easily backtrack into the Alhambra grounds after leaving the
gardens).*

*If you do go from the Partal Gardens to the Generalife Gardens,
it's a delightful 15-to-20-minute stroll through lesser (but still pleasant)
gardens, along a row of fortified towers—just follow signs for* Torres
Generalife. *Just before reaching Generalife, you'll cross over a bridge
and look down on the dusty lane called Cuesta de los Chinos (a handy
shortcut for returning to downtown later).*

▲Generalife Gardens

If you have a long wait before your entry to Palacios Nazaries, tour
these gardens first, then the Alcazaba fort and Charles V's Palace.

The sultan's vegetable
and fruit garden and summer
palace, called the Generalife
(hen-eh-raw-LEEF-ay),
are a short hike uphill past
the ticket office. The 2,000
residents of the Alhambra
enjoyed the fresh fruit and
veggies grown here. But
most importantly, this little
palace provided the sultan with a cool and quiet summer escape.

Follow the simple one-way path through the sprawling gardens (planted only in the 1930s—in Moorish times, there were no
cypress trees here). The sleek, modern amphitheater has been renovated and continues to be an important concert venue for Granada.
It sees most activity during the International Festival of Music

The Alhambra Grounds

As you wander the grounds, remember that the Alhambra was once a city of 2,000 people fortified by a 1.5-mile rampart and 30 towers. The zone within the walls was the medina, a town with a general urban scene. As you stroll from the ticket booth down the garden-like Calle Real de la Alhambra to the palace, you're walking through the ruins of the medina (destroyed by the French in 1812).

The Palacios Nazaries, Alcazaba fort, and Generalife Gardens all have turnstiles. But the medina—with Charles V's Palace, a line of shops showing off traditional woodworking techniques, and the fancy Alhambra parador—is wide open to anyone with an Alhambra ticket.

It's especially fun to snoop around the historic **Parador de Granada San Francisco,** which—as a national monument—is legally required to be open to the public. Once a Moorish palace within the Alhambra, it was later converted into a Franciscan monastery, with a historic claim to fame: Its church is where the Catholic Monarchs (Ferdinand and Isabel) chose to be buried. For a peek, step in through the arch leading to a small garden area and reception. Enter to see the tomb, located in the open-air ruins of the church (just before the reception desk and the guests-only-beyond-this-point sign). The slab on the ground near the altar—a surviving bit from the mosque that was here before the church—marks the place where the greatest king and queen of Spain were buried until 1521 (when they were moved to the Royal Chapel—see page 536). The next room is a delightful former cloister. Now a hotel, the parador has a restaurant and café open to non-guests.

The medina's main road dead-ended at the **Wine Gate** (Puerta del Vino), which protected the fortress. When you pass through the Wine Gate, you enter a courtyard that was originally a moat, then a reservoir (in Christian times). The well—now encased in a bar-kiosk—is still a place for cold drinks. If you're done with your Alhambra visit, you can exit down to the city from the Wine Gate.

and Dance (described on page 506). Many of the world's greatest artists have performed here, including Arthur Rubenstein, Rudolf Nureyev, and Margot Fonteyn. Head for the top of the amphitheater, then walk through the manicured hedge gardens, along delightful ponds and fountains, to the palace.

At the small palace, pass through the dismounting room (imagine dismounting onto the helpful stone ledge, and letting your horse drink in the trough here). Show your ticket and enter the most exceptional Arabian garden in Andalucía.

Here in the summer home of the Moorish kings, this garden is the closest thing on earth to the Quran's description of heaven. It was planted more than 600 years ago—that's remarkable longevity for a European garden. Five-hundred-year-old paintings show it looking essentially the same as it does today. The flowers, herbs, aromas, and water are exquisite...even for a sultan. Up the Darro River, the royal aqueduct diverted a life-giving stream of water into the Alhambra. It was channeled through this extra-long decorative fountain to irrigate the bigger garden outside, then along an aqueduct into the Alhambra for its 2,000 thirsty residents. And though the splashing fountains are a delight, they are a 19th-century addition. The Moors liked a peaceful pond instead.

At the end of the pond you enter the sultan's tiny three-room summer palace. From the end, climb 10 steps into the Christian Renaissance gardens. The ancient decrepit tree rising over the pond inspired Washington Irving, who wrote that this must be the "only surviving witness to the wonders of that age of Al-Andalus."

Climbing up and going through the turnstile, you have two options for where to head next. If you're exhausted, just head to the right and follow *salida* signs toward the gardens' exit (next to the Alhambra's main entrance). But if you want a little more exercise (and views), turn left and huff up the staircase called Escalera del Agua, whose banisters double as little water canals. From the top, you'll have a chance to enter the "Romantic Viewpoint"—climb up the stairs for a top-floor view over the gardens (pleasant enough, but less impressive than other views at the Alhambra). Then hike back down through the garden and follow *salida* signs to the exit.

Your visit to the Alhambra is complete, and you've earned your reward. "Surely Allah will make those who believe and do good deeds enter gardens beneath which rivers flow; they shall be adorned therein with bracelets of gold and pearls, and their garments therein shall be of silk" (Quran 22.23).

▲▲Royal Chapel (Capilla Real)

Without a doubt Granada's top Christian sight, this lavish chapel holds the dreams—and bodies—of Queen Isabel and King Ferdinand. The "Catholic Monarchs" were all about the

Reconquista. Their marriage united the Aragon and Castile king-doms, allowing an acceleration of the Christian and Spanish push south. In its last 10 years, the Reconquista snowballed. This last Moorish capital—symbolic of their victory—was their chosen burial place. While smaller and less architecturally striking than the cathedral (described next), the chapel is far more historically significant.

Cost and Hours: €3.50; March-Oct daily 10:15-13:30 & 16:00-19:30 except opens at 11:00 on Sun; in Nov-Feb daily 10:15-13:30 & 15:30-18:30 except opens at 11:00 on Sun; no photos, entrance on Calle Oficios, just off Gran Vía del Colón—go through iron gate, tel. 958-227-848.

➲ **Self-Guided Tour:** In the lobby, before you show your ticket and enter the chapel, notice the **painting of Boabdil** (on the black horse) giving the key of Granada to the conquering King Ferdinand. Boabdil wanted to fall to his knees, but the Spanish king, who had great respect for his Moorish foe, embraced him instead. They fought a long and noble war (for instance, respect-fully returning the bodies of dead soldiers). Ferdinand is in red, and Isabel is behind him wearing a crown. The painting is flanked high on the wall by portraits of Ferdinand and Isabel. Two small exhibits celebrate the 500th anniversaries of the death of Isabel in 2004 and of Philip the Fair (her son-in-law) in 2006.

Isabel decided to make Granada the capital of Spain (and burial place for Spanish royalty) for three reasons: 1) With the conquest of this city, Christianity had finally overcome Islam in Europe; 2) her marriage with Ferdinand, followed by the conquest of Granada, had marked the beginning of a united Spain; and 3) in Granada, she agreed to sponsor Columbus.

Show your ticket and step into the **chapel.** It's Plateresque Gothic—light and lacy silver-filigree style, named for and inspired by the fine silverwork of the Moors. The chapel's interior was orig-inally austere, with fancy touches added later by Ferdinand and Isabel's grandson Charles V. Five hundred years ago, this was the most lavish interior money could buy. Ferdinand and Isabel spent a quarter of their wealth on it. Because of its speedy completion (1506-1521), the architecture is unusually harmonious.

In the center of the cha-pel (in front of the main altar), the **four royal tombs** are Renaissance-style. Carved in Italy in 1521 out of Carrara marble, they were sent by ship to Spain. The faces—based on death masks—are considered accurate. If you're looking at the altar, **Ferdinand** and **Isabel** are on the right. (Isabel fans attribute the bigger dent she puts in the pillow to her larger brain.) Isabel's contemporaries described the queen as being of medium height, with auburn hair and blue eyes, and possessing a serious, modest, and gentle personality. (Compare Ferdinand and Isabel's tomb statues with the painted and gilded wood statues of them kneeling in prayer, flanking the altarpiece.)

Philip the Fair and **Juana the Mad** (who succeeded Ferdinand and Isabel) lie on the left. Philip was so "Fair" that it drove the insanely jealous Juana "Mad." Philip died young, and for two years Juana kept his casket at her bedside, kissing his embalmed body good night. Philip and Juana's son, Charles V (known as Carlos I in Spain), was a key figure in European history, as his coronation merged the Holy Roman Empire (Philip the Fair's Habsburg domain) with Juana's Spanish empire. Europe's top king, Charles V ruled a vast empire stretching from Holland to Sicily, from Bohemia to Bolivia (1519-1556, see listing for his palace within the Alhambra on page 526).

When Philip II, the son of Charles V, decided to build El Escorial (his palace outside Madrid) and establish Madrid as the single capital of a single Spain, Granada lost power and importance. More importantly, Spain began to decline. After the reign of Charles V, Spain squandered her vast wealth trying to maintain this impossibly huge empire. The country's rulers did it not only for material riches, but to defend the romantic, quixotic dream of a Catholic empire—ruled by one divinely ordained Catholic monarch—against an irrepressible tide of nationalism and Protestantism that was sweeping across the vast Habsburg holdings in Central and Eastern Europe. Spain's relatively poor modern history can be blamed, in part, on its people's stubborn unwillingness to accept the end of this old-regime notion. Even Franco borrowed symbols from the Catholic Monarchs to legitimize his dictatorship and keep the 500-year-old legacy alive. Today's Spaniards reflect that the momentous marriage that created their country also sucked them into centuries of European squabbling, eventually leaving Spain impoverished.

Look at the intricate carving on the tombs. It's a humanistic statement, with these healthy, organic, realistic figures rising out of the Gothic age.

From the feet of the marble tombs, step downstairs to see the actual **coffins.** They are plain. Ferdinand and Isabel were originally buried in the Franciscan monastery (in what is today the parador, up at the Alhambra). You're standing in front of the two people who created Spain. The fifth coffin (on right, marked *PM*) belongs to a young Prince Michael, who would have been king of a united Spain and Portugal. (A sad—but too long—story....)

The **high altar** is one of the finest Renaissance works in Spain. It's dedicated to two Johns: the Baptist and the Evangelist. In the center you can see the Baptist and the Evangelist chatting as if over tapas—an appropriately humanistic scene. Scenes from the Baptist's life are on the left: John beheaded after Salomé's fine dancing, and (below) John baptizing Jesus. Scenes from the Evangelist's life are on the right: John's martyrdom (a failed attempt to boil him alive in oil), and, below, John on Patmos (where he may have written the last book of the Bible, Revelation). John is talking to the eagle that, according to tradition, flew him to heaven. A colorful series of reliefs at the bottom level recalls the Christian conquest of the Moors (left to right): Ferdinand, Boabdil with army and key to Alhambra, Moors expelled from Alhambra (right of altar table), conversion of Muslims by tonsured monks, and Ferdinand again.

A finely carved Plateresque arch, with the royal initials *F* and *Y*, leads to a small glass pyramid in the **treasury**. This holds Queen Isabel's silver crown ringed with pomegranates (symbolizing

Granada), her scepter, and King Ferdinand's sword. Do a counterclockwise spin around the room to see it all, starting to the right of the entry arch. There you'll see the devout Isabel's prayer book, in which she followed the Mass. The book and its sturdy box date from 1496. According to legend, the fancy box on the other side of the door is supposedly the one that Isabel filled with jewels and gave to Columbus (her military expenses had made her cash-poor). Columbus sold these to finance his journey. In the corner (and also behind glass) is the ornate silver-and-gold cross that Cardinal Mendoza, staunch supporter of Queen Isabel, carried into the Alhambra on that historic day in 1492. Next, the big silver-and-gold silk tapestry is the altar banner for the mobile campaign chapel of Ferdinand and Isabel, who always traveled with their army. In the case to its left, you'll see the original Christian army flags raised over the Alhambra in 1492.

The next zone of this grand hall holds the first great art collection ever established by a woman. Queen Isabel amassed more than 200 important paintings. After Napoleon's visit, only 30 remained. Even so, this is a fine collection, all on wood, featuring works by Sandro Botticelli, Pietro Perugino, the Flemish master Hans Memling, and some less-famous Spanish masters.

Finally, at the end of the room, the two carved sculptures of Ferdinand and Isabel were the originals from the high altar. Charles V considered these primitive and replaced them with the ones you saw earlier.

To reach the cathedral (described next), exit behind Isabel, out through one iron gate and then immediately through the neighboring iron gate.

▲Cathedral

One of only two Renaissance churches in Spain (the other is in Córdoba), Granada's cathedral is the second-largest in Spain after Sevilla's. While it was started as a Gothic church, it was built using Renaissance elements, and then decorated in Baroque style.

Cost and Hours: €3.50; April-Oct Mon-Sat 10:45-13:30 & 16:00-20:00, Sun 16:00-20:00; Nov-March until 19:00; 45-minute audioguide-€3, entrance off Gran Vía del Colón through the iron gateway next to the "Gran Vía 1" bus stop, tel. 958-222-959.

❍ Self-Guided Tour: Your visit starts in the priests' wardrobe room (after the ticket checker, step right). It's lush and wide-open; the gilded ceilings, mirrors, and wooden cabinets give this room a light, airy feel. Two grandfather clocks made in London (one with Asian motifs) ensured that everyone got dressed on time. The highlight of this room: the small, delicate painted wood statue of the *Immaculate Conception* by Granada's own Alonso Cano (1601-1667).

Wandering out, you'll be behind the main altar. A fine series of paintings by Cano, moved from under arches high above, now encircle the back of the altar. Their distortion was intentional, since the paintings were designed to look natural when viewed from floor level. As you walk around the pews and gigantic Baroque organs, you'll see the cathedral at its most beautiful.

Standing in front of the high altar, look up at the spread of vacant niches (with squares now filled with paintings). These were intended to hold the royal coffins. But Phillip II changed focus, abandoning Granada for El Escorial, and these sit empty to this day. Only four royals are buried in Granada (at the Royal Chapel). The cathedral's cool, spacious, bright interior is a refreshing break from the dark Gothic of so many Spanish churches. In a move that was modern back in the 18th century, the walls of the choir (the big, heavy wooden box that dominates the center of most Spanish churches) were taken out so that people could be involved in the worship. At about the same time, a bishop ordered the interior painted with lime (for hygienic reasons, during a time of disease). The people liked it, and it stayed white. As you explore, remember that the abundance of Marys is all part of the Counter-

Reformation. Most of the side chapels are decorated in Baroque style. On the outer wall, directly to the right of the high altar, is a politically incorrect version of St. James the Moor-Slayer, with his sword raised high and an armored Moor trampled under his horse's hooves.

Wander back through the pews toward the cathedral's main doors. A small sacristy museum is tucked away in the right corner (as you face the doors). There may be no detailed descriptions for any of the items, but a beautiful bust of St. Pablo (Paul, with a flowing beard) by Cano is worth seeking out. As you head out, look for the music sheets behind the main altar; they're mostly 16th-century Gregorian chants. Notice the sliding C clef. Rather than a fixed G or F clef, the monks knew that this clef—which could be located wherever worked best on the staff—marked middle C, and they chanted to notes relative to that. Go ahead—try singing a few verses of the Latin.

Immediately in front of the cathedral is the stop for minibus #32 to the Alhambra. And four blocks away (if you head left up the busy street, then turn right) is the Albayzín.

Near Plaza Nueva

Hammam Baños Árabes (Arab Baths)—For an intimate and subdued experience, consider some serious relaxation at the Arab Baths, where you can enjoy the three different-temperature pools and a steam room. A maximum of 30 people are allowed in the baths at one time.

Cost and Hours: If you just want a 90-minute soak in the baths, the cost is €22; it costs more to add a 15-minute massage: a regular massage is €32, a traditional scrubbing massage is €39, and to have both costs €49. Daily 10:00-24:00, appointments scheduled every even-numbered hour, co-ed with mandatory swimsuits, quiet atmosphere encouraged, free lockers and towels available, no loaner swimsuits but you can buy one for €12, just off Plaza Nueva and a few doors down from the TI at Santa Ana 16, 50 percent paid reservation required, tel. 958-229-978, www.hammamspain.com/granada.

▲The Albayzín

Explore Spain's best old Moorish quarter, with countless colorful corners, flowery patios, and shady lanes. While the city center of Granada—which is pleasant enough—feels more or less like many other Spanish cities, the Albayzín is unique. You can't say you've really seen Granada until you've at least strolled a few of its twisty lanes. It's an odd mix of very touristy and gritty—with very little in between. Climb high to the San Nicolás church for the best view of the Alhambra. Then wander through the mysterious back streets. (I've listed these sights roughly in order from the San Nicolás viewpoint.)

Getting to the Albayzín: A handy city **minibus** threads its way around the Albayzín from Plaza Nueva (see "Albayzín Circular Bus Tour," next), getting you scenically and sweatlessly to the San Nicolás viewpoint. You can also **taxi** to the San Nicolás church and explore from there. (Consider having your cabbie take you on a detour to the Sacromonte enclave of cave-dwelling Gypsies, described later.)

It's a steep but fascinating 20-minute walk up: Leave the west end of Plaza Nueva on Calle de Elvira. After about 50 yards, at the pharmacy and newsstand, bear right on Calle Calderería Vieja. Follow this stepped street past Moroccan eateries and pastry shops, vendors of imported North African goods, halal butchers, and *teterías* (Moorish tea rooms). The lane bears right, then passes to the left of the church (becoming Cuesta de San Gregorio), and slants, winds, and zigzags uphill. Cuesta de San Gregorio eventually curves left and is regularly signposted. When you reach the Moorish-style house, La Media Luna (with the tall trees and keyhole-style doorway), stop for a photo and a breather, then follow the wall, continuing uphill. At the next intersection (with the black cats), turn right on Aljibe del Gato. Farther on, this street takes a 90-degree turn to the right; at this point, turn left onto Calle Atarasana Vieja. It's confusing, but keep going up, up, up. At the crest (and the dead-end), turn right on Camino Nuevo de San Nicolás, then walk 200 yards to the street that curves up left (look for a bus-stop sign—this is where the minibus would have dropped you off). Continue up the curve and soon you'll see feet hanging from the plaza wall. Steps lead up to the church's viewpoint. Whew! You made it!

Albayzín Circular Bus Tour—The handy Albayzín minibus #31 gallops the 15-minute loop as if in a race, departing from Plaza Nueva about every 15 minutes (pay driver €1.20, minibus #32 does the same loop, but—depending on where you catch it—goes to the Alhambra first). While good for a lift to the top of the Albayzín (buzz when you want to get off), I'd stay on for an entire circle and return to the Albayzín later for dinner—either on foot or by bus again. (Note: The less frequent minibus #35, departing every 40 minutes, does same trip with a side-trip up into Sacromonte.)

Here's the route: Go along up above the Darro River, past the ruins of a bridge and gate and the Paseo de los Tristes square (see page 517). Turning uphill, pass Sacromonte on the right (entrance

Albayzín Neighborhood

STREET WIDTH IS EXAGGERATED FOR CLARITY

NOTE: NOT TO SCALE

➡ 20 MIN. UPHILL WALK FROM PLAZA NUEVA TO SAN NICOLÁS

♥ VIEW

DCH

❶ Hotel Santa Isabel la Real

❷ El Numero 8 "Casa de Rafa" (Apts.)

❸ Makuto Guesthouse

❹ Plaza S. Miguel el Bajo Eateries

❺ Casa Torcuato (2 locations)

❻ Restaurante El Ladrillo

❼ Rest. Estrellas de S. Nicolás & Great Mosque of Granada

❽ Bar Kiki

❾ Paseo de los Tristes Bars

❿ Carmen Mirador de Aixa & Carmen de las Tomasas Rests.

⓫ Carmen de Aben Humeya Rest.

⓬ Carmen de la Media Luna (Landmark)

⓭ Hammam El Bañuelo (Moorish Baths)

⓮ Hammam Baños Árabes (Arab Baths)

⓯ To Cave Museum of Sacromonte, Roma Caves & Zambra Dance Clubs

GRANADA

to the neighborhood marked by a statue of a popular Gypsy guide). Then, turning left, enter the actual Albayzín. After stopping at the church of San Salvador, plunge into the thick of it, with stops below the San Nicolás church (famous viewpoint, and the jumping-off point for my suggested "Exploring the Albayzín" stroll, described later) and at Plaza San Miguel Bajo (cute square with recommended eateries and another viewpoint). Then descend, enjoying a commanding view of Granada on the left as you swing through the modern city. Hitting the city's main drag, Gran Vía del Colón,

Safety in the Albayzín

With tough economic times, young ruffians are hanging out in the dark back lanes of the labyrinthine Albayzín quarter. While this charming Moorish district is certainly safe by day, it can be edgy after dark. Most of the area is fine to wander, though many streets are poorly lit, and the maze of lanes can make it easy to get lost and wind up somewhere you don't want to be. Some nervous travelers choose to avoid the neighborhood entirely after dark, but I recommend venturing into the Albayzín to enjoy its restaurants, ideal sunset views, and charming ambience. Just be sure to exercise normal precautions: Leave your valuables at your hotel, stick to better-lit streets, and take a minibus or taxi home if you're unsure of your route. Violent crime is rare, but pickpocketing is epidemic. Keep a very close eye on your stuff. Some visitors mistakenly think that the danger in this historic "Moorish" district is from Arabs, but the real crooks can be Northern and Eastern European hippies loitering in the squares.

Locals say the biggest hazard when walking in the Albayzín are the many deposits left by its animal inhabitants (and not cleaned up by their poorly trained owners). If you bury your nose in a guidebook while you walk, you'll likely wind up burying your shoe in something else.

make a U-turn at the Gardens of the Triumph, celebrating the Immaculate Conception of the Virgin Mary (notice her statue atop a column). Behind Mary stands the old Royal Hospital—built in the 16th century for Granada's poor by the Catholic kings after the Reconquista, in hopes of winning the favor of the city's conquered residents. From here, zip back into town, stopping at the cathedral, and back home to Plaza Nueva.

▲▲**San Nicolás Viewpoint (Mirador de San Nicolás)**—For

one of Europe's most romantic viewpoints, be here at sunset, when the Alhambra glows red and the Albayzín widows share the benches with local lovers, hippies, and tourists (free, always open). In 1997 President Clinton made a point to bring his family here—a favorite spot from a trip he made as a student. But this was hardly an original idea; generations of visitors have been drawn here. For an affordable (€3-6) drink with the same million-euro view, step into the El Huerto de Juan Ranas Bar (just below and to the left, at Calle de Atarazana 8).

Great Mosque of Granada—Granada's Muslim population is on the rebound, and now numbers 8 percent of the city's residents.

A striking and inviting mosque is just next to the San Nicolás viewpoint (to your left as you face the Alhambra). Local Muslims write, "The Great Mosque of Granada signals, after a hiatus of 500 years, the restoration of a missing link with a rich and fecund Islamic contribution to all spheres of human enterprise and activity."

Built in 2003 (with money from the local community and Islamic Arab nations), it has a peaceful view courtyard and a minaret that comes with a live call to prayer five times a day (printed schedule inside). It's stirring to see the muezzin holler "God is Great" from the minaret without amplification (locals didn't want it amplified). Visitors are welcome in the courtyard, which offers Alhambra views without the hedonistic ambience of the more famous San Nicolás viewpoint.

Cost and Hours: Free, daily 11:00-14:00 & 18:00-20:30.

Background: While tourists come to Granada to learn about the expulsion of the Moors in 1492, local Muslims are frustrated by what a flier at the mosque calls the "errors, nonsense, and lies local guides perpetuate without knowledge nor shame which flocks of passive tourists accept without questioning." The flier tries to set the record straight, from the Muslim perspective: Muslims were as indigenous as any other group. After living here for seven centuries, the Muslims of Granada and Andalucía were as Iberian as the modern Spaniards of today. Islam is not a religion of immigrants; Islam is not a culture of the Orient and Arabs. "Muslim" and "Arab" are not interchangeable terms. The Muslims of Al-Andalus were not hedonistic. The Reconquista did not "liberate" Spain. Harems were not just full of sexy women. (For more on the Muslim perspective, visit the info desk at the mosque.)

The European Union sees Granada as a center for Muslim-Christian integration—or, at least, co-existence. To Muslims, the city is a symbol of the "holocaust" of the Reconquista, when 135,000 of their people were brutally expelled and many more suffered "forced conversion" in the 16th century. Today there are about 700,000 Muslims in Spain (and about 5 million in France).

Exploring the Albayzín—From the San Nicolás viewpoint and the Great Mosque, you're at the edge of a hilltop neighborhood even the people of Granada recognize as a world apart. Each of the district's 20 churches sits on a spot once occupied by a mosque. When the Reconquista arrived in Granada, the Christians attempted to coexist with the Muslims. But after seven years, this idealistic attempt ended in failure, and the Christians forced the Muslims to convert. In 1567 Muslims were expelled, leading to 200 years of economic depression for the city. Eventually, large walled noble manor houses with private gardens were built here in the depopulated Albayzín. These survive today in the form of the characteristic *carmen* restaurants so popular with visitors.

From the San Nicolás viewpoint, turn your back to the Alhambra and walk north (passing the church on your right and the Biblioteca Municipal on your left). A lane leads past a white stone arch (on your right)—now a chapel built into the old Moorish wall. You're walking past the scant remains of the pre-Alhambra fortress of Granada. At the end of the lane, step down to the right through the 11th-century "New Gate" (Puerta Nueva—older than the Alhambra) and into **Plaza Larga.** In medieval times this tiny square (called "long," because back then it was) served as the local marketplace. It still is a busy market each morning. Casa Pasteles, at the near end of the square, serves good coffee and cakes.

Leave Plaza Larga on **Calle Agua de Albayzín** (as you face Casa Pasteles, it's to your right). The street, named for the public baths that used to line it, shows evidence of the Moorish plumbing system: gutters. Back when Europe's streets were filled with muck, Granada actually had Roman Empire–style gutters with drains leading to clay and lead pipes.

You're in the heart of the Albayzín. Explore. Poke into an old church. They're plain by design to go easy on the Muslim converts, who weren't used to being surrounded by images as they worshipped. You'll see lots of real Muslim culture living in the streets, including many recent Spanish converts.

Sacromonte

The Sacromonte district is home to Granada's thriving Roma community. Marking the entrance to Sacromonte is a statue of Chorrohumo (literally, "exudes smoke," and a play on the slang word for "thief": *chorro*). He was a Roma from Granada, popular in the 1950s for guiding people around the city.

While the neighboring Albayzín is a sprawling zone blanketing a hilltop, Sacromonte is much smaller—very compact and very steep. Most houses are burrowed into the wall of a cliff. Sacromonte has one main street: Camino del Sacromonte, which is lined with caves primed for tourists and restaurants ready to

Granada's Roma (Gypsies)

Both the English word "Gypsy" and its Spanish counterpart, *gitano,* come from the word "Egypt"—where Europeans once believed these nomadic people had originated. Today the preferred term is "Roma," since "Gypsy" has acquired negative connotations (though for clarity's sake, I've used both terms throughout this book).

After migrating from India in the 14th century, the Roma people settled mostly in the Muslim-occupied lands in southern Europe (such as the Balkan Peninsula, then controlled by the Ottoman Turks). Under medieval Muslims, the Roma enjoyed relative tolerance. They were traditionally good with crafts and animals.

The first Roma arrived in Granada in the 15th century—and they've remained tight-knit ever since. Today 50,000 Roma call Granada home, many of them in the district called Sacromonte. In most of Spain, Roma are more assimilated into the general population, but Sacromonte is a large, distinct Roma community. (After the difficult Civil War era, they were joined by many farmers who, like the Roma, appreciated Sacromonte's affordable, practical cave dwellings—warm in the winter and cool in the summer.)

Spaniards, who generally consider themselves to be tolerant and not racist, claim that in maintaining such a tight community, the Roma segregate themselves. The Roma call Spaniards *payos* ("whites"). Recent mixing of Roma and *payos* has given birth to the term *gallipavo* (rooster-duck), although who's who depends upon whom you ask.

Are Roma thieves? Sure, some of them are. But others are honest citizens, trying to make their way in the world just like anyone else. Because of the high incidence of theft, it's wise to be cautious when dealing with a Roma person—but it's also important to keep an open mind.

fight over the bill. (Don't come here expecting to get a deal on anything.) Intriguing lanes run above and below this main drag—a steep hike above Camino del Sacromonte is the cliff-hanging, parallel secondary street, Vereda de Enmedio, which is less touristy, with an authentically residential vibe.

▲**Cave Museum of Sacromonte (Museo Cuevas del Sacromonte)** —This hilltop complex, also known as the Center for the Interpretation of Sacromonte (Centro de Interpretación del Sacromonte), is a kind of open-air folk museum about Granada's unique Roma cave-dwelling tradition (though doesn't have much on the Gypsies themselves). The exhibits, with good English descriptions, are spread through a series of whitewashed caves along a ridge, with spectacular views to the Alhambra. As you stroll from cave to cave, you'll learn about the local geology (rocks, flora, and fauna); crafts (basket-weaving, pottery-making, metalworking, and weaving); and lifestyles (including a look into a typical home and kitchen). There's also an exhibit about other cave-dwelling cultures from around the "troglodyte world," and one about Sacromonte's vital role in the development of Granada's local brand of flamenco. As you wander, imagine this in the 1950s, when it was still a bustling community of Roma cave-dwellers. Today, hippies squat in abandoned caves higher up.

Cost and Hours: €5; April-Oct Tue-Sun 10:00-14:00 & 17:00-20:30, Nov-March Tue-Sun 10:00-14:00 & 16:00-19:00, closed Mon year-round; Barranco de los Negros, tel. 958-215-120, www.sacromontegranada.com.

Getting There: You can ride minibus #35 from Plaza Nueva (ask driver, "*¿Museo Cuevas?*," departs only every 40 minutes) or a taxi. You'll get off at the "Sacromonte 2" bus stop, next to the Venta El Gallo restaurant, at the bottom of the hill along the main road. From there, it's a very steep but interesting 10-minute hike past cave dwellings up to the top of the hill—follow the signs. If you don't want to wait for minibus #35, you can ride #31 or #32 to the entrance of Sacromonte, and walk from there—giving you a good look at the whole area.

Performances: In summer (July-Aug), the center also features flamenco shows and classical guitar concerts in its wonderfully scenic setting (prices and schedules vary—see website above for details).

Zambra Dance—A long flamenco tradition exists in Granada, and the Gypsies of Sacromonte are credited with developing this city's unique flavor of this Andalusian art form. Sacromonte is a good place to see *zambra*, a flamenco variation with a more Oriental feel in which the singer also dances. A half-dozen cave-bars offering *zambra* in the evenings line Sacromonte's main drag. Two well-established venues are Zambra Cueva de la Rocío (€25, includes a drink and a bus ride from hotel, €20 without transport, daily show at 22:00, 1 hour, Camino del Sacromonte 70, tel. 958-227-129) and María la Canastera (€25, includes a drink and transportation from hotel, €17 without transport, daily show at 22:00, 1 hour, Camino del Sacromonte 89, tel. 958-121-183, www.granadainfo.com /canastera). The biggest operation here is the restaurant Venta El Gallo, which has performances of more straightforward flamenco (not specifically *zambra*). Or consider the summer performances at the museum (explained earlier). I'd just go and explore late at night (with no wallet and €30 in my pocket) rather than book an evening through my hotel (they'll likely offer to reserve for you).

Near Granada

Carthusian Monastery (La Cartuja)—A church with an interior that looks as if it squirted out of a can of whipped cream, La Cartuja is nicknamed the "Christian Alhambra" for its elaborate white Baroque stucco work. In the rooms just off the cloister, notice the gruesome paintings of martyrs placidly meeting their grisly fates.

Cost and Hours: €3.50, daily April-Oct 10:00-13:00 & 16:00-20:00, Nov-March 10:00-13:00 & 15:00-18:00, catch bus #8 from Gran Vía del Colón, tel. 958-161-932. The monastery is a mile north of town on the way to Madrid; drivers take the *Méndez Núñez* exit from the A-44 expressway and follow signs.

Sleeping in Granada

In July and August, when Granada's streets are littered with sunstroke victims, rooms are plentiful and prices soft. In the crowded months of April, May, September, and October, prices can spike up 20 percent. (If you see a price range below, it indicates low- to high-season rates—though I've excluded Holy Week and other inflated prices.) Except for the hotels in the Albayzín and near the Alhambra, most of my listings are within a 5-to-10-minute walk of Plaza Nueva (see map on page 551).

Given all the restrictions, it's difficult to drive into Granada even when you know the system (see "Arrival in Granada" on page 504). While few hotels have parking facilities, any of them can direct you to a garage (such as Parking San Agustín, just off Gran Vía del Colón, €25/day).

On or near Plaza Nueva

Each of these (except the hostel) is big, professional, plenty comfortable, and perfectly located. Prices vary with demand.

$$$ Casa del Capitel Nazarí, just off the church end of Plaza Nueva, is a restored 16th-century Renaissance palace transformed into 18 small but tastefully decorated rooms, all facing a courtyard that hosts changing art exhibits (Sb-€60-88, Db-€75-118, extra bed-€35-38, breakfast-€9, includes afternoon tea/coffee, aircon, free Internet access and Wi-Fi, parking-€18.50/day, Cuesta Aceituneros 6, tel. 958-215-260, fax 958-215-806, www.hotelcasa capitel.com, info@hotelcasacapitel.com).

$$$ Hotel Casa 1800 Granada, with 25 rooms around a beautiful, airy old courtyard in the lower part of the Albayzín

Sleep Code

(€1 = about $1.40, country code: 34)

S = Single, **D** = Double/Twin, **T** = Triple, **Q** = Quad, **b** = bathroom, **s** = shower only. Unless otherwise noted, credit cards are accepted and English is spoken. Prices include the IVA hotel tax. Breakfast may or may not be included.

To help you easily sort through these listings, I've divided the accommodations into three categories based on the price for a standard double room with bath during high season:

$$$ Higher Priced—Most rooms €100 or more.
  $$ Moderately Priced—Most rooms between €50-100.
    $ Lower Priced—Most rooms €50 or less.

Prices can change without notice; verify the hotel's current rates online or by email. For other updates, see www.ricksteves.com/update.

GRANADA

(just steps above the Paseo de los Tristes), sets the bar for affordable class. It's tidy and well-run, and offers special extras, such as a complimentary tea and coffee bar each afternoon (standard Db-€135, pricier "superior" and "deluxe" rooms are available but not much different, big buffet breakfast-€11, air-con, elevator, free Wi-Fi, Benalúa 11, tel. 958-210-700, www.hotelcasa1800granada.com, info@hotelcasa1800granada.com).

$$$ Hotel Maciá Plaza, right on the colorful Plaza Nueva, has 44 smallish, clean, modern, and classy rooms. Choose between an on-the-square view or a quieter interior room (Sb-€60-75, Db-€120, €20 extra for a square view, extra bed-€15, 10 percent discount in 2012 when you show this book at check-in—but you must book direct, good buffet breakfast-€7.50, air-con, elevator, free Wi-Fi, Plaza Nueva 5, tel. 958-227-536, fax 958-227-533, www.maciahoteles.com, maciaplaza@maciahoteles.com).

$$ Hotel Anacapri is a bright, cool marble oasis with 49 modern rooms and a quiet lounge (Sb-€55-65, Db-€75-97, Tb-€95-117, extra bed-€20, includes breakfast with direct bookings in 2012 except with promotional rates, air-con, elevator, free limited Internet access and free Wi-Fi in lobby with this book, parking-€15, 2 blocks toward Gran Vía from Plaza Nueva at Calle Joaquín Costa 7, just a block from cathedral bus stop, tel. 958-227-477, fax 958-228-909, www.hotelanacapri.com, reservas@hotelanacapri.com, helpful Kathy speaks Iowan).

$$ NH Hotel Inglaterra is a modern and peaceful chain hotel, with 36 rooms offering all the comforts (Db-€55-90, extra bed-€20-30, buffet breakfast-€13, air-con, elevator to third floor

Granada Hotels & Restaurants

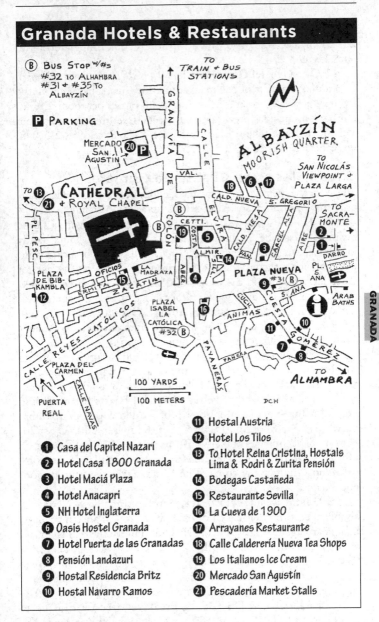

1. Casa del Capitel Nazarí
2. Hotel Casa 1800 Granada
3. Hotel Maciá Plaza
4. Hotel Anacapri
5. NH Hotel Inglaterra
6. Oasis Hostel Granada
7. Hotel Puerta de las Granadas
8. Pensión Landazuri
9. Hostal Residencia Britz
10. Hostal Navarro Ramos
11. Hostal Austria
12. Hotel Los Tilos
13. To Hotel Reina Cristina, Hostals Lima & Rodri & Zurita Pensión
14. Bodegas Castañeda
15. Restaurante Sevilla
16. La Cueva de 1900
17. Arrayanes Restaurante
18. Calle Calderería Nueva Tea Shops
19. Los Italianos Ice Cream
20. Mercado San Agustín
21. Pescadería Market Stalls

only, free Wi-Fi in lobby, parking-€14, Cetti Merien 6, tel. 958-221-559, fax 958-227-100, www.nh-hotels.com, nhinglaterra@nh-hotels.com).

$ Oasis Hostel Granada offers 90 beds in 11 rooms (all with bathrooms) and lots of backpacker bonding, just a block above the lively Moorish-flavored tourist drag (6-10 bunks per room, €16-20 per person, includes breakfast and sheets, free Internet access and Wi-Fi, shared kitchen, Placeta Correo Viejo 3, tel. 958-215-848, www.hostelsoasis.com).

Cheap Sleeps on Cuesta de Gomérez

These are inexpensive and ramshackle lodgings on this pedestrian-only street leading from Plaza Nueva up to the Alhambra.

$$ Hotel Puerta de las Granadas has 16 rooms with a sterile business-class vibe, an inviting cafeteria courtyard, and a handy location (basic patio-view Db-€59-89, €5-10 more for street view, €15 more for cathedral view, €25 more for Alhambra view, ask for 5 percent Rick Steves discount in 2012 if you book direct, breakfast-€8 or included during slow times, air-con, free Internet access and Wi-Fi, free tea in cafeteria all day, Cuesta de Gomérez 14, tel. 958-216-230, fax 958-216-231, www.hotelpuertadelasgranadas.com, reservas@hotelpuertadelasgranadas.com).

$ Pensión Landazuri is run by friendly English-speaking Matilde Landazuri, her son Manolo, and daughters Margarita and Elisa. Their characteristic old house has 18 rooms—some are well-worn, while others are renovated. It boasts hardworking, helpful management and a great roof garden with an Alhambra view (S-€24, Sb-€36, D-€34, Db-€45, Tb-€60, Qb-€70, eggs-and-bacon breakfast-€3.50, parking-€10/day, Cuesta de Gomérez 24, tel. & fax 958-221-406, www.hostallandazuri.com, info@hostallandazuri.com). The Landazuris also run a good, cheap café.

$ Hostal Residencia Britz, overlooking Plaza Nueva, is simple and no-nonsense. All of its 22 basic rooms are streetside—bring earplugs (S-€25, D-€36, Db-€48, no breakfast, fans but no air-con, elevator, free Wi-Fi, Plaza Nueva y Gomérez 1, tel. & fax 958-223-652, www.lisboaweb.com, reservasbritz@hotmail.com).

$ Hostal Navarro Ramos is a little cash-only cheapie, renting seven rooms (five with private baths) facing an interior air-shaft (S-€20, D-€27, Db-€36, no breakfast, free Wi-Fi, Cuesta de Gomérez 21, tel. 958-250-555, www.pensionnavarroramos.com, Carmen).

$ Hostal Austria, run by English-speaking Austrian Irene (ee-RAY-nay), rents 16 basic but tidy backpacker-type rooms (Sb-€25-30, Db-€35-40, Tb-€50-60, Qb-€65-75, Quint/b-€80-90, family rooms, no breakfast, air-con, free Wi-Fi, Cuesta de

Gomérez 4, tel. & fax 958-227-075, www.pensionaustria.com, pensionaustria@pensionaustria.com).

Near the Cathedral

$$ Hotel Los Tilos offers 30 comfortable, business-like rooms (some with balconies) on the charming traffic-free Plaza de Bib-Rambla behind the cathedral. Guests are welcome to use the fourth-floor terrace with views of the cathedral and the Alhambra (Sb-€45-55, Db-€55-80, Tb-€77-100, prices may be cheaper if you reserve online, free breakfast when you book direct and show the 2012 edition of this book at check-in, air-con, free Wi-Fi, parking-€18/day, Plaza de Bib-Rambla 4, tel. 958-266-712, fax 958-266-801, www.hotellostilos.com, clientes@hotellostilos.com, friendly José María).

On or near Plaza de la Trinidad

The charming, park-like square called Plaza de la Trinidad is just a short walk west of the cathedral area (Pescadería and Bib-Rambla squares). It's also home to several good accommodations.

$$$ Hotel Reina Cristina has 55 quiet, elegant rooms a few steps off Plaza de la Trinidad. Check out the great Mudejar ceiling and the painting at the entrance of this house, where the famous Spanish poet Federico García Lorca hid until he was captured and executed by the Guardia Civil (Sb-€46-90, Db-€66-139, Tb-€81-169, skip breakfast to save €13 per person, air-con, elevator, pay Internet access, free Wi-Fi in lobby, parking-€18/day, near Plaza de la Trinidad at Tablas 4, tel. 958-253-211, fax 958-255-728, www.hotelreinacristina.com, clientes@hotelreinacristina.com).

$ Hostal Lima, run with class by Manolo, has 25 small but well-appointed rooms in two buildings a block off the square. The public areas are decorated with flamboyant medieval flair—colorful tiles, wood-carved life-sized figures, and so on (Sb-€33, Db-€42, Tb-€65, breakfast-€6, air-con, elevator in one building only, free Wi-Fi, parking-€12, Laurel de las Tablas 17, tel. 958-295-029, www.hostallimagranada.com).

$ Hostal Rodri, run by Manolo's brother José, has 10 similarly good rooms a few doors down that feel new and classy for their price range (Sb-€30, Db-€43, breakfast-€6, air-con, free cable Internet, parking-€12, Laurel de las Tablas 9, tel. 958-288-043, www.hostalrodri.com, info@hostalrodri.com).

$ Zurita Pensión, well-run by Francisco and Loli, faces Plaza de la Trinidad. Eight of the 14 rooms have small balconies, but even with their double-paned windows, they may come with night noise (S-€21, D-€34, Db-€42, Tb-€63, air-con, free Wi-Fi, parking-€12-15/day, Plaza de la Trinidad 7, tel. 958-275-020, www.pensionzurita.com, pensionzurita@gmail.com).

In the Albayzín

Note that some consider this area sketchy after dark (see sidebar on page 544).

$$ Hotel Santa Isabel la Real, an elegant medieval mansion, has 11 rooms ringing a noble courtyard. Each room is a bit different; basic rooms look to the patio, while various pricier rooms have better exterior views. Buried deep in the Albayzín and furnished in a way that gives you the old Moorish Granada ambience, it offers a warm welcome and rich memories (Db-€85-105 with breakfast, air-con, elevator, free Internet access and Wi-Fi, parking-€14/day, midway between San Nicolás viewpoint and Plaza San Miguel Bajo on Calle Santa Isabel la Real, immediately at a bus stop, tel. 958-294-658, fax 958-294-645, www.hotelsantaisabellareal.com, info@hotelsantaisabellareal.com).

$$ El Numero 8 "Casa de Rafa" is a traditional house in the heart of the Albayzín that's been converted into four small, funky kitchenette apartments with an eclectic, ever-evolving artistic feel. Chicago-raised, easygoing owner Rafa lives on-site. You'll share two tiny patios and a rooftop terrace with a spectacular, in-your-face view of the Alhambra. Contact Rafa in advance to set up a time to check in. He'll ease your arrival by meeting you at a taxi or bus drop-off point and walking you back to the apartment (Sb-€40-50, Db-€50-65, extra person-€10, 2-night minimum, fans but no air-con, free Wi-Fi, 5-minute walk from Plaza Nueva at tiny Plaza Virgen del Carmen—see map on page 543, tel. 958-220-682, mobile 610-322-216, www.elnumero8.com, casaocho@gmail.com).

$$ 1001 Nights Granada, run by American Frederick and his Spanish wife, rents 15 renovated and fully furnished duplexes and apartments in traditional Moorish houses situated in the Albayzín district, many with grand Alhambra views (Db-€90 in March-May and Sept-Oct, €72 in July-Aug and Jan-Feb, prices vary with size—see photos and videos on website, 2-night minimum—longer during holidays, 20 percent deposit required to reserve online, pay the balance in cash after you arrive, electronic check-in so arrive when you like, no breakfast, air-con, free Wi-Fi, some units have private terraces and swimming pools, mobile 620-585-594, www.1001nights.es, info@1001nights.es).

$ Makuto Guesthouse, a hostel tucked deep in the Albayzín, feels like a hippie commune you can pay to join for a couple of days. With 40 beds in seven rooms clustered around a lush garden courtyard that feels made for hanging out—including several hammock-and-lounge-sofa "hang-out zones"—it exudes an easygoing Albayzín vibe (Db-€50-60, bunk in 4-to-6-bed room-€15-18, includes breakfast, free Internet access and Wi-Fi, din-

ners available most nights, Calle Tiña 18, tel. 958-805-876, www
.makutoguesthouse.com).

In or near the Alhambra

If you want to stay on the Alhambra grounds, you have two popular options (famous, overpriced, and generally booked up long in
advance) and one practical and economic place above the parking
lot. All are a half-mile up the hill from Plaza Nueva.

$$$ Parador de Granada San Francisco offers 40 designer
rooms in a former Moorish palace that was later transformed into
a 15th-century Franciscan monastery. It's considered Spain's pre-
mier parador...and that's saying something (standard Db-€320,
breakfast-€20, air-con, free Wi-Fi, free parking, Calle Real de la
Alhambra, tel. 958-221-440, fax 958-222-264, www.parador.es,
granada@parador.es). You must book months ahead to spend the
night in this lavishly located, stodgy, and historic palace. Any peas-
ant, however, can drop in for a coffee, drink, snack, or meal. For
details about the history of the building, see sidebar on page 535.

$$$ Hotel América is classy and cozy, with 17 rooms in an
early-19th-century house next to the parador (Sb-€74, Db-€120,
€25-40 more for a bigger room with a terrace, breakfast-€8, free
Wi-Fi, parking-€14/day, closed Dec-Feb, Calle Real de la Alhambra 53, tel. 958-227-471, fax 958-227-470, www.hotelamerica
granada.com, reservas@hotelamericagranada.com, friendly Isabel).
Book well in advance.

$$ Hotel Guadalupe, big and modern with 57 sleek rooms,
is quietly and conveniently located overlooking the Alhambra
parking lot. While a 30-minute hike above the town, many
(especially drivers) find this to be a practical option (Sb-€50-72,
Db-€55-115, Tb-€80-135, bigger "superior" rooms with Jacuzzis
and balconies aren't worth the extra cost, breakfast-€9, air-con,
elevator, free Wi-Fi in lobby, parking in Alhambra lot-€14, Paseo
de la Sabica 30, tel. 958-225-730, www.hotelguadalupe.es, info
@hotelguadalupe.es).

Eating in Granada

Restaurants generally serve lunch from 13:00 to 16:00 and din-
ner from 20:00 until very late (Spaniards don't start dinner until
about 21:00). Many of Granada's bars still serve a small tapas
plate free with any beer or wine—a tradition that's dying out in
most of Spain. Save on your food expenses by doing a tapas crawl
(especially good along Calle Navas, right off Plaza del Carmen)
and claim your "right" to a free tapa with every drink. For more
budget-eating thrills, buy picnic supplies near Plaza Nueva, and

sling them up to the Albayzín. This makes for a great cheap date at the San Nicolás viewpoint or on one of the scattered squares and lookout points.

In search of an edible memory? A local specialty, *tortilla Sacromonte*, is a spicy omelet with pig's brain and other organs. *Berenjenas fritas* (fried eggplant) and *habas con jamón* (small green fava beans cooked with cured ham) are worth seeking out. *Tinto de verano*—a red-wine spritzer with lemon and ice—is refreshing on a hot evening. For tips on eating near the Alhambra, see page 523.

In the Albayzín

The most interesting meals hide out deep in the Albayzín (Moorish quarter). The easy way to get there is by taking minibus #31 from Plaza Nueva or #32 from Plaza Isabel La Católica. To find a particular square, ask any local, or follow my directions and the full-color Granada map at the front of this book. If dining late, take the minibus or a taxi back to your hotel; Albayzín back streets can be poorly lit, confusing to follow, and plagued by pickpockets.

Part of the charm of the quarter is the lazy ambience on its squares: **Plaza Larga** is extremely characteristic, with tapas bar tables spilling out onto the square, a morning market, and a much-loved pastry shop. But the next area is even more enticing...

Plaza San Miguel el Bajo: The farthest hike into the Albayzín, this neighborhood square boasts my favorite funky local scene—kids kicking soccer balls, old-timers warming benches, and women gossiping under the facade of a humble church. It's circled by inviting little bars and restaurants. **El Acebuche** promises "Andalusian flavor with a light dash of the Orient" (€11-16 meals, daily). **Rincón de la Aurora** has a €10 weekday fixed-price meal and €6-12 meals anytime, plus tapas (closed Wed and Sun afternoon). **El Ají** is a sit-down restaurant with a mod vibe and a bit of Argentinian flair (€10-14 starters, €12-20 main dishes, closed Tue). And just down the street (beyond El Ají) is a little hole-in-the-wall **take-away shop** selling empanadas and pizza by the slice to munch out on the square (closed Tue). This is a great spot to end your Albayzín visit, as there's a viewpoint overlooking the modern city a block away. Minibuses #31 and #32 rumble by every few minutes, ready to zip you back to Plaza Nueva.

Casa Torcuato is a hardworking eatery serving straightforward yet creative food in a smart upstairs dining room. They serve good fixed-price meals for lunch (€10) and dinner (€15).

Plates of fresh fish run €8-12 and their tropical salad includes a Tahitian wonderland of fruits (closed Sun, 2 blocks beyond Plaza Larga at Calle Aqua 20, second location on nearby Calle Pagés, tel. 958-202-039).

Restaurante El Ladrillo, with outdoor tables on a peaceful square, is *the* place for piles of fish. Their popular €12 *barco* ("boat-load" of mixed fried fish) is a fishy feast that stuffs two to the gills. The smaller €7.50 *canoa* ("canoe") fills one person adequately, or, when combined with a salad, can feed two (€5 salads, €9-12 fish dishes, daily 12:00-24:00, on Placeta de Fátima, just off Calle Pagés).

Near the San Nicolás Viewpoint

This area is thoroughly touristy, so don't expect any local hangouts here. But these two options are suitable for a good meal.

Restaurante Estrellas de San Nicolás, in the former home of a well-loved Albayzín bigwig, immediately next to the view terrace, features similar views from its two floors of indoor seating. Serving well-regarded food, this splurge has quickly acquired a loyal local following (€10-20 starters, €20-27 main dishes, €31 fixed-price diner, €20 or €27 fixed-price lunch, Atrazana Vieja 1, tel. 958-288-739).

Bar Kiki, a laid-back and popular bar-restaurant on an unpretentious square, serves simple tapas. Try their tasty fried eggplant (random hours, closed Wed, just behind viewpoint at Plaza de San Nicolás 9).

Paseo de los Tristes: This spot is like a stage set of outdoor bars on a terrace over the river gorge. While it lacks a serious restaurant and the food values are mediocre at best, the scene—cool along a stream under trees, with the floodlit Alhambra high above, and a happy crowd of locals enjoying a meal or drink out—is a winner. As this is at the base of the Albayzín, there's no issue of danger after dark here. It's a simple, level five-minute walk back to Plaza Nueva.

Carmens in the Albayzín

For a more memorable but expensive experience, consider fine dining with Alhambra views in a *carmen*, a typical Albayzín house with a garden (buzz to get in). After the Reconquista, the Albayzín became depopulated. Wealthy families took larger tracts of land and built fortified mansions with terraced gardens within their walls. Today, rather than growing produce, the gardens of many of these *carmens* host dining tables and pricey, romantic restaurants.

Carmen Mirador de Aixa, small and elegant, has the dreamiest Alhambra views among the *carmens*. You'll pay a little more, but the food is exquisitely presented and the view makes the splurge worthwhile (€10-20 starters, €20-27 main dishes; closed Sun dinner, all day Mon, and Tue lunch; next to Carmen de las Tomasas at Carril de San Agustín 2, tel. 958-223-616).

Carmen de las Tomasas serves gourmet traditional Andalusian cuisine with killer views in a dressy/stuffy atmosphere (€9-17 starters, €20-26 main dishes, Wed-Sun 13:00-16:00 & 20:15-23:30, generally—but not always—closed Mon-Tue, reservations required, Carril de San Agustín, tel. 958-224-108, Cristina).

Carmen de Aben Humeya is the least expensive, least stuffy, and least romantic. Its outdoor-only seating lets you enjoy a meal or just a long cup of coffee while gazing at the Alhambra. This is a rare place enthusiastic about dinner salads (€10-18 starters and main dishes, daily 13:00-24:00, food served 13:30-15:30 & 20:30-23:30, closed Wed, also closed Tue evenings in winter, Cuesta de las Tomasas 12, tel. 958-226-665).

Near Plaza Nueva

For people-watching, consider the many restaurants on Plaza Nueva or Plaza de Bib-Rambla (south of cathedral). For a happening scene, check out the bars on and around Calle de Elvira. It's best to wander and see where the biggest crowds are.

Bodegas Castañeda is the best mix of lively, central, and cheap among the tapas bars I visited. Just a block off Plaza Nueva, it requires a bit of self-service: When crowded, you need to power your way to the bar to order; when quiet, you can order at the bar and grab a little table (same budget prices). Consider their *tablas combinadas*—variety plates of cheese, meat, and *ahumados* (four different varieties of smoked fish)—and tasty *croquetas* (breaded and fried mashed potatoes and ham). Order a glass of their gazpacho. The big kegs tempt you with different local sherries. Tapas can be ordered from an easy menu and cost €2-3 apiece (€6-11 half-*raciones*, €10-15 *raciones*, daily 11:30-16:30 & 19:00-1:00 in the morning, Calle Almireceros 1, tel. 958-215-464). Don't be confused by the neighboring, similar "Antigua Bodega Castañeda" restaurant nearby (run by a relative and not as good).

Restaurante Sevilla, with its tight and charming little dining room behind a high-energy tapas bar, has been a favorite of well-dressed natives for 75 years. Specialties include paella, other rice dishes, soups, and salads. You'll eat surrounded by old photos of local big shots who've dined here. On hot nights, tables pour out onto the little square facing the Royal Chapel. It's a local-feeling, elegant, urban scene. In the evenings, the bar displays a yummy spread of tapas—you get one free with any drink you buy, and can pay €0.50 for each additional one (€8-12 starters, €14-20 main dishes, daily 9:00-24:00 except closed Sun evenings in summer, may close for renovation in 2012; across from Royal Chapel at

Calle Oficios 12, tel. 958-221-223).

La Cueva de 1900 is a fresh, family-friendly deli-like place on the main drag appreciated for its simple dishes and quality ingredients. It's proud of its homemade hams, sausages, and cheeses—sold in 100-gram lots and served with checkered-tablecloth style. Their fixed-price lunch is €10, but if you've had enough meat, try one of their good €5-7 salads (€3-4 *bocadillo* sandwiches, €8-16 meaty meals, daily 12:00-24:00, Calle Reyes Católicos 42, tel. 958-229-327).

At **Arrayanes,** a good Moroccan restaurant, Mostafa will help you choose among the many salads, the *briwat* (a chicken-and-cinnamon pastry appetizer), the *pastela* (a first-course version of *briwat*), the couscous, or *tajin* dishes. He treats his guests like old friends...especially the ladies (€4-10 starters, €10-14 main dishes, Wed-Mon 13:30-16:30 & 19:30-23:30, closed Tue, Cuesta Marañas 4, where Calles Calderería Nueva and Vieja meet, tel. 958-228-401, mobile 619-076-862).

Hippie Options on Calle Calderería Nueva: From Plaza Nueva, walk two long blocks down Calle de Elvira and turn right onto the wonderfully hip and Arabic-feeling Calle Calderería Nueva, which leads uphill into the Albayzín. The street is lined with trendy *teterías.* These small tea shops, open all day, are good places to linger, chat, and imagine you're in Morocco. Many also have the opportunity to rent a hookah (water pipe) to smoke some fruit-flavored tobacco with friends. Some are conservative and unmemorable, and others are achingly romantic, filled with incense, beaded cushions, live African music, and effervescent young hippies. They sell light meals such as crêpes, and a worldwide range of teas, all marinated in a candlelit snake-charmer ambience.

Dessert: **Los Italianos,** Italian-run and teeming with locals, is popular for its ice cream, *horchata* (*chufa*-nut drink), and shakes. When Michelle Obama visited Granada in 2010, this is where she got her ice-cream fix (mid-March-mid-Oct daily 8:00-24:00, closed off-season, across the street from cathedral and Royal Chapel at Gran Vía 4, tel. 958-224-034).

Markets: Though heavy on meat, **Mercado San Agustín** also sells fruits and veggies. Throughout the EU, locals lament the loss of the authentic old market halls as they are replaced with new hygienic versions. If nothing else, it's as refreshingly cool as a meat locker (Mon-Sat 9:00-15:00, closed Sun, very quiet on Mon, a block north of cathedral and a half-block off Gran Vía on Calle Cristo San Agustín). Tucked away in the back of the market is a very cheap and colorful little eatery: **Cafetería San Agustín.** They make their own *churros* and give a small tapa free with each drink (menu on wall). If waiting for the cathedral or Royal Chapel to open, kill time in the market. The stalls around the market and the

Pescadería square, downhill from the actual market and a block from Plaza de Bib-Rambla, are actually more popular with locals looking to buy produce.

Granada Connections

From Granada by Train to: Barcelona (1/day Wed, Thu, and Sat only, 11.5 hours; also 1/night daily, 12.5 hours), **Madrid** (2/day on Altaria, 4.5 hours), **Toledo** (all service is via Madrid, nearly hourly AVE connections to Toledo), **Algeciras** (3/day, 4.25 hours), **Ronda** (3/day, 2.5 hours), **Sevilla** (4/day, 3 hours), **Córdoba** (2/day, 2.5 hours), **Málaga** (3/day, 2.5-3.25 hours on AVE, transfer in Bobadilla or Antequera). Train info: toll tel. 902-320-320, www.renfe.com. Many of these connections have a more frequent (and sometimes much faster) bus option—see below.

By Bus to: Nerja (7/day, 2-2.5 hours, more possible with transfer in Motril), **Sevilla** (to Plaza de Armas Station: 8/day, 3 hours *directo*, 4 hours *ruta*; to El Prado Station: 2/day, 3.25 hours), **Córdoba** (8/day, 2.5-3 hours), **Madrid** (roughly hourly, 5 hours, most to Estación Sur, a few to Intercambiador de Avenida de América, one direct to Barajas Airport), **Málaga** (hourly, 1.5-2 hours), **Algeciras** (4/day *directo*, 4 hours; 1/day *ruta*, 5.5 hours), **La**

Línea de la Concepción/Gibraltar (2/week on Fri and Sun, 5.5 hours; otherwise change in Algeciras), **Jerez** (1/day, 4.75 hours), **Barcelona** (4/day, 12.75-15 hours, often at odd times, only one fully daytime connection departs Granada at 10:00 and arrives Barcelona at 24:15). To reach **Ronda,** change in Málaga or Antequera; to reach **Tarifa,** change in Algeciras or Málaga. All of these buses are run by Alsa (tel. 902-422-242, www.alsa.es). If there's a long line at the ticket windows, you can use the automated machines (press the flag for English)—but these only sell tickets for some major routes (such as Málaga), and sometimes eat credit cards like a Spaniard eats *jamón*.

By Car: To drive to **Nerja** (1.5 hours away), take the exit for the coastal town of Motril. You'll wind through 50 scenic miles south of Granada, then follow signs for Málaga. You can also hop a taxi to Nerja (€125 fixed rate).

SEVILLA

Flamboyant Sevilla thrums with flamenco music, sizzles in the summer heat, and pulses with the passion of Don Juan and Carmen. It's a place where bullfighting is still politically correct and little girls still dream of growing up to become flamenco dancers. While Granada has the great Alhambra and Córdoba has the remarkable Mezquita, Sevilla has a soul. (Soul—or *duende*—is fundamental to flamenco.) It's a wonderful-to-be-alive-in kind of place.

The gateway to the New World in the 16th century, Sevilla boomed when Spain did. The explorers Amerigo Vespucci and Ferdinand Magellan sailed from its great river harbor, discovering new trade routes and abundant sources of gold, silver, cocoa, and tobacco. In the 17th century, Sevilla was Spain's largest and wealthiest city. Local artists Diego Velázquez, Bartolomé Murillo, and Francisco de Zurbarán made it a cultural center. Sevilla's Golden Age—and its New World riches—ended when the harbor silted up and the Spanish empire crumbled.

In the 19th century, Sevilla was a big stop on the Romantic "Grand Tour" of Europe. To build on this tourism and promote trade among Spanish-speaking nations, Sevilla planned a grand exposition in 1929. Bad year. The expo crashed along with the stock market. In 1992 Sevilla got a second chance at a world's fair. This expo was a success, leaving the city with an impressive infrastructure: a new airport, a train station, sleek bridges, and the super AVE bullet train (making Sevilla a 2.5-hour side-trip from Madrid). In 2007, the main boulevards—once thundering with noisy traffic and mercilessly cutting the city in two—were

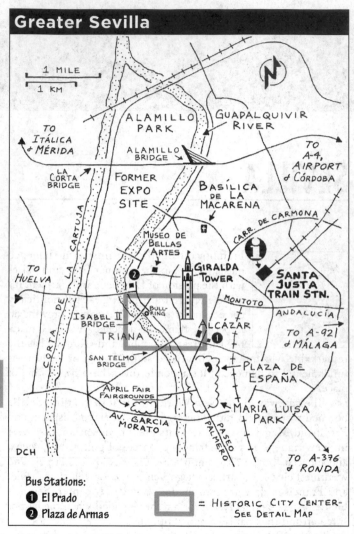

Greater Sevilla

1 MILE
1 KM

ALAMILLO PARK

GUAPALQUIVIR RIVER

TO ITÁLICA & MÉRIDA

ALAMILLO BRIDGE

TO A-4, AIRPORT & CÓRDOBA

LA CORTA BRIDGE

FORMER EXPO SITE

BASÍLICA DE LA MACARENA

CARR. DE CARMONA

LA CARTUJA

MUSEO DE BELLAS ARTES

GIRALDA TOWER

SANTA JUSTA TRAIN STN.

TO HUELVA

CORTA DE

MONTOTO

ANDALUCÍA

ISABEL II BRIDGE

BULL-RING

ALCÁZAR

TO A-921 & MÁLAGA

TRIANA

SAN TELMO BRIDGE

PLAZA DE ESPAÑA

APRIL FAIR FAIRGROUNDS

MARÍA LUISA PARK

AV. GARCIA MORATO

PASEO PALMERO

DCH

TO A-376 & RONDA

Bus Stations:
❶ El Prado
❷ Plaza de Armas

☐ = HISTORIC CITY CENTER—
SEE DETAIL MAP

pedestrianized, dramatically enhancing Sevilla's already substantial charm.

Today, Spain's fourth-largest city (pop. 704,000) is Andalucía's leading destination, buzzing with festivals, color, guitars, castanets, and street life, and enveloped in the fragrances of orange trees, jacaranda, and myrtle. James Michener wrote, "Sevilla doesn't *have* ambience, it *is* ambience." Sevilla also has its share of impressive sights. Its cathedral is Spain's largest. The Alcázar is a fantastic royal palace and garden ornamented with Mudejar (Islamic) flair. But the real magic is the city itself, with its tangled former Jewish Quarter, riveting flamenco shows, thriving bars, and teeming evening paseo.

Planning Your Time

On a three-week trip, spend two nights and two days here. On even the shortest Spanish trip, I'd zip here on the slick AVE train for a day trip from Madrid. With more time, if ever there was a Spanish city to linger in, it's Sevilla.

The major sights are few and simple for a city of this size. The cathedral and the Alcázar are worth about three hours, and a

wander through the Santa Cruz district takes about an hour. You could spend half a day touring Sevilla's other sights. Stroll along the bank of the Guadalquivir River and cross Isabel II Bridge (also known as the Bridge of Triana) for a view of the cathedral and Torre del Oro. An evening here is essential for the paseo and a flamenco show. Stay up at least once until midnight (or later) to appreciate Sevilla on a warm night—one of its major charms.

Bullfights take place on most Sundays in May and June, on Easter and Corpus Christi, daily through the April Fair, and in late September. The Museo de Bellas Artes is closed on Monday. Tour groups clog the Alcázar and cathedral in the morning; go late in the day to avoid the lines.

Córdoba (see next chapter) is a convenient and worthwhile side-trip from Sevilla, or a handy stopover if you're taking the AVE to or from Madrid.

Orientation to Sevilla

For the tourist, this big city is small. The bull's-eye on your map should be the cathedral and its Giralda Bell Tower, which can be seen from all over town. Nearby

are Sevilla's other major sights, the Alcázar (palace and gardens) and the lively Santa Cruz district. The central north–south pedestrian boulevard, Avenida de la Constitución (with TIs, banks, a post office, and other services), stretches north a few blocks to Plaza Nueva, gateway to the shopping district. A few blocks west of the cathedral are the bullring and the Guadalquivir River, while Plaza de España is a few blocks south. Triana, the area on the west bank of the Guadalquivir River, is working-class and colorful, but lacks tourist sights. With most sights walkable, and taxis so friendly, easy, and affordable, I rarely bother with the bus.

Sevilla is an easy city to get turned around in. Be aware that city maps from the tourist office are oriented with north to the left, while this book's maps put north on top.

Tourist Information

Sevilla has tourist offices wherever you need them—at the **airport** (Mon-Fri 9:00-19:30, Sat-Sun 9:30-15:00, tel. 954-782-035), **train station** (overlooking tracks 6-7, Mon-Fri 9:00-19:30, Sat-Sun 9:30-15:00, tel. 954-782-003), and in three central locations near Avenida de la Constitución: near the river side of the **Alcázar** (Mon-Fri 9:00-19:30, Sat-Sun 9:30-15:00, Avenida de la Constitución 21, tel. 954-787-578); across the small square from the **cathedral** entrance (Mon-Sat 10:30-14:30 & 15:30-19:30, Sun 10:30-14:30, Plaza del Triunfo, tel. 954-210-005); and near **Plaza Nueva** (Mon-Fri 9:00-19:30, Sat-Sun 10:00-14:00, a block north of the square on Plaza San Francisco, tel. 954-595-288, free Internet access for one hour at certain times—see "Helpful Hints," later).

At any TI, ask for the city map, the English-language magazines *Welcome Olé* and *The Tourist,* and a current listing of sights with opening times. The free monthly events guide—*El Giraldillo,* written in Spanish basic enough to be understood by travelers— covers cultural events throughout Andalucía, with a focus on Sevilla. The Alcázar and airport TIs cover all of Andalucía as well as Sevilla; if you stop at one of these, ask for information you might need for elsewhere in the region (for example, if heading south, ask for the free *Route of the White Towns* brochure and a Jerez map). Helpful websites are www.turismosevilla.org and www.andalucia.org.

The **Sevilla Card** (sold at the ICONOS shop next to the Alcázar TI, Mon-Sat 10:00-20:30, Sun 11:00-19:00; or at the train station's hotel room–finding booth overlooking track 11) covers admission to most of Sevilla's sights (including the cathedral, Alcázar, Flamenco Dance Museum, Basílica de la Macarena, Bullfight Museum, and more), and gives discounts at some hotels and restaurants. It's doubtful whether any but the busiest sightseer would save much money using the card (€29/24 hours—includes choice of 2 museums and river cruise; €47/48 hours—includes all sights and choice of river cruise or bus tour; €60/72 hours or €80/120 hours—includes all sights plus cruise and bus tour; www .sevillacard.es). If you're over 65, keep in mind that even without the Sevilla Card, you'll get into the Alcázar free and into the cathedral almost free.

Arrival in Sevilla

By Train: Trains arrive at the sublime Santa Justa station, with banks, ATMs, and a TI. Baggage storage *(cosigna)* is below track 1 (€3-5/day depending on size of bag, security checkpoint). The TI overlooks tracks 6-7. If you don't have a hotel room reserved, the room-finding booth above track 11 can help; you can also get maps and other tourist information here if the TI line is long (Mon-Fri 10:00-20:30, Sat 10:00-14:30 & 16:30-20:30, Sun 9:30-14:30). The plush little AVE Sala Club, designed for business travelers, welcomes those with a first-class AVE ticket and reservation (across the main hall from track 1).

The town center is marked by the ornate Giralda Bell Tower, pecking above the apartment flats (visible from the front of the station—with your back to the tracks, it's at 1 o'clock). To get into the center, it's a flat and boring 25-minute walk (longer if you get lost) or a €5 taxi ride. By city bus, it's a short ride on #C1 to the El Prado bus station (€1.30, pay driver, find bus stop 100 yards in front of the train station), then a 10-minute walk.

By Bus: Sevilla's two major bus stations both have information offices, basic eateries, and baggage storage. The **El Prado station** covers most of Andalucía (daily 7:00-22:00, information tel. 954-417-111, no English spoken; baggage storage/*consigna* at the far end of station—€2/day, daily 9:00-21:00). From the bus station to downtown (and Barrio Santa Cruz hotels), it's about a 10-minute walk: Exit the station to the right, and cross the busy street at the big roundabout. Turn right and keep the fenced-in gardens on your left. At the end of the fence, duck left through the Murillo Gardens and into the heart of Barrio Santa Cruz (use the color map in the front of this book to navigate). To cut a few minutes off the walk—or to reach the hotels near Plaza Nueva—take the city's short tram from the El Prado station (€1.30, buy ticket at machine before boarding; ride it two stops to Archivo de Indias to reach the cathedral area, or three stops to Plaza Nueva).

The **Plaza de Armas station** (near the river, opposite the Expo '92 site) serves long-distance destinations such as Madrid, Barcelona, Lagos, and Lisbon. Ticket counters line one wall, an information kiosk is in the center, and at the end of the hall are luggage lockers (€3.50/day). As you exit onto the main road (Calle Arjona), the bus stop is to the left, in front of the taxi stand (bus #C4 goes downtown, €1.30, pay driver, get off at Puerta de Jerez near main TI). Taxis to downtown cost around €5.

By Car: To drive into Sevilla, follow *centro ciudad* (city center) signs and stay along the river. For short-term parking on the street, the riverside Paseo de Cristóbal Colón has two-hour meters and hardworking thieves. Ignore the bogus traffic wardens who direct you to an illegal spot, take a tip, and disappear later when your car gets towed. For long-term parking, hotels charge as much as a normal garage. For simplicity, I'd just park at a central garage (€15-20/day) and catch a taxi to my hotel. Try the big one under the bus station at Plaza de Armas, the Cristóbal Colón garage by the bullring and river, the Plaza Nueva garage on Albareda, or the one at Avenida Roma/Puerta de Jerez (cash only). For hotels in the Santa Cruz area, the handiest parking is the Cano y Cueto garage near the corner of Calle Santa María la Blanca and Menéndez Pelayo (open 24/7, at edge of big park, unsigned and underground).

By Plane: The Especial Aeropuerto (EA) bus connects the airport with the train station and town center, terminating south of the Alcázar gardens on Avenida del Cid (€2.40, 2/hour, 30 minutes, buy ticket from driver). If you're going from downtown Sevilla to the airport, ask your hotelier or the TI where to catch the bus; the stop is usually on Avenida del Cid by the Portugal Pavilion but can change because of religious processions, construction, and other factors. (The return bus also stops at the Santa Justa train station and the El Prado bus station.) To taxi into town, go to one of the airport's taxi stands to ensure a fixed rate (€22 by day, €24 at night and on weekends, €29 during Easter week, extra for luggage, confirm price with the driver before your journey). For flight information, call 954-449-000.

Getting Around Sevilla

Most visitors have a full and fun experience in Sevilla without ever riding public transportation. The city center is compact, and most of the major sights are within easy walking distance (the Basílica de la Macarena is a notable exception). On a hot day, air-conditioned buses can be a blessing.

By Taxi: Sevilla is a great taxi town. You can hail one anywhere, or find them parked by major intersections and sights (weekdays: €1.22 drop rate, €0.85/kilometer, €3.33 minimum; Sat-Sun, weekends, and nights between 21:00 and 7:00: €1.49 drop rate, €1.04/kilometer, €4.17 minimum; calling for a cab adds about €2-3. A quick daytime ride in town will be at or around the €3.33 minimum. Although I'm quick to take advantage of a taxi, thanks to one-way streets and traffic congestion it's often just as fast to hoof it between central points.

By Bus, Tram, and Metro: Due to ongoing construction projects in the city center, bus routes often change. It's best to check with your hotel or the TI for the latest updates.

A single trip on any form of city transit costs €1.30. You can also buy a Tarjeta Multiviajes card that's rechargeable and shareable (€6.40 for 10 trips without transfers, €7 with transfers, €1.50 deposit, buy at kiosks; for transit details, see www.tussam.es).

The various #C **buses,** which are handiest for tourists, make circular routes through town (note that all of them eventually wind up at Basílica de La Macarena). For all buses, buy your ticket from the driver. The #C3 stops at Murillo Gardens, Triana (district on the west bank of the river), then La Macarena. The #C4 goes the opposite direction without entering Triana. And the spunky little #C5 is a minibus that winds through the old center of town, including Plaza del Salvador, Plaza de San Francisco, the bullring, Plaza Nueva, the Museo de Bellas Artes, La Campana, and La Macarena, providing a fine and relaxing joyride that also connects some farther-flung sights.

A new **tram** *(tramvia)* makes just a few stops in the heart of the city, but can save you a bit of walking. Buy your ticket at the machine on the platform before you board (runs every 6-7 minutes until 1:45 in the morning). The handiest stops include (from south to north) Prado San Sebastián (El Prado Bus station), Puerta Jerez (the south end of Avenida de la Constitución), Archivo de Indias (next to the cathedral), and Plaza Nueva. Eventually the tram will reach the Santa Justa train station.

Sevilla also has a brand-new underground **metro,** but tourists won't need to use it. It's designed to connect the suburbs with the center and is only partially finished.

Helpful Hints

Festivals: Sevilla's peak season is April and May, and it has two one-week festival periods when the city is packed: Holy Week and April Fair.

While **Holy Week** (Semana Santa) is big all over Spain, it's biggest in Sevilla. It's held the week between Palm Sunday and Easter Sunday (April 1-8 in 2012). Locals start preparing for the big event up to a year in advance. What would normally be a five-minute walk can take an hour and a half if a procession crosses your path. But even these hassles seem irrelevant as you listen to the *saetas* (spontaneous devotional songs) and let the spirit of the festival take over.

Then, after Easter—after taking enough time off to catch its communal breath—Sevilla holds its **April Fair** (April 24-29 in 2012). This is a celebration of all things Andalusian, with plenty of eating, drinking, singing, and merrymaking (though most of the revelry takes place in private parties at a

Holy Week *(Semana Santa)* in Andalucía

Holy Week—the week between Palm Sunday and Easter (April 1-8 in 2012)—is a major holiday throughout the Christian world, but nowhere is it celebrated with as much fervor as in Andalucía, especially Sevilla. Holy Week is all about the events of the Passion of Jesus Christ: his entry into Jerusalem, his betrayal by Judas and arrest, his crucifixion, and his resurrection. In Sevilla, on each day throughout the week, 60 neighborhood groups (brotherhoods) parade from their neighborhood churches to the cathedral with floats depicting some aspect of the Passion story.

As the week approaches, the anticipation grows: Visitors pour into town, grandstands are erected along the parade routes, and TV stations anxiously monitor the weather report. The floats are so delicate that rain would force the processions (and live broadcasts) to be called off—a crushing disappointment.

By mid-afternoon of any day during Holy Week, thousands line the streets. The parade begins. First comes a line of "penitents" *(penitentes)*, carrying a big cross, candles, and incense. The penitents perform their penance publically but anonymously, their identities obscured by hooded robes. (The penitents' traditional hooded garb has been worn for centuries—long before such hoods became associated with racism in the American South.) Some processions are silent, but others are accompanied by beating drums, brass bands, or wailing singers.

A hush falls over the crowd as the floats approach. First comes a Passion float, showing Christ in some stage of the

large fairground).

Book rooms well in advance for these festival times. Prices can go sky-high, many hotels have four-night minimums, and food quality at touristy restaurants can plummet.

Internet Access: Almost every hotel in town has Wi-Fi, and many also have Internet terminals or loaner laptops for guests to use. Otherwise, try **Internetia,** a thriving-with-students Internet café with two dozen terminals (€2.30/hour, Wi-Fi, disc-burning, daily 10:00-23:00, about three blocks beyond the eastern edge of Santa Cruz at Avenida Menéndez Pelayo 43-45, tel. 954-534-003). The **TI at Plaza Nueva** (near Plaza San Francisco) offers up to one hour of free Internet access at eight terminals, as well as free Wi-Fi (Internet available only Mon-Fri 10:00-14:00 & 17:00-20:00, none Sat-Sun).

drama—being whipped, appearing before Pilate, or carrying the cross to his execution. More penitents follow—with dozens or even hundreds of participants, a procession can stretch out over a half-mile. All this sets the stage for the finale—typically a float of the Virgin Mary, who represents the hope of resurrection.

The elaborate floats feature carved wooden religious sculptures, some embellished with gold leaf and silverwork. They can be adorned with fresh flowers, rows of candles, and even jewelry on loan from the congregation. Each float is carried by 30 to 50 men, who labor unseen (you might catch a glimpse of their shuffling feet). The bearers wear turban-like headbands to protect their heads and necks from the crushing weight (the floats can weigh as much as two tons). Two "shifts" of float carriers rotate every 20 minutes. As a sign of their faith, some men carry the float until they collapse.

As the procession nears the cathedral, it passes through the square called La Campana, south along Calle Sierpes, and through Plaza de San Francisco. (Some parades follow a parallel route a block or two east.) Grandstands and folding chairs are filled by VIPs and Sevilla's prominent families. Thousands of candles drip wax along the well-trod parade routes, forming a waxy buildup that causes car tires to squeal for days to come.

Being in Sevilla for Holy Week is both a blessing and a curse. It's a remarkable spectacle, but it's extremely crowded. Parade routes can block your sightseeing for hours. Check printed schedules if you want to avoid them. If you do find a procession blocking your way, look for a crossing point marked by a red-painted fence, or ask a guard. Regardless of your own faith, the intense devotion of the Andalusian people is reason enough to appreciate their Holy Week traditions.

SEVILLA

Post Office: The post office is at Avenida de la Constitución 32, across from the cathedral (Mon-Fri 8:30-20:30, Sat 9:30-14:00, closed Sun).

Laundry: Lavandería Roma offers quick and economical drop-off service (€6/load wash-and-dry, Mon-Fri 9:30-14:00 & 17:30-20:30, Sat 9:00-14:00, closed Sun, 2 blocks inland from bullring at Castelar 2, tel. 954-210-535). Near the recommended Santa Cruz hotels, **La Segunda Vera Tintorería** has two machines for self-service (€6/load wash-and-dry, €10/load drop-off service, Mon-Fri 9:30-13:45 & 17:30-20:00, closed Sat-Sun, about a block from the eastern edge of Santa Cruz at Avenida Menéndez Pelayo 11, tel. 954-534-219).

Train Tickets: For schedules and tickets, visit the RENFE Travel Center at the **train station** (daily 8:00-22:00, take a number

Sevilla at a Glance

▲▲▲**Flamenco** Flamboyant, riveting music-and-dance performances, offered at clubs throughout town. **Hours:** Shows start as early as 19:00. See page 609.

▲▲**Cathedral and Giralda Bell Tower** The world's largest Gothic church, with Columbus' tomb, a treasury, and climbable tower. **Hours:** July-Aug Mon-Sat 9:30-17:00, Sun 14:30-18:00; Sept-June Mon-Sat 11:00-17:00, Sun 14:30-18:00. See page 580.

▲▲**Alcázar** Palace built by the Moors in the 10th century, revamped in the 14th century, and still serving as royal digs. **Hours:** April-Sept daily 9:30-19:00, Oct-March daily 9:30-17:00. See page 588.

▲▲**Basílica de la Macarena** Church and museum with the much-venerated Weeping Virgin statue and two significant floats from Sevilla's Holy Week celebrations. **Hours:** Mon-Sat 9:00-14:00 & 17:00-21:00, Sun from 9:30. See page 603.

▲▲**Bullfight Museum** Guided tour of the bullring and its museum. **Hours:** Daily May-Oct 9:30-20:00, Nov-April 9:30-19:00, on fight days until 14:00. See page 606.

▲▲**Evening Paseo** Locals strolling in the cool of the evening, mainly along Avenida de la Constitución, Barrio Santa Cruz, the Calle Sierpes and Tetuán shopping pedestrian zone, and the Guadalquivir River. **Hours:** Spring through fall, until very late at night in summer. See page 611.

▲**Museo Palacio de la Condesa de Lebrija** A fascinating 18th-century aristocratic mansion. **Hours:** July-Aug Mon-Fri 9:00-15:00, Sat-Sun 10:00-14:00; Sept-June Mon-Fri 10:30-19:30, Sat-Sun 10:00-14:00. See page 598.

▲**Flamenco Dance Museum** High-tech museum explaining the history and art of Sevilla's favorite dance. **Hours:** Daily 9:30-19:00. See page 598.

▲**Museo de Bellas Artes** Andalucía's top paintings, including works by Spanish masters Murillo and Zurbarán. **Hours:** Tue-Sat 9:00-20:30, Sun 9:00-14:30, closed Mon. See page 599.

▲**Bullfights** Some of Spain's best bullfighting, held at Sevilla's arena. **Hours:** Fights generally at 18:30 on most Sundays in May and June, on Easter and Corpus Christi, and daily through the April Fair and in late September. Rookies fight small bulls on Thursdays in July. See page 605.

and wait, tel. 902-320-320 for reservations and info) or the one near **Plaza Nueva** in the center (Mon-Fri 9:30-13:30 & 17:30-19:30, Sat 10:00-13:00, closed Sun, Calle Zaragoza 29, tel. 954-211-455). You can also check schedules at www.renfe .com; see page 625 for details. Many travel agencies sell train tickets; look for a train sticker in agency windows.

Warning: You may encounter women thrusting sprigs of rosemary into the hands of passersby, grunting, *"Toma! Es un regalo!"* ("Take it! It's a gift!"). If you take one of these sprigs, you'll be harassed for money in return. Just walk on by if you are approached.

Tours in Sevilla

Guided City Walks by Concepción—Concepción Delgado, an enthusiastic teacher who's a joy to listen to, takes small groups

on English-language walks. Using me as her guinea pig, Concepción has designed a fine two-hour **Sevilla Cultural Show & Tell.** This introduction to her hometown, sharing important insights the average visitor misses, is worthwhile even on a one-day visit (€15/person, minimum 4 people, Feb-July and Sept-Dec Mon-Sat at 10:30; Jan and Aug on Mon, Wed, and Fri only; meet at statue in Plaza Nueva).

For those wanting to really understand the city's two most important sights—which are tough to fully appreciate—Concepción also offers in-depth tours of the **cathedral** and the **Alcázar** (both tours last 1.25 hours, cost €7—not including entrance fees, €2 discount if you also take the Show & Tell tour; meet at 13:00 at statue in Plaza del Triunfo; minimum 4 people; cathedral tours—Mon, Wed, and Fri; Alcázar tours—Tue, Thu, and Sat; no Alcázar tours Jan and Aug).

Although you can just show up for Concepción's tours, it's smart to confirm the departure times and reserve a spot (tel. 902-158-226, mobile 616-501-100, www.sevillawalkingtours.com, info@sevillawalkingtours.com). Concepción does no tours on Sundays or holidays. Because she's a busy mom of two young kids, Concepción sometimes sends her colleague Alfonso (who's also excellent) to lead these tours.

Hop-on, Hop-off Bus Tours—Two competing city bus tours leave from the curb near the riverside Torre del Oro (Gold Tower). You'll see the parked buses and salespeople handing out fliers. Each tour does about an hour-long swing through the city with

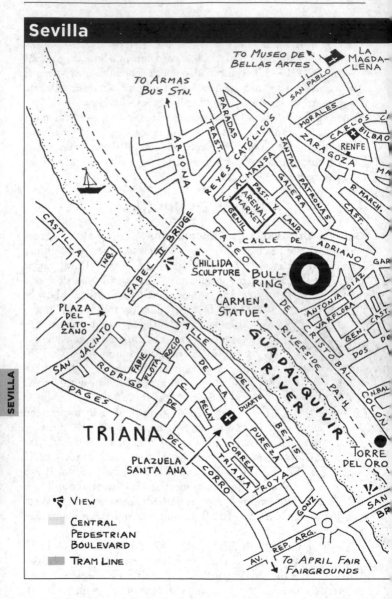

Sevilla

TO MUSEO DE BELLAS ARTES
LA MAGDALENA
TO ARMAS BUS STN.
SAN PABLO
PARADAS
TRAST.
ARJONA
MORALES
CARLOS C
BILBAO
RENFE
REYES CATÓLICOS
ZARAGOZA
SANTAS PATRONAS
ALMANSA
PAST Y LAND.
GALERA
ARENAL MARKET
GENIL
P. MARCH.
CAST.
MA
CASTILLA
INQ.
ISABEL II BRIDGE
PASEO
CALLE DE ADRIANO
GAR
CHILLIDA SCULPTURE
BULL-RING
DE
ANTONIA DIAZ
VARFLORA
GEN. CAST.
DE
PLAZA DEL ALTOZANO
CARMEN STATUE
CRISTOBAL
DOS
SAN JACINTO
CALLE
GUADALQUIVIR
RIVER-SIDE PATH
CNBAL
COLÓN
FABIE
ROCIO
C. DE
DEL
RODRIGO
FLOTA
PAGES
DE
DE LA
PELAY
DUARTE
BETIS
TORRE DEL ORO
TRIANA
DEL
PUREZA
SAN BR
PLAZUELA SANTA ANA
CORREA
TRIANA
TROYA
CORRO
GONZ.
REP. ARG.
AV.
TO APRIL FAIR FAIRGROUNDS

VIEW
CENTRAL PEDESTRIAN BOULEVARD
TRAM LINE

SEVILLA

recorded narration (€16-17, daily 10:00-21:00, green route has shorter option). The tours, which allow hopping on and off at four stops, are heavy on Expo '29 and Expo '92 neighborhoods—both zones of little interest in 2012. While the narration does its best, Sevilla is most interesting where buses can't go.

Horse and Buggy Tours—A carriage ride is a classic, popular way to survey the city and a relaxing way to enjoy María Luisa Park

(€50 for a 45-minute clip-clop, find a likable English-speaking driver for better narration). Look for rigs at Plaza América, Plaza del Triunfo, Torre del Oro, Alfonso XIII Hotel, and Avenida Isabel la Católica.

Boat Cruises—Boring one-hour panoramic tours leave every 30 minutes from the dock behind Torre de Oro. The low-energy recorded narration is hard to follow, but there's little to see anyway

Barrio Santa Cruz Self-Guided Walk

(overpriced at €15, tel. 954-561-692).

More Tours—Visitours, a typical big-bus tour company, does €95 all-day trips to Córdoba (Tue, Thu, and Sat; tel. 955-999-760, mobile 686-413-413, www.visitours.es, visitours@visitours.es). For other guides, contact one of the **Guide Associations of Sevilla:** AUITS (tel. 699-494-204, www.auits.com, guias@auits.com) or APIT (tel. 954-210-037, www.apitsevilla.com, visitas@apitsevilla .com).

Self-Guided Walk

Barrio Santa Cruz

Of Sevilla's once-thriving Jewish Quarter, only the tangled street plan and a wistful Old World ambience survive. This classy maze of lanes (too slender for cars), small plazas, tile-covered patios, and whitewashed houses with wrought-iron latticework draped in flowers is a great refuge from the summer heat and bustle of

S. MARIA
LA BLANCA

❶ Plaza de la Virgen de los Reyes
❷ Plaza del Triunfo
❸ Patio de Banderas
❹ Calle Agua
❺ Plaza de la Santa Cruz
❻ Plaza de Refinadores
❼ Casa de Murillo
❽ Monasterio de San José del Carmen
❾ Plaza de los Venerables
❿ Plaza de Doña Elvira
⓫ Plaza de la Alianza

PLAZA SANTA CRUZ

❻ PLAZA DE REFINADORES

❺

PLAZA DE ALFARO

MURILLO GARDENS

50 YARDS
50 METERS

⬅ WALKING TOUR

DCH

SEVILLA

Sevilla. The streets are narrow—some with buildings so close they're called "kissing lanes." A happy result of the narrowness

is shade: Locals claim the Barrio Santa Cruz is three degrees cooler than the rest of the city.

Orange trees abound— because they never lose their leaves, they provide constant shade. But forget about eating any of the oranges. They're bitter and used only to make vitamins, perfume, cat food, and that marmalade you can't avoid in British B&Bs. But when they blossom (for three weeks in spring, usually in March), the aroma is heavenly.

The Barrio is made for wandering. Getting lost is easy, and I recommend doing just that. But to get started, here's a plaza-to-plaza walk that loops you through the *corazón* (heart) of the neighborhood and back out again. Ideally, don't do the walk in the morning, when the Barrio's charm is trampled by tour groups. Early evening (around 18:00) is ideal.

❶ Plaza de la Virgen de los Reyes: Start in the square in front of the cathedral, at the base of the Giralda Bell Tower. This square is dedicated to the Virgin of the Kings. See her tile on the white wall facing the cathedral. She is one of several different versions of Mary you'll see in Sevilla, each appealing to a different type of worshipper. This one is big here because the Spanish king reportedly carried her image with him when he retook the town from the Moors in 1248. The fountain dates from 1929. From this peaceful square, look up the street leading away from the cathedral and notice the characteristic (government-protected) 19th-century architecture. The ironwork is typical of Andalucía and the pride of Sevilla. You'll see it and the traditional color scheme of white-wash-and-goldenrod all over the town center.

Another symbol you'll see throughout Sevilla is the city insignia: "NO8DO," the letters "NODO" with a figure-eight-like shape at their center. *Nodo* meant "knot" in the old dialect, and this symbol evokes the strong ties between the citizens of Sevilla and King Alfonso X (during a succession dispute in the 13th century, the Sevillans remained loyal to their king).

• *Walk with the cathedral on your right into the...*

❷ Plaza del Triunfo: The "Plaza of Triumph" is named for the 1755 earthquake that destroyed Lisbon and rattled Sevilla, but left most of the city intact. Find the statue thanking the Virgin, located at the far end of the square, under a stone canopy. That Virgin faces another one (closer to you), atop a tall pillar honoring Sevillan artists, including the painter Murillo (see "Casa de Murillo," later).

• *Pass through the opening in the crenellated Alcázar wall under the arch. You'll emerge into a courtyard called the...*

❸ Patio de Banderas: Named for "flags," not Antonio, the Banderas Courtyard was once a kind of military parade ground for the royal guard. The barracks sur-rounding the square once housed the king's bodyguards. Today, the far end of this square is a favor-ite spot for a postcard view of the Giralda Bell Tower.

• *Exit the courtyard at the far corner, through the Judería arch. Go down the long, narrow passage. Emerging into the light, you'll be walking alongside the Alcázar wall. Take the first left, then right, through a small square and follow the narrow alley-way called...*

❹ **Calle Agua:** As you walk along the street, look to the left, peeking through iron gates for occasional glimpses of the flower-smothered patios of exclusive private residences. The patio at #2 is a delight—ringed with columns, filled with flowers, and colored with glazed tiles. The tiles are not only decorative; they keep buildings cooler in the summer heat. Emerging at the end of the street, turn around and look back at the openings of two old pipes built into the wall. These pipes once carried water to the Alcázar (and today give the street its name). You're standing at an entrance into the pleasant Murillo Gardens (to the right), formerly the fruit-and-vegetable gardens for the Alcázar.

• *Don't enter the gardens now, but instead cross the square diagonally and continue 20 yards down a lane to the...*

❺ **Plaza de la Santa Cruz:** Arguably the heart of the Barrio, this is a pleasant square of orange and olive trees and draping vines. It was once the site of a synagogue (the Barrio had three; now there are none), which Christians destroyed. They replaced the synagogue with a church, which the French (under Napoleon) then demolished. It's a bit of history that locals remember when they see the blue, white, and red French flag marking the French consulate, now overlooking this peaceful square. The Sevillan painter Murillo, who was buried in the now-gone church, lies somewhere below you. On the square you'll find the recommended Los Gallos flamenco bar, which combusts nightly after midnight with impromptu flamenco (described on page 611).

• *At the far end of the square, a one-block (optional) detour along Calle Mezquita leads to the nearby...*

❻ **Plaza de Refinadores:** Sevilla's most famous (if fictional) 17th-century citizen is honored here with a statue. Don Juan Tenorio—the original Don Juan—was a notorious sex addict and atheist who proudly thumbed his nose at the stifling Church-driven morals of his day.

• *Backtrack to Plaza de la Santa Cruz and turn right (north) on Calle Santa Teresa. At #8 (on the left) is...*

❼ **Casa de Murillo:** One of Sevilla's famous painters, Bartolomé Esteban Murillo (1618-1682), lived here, soaking in the ambience of street life and reproducing it in his paintings of cute beggar children (see sidebar on page 582).

• *Directly across from Casa de Murillo is the...*

❽ **Monasterio de San José del Carmen:** This is where St. Teresa stayed when she visited from her hometown of Ávila. The convent (closed to the public) keeps artifacts of the mystic nun, such as her spiritual manuscripts.

Continue north on Calle Santa Teresa, then take the first left on Calle Lope de Rueda, then left again, then right on **Calle Reinoso.** This street—so narrow that the buildings almost

Sevilla's Jews

In the summer of 1391, smoldering anti-Jewish sentiment flared up in Sevilla. On June 6 Christian mobs ransacked the city's Jewish Quarter (Judería). Around 4,000 Jews were killed, and 5,000 Jewish families were driven from their homes. Synagogues were stripped and transformed into churches. The former Judería eventually became the neighborhood of the Holy Cross—Barrio Santa Cruz. Sevilla's uprising spread through Spain (and Europe), the first of many nasty pogroms during the next century.

Before the pogrom, Jews had lived in Sevilla for centuries as the city's respected merchants, doctors, and bankers. They flourished under the Muslim Moors. After Sevilla was "liberated" by King Ferdinand III (1248), Jews were given protection by Spain's kings and allowed a measure of self-government, though they were confined to the Jewish neighborhood.

But by the 14th century, Jews were increasingly accused of everything from poisoning wells to ritually sacrificing Christian babies. Mobs killed suspected Jews, and some of Sevilla's most respected Jewish citizens had their fortunes confiscated.

After 1391, Jews faced a choice: Be persecuted (even killed), relocate, or convert to Christianity. Those who converted—called *conversos*, New Christians, or *marranos* (swine)—were always under suspicion of practicing their old faith in private, undermining true Christianity. Longtime Christians were threatened by this new social class of converted Jews, who now had equal status, fanning the mistrust.

To root out the perceived problem of underground Judaism, the "Catholic Monarchs," Ferdinand and Isabel, established the Inquisition in Spain (1478). Under the direction of Grand Inquisitor Tomás de Torquemada, these religious courts arrested and interrogated *conversos* suspected of practicing Judaism. Using long solitary confinement and torture, they extracted confessions.

On February 6, 1481, Sevilla hosted Spain's first auto-da-fé ("act of faith"), a public confession and punishment for heresy. Six accused *conversos* were paraded barefoot into the cathedral, made to publicly confess their sins, then burned at the stake. Over the next three decades, thousands of *conversos* (some historians say hundreds, some say tens of thousands) were tried and killed in Spain.

In 1492, the same year the last Moors were driven from Spain, Ferdinand and Isabel decreed that all remaining Jews convert or be expelled (to Portugal and ultimately to Holland). Spain emerged as a nation unified under the banner of Christianity.

touch—is one of the Barrio's "kissing lanes." A popular explanation suggests the buildings were built so close together to provide maximum shade. But remember this was the Jewish ghetto, where all the city's Jews were forced to live in a very small area. That's why the streets of Santa Cruz are so narrow.

• *The street spills onto the...*

❾ Plaza de los Venerables: This square is another candidate for "heart of the Barrio." The streets branching off it ooze local ambience. When the Jews were expelled from Spain in 1492, this area became deserted and run-down. But in 1929, for its world's fair, Sevilla turned the plaza into a showcase of Andalusian style, adding the railings, tile work, orange trees, and other too-cute Epcot-like adornments. A different generation of tourists enjoys the place today, likely unaware that what they're seeing in Santa Cruz is far from "authentic" (or, at least, not as old as they imagine).

The large, harmonious Baroque-style Hospital de los Venerables (1675), once a retirement home for old priests (the "venerables"), is now a cultural foundation and museum (€4.75, includes audioguide). The highlight is the church and courtyard, featuring a round, sunken fountain. The museum also has a small Velázquez painting of Santa Rufina, one of two patron saints protecting Sevilla. The painting was acquired at a 2007 auction for more than €12 million.

• *Continuing west on Calle Gloria, you soon reach the...*

❿ Plaza de Doña Elvira: This small square—with orange trees, tile benches, and a stone fountain—sums up our Barrio walk. Shops sell work by local artisans, such as ceramics, embroidery, and fans.

• *Cross the plaza and head north along Calle Rodrigo Caro into the...*

⓫ Plaza de la Alianza: Ever consider a career change? Gain inspiration at the site that once housed the painting studio of John Fulton (1932-1998; find the small plaque on the other side of the square), an American who pursued two dreams. Though born in Philadelphia, Fulton got hooked on bullfighting. He trained in the tacky bullrings of Mexico, then in 1956 he moved to Sevilla, the world capital of the sport. His career as matador was not top-notch, and the Spaniards were slow to warm to the Yankee, but his courage and persistence earned their grudging respect. After he put down the cape, he picked up a brush, making colorful paintings in his Sevilla studio.

• *From Plaza de la Alianza, you can return to the cathedral by turning left (west) on Calle Joaquin Romero Murube (along the wall). Or head northeast on Callejón de Rodrigo Caro, which intersects with Calle Mateos Gago, a street lined with tapas bars.*

Sights in Sevilla

▲▲Cathedral and Giralda Bell Tower

Sevilla's cathedral is the third-largest church in Europe (after St. Peter's at the Vatican and St. Paul's in London), and the largest Gothic church anywhere.

When they ripped down a mosque of brick on this site in 1401, the Reconquista Christians bragged, "We'll build a cathedral so huge that anyone who sees it will take us for madmen." They built for 120 years. Even today, the descendants of those madmen proudly display an enlarged photocopy of their *Guinness Book of Records* letter certifying, "Santa María de la Sede in Sevilla is the cathedral with the largest area: 126.18 meters x 82.60 meters x 30.48 meters high."

Cost and Hours: €8, €2 for those over age 65 (must show ID), kids under age 18 free, includes free entry to the Church of the Savior; July-Aug Mon-Sat 9:30-17:00, Sun 14:30-18:00; Sept-June Mon-Sat 11:00-17:00, Sun 14:30-18:00; last entry to cathedral one hour before closing, last entry to bell tower 30 minutes before closing; WC and drinking fountain just inside entrance and in courtyard near exit, tel. 954-214-971. Most of the website www.catedraldesevilla.es is in Spanish, but following the "vista virtual" links will take you to a virtual tour with an English option.

Crowd-Beating Tip: Though there's usually not much of a line to buy tickets, you can avoid it altogether by buying the €8 ticket at the Church of the Savior (Iglesia de Salvador), a few blocks north. See that church first, then come to the cathedral and waltz past the line to the turnstile.

Tours: My self-guided tour covers the basics. The €3 audio-guide explains each side chapel for anyone interested in all the old paintings and dry details. For €6 you can enjoy Concepción Delgado's tour instead (see "Tours in Sevilla," earlier).

❂ Self-Guided Tour: Enter the cathedral at the south end (closest to the Alcázar, with a full-size replica of the Giralda's weathervane statue in the patio).

• *First, you pass through the...*

❶ Art Pavilion: Just past the turnstile, you step into a room of paintings that once hung in the church, including works by Sevilla's two 17th-century masters—Bartolomé Murillo (*St. Ferdinand*—the king who freed Sevilla from the Moors) and Francisco de Zurbarán *(St. John the Baptist in the Desert).* Find a

Sevilla's Cathedral

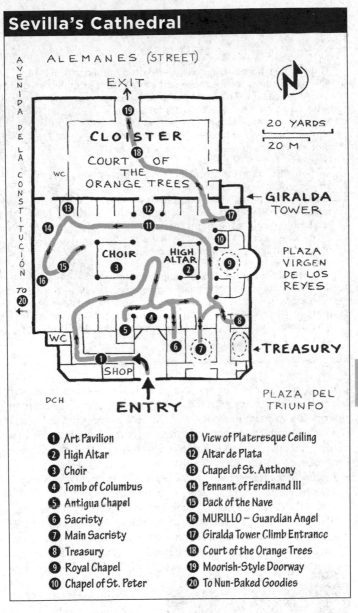

ALEMANES (STREET)

EXIT

A V E N I D A   D E   L A   C O N S T I T U C I Ó N

TO **20**

CLOISTER

COURT OF THE ORANGE TREES

WC

19

18

20 YARDS

20 M

← GIRALDA TOWER

CHOIR **3**

HIGH ALTAR **2**

13

14

15

16

12

11

17

10

9

PLAZA VIRGEN DE LOS REYES

WC

5

4

6

7

8

1

SHOP

DCH

ENTRY

← TREASURY

PLAZA DEL TRIUNFO

1 Art Pavilion
2 High Altar
3 Choir
4 Tomb of Columbus
5 Antigua Chapel
6 Sacristy
7 Main Sacristy
8 Treasury
9 Royal Chapel
10 Chapel of St. Peter

11 View of Plateresque Ceiling
12 Altar de Plata
13 Chapel of St. Anthony
14 Pennant of Ferdinand III
15 Back of the Nave
16 MURILLO – Guardian Angel
17 Giralda Tower Climb Entrance
18 Court of the Orange Trees
19 Moorish-Style Doorway
20 To Nun-Baked Goodies

SEVILLA

Bartolomé Murillo
(1617-1682)

The son of a barber of Seville, Bartolomé Murillo got his start selling paintings meant for export to the frontier churches of the Americas. In his 20s, he became famous after he painted a series of saints for Sevilla's Franciscan monastery. By about 1650, Murillo's sugary, simple, and accessible religious style was spreading through Spain and beyond.

Murillo painted street kids with cute smiles and grimy faces, and radiant young Marías with Ivory-soap complexions and rapturous poses (Immaculate Conceptions). His paintings view the world through a soft-focus lens, wrapping everything in warm colors and soft light, with a touch (too much, for some) of sentimentality.

Murillo became rich, popular, a family man, and the toast of Sevilla's high society. In 1664 his wife died, leaving him heartbroken, but his last 20 years were his most prolific. At age 65, Murillo died painting, after falling off a scaffold. His tomb is lost somewhere under the bricks of Plaza de la Santa Cruz.

painting showing two of Sevilla's patron saints—Santa Justa and Santa Rufina. Potters by trade, these two are easy to identify by their pots and palm branches, and the bell tower symbolizing the town they protect. As you tour the cathedral, keep track of how many depictions of this dynamic and saintly duo you spot. They're everywhere.

• *Walking past a rack of church maps and a WC, enter the actual church. In the center of the church, sit down in front of the...*

❷ **High Altar:** Look through the wrought-iron Renaissance grille at what's called the largest altarpiece *(retablo mayor)* ever made—65 feet tall, with 44 scenes from the life of Jesus carved from walnut and chestnut, blanketed by a staggering amount of

gold leaf (and dust). The work took three generations to complete (1481-1564). The story is told left to right, bottom to top. Find Baby Jesus in the manger, in the middle of the bottom row, then follow his story through the miracles, the

Passion, and the Pentecost. Crane your neck to look way up to the tippy-top, where a Crucifixion adorns the dizzying summit.

• *Turn around and check out the...*

❸ **Choir:** Facing the high altar, the choir features an organ of 7,000 pipes (played at the 10:00 Mass Mon-Fri, 10:00 & 13:00 Mass Sun, not in July-Aug, free for worshippers). A choir area like this one (an enclosure within the cathedral for more intimate services) is common in Spain and England, but rare in churches elsewhere. The big, spinnable book holder in the middle of the room held giant hymnals—large enough for all to chant from in a pre-Xerox age when there weren't enough books for everyone.

• *Now turn 90 degrees to the left and march to find the...*

❹ **Tomb of Columbus:** In front of the cathedral's entrance for pilgrims are four kings who carry the tomb of Christopher Columbus. His pallbearers represent the regions of Castile, Aragon, León, and Navarre (identify them by their team shirts). Columbus even traveled a lot posthumously. He was buried first in Spain, then in Santo Domingo in the Dominican Republic, then Cuba, and finally—when Cuba gained independence from Spain, around 1900—he sailed home again to Sevilla. Are the

remains actually his? Sevillans like to think so. (Columbus died in 1506. Five hundred years later, to help celebrate the anniversary of his death, DNA samples gave Sevillans the evidence they needed to substantiate their claim.) On the left is a mural of St. Christopher—patron saint of travelers—from 1584. The clock above has been ticking since 1788.

• *Facing Columbus, turn right and duck into the first chapel (on your left) to find the...*

❺ **Antigua Chapel:** Within this chapel is the gilded fresco of the Virgin Antigua, the oldest art in the church. It was actually painted onto a horseshoe-shaped prayer niche of the mosque formerly on this site. After Sevilla was reconquered in 1248, the mosque served as a church for about 120 years—until it was torn down to make room for this huge cathedral. Builders, captivated by the beauty of the Virgin holding the rose and the Christ Child holding the bird (and knowing that she was considered the protector of sailors in this port city), decided to save the fresco.

• *Exiting the chapel, we'll tour the cathedral counterclockwise. As you explore, note that its many chapels are described in English, and many of the windows have their dates worked into the design. Just on the other side of Columbus, walk through the small chapel and into the...*

❻ Sacristy: This space is where the priests get ready each morning before Mass. The Goya painting above the altar features Justa and Rufina—patron saints of Sevilla who were martyred in ancient Roman times. They're always shown with their trademark attributes: the town bell tower, pots, and palm leaves. I say they're each holding a bowl of gazpacho (particularly refreshing on hot summer days) and sprigs of rosemary from local Gypsies (an annoyance even back then). Art historians claim that since they were potters, they are shown with earthenware, and the sprigs are palm leaves—symbolic of their martyrdom. Whatever.

• *Two chapels down is the entrance to the...*

❼ Main Sacristy: Marvel at the ornate, 16th-century Plateresque dome of the main room, a grand souvenir from Sevilla's Golden Age. The intricate masonry resembles lacy silverwork (it's named for *plata*—silver). God is way up in the cupola. The three layers of figures below him show the heavenly host; relatives in purgatory—hands folded—looking to heaven in hope of help; and the wretched in hell, including a topless sinner engulfed in flames and teased cruelly by pitchfork-wielding monsters. Locals use the 110-pound silver religious float that dominates this room to parade the holy host (communion wafer) through town during Corpus Christi festivities.

• *At the far end of the main sacristy, at the left-hand corner, is a door leading to our next stop. (If it's closed, you can backtrack to the main part of the church and head next door.)*

❽ Treasury: The *tesoro* fills several rooms in the corner of the church. Wander deeper into the treasury to find a unique oval dome. It's in the 16th-century chapter room *(sala capitular)*, where monthly meetings take place with the bishop (he gets the throne, while the others share the bench). The paintings here are by

Murillo: a fine *Immaculate Conception* (1668, high above the bishop's throne) and portraits of saints important to Sevillans.

The wood-paneled "room of ornaments" shows off gold and silver reliquaries, which hold hundreds of holy body parts, as well as Spain's most valuable crown. The jeweled crown by Manuel de la Torres (the Corona de la Virgen de los Reyes) sparkles with 11,000 precious stones and the world's largest pearl—used as the torso of an angel. Opposite the crown is a reliquary featuring what is said to be a

Immaculate Conception

Throughout Sevilla and Spain you'll see paintings titled *The Immaculate Conception,* all looking quite similar (see example on page 582). Young, lovely, and beaming radiantly, these virgins look pure, untainted...you might even say "immaculate." According to Catholic doctrine, Mary, the future mother of Jesus, entered the world free from the original sin that other mortals share. When she died, her purity allowed her to be taken up directly to heaven (the Assumption).

The doctrine of Immaculate Conception can be confusing, even to Catholics. It does not mean that the Virgin Mary herself was born of a virgin. Rather, Mary's mother and father conceived her in the natural way. But at the moment Mary's soul animated her flesh, God granted her a special exemption from original sin. The doctrine of Immaculate Conception had been popular since medieval times, though it was not codified until 1854. It was Sevilla's own Bartolomé Murillo (1617-1682) who painted the model of this goddess-like Mary, copied by so many lesser artists. In Counter-Reformation times (when Murillo lived), paintings of a fresh-faced, ecstatic Mary made abstract doctrines like the Immaculate Conception and the Assumption tangible and accessible to all.

Most images of the Immaculate Conception show Mary wearing a radiant crown and with a crescent moon at her feet; she often steps on the heads of cherubs. Paintings by Murillo frequently portray Mary in a blue robe with long, wavy hair—young and innocent.

piece of the "true cross"—the cross to which Christ was nailed.

• *Leave the treasury and cross through the church to see...*

More Church Sights: First you'll pass the closed-to-tourists ❾ **Royal Chapel,** the burial place of several of the kings of Castile (open for worship only—access from outside), then the ❿ **Chapel of St. Peter,** which is dark but filled with paintings by Francisco de Zurbarán (showing scenes from the life of St. Peter). At the far corner—past the glass case displaying the *Guinness* certificate declaring that this is indeed the world's largest church by area—is the entry to the Giralda Bell Tower. You'll finish your visit here. But for now, continue your counterclockwise circuit. Near the middle (and high) altar, crane your neck skyward to admire the ⓫ **Plateresque tracery** on the ceiling, and take in the enormous ⓬ **Altar de Plata** rising up in a side chapel. The gleaming silver altarpiece adorned with statues looks like a big monstrance, those vessels for displaying the communion wafer.

The ⓭ **Chapel of St. Anthony** (Capilla de San Antonio), the last chapel on the right, is used for baptisms. The Renaissance baptismal font has delightful carved angels dancing along its base.

In Murillo's painting, *Vision of St. Anthony* (1656), the saint kneels in wonder as a Baby Jesus comes down surrounded by a choir of angels. Anthony is one of Iberia's most popular saints. As he is the patron saint of lost things, people come here to pray for Anthony's help in finding jobs, car keys, and life partners. Above the *Vision* is *The Baptism of*

Christ, also by Murillo. You don't need to be an art historian to know that the stained glass dates from 1685. And by now you must know who the women are....

Nearby, a glass case displays the ❹ **pennant of Ferdinand III,** which was raised over the minaret of the mosque on November 23, 1248, as Christian forces finally expelled the Moors from Sevilla. For centuries, it was paraded through the city on special days.

Continuing on, stand at the ❺ **back of the nave** (behind the choir) and appreciate the ornate immensity of the church. Can you see the angels trumpeting on their Cuban mahogany? Any birds?

Turn around. The massive candlestick holder dates from 1560. To the left is a niche with ❻ **Murillo's *Guardian Angel*** pointing to the light and showing an astonished child the way.

• *Backtrack the length of the church toward the Giralda Bell Tower, and notice the back of the choir's Baroque pipe organ. The exit sign leads to the Court of the Orange Trees and the exit. But first, some exercise.*

❼ **Giralda Tower Climb:** Your church admission includes entry to the bell tower. Notice the beautiful Moorish simplicity as you climb to its top, 330 feet up, for a grand city view. The spiraling ramp was designed to accommodate riders on horseback, who galloped up five times a day to give the Muslim call to prayer.

• *Go back down into the cathedral interior, then visit the...*

❽ **Court of the Orange Trees:** Today's cloister was once the mosque's Court of the Orange Trees (Patio de los Naranjos).

Twelfth-century Muslims stopped at the fountain in the middle to wash their hands, face, and feet before praying. The ankle-breaking lanes between the bricks were once irrigation streams—a reminder that the Moors introduced irrigation to Iberia. The mosque was made of bricks; the church is built of stone. The only remnants of the mosque today are the Court of the Orange Trees, the Giralda Bell Tower, and the site itself.

• *You'll exit the cathedral through the Court of the Orange Trees (if you need to use the WCs, they're at the far end of the courtyard, downstairs). As you leave, look back from the outside and notice the arch over the...*

⑲ Moorish-Style Doorway: As with much of the Moorish-looking art in town, it's actually Christian—the two coats of arms are a giveaway. The relief above the door shows the Bible story of Jesus ridding the temple of the merchants...a reminder to contemporary merchants that there will be no retail activity in the church. The plaque on the right honors Miguel de Cervantes, the great 16th-century Spanish writer. It's one of many plaques scattered throughout town showing places mentioned in his books. (In this case, the topic was pickpockets.) The huge green doors predate the church. They are a bit of the surviving pre-1248 mosque—wood covered with bronze. Study the fine workmanship.

Giralda Tower Exterior: Step across the street from the exit gate and look at the bell tower. Formerly a Moorish minaret from

which Muslims were called to prayer, it became the cathedral's bell tower after the Reconquista. A 4,500-pound bronze statue symbolizing the Triumph of Faith (specifically, the Christian faith over the Muslim one) caps the tower and serves as a weather vane (in Spanish, *girar* means "to rotate"—so a *giraldillo* is something that rotates). Locals actually use it to predict the weather. (If the wind is blowing from the southwest, it means moist ocean air will soon bring rain.) In 1356, the original top of the tower fell. You're looking at a 16th-century Christian-built top with a ribbon of letters proclaiming, "The strongest tower is the name of God" (you can see *Fortísima*—"strongest"—from this vantage point).

Now circle around for a close look at the corner of the tower at ground level. Needing more strength than their bricks could provide for the lowest section of the tower, the Moors used Roman-cut stones. You can actually read the Latin chiseled onto one of the stones 2,000 years ago. The tower offers a brief recap of the city's history—sitting on a Roman foundation, a long Moorish period capped by our Christian age. Today, by law, no building can be higher than the statue atop the tower.

• *Your cathedral tour is finished. If you've worked up an appetite, get out your map and make your way a few blocks for some...*

⑳ Nun-Baked Goodies: Stop by the El Torno Pasteleria de Conventos, a co-op where the various orders of cloistered nuns send their handicrafts (such as babies' baptismal dresses) and baked goods to be sold. "El Torno" is the lazy Susan that the cloistered nuns spin to sell their cakes and cookies without being seen. You won't actually see the *torno* (this shop is staffed by non-nuns), but this humble little hole-in-the-wall shop is worth a peek, and definitely serves the best cookies, bar nun. It's located through the passageway at 24 Avenida de la Constitución, immediately in front of the cathedral's biggest door: Go through the doorway marked *Plaza del Cabildo* into the quiet courtyard (Sept-July Mon-Fri 10:00-13:30 & 17:00-19:30, Sat-Sun 10:30-14:00, closed Aug, Plaza del Cabildo 2, tel. 954-219-190).

▲▲ Alcázar

Originally a 10th-century palace built for the governors of the local Moorish state, this building still functions as a royal palace—the

oldest in use in Europe. The core of the palace features an extensive 14th-century rebuild, done by Muslim workmen for the Christian king, Pedro I (1334-1369). Pedro was nicknamed either "the Cruel" or "the Just," depending on which end of his sword you were on. Pedro's palace embraces both cultural traditions.

Today, visitors can enjoy several sections of the Alcázar. Spectacularly decorated halls and courtyards have distinctive Islamic-style flourishes. Exhibits call up the era of Columbus and Spain's New World dominance. The lush, sprawling gardens invite exploration. Even the palatial rooms used by today's king and queen can be visited (reservations required).

Cost and Hours: €8.50; €2 for students and seniors over 65—must show ID, free for children under 16; ticket also includes Antiquarium at Plaza de la Encarnación, April-Sept daily 9:30-19:00, Oct-March daily 9:30-17:00; tel. 954-502-323, www.patronato-alcazarsevilla.es.

Crowd-Beating Tips: Tour groups clog the palace and rob it of any mystery in the morning (especially on Tue); come as late as possible.

Tours: The fast-moving €3.60 audioguide gives you an hour of information as you wander. My self-guided tour hits the highlights, or consider Concepción Delgado's Alcázar tour (described on page 571).

The **Upper Royal Apartments** can only be visited with a separate tour, reserved in advance (€4.20, includes audioguide, must check bags in provided lockers.) Groups leave every half-hour from 10:00 to 13:30—if interested, book a spot as soon as you arrive at the Alcázar. You tour in a small group of 15 people, escorted by a

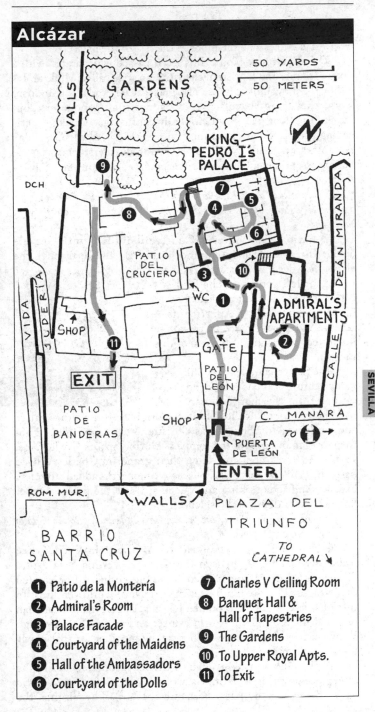

Alcázar

1. Patio de la Montería
2. Admiral's Room
3. Palace Facade
4. Courtyard of the Maidens
5. Hall of the Ambassadors
6. Courtyard of the Dolls
7. Charles V Ceiling Room
8. Banquet Hall & Hall of Tapestries
9. The Gardens
10. To Upper Royal Apts.
11. To Exit

security guard, following a 25-minute audioguide. For some it's worth it just to escape the mobs in the rest of the palace.

➋ Self-Guided Tour: This royal palace is decorated with a mix of Islamic and Christian elements—a style called Mudejar. It's a thought-provoking glimpse of a graceful Al-Andalus (Moorish) world that might have survived its Castilian conquerors...but didn't. The floor plan is intentionally confusing, to make experiencing the place more exciting and surprising. While Granada's Alhambra was built by Moors for Moorish rulers, what you see here is essentially a Christian ruler's palace, built in the Moorish style.

• *Buy your ticket and enter through the turnstiles. Pass through the garden-like Patio of the Lions and through the arch into a courtyard called the . . .*

❶ Patio de la Montería (Courtyard of the Hunt): Get oriented. The palace's main entrance is directly ahead, through the elaborately decorated facade. WCs are in the far-left corner. In the far-right corner is the staircase (and ticket booth) for the Upper Royal Apartments—reserve an entry time now, if you're interested (see details at the end of this tour).

The palace complex was built over many centuries. It has rooms and decorations from the many rulers who've lived here. Moorish caliphs built the original 10th-century palace and gardens. After Sevilla was Christianized, King Pedro I built the most famous part of the complex. During Spain's Golden Age, Ferdinand and Isabel and, later, their grandson Charles V lived here; they all left their mark. Successive monarchs added still more luxury. And today's king and queen still use the palace's upper floor as one of their royal residences.

• *Before entering the heart of the palace, start in the wing to the right of the courtyard. Step inside.*

❷ Admiral's Room (Cuarto del Almirante): When Queen Isabel debriefed Columbus at the Alcázar after his New World discoveries, she realized this could be big business. She created this wing in 1503 to administer Spain's New World ventures. In these halls, Columbus recounted his travels, Ferdinand Magellan planned his around-the-world cruise, and mapmaker Amerigo Vespucci tried to come up with a catchy moniker for that newly discovered continent.

In the pink-and-red Audience Chamber (once a chapel), the **altarpiece painting** is of St. Mary of the Navigators (*Santa María de los Navegantes*, by Alejo Fernández, 1530s). The Virgin—the

Christopher Columbus
(1451-1506)

This Italian wool-weaver ran off to sea, was shipwrecked in Portugal, married a captain's daughter, learned Portuguese and Spanish, and convinced Spain's monarchs to finance his bold scheme to trade with the East by sailing west. On August 3, 1492, Columbus set sail from Palos (near Huelva, 60 miles west of Sevilla) with 3 ships and 90 men, hoping to land in Asia, which Columbus estimated was 3,000 miles away. Three thousand miles later—with the superstitious crew ready to mutiny, having seen evil omens like a falling meteor and a jittery compass—Columbus landed on an island in the Bahamas (October 12, 1492), convinced he'd reached Asia. They traded with the "Indians" and returned home to Palos harbor, where they were received as heroes.

Columbus made three more voyages to the New World and became rich with gold. He gained a bad reputation among the colonists, was arrested, and returned to Spain in chains. Though pardoned, Columbus fell out of favor with the court. On May 20, 1506, he died in Valladolid. His son said he was felled by "gout and by grief at seeing himself fallen from his high estate," but historians speculate that diabetes or syphilis may have contributed. Columbus died thinking he'd visited Asia, unaware he'd opened up Europe to a New World.

patron saint of sailors and a favorite of Columbus—keeps watch over the puny ships beneath her. Her cape seems to protect everyone under it—even the Native Americans in the dark background (the first time "Indians" were painted in Europe).

Standing beside the Virgin (on the right, dressed in gold, joining his hands together in prayer) is none other than Christopher Columbus. He stands on a cloud, because he's now in heaven (as this was painted a few decades after his death). Notice that Columbus is blond. Columbus' son said of his dad: "In his youth his hair was blond, but when he reached 30, it all turned white." Many historians believe this to be the earliest known portrait of Columbus. If so, it also might be the most accurate. On the left side of the painting, the man with the gold cape is King Ferdinand.

Left of the painting is a **model** of Columbus' *Santa María*, his flagship and the only one of his three ships not to survive the 1492 voyage. Columbus complained that the *Santa María*—a big cargo ship, different from the sleek *Niña* and *Pinta* caravels—was too slow. On Christmas Day it ran aground off present-day Haiti and tore a hole in its hull. The ship was dismantled to build the first permanent structure in America, a fort for 39 colonists. (After Columbus left, the natives burned the fort and killed the colonists.) Opposite the altarpiece (in the center of the back wall) is the family **coat of arms** of Columbus' descendants, who now live in Spain and Puerto Rico. Using Columbus' Spanish name, it reads: "To Castile and to León, Colón gave a new world."

Return to the still-used reception room, filled with big canvases. The **biggest painting** (and most melodramatic) shows the turning point in Sevilla's history: King Ferdinand III humbly kneels before the bishop, giving thanks to God for helping him liberate the city from the Muslims (in 1248). Ferdinand promptly turned the Alcázar of the caliphs into the royal palace of Christian kings.

Pop into the room beyond the grand piano for a look at ornate **fans** (mostly foreign and well-described in English). A long painting shows 17th-century Sevilla during Holy Week. Follow the procession, which is much like today's, with traditional floats carried by teams of men and followed by a retinue of penitents.

• *Return to the Patio de la Montería. Face the impressive entrance facade of the...*

❸ **Palace of King Pedro I (Palacio del Rey Pedro I):** This is the entrance to the 14th-century nucleus of the complex. The facade's elaborate blend of Islamic tracery and Gothic Christian elements introduces us to the Mudejar style seen throughout Pedro's part of the palace.

• *Enter the palace. Pass through the Vestibule (impressive, yes, but we'll see better), and continue through the maze of rooms and passageways until you emerge into the big courtyard with a long pool in the center. This is the...*

❹ **Courtyard of the Maidens (Patio de las Doncellas):** You've reached the center of King Pedro's palace. It's an open-air courtyard, surrounded by rooms. In the center is a long, rectangular reflecting pool. Like the Moors who preceded him, Pedro built his palace around water. The pool has four (covered) cisterns, two at each end. They distribute water to the four quadrants of the palace and—symbolically—to the four corners of the world.

King Pedro cruelly abandoned his wife and moved into the Alcázar with his mistress, then hired Muslim workers from

Granada to re-create the romance of that city's Alhambra in Sevilla's stark Alcázar. The designers created a microclimate engineered for coolness: water, plants, pottery, thick walls, and darkness. This palace is considered Spain's best example of the Mudejar style. Stucco panels with elaborate designs, colorful ceramic tiles, coffered wooden ceilings, and lobed arches atop slender columns create a refined, pleasing environment. The elegant proportions and symmetry of this courtyard are a photographer's delight.

• *Explore the rooms branching off the courtyard. Through the door at the end of the long reflecting pool is the palace's most important room, called the...*

❺ **Hall of the Ambassadors (Salón de Embajadores):** Here, in his throne room, Pedro received guests and caroused in luxury.

The room is a cube topped with a half-dome, like many important Islamic buildings. In Islam, the cube represents the earth, and the dome is the starry heavens. In Pedro's world, the symbolism proclaimed that he controlled heaven and earth. Islamic horseshoe arches stand atop columns with golden capitals. Lattice windows (a favorite of Pedro's) are above those.

The stucco on the walls is molded with interlacing plants, geometrical shapes, and Arabic writing. Imagine, here in a Christian palace, that the walls are inscribed with unapologetically Muslim sayings: "None but Allah conquers" and "Happiness and prosperity are benefits of Allah, who nourishes all creatures." The artisans added propaganda phrases such as "Dedicated to the magnificent Sultan Pedro—thanks to God!"

The Mudejar style also includes Christian motifs. Find the row of kings, high up at the base of the dome, chronicling all of Spain's ruler from the 600s to the 1600s. Throughout the palace, you'll see coats of arms—including the castle of Castile and the lion of León. There are also natural objects (shells and birds) you wouldn't normally find in Islamic decor, which traditionally avoids realistic images of nature.

Wander through adjoining rooms. Straight ahead from the Hall of the Ambassadors, in the **Philip II Ceiling Room** (Salón del Techo de Felipe II), look above the arches to find peacocks, falcons, and other birds amid interlacing vines. Imagine day-to-day life in the palace—with VIP guests tripping on the tiny but jolting steps.

• *Make your way to the second courtyard, nearby (in the Hall of the Ambassadors, face the Courtyard of the Maidens, then walk to the left). This smaller courtyard is the...*

❻ Courtyard of the Dolls (Patio de las Muñecas): This delicate courtyard was for the king's private and family life. Originally, the center of the courtyard had a pool, cooling the residents and reflecting the decorative patterns once brightly painted on the walls. The columns are different colors—alternating white, black, and pink marble. (Pedro's original courtyard was a single story. The upper floors and skylight were added centuries later.) The courtyard's name comes from the tiny doll faces found at the base of one of the arches. Circle the room and try to find them.

• *The long adjoining room with the gilded ceiling, the* **Prince's Room** *(Cuarto del Príncipe), was Queen Isabel's bedroom, where she gave birth to a son, Prince Juan.*

Return to the Courtyard of the Maidens. Look up and notice the second story. Isabel's grandson, Charles V, added it in the 16th century. See the difference in styles: Mudejar below (lobed arches and elaborate tracery), and Renaissance above (round arches and less decoration).

As you stand in the courtyard with your back to the Hall of the Ambassadors, the door in the middle of the right side leads to the...

❼ Charles V Ceiling Room (Salón del Techo del Carlos V): Emperor Charles V, who ruled Spain at its peak of New World wealth, expanded the palace. The reason? His marriage to his beloved Isabel, which took place in this room. Devoutly Christian, Charles celebrated his wedding night with a midnight Mass, and later ordered the Mudejar ceiling in this room to be replaced with a less Islamic (but no less impressive) one.

• *We've seen the core of King Pedro's palace, with the additions by his successors. Return to the Courtyard of the Maidens, turn right, and find the staircase in the corner. This leads up to rooms decorated with bright ceramic tiles. Pass through the chapel and into two big, long, parallel rooms, the...*

❽ Banquet Hall (Salón Gótico) and **Hall of Tapestries (Salón Tapices):** Charles and Isabel's wedding reception was held in this big, airy banquet hall. Tiles of yellow, blue, green, and orange line the room, some decorated with whimsical human figures with vase-like bodies. The windows open onto views of the gardens.

Next door, the walls are hung with large Brussels-made tapestries showing the conquests, trade, and industriousness of Charles' prosperous reign. (The highlights are described in Spanish along the top and in Latin along the bottom.) The map tapestry of the Mediterranean world has south pointing up. Find Genova, Italy, on the bottom; Africa on top;

Lisbon on the far right; and the large city of Barcelona in between. The artist included himself holding the legend—with a scale in both leagues and miles.

• *At the far end of the Banquet Hall, head outside to...*

❾ **The Gardens:** This space is full of tropical flowers, feral cats, cool fountains, and hot tourists. The intimate geometric

zone nearest the palace is the Moorish garden. The far-flung garden beyond that was the backyard of the Christian ruler. The **elevated walkway** (Galería del Grutesco—the Grotto Gallery) along the left side of the gardens provides fine views. (Enter it from the palace end.)

Descending to the lower garden, find the entrance to the **Baths of María de Padilla**—an underground rainwater cistern named for Pedro's mistress.

Garden lovers could linger here for hours. Even aborophobes will find it fascinating. Here in the gardens, the Christian and Islamic traditions merge. Both cultures used water and nature as essential parts of their architecture. The garden's pavilions and fountains only enhance this. Wander among palm trees, myrtle hedges, and fragrant roses, and experience a small sample of the heavenly paradise that both cultures believed lay beyond.

• *If you'd like to see more, return to the Patio de la Montería and go upstairs to visit the Upper Royal Apartments (requires reservation and separate entry fee—see "Tours" on page 588). Otherwise, skip to the conclusion of this tour, below.*

❿ **Upper Royal Apartments (Cuarto Real Alto):** This is the royal palace of today's monarchs. Fifteen public reception rooms are open to visitors: the official dining room, Audience Hall, and so on. The rooms are amply decorated with Versailles-like furniture, chandeliers, carpets, and portraits of 19th-century nobility. The highlight is the Audience Room, a Mudejar-style room overlooking the Patio de la Montería. You don't get to see the actual living quarters of the present king and queen, but they're just down the hall.

• *When you're ready to go, head for the exit, through the **Patio de Banderas**—enjoying a classic Giralda Bell Tower view as you leave. In former times, this courtyard was the entrance for those arriving by horse carriage.*

Your Royal Alcázar tour is over. From Moors to Pedro the Cruel to Isabel and Charles to King Juan Carlos and Queen Sofia, we've seen the home of a millennium of kings and queens. After digesting all those names, I need some Alcaseltzer.

Near the Cathedral and Alcázar

Archivo de Indias—The Lonja Palace, across the street from the Alcázar, was designed by royal architect Juan de Herrera, the same person who planned El Escorial. Originally a market for traders, this is the top building from Sevilla's 16th-century glory days. Today, it houses the archive of documents from the discovery and conquest of the New World, which are shown in rotating exhibits. This could be fascinating, but generally little of importance makes it on display (old maps of Havana, anyone?). The displays are in Spanish, with limited English information.

Cost and Hours: Free, Mon-Sat 9:30-17:00, Sun 10:00-14:00, Avenida de la Constitución 3, tel. 954-500-528.

Avenida de la Constitución—Old Sevilla is bisected by this grand boulevard. Its name celebrates the country's 1978 adoption of a democratic constitution, as the Spanish people moved quickly to re-establish their government after the 1975 death of longtime dictator Francisco Franco. Long a commercial street, the avenue was converted into a pedestrian boulevard in 2007. Overnight, the city's paseo route took on a new dimension. And suddenly cafés and shops here had fresh appeal. (Two Starbucks moved in, strategically bookending the boulevard, but they're having a tough time winning over locals who like small €1 coffees rather than mammoth €4 ones.) The new tram line (infamously short at only three-quarters of a mile) is controversial, as it violates what might have been a more purely pedestrian zone.

Between the River and the Cathedral

Hospital de la Caridad—This Charity Hospital was founded by a nobleman in the 17th century. Peek into the fine courtyard. On the left, the chapel has some gruesome art (above both doors) illustrating that death is the great equalizer, and an altar so sweet only a Spaniard could enjoy it. The Dutch tiles depicting scenes of the Old and New Testament are a reminder that the Netherlands was under Spanish rule in the mid-16th century.

Cost and Hours: €5, includes slightly interesting audio-guide, erratic hours, but typically Mon-Sat 9:00-13:00 & 15:30-19:00, Sun 9:00-12:30, last entry 30 minutes before closing, tel. 954-223-232.

Torre del Oro (Gold Tower) and Naval Museum—Sevilla's historic riverside Gold Tower was the starting and ending point for all shipping to the New World. It's named for the golden tiles that once covered it—not for all the New World booty that landed here. Since the Moors built it in the 13th century, it has been part of the city's fortifications, with a heavy chain draped across the river to protect the harbor. Today it houses a dreary little naval museum. Looking past the dried fish and charts of knots, find the mural showing the world-spanning journeys of Vasco da Gama, the model of Columbus' *Santa María* (the first ship to land in the New World), and an interesting mural of Sevilla in 1740. Enjoy the view from the balconies upstairs. The Guadalquivir River is now just a trickle of its former self, after canals built in the 1920s siphoned off most of its water to feed ports downstream.

Cost and Hours: €2, includes audioguide, Tue-Fri 9:30-13:30, Sat-Sun 10:30-13:30, closed Mon and Aug, tel. 954-222-419.

North of the Cathedral

Plaza Nueva—This "New Square" is marked by a statue of King Ferdinand III, who liberated Sevilla from the Moors in the 13th century and was later sainted. This is the end of the line for Sevilla's short tram system (which zips down Avenida de la Constitución to the El Prado bus station). Running along the top of the square is the relatively modern **City Hall.** For a more interesting look at this building, circle around to the other end (on the smaller square, called Plaza San Francisco) where you can see how the structure has expanded right along with the city it governs: architectural styles evolve, from left to right, along the facade. The newest, right part of the facade is more or less undecorated—a blank canvas for future artists to leave their mark. This square has been used for executions, bullfights, and (today) big city events.

▲**Church of the Savior (Iglesia del Salvador)**—Sevilla's second-biggest church after its cathedral was built on the site of a mosque dating from the ninth century. (In the courtyard next to the church, you can still see the remains of the mosque's patio and the foot of the former minaret.) The spacious interior, which was recently renovated, now gleams with freshly scrubbed Baroque pride. Explore its 14 richly decorated altarpieces, many from the 18th century. You'll also find sculptures by some of Sevilla's most celebrated Baroque artists, such as *Jesus of the Passion* by Martinez Montañés and *Christ of Love* by Juan de Mena. Plaza del Salvador, the pleasant square in front of the church, is cozy and intimate—a favorite meeting point for locals.

Cost and Hours: €3, free with €8 cathedral ticket, audioguide-€2.50; Mon-Sat July-Aug 10:00-17:00, Sept-June 11:30-18:00; Sun 15:00-19:00 year-round; Plaza del Salvador, tel. 954-211-679. If you plan to visit this church and later go to the cathedral, avoid possible lines there by buying your cathedral ticket here.

▲**Museo Palacio de la Condesa de Lebrija**—This aristocratic mansion takes you back into the 18th century like no other place in town. The Countess of Lebrija was a passionate collector of antiquities. Her home's ground floor is paved with Roman mosaics (that you can actually walk on) and lined with musty old cases of Phoenician, Greek, Roman, and Moorish artifacts—mostly pottery. To see a plush world from a time when the nobility had a private priest and their own chapel, take a quickie tour (in both English and Spanish) of the upstairs, which shows the palace as the countess left it when she died in 1938.

Cost and Hours: €5 for unescorted visit of ground floor, €8 includes tour of "lived-in" upstairs offered every 45 minutes; July-Aug Mon-Fri 9:00-15:00, Sat-Sun 10:00-14:00; Sept-June Mon-Fri 10:30-19:30, Sat-Sun 10:00-14:00; free and obligatory bag check, Calle Cuna 8, tel. 954-227-802, www.palaciodelebrija.com.

Plaza de la Encarnación—This formerly nondescript square recently underwent a dramatic renovation and now makes a bold architectural statement in the heart of old Sevilla. A gigantic undulating canopy of five waffle-patterned, mushroom-shaped, hundred-foot-tall structures provides shade to the formerly sun-baked square. Under the canopy is a gazebo for performances, and in the concrete structure below are  a food market and an *antiquarium* (a museum displaying Roman ruins found during the excavation of the site). The canopy, named the Metropol Parasol, was designed by German architect Jürgen Mayer H., who won a contest to create a new iconic structure for Sevilla (trendy-to-the-max Jürgen shifted his middle initial to become his last name). The dynamic vaulting is intended to echo the interior of Sevilla's vast cathedral. The wooden structure, unbelievably, is held together with glue. And—as you might guess for a cutting-edge architectural work with a hefty price tag (reportedly €86 million) completed several years behind deadline—it has been controversial. Architecture critics greeted its March 2011 unveiling with a mix of appreciation and puzzlement, and the structure has yet to win over the hearts of most Sevillans. Fans of modern architecture (or experimental civic projects) will find it worth the short walk from Plaza Nueva to take a peek (especially handy if you're visiting the Museo Palacio de la Condesa de Lebrija, just a block away).

▲**Flamenco Dance Museum (Museo del Baile Flamenco)**—If you want to understand more about the dance that embodies the spirit of southern Spain, this small but good museum—overpriced at €10—does the trick. The grande dame of flamenco, Cristina Hoyos, has collected a few artifacts and costumes and put together a series of well-produced videos explaining the art of flamenco. Ride the red elevator to floor 1 to tour the main exhibition, with videos, flamenco dresses and other objects, and posters celebrating notable flamenco artists over time. The place is heavy on evocative video clips, but a bit light on actual information. One particularly interesting film illustrates the key elements of the dance form: pain, joy, elegance, seduction, soul, and—I believe—love of ham. Floor 2 and the basement (-1) feature temporary exhibits—mostly artwork relating to flamenco. On the ground floor and in the basement, you can watch flamenco lessons in progress—or even take one yourself.

Cost and Hours: €10, 10 percent discount with this book in 2012, daily 9:30-19:00, last entry 30 minutes before closing, Manuel Rojas Marcos 3, about 3 blocks east of Plaza Nueva, tel. 954-340-311, www.museoflamenco.com.

Classes: You can participate in a one-hour lesson and take a little *olé* home (up to €60/person, prices go down with more people, shoes not provided).

Performances: Regular dance shows run Sun-Thu at 19:00 (€15) and Fri-Sat at 19:30 (€23). A combo-ticket includes the museum and a show (€20 weekday or €28 weekend; 10 percent discount off museum, show, or combo-ticket with this book in 2012).

▲Museo de Bellas Artes

Sevilla's passion for religious art is preserved and displayed in its Museum of Fine Arts. While most Americans go for El Greco,

Goya, and Velázquez (not a forte of this collection), this museum gives a fine look at other, less-appreciated Spanish masters: Zurbarán and Murillo. Rather than exhausting, the museum is pleasantly enjoyable.

Cost and Hours: €1.50, Tue-Sat 9:00-20:30, Sun 9:00-14:30, closed Mon, last entry 15 minutes before closing, tel. 954-786-500, www.juntadeandalucia.es/cultura/museos.

Getting There: The museum is at Plaza Museo 9; it's a 15-minute walk from the cathedral, or a short ride on bus #C5 from Plaza Nueva. If coming from the Basílica de La Macarena, take bus #C4 to the Torneo stop and walk inland four blocks. Pick up the English-language floor plan, which explains the theme of each room.

Background: Sevilla was Spain's wealthy commercial capital, similar to New York City, whereas Madrid was a newly built center of government, like Washington, D.C. In the early 1800s, Spain's liberal government was disbanding convents and monasteries, and secular fanatics were looting churches. Thankfully, the region's religious art was rescued and hung safely here in this convent-turned-museum.

Spain's economic Golden Age (the 1500s) blossomed into the Golden Age of Spanish painting (the 1600s). Several of Spain's top artists—Zurbarán, Murillo, and Velázquez—lived in Sevilla during the 1600s. Artists labored to make the spiritual world tangible, and forged the gritty realism that marks Spanish painting. You'll see balding saints and monks with wrinkled faces and sunburned hands. The style suited Spain's spiritual climate, as the Catholic Church used this art in its Counter-Reformation battle against the Protestant rebellion.

◐ Self-Guided Tour: The permanent collection features 20 rooms in neat chronological order. It's easy to breeze through once with my tour, then backtrack to what appeals to you.

• *Enter and follow signs to the permanent collection, which begins in Sala I (Room 1).*

Rooms 1-4: Medieval altarpieces of gold-backed saints, Virgin-and-babes, and Crucifixion scenes attest to the religiosity that nurtured Spain's early art. Spain's penchant for unflinching realism culminates in Room 2 with Pedro Torrigiano's 1525 statue of an emaciated San Jerónimo, and in Room 3 with the painted clay head of St. John the Baptist—complete with severed neck muscles, throat, and windpipe. This kind of warts-and-all naturalism would influence the great Sevillan painter Velázquez (whose few works are often displayed in Room 4).

• *Continue through the pleasant outdoor courtyard to the former church that is now Room 5.*

Room 5—Murillo: The works of another hometown boy, Bartolomé Murillo (mur-EE-oh, 1617-1682), are displayed here. His signature subject is the Immaculate Conception, the doctrine that holds that Mary was

exempt from original sin. Several *Inmaculadas* may be on display. Typically, Mary is depicted as young, dressed in white and blue, standing atop the moon (crescent or full). She clutches her breast and gazes up rapturously, surrounded by tumbling winged babies. Murillo's tiny *Madonna and Child* (*Virgen de la Servilleta,*

1665; at the end of the room in the center, where the church's altar would have been) shows the warmth and appeal of his work.

Murillo's sweetness is quite different from the harsh realism of his fellow artists, but his work was understandably popular. For many Spaniards, Mary is their main connection to heaven. They pray directly to her, asking her to intercede on their behalf with God. Murillo's Marys are always receptive and ready to help. (For more on Murillo, see page 582.)

Besides his *Inmaculadas*, Murillo painted popular saints. They often carry sprigs of plants, and cock their heads upward, caught up in a heavenly vision of sweet Baby Jesus. Murillo is also known for his "genre" paintings—scenes of common folk and rascally street urchins—but the museum has few of these.

• *Now head upstairs to the first floor.*

Rooms 6-9: In rooms 6 and 7, you'll see more Murillos and Murillo imitators. Room 8 is dedicated to yet another native Sevillan (and friend of Murillo), Juan de Valdés Leal (1622-1690). He adds Baroque motion and drama to religious subjects. His surreal colors and feverish, unfinished style create a mood of urgency.

Room 10—Zurbarán: Francisco de Zurbarán (thoor-bar-AHN, 1598-1664) painted saints and monks, and the miraculous things they experienced, with an unblinking, crystal-clear, brightly lit, highly detailed realism. Monks and nuns could meditate upon Zurbarán's meticulous paintings for hours, finding God in the details.

In Zurbarán's *St. Hugo Visiting the Refectory (San Hugo en el Refectorio)*, white-robed Carthusian monks gather together for their

simple meal in a communal dining hall. Above them hangs a painting of Mary, Baby Jesus, and John the Baptist. Zurbarán created paintings for monks' dining halls like this. His audience: celibate men and women who lived in isolation, as in this former convent, devoting their time to quiet meditation, prayer, and Bible study. Zurbarán shines a harsh spotlight on many of his subjects, creating strong shadows. Zurbarán's people often stand starkly isolated against a single-color background—a dark room or the gray-white of a cloudy sky. He was the ideal painter of the austere religion of 17th-century Spain.

Find *The Virgin of the Caves (La Virgen de las Cuevas)* and study the piety and faith in the monks' weathered faces. Zurbarán's Mary is protective, with her hands placed on the heads of two monks. Note the loving detail on the cape embroidery, the brooch, and the flowers at her feet. But also note the angel babies holding the cape, with their painfully double-jointed arms. Zurbarán was no Leonardo.

The Apotheosis of St. Thomas Aquinas (*Apteosis de Santo Tomás de Aquino,* may be displayed on ground level, Room 5) is considered Zurbarán's most important work. It was done at the height of his career, when stark realism was all the rage. In a believable, down-to-earth way, Zurbarán presents the pivotal moment when the great saint-theologian experiences his spiritual awakening.

The Rest of the Museum: Spain's subsequent art, from the 18th century on, generally followed the trends of the rest of Europe. Room 12 has creamy Romanticism and hazy Impressionism. You'll see typical Sevillan motifs such as matadors, cigar-factory girls, and river landscapes. Enjoy these painted slices of Sevilla, then exit to experience similar scenes today.

South of the Cathedral, near Plaza de España

University—Today's university was yesterday's *fábrica de tabacos* (tobacco factory), which employed 10,000 young female *cigareras*— including the saucy femme fatale of Bizet's opera *Carmen.* In the 18th century, it was the second-largest building in Spain, after El Escorial. Wander through its halls as you walk to Plaza de España. The university's bustling café is a good place for cheap tapas, beer, wine, and conversation (Mon-Fri 8:00-21:00, Sat 9:00-13:00, closed Sun).

Plaza de España—This square, the surrounding buildings, and the nearby María Luisa Park are the remains of the 1929 inter-

national fair, where for a year the Spanish-speaking countries of the world enjoyed a mutual-admiration fiesta. When they finish the restoration work here (it's taking years), this delightful area—the epitome of world's fair–style architecture—will once again be great for people-watching (especially during the 19:00-20:00 peak paseo hour). The park's highlight is the former Spanish Pavilion. Its tiles (a trademark of Sevilla) show historic scenes and maps from every province of Spain (arranged in alphabetical order, from Álava to Zaragoza). Climb to one of the balconies for a fine view. Beware: This is a classic haunt of thieves and con artists. Believe no one here. Thieves, posing as lost tourists, will come at you with a map unfolded to hide their speedy, greedy fingers.

Away from the Center

▲▲Basílica de la Macarena

Sevilla's Holy Week (Semana Santa) celebrations are Spain's grandest. During the week leading up to Easter, the city is packed

with pilgrims witnessing 60 processions carrying about 100 religious floats. If you miss the actual event, you can get a sense of it by visiting the Basílica de la Macarena and its accompanying museum to see the two most impressive floats and the darling of Holy Week, the statue of the Virgen de la Macarena.

Cost and Hours: Church-free, treasury museum-€5, audioguide-€1, Mon-Sat 9:00-14:00 & 17:00-21:00, Sun from 9:30. Although far from the

city center, it's located on Sevilla's ring road and easy to reach. Wave down a taxi and say "Basilica Macarena" (about €7 from city center). All the #C buses go there, including bus #C3 or #C4 from Puerta de Jerez (near the Torre de Oro) or Menéndez Pelayo (the ring road east of the cathedral), tel. 954-901-800, www.hermandad delamacarena.es.

◒ Self-Guided Tour: Despite the long history of the Macarena statue, the Neo-Baroque church was only built in 1949 to give the oft-moved sculpture a permanent home.

• Grab a pew and study the...

Weeping Virgin: La Macarena is known as the "Weeping Virgin" for the five crystal teardrops trickling down her cheeks.

She's like a Baroque doll with human hair and articulated arms, and is even dressed in underclothes. Sculpted in the late 17th century (probably by Pedro Roldán), she's become Sevilla's most popular image of Mary.

Her beautiful expression—halfway between smiling and crying—is ambiguous, letting worshippers project their own emotions onto her. Her weeping can be contagious—look around you. She's

also known as La Esperanza, the Virgin of Hope, and she promises better times after the sorrow.

Installed in a side chapel (on the left) is the **Christ of the**

Judgment (from 1654), showing Jesus on the day he was condemned. This statue and La Macarena stand atop the two most important floats of the Holy Week parades.

• *To see the floats and learn more, visit the treasury museum to the left of the church.*

Tesoro (Treasury Museum): This small three-floor museum tells the history of the Virgin statue and the Holy Week parades. Though rooted in medieval times, the current traditions developed around 1600, with the formation of various fraternities (*hermandades*). During Holy Week, they demonstrate their dedication to God by parading themed floats throughout Sevilla to retell the story of the Crucifixion and Resurrection of Christ (for more, see "Holy Week in Andalucía," sidebar, page 568). The museum displays ceremonial banners, scepters, and costumed mannequins; videos show the parades in action (some displays in English).

The three-ton float that carries the Christ of the Judgment is slathered in gold leaf and shows a commotion of figures acting out the sentencing of Jesus. (The statue of Christ—the one you saw in the church—is placed before this crowd for the Holy Week procession.) Pontius Pilate is about to wash his hands. Pilate's wife cries as a man reads the death sentence. During the Holy Week procession, pious Sevillan women wail in the streets while relays of 48 men carry this float on the backs of their necks—only their feet showing under the drapes—as they shuffle through the streets from midnight until 14:00 in the afternoon every Good Friday. The men rehearse for months in advance to get their choreographed footwork in sync.

La Macarena follows the Christ of the Judgment in the procession. Mary's smaller 1.5-ton float seems all silver and candles— "strong enough to support the roof, but tender enough to quiver in the soft night breeze." Mary has a wardrobe of three huge mantles, worn in successive years. They are about 100 years old. Her six-pound gold crown/halo is from 1913. This float has a mesmerizing effect on the local crowds. They line up for hours, clapping, weeping, and throwing roses as it slowly sways along the streets, working its way through town. My Sevillan friend explained, "She knows all the problems of Sevilla and its people. We've been confiding in her for centuries. To us, she is hope. That's her name—Esperanza."

The museum collection also contains some matador paraphernalia. La Macarena is the patron saint of bullfighters, and they give thanks for her protection. Copies of her image are popular in bullring chapels. In 1912 the bullfighter José Ortega, hoping for protection, gave La Macarena the five emerald brooches she wears. It worked for eight years...until he was gored to death in the ring. For a month, La Macarena was dressed in widow's black—the only time that has happened.

• *Exit the church into the...*

Macarena Neighborhood: Outside, notice the best surviving bit of Sevilla's old walls. Originally Roman, what remains today was built by the Moors in the 12th century to (unsuccessfully) keep the Christians out. And yes, it's from this city that a local dance band (Los del Río) changed the world by giving us the popular 1990s song "The Macarena." He-e-y-y, Macarena!

Near Sevilla

Itálica—One of Spain's most impressive Roman ruins is found outside the sleepy town of Santiponce, about six miles northwest of Sevilla. Founded in 206 B.C. for wounded soldiers recuperating from the Second Punic War, Itálica became a thriving town of great agricultural and military importance. It was the birthplace of famous Roman emperors Trajan and Hadrian. Today its best-preserved ruin is its amphitheater—one of the largest in the Roman Empire—with a capacity for 30,000 spectators. Other highlights include beautiful floor mosaics, such as the one in Casa de los Pájaros (House of the Birds) that shows more than 30 species of birds. To avoid the midday heat in summer, plan your visit to arrive early or late, and definitely bring water.

Cost and Hours: €1.50; April-Sept Tue-Sat 8:30-21:00, Sun 9:00-15:00; Oct-March Tue-Sat 9:00-18:30, Sun 10:00-15:00; closed Mon year-round; last entry 30 minutes before closing; tel. 955-622-266, www.juntadeandalucia.es/cultura/italica.

Getting There: You can get to Itálica on bus #M-172A (30-minute trip, frequent departures from Sevilla's Plaza de Armas station). If you're driving, head west out of Sevilla in the direction of Huelva; after you cross the second branch of the river, turn north on SE-30/A-66, and after a few miles, get off at Santiponce. Drive past pottery warehouses and through the town to the ruins at the far (west) end.

Experiences in Sevilla

Bullfighting

▲**Bullfights**—Some of Spain's best bullfighting is done in Sevilla's 14,000-seat bullring, Plaza de Toros. Fights are held (generally at 18:30) on most Sundays in May and June; on Easter and Corpus Christi; daily during the April Fair (April 24-29 in 2012); and at the

end of September (during the Feria de San Miguel). These serious fights, with adult matadors, are called *corrida de toros* and often sell out in advance. On many Thursday evenings in July, there are *novillada* fights, with teenage novices doing the killing and smaller bulls doing the dying. *Corrida de toros* seats range from €25 for high seats looking into the sun to €150 for the first three rows in the shade under the royal box; *novillada* seats are half that—and easy to buy at the arena a few minutes before show time (ignore scalpers outside; get information at a TI, your hotel, by phone, or online; tel. 954-210-315, www.lamaestranza.es).

▲▲**Bullring (Plaza de Toros) and Bullfight Museum (Museo Taurino)**—Follow a bilingual (Spanish and English) 40-minute guided tour through the bullring's strangely quiet and empty arena, its museum, and the chapel where the matador prays before the fight. (Thanks to readily available blood transfusions, there have been no deaths in nearly three decades.) The two most revered figures of Sevilla, the Virgen de la Macarena and the Jesús del Gran Poder (Christ of All Power), are represented in the chapel. In the museum, you'll see great classic scenes and the heads of a few bulls—awarded the bovine equivalent of an Oscar for a particularly good fight. The city was so appalled when the famous matador Manolete was killed in 1947 that even the mother of the bull that gored him was destroyed. Matadors—dressed to kill—are heartthrobs in their "suits of light." Many girls have their bedrooms wallpapered with posters of cute bullfighters. See page 814 for more on the "art" of bullfighting.

Cost and Hours: €6.50, entrance with escorted tour only—no free time inside, 3/hour, daily May-Oct 9:30-20:00, Nov-April 9:30-19:00, until 14:00 on fight days, when chapel and horse room are closed. The last tour departs 15 minutes before closing. While they take groups of up to 50, it's still wise to call or drop by to reserve a spot in the busy season (tel. 954-210-315, www.realmaestranza.com).

The April Fair

For a seven-day period that falls a week or two after Easter, much of Sevilla is packed into its vast fairgrounds for a grand party (April 24-29 in 2012). The fair, seeming to bring all that's Andalusian together, feels friendly, spontaneous, and very real. The local passion for horses, flamenco, and sherry is clear—riders are ramrod straight, colorfully clad girls ride sidesaddle,

and everyone's drinking sherry spritzers. Women sport outlandish dresses that would look clownish elsewhere, but are somehow brilliant here en masse. Horses clog the streets in an endless parade until about 20:00, when they clear out and the streets fill with exuberant locals. The party goes for literally 24 hours a day for the entire week.

Countless private party tents, or *casetas,* line the lanes. Each tent is the private party zone of a family, club, or association. You need to know someone in the group—or make friends quickly—to get in. Because of the exclusivity, it has a real family-affair feeling. In each *caseta,* everyone knows everyone. It seems like a thousand wedding parties being celebrated at the same time.

Any tourist can have a fun and memorable evening by simply crashing the party. The city's entire fleet of taxis (who'll try to charge double) and buses seems dedicated to shuttling people from downtown to the fairgrounds. Given the traffic jams and inflated prices, you may be better off hiking: From the Torre del Oro, cross the San Telmo Bridge to Plaza de Cuba and hike down Calle Asunción. You'll see the towering gate to the fairgrounds in the distance. Just follow the crowds (there's no admission charge). Arrive before 20:00 to see the horses, but stay later, as the ambience improves after the *caballos* giddy-up on out. Some of the larger tents are sponsored by the city and open to the public, but the best action is in the streets, where party-goers from the livelier *casetas* spill out. Although private tents have bouncers, everyone is so happy that it's not tough to strike up an impromptu friendship, become a "special guest," and be invited in. The drink flows freely, and the food is fun and cheap.

Shopping in Sevilla

For the best local shopping experience, follow my shopping stroll (described next). The popular pedestrian streets Sierpes and

Tetuán/Velázquez—along with the surrounding lanes near Plaza Nueva— are packed with people and shops. Small shops close between 13:30 and 16:00 or 17:00 on weekdays, as well as on Saturday afternoons and all day Sunday. But big ones such as El Corte Inglés stay open (and air-conditioned) right through the siesta. El Corte Inglés also has a supermarket downstairs and a good but expensive restaurant (Mon-Sat 10:00-22:00, closed Sun). Popular souvenir items include ladies' fans, shawls, *mantillas,* other items related to flamenco (castanets, guitars, costumes), ceramics, and bullfighting posters.

Collectors' markets hop on Sunday: stamps and coins at Plaza del Cabildo (near the cathedral) and art on Plaza del Museo (by the Museo de Bellas Artes).

Mercado del Arenal, the covered fish-and-produce market, is perfect for hungry photographers (Mon-Sat 9:00-14:30, closed Sun, least lively on Mon, on Calle Pastor y Landero at Calle Arenal, just beyond bullring). For suggestions on dining here (including a small café-bar for breakfast and a fish restaurant inside), see page 622.

▲▲Shopping Paseo Tour

Although many tourists never get beyond the cathedral and the Santa Cruz neighborhood, it's important to wander west into the lively pedestrian shopping center of town. These streets—Calle Tetuán (which becomes Velázquez), Calle Sierpes, and Calle Cuna—also happen to be part of the oldest section of Sevilla. A walk here is a chance to join one of Spain's liveliest paseos—that bustling celebration of life that takes place before dinner each evening, when everyone is out strolling, showing off their fancy shoes and making the scene. This walk (if done between 18:00 and 20:00) gives you a look at the paseo scene and the town's most popular shops. You'll pass windows displaying the best in both traditional and trendy fashion. The walk ends at a plush mansion of a local countess (open to the public).

Start on the pedestrianized **Plaza Nueva,** a 19th-century square facing the ornate city hall, which features a statue of Ferdinand III, a local favorite because he freed Sevilla from the Moors in 1248. From here wander the length of **Calle Tetuán** (notice the latest in outrageous shoes). Calle Tetuán becomes **Velázquez,** and ends at La Campana (a big intersection and popular meeting point, with the super department store, El Corte Inglés, just beyond, on Plaza del Duque de la Victoria). At La Campana, tempt yourself with sweets at the venerable Confitería La Campana.

Next, take two rights to get to **Calle Sierpes,** great for shopping and strolling. Calle Sierpes is the main street of the Holy Week processions—imagine it packed with celebrants and its balconies bulging with spectators. At the corner of Sierpes and Jovellanos/Sagasta, you're near several fine shops featuring Andalusian accessories. Drop in to see how serious local women are about their fans, shawls, *mantillas* (ornate head scarves), and *peinetas* (combs designed to secure and prop up the *mantilla*). The most valuable *mantillas* are silk, and the top-quality combs are made of tortoise shell (though most women opt for much more affordable polyester and plastic). Andalusian women have various fans to match different dresses—they are considered an accessory. The *mantilla* comes in black (worn only on Good Friday and by the mother of the groom at weddings) and white (worn at bullfights during the April Fair).

From here turn left down **Calle Sagasta.** Notice that the street has two names—the modern version and a medieval one: Antigua Calle de Gallegos ("Ancient Street of the Galicians"). With the Christian victory in 1248, the Muslims were given one month to evacuate. To consolidate Christian control, settlers from the northwest corner of Iberia were planted here. This street was home to the Galicians.

Finally, you'll arrive at the charming Plaza del Salvador. It's teeming with life again, now that the Church of the Savior is completely restored. Backtrack left along **Calle Cuna,** famous for its exuberant flamenco dresses and classic wedding dresses. Local women save up to have flamenco dresses custom made for the April Fair: They're considered an important status symbol. (Flamenco miniskirts have been popular in recent years, but now hemlines are falling again.) If all this shopping makes you feel like a countess, Calle Cuna leads to the Museo Palacio de la Condesa de Lebrija, and nearby is the super-modern Metropol Parasol structure towering over Plaza de la Encarnación (both described on page 598).

Nightlife in Sevilla

▲▲▲Flamenco

This music-and-dance art form has its roots in the Roma (Gypsy) and Moorish cultures. Even at a packaged "flamenco evening,"

sparks fly. The men do most of the flamboyant machine-gun footwork. The women often concentrate on the graceful turns and smooth, shuffling step of the *soléa* version of the dance. Watch the musicians. Flamenco guitarists, with their lightning-fast finger-roll strums, are among the best in the world. The intricate rhythms are set by castanets or the hand-clapping (called *palmas*) of those who aren't dancing at the moment. In the raspy-voiced wails of the singers, you'll hear echoes of the Muslim call to prayer.

Like jazz, flamenco thrives on improvisation. Also like jazz, good flamenco is more than just technical proficiency. A singer or dancer with "soul" is said to have *duende.* Flamenco is a happening, with bystanders clapping along and egging on the dancers with whoops and shouts. Get into it. For a tourist-oriented flamenco show, your hotel can get you nightclub show tickets (happily, since they snare a hefty commission for each sale). But it's easy to book a place on your own. Aficionados will likely enjoy the Flamenco Dance Museum as well, which also has performances (page 598).

You basically have three options: serious—yet still touristy—flamenco shows, where the singing and dancing take center stage; even more touristy shows that have a bar and/or food (scurrying waiters can distract from the performers); and casual bars—the least touristy—where you can catch impromptu or semi-impromptu musicians at play.

Serious Flamenco Shows—Touristy flamenco shows give you all the clichés; at **Casa de la Memoria de Al-Andalus** (House of the Memory of Al-Andalus) you'll enjoy an elegant and classy musical experience with a small cast and classic solos. In an alcohol-free atmosphere, 90 tourists sit on 3 rows of folding chairs circling a small stage for an intimate concert featuring flamenco and other Andalusian music. It's all acoustic, and the nightly musical mix varies according to the personalities of the performers. It's also a perfect place to practice your Spanish fan *(abanico)* skills on warm nights. One-hour concerts are nightly all year at 21:00; with demand, shows are added at 19:30 and/or 22:30 (€15, reservations smart, box office open Mon-Sat 10:00-14:00 and daily 18:00-22:00. Same-day tickets generally available but better to buy tickets a day or more beforehand, arrive early for front-row seats, in Barrio Santa Cruz, adjacent to Hotel Alcántara at Ximénez de Enciso 28, tel. 954-560-670, www.casadelamemoria .es, memorias@terra.es).

Auditorio Álvarez Quintero, another good option just a block from the cathedral, fills a small atrium with 85 folding chairs and good performers that change each evening (€17, nightly at 21:00, doors open at 20:30—worth arriving early to get a good seat, Álvarez Quintero 48, tel. 954-293-949, www.alvarezquintero .com).

Shows with Drinks and/or Food—These packaged shows can be a bit sterile, and an audience of tourists doesn't help, but I find both Los Gallos and El Arenal entertaining and riveting. While El Arenal may have a slight edge on talent and feels slicker, Los Gallos has a cozier setting, with cushy rather than hard chairs—and it's cheaper.

Los Gallos presents nightly two-hour shows at 20:00 and 22:30 (€30 ticket includes a drink, €3/person discount with this book in 2012—but limited to two admissions, arrive 30 minutes early for best seats, noisy bar but no food served, Plaza de la Santa Cruz 11, tel. 954-216-981, www.tablaolosgallos.com, owners José and Nuria promise goose bumps).

Tablao El Arenal has arguably more professional performers and a classier setting for its show—but dinner customers get the preferred seating, and waiters are working throughout the performance (€37 ticket includes a drink, €59 includes tapas, €72 includes dinner, shows at 20:00 and 22:00, near bullring at Calle Rodó 7, tel. 954-216-492, www.tablaoelarenal.com).

El Patio Sevillano is more of a variety show, with flamenco as well as other forms of song and dance. At this venue, in a big hall with hard chairs, diners have the worst seats rather than the best (€38 ticket includes a drink, €60 with tapas, €72 with dinner, 1.5-hour shows at 19:00 and 21:30, next to bullring on busy riverfront road at Paseo de Cristóbal Colón, tel. 954-214-120, www .elpatiosevillano.com).

Impromptu Flamenco in Bars—Spirited flamenco singing still erupts spontaneously in bars throughout the old town after midnight. Head across the river to Triana and just follow your ears as you wander down Calle Betis, the riverfront street leading off Plaza de Cuba across the bridge. The **Lo Nuestro** and **Rejoneo** bars are local favorites (at Calle Betis 31A and 31B).

Or try **La Carbonería Bar,** the sangria equivalent of a beer garden. It's a sprawling place with a variety of rooms leading to a big, open tented area filled with young locals, casual guitar strummers, and nearly nightly flamenco music after about 23:00 (no dancing). Located just a few blocks from most of my recommended hotels, this is worth finding if you're not quite ready to end the day (no cover, €2.50 sangria, daily 20:00-3:00 in the morning; near Plaza Santa María—find Hotel Fernando III, the side alley Céspedes dead-ends at Levies, head left to Levies 18, unsigned door; for location, see map on page 614).

▲▲Evening Paseo

Sevilla is meant for strolling. The paseo thrives every non-winter evening in these areas: along either side of the river between the San Telmo and Isabel II bridges (Paseo de Cristóbal Colón and Triana district; see "Eating in Sevilla," page 619), up Avenida de la Constitución, around Plaza Nueva, at Plaza de España, and throughout the Barrio Santa Cruz. On hot summer nights, even families with toddlers are out and about past midnight. Spend some time rafting through this sea of humanity. Savor the view of floodlit Sevilla by night from the far side of the river—perhaps over dinner.

Sleeping in Sevilla

All of my listings are centrally located, mostly within a five-minute walk of the cathedral. The first are near the charming but touristy Santa Cruz neighborhood. The last group is just as central but

Sleep Code

(€1 = about $1.40, country code: 34)
S = Single, **D** = Double/Twin, **T** = Triple, **Q** = Quad, **b** = bathroom, **s** = shower only. Unless otherwise noted, credit cards are accepted, hoteliers speak enough English, tax is usually included, and breakfast generally costs extra.

To help you easily sort through these listings, I've divided the accommodations into three categories based on the price for a double room with bath during high season:

$$$ Higher Priced—Most rooms €110 or more.
$$ Moderately Priced—Most rooms between €60-110.
$ Lower Priced—Most rooms €60 or less.

Prices can change without notice; verify the hotel's current rates online or by email. For other updates, see www.ricksteves.com/update.

closer to the river, across the boulevard in a more workaday, less touristy zone.

Room rates as much as double during the two Sevilla fiestas (Holy Week; and the weeklong April Fair, held a week or two after Easter). In general, the busiest and most expensive months are April, May, September, and October. Hotels put rooms on the discounted push list in July and August—when people with good sense avoid this furnace—and from November through February. Prices generally include the IVA hotel tax. A price range indicates low- to high-season prices (but I have not listed festival prices).

If you do visit in July or August, the best values are central business-class places. They offer summer discounts and provide a (necessary) cool, air-conditioned refuge. But be warned that Spain's air-conditioning often isn't the icebox you're used to, especially in Sevilla.

Santa Cruz Neighborhood

These places are off Calle Santa María la Blanca and Plaza Santa María. The most convenient parking lot is the underground Cano y Cueto garage near the corner of Calle Santa María la Blanca and Menéndez Pelayo (about €18/day, open 24/7, at edge of big park, unsigned). A fine Internet café and self-service launderette are a couple of blocks away up Menéndez Pelayo (see "Helpful Hints" on page 568).

$$$ Hotel Casa 1800, well-priced for its elegance, is worth the extra euros. Located dead-center in Santa Cruz (facing a boisterous tapas bar that quiets down after midnight), its 24 rooms circle an elegant chandeliered patio lounge that hosts a daily free afternoon tea for guests. With a rooftop terrace offering an impressive cathedral view and elegantly appointed rooms with high, beamed ceilings, it's a winner (standard Db-€138, superior Db with private patio-€150, deluxe Db with patio and Jacuzzi-€184, "grand deluxe" Db with all of the above and more-€220, breakfast-€12, air-con, elevator, free Internet access and Wi-Fi, Rodrigo Caro 6, tel. 954-561-800, www.hotelcasa1800.com, info@hotelcasa1800 .com).

$$$ Hotel Las Casas de la Judería has 178 quiet, elegant rooms and suites, many of them tastefully decorated with hardwood floors and a Spanish flair. The rooms, which surround a series of peaceful courtyards, are a romantic splurge. Ask for one of the newer rooms to avoid the dated ones. The service can be stiff and stuffy (Sb-€100-160, Db-€120-200, extra bed-€45; low-season prices—July-Aug and late-Nov-Feb—are discounted a further 10 percent to those with this book who ask in 2012, but check their website for even better rates; expensive but great buffet breakfast-€19, air-con, elevator, free Wi-Fi in lobby, pool in summer, valet parking-€19/day, Plaza Santa María 5, tel. 954-415-150, fax 954 422-170, www.casasypalacios.com, juderia@casasypalacios .com).

$$ Hotel Amadeus is a little gem that music lovers will appreciate (it even has a couple of soundproof rooms with pianos—something I've never seen anywhere else in Europe). It's lovingly decorated with a music motif around small courtyards, with elevators that take you to your choice of two roof terraces (one with an under-the-stars Jacuzzi). Though small, this 24-room place is classy and comfortable, with welcoming public spaces and a very charming staff. The €8.50 breakfast comes on a trolley—enjoy it in your room, in the lounge, or on a terrace (Sb-€85, Db-€98, big Db-€115, suites-€165-195, cheaper July-Aug, air-con, elevator, free Internet access and Wi-Fi, laundry-€15, parking-€16, Calle Farnesio 6, tel. 954-501-443, fax 954-500-019, www.hotelamadeus sevilla.com, reservas@hotelamadeussevilla.com, wonderfully run by María Luisa and her staff—Zaida and Cristina). They'll even loan you a free laptop to access Wi-Fi in your room. Their next-door annex is every bit as charming and a similarly good value: **$$$ La Música de Sevilla** offers six additional, beautifully appointed rooms; three rooms face the interior patio, and three are streetside with small balconies (patio Db-€110, exterior Db-€130, air-con, reserve and check in at Hotel Amadeus).

$$ El Rey Moro encircles its spacious, colorful patio (which tourists routinely duck into for a peek) with 19 rooms. Colorful and dripping with quirky Andalusian character, and thoughtful about including extras (such as free loaner bikes), it's a class act

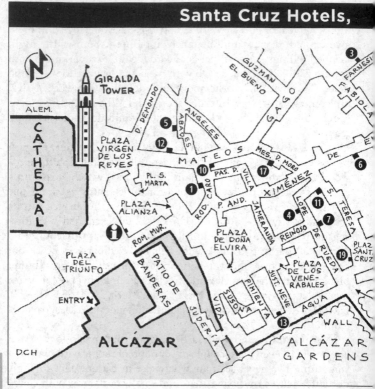

Santa Cruz Hotels,

(Sb-€39-79, Db-€69-100, breakfast-€9—or free if you reserve on their website, check their site for other specials, air-con, elevator, free Internet access and Wi-Fi, Lope de Rueda 14, tel. 954-563-468, www.hotelelreymoro.com, hotel@elreymoro.com).

$$ YH Giralda, once an 18th-century abbots' house, is now a charming 14-room hotel tucked away on a little street right off Mateo Gagos, just a couple of blocks from the cathedral. The exterior rooms have windows onto a pedestrian street, and a few of the interior rooms have small windows that look into the inner courtyard; all rooms are neatly appointed (Sb-€50-84, Db-€50-94, Tb-€75-115, Qb-€85-135, higher rates are for weekends, no breakfast, air-con, pay Wi-Fi, Calle Abades 30, tel. 954-228-324, fax 954-227-019, www.yh-hoteles.com, yhgiralda@yh-hoteles.com).

$$ Hotel Alcántara offers more no-nonsense comfort than character. Well-located but strangely out of place in the midst of the Santa Cruz jumble, it rents 21 slick rooms at a good price (Sb-€71, small Db-€82, bigger Db twin-€93, fancy Db-€117, 10 percent discount or a free breakfast—your choice—if you book direct, pay

Restaurants, & Flamenco

50 YARDS

50 METERS

1 Hotel Casa 1800
2 Hotel Las Casas de la Judería
3 Hotel Amadeus, La Música de Sevilla & Pensión Córdoba
4 El Rey Moro
5 YH Giralda
6 Hotel Alcántara & Casa de la Memoria de Al-Andalus (Flamenco, Music)
7 Hotel Murillo
8 Pensión San Benito Abad
9 To Samay Hostel, Internet Café & Launderette
10 Bodega Santa Cruz
11 Las Teresas Bar
12 Cervecería Giralda
13 Corral del Agua Restaurante
14 Restaurante Modesto (2)
15 Freiduría Puerta de la Carne
16 Bar Restaurante El 3 de Oro
17 Restaurante San Marco
18 Café Bar Carmela
19 Los Gallos (Flamenco)
20 To La Carbonería Bar

SEVILLA

cash, and show this book in 2012—not valid during Holy Week or April Fair, breakfast-€6, air-con, elevator, free Wi-Fi, rentable laptop, outdoor patio, Ximénez de Enciso 28, tel. 954-500-595, fax 954-500-604, www.hotelalcantara.net, info@hotelalcantara.net). The hotel is adjacent to Casa de la Memoria de Al-Andalus, which offers concerts (described earlier under "Flamenco").

$$ Hotel Murillo enjoys one of the most appealing locations in Santa Cruz, along one of the very narrow "kissing lanes." Above its elegant, antiques-filled lobby are 57 nondescript rooms with marble floors (Sb-€65-90, Db-€80-105, about €25 more for "superior" rooms with fancier decor, breakfast-€8.50, air-con, elevator, free Wi-Fi in lobby, bar across the street closes at midnight, Lope de Rueda 7, tel. 954-216-095, www.hotelmurillo.com, reservas @hotelmurillo.com). They also rent apartments with kitchens (Db-€90-120, see website for details).

$ Pensión Córdoba, a homier and cheaper option, has 12 tidy, quiet rooms, solid modern furniture, and a showpiece tiled courtyard (S-€30-40, Sb-€40-50, D-€45-55, Db-€60-70, no breakfast,

Sevilla Hotels,

Hotels

1 Hotel Alminar & Auditorio Álvarez Quintero
2 Hotel San Francisco
3 Hotel Vincci La Rábida & Laundry
4 Hotel Taberna del Alabardero
5 Hotel Maestranza
6 To Oasis Backpackers Hostel

Restaurants & Flamenco

7 Bar Bistec & Taberna La Plazuela
8 Bar Santa Ana
9 Restaurante Río Grande
10 El Faro de Triana & La Taberna del Pescador
11 Bodega Restaurante La María

Restaurants, & Flamenco

To MUSEO PALACIO, PLAZA DE LA ENCARNACIÓN & ⑥

200 YARDS
200 METERS

IGLESIA DEL SALVADOR

PLAZA NUEVA

CITY HALL ②

①

FLAMENCO DANCE MUSEUM

GIRALDA

CATHEDRAL

BARRIO SANTA CRUZ
(SEE DETAIL MAPS)

ARCHIVO DE INDIAS

HOSPITAL DE LA CARIDAD

ALCÁZAR

ALCÁZAR GARDENS

PUERTA DE JEREZ

SAN FERNANDO

HOTEL ALF XIII

TO EL PRADO BUS STN.

TO PLAZA DE ESPAÑA

UNIV.

SEVILLA

⑫ Horno San Buenaventura
⑬ Bodega Morales & Freiduría La Isla
⑭ Bodega Paco Góngora
⑮ Cafetería Mesón Serranito
⑯ Marisquería Arenal Sevilla & Mercado del Arenal
⑰ Bar Restaurante Pepe Hillo

⑱ La Societé
⑲ Restaurante Enrique Becerra
⑳ Taberna del Alabardero
㉑ Tablao El Arenal (Flamenco)
㉒ El Patio Sevillano (Flamenco)
㉓ Lo Nuestro & Rejoneo Bars
㉔ El Torno Pasteleria de Conventos

cash only, air-con, free Internet access and Wi-Fi in lobby, on a tiny lane off Calle Santa María la Blanca at Farnesio 12, tel. 954-227-498, www.pensioncordoba.com, reservas@pensioncordoba.com, Ana and María).

$ Pensión San Benito Abad, with eight humble rooms, faces a traditional Sevilla courtyard buried at the end of a dead-end lane just off Plaza Santa María. The rooms are dark, with windows that open onto an inner courtyard. The hardworking owners don't speak English, but offer some of the most conveniently located cheap rooms in town (S-€25, D-€40, Db-€50, slightly cheaper if you don't use the air-con or heat, no breakfast, parking-€15, on a tiny lane next to Cano y Cueto garage at Calle Canarios 4, tel. 954-415-255, www.hostalsanbenito.com, hostalsanbenito@gmail.com, Charo and Tomás).

$ Samay Hostel, on a busy street a block from the edge of the Barrio Santa Cruz, is a youthful, well-run slumbermill with 90 beds in 23 rooms (Db-€25-32/person, bunk in 4- to 10-bed dorm-€15-18, includes linens, no breakfast but shared kitchen, air-con, elevator, free Internet access and Wi-Fi, laundry service, 24-hour reception, rooftop terrace, Menéndez Pelayo 13, tel. 955-100-160, www.samayhostels.com, Pablo).

Near the Cathedral

$$$ Hotel Alminar, plush and elegant, rents 12 fresh, slick, minimalist rooms (Sb-€60-95, Db-€95-125, superior Db with terrace-€115-155, extra bed-€25, breakfast-€6, air-con, elevator, free Internet access and Wi-Fi, just 100 yards from the cathedral at Álvarez Quintero 52, tel. 954-293-913, fax 954-212-197, www.hotelalminar.com, reservas@hotelalminar.com, run by well-dressed, never-stressed Francisco).

$$ Hotel San Francisco may have a classy facade, but inside its 17 rooms are sparsely decorated, with metal doors. It's centrally located, clean, and quiet, except for the noisy ground-floor room next to the TV and reception (Sb-€40-55, Db-€50-68, Tb-€62-80, no breakfast, air-con, elevator, small rooftop terrace with cathedral view, free Wi-Fi in lobby with loaner netbook, located on pedestrian street at Álvarez Quintero 38, tel. 954-501-541, www.sanfranciscoh.com, info@sanfranciscoh.com, Carlos).

West of Avenida de la Constitución

$$$ Hotel Vincci La Rábida, part of a big, impersonal hotel chain, offers four-star comfort with its 113 rooms, huge and inviting courtyard lounge, and powerful air-conditioning. Its pricing is dictated by a magical computer that has perfect price discrimination down to a science (see website for prices—rates can spike to €400 with high demand and dip to €80 during slow times, when that air-con is most welcome; elevator, pay Wi-Fi, Castelar 24, tel. 954-501-280, fax 954-216-600, www.vinccihoteles.com, larabida @vinccihoteles.com).

$$$ Hotel Taberna del Alabardero is unique, with only seven rooms occupying the top floor of a poet's mansion (above the recommended classy restaurant, Taberna del Alabardero). It's nicely located, a great value, and the ambience is perfectly circa 1900 (Db-€130-160, Db suite-€200-250, tax not included, 10 percent discount with this book in 2012, includes breakfast, air-con, elevator, free Wi-Fi, parking-€20, closed in Aug, Zaragoza 20, tel. 954-502-721, fax 954-563-666, www.tabernadelalabardero.es, hotel.alabardero@esh.es).

$$ Hotel Maestranza, sparkling with loving care and charm, has 18 small, clean, simple rooms well-located on a street just off Plaza Nueva. It feels elegant for the price. To escape the noise from the tapas bars below, ask for an interior room, especially on weekends (Sb-€41-53, Db-€57-87, family suite-€104-135, extra bed-€20, 5 percent cash discount, no breakfast, air-con, elevator, free Wi-Fi, Gamazo 12, tel. 954-561-070, fax 954-214-404, www.hotel maestranza.es, sevilla@hotelmaestranza.es, Antonio).

North of Plaza Nueva, Between Plaza de la Encarnación and Plaza de la Alfalfa

$ Oasis Backpackers Hostel is a good place for cheap beds and for hanging out and connecting with young backpackers. Each of the eight rooms, with four double bunks, comes with a modern bathroom and individual lockers. The rooftop terrace—with lounge chairs, a small pool, and adjacent kitchen—is well-used (€15-20/bed, includes breakfast, free Internet access, just off Plaza de la Encarnación behind the church at #29 1/2 on the tiny and quiet lane, tel. 954-293-777, www.hostelsoasis.com, sevilla@hostelsoasis .com). They also have popular branches in Granada, Málaga, and Lisbon.

Eating in Sevilla

Local soups, such as *salmorejo* (Córdoba-style super-thick gazpacho) and *ajo blanco* (almond-based with garlic), are tasty. A popular Andalusian meal is fried fish, particularly marinated *adobo*. I like *taquitos de merluza* (hake fish), but for a mix of fish, ask for *frito variado*.

Restaurants generally serve lunch from 13:00 to 16:00 and dinner from 20:00 until very late (Spaniards don't start dinner until about 21:00). If you're hungry for dinner before the locals are, do the tapas tango, using the tapas tips on page 30. Wash down your tapas with *fino* (chilled dry sherry) or the more refreshing *tinto de verano* ("summer red wine"), an Andalusian red wine with soda, like a mild sangria. A good, light white wine is *barbadillo*. And for a heavy red, always go for the Rioja.

Across the River in Triana

The colorful Triana district—on the west bank of the river, between the San Telmo and Isabel II bridges—is filled with rustic and fun eateries. The riverside and traffic-free Calle Betis is lined with a variety of places to eat, from fine riverside restaurants to sloppy fish joints. It also comes with good picnic and take-out opportunities for romantics.

Tapas in a Triana Neighborhood Joint

Bars along the river and the parallel street one block inland are good for tapas. Before sitting down, walk to the Santa Ana church (midway between the bridges, two blocks off the river), where tables spill onto the square behind the church (Plazuela de Santa Ana) in the shadow of the floodlit spire. It feels like the whole neighborhood is out celebrating.

Bar Bistec, with most of the square's tables, does grilled fish with gusto. They're enthusiastic about their cod fritters and calamari, and brag about their pigeon, quail, and snails in sauce. Consider the indoor seating and the fun at the bar before sitting out on the square (€8 half-*raciones,* €14 *raciones,* daily 11:30-16:00 & 20:00-24:00, Plazuela de Santa Ana, tel. 954-274-759).

Taberna La Plazuela is self-service, doing simpler fare with enticing €10 *tostones* (giant fancy Andalusian bruschetta, good for 3-4 people) and €2.30 *montaditos* (little sandwiches). Get what you want and grab a table on the leafy square. Ignore the printed menu and read the daily specials board (same hours and owners as Bar Bistec, above).

Bar Santa Ana, just a block away alongside the church, is a rustic neighborhood sports-and-bull bar with great seating on the street. Peruse the interior, draped in bullfighting and Weeping Virgin memorabilia. It's always busy with the neighborhood gang enjoying fun tapas like *delicia de solomillo* (tenderloin) and the bar's willingness to serve even cheap tapas at the outdoor tables. If you stand at the bar, they'll keep track of your bill by chalking it directly on the counter in front of you (long hours, typically closed one day per week—closed Sun during April Fair, facing the side of the church at Pureza 82, tel. 954-272-102).

Riverside Dinners in Triana

Restaurante Río Grande is your stuffy, candlelit-fancy option—*the* place for a restaurant dinner with properly attired waiters and a full menu rather than tapas. Dining on the terrace is less expensive and more casual (€10-20 starters, €15-25 main dishes, daily 13:00-16:00 & 20:00-24:00, air-con, 2-person minimum for house specialties—paella and rice dishes, also lots of seafood, next to the San Telmo Bridge, tel. 954-273-956).

El Faro de Triana is actually the old yellow bridge tower overlooking the Isabel II Bridge. While professional, it's less formal and quirkier than Río Grande. They offer inexpensive tapas, €7-9 half-*raciones*, €12-18 *raciones*, and grand views over the river from the top floor (the views are better than the food; some diners object to strong river aroma). Choose from four dining zones: rooftop, outdoor terrace just below the rooftop (perhaps the best), riverside metal tables on the sidewalk, and the bar. There's no cover charge, but they don't serve tapas on the roof or riverside (open daily, bar—8:00-24:00, restaurant—13:00-16:30 & 20:15-24:00, tel. 954-336-192).

La Taberna del Pescador, with tablecloths on its riverside tables, is a fancy dining option (€6-10 half-*raciones*, €12-15 *raciones*, daily 8:00-24:00, 50 yards from Puente de Isabel II on Calle Betis, tel. 954-330-069).

Bodega Restaurante La María also offers fine tablecloth type restaurant seating on the riverside, but with a formal menu focusing on fresh fish and grilled meat rather than tapas (€5-10 half-*raciones*, €9-16 *raciones*, Wed-Mon 13:00-16:00 & 20:00-24:00, closed Tue, Calle Betis 12, tel. 954-338-461).

Near Recommended Hotels in Barrio Santa Cruz

These eateries—for tapas, dining, and cheaper eats—are handy to my recommended Barrio Santa Cruz accommodations.

Tapas

For tapas, the Barrio Santa Cruz is trendy and *romántico*. Plenty of atmospheric-but-touristy restaurants fill the neighborhood near the cathedral and along Calle Santa María la Blanca. From the cathedral, walk up Mateos Gago, where several classic old bars—with the day's tapas scrawled on chalkboards—keep tourists and locals well fed and watered. (Turn right at Mesón del Moro for several more.)

A block farther, you'll find **Bodega Santa Cruz** (a.k.a. **Las Columnas**), a popular, user-friendly standby with cheap, unpretentious tapas. You're not coming here for the food (which is basic), but for the bustling atmosphere, as locals and tourists alike crowd the place, inside and out, for hours on end. You can keep an eye on the busy kitchen from the bar, or hang out like a cowboy at the tiny stand-up tables out front. Separate chalkboards list €2 tapas and €2 *montaditos* (little sandwiches served on a bun).

Las Teresas is a characteristic small bar draped in fun photos. It serves good tapas from a tight little menu. Prices at the bar and outside tables (for fun tourist-watching) are the same, but they serve tapas only at the bar. The hams (with little upside-down umbrellas that catch the dripping fat) are a reminder that the Spanish are enthusiastic about their cured-meat dishes (€3-4 tapas, €8-10 half-*raciones*, €14-19 *raciones*, open daily but sometimes closed during siesta, Calle Santa Teresa 2, tel. 954-213-069).

Cervecería Giralda is a long-established meeting place for locals. With an almost genteel tiled setting and stiff waiters, it has an upscale air. It's famous for its fine tapas, but feels particularly touristy (confirm prices, stick with straight items on menu rather than expensive trick specials proposed by waiters; daily 9:00-24:00, Mateos Gago 1).

Dining

Corral del Agua Restaurante, a romantic pink-tablecloth place with a smart interior and charming courtyard seating, serves fine Andalusian cuisine deep in the Barrio Santa Cruz (€7-12 starters, €16-23 main dishes, three-course lunch special with a glass of wine—€20, Mon-Sat 12:00-16:00 & 20:00-24:00, closed Sun, arrive early or reserve ahead, Calle Agua 6, tel. 954-224-841).

Restaurante Modesto is a local favorite serving pricey but top-notch Andalusian fare—especially fish—with a comfortable dining room and atmospheric outdoor seating in the bright, bustling square just outside the Barrio Santa Cruz. They offer creative, fun meals—look around before ordering—and a good €20 fixed-price lunch or dinner served by energetic, occasionally pushy waiters. Their €9 house salad is a meal, and their €15.10 *fritura modesto* (fried seafood plate) is popular (€7-15 starters, €12-20 main dishes, inside open daily 12:00-17:00 & 20:00-24:00, outside tables open daily 12:00-24:00, near Santa María la Blanca at Cano y Cueto 5, tel. 954-416-811). Across the street is the related **Modesto Tapas,** with stand-up tables and a more basic all-tapas menu (also with outdoor seating; at Cano y Cueto 2).

Eating Casually in Barrio Santa Cruz and Plaza Santa María la Blanca

Freiduría Puerta de la Carne and **Bar Restaurante El 3 de Oro** are a two-for-one operation. Freiduría is a fried-fish-to-go place, with great outdoor seating, while El 3 de Oro is a fancier restaurant across the street that serves fine wine or beer to the fry shop's outdoor tables. First go into the fry shop and order a cheap cone of tasty fried fish with a tomato salad. Study the photos of the various kinds of seafood available; *un quarto* (250 grams for €5-7) serves one person. Then head out front and flag down a server to order a drink (technically from the restaurant), all while enjoying a great outdoor setting—almost dining for the cost of a picnic (Freiduría open Mon-Sat 13:00-24:00, Sun lunch only; El 3 de Oro open Mon-Sat 13:00-16:30 & 19:30-24:00, Sun lunch only; Santa María la Blanca 34, tel. 954-426-820).

Restaurante San Marco offers reasonably priced pizza and fun, basic Italian cuisine under the arches of what was a Moorish bath in the Middle Ages (and a disco in the 1990s). The air-conditioned atmosphere feels upscale but is easygoing and family-friendly (€7-9 salads, pizza, and pasta; €10-17 meat dishes; daily 13:00-16:15 & 20:00-24:00, Calle Mesón del Moro 6, tel. 954-564-390).

Breakfast on Plaza Santa María la Blanca: Several nondescript places seem to keep travelers happy at breakfast time on the sunny main square near most of my recommended hotels. I like **Café Bar Carmela.** For the cost of a continental breakfast at your hotel (€5.50-7.50), you can have a hearty American-style breakfast on the square (easy menus, open from 9:30, Calle Santa María la Blanca 6, tel. 954-540-590).

Between the Cathedral and the River

I don't like the restaurants surrounding the cathedral, but many good places are just across Avenida de la Constitución. In the area between the cathedral and the river, you can find tapas, cheap eats, and fine dining.

Tapas

Calle García de Vinuesa leads past several colorful and cheap tapas places to a busy corner surrounded with happy eateries.

Horno San Buenaventura, across from the cathedral on the corner of García de Vinuesa and the Avenida, is a big, venerable bakery with a quiet dining room upstairs. Its slick, chrome-filled, spacious main floor is lined with long display cases of sandwiches and desserts. The tapas bar upstairs has table service only (open daily, light meals are posted by the door, avoid the frozen paella).

Bodega Morales, farther up Calle García de Vinuesa (at #11), oozes old Sevilla ambience. The front area is more of a drinking bar; for food, go in the back section (if it's crowded, use the separate entrance around the corner). Here, sitting among huge adobe jugs, you can munch tiny sandwiches *(montaditos)* and tapas. Both are the same price (€2 *montaditos,* €2 tapas, €6 half-*raciones*—order at the bar, Mon-Sat 12:00-16:00 & 20:00-24:00, closed Sun, tel. 954-22-1242).

Freiduría La Isla, across the street, has been frying fish since 1938 (they renovated a few years ago...and changed the oil). Along with *pescado frito* (€5.50-7.50), they also sell wonderful homemade potato chips and fried almonds. It's family-friendly, with an easy English menu. Try their €5.50 *adobo* (marinated shark) or *frito variado* for a fish sampler. It's pretty much all fried fish, except for a tomato and pepper dish and their €1.20 gazpacho, offered only in the summer (Mon 20:00-23:00, Tue-Sat 13:00-15:30 & 20:00-23:00, closed Sun).

Bodega Paco Góngora is colorful and a bit classier than most tapas bars, with a tight dining area and delightful tapas served at the bar. Its sit-down meals are well presented and reasonably priced (€2-5 tapas, €8-10 half-*raciones*, daily 12:00-16:00 & 20:00-24:00, ask for the English menu, off Plaza Nueva at Calle Padre Marchena 1, tel. 954-214-139).

Mesón Serranito has a long hall with a mural-tile bar and ham hocks on one side, and bulls' heads over tables on the other. It's relatively spacious and typically full of happily munching locals (€8-9 *platos combinados,* daily 12:00-24:00, Antonia Díaz 11, tel. 954-211-243).

Cheap Eats at the Market Hall

Mercado del Arenal, the covered fish-and-produce market, is ideal for both snapping photos and grabbing a cheap lunch. As with most markets, you'll find characteristic little diners with prices designed to lure in savvy shoppers, not to mention a crispy fresh world of picnic goodies—and a riverside promenade with benches just a block away (Mon-Sat 9:00-14:30, closed Sun, sleepy on Mon, on Calle Pastor y Landero at Calle Arenal, just beyond bullring). There's also a fancier fish restaurant in the market with a great lunch deal (see Taberna del Alabardero, in next section).

Dining Between the Cathedral, Plaza Nueva, and the River

Marisquería Arenal Sevilla is a popular fish restaurant that thrives in the middle of the Arenal Market. When the market closes (daily at 14:30), this eatery stays open. You'll be eating in the empty Industrial Age market with workers dragging their crates around. It's a great family-friendly, finger-licking-good scene much appreciated by its enthusiastic local following. Fish is priced by weight, so be careful when ordering, and always double-check the bill (€6-18 fish plates, generally open 13:00-17:00 & 21:00-24:00, closed Sun night and all day Mon, reservations smart for dinner, Mercado del Arenal, enter on Calle Pastor y Landero 9, tel. 954-220-881).

Bar Restaurante Pepe Hillo is an appealing, trendy-yet-accessible hangout serving upscale bar food with a bull motif, across from the bullring (and, therefore, riotous after fights). One side is a youthful tapas bar, while the other side is a delightful, relatively calm oasis. Both share the same inviting menu (in English), with big €8 half-*raciones*, €10-13 *raciones*, creative house specialties, and a good wine list—but no tapas (daily 12:00-24:00 but dining room closes in mid-afternoon, enter on Calle Pastor y Landero, Adriano 24, tel. 954-215-390).

La Societé is an antidote for the same old variations-on-a-theme Sevillan tapas bars. With a sleek, Ikea-mod ambience and a long chalkboard menu of €3 *montaditos* (sandwiches), it's a welcome break (€3-5 tapas, €6-9 half-*raciones*, €10-12 *raciones*, daily 12:00-17:00 & 20:00-24:00, Adriano 8).

Restaurante Enrique Becerra is a fancy little 10-table place popular with local foodies. It's well known for its gourmet Andalusian cuisine and fine wine. Muscle past the well-dressed locals at the tapas bar for gourmet snacks and wine by the glass, or head to the quieter upstairs dining room. While the restaurant satisfies its guests with quality food, given the tight seating and its popularity with tourists, it can feel like a trap (€3-4 tapas available only at the bar, otherwise €11-18 starters and €18-26 main dishes, Mon-Sat 13:00-16:30 & 20:00-24:00, closed Sun, reservations essential, Gamazo 2, tel. 954-213-049).

Taberna del Alabardero, one of Sevilla's finest restaurants, serves refined Spanish cuisine in chandeliered elegance just a couple of blocks from the cathedral. If you order à la carte, it adds up to about €45 a meal, but for €48 (or €58 with wine) you can have a fun seven-course fixed-price meal with lots of little surprises from the chef. Or consider their €18/person (no sharing) starter sampler, followed by an entrée. The service in the fancy upstairs dining rooms gets mixed reviews (carefully read and understand your bill)...but the setting is stunning (daily 13:00-16:30 & 20:00-24:00, closed Aug, air-con, reservations smart, Zaragoza 20, tel. 954-502-721).

Taberna del Alabardero Student-Served Lunch: The ground-floor dining rooms (elegant but nothing like upstairs) are popular with local office workers for a great-value, student-chef-prepared, fixed-price lunch sampler (three delightful courses-€13 Mon-Fri, €18 Sat-Sun; €20 dinner available daily, drinks not included, open daily 13:00-16:30 & 20:00-23:30). To avoid a wait, arrive before 14:00 (no reservations possible).

Sevilla Connections

Note that many destinations are well served by both trains and buses.

By Train
From Sevilla by AVE Train to Madrid: The AVE express train is expensive (€81, €8 cheaper during off-peak times, minimum €10.35

reservation fee with railpass) but fast (2.5 hours to Madrid; hourly departures 7:00-23:00, see page 429 for more on the Sevilla–Madrid train route). Departures between 16:00 and 19:00 can book up far in advance, but surprise holidays and long weekends can totally jam up trains as well—reserve as far ahead as possible.

From Sevilla by Train to Córdoba: There are three options for this journey: slow and cheap **regional** trains (8/day, 80 minutes, €11), fast and cheap regional high-speed **Avant** trains (9/day, 45 minutes, €17, requires reservation), and fast and expensive **AVE** trains en route to Madrid (19/day, 45 minutes, €34, requires reservation). Unless you must be on a particular departure, there's no reason to pay double for AVE; Avant is just as quick and half the price. (If you have a railpasss, you still must buy a reservation: €6.50 for Avant or €10.35 for AVE.)

Other Trains from Sevilla to: Málaga (6/day, 2 hours on AVE or Avant; 6/day, 2.5 hours on slower regional trains), **Ronda** (2/day, 4 hours, transfer in Bobadilla), **Granada** (4/day, 3 hours), **Jerez** (12/day, 1.25 hours), **Barcelona** (2/day, 5.5 hours; plus one slow train, 12 hours), **Algeciras** (3/day, 5 hours, transfer at Córdoba, Antequera, or Bobadilla). Trains run to **Lisbon,** Portugal, but they take a long time, since they go through Madrid; buses to Lisbon are far better (see later). Train info: toll tel. 902-320-320, www.renfe.com.

By Bus

Sevilla has two bus stations: The El Prado station, just south of the Alcázar, primarily serves regional destinations; the Plaza de Armas station, farther north (near the bullring), handles most long-distance buses. Bus info: tel. 954-908-040 but rarely answered, go to TI for latest schedule info.

From Sevilla's El Prado station to Andalucía and the South Coast: Regional buses are operated by Comes (www.tgcomes.es), Los Amarillos (www.losamarillos.es), and Linesur (www.linesur.com). Connections to **Jerez** are frequent, as many southbound buses head there first (7-10/day, 1.5 hours, run by all three companies; note that train is also possible—see above). Los Amarillos runs buses to some of Andalucía's hill towns, including **Ronda** (3 *directo* buses/day take 2 hours, 5 others go via Villamartín and take 2.5 hours) and **Arcos** (2/day, 2 hours; many more departures possible with a transfer in Jerez). For the South Coast, a handy Comes bus departs Sevilla four times a day and heads for **Tarifa** (2.5-3.25 hours), **Algeciras** (3.5-4 hours), and **La Línea/Gibraltar** (4-4.5 hours). However, if **Algeciras** is your goal, Linesur has a much faster direct connection (7-8/day, 2.5 hours). There's also one bus a day from this station to **Granada** (2.5 hours); the rest depart from the Plaza de Armas station.

From Sevilla's Plaza de Armas station to: Madrid (departures generally on the hour, 6 hours, €20, tel. 902-229-292), **Córdoba** (7/day, 2.5 hours), **Granada** (9/day, 3.5 hours *directo, ruta* buses take about 10 minutes more), **Málaga** (6/day direct, 2.5-3 hours, connects to Nerja), **Nerja** (2/day, 4.75 hours), **Barcelona** (2/day, 16.5 hours, including one overnight bus). Information: tel. 902-450-550.

By Bus to Portugal: The best way to get to **Lisbon,** Portugal, is by bus (Alsa and Eurolines share a twice-daily service, departures at 15:00 and 24:00, 7 hours, €35, departs Plaza de Armas station, tel. 954-905-102, www.alsa.es). The midnight departure continues past Lisbon to **Coimbra** (arriving 10:30) and **Porto** (arriving 12:15). Sevilla also has direct bus service to **Lagos,** Portugal, on the Algarve (4/day in summer, 2/day off-season, about 6 hours, €20, buy ticket a day or two in advance May-Oct, tel. 954-907-737, www.damas-sa.es). The bus departs from Sevilla's Plaza de Armas bus station and arrives at the Lagos bus station. If you'd like to visit Tavira on the way to Lagos, purchase a bus ticket to Tavira, have lunch there, then take the train to Lagos.

CÓRDOBA

Straddling a sharp bend of the Guadalquivir River, Córdoba has a glorious Roman and Moorish past, once serving as a regional capital for both empires. It's home to Europe's best Islamic sight after Granada's Alhambra: the Mezquita, a splendid and remarkably well-preserved mosque that dates from A.D. 784. When you step inside the mosque, which is magical in its grandeur, you can imagine Córdoba as the center of a thriving and sophisticated culture. During the Dark Ages, when much of Europe was barbaric and illiterate, Córdoba was a haven of enlightened thought—famous for religious tolerance, artistic expression, and dedication to philosophy and the sciences.

Beyond the magnificent Mezquita, the city of Córdoba has two sides: The extremely touristy maze of streets immediately surrounding the giant main attraction, lined with trinket shops, hotels, and restaurants; and the workaday part of town (centered on Plaza de las Tendillas). While the over-commercialized vibe of the touristy area can be off-putting, a quick walk takes you to real-life Córdoba.

Planning Your Time

Ideally, Córdoba is worth two nights and a day. Don't rush the magnificent Mezquita, but also consider sticking around to experience the city's other pleasures: Wander the evocative Jewish Quarter, enjoy the tapas scene, and explore the modern part of town.

However, if you're tight on time, it's possible to do Córdoba more quickly—especially since it's conveniently located on the AVE bullet-train line (and because, frankly, Córdoba is less interesting than the other two big Andalusian cities, Sevilla and Granada). To see Córdoba as an efficient stopover between Madrid and Sevilla (or as a side-trip from Sevilla—frequent trains, 45-minute trip), focus on the Mezquita: Taxi from the station, spend two hours there, explore the old town for an hour...and then scram.

Orientation to Córdoba

Córdoba's big draw is the mosque-turned-cathedral called the Mezquita (for pronunciation ease, think female mosquito). Most of the town's major sights are nearby, including the Alcázar, a former royal castle. And though the town seems to ignore its marshy Guadalquivir River (a prime bird-watching area), the riverbank sports a Renaissance triumphal arch next to a stout "Roman Bridge." The bridge leads to the town's old fortified gate (which now houses a museum on Moorish culture, the Museum of Al-Andalus Life). The Mezquita is buried in the characteristic medieval town. Around that stretches the Jewish Quarter, then the modern city—which feels much like any other in Spain, but with some striking Art Deco buildings at Plaza de las Tendillas and lots of Art Nouveau lining Avenida del Gran Capitán.

Tourist Information

Córdoba has helpful TIs at the train station, Alcázar, and Plaza de las Tendillas (all open daily 9:30-14:00 & 17:00-19:30, tel. 902-201-774, www.turismodecordoba.org). Another TI, near the Mezquita, is run separately and covers all of Andalucía (Mon-Fri 9:30-19:30, Sat-Sun 9:30-15:00, Torrijos 10, tel. 957-355-179).

Arrival in Córdoba

By Train or Bus: Córdoba's train station is located on Avenida de América. Built in 1991 to accommodate the high-speed AVE train line, the slick train station has ATMs, restaurants, a variety of shops, a TI booth (on the concourse above the track), an information counter, and a small lounge for first-class AVE passengers. Taxis and local buses are just outside.

The bus station is across the street from the train station (on Avenida Vía Augusta, to the north). It's about a 25-minute walk from either station to the old town. There's no luggage storage at the train station, but the bus station has lockers (€3.50, look for *consigna* sign and buy token at machine).

To get to the old town, hop a **taxi** (€6 to the Mezquita) or catch **bus** #3 or #16 (buy €1.15 ticket on board, ask driver for *"mezquita,"* get off at Calle San Fernando, and take Calle del Portillo, following the twists and turns—and occasional signs—to the Mezquita).

Córdoba

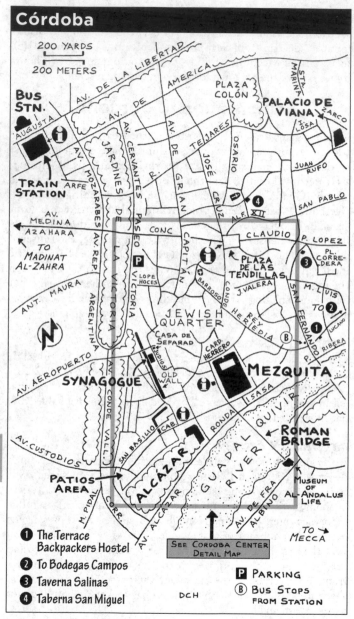

CÓRDOBA

1 The Terrace
Backpackers Hostel

2 To Bodegas Campos

3 Taverna Salinas

4 Taberna San Miguel

See Cordoba Center
Detail Map

P Parking
B Bus Stops
From Station

DCH

To **walk** the 25 minutes from the train station to the Mezquita, turn left onto Avenida de América, then right on Avenida del Gran Capitán, which becomes a pedestrian zone. At the end, ask someone, *"¿Dónde está la Mezquita?"* You'll be directed downhill, through the whitewashed old Jewish Quarter.

Helpful Hints

Closed Days: The synagogue, Madinat Al-Zahra, and Palacio de Viana are closed on Monday. The Mezquita is open daily.

Festival: During the first half of May, Córdoba hosts the Concurso Popular de Patios Cordobeses—a patio contest.

Cheap Tricks: The Alcázar de los Reyes Cristianos and related Baths of the Caliphate Alcázar are free all day Wednesday.

Laundry: The helpful staff at **Sol y Mar** will wash, dry, and fold your laundry (€13.10/load, usually same-day service if you drop off in the morning, cheaper for self-service, Mon-Fri 9:30-13:30 & 17:00-20:30, Sat 9:30-13:30, closed Sun, Calle del Doctor Fleming 8, tel. 957-298-929).

Local Guides: Isabel Martinez Richter is a charming archaeologist who loves to make the city come to life for curious Americans (mobile 669-369-645, isabmr@terra.es). **Angel Lucena** is also a good teacher and a joy to be with (€100/3 hours, mobile 607-898-079, lucenaangel@hotmail.com).

Sights in Córdoba

▲▲▲The Mezquita

This massive former mosque—now with a 16th-century church rising up from the middle—was once the center of Western Islam and the heart of a cultural capital that rivaled Baghdad and Istanbul. A wonder of the medieval world, it's remarkably well-preserved, giving today's visitors a chance to soak up the ambience of Islamic Córdoba in its 10th-century prime.

Cost and Hours: €8, ticket kiosk inside the Patio de los Naranjos, Mon-Sat free entry until 10:00 (because they don't want to charge a fee to attend the 9:30 Mass), dry €3.50 audioguide; open March-Oct Mon-Sat 8:30-19:00, Sun 8:30-10:30 & 14:00-19:00; Nov-Feb Mon-Sat 10:00-18:00, Sun 8:30-10:30 & 14:00-18:00; last entry 30 minutes before closing, Christian altar accessible only after 10:30 unless you attend Mass, try to avoid midday crowds (11:00-15:00) by coming early or late; tel. 957-470-512, www.catedraldecordoba.es.

◉ Self-Guided Tour: Before entering the patio, take in the exterior of the Mezquita. The mosque's massive footprint is clear when you survey its sprawling walls from outside. At 600 feet by 400 feet, it seems to dominate the higgledy-piggledy medieval

The Mezquita

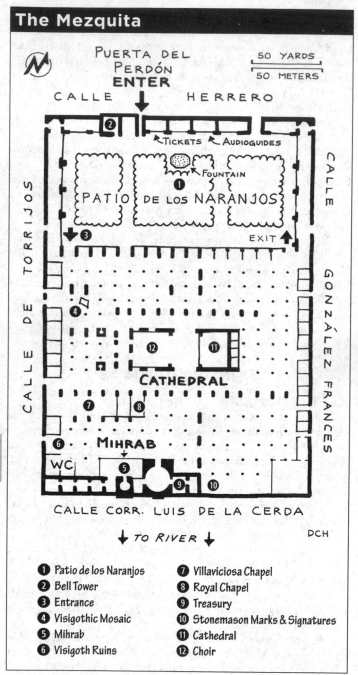

PUERTA DEL PERDÓN
ENTER

CALLE   HERRERO

50 YARDS
50 METERS

2

Tickets   Audioguides

Fountain

1

PATIO DE LOS NARANJOS

CALLE DE TORRIJOS

CALLE GONZÁLEZ FRANCES

3

EXIT

4

12   11

CATHEDRAL

7   8

6   **MIHRAB**

WC   5   9   10

CALLE CORR. LUIS DE LA CERDA

↓ TO RIVER ↓

CÓRDOBA

DCH

1 Patio de los Naranjos
2 Bell Tower
3 Entrance
4 Visigothic Mosaic
5 Mihrab
6 Visigoth Ruins
7 Villaviciosa Chapel
8 Royal Chapel
9 Treasury
10 Stonemason Marks & Signatures
11 Cathedral
12 Choir

town that surrounds it.

Patio de los Naranjos: The Mezquita's big, welcoming courtyard is free to enter. When this was a mosque, the Muslim faithful would gather in this courtyard to perform ablution—ritual washing before prayer, as directed by Muslim law. Historians believe this was the first such courtyard with trees for shade. The trees (probably olive, palm, or orange) were planted in rows that line up with the colonnades inside the mosque, symbolically extending the place of worship through the courtyard. The courtyard walls display many of the mosque's carved ceiling panels and beams, which date from

the 10th century. Gaze up through the trees for views of the **bell tower** (c. 1600), built over the remains of the original Muslim minaret. For four centuries, five times a day, a cleric (called a muezzin) would climb the minaret that once stood here to call Muslims to face Mecca and pray.

• *Buy your ticket (and, if you wish, rent an audioguide at a separate kiosk to the right). Enter the building by passing through the keyhole gate at the far right corner (pick up an English map-brochure as you enter).*

Interior: Entering the former mosque from the patio, you pass from an orchard of orange trees into a forest of delicate columns dating from 786. The 850 red-and-blue columns are

topped with double arches—a round Romanesque arch above a Visigothic horseshoe arch—made from alternating red brick and white stone. The columns and capitals (built of marble, granite, and alabaster) were recycled from ancient Roman ruins and conquered Visigothic churches.

(Golden Age Arabs excelled at absorbing both the technology and the building materials of the people they conquered.) The columns seem to recede to infinity, as if reflecting the immensity and complexity of Allah's creation. Supporting such a tall ceiling with thin columns required extra bracing with the double arches you see—a beautiful solution to a practical problem.

Although it's a vast room, the low ceilings and dense columns create an intimate and worshipful atmosphere. The original mosque was brighter, before Christians renovated the place for their use and closed in the arched entrances from the patio and street. The

Islamic Córdoba (756-1236):
Medieval Europe's Cultural Capital

After his family was slaughtered by political rivals (A.D. 750), 20-year-old Prince Abd Al-Rahman fled the royal palace at Damascus, headed west across North Africa, and went undercover among the Berber tribesmen of Morocco. For six years he avoided assassination while building a power base among his fellow Arab expatriates and the local Muslim Berbers. As an heir to the title of "caliph," or ruler of Islam, he sailed north and claimed Moorish Spain as his own, confirming his power by decapitating his enemies and sending their salted heads to the rival caliph in Baghdad. This split in Islam is somewhat like the papal schism of medieval Christian Europe, when the Church split into factions over who was the rightful pope.

Thus began an Islamic flowering in southern Spain under Abd Al-Rahman's family, the Umayyads. They dominated Sevilla and Granada, ruling the independent state of "Al-Andalus," with their capital at Córdoba.

By the year 950—when the rest of Europe was mired in poverty, ignorance, and superstition—Córdoba was Europe's greatest city, rivaling Constantinople and Baghdad. It had well over 100,000 people (Paris had a third that many), with hundreds of mosques, palaces, and public baths. The streets were paved and lighted at night with oil lamps, and running water was piped in from the outskirts of the city. Medieval visitors marveled at the size and luxury of the Mezquita mosque, a symbol that the Umayyads of Spain were the equal of the caliphs of Baghdad.

This Golden Age was marked by a remarkable spirit of tolerance and cooperation in this region among the three great monotheistic religions: Islam, Judaism, and Christianity. Giving that society a positive spin, my guide explained, "Umayyad

giant cathedral sits in the center of the mosque. For now, pretend it doesn't exist. We'll visit it after exploring the mosque.

The mosque sits on the site of an early-Christian church built during the Visigothic period (sixth century). Five columns in from the entrance, a wooden railing marks a hole where you can look down to see a Visigothic **mosaic** from that original church. This is important to the locals, proving there was a church here before the mosque, and making it defensible for this newer church to have "violated" the great mosque. When modern-day Muslims called to have the Mezquita become a mosque again, the local bishop responded by changing the tourist information to make it clear: This is a living church and will stay that way.

• *Walk to the center of the far wall (opposite the entrance), where you'll find the focal point of the mosque, the...*

Mihrab: The mosque equivalent of a church's high altar, this

Al-Andalus was not one country with three cultures. It was one culture with three religions...its people shared the same food, dress, art, music, and language. Different religious rituals within the community were practiced in private. But clearly, Muslims ruled. No church spire could be taller than a minaret, and while the call to prayer rang out five times daily, there was no ringing of church bells."

The university rang with voices in Arabic, Hebrew, and Latin, sharing their knowledge of *al-jibra* (algebra), medicine, law, and literature. The city fell under the enlightened spell of the ancient Greeks, and Córdoba's 70 libraries bulged with translated manuscripts of Plato and Aristotle, works that would later inspire medieval Christians.

Ruling over the Golden Age were two energetic leaders—Abd Al-Rahman III (912-961) and Al-Hakam II (961-976)—who conquered territory, expanded the Mezquita, and boldly proclaimed themselves caliphs.

Córdoba's Y1K crisis brought civil wars that toppled the caliph (1031), splintering Al-Andalus into several kingdoms. Córdoba came under the control of the Almoravids (Berbers from North Africa), who were less sophisticated than the Arab-based Umayyads. Then a wave of even stricter Islam swept through Spain, bringing the Almohads to power (1147) and driving Córdoba's best and brightest into exile. The city's glory days were over, and it was replaced by Sevilla and Granada as the centers of Spanish Islam. On June 29, 1236, Christians conquered the city. That morning Muslims said their last prayers in the great mosque. That afternoon, the Christians set up their portable road altar and celebrated the church's first Mass. Córdoba's days as a political and cultural superpower were over.

was the focus of the mosque and is the highlight of the Mezquita today. Picture the mosque at prayer time. Each floor stone is about the size of a prayer rug...more than 20,000 people could pray at once here. Imagine the multitude kneeling in prayer, facing the mihrab, rocking forward to touch their heads to the ground, and saying, *"Allahu Akbar, La illa a il Allah, Muhammad razul Allah"*—"Allah is great, there is no god but Allah, and Muhammad is his prophet."

The mihrab, a feature in all mosques, is a decorated "niche"—in this case, more like a small room with a golden-arch entrance. During a service, the imam (prayer leader) would stand here to read scripture and give sermons. He spoke loudly into the niche, his back to the assembled crowd, and the architecture worked to amplify his voice so all could hear. Built in the mid-10th century by Al-Hakam II, the exquisite room reflects the wealth of Córdoba in its prime. Three thousand pounds of multicolored glass-and-enamel cubes panel the walls and domes in mosaics designed by Byzantine craftsmen, depicting flowers and quotes from the Quran. Gape up. Overhead rises a colorful, starry dome with skylights and interlocking lobe-shaped arches.

• *In the far-right corner, you'll find...*

Visigoth Ruins: On display in the corner to the right of the mihrab are bits of carved stone from the Visigothic Christian church of San Vicente that stood here in the sixth century. (The Christian symbolism was scratched off so the stones could be reused by Muslims.) Abd Al-Rahman I bought the church from his Christian subjects before leveling it to build the mosque. From here pan 90 degrees to enjoy a view that reveals the vastness of the mosque. (Perhaps you might also appreciate a hidden WC and drinking fountain—in the corner.)

• *In front of the mihrab and a bit to the left is a roped-off open area that was the...*

Villaviciosa Chapel: In 1236, Saint-King Ferdinand III con-quered the city and turned the mosque into a church. Still, the locals continued to call it "La Mezquita," and left the structure virtually unchanged (70 per-cent of the original mosque structure sur-vives to this day). Sixteen columns were removed and replaced by Gothic arches to make this chapel. It feels as if the church architects appreciated the opportunity to incorporate the sublime architecture of the pre-existing mosque into their church. Notice how the floor was once almost entirely covered with the tombs of

nobles and big shots eager to make this their final resting place.

• *Immediately to your right (as you face the main entrance of the Mezquita), you'll see the...*

Royal Chapel: The chapel—designed for the tombs of Christian kings—is completely closed off. While it was never open to the public, the tall, well-preserved Mudejar walls and dome are easily visible. The lavish Arabic-style decor dates from the 1370s, done by Muslim artisans after the Reconquista. The fact that a Christian king chose to be buried in a tomb so clearly Moorish in design indicates the mutual respect between the cultures (before the Inquisition changed all that).

• Return to the mihrab, then go through the big door to your immediate left, which leads into the Baroque...

Treasury (Tesoro): The treasury is filled with display cases of religious artifacts and the enormous monstrance that is paraded through the streets of Córdoba each Corpus Christi, 60 days after Easter (notice the handles). The monstrance was an attempt by 16th-century Christians to create something exquisite enough to merit being the holder of the Holy Communion wafer. As they believed the wafer actually was the body of Christ, this trumped any relics. The monstrance is designed like a seven-scoop ice-cream cone, held together by gravity. While the bottom is silver-plated 18th-century Baroque, the top is late Gothic—solid silver with gold plating courtesy of 16th-century conquistadors.

The big canvas nearest the entrance shows Saint-King Ferdinand III, who conquered Córdoba in 1236, accepting the keys to the city's fortified gate from the vanquished Muslims. The victory ended a six-month siege and resulted in a negotiated settlement: The losers' lives were spared, providing they evacuated. Most went to Granada, which remained Muslim for another 250 years. The same day, the Spaniards celebrated Mass in a makeshift chapel right here in the great mosque.

Among the other Catholic treasures, don't miss the ivory crucifix (next room, body carved from one tusk, arms carefully fitted on) from 1665. Get close to study Jesus' mouth—it's incredibly realistic. The artist? No one knows.

Just outside the treasury exit, a glass case shows off casts of the many **stonemason marks and signatures** found in this one building. Try to locate the actual ones on nearby columns. (I went five for six.) This part of the mosque has the best light for photography, thanks to skylights put in by 18th-century Christians.

The mosque grew over several centuries under a series of rulers. Remarkably, each ruler kept to the original vision—rows and rows of multicolored columns topped by double arches. Then came the Christians.

Cathedral: Rising up in the middle of the forest of columns is the bright and newly restored cathedral, oriented in the Christian tradition, with its altar at the east end. This doesn't jibe with the mihrab, which normally also faces east (but to Mecca, not Jerusalem), because this mihrab actually faces south—as mosques in Syria do in order to face Mecca. (Syria was the ancestral home of Córdoba's zealous Umayyad branch of Islam.) Gazing up at the rich decoration,

it's easy to forget that you were in a former mosque just seconds ago. While the mosque is about 30 feet high, the cathedral's ceiling soars 130 feet up. Look at the glorious ceiling.

In 1523 Córdoba's bishop proposed building this grand church in the Mezquita's center. The town council opposed it, but King Charles V ordered it done. According to a false but believable legend, when the king saw the final product, he declared that they'd destroyed something unique to build something ordinary. For a more positive take on this, acknowledge that it would have been quicker and less expensive for the Christian builders to destroy the mosque, but they respected its beauty and built their church into it.

It's interesting to ponder the aesthetics and psychology of the Catholic Church versus Islam in the styles of these two great places of worship (horizontal versus vertical, intimate versus powerful, fear-inspiring versus loving, dark versus bright, simple versus elaborate, feeling close to God versus feeling small before God).

The basic structure is late-Gothic, with fancy Isabelline-style columns. The nave's towering Renaissance arches and dome emphasize the triumph of Christianity over Islam in Córdoba. The twin pulpits feature a marble bull, eagle, angel, and lion—symbols of the four evangelists. The cathedral's new Carrara marble throne (cátedra) is the seat of the bishop.

Choir: The Baroque-era choir stalls were added much later—made in 1750 of New World mahogany. While cluttering up a previously open Gothic space, the choir is considered one of the masterpieces of 18th-century Andalusian Baroque. Each of the 109 stalls (108 plus the throne of the bishop) features a scene from the Bible: Mary's life on one side facing Jesus' life on the other. The lower chairs feature carved reliefs of the 49 martyrs of Córdoba (from Roman, Visigothic, and Moorish times), each with a palm frond symbolizing martyrdom and the scene of their death in the background. The medieval church strayed from the inclusiveness taught by Jesus. Choirs (which seem to consume otherwise-spacious church interiors throughout Spain) were only for canons, priests, and the bishop. Those days are long gone. In fact, a public Mass is now held right here (Mon-Sat mornings at 9:30).

Near the Mezquita

All of these sights are within a few minutes' walk of the Mezquita.

On and near the River

Just downhill from the Mezquita is the Guadalquivir River (which flows on to Sevilla and eventually out to the Atlantic). While silted

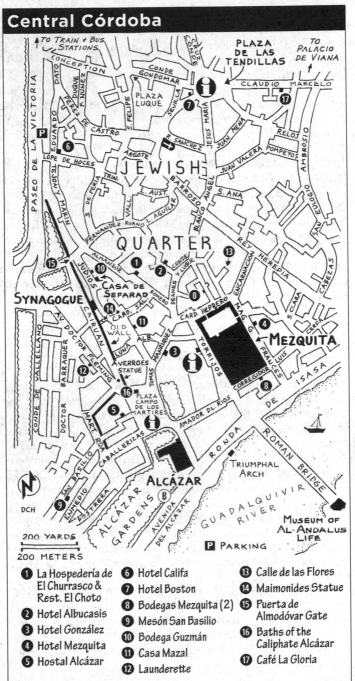

Central Córdoba

- ❶ La Hospedería de El Churrasco & Rest. El Choto
- ❷ Hotel Albucasis
- ❸ Hotel González
- ❹ Hotel Mezquita
- ❺ Hostal Alcázar
- ❻ Hotel Califa
- ❼ Hotel Boston
- ❽ Bodegas Mezquita (2)
- ❾ Mesón San Basilio
- ❿ Bodega Guzmán
- ⓫ Casa Mazal
- ⓬ Launderette
- ⓭ Calle de las Flores
- ⓮ Maimonides Statue
- ⓯ Puerta de Almodóvar Gate
- ⓰ Baths of the Caliphate Alcázar
- ⓱ Café La Gloria

up today, it was once navigable from here. The town now seems to turn its back on the Guadalquivir, but the arch next to the Roman Bridge (with its ancient foundation surviving) and the fortified gate on the far bank (now housing a museum, described later) evoke a day when the river was key to the city's existence.

Triumphal Arch and Plague Monument—The unfinished Renaissance arch was designed to give King Philip II a royal welcome, but he arrived before its completion—so the job was canceled. The adjacent monument with the single column is an 18th-century plague monument dedicated to St. Raphael (he was in charge of protecting the population from the main scourges in this region at that time: plague, hunger, and floods).

Roman Bridge—The bridge sits on its first-century-A.D. foundations and retains its 16th-century arches, but was poorly restored in 2009. It feels like so much other modern work along this riverbank—done on the cheap. As it was the first bridge over this river, it established Córdoba as a strategic point. Walk across the bridge for a fine view of the city—especially the huge mosque with its cathedral busting through the center. You'll be steps away from the museum described next.

▲Museum of Al-Andalus Life—The Museo Vivo de Al-Andalus fills the fortified gate (built in the 14th century to protect the Christian city) at the far side of the Roman Bridge. It is a velvety, philosophical, almost evangelical attempt to humanize the Muslim Moorish culture, and is funded by a foundation started by Roger Garaudy, a former French politician and writer controversial for Holocaust revisionism. Don a headset and wander through simple displays as the clear, engrossing soundtrack lets you sit at the feet of the great poets and poke into Moorish living rooms. It's worth the climb up to the rooftop terrace for the best panoramic view of Córdoba. Garaudy's one-hour "Multivision" video is a flowery story taking you from prehistory to the formation of the great monotheistic religions...the greatest of which—in his opinion—is Islam.

Cost and Hours: €4.50, daily May-Sept 10:00-14:00 & 16:30-20:30, Oct-April 10:00-18:00; "Multivision" video is €1.20 extra, played in English, 5-6/day, generally at the top of the hour, or at :30 past the hour on summer mornings—ask about next showing as you enter; Torre de la Calahorra, tel. 957-293-929, www.torrecalahorra.com.

Jewish Córdoba

Córdoba's Jewish Quarter dates from the late Middle Ages, after Muslim rule and during the Christian era. Now little remains. For a sense of it in its thriving heyday, visit the synagogue and the cultural center located a few steps away (both described in this section). For a pretty picture, find **Calle de las Flores** (a.k.a. "Blossom Lane"). This narrow flower-bedecked street frames the cathedral's bell tower as it hovers in the distance (the view is a favorite for local guidebook covers).

Synagogue (Sinagoga)—The small yet beautifully preserved synagogue was built in 1315, under Christian rule, but the Islamic decoration has roots way back to Abd Al-Rahman I (see sidebar on page 634). During Muslim times, Córdoba's sizable Jewish community was welcomed, though they paid substantial taxes to the city—money that enlarged the Mezquita and generated goodwill. That goodwill came in handy when Córdoba's era of prosperity and mutual respect ended with the arrival of the intolerant Almohad Berbers. Christians and Jews were repressed, and brilliant minds—such as the rabbi and philosopher Maimonides—fled for their own safety.

The Christian Reconquista of Córdoba (1236) brought another brief period of religious tolerance. That's when this synagogue was built—the result of a joint effort by Christians, Jews, and Muslim (Mudejar) craftsmen. By the end of the 14th century, however, Spain's Jews were again persecuted. They were finally expelled or forced to convert in 1492; this is one of only three surviving synagogues in Spain built before that year.

Rich Mudejar decorations of intertwined flowers, arabesques, and Stars of David plaster the walls. What appear to be quotes from the Quran in Arabic are actually quotes from the Bible in Hebrew. On the east wall (the symbolic direction of Jerusalem), find the niche for the Ark, which held the scrolls of the Torah (the Jewish scriptures). The upstairs gallery was reserved for women. This synagogue, the only one that survives in Córdoba, was left undisturbed because it was used as a church until the 19th century—in fact, you can see a cross painted into a niche.

Cost and Hours: €0.30—but since it's free for EU residents, they rarely accept payment; Tue-Sun 9:30-14:00 & 15:30-17:30, closed Mon, Calle de los Judíos 20, tel. 957-202-928. To learn more about the synagogue and its community, head next to the Casa de Sefarad, just 10 steps uphill.

Córdoba's Jewish Quarter: A Ten-Point Scavenger Hunt

Whereas most of the area around the Mezquita is commercial and touristy, the neighborhood to the east seems somehow almost untouched by tourism and the modern world (as you leave the Mezquita, turn right and exit the orange-grove patio). To catch a whiff of Córdoba as it was before the onslaught of tourism and the affluence of the 21st century, explore this district. Just wander and observe. Here are a few characteristics to look for:

1. **Narrow streets.** Skinny streets make sense in hot climates, as they provide much-appreciated shade. Skinny streets were also a practical necessity, since the city's Jews had to make the most of the limited space in which they were allowed to live.

2. **Thick, whitewashed walls.** Both features serve as a kind of natural air-conditioning—and the chalk ingredient in the whitewash "bugs" bugs.

3. **Colorful doors and windows.** What little color there is in this famously white city helps counter the boring whitewash.

4. **Iron grilles.** Historically, these were more artistic, but modern ones are more practical. Their continued presence is a reminder of the persistent gap through the ages between rich and poor. The wooden latticework covering many windows is a holdover from days when women were extremely modest and wanted privacy.

5. **Stone bumpers on corners.** These protected buildings against reckless drivers. Scavenged secondhand ancient Roman pillars worked well.

6. **Scuff guards.** Made of harder materials, these guards sit at the base of the whitewashed walls—and, from the looks of it, are serving their purpose.

7. **Riverstone cobbles.** These stones were cheap and local, and provided drains down the middle of a lane. They were flanked by smooth stones that stayed dry for walking (and now aid the rolling suitcases of modern-day tourists).

8. **Pretty patios.** Córdobans are proud of their patios. Walk up to the inner iron gates of the wide-open front doors and peek in (see "Patios" sidebar, later).

9. **Remnants of old towers from minarets.** Muslim Córdoba peaked in the 10th century with an estimated 400,000 people, which meant lots of neighborhood mosques.

10. **A real neighborhood.** People really live here. There are no tacky shops, and just about the only tourist is…you.

Casa de Sefarad—Set inside a restored 14th-century home directly across from the synagogue, this interpretive museum brings to life Córdoba's rich Jewish past. Eight rooms around a central patio are themed to help you understand different aspects of daily life for Spain's former Jewish community. The rooms focus on themes such as contributions from women in the community, Jewish holidays, and musical traditions. Upstairs is an interpretive center for the synagogue, along with rooms dedicated to Maimonides, the Inquisition, and the synagogue. The Casa de Sefarad is a cultural center for Sephardic (the Hebrew word for "Spanish") Jewish heritage. Jaime and his staff stress that the center's purpose is not political or religious, but cultural. Along with running this small museum, they teach courses, offer a library, and promote an appreciation of Córdoba's Jewish heritage.

Cost and Hours: €6, includes audioguide, Mon-Sat 11:00-18:00, Sun 11:00-14:00, 30-minute guided tours in English available by request if a guide is available, next to the synagogue at the corner of Calle de los Judíos and Calle Averroes, tel. 957-421-404, www.casadesefarad.es. The Casa de Sefarad hosts weekly concerts—acoustic, Sephardic, Andalusian, and flamenco—on its patio (€15, most Saturdays in season at 20:00, reservations smart).

City Wall—Built upon the foundation of Roman Córdoba's wall, these fortifications date mostly from the 12th century. While the city stretched beyond the wall in Moorish times, this wall protected its political, religious, and commercial center. Of the seven original gates, the Puerta de Almodóvar (near the synagogue) is best preserved today. Just outside this gate, you'll find statues of Córdoba's great thinkers: Seneca (the Roman philosopher and adviser to Nero), Maimonides, and Averroes.

Statues of Maimonides and Averroes—Statues honor two of Córdoba's deepest-thinking homeboys—one Jewish, one Muslim, both driven out during the wave of Islamic intolerance after the fall of the Umayyad caliphate. (Maimonides is 30 yards downhill from the synagogue; Averroes is at the end of the old wall, where Cairuán and Doctor Fleming streets meet.)

Maimonides (1135-1204) was born in Córdoba and raised on both Jewish scripture and Aristotle's philosophy. Like many tolerant Córdobans, he saw no conflict between the two. Maimonides—sometimes called the "Jewish Aquinas"—wrote the *Guide of the Perplexed* (in Arabic), in which he asserted (as the Christian philosopher St. Thomas Aquinas later would) that secular knowledge and religious faith could go hand-in-hand.

Córdoba changed in 1147, when the fundamentalist Almohads assumed power. Maimonides was driven out, eventually finding work in Cairo as the sultan's doctor. Today tourists, Jewish scholars, and fans of Aquinas rub the statue's foot in the hope that some of Maimonides' genius and wisdom will rub off on them.

The story of **Averroes** (1126-1198) is a near match of Maimonides', except that Averroes was a Muslim lawyer, not a Jewish doctor. He became the medieval world's number-one authority on Aristotle, influencing Aquinas. Averroes' biting tract *The Incoherence of the Incoherence* attacked narrow-mindedness, asserting that secular philosophy (for the elite) and religious faith (for the masses) both led to truth. The Almohads banished him from the city and burned his books, ending four centuries of Córdoban enlightenment.

The Alcázar

Alcázar de los Reyes Cristianos—Tourists line up to visit Córdoba's overrated fortress, the "Castle of the Christian Monarchs," which sits strategically next to the Guadalquivir River. Upon entering, look to the right to see a big, beautiful garden rich with flowers and fountains. To the left is a modern-feeling, unimpressive fort. While it was built along the Roman walls in Visigothic times, constant reuse and recycling has left it sparse and barren (with the exception of a few interesting Roman mosaics on the walls). Crowds squeeze up and down the congested spiral staircases of "Las Torres" for meager views. Ferdinand and Isabel donated the castle to the Inquisition in 1482, and it became central in the church's effort to discover "false converts to Christianity"—mostly Jews who had decided not to flee Spain in 1492.

Cost and Hours: €4, free on Wed; open mid-June-mid-Sept Tue-Sat 8:30-14:30, Sun 9:30-14:30, closed Mon; off-season Tue-Fri 8:30-19:30, Sat 9:30-16:30, Sun 9:30-14:30, closed Mon; last entry 30 minutes before closing. On Fridays and Saturdays you're likely to see civil wedding parties here.

Baths of the Caliphate Alcázar (Baños Califales)—The scant but evocative remains of these 10th-century royal baths are all that's left from the caliph's palace complex. They date from a time when the city had hundreds of baths and a population of several hundred thousand. The exhibit teaches about Arabic baths in general and the caliph's in particular. A 10-minute video (normally in Spanish, English on request) tells the story well.

Cost and Hours: €2, free on Wed; open mid-June-mid-Sept Tue-Sat 8:30-14:30, Sun 9:30-14:30, closed Mon; off-season Tue-Fri 8:30-19:30, Sat 9:30-16:30, Sun 9:30-14:30, closed Mon; last entry 30 minutes before closing, just outside the wall near the Alcázar.

Away from the Mezquita

Plaza de las Tendillas—While most tourists leave Córdoba having seen only the Mezquita and the cute medieval quarter that surrounds it, the modern city offers a good peek at urban Andalucía. Perhaps the best way to sample this is to browse Plaza de las Tendillas and the surrounding streets. The square, with an Art Deco charm, acts like there is no tourism in Córdoba. On the hour, a clock here chimes the guitar chords of Juan Serrano—a Córdoban classic.

Characteristic cafés and shops abound. For example, **Café La Gloria** provides an earthy Art Nouveau experience. Located just down the street from Plaza de las Tendillas, it has an unassuming entrance, but a sumptuous interior. Carved floral designs wind around the bar, mixing with *feria* posters and bullfighting memories. Pop in for a quick beer or coffee (daily from 8:00 until late, quiet after lunch crowd clears out, Calle Claudio Marcelo 15, tel. 957-477-780).

Palacio de Viana   Decidedly off the beaten path, this former palatial estate is a 25-minute walk northeast from the cluster of sights near the Mezquita. A guided tour whisks you through each room of an exuberant 16th-century estate, while an English handout drudges through the dates and origin of each important piece. But the house is best enjoyed by ignoring the guide and gasping at the massive collection of—for lack of a better word—stuff. Decorative-art fans will have a field day. The sight is known as the "patio museum" for its 12 connecting patios, each with a different theme:

Cost and Hours: House—€6, patios only €3; July-Aug Tue-Sun 9:00-15:00; Sept-June Tue-Fri 10:00-19:00, Sat-Sun 10:00-15:00; closed Mon year-round, last entry one hour before closing, no photos inside, Plaza Don Gome 2, tel. 957-496-741.

Near Córdoba

Madinat Al-Zahra (Medina Azahara)—Five miles northwest of Córdoba, these ruins of a once-fabulous palace of the caliph were completely forgotten until excavations began in the early 20th century. Built in A.D. 929 as a power center to replace Córdoba,

Patios

In Córdoba, patios are taken very seriously, as shown by the fiercely fought contest that takes place the first half of every May to pick the city's most pic-

turesque. Patios, a common feature of houses throughout Andalucía, have a long history here. The Romans used them to cool off, and the Moors added lush, decorative touches. The patio functioned as a quiet out-door living room, an oasis from the heat. Inside elaborate iron-work gates, roses, geraniums, and jasmine spill down white-washed walls, while fountains play and caged birds sing. Some patios are owned by individuals, some are communal courtyards for several homes, and some grace public buildings like museums or convents.

Today homeowners take pride in these mini-paradises, and have no problem sharing them with tourists. Keep an eye out for square metal signs that indicate historic homes. As you wander Córdoba's back streets, pop your head into any wooden door that's open. The proud owners (who keep inner gates locked) enjoy showing off their picture-perfect patios. A concentration of patio-contest award-winners runs along Calle de San Basilio and Calle Martín Roa, just across from the Alcázar gardens.

Madinat Al-Zahra was both a palace and an entirely new capital city—the "City of the Flower"—covering nearly half a square mile (only about 10 percent has been uncovered). Extensively planned

with an orderly design, Madinat Al-Zahra was meant to symbol-ize and project a new discipline on an increasingly unstable Moorish empire in Spain. It failed. Only 75 years later, the city was looted and destroyed.

The site is underwhelm-ing—a jigsaw puzzle waiting to be reassembled by patient archaeologists. Upper terrace exca-vations have uncovered stables and servants' quarters. Farther downhill, the house of a high-ranking official has been partially reconstructed. At the lowest level, you'll come to the remains of the mosque—placed at a diagonal, facing true east. The highlight of the visit is an elaborate reconstruction of the caliph's throne room, capturing a moody world of horseshoe arches and delicate stucco.

Legendary accounts say the palace featured waterfall walls, lions in cages, and—in the center of the throne room—a basin filled with mercury, reflecting the colorful walls. The effect likely humbled anyone fortunate enough to see the caliph.

Cost and Hours: €1.50, Tue-Sat 10:00-18:30, Sun 10:00-14:00, closed Mon, tel. 957-352-860.

Getting There: Madinat Al-Zahra is located on a back road five miles from Córdoba. By **car,** head to Avenida de Medina Azahara (one block south of the train station), following signs for *A-431*; the site is well-signposted from the highway. Though the ruins aren't accessible by regular public transportation, the TI runs a **shuttle bus** that leaves each morning and returns two hours later (€7, buy ticket at any of the city TIs— train station, Alcázar, or Plaza de las Tendillas; runs year-round Tue-Fri and Sun at 9:30 and 10:15; Sat at 9:30, 10:15, and 15:00; informative English booklet provided). Catch the bus near the Cruz Roja Hospital at Paseo de la Victoria.

Sleeping in Córdoba

I've listed prices for the high season; most of these are cheaper outside peak times. If it's hot and you've got a lot of luggage, don't bother with the inconvenient city buses; just hop in a taxi.

Near the Mezquita

These are all within a five-minute stroll of the Mezquita.

$$$ La Hospedería de El Churrasco is a nine-room jewel box of an inn, featuring plush furniture, tasteful traditional decor, and hardwood floors. Quiet and romantic, it's tucked in the old quarter just far enough away from the tourist storm, yet still handy for sightseeing (Sb-€120, Db-€140, superior Db-€180, €20 more per room in April-May and Oct, website shows off each distinct room, no twin rooms, includes breakfast, air-con, free Internet access, free cable Internet in rooms, parking-€20, midway between Puerta de Almodóvar and the Mezquita at Calle Romero 38, tel. 957-294-808, fax 957-421-661, www.elchurrasco.com, hospederia @elchurrasco.com).

$$ Hotel Albucasis, at the edge of the tourist zone, features 15 basic, clean rooms, all of which face quiet interior patios. The friendly, accommodating staff and cozy setting make you feel right at home (Sb-€55, Db-€85, breakfast-€6, air-con, elevator, free

Sleep Code

(€1 = about $1.40, country code: 34)
S = Single, **D** = Double/Twin, **T** = Triple, **Q** = Quad, **b** = bathroom, **s** = shower only. Unless otherwise noted, credit cards are accepted, English is spoken, and breakfast generally costs extra.

To help you easily sort through these listings, I've divided the accommodations into three categories, based on the price for a standard double room with bath during high season:

$$$ Higher Priced—Most rooms €100 or more.
  $$ Moderately Priced—Most rooms between €60-100.
    $ Lower Priced—Most rooms €60 or less.

Prices can change without notice; verify the hotel's current rates online or by email. For other updates, see www.ricksteves.com/update.

Wi-Fi in lobby, parking-€12 but free in off-season, Buen Pastor 11, tel. 957-478-625, www.hotelalbucasis.com, hotelalbucasis@hotmail.com).

$$ Hotel Mezquita, just across from the main entrance of the Mezquita, rents 31 modern and comfortable rooms. The grand entrance lobby elegantly recycles an upper-class mansion (Sb-€46, Db-€79, Tb-€117, breakfast-€4, air-con, elevator, free Wi-Fi in lobby, Plaza Santa Catalina 1, tel. 957-475-585, fax 957-476-219, www.hotelmezquita.com, hotelmezquita@wanadoo.es).

$$ Hotel González, with many of its 17 basic rooms facing its cool and peaceful patio, is sparse but sleepable. It's clean and well-run, with a good location and price (Sb-€42, Db-€75, Tb-€110, higher prices for busy times—especially weekends, breakfast-€4, air-con, elevator, free Wi-Fi in lobby, Manríquez 3, tel. 957-479-819, fax 957-486-187, www.hotel-gonzalez.com, hotelgonzalez @wanadoo.es).

$ Hostal Alcázar is your best cheapie. Run-down and budget-priced, without a real reception desk, this friendly place is just outside the old city wall on a quiet cobbled traffic-free street known for its prizewinning patios. Its 16 rooms are split between 2 homes on opposite sides of the lane, conveniently located 50 yards from a taxi and bus stop (Sb-€20, small Db-€36, bigger Db-€45, Tb-€60, 2-room apartment-€60 for 3 or €80 for 4, breakfast-€4, air-con, free Wi-Fi on patio, parking-€6, near Alcázar at Calle de San Basilio 2, tel. 957-202-561, www.hostalalcazar.com, hostalalcazar@hotmail.com, ladies' man Fernando and family, son Demitrio speaks English).

CÓRDOBA

In the Modern City

While still within easy walking distance of the Mezquita, these places are outside of the main tourist zone—not buried in all that tangled medieval cuteness.

$$ Hotel Califa, a modern 65-room business-class hotel from the NH chain, sits on a quiet street a block off busy Paseo Victoria, on the edge of the jumbled old quarter. Still close enough to the sights, its slick modern rooms can be a great value if you get a deal (vast price range depending on demand but Db generally €80-90 during the week, €120 weekends, around €70 in heat of summer, Tb generally €20-25 more, air-con, elevator, free Internet access, pay Wi-Fi, parking-€15, Lope de Hoces 14, tel. 957-299-400, www.nh-hotels.com, nhcalifa@nh-hotels.com).

$$ Hotel Boston, with 39 rooms, is a decent budget bet if you want a reliable, basic hotel away from the touristy Mezquita zone. It's a taste of workaday Córdoba (Sb-€40-48, Db-€55-76, Tb-€75-90, breakfast-€5, air-con, elevator, pay Internet access, free Wi-Fi, parking-€12, Málaga 2, just off Plaza de las Tendillas, tel. 957-474-176, www.hotel-boston.com, info@hotel-boston.com).

$ The Terrace Backpackers Hostel rents dorm beds and simple doubles in a great neighborhood (dorm beds-€15-19, D-€40-50, air-con, free Wi-Fi, terrace, kitchen, self-service laundry, lots of hostel-type info and help, at Potro bus stop—take #3 from station—at Calle Lucano 12, tel. 957-492-966, theterracebackpackers hostel@yahoo.com).

Eating in Córdoba

Córdoba is a great dining town, with options ranging from obvious touristy bars in the old center to enticing, locals-only hangouts a few blocks away. Specialties include *salmorejo*, Córdoba's version of gazpacho. It's creamier, with more bread and olive oil and generally served with pieces of ham and hard-boiled egg. Most places serve white wines from the nearby Montilla-Moriles region; these *finos* are slightly less dry but more aromatic than the sherry produced in Jerez de la Frontera. For a good value and truly local scene, explore the little characteristic bars in the lanes around Plaza de la Corredera.

Near the Mezquita

There are plenty of touristy options around the Mezquita, designed for out-of-towners and tour groups. By walking a couple blocks away along Calle del Cardenal González, you get into a district of cheap, accessible little places offering a better value. Listed here, in order, are a bright and efficient diner about 50 yards from the mosque, a colorful neighborhood restaurant, a down-and-dirty wine bar, a Jewish restaurant, and a steak house.

Bodegas Mezquita is a good bet for a bright, air-conditioned place a block from the mosque. They have a good *menú del día*, or you can order from their menu of €3-4 tapas, €4-10 half-*raciones*, and €8-16 *raciones* (long hours daily, one block above the Mezquita garden at Céspedes 12, tel. 957-490-004). They have a second location below the Mezquita (Corregidor Luis de la Cerda 73, tel. 957-498-117).

Mesón San Basilio is the local hangout on Calle de San Basilio, just outside the wall. Although there's no seating outside, the restaurant still offers great "patio ambience"—with a view of the kitchen action. No tourists, no pretense...it's understandably the neighborhood favorite (classic €18.50 fixed-priced meal, €8 lunch special weekdays, lots of €9-15 fish and meat dishes, Mon-Sat 13:00-16:00 & 20:00-24:00, Sun 13:00-16:00 only, Calle de San Basilio 19, tel. 957-297-007). For something rougher—rustic meals, tapas, and crowds—go to the church and head a block left to **Bodega San Basilio** (Calle de Enmedio, tel. 957-297-832).

Bodega Guzmán, which proudly displays the heads of brave-but-unlucky bulls, serves cold, very basic tapas to locals who call the waiters by their first names and burst into song when they feel the flamenco groove. Arrive early to get a table. While it feels like a drinks-only place, they do have rustic €2 tapas and €6 *raciones* (ask for the list in English). Choose a table or belly up to the bar and try a local Montilla-Moriles white wine: dry *(blanco seco)* or sweet *(blanco dulce)* for €1 a glass. For grape juice, ask for *mosto* (closed Thu; if entering the old town from Puerta de Almodóvar take the first right—it's 100 yards from the gate at Calle de los Judíos 7).

Casa Mazal, run by the nearby Casa de Sefarad Jewish cultural center, serves updated, modern Jewish cuisine. Small dining rooms sprawl around the charming medieval courtyard of a former house. With a seasonal menu that includes several vegetarian options, it offers a welcome dose of variety from the typical Spanish standards (€7-9 starters, €10-15 main dishes, Wed-Mon 12:00-17:00 & 20:00-24:00, closed Tue, also closed Mon off-season, Tomás Conde 3, tel. 957-941-888).

Restaurante El Choto is bright, formal, and dressy, with a small leafy patio, buried deep in the Jewish Quarter. It's touristy yet intimate, serving well-presented international dishes with an emphasis on grilled meat. The favorite is kid goat with garlic—*choto al ajillo* (€23 house fixed-price meal, €36 tasting-menu fixed-price meal, €15-25 main dishes, closed Sun evening and all day Mon, Calle de Almanzor 10, tel. 957-760-115).

Just East of the Mezquita Zone

Bodegas Campos, my favorite place in town, is a historic and venerable house of eating, attracting so many locals it comes with its own garage. It's worth the 10-minute walk from the tourist zone. They have a stuffy and expensive formal restaurant upstairs (€12-20 starters, €17-27 main dishes), but I'd eat in the more relaxed and affordable tavern on the ground floor (€6-9 half-*raciones*). The service is great and the menu is inviting. In two visits I nearly ate my way through the offerings, a half-*ración* at a time, and enjoyed each dish. Experiment—you can't go wrong. House specialties are bull-tail stew (*rabo de toro*—rich, tasty, and a good splurge) and anything with *pisto*, the local ratatouille-like vegetable stew. Don't leave without exploring the sprawling complex, which fills 14 old houses that have been connected to create a network of dining rooms and patios, small and large. The place is a virtual town history museum: Look for the wine barrels signed by celebrities and VIPs, the old refectory from a convent, and a huge collection of classic, original *feria* posters and great photos (Mon-Sat 12:00-17:00 & 20:00-24:00, Sun 12:00-17:00 only; from river end of Mezquita walk east along Cardenal González, continue 10 minutes straight to Calle de Lineros 32; tel. 957-497-500).

In the Modern City

These are worth the 10-to-15-minute walk from the main tourist zone—walking here, you feel a world apart from the touristy scene. Combine a meal here with a paseo through the Plaza de las Tendillas area to get a good look at modern Córdoba.

Taverna Salinas seems like a movie set designed to give you the classic Córdoba scene. Though all the seating is indoors, it's still pleasantly patio-esque, and popular with locals for its traditional cuisine and exuberant bustle. The seating fills a big courtyard and sprawls through several smaller, semi-private rooms. The fun menu features a slew of enticing €6-7 plates (spinach with chickpeas is a house specialty). Study what locals are eating before ordering. There's no drinks menu—just basic beer or inexpensive wine. If there's a line (as there often is later in the evening), leave your name and throw yourself into the adjacent tapas-bar mosh pit for a drink (Mon-Sat 12:30-16:00 & 20:00-23:30, closed Sun and Aug; from Plaza de las Tendillas walk 3 blocks to the Roman temple, then go 1 more block and turn right to Tundidores 3; tel. 957-480-135).

Taberna San Miguel is nicknamed "Casa el Pisto" for its famous vegetable stew *(pisto)*. Well-respected, it's packed with locals who appreciate regional cuisine, a good value, and a place with a long Córdoban history. Go to the bar to be seated (€2-3 tapas, €6-10 half-*raciones*, €7-14 *raciones*, 20 percent extra to sit in patio or outside, closed Sun-Mon and Aug, 2 blocks north of Plaza de las Tendillas at Plaza San Miguel 1, tel. 957-478-328).

Córdoba Connections

From Córdoba by Train: Córdoba is on the slick AVE train line (reservations required), making it an easy stopover between **Madrid** (2-3/hour, 1.75 hours, €69, railpass-holders pay €10.35 for required reservation) and **Sevilla** (2-3/hour, 45 minutes, €34, railpass-holders pay €10.35 for required reservation). The Avant train connects Córdoba to Sevilla just as fast for half the price (9/day, 45 minutes, €17, railpass-holders pay €6.50 for required reservation). The slow regional train to Sevilla takes nearly twice as long, but doesn't require a reservation and is even cheaper (8/day, 80 minutes, €11 one-way).

Other trains go to **Granada** (2/day on Altaria, 2.5 hours, €36—bus is more frequent, cheaper, and nearly as fast), **Ronda** (2/day direct on Altaria, 1.75 hours, €40; 1/day much cheaper but much longer with transfer in Bobadilla, 4 hours, €17), **Jerez** (to transfer to Arcos; 8/day, 2.5-3 hours, €24 on regional train, €30-40 on fast train), **Málaga** (fast and cheap Avant train, 6/day, 1 hour, €23; fast and expensive AVE train, 11/day, 1 hour, €44), and **Algeciras** (2/day, 3.5 hours). Train info: toll tel. 902-320-320.

By Bus to: Granada (5/day *directo*, 2.75 hours, €13; 2/day *ruta*, 4 hours, €17), **Sevilla** (6/day, 2 hours, €11), **Madrid** (6/day, 5 hours, €16), **Málaga** (4/day, 3-3.5 hours, €13), **Barcelona** (2/day, 10 hours). The efficient staff at the information desk prints bus schedules for you—or you can check all schedules at www.estacionautobuses cordoba.es. Bus info: tel. 957-404-040.

ANDALUCÍA'S WHITE HILL TOWNS

Arcos de la Frontera • Ronda •
Zahara and Grazalema • Jerez

Just as the American image of Germany is Bavaria, the Yankee dream of Spain is Andalucía. This is the home of bullfights, flamenco, gazpacho, pristine whitewashed hill towns, and glamorous Mediterranean resorts. The big cities of Andalucía (Granada, Sevilla, and Córdoba) and the South Coast (Costa del Sol) are covered in separate chapters. This chapter explores Andalucía's hill-town highlights.

The Route of the White Hill Towns (Ruta de los Pueblos Blancos), Andalucía's charm bracelet of cute towns perched in the sierras, gives you wonderfully untouched Spanish culture. Spend a night in the romantic queen of the white towns, Arcos de la Frontera. (Towns with "de la Frontera" in their names were established on the front line of the centuries-long fight to recapture Spain from the Muslims, who were slowly pushed back into Africa.) Farther east, the larger town of Ronda stuns visitors with its breathtaking setting—straddling a gorge that thrusts deep into the Andalusian bedrock. Ronda's venerable old bullring, smattering of enjoyable sights, and thriving tapas scene round out its charms. Smaller hill towns, such as Zahara and Grazalema, offer plenty of beauty. As a whole, the hill towns—no longer strategic, no longer on any frontier—are now just passing time peacefully. Join them.

Between Sevilla and the hill towns, the city of Jerez—teeming with traffic and lacking in charm—is worth a peek for its famous Horse Symphony and a glass of sherry on a sherry bogeda tour.

To study ahead, visit www.andalucia.com for information on hotels, festivals, museums, nightlife, and sports in the region.

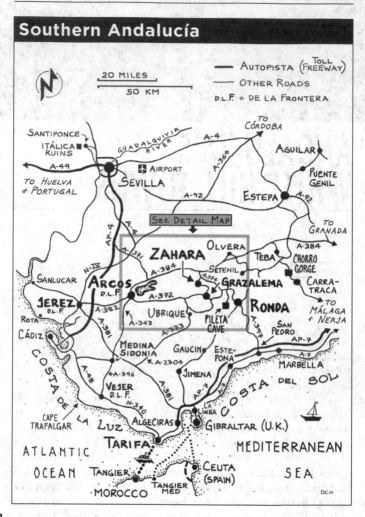

Southern Andalucía

AUTOPISTA (FREEWAY) — TOLL
OTHER ROADS
D.L.F. = DE LA FRONTERA

20 MILES
50 KM

SANTIPONCE
ITÁLICA RUINS
A-49
TO HUELVA & PORTUGAL
SEVILLA
AIRPORT
GUADALQUIVIR RIVER
A-4
TO CÓRDOBA
A-364
AGUILAR
PUENTE GENIL
ESTEPA
A-92
A-92
TO GRANADA
SEE DETAIL MAP
ZAHARA
OLVERA
A-384
TEBA
CHORRO GORGE
A-331
SETENIL
A-374
GRAZALEMA
CARRA-TRACA
AP-4
A-4
N-IV
SANLUCAR
ARCOS D.L.F.
A-384
A-372
RONDA
TO MÁLAGA & NERJA
JEREZ D.L.F.
A-382
UBRIQUE
A-343
PILETA CAVE
A-373
A-397
SAN PEDRO
ROTA
A-381
MEDINA SIDONIA
GAUCIN
ESTE-PONA
AP-7
A-7
MARBELLA
CÁDIZ
COSTA DE LA LUZ
A-48
A-2304
JIMENA
COSTA DEL SOL
VEJER D.L.F.
A-396
A-381
AP-7
A-7
N-340
LA LINEA
CAPE TRAFALGAR
ALGECIRAS
GIBRALTAR (U.K.)
MEDITERRANEAN
TARIFA
ATLANTIC OCEAN
TANGIER
CEUTA (SPAIN)
SEA
MOROCCO
TANGIER MED
DCH

Planning Your Time

On a three-week vacation in Spain, the Andalucía region is worth two nights and up to two days sandwiched between visits to Sevilla and Tarifa. Arcos makes the best home base, as it's close to interesting smaller towns, near Jerez, and conveniently situated halfway between Sevilla and Tarifa. The towns can also be accessed from the Costa del Sol resorts via Ronda.

See Jerez on your way in or out, spend a day hopping from town to town in the more remote interior (including Grazalema and Zahara), and enjoy Arcos early and late in the day. For more details on exploring this region by car, see "Route Tips for Drivers" at the end of this chapter.

Without a car, keep things simple and focus only on Arcos and Jerez (both well-served by frequent-enough public buses from Sevilla). If you're more interested in Ronda, it's easy to visit, right on a train line.

Spring and fall are high season throughout this area. In summer you'll encounter intense heat, but empty hotels, lower prices, and no crowds.

Arcos de la Frontera

Arcos smothers its long, narrow hilltop and tumbles down the back of the ridge like the train of a wedding dress. It's larger than most other Andalusian hill towns, but equally atmospheric. Arcos consists of two towns: the fairy-tale old town on top of the hill and the fun-loving lower, or new, town. The old center is a labyrinthine wonderland, a photographer's feast. Viewpoint-hop through town. Feel the wind funnel through the narrow streets as cars inch around tight corners. Join the kids' soccer game on the churchyard patio. Enjoy the moonlit view from the main square.

Though it tries, Arcos doesn't have much to offer other than its basic whitewashed self. The locally produced English guidebook on Arcos waxes poetic and at length about very little. You can arrive late and leave early and still see it all.

Orientation to Arcos

Tourist Information

The TI, on the main road leading up into the old town, is helpful and loaded with information, including bus schedules (March-Nov daily 9:30-14:00 & 15:00-19:30, Sun from 10:00; Dec-Feb daily until 18:30; Cuesta de Belén 5, tel. 956-702-264, www.ayuntamientoarcos.org).

On the floors above the TI is a skippable local history museum called Centro de Interpretación Ciudad de Arcos (CICA), with few artifacts and sparse exhibits described only in Spanish.

The TI organizes a one-hour **walking tour,** which includes a tour of CICA and a walk through the old town, learning about Arcos' history, lifestyles, and Moorish influences. You also get a peek at some private courtyard patios (€6, Mon-Fri at 11:00 and 18:00, Sat only at 11:00, none on Sun, meet at TI, in Spanish and/or English; for private tours call TI).

HILL TOWNS

Arrival in Arcos

By Bus: The bus station is on Calle Corregidores, at the foot of the hill. To get up to the old town, catch the shuttle bus marked *Centro* (€1, pay driver, 2/hour, runs roughly Mon-Fri 7:00-22:00, Sat 9:00-22:00, none on Sun), hop a taxi (€5 fixed rate; if there are no taxis waiting, call 956-704-640), or hike 20 uphill minutes (see map).

By Car: The old town is a tight squeeze with a one-way traffic flow from west to east (coming from the east, circle south under town). The TI and my recommended hotels are in the west. If you miss your target, you must drive out the other end, double back, and try again. Driving in Arcos is like threading needles (many drivers pull in their side-view mirrors to buy a few extra precious inches). Turns are tight, parking is frustrating, and congestion can lead to long jams.

Small cars can park in the main square of the old town at the top of the hill (Plaza del Cabildo). Get a €3.50 all-day pass from your hotel or buy a ticket from the machine (€0.70/hour, 2-hour maximum, only necessary Mon-Fri 9:00-14:00 & 17:00-21:00 and Sat 9:00-14:00—confirm times on machine). If staying overnight, tell the uniformed parking attendant the name of your hotel. If there's no spot, wait until one opens up (he'll help...for a little tip). Once you grab a spot, tell him you'll be back from your hotel with a ticket.

It's less stressful (and better exercise) to park in the modern underground pay lot at Plaza de España in the new town. From this lot, catch a taxi or the shuttle bus up to the old town (2/hour; as you're looking uphill, the bus stop is to the right of the traffic circle), or hike 15 minutes.

Getting Around Arcos

The old town is easily walkable, but it's fun and relaxing to take a circular **minibus** joyride. The little shuttle bus (also mentioned in "Arrival," above) constantly circles through the town's one-way system and around the valley (€1, 2/hour, runs roughly Mon-Fri 7:00-22:00, Sat 9:00-22:00, none on Sun). For a 30-minute tour, hop on. You can catch it just below the main church in the old town near the mystical stone circle (generally departs roughly at :20 and :50 past the hour). Sit in the front seat for the best view of the tight squeezes and the school kids hanging out in the plazas as you wind through the old town. After passing under a Moorish gate, you enter a modern residential neighborhood, circle under the eroding cliff, and return to the old town by way of the bus station and Plaza de España.

Arcos de la Frontera

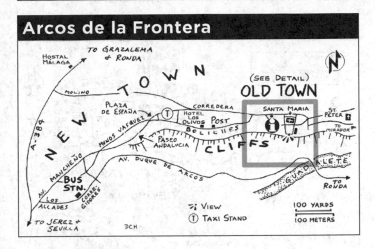

Helpful Hints

Internet Access: Most hotels have Wi-Fi for guests, and some also have Internet terminals. There's no real Internet café in Arcos' old town, but the TI may have a terminal where you can pay to get online.

Post Office: It's at the lower end of the old town at Paseo de los Boliches 24, a few doors up from Hotel Los Olivos (Mon-Fri 8:30-14:30, Sat 9:30-13:00, closed Sun).

Viewpoint: For drivers, the best town overlook is from a tiny park just beyond the new bridge on the El Bosque road. In town, there are some fine viewpoints (for instance, from the main square), but the church towers are no longer open to the public.

Self-Guided Walk

Welcome to Arcos' Old Town

This walk will introduce you to virtually everything worth seeing in Arcos.

• *Start at the top of the hill, in the main square dominated by the church. (Avoid this walk during the hot midday siesta.)*

Plaza del Cabildo: Stand at the viewpoint opposite the church on the town's main square. Survey the square, which in the old days doubled as a bullring. On your right is the parador, a former

HILL TOWNS

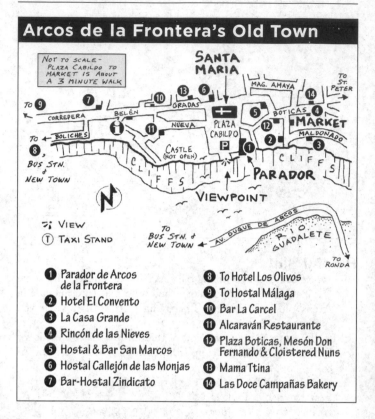

Arcos de la Frontera's Old Town

NOT TO SCALE -
PLAZA CABILDO TO
MARKET IS ABOUT
A 3 MINUTE WALK

SANTA MARIA

MAG. AMAYA

TO ST. PETER

CORREDERA

BELÉN

GRADAS

BOTICAS

MARKET

TO BOLICHES

NUEVA

PLAZA CABILDO

MALDONADO

CASTLE (NOT OPEN)

CLIFFS

PARADOR

CLIFFS

BUS STN. & NEW TOWN

VIEWPOINT

N

TO BUS STN. & NEW TOWN

AV. DUQUE DE ARCOS

RIO GUADALETE

TO RONDA

VIEW

TAXI STAND

1 Parador de Arcos de la Frontera
2 Hotel El Convento
3 La Casa Grande
4 Rincón de las Nieves
5 Hostal & Bar San Marcos
6 Hostal Callejón de las Monjas
7 Bar-Hostal Zindicato

8 To Hotel Los Olivos
9 To Hostal Málaga
10 Bar La Carcel
11 Alcaraván Restaurante
12 Plaza Boticas, Mesón Don Fernando & Cloistered Nuns
13 Mama Ttina
14 Las Doce Campañas Bakery

palace of the governor. It flies three flags: green for Andalucía, red-and-yellow for Spain, and blue-and-yellow for the European Union. On your left are the City Hall and the TI, below the 11th-century Moorish castle where Ferdinand and Isabel held Reconquista strategy meetings (castle privately owned and closed to the public).

Now belly up to the railing and look down. The people of Arcos boast that only they see the backs of the birds as they fly. Ponder the parador's erosion concerns (it lost part of its lounge in the 1990s when it dropped right off), the orderly orange groves, and fine views toward Morocco. The city council considered building an underground parking lot to clear up the square, but nixed it because of the land's fragility. You're 330 feet above the Guadalete River. This is the town's suicide departure point for men (women jump from the other side).

• Looming over the square is the...

HILL TOWNS

Church of Santa María: After Arcos was retaken from the Moors in the 13th century, this church was built atop a mosque.

Notice the church's fine but chopped-off bell tower. The old one fell in the earthquake of 1755 (famous for destroying Lisbon). The replacement was intended to be the tallest in Andalucía after Sevilla's—but money ran out. It looks like someone lives on an upper floor. Someone does—the church guardian resides there in a room strewn with bell-ringing ropes.

Buy a ticket (€2, Mon-Fri 10:00-13:00 & 16:00-19:00, Sat 10:00-14:00, closed Sun and Jan-Feb), and step into the center, where you can see the beautifully carved choir. The organ was built in 1789 with that many pipes. At the very front of the church, the nice Renaissance high altar—carved in wood—covers up a Muslim prayer niche that survived from the older mosque. The altar shows God with a globe in his hand (on top), and scenes from the life of Jesus (on the right) and Mary (left). Circle the church counterclockwise and notice the elaborate chapels. Although most of the architecture is Gothic, the chapels are decorated in Baroque and Rococo styles. The ornate statues are used in Holy Week processions. Sniff out the "incorruptible body" (miraculously never rotting) of St. Felix—a third-century martyr (directly across from the entry). Felix may be nicknamed "the incorruptible," but take a close look at his knee. He's no longer skin and bones...just bones and the fine silver mesh that once covered his skin. Rome sent his body here in 1764, after recognizing this church as the most important in Arcos. In the back of the church, under a huge fresco of St. Christopher (carrying his staff and Baby Jesus), is a gnarly Easter candle from 1767.

• Back outside, examine the...

Church Exterior: Circle clockwise around the church, down four steps, to find the third-century Roman votive altar with a carving of the palm tree of life. Though the Romans didn't build this high in the mountains, they did have a town and temple at the foot of Arcos. This carved stone was discovered in the foundation of the original Moorish mosque, which stood here before the first church was built.

Head down a few more steps and come to the main entrance (west portal) of the church (closed until restoration is complete). This is a good example of Plateresque Gothic—Spain's last and most ornate kind of Gothic.

In the pavement, notice the 15th-century magic circle with 12 red and 12 white stones—the white ones have various "constellations" marked (though they don't resemble any of today's star charts). When a child would come to the church to be baptized, the parents would stop here first for a good Christian exorcism. The exorcist would stand inside the protective circle and cleanse the baby of any evil spirits. While locals no longer do this (and a modern rain drain now marks the center), Sufis, members of a sect of Islam, still come here in a kind of pilgrimage every November. (Down a few more steps and 10 yards to the left, you can catch the public bus for a circular minibus joyride through Arcos; see "Getting Around Arcos," earlier.)

Continue around the back of the church. On your left, look for **Señor González Oca's tiny barbershop,** with some exciting posters of bulls running Pamplona-style through the streets of Arcos during Holy Week—an American from the nearby Navy base at Rota was killed here by a bull in 1994. (Señor González Oca is now semi-retired, but if he's in, he's happy to show off his posters; drop in and say, "Hola." Need a haircut, guys? €9.)

Continuing along under the **flying buttresses,** notice the scratches of innumerable car mirrors on each wall (and be glad you're walking). The buttresses were built to shore up the church when it was damaged by an earthquake in 1699. (Thanks to these supports, the church survived the bigger earthquake of 1755.) The security grille (over the window above) protected cloistered nuns when this building was a convent. Look at the arches that prop up the houses downhill on the left; all over town, arches support earthquake-damaged structures.

• *Now make your way...*

From the Church to the Market: Completing your circle around the church (huffing back uphill), turn left under more arches built to repair earthquake damage and walk east down the bright, white Calle Escribanos. From now to the end of this walk, you'll basically follow this lane until you come to the town's second big church (St. Peter's). After a block, you hit Plaza Boticas.

On your right is the last remaining **convent** in Arcos. Notice the no-nunsense, spiky window grilles high above, with tiny peepholes in the latticework for the cloistered nuns to see through. Step into the lobby under the fine portico to find their one-way mirror and a spinning cupboard that hides the nuns from view. Push the buzzer, and one of the eight sisters (several are from Kenya and speak English well) will spin out some boxes of excellent, freshly baked cookies—made from pine nuts, peanuts, almonds, and other nuts—for you to consider buying (€6-7, open daily but not reliably 8:30-14:30 & 17:00-19:00; be careful—if you stand big and tall to block out the light, you can actually see the sister through the glass). If you ask for *magdalenas,* bags of cupcakes will swing around (€1.50). These are traditional goodies made from natural ingredients. Buy some goodies to support their church work, and give them to kids as you complete your walk.

The **covered market** *(mercado)* at the bottom of the plaza (down from the convent) resides in an unfinished church. At the entry, notice what is half of a church wall. The church was being built for the Jesuits, but construction stopped in 1767 when King Charles III, tired of the Jesuit appetite for politics, expelled the order from Spain. The market is closed on Sunday and Monday— they rest on Sunday, so there's no produce, fish, or meat ready for Monday. Poke inside. It's tiny but has everything you need. Pop into the *servicio público* (public WC)—no gender bias here.

• *Continue straight down Calle Botica...*

From the Market to the Church of St. Peter: As you walk, peek discreetly into private patios. These wonderful, cool-tiled courtyards filled with plants, pools, furniture, and happy family activities are typical of Arcos. Except in the mansions, these patios are generally shared by several families. Originally, each courtyard served as a catchment system, funneling rainwater to a drain in the middle, which filled the well. You can still see tiny wells in wall niches with now-decorative pulleys for the bucket.

On the left (at #11), look for **Las Doce Campanas bakery,** where Juan Miguel or Encarni sells traditional and delicious sultana cookies (€1.20 each). These big, dry macaroons (named for the wives of sultans) go back to Moorish times. At the next corner, squint back above the bakery to the corner of the tiled rooftop. The tiny stone—where the corner hits the sky—is a very eroded mask, placed here to scare evil spirits from the house. This is Arcos' last surviving mask from a tradition that lasted until the mid-19th century.

Also notice the ancient columns on each corner. All over town, these columns—many actually Roman, appropriated from their original ancient settlement at the foot of the hill—were put up to protect buildings from reckless donkey carts and tourists in rental cars.

As you continue straight, notice that the walls are scooped out on either side of the windows. These are a reminder of the days when women stayed inside but wanted the best possible view of any people action in the streets. These "window ears" also enabled boys in a more modest age to lean inconspicuously against the wall to chat up eligible young ladies.

Across from the old facade ahead, find the **Association of San Miguel.** Duck right, past a bar, into the oldest courtyards in town—you can still see the graceful Neo-Gothic lines of this

HILL TOWNS

noble home from 1850. The bar is a club for retired men—always busy when a bullfight's on TV or during card games. The guys are friendly, and drinks are cheap. You're welcome to flip on the light and explore the old-town photos in the back room.

Just beyond, facing the elegant front door of that noble house, is Arcos' second church, **St. Peter's** (€1 donation, Mon-Fri 9:00-14:00 & 15:30-18:30, Sat 9:00-12:00, closed Sun). You know it's St. Peter's because St. Peter, mother of God, is the centerpiece of the facade. Let me explain. It really is the second church, having had an extended battle with Santa María for papal recognition as the leading church in Arcos. When the pope finally favored Santa María, St. Peter's parishioners changed their prayers. Rather than honoring "María," they wouldn't even say her name. They prayed "St. Peter, mother of God." Like Santa María, it's a Gothic structure, filled with Baroque decor, many Holy Week procession statues, humble English descriptions, and relic skeletons in glass caskets (two from the third century A.D.).

In the cool of the evening, the tiny square in front of the church—about the only flat piece of pavement around—serves as the old-town soccer field for neighborhood kids. Until a few years ago, this church also had a resident bellman—notice the cozy balcony halfway up. He was a basket-maker and a colorful character, famous for bringing a donkey into his quarters, which grew too big to get back out. Finally, he had no choice but to kill and eat the donkey.

Twenty yards beyond the church, step into the nice **Galería de Arte San Pedro,** featuring artisans in action and their reasonably priced paintings and pottery. Walk inside. Find the water drain and the well.

Across the street, a sign directs you to **Mirador**—a tiny square 100 yards downhill that affords a commanding view of Arcos. The reservoir you see to the east of town is used for water sports in the summertime, and forms part of a power plant that local residents protested—to no avail—based on environmental concerns.

From the Church of St. Peter, circle down and around back to the main square, wandering the tiny neighborhood lanes. Just below St. Peter's is a delightful little Andalusian garden (formal Arabic style, with aromatic plants such as jasmine, rose, and lavender, and water in the center). The lane called Higinio Capote, below Santa María, is particularly picturesque with its many geraniums. Peek into patios, kick a few soccer balls, and savor the views.

Nightlife in Arcos

Evening Action in the New Town—The newer part of Arcos has a modern charm. In the cool of the evening, all generations enjoy life out around Plaza de España (10-minute walk from the old town). Several good tapas bars border the square or are nearby.

The big park (Recinto Ferial) below Plaza de España is the late-night fun zone in the summer (June-Aug) when *carpas* (restaurant tents) fill with merrymakers, especially on weekends. The scene includes open-air tapas bars, disco music, and dancing. There are sometimes free evening events here in the summer—ask at the TI.

Sleeping in Arcos

Hotels in Arcos consider April, May, August, September, and October to be high season. Note that some hotels double their rates during the motorbike races in nearby Jerez (usually April or May, varies yearly, call TI or ask your hotel) and during Holy Week (the week leading up to Easter); these spikes are not reflected in the prices below.

In the Old Town

For all of these (except Zindicato), the nearest parking is at Plaza Cabildo, the main square in front of the church (buy €3.50 parking pass from your hotel).

$$$ Parador de Arcos de la Frontera is royally located, with 24 elegant, recently refurbished and reasonably priced rooms (8 have balconies). If you're going to experience a parador, this is a good one (Sb-€120-131, Db-€150-163, Db with terrace-€174-196, cheaper rates are for Nov-Feb, breakfast-€16, air-con, elevator, free Internet access, free parking, Plaza del Cabildo, tel. 956-700-500, fax 956-701-116, www.parador.es, arcos@parador.es).

$$ Hotel El Convento, deep in the old town just beyond the parador, is the best value in town. Run by a hardworking family and their wonderful staff, this cozy hotel offers 13 fine rooms—all with great views, most with balconies. In 1998 I enjoyed a big party with most of Arcos' big shots as they dedicated a fine room with a grand-view balcony to "Rick Steves, Periodista Turístico." Guess where I sleep when in Arcos... (Sb with balcony-€56, Sb with terrace-€69, Db with balcony-€71, Db with terrace-€86, extra person-€19; 10 percent discount in 2012 when you book direct, pay in cash, and show this book; usually closed Nov-Feb;

HILL TOWNS

Sleep Code

(€1 = about $1.40, country code: 34)
S = Single, **D** = Double/Twin, **T** = Triple, **Q** = Quad, **b** = bathroom, **s** = shower only. Unless otherwise noted, you can assume credit cards are accepted, English is spoken, and the IVA tax is included in the price, but breakfast is not included.

To help you easily sort through these listings, I've divided the accommodations into three categories, based on the price for a standard double room with bath during high season:

$$$ Higher Priced—Most rooms €100 or more.
  $$ Moderately Priced—Most rooms between €50-100.
    $ Lower Priced—Most rooms €50 or less.

Prices can change without notice; verify the hotel's current rates online or by email. For other updates, see www.ricksteves.com/update.

Maldonado 2, tel. 956-702-333, fax 956-704-128, www.hotelel convento.es, reservas@hotelelconvento.es). Over an à la carte breakfast, bird-watch on their view terrace, with all of Andalucía spreading beyond your *café con leche*.

$$ La Casa Grande is a lovingly appointed *Better Homes and Moroccan Tiles* kind of place that rents eight rooms with big-view windows. Like in a lavish yet very authentic old-style B&B, you're free to enjoy its fine view terrace, homey library, and atrium-like patio, where you'll be served a traditional breakfast. They also offer guided visits and massage services (Db-€71-85; junior suites: Db-€82-119, Tb-€106-119, Qb-€123-140; breakfast-€9, air-con, free Internet access, Maldonado 10, tel. 956-703-930, fax 956-717-095, www.lacasagrande.net, info@lacasagrande.net, Elena).

$$ Rincón de las Nieves, with simple Andalusian style, has a cool inner courtyard surrounded by three rooms and a sprawling apartment which can accommodate up to seven people. Two of the rooms have their own outdoor terraces with obstructed views, and all have access to the rooftop terrace (Db-€50-65, higher for Holy Week and Aug, apartment-€20-24/person, air-con, Boticas 10, tel. 956-701-528, mobile 656-886-256, rincondelasnieves@gmail.com).

$ Hostal San Marcos, above a neat little bar in the heart of the old town, offers four air-conditioned rooms and a great sun terrace with views of the reservoir (Sb-€25, Db-€35, Tb-€45, air-con, Marqués de Torresoto 6, best to reserve by phone, tel. 956-700-721, mobile 615-375-077, www.hsanmarcos.es, info@hsanmarcos.es). Loli speaks no English.

   $ Hostal Callejón de las Monjas (a.k.a. Hostal El Patio) offers the best cheap beds in the old town. With a tangled floor plan and nine simple rooms, it's on a sometimes-noisy street behind the Church of Santa María (Sb-€20, D-€27, Db-€33, Db with terrace-€39, Tb-€44, Qb apartment-€66, air-con, Calle Deán Espinosa 4, tel. & fax 956-702-302, mobile 605-839-995, www.mesonelpatio .com, padua@mesonelpatio.com, staff speak no English). There's a bar-restaurant with bullfighting posters in the cellar.

   $ At Bar-Hostal Zindicato, the bar comes first, but they also rent four tidy, modern, air-conditioned rooms really cheap out back on the ground floor (Db-€30, Calle Corredera 2, tel. 956-701-841, mobile 657-911-851). It's in a less quaint zone at the bottom end of the old town.

In the New Town
$$ Hotel Los Olivos is a bright, cool, and airy place with 19 rooms, an impressive courtyard, roof garden, generous public spaces, bar, view, friendly folks, and easy parking. The seven view rooms can be a bit noisy in the afternoon, but—with double-paned windows—are usually fine at night (Sb-€43-48, Db-€65-80, Tb-€80-95, extra bed €15, breakfast-€8.50; 10 percent discount when you book direct, pay in cash, and show this book; free Internet access and Wi-Fi, Paseo de los Boliches 30, tel. 956-700-811, fax 956-702-018, www.hotel-losolivos.es, reservas@hotel-losolivos.es, Raquel and Miguel Ángel).

   $ Hostal Málaga is surprisingly nice, if for some reason you want to stay on the big, noisy road at the Jerez edge of town. Nestled on a quiet lane between truck stops on A-382, it offers 18 clean, attractive rooms and a breezy two-level roof garden (Sb-€20-25, Db-€35-38, Qb apartment-€50, air-con, Wi-Fi, easy parking, Ponce de León 5, tel. & fax 956-702-010, www.hostalmalaga.com, hostal malagaarcos@hotmail.com, Josefa speaks German if that helps).

Eating in Arcos

Restaurants generally serve lunch from 13:00 to 16:00 and dinner from 20:00 until very late (Spaniards don't start dinner until about 21:00).

Dining
The **Parador** (described earlier, under "Sleeping in Arcos") has an expensive restaurant with a cliff-edge setting. A costly drink on the million-dollar-view terrace can be worth the price (€13-14 starters, €16-19 main dishes, €24 lunch deal, €32 three-course fixed-price meal at lunch or dinner, daily 13:30-16:00 & 20:30-23:00, on main square).

Cheaper Eating in the Old Town

Several decent, rustic bar-restaurants are in the old town, within a block or two of the main square and church. Most serve tapas at the bar and *raciones* at their tables. Prices are fairly consistent (€2 tapas, €5 *media-raciones*, €8 *raciones*).

Bar La Carcel ("The Prison") is run by a hardworking family that brags about its exquisite tapas and small open-faced sandwiches. I agree. The menu is accessible; prices are the same at the bar or at the tables; and the place has a winning energy, giving the traveler a fun peek at this community (Tue-Sun 12:00-16:00 & 20:00-24:00, closed Mon; July-Aug it's open Mon and closed Sun; Calle Deán Espinosa 18, tel. 956-700-410).

Alcaraván tries to be a bit trendier yet *típico,* with a hibachi hard at work out front. A flamenco ambience fills its medieval vault in the castle's former dungeon. This place attracts French and German tourists who give it a cool vibe. Francisco and his wife cook from 13:00 and from 21:00 (closed Mon, Calle Nueva 1).

Bar San Marcos is a tiny, homey bar with five tables, an easy-to-understand menu offering hearty, simple home cooking, and cheap €5 plates and €7 fixed-price meals (kitchen open long hours daily, Marqués de Torresoto 6).

Mesón Don Fernando gives rustic a feminine twist with an inviting bar and both indoor and great outdoor seating on the square just across from the little market (Tue-Thu 13:30-16:00 & 20:15-23:00 for food, closed Wed, longer hours for drinks on the square, on Plaza Boticas).

Mama Ttina gives you an Italian break from Andalucía, with pizza and pastas to go along with the Italian pop music and international Italian/Andaluz/Moroccan/British staff (€7-12 pizzas and pastas, daily 14:00-16:00 & 20:00-24:00 except closed for lunch Tue-Wed, Deán Espinosa 10, tel. 956-703-937).

Tapas in the New Town

Plaza de España, in the lower new town, is lined with tapas bars and restaurants. There's even an Egyptian restaurant if you're in the mood for a change. For a great perch while enjoying the local family scene, consider the busy **Restaurante Bar Terraza** (€12 plates) at the end of Plaza de España.

Arcos Connections

By Bus

Leaving Arcos by bus can be frustrating (especially if you're going to Ronda)—buses generally leave late, the schedule information boards are often inaccurate, and the ticket window usually isn't open (luckily, you can buy your tickets on the bus). But local buses do give you a glimpse at *España profunda* ("deep Spain"), where everyone seems to know each other, no one's in a hurry, and despite any language barriers, people are quite helpful when approached.

Two bus companies (Los Amarillos and Comes) share the Arcos bus station. Call the Jerez offices for departure times, or ask your hotelier for help. If you want to find out about the Arcos–Jerez schedule, make it clear you're coming from Arcos (Los Amarillos tel. 902-210-317; Comes toll tel. 902-199-208, www.tgcomes.es). Also try the privately run www.movelia.es for bus schedules and routes.

From Arcos by Bus to: Jerez (hourly, 30 minutes), **Ronda** (2-3/day, 2 hours, 4 hours with transfer in Villamartín—when transferring, confirm with driver what the final destination is—bus could be headed to Ronda or Sevilla, and dashboard destination signs are often inaccurate), **Cádiz** (4-5/day, 1.25 hours), **Sevilla** (2/day, 2 hours, more departures with transfer in Jerez). Buses run less frequently on weekends. The closest train station to Arcos is Jerez.

Route Tips for Drivers

The trip to **Sevilla** takes just over an hour if you pay €5 for the toll road. To reach **southern Portugal,** follow the freeway to Sevilla, skirt the city by turning west on C-30 in the direction of Huelva, and it's a straight shot from there.

For more driving tips for the region, see the end of this chapter.

Ronda

With nearly 40,000 people, Ronda is one of the largest white hill towns. It's also one of the most spectacular, thanks to its gorge-straddling setting. Approaching the town from the train or bus station, it seems flat...until you reach the New Bridge and realize that it's clinging to the walls of a canyon.

While day-trippers from the touristy Costa del Sol clog Ronda's streets during the day, locals retake the town in the early evening, making nights peaceful. If you liked Toledo at night, you'll love the local feeling of evenings in Ronda. Since it's served by train and bus, Ronda makes a relaxing break for non-drivers traveling between Granada, Sevilla, and Córdoba. Drivers can use

Ronda as a convenient base from which to explore many of the other *pueblos blancos*.

Ronda's main attractions are its gorge-spanning bridges, the oldest bullring in Spain, and an intriguing old town. The cliff-side setting, dramatic today, was practical back in its day. For the Moors, it provided a tough bastion, taken by the Spaniards only in 1485, seven years before Granada fell. Spaniards know Ronda as the cradle of modern bullfighting and the romantic home of 19th-century *bandoleros*. The real joy of Ronda these days lies in exploring its back streets and taking in its beautiful balconies, exuberant flowerpots, and panoramic views. Walking the streets, you feel a strong local pride and a community where everyone seems to know everyone.

Orientation to Ronda

Ronda's breathtaking ravine divides the town's labyrinthine Moorish quarter and its new, noisier, and more sprawling Mercadillo quarter. A massive-yet-graceful 18th-century bridge connects these two neighborhoods. Most things of touristic importance (TI, post office, hotels, bullring) are clustered within a few blocks of the bridge. The paseo (early evening stroll) happens in the new town, on Ronda's major pedestrian and shopping street, Carrera Espinel.

Tourist Information

Ronda has two competing TIs. The **city TI** is across the square from the bullring. It gives out a decent town map (free), sells the Bono Turístico city pass (described below), and organizes walking tours (Mon-Fri 10:00-19:00, until 18:00 late-Oct-late March; Sat-Sun 10:00-14:00 & 15:00-17:00; Paseo Blas Infante, tel. 952-187-119, www.turismoderonda.es). The **regional TI**—on the main square, Plaza de España, opposite the bridge—covers all of Andalucía (Mon-Fri 9:00-19:30, Sat-Sun 9:30-15:00, longer hours in summer, tel. 952-169-311). It hands out several free maps, including a better Ronda map, an excellent Andalusian road map, and maps of Granada, Sevilla, and the Route of the White Towns. Both TIs have listings of the latest museum hours.

If you're an avid sightseer, consider getting the **Bono Turístico** city pass. The €9 version gets you into five sights (including the Arab Baths, Museo Joaquín Peinado, and Mondragón Palace); the €14 version covers eight sights (adding the Lara Museum and others). Both are valid for one week and are sold only at the city TI and a few participating sights (such as the Arab Baths and Museo Joaquín Peinado).

HILL TOWNS

Ronda

To Pileta Cave, Arcos, Sevilla & ④

200 YARDS
200 METERS

Ⓣ TAXI STAND
View
Ⓟ PARKING

① Hotel San Gabriel
② Hotel Ronda
③ Hotel Alavera de los Baños
④ To Hotel Reina Victoria
⑤ Hotel Enfrente Arte Ronda
⑥ Hotel Don Miguel
⑦ Hotel El Tajo & Spar Market
⑧ Hotel San Francisco
⑨ Hotel Royal
⑩ To Hostal Andalucía
⑪ Hostal Doña Carmen
⑫ To Hotel Bandolero
⑬ Confitería Daver
⑭ Tragatapas
⑮ Bar Lechuguita
⑯ Café & Bar Faustino
⑰ La Tradicional
⑱ To Almocábar Gate, Bar-Restaurante Almocábar, Casa Maria & Bodega San Francisco
⑲ Restaurante del Escudero
⑳ Restaurante Pedro Romero
㉑ Rest. Casa Santa Pola
㉒ Casa del Rey Moro Garden
㉓ Palacio del Marqués de Salvatierra
㉔ Lara Museum
㉕ Museo Joaquín Peinado

HILL TOWNS

Arrival in Ronda

By Train: From the station, it's a 15-to-20-minute **walk** to the center: Turn right out of the station on Avenida de Andalucía, and go through the roundabout (you'll see the bus station on your right). Continue straight down the street (now called San José) until it dead-ends. Turn left and walk downhill past a church and the Alameda del Tajo park. Keep going down this street, passing the bullring, to get to the TI and the famous bridge. A **taxi** to the center costs about €6.50.

By Bus: To get to the center from the bus station, leave the station walking to the right of the roundabout, then follow the directions for train travelers (described above). To use the station's baggage lockers, buy a token *(ficha)* at the kiosk by the exit (€4).

By Car: Street parking away from the center is often free. The handiest place to park in the center of Ronda is the underground lot at Plaza del Socorro (one block from bullring, €18/24 hours).

Tours in Ronda

Walking Tours—The TI opposite the bullring offers two-hour guided walks of the city on Saturdays and Sundays, starting at 12:30. Reserve at the TI, then pay the guide (€10 includes Mondragón Palace, €15 adds the bullring, sometimes in two languages). Tours can be canceled if there aren't enough sign-ups.

Local Guide—Energetic and knowledgeable **Antonio Jesús Naranjo** will take you on a two-hour walking tour of the city's sights. He showed Michelle Obama around when she was in town (from €118 Mon-Fri, from €130 Sat-Sun and holidays, reserve early, tel. 952-870-614, mobile 639-073-763, www.guiaoficialderonda.com, guiajesus@yahoo.es). The TI has a list of other local guides.

Sights in Ronda

Ronda's New Town

HILL TOWNS

▲▲▲The Gorge and New Bridge (Puente Nuevo)—The ravine, called El Tajo—360 feet down and 200 feet wide—divides Ronda into the whitewashed old Moorish town (La Ciudad) and the new town (El Mercadillo) that was built after the Christian reconquest in 1485. The New Bridge mightily spans the gorge. A different bridge was built here in 1735, but fell after six years. This one was built from 1751 to 1793. Look down...carefully.

You can see the foundations of the

original bridge (and a super view of the New Bridge) from the Jardines de Cuenca park (daily in summer 9:30-21:30, winter 9:30-18:30): From Plaza de España, walk down Calle Rosario, turn right on Calle Los Remedios, and then take another right at the sign for the park. There are also good views from the parador, which overlooks the gorge and bridge from the new-town side.

From the new-town side of the bridge, on the right, you'll see the entrance to the **New Bridge Interpretive Center,** where you can pay to climb down and enter the structure of the bridge itself. Inside the mostly empty-feeling hall are modest audio-visual displays about the bridge's construction and famous visitors to Ronda. But the views of the bridge and gorge from the outside are far more thrilling than anything you'll find within (€2; Mon-Fri 10:00-19:00, late Oct-late March until 18:00; Sat-Sun 10:00-15:00 year-round; mobile 649-965-338).

▲▲▲**Bullring**—Ronda is the birthplace of modern bullfighting, and this was the first great Spanish bullring. Philip II initi-

ated bullfighting as war training for knights in the 16th century. Back then, there were two kinds of bullfighting: the type with noble knights on horseback, and the coarser, man-versus-beast entertainment for the commoners (with no rules...much like when the WWF wrestlers bring out the folding chairs). Ronda practically worships Francisco Romero, who melded the noble and chaotic kinds of bullfighting with rules to establish modern bullfighting right here in the early 1700s. He introduced the scarlet cape, held unfurled with a stick. His son Juan further developed the ritual (local aficionados would never call it a "sport"—you'll read newspaper coverage of fights not on the sports pages but in the culture section), and his grandson Pedro was one of the first great matadors (killing nearly 6,000 bulls in his career).

Ronda's bullring and museum are Spain's most interesting to tour (even better than Sevilla's). To tour the ring, stables, chapel, and museum, buy a ticket at the back of the bullring, the farthest point from the main drag.

Cost and Hours: €6, daily April-Sept 10:00-20:00, March and Oct 10:00-19:00, Nov-Feb 10:00-18:00, tel. 952-874-132. The excellent €2 audioguide describes everything and is essential to fully enjoy your visit.

Bullfights: Bullfights are scheduled only for the first weekend of September during the *feria* (fair) and occur rarely in the spring. Whereas every other *feria* in Andalucía celebrates a patron saint, the Ronda fair glorifies legendary bullfighter Pedro Romero. For September bullfights, tickets go on sale the preceding July. (As these sell out immediately, Sevilla and Madrid are more practical places for a tourist to see a bullfight.)

Visiting the Bullring: I'd visit in this order. Directly to the right as you enter is the bullfighters' **chapel.** Before going into the ring, every matador would stop here to pray to Mary for safety—and hope to see her again.

• *Just beyond the chapel are the doors to the museum exhibits: horse gear and weapons on the left, and the story of bullfighting on the right, with some English translations.*

The **horse gear and guns exhibit** makes the connection with bullfighting and the equestrian upper class. As through-out Europe, "chivalry" began as a code among the sophisticated, horse-riding gentry. (In Spanish, the word for "gentleman" is the same as the word for "horseman" or "cowboy"—*caballero*.) And, of course, nobles are into hunting and dueling, hence the fancy guns. Don't miss the well-described

dueling section with gun cases for two, as charming as a picnic basket with matching wine glasses.

Backtrack past the chapel to see Spain's best **bullfighting exhibit.** It's a shrine to bullfighting and the historic Romero family. First it traces the long history of bullfighting, going all the way back to the ancient Minoans on Crete. Historically, there were only two arenas built solely for bullfighting: in Ronda and Sevilla. Elsewhere, bullfights were held in town squares—you'll see a painting of Madrid's Plaza Mayor filled with spectators for a bull-fight. (For this reason, to this day, even a purpose-built bullring is generally called *plaza de toros*—"square of bulls.") You'll also see stuffed bull heads, photos, "suits of light" worn by bullfighters, and capes (bulls are actually colorblind, but the traditional red cape was designed to disguise all the blood). One section explains some of the big "dynasties" of fighters. At the end of the hall are historic posters from Ronda's bullfights (all originals except the Picasso). Running along the left wall are various examples of artwork glori-fying bullfighting, including original Goya engravings.

• *From the museum, take advantage of the opportunity to walk in the actual arena.*

Here's your chance to play *toro*, surrounded by 5,000 empty seats. The two-tiered arena was built in 1785—on the 300th anni-versary of the defeat of the Moors in Ronda. Notice the 136 classy Tuscan columns, creating a kind of 18th-century Italian theater.

Lovers of the "art" of bullfighting will explain that the event is much more than the actual killing of the bull. It celebrates the noble heritage and the Andalusian horse culture. When you leave the museum and walk out on the sand, look across to see the ornamental columns and painted doorway where the dignitaries sit (over the gate where the bull enters). On the right is the place for the band (marked *música*), which in the case of a small town like Ronda, is most likely a high school band.

• *Just beyond the arena are more parts of the complex.*

From the arena, walk through the bulls' entry into the bullpen and the **stables.** There are six bulls per fight (and three matadors). The bulls are penned up here beforehand, and ropes and pulleys safely open the right door at the right time. Climb upstairs and find the indoor arena (Picadero) and see Spanish thoroughbred horses training from the **Equestrian School** of the Real Maestranza (Mon-Fri).

Alameda del Tajo—One block away from the bullring, the town's main park is a great place for people-watching, a snooze in the shade, or practicing your Spanish with seniors from the old folks' home.

Ronda's Old Town

▲ **Santa María la Mayor Colleglate Church**—This 15th-century church with a fine Mudejar bell tower shares a park-like square with orange trees and the City Hall. It was built on and around the remains of Moorish Ronda's main mosque (which was itself built on the site of a temple to Julius Caesar). With a pleasantly eclectic interior that features some art with unusually modern flair, and a good audioguide to explain it all, it's worth a visit.

Cost and Hours: €4, includes audioguide, daily April-Sept 10:00-20:00, March and Oct 10:00-19:00, Nov-Feb 10:00-18:00, closed Sun 12:30-14:00 for Mass, Plaza Duquesa de Parcent in the old town.

Visiting the Church: In the room where you purchase your ticket, look for the only surviving mosque prayer niche (that's a mirror; look back at the actual mihrab, which faces not Mecca, but Gibraltar—where you'd travel to get to Mecca). Partially destroyed by an earthquake, the reconstruction of the church resulted in the Moorish/Gothic/Renaissance/Baroque fusion (or confusion) you see today.

HILL TOWNS

The front of the church interior is dominated by a magnificent Baroque high altar with the standard statue of the *Immaculate Conception* in the center. The even more ornate chapel directly to the right is a good example of Churrigueresque architecture, a kind of Spanish Rococo in which decoration obliterates the architecture—notice that you can hardly make out the souped-up columns. This chapel's fancy decor provides a frame for an artistic highlight of the town, the "Virgin of the Ultimate Sorrow." The big fresco of St. Christopher with Baby Jesus on his shoulders (on the left, where you entered) shows the patron saint both of Ronda and of travelers.

Facing the altar is an elaborately carved choir with a wall of modern bronze reliefs depicting scenes from the life of the Virgin Mary. Similar to the Via Crucis (Way of the Cross), this is the Via Lucis (Way of the Light), with 14 stations (such as #13—the Immaculate Conception, and #14—Mary's assumption into heaven) that serve as a worship  aid to devout Catholics. The centerpiece is Mary as the light of the world (with the moon, stars, and sun around her).

Head to the left around the choir, noticing the bright paintings along the wall by French artist Raymonde Pagegie, who gave sacred scenes a fresh twist—like the Last Supper attended by female servants, or the scene of Judgment Day, when the four horsemen of the apocalypse pause to adore the Lamb of God.

The treasury (at the far-right corner, with your back to the high altar) displays vestments that look curiously like matadors' brocaded outfits—appropriate for this bullfight-crazy town.

Mondragón Palace (Palacio de Mondragón)—This beautiful Moorish building was erected in the 14th century, possibly as the residence of Moorish kings, and was carefully restored in the 16th century. At the entrance (free to view without a ticket) is a topographic model of Ronda, which helps you envision the fortified old town apart from the grid-like new one. The rest of the building houses Ronda's Municipal Museum, focusing on prehistory and geology. Wander through its many rooms to find the kid-friendly prehistory section, with exhibits on Neolithic toolmaking and early metallurgy (described in English). If you plan to visit the Pileta Cave (see page 677), find the panels that describe the cave's formation and shape. Even if you have no interest in your ancestors or speleology, the building's architecture is impressive; linger in the two small gardens, especially the shaded one.

Cost and Hours: €3; Mon-Fri 10:00-19:00, late Oct-late

March until 18:00; Sat-Sun 10:00-15:00, on Plaza Mondragón in old town, tel. 952-870-818.

Nearby: Leaving the palace, wander left a few short blocks to the nearby Plaza de María Auxiliadora for more views and a look at the two rare *pinsapos* (resembling extra-large Christmas trees) in the middle of the park; this part of Andalucía is the only region in Europe where these ancient trees still grow. For an intense workout but a picture-perfect view, find the *Puerta de los Molinos* sign and head down, down, down. (Just remember you have to walk back up, up, up.) Not for the faint of heart or in the heat of the afternoon sun, this pathway leads down to the viewpoint where windmills once stood. Photographers go crazy reproducing the most famous postcard view of Ronda—the entirety of the New Bridge. Wait until just before sunset for the best light and cooler temperatures.

Lara Museum—This discombobulated collection of Ronda's history in dusty glass cases displays everything from sewing machines to fans to old movie projectors to matador outfits (with decent English explanations). The highlight for many is the basement, with juvenile displays showing torture devices from the Inquisition and local witchcraft (€4, daily 11:00-20:00, mid-Oct-mid-March until 19:00, Calle Arminan 29, tel. 952-871-263, www.museolara .org).

Museo del Bandolero—This tiny museum, while not as intriguing as it sounds, is an interesting assembly of *bandolero* photos, guns, clothing, knickknacks, and old documents and newspaper clippings. The Jesse Jameses and Billy el Niños of Andalucía called this remote area home. One brand of romantic bandits fought Napoleon's army—often more effectively than the regular Spanish troops. The exhibits profile specific *bandoleros* and display books (from comics to pulp fiction) that helped romanticize these heroes of Spain's "Old West." The museum feels a bit like a tourist trap (with a well-stocked gift shop), but brief but helpful English descriptions make this a fun stop. Next door is a free 22-minute movie about *bandoleros*, but it's only in Spanish.

Cost and Hours: €3.50, daily May-Sept 10:30-20:00, Oct-April until 19:00, across main street below Church of Santa María la Mayor at Calle Armiñán 65, tel. 952-877-785, www.museo bandolero.com.

▲Museo Joaquín Peinado—Housed in an old palace, this fresh museum features an impressively large professional overview of the life's work of Joaquín Peinado (1898-1975), a Ronda native and pal of Picasso. Because Franco killed creativity in Spain for much of the last century, nearly all of Peinado's creative work was done in Paris. His style evolved through the big "isms" of the 20th century, ranging from Expressionist to Cubist, and even to erotic. While

Peinado's works seem a bit derivative, perhaps that's understandable as he was friends with one of the art world's biggest talents. The nine-minute movie that kicks it off is only in Spanish, though there are good English explanations throughout the museum. You'll have an interesting modern-art experience here, without the crowds of Madrid's museums. It's fun to be exposed to a lesser-known but very talented artist in his hometown.

Cost and Hours: €4, Mon-Fri 10:00-18:00, Sat-Sun 10:00-15:00, Plaza del Gigante, tel. 952-871-585.

Walk Through Old Town to Bottom of Gorge—From the New Bridge you can descend down Cuesta de Santo Domingo (crossing the bridge from the new town into the old, take the first left at the former Dominican Church, once the headquarters of the Inquisition in Ronda) into a world of whitewashed houses, tiny grilled balconies, and winding lanes—the old town.

A couple of blocks steeply downhill (on the left), you'll see the **Casa del Rey Moro** (House of the Moorish King). It was never the home of any king; it was given its fictitious name by the grandson of President McKinley, who once lived here. It offers visitors entry to the fine "Moorish-Hispanic" belle époque garden, designed in 1912 by a French landscape architect (the house interior is not open to visitors). Follow signs to "the Mine," an exhausting series of 280 slick, dark, and narrow stairs (like climbing down and then up a 20-story building) leading to the floor of the gorge. The Moors cut this zigzag staircase into the wall of the gorge in the 14th century to access water when under siege, then used Spanish slaves to haul water up to the thirsty town (€4, generally daily 10:00-19:00, June-Aug until 20:00).

Fifty yards downhill from the garden is **Palacio del Marqués de Salvatierra** (closed to public). As part of the "distribution" following the Reconquista here in 1485, the Spanish king gave this grand house to the Salvatierra family (who live here to this day). The facade is rich in colonial symbolism from Spanish America—note the pre-Columbian-looking characters (four Peruvian Indians) flanking the balcony above the door and below the family coat of arms.

Just below the palace, stop to enjoy the view terrace. Look below. A series of square vats are all that remains of the old tanneries. There are two old bridges, with the Arab Baths just to the right, and at the edge of town is a rectangular horse-training area.

Twenty steps farther down, you'll pass through the Philip V

HILL TOWNS

gate, for centuries the main gate to the fortified city of Ronda. Continuing downhill, you come to the **Old Bridge** (Puente Viejo),

rebuilt in 1616 upon the ruins of an Arabic bridge. Enjoy the views from the bridge (but don't cross it yet), then continue down the old stairs. From the base of the staircase, look back up to glimpse some of the surviving highly fortified Moorish city walls. You've now reached

the oldest bridge in Ronda, the Arab Bridge (also called the San Miguel Bridge). Sometimes given the misnomer of Puente Romano (Roman Bridge), it was more likely built long after the Romans left. For centuries, this was the main gate to the fortified city. In Moorish times, you'd purify both your body and your soul here before entering the city, so just outside the gate was a little mosque (now the ruined chapel) and the Arab Baths.

The **Arab Baths**, worth ▲, are evocative ruins that warrant a quick look. They were located half underground to maintain the

temperature and served by a horse-powered water tower. You can still see the top of the shaft (30 yards beyond the bath rooftops, near a Cyprus tree, connected to the baths by an aqueduct). Water was hoisted from the river below to the aqueduct by ceramic containers that were attached to a belt powered by a horse walking in circles. Inside, two of the original eight columns scavenged from the Roman ruins still support brick vaulting. A delightful 10-

minute video brings the entire complex to life—Spanish and English versions run alternately (€3, free on Mon; open Mon-Fri 10:00-19:00, Nov-April until 18:00; Sat-Sun 10:00-15:00 year-round; sometimes open later in summer, call ahead before making the trip, mobile 656-950-937).

From here, hike back to the new town along the other side of the gorge: Return to the bridge just uphill. Cross it and take the stairs immediately on the left, which lead scenically along the gorge up to the New Bridge.

Near Ronda: Pileta Cave

The Pileta Cave (Cueva de la Pileta) offers Spain's most intimate look at Neolithic and Paleolithic paintings that are up to 25,000 years old. Set in a dramatic, rocky limestone ridge at the eastern edge of Sierra de Grazalema Natural Park, Pileta Cave is 14 miles from Ronda, past the town of Benaoján, at the end of an access road. It's particularly handy if you're driving between Ronda and Grazalema.

Farmer José Bullón and his family live down the hill from the cave, and because they strictly limit the number of visitors, Pileta's rare paintings are among the best-preserved in the world. Señor Bullón and his son lead up to 25 people at a time through the cave, which was discovered by Bullón's grandfather in 1905. Call the night before to see if there's a tour and space available at the time you want. Note that if you simply show up for the 13:00 tour and it is full, it'll be another three hours before the next one starts. Bring a sweater and good shoes. You need a good sense of balance to take the tour. The 10-minute hike, from the parking lot up a trail with stone steps to the cave entrance, is moderately steep. Inside the cave, there are no handrails, and it can be difficult to keep your footing on the slippery, uneven floor while being led single-file, with only a lantern light illuminating the way.

Señor Bullón is a master at hurdling the language barrier. As you walk the cool half-mile, he'll spend an hour pointing out lots of black, ochre, and red drawings, which are five times as old as the Egyptian pyramids. Mostly it's just lines or patterns, but there are also horses, goats, cattle, and a rare giant fish, made from a mixture of clay and fat by finger-painting prehistoric *hombres*. The 200-foot main cavern is impressive, as are some weirdly recognizable natural formations such as the Michelin man and a Christmas tree.

Cost and Hours: €8, 60-minute tours generally on the hour but depends on the number of people, daily 10:00-13:00 & 16:00-18:00, Nov-mid-April until 17:00, closing times indicate last tour, €10 guidebook, no photos, tel. 952-167-343, www.cuevadelapileta .org.

Getting There: It's possible to get here without wheels, but I wouldn't bother (you'd have to take the Ronda–Benaoján bus—2/day, departs at 8:30 and 13:00, 30 minutes—and then it's a 2-hour, 3-mile uphill hike). You can get from Ronda to the cave by taxi—it's about a half-hour drive on twisty roads—and have the driver wait (€60 round-trip). If you're driving, it's easy: Leave Ronda through the new part of town, and take A-374. After a few miles, passing Cueva del Gato, exit left toward Benaoján on MA-555. Go through Benaoján and follow the numerous signs to the cave. Leave nothing of value in your car.

Eating near the Cave: Nearby Montejaque has several good restaurants clustered around the central square.

Sleeping near the Cave: A good base for visiting Ronda and the Pileta Cave (as well as Grazalema) is **$$ Cortijo las Piletas.** Nestled at the edge of Sierra de Grazalema Natural Park (just a 15-minute drive from Ronda, with easy access from the main highway), this spacious family-run country estate has nine rooms and plenty of opportunities for swimming, hiking, bird-watching, and exploring the surrounding area. They can also arrange for biking and horseback riding (Sb-€68-74, Db-€84-90, extra bed-€15-18, includes breakfast but not tax, dinner offered some days—book in advance, mobile 605-080-295, www.cortijolaspiletas.com, info @cortijolaspiletas.com, Pablo and Elisenda). Another countryside option is **$$ Finca La Guzmana,** run by expat Brit Peter. Seven beautifully appointed pastel rooms surround an open patio at this renovated estate house. Bird-watching, swimming, and trekking are possible (Db-€70-80, includes breakfast, mobile 600-006-305, www.laguzmana.com, info@laguzmana.com).

Sleeping in Ronda

(€1 = about $1.40, country code: 34)
Ronda has plenty of reasonably priced, decent-value accommodations. It's crowded only during Holy Week (the week leading up to Easter) and the first week of September (for bullfighting season). Most of my recommendations are in the new town, a short stroll from the New Bridge and about a 10-minute walk from the train station. In the cheaper places, ask for a room with a *ventana* (window) to avoid the few interior rooms. Breakfast is usually not included.

In the Old Town

Clearly the best options in town, these hotels are worth reserving early. The first two are right in the heart of the Old Town, while the Alavera de los Baños is a steep 15-to-20-minute hike below, but still easily walkable to all the sights (if you're in good shape) and in a bucolic setting.

$$ Hotel San Gabriel has 22 pleasant rooms, a kind staff, public rooms filled with art and poetry books, a cozy wine cellar, and a fine garden terrace. It's a large 1736 townhouse, once the family's home, that's been converted to a characteristic hotel, marinated in history. If you're a cinephile, kick back in the charming TV room—with seats from Ronda's old theater and a collection of DVD classics—then head to the breakfast room to check out photos of big movie stars (and, ahem, bespectacled travel writers) who have stayed here (Sb-€66, Db-€85, bigger superior Db-€95, Db junior suite-€109, lavish honeymoon suite-€150, breakfast-€6, air-con, incognito elevator, free Internet access and Wi-Fi, double-park in front and they'll direct you to a €9 parking spot, follow signs on the main street of old town to Calle Marqués de Moctezuma 19, tel. 952-190-392, fax 952-190-117, www.hotelsangabriel.com, info @hotelsangabriel.com, family-run by José Manuel and Ana).

$$ Hotel Ronda provides an interesting mix of minimalist and traditional Spanish decor, with five rooms located in the old town. Although there are no views, the refurbished mansion is quiet and homey (Sb-€52, Db-€67, additional bed-€21, no breakfast, air-con, free Internet access and Wi-Fi, Ruedo Doña Elvira 12, tel. 952-872-232, www.hotelronda.net, laraln@telefonica.net, no English spoken).

$$ Alavera de los Baños, a delightful oasis located next to ancient Moorish baths at the bottom of the hill, has nine small rooms and big inviting public places, with appropriately Moorish decor. This hotel offers a swimming pool, a peaceful Arabic garden, and a restaurant open every day for a €15 tapas lunch and sporadically at dinner for guests who've made reservations. The artistic ambience urges, "Relax!" You're literally in the countryside, with sheep and horses outside near the garden (Sb-€60-70, Db-€80-95, Db with terrace-€90-105, includes breakfast, free Wi-Fi in some rooms, free and easy parking, closed Jan, steeply below the heart of town at Calle San Miguel, tel. & fax 952-879-143, www .alaveradelosbanos.com, alavera@telefonica.net, well-run by personable Christian and Inma).

In the New Town

More convenient than charming (except the Hotel Enfrente Arte Ronda—in a class all its own), these hotels put you in the thriving new town.

$$$ Hotel Reina Victoria, with 89 rooms, hangs royally over the gorge at the edge of town and has a marvelous view—Hemingway loved it. While it feels a bit past its prime, and the service is spotty, I'd choose this—with all its romantic Old World elegance—over the more central parador (Sb-€97-117, Db-€112-156, breakfast-€9, air-con, elevator, free Wi-Fi in lobby, pool, free parking, 10-minute walk from city center; easy to miss—look for intersection of Avenida Victoria and Calle Jerez, Jerez 25; tel. 952-871-240, fax 952-871-075, www.hotelreinavictoria.es, info@hotel reinavictoria.es).

$$ Hotel Enfrente Arte Ronda, on the edge of things a steep 10-to-15-minute walk below the heart of the new town, is relaxed, funky, and friendly. The 12 rooms are spacious and exotically decorated, but dimly lit. It features a sprawling maze of exuberantly decorated public spaces, including a peaceful bamboo garden, game and reading room, small swimming pool, sauna, and terraces with sweeping countryside views. Guests can enjoy themed dinners on certain nights (€15, confirm with reception in

HILL TOWNS

advance), and can help themselves to free drinks from the self-service bar. This one-of-a-kind place is in all the guidebooks, so reserve early (Db-€80-105, extra bed-€28, prices do not include tax, includes buffet breakfast, air-con, elevator, free Internet access and Wi-Fi in lobby, Real 40, tel. 952-879-088, fax 952-877-217, www.enfrentearte.com, reservations@enfrentearte.com).

$$ Hotel Don Miguel, facing the gorge just left of the bridge, has disinterested staff and all the charm of a tour-group hotel, but it couldn't be more central. Of its 30 sparse but comfortable rooms, 20 have balconies and/or gorgeous views at no extra cost. Street rooms come with a little noise (Sb-€55-65, Db-€85-100, Tb-€110-135, tax not included, includes buffet breakfast, air-con, elevator, free Wi-Fi in lobby, parking garage a block away-€9/day, Plaza de España 4, tel. 952-877-722, fax 952-878-377, www.dmiguel.com, reservas@dmiguel.com).

$$ Hotel El Tajo has 33 decent, quiet rooms—once you get past the tacky faux-stone Moorish decoration in the foyer (Sb-€43, Db-€65, breakfast-€6, air-con, elevator, free Wi-Fi in some rooms, parking-€10, Calle Cruz Verde 7, a half-block off the pedestrian street, tel. 952-874-040, fax 952-875-099, www.hoteleltajo.com, reservas@hoteleltajo.com).

$$ Hotel San Francisco offers 27 small, nicely decorated rooms a block off the main pedestrian street in the town center (Sb-€35-40, Db-€50-65, Tb-€70-80, breakfast-€4, air-con, elevator, parking-€8.50, María Cabrera 20, tel. 952-873-299, fax 952-874-688, hotelronda@terra.es).

$ Hotel Royal has a dreary reception and 29 clean, spacious, simple rooms—many on the main street that runs between the bullring and bridge. Thick glass keeps out most of the noise, while the tree-lined Alameda del Tajo park across the street is a treat. Some rooms and hallways are dimly lit (Sb-€38, Db-€45-50, Tb-€55-60, breakfast-€4, air-con, free Wi-Fi, parking-€13, Calle Virgen de la Paz 42, 3 blocks off Plaza de España, tel. 952-871-141, fax 952-878-132, www.ronda.net/usuar/hotelroyal, hroyal@ronda.net, some English spoken).

$ Hostal Andalucía has 11 clean, comfortable, and recently renovated rooms immediately across the street from the train station (Sb-€27, Db-€42, Tb-€53, breakfast-€2, air-con, free Wi-Fi, easy street parking, Martínez Astein 19, tel. 952-875-450, www.hostalandalucia.net, info@hostalandalucia.net).

$ Hostal Doña Carmen, a basic cheapie, rents 32 bare-bones rooms in two sections. The rooms sharing a shower down the hall, with no air-con or TV, are especially reasonable (S-€17, Sb-€25, D-€28, Db-€45, T-€40, Tb-€55, no breakfast, air-con and TV only in rooms with bath, free Wi-Fi in lobby, Calle Naranja 28, tel. 952-871-994).

Near Ronda

$$ Hotel Bandolero, about 12 miles south of Ronda in the village of Júzcar, is for nature-lovers. Settle into the rustic rooms, go hiking and bird-watching, or take a dip in the pool (Sb-€40-45, standard Db-€58-96, superior Db-€68-106, Db suite-€79-117, higher prices are for half-board, restaurant, Avenida Havaral 43, tel. 952-183-660, www.hotelbandolero.com, reservas@hotelbandolero.com, David).

Eating in Ronda

Plaza del Socorro, a block in front of the bullring, is an energetic scene, bustling with tourists and local families enjoying the square and its restaurants. The pedestrian-only **Calle Nueva** is lined with hardworking eateries. To enjoy a drink or a light meal with the best view in town, consider the terraces of Hotel Don Miguel just under the bridge. For coffee and pastries, locals like the elegant little **Confiteria Daver** (café open daily 8:00-20:30, take-away until 21:00, Calle Los Remedios 6). Picnic shoppers find the **Spar** supermarket convenient, opposite Hotel El Tajo (Mon-Sat 9:00-21:00, closed Sun, Calle Cruz Verde 18). The Alameda del Tajo park (with WC) near the bullring is a good picnic spot.

Tapas in the City Center

Ronda has a fine tapas scene. You won't get a free tapa with your drink as in some other Spanish towns, but these bars have accessible tapas lists, and they serve bigger plates. Each of the following places could make a fine solo destination for a meal, but they're close enough that you can easily try more than one.

Tragatapas, the accessible little brother of the acclaimed gourmet Restaurante Tragabuches, serves super-creative and always-tasty tapas in a stainless-steel minimalist bar. There's just a handful of tall tiny tables and stools, and an enticing blackboard of the day's specials. If you want to sample Andalusian gourmet (e.g., a variety of €1.50-3 tapas such as asparagus on a stick sprinkled with manchego cheese grated coconut-style) without going broke, this is the place to do it (also €6-12 larger plates, daily 12:00-17:00 & 20:00-24:00, closed Sun evenings off-season, Calle Nueva 4, tel. 952-877-209).

Bar Lechuguita, a hit with older locals early and younger ones later, serves a long and tasty list of tapas for a good price. Rip off a tapas inventory sheet and mark which ones you want (most cost €0.75; €5 plates also available). Be adventurous and don't miss the bar's namesake, #15, *Lechuguita* (a wedge of lettuce with vinegar, garlic, and a secret ingredient). The order-form routine makes it easy to communicate and get exactly what you like, plus you know the exact price (Mon-Sat 13:00-15:15 & 20:15-23:30, closed Sun, no chairs or tables, just a bar and tiny stand-up ledges, Calle los Remedios 35).

Café & Bar Faustino is a place Brueghel would paint—a festival of eating with a fun and accessible menu that works both at the bar and at tables. The atmosphere makes you want to stay, and the selection makes you wish your appetite was even bigger (lots of €1 tapas, €3 sandwiches, €5-8 *raciones,* Tue-Sun 12:00-24:00, closed Mon, just off Plaza Carmen Abela at Santa Cecilia 4, tel. 952-190-307).

La Tradicional, run by Elias (from Casa María—described below), serves up €1.20 tapas and €4-11 *raciones* with an emphasis on meats (Thu-Tue 12:00-17:00 & 18:30-24:00, closed Wed, Las Tiendas 2, tel. 952-875-683).

Outside the Almocábar Gate

To entirely leave the quaint old town and bustling city center with all of its tourists and grand gorge views, hike 10 minutes out to the far end of the old town, past the Church of the Holy Ghost, to a big workaday square that goes about life as if the world didn't exist outside Andalucía. Among the numerous eateries here are two of special note: The tiny, quirky Casa María is the ultimate in an intimate home-cooking experience, and Bodega San Francisco is a cheap tapas bar and a more normal little restaurant.

Bar-Restaurante Almocábar is a favorite eatery for many Ronda locals. Its restaurant—a cozy eight-table room with Moorish tiles and a window to the kitchen—serves up tasty, creative, well-presented meals from a menu that's well-described in English (plus a handwritten list of the day's specials). Many opt for the good €8-15 salads—rare in Spain. At the busy bar up front, you can order anything from the dining room menu, or choose from the list of €1.50-2 tapas (€5-15 starters, €12-20 main dishes, closed Tue, Calle Ruedo Alameda 5, tel. 952-875-977).

Casa María is like eating in the home of Elias and Isabel and their daughter María. There's little English spoken and no menu, so this is the adventure—you trust Elias to cook up whatever's seasonal for a four-course rustic fiesta for €28 to €35, including drinks (Elias loves red meat). Show Elias this book and you'll get more than the standard glass of house wine, although wine-lovers will want to pay a bit more for a better bottle (Thu-Tue 12:30-16:30 & 19:30-24:00, closed Wed, facing Plaza Ruedo Alameda at #27, tel. 952-876-212).

Bodega San Francisco is a rustic bar with tables upstairs and a homey restaurant across the street. The bar is your budget option with an accessible list of €4-9 *raciones* and €1.50 tapas; the restaurant, while also rustic, comes with serious plates and big splittable portions (from the same menu). This place is understandably a neighborhood favorite (closed Thu, Ruedo de Alameda 32, tel. 952-878-162).

Dining in the City Center

Ronda is littered with upscale-seeming restaurants that toe the delicate line between a good dinner spot and a tourist trap. While (admittedly) none of the following could be called "untouristy," they each offer decent food with either a striking setting, a venerable ambience, or both. For a more authentic dining experience, do a tapas crawl through town, or head for the far more characteristic eateries just outside the Almocábar Gate (both described above).

Restaurante del Escudero serves lovingly presented Spanish food with a posh modern touch in a crystal- and cream-colored dining room or on a terrace overlooking the gorge (€12-18.50 fixed-price meals, €29 gourmet tasting meals, €7-13 starters, €16-20 main dishes, daily 12:00-22:30 except closed Sun eve in summer, behind bullring at Paseo Blas Infante 1, tel. 952-871-367).

Restaurante Pedro Romero, though touristy and overpriced, is a venerable institution in Ronda. Assuming a shrine to bullfighting draped in *el toro* memorabilia doesn't ruin your appetite, it gets good reviews. Rub elbows with the local bullfighters or dine with the likes (well, photographic likenesses) of Orson Welles, Ernest Hemingway, and Francisco Franco (€15-25 fixed-price meals, €7-12 starters, €16-20 main dishes, daily 12:00-16:00 & 19:30-23:00, air-con, across the street from bullring at Calle Virgen de la Paz 18, tel. 952-871-110).

Restaurante Casa Santa Pola offers gourmet versions of traditional food with friendly, professional service, with several small dining rooms and a delightful terrace perched on the side of the gorge—worth reserving ahead (€15-18 fixed-price meals, €7-12 starters, €14-24 main dishes; good oxtail stew, roasted lamb, and honey-tempura eggplant; daily 12:30-16:30 & 19:00-22:30; after crossing New Bridge from the bullring, take the first left downhill and you'll see the sign, Calle Santo Domingo 3; tel. 952-879-208).

Ronda Connections

Note that some destinations are linked with Ronda by both bus and train. Direct bus service to other hill towns can be sparse (as few as one per day), and train service usually involves a transfer in Bobadilla. It's worth spending a few minutes in the bus or train station on arrival to plan your departure. Your options improve from major transportation hubs such as Málaga.

From Ronda by Bus to: Algeciras (6/day, 2 hours, Comes), **La Línea/Gibraltar** (no direct bus, transfer in Algeciras;

Algeciras to Gibraltar—2/hour, 45 minutes, can buy ticket on bus), **Arcos** (2-3/day, 2 hours, Comes), **Benaoján** (2/day, 30 minutes, Los Amarillos), **Jerez** (4/day, 2.5-3 hours, Comes), **Grazalema** (2/day, 45 minutes, Los Amarillos), **Zahara** (1/day, Mon-Fri only, 1 hour, Comes), **Sevilla** (8/day, 2-2.5 hours, fewer on weekends, Los Amarillos; also see trains below), **Málaga** (*directo* 10/day, less on weekends, 1.75 hours, Los Amarillos; *ruta* 2/day, 4 hours, Portillo; access other Costa del Sol points from Málaga), **Marbella** (5/day, 1.25 hours, Portillo), **Fuengirola** (5/day, 1.75 hours, Portillo), **Nerja** (4 hours, transfer in Málaga; can take train or bus from Ronda to Málaga). If traveling to **Córdoba,** it's easiest to take the train since there are no direct buses (see below). There's no efficient way to call "the bus company" because four share the same station: Los Amarillos (tel. 952-187-061, www.losamarillos.es), Portillo (tel. 902-450-550, www.ctsa-portillo.es), Comes (tel. 902-199-208, www.tgcomes.cs), and GPP (tel. 952-875-435). It's best to just drop by and compare schedules (on Plaza Concepción García Redondo, several blocks from train station).

By Train to: Algeciras (3-4/day, 1.5-2 hours), **Bobadilla** (4/day, 1 hour), **Málaga** (2/day, 2-3 hours—morning train direct, evening train with transfer in Bobadilla), **Sevilla** (2/day, 4 hours, transfer in Bobadilla), **Granada** (3/day, 2.5 hours), **Córdoba** (2/day direct, 1.75 hours; more with transfer in Bobadilla, 3.5 hours), **Madrid** (2/day, 4 hours). Transfers are a snap and time-coordinated in Bobadilla; with four trains arriving and departing simultaneously, double-check that you're jumping on the right one. Train info: toll tel. 902-320-320, www.renfe.com.

More Hill Towns: Zahara and Grazalema

There are plenty of undiscovered and interesting hill towns to explore. About half of the towns I visited were memorable. Unfortunately, public transportation is frustrating, so I'd do these towns only by car. Useful information on the area is rare. Fortunately, a good map, the tourist brochure (pick it up in Sevilla or Ronda), and a spirit of adventure work fine.

Along with Arcos, Zahara and Grazalema are my favorite white villages.

Zahara

This tiny town in a tingly setting under a Moorish castle (worth the climb) has a spectacular view. While the big church facing the town square is considered one of the richest in the area, the smaller church has the most-loved statue. The Virgin of Dolores is Zahara's answer to Sevilla's Virgin of Macarena (and is similarly paraded through town during Holy Week). While Grazalema is a better overnight stop, Zahara is a delight for those who want to hear only the sounds of the wind, birds, and elderly footsteps on ancient cobbles.

Orientation to Zahara

Tourist Information

The TI is located in the main plaza (Mon-Fri 10:00-13:30, Sat-Sun 10:00-12:30, gift shop, Plaza del Rey 3, tel. 956-123-114). It has a single computer with Internet access (€1.50, one-hour limit). Upstairs from the TI are Spanish-only displays about the flora and fauna of nearby Sierra de Grazalema Natural Park.

Drivers can park for free in the main plaza, or continue up the hill to the parking lot at the base of the castle, just past the cliffside Hotel Arco de la Villa, the town's only real hotel (16 small modern rooms, Db-€60, breakfast-€3, tel. 956-123-230, www.tugasa.com).

Sights in Zahara

▲**Zahara Castle**—During Moorish times, Zahara lay within the fortified castle walls above today's town. It was considered the gateway to Granada and a strategic stronghold for the Moors by the Christian forces of the Reconquista. Locals tell of the Spanish conquest of the Moors' castle (in 1482) as if it happened yesterday: After the Spanish failed several times to seize the castle, a clever Spanish soldier noticed that the Moorish sentinel would check if any attackers were hiding behind a particular section of the wall by tossing

HILL TOWNS

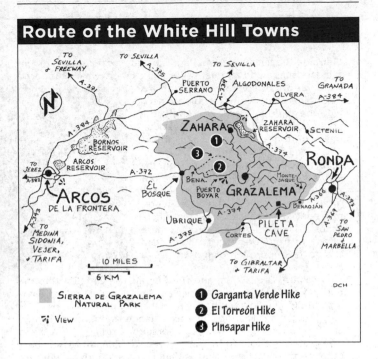

Route of the White Hill Towns

❶ Garganta Verde Hike
❷ El Torreón Hike
❸ Pinsapar Hike

SIERRA DE GRAZALEMA NATURAL PARK

View

a rock and setting the pigeons in flight. If they flew, the sentinel figured there was no danger. One night a Spaniard hid there with a bag of pigeons and let them fly when the sentinel tossed his rock. Upon seeing the birds, the guard assumed he was clear to enjoy a snooze. The clever Spaniard then scaled the wall and opened the door to let in his troops, who conquered the castle. Ten years later Granada fell, the Muslims were back in Africa, and the Reconquista was complete.

It's a fun climb up to the remains of the castle. Start at the paved path across from the town's upper parking lot. It's a moderately easy 15-minute hike past some Roman ruins and along a cactus-rimmed ridge to the top, where you can enter the tower. Use your penlight or feel along the stairway to reach the roof, and enjoy spectacular views from this almost impossibly high perch far above the town. As you pretend you're defending the tower, realize that what you see is quite different from what the Moors saw: The huge lake dominating the valley is a reservoir—before 1991, the valley had only a tiny stream.

Cost and Hours: Free, tower always open.

HILL TOWNS

Sierra de Grazalema Natural Park

Sierra de Grazalema Natural Park is unique for its rugged mountain landscape and its relatively rainy climate, which support a wide variety of animals and plant life.

One-third of Spain's flowers bloom here, wild ibex (mountain goats) climb the steep slopes, and Europe's largest colony of griffon vultures soars high above. The park's plant poster child is the *pinsapo,* a type of fir tree left over from the last Ice Age (the park is one of the few places in Europe where these trees still grow). About a fifth of the 200-square-mile park is a special reserve area, where access is limited, largely to protect these rare trees from forest fires. Hikers need to get (free) permits for most trails in the reserve.

Zahara, Grazalema, and the Pileta Cave all fall within the park boundaries. Drivers will get an eyeful of scenery just passing through the park on their way to these sights.

If you want to more fully experience the park—by hiking, caving, canoeing, kayaking, or horseback riding—the easiest way is to take a tour from Zahara Catur (in Zahara, www.zahara catur.com) or Horizon (in Grazalema, www.horizonaventura .com). They also handle the permit procedure for you.

If you want to hike in the park on your own, you'll need a park map, a permit for most hikes within the reserve area (see permit procedure on next page), and a car to get to the trailhead. From July through September, you may have to go with a guided group anyway, if you want to hike in the reserve (about €13/per-

Grazalema

A beautiful postcard-pretty hill town, Grazalema offers a royal balcony for a memorable picnic, a square where you can watch old-timers playing cards, and plenty of quiet whitewashed streets and shops to explore. Situated within Sierra de Grazalema Natural Park, Grazalema is graced with lots of scenery and greenery. Driving here from Ronda on A-372, you pass through a beautiful park-like grove of cork trees. While the park is known as the rainiest place in Spain, the clouds seem to wring themselves

son for a half-day hike, offered by Zahara Catur and Horizon).

Popular hikes in the reserve (all requiring permits) include:

Garganta Verde: Explore a canyon with a huge open cave near vulture breeding grounds (1.5 miles each way, initially gentle hike then very steep descent, allow 4-5 hours).

El Torreón: Climb the park's highest mountain, at 5,427 feet (1.75 miles each way, steep incline to summit, allow 4-5 hours).

Pinsapar: Hike on mountain slopes forested with *pinsapo* trees (8.5 miles each way, steep climb for first third of trail then downhill, allow 6 hours).

Information: The TIs in Grazalema and Zahara sell a Spanish-only park guide with descriptions and trail maps (€15).

Getting a Hiking Permit: A permit is free but required; a ranger will fine you if you don't have one. To get a permit, email, call, or visit the park office in the town of El Bosque, a gateway to the park. You can request a permit for a specific hike up to 30 days in advance. Pick up the permit in El Bosque, or have them fax it to the TI in Grazalema or Zahara (El Bosque park office hours generally Mon-Sat 10:00-14:00 & 17:00-19:00, Sun 9:00-14:00, Avenida de la Diputación, tel. 956-727-029, cv_elbosque @egmasa.es). Include the date, the number of people in your group, the hike you want to do, and your passport number (allow plenty of time for this process). If you're staying at the recommended La Mejorana Guest House in Grazalema, your host will help you with the paperwork.

Hikes from Grazalema (No Permit Required): If you'd rather not hassle with getting a permit, or if you don't have a car to reach the trailheads, try one of several hikes that start from the town of Grazalema. You'll find descriptions in pamphlets available at the Grazalema TI or Horizon (€1).

out before they reach the town—I've only ever had blue skies. If you want to sleep in a small Andalusian hill town, this is a good choice.

The TI is located at the car park at the cliffside viewpoint, Plaza de los Asomaderos (tel. 956-132-052, www.centrode informaciongrazalema.info). Enjoy the view, then wander into the town. A tiny lane leads a block from the center rear of the plaza to Plaza de Andalucía (filled by the tables of a commotion of tapas bars). Shops sell the town's beautiful and famous handmade wool blankets and good-quality leather items from nearby Ubrique. A block farther uphill takes you to the main square with the church, Plaza de España. A coffee on the square here is a joy. Small lanes stretch from here into the rest of the town.

Popular with Spaniards, the town makes a good home base for exploring Sierra de Grazalema Natural Park—famous for its

HILL TOWNS

Grazalema

1. La Mejorana Guest House
2. Hotel Peñón Grande
3. Casa de Las Piedras
4. Plaza de Andalucía Eateries
5. El Torreón Restaurante
6. El Pinsapar Restaurante
7. Meson el Simancon Rest.
8. Horizon Adventure Tours

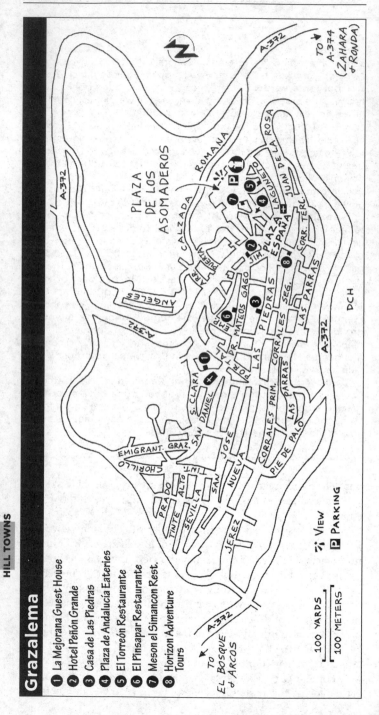

👁 VIEW
🅿 PARKING

100 YARDS
100 METERS

spectacularly rugged limestone landscape of cliffs, caves, and gorges (see sidebar). For outdoor gear and adventures, including hiking, caving, and canoeing, contact **Horizon** (summer Tue-Sat 9:00-14:00 & 17:00-20:00, rest of year Tue-Sat 9:00-14:00 & 16:00-19:00, closed Sun-Mon year-round, off Plaza de España at Corrales Terceros 29, tel. & fax 956-132-363, mobile 655-934-565, www.horizonaventura.com, grazalema@horizonaventura.com).

Sleeping in Grazalema

$$ La Mejorana Guest House is the best bet in town—if you can manage to get one of its six rooms. You won't want to leave this beautifully perched garden villa, with its royal public rooms overlooking the valley from the upper part of town. Helpful Ana and Andres will help you get a hiking permit in the park (Db-€58, includes breakfast, Wi-Fi, pool, located at top of town on tiny lane below Guardia Civil headquarters at Santa Clara 6, tel. 956-132-327, mobile 649-613-272, www.lamejorana.net, info@lamejorana .net).

$$ Hotel Peñón Grande, named for a nearby mountain, is just off the main square and rents 16 comfortable business-class rooms (Sb-€38, Db-€55, extra bed-€14, air con, Plaza Pequeña 7, tel. 956-132-434, fax 956-132-435, www.hotelgrazalema.es, hotel @hotelgrazalema.es).

$ Casa de Las Piedras, just a block from the main square, has 16 comfortable rooms with private baths (Sb-€35, Db-€48); 2 other rooms that share 1 bathroom and have access to a kitchen and washing machine (D-€40); and 14 super-cheap basic rooms that share 5 bathrooms (D-€28, no access to kitchen or washing machine). The beds feature the town's locally made wool blankets (10 percent discount with this book and two-night minimum stay, buffet breakfast-€6, Calle Las Piedras 32, tel. & fax 956-132-014, www.casadelaspiedras.org, reservas@casadelaspiedras.net, Katy and Rafi).

Eating in Grazalema

Grazalema offers many restaurants and bars. Tiny Plaza de Andalucía has several good bars for tapas with umbrella-flecked tables spilling across the square, including **Zulema** (big salads, tel. 956-132-402) and **La Posadilla** (tel. 956-132-051).

El Torreón specializes in local lamb and game dishes, and also has many vegetarian options (closed Wed, Calle Agua 44, tel. 956-132-313).

El Pinsapar, up the hill from the main plaza, is appreciated for its good prices and local specialties, including fresh trout

HILL TOWNS

(closed Wed, air-con, Dr. Mateos Gago 22, tel. 956-132-202).

Meson el Simancon serves well-presented cuisine typical of the region in a romantic setting. While a bit more expensive, it's considered the best restaurant in town (closed Tue, facing Plaza de los Asomaderos and the car park, tel. 956-132-421).

Grazalema Connections

From Grazalema by Bus to: Ronda (2/day, 45 minutes), **El Bosque** (2/day, 45 minutes). Bus service is provided by Los Amarillos (www.losamarillos.es).

Jerez

With nearly 200,000 people, Jerez (*h*ay-RETH, with a guttural *h*) is your typical big-city mix of industry and dusty concrete suburbs, but it has a lively old center and two claims to touristic fame: horses and sherry. Jerez is ideal for a noontime visit on a weekday. See the famous horses, sip some sherry, wander through the old quarter, and swagger out.

Orientation to Jerez

There is no easy way to feel oriented in Jerez due to the complicated, medieval street plan, so ask for directions liberally.

Tourist Information
The helpful TI, on Plaza Alameda Cristina, gives out free maps and info on the sights (June-Sept Mon-Fri 9:00-15:00 & 17:00-19:00, Sat-Sun 9:30-14:30; Oct-May Mon-Fri 9:00-15:00 & 16:30-18:30, Sat-Sun 9:30-14:30; tel. 956-338-874, www.turismojerez.com).

Arrival in Jerez
By Bus or Train: Both the bus and train stations are by the enormous headless statue at Glorieta del Minotauro. Unfortunately, you can't store luggage at either one. However, you can stow bags for free in the Royal Andalusian School's *guardaropa* (coat room), if you attend their Horse Symphony show, described later under "Sights in Jerez."

The center of town and the TI are a 20-minute walk from both stations. When exiting either station, keep the large parking lot on your left. You'll soon be greeted by the gigantic Glorieta del Minotauro statue at a traffic circle. Take the crosswalk straight

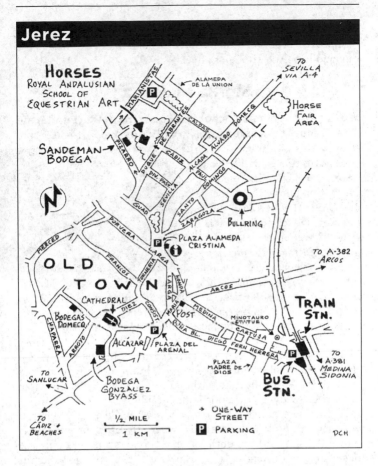

Jerez

HORSES
ROYAL ANDALUSIAN
SCHOOL OF
EQUESTRIAN ART

SANDEMAN
BODEGA

MARIANISTAS

ALAMEDA
DE LA UNION

TO
SEVILLA
VIA A-4

HORSE
FAIR
AREA

PIZARRO

DUQUE DE ABRANTES

CABEZAS

CABIZ

ALVARO DOMECQ

ALCADA

PN PASTA

SANTO DOMINGO

PAUL

SEVILLA

GUAD

PORVERA

N

ZARAGOZA

BULLRING

MERCED

LARGA

PLAZA ALAMEDA
CRISTINA

i

FRANCOS

TORNERIA

TO A-382
ARCOS

O L D
T O W N

LARGA

ARGA

TONIA V

ARCOS

CATHEDRAL

BODEGAS
DOMECQ

CHAVARRA

ARROYO

DIEZ

CONSIST.

MARIA

MEDINA

MINOTAURO
STATUE

TRAIN
STN.

PLAZA DEL
ARENAL

ALCÁZAR

TNA BL.

CARTUJA

DIEGO FERN HERRERA

TO
SANLUCAR

BODEGA
GONZALEZ
BYASS

PLAZA
MADRE DE
DIOS

TO
A-381
MEDINA
SIDONIA

BUS
STN.

TO
CÁDIZ +
BEACHES

½ MILE

1 KM

➜ ONE-WAY
STREET

P PARKING

DCH

over to Calle Medina and follow it faithfully. At the confusing five-way intersection, angle right on Honda, continue past a small roundabout decorated with empty sherry barrels, and go straight until you reach Plaza Alameda Cristina—the TI is tucked away on your right.

By Car from Arcos: Driving in Jerez can be frustrating. The outskirts are filled with an almost endless series of roundabouts. Continuing straight through each one will eventually bring a rail bridge into sight. Continue to follow traffic and signs to *centro ciudad*. The route may seem circuitous (it is), but it will eventually take you past the main TI on Plaza Alameda Cristina.

If you're going straight to see the horses, follow the directions in the listing on page 694; otherwise it's best to park in one of the many underground garages and catch a cab or walk. Plaza Arenal (€1.30/hour) is the most centrally located lot, or there's the handy underground parking lot at Plaza Alameda Cristina. For street parking, blue-line zones require prepaid parking tickets on your dashboard (Mon-Fri 9:00-13:30 & 17:00-20:00, Sat 9:00-14:00, Sun and July-Aug afternoons free).

Sights in Jerez

▲▲Royal Andalusian School of Equestrian Art (Fundación Real Escuela Andaluza del Arte Ecuestre)—If you're into

horses, this is a must. Even if you're not, this is art like you've never seen. The school does its Horse Symphony show Tuesday and Thursday at 12:00 during most of the year (also on Fri in Aug, Nov-Feb Thu only; €19 general seating, €25 "preference" seating, 1.5 hours with 15-minute

intermission; no photos in show, stables, or museum; tel. 956-318-008, fax 956-318-015, tickets available online at www.realescuela .org). General seating is fine; some "preference" seats are too close for good overall views. The show explanations are in Spanish.

This is an equestrian ballet with choreography, purely Spanish music, and costumes from the 19th century. The stern riders and their talented, obedient steeds prance, jump, hop on their hind legs, and do-si-do in time to the music, all to the delight of an arena filled with mostly tourists and local horse aficionados.

The riders, trained in dressage (dreh-SAZH), cue the horses with the slightest of commands, whether verbal or with body movements. You'll see both purebred Spanish horses (of various colors, with long tails, calm personalities, and good jumping ability) and the larger mixed breeds (with short tails and a walking—not prancing—gait). The horses must be three years old before their three-year training begins, and most performing horses are male (stallions or geldings), since mixing the sexes brings problems.

The equestrian school is a university, open to all students in the EU, and with all coursework in Spanish. Although still a male-dominated activity, there have recently been a few female graduates. Tight-fitted mushroom hats are decorated with different stripes to show each rider's level. Professors often team with students and evaluate their performance during the show.

Training sessions on non-performance days offer the public a sneak preview (€10; Mon, Wed, and Fri—except no Fri in Aug, also on Tue in Nov-Feb; arrive anytime between 11:00-13:00). Big tour groups crowd in at 11:00 and schedules may vary, so it's wise to call ahead. Sessions can be exciting or dull, depending on what the trainers are working on. After the training session, you can take a 1.5-hour guided tour of the stables, horses, multimedia and carriage museums, tack room, gardens, and horse health center. Sip sherry in the arena's bar to complete this Jerez experience.

Getting There: After passing the TI on Plaza Alameda Cristina, follow pink signs with arrows pointing to the *Real Escuela de Arte Ecuestre*. Parking is located behind the horse school, and one-way streets mean there is only one way to arrive. Expect to make at least one wrong turn, so allow a little extra time.

From the bus or train stations to the horses, it's about a €5 taxi ride or a 40-minute walk.

▲▲**Sherry Bodega Tours**—Spain produces more than 10 million gallons per year of this fortified wine. The name "sherry" comes from English attempts to pronounce Jerez. Although traditionally the drink of England's aristocracy, today it's more popular with Germans. Your tourist map of Jerez is speckled with *venencia* symbols, each representing a sherry bodega that offers tours and tasting. *Venencias* are specially designed ladles for dipping inside the sherry barrel, breaking through the yeast layer, and getting to the good stuff.

Sandeman: Just around the corner from the horse school is the venerable Sandeman winery, founded in 1790 and the longtime

choice of English royalty. This tour is the aficionado's choice for its knowledgeable guides and their quality explanations of the process. Each stage is explained in detail, with visual examples of *flor* (the yeast crust) in backlit barrels, graphs of how different blends are made, and a quick walk-through of the bottling plant. The finale is a chance to taste three varieties (€7 for regular sherries, up to €21 for rare sherries, €7.50 adds tapas to the tasting, tour/tasting lasts 60-90 minutes; English tours Mon, Wed, and Fri at 11:30, 12:30, and 13:30 plus April-Oct also at 14:30; Tue and Thu at 10:30, 12:00, 13:00, and 14:00 plus April-Oct also at 15:00; closed Sun; tour times adjust with the horse show, call to confirm, reservations not required, tel. 956-151-710, www.sandeman.eu). For efficiency, first see the Horse Symphony, which ends at 13:30, then walk to Sandeman's for the

HILL TOWNS

Sherry

Spanish sherry is not the sweet dessert wine sold in the States as sherry. In Spain, sherry is (most commonly) a chilled very dry fortified white wine, often served with appetizers such as tapas, seafood, and cured meats.

British traders invented the sherry-making process as a way of transporting wines so they wouldn't go bad on a long sea voyage. Some of the most popular brands (such as Sandeman and Osbourne) were begun by Brits, and for years it was a foreigners' drink. But today, sherry is typically Spanish.

Sherry is made by blending wines from different grapes and vintages, all aged together. Start with a strong, acidic wine (from grapes that grow well in the hot, chalky soil around Jerez). Mature it in large vats until a yeast crust *(flor)* forms on the surface, protecting the wine from the air. Then fortify it with distilled alcohol.

Next comes sherry-making's distinct *solera* process. Pour the young fortified wine into the top barrel of a unique contraption—a stack of oak barrels called a *criadera*. Every year, one-third of the oldest sherry (in the barrels on the ground level) is bottled. To replace it, one-third of the sherry in the barrel above is poured in, and so on. This continues until the top barrel is one-third empty, waiting to be filled with the new year's vintage.

Fino is the most popular type of sherry (and the most different from Americans' expectations)—white, dry, and chilled. The best-selling commercial brand of *fino* is Tío Pepe; *manzanilla* is a regional variation of *fino,* as is *montilla* from Córdoba. Darker-colored and sometimes sweeter varieties of sherry include *amontillado* and *oloroso.* And yes, Spain also produces the thick, sweet cream sherries served as dessert wines. A good raisin-y, syrupy-sweet variety is Pedro Ximénez, made from sun-dried grapes of the same name.

next English tour. Or do the 10:30 Sandeman's tour before the Horse Symphony.

González Byass: The makers of the famous Tío Pepe offer a tourist-friendly tour, with more pretense and less actual sherry-making on display (that's done in a new, enormous plant outside of town). The tourist train through fake vineyards and a video presentation are forgettable, but the grand circle of sherry casks signed by a *Who's Who* of sherry-drinkers is worthwhile. Taste two sherries at the end of the 1.5-hour tour (€11, light tapas lunch with tour-€16;

tours run Mon-Sat at 12:00, 13:00, 14:00, 17:00, and 18:30; Sun at 12:00, 13:00, and 14:00; Manuel María González 12, tel. 902-440-077, www.bodegastiopepe.com).

Others: You'll come across many other sherry bodegas in town, including **Fundador Pedro Domecq,** located near the cathedral (Calle San Ildefonso 3, tel. 956-346-000, www.bodegas fundadorpedrodomecq.com).

Alcázar—This gutted castle looks tempting, but don't bother. The €3 entry fee doesn't even include the Camera Obscura (€5.40 combo-ticket covers both, Mon-Fri 10:00-18:00—or until 20:00 in mid-July-mid-Sept, Sat-Sun 10:00-15:00). Its underground parking is convenient for those touring González Byass (€1.30/hour).

Jerez Connections

Jerez's bus station is shared by six bus companies, each with its own schedule. Some specialize in certain destinations, while others share popular destinations such as Sevilla and Algeciras. The big ones serving most southern Spain destinations are Los Amarillos (toll tel. 902-210-317, www.losamarillos.es), Comes (toll tel. 902-199-208, www.tgcomes.es), and Linesur (tel. 956-341-063, www.linesur.com). Shop around for the best departure time and most direct route. While here, clarify routes for any further bus travel you may be doing in Andalucía—especially if you're going through Arcos de la Frontera, where the ticket office is often closed. Also try the privately run www.movelia.es for bus schedules and routes.

From Jerez by Bus to: Tarifa (1/day on Algeciras route with Comes, 2 hours, more frequent with transfer in Cádiz), **Algeciras** (1/day with Comes, 8/day with Linesur, fewer on weekends 1.5 hours), **Arcos** (hourly, 30 minutes), **Ronda** (4/day, 2.5-3 hours), **La Línea/Gibraltar** (1/day, 3 hours), **Sevilla** (7-10/ day, 1.5 hours), **Málaga** (2/day Mon-Sat, 1/day Sun, 4.5 hours), **Granada** (1/day, 4.75 hours), **Madrid** (3/day, more service on weekends, 7 hours).

By Train to: Sevilla (nearly hourly, 1.25 hours), **Madrid** (2/day, 4.5 hours), **Barcelona** (1/day, 7 hours). Train info: toll tel. 902-320-320, www.renfe.com.

By Car: It's a zippy 30 minutes from Jerez to Arcos.

Near the Hill Towns

If you're driving between Arcos and Tarifa, here are several sights to explore.

Yeguada de la Cartuja

This breeding farm, which raises Hispanic Arab horses according to traditions dating back to the 15th century, offers shows on Saturday at 11:00 (€19 for best seats in *tribuna* section, €14 for seats in the stands, Finca Fuente del Suero, Carretera Medina–El Portal, km 6.5, Jerez de la Frontera, tel. 956-162-809, www.yeguada cartuja.com). From Jerez, take the road to Medina Sidonia, then turn right in the direction of El Portal—you'll see a cement factory on your right. Drive for five minutes until you see the farm. A taxi from Jerez will cost about €14 one-way.

Medina Sidonia

This town is as whitewashed as can be, surrounding its church and hill, which is topped with castle ruins. I never drive through here without a coffee break and a quick stroll. Signs to *centro urbano* route you through the middle to Plaza de España (lazy cafés, bakery, plenty of free parking just beyond the square out the gate). If it's lunchtime, consider buying a picnic, as all the necessary shops are nearby and the plaza benches afford a solid workaday view of a perfectly untouristy Andalusian town. According to its own TI, the town is "much appreciated for its vast gastronomy." Small lanes lead from the main square up to Plaza Iglesia Mayor (church and TI open daily 10:30-14:00 & 16:30-18:30, tel. 956-412-404, www.medinasidonia.com). At the church, a man will show you around for a tip. Even without giving a tip, you can climb yet another belfry for yet another vast Andalusian view. The castle ruins just aren't worth the trouble.

Vejer de la Frontera

Vejer, south of Jerez and just 30 miles north of Tarifa, will lure all but the very jaded off the highway. Vejer's strong Moorish roots give it a distinct Moroccan (or Greek Island) flavor—you know, black-clad women whitewashing their homes, and lanes that can't decide if they're roads or stairways. Only a generation ago, women here wore veils. The town has no real sights—other than its women's faces—and very little tourism, making it a pleasant stop. The TI is at Remedios 2 (tel. 956-451-736, www.turismovejer.es).

The coast near Vejer has a lonely feel, but its pretty, windswept beaches are popular with windsurfers and sand flies. The Battle of Trafalgar was fought just off Cabo de Trafalgar (a nondescript lighthouse today). I drove the circle so you don't have to.

Sleeping in Vejer: A newcomer on Andalucía's tourist map, the old town of Vejer has just a few hotels.

$$ Hotel Convento San Francisco is a poor man's parador in a refurbished convent with pristine, spacious rooms and elegant public lounges (Sb-€51, Db-€72, breakfast-€3.35, air-con, free Wi-Fi in lobby, La Plazuela, tel. 956-451-001, fax 956-451-004, www.tugasa.com, convento-san-francisco@tugasa.com).

$ Hostal La Posada's 10 clean and charming rooms, in a modern apartment flat, are cheap and funky. This family-run place has no reception (S-€20-25, Db-€35-50, higher prices are for mid-July-Aug, Los Remedios 21, tel. & fax 956-450-258, www.hostal-laposada.com, no English spoken).

Route Tips for Drivers

Sevilla to Arcos (55 miles): The remote hill towns of Andalucía are a joy to tour by car with Michelin map 578 or any other good map. Drivers can zip south on N IV from Sevilla along the river, following signs to *Cádiz.* Take the fast toll expressway (blue signs, E-5, A-4); the toll-free N-IV is curvy and dangerous. About half-way to Jerez, at Las Cabezas, take CA 403 to Villamartín. From there, circle scenically (and clockwise) through the thick of the Pueblos Blancos—Zahara and Grazalema—to Arcos.

It's about two hours from Sevilla to Zahara. You'll find decent but winding roads and sparse traffic. It gets worse (but very scenic) if you take the tortuous series of switchbacks over the 4,500-foot summit of Puerto de Las Palomas (Pass of the Pigeons, climb to the viewpoint) on the direct but difficult road from Zahara to Grazalema (you'll see several hiking trailheads into Sierra de Grazalema Natural Park, though most require free permits—see sidebar on page 688).

Another scenic option through the park from Grazalema to Arcos is the road that goes up over Puerto del Boyar (Pass of the Boyar), past the pretty little valley town of Benamahoma, and down to El Bosque. The road from Ronda to El Gastor, Setenil (cave houses and great olive oil), and Olvera is another picturesque alternative.

Arcos to Tarifa (80 miles): You can drive from Arcos to Jerez in 30 minutes. If you're going to Tarifa, take the tiny C-343 road at the Jerez edge of Arcos toward Paterna and Vejer. Later, you'll pick up signs to *Medina Sidonia,* and then to *Vejer* and *Tarifa.*

Costa del Sol to Ronda and Beyond: Drivers coming up from the coast catch A-397 at San Pedro de Alcántara and climb about 20 miles into the mountains. A-369 offers a much longer, winding, but scenic alternative that takes you through a series of white-washed villages.

Beware if you have old maps. The road-numbering system from the coast into Sevilla was changed a couple of years ago: From Marbella to Ronda, take A-397 (formerly A-376). From Ronda to Jerez, start on A-374 (formerly A-376) then get on A-384 (which at Arcos may still be labeled with its old number, A-382). To head to Sevilla, branch off from A-384 onto A-375.

SPAIN'S SOUTH COAST

Nerja • Gibraltar • Tarifa

Spain's famous Costa del Sol is so bad, it's interesting. To northern Europeans, the sun is a drug, and this is their needle. Anything resembling a quaint fishing village has been bikini-strangled and Nivea-creamed. Oblivious to the concrete, pollution, ridiculous prices, and traffic jams, tourists lie on the beach like game hens on skewers—cooking, rolling, and sweating under the sun.

Where Europe's most popular beach isn't crowded by high-rise hotels, most of it's in a freeway choke hold. Wonderfully undeveloped beaches between Tarifa and Cádiz, and east of Almería, are ignored, while human lemmings make the scene where the coastal waters are so polluted that hotels are required to provide swimming pools. It's a fascinating study in human nature. The Costa del Sol has suffered through the recent economic crisis: Real estate, construction, and tourism had powered the economy, and the effects of its decline are still apparent. Crime and racial tension have risen, as many once-busy individuals are now without work.

Particularly in the resorts west of Málaga, most of the foreign visitors are British—you'll find beans on your breakfast plate and Tom Jones for Muzak. Spanish visitors complain that some restaurants have only English menus, and indeed, the typical expats here actually try *not* to integrate. I've heard locals say of the British, "If they could, they'd take the sun back home with them—but they can't, so they stay here." They enjoy English TV and radio, and many barely learn a word of Spanish. (Special school buses take British children to private English-language schools that connect with Britain's higher-education system.) For an insight into this British community, read the free local expat magazines.

Laugh with Ronald McDonald at the car-jammed resorts. But if you want a place to stay and play in the sun, unroll your beach towel at Nerja, the most appealing beach-resort town on the coast. And don't forget that you're surprisingly close to jolly olde England: The land of tea and scones, fish-and-chips, pubs and bobbies awaits you—in Gibraltar. Although a British territory, Gibraltar has a unique cultural mix that makes it far more interesting than the anonymous resorts that line the coast. Beyond "The Rock," the whitewashed port of Tarifa—the least-developed piece of Spain's generally overdeveloped southern coast—is a workaday town with a historic center, broad beaches, and good hotels and restaurants. Most importantly, Tarifa is the perfect springboard for a quick trip to Morocco (see next chapter). These three places alone—Nerja, Gibraltar, and Tarifa—make the Costa del Sol worth a trip.

Planning Your Time

My negative opinions on the "Costa del Turismo" are valid for peak season (mid-July–mid-Sept). If you're there during a quieter time and you like the ambience of a beach resort, it can be a pleasant stop. Off-season it can be neutron-bomb quiet.

The whole 150 miles of coastline takes six hours by bus or three hours to drive with no traffic jams. You can resort-hop by bus across the entire Costa del Sol and reach Nerja for dinner. If you want to party on the beach, it can take as much time as Mazatlán.

To day-trip to Tangier, Morocco, head for Tarifa.

Nerja

While cashing in on the fun-in-the-sun culture, Nerja (NEHR-*h*ah, with a guttural *h*) has actually kept much of its quiet Old World charm. It has good beaches, a fun evening paseo (strolling scene) that culminates in the proud Balcony of Europe terrace, enough pastry shops and nightlife, and locals who get more excited about their many festivals than the tourists do.

Although Nerja's population swells from about 22,000 in winter to about 90,000 in the summer, it's more of a year-round destination and a real town than many other resorts. Thanks to cheap airfares and the completion of the expressway, real estate boomed here in the last decade (property values doubled in six years). The bubble collapsed to some extent with the recent financial crisis, but Nerja has remained hardier than other parts of the Costa del Sol. New restaurants and hotels are still opening here all the time.

Nerja is more diverse than many of the rival resorts—in addition to British accents, you'll overhear French, German, Dutch, and Scandinavian being spoken on the beaches. There's also a long tradition of Spanish people retiring and vacationing here. Pensioners from northern Spain move here—enjoying long life spans, thanks in part to the low blood pressure that comes from a diet of fish and wine. While they could afford to travel elsewhere, an inertia remains from Franco's day, when people generally vacationed within the country. In summer, to escape the brutal heat of inland Spain and the exhaustion that comes with having kids home from school all day, many Spanish moms take the kids to condos on the south coast, while dads stay home to work. This is a time when many husbands get to "be Rodriguez" (i.e., anonymous and free), and enjoy (at a minimum) a break from the rigors of family life.

Nerja

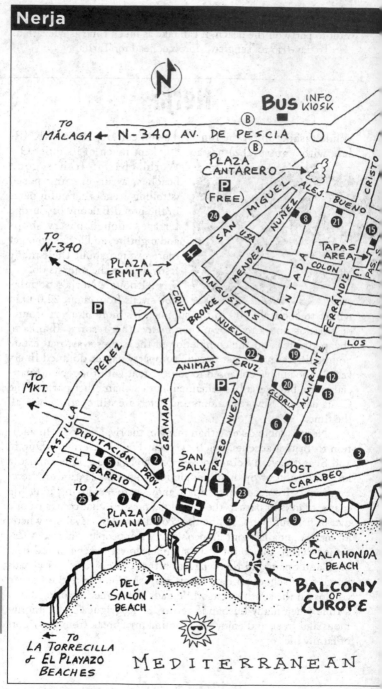

1. Hotel Balcón de Europa
2. Hotel Plaza Cavana
3. Hotel Carabeo & Restaurant 34
4. Hostal Marissal & Cochran's Terrace
5. Hostal Don Peque
6. Hostal Miguel
7. Pensión Mena
8. Hostal Lorca
9. Papagayo Beach Rest.
10. Casa Luque Restaurante
11. Pepe Rico & El Pulguilla Restaurante
12. Pinocchio Restaurante
13. Haveli Restaurante
14. El Chispa/Bar Dolores
15. La Puntilla Bar Restaurante
16. Los Cuñaos
17. La Taberna de Pepe
18. To Ayo's Café
19. Bar El Molino
20. El Burro Blanco
21. Bodega Los Bilbainos
22. Black and White Bar
23. El Valenciano Helados Ice Cream
24. Mercadona Supermarket
25. To Internet Café

* NOT TO SCALE—
BUS INFO KIOSK TO
BALCONY OF EUROPE
IS A 10 MIN. WALK

Ⓑ BUS STOP
◄ VIEW
Ⓟ PARKING

SPAIN'S SOUTH COAST

Orientation to Nerja

The tourist center of Nerja is right along the water and crowds close to its famous bluff, the "Balcony of Europe" (Balcón de Europa). Fine strings of beaches flank the bluff, stretching in either direction. The old town is just inland from the Balcony, while the more modern section slopes up and away from the water.

Tourist Information

The helpful English-speaking TI has bus schedules, tips on beaches and side-trips, and brochures for nearby destinations, such as the Caves of Nerja, Frigiliana, Málaga, and Ronda (July-Aug Mon-Sat 10:00-14:00 & 18:00-22:00, Sun 18:00-22:00; April-June and Sept-Oct Mon-Sat 10:00-14:00 & 17:00-20:00, Sun 10:00-14:00; Nov-March daily 10:00-14:00; 100 yards from the Balcony of Europe and half a block inland from the big church, tel. 952-521-531, www.nerja.org). Ask for a free city map and the *Leisure Guide*, which has a comprehensive listing of activities. Their *Hiking the Sierra of Nerja and Cliffs of Maro* booklet describes good local walks.

Arrival in Nerja

By Bus: The Nerja bus station is actually just a bus stop with an info kiosk on Avenida de Pescia (Mon-Tue and Fri 6:00-20:15, Wed-Thu and Sat-Sun 7:00-12:00 & 14:45-19:15, schedules posted, tel. 952-521-504). To travel from Nerja, buy tickets at the kiosk—don't assume they're available on the bus. Because many buses leave at the same times, arrive at least 15 minutes before departure to avoid having to elbow other tourists.

By Car: For the most central parking, follow *Balcón de Europa* signs, and then pull into the big underground parking lot (which deposits you 200 yards from the Balcony of Europe; €1.80/hour, €18.30/24 hours). Other relatively central parking lots (including the enormous Municipal Parking Carabeo, just east of the Balcony) cost nearly as much. The handiest free parking is about a 10-minute walk farther out, next to the bridge over the dry riverbed (near the town bus stop, just off N-340). Street parking in Nerja is free and unlimited, but it's very tight. If you do find a space, avoid parking next to yellow lines, and read signs carefully—on certain days of the month you're required to move your car.

Helpful Hints

Internet Access: Nerja's scenically situated Internet café, **Europ@ Web,** is on a square overlooking Playa la Torrecilla, where Calle de Castilla Pérez meets Calle Málaga (daily 10:00-22:00, until 24:00 in summer, 24 computers, tel. 952-526-147).

Radio: For a taste of the British expat scene, pick up the monthly *Street Wise* magazine or tune in to Coastline Radio at 97.6 FM.

Local Guide: Carmen Fernandez is good, with knowledge of the entire region (standard rate €125/5-hour day, mobile 610-038-437, mfeyus@yahoo.es).

Massage: Tiny yet muscular Marie, who moved here from France, runs a massage parlor out of her apartment. She does an excellent one-hour massage for €40 (€10 more on weekends)—just give her a call (**Amarilys Masaje,** Calle de Castilla Perez 10, mobile 667-825-828).

Getting Around Nerja

You can easily **walk** anywhere you need to go.

Nerja's **taxis** are pricey—the in-town minimum is €6, even for a short trip. They don't use meters—instead, most journeys have a set fee (e.g., €7 to Burriana Beach, €12 to Frigiliana, tel. 952-524-519 or 952-520-537).

To clip-clop in a **horse and buggy** through town, it's €35 for about 25 minutes (you'll usually find these at the Plaza de los Cangrejos above Playa la Torrecilla).

Sights in Nerja

▲▲**Balcony of Europe (Balcón de Europa)**—The bluff, jutting happily into the sea, was completely pedestrianized in 2010. It's

the center of Nerja's *paseo* and a magnet for street performers. The mimes, music, and puppets can draw bigger crowds than the Balcony itself, which overlooks the Mediterranean, miles of coastline, and little coves and caves below. A castle, and later a fort, occupied this spot from the ninth century until the earthquake of 1884. Now it's a people-friendly view terrace.

Built in the early 1800s to defend against Napoleon, the English-Spanish fort here protected the harbor with the help of seven cannons. When the 1884 earthquake destroyed the castle and fort, it sent the cannons into the sea. A century later, two were salvaged, cleaned up, and placed here. Study the beautifully aged metal work.

The cute statue of King Alfonso XII reminds locals of how this popular sovereign (the great-grandfather of today's King Juan Carlos) came here after the devastating earthquake (a huge

Costa del Sol History

Many Costa del Sol towns come in pairs: the famous beach town with little history, and its smaller yet much more historic partner established a few miles inland—safely out of reach of the Barbary pirate raids that plagued this coastline for centuries. Nerja is a good example of this pattern. Whereas it has almost no history and was just an insignificant fishing village until tourism hit, its more historic sister, Frigiliana, hides out in the nearby hills. The Barbary pirate raids were a constant threat. In fact, the Spanish slang for "the coast is clear" is *"no hay moros en la costa"* (there are no Moors on the coast).

Nerja was overlooked by the tourism scene until about 1980, when the phenomenal Spanish TV show *Verano Azul (Blue Summer)* was set here. This post-Franco program featured the until-then off-limits topics of sexual intimacy, marital problems, adolescence, and so on in a beach-town scene (imagine combining *All in the Family, Baywatch,* and *The Hills*). To this day, when Spaniards hear the word "Nerja," they think of this TV hit.

Despite the fame, development didn't really hit until about 2000, when the expressway finally and conveniently connected Nerja with the rest of Spain. Thankfully, a building code prohibits any new buildings higher than three stories in the old town.

number of locals had died). He mobilized the local rich to dig out the community and put things back together. Standing on this promontory amid the ruins of the earthquake-devastated castle, he marveled at the view and coined its now-famous name, "Balcón de Europa."

The Nerja castle was part of a 16th-century lookout system. After the Christian Reconquista in 1492 drove Muslim Moors into exile, pirate action from Muslim countries in North Africa picked up. Lookout towers were stationed within sight of one another all along the coast. Warnings were sent whenever pirates threatened (smoke by day, flames by night). Look to the east—you can see three towers crowning bluffs in the distance.

Also to the east you can just see the tip of Burriana Beach. Spaniards love their *chiringuitos*, as local beach restaurants are called. The *chiringuito* immediately below you, Papagayo, is understandably popular.

Scan the horizon. Until recently this was a favored landing spot (just beyond the tighter security zone near Gibraltar) for illegal immigrants and drug runners coming in from Africa. Many Moroccan teens try to sneak into Europe here, as local laws prohibit turning away undocumented children (the police use DNA tests to determine the age of recent arrivals—if they're under 18, they stay). Laws also grant automatic EU citizenship to anyone born in Europe, so many pregnant women try to slip in (once the baby's born, the mother's legal, too). However, illegal immigration is down: With the help of a new high-tech satellite-scanning system, the Guardia Civil can now detect floating objects as small as makeshift rafts and intercept them before they reach land.

Walk beneath the Balcony for views of the scant remains (bricks and stones) of the ninth-century Moorish castle. Locals claim an underground passage connected the Moorish fortress with the mosque that stood where the San Sebastián church stands today.

Church of San Salvador—Just a block inland from the Balcony, this church was likely built upon the ruins of a mosque (c. 1600). Its wooden ceiling is Mudejar—made by Moorish artisans working in Christian times. The woodworking technique is similar to that featured in the Alhambra in Granada. The modern fresco of the *Annunciation* (in the rear of the nave) is by Paco Hernandez, the top local artist of this generation. In front, on the right, is a niche featuring Jesus with San Isidoro (as a little boy). Isidoro is the patron saint of Madrid, Nerja, and farmers (sugar-cane farming was the leading industry here before tourism hit). From the porch of the church, look inland to see City Hall, marked by four flags (Andalucía's is green for olive trees and white for the color of the houses in this part of Spain).

Town Strolls—Nerja was essentially destroyed after the 1884 earthquake—and at the time there was little more here beyond the castle anyway—so there's not much to see in the town itself. However, a few of its main streets are worth a quick look. From the Balcony of Europe head inland. Consider first grabbing some ice cream at El Valenciano Helados, a local favorite run by a Valencia family. Try the refreshing *chufa*-nut Valencian specialty called *horchata*.

A block farther inland, the old town's three main streets come together. The oldest street, Calle Carabeo, heads off to your right (notice how buildings around here are wired on the outside). On the left, Calle Pintada heads inland. Its name means "the painted street," as it was spiffed up in 1885 for the king's visit. Today it's the town's best shopping street. And between those streets runs Calle Almirante Ferrandiz, Nerja's restaurant row, which is particularly lively in the evenings.

Beaches *(Playas)*

The single best thing to do on a sunny day in Nerja is to hit the beach: swim, sunbathe, sip a drink, go for a hearty hike along the rocky coves...or all of the above.

Nerja's many beaches are well-equipped, with bars and restaurants, free showers, and rentable lounge chairs and umbrellas (about €4/person for chair and umbrella, same cost for 10 minutes or all day). Nearby restaurants rent umbrellas, and you're welcome to take drinks and snacks out to your spot. Spanish law requires that all beaches are open to the public (except the one in Rota, which is reserved for American soldiers). While there are some nudist beaches (such as Cantarriján, described on page 712), keep in mind that in Europe, any beach can be topless. During the summer, Spanish sun-worshippers pack the beach from about 11:00 until around 13:30, when they move into the beach restaurants for relief from the brutal sun. Watch out for red flags on the beach, which indicate when the seas are too rough for safe swimming (blue = safe, orange = caution, red = swimming prohibited). Don't take valuables to the beach, as thieves have fast fingers.

Beaches lie east and west of the Balcony of Europe. For each area, I've listed beaches from nearest to farthest. Even if you're not swimming or sunbathing, walking along these beaches (and the trails that connect them, if open) is a delightful pastime.

East of the Balcony of Europe

Paseo de los Carabineros—One of Nerja's most appealing draws has been the walkway called the Paseo de los Carabineros, which scampers up and down cliffs, just above the pebbles and sand, to connect the enticing beaches east of the Balcony. Unfortunately, due to erosion concerns and a lack of funds (and municipal motivation), the path has been closed for the past few years. For now, only the first little bit, to Calahonda Beach (described next), is completely open. To reach the other beaches east of the Balcony of Europe, you'll have to walk through the modern town above the beaches...less fun.

To discourage people from using the Paseo de los Carabineros, city officials have erected concrete barriers in a few places along the walkway, removed guardrails (so in some cases you're walking precariously along the cliffs), and allowed the path to become overgrown with plants. While it's possible to follow this pathway at your own risk, it's quite treacherous—in a couple of places you have to actually scale a wall. (Because the path closure is well-advertised at both ends, you're completely liable if anything happens.) Gung-ho travelers still make this walk (I did...carefully), and in summer and at low tide, you can likely walk along the sand and pebbles around the giant rocks (slow going)—but it's not recommended if a pleasant stroll is what you want. The good news is that plans are afoot to restore and reopen the Paseo de los Carabineros. Ask locally, but don't be disappointed if this often-delayed project fails to materialize.

Calahonda Beach (Playa Calahonda)—Directly beneath the Balcony of Europe (to the left as you face the sea) is one of Nerja's most characteristic little patches of sun. This pebbly beach is full of fun pathways, crags, and crannies, and its humble Papagayo restaurant is open all day. Antonio can be seen each morning working with his nets and sorting through his fish. His little pre-tourism beach hut—a stuccoed-and-whitewashed marshmallow bulge with blue trim burrowed into the cliff—is wonderfully photogenic. To get here from the Balcony, simply head down through the arch across from the El Valenciano Helados ice-cream stand...you'll be on the beach in seconds.

Carabeo Beach (Playa Carabeo)—Less developed than the others listed here, Carabeo is wedged into a cove between the bustling Calahonda and Burriana beaches. For many, its lack of big restaurants is a plus. If the Paseo de los Carabineros is closed, you can reach the beach by walking along Calle Carabeo and taking the stairs down from the viewpoint at the park.

Burriana Beach (Playa de Burriana)—Nerja's leading beach is a 20-minute walk east from the Balcony of Europe. Big, bus-

tling, crowded, and fun, it's understandably a top attraction. Burriana is fun for families, with paddleboats, playgrounds, volleyball courts, and other entertainment options. The beach is also lined with a wide range of cafés and restaurants—but the best is clearly Ayo's, whose paella feast is a destination in itself (see listing on page 720).

Getting There: Assuming Paseo de los Carabineros is closed, from Nerja's main intersection (with the triple fork), follow the right fork and walk along Calle Carabeo. You'll pass the viewpoint park with the stairs leading down to Carabeo Beach; keep going until you're forced to jog left (up Cómpeta) into a dull modern part of town. You'll see the boxy parador on your right; circle around behind it, following the low-profile signs for *Playa Burriana* (near the parador entrance) to the right. Curl around to the right, then twist down the switchback road to the beach. It's a €7 taxi ride.

Cantarriján Beach—The only beach listed here not within easy walking distance of Nerja, this is the place if you're craving a more desolate beach (and have a car). Drive about 4.5 miles (15 minutes) east (toward Herradura) to the Cerro Gordo exit, and follow *Playa Cantarriján* signs (paved road, just before the tunnel). Park at the viewpoint and hike 30 minutes down to the beach (or, in mid-June-Sept, ride the shuttle bus down). Down below, rocks and two restaurants separate two pristine beaches—one for people with bathing suits (or not); the other, more secluded, more strictly for nudists. As this beach is in a natural park and requires a long hike, it provides a fine—and rare—chance to experience the Costa del Sol in some isolation.

West of the Balcony of Europe

Unlike the walkways east of the Balcony, the promenades to the west are open for business—making this a delightful place to stroll.

Del Salón Beach (Playa del Salón)—The sandiest—and most crowded—beach in Nerja is down the walkway to the right of Cafetería Marissal, just west of the Balcony of Europe (to the right as you look out to sea). For great drinks with a view, stop by the recommended Cochran's Terrace or Casa Luque on the way down. Continuing farther west, you'll reach another sandy beach, **Playa la Torrecilla,** at the end of Calle Málaga.

El Playazo ("Big Beach")—A short hike on a promenade west of Playa la Torrecilla, this beach is preferred by locals, as it's less developed than the more central ones, offering a couple of miles of wide-open spaces that allow for fine walks and a chance to "breathe in the beach."

Near Nerja

▲Caves of Nerja (Cuevas de Nerja)—These caves (2.5 miles east of Nerja, exit 295), with an impressive array of stalactites and stalagmites, are a classic roadside attraction. The huge caverns are filled with backlit formations and a big hit with cruise-ship groups and Spanish families. The visit involves a 30-minute unguided ramble deep into the mountain, up and down 400 dark stairs. At the end you reach the Hall of the Cataclysm, where you'll circle the world's largest stalactite column (certified by *Guinness Book of World Records*). Someone figured out that it took one trillion drops to make the column.

The free exhibit in the Centro de Interpretación explains the cave's history and geology (in house next to bus parking; exhibit in Spanish, but includes free English brochure).

Cost and Hours: €8.50, daily 10:00-14:00 & 16:00-18:30, July-

Aug until 19:30, easy parking–€1, tel. 952-529-520.

Concerts: During the festival held here the third week of July, the caves provide a cool venue for hot flamenco and classical concerts (tickets sold out long in advance).

Services: The restaurant offers a view and three-course fixed-price meals for €8, and the picnic spot (behind the ticket office) offers pine trees, benches, and a kids' play area.

Getting There: To reach the caves, catch a bus from Nerja's main bus stop (€1, 13/day, 10 minutes).

Frigiliana—The picturesque whitewashed village of Frigiliana (free-*h*ee-lee-AH-nah, with a guttural *h*), only four miles inland from Nerja, is easily reached by bus (€1, 9/day, none on Sun, 15 minutes) or taxi (€12 one-way). While it doesn't match up to the striking White Towns listed in the preceding chapter, its proximity to Nerja makes it an enticing side-trip if this is the nearest you'll get to hill towns on your trip.

The bus stop is in the middle of town, on Plaza del Ingenio. This is also the point that separates the new town from the old town (the steep old Moorish quarter climbing the hill up ahead). The **TI** is a 100-yard walk uphill, in the new town (Mon-Fri 10:00-17:00, Sat-Sun 10:00-14:00 & 16:00-19:30, tel. 952-534-261, www.frigiliana.com). Pick up a map and the translations of the tile you'll see displayed around town. The TI shares a building with the local archaeological museum, with artifacts unearthed near Frigiliana; their prized piece is the fifth-century B.C. skull of a 10-year-old child (free, same hours as TI).

Focus your visit on the old town. Begin by climbing up to the terrace in front of the factory *(ingenio)*—the blocky, un-white-washed, double-smokestack building that dominates the town. Dating from the 16th century, this still produces sugarcane honey. From the end of the terrace, hike up the steep street, bearing right at the fork up Calle Hernando el Darra. At #10 (on the right), notice the tile in the wall—the first in a series of a dozen around town that describe, in poetic Spanish, the story of the 1568 Battle of Peñón. At the next fork, bear right (uphill) on Calle Amargura and walk steeply uphill, enjoying the  flowerpot-lined lane. Notice the distinctive traditional door-knockers, shaped like a woman's hand. More common in Morocco, these are the "hand of Fatima"—the daughter of the Prophet Muhammad—and are intended to ward off evil.

After turning the corner, take the left/downhill road at the next fork, than head right up Calle Sta. Teresa de Ávila. Then head left down the steep, stepped Calle del Garral. You'll pop out just below the main church. Before going there, detour a few steps to the right, then head left to Plaza de la Fuente Vieja—home of a 17th-century fountain that's one of the town's trademarks. Then head back up the way you came to find your way to the inviting café-lined plaza in front of the Church of San Antonio of Padua (with a stark interior). From here, you can follow the main drag back to where you entered town, or enjoy exploring Frigiliana's back lanes.

Hiking—Europeans visiting the region for a longer stay generally use Nerja as a base from which to hike. The TI can describe a variety of hikes. One of the most popular includes a refreshing two-to-three-hour walk up a river (at first through a dry riverbed, and later up to your shins in water; 7.5 miles one-way). Another, more demanding hike takes you to the 5,000-foot summit of El Cielo for the best memorable king-of-the-mountain feeling this region offers.

Nightlife in Nerja

Bar El Molino offers live Spanish folk singing nightly in a rustic cavern that's actually an old mill—the musicians perform where the mule once tread. It's touristy but fun (starts at 22:00 but pretty dead before 23:00, no cover—just buy a drink, Calle San José 4). The local sweet white wine, *vino del terreno*—made up the hill in Frigiliana—is popular here (€3/glass).

El Burro Blanco is a touristy flamenco bar with shows nightly from 22:30. Keeping expectations pretty low, they advertise "The Best One in Nerja" (no cover—just buy a drink, on corner of Calle Pintada and Calle de la Gloria).

Bodega Los Bilbainos is a classic dreary old dive—a favorite with local men and communists (tapas and drinks, Calle Alejandro Bueno 8).

For more trendy and noisy nightlife, check out the **Black and White Bar** karaoke bar on Pintada (karaoke nightly, near El Burro Blanco at Calle Pintada 35) and the bars and dance clubs on Antonio Millón and Plaza Tutti Frutti.

Sleeping in Nerja

The entire Costa del Sol is crowded during August and Holy Week (the week leading up to Easter), when prices are at their highest. Reserve in advance for peak season—basically mid-July through mid-September—which is prime time for Spanish workers to hit the beaches. Any other time of year, you'll find that Nerja has

Sleep Code

(€1 = about $1.40, country code: 34)

S = Single, **D** = Double/Twin, **T** = Triple, **Q** = Quad, **b** = bathroom, **s** = shower only. Unless otherwise noted, credit cards are accepted and English is spoken, but breakfast is not included.

To help you easily sort through these listings, I've divided the accommodations into three categories, based on the price for a standard double room with bath during high season:

$$$ Higher Priced—Most rooms €100 or more.

$$ Moderately Priced—Most rooms between €50-100.

$ Lower Priced—Most rooms €50 or less.

Prices can change without notice; verify the hotel's current rates online or by email. For other updates, see www .ricksteves.com/update.

plenty of comfy, easygoing low-rise resort-type hotels and rooms. Room rates are generally three-tiered: low season (Nov-March), middle season (April-June and Oct), and high season (July-Sept).

Compared to the pricier hotels, the better *hostales* are an excellent value. Hostal Don Peque, Hostal Miguel, and Pensión Mena are all within a few blocks of the Balcony of Europe.

Breakfast: Some hotels here overcharge for breakfast. Don't hesitate to go elsewhere, as many places serve breakfast for more reasonable prices. For a cheap breakfast with a front-row view of the promenade action on the Balcony of Europe, head to **Cafetería Marissal** (in the *hostal* of the same name) and grab a wicker seat under the palm trees (€3-5.50 options include English breakfasts, daily from 9:00). **Papagayo** serves breakfast on the beach, just below the Balcony of Europe, to those who don't mind a little sand in their coffee (from 10:00). If you're up for a short hike before breakfast, consider the recommended **Ayo's** on Burriana Beach (daily from 9:00).

Close to the Balcony of Europe

$$$ Hotel Balcón de Europa is the most central place in town. It's right on the water and the square, with the prestigious address Balcón de Europa 1. It has 110 rooms, recently renovated with modern style, plus all the comforts—including a pool and an elevator down to the beach. It's popular with groups. All the suites have seaview balconies, and most regular rooms also come with views (Sb-€72/83/109, standard Db-€100/117/142, about €30 extra for sea view and balcony, prices don't include tax, breakfast-€12, air-con, elevator, pay Internet access, free Wi-Fi, parking-€11, tel. 952-520-800, fax 952-524-490, www.hotelbalconeuropa.com, reservas@hotelbalconeuropa.com).

$$$ Hotel Plaza Cavana, with 39 rooms, overlooks a plaza lily-padded with cafés. It feels a bit institutional, but if you'd like a central location, marble floors, modern furnishings, an elevator, and a small unheated rooftop swimming pool, dive in (Sb-€39-119, Db-€49-129, bigger superior Db-€10 more, Tb-20 percent more, Qb-30 percent more; 10 percent discount for my readers for 1-to-2-night stays, 15 percent for stays of 3 nights or more, and free breakfast for those booking direct with this guidebook in 2012; some view rooms, air-con, elevator, pay Internet access, free Wi-Fi in lobby, second small unheated pool in basement, parking-€10-15, 2 blocks from Balcony of Europe at Plaza de Cavana 10, tel. 952-524-000, fax 952-524-008, www.hotelplazacavana.com, info @hotelplazacavana.com).

$$$ Hotel Carabeo, a boutique-hotel splurge, has seven classy rooms on the cliff east of downtown—less than a 10-minute walk away, but removed from the bustle of the Balcony of Europe (non-view Db-€75-85/80-90/85-100; seaview Db-€100-155/130-175/145-195, price range depends on type of room, prices don't include tax, air-con, free Wi-Fi in lobby, Calle Carabeo 34, tel. 952-525-444, www.hotelcarabeo.com, info@hotelcarabeo.com). This is also home to the recommended Restaurant 34.

$$ Hostal Marissal has an unbeatable location next door to the fancy Balcón de Europa hotel, and 23 modern, spacious rooms with old-fashioned furniture and clever gadgets on the doors to prevent them from slamming. Some rooms have small view balconies overlooking the Balcony of Europe action. Their cafeteria and bar, run by helpful staff, make the Marissal even more welcoming (Sb-€30/35/45-50, Db-€40/50/60-70, apartment for up to 4 people-€80-155, breakfast-€3-5.50, double-paned windows, air-con, elevator, free Wi-Fi, Balcón de Europa 3, reception at Marissal café, tel. 952-520-199, fax 952-526-654, www.hostal marissal.com, reserva@hostalmarissal.com, Carlos and María).

$$ Hostal Don Peque sits in a dull urban zone an easy couple of blocks' walk from the Balcony of Europe—but it compensates with 10 bright, colorful, and cheery rooms (eight with balconies—a few with sea views). Owners Roberto and Clara moved here from France and have infused the place with their personality. They rent beach equipment at reasonable prices, but their bar-terrace with rooftops-and-sea views may be more enticing (Sb-€35/48/55, Db-€40/55/70, Tb-€55/70/90, bunk-bed family room for up to 4-€15 more than Tb, rates decrease for extended stays and increase for holidays, prices include basic breakfast—or pay €6 extra for a much fancier one, air-con, thin walls, free Wi-Fi, Diputación 13,

tel. 952-521-318, www.hostaldonpeque.com, info@hostaldonpeque
.com).

$ Hostal Miguel offers nine sunny and airy rooms in the heart
of "Restaurant Row" (so expect some street noise). Top-floor rooms
have mountain views, and breakfast is served on the pretty green
terrace. The owners—British expats Ian, Jane, and Hannah—are
long-time Nerja devotees (Sb-€29-40, Db-€36-54, book direct
for these prices, 4 percent more if paying with credit card, break-
fast-€5, family suite, no air-con but fans and fridges, free Wi-Fi
in most rooms, laundry service-€5, beach equipment available on
request, Almirante Ferrándiz 31, tel. 952-521-523, mobile 696-799-
218, www.hostalmiguel.com, hostalmiguel@gmail.com).

$ Pensión Mena rents 11 nice rooms—four with seaview
terraces (€5 extra and worth it)—and offers a quiet, breezy garden (Sb-€18-28, Db-€27-43, no breakfast, some street noise, free
Wi-Fi in lobby, El Barrio 15, tel. & fax 952-520-541, www.hostal
mena.es, info@hostalmena.es, María). The reception has limited
hours (daily 9:30-13:30 & 17:00-20:30); if they're closed when you
arrive to check in, report to their sister hotel, Hotel Mena Plaza, a
few blocks away at Plaza de España 2.

In a Residential Neighborhood

$ Hostal Lorca is located in a quiet residential area five minutes
from the center, three blocks from the bus stop, and close to a
small, handy grocery store. Run by a friendly young Dutch couple,
Femma and Rick, this *hostal* has nine modern, comfortable rooms
and an inviting compact backyard with a terrace, a palm tree, and
a small pool. You can use the microwave and take drinks (on the
honor system) from the well-stocked fridge. This quiet, homey
place is a winner (Sb-€25-33, Db-€29-52, extra bed-€12, cash only,
no air-con but fans, free Wi-Fi, look for yellow house at Mendez
Nuñez 20, tel. 952-523-426, www.hostallorca.com, info@hostal
lorca.com).

Eating in Nerja

There are three Nerjas: the private domain of the giant beachside
hotels; the central zone, packed with fun-loving (and often tipsy)
expats and tourists eating and drinking from trilingual menus; and
the back streets, where local life goes on as if there were no tourists. The whole old town (around the Balcony of Europe) is busy
with lively restaurants. Wander around and see who's eating best.

To pick up picnic supplies, head to the **Mercadona** supermarket (Mon-Sat 9:15-21:15, closed Sun, inland from Plaza Ermita
on Calle San Miguel).

Near the Balcony of Europe

Papagayo, a classic *chiringuito* (beach restaurant), lounges in the sand a few steps below the Balcony of Europe. You may be paying for the location, but it's quite a location. They serve drinks and snacks to those enjoying their beach umbrellas (€2-8 breakfasts, €4-12 snacks and meals, open with demand, daily breakfast from 10:00, lunch 12:00-17:00, tel. 952-523-816, "moon beach parties" on summer evenings).

Cochran's Terrace serves mediocre meals in a wonderful seaview setting, overlooking Del Salón Beach (€7-12 main dishes, daily all day for drinks, 12:00-15:00 & 19:00-23:00 for meals, just behind Hostal Marissal).

Casa Luque, between the Church of San Salvador and the cliffside, is a worthwhile splurge, featuring a terrace in back with wicker furniture, sea views, a stiffly formal vibe, and enough ambience to justify the price. Its dining room, despite its lack of view, is the most high-end and romantic I've seen in town (€6-12 small plates, €22 for 7-tapas tasting meal, wines can be purchased by the glass, Thu-Sat and Mon-Tue 12:30-15:30 & 19:30-23:30, Sun 19:30-23:30 only, closed Wed, tel. 952-521-004).

Restaurant 34, in Hotel Carabeo, manages white-tablecloth elegance in a relaxed atmosphere that successfully mixes eclectic antiques with modern accents. More tables sprawl outside, along the swimming pool and toward sweeping sea views (call ahead to reserve a seaview table). The staff is friendly, and the cuisine features seasonal local produce (€9-15 starters, €17-24 main dishes, €25 three-course fixed-price meal, Tue-Sun from 19:00, closed Mon, Calle Carabeo 34, tel. 952-525-444).

Along Restaurant Row

Strolling up Calle Almirante Ferrándiz (which changes its name farther uphill to "Cristo"), you'll find a good variety of eateries, albeit filled with tourists. On the upside, the presence of expats means you'll find places serving food earlier in the evening than the Spanish norm. Here are my choices in four categories: Romantic, Italian, Indian, and Spanish seafood and tapas.

Pepe Rico is the most romantic (in a schlocky adult-contemporary way) along this street, with a big terrace and a cozy dining room (€6-12 starters, €16-20 main dishes, €28 four-course meals, Mon-Sat 12:30-15:00 & 19:00-23:00, closed Sun, Calle Almirante Ferrándiz 28, tel. 952-520-247).

Pinocchio seems to be the local favorite for Italian (€7-9 pizzas and pastas, daily, Calle Almirante Ferrándiz 51, tel. 952-527-248).

Haveli, run by Amit and his Swedish wife, Eva, serves good Indian food in a nondescript atmosphere. For more than two decades, it's been a hit with Brits, who know their Indian food (€10-12 plates, daily 19:00-24:00 in summer, closed Mon off-season, Cristo 42, tel. 952-524-297).

El Pulguilla is a great, high-energy place for Spanish cuisine, fish, and tapas. Its two distinct zones (tapas bar up front and more formal restaurant out back) are both jammed with enthusiastic locals and tourists. The lively no-nonsense stainless-steel tapas bar doubles as a local pick-up joint later in the evening. Drinks come with a free small plate of clams, mussels, shrimp, chorizo sausage, or seafood salad. For a sit-down meal, head back to the gigantic terrace. Though not listed on the menu, half-portions *(media-raciones)* are available for many items, allowing you to easily sample different dishes (€10-15 dinners, closed Mon, Almirante Ferrándiz 26, tel. 952-521-384).

Tapas Bars near Herrera Oria

A 10-minute gently uphill hike from the water takes you into the residential thick of things, where the sea views come thumbtacked to the walls, prices are lower, and locals fill the tables. The first three are tapas bars within a block of one another. Each is a colorful local hangout with different energy levels on different nights. Survey all three before choosing one, or have a drink and tapa at each. These places are generally open all day for tapas and drinks, and serve table-service meals during normal dining hours. If you prefer a restaurant setting to a bar, try the last listing, La Taberna de Pepe.

Remember that in Nerja, tapas are snack-size portions, generally not for sale but free with each drink. To turn them into more of a meal, ask for the menu and order a full-size *ración*, or half-size *media-ración*. The half-portions are generally bigger than you'd expect.

El Chispa (a.k.a. Bar Dolores) is big on seafood, which locals enjoy on an informal terrace. Their *tomate ajo* (garlic tomato) is tasty, and their *berenjenas* (fried and salted eggplant) comes piping hot and is also worth considering. They'll want you to try the molasses-like sugar-cane syrup on the eggplant. They serve huge portions—*media-raciones* are enough for two (€5-12 *raciones*, daily, San Pedro 12, tel. 952-523-697).

La Puntilla Bar Restaurante is a boisterous little place, with its rickety plastic furniture spilling out onto the cobbles on hot summer nights (generous €4-6 splittable salads, €4-7 half-*raciones*, €7-13 *raciones*, daily 12:00-24:00, a block in front of Los Cuñaos at Calle Bolivia 1, tel. 952-528-951).

Los Cuñaos hangs the banners of the entire soccer league on the walls. Local women hang out to chat, and kids wander around like it's home. Although it has the least interesting menu, it has the most interesting business card (€7.50 meals, €16-17 two-person meals, closed Sat, Herrera Oria 19, tel. 650-359-226).

La Taberna de Pepe is more of a sit-down restaurant, though it does have a small bar with tapas. The tight, cozy (almost cluttered) eight-table interior is decorated with old farm tools and crammed with happy eaters choosing from a short menu of well-executed seafood. It feels classier than the rough-and-tumble tapas bars listed above, but isn't pretentious (€6-12 dishes, Fri-Wed 12:15-16:00 & 19:00-24:00, closed Thu, Herrera Oria 30, tel. 952-522-195).

Paella Feast on Burriana Beach

Ayo's is famous for its character of an owner and its €6 beachside all-you-can-eat paella feast at lunchtime. For 30 years, Ayo—a lovable ponytailed bohemian who promises to be here until he dies—has been feeding locals. Ayo is a very big personality—one of the five kids who discovered the Caves of Nerja, formerly a well-known athlete, and now someone who makes it a point to hire hard-to-employ people as a community service. The paella fires get stoked up at about noon and continue through mid-afternoon. Grab one of a hundred tables under the canopy next to the rustic open-fire cooking zone, and enjoy the beach setting in the shade with a jug of sangria. For €6, you can fill your plate as many times as you like. It's a 20-minute walk from the Balcony of Europe, at the east end of Burriana Beach—look for Ayo's rooftop pyramid (daily "sun to sun," for breakfast—see below, paella served only at lunch, Playa de Burriana, tel. 952-522-289).

Breakfast at Ayo's: Consider arriving at Ayo's at 9:00. Locals order the *tostada con aceite de oliva* (toast with olive oil and salt-€0.50). Ayo also serves toasted ham-and-cheese sandwiches and good coffee.

Nerja Connections

While there are some handy direct bus connections from Nerja to major destinations, many others require a transfer in the town of **Málaga**. The closest train station to Nerja is in Málaga. Fortunately, connections between Nerja and Málaga are easy, and the train and bus stations in Málaga are right next to each other.

Nerja

From Nerja by Bus to: Málaga (1-2/hour, 1 hour *directo*, 1.5 hours *ruta*), **Caves of Nerja** (13/day, 10 minutes), **Frigiliana** (9/day, 20 minutes), **Granada** (6/day, 2-2.5 hours, more with transfer in Motril—but check the departure time from Motril to Granada to make sure you're really saving time; Nerja to Motril, 1 hour, Motril to Granada, 1.25 hours), **Córdoba** (2/day, 4.5 hours), **Sevilla** (2/day, 4.75 hours), **Algeciras** (with connections to La Línea de la Concepción/Gibraltar and Tarifa; 1/day direct, 3.5 hours, more with transfer in Málaga; there are also connections to La Línea de la Concepción/Gibraltar and Tarifa via Málaga). To reach **Ronda**, you'll transfer in Málaga. Remember to double-check the codes on bus schedules—for example, 12:00*S* means 12:00 daily except Saturday. Almost all buses from Nerja are operated by Alsa (toll tel. 902-422-242, www.alsa.es), except the local bus to Frigiliana (Autocares Nerja, tel. 952-520-984).

To Málaga Airport (about 40 miles west): Catch the bus to Málaga (€4, 18/day, 1.25-1.5 hours), then take a local bus (€2, buy ticket on board, about 2/hour, 30 minutes) to the airport (airport tel. 952-048-804). If you'd rather take a taxi from Nerja to the airport, figure on paying about €65, or ask your Nerja hotelier about airport shuttle transfers (operated by various companies in town, generally less expensive than a taxi).

Málaga

This seaside city's busy airport is the gateway to the Costa del Sol. Málaga's bus and train stations—a block apart at the western edge of Málaga's town center—both have pickpockets and lockers (the train station's lockers are more modern).

Málaga's big, airy U-shaped **bus station**, on Paseo de los Tilos, has long rows of counters for the various bus companies. In the center of the building is a helpful info desk that can print out schedules for any destination and point you to the right ticket window (daily 7:00-10:00 & 10:30-19:00 & 19:30-22:00, tel. 952-350-061, www.estabus.emtsam.es). Flanking the information desk on either side are old-fashioned lockers (buy a €3.20 token, or *ficha*, from the automated machine). The station also has several basic eateries, newsstands, WCs, and so on. The train station is just a five-minute walk away: As you stand near the bus stalls, facing the building (with the buses behind you), the train station is over your right shoulder (exit at the far corner of the station, cross the street, and enter the big shopping mall labeled *Estación María Zambrano*—walk a few minutes through the mall to the train station). If you have time to kill near the bus station, explore the train station mall, or visit the mall across from the bus-station roundabout.

The **train station** (called Estación María Zambrano) is slick and modern, inside a big shopping mall (with a food court upstairs). Modern lockers are by the entrance to tracks 10-11 (€3-5 depending on size, security checkpoint), and car-rental offices are by the entrance to tracks 1-9 (Hertz, Avis, Europcar, and National/Atesa). A TI kiosk is in the main hall, just before the shopping mall. To reach the bus station, enter the mall by the TI kiosk and follow signs to *estación de autobuses*—it's across the street, a five-minute walk away.

From Málaga by Bus to: Nerja (1-2/hour, 1 hour *directo*, 1.5 hours *ruta*), **Ronda** (*directo* buses by Los Amarillos: 10/day Mon-Fri, 6/day Sat-Sun, 1.75 hours; avoid the *ruta* buses by Portillo: 2/day, 4 hours), **Algeciras** (4/day *directo*, 1.75 hours; 7/day *semi-directo*, 2.5 hours; 9/day *ruta*, 3 hours; all Portillo), **La Línea de Concepción/Gibraltar** (6/day, 3 hours, *ruta* only, Portillo), **Tarifa** (2/day direct, 3.5 hours, Portillo, many more possible with transfer in Algeciras), **Sevilla** (6/day, 2.5-3.5 hours, Alsa), **Jerez** (2/day Mon-Sat, 1/day Sun, 4.5 hours, Los Amarillos), **Granada** (hourly, 1.5-2 hours, Alsa), **Córdoba** (4/day, 3-3.5 hours *directo*, Alsa), **Madrid** (5/day, 6 hours, run by Daibus, tel. 902-277-999, www.daibus.es), **Barcelona** (4/day, 17 hours, Alsa), **Marbella** (at least hourly, 55 minutes *directo*, 1.25 hours *ruta*). Most buses are operated by Alsa (tel. 902-422-242, www.alsa.es), Portillo (tel. 902-450-550, www.ctsa-portillo.es), or Los Amarillos (tel. 952-363-024, www.losamarillos.es).

From Málaga by Train to: Ronda (1/day direct in evening, 2 hours; 2/day with transfer in Bobadilla, 2-3 hours), **Algeciras** (2/day, 4 hours, transfer in Bobadilla—same as Ronda train, above), **Madrid** (12/day, 2.5-3 hours on AVE), **Córdoba** (best option: 6/day on AVANT, 1 hour, €23; also possible for double the price but no faster on AVE: 11/day, 1 hour, €46), **Granada** (4/day, 3.25-5 hours, requires transfer in Bobadilla, Pedrera, or Osuna—bus is better), **Sevilla** (6/day on fast AVANT, 2 hours, €39; or 5/day on slower regional trains, 2.5 hours, €19), **Jerez** (4-5/day, 4.5 hours, transfer in Dos Hermanas), **Barcelona** (2/day on AVE, 5.5 hours, €145, trains leave at 8:20 and 16:50; or 1/day on slow Arco, 13.5 hours, €66). Train info: toll tel. 902-320-320, www.renfe.com.

Between Nerja and Gibraltar

Buses take five hours to make the Nerja–Gibraltar trip, including a transfer in Málaga, where you may have to change bus companies (they leave nearly hourly from Nerja to Málaga). Along the way, buses stop at each of the following towns (see map on page 702).

Fuengirola and Torremolinos—The most built-up part of the region, where those most determined to be envied settle down, is a bizarre world of Scandinavian package tours, flashing lights, pink flamenco, multilingual menus, and all-night happiness. Fuengirola is like a Spanish Mazatlán with a few older, less-pretentious budget hotels between the main drag and the beach. The water here is clean and the nightlife fun and easy. James Michener's idyllic Torremolinos has been strip-malled and parking-metered.

Marbella—This is the most polished and posh town on the Costa del Sol. High-priced boutiques, immaculate streets set with intricate pebble designs, and beautifully landscaped squares testify to Marbella's arrival on the world-class-resort scene. Have a *café con leche* on the beautiful Plaza de Naranjos in the old city's pedestrian section. Wander down to new Marbella and the high-rise beachfront apartment buildings to walk along the wide promenade lined with restaurants. Check out the beach scene. Marbella is an easy stop on the Algeciras–Málaga bus route (as you exit the bus station, take a left to reach the center of town). You can also catch a handy direct bus here from the Málaga airport (20/day, fewer off-season, 45 minutes, www.ctsa-portillo.com).

San Pedro de Alcántara—This town's relatively undeveloped sandy beach is popular with young travelers. San Pedro's neighbor, Puerto Banús, is "where the world casts anchor." This luxurious, Monaco-esque jet-set port, complete with casino, is a strange mix of Rolls-Royces, yuppies, boutiques, rich Arabs, and budget browsers.

Gibraltar

One of the last bits of the empire upon which the sun never set, Gibraltar is a quirky mix of Anglican propriety, "God Save the  Queen" tattoos, English bookstores, military memories, and tourist shops. It's understandably famous for its dramatic Rock of Gibraltar, which rockets improbably into the air from an otherwise flat terrain, dwarfing everything around it. If the Rock didn't exist, some clever military tactician would have tried to build it to keep an eye on the Strait of Gibraltar.

Britain has controlled this highly strategic spit of land since they took it by force in 1704, in the War of Spanish Succession. In 1779, while Britain was preoccupied with its troublesome overseas colonies, Spain (later allied with France) declared war and tried to retake Gibraltar; a series of 14 sieges became a way of life, and the already imposing natural features of the Rock were used for

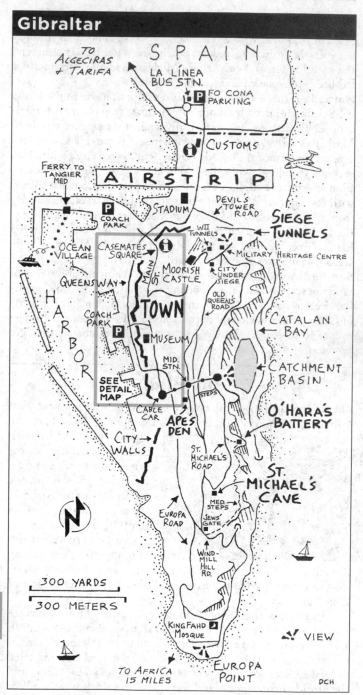

Gibraltar

SPAIN

TO ALGECIRAS + TARIFA

LA LÍNEA BUS STN.

FO CONA PARKING

CUSTOMS

FERRY TO TANGIER MED

AIRSTRIP

DEVIL'S TOWER ROAD

SIEGE TUNNELS

STADIUM

COACH PARK

WII TUNNELS

Military Heritage Centre

OCEAN VILLAGE

CASEMATES SQUARE

CITY UNDER SIEGE

MOORISH CASTLE

QUEENSWAY

MAIN ST.

TOWN

OLD QUEEN'S ROAD

HARBOR

COACH PARK

MUSEUM

CATALAN BAY

CATCHMENT BASIN

MID. STN.

SEE DETAIL MAP

STEPS

O'HARA'S BATTERY

CABLE CAR

APE'S DEN

CITY WALLS

ST. MICHAEL'S ROAD

ST. MICHAEL'S CAVE

MED. STEPS

EUROPA ROAD

JEWS' GATE

N

WIND-MILL HILL RD.

300 YARDS

300 METERS

SPAIN'S SOUTH COAST

KING FAHD MOSQUE

VIEW

TO AFRICA 15 MILES

EUROPA POINT

DCH

defensive purposes. During World War II, the Rock was further fortified and dug through with more and more strategic tunnels. As recently as the mid- to late 20th century, during the Franco period, tensions ran high—and Britain's grasp on the Rock was tenuous.

Strolling Gibraltar, you can see that it was designed as a modern military town (which means it's not particularly charming). But over the last 20 years the economy has gone from one dominated by the military to one based on tourism (as, it seems, happens to many empires). On summer days and weekends, the tiny colony is inundated by holiday-goers, primarily the Spanish (who come here for tax-free cigarettes and booze) and British (who want a change in weather but not in culture). As more and more glitzy high-rise resorts squeeze between the stout fortresses and ramparts—as if trying to create a mini-Monaco—there's a sense that this is a town in transition.

Though it may be hard to imagine a community of 30,000 that feels like its own nation, real Gibraltarians, as you'll learn when you visit, are a proud bunch. They were evacuated during World War II, and it's said that after their return, a national spirit was forged. If you doubt that, be here on Gibraltar's national holiday— September 10—when everyone's decked out in red and white, the national colors.

Gibraltarians have a mixed and interesting heritage. Spaniards call them Llanitos (yah-NEE-tohs), meaning "flat" in Spanish, though the residents live on a rock. The locals—a fun-loving and tolerant mix of British, Spanish, and Moroccan, virtually all of whom speak the Queen's English—call their place "Gib."

From a traveler's perspective, Gibraltar—with its quirky combination of Brits, monkeys, and that breathtaking Rock—is an offbeat detour that adds some variety to a Spanish itinerary. If you're heading to Gibraltar from Spain (as you almost certainly are), be aware most Spaniards still aren't thrilled with this enclave of the Commonwealth on their sunny shores. They basically ignore the place—so, for example, if you're inquiring about bus schedules, don't ask how to get to Gibraltar, but rather to La Línea de la Concepción, the neighboring Spanish town. A passport is required to cross the border (you'll only get a stamp if you need a visa— otherwise, you'll just get a wave-through).

Planning Your Time

Make Gibraltar a day trip (or just one overnight); rooms are expensive compared to Spain.

For the best day trip to Gibraltar, consider this plan: Walk across the border, catch bus #3, and ride it to the end, following my self-guided tour. Ride bus #3 back to the cable-car station, then catch the cable car to the peak for Gibraltar's ultimate top-of-the-rock view. From there, either walk down or take the cable car back into town. From the cable-car station, follow my self-guided town walk all the way to Casemates Square. Spend your remaining free time in town before returning to Spain. Note that, with all the old walls and fortresses, Gibraltar can be tricky to navigate. Ask for directions: Locals speak English.

Tourists who stay overnight find Gibraltar a peaceful place in the evening, when the town can just be itself. No one's in a hurry. Families stroll, kids play, seniors window-shop, and everyone chats...but the food is still pretty bad.

There's no reason to take a ferry from Gibraltar to visit Morocco—for many reasons, it's a better side-trip from Tarifa (specifics covered on page 771).

Orientation to Gibraltar

(tel. code: 350-200)
Gibraltar is a narrow peninsula (three miles by one mile) jutting into the Mediterranean. Virtually the entire peninsula is domi-

nated by the steep-faced Rock itself. The locals live down below in the long, skinny town at the western base of the mountain (much of it on reclaimed land).

For information on all the little differences between Gibraltar and Spain—from area codes to electricity—see "Helpful Hints," later.

Tourist Information

Gibraltar's helpful TI is at Casemates Square, the grand square at the Spain end of town. Pick up a free map and—if it's windy—confirm that the cable car is running (Mon-Fri 9:00-17:30, Sat 10:00-15:00, Sun 10:00-13:00, tel. 74982, www.visitgibraltar.gi). There's also a TI window at the border in the customs building (Mon-Fri 9:00-16:30, closed Sat-Sun).

Arrival in Gibraltar

No matter how you arrive, you'll need your passport to cross the border. These directions will get you as far as the border; from there, see "Getting from the Border into Town," later.

By Bus: Spain's La Línea de la Concepción bus station is a five-minute walk from the Gibraltar border (baggage storage-€3/day; buy a token, or *ficha* from the security guard—if you can't find

Spain vs. Gibraltar

Spain has been annoyed about Gibraltar ever since Great Britain nabbed this prime 2.5-square-mile territory in 1704

(during the War of Spanish Succession) and was granted it through the Treaty of Utrecht in 1713. Although Spain long ago abandoned efforts to reassert its sovereignty by force, it still tries to make Gibraltarians see the error of their British ways. Over the years Spain has limited Gibraltar's air and sea connections, choked traffic at the three-quarter-mile border, and even messed with the local phone system in efforts to convince Britain to give back the Rock. Still, given the choice—which they got in referenda in 1967 and 2002—Gibraltar's residents steadfastly remain Queen Elizabeth's loyal subjects, voting overwhelmingly (99 percent in the last election) to continue as a self-governing British dependency. Gibraltar's governor is popular for dealing forcefully and effectively with Spain on these issues.

him, ask around; station closed, and lockers inaccessible, 22:00-6:00). To reach the border, exit the station and bear left toward the Rock (you can't miss it).

By Car: Customs checks at the border create a bit of a bottleneck for drivers. But at worst there's a 15-minute wait during the morning rush hour into Gibraltar and the evening rush hour back out. Parking in town is free and easy except for weekday working hours, when it's tight and frustrating. It's simpler to park in La Línea (explained below) and just walk across the border.

Freeway signs in Spain say *Algeciras* and *La Línea*, pretending that Gibraltar doesn't exist until you're very close. After taking the La Línea–Gibraltar exit off the main Costa del Sol road, continue as the road curves left (with the Rock to your right). Enter the left-hand lane at the traffic circle before the border and you'll end up in La Línea. The Fo Cona underground parking lot is handy (€1/hour, €6/day, on "20th of April" street). You'll also find blue-lined parking spots in this area (€1/hour from meter, 6-hour limit 9:00-20:00, free before and after that, bring coins, leave ticket on dashboard). From La Línea, it's a five-minute stroll to the border, where you can catch a bus or taxi into town (see "Getting from the Border into Town," below).

If driving into Gibraltar, drive along the sea side of the ramparts (on Queensway—but you'll see no street name). There are big parking lots here and at the cable-car terminal. Parking is generally free—if you can find a spot. By the way, while you'll still find English-style roundabouts, cars here stopped driving on the British side of the road in the 1920s.

Getting from the Border into Town

The "frontier" (as the border is called) is a chaotic hubbub of travel agencies, confused tourists, crafty pickpockets, and duty-free shops (you may see people standing in long lines, waiting to buy cheap cigarettes). The guards barely even look up as you flash your passport. Before exiting the customs building, pick up a map at the TI window on your left (Mon-Fri 9:00-16:30, closed Sat-Sun).

To reach downtown, you can walk (30 minutes), catch a bus (€0.80/£0.60 one-way, runs every 15 minutes), or take a taxi (pricey at €9/£6 to the cable-car station).

To get into town by **foot,** walk straight across the runway (look left, right, and up), then head down Winston Churchill Avenue, angling right at the Shell station on Smith Dorrien Avenue.

Catch either the blue **bus** #3 to Cathedral Square (you can stay on to cable-car station or to continue my self-guided tour—see page 730) or the London-style double-decker bus #10 to Casemates Square (with the TI).

If you plan to join a **taxi tour** up to the Rock (see page 735), note that you can book one right at the border.

Helpful Hints

Gibraltar Isn't Spain: Gibraltar, a British colony, uses different coins, currency (see below), stamps, and phone cards than those used in Spain. Note that British holidays such as the Queen's (official) Birthday (June 11 in 2012) and Bank Holidays (May 7, June 4, and Aug 27 in 2012) are observed, along with local holidays such as Gibraltar's National Day (Sept 10).

Use Pounds, not Euros: Gibraltar uses the British pound sterling (£1 = about $1.60). A pound is broken into 100 pence (abbreviated p). Like other parts of the UK (such as Scotland, Wales, and Northern Ireland), Gibraltar mints its own Gibraltar-specific banknotes and coins featuring local landmarks, people, and historical events—offering a colorful history lesson. Gibraltar's pounds are interchangeable with other British pounds.

Merchants in Gibraltar also accept euros...but at about a 20 percent extra cost to you. Gibraltar is expensive even at fair exchange rates. You'll save money by hitting up an ATM and taking out what you'll need. But before you leave, stop at an exchange desk and change back what you don't spend (at about a 5 percent loss), since Gibraltar currency is hard to change in Spain. (If you'll be making only a few purchases, you can try to avoid this problem by skipping the ATM and buying things with your credit card.) Be aware that if you pay for anything in euros, you may get pounds back in change.

Hours: This may be the United Kingdom, but Gibraltar follows a siesta schedule, with some businesses closing from 13:00 to 15:00 on weekdays, and shutting down at 14:00 on Saturdays until Monday morning.

Electricity: If you have electrical gadgets, note that Gibraltar uses the British three-pronged plugs (not the European two-pronged ones). Your hotel may be able to loan you an adapter.

Telephone: To telephone Gibraltar from anywhere in Europe, dial 00-350-200 and the five-digit local number. To call Gibraltar from the US or Canada, dial 011-350-200-local number.

Internet Access: The **King's Bastion Leisure Centre** has free Wi-Fi, but no terminals (see later). **Café Cyberworld** has several terminals with pricey Internet access (£0.10/minute, £2.50/30 minutes, £4.50/hour, daily 12:00-24:00, Queensway 14, in Ocean Heights Gallery, an arcade 100 yards toward the water from Casemates Square, tel. 51416). There's also Internet access at the cultural center, listed next.

John Mackintosh Cultural Centre: This is your classic British effort to provide a cozy community center. Without a hint of tourism, the upstairs library welcomes drop-ins to enjoy local newspapers and publications, and to check their email (Mon-Fri 9:30-19:30, closed Sat-Sun).

Activities: The recently opened **King's Bastion Leisure Centre** fills an old fortification (the namesake bastion) with a modern entertainment complex. On the ground floor is a huge bowling alley; upstairs are an ice-skating rink and a three-screen cinema (www.leisurecinemas.com). Rounding out the complex are bars, restaurants, discos, and lounges. Many of the activities are geared for families, especially tweens and teens. It's easy to find, just outside Cathedral Square (daily 10:00-24:00, air-con, free Wi-Fi).

Side-Trip to Tangier, Morocco: While a very sporadic ferry does run from Gibraltar directly to Tangier, it's designed for Moroccan workers (returning home to Tangier for the weekend) and doesn't work for a same-day round-trip. Instead, either go via Tarifa (best choice, with direct connections to downtown Tangier—see page 747) or via Algeciras (closer to Gibraltar, but ferries drop you at a port farther from downtown Tangier). Various travel agencies in town sell package tours that include a bus transfer to the boat in Algeciras.

Self-Guided Bus Tour

Gibraltar Town Bus #3 Orientation Tour

Leaving the "frontier," walk straight ahead for 200 yards to the bus stop on the right. Catch bus #3 and enjoy this three-mile orientation ride that takes you from one end of the colony to the other (Mon-Fri 4/hour, Sat-Sun 2-3/hour, buy ticket from driver, ride 20 minutes to the end of the line: Europa Point). Your ticket options: one-way (£0.60/€0.80), round-trip (£0.90/€1.20—get this one if you're riding all the way out to Europa Point, then back into town), or all day (£1.50/€1.90).

This tour will zip you through town, including the touristy areas and some parts of workaday Gibraltar. It goes quickly. Read fast...

Airstrip: You enter Gibraltar by crossing an airstrip. Three or four times a day, the entry road into Gibraltar is closed to allow planes to land or take off. Originally a horse-racing stadium, this area was later filled in with stones excavated from the 30 miles of military tunnels carved into the Rock. This airstrip was a vital lifeline in the days when Spain and Britain were quarreling over Gibraltar (especially 1970-1985) and the border was closed. If you look at the face of the Rock, you can see the tiny windows that were once perches from where big cannons could fire. Behind them lie siege tunnels, open as a tourist attraction (described later in this chapter).

Moorish Castle: Just after the airstrip, at the first roundabout, the bus passes a road leading left (which heads clockwise around the Rock to the town of Catalan Bay, peaceful beaches, and the huge mountainside rainwater-catchment wall). The Moorish Castle above dates back over a thousand years. On the right is land reclaimed in 1989, filled mostly with government-subsidized apartments.

Ramparts: You'll cross the bridge and drive onto the ramparts. Water once came all the way up to the ramparts—50 percent of the city is on reclaimed land. Gibraltar's heritage shows in the architecture: tiles (Portuguese), shutters (Genoese Italian), and wrought iron (Georgian English).

On the right after the next stop you'll see World War memorials. The first is the American War Memorial (the building-like structure with a gold plaque and arch), built in 1932 to commemorate American sailors based here in World War I. Farther along you'll see 18th-century cannons and a memorial to Gibraltarians who died in World War II.

Downtown: The following sights come up quickly: Passing the NatWest House office tower on the left, you'll immediately see a **synagogue** (only the top peeks out above a wall; the wooden doors in the wall bear the Star of David). In the 19th century, half of Gibraltar was Jewish. The Jewish community now numbers 600. Just after the synagogue is little **Cathedral Square,** with a playground, TI, and the Moorish-looking Anglican cathedral (behind the playground). Gibraltar is the European headquarters of the Anglican Church. Now you'll pass a long wall; most of it is the back of the Governor's Residence (a.k.a. The Convent).

Charles V Wall: The next bus stop is at the old Charles V wall, built in response to a 1552 raid in which the pirate Barbarossa captured 70 Gibraltarians into slavery. Notice the classic red telephone box near the bus stop. Immediately after you pass under the wall you'll see a green park on your left that contains the **Trafalgar cemetery.** Buried here are some British sailors who died defeating the French off the coast of Spain's Cape Trafalgar in 1805.

Cable-Car Lift and Botanical Gardens: The next stop is at the big parking lot for the cable car to the top of the Rock, as well as for the botanical gardens (free, daily 8:00-sunset), located at the base of the lift. You can get off to do this now—or finish the tour and come back here later, on the way back into town.

Out of Town: Heading uphill out of town, your best views are on the right. It's believed that the body of Admiral Nelson was pickled in a barrel of spirits in a harbor just below you after his victorious (yet fatal) Battle of Trafalgar. After riding through nondescript residential neighborhoods for several minutes, you'll go by the big former naval hospital and barracks. Reaching the end of the Rock, you'll pass modern apartments and the mosque.

King Fahd Mosque: This $20 million gift from the Saudi sultan was completed in 1997, and Gibraltar's 900 Muslims worship here each Friday. Five times a day—as across the strait in Morocco—an imam sings the call to prayer.

Europa Point: The lighthouse marks windy Europa Point—the end of the line. Buses retrace the route you just traveled, departing about every 15 minutes (every 20-30 minutes on weekends). This whole area is slated for a huge beautification project, so you may see lots of construction. Europa Point, up the mound from the bus stop and tourist shop (on right), is an observation post. A plaque here identifies the mountains of Morocco 15 miles across the strait. The glow of the lighthouse (150 feet tall, from 1841, closed to visitors) can be seen from Morocco. The playground is a favorite for local kids.

Your tour is finished. Enjoy the views before catching a bus back into town (departs from where you got off). Hop off at the cable-car station to ride to the top of the Rock, tour the botanical gardens, or begin the town walk described next.

Self-Guided Walk

Welcome to Gibraltar

Gibraltar town is long and skinny, with one main street (called Main Street). Stroll the length of it from the cable-car station to Casemates Square, following this little tour. A good British pub and a room-temperature pint of beer await you at the end.

From the cable-car terminal, turn right (as you face the sea) and head into town. Soon you'll come to the **Trafalgar cemetery,** a reminder of the colony's English military heritage. Next you come to the **Charles V wall**—a reminder of its Spanish military heritage—built in 1552 by the Spanish to defend against marauding pirates. Gibraltar was controlled by Moors (711-1462), Spain (1462-1704), and then the British (since 1704). Passing through the Southport Gates, you'll see one of the many red history plaques posted about town.

Heading into town, you pass the tax office, then the **John Mackintosh Cultural Centre,** which has Internet access and a copy of today's *Gibraltar Chronicle* upstairs in its library. The *Chronicle* comes out Monday through Friday and has covered the local news since 1801. The Methodist church sponsors the cheap and cheery **Carpenter's Arms** tearoom just above one of several fish-and-chips joints (rare in Iberia).

The pedestrian portion of Main Street begins near the **Governor's Residence.** The British governor of Gibraltar took over a Franciscan convent, hence the name of the local white house: The Convent. The **Convent Guard Room,** facing the Governor's Residence, is good for photos.

Gibraltar's courthouse stands behind a **small tropical garden,** where John and Yoko got married back in 1969 (as the ballad goes, they "got married in Gibraltar near Spain"). Sean Connery did, too. Actually, many Brits like to get married here because weddings are cheap, fast (only 48 hours' notice required), and legally recognized as British.

Main Street now becomes a **shopping drag.** You'll notice lots of colorful price tags advertising tax-free booze, cigarettes, and sugar (highly taxed in Spain). Lladró porcelain, while made in Valencia, is popular here

Gibraltar Town

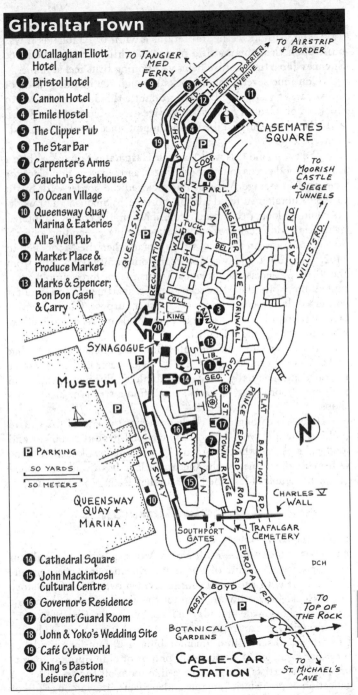

1. O'Callaghan Eliott Hotel
2. Bristol Hotel
3. Cannon Hotel
4. Emile Hostel
5. The Clipper Pub
6. The Star Bar
7. Carpenter's Arms
8. Gaucho's Steakhouse
9. To Ocean Village
10. Queensway Quay Marina & Eateries
11. All's Well Pub
12. Market Place & Produce Market
13. Marks & Spencer; Bon Bon Cash & Carry

14. Cathedral Square
15. John Mackintosh Cultural Centre
16. Governor's Residence
17. Convent Guard Room
18. John & Yoko's Wedding Site
19. Café Cyberworld
20. King's Bastion Leisure Centre

TO TANGIER MED FERRY

TO AIRSTRIP & BORDER

SMITH DORRIEN AVENUE

CASEMATES SQUARE

TO MOORISH CASTLE & SIEGE TUNNELS

FISH MKT. RD.

FISH MKT. ROAD

COOP.

PARL.

TOWN

QUEENSWAY

RECLAMATION RD.

LINE WALL RD.

IRISH TOWN

ENGINEER LANE

MAIN

BELL LANE

CORNWALL

CASTLE RD.

WILLIS'S RD.

COLL

KING

CANNON

SYNAGOGUE

MUSEUM

KING STREET

LIB.

GOV.

GEO.

ST.

PRINCE EDWARD'S ROAD

FLAT BASTION RD.

P Parking

50 YARDS
50 METERS

QUEENSWAY

MAIN

TOWN RANGE

CHARLES V WALL

QUEENSWAY QUAY & MARINA

SOUTHPORT GATES

TRAFALGAR CEMETERY

DCH

EUROPA RD.

BOYD

ROSIA

BOTANICAL GARDENS

CABLE-CAR STATION

TO TOP OF THE ROCK

TO ST. MICHAEL'S CAVE

SPAIN'S SOUTH COAST

(because it's sold without the hefty Spanish VAT—Value-Added Tax). The Catholic cathedral retains a whiff of Arabia (as it was built upon the remains of a mosque), while the big **Marks & Spencer department store** helps vacationing Brits feel at home.

Continue several more blocks through the bustling heart of Gibraltar. If you enjoy British products, this is your chance to stock up on Cadbury chocolates, digestive biscuits, wine gums, and Weetabix—but you'll pay a premium, since it's all "imported" from the UK.

The town (and this walk) ends at **Casemates Square.** While a lowbrow food circus today, it originated as a barracks and place for ammunition storage. When Franco closed the border with Spain in 1969, Gibraltar suffered a labor shortage, as Spanish guest workers could no longer commute into Gibraltar. The colony countered by inviting Moroccan workers to take their place—ending a nearly 500-year Moroccan absence, which began when the Moors fled in 1462. As a result, today's Moroccan community dates only from the 1970s. Whereas the previous Spanish labor force simply commuted into work, the Moroccans needed apartments, so Gibraltar converted the Casemates barracks for that purpose. Cheap Spanish labor has crept back in, causing many locals to resent store clerks who can't speak proper English.

At the far end of Casemates Square is a crystal shop that makes its own crystal right there (you can watch). They claim it's the only thing actually "made in Gibraltar." But just upstairs, on the upper floor of the barracks, you'll find a string of local crafts shops.

If you go through the triple arches at the end of the square (behind the TI), you'll reach the covered **produce market** and food stalls. Across the busy road a few minutes' walk farther is the well-marked entrance to the **Ocean Village** boardwalk and entertainment complex (described later, under "Eating in Gibraltar.")

Sights in Gibraltar

In Gibraltar Town

▲**Gibraltar Museum**—Built atop a Moorish bath, this museum tells the story of a chunk of land that has been fought over for centuries. Start with the fine 15-minute video overview of the story of the Rock—a worthwhile prep for the artifacts (such as ancient Roman anchors made of lead) you'll see in the museum. Then wander through the scant remains of the 14th-century Moorish baths. Upstairs you'll see military memorabilia, a 15-foot-long model of the Rock, wonderful century-old photos of old Gibraltar, paintings by local artists, and, in a cave-like room off the art gallery, a collection of prehistoric remains and artifacts. The famous skull of a Neanderthal woman found in Forbes' Quarry is a copy (the original is in the British Museum in London). Found in Gibraltar in 1848, this was the first Neanderthal skull ever discovered. No one realized its significance until a similar skull found years later in Germany's Neanderthal Valley was correctly identified—stealing the name, claim, and fame from Gibraltar (£2, Mon-Fri 10:00-18:00, Sat 10:00-14:00, last entry 30 minutes before closing, closed Sun, no photos, on Bomb House Lane near the cathedral).

Up on the Rock

The actual Rock of Gibraltar is the colony's best sight. Its attractions: the stupendous view from the very top, quirky apes, a hokey cave (St. Michael's), and the impressive Siege Tunnels drilled through the rock face for military purposes. Frankly, the sights that charge admission aren't that exciting; the Rock's best attractions—enjoying views from the top and seeing the monkeys—are free. Hikers can ride the lift up and take a long, steep, scenic walk down, connecting the various sights by strolling along paved military lanes.

Cost: There's a £0.50 fee to enter the grounds of the Rock, technically called the "Upper Rock Nature Reserve"—that's just to walk around and enjoy the views and the monkeys. A £10 ticket is required to visit any or all of these major sights within the reserve: St. Michael's Cave, Siege Tunnels, Moorish Castle, Military Heritage Centre, and City Under Siege exhibit (includes the £0.50 nature-reserve entrance fee). If you take a taxi tour, entry to the nature reserve and sights is included; if you ride the cable car, the nature-reserve entry fee is included, but you'll have to buy the £10 ticket to go in the sights. (Both options are explained below).

Hours: Daily 9:30-19:15, until 18:15 late Oct-late March, last entry 30 minutes before closing.

Additional Sights at the Rock: Two sights at the Rock are not part of the official reserve ticket, and have their own separate tickets and hours: O'Hara's Battery and the World War II Tunnels (both described later).

Visiting the Rock: You have two options for touring the Rock: Take a 1.5-hour taxi tour (£22/person) or ride the cable car (£9 round-trip; or £7.50 one-way plus £10 to see the sights as you hike back down).

The **taxi tour** includes entry to St. Michael's Cave and the Siege Tunnels, a couple of extra stops, and the running commentary of your licensed cabbie/guide. Because the cable car doesn't get you very close to the cave and tunnels (and doesn't cover cave and tunnel admission), take the taxi tour if you'll be visiting these sights and don't want to walk. On the other hand, the **cable car** takes you to the very top of the Rock (which the taxi tours don't).

You can still see the sights, but you'll have to pay £10 and connect them by foot (not a bad thing—it's a pleasant walk down).

There's certainly no reason to take a big-bus tour (advertised and sold all over town) considering how fun and easy the taxi tours are. Private cars are not allowed high on the Rock.

Here are more details on each option:

Taxi Tours: Minibuses driven by cabbies trained and licensed to lead these little trips are standing by at the border and at various points in town (including Cathedral Square, John Mackintosh Square, Casemates Square, and Trafalgar Cemetery near the cable-car station). They charge £22/person (4-person minimum, or £65 for only 2 people in one taxi, includes £10 reserve sights ticket, tel. 70027). Taxi tours and big buses

do the same 1.5-hour loop tour with four stops: a Mediterranean viewpoint (called the Pillar of Hercules), St. Michael's Cave (15-minute visit), a viewpoint near the top of the Rock where you can get up close to the monkeys, and the Siege Tunnels (20-minute visit). Buddy up with other travelers and share the cost.

Cable Car to the Summit: A dizzying array of colorfully named combo-tickets are offered for the cable car and its partner attractions. The only ones worth considering are the "Skyline Supreme" (just a ticket for the cable car: £7.50 one-way, £9 round-trip) and the "SkyWalk Combo" (combining the cable car and the £10 reserve sights ticket—this doesn't save any money over buying the tickets separately, and only makes sense one-way—£17.50). The cable car runs every 10-15 minutes (daily from 9:30, last ascent at 19:15, last descent at 19:45), or continuously in busy times. Lines can be long if a cruise ship is in town. The cable car won't run if it's windy or rainy; if the weather is questionable, ask at the TI before heading to the station. The cable-car ride includes a hand-held audio/videoguide that explains what you're seeing from the spectacular viewpoints (pick it up at the well-marked booth when you disembark at the top, must leave ID as a deposit). In the winter (Oct-March), the cable car stops halfway down for those who want to get out, gawk at the monkeys, and take a later car down—but you'll probably see monkeys at the top anyway.

To take in all of the sights, you'll need to **hike down,** rather than taking the cable car back (be sure to specify you want a one-way ticket up). Simply hiking down without visiting the sights is enjoyable, too. Approximate hiking times: from the top of the cable car to St. Michael's Cave—25 minutes; from the cave to the Apes' Den—20 minutes; from the Apes' Den to the Siege Tunnels—30 minutes; from the tunnels back into town, passing the Moorish Castle—20 minutes. Total from top to bottom: about 1.5 hours (on paved roads with almost no traffic), not including sightseeing. For hikers, I've connected the dots with directions below.

▲▲▲**The Summit of the Rock**—The cable car takes you to the real highlight of Gibraltar: the summit of the spectacular Rock itself. (Taxi tours don't go here; they stop on a ridge below the summit, where you enjoy a commanding view—but one that's nowhere near as good.) The limestone massif, or large rock mass, is nearly a mile long, rising 1,400 feet high with very sheer faces. According to legend, this was one of the Pillars of Hercules (paired with Djebel Musa, another mountain across the strait in Morocco), marking the edge of the known world in ancient times. Local guides say that these pillars are the only places on the planet where you can see two seas and two continents at the same time.

In A.D. 711, the Muslim chieftain Tarik ibn Ziyad crossed over from Africa and landed on the Rock, beginning the Moorish conquest of Spain and naming the Rock after himself—Djebel-Tarik ("Rock of Tarik"), which became "Gibraltar."

At the top of the Rock (the cable-car terminal) there's a view terrace and a restaurant. From here you can explore old ramparts and drool at the 360-degree view of Morocco (including the Rif Mountains and Djebel Musa), the Strait of Gibraltar, the bay stretching west toward Algeciras, and the twinkling Costa del Sol arcing eastward. The views are especially crisp on brisk off-season days. Below you (to the east) stretches the giant catchment system that the British built to collect rainwater in the not-so-distant past, when Spain allowed neither water nor tourists to cross its disputed border. Broad sheets catch the rain, sending it through channels to reservoirs located inside the rock.

• *Up at the summit, you'll likely see some of the famed...*

▲▲**Apes of Gibraltar**—The Rock is home to about 200 "apes" (actually, tailless Barbary macaques—a type of monkey). Taxi tours come with great monkey fun, but if you're on your own, you'll probably see them at the top and at various points on the walk back down (basically, the monkeys congregate anywhere that tourists do—hoping to get food). The males are bigger, females have beards, and newborns are black. They live about 15-20 years. Legend has it that as long as the monkeys remain here, so will the Brits. (According to a plausible local legend, when word came a few decades back that the ape population was waning, Winston

Churchill made a point to import reinforcements.) Keep your distance from the monkeys. (Guides say that for safety reasons, "They can touch you, but you can't touch them." And while guides feed them, you shouldn't—it disrupts their diet.) Beware of the monkeys' kleptomaniac tendencies; they'll ignore the peanut in your hand and claw after the full bag in your pocket. Because the monkeys associate plastic bags with food, keep your bag close to your body: Tourists who wander by absent-mindedly, loosely clutching a bag, are apt to have it stolen by a purse-snatching simian. If there's no ape action, wait for a banana-toting taxi tour to stop by and stir some up. Guides love to get the monkeys to actually climb onto the backs and shoulders of their tour members—always a crowd-pleaser.

• *If you're hiking down, you'll find that your options are clearly marked at most forks. I'll narrate the longest route down, which passes all of the sights en route.*

From the top cable-car station, exit and head downhill on the well-paved path (toward Africa). You'll pass the viewpoint for taxi tours (with monkeys hanging around, waiting for tour groups to come feed them), pass under a ruined observation tower, and eventually reach a wide part of the road. Most will want to continue to St. Michael's Cave (skip down to that section), but you also have an opportunity to hike (or ride a shuttle bus) steeply up to...

O'Hara's Battery—At 1,400 feet, this is the actual highest point on the Rock. A massive 9.2-inch gun sits on the summit, where a Moorish lookout post once stood. The battery was built after World War I, and the last test shot was fired in 1974. Locals are glad it's been mothballed—during test firings, they had to open their windows, which might otherwise have shattered from the pressurized air blasted from this gun. The battery was recently opened to the public; you can go inside to see not only the gun, but also the powerful engines underneath that were used to move and aim it. The iron rings you see every 30 yards or so along the military lanes around the Rock once anchored pulleys used to haul up guns like the huge one at O'Hara's Battery (£3.50, not covered by reserve sights ticket, shuttle runs up when open, Mon-Fri 10:30-17:00, closed Sat-Sun).

• *From the crossroads below O'Hara's Battery, taking the right (downhill) fork leads you down to a restaurant and shop, then the entrance to...*

▲**St. Michael's Cave**—Studded with stalagmites and stalactites, eerily lit, and echoing with classical music, this cave is dramatic, corny, and slippery when wet. Considered a one-star sight since Neolithic times, these caves were alluded to in ancient Greek legends—when the caves were believed to be the Gates of Hades (or the entrance of a tunnel to Africa). All taxi tours stop here (entry included in cost of taxi tour). This sight requires a long walk for cable-car riders (who must have the £10 reserve sights ticket to enter; same hours as other reserve sights). Walking through takes about 15 minutes; you'll pop out at the gift shop.

• *From here, most will head down to the Apes' Den (see next paragraph), but serious hikers have the opportunity to curl around to Jews' Gate at the tip of the Rock, then circle around the back of the Rock on the strenuous* **Mediterranean Steps** *(leading back up to O'Hara's Battery). To do this, turn sharply left after St. Michael's Cave and head for Jews' Gate. Since it's on the opposite side from the town, it's the closest thing in Gibraltar to "wilderness." If this challenging 1.5-to-2-hour hike sounds enjoyable, ask for details at the TI.*

The more standard route is to continue downhill. At the three-way fork, you can take either the middle fork (more level) or the left fork (hillier, but you'll see monkeys at the Apes' Den) to the Siege Tunnels. The **Apes' Den**, *at the middle station for the cable car, is a scenic terrace where monkeys tend to gather, and where taxi tours stop to do some monkeying around.*

Continue on either fork (they converge), following signs for Siege Tunnels, *for about 30 more minutes. Eventually you'll reach a terrace with three flags (from highest to lowest: United Kingdom, Gibraltar, EU) and a fantastic view of Gibraltar's airport, "frontier" with Spain, and the Spanish city of La Línea de la Concepción. From here, the Military Heritage Centre is beneath your feet (described later), and it's a short but steep hike up to the...*

▲**Siege Tunnels**—Also called the Upper Galleries, these chilly

tunnels were blasted out of the rock by the Brits during the Great Siege by Spanish and French forces (1779-1783). The clever British, safe inside the Rock, wanted to chip and dig to a highly strategic outcrop called "The Notch," ideal for mounting a big gun. After blasting out some ventilation holes for the miners, they had an even better idea: Use gunpowder to carve out a whole network of tunnels with shafts that would be ideal for aiming artillery. Eventually they excavated "St. George's Hall," a huge cavern that housed seven guns. These were the first tunnels inside the Rock; more than a century and a half later, during World War II, 30 more miles of tunnels were blasted out. Hokey but fun dioramas help recapture a time when Brits were known more for conquests than for crumpets. All taxi tours stop here (entry included in cost of taxi tour); hikers must have or buy the £10 reserve sights ticket to enter (same hours as other reserve sights).

• *Hiding out in the bunker below the three flags (go down the stairs and open the heavy metal door—it's unlocked) is the...*

Military Heritage Centre—This small one-room collection features old military photographs from Gibraltar. The second room features a poignant memorial to the people who "have made the supreme sacrifice in defence of Gibraltar" (covered by £10 reserve sights ticket—but tickets rarely checked, same hours as other reserve sights).

• *From here, the road switchbacks down into town. At each bend in the road you'll find one of the next three sights.*

City Under Siege—This hokey exhibit is worth a quick walkthrough if you've been fascinated by all this Gibraltar military history. Displayed in some of the first British structures built on Gibraltar soil, it re-creates the days of the Great Siege, which lasted for more than three and a half years (1779-1783)—one of 14 sieges that attempted but failed to drive the Brits off the Rock. With evocative descriptions, some original "graffiti" scratched into the wall by besieged Gibraltarians, and some borderline-hokey dioramas, the exhibit explains what it was like to live on the Rock, cut off from the outside world, during those challenging times (covered by £10 reserve sights ticket—but tickets rarely checked, same hours as other reserve sights).

World War II Tunnels—This privately run operation takes you through some of the tunnels carved out of the Rock during a much later conflict than the others described here. You'll emerge back up at the Military Heritage Centre (£8, not covered by reserve sights ticket, Mon-Sat 10:00-17:00, closed Sun).

Moorish Castle—Actually more a tower than a castle, this recently restored building is basically an empty shell. (In the interest of political correctness, the tourist board recently tried to change the name to "Medieval Castle"...but it *is* Moorish, so the name didn't stick.) It was constructed on top of the original castle built in A.D. 711 by the Moor Tarik ibn Ziyad, who gave his name to Gibraltar.

• *The tower marks the end of the Upper Rock Nature Reserve. Heading downhill, you begin to enter the upper part of modern Gibraltar. While you could keep on twisting down the road, keep an eye out for staircase shortcuts into town (most direct are the well-marked Castle Steps).*

Nightlife in Gibraltar

If you're coming from the late-night bustle of Spain, where you'll see young parents out strolling with their toddlers at midnight, you'll find Gibraltar extremely quiet after-hours. Main Street is completely dead (with the exception of a few lively pubs, mostly a block or two off the main drag). Head instead to the Ocean Village complex, a five-minute walk from Casemates Square, where the boardwalk is lined with bars, restaurants, and a casino. Another waterfront locale—a bit more sedate—is the Queensway Quay Marina. (Both areas are described later, under "Eating in Gibraltar.") Kids love the King's Bastion Leisure Centre (described earlier, under "Helpful Hints").

Some pubs, lounges, and discos—especially on Casemates Square—offer live music (look around for signs, or ask at the TI). O'Callaghan Eliott Hotel hosts free live jazz on Thursday evenings.

Sleeping in Gibraltar

Gibraltar is not a good value for accommodations. There are only a handful of hotels and (disappointingly) no British-style B&Bs. As a general rule, the beds are either bad or overpriced. Remember, you'll pay a 20 percent premium if paying with euros—pay with local cash or your credit card.

$$$ O'Callaghan Eliott Hotel, with four stars, boasts a roof-top pool with a view, a fine restaurant, bar, terrace, inviting sit-a-bit public spaces, and 121 modern, mildly stylish business-class

Sleep Code

(£1 = about $1.60, tel. code: 350-200)
S = Single, **D** = Double/Twin, **T** = Triple, **Q** = Quad, **b** = bathroom, **s** = shower only. All of these places accept credit cards, and their staffs speak English.

To help you easily sort through these listings, I've divided the accommodations into three categories, based on the price for a standard double room with bath during high season:

  $$$ Higher Priced—Most rooms £75 or more.
   $$ Moderately Priced—Most rooms between £35-75.
    $ Lower Priced—Go back to Spain.

Prices can change without notice; verify the hotel's current rates online or by email. For other updates, see www.ricksteves.com/update.

rooms—all with balconies (sky-high rack rates of Db-£240-270, but often around Db-£100 with Web booking for non-peak days, breakfast-£14, non-smoking, air-con, elevator, pay Wi-Fi, free parking, centrally located at Governor's Parade 2, up Library Street from main drag, tel. 70500, fax 70243, www.ocallaghan hotels.com, eliott@ocallaghanhotels.com).

$$$ Bristol Hotel offers 60 basic, slightly worn English rooms in the heart of Gibraltar (Sb-£63-68, Db-£81-87, Tb-£93-99, higher prices for exterior rooms, breakfast-£5, air-con, elevator, free Wi-Fi in lobby, swimming pool, limited free parking—first come, first served, Cathedral Square 10, tel. 76800, fax 77613, www.bristolhotel.gi, reservations@bristolhotel.gi).

$$ Cannon Hotel is a run-down dive. But it's also well-located and friendly and has the only cheap hotel rooms in town. Its 18 rooms (most with wobbly cots and no private bathrooms) look treacherously down on a little patio (S-£30, D-£42, Db-£53, T-£52.50, Tb-£60, includes full English breakfast, free Wi-Fi, behind cathedral at Cannon Lane 9, tel. 51711, fax 51789, www .cannonhotel.gi, cannon@sapphirenet.gi).

$ Emile Hostel, simple and the cheapest place in town, welcomes people of any age (42 beds, bunk in 6-bed dorm-£17, S-£25, D-£40, à la carte breakfast—full English is £3.50, cash only, free Wi-Fi, on Montagu Bastion diagonally across the street from Shell station, ramped entrance on Line Wall Road, tel. & fax 51106, www.emilehostel.net, emilehostel@yahoo.co.uk).

Eating in Gibraltar

Take a break from *jamón* and sample some English pub grub: fish-and-chips, meat pies, jacket potatoes (baked potatoes with fillings), or a good old greasy English breakfast. English-style beers include chilled lagers and room-temperature ales, bitters, and stouts. In general, the farther you venture away from Main Street, the cheaper and more local the places become. Since budget-priced English food isn't exactly high cuisine, the best plan may be to stroll the streets and look for the pub with the ambience you like best (various options: lots of chatting, sports fans riveted to a football match, noisy casino machines, or whatever). I've listed a few of my favorites below. Or venture to one of Gibraltar's more upscale recent developments at either end of the old town: Ocean Village or Queensway Quay.

If you're bothered by smoke, be aware that Gibraltar (unlike

Britain and Spain) has not imposed a smoking ban—so many places can still be smoky.

Downtown, Near Main Street

The Clipper, my favorite pub for dinner, offers filling £7 meals and Murphy's stout on tap (English breakfast-£5, Mon-Sat 9:30-22:00, Sun 13:00-22:00, on Irish Town Lane, tel. 79791).

The Star Bar, which brags that it's "Gibraltar's Oldest Bar," is on a quiet street with a pubby interior and good £6-9 plates (daily 7:00-24:00, food served till 22:00, on Parliament Lane off Main Street, across from Corner House Restaurant, tel. 75924).

Carpenter's Arms is a fast, cheap-and-cheery café run by the Methodist church, serving £3 meals with a missionary's smile. It's upstairs in the Methodist church on Main Street (Mon-Fri 9:00-14:00, closed Sat-Sun and Aug, volunteer-run, 100 yards past the Governor's Residence at 297 Main Street).

Gaucho's is a classy, atmospheric steakhouse actually inside the casemates, just outside Casemates Square (£5 salads, £5-6 starters, £16-22 steaks, daily 12:00-15:00 & 19:00-23:00, Waterport Casemates, tel. 59700).

Casemates Square Food Circus: The big square at the entrance of Gibraltar contains a variety of restaurants, ranging from fast food (fish-and-chips joint, Burger King, and Pizza Hut) to inviting pubs spilling out onto the square. The **All's Well** pub serves £8-10 meals (Moroccan *tajine,* salads, burgers, fish-and-chips, and more) and offers pleasant tables with umbrellas under leafy trees (daily 10:00-19:00). Fruit stands and cheap take-out food stalls bustle just outside the entry to the square at the **Market Place** (Mon-Sat 9:00-15:00, closed Sun).

Groceries: The **Bon Bon Cash & Carry** minimarket is on the main drag, off Cathedral Square (daily 9:30-19:00, Main Street 239). Nearby, **Marks & Spencer** has a small food market on the ground floor, with pre-made meals and fresh-baked cookies (Mon-Thu 9:00-19:00, Fri 11:00-18:00, Sat 9:30-17:00, closed Sun).

Ocean Village

This brand-new development is the best place to get a look at

the bold new face of Gibraltar. Formerly a dumpy port, it's been turned into a swanky marina fronted by glassy high-rise condo buildings. The boardwalk arcing around the marina is packed with shops, restaurants, and bars—Indian, Mexican, sports bar, pizza parlor, Irish pub, fast food, wine bar, and more. Anchoring the development is Gibraltar's casino. While the whole thing can feel a bit corporate, it offers an enjoyable 21st-century contrast to the "English village" vibe of Main Street (which can be extremely sleepy after-hours).

Queensway Quay Marina

To dine in yacht-club ambience, stroll the marina and choose from a string of restaurants serving the boat-owning crowd. When the sun sets, the quay-side tables at each of these places are prime dining real estate. **Waterfront Restaurant** has a lounge-lizard interior and great marina-side tables outside (£5-7 starters, £10-16 main dishes, daily specials, Indian, and classic British; daily 9:00-24:00, last orders 22:45, tel. 45666). Other options include Indian, Italian, trendy lounges, and (oh, yeah) Spanish.

Gibraltar Connections

By Bus

Bus travelers walk five minutes from Gibraltar's border into Spain to reach La Línea de la Concepción, the nearest bus station (tel. 902-199-208 or 956-172-396). The nearest train station is at Algeciras, which is the region's main transportation hub (for Algeciras connections, see page 759).

From La Línea de la Concepción by Bus to: **Algeciras** (2/ hour, less on weekends, 45 minutes, can buy €2.10 ticket on bus), **Tarifa** (6/day direct, 1 hour; more possible with change in Algeciras, 1.5 hours), **Málaga** (5/day, 3 hours), **Ronda** (no direct bus, transfer in Algeciras; Algeciras to Ronda: 3-4/day, 2 hours), **Granada** (1/day, 5.25 hours), **Sevilla** (4/day, 4-4.5 hours), **Jerez** (1/day, 3 hours), **Córdoba** (1/day, 5.25 hours), **Madrid** (1/day, 8 hours).

By Plane

From Gibraltar, you can fly to various points in Britain: British Airways flies to London Heathrow (www.ba.com); easyJet connects to London Gatwick and Liverpool (www.easyjet.com); and Monarch Airlines goes to London Luton and Manchester (www.flymonarch.com). The airport is easy to reach; after all, you can't enter town without crossing its runway, one way or another.

Tarifa

Mainland Europe's southernmost town is whitewashed and Arab-feeling, with a lovely beach, an old castle, restaurants swimming  in fresh seafood, inexpensive places to sleep, enough windsurfers to sink a ship, and, best of all, hassle-free boats to Morocco.

As I stood on Tarifa's town promenade under the castle, looking out at almost-touchable Morocco across the Strait of Gibraltar, my only regret was that I didn't have this book to steer me clear of gritty Algeciras on earlier trips. Tarifa, with hourly 35-minute boat transfers to Tangier, is the best jumping-off point for a Moroccan side-trip, as its ferry route goes directly to Tangier's city-center Medina Port—for details, see the Tangier chapter. The other routes, from Algeciras and Gibraltar, take you to the Tangier MED Port, 25 miles east of Tangier city. (It's possible that in the future Tarifa boats may also be steered to the MED Port—but even if this happens, Tarifa is still a much more appealing home base than Algeciras.)

Tarifa has no blockbuster sights (and can be quiet off-season), but it's a town where you just feel good to be on vacation. Don't expect a snazzy Riviera-style beach resort, à la Nerja. Tarifa is a functional, dreary-in-parts port city with an atmospheric old town and a long, broad stretch of relatively undeveloped but wildly popular sandy beach. The town is a hip and breezy mecca among windsurfers, drawn here by the strong winds created by the bottleneck at the Strait of Gibraltar. Tarifa is mobbed with young German and French adventure-seekers in July and August. This crowd from all over Europe (and beyond) makes Tarifa one of Spain's trendiest-feeling towns. It has far more artsy boutique hotels than most Spanish towns its size, and its restaurant offerings are atypically eclectic for normally same-Jane Spain—you'll see vegetarian and organic, Italian and Indian, gourmet burgers and tea houses, and on each corner, it seems, there's a stylish bar-lounge with techno music, mood lighting, and youthful Europeans just hanging out.

Orientation to Tarifa

The old town, surrounded by a wall, slopes gently up from the water's edge (and the port to Tangier). The modern section stretches farther inland from Tarifa's fortified gate.

Tourist Information

The TI is on Paseo de la Alameda (Mon-Fri 9:30-13:30 & 16:00-18:00, Sat-Sun 9:30-13:30; hours may be slightly longer in summer, or slightly shorter on slow or bad-weather days, tel. 956-680-993, www.aytotarifa.com, turismo@aytotarifa.com).

Experiencia Tarifa: This organization, run by can-do Quino of the recommended Hostal Alborada, produces a good free magazine and town map featuring hotels, restaurants, and a wide array of activities (also online at www.experienciatarifa.com).

Arrival in Tarifa

By Bus: The bus station (actually a couple of portable buildings with an outdoor sitting area) is on Batalla del Salado, about a five-minute walk from the old town. (The more central TI also has bus schedules.) Buy tickets directly from the driver if the ticket booth is closed (Mon-Fri 7:30-9:30 & 10:00-11:00 & 14:30-18:30, Sat-Sun 15:00-19:30, hours vary slightly depending on season, tel. 956-684-038, toll tel. 902-199-208). To reach the old town, walk away from the wind turbines perched on the mountain ridge.

By Car: If you're staying in the center of town, follow signs for *Alameda* or *Puerto*, and continue along Avenida de Andalucía. Follow signs to make an obligatory loop to the port entrance, then swing right and park for free in the lot at the far end of Calle Juan Núñez (on the harbor, at the base of the castle). During the busiest summer months (July-Aug), this parking lot can fill up, in which case you'll need to use one of the pay lots on either side of the old-town wall (to the west, just off of Avenida de la Constitución on Calle Joaquín Tena Artigas; or to the east, off of Camino del Olivar). Or you can try finding street parking, which is most abundant in the new town just north of the old-town walls. Blue lines indicate paid parking, and yellow lines are no-parking areas.

Helpful Hints

Internet Access: Pandor@, in the heart of the old town, has 16 computers across from Café Central, near the church (€2.50/1 hour, generally daily in summer 10:00-23:00, in winter 10:00-14:30 & 16:30-21:30, tel. 956-680-816).

Ferry Tickets: You can buy Morocco ferry tickets right at the port, but if you want to avoid that short walk, FRS (the more established of the two ferry companies) also has an office just outside the old-town wall, at the corner of Avenida de Andalucía and Avenida de la Constitución. You can buy tickets or book a seat on one of their tours here (Mon-Fri 8:00-21:00, Sat 8:00-15:00, closed Sun, tel. 956-684-847,

Side-Tripping to Morocco

Tangier, worth ▲▲, is the main reason to go to Tarifa. The ride on fast, modern catamarans (huge car ferries that zip over every hour all year long) takes less than an hour and drops you off in the city center (unlike boats from Algeciras and Gibraltar that dock at the Tangier MED Port, about 25 miles from downtown Tangier). You walk from the Tangier port into a remarkable city—the fifth-largest in Morocco—which is no longer the Tijuana of Africa, but a booming town enjoying the enthusiastic support and can-do vision of a new and activist king.

Most tourists do the mindless belly-dancing-and-shopping excursion (which costs about €60 including the ferry ride—actually cheaper than the round-trip ferry ride sans tour). They're met by a guide, taken on a bus tour and a walk through the old-town market, offered a couple of crass Kodak moments with snake charmers and desert dancers, and given lunch with live music and belly-dancing. Then they visit a big shop and are hustled back down to their boat where—five hours after they landed—they return to the First World thankful they don't have diarrhea.

The alternative is to simply take the ferry on your own and leave the tourist track. Things are cheap and relatively safe. Since more than 90 percent of visitors choose the comfort of a tour, independent adventurers rarely see another tourist and avoid all the kitsch. You can catch a morning boat and spend the entire day, returning that evening; extend with an overnight in Tangier; or even head deeper into Morocco.

Whether you're planning a day trip or an overnight stay, see the Tangier chapter for all the details. If you're going to stay longer in Morocco, you'll need the help of another guidebook.

www.frs.es). For specifics on side-tripping to Morocco, see the Tangier chapter.

Excursions: Girasol Adventure offers a variety of outdoor excursions, including mountain-bike rentals (€18/day with helmet), guided bike tours, hikes in the national park, rock-climbing classes, tennis lessons, and, when you're all done...a massage (€50/hour). The various activities generally last a half-day and cost around €25-35. Ask Sabine or Chris for details (Mon-Fri 10:15-14:00 & 18:30-20:30, Sat 11:00-14:00, closed Sun, Calle Colón 12, tel. 956-627-037, www.girasol-adventure.com).

Tarifa

ATLANTIC OCEAN

BEACH

1. Hostal Alborada
2. Hotel La Mirada
3. La Sacristía
4. Casa Blan+co
5. Hotel Misiana
6. La Casa Amarilla
7. Hostal La Calzada
8. Hostal Alameda
9. Hostal Africa
10. Pensión Correo
11. Hostal/Rest. Villanueva
12. Restaurante Morilla
13. To El Puerto Restaurante
14. La Oca da Sergio
15. Ristorante La Trattoria
16. To Restaurante Souk & Surfing Sushi
17. Bar El Francés
18. Café Bar Los Melli & Bar El Pasillo
19. El Otro Melli
20. La Posada
21. Café Central & FIRMM
22. Casino Tarifeno
23. Confitería La Tarifeña
24. Churrería La Palmera
25. Supermarket
26. Mercado (Farmers Market)
27. Internet Café
28. Girasol Adventure
29. Whale Watch Tarifa & Baelo Tour
30. FRS Ferry Office
31. Tarifa Travel
32. Travelsur

TO BEACH

BULLRING

BERING

CASTILLE 30S

ALMADRABA

31

AVENIDA   DE

AV. FUERZAS ARMADAS

HUERTA DEL REY

PADRE FONT

J.T. ARTIGAS

CRUZ ROJA

CALLE ALCALDE JUAN NÚÑEZ

DOUBLE ARCH

BOAT TO TANGIER (MOROCCO)

TO 13, BEACH FREE P & ISLA DE LAS PALOMAS

HARBOR

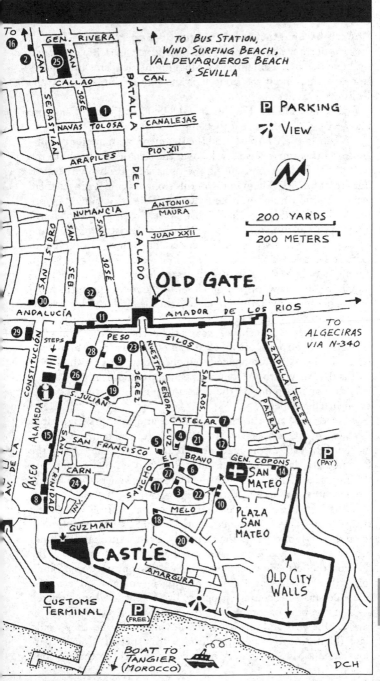

SPAIN'S SOUTH COAST

Sights in Tarifa

Church of St. Matthew (Iglesia de San Mateo)—Tarifa's most important church, facing its main drag, is richly decorated for being in such a small town. Most nights, it seems life squirts from the church out the front door and into the fun-loving Calle El Bravo. Wander inside.

Cost and Hours: Free, daily 9:00-13:00 & 17:30-20:30; there may be English-language leaflets inside on the right.

Visiting the Church: Find the fragment of an **ancient tombstone**—a tiny square (eye-level, about the size of this book) in the wall just before the transept on the right side. Probably the most important historical item in town, this stone fragment proves there was a functioning church here during Visigothic times, before the Moorish conquest. The tombstone reads, in a kind of Latin Spanish (try reading it), "Flaviano lived as a Christian for 50 years, a little more or less. In death he received forgiveness as a servant of God on March 30, 674. May he rest in peace." If that gets you in the mood to light a candle, switch on an electric "candle" by dropping in a coin. (It works.) A bit closer to the main entrance, you'll see a sign offering you the chance to light a digital candle by sending a text message (for a pricey €1.50).

Step into the side chapel around the corner, in the right transept. The centerpiece of the **altar** is a boy Jesus. By Andalusian tradition, he used to be naked, but these days he's clothed with outfits that vary with the Church calendar. Underneath the dome, cherubs dance around on the pink-and-purple interior above an exquisite chandelier.

Head back out into the main nave, and face the high altar. A statue of **St. James the Moor-Slayer** (missing his sword) is on the right wall of the main central altar. Since the days of the Reconquista, James has been Spain's patron saint. For more on this important figure—and why he's fighting invaders that came to Spain centuries after his death—see page 301.

The left side of the nave harbors several **statues**—showing typically over-the-top Baroque emotion—that are paraded through town during Holy Week. The **Captive Christ** (with hands bound) evokes a time when Christians were held captive by Moors. The door on the left side of the nave is the **"door of pardons."** For a long time Tarifa was a dangerous place—on the edge of the Reconquista. To encourage people to live here, the Church offered a second helping of forgiveness to anyone who lived in Tarifa for a year. One year and one day after moving to Tarifa, they would have the privilege of passing through this special "door of pardons," and a Mass of thanksgiving would be held in that person's honor.

Castle of Guzmán el Bueno—This castle, recently reopened after a long restoration, is a concrete hulk in a vacant lot, interesting only for the harbor views from its ramparts. It was named after a 13th-century Christian general who gained fame in a sad show of courage while fighting the Moors. Holding Guzmán's son hostage, the Moors demanded he surrender the castle or they'd kill the boy. Guzmán refused, even throwing his own knife down from the ramparts. It was used on his son's throat. Ultimately, the Moors withdrew to Africa, and Guzmán was a hero. *Bueno.*

Cost and Hours: €2; Tue-Sat 11:00-14:00 & 18:00-20:00, Oct-April evening hours shift from 17:00-19:00 to 16:00-18:00; Sun 11:00-14:00 year-round, closed Mon).

Nearby: If you skip the castle, you'll get equally good views from the plaza just left of the town hall. Follow *ayto* signs to the ceramic frog fountain in front of the Casa Consistorial and continue left.

Bullfighting—Tarifa has a third-rate bullring where novices botch fights on occasional Saturdays through the summer. Professional bullfights take place the first week of September. The ring is a short walk from town. You'll see posters everywhere.

▲Whale-Watching—Several companies in Tarifa offer daily whale- and dolphin-watching excursions. Over the past four decades, people in this area went from eating whales to protecting them and sharing them with 20,000 visitors a year. Talks are under way between Morocco and Spain to protect the Strait of Gibraltar by declaring it a national park.

For any of the tours, it's wise (but not always necessary) to reserve one to three days in advance. You'll get a multilingual tour and a two-hour boat trip. Sightings occur on nearly every trip: Dolphins and pilot whales frolic here any time of year (they like the food), sperm whales visit from March through July, and orcas pass through in July and August. In bad weather, trips may be canceled or boats may leave instead from Algeciras (in which case, drivers follow in a convoy, people without cars usually get rides from staff, and you'll stand a lesser chance of seeing whales).

The best company is the Swiss nonprofit **FIRMM** (Foundation for Information and Research on Marine Mammals), which gives a 30-minute educational talk before departure. To reserve it's best to call ahead or stop by one of their two offices (€30/person, 1-5 trips/day April-Oct, sometimes also Nov, also offers intensive week-long courses that include boat trips, one office around the corner from Café Central—one door inland at Pedro Cortés 4, second office inside the ferry port, tel. 956-627-008, mobile 619-459-441, www.firmm.org, mail@firmm.org). If you don't see any whales or dolphins on your tour, you can join another trip for free.

Whale Watch Tarifa is another good option. In addition to a two-hour whale-watching trip (€30), they offer a three-hour orca trip in July and August (€45, Avenida de la Constitución 6, tel. 956-627-013, mobile 639-476-544, www.whalewatchtarifa.net, whalewatchtarifa@whalewatchtarifa.net, run by Lourdes and Ana).

Isla de las Palomas—Extending out between Tarifa's port and beaches, this island connected by a spit is the actual "southernmost point in mainland Europe." Walk along the causeway, with beaches stretching to your right and a bustling port to your left, to the tip, which was fortified in the 19th century to balance the military might of Britain's nearby Rock of Gibraltar. The actual tip, still owned by the Ministry of Defense, is closed to the public, but a sign at the gate still gives you that giddy "edge of the world" feeling.

▲▲**Beach Scene**—Tarifa's vast, sandy beach stretches west for about five miles. You can walk the beach from Tarifa, while

those with a car can explore farther (following Cádiz Road). On windy summer days, the sea is littered with sprinting windsurfers, while kitesurfers flutter in the sky. "Paddleboarding" (standing on a surfboard while maneuvering with a long, kayak-like paddle) is also becoming popular. It's a fascinating scene: A long string of funky beach resorts is packed with vans and fun-mobiles from northern Europe under mountain ridges lined with modern energy-generating windmills. The various resorts each have a sandy access road, parking, a cabana-type hamlet with rental gear, beachwear shops, a bar, and a hip, healthy restaurant. I like Valdevaqueros beach (five miles from Tarifa), with a wonderful thatched restaurant serving hearty salads, paella, and burgers. Camping Torre de la Peña also has some fun beach eateries.

In July and August, inexpensive buses do a circuit of nearby campgrounds, all on the waterfront (€2, departures about every 1-2 hours, confirm times with TI). Trying to get a parking spot in August can take the joy out of this experience.

Nightlife in Tarifa

You'll find plenty of enjoyable nightspots—the entire town seems designed to cater to a young, international crowd of windsurfers and other adventure travelers. Just stroll the streets of the old town and dip into whichever trendy lounge catches your eye. For something more sedate, the evening paseo fills the park-like boulevard called Pasco Alameda (just outside the old-town wall); the Almedina bar hosts flamenco shows every Thursday (at the south end of town, just below Plaza de Santa María); and the new theater next to the TI sometimes has musical performances (ask at the TI or look for posters).

Sleeping in Tarifa

Room rates vary with the season. For many hotels, I've listed the three seasonal tiers (highest prices—mid-June-Sept; medium prices—spring and fall; and lowest prices—winter).

Outside the City Wall

These hotels are about five blocks from the old town, right off the main drag, Batalla del Salado, in the plain, modern part of town. While in a drab area, both are well-run oases that are close to the beach and the bus station, with free and easy street parking.

$$ Hostal Alborada is a squeaky-clean, family-run 37-room place with two attractive courtyards and modern conveniences. Father Rafael, sons Quino (who speaks English and is generous

---

Sleep Code

(€1 = about $1.40, country code: 34)
S = Single, **D** = Double/Twin, **T** = Triple, **Q** = Quad, **b** = bathroom, **s** = shower only. Unless otherwise noted, credit cards are accepted and English is spoken. Breakfast is not included (unless noted).

To help you easily sort through these listings, I've divided the accommodations into three categories, based on the price for a standard double room with bath during high season:

$$$ Higher Priced—Most rooms €100 or more.
$$ Moderately Priced—Most rooms between €50-100.
$ Lower Priced—Most rooms €50 or less.

Prices can change without notice; verify the hotel's current rates online or by email. For other updates, see www.ricksteves.com/update.

with travel tips) and Carlos, and their family are happy to help make your Morocco tour or ferry reservation, or arrange any other activities you're interested in. If they're not too busy, they'll even give you a free lift to the port (Sb-€40/55/65, Db-€50/70/85, Tb-€80/90/110, pay for first night when reserving, upon arrival show this book for a 10 percent discount in 2012—not valid July-Sept, strict 15-day cancellation policy, basic breakfast-€2.50, breakfast with delicious tomato bread-€5, air-con, pay Internet access, free Wi-Fi, laundry-€14, Calle San José 40, tel. 956-681-140, fax 956-681-935, www.hotelalborada.com, info@hotel alborada.com).

$$ Hotel La Mirada, which feels sleek and stark, has 25 mod and renovated rooms—most with sea views at no extra cost. While the place lacks personality, it's well-priced and comfortable (Sb-€45/55/60, Db-€65/75/90, breakfast-€5, elevator, free Wi-Fi, expansive sea views from large roof terrace with inviting lounge chairs, Calle San Sebastián 41, tel. 956-684-427, fax 956-681-162, www.hotel-lamirada.com, reservas@hotel-lamirada.com, Antonio and Salvador).

Inside or next to the City Wall

The first three listings are funky, stylish boutique hotels in the heart of town—*muy* trendy and a bit full of themselves.

$$$ La Sacristía, formerly a Moorish stable, now houses travelers who want stylish surroundings. It offers 10 fine and uniquely decorated rooms, mingling eclectic elements of chic Spanish and Asian style. They offer spa treatments, custom tours of the area, and occasional special events—join the party since you won't sleep (Db-€117, superior Db-€137, extra bed-€35, can be cheaper off-season, includes breakfast, some superior rooms have air-con but most rooms have fans, massage room, sauna, roof terrace, TV on request, very central at San Donato 8, tel. 956-681-759, fax 956-685-182, www.lasacristia.net, tarifa@lasacristia.net, helpful Teresa). They also rent 10 apartments at a separate location.

$$$ Casa Blan+co, where minimalist meets Moroccan, is the newest reasonably priced designer hotel on the block. Each of its seven rooms (with double beds only—no twins) is decorated (and priced) differently. The place is decked out with practical amenities (mini-fridge and stovetop) as well as romantic touches—loft beds, walk-in showers, and subtle lighting (high-season Db-€92-133, low-season Db-€52-69, includes breakfast, small roof terrace, free Wi-Fi in lobby, off main square at Calle Nuestra Señora de la Luz 2, tel. 956-681-515, fax 956-681-990, www.casablan-co.com, info @casablan-co.com).

$$$ Hotel Misiana has 13 comfortable, newly remodeled, spacious rooms above a bar-lounge. Their designer gave the place

a mod pastel boutique-ish ambience. To avoid noise from the lounge below (open until 3:00 in the morning), request a room on a higher floor (Sb-€50/60/115, Db-€70/85/135, fancy top-floor Db suite-€110/140/250, low- and mid-season rates are €10-20 more on weekends, includes breakfast, double-paned windows, elevator, free Wi-Fi in bar, 100 yards directly in front of the church at Calle Sancho IV El Bravo 16, tel. 956-627-083, fax 956-627-055, www .misiana.com, reservas@misiana.com).

$$ La Casa Amarilla ("The Yellow House") offers 10 posh apartments with tiny kitchens, plus three smaller studios with modern decor (studio Db-€57/78/114, apartment Db-€76/91/130, reserve with credit card, no breakfast, free Wi-Fi, across street from Café Central, Calle Sancho IV El Bravo 9, tel. 956-681-993, fax 956-684-029, www.lacasaamarilla.net, info@lacasaamarilla .net).

$$ Hostal La Calzada has eight airy, well-appointed rooms right in the lively old-town thick of things, though the management is rarely around (Db-€50-75, extra bed-€10, higher in Aug, closed Dec-March, air-con, free Wi-Fi in lobby, 20 yards from church at Calle Justino Pertinez 7, tel. 956-681-492, fax 956-680 366, www.hostallacalzada.com, info@hostallacalzada.com).

$$ Hostal Alameda, overlooking a square where the local children play, glistens with pristine marble floors and dark red decor. The main building has 11 bright rooms and the annex has 16 more-modern rooms; both face the same delightful square (Db-€60/70/90, extra bed-€20-30, à la carte breakfast, air-con, free Wi-Fi, Paseo de la Alameda 4, tel. 956-681-181, fax 956-680-264, www.hostalalameda.com, reservas@hostalalameda.com, Antonio).

$$ Hostal Africa, with 13 bright rooms and an inviting roof terrace, is buried on a very quiet street in the center of town. Its dreamy blue-and-white color scheme and stripped-down feel give it a Moorish ambience (S-€20/25/35, Sb-€25/35/50, D-€30/40/50, Db-€35/50/65, Tb-€50/75/100, no breakfast, laundry-€10—or €20 in high season, free Wi-Fi in public spaces, storage for boards and bikes, Calle María Antonia Toledo 12, tel. 956-680-220, mobile 606-914-294, www.hostalafrica.com, hostal_africa@hotmail.com, Miguel and Eva keep the reception desk open only 9:00-24:00).

$$ Pensión Correo rents nine simple rooms (three sharing a bathroom) at a fair value—especially Room 8, with its private roof terrace (S-€20-35, D-€35-60, Db-€45-80, Tb-€50-90, Qb-€60-110, extra bed-€15-20, reservations more than 24 hours in advance require first night prepaid by credit card—refundable up to 48 hours in advance, no breakfast, roof garden, free Wi-Fi in some rooms, Coronel Moscardo 8, tel. 956-680-206, www.pension correo.com, welcome@pensioncorreo.com, María José and Luca).

$ **Hostal Villanueva** offers 12 remodeled rooms at budget prices over a good restaurant. It's simple, clean, and friendly. It lacks indoor public areas, but has an inviting terrace overlooking the old town. On a busy street, it's dominated by its restaurant. Pepe (who speaks a smidgen of English) asks that you reconfirm your reservation by phone the day before you arrive (Sb-€25-30, Db-€35-55, cash only, no breakfast, just west of the old-town gate at Avenida de Andalucía 11, access from outside the wall, tel. & fax 956-684-149, hostalvillanueva@hotmail.com).

Eating in Tarifa

I've grouped my recommendations below into two categories: Sit down to a real restaurant meal, or enjoy a couple of the many characteristic tapas bars in the old town.

Dining

Seafood

Restaurante Morilla, facing the church and on the town's prime piece of people-watching real estate, serves tasty local-style fish—grilled or baked. This is a real restaurant (€1.50 tapas sold only at the stand-up bar and sometimes at a few tables), with good indoor and outdoor seating. The waiter will tell you about today's fish; it's sold by weight, so confirm the price carefully (€4-11 starters, €10-16 main dishes, daily 9:00-24:00, Calle Sancho IV El Bravo, tel. 956-681-757).

El Puerto, in a dreary and untouristy area between the port and the beach (near the causeway out to Isla de las Palomas), has a great reputation for its pricey but very fresh seafood. Locals swear that it's a notch or two above the seafood places in town (€8-14 starters, €10-20 seafood dishes and some meats, Thu-Mon 12:00-16:00 & 20:00-24:00, Tue-Wed 12:00-16:00 only, Avenida Fuerzas Armadas 13, tel. 956-681-914).

Restaurante Villanueva is a homey-feeling, affordable seafood option, with a sprawling interior and outdoor tables on a busy street just outside the old-town wall (€7.50 lunch, €4-7 starters, €9-15 main dishes, Tue-Sun 13:00-16:00 & 19:45-23:00, closed Mon, Avenida de Andalucía 11, tel. 956-684-149).

Italian

La Oca da Sergio, cozy and fun, is one of the numerous pizza-and-pasta joints supported by the large expat Italian community. Sergio prides himself on importing actual Italian ingredients (€7-11 starters, €9-14 pastas, €7-10 pizzas, €14-16 meat and fish dishes, indoor and outdoor seating, daily 13:00-16:00 & 20:00-24:00 except closed Tue in winter; around the left side of the church and straight back, just before the Moorish-style old-folks' home at Calle General Copons 6; tel. 956-681-249, mobile 615-686-571).

Ristorante La Trattoria, on the Alameda, is another good Italian option, with cloth-napkin class, friendly staff, and ingredients from Italy. Sit inside, near the wood-fired oven, or out along the main strolling street (€9-15 starters and pastas, €6-12 pizzas, €16-20 meat dishes; Thu-Tue 19:30-24:00, closed Wed; July-Aug open daily plus Sat-Sun 13:00-16:00; Paseo de la Alameda, tel. 956-682-225).

In the New Town

These two restaurants are in a residential area just above the beach, about a 15-minute walk (or easy car or taxi ride) from the old town. They're worth a detour for their great food, and for the chance to see an area away from the main tourist zone (though the sushi bar is on the beach and is no stranger to tourists). To get to either, begin by heading up Calle San Sebastián, which turns into Calle Pintor Pérez Villalta. When you see a big staircase on your right, head up the stairs to reach Restaurante Souk, or turn left toward the beach to find Surfing Sushi.

Restaurante Souk serves a tasty fusion of Moroccan, Indian, and Thai cuisine in a dark, exotic, romantic, purely Moroccan ambience. The ground floor (where you enter) is a bar and atmospheric tea house, while the dining room is downstairs (€6-9 starters, €12-17 main dishes; July-Sept daily 20:00-3:00 in the morning; Oct-June Wed-Mon 20:00-1:00, closed Tue; good wine list, Mar Tirreno 46, tel. 956-627-065, friendly Claudia).

Surfing Sushi, part of a cool surfer bar called Surla, serves up wonderfully executed sushi using only the freshest of ingredients. Situated just a few steps above the beachfront walkway, it's at the center of a sprawling zone of après-surf hangouts. They also offer delivery (€16-21 shareable sushi platters, mid-June-mid-Sept daily 20:00-24:00, closed Wed off-season, possible to order delivery sushi by phone at other times, Calle Pintor Pérez Villalta 1, tel. 956-685-175, www.surfingsushi.com).

Tapas

Bar El Francés is a thriving hole-in-the-wall where "Frenchies" (as the bar's name implies) Marcial and Alexandra serve tasty little plates of tapas. From Café Central, follow the cars 100 yards to the first corner on the left to reach this simple, untouristy standing-and-stools-only eatery. This spot is popular for its fine *raciones* (€6-10) and tapas (€1.30-1.50)—especially oxtail *(rabo del toro)*, pork with tomato sauce *(carne con tomate)*, pork with spice *(chicharrones)*, and garlic-grilled tuna *(atún a la plancha)*. The outdoor terrace with restaurant-type tables (no tapas served here) is an understandably popular spot to enjoy a casual meal. Show this book and Marcial will be happy to bring you a free glass of sherry (Mon-Sat open long hours, especially April-Sept, closed Sun; daily June-Aug; closed Dec-Feb; Calle Sancho IV El Bravo 21A, mobile 685-867-005).

Café Bar Los Melli is a local favorite for feasts on rickety tables set on cobbles. This family-friendly place, run by José, offers a good chorizo sandwich and *patatas bravas*—potatoes with a hot tomato sauce served on a wooden board (€5 half-*raciones*, €8 *raciones*, Thu-Tue 20:00-24:00, Sat-Sun also 13:00-16:00, closed Wed; from Bar El Francés, cross parking lot and take Calle del Legionario Ríos Moya up one block; mobile 605-866-444). **Bar El Pasillo,** next to Los Melli, also serves tapas (closed Mon-Tue). **El Otro Melli,** run by José's brother Ramón, is a few blocks away on Plaza de San Martín.

La Posada, a local-feeling place a block beyond the main tourist zone (and just up the street from Los Melli), takes prides in its fresh ingredients. There's a small dining room, a nondescript bar with a giant stone beer tap that's a replica of the city's first communal faucet, and tables out front near the real thing (€1.50 *montaditos*, €3 *tostadas*, €4-6 half-*raciones*, €7-11 *raciones;* July-Aug daily 13:00-16:30 & 20:00-24:00; Sept-June Mon and Wed-Fri 20:00-24:00, Sat-Sun 13:00-16:30 & 20:00-24:00, closed Tue; Calle Guzman el Bueno 3A, mobile 636-929-449).

Café Central is *the* happening place nearly any time of day—it's the perch for all the cool tourists. Less authentically Spanish than the others I've listed, it has a hip, international vibe. The bustling ambience and appealing setting in front of the church are better than the food (€1.30 tapas, €5 half-*raciones*), but they do have breakfast with eggs (€2-4), good €6 salads (study the menu), and impressively therapeutic healthy fruit drinks (daily 8:30-24:00, off Plaza San Mateo, near church, tel. 956-682-877).

Casino Tarifeno is just to the sea side of the church. It's an old-boys' social club "for members only," but it offers a musty Andalusian welcome to visiting tourists, including women. Wander through. There's a low-key bar with tapas, a TV room, a card room, and a lounge. There's no menu, but prices are standard. Just point and say the size you want: tapa (€1.20), *media-ración* (€4), or *ración* (€7). A far cry from some of the trendy options around town, this is a local institution (daily 12:00-24:00).

Pastries, Beach Bars, and Picnics

Breakfast or Dessert: **Confitería La Tarifeña** serves super pastries and flan-like *tocino de cielo* (daily 9:00-21:00, at the top of Calle Nuestra Señora de la Luz, near the main old-town gate).

Churrería La Palmera serves breakfast before most hotels and cafés have even turned on the lights—early enough for you to get your coffee fix, and/or bulk up on *churros* and chocolate, before hopping the first ferry to Tangier (Sanchez IV El Bravo 34).

Windsurfer Bars: If you have a car, head to the string of beaches. Many have bars and fun-loving thatched restaurants that keep the wet-suited gang fed and watered (see "Beach Scene" on page 752).

Picnics: Stop by the *mercado municipal* (farmers' market, Mon-Sat 8:00-14:00, closed Sun, in old town, inside gate nearest TI), any grocery, or the **superSol supermarket** (Mon-Sat 9:30-21:30, closed Sun, has simple cafeteria, near the hotels in the new town at Callao and San José).

Tarifa Connections

Tarifa

From Tarifa by Bus to: La Línea de la Concepción/Gibraltar (6/day direct, 1 hour, starting around 12:00; more possible with transfer in Algeciras, 1.5 hours), **Algeciras** (10/day, 30 minutes, first departure from Tarifa weekdays at 6:30, on Sat 8:15, on Sun 10:00; return from Algeciras as late as 21:00), **Jerez** (1/day, 2 hours, more frequent with transfer in Cádiz), **Sevilla** (4/day, 2.5-3.25 hours), and **Málaga** (3/day, 3.5 hours). All bus service from Tarifa is by Comes (tel. 956-684-038, www.tgcomes.es).

Algeciras

Algeciras (ahl-*h*eh-THEE-rahs, with a guttural *h*) is only worth leaving. It's useful to the traveler mainly as a transportation hub, with trains and buses to destinations in southern and central Spain (it also has a ferry to Tangier, but it takes you to the Tangier MED port about 25 miles from Tangier city—going from Tarifa is much better). If you're headed for Gibraltar or Tarifa by public transport, you'll almost certainly change in Algeciras at some point.

Everything of interest is on Juan de la Cierva, which heads inland from the port. The **TI** is about a block in (Mon-Fri 9:00-19:30, Sat-Sun 9:30-15:00, tel. 956-784-131), followed by the side-by-side **train station** (opposite Hotel Octavio) and **bus station** three more blocks later.

Trains: If arriving at the train station, head out the front door: The bus station (called San Bernardo Estación de Autobuses) is ahead and on the right; the TI is another three blocks ahead (the road becomes Juan de la Cierva when the road jogs), also on the right; and the port is just beyond.

From Algeciras by Train to: Madrid (2/day, 5.5 hours, arrives at Atocha), **Ronda** (3-4/day, 1.5-2 hours), **Granada** (3/day, 4.25-5 hours), **Sevilla** (3/day, 5 hours, transfer at Bobadilla; bus is better), **Córdoba** (2/day direct on Altaria, 3.5 hours; plus 1/day with transfer in Bobadilla, 5.25 hours), **Málaga** (2/day, 4 hours, transfer in Bobadilla; bus is faster). With the exception of the route to Madrid, these are particularly scenic trips; the best (though slow) is the mountainous journey to Málaga via Bobadilla.

Buses: Algeciras is served by three different bus companies (Comes, Portillo, and Linesur), all located in the same terminal (called San Bernardo Estación de Autobuses) next to Hotel Octavio and directly across from the train station. The companies generally serve different destinations, but there is some overlap. Compare schedules and rates to find the most convenient bus for you. By the ticket counter you'll find an easy red letter board that lists departures. Lockers are near the platforms—purchase a token at the machines.

From Algeciras by Bus: Comes (tel. 902-199-208, www .tgcomes.es) runs buses to **La Línea/Gibraltar** (2/hour, less on weekends, 45 minutes, 7:00-22:30), **Tarifa** (11/day, less on weekends, 30 minutes), **Ronda** (3-4/day, 2 hours), **Sevilla** (4/day, 3.5 hours), **Jerez** (1/day, 2.5 hours), and **Madrid** (3/day, 8 hours).

Portillo (tel. 956-654-304, www.ctsa-portillo.com) offers buses to **Málaga** (17/day, 1.75 hours *directo*, 3 hours *ruta*) and **Granada** (4/day, 4-5 hours).

Linesur (tel. 956-667-649, www.linesur.com) runs the most frequent direct buses to **Sevilla** (8/day, fewer on weekends, 2.75-3 hours) and **Jerez** (8/day, fewer on weekends, 1.5 hours).

Ferries from Algeciras to Tangier, Morocco: Although it's possible to sail from Algeciras to Tangier, the ferry takes you to the Tangier MED Port, which is 25 miles east of Tangier city and a hassle. You're better off taking a ferry from Tarifa: They sail direct to the port in Tangier. If you must sail from Algeciras, buy your ticket at the port (skip the divey-looking travel agencies littering the town). Official offices of the seven boat companies are inside the main port building, directly behind the helpful little English-speaking info kiosk (8-22 ferries/day, port open daily 6:45-21:45, tel. 956-585-463).

Route Tips for Drivers

Tarifa to Gibraltar (45 minutes): This short drive takes you past a silvery-white forest of windmills, from peaceful Tarifa past Algeciras to La Línea (the Spanish town bordering Gibraltar). Passing Algeciras, continue in the direction of Estepona. At San Roque, take the La Línea–Gibraltar exit.

Gibraltar to Nerja (130 miles): Barring traffic problems, the trip along the Costa del Sol is smooth and easy by car—much of it on a new highway. Just follow the coastal highway east. After Málaga, follow signs to *Almería* and *Motril*.

Nerja to Granada (80 miles, 1.5 hours, 100 views): Drive along the coast to Motril, catching N-323 north for about 40 miles to Granada. While scenic side-trips may beckon, don't arrive late in Granada without a confirmed hotel reservation.

MOROCCO

MOROCCO

Al-Maghreb

A young country with an old history, Morocco is a photographer's delight and a budget traveler's dream. It's cheap, exotic, and easier and more appealing than ever. Along with a rich culture, Morocco offers plenty of contrast—from beach resorts to bustling desert markets, from jagged mountains to sleepy, mud-brick oasis towns. And there's a distinct new energy as its popular activist king asserts his vision.

Morocco (*Marruecos* in Spanish; *Al-Maghreb* in Arabic) also provides a good dose of culture shock—both bad and good. It makes Spain seem meek and mild. You'll encounter oppressive friendliness, brutal heat, the Arabic language, the Islamic faith, ancient cities, and aggressive beggars.

While Morocco is clearly a place apart from Mediterranean Europe, it doesn't really seem like Africa either. It's a mix, reflecting its strategic position between the two continents. Situated on the Strait of Gibraltar, Morocco has been flooded by waves

of invasions over the centuries. The Berbers, the native population, have had to contend with the Phoenicians, Carthaginians, Romans, Vandals, and more.

The Arabs brought Islam to Morocco in the seventh century A.D. and stuck around, battling the Berbers in various civil wars. A series of Berber and Arab dynasties rose and fell; the Berbers won out and still run the country today.

From the 15th century on, European countries carved up much of Africa. By the early 20th century, most of Morocco was under French control, and strategic Tangier was jointly ruled by multiple European powers. The country wasn't granted independence until 1956. In the late 1970s, Morocco itself became an invading country, grabbing Spain's Western Sahara territory and causing

Morocco

the relatively few inhabitants to clamor for independence. Western Sahara's claim still has not been settled by the United Nations.

Unfortunately, most of the English-speaking Moroccans the typical tourist meets are hustlers. Many visitors develop some intestinal problems by the end of their visit. Most women are harassed on the streets by horny but generally harmless men. And in terms of efficiency, Morocco makes Spain look like Sweden.

When you cruise south across the Strait of Gibraltar, leave your busy itineraries and split-second timing behind. Morocco must be taken on its own terms. In Morocco things go smoothly only *"Inshallah"*—if God so wills.

Helpful Hints

Politics: Americans pondering a visit understandably wonder how they'll be received in this Muslim nation. Al Jazeera blares from televisions in all the bars, but I've seen no angry graffiti or posters and felt no animosity toward American individuals there (even on my last visit, literally days after US forces killed Osama bin Laden). Western visitors feel a warm welcome in post-9/11 Morocco. And it's culturally enriching for Westerners to experience Morocco—a Muslim monarchy with women still in traditional dress and roles, succeeding on

Islam 101

Islam has more than a billion adherents worldwide, and traveling in an Islamic country is an opportunity to better understand the religion. This admittedly basic and simplistic outline (written by a non-Muslim) is meant to help travelers from the Christian West understand a very rich but often misunderstood culture.

Muslims, like Christians and Jews, are monotheistic. They call God "Allah." The most important person in the Islamic faith is the prophet Muhammad, who lived in the sixth and seventh centuries A.D. The holy book of Islam is the Quran, believed by Muslims to be the word of Allah as revealed to Muhammad.

The "five pillars" of Islam are the core tenets of the faith. Followers of Islam should:

1. Say and believe, "There is only one God, and Muhammad is his prophet."

2. Pray five times a day, facing Mecca. Modern Muslims explain that it's important for this ritual to include washing, exercising, stretching, and thinking of God.

3. Give to the poor (one-fortieth of your wealth, if you are not in debt).

4. Fast during daylight hours through the month of Ramadan. Fasting is a great social equalizer and helps everyone to feel the hunger of the poor.

5. Make a pilgrimage to Mecca. Muslims who can afford it, and who are physically able, are required to travel to the sacred sites in Mecca and Medina at least once in their lifetimes.

Just as it helps to know about spires, feudalism, and the saints to comprehend European sightseeing, a few basics on Islam help make your sightseeing in Morocco more meaningful.

its own terms without embracing modern Western "norms."

Hustler Alert: Moroccans may be some of Africa's wealthiest people, but you are still incredibly rich to them. This imbalance causes predictable problems. Wear your money belt. Assume con artists are more clever than you. Haggle when appropriate; prices skyrocket for tourists (see "Bargaining Basics," page 789). You'll attract hustlers like flies at every famous tourist sight or whenever you pull out your guidebook or a map. In the worst-case scenario, they'll lie to you, get you lost, blackmail you, and pester the heck out of you. Never leave your car or baggage where you can't get back to it without someone else's "help." Anything you buy in a guide's company gets him a 20 percent commission. Normally locals, shop-keepers, and police will come to your rescue if the hustlers' heat becomes unbearable. Consider hiring a guide, since it's helpful to have a trans-lator, and once you're "taken," the rest seem to leave you alone.

Marijuana Alert: In Morocco, marijuana *(kif)* is as illegal as it is popular, a fact that many Westerners in local jails would love to remind you of. As a general rule, just walk right by those hand-carved pipes in the marketplace. Some dealers who sell it cheap make their profit after you get arrested. Cars and buses are stopped and checked by police routinely throughout Morocco—especially in the north and in the Chefchaouen region, which is Morocco's *kif* capital.

Health: Morocco is much more hazardous to your health than Spain. Eat in clean—not cheap—places. Peel fruit, eat only cooked vegetables, and drink reliably bottled water (Sidi Ali or Sidi Harazem). When you do get diarrhea—and you should plan on it—adjust your diet (small and bland meals, no milk or grease) or fast for a day, but make sure you replenish lost fluids. Relax: Most diarrhea is not serious, just an adjustment that will run its course.

Closed Days: Friday is the Muslim day of rest, when most of the country (except Tangier) closes down.

Ramadan: During this major month-long religious holiday (July 20-Aug 18 in 2012), Muslims focus on prayer and reflection. Following Islamic doctrine, they refrain during daylight hours from eating, drinking (including water), smoking, and having sex. On the final day of Ramadan, Muslims celebrate *Eid* (an all-day feast and gift-giving party, similar to Christmas), and travelers may find some less-touristy stores and restaurants closed.

Money: Euros work here (as do dollars and pounds). If you're on a five-hour tour, bring along lots of €1 and €0.50 coins for tips, small purchases, and camel rides. But if you plan to do any-thing independently, change some money into Moroccan dir-hams upon arrival (8 dh = about $1). Banks and ATMs have uniform rates. If you use an exchange desk, just be sure you can see the buying and selling rates; they should be within 10 percent of one another with no extra fees. Don't leave the country with Moroccan money unless you want a souvenir, since few places in Spain are willing to change dirhams to euros or dollars.

Information: Travel information, English or otherwise, is rare here. For an extended trip, bring guidebooks from home or Spain—Lonely Planet and Rough Guide both publish good ones. Buy the best map you can find locally—names are always changing, and if you need to ask someone, it's helpful to have towns, roads, and place names written in Arabic.

Language: With its unique history of having been controlled by so many different foreign and domestic rulers, Tangier is a babel of languages. Most locals speak Arabic first and French second (all Moroccans must learn it in schools); sensing that you're a foreigner, they'll most likely address you in French. Spanish ranks third, and English a distant fourth. The Arabic squiggle-script, its many difficult sounds, and the fact that French is Morocco's second language combine to make communication tricky for English-speaking travelers. A little French goes a long way, but learn a few words in Arabic. Have your first local friend help you with the pronunciation:

English	Arabic	Pronounced
Hello. ("Peace be with you")	*Salaam alaikum.*	sah-LAHM ah-LAY-koom
Hello. (response: "Peace also be with you")	*Wa alaikum salaam.*	wah ah-LAY-koom sah-LAHM
Please.	*Min fadlik.*	meen FAHD-leek
Thank you.	*Shokran.*	SHOH-kron (like "sugar on")
Excuse me.	*Ismahli.*	ees-SMAH-lee
Yes.	*Yeh.*	EE-yeh
No.	*Lah.*	lah
Give me five. (kids enjoy this...not above but straight ahead)	*Ham sah.*	hahm sah
OK.	*Wah hah.*	wah hah
Very good.	*Miz yen biz ef.*	meez EE-yehn beez ehf
Goodbye.	*Maa salama.*	mah sah-LEM-ah

Moroccans are more touchy-feely than their Spanish neighbors. Expect lots of hugs if you make an effort to communicate. When greeting someone, a handshake is customary, followed by placing your right hand over your heart. Listen carefully and write new words phonetically. Bring an Arabic phrase book. In markets, I sing, "la la la la la" to my opponents. *Lah shokran* means "No, thank you."

Getting Around Morocco: Moroccan trains are quite good. Second class is cheap and comfortable. Buses connect all smaller towns very well. By car, Morocco is easy, but drive defensively and never rely on the oncoming driver's skill. Night driving is dangerous. Pay a guard to watch your car overnight.

Keeping Your Bearings: Navigate the labyrinthine *medinas* (old towns) by altitude, gates, and famous mosques or buildings. Write down what gate you came in, so you can enjoy being lost—temporarily. *Souk* is Arabic for a particular market (such as leather, yarn, or metalwork). A *kasbah* is loosely defined as a fortress (or a town within old fortress walls).

MOROCCO

TANGIER

Tanja

Go to Africa. As you step off the boat, you realize that the crossing (less than an hour) has taken you further culturally than did the trip from the US to Spain. Morocco needs no museums; its sights are living in the streets. For decades its once-grand coastal city of Tangier deserved its reputation as the "Tijuana of Africa." But that has changed. The current king is enthusiastic about Tangier, and there's a fresh can-do spirit in the air. The town is as Moroccan as ever...yet more enjoyable and less stressful.

Morocco in a Day?

Though Morocco certainly deserves more than a day, many visitors touring Spain see it in a quick side-trip. And, though such a short sprint through Tangier is only a tease, it's far more interesting than another day in Spain. A day in Tangier gives you a good introduction to Morocco, a legitimate taste of North Africa, and a nonthreatening slice of Islam. All you need is a passport (no visa or shots required) and €67 for the round-trip ferry crossing. Your big decisions: where to sail from; whether to go on your own or buy a ferry/guided tour day-trip package; and whether to make it a day trip or spend the night. Of these, the biggest decision is:

With a Tour or On My Own?: Because the ferry company expects you to do a lot of shopping (providing them with kickbacks), it's actually a bit cheaper to join a one-day tour than to buy a round-trip ferry ticket. The question is: Do you want the safety and comfort of having Morocco handed to you on a user-friendly platter; or do you want the independence to see what you want to see, with a more authentic experience, fewer cultural clichés, and less forced shopping? There are pros and cons to each approach, depending on your travel style. My preferred approach is sort of a hybrid: Go to Morocco "on your own," but arrange in advance to meet up with a local guide to ease your culture shock and accompany you to your choice of sights (I've listed several guides on page 782, or you can book a tour with the ferry company and pay for the "VIP" option). While this costs a bit more than joining a package tour, ultimately the cost difference (roughly €10-20 more per person) is pretty negligible, considering the dramatically increased cultural intimacy. Doing it entirely on your own (no guide at all) can be a great adventure, but potentially more stressful.

Time Difference: Morocco is on Greenwich Mean Time (like Great Britain)—that means one hour behind Spain. It typically observes Daylight Saving Time, but "springs forward" and "falls back" at different times than Europe. In general, Moroccans change their clocks in early April (a week after Spain), then again just before Ramadan (in 2011, that date was July 31—nearly three months before Spain). Therefore, during the summer months, Morocco is either one hour (if they've changed) or two hours (if they haven't changed, or have already changed back) behind Spain. In general, ferry and other schedules use the local time (if your boat leaves Tangier "at 17:00," that means 5:00 p.m. Moroccan time—not Spanish time)...be sure to change your watch when you get off the boat.

Terminology: Note that the Spanish refer to Morocco as "Marruecos" (mar-WAY-kohs) and Tangier as "Tánger" (TAHN-hair, with a guttural *h*).

Going on Your Own, by Ferry from Tarifa

While the trip to Tangier can be made from various ports, only the ferry from Tarifa takes you to Tangier's city-center port, called the Tangier Medina Port (Spaniards call it the *Puerto Viejo*, "Old Port"). Boats from Algeciras or Gibraltar dock instead at the Tangier MED Port (Spaniards call it the *Puerto Nuevo*, "New Port"), about 25 miles east of the city center. (Note: Confusingly, because the city-center port is being remodeled, some Moroccans call it the "new port"—exactly the opposite of the Spaniards.) Tangier's city-center port has been closed to cargo shipping, and is in the midst of a massive renovation and beautification project, which will extend the pier to accommodate large cruise ships and create a marina for yachts. Most sources indicate that ferries from Tarifa will continue to use the city-center port, though it's possible (temporarily—due to construction at the port) that Tarifa ships could be sent to the MED port. I'll describe the trip assuming you're sailing from Tarifa to Tangier's city-center Medina Port—the most logical route for the typical traveler.

Ferry Crossing: Two different companies make essentially

the same 35-minute cross-
ing from Tarifa to Tangier,
on alternating hours: **FRS**
(tel. 956-684-847, www.frs
.es) and **Comarit** (tel. 956-
657-462, www.comarit.es).
Prices are about the same
with either company (€37 one-way, €67 round-trip). Between
them, boats leave Tarifa at the top of every hour from about 8:00
to 22:00—so go with the boat that best suits your schedule. For
the return trip from Tangier to Tarifa, boats run from about 7:00
to 21:00.

Tickets are very easy to get: You can buy one at the port,
through your hotel in Tarifa, from a local travel agency, or at FRS's
ticket office in town (see page 746). You can almost always just buy
a ticket and walk on, though in the busiest summer months (July-
Aug), the popular 9:00 departure could be booked up with tours.
Boats are most crowded in July (when Moroccans in Spain go
home for Ramadan) and in August (when the Costa del Sol groups
come en masse). A few crossings a year are canceled because of
storms or wind, mostly in winter.

Procedure: The ferry from Tarifa is a fast Nordic hydrofoil
that theoretically takes 35 minutes to cross. It often leaves late.

You'll go through Spanish customs at
the port and Moroccan customs on
the ferry. Whether taking a tour or
traveling on your own, you *must* get
a stamp (available on board) from the
Moroccan immigration officer. After
you leave Spain, find the customs desk
on the boat, line up, and get your passport and entry paper stamped. If you're
coming back the same day and know
your return time, the immigration official may also give you an exit stamp
(for your return from Morocco), which
prevents delays at the port at departure time. The ferry is equipped
with WCs, a shop, and a snack bar. Tarifa's modern little terminal
has a cafeteria and WCs.

Hiring a Guide: Even if you're visiting Morocco independently, I recommend hiring a local guide to show you around
Tangier (for a list of recommended guides, see "Guides," on page
782).

Tangier MED Port: Ferries from Algeciras and Gibraltar
(and, potentially but unlikely, ferries from Tarifa) arrive at the
Tangier MED Port, 25 miles from downtown. While this wastes

time (it's about an hour each way from the boat to downtown Tangier), the connection is simple: A free shuttle bus picks up passengers at the Tangier MED Port terminal and brings them right to the entrance of the Tangier Medina Port, in the city center. Remember that if you're coming from Tarifa, your ship will most likely dock at the Tangier Medina Port (covered under "Arrival in Tangier—By Ferry," page 778).

Returning to Tarifa: It's smart to return to the port about 20 minutes before your ferry departs. If you didn't get your passport's exit stamp on the way over, you must wait in line to get it stamped at the Tangier ferry terminal before you board the boat.

Taking a Tour

Taking a tour is easier but less rewarding than doing it on your own or with a private guide. A typical day-trip tour includes a round-trip crossing and a guide who meets your big group at a prearranged point in Tangier, then hustles you through the hustlers and onto your tour bus. Several guides await the arrival of each ferry in Tangier and assemble their groups. (Tourists wear stickers identifying which tour they're with.) All offer essentially the same five-hour Tangier experience: a city bus tour, a drive

through the ritzy palace neighborhood, a walk through the Medina (old town), and an overly thorough look at a sales-starved carpet shop (where prices include a 20 percent commission for your guide and tour company; some carpet shops are actually owned by the ferry companies). Longer tours may include a trip to the desolate Atlantic Coast for some rugged African scenery, and the famous ride-a-camel stop (five-minute camel ride for a couple of euros). Any tour wraps up with lunch in a palatial Moroccan setting with live music (and non-Moroccan belly dancing), topped off by a final walk back to your boat through a gauntlet of desperate merchants.

Sound cheesy? It is. But no amount of packaging can gloss over this exotic and different culture. This kind of cultural voyeurism is almost embarrassing, but it's nonstop action.

The day trip is so tightly organized that tourists have hardly any time alone in Tangier. For many people, that's just fine. But frankly, seeing a line of day-trippers clutching their bags nervously like paranoid kangaroos reminded me of a self-imposed hostage crisis. It was pathetic.

You rarely need to book a tour more than a day in advance, even during peak season. Tours generally cost about €60 (less than a round-trip ferry ticket alone—they make their money off commissions if you shop, and get a group rate on the ferry tickets). Prices are roughly the same no matter where you buy. While some agencies run their own tours, others simply sell tickets on excursions operated by the two big ferry companies, FRS and Comarit. If you're choosing between these two companies, the more-established FRS has a better reputation for tours than the cheaper, newer Comarit. But ultimately, it's the luck of the draw as to which guide you're assigned. Don't worry about which tour company you select. (They're all equally bad.)

Tours leave Tarifa on a variable schedule: For example, one tour may depart at 9:00 and return at 15:00, the next could run 11:00-19:00 (offering a longer experience), and the next 13:00-19:00. If you're an independent type on a one-day tour, you could stay with your group until you return to the ferry dock, and then just slip back into town on your own, thinking, "Freedom!" You're welcome to use your return ferry ticket on any later boat run by the same company (FRS or Comarit; each has departures every two hours).

You can pay extra for various add-ons. For an extra €15 per person beyond the cost of a standard tour, they will arrange a **"VIP tour"** for up to four people—you'll get a private guide and vehicle, plus lunch. This is actually quite economical, especially if you're traveling as a foursome and would prefer a more personalized experience.

If you want a longer visit, it's cheap to book a package through the ferry company that includes staying in a Tangier hotel for one night (only €30-35 more than the regular tour, €10 extra in peak season, includes guiding and 2 lunches and 1 dinner). If you stay overnight, the first day is the same as the one-day tour, but rather than catching the boat that afternoon, you take the same boat—on your own—24 hours later. There's also a two-day option that includes no guiding or meals (€25-30 more than regular tour, €12 extra in peak season).

Booking a Tour: If you're taking one of these tours, you may as well book direct with the **ferry company** (see contact information earlier, under "Ferry Crossing," or visit their offices at the port in Tarifa), or through your **hotel** (you'll pay the same, but the hotel gets a commission; if you know you want to visit Morocco with a tour, ask your hotel to book it when you reserve). There's not much reason to book with a **travel agency,** but offices all over southern Spain and in Tarifa sell ferry tickets and seats on tours. In Tarifa, Luís and Antonio at Baelo Tour offer my readers a 10 percent discount (daily in summer 7:40-21:00, across from TI at Avenida de la Constitución 5, tel. 956-681-242); other Tarifa-based agencies are Tarifa Travel and Travelsur (both on Avenida de Andalucía, above the old-town walls).

Tangier

Artists, writers, and musicians have always loved Tangier. Delacroix and Matisse were drawn by its evocative light. The Beat generation, led by William S. Burroughs and Jack Kerouac, sought the city's multicultural, otherworldly feel. Paul Bowles found his sheltering sky here. From the 1920s through the 1950s, Tangier was an "international city," too strategic to give to any one nation, and jointly governed by as many as nine different powers, including France, Spain, Britain, Italy, Belgium, the Netherlands...and Morocco. The city was a tax-free zone (since there was no single authority to collect taxes), which created a booming free-for-all atmosphere, attracting playboy millionaires, bon vivants, globe-trotting scoundrels, con artists, and expat romantics. Tangier enjoyed a cosmopolitan golden age that, in many ways, shaped the city visitors see today.

Tangier is always defying expectations. Ruled by Spain in the 19th century and France in the 20th, it's a rare place where signs are in three languages...and English doesn't make the cut. In this Muslim city, you'll find a synagogue, Catholic and Anglican churches, and the town's largest mosque in close proximity.

Because of its "international zone" status, Morocco's previous king effectively disowned the city, denying it national funds for improvements. Over time, neglected Tangier became the arm-

pit of Morocco. But when the new king—Mohammed VI—was crowned in 1999, the first city he visited was Tangier. His vision is to restore Tangier to its former glory. Prodding his countrymen with the slogan "Morocco is moving," he's nudging the country into the future.

Thanks to King Mohammed VI, Tangier (with a population of 700,000 and growing quickly) is experiencing a rebirth. While the city has a long way to go, restorations are taking place on a grand scale: The beach has been painstakingly cleaned, pedestrian promenades are popping up, and gardens bloom with lush new greenery. A brand-new futuristic soccer stadium opened in 2011, and the city-center port is being converted into a huge, slick leisure-craft complex that will handle cruise megaships, yachts, and ferries from Tarifa.

I'm uplifted by the new Tangier—it's affluent and modern without having abandoned its roots and embraced Western values. Many visitors are impressed by the warmth of the Moroccan people. Notice how they touch their right hand to their heart after shaking hands or saying, "thank you"—a kind gesture meant to emphasize sincerity. (In Islam, the right hand is holy, while the left hand is evil. Moroccans who eat with their hands—as many civilized people do in this part of the world—always eat with their right hand; the left hand is for washing.)

A visit to Morocco—so close to Europe, yet embracing the Arabic language and script and Muslim faith—lets a Westerner marinated in anti-Muslim propaganda see what Islam aspires to be and can be...and realize it is not a threat.

TANGIER

Planning Your Time

If you're not on a package tour, pre-arrange for a guide to meet you at the ferry dock (see "Guides," later), hire a guide upon arrival, or head on your own to the big square called the Grand Socco to get oriented (you can walk or catch a Petit Taxi from the port to the Grand Socco). Get your bearings with my Grand Socco spin-tour, then delve into the old town (the lower Medina, with the Petit Socco, market, and American Legation Museum; and the upper Medina's Kasbah, with its museum and residential lanes). With more time, take a taxi to sightsee along the beach and then along Avenue Mohammed VI, through the urban new town, and back to the port. You'll rarely see other tourists outside the tour-group circuit.

After Dark: Nighttime is great in Tangier. If you're spending the night, don't relax in a fancy hotel restaurant. Get out and about in the old town after dark. It's an entirely different experience and a highlight of any visit. (But remember, this isn't night-owl Spain—things die down by around 22:00.)

Orientation to Tangier

Like almost every city in Morocco, Tangier is split in two: old and new. From the ferry dock you'll see the old town (Medina)—encircled by its medieval wall—on your right, behind Hotel Continental. The old town has the markets, the Kasbah (with its palace and the mosque of the Kasbah—marked by the higher of the two minarets you see), cheap hotels, characteristic guest houses, homes both decrepit and recently  renovated, and 2,000 wannabe guides. The twisty, hilly streets of the old town are caged within a wall accessible by keyhole gates. The larger minaret (on the left) belongs to the modern Mohammed

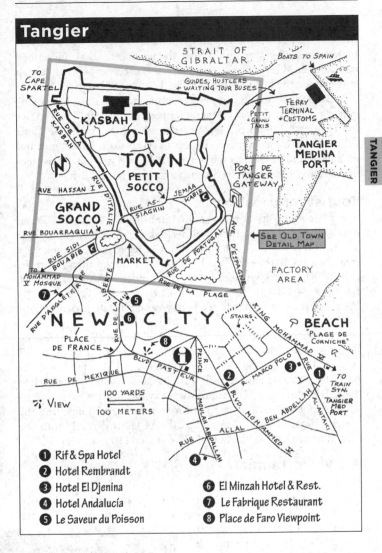

Tangier

TANGIER

STRAIT OF GIBRALTAR

BOATS TO SPAIN

TO CAPE SPARTEL

GUIDES, HUSTLERS & WAITING TOUR BUSES

FERRY TERMINAL + CUSTOMS

PETIT + GRAND TAXIS

KASBAH

OLD TOWN

PETIT SOCCO

PORT DE TANGER GATEWAY

TANGIER MEDINA PORT

RUE DE LA KASBAH

RUE D'ITALIE

AVE HASSAN I

JEMAA KABIR

RUE AS-SIAGHIN

GRAND SOCCO

RUE BOUARRAQUIA

AVE D'ESPAGNE

SEE OLD TOWN DETAIL MAP

RUE SIDI BOUABIB

MARKET

RUE DE PORTUGAL

FACTORY AREA

TO MOHAMMAD V MOSQUE

RUE DE LA PLAGE

❼

❺

RUE D'ANGLETERRE

RUE DE LIBERTE

❻

N E W C I T Y

STAIRS

KING MOHAMMED VI

BEACH "PLAGE DE CORNICHE"

PLACE DE FRANCE

❽

BLVD PASTEUR

PRINCE

RUE DE MEXIQUE

❷

R. MARCO POLO

❸

❶

TO TRAIN STN. & TANGIER MED PORT

BLVD. MOHAMMED

BEN ABDELLAH

RUE AL ANTAKI

MOULAN ABDALLAN

ALLAL

RUE

❹

📷 VIEW

100 YARDS
100 METERS

❶ Rif & Spa Hotel
❷ Hotel Rembrandt
❸ Hotel El Djenina
❹ Hotel Andalucía
❺ Le Saveur du Poisson

❻ El Minzah Hotel & Rest.
❼ Le Fabrique Restaurant
❽ Place de Faro Viewpoint

V mosque—the biggest one in town.

The new town, with the TI and modern international-style hotels, sprawls past the industrial port zone to your left. The big square, Grand Socco, is the hinge between the old and new parts of town.

Note that while tourists (and this guidebook) refer to the twisty old town as "the Medina," locals consider both the old and new parts of the city center to be medinas.

Tangier is the fifth-largest city in Morocco, and many visitors assume they'll get lost here. While the city could use more street signs, it's laid out simply—although once you enter the mazelike Medina, all bets are off. Nothing listed under "Sights in Tangier" is more than a 20-minute walk from the port. Petit Taxis (described later, under "Getting Around Tangier") are a remarkably cheap godsend for the hot and tired tourist. Use them liberally.

Because so many different colonial powers have had a finger in this city, it goes by many names: In English, it's Tangier (or Tangiers); in French, Tanger (tahn-zhay); in Arabic, it's Tanja (TAHN-zhah); in Spanish, Tánger (TAHN-*h*air, with a guttural *h*); and so on. Unless you speak Arabic, French is the handiest second language, followed by Spanish and (finally) English.

Tourist Information

The TI, about a 15-minute gradual uphill walk from the Grand Socco, is not particularly helpful (English is in short supply, but a little French goes a long way). But at least you can pick up a free town brochure—in French only—with a town map (Mon-Fri 8:30-16:30, closed Sat-Sun, in new town at Boulevard Pasteur 29, tel. 0539-94-80-50). There's also a TI desk at the Tangier MED Port, and there may be one at the city-center Tangier Medina Port in the future.

The urban area around the Tangier TI has a few interesting features. The yellow building across the small street from the TI (toward the Grand Socco) is a synagogue. A block farther is the beautiful Place de Faro terrace, with its cannons and views back to Spain. (Nicknamed "Terrace of the Lazy Ones," this momentum-killing spot is usually lined with men relaxing and enjoying the views.) Beyond that, Rue de la Liberté leads directly into the Grand Socco square, the hub of old Tangier.

Arrival in Tangier

By Ferry

If you're taking a tour, just follow the leader. If you're on your own, you'll want to head for the Grand Socco to get oriented. You can either take a taxi (cheap) or walk (about 10 gently uphill minutes through the colorful but confusing lanes of the Medina). Note that the entire port area is slated for an extensive reconstruction in the coming years, so you may find some changes from the way things are described here.

A small blue **Petit Taxi** is your easiest way to get from the port into town (described later, under "Getting Around Tangier");

unfortunately, prices are not regulated from the port. An honest cabbie will charge you 10 dh (about $1.25) for a ride from the ferry into town; less scrupulous drivers will try to charge closer to 100 dh. Set your price before hopping in.

To **walk** into town, head out through the port entrance checkpoint (by the mosque) and bear left at the stubby wall, passing the big bus parking lot and the white Hotel Continental on your right-hand side. After a few minutes, at the end of the bus lot, look for a mosque's white minaret with green tile high on the hill, and head toward it by going up the street just beyond the long, high white wall (behind the buses). Go through the yellow gateway (Bab Dar Dbagh) marked *1921* and *1339*. Bear right/uphill at the T-intersection, then turn left/uphill on Rue de la Marine. You'll pass a school on the right, then the mosque with the green minaret on your left. Continue straight up to the café-lined Petit Socco square, then continue to the top of the street and turn left before the white gate to enter the Grand Socco. Leave mental breadcrumbs as you walk, so you can find your way back to your boat.

By Plane

The Tangier Airport (Aeroport Ibn Battouta) is very new-feeling, slick, and well-organized, with ATMs, cafés, and other amenities. Iberia, Royal Air Maroc, easyJet, and Ryanair fly from here to Madrid (easyJet also has a route to Paris). Jet4you, another low-cost airline, is based in Casablanca, but offers flights from Tangier to Barcelona and Brussels (www.jet4you.com). To get into downtown Tangier, taxis should run you about 150 dh and take 30-45 minutes.

Getting Around Tangier

There are two types of taxis: Avoid the big, beige Mercedes "Grand Taxis," which are the most aggressive and don't use their meters (they're designed for longer trips outside of the city center, but have been known to take tourists for a ride in town...in more ways than one). Look instead for Petit Taxis—blue with a yellow stripe (they fit up to three people). These generally use their meters, are very cheap, and only circulate within the city. However, at the port, Petit Taxis are allowed to charge whatever you'll pay without using the meter, so it's essential to agree on a price up front (see "Arrival in Tangier," earlier).

Be aware that Tangier taxis "double up"—if you're headed somewhere, the driver may pick up someone else who's going in the same direction. However, in this case you don't get to split the fare—each of you pays full price (even though sometimes the other passenger's route takes you a bit out of your way).

Helpful Hints

Money: The exchange rate is 8 dh = about $1; 11 dh = about €1. While most businesses happily take euros or dollars, it's classier to use the local currency—and you'll save money. If you're on a tour, they'll rip you off anyway, so just stick with euros. If you're on your own, it's fun to get a pocket full of dirhams.

A few ATMs are around the Grand Socco (look for one just to the left of the archway entrance into the Medina); more are opposite the TI along Boulevard Pasteur. ATMs work as you expect them to.   Exchange desks are quick, easy, and fair. (Just understand the buy-and-sell rates—there should be no other fee. If you change €50 into dirhams and immediately change the dirhams back, you should have about €45.) Look for the official *Bureaux de Change* offices, where you'll get better rates than at the banks. There are some on Rue Pasteur, and a handful between the Grand and Petit Soccos. The official change offices all offer the same rates, so there's no need to shop around.

Convert your dirhams back to euros before catching the ferry—it's cheap and easy to do here (change desks at the port keep long hours), but very difficult once you're back in Spain.

Telephone: To call Tangier from Spain, dial 00 (Europe's international access code), 212 (Morocco's country code), then the local number (dropping the initial zero). To dial Tangier from elsewhere in Morocco, dial the local number in full (keeping the initial zero).

Navigation: Tangier's maps and street signs are frustrating. I ask in French for the landmark: *Où est...?* ("Where is...?," pronounced oo ay, as in *"oo ay Medina?"* or *"oo ay Kasbah?"*). It can be fun to meet people this way. However, most people who offer to help you (especially those who approach you) are angling for a tip—young and old, locals see dollar signs when a traveler approaches. To avoid getting unwanted company, ask for directions only from people who can't leave what they're doing (such as the only clerk in a shop) or from women who aren't near men. There are fewer hustlers in the new (but less interesting) part of town. Be aware that most people don't know the names of the smaller streets (which don't usually have signs), and tend to navigate by landmarks. In case you get the wrong directions, ask three times and go with the consensus. If there's no consensus, it's time to hop into a Petit Taxi.

Mosques: Tangier's mosques (and virtually all of Morocco's) are closed to non-Muslim visitors.

Women in Morocco

Most visitors to Tangier expect to see the women completely covered head-to-toe by their kaftan. In fact, only about one-quarter of Moroccan women still adhere strictly to this religious code. Some just cover their head (allowing their face to be seen), while others eliminate the head scarf altogether. Some women wear only Western-style clothing. This change in dress visibly reflects deeper, more fundamental shifts in Moroccan attitudes about women's rights.

Morocco happens to be one of the most progressive Muslim countries around. As in any border country, contact with other cultures fosters the growth of new ideas. Bombarded with Spanish television and visitors like you, change is inevitable. Another proponent of change is King Mohammed VI, who was only 35 years old when he rose to the throne in 1999. For the first time in the country's history, the king personally selected a female adviser to demonstrate his commitment to change. The king also married a commoner for...get this...*love*. And even more shocking, she's seen in public. (It's a first—locals don't even know what King Mohammed VI's mother looks like, as she is never in the public view.)

Recent times have brought even more sweeping transformations to Moroccan society. In order to raise literacy levels and understanding between the sexes, schools are now co-ed—something taken for granted in the West for decades. In 2004, the Mudawana, or judiciary family code, was shockingly overhauled. The legal age for women to marry is now 18 (just like men) instead of 15. Other changes make it more difficult to have a second wife. Verbal divorce and abandonment are no longer legal—disgruntled husbands must now take their complaints to court before divorce is granted. And for the first time, women can divorce their husbands. If children are involved, whoever takes care of the kids gets the house. Of course, not everyone has been happy with the changes, and Islamic fundamentalists were blamed for a series of bombings in Casablanca in 2003. But the reforms became law, and Morocco became a trendsetter for women's equality in the Islamic world.

Guides

If you're on your own, you'll be to street guides what a horse's tail is to flies...all day long. Seriously—it can be exhausting to constantly deflect come-ons from anyone who sees you open a guidebook. In order to have your own translator, and a shield from less scrupulous touts who hit up tourists constantly throughout the old town, I recommend hiring a guide. Stress your interest in the people and culture rather than shopping. Guides, hoping to get a huge commission from your purchases, can cleverly turn your Tangier day into the Moroccan equivalent of the Shopping Channel. Truth be told, some of these guides would work for free, considering all the money they make on commissions when you buy stuff.

I've worked with a variety of guides who speak great English, are easy to get along with, will meet you at the ferry dock, and charge fixed rates. They've promised me they won't make you do any more shopping than you want to—so be very clear about your interests. If one of these guides is busy (or takes a long time responding to your email), try the others. Any of these guides will make your Tangier experience more enjoyable for a negligible cost. They can also book your ferry tickets for the same cost as booking direct: They'll give you a reference number to give at the ticket office in Tarifa, then you'll pay them for the tickets when you meet in Tangier. While each has their own specific itineraries, the two basic options are more or less the same: a half-day walking tour around the Medina and Kasbah (generally 3-5 hours); or a full-day "grand tour" that includes the walk around town as well as a mini-bus ride to outlying viewpoints—the Caves of Hercules and Cape Spartel (7-8 hours, generally also includes lunch at your expense in a restaurant the guide suggests). Prices are fairly standard from guide to guide. If you're very pleased with your guide, he'll appreciate a tip.

Aziz Begdouri, who enjoys teaching about Moroccan society and culture, has been a big help to me with my guidebook-writing and TV production in Tangier (half-day walking tour-€15/person, groups limited to 4-5 people; 8-hour grand tour-€35/person; mobile 06-6163-9332, from Spain dial 00-212-6-6163-9332, aziz tour@hotmail.com).

Ahmed Taoumi, who has been guiding for more than 30 years, is a great teacher—almost professorial—but also a good storyteller and fun to be around. He takes pride in tailoring his tours to his customers' interest (half-day walking tour-€18/person,

full-day grand tour with minibus-€35/person, also offers minibus side-trips to nearby destinations and discounted ferry tickets,
mobile 06-6166-5429, from Spain dial 00-212-6-6166-5429, www
.visitangier.com, taoumitour@hotmail.com,).

If Aziz Begdouri and Ahmed are both busy, consider one of
the following youthful go-getters who are a bit lighter on information, but enjoyable to spend time with and dedicated to making
visitors comfortable: **Aziz Benami** (half-day walking tour-€15/per-
son; all-day minibus and walking tour-€79/person, price includes
ferry tickets from Spain; mobile 06-6126-3335, from Spain dial
00-212-6-6126-3335, www.tangierprivateguide.com, info@tangier
privateguide.com) and **Abdellatif ("Latif") Chebaa** (half-day
walking tour-€15/person, grand tour-€35/person, mobile 06-6107-
2014, from Spain dial 00-212-6-6107-2014, visittangier@gmail
.com).

Other Options: If you don't want to plan too far ahead, and
any guide will do, you can book a **"VIP" tour** through the ferry
companies in Tarifa for approximately the same prices listed above
(for details, see page 774). I've also had good luck with the **private
guides who meet the boat.** If you're a decent judge of character, try interviewing guides when you get off the ferry to find one
you click with, then negotiate a good price. These hardworking,
English-speaking, and licensed guides offer their services for the
day for €15.

Sights in Tangier

▲▲The Grand Socco

This big, bustling square is a transportation hub, market, popular
meeting point, and the fulcrum between the new town and the
old town (Medina). Five
years ago, it was a pedestrian nightmare and a per-
petual traffic jam. But now,
like much of Tangier, it's on
the rise. Many of the sights
mentioned in this spin-tour
are described in more detail
later in this chapter.

○ Self-Guided Spin Tour: The Grand Socco is a good place
to get oriented to the heart of Tangier. Stand on the square between
the fountain and the mosque (the long building with arches and
the tall tower). We'll do a slow clockwise spin.

Start by facing the **mosque**—newly remodeled with a long
arcade of keyhole arches, and with a colorfully tiled minaret.
Morocco is a decidedly Muslim nation, though its take on Islam

Tangier's Old Town

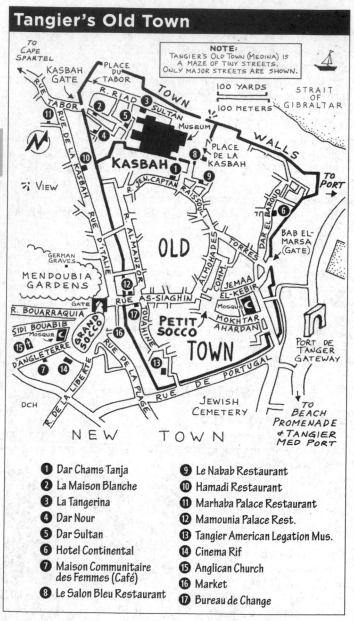

NOTE: Tangier's Old Town (Medina) is a maze of tiny streets. Only major streets are shown.

100 YARDS
100 METERS

TO CAPE SPARTEL

KASBAH GATE

PLACE DU TABOR

R. RIAD SULTAN

TOWN WALLS

STRAIT OF GIBRALTAR

Museum

KASBAH

PLACE DE LA KASBAH

RUE TABOR

RUE DE LA KASBAH

RUE D'ITALIE

VIEW

R. JEN. CAPTAN RAISSOULI

TO PORT

BAB EL-MARSA (GATE)

DAR EL BAROUD

GERMAN GRAVES

MENDOUBIA GARDENS

OLD

R. ALMANZOR

ALMOHADES

TORRES

COMM.

Gate

R. BOUARRAQUIA

RUE AS-SIAGHIN

PETIT SOCCO

JEMAA EL-KEBIR

Mosque

MOKHTAR AHARDAN

TOUAHINE

PORT DE TANGER GATEWAY

SIDI BOUABIB Mosque

GRAND SOCCO

Market

TOWN

D'ANGLETERRE

RUE DE LA PLAGE

RUE DE PORTUGAL

DCH

R. DE LA LIBERTE

JEWISH CEMETERY

TO BEACH PROMENADE & TANGIER MED PORT

NEW   TOWN

1 Dar Chams Tanja
2 La Maison Blanche
3 La Tangerina
4 Dar Nour
5 Dar Sultan
6 Hotel Continental
7 Maison Communitaire des Femmes (Café)
8 Le Salon Bleu Restaurant
9 Le Nabab Restaurant
10 Hamadi Restaurant
11 Marhaba Palace Restaurant
12 Mamounia Palace Rest.
13 Tangier American Legation Mus.
14 Cinema Rif
15 Anglican Church
16 Market
17 Bureau de Change

TANGIER

(see "Islam 101," page 766) is progressive, likely owing to the country's crossroads history. For example, women are relatively free to dress as they like. Five times a day, you'll hear the call to prayer echo across the rooftops of Tangier, from minarets like this one. Unlike many Muslim countries, Morocco doesn't allow non-Muslims to enter its mosques (with the exception of its biggest and most famous one, in Casablanca). This custom may have originated decades ago, when occupying French foreign legion troops spent the night in a mosque, entertaining themselves with wine and women. Following this embarrassing desecration, it was the French government—not the Moroccans—who instituted the ban that persists today.

Locals say that in this very cosmopolitan city, any time you see a mosque, you'll find a church nearby. Sure enough, peeking up behind the mosque, you can barely make out the white, crenellated top of the **Anglican Church**'s tower (or at least the English flag above it—a red cross on a white field). A fascinating architectural hybrid of Muslim and Christian architecture, this house of worship is well worth a visit.

Also behind the mosque, you can see parts of a sprawling **market.** (This features mostly modern goods; the far more colorful produce, meat, and fish market is across the square.) Those market stalls used to fill the square you're standing in; traditionally the Grand Socco was Tangier's hub for visiting merchants. The gates of town would be locked each evening, and vendors who did not arrive in time spent the night in this area. (Nearby were many caravanserai, old-fashioned inns.) But a few years ago, this square was dramatically renovated by the visionary king, Mohammed VI, and given a new name: "April 9th Square," commemorating the date in 1947 when an earlier king, Mohammed V, appealed to his French overlords to grant his country its independence. (France eventually complied, peacefully, in 1956.) In just the last few years, Mohammed VI tamed the traffic, added the fountain you're standing next to (there was never a fountain here before), and turned this into a delightfully people-friendly space.

Spin a few more degrees to the right, where you'll see the crenellated gateway marked *Tribunal de Commerce*—the entrance to the **Mendoubia Garden,** a pleasant park with a gigantic tree and a quirky history that reflects the epic story of Tangier (particularly from the 1920s to the 1950s, when multiple foreign powers shared control of this city). At the top of the garden gateway, notice the Moroccan flag: a green five-pointed star on a red field.

The five points of the star represent the five pillars of Islam (see "Islam 101" sidebar, page 766); green is the color of peace; and red represents the struggles of hard-fought Moroccan history.

Spinning farther right, you'll see the **keyhole arch** marking the entrance to the Medina. (If you need cash, notice the exchange booths and ATM just to the left of this gateway.) To reach the heart of the Medina—the Petit Socco (the café-lined little brother of the square you're on now)—go through this arch and take the first right.

In front of the arch, you'll likely see **day laborers** looking for work. Each one stands next to a symbol of the kind of work he specializes in: a bucket of paintbrushes for a painter, a coil of wiring for an electrician, and a loop of hose for a plumber.

Speaking of people looking for work, how many locals have offered to show you around ("Hey! What you looking for? I help you!") since you've been standing here, holding this guidebook? Get used to it. While irritating, it's understandable. To these very poor people, you're impossibly rich—your pocket change is at least a good day's wage. If someone pesters you, you can simply ignore them, or say *"Lah shokran"* (No, thank you). But be warned: The moment you engage them, you've just prolonged the sales pitch.

Back to our spin-tour: To the right of the main arch, and just before the row of green rooftops, is the low-profile entrance to the **market** *(souk)*. A barrage on all the senses, this is a fascinating place to explore. The row of green rooftops leads toward Rue de la Plage, with more market action.

Continue spinning another quarter-turn to the tall, white building at the top of the square labeled **Cinema Rif.** This historic movie house still plays films (in Arabic and French). The street to the left of the cinema takes you to Rue de la Liberté, which eventually leads through the modern town to the TI (about a 15-minute walk). Just to the right of the cinema, notice the yellow terrace, which offers the best view over the Grand Socco (just go up the staircase). It's also part of a café, where you can order a Moroccan tea (green tea, fresh mint, and lots of sugar), enjoy the view over the square, and plot your next move.

Near the Grand Socco

These sights are near the Grand Socco, but still outside the Medina (old town).

▲**Anglican Church**—St. Andrew's Anglican Church, tucked behind a showpiece mosque, embodies Tangier's mingling of Muslim and Christian tradition. The land on which the church sits was a gift from the sultan to the British community in 1881, during Queen Victoria's era. Shortly thereafter, this church was built. Although fully Christian, the church is designed in the style of a Muslim mosque. The Lord's Prayer rings the arch in Arabic, as verses of the Quran would in a mosque. Knock on the door—Ali or his son Yassin will greet you and give you a "thank you very much" tour (a tip of about 20 dh is appreciated; daily 9:00-18:00 except closed during Sunday services). The garden surrounding the church is a tranquil, parklike cemetery.

Mendoubia Garden—This pleasant park, through the castle-like archway off of the Grand Socco, is a favorite place for locals to

hang out, but also has a surprising history. Walk through the gateway to see the trunk of a gigantic banyan tree, which, according to local legend, dates from the 12th century. Notice how the extra supportive roots have grown from the branches down to the ground. The large building to the left—today the business courthouse (*Tribunal de Commerce*)—was built to house the representative of the Moroccan king, back in the early 20th century when Tangier was ruled as a protectorate of various European powers and needed an ambassador of sorts to keep an eye out for Moroccan interests. The smaller house on the right (behind the giant tree) is currently the marriage courthouse (used exclusively for getting married or divorced), but it was once the headquarters of the German delegation in Tangier. France originally kept Germany out of the protectorate arrangement by giving them the Congo. But in 1941, when Germany was on the rise in Europe and allied with Spain's Franco, it joined the mix of ruling powers in Tangier. Although Germans were only here for a short time (until mid-1942), they had a small cemetery in what's now the big park in front of you. If you go up the stairs and around the blocky Arabic monument, at the bases of the trees beyond it you'll find headstones of German graves...an odd footnote in the very complex history of this intriguing city.

The Medina (Old Town)

Tangier's Medina is its convoluted old town—a twisty mess of narrow stepped lanes, dead-end alleys, and lots of local life spilling out into the streets. It's divided roughly into two parts: the lower Medina, with the Petit Socco, market, American Legation, and bustling street life; and, at the top, the more tranquil Kasbah.

The Lower Medina and Petit Socco

A maze of winding lanes and tiny alleys weave through the old-town market area.

Petit Socco—This little square, also called Souk Dahel ("Inner Market"), is the center of the lower Medina. Lined with tea shops and cafés, it has a romantic quality that has long made it a people magnet. In the 1920s, it was the meeting point for Tangier's wealthy and influential elite; by the 1950s and '60s, it drew Jack Kerouac and his counterculture buddies. Nursing a coffee or a mint tea here, it's easy to pretend you're a Beat Generation rebel, dropping out from Western society and delving deeply into an exotic, faraway culture. More recently, filmmakers have been drawn here. Scenes from both *The Bourne Ultimatum* and *Inception* were filmed on the streets between the Grand and Petit Soccos.

The Petit Socco is ideal for some casual people-watching over a drink. You can go to one of the more traditional cafés, but Café Central—with the modern awning—is the most accessible, and therefore the most commercialized and touristy (7-12-dh coffee drinks, 20-45-dh meals, daily 6:00-24:00).

▲▲Market (Souk)—The Medina's market, just off the Grand Socco, is a highlight. Wander past piles of fruit, veggies, and olives, countless varieties of bread, and fresh goat cheese wrapped in palm leaves. Phew! You'll find everything but pork.

Entering the market through the door from the Grand Socco, turn right to find butchers, a cornucopia of produce (almost all of it from Morocco), more butchers, piles of olives, and yet more butchers. The chickens are plucked and hung to show they have been killed according to Islamic guidelines (Halal): Animals are slaughtered with a sharp knife in the name of Allah, head to Mecca, and drained of their blood. The far aisle (parallel and to the left of where you're walking) has more innards and is a little harder to stomach.

You'll see women vendors wearing straw hats decorated with ribbons, and often also striped skirts, scattered around the mar-

TANGIER

Bargaining Basics

No matter what kind of merchandise you buy in Tangier, the shopping is...Moroccan. Bargain hard! The first price you're offered is simply a starting point, and it's expected that you'll try to talk the price way down. Bargaining can become an enjoyable game if you follow a few basic rules:

Determine what the item is worth to you. Before you even ask a price, decide what the item's value is to you. Consider the hassles involved in packing it or shipping it home.

Determine the merchant's lowest price. Many merchants will settle for a nickel profit rather than lose the sale entirely. Work the cost down to rock bottom, and when it seems to have fallen to a record low, walk away. That last price the seller hollers out as you turn the corner is often the best price you'll get. If the price is right, go back and buy.

Look indifferent. As soon as the merchant perceives the "I gotta have that!" in you, you'll never get the best price.

Employ a third person. Use your friend who is worried about the ever-dwindling budget or who doesn't like the price or who is bored and wants to return to the hotel. This trick can work to bring the price down faster.

Show the merchant your money. Physically hold out your money and offer him "all you have" to pay for whatever you are bickering over. He'll be tempted to just grab your money and say, "Oh, OK."

If the price is too much, leave. Never worry about having taken too much of the merchant's time. They are experts at making the tourist feel guilty for not buying. It's all part of the game.

ket; these are Berbers from the nearby Rif mountains. (Before taking photos of these women, or any people you see here, it's polite to ask permission.)

Eventually you'll emerge into the large white market of fish-sellers; with the day's catch from both the Mediterranean and the Atlantic, this is like a textbook of marine life. The door at the far end of the fish market pops you out on the Rue Salah El-dine Al Ayoubi; a right turn takes you back to the Grand Socco, but a left turn

leads to the (figurative and literal) low end of the market—a world of very rustic market stalls under a corrugated plastic roof. While just a block from the main market, this is a world apart, and not to everyone's taste. Here you'll find cheap produce, junk shops, electronics (such as recordable CDs and old remote controls), old ladies sorting bundles of herbs from crinkled plastic bags, and far less sanitary-looking butchers than the ones inside the main market hall (if that's possible). Peer down the alley filled with a twitching poultry market, which encourages vegetarianism.

The upper part of the market (toward the Medina and Petit Socco) has a few food stands, but more non-perishable items, such as clothing, cleaning supplies, toiletries, and prepared foods. Scattered around this part of the market are spice and herb stalls (usually marked *hérboriste*), offering a fragrant antidote to the meat stalls. In addition to cooking spices, these sell homegrown Berber cures for ailments. Pots hold a dark-green gelatinous goo—a kind of natural soap.

If you're looking for souvenirs, you won't have to find them... they'll find you, in the form of aggressive salesmen who approach you on the street and push their conga drums, T-shirts, and other trinkets in your face. Most of the market itself is more focused on locals, but the Medina streets just above the market are loaded with souvenir shops. Aside from the predictable trinkets, the big-ticket items here are tilework (such as vases) and carpets. You'll notice many shops have tiles and other, smaller souvenirs on the ground floor, and carpet salesrooms upstairs.

▲▲▲**Exploring the Medina**—Appealing as the market is, one of the most evocative Tangier experiences is to simply lose yourself in the lanes of the Medina. A first-time visitor cannot stay oriented—so don't even try. I just wander, knowing that uphill will eventually get me to the Kasbah and downhill will eventually lead me to the port. Expect to get a little lost...going around in circles is part of the fun. Pop in to see artisans working in their shops: mosaic

tile-makers, thread spinners, tailors. While shops are on the ground level, the family usually lives upstairs.

Many people can't afford private ovens, phones, or running water, so there are economical communal options: phone desks (called *telebou-tiques*), baths, and bakeries. If you smell the aroma of baking bread, look for a hole-in-the-wall bakery, where locals drop off their ready-to-cook dough (as well as meat, fish, or nuts to roast). You'll also stumble upon communal taps, with water provided by the government, where people come to wash. Cubby-hole rooms are filled with kids playing video games on old TVs—they can't afford their own at home, so they come here instead.

Go on a photo safari for ornate "keyhole" doors, many of which lead to neighborhood mosques. Green doors are the color of Islam and symbolize peace. The ring-shaped door knockers double as a place to hitch a donkey.

As you explore, notice that some parts of the Medina seem starkly different, with fancy wrought-iron balconies. This is the approximately 20 percent of the town that was built and controlled by Spaniards and Portuguese living here (with the rest being Arabic and Berber). The two populations were separated by a wall, the remains of which you can still trace running through the Medina. It may seem at first glance that these European zones are fancier and "nicer" compared to the poorer-seeming Arabic/Berber zones. But the Arabs and Berbers take more care with the inside of their homes—if you went behind these hum-

ble walls, you'd be surprised how pleasant the interiors are. While European cultures externalize resources, Arab and Berber cultures internalize them.

Tangier American Legation Museum—Located at the bottom end of the Medina (just above the port), this unexpected museum

is worth a visit. Morocco was one of the first countries to recognize the newly formed United States as an independent country (in 1777). The original building, given to the United States by the sultan of Morocco, became the fledgling government's first foreign acquisition. This was the US embassy (or consulate) in Morocco from 1821 to 1961, and it's still American property—our only National Historic Landmark overseas. Today this nonprofit museum and research center, housed in a 19th-century mansion, is a strangely peaceful oasis within Tangier's intense old town. It offers a warm welcome and lots of interesting artifacts—all well-described in English in an evocative building. The ground floor is filled with an art gallery. In the stairwell, you'll see photos of kings with presidents, and a letter with the news of Lincoln's assassination. Upstairs are more paintings, as well as model soldiers playing out two battle scenes from Moroccan history. These belonged to American industrialist Malcolm Forbes, who had a home in Tangier (his son donated these dioramas to the museum). Rounding out the upper floor are more paintings, and evocative old maps of Tangier and Morocco. A visit here is a fun reminder of how long the US and Morocco have had good relations (free entry but donations appreciated, Mon-Thu 10:00-13:00 & 15:00-17:00, Fri 10:00-12:00 & 15:00-17:00, during Ramadan holiday 10:00-15:00, closed Sat-Sun, ring bell, Rue d'Amérique 8, tel. 0539-935-317, www.legation.org).

• *When you've soaked in enough old-town atmosphere, make your way to the Kasbah (see map). Within the Medina, head uphill, or exit the Medina gate and go right on Rue de la Kasbah, which follows the old wall uphill to Bab Kasbah (a.k.a. Porte de la Kasbah), a gateway into the Kasbah.*

Kasbah

Loosely translated as "fortress," a *kasbah* is an enclosed, protected residential area near a castle that you'll find in hundreds of Moroccan towns. Originally this was a place where a king or other leader could protect his tribe. Tangier's Kasbah comprises the upper quarter of the old town. A residential area with twisty lanes and some nice guest houses, this area is a bit more sedate and less claustrophobic than parts of the Medina near the market below.

▲**Kasbah Museum**—On Place de la Kasbah, you'll find the Dar el-Makhzen, a former sultan's palace that now houses a history

museum with a few historical artifacts. While there's not a word of English, some of the exhibits are still easy to appreciate, and the building itself is beautiful. Most of the exhibits surround the central, open-air courtyard; rooms proceed roughly chronologically as you move counter-clockwise, from early hunters and farmers to prehistoric civilizations, Roman times, the region's conversion to Islam, and the influence of European powers. The two-story space at the far end of the courtyard focuses on a second-century mosaic floor depicting the journey of Venus. The big 12th-century wall-size map (in Arabic) shows the Moorish view of the world: with Africa on top (Spain is at the far right). Nearby is an explanation of terra-cotta production (a local industry), and upstairs is an exhibit on funerary rituals. Near the entrance, look for signs to *jardin* and climb the stairs to reach a chirpy (if slightly overgrown) garden courtyard. While the building features some striking tilework, you just can't shake the feeling that the best Moorish sights are back in Spain.

Cost and Hours: 10 dh, Wed-Mon 9:00-16:00, closed for prayer Fri 12:30-14:30, closed all day Tue, tel. 0539-932-097.

Place de la Kasbah—Because the Kasbah Museum (while modest) is the city's main museum, the square in front of the palace

attracts more than its share of tourists. That means it's also a vivid gauntlet of amusements waiting to ambush parading tour groups: snake charmers, squawky dance troupes, and colorful water vendors. These colorful Kodak-moment hustlers make their living off the many tour groups passing by daily. (As you're cajoled, remember that the daily minimum wage here for men as skilled as these beggars is $10. That's what the gardeners you'll pass in your walk earn each day. In other words, a €1 tip is an hour's wage for these people.) If you draft behind a tour group, you won't be the focus of the hustlers. But if you take a photo, you must pay.

Before descending out of the Kasbah, don't miss the ocean viewpoint—as you stand in the square and face the palace, look to the right to find the hole carved through the thick city wall (Bab Dhar, "Sea Gate"). This leads out to a large natural terrace with fine views over the port, the Mediterranean, and Spain.

The lower gate of the Kasbah (as you stand in Place de la Kasbah facing the palace, it's on your left) leads to a charming little alcove, between the gates, where you can see a particularly fine tile fountain: The top part is carved cedarwood, below that is carved plaster, and the bottom half is

hand-laid tiles. In this area, poke down the tiny lane to the left of the little shop—you'll find that it leads to a surprisingly large courtyard ringed by fine homes.

Matisse Route—The artist Matisse, who traveled to Tangier in 1912, was inspired by his wanderings through this area, picking up themes that show up in much of his art. The diamond-shaped stones embedded in the street (you'll see them on the narrow lane leading up along the left side of the palace) mark a "Matisse

Route" through the Kasbah, from the lower gate to the upper; those familiar with his works will recognize several scenes along this stretch.

Tangier Beach (Plage de Corniche, a.k.a. Playa)

Lined with lots of fishy eateries and entertaining nightclubs, this fine, wide, white-sand crescent beach stretches eastward from the port. The locals call it by the Spanish word *playa*. It's packed with locals doing what people around the world do at the beach—with a few variations. Traditionally clad moms let their kids run wild. Along with lazy camels, you'll see people—young and old—covered in hot sand to combat rheumatism. Early, late,

and off-season, the beach becomes a popular venue for soccer teams. The palm-lined pedestrian street along the waterfront was renamed for King Mohammed VI, in appreciation for recent restorations. While the beach is cleaner than it once was, it still has more than its share of litter—great for a stroll, but maybe not for sunbathing or swimming. If you have a beach break in mind, do it on Spain's Costa del Sol.

Just past the beach on the port side (between here and the Medina) is a zone of nondescript factories. Here local women sew clothing for big, mostly European companies that pay about $8 a day. Each morning and evening rush hour, the street is filled with these women commuters...on foot.

Nightlife in Tangier

Most important: Be out in the **Medina** around 21:00. In the cool of the evening, the atmospheric squares and lanes become even more evocative. Then at about 22:00 things get dark, lonely, and foreboding.

El Minzah Hotel hosts **traditional music** most nights for those having dinner there (see "Eating in Tangier," later; 85 Rue de la Liberté, tel. 0539-935-885).

The **Rif Cinema,** the landmark theater at the top of the Grand Socco, shows movies in French—which the younger generation must learn—and Arabic. The cinema is worth popping into, if only to see the Art Deco interior. As movies cost only 20 dh, consider dropping by to see a bit of whatever's on...in Arabic (closed Mon, tel. 0539-934-683).

Sleeping in Tangier

I've recommended two vastly different types of accommodations in Tangier: cozy Moroccan-style (but mostly French-run) guest houses in the maze of lanes of the Kasbah neighborhood, at the top of the Medina (old town); and big, modern international-style hotels in the urban-feeling new town, a 10-to-20-minute walk from the central sights.

Remember, if you want to call Tangier from Europe, dial 00 (Europe's international access code), 212 (Morocco's country code), then the local number (dropping the initial zero). June through mid-September is high season, when rooms may be a bit more expensive and reservations are wise. Most hotels charge an extra tax of 15-25 dh per person per night (typically not included in the prices I've listed here).

Moroccan-Style Guest Houses in the Kasbah

In Arabic, *dar* means "guest house." You'll find these in the Medina, or atmospheric old quarter. While the lower part of the Medina is dominated by market stalls and tourist traps, and can feel a bit seedy after dark, the upper part (called the Kasbah, for the castle that dominates this area) is more tranquil and feels very residential. All of these are buried in a labyrinth of lanes that can be very difficult to navigate; the map on page 784 gives you a vague sense of where to go, but it's essential to ask for very clear directions when you reserve. If you're hiring a guide in Tangier, ask them to help you find your *dar*. (If you're on your own, you can try asking directions when you arrive—but many local residents

---

Sleep Code

(8 dh = about $1, country code: 212, area code: 539)
S = Single, **D** = Double/Twin, **T** = Triple, **Q** = Quad, **b** = bathroom, **s** = shower only. Unless otherwise noted, credit cards are accepted, English is spoken, and breakfast is included.

To help you easily sort through these listings, I've divided the accommodations into three categories, based on the price for a standard double room with bath (during high season):

  $$$ **Higher Priced**—Most rooms 1,000 dh or more.
   $$ **Moderately Priced**—Most rooms between 500-1,000 dh.
    $ **Lower Priced**—Most rooms 500 dh or less.

Prices can change without notice; verify the hotel's current rates online or by email. For other updates, see www .ricksteves.com/update.

take that as an invitation to tag along and hound you for tips.) All of these are in traditional old houses, with rooms surrounding a courtyard atrium, and all have rooftop terraces where you can relax and enjoy sweeping views over Tangier. There are rarely stand-alone showers; instead, in Moroccan style, you'll find a handheld shower in a corner of the bathroom.

$$$ Dar Chams Tanja, just below the Kasbah gate, has seven elegant, new-feeling rooms with all the comforts surrounding a clean-white inner courtyard with lots of keyhole windows. While pricey, it's impeccably decorated, calm, and stylish (five big Db-1,580 dh, two small Db-1,240 dh, sometimes discounts in slow times—check website, air-con, free Wi-Fi, hammam—Turkish-style bath, massage service, Rue Jnan Kabtan 2, tel. 0539-332-323, www.darchamstanja.com, darchamstanja@gmail.com).

$$$ La Maison Blanche ("The White House"), run by tour guide Aziz Begdouri, has nine rooms in a traditional Moroccan house with modern amenities in the Kasbah (Sb-1,000 dh, Db-1,100 dh, all with bathtubs, air-con, free Wi-Fi, just inside the upper gate of the Kasbah at Rue Ahmed Ben Ajiba 2, tel. 0539-373-545, www.lamaisonblanchetanger.com, info@ lamaison blanchetanger.com).

$$ La Tangerina, run by Jürgen (who's German) and his Moroccan wife Farida, has 10 comfortable rooms that look down into a shared atrium. At the top is a gorgeous rooftop seaview balcony (Db-600-935 dh in April and June-mid-Sept, otherwise Db-500-770; suite-1,520-1,650 dh in April and June-mid-Sept, otherwise 1,100-1,320 dh; prices depend on size and include tax, cash only, free Wi-Fi, wood-fired hammam, Riad Sultan 19, tel. 0539-947-731, www.lantangerina.com, info@latangerina.com).

$$ Dar Nour, run with funky French style by Philippe, Jean-Olivier, and Catherine, has an "Escher-esque" floor plan that sprawls through five interconnected houses (it's "labyrinthine like the Medina," says Philippe). The 10 homey rooms feel very traditional, with lots of books and lounging areas spread throughout (Db-735 dh, junior suite Db-970 dh, suite Db-1,330 dh, cash only, free Wi-Fi in lobby, Rue Gourna 20, mobile 06-6211-2724, www .darnour.com, contactdarnour@yahoo.fr).

$$ Dar Sultan rents six romantically decorated rooms on a pleasant street in the heart of the Kasbah (Db-990 dh, larger Db-1,210 dh, Db with terrace-1,320 dh, free Wi-Fi in lobby and cable Internet in rooms, Rue Touila 49, tel. 0539-336-061, www .darsultan.com, dar-sultan@menara.ma).

Modern Hotels in the Modern City

These hotels are centrally located, near the TI, and within walking distance of the Grand Socco, Medina, and market. The first two are three-star hotels and take credit cards; the others are cash-only.

$$$ Rif & Spa Hotel, recently restored to its 1970s glamour, is a worthy splurge. Offering 127 plush, modern rooms, sprawling public spaces, a garden, a pool, and grand views, it feels like an oversized boutique hotel. The great Arabic lounge—named for Winston Churchill—with a harbor view compels you to relax (Sb-1,200 dh, Db-1,400 dh, 200-dh more July-Aug, 200-dh extra for sea view, see website for specials, breakfast-100 dh, air-con, elevator, free Wi-Fi in lobby, 3 restaurants, spa and sauna, Avenue Mohammed VI 152, tel. 0539-349-300, fax 0539-944-569, www .hotelsatlas.com, riftanger@menara.ma).

$$ Hotel Rembrandt feels just like the 1940s, with a restaurant, a bar, and a swimming pool surrounded by a great grassy garden. Its 70 rooms are outdated and simple, but clean and comfortable, and some come with views (Sb-450-550 dh, Db-600-710 dh, higher prices are for June-Aug, sea view-100 dh extra, includes tax, breakfast often included, otherwise-80 dh, air-con, elevator, free Wi-Fi, a 5-minute walk above the beach in a busy urban zone at Boulevard Mohammed VI 1, tel. 0539-937-870, fax 0539-930-443, www.hotel-rembrandt.com, hotelrembrandt@menara.ma).

$$ Hotel Continental—actually in the Medina (at the bottom of the old town, facing the port)—is the Humphrey Bogart option, a grand old place sprawling along the old town. It has lavish, atmospheric, and recently renovated public spaces, a chandeliered breakfast room, and 70 spacious bedrooms with rough hardwood floors and new bathrooms. Jimmy, who's always around and runs the shop adjacent to the lobby, says he offers everything but Viagra. When I said, "I'm from Seattle," he said, "206." Test him—he knows your area code (Sb-495 dh, Db-635 dh, about 100 dh more July-Sept, includes tax and breakfast, free Wi-Fi, Dar Baroud 36, tel. 0539-931-024, fax 0539-931-143, hcontinental @iam.net.ma). This hotel's terrace aches with nostalgia. Back during the city's glory days, a ferry connected Tangier and New York. American novelists would sit out on the terrace of Hotel Continental, never quite sure when their friends' boat would arrive from across the sea...

$ Hotel El Djenina is a local-style business-class hotel—extremely plain, reliable, safe, and well-located. Its 40 rooms are a block off the harbor, midway between the port and the TI. Request a room on the back side to escape the street noise (Sb-319-357 dh, Db-382-463 dh, higher prices are for mid-May-Sept, cash only, no breakfast, no air-con, elevator, free Wi-Fi, tel. 0539-942-244, fax 0539-942-246, Rue al-Antaki 8, eldjenina@menara.ma).

$ Hotel Residencia Andalucía is solid, clean, and minimal. It's buried in a totally non-touristy area in the new town, about a 20-minute walk from the Grand Socco. It has 19 rooms, a small reception, and a peaceful lobby (Sb-200-230 dh, Db-230-260 dh, higher prices are for mid-June-mid-Sept, cash only, Rue Omar Ben Abdelaziz 14, tel. 0539-941-334, Azdeen speaks a little English). Don't confuse it with the similarly named but very exclusive Hotel Andalucía Golf across town.

Eating in Tangier

Moroccan food is a joy to sample. First priority is a glass of the refreshing "Moroccan tea"—green tea that's boiled and steeped once, then combined with fresh mint leaves to boil and steep some more, before being loaded up with sugar. Tourist-oriented restaurants have a predictable menu. For starters, you'll find Moroccan vegetable soup (harira) or Moroccan salad (a combination of fresh and stewed vegetables). Main dishes include couscous (usually with chicken, potatoes, carrots, and other vegetables and spices); tangine (stewed meat served in a fancy dish with a cone-shaped top); and briouates (small savory pies). Everything comes with Morocco's distinctive round, flat bread. For dessert, it's pastries—typically, almond cookies.

I've mostly listed places in or near the Medina. (If you'd prefer the local equivalent of a yacht-club restaurant, survey the places along the beach.) Moroccan waiters expect about a 10 percent tip.

Le Saveur du Poisson is an excellent bet for the more adventurous, featuring one room cluttered with paintings adjoining a busy kitchen. There are no choices here. Just sit down and let owner Muhammad or his son, Hassan, take care of the rest. You get a rough hand-carved spoon and fork. Surrounded by lots of locals and unforgettable food, you'll be treated to a multicourse menu. Savor the delicious fish dishes—Tangier is one of the few spots in Morocco where seafood is a major part of the diet. The fruit punch—a mix of seasonal fruits brewed overnight in a vat—simmers in the back room. Ask for an explanation, or even a look. The desserts are full of nuts and honey. The big sink in the room is for locals who prefer to eat with their fingers (150-dh fixed-price meal, Sat-Thu 13:00-17:00 & 20:00-23:00, closed Fri and during Ramadan; walk down Rue de la Liberté roughly a block toward the Grand Socco from El Minzah Hotel, look for the stairs leading down to the market stalls and go down until you see fish on the grill; Escalier Waller 2, tel. 0539-336-326).

Maison Communitaire des Femmes, a community center for women, hides an inexpensive, hearty lunch spot that's open to everyone. A tasty three-course lunch is only 60 dh. Profits support the work of the center (Mon-Sat 12:00-16:00, last order at 15:30, also open 8:00-11:00 & 15:30-18:00 for cakes and tea, closed Sun, pleasant terrace out back, near slipper market just outside Grand

Socco, Place du 9 Avril).

El Minzah Hotel offers a fancier yet still authentic experience. The atmosphere is classy but low-stress. It's where unadventurous tourists and local elites dine. Dress up and choose between two dining zones: The white-tablecloth continental (French) dining area, called El Erz, is stuffy (80-150-dh starters, 120-240-dh main dishes); while in the Moroccan lounge, El Korsan, you'll be serenaded by live traditional music (music nightly 20:00-23:30, belly-dance show at 20:30 and 22:30, no extra charge for music; 70-120-dh starters, 170-260-dh main dishes). There's also a cozy wine bar here—a rarity in a Muslim country (50-120-dh starters, 120-190-dh main dishes, decorated with photos of visiting celebrities). At lunch, light meals and salads are served poolside (all dining areas open daily 13:00-16:00 & 20:00-22:30, Rue de la Liberté 85, tel. 0539-935-885, www.elminzah.com).

Le Salon Bleu has decent Moroccan food and some of the most spectacular seating in town: perched on a whitewashed terrace overlooking the square in front of the Kasbah Museum, with 360-degree views over the rooftops. Hike up the very tight spiral staircase to the top level, with the best views and lounge-a-while sofa seating. French-run (by the owners of Dar Nour guest house), it offers a simple menu of Moroccan fare—the 80-dh appetizer plate is a good sampler for lunch or to share for an afternoon snack. While there is some indoor seating, I'd skip this place if the weather's not ideal for lingering on the terrace (30-40-dh starters, 80-120-dh main dishes, Place de la Kasbah, mobile 06-5432-7618). You'll see it from the square in front of the Kasbah; to reach it, go through the gate to the left (as you face it), then look right for the stairs up.

Le Fabrique has nothing to do with old Morocco. But if you want a break from couscous and keyhole arches, this industrial-mod brasserie with concrete floors and exposed brick has a menu of purely French classics—a good reminder that in the 20th century, Tangier was nearly as much a French city as a Moroccan one (70-140-dh starters, 130-230-dh main dishes, Tue-Sat 12:00-14:30 & 20:00-23:00, closed Sun-Mon, Rue d'Angleterre 7, tel. 0539-374-057). It's a steep 10-minute walk up from the Grand Socco: Head up Rue d'Angleterre (left of Cinema Rif) and hike up the hill until the road levels out—it's on your left.

Le Nabab is geared for tourists, but offers more style and less crass commercialism than the tourist traps listed below. Squirreled away in a mostly residential neighborhood just below the lower Kasbah gate (near the top of the Medina), it has a menu of predictable Moroccan favorites in a sleek concrete-and-white-tablecloths dining room with a few echoes of traditional Moroccan decor (170-dh three-course meal is a good deal to sample several items,

40-55-dh starters, 100-150-dh main dishes, Mon-Sat 12:00-15:30 & 19:30-23:30, closed Sun; below the lower Kasbah gate—bear left down the stairs, then right, and look for signs; Rue Al Kadiria 4, mobile 06-6144-2220).

Tourist Traps

Tangier seems to specialize in very touristy Moroccan restaurants that are designed to feed and entertain dozens or even hundreds of tour-group members with overpriced and predictable menus of Moroccan classics, and often live music and belly-dancing. The only locals you'll see here are the waiters. For day-trippers who just want a safe, comfortable break in the heart of town, these restaurants' predictability and Moroccan clichés are just perfect. For other travelers, these places are tour-group hell and make you thankful to be free. Each local guide has their own favorite, but these are the best-known.

Hamadi is as luxurious a restaurant as a tourist can find in Morocco, with good food at reasonable prices (25-40-dh starters, 60-80-dh main dishes, long hours daily, Rue Kasbah 2, tel. 0539-934-514).

Marhaba Palace has the most impressive interior, with huge keyhole arches ringing a grand upstairs hall slathered in colorful tilework. It also has the highest prices—hardly a good value. It's near the upper gate to the Kasbah, so it's convenient for a meal just before heading downhill through town to the Medina and market (170-240-dh fixed-price meals, daily 10:00-23:00, Rue Kasbah, tel. 0539-937-927).

Mamounia Palace, considered by most the bottom of the barrel, is right on the Petit Socco and more in the middle of the action. At least it has a Hollywood connection: The Moroccan tea-house scenes from the movie *Inception* were filmed on its upstairs balcony. A meal here will cost you about 100 dh for four courses (no à la carte, daily 11:00-22:00, tel. 0539-935-099).

Tangier Connections

In Tangier, all train traffic comes and goes from the suburban Gare Tanger Ville train station, one mile from the city center and a short Petit Taxi ride away (10-20 dh). If you're traveling inland, check the information booth at the entrance of the train station for schedules (www.oncf.ma).

From Tangier by Train to: Rabat (5/day, 5 hours), **Casablanca** (station also called **Casa Voyageurs,** 6/day, 5 hours; a new train line will cut the trip to about 2 hours by 2014), **Marrakech** (4/day, 12 hours), **Fès** (4/day, 4.5 hours).

From Tangier by Bus to: Ceuta and **Tétouan** (hourly, 1 hour).

From Fès to: Casablanca (9/day, 4.5 hours), **Marrakech** (7/day, 7 hours), **Rabat** (9/day, 4 hours), **Meknès** (10/day, 45 minutes), **Tangier** (5/day, 5.5 hours).

From Rabat to: Casablanca (2/hour, 45 minutes), **Fès** (9/day, 3.5 hours), **Tétouan** (2 buses/day, 4.5 hours, 3 trains/day, 6 hours).

From Casablanca to: Marrakech (9/day, 3.5 hours).

From Marrakech to: Meknès (7/day, 7 hours), **Ouarzazate** (4/day, 4 hours).

By Plane: Flights within Morocco are convenient and reasonable (about $180 one-way from Tangier to Casablanca).

Extended Tour of Morocco

Morocco gets much better as you go deeper into the interior. The country is incredibly rich in cultural thrills, though you'll pay a

price in hassles and headaches—it's a package deal. But if adventure is your business, Morocco is a great option. Invest in a good Morocco guidebook to make this trip. Here are a few tips and insights to get you started.

To get a fair look at Morocco, you must get past the hustlers and con artists of the north coast (Tangier, Tétouan). It takes a minimum of four or five days to make a worthwhile visit—ideally seven or eight. Plan at least two nights in either Fès or Marrakech. A trip over the Atlas Mountains gives you an exciting look at Saharan Morocco. If you need a vacation from your vacation, check into one of the idyllic Atlantic beach resorts on the south coast. Above all, get past the northern day-trip-from-Spain, take-a-snapshot-on-a-camel fringe. (Oops, that's us. Oh well.)

If you're relying on public transportation for your extended tour, sail to Tangier, blast your way through customs, ignore any hustler who tells you there's no way out until tomorrow, and hop in a Petit Taxi for the Tanger Ville train station one mile away. From there set your sights on Rabat, a dignified European-type town with fewer hustlers, and make it your get-acquainted stop in Morocco. Trains go farther south from Rabat.

If you're driving a car, crossing the border can be a bit unnerving, since you'll be forced to jump through several bureaucratic hoops. You'll go through customs at both borders, buy Moroccan insurance for your car (cheap and easy), and feel at the mercy of a bristly bunch of shady-looking people you'd rather not be at the mercy of. Don't pay anyone on the Spanish side. Consider tipping a guy on the Moroccan side if you feel he'll shepherd you through. Relax and let him grease those customs wheels. He's worth it. As soon as possible, hit the road and drive to Chefchaouen, the best first stop for those with their own wheels.

Moroccan Towns

▲▲**Chefchaouen**—Just two hours by bus or car from Tétouan, this is the first pleasant town beyond the north coast. Monday and Thursday are colorful market days. Stay in the classy old Hotel Chaouen on Place el-Makhzen. The Hotel Parador (historic inn, but not the same as the Spanish government-run chain) faces the old town and offers good meals and a refuge from hustlers. Wander deep into the whitewashed old town from here.

▲▲**Rabat**—Morocco's capital and most European city, Rabat is the most comfortable and least stressful place to start your North African trip. You'll find a colorful market (in the old neighboring town of Salé), bits of Islamic architecture (Mausoleum of Mohammed V), the king's palace, mellow hustlers, and fine hotels.

▲▲▲**Fès**—More than just a funny hat that tipsy Shriners wear, Fès is Morocco's religious and artistic center, bustling with craftspeople, pilgrims, shoppers, and shops. Like most large Moroccan cities, it has a distinct new town from the French colonial period, as well as an exotic (and stressful) old walled Arabic town (the Medina), where you'll find the market.

For 12 centuries traders have gathered in Fès, founded on a river at the crossroads of two trade routes. Soon there was an irrigation system; a university; resident craftsmen from Spain; and a diverse population of Muslims, Christians, and Jews. When France claimed Morocco in 1912, they made their capital in Rabat, and Fès fizzled. But the Fès marketplace is still Morocco's best.

▲▲▲**Marrakech**—Morocco's gateway to the south, Marrakech is where the desert, mountain, and coastal regions merge. This market city is a constant folk festival, bustling with Berber tribespeople and a colorful center. The new city has the train station, and the main boulevard (Mohammed V) is lined with banks, airline offices, a post office, a tourist office, and comfortable hotels. The old city features the maze-like market and the huge Djemaa el-Fna, a square seething with people—a 43-ring Moroccan circus.

▲▲▲**Over the Atlas Mountains**—Extend your Moroccan trip several days by heading south over the Atlas Mountains. Take a bus from Marrakech to Ouarzazate (short stop), and then to Tinerhir (great oasis town, comfy hotel, overnight stop). The next day go to Er Rachidia and take the overnight bus to Fès.

By car, drive from Fès south, staying in the small mountain town of Ifrane, and then continue deep into the desert country past Er Rachidia and on to Rissani (market days: Sun, Tue, and Thu). Explore nearby mud-brick towns still living in the Middle Ages. Hire a guide to drive you past where the road stops, and head cross-country to an oasis village (Merzouga), where you can climb a sand dune and watch the sun rise over the vastness of Africa. Only a sea of sand separates you from Timbuktu.

SPAIN: PAST & PRESENT

The distinctive Spanish culture has been shaped by the country's parade of rulers. Roman emperors, Muslim sultans, hard-core Christians, conquistadors, French dandies, and Fascist dictators have all left their mark on Spain's art, architecture, and customs. Start by understanding the country's long history of invasions and religious wars, and you'll better appreciate the churches, museums, and monuments you'll visit today.

History

In 1492, Columbus sailed the ocean blue—and Spain became a nation, too. The sunny weather, fertile soil, and Mediterranean ports of the Iberian Peninsula made it a popular place to call home. A mix from various migrations and invasions, the original "Iberians" crossed the Pyrenees around 800 B.C. The Phoenicians established the city of Cádiz around 1100 B.C., and Carthaginians settled around 250 B.C.

Romans (c. 200 B.C.-A.D. 400)

The future Roman Emperor Augustus finally quelled the last Iberian resistance (19 B.C.), making the province of "Hispania" an agricultural breadbasket (olives, wine) to feed the vast Roman Empire. The Romans brought the Latin language, a connection to the wider world, and (in the fourth century) Christianity. When the empire began crumbling around A.D. 400, Spain made a peaceful transition, ruled by Christian Visigoths from Germany who had strong Roman ties. Roman influence remained for centuries after, in the Latin-based Spanish language, irrigation methods, and building materials and techniques. The Romans' large farming estates would change hands over the years, passing from Roman senators to Visigoth kings to Islamic caliphs to Christian nobles. And, of course, the Romans left wine.

Moors (711-1492)

In A.D. 711, 12,000 zealous members of the world's newest religion—Islam—landed on the Rock of Gibraltar and, in three short years, conquered the Iberian Peninsula. These North African Muslims—generically called "Moors"—dominated Spain for the next 700 years. Though powerful, they were surprisingly tolerant of the people they ruled, allowing native Jews and Christians to practice their faiths, so long as the infidels paid extra taxes.

The Moors themselves were an ethnically diverse culture, including both crude Berber tribesmen from Morocco and sophisticated rulers from old Arab families. From their capital in Córdoba, various rulers of the united Islamic state of "Al-Andalus" pledged allegiance to foreign caliphs in Syria, Baghdad, or Morocco.

With cultural ties that stretched from Spain to Africa to Arabia to Persia and beyond, the Moorish culture in Spain (especially around A.D. 800-1000) was perhaps Europe's most advanced, a beacon of learning in Europe's so-called "Dark" Ages. Mathematics, astronomy, literature, and architecture flourished. Even winemaking was encouraged, though for religious reasons the Muslims didn't drink alcohol. The Moorish legacy lives on today in architecture (horseshoe arches, ceramic tiles, fountains, and gardens), language (the Spanish *el* comes from Arabic *al*)...and wine.

Reconquista (711-1492)

The Moors ruled for more than 700 years, but throughout that time they were a minority ruling a largely Christian populace.

Pockets of independent Christians remained, particularly in the mountains in the peninsula's north. Local Christian kings fought against the Moors whenever they could, whittling away at the Muslim empire, "reconquering" more and more land in what's known as the Reconquista. The last Moorish stronghold, Granada, fell to the Christians in 1492.

The slow, piecemeal process of the Reconquista split the peninsula into many independent kingdoms and dukedoms, some Christian, some Moorish. The Reconquista picked up steam after A.D. 1000, when Al-Andalus splintered into smaller regional states—Granada, Sevilla, Valencia—ruled by local caliphs. Toledo fell to the Christians in 1085. By 1200 the neighboring Christian state

Notable Spaniards

Hadrian (A.D. 76-138)—Roman emperor, one of three born in Latin-speaking Hispania (along with Trajan, reigned 98-117, and Marcus Aurelius, reigned 161-180), who ruled Rome at its peak of power.

El Cid (1040?-1099)—A real soldier-for-hire who inspired fictional stories and Spain's oldest poem, El Cid (literally, "The Lord") fought for both Christians and Muslims during the wars of the Reconquista. He's best known for liberating Valencia from the Moors.

St. Teresa of Ávila (1515-1582)—Mystic nun whose holiness and writings led to convent reform and to her sainthood. Religiously intense Spain produced other saints, too, including Dominic (1170-1221), who founded an order of wandering monks, and Ignatius of Loyola (1491-1556), who founded the Jesuits, an order of "intellectual warriors."

Ferdinand (1452-1516) and Isabel (1451-1504)—Their marriage united most of Spain, ushering in its Golden Age. The "Catholic Monarchs" drove out Moors and Jews, and financed Columbus' lucrative voyages to the New World.

Hernán Cortés (1485-1547)—Conquered Mexico in 1521. Along with Vasco Núñez de Balboa, who discovered the Pacific, and Francisco Pizarro, who conquered Peru, Cortés and other Spaniards explored and exploited the New World.

El Greco (1541-1614)—The artist is known for his ethereal paintings of "flickering" saints.

Diego Velázquez (1599-1660)—Velázquez painted camera-eye realistic portraits of the royal court.

Francisco de Goya (1746-1828)—The artist is best known for his expressionistic nightmares (see page 390 for more).

of Portugal had the borders it does today, making it the oldest unchanged state in Europe. The rest of the peninsula was a battleground, a loosely knit collection of small kingdoms, some Christian, some Muslim. Heavy stone castles dotted the interior region of Castile, as lords and barons duked it out. Along the Mediterranean coast (from the Pyrenees to Barcelona to Valencia), three Christian states united into a sea-trading power, the kingdom of Aragon.

In 1469, Isabel of Castile married Ferdinand II of Aragon. These so-called Catholic Monarchs (Reyes Católicos) united the peninsula's two largest kingdoms, instantly making Spain a European power. In 1492, while Columbus explored the seas under Ferdinand and Isabel's flag, the Catholic Monarchs drove the Moors out of Granada and expelled the country's Jews, creating a

Francisco Franco (1892-1975)—The general who led the military uprising against the elected Republic, sparking Spain's Civil War (1936-1939). After victory, he ruled Spain for more than three decades as an absolute dictator, maintaining its Catholic, aristocratic heritage while slowly modernizing the country (see page 68).

Salvador Dalí (1904-1989)—A flamboyant, waxed-mustachioed Surrealist painter, Dalí and a fellow Spaniard, filmmaker Luis Buñuel, made one of the first art films, *An Andalusian Dog* (see sidebar on page 134).

Pablo Picasso (1881-1973)—Though he lived most of his adult life in France, the 20th century's greatest artist explored Spanish themes, particularly in his famous work *Guernica*, which depicts Civil War destruction (see sidebar on page 396).

Placido Domingo (b. 1941)—The son of *zarzuela* singers in Madrid (but raised in Mexico), this operatic tenor is just one of many classical musicians from Spain, including fellow "Three Tenors" singer José Carreras, composer Manuel de Falla, cellist Pablo Casals, and guitarist Andrés Segovia.

Spaniards in the News Today—King Juan Carlos I and his Greek-born wife, Queen Sofía; their son Felipe and his wife, Letizia; left-of-center prime minister José Luis Rodríguez Zapatero (until elections in March 2012); bicyclists Oscar Pereiro, Igor Astarloa, and Tour de France cyclist Alberto Contador; golfer Sergio Garcia; tennis star Rafael Nadal; pop singer Julio Iglesias (father of pop singer Enrique Iglesias); Oscar Award–winning actors Javier Bardem and Penélope Cruz; and movie directors Pedro Almodóvar and Pedro Amenábar.

unified, Christian, militaristic nation-state, fueled by the religious zeal of the Reconquista.

The Golden Age (1500-1600)

Spain's bold sea explorers changed the economics of Europe, opening up a New World of riches and colonies. The Spanish flag soon flew over most of South and Central America. Gold, silver, and agricultural products (grown on large estates with cheap labor) poured into Spain. In return, the stoked Spaniards

exported Christianity, converting the American natives with persistent Jesuit priests and cruel conquistadors.

Ferdinand and Isabel's daughter (Juana the Mad) wed a German prince (Philip the Fair), and their son inherited both crowns. Charles V (1500-1558, called Carlos I in Spain) was the most powerful man in the world, ruling an empire that stretched from Holland to Sicily, from Bohemia to Bolivia. The aristocracy and the clergy were swimming in money. Art and courtly life flourished during this Golden Age, with Spain hosting the painter El Greco and the writer Miguel de Cervantes.

But Charles V's Holy Roman Empire was torn by different languages and ethnic groups, and by protesting Protestants. He spent much of the nation's energies at war with Protestants, encroaching Muslim Turks, and Europe's rising powers. When an exhausted Charles announced his abdication (1555) and retired to a monastery, his sprawling empire was divvied up among family members, with Spain and its possessions going to his son, Philip II (1527-1598).

Philip II conquered Portugal (1580, his only successful war), moved Spain's capital to Madrid, built El Escorial, and continued fighting losing battles across Europe (the Netherlands, France) that drained the treasury of its New World gold. In the summer of 1588, Spain's seemingly unbeatable royal fleet of 125 ships—the Invincible Armada—sailed off to conquer England, only to be unexpectedly routed in battle by bad weather and Sir Francis Drake's cunning. Just like that, Britannia ruled the waves, and Spain spiraled downward, becoming a debt-ridden, overextended, flabby nation.

Slow Decline (1600-1900)

The fast money from the colonies kept Spain from seeing the dangers at home. The country stopped growing its own wheat and neglected its fields. Great Britain and the Netherlands were the rising sea-trading powers in the new global economy. During the centuries when science and technology developed as never before in other European countries, Spain was preoccupied by its failed colonial politics. (Still, 1600s Spain produced the remarkable painter Diego Velázquez.)

By 1700, once-mighty Spain lay helpless while rising powers France, England, and Austria fought over the right to pick Spain's next king in the War of the Spanish Succession (1701-1714), which was fought partly on Spanish soil (Britain held out against the French in the Siege of Gibraltar). Spanish king Charles II didn't

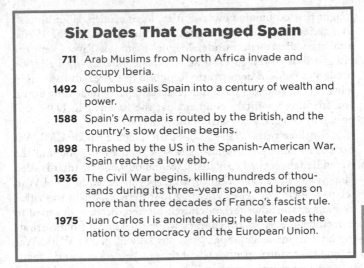

Six Dates That Changed Spain

711 Arab Muslims from North Africa invade and occupy Iberia.

1492 Columbus sails Spain into a century of wealth and power.

1588 Spain's Armada is routed by the British, and the country's slow decline begins.

1898 Thrashed by the US in the Spanish-American War, Spain reaches a low ebb.

1936 The Civil War begins, killing hundreds of thousands during its three-year span, and brings on more than three decades of Franco's fascist rule.

1975 Juan Carlos I is anointed king; he later leads the nation to democracy and the European Union.

have an heir, so he willed his kingdom to Louis XIV's grandson, Philip of Anjou, who was set to inherit both France and Spain. But the rest of Europe didn't want powerful France to become even stronger. The war ended in compromise: Philip become king of Spain (Spain lost several possessions), but he had to renounce claims to any other thrones. The French-born, French-speaking Bourbon King Philip V (1683-1746) ruled Spain for 40 years. He and his heirs made themselves at home, building the Versailles-like Royal Palace in Madrid and La Granja near Segovia.

The French invaded Spain under Napoleon, who installed his brother as king in 1808. The Spaniards rose up (chronicled by Goya's paintings of the second and third of May 1808), sparking the Peninsular War—called the War of Independence by Spaniards—that finally won Spain's independence from French rule.

Nineteenth-century Spain was a backward nation, with internal wars over which noble family should rule (the Carlist Wars), liberal revolutions put down brutally, and political assassinations. Spain gradually lost its global possessions to other European powers and to South American revolutionaries. Spain hit rock bottom in 1898, when the upstart United States picked a fight and thrashed them in the Spanish-American War, taking away Spain's last major possessions: Cuba, Puerto Rico, and the Philippines.

The 20th Century

A drained and disillusioned Spain was ill-prepared for modern technology and democratic government.

The old ruling class (the monarchy, church, and landowners)

fought new economic powers (cities, businessmen, labor unions) in a series of coups, strikes, and sham elections. In the 1920s, a military dictatorship under Miguel Primo de Rivera kept the old guard in power. In 1930 he was ousted and an open election brought a modern democratic Republic to power. But the right wing regrouped under the Falange (fascist) party, fomenting unrest and sparking a military coup against the Republic in 1936, supported by General Francisco Franco (1892-1975).

For three years (1936-1939), Spain fought a bloody Civil War between Franco's Nationalists (also called Falangists) and the Republic (also called Loyalists). Some 600,000 Spaniards died (due to all causes), and Franco won. (For more on the Civil War, see page 445.) For nearly the next four decades, Spain was ruled by Franco, an authoritarian, church-blessed dictator who tried to modernize the backward country while shielding it from corrupting modern influences. Spain was officially neutral in World War II, and the country spent much of the postwar era as a world apart. (On my first visit to Spain, in 1973, I came face-to-face with fellow teenagers—me in backpack and shorts, the Spaniards in military uniforms, brandishing automatic weapons.)

Before Franco died, he handpicked his protégé, King Juan Carlos I, to succeed him. But to everyone's surprise, the young, conservative, mild-mannered king stepped aside, settled for a figurehead title, and guided the country quickly and peacefully toward democratic elections (1977).

Spain had a lot of catching up to do. Culturally, the once-conservative nation exploded and embraced new ideas, even plunging to wild extremes. In the 1980s Spain flowered under left-leaning prime minister Felipe González. Spain showed the world its new modern face in 1992, hosting both a World Exhibition at Sevilla and the Summer Olympics at Barcelona.

Spain Today

From 1996 to 2004, Spain was led by the centrist prime minister José María Aznar. He adopted moderate policies to minimize the stress on the country's young democracy, fighting problems such as unemployment and foreign debt with reasonable success. However, his support of the United States' war in Iraq was extremely unpopular. In spring 2004, the retiring Aznar supported a similarly centrist successor, Mariano Rajoy, who seemed poised to win the election. On the eve of the election, on March 11, three Madrid train stations were bombed at the height of rush hour, killing 191 people. The terrorist group claiming responsibility denounced Spain's Iraq policy, and three days later, Aznar's party lost the election. The new prime minister, left-of-center José Luis Rodríguez Zapatero, quickly began pulling Spain's troops out of Iraq, as well as enacting sweeping social changes in Spain. Zapatero and his party were reelected in 2008. The next elections are set for March of 2012, but Zapatero has decided not to run again.

Spain enjoyed a strong economy through the late 1990s and early 2000s, thanks in part to a thriving tourism industry and a boom in housing construction. But the country was hit hard by the global economic downturn in 2009. Spain's real-estate bubble burst, banks stopped lending, and by 2010 unemployment soared to 20 percent. So many young Spaniards are out of work (one-fourth of those under 30, and nearly 40 percent of those under 25) that a new name was coined to describe them: *"generación ni-ni"* (the neither-nor generation). Under pressure from the European Union to cut its national debt, Spain's government has adopted plans to cut payouts to new parents and scale back government pensions and salaries. These "austerity measures" have drawn criticism from unions and the public.

Artists

El Greco (1541-1614) exemplifies the spiritual fervor of much Spanish art. The drama, surreal colors, and intentionally unnatural distortion of his compositions have the intensity of a religious vision. (For more on El Greco, see page 485.)

Diego Velázquez (1599-1660) went to the opposite extreme. His masterful court portraits are studies in camera-eye realism and cool detachment from his subjects. Velázquez was unmatched in using a few strokes of paint to suggest details.

Francisco de Goya (1746-1828) lacked Velázquez's detachment. He let his liberal tendencies shine through in unflattering portraits of royalty and in emotional scenes of abuse of power. He unleashed his inner passions in the eerie, nightmarish canvases of his last, "dark" stage. (For more on Goya, see page 390.)

Bartolomé Murillo (1617-1682) painted a dreamy world of religious visions. His pastel soft-focus works of cute Baby Jesuses and radiant Virgin Marys helped make Catholic doctrine palatable to the common folk at a time when many were defecting to Protestantism. (For more on Murillo, see page 582.)

In the 20th century, **Pablo Picasso** (see his inspirational antiwar *Guernica* mural in Madrid, described on page 396), **Joan Miró,** and Surrealist **Salvador Dalí** (see sidebar on page 134) made their marks. Great museums featuring all three are in or near Barcelona.

Besides the works of its native sons, Spain's museums have plenty of foreign art. During its Golden Age, wealthy Spanish aristocrats bought wagonloads of the most popular art of the time—

Italian Renaissance and Baroque works by Titian, Tintoretto, Veronese, and others. They also loaded up on paintings by Peter Paul Rubens, Hieronymus Bosch, and Pieter Brueghel from the Low Countries, which were then under Spanish rule.

Architecture

Spanish History Set in Stone

The two most fertile periods of architectural innovation in Spain were during the Moorish occupation and in the Golden Age. Otherwise, Spanish architects marched obediently behind the rest of Europe. Modern architects have finally brought Spain back to the forefront of construction and design.

Spain's history is dominated by 700 years of pushing the Muslim Moors back into Africa (711-1492). Throughout Spain, it seems every old church was built upon a mosque (Sevilla's immense cathedral, for one, and Córdoba's remarkable Mezquita, which preserved the mosque but plopped a cathedral right in the middle of it). Granada's Alhambra is the best example of the secular Moorish style. It's an *Arabian Nights* fairy tale: finely etched domes, lacy arcades, stalactite-studded ceilings, keyhole arches, and lush gardens. At its heart lies an elegantly proportioned court-yard, where the designers created an ingenious microclimate: water, plants, pottery, thick walls, and darkness...all to be cool. The stuccoed walls are ornamented with a stylized Arabic script, creating a visual chant of verses from the Quran. Meanwhile, sim-ple Romanesque churches dotted the northern part of Spain not controlled by the Moors (such as along the Camino de Santiago and in the folds of the Picos de Europa).

As the Christians slowly reconquered Iberian turf, they turned their fervor into stone, building churches in the lighter, heaven-reaching stained-glass Gothic style (Toledo and Sevilla). Gothic was a French import, trickling into conservative Spain long after it had swept through Europe.

As Christians moved in, many Muslim artists and archi-tects stayed, giving the new society the Mudejar style—Moorish in appearance, but commissioned by Catholics. (Mudejar means "those who stayed.") In Sevilla's Alcázar, the Arabic script on the walls relates not the Quran, but New Testament verses and Christian propaganda, such as "Dedicated to the magnificent Sultan, King Pedro—thanks to God!" (In contrast, the style of Christians living under Moorish rule is called Mozarabic.)

The money reaped and raped from Spain's colonies in the Golden Age (1500-1600) spurred new construction. Churches and palaces borrowed from the Italian Renaissance and the more elab-orate Baroque. Ornamentation reached unprecedented heights in

Church Architecture

History comes to life when you visit a centuries-old church. Even if you don't know your apse from a hole in the ground, learning a few simple terms will enrich your experience. Note that not every church will have every feature. Also, a "cathedral" isn't a type of architecture, but rather a designation for a church that's a governing center for a local bishop.

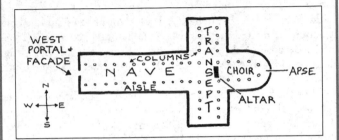

SPAIN: PAST & PRESENT

Aisles: The long, generally low-ceilinged arcades that flank the nave.

Altar: The raised area with a ceremonial table (often adorned with candles or a crucifix), where the priest prepares and serves the bread and wine for Communion.

Apse: The space beyond the altar, generally bordered with small chapels.

Barrel Vault: A continuous round-arched ceiling that resembles an extended upside-down U.

Choir: A cozy area, often screened off, located within the church nave and near the high altar, where services are sung in a more intimate setting.

Cloister: A square-shaped series of hallways surrounding an open-air courtyard, where monks and nuns got fresh air.

Facade: The outer wall of the church's main (west) entrance, viewable from outside and generally highly decorated.

Groin Vault: An arched ceiling formed where two equal barrel vaults meet at right angles. Less common usage: term for a medieval jock strap.

Narthex: The area (portico or foyer) between the main entry and the nave.

Nave: The long, central section of the church (running west to east, from the entrance to the altar) where the congregation stood during the service.

Transept: The north–south part of the church, which crosses (perpendicularly) the east–west nave. In a traditional Latin cross-shaped floor plan, the transept forms the "arms" of the cross.

West Portal: The main entry to the church (on the west end, opposite the main altar).

Spain, culminating in the Plateresque style of stonework, so called because it resembles intricate silver *(plata)* filigree work (see, for example, the facade of the University of Salamanca).

The 1500s were also the era of religious wars. The monastery/palace of El Escorial, built in sober geometric style, symbolizes the austerity of a newly reformed Catholic Church ready to strike back. King Philip II ruled his empire and directed the Inquisition from here, surrounded by plain white walls, well-scrubbed floors, and simple furnishings. El Escorial was built at a time when Catholic Spain felt threatened by Protestant heretics, and its construction dominated the Spanish economy for a generation (1563-1584). Because of this bully in the national budget, Spain has almost nothing else to show from this most powerful period of her history.

For the next three centuries (1600-1900), backward-looking Spain recycled old art styles.

As Europe leapt from the 19th into the 20th century, it celebrated a rising standard of living and nearly a hundred years without a major war. Art Nouveau architects forced hard steel and concrete into softer organic shapes. Barcelona's answer to Art Nouveau was Modernisme, and its genius was Antoni Gaudí, with his asymmetrical "cake-in-the-rain" Barcelona buildings like Casa Milà and Sagrada Família.

Much of Spain's 20th-century architecture—the minimal fascist style of the Valley of the Fallen and ugly concrete apartments—follows patterns seen elsewhere in Europe. But Spain today produces some of Europe's most interesting structures. Santiago Calatrava (from Valencia, born 1951) uses soaring arches and glass to create bridges (such as the iconic one in Sevilla, and a brand-new one in Venice), airports, and performance halls (including Valencia's Opera House). One of the world's most striking and well-known buildings in recent years—Frank Gehry's Guggenheim Museum—is in Bilbao, and similarly innovative structures are popping up everywhere.

Bullfighting

An Authentic Ritual or a Cruel Spectacle?

The Spanish bullfight is as much a ritual as it is a sport. Not to acknowledge the importance of the bullfight is to censor a venerable part of Spanish culture. But it also makes a spectacle out of the cruel killing of an animal. Should tourists boycott bullfights? I don't know.

When the day comes that bullfighting is kept alive by tourist dollars rather than by the local culture, then I'll agree with those who say it's immoral and that tourists shouldn't encourage it by

Man vs. Bull Through History

The exact origins of bullfighting are impossible to trace, but men have battled bulls since ancient times. In ancient Crete, Minoan athletes sprang somersaults over bulls' horns (c. 1500 B.C.). In Asia and Italy, worshippers of Mithras and Artemis slaughtered bulls in ritual sacrifice (c. 500 B.C.-A.D. 500). And in ancient Rome, animal fights were popular warm-up acts for the gladiator games, performed in large arenas while thousands cheered. (In an interesting counterpoint, in many cultures—including, some would argue, Spain—bulls are respected or even revered, from those who would worship a golden calf in Moses' time, to the people of contemporary India.)

The Romans likely introduced bullfights to Spain. In the Middle Ages (historians speculate), bullfighting became a sport for knights, both Christian and Moorish, who held tournaments on feast days. They fought on horseback with lances, assisted by squires.

It was in the town of Ronda, around 1726, that the charismatic Francisco Romero transformed bullfighting from a sport of nobles on horseback to one of commoners on foot, armed only with a sword and cape. The mounted *picador* became the support player, and the matador became the star. Successive matadors thrilled crowds by allowing the bull to come ever closer.

From Spain bullfighting spread to southern France and Latin America (where it continues today). In the 20th century, the dictator Franco made bullfighting the national pastime. Since Franco it's become increasingly unpopular. Today, only a third of Spaniards follow it at all. Calling bullfights unsuitable for children, the government has banned live broadcasts on state-run TV, though private channels continue to cover the events. Today's matadors remain the brave-but-pretty cover boys gracing tabloids. In 2010 a couple of top matadors were gored, making the sport appear even more brutal, tragic, and edgy. Starting in 2012, bullfighting will be banned in Catalunya.

buying tickets. Consider the morality of supporting this gruesome aspect of Spanish culture before buying a ticket.

While no two bullfights are the same, they unfold along a strict pattern. The punctual ceremony begins with a parade of participants across the ring. Then the trumpet sounds, the "Gate of Fear" opens, and the leading player—*el toro*—thunders in. A ton of angry animal is an awesome sight, even from the cheap seats (with the sun in your eyes).

The fight is divided into three acts. Act I is designed to size up the bull and wear him down. With help from his assistants, the matador (literally, "killer") attracts the bull with a shake of the cape, then directs the animal past his body, as close as his bravery allows. The bull sees only things in motion and (some think) in red. After a few passes, the *picadores* enter, mounted on horseback, to spear the swollen lump of muscle at the back of the bull's neck. This tests the bull, causing him to lower his head and weakening the thrust of his horns. (Until 1927, the horses had no protective pads and were often killed.)

In Act II, the matador's assistants *(banderilleros)* continue to enrage and weaken the bull. They charge the charging bull and—leaping acrobatically across its path—plunge brightly colored barbed sticks into the bull's vital neck muscle.

After a short intermission, during which the matador may, according to tradition, ask permission to kill the bull and dedicate the kill to someone in the crowd, the final and lethal Act III begins.

The matador tries to dominate and tire the bull with hypnotic cape work. A good pass is when the matador stands completely still while the bull charges past.

Then the matador thrusts a sword between the animal's shoulder blades for the kill. A quick kill is not always easy, and the matador may have to make several bloody thrusts before the sword stays in and the bull finally dies. (One of the matador's assistants may go in at the end to finish the job with a dagger between the eyes.) Mules drag the dead bull out, and his meat is in the market *mañana* (barring "mad cow" concerns—and if ever there was a mad cow...). *Rabo del toro* (bull-tail stew) is a delicacy.

Throughout the fight, the crowd shows its approval or impatience. Shouts of *"¡Olé!"* or *"¡Torero!"* mean they like what they see. Whistling or rhythmic hand-clapping greets cowardice and incompetence.

You're not likely to see much human blood spilled. In 200 years of bullfighting in Sevilla, only 30 fighters have died (and only three were actually matadors). If a bull does kill a fighter, the next matador comes in to kill him. Historically, even the bull's mother is killed, since the evil qualities are assumed to have come from her.

After an exceptional fight, the crowd may wave white handkerchiefs to ask that the matador be awarded the bull's ear or tail. A brave bull, though dead, gets a victory lap from the mule team on his way to the slaughterhouse. Then the trumpet sounds, and a new bull charges in to face a fresh matador.

Fights are held on most Sundays from Easter through September (at 18:30 or 19:30). Serious fights with adult matadors are called *corrida de toros*. These are often sold out in advance. Summer fights are often *novillada*, with teenage novices doing the killing. *Corrida de toros* seats range from €20 for nosebleed seats in the sun to €140 for front-row seats in the shade. *Novillada* seats are half that, and generally easy to get at the arena a few minutes before showtime. Many Spanish women consider bullfighting sexy. They swoon at the dashing matadors who are sure to wear tight pants (with their *partas nobles*—noble parts—in view, generally organized to one side, farthest from the bull).

A typical bullfight lasts about two hours and consists of six separate fights—three matadors (each with his own team of *picadores* and *banderilleros*) fighting two bulls each. If you're curious to see a bullfight without making an expensive and time-consuming trip to the ring, keep an eye out for televised bullfights in bars. For a closer look at bullfighting by an American aficionado, read Ernest Hemingway's classic, *Death in the Afternoon*.

APPENDIX

Contents

Tourist Information

Spain has a national tourist office in the **US:** tel. 212/265-8822, www.spain.info. Before you go, scan its website or call to briefly describe your trip and request information. They'll mail you a general-interest brochure, and you can download many other brochures free of charge.

In **Spain** your best first stop in a new city is the *Turismo*, the tourist information office (abbreviated **TI** in this book). TIs are good places to get city maps, advice on public transportation (including bus and train schedules), walking-tour information, tips on special events, and recommendations for nightlife. Many TIs have information on the entire country or at least the region, so try to pick up maps for destinations you'll be visiting later in your trip. If you're arriving in town after the TI closes, call ahead or pick up a map in a neighboring town.

While the TI is eager to book you a room, use its room-finding service only as a last resort. They are unable to give hard opinions on the relative value of one place over another. The accommodations stakes are too high to go potluck through the TI. Even if there's no "fee," you'll save money by going direct with the listings in this book.

Websites for Spain: In addition to the Spanish Tourist Board site (www.spain.info), consider visiting www.mcu.es (museums and historic sites in Spain) and www.renfe.com (train info and schedules).

For Gibraltar: Try the Gibraltar Information Bureau (from the US, dial 011-350-74950; www.gibraltar.gov.uk).

For Morocco: Contact the Moroccan National Tourist Office (from the US, dial 011-212-537-674-013; www.visitmorocco.com).

Communicating

Hurdling the Language Barrier

Spain presents the English-speaking traveler with one of the most formidable language barriers in Western Europe. Many Spanish people—especially those in the tourist trade and in big cities—speak English. Still, many people don't. Locals visibly brighten when you know and use some key Spanish words (see "Spanish Survival Phrases" on page 855). Learn the key phrases. Travel with a phrase book, particularly if you want to interact with the Spanish people. You'll find that doors open more quickly and with more smiles when you can speak a few words of the language.

Telephones

Smart travelers use the telephone to reserve or reconfirm rooms, get tourist information, reserve restaurants, confirm tour times, or phone home. Generally the easiest, cheapest way to call home is to use an international phone card purchased in Spain. This section covers dialing instructions, phone cards, and types of phones (for more in-depth information, see www.ricksteves.com/phoning).

How to Dial

Calling from the US to Spain, or vice versa, is simple—once you break the code. The European calling chart in this chapter will walk you through it.

Dialing Domestically Within Spain

About half of all European countries use area codes; the other half, including Spain, use a direct-dial system without area codes.

Land lines start with 9, and mobile lines start with 6. All phone numbers in Spain are nine digits (no area codes) that can be dialed direct throughout the country. For example, the phone number of one of my recommended Madrid hotels is 915-212-941. That's exactly what you dial, whether you're calling the hotel from the Madrid train station or from Barcelona.

Dialing Internationally to or from Spain

If you want to make an international call, follow these steps:

• Dial the international access code (00 if you're calling from Europe, 011 from the US or Canada).

• Dial the country code of the country you're calling (34 for Spain, or 1 for the US or Canada).

• Dial the local number, keeping in mind that calling many countries requires dropping the initial zero of the phone number. (The European calling chart lists specifics per country.)

Calling from the US to Spain: Dial 011 (the US international access code), 34 (Spain's country code), then the nine-digit number. For example, if you're calling the Madrid hotel I mentioned above, you'd dial 011-34-915-212-941.

Calling from any European country to the US: To call my office in Edmonds, Washington, from anywhere in Europe, I dial 00 (Europe's international access code), 1 (the US country code), 425 (Edmonds' area code), and 771-8303.

Note: You might see a + in front of a European number. When dialing the number, replace the + with the international access code of the country you're calling from (00 from Europe, 011 from the US or Canada).

Public Phones and Hotel-Room Phones

To make calls from public phones, you'll need a prepaid phone card. There are two kinds of phone cards: insertable and international. Both types work in Spain. (If you have a live card at the end of your trip, give it to another traveler to use up.) Coin-op phones are virtually extinct.

Insertable Phone Cards: These cards, called *tarjetas telefónicas*, can be used only at pay phones for domestic or international calls. They're sold at post offices and many newsstand kiosks. Spanish pay phones are easy to find but refuse to be rushed. After you "*inserta*" your "*tarjeta*" into the phone, wait until the digital display says "*Marque número*," and then dial. Dial slowly and deliberately. Push the square R button to get a dial tone for a new call. The phone doesn't beep to remind you that you've left the card in, so don't forget to remove it when you're done. The cost of the call is automatically deducted from your card.

International Phone Cards: These prepaid cards, called *tarjetas telefónicas con código*, are the cheapest way to make international calls from Europe—with the best cards, it costs literally pennies a

European Calling Chart

Just smile and dial, using this key:
AC = Area Code, LN = Local Number.

European Country	Calling long distance within ...	Calling from the US or Canada to ...	Calling from a European country to ...
Austria	AC + LN	011 + 43 + AC (without the initial zero) + LN	00 + 43 + AC (without the initial zero) + LN
Belgium	LN	011 + 32 + LN (without initial zero)	00 + 32 + LN (without initial zero)
Bosnia-Herzegovina	AC + LN	011 + 387 + AC (without initial zero) + LN	00 + 387 + AC (without initial zero) + LN
Britain	AC + LN	011 + 44 + AC (without initial zero) + LN	00 + 44 + AC (without initial zero) + LN
Croatia	AC + LN	011 + 385 + AC (without initial zero) + LN	00 + 385 + AC (without initial zero) + LN
Czech Republic	LN	011 + 420 + LN	00 + 420 + LN
Denmark	LN	011 + 45 + LN	00 + 45 + LN
Estonia	LN	011 + 372 + LN	00 + 372 + LN
Finland	AC + LN	011 + 358 + AC (without initial zero) + LN	999 (or other 900 number) + 358 + AC (without initial zero) + LN
France	LN	011 + 33 + LN (without initial zero)	00 + 33 + LN (without initial zero)
Germany	AC + LN	011 + 49 + AC (without initial zero) + LN	00 + 49 + AC (without initial zero) + LN
Gibraltar	LN	011 + 350 + LN	00 + 350 + LN
Greece	LN	011 + 30 + LN	00 + 30 + LN
Hungary	06 + AC + LN	011 + 36 + AC + LN	00 + 36 + AC + LN
Ireland	AC + LN	011 + 353 + AC (without initial zero) + LN	00 + 353 + AC (without initial zero) + LN

APPENDIX

to make or receive calls, and 20-50 cents to send or receive text messages.

You'll pay lower rates if your phone is electronically "unlocked" (ask your provider about this); then in Europe you can simply buy a tiny **SIM card,** which gives you a European phone number. SIM cards are sold at mobile-phone stores and some newsstand kiosks for about $5-15, and generally include several minutes' worth of prepaid domestic calling time. When you buy a SIM card, you may need to show ID, such as your passport. Insert the SIM card in your phone (usually in a slot on the side or behind the battery), and it'll work like a European mobile phone. When purchasing a SIM card, always ask about fees for domestic and international calls, roaming charges, and how to check your credit balance and buy more time. When you're in the SIM card's home country, domestic calls are reasonable, and incoming calls are free. You'll pay more if you're roaming in another country.

Many **smartphones,** such as the iPhone (AT&T version—not Verizon), Android, and BlackBerry, work in Europe. For voice calls and text messaging, smartphones function the same as other US mobile phones (explained earlier). But beware of sky-high fees for data downloading (checking email, browsing the Internet, streaming videos, and so on). To avoid this expense, disable data roaming on your phone, and use its wireless function to get online at Wi-Fi hotspots instead. Ask your mobile-phone service provider to cut off your account's data-roaming capability, or turn it off manually on your phone (look under the "Network" menu). If you want Internet access without being limited to Wi-Fi, reduce your data charges by signing up for a limited international data-roaming plan through your carrier, then use data roaming selectively (if a particular task gobbles bandwidth, wait until you're on Wi-Fi). In general, ask your provider in advance how to avoid unwittingly roaming your way to a huge bill. If your smartphone is on Wi-Fi, you can use certain apps to make cheap or free voice calls (see "Calling over the Internet," later).

Buying a European Mobile Phone: Mobile-phone shops all over Europe sell basic phones. Big department stores are another good source. Phones that are "locked" to work with a single provider start around $40; "unlocked" phones (which allow you to switch out SIM cards to use your choice of provider) start around $60. Along with the phone, you'll need to buy a SIM card and prepaid credit for making calls.

Renting a European Mobile Phone: Car-rental companies and mobile-phone companies offer the option to rent a mobile phone with a European number. While this seems convenient, hidden fees (such as high per-minute charges or expensive shipping costs) can really add up—which usually makes it a bad value.

One exception is Verizon's Global Travel Program, available only to Verizon customers.

Calling over the Internet

Some things that seem too good to be true...actually are true. If you're traveling with a laptop, you can make calls using VoIP (Voice over Internet Protocol). With VoIP, two computers act as the phones, and the Internet-based calls are free (or you can pay a few cents to call from your computer to a telephone). If both computers have webcams, you can even see each other while you chat. The major providers are Skype (www.skype.com) and Google Talk (www.google.com/talk).

For people traveling with a smartphone, various apps allow you to make VoIP calls from a Wi-Fi hotspot. A Skype app is available for most smartphones (including the iPhone, Android, and BlackBerry), while Fring (www.fring.com) allows you to use other VoIP providers—including Google Talk—on your smartphone. These apps also work on the iPod Touch (if you have an older model, you'll need to attach an external microphone).

Useful Phone Numbers

In Spain, numbers that start with 900 are toll-free; numbers that start with 901 and 902 cost money and can sometimes be expensive to call. Note that you can't call Spain's toll-free numbers from America, nor can you count on reaching America's toll-free numbers from Spain.

Emergency Needs
Police: Spain—tel. 091, Morocco—tel. 19
Ambulance: Spain—tel. 112, Morocco—tel. 15

Embassies and Consulates
US Embassy in Madrid, Spain: tel. 915-872-240, after-hours emergency tel. 915-872-200 (Calle Serrano 75, http://madrid.us embassy.gov/)
US Embassy in Gibraltar: Call US Embassy in Madrid
US Consulate General in Casablanca, Morocco: tel. 0522-264-550 or 0522-267-151, after-hours emergency tel. 0661-172-367 (Boulevard Moulay Youssef 8, http://casablanca.usconsulate.gov)
Canadian Embassy in Madrid, Spain: tel. 913-828-400 (Paseo de la Castellana 259 D, www.espana.gc.ca)
Canadian Embassy in Rabat, Morocco: tel. 0537-687-400 (13 bis rue Jaâfa-as-Sadik, www.morocco.gc.ca)

Travel Advisories
US Department of State: tel. 202/647-5225, www.travel.state.gov

Canadian Department of Foreign Affairs: Canadian tel. 800-267-6788, www.dfait-maeci.gc.ca
US Centers for Disease Control and Prevention: tel. 800-CDC-INFO (800-232-4636), www.cdc.gov/travel

Directory Assistance
In Spain, dial 11811 (€0.40/min) or 11818 (€0.55/call from private numbers, free from phone booths).

Trains
Train (RENFE) Reservation and Information: toll tel. 902-320-320, www.renfe.com

Airports
The following airports share a customer-assistance line, toll tel. 902-404-704, and a website, www.aena.es.
> **Barcelona:** El Prat de Llobregat Airport
> **Madrid:** Barajas Airport
> **Sevilla:** San Pablo Airport

Internet Access
It's useful to get online periodically as you travel—to confirm trip plans, check train or bus schedules, get weather forecasts, catch up on email, blog or post photos from your trip, or call folks back home (explained earlier, under "Calling over the Internet").

Some hotels offer a computer in the lobby with Internet access for guests. If you ask politely, smaller places may sometimes let you sit at their desk for a few minutes just to check your email. If your hotel doesn't have access, ask your hotelier to direct you to the nearest place to get online. Internet cafés are easy to find in Spain; for specific listings, check the various "Helpful Hints" sections in this book.

Traveling with a Laptop or Other Wireless Device: These days, almost every Spanish hotel has Wi-Fi (wireless Internet access)—which Spaniards call "wee-fee." Many accommodations in Spain are located in historic old buildings with thick walls, and Wi-Fi signals often can't penetrate past the lobby area—don't be surprised if you can't log on from your room. Most hotels offer Wi-Fi for free; others (especially expensive hotels) charge by the minute or hour. Instead of Wi-Fi, a few hotels have a port in the room for plugging in a cable.

A cellular modem—which lets your laptop access the Internet over a mobile phone network—provides more extensive coverage, but is much more expensive than Wi-Fi. Movistar, the Spanish telecom, offers Wi-Fi hot spots at some hotels, restaurants, and cafés (www.movistar.es/on/es/wifi).

Warning: While using a public Internet terminal or free Wi-Fi is convenient, it can come with security risks. Some computers are loaded with damaging "malware," such as "key logger" programs that keep track of what you're typing—including passwords. You can ask the Internet café or hotel what sort of security software their machines and Wi-Fi routers are running. If you're not convinced it's secure, don't access any sites (such as online banking) that could be sensitive to fraud. Be careful about storing personal information (such as passport and credit-card numbers) online.

Mail

Although you can arrange for mail delivery to your hotel (allow 10 days for a letter to arrive), phoning and emailing are so easy that I've dispensed with mail stops altogether.

You can mail one package per day to yourself worth up to $200 duty-free from Europe to the US (mark it "personal purchases"). If you're sending a gift to someone, mark it "unsolicited gift." For details, visit www.cbp.gov and search for "Know Before You Go."

Transportation

By Car or Public Transportation?

Trains and buses work best for solo travelers, blitz tourists, and city-to-city travelers; those with an ambitious multicountry itinerary; and those who don't want to drive. Cars are best for three or more traveling together (especially families with small kids), those packing heavy, and those scouring the countryside. But they're an expensive headache in bigger cities.

Though a car gives you more freedom—enabling you to search for hotels more easily and carrying your bags for you—trains and buses zip you scenically from city to city, usually dropping you in the center, often near a TI.

In this section, I'll cover specifics on traveling by train, bus, and car in Spain.

Public Transportation

Public transportation in Spain is slick, modern, and efficient. The best option is to mix bus and train travel. Always verify schedules before your departure. Don't leave a station without your next day's schedule options in hand. To ask for a schedule at an information window, say, *"Horario para* (fill in names of cities), *por favor."* (The local TI will sometimes have schedules available for you to take or copy.) To study train schedules in advance, visit Germany's excellent all-Europe website, http://bahn.hafas.de/bin/query.exe/en, or Spain's site, www.renfe.com. Bus schedules are more difficult to track down because routes are operated by different companies; for the names of regional carriers, check the "Connections" section of each destination chapter in this book. You can also try www.movelia.es, a third-party site listing several (but not all) bus companies.

Trains

You can buy a Spain "flexi" railpass that allows travel for a given number of days over a longer period of time, but you'll pay separately ($10-35) for seat reservations on all trains. Buying individual train tickets in advance or as you go in Spain can be less expensive, and gives you better access to seat reservations (which are limited for railpass holders). Some individual ticket prices already include seat reservations when required (for instance, for fast trains).

If your trip also includes a neighboring country, consider the France–Spain, Portugal–Spain, or Italy–Spain passes (see chart in this chapter). A Eurail Selectpass lets you travel even farther. Spain also offers a rail-and-drive pass, which gives you the ease of big-city train hops and the flexibility of a car for rural areas such as the Andalusian hill towns. These passes are sold only outside Europe. For specifics, check the railpass chart, contact your travel agent, or see my *Guide to Eurail Passes* at www.ricksteves.com/rail. Even if you have a railpass, use buses when they're more convenient and direct than the trains. Remember to reserve ahead for the fast AVE trains and overnight journeys.

RENFE (the acronym for the Spanish national train system) used to mean "Really Exasperating, and Not For Everyone," but it has moved into the 21st century. For information and reservations, dial RENFE's national number (toll tel. 902-320-320) from anywhere in Spain, or visit www.renfe.com. For tips on buying tickets, see the sidebar.

Spain categorizes trains this way:

The high-speed train called the **AVE** (AH-vay, stands for *Alta Velocidad Española*) whisks travelers between Madrid and Toledo in 30 minutes, Madrid and Sevilla or Barcelona in less than three hours, and Madrid and Málaga in three hours. For decades, Spain's

trains didn't fit on Europe's tracks, but AVE trains run on standard European-gauge rails. AVE trains can be priced differently according to their time of departure. Peak hours *(punta)* are most expensive, followed by *llano* and *valle* (quietest and cheapest times). AVE is almost entirely covered by the Eurailpass (book ahead, a seat reservation fee

Buying Train Tickets

Trains can sell out, so it's smart to buy your tickets a day in advance, even for short rides. You have four options for buying train tickets: at the station, at a travel agency, online, or by phone. Since station ticket offices can get very crowded, most travelers will find it easiest to go to a travel agency, most of which charge only a nominal service fee.

At the Station: You will likely have to wait in a line to buy your ticket. First find the correct line—at bigger stations, there might be separate windows for short-distance, long-distance, advance, and "today" (para hoy) tickets. To avoid wasting time in the wrong line, read the signs carefully, and ask a local (or a clerk at an information window) which line you need. You might have to take a number—watch others and follow their lead.

As another option, you could buy tickets or reservations at the RENFE offices located in more than 100 city centers. These are more central and multilingual—also less crowded and confusing—than the train station.

Travel Agency: The best choice for most travelers is to buy tickets at an English-speaking travel agency. The El Corte Inglés department stores (with locations in most Spanish cities) often have handy travel agencies inside. I've recommended these and other travel agencies throughout this book. Look for a train sticker in agency windows.

Online: Although the website www.renfe.com is useful for

from Madrid to Sevilla costs Eurailers about $23 in second class; $38 for first class, includes meal).

A related high-speed train, the Alvia, runs on AVE lines but can switch to Iberian track without stopping. On the Madrid–San Sebastián route, for example, it reaches the Basque Country in five hours.

Avant trains are also high-speed—typically about as fast as AVE—but designed for shorter distances. These tend to be much cheaper than AVE, even on the same route (sample second-class fares: between Madrid and Toledo—€16 on AVE, €11 on Avant; between Sevilla and Córdoba—€34 on AVE, €17 on Avant). Railpass reservations also cost about half as much for Avant as for AVE. If you're on a tight budget, compare your options before buying.

The **Talgo** is fast, air-conditioned, and expensive, and runs on AVE rails. **Intercity** and **Electro** trains fall just behind Talgo in speed, comfort, and expense. **Rápido, Tranvía, Semidirecto,** and **Expreso** trains are generally slower. **Cercanías** are commuter trains for big-city workers and small-town tourists. **Regional** and **Correo** trains are slow, small-town milk runs. Trains get more

confirming schedules and prices, you cannot dependably buy tickets online unless you have a European credit card. The website rejects nearly every attempt to use a US card, but if you have the patience and enough Spanish language skill, you might nab an online discount of up to 60 percent (available two weeks to two months ahead of travel). US agents can't match these rates. Another option is go through www.rumbo.es. This travel website (select English at the very bottom of the page) sells discounted tickets online for a small service fee (about €5).

By Phone: Tickets can be purchased over the phone with an American Express card (toll tel. 902-240-202). Pick up your ticket at the station by punching your confirmation code (*localizador*) into one of the automated machines. Discounts up to 40 percent off are offered a week or more ahead by phone (and at stations).

You can also reserve tickets by phone, then buy them at the station, which you must do a few days before departure (at a ticket window, usually signed "*venta anticipada*"). You can't pay for reserved tickets at the station on your day of travel.

The Fine Print: First-class tickets cost 50 percent more than second class—often as much as a domestic flight (see "Cheap Flights" on page 840). Discounted tickets come with restrictions, such as being nonrefundable and nonchangeable. Be sure to read all the details carefully at time of purchase.

expensive as they pick up speed, but all are cheaper per mile than their northern European counterparts. Spain loves to name trains, so you may encounter types of trains not listed here. The names Euromed, Alaris, Altaria, and Arco all indicate faster trains that require reservations. These can cost significantly less than AVE on some routes (for example, on the Córdoba–Sevilla route, AVE costs nearly double Altaria, but they take the same amount of time). Ask about the travel time for each option when buying your tickets.

Salidas means "departures," and *llegadas* is "arrivals." On train schedules, "LMXJVSD" stands for the days of the week in Spanish, starting with Monday. A train that runs "LMXJV-D" doesn't run on Saturdays. *Laborables* can mean Monday through Friday or Monday through Saturday.

Overnight Trains: For long trips, I go overnight on the train or I fly (domestic shuttle flights are generally less than $100). Overnight trains (and buses) are usually less expensive and slower than the daytime rides. Most overnight trains have berths and beds that you can rent (not included in the cost of your train ticket or railpass). A sleeping berth (*litera*) costs extra, with the price

Railpasses

Prices listed are for 2011 and are subject to change. For the latest prices, details, and train schedules (and easy online ordering), see my comprehensive *Guide to Eurail Passes* at www.ricksteves.com/rail.

"Saver" prices are per person for two or more people traveling together. "Youth" means under age 26. The fare for children 4–11 is half the adult individual fare or Saver fare. Kids under age 4 travel free.

SPAIN RAIL & DRIVE PASS

Any 3 rail days and 2 car days in 2 months.

Car Category	1st Class	2nd Class	Extra car day
Economy	$354	$293	$48
Compact	361	300	55
Intermediate	389	328	83
Intermediate auto.	426	365	119
Full size	454	393	147

Prices are per person, two traveling together. Solo travelers pay about $100 extra. Third and fourth people sharing the car buy only the railpass. Extra rail days (max 7) cost $34–$42 per day. To order Rail & Drive passes, call your travel agent or Rail Europe at 800-438-7245. *This pass is not sold by Europe Through the Back Door.*

Map key:

Approximate point-to-point one-way second-class rail fares in US dollars. First class costs 50 percent more. Add up fares for your itinerary to see whether a railpass will save you money. Dashed lines are buses.

SPAIN PASS

	1st Class	2nd Class
3 days in 2 months	$304	$244
Extra rail days (max 7)	39–43	30–35

SPAIN-PORTUGAL PASS

	Individual 1st Class	Saver 1st Class
3 days in 2 months	$347	$295
Extra rail days (max 7)	45–48	38–42

SELECTPASS

This pass covers travel in three adjacent countries. Please visit **www.ricksteves.com/rail** for four- and five-country options.

	Individual 1st Class	Saver 1st Class	Youth 2nd Class
5 days in 2 months	$499	$424	$325
6 days in 2 months	551	469	359
8 days in 2 months	651	554	424
10 days in 2 months	755	643	492

FRANCE–SPAIN PASS

	Individual 1st Class	Individual 2nd Class	Saver 1st Class	Saver 2nd Class	Youth 2nd Class
4 days in 2 months	$409	$349	$349	$297	$265
Extra rail days (max 6)	46–49	39–42	39–42	33–37	29–33

depending on the route and type of compartment. Night trains are popular, so it's smart to reserve in advance, even from home. Travelers with first-class reservations are entitled to use comfortable "Intercity" lounges in train stations in Spain's major cities.

Hotel Trains: The term "Hotel Train" (Trenhotel) usually means fancy and expensive. The pricey overnight Hotel Train between Madrid and Lisbon is called the Lusitania (approximate prices: first class-$225, including a bed in a double compartment; second class-$125 in a quad; about $55 or more for a sleeper if you have a railpass, additional cost for singles or a shower in your compartment; advance-purchase deals available at stations and www.renfe.com). Unfortunately, no cheaper rail option exists between these two capital cities. You can save money by taking a bus, or save time by taking a plane. Hotel Train prices are at least as high between other major cities, such as Barcelona–Valencia or Barcelona–Madrid.

High-priced international Hotel Trains connect France, Italy, and Switzerland with Spain. All of these spendy overnight trains (known collectively as Elipsos) have names: Francisco de Goya (Madrid–Paris), Joan Miró (Barcelona–Paris), Pau Casals (Barcelona–Zürich), and Salvador Dalí (Barcelona–Milan). Full fares range from about $250 in a quad to $700 for a Gran Clase single compartment. Travelers with any railpass that covers at least one country on the route of travel (including Swiss Passes but not Swiss Cards) can use a railpass travel day and pay about half the full fare. For more information on international Hotel Trains, see www.elipsos.com. Even if you can easily afford to take a Hotel Train, consider flying instead to save time (see "Cheap Flights," later).

To avoid the expense of an international Hotel Train, you can take a cheaper train trip that involves a transfer at the Spanish border (at Irún on Madrid–Paris runs, at Cerbère on the eastern side). You'll connect to a normal night train with $35 sleeping berths *(literas/couchettes)* on one leg of the trip. This plan is more time-consuming, and may take two days of a flexipass.

Buses

Spain's bus system is confusing. There are a number of different bus companies (though usually clustered within one building), sometimes running buses to the same destinations and using the same transfer points. If you have to transfer, make sure to look for a bus with the same name/logo as the company you bought the ticket from. The larger stations have a consolidated information desk with all the schedules. In smaller stations, check the destinations and schedules posted on each office window. (If your connection requires a transfer to another company's bus in a different city,

Public Transportation Routes in Iberia

don't count on getting help from the originating clerk to figure out the onward connection.) Bus service on holidays, Saturdays, and especially Sundays can be less frequent.

If you arrive in a city by bus and plan to leave by bus, stick around the station upon your arrival to check your departure options and buy a ticket in advance if necessary (and possible). If you're downtown, need a ticket, and the bus station isn't central, save time by asking at the tourist office about travel agencies that sell bus tickets.

You can (and most likely will be required to) stow your luggage under the bus. Your ticket comes with an assigned seat; if the bus is full, you should take that seat, but if it's uncrowded, most

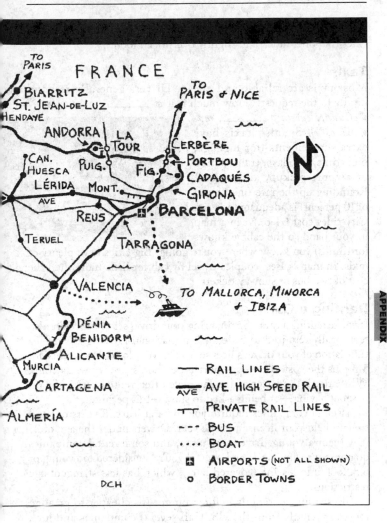

TO PARIS

FRANCE

TO PARIS & NICE

BIARRITZ
ST. JEAN-DE-LUZ
HENDAYE
ANDORRA
LA TOUR
CERBÈRE
PORTBOU
CAN. HUESCA
PUIG.
FIG.
CADAQUÉS
LÉRIDA
MONT.
GIRONA
AVE
BARCELONA
REUS
TERUEL
TARRAGONA
VALENCIA
TO MALLORCA, MINORCA & IBIZA
DÉNIA
BENIDORM
ALICANTE
MURCIA
CARTAGENA
ALMERÍA

—— RAIL LINES
AVE AVE HIGH SPEED RAIL
TT PRIVATE RAIL LINES
--- BUS
.... BOAT
Airports (NOT ALL SHOWN)
o BORDER TOWNS

DCH

people just sit where they like. For longer rides, give some thought to which side of the bus will get the most sun, and sit on the opposite side, even if the bus is air-conditioned and has curtains. Your ride likely will come with a soundtrack: taped Spanish pop music, radio, or sometimes videos. If you prefer silence, bring earplugs. Buses are non-smoking.

Drivers and station personnel rarely speak English. Buses generally lack WCs, but they stop every two hours or so for a break (usually 15 minutes, but can be up to 30). Drivers announce how long the stop will be, but if in doubt, ask the driver, "How many minutes here?" *("¿Cuántos minutos aquí?")* so you know if you have time to get out. Listen for the bus horn as a final call before departure. Bus stations have WCs (rarely with toilet paper) and cafés that offer quick and slightly overpriced food.

Taxis

Most taxis are reliable and cheap. Drivers generally respond kindly to the request, "How much is it to _____, more or less?" ("¿Cuánto cuesta a _____, más o menos?"). Spanish taxis have extra supplements (for luggage, nighttime, Sundays, train-station or airport pickup, and so on). Rounding up the fare (maximum of 10 percent) is adequate for a tip. City rides cost €4-6. Keep a map in your hand so the cabbie knows  (or thinks) you know where you're going. Big cities have plenty of taxis. In many cases, couples travel by cab for little more than the cost of two bus or subway tickets.

Renting a Car

APPENDIX

If you're renting a car in Spain, bring your driver's license. You're also technically required to have an International Driving Permit—a translation of your driver's license (sold at your local AAA office for $15 plus the cost of two passport-type photos; see www.aaa.com). While that's the letter of the law, I've often rented cars in Spain without having—or being asked to show—this permit.

Rental companies require you to be at least 18 years old and to have held your license for one year. Drivers under the age of 25 may incur a young-driver surcharge, and some rental companies do not rent to anyone 75 and over. If you're considered too young or old, look into leasing (covered later), which has less stringent age restrictions.

Research car rentals before you go. It's cheaper to arrange most car rentals from the US. Call several companies and look online to compare rates, or arrange a rental through your home-town travel agent.

Most of the major US rental agencies (such as Alamo/National, Avis, Budget, Dollar, Hertz, and Thrifty) have offices throughout Europe. It can be cheaper to use a consolidator, such as Auto Europe (www.autoeurope.com) or Europe by Car (www.ebctravel.com), which compares rates at several companies to get you the best deal. However, my readers have reported problems with consolidators ranging from misinformation to unexpected fees; because you're going through a middleman, it can be more challenging to resolve disputes that might arise with the rental agency.

Driving in Spain: Distance and Time

Note: Your times may vary based on traffic, construction, and road conditions.

m = miles
h = hours
···· = ferry

Regardless of the car-rental company you choose, always read the contract carefully. The fine print can conceal a host of common add-on charges—such as one-way drop-off fees, airport surcharges, or mandatory insurance policies—that aren't included in the "total price," but can be tacked on when you pick up your car.

For the best rental deal, rent by the week with unlimited mileage. To save money on gas, ask for a diesel car. I normally rent the smallest, least-expensive model with a stick shift (cheaper than an automatic). Almost all rentals are manual by default, so if you need an automatic, you must request one in advance; beware that these cars are usually larger models and not as maneuverable on narrow, winding roads (such as in Andalucía's hill towns). An automatic transmission adds about 50 percent to the car-rental cost over a manual transmission.

For a three-week rental, allow $900 per person (based on two people sharing a car), including insurance, tolls, gas, and parking. But for trips of this length, look into leasing (see below); you'll save money on insurance and taxes. Compare pick-up costs (downtown can be cheaper than the airport) and explore drop-off options.

You can sometimes get a GPS unit with your rental car or leased vehicle for an additional fee (around $15/day; be sure it's set to English and has all the maps you need before you drive off). Or, if you have a portable GPS device at home, consider taking it with you to Europe (buy and upload European maps before your trip). GPS apps are also available for smartphones, but roaming charges in Europe can lead to exorbitant charges.

When you pick up the rental car, check it thoroughly and make sure any damage is noted on your rental agreement. Find out how your car's lights, turn signals, wipers, and gas cap function, and know what kind of gas the car takes.

Returning a car at a big-city train station can be tricky; get precise details on the car drop-off location and hours. Note that rental offices usually close from midday Saturday until Monday. When you return the car, make sure the agent verifies its condition with you.

Car Insurance Options

When you rent a car, you are liable for a very high deductible, sometimes equal to the entire value of the car. Limit your financial risk by choosing one of these three options: Buy Collision Damage Waiver (CDW) coverage from the car-rental company, get coverage through your credit card (free, if your card automatically includes zero-deductible coverage), or buy coverage through Travel Guard.

CDW includes a very high deductible (typically $1,000-1,500). Though each rental company has its own variation, basic CDW costs $15-25 a day (figure roughly 25 percent extra) and reduces your liability, but does not eliminate it. When you pick up the car, you'll be offered the chance to "buy down" the basic deductible to zero (for an additional $15-30/day; this is sometimes called "super CDW").

If you opt for **credit-card coverage,** there's a catch. You'll technically have to decline all coverage offered by the car-rental company, which means they can place a hold on your card (which can be up to the full value of the car). In case of damage, it can be time-consuming to resolve the charges with your credit-card company. Before you decide on this option, quiz your credit-card company about how it works.

Finally, you can buy collision insurance from **Travel Guard** ($9/day plus a one-time $3 service fee covers you for up to $35,000, $250 deductible, tel. 800-826-4919, www.travelguard.com). It's valid everywhere in Europe except the Republic of Ireland, and some Italian car-rental companies refuse to honor it. Note that various states differ on which products and policies are available to their residents.

For more on car-rental insurance, see www.ricksteves.com /cdw.

Leasing

For trips of two-and-a-half weeks or more, consider leasing (which automatically includes zero-deductible collision and theft insurance). By technically buying and then selling back the car, you save lots of money on tax and insurance. Leasing provides you a brand-new car with unlimited mileage and a 24-hour emergency assistance program. You can lease for as little as 17 days to as long as 6 months. Car leases must be arranged from the US. One of many companies offering affordable lease packages is Europe by Car (US tel. 800-223-1516, www.ebctravel.com).

Driving

Driving in rural Spain is great—traffic is sparse and roads are generally good. But a car is a pain in big cities such as Madrid. Drive defensively. If you're involved in an accident, you will be in for a monumental headache.

Good maps are available and inexpensive throughout Spain. In smaller towns, following signs to *centro ciudad* will get you to the heart of things.

Freeways and Tolls: Spain's freeways come with tolls (about $4 for every hour of driving), but save huge amounts of time. Always pick up a ticket as you enter a toll freeway. On freeways, navigate by direction *(norte, oeste, sur, este)*. And because road numbers can be puzzling and inconsistent, navigate by city names. Mileage signs are in kilometers (see page 849 for conversion formula into miles).

Road Rules: Seatbelts are required by law. Children under 12 must ride in the back seat, and children up to age 3 must have a child seat. You must put on a reflective safety vest any time you get out of your car on the side of a highway or unlit road (most

STOP AND LEARN THESE ROAD SIGNS

(50) Speed Limit (km/hr)	▽ Yield	No Passing	End of No Passing Zone
DIRECCIÓN ÚNICA One Way	⊗ Intersection	◆ Main Road	Freeway
⚠ Danger	No Entry	No Entry for Cars	All Vehicles Prohibited
P Parking	No Parking	ADUANA DOUANE Customs	Peace

rental-car companies provide one—but check when you pick up the car). Those who use eyeglasses are required by law to have a spare pair in the car. It is illegal to talk on a cell phone while driving (unless it's hands-free).

Drivers must turn on headlights during daylight hours if visibility is poor. Spain does not allow a right turn at a red light. For more on road rules, ask your car-rental company, or check the US State Department website (www.travel.state.gov, click on "International Travel," "Spain," and "Traffic Safety and Road Conditions").

Traffic Cops: Watch for traffic radars and expect to be stopped for a routine check by the police (be sure your car-insurance form is up to date). Small towns come with speed traps and corruption. Tickets, especially for foreigners, are issued and paid for on the spot. Insist on a receipt *(recibo)*, so the money is less likely to end up in the cop's pocket.

Fuel: Gas and diesel prices are controlled and the same everywhere—about $6 a gallon for gas, less for diesel (gas is priced by the liter in Spain). Unleaded gas *(gasolina sin plomo)* is either *normal* or *super*. Note that diesel is called *diesel* or *gasóleo*—pay attention when filling your tank.

Theft: Choose parking places carefully. Stow valuables in the trunk during the day and leave nothing worth stealing in the car overnight. While you should avoid parking lots with twinkly asphalt, thieves break car windows anywhere, even at stoplights. If your car's a hatchback, take the trunk cover off at night so thieves can look in without breaking in. Try to make your car look locally owned by hiding the "tourist-owned" rental-company decals and putting a local newspaper in your front or back window. Parking attendants all over Spain holler, *"Nada en el coche"* ("Nothing in the car"). And they mean it. Ask your hotelier for advice on parking. In cities you can park safely but expensively in guarded lots.

Cheap Flights

While trains are still the best way to connect places that are close together, a flight can save both time and money on long journeys. When comparing a flight versus a train trip, consider the time it takes to get to the airport and how early you'll need to arrive to check in before the flight. Most flights make sense only as an alternate to a train ride five or more hours in length.

One of the best websites for comparing inexpensive flights is www.skyscanner.net. Other comparison search engines include www.wegolo.com and www.whichbudget.com.

For flights within Spain and around Europe, try the national carriers Vueling (www.vueling.com), Iberia (www.iberia.com), or Spanair (www.spanair.com). Other well-known cheapo airlines

include easyJet (www.easyjet.com) and RyanAir (www.ryanair
.com). Airport websites may list small airlines that serve your
destination.

Be aware of the potential drawbacks of flying on the cheap:
nonrefundable and nonchangeable tickets, minimal or nonexistent customer service, treks to airports far outside town, early or
late departure/arrival times when there is no public transportation
(forcing you to take expensive taxis), and pricey baggage fees. If
you're traveling with lots of luggage, a cheap flight can quickly
become a bad deal. To avoid unpleasant surprises, read the small
print before you book.

Resources

Resources from Rick Steves

Rick Steves' Spain 2012 is one of many books in my series on
European travel, which includes country guidebooks, city guide-

books (Rome, Florence, Paris, London, and
others), Snapshot Guides (excerpted chapters
from my country guides), Pocket Guides
(full-color little books on big cities), and my
budget-travel skills handbook, *Rick Steves'
Europe Through the Back Door*. Some of my
books are available in electronic format. My
phrase books—for Italian, French, German,
Spanish, and Portuguese—are practical and
budget-oriented. My other books include
Europe 101 (a crash course on art and history),
Mediterranean Cruise Ports (how to make the
most of your time in port), and *Travel as a
Political Act* (a travelogue sprinkled with tips
for bringing home a global perspective). A more complete list
of my titles appears near the end of this book.

Video: My public television series, *Rick Steves' Europe*, covers
European destinations in 100 shows, with 10 episodes on Spain.
To watch episodes, visit www.hulu.com/rick-steves-europe; for
scripts and other details, see www.ricksteves.com/tv.

Audio: My weekly public radio
show, *Travel with Rick Steves*, features
interviews with travel experts from
around the world. All of this audio
content is available for free at Rick
Steves Audio Europe, an extensive
online library organized by destination.
Choose whatever interests you, and
download it for free to your computer or

mobile device via www.ricksteves.com/audioeurope, iTunes, or the
Rick Steves Audio Europe smartphone app.

Maps

The black-and-white maps in this book, designed by David
Hoerlein, are concise and simple. The maps are intended to help
you locate recommended places and get to TIs, where you can pick
up more in-depth maps of cities or regions (usually free). Better
maps are available—and cheaper than in the US—throughout
Spain at newsstands, bookstores, and gas stations. Before you
buy a map, look at it to be sure it has the level of detail you want.
Drivers will want to pick up a good, detailed map in Europe (I'd
recommend a 1:200,000- or 1:300,000-scale map).

Other Guidebooks

If you're like most travelers, this book is all you need. But if you're
heading beyond my recommended destinations, $40 for extra maps
and books can be money well spent.

The following books are worth considering, but are not
updated annually; check the publication date before you buy.
Lonely Planet's guide to Spain is well researched, with good maps
and hotel recommendations for low- to moderate-budget travelers.
The similar *Rough Guide to Spain* is hip and insightful, written by
British researchers. Students and vagabonds like the highly opin-
ionated *Let's Go: Spain & Portugal*, updated by Harvard students.
Let's Go is best for backpackers who stay at hostels, use railpasses,
and dive into the youth and nightlife scene.

The Eyewitness series has about a dozen editions covering
Spain, including Barcelona, Madrid, and Sevilla/Andalucía.
They're extremely popular for great, easy-to-grasp graphics and
photos, but the written content in Eyewitness is relatively skimpy,
and the books weigh a ton. I simply borrow them for a minute
from other travelers at certain sights to make sure I'm aware of that
place's highlights. Time Out travel guides provide good, detailed
coverage of Madrid, Barcelona, and Andalucía, particularly on
arts and entertainment.

The popular skinny Michelin Green Guides to Spain are
excellent, especially if you're driving. They're known for their city
and sightseeing maps, dry but concise and helpful information on
major sights, and good cultural and historical background. English
editions, covering most of the regions you'll want to visit, are sold
in Spain.

I like Cadogan guides for their well-presented background
information and coverage of cultural issues. Their recommendations suit upscale travelers. Older travelers enjoy Frommer's
Spain guides, even though these, like the Fodor's guides, ignore

Begin Your Trip at www.ricksteves.com

At ricksteves.com, you'll discover a wealth of free information on European destinations, including fresh monthly news and helpful tips from thousands of fellow travelers. You'll find my latest guidebook updates (www.ricksteves.com/update), a monthly travel e-newsletter (easy and free to sign up), my personal travel blog, and my free Rick Steves Audio Europe smartphone app (if you don't have a smartphone, you can access the same content via podcasts). You can also follow me on Facebook and Twitter.

Our **online Travel Store** offers travel bags and accessories specially designed by me to help you travel smarter and lighter. These include my popular carry-on bags (roll-aboard and backpack versions), money belts, totes, toiletries kits, adapters, other accessories, and a wide selection of guidebooks, planning maps, and DVDs.

Choosing the right **railpass** for your trip—amid hundreds of options—can drive you nutty. We'll help you choose the best pass for your needs and ship it to you for free, plus give you a bunch of free extras.

Rick Steves' Europe Through the Back Door travel company offers **tours** with more than three dozen itineraries and 450 departures reaching the best destinations in this book... and beyond. Our Spain tours include Barcelona and Madrid in 8 days, the Basque Country of Spain and France in 8 days, and Spain with Morocco in 16 days. You'll enjoy great guides, a fun bunch of travel partners (with small groups of generally around 24-28), and plenty of room to spread out in a big, comfy bus. You'll find European adventures to fit every vacation length. For all the details, and to get our Tour Catalog and a free Rick Steves Tour Experience DVD (filmed on location during an actual tour), visit www.ricksteves.com or call us at 425/608-4217.

alternatives that enable travelers to save money by dirtying their fingers in the local culture. The encyclopedic Blue Guides to Spain are dry as the plains in Spain, but just right for scholarly types.

If you'll be traveling to neighboring countries, consider *Rick Steves' Portugal* and *Rick Steves' France*.

Recommended Books and Movies

Spain is overwhelmingly rich in history, art, and culture. To learn more about Spain's past and present, check out a few of these books or films.

Nonfiction

Spain has undergone incredible changes since the death of Franco in 1975 and the end of his nearly four-decade dictatorship. *The New Spaniards* (Hooper) is a survey of all aspects of modern Spain, including its politics, economy, demographics, education, religion, and popular culture.

For a sympathetic cultural history of the Basque people, their language, and contributions from Roman times to the present, read *The Basque History of the World* (Kurlansky).

George Orwell traded his press pass for a uniform, fought against Franco's Fascists in the Spanish Civil War of 1936-1939, and then wrote an account of his experiences in his gripping *Homage to Catalonia*. *The Battle for Spain* (Beevor) re-creates the political climate during the Civil War.

James Michener traveled to Spain for several decades, and his tribute, *Iberia*, describes how Spain's dark history created a contradictory and passionately beautiful land.

Hemingway shows his journalistic side in two books on bull-fighting: *Death in the Afternoon* and *The Dangerous Summer*.

How Muslims, Jews, and Christians created a culture of tolerance in medieval Spain is vividly brought to life in *The Ornament of the World* (Menocal).

Travelers' Tales: Spain (McCauley) offers dozens of essays about Spain and its people from numerous authors.

Penelope Casas has written many popular books on the food of Spain, including tapas, paella, and regional cooking. Her *Discovering Spain: An Uncommon Guide* blends references to history, culture, and food with travel information. For deciphering menus in restaurants, foodies like *The Marling Menu-Master for Spain*.

The nature of pilgrimage is explored along the famous Camino de Santiago trail in northern Spain in *Following the Milky Way* (Aviva) and *On Pilgrimage* (Lash).

The eccentricities of village life in the mountains south of Granada are lovingly detailed in a British expat's 1920s experiences in *South from Granada* (Brenan). A contemporary family's adjustments to living in the same region are described in *Driving Over Lemons: An Optimist in Spain* (Stewart) and the author's later books.

Fiction

Fans of classic literature will want to read Cervantes' *Don Quixote*. Another classic, Irving's *Tales of the Alhambra*, weaves fact, mythical tales, and descriptions of Granada and its beautiful Moorish castle complex—the Alhambra—during the author's 19th-century visit.

Hemingway fans will enjoy *The Sun Also Rises;* this story of expats living in post-WWI France and Spain introduced many readers to bullfighting. Hemingway's *For Whom the Bell Tolls*, a tale of idealism and harsh reality, is set against the complexity of the Spanish Civil War.

That ugly period of Spanish history is also the subject of *The Carpenter's Pencil* (Rivas), an unsentimental tale of an imprisoned revolutionary haunted by his past.

The brutality and intolerance of the dark years of the Spanish Inquisition are illuminated in Winstein's *The Heretic*, with Sevilla as the backdrop. *The Last Jew* (Gordon) is one man's story of survival in Inquisition-era Spain. *Stories from Spain* (Barlow and Stivers) relates well-known Spanish legends that chronicle nearly 1,000 years of Spanish history.

The 2005 bestselling thriller *The Shadow of the Wind* (Zafón) takes place in 1950s Barcelona; the same author's 2009 novel, *The Angel's Game*, takes you back to Barcelona in the 1920s. Robert Wilson's popular police thrillers, including *The Blind Man of Seville*, are set in Spain and Portugal.

Films

In *The Mystery of Picasso* (1956), Picasso is filmed painting from behind a transparent canvas, allowing a unique look at his creative process.

Peter O''Toole and Sophia Loren star in the musical version of Don Quixote, *Man of La Mancha* (1972).

In the first of Carlos Saura's flamenco dance trilogy, *Blood Wedding* (1981), he adapts Federico García Lorca's play about a wedding imposed on a bride in love with another man. *Carmen* (1983) shows a Spanish cast rehearsing the well-known French novel and opera. *El Amor Brujo* (1986) is a ghostly love story.

L'auberge Espagnole (2002) tells the story of the loves and lives of European students sharing an apartment in Barcelona.

In *Barcelona* (1994) two Americans in Spain try to navigate the Spanish singles scene and the ensuing culture clash.

The Spanish film *Open Your Eyes* (1997) inspired the 2001 Tom Cruise thriller *Vanilla Sky*, where a car accident sets off an intricate series of events.

Woody Allen's *Vicky Cristina Barcelona* (2008) stars Javier Bardem as a macho Spanish artist romancing two American women, when suddenly his stormy ex-wife (Penélope Cruz, in an Oscar-winning role) re-enters his life.

Pedro Almodóvar's piquant films about relationships in the post-Franco era have garnered piles of international awards. Spanish actors Bardem, Cruz, and Antonio Banderas have starred in his films. Almodóvar's best-known films include *Women on the Verge of a Nervous Breakdown* (1988), *All About My Mother* (1999), *Talk to Her* (2002), *Volver* (2006), and *Broken Embraces* (2009).

Holidays and Festivals

Religious holidays are big in Spain, and the country erupts with fiestas and celebrations throughout the year. This list includes many—but not all—big festivals celebrated in major cities, plus national holidays observed throughout Spain. Many sights and banks close down on national holidays—keep this in mind when planning your itinerary. Before arranging a trip around a festival, make sure to verify its dates—check the festival or TI website, or contact the Spanish Tourist Office (www.spain.info, US tel. 212/265-8822).

Popular places are even busier on weekends, and inundated on three-day weekends, when hotels, trains, and buses can get booked up before, during, and after the actual holiday. Plan ahead and reserve your accommodations and transportation (particularly for AVE trains) well in advance.

In 2012, be prepared for big crowds during these holiday periods: Holy Week (Semana Santa) and Easter weekend, especially in Sevilla; April Fair in Sevilla; the San Isidro festival in Madrid; Labor Day; Dos de Mayo, Madrid; Ascension; Pentecost weekend; Assumption weekend; Spanish National Day; Constitution Day, followed closely by the Feast of the Immaculate Conception—both the previous and following weekends may be busy; and Christmas and New Year's. Look out  for any local holiday that falls on a Tuesday or Thursday—the Spanish will often take Monday or Friday off as well to have a four-day weekend.

2012

JANUARY						
S	M	T	W	T	F	S
1	2	3	4	5	6	7
8	9	10	11	12	13	14
15	16	17	18	19	20	21
22	23	24	25	26	27	28
29	30	31				

FEBRUARY						
S	M	T	W	T	F	S
			1	2	3	4
5	6	7	8	9	10	11
12	13	14	15	16	17	18
19	20	21	22	23	24	25
26	27	28	29			

MARCH						
S	M	T	W	T	F	S
				1	2	3
4	5	6	7	8	9	10
11	12	13	14	15	16	17
18	19	20	21	22	23	24
25	26	27	28	29	30	31

APRIL						
S	M	T	W	T	F	S
1	2	3	4	5	6	7
8	9	10	11	12	13	14
15	16	17	18	19	20	21
22	23	24	25	26	27	28
29	30					

MAY						
S	M	T	W	T	F	S
		1	2	3	4	5
6	7	8	9	10	11	12
13	14	15	16	17	18	19
20	21	22	23	24	25	26
27	28	29	30	31		

JUNE						
S	M	T	W	T	F	S
					1	2
3	4	5	6	7	8	9
10	11	12	13	14	15	16
17	18	19	20	21	22	23
24	25	26	27	28	29	30

JULY						
S	M	T	W	T	F	S
1	2	3	4	5	6	7
8	9	10	11	12	13	14
15	16	17	18	19	20	21
22	23	24	25	26	27	28
29	30	31				

AUGUST						
S	M	T	W	T	F	S
			1	2	3	4
5	6	7	8	9	10	11
12	13	14	15	16	17	18
19	20	21	22	23	24	25
26	27	28	29	30	31	

SEPTEMBER						
S	M	T	W	T	F	S
						1
2	3	4	5	6	7	8
9	10	11	12	13	14	15
16	17	18	19	20	21	22
23/30	24	25	26	27	28	29

OCTOBER						
S	M	T	W	T	F	S
	1	2	3	4	5	6
7	8	9	10	11	12	13
14	15	16	17	18	19	20
21	22	23	24	25	26	27
28	29	30	31			

NOVEMBER						
S	M	T	W	T	F	S
				1	2	3
4	5	6	7	8	9	10
11	12	13	14	15	16	17
18	19	20	21	22	23	24
25	26	27	28	29	30	

DECEMBER						
S	M	T	W	T	F	S
						1
2	3	4	5	6	7	8
9	10	11	12	13	14	15
16	17	18	19	20	21	22
23/30	24/31	25	26	27	28	29

Jan 1	New Year's Day
Jan 6	Epiphany
Early Feb	La Candelaria (religious festival), Madrid
Feb 28	Day of Andalucía (some closures), Andalucía
April 1-8	Holy Week
April 9	Easter Monday
April 24-29	April Fair, Sevilla
Early May	Feria del Caballo (horse pageantry), Jerez
May 1	Labor Day (closures)
May 2	Dos de Mayo, Madrid
May 17	Ascension
May 25-27	Pentecost weekend
Throughout May	San Isidro (religious festival on May 15; also bullfights and zarzuelas all month long), Madrid

June	La Patum (Moorish battles), Barcelona
June 7	Corpus Christi
June 23	Feast of St. Joan
June 23-24	Festival of St. John the Baptist
Late June-Early July	International Festival of Music and Dance, Granada
July 6-14	Running of the Bulls (Fiesta de San Fermín), Pamplona
July 25	Feast of St. James, Santiago de Compostela
Aug	Gràcia Festival, Barcelona
Mid-Aug	Verbena de la Paloma (folk festival), Madrid
Aug 15	Assumption of Mary (religious festival)
Aug 24	Festival of St. Batholomew, Sitges
Sept	Autumn Festival (flamenco, bullfights), Jerez
Sept 23	Festival of St. Tecla, Sitges
Sept 24	La Mercé (parade), Barcelona
Late Sept	San Miguel Fair (bullfights), Sevilla
Late Sept (last weekend)	Little San Fermín (concerts, parades), Pamploma
Oct 12	Spanish National Day
Late Oct-Nov	International Jazz Festival, Madrid
Nov 1	All Saints' Day
Nov 9	Virgen de la Almudena, Madrid
Dec 6	Constitution Day
Dec 8	Feast of the Immaculate Conception
Dec 13	Feast of Santa Lucía
Dec 25	Christmas
Dec 31	New Year's Eve

Conversions and Climate

Numbers and Stumblers

- Europeans write a few of their numbers differently than we do. 1 = $\mathcal{1}$, 4 = $\mathcal{4}$, 7 = $\mathcal{7}$.
- In Europe, dates appear as day/month/year, so Christmas is 25/12/12.
- Commas are decimal points and decimals commas. A dollar and a half is 1,50, and there are 5.280 feet in a mile.
- When pointing, use your whole hand, palm down.
- When counting with fingers, start with your thumb. If you hold up your first finger to request one item, you'll probably get two.
- What Americans call the second floor of a building is the first floor in Europe.
- On escalators and moving sidewalks, Europeans keep the left "lane" open for passing. Keep to the right.

Metric Conversions (approximate)

A kilogram is 2.2 pounds, and 1 liter is about a quart (almost four to a gallon). A kilometer is six-tenths of a mile. I figure kilometers to miles by cutting them in half and adding back 10 percent of the original (120 km: 60 + 12 = 72 miles, 300 km: 150 + 30 = 180 miles).

1 foot = 0.3 meter	1 square yard = 0.8 square meter
1 yard = 0.9 meter	1 square mile = 2.6 square kilometers
1 mile = 1.6 kilometers	1 ounce = 28 grams
1 centimeter = 0.4 inch	1 quart = 0.95 liter
1 meter = 39.4 inches	1 kilogram = 2.2 pounds
1 kilometer = 0.62 mile	32°F = 0°C

Clothing Sizes

When shopping for clothing, use these US-to-European comparisons as general guidelines (but note that no conversion is perfect).

- Women's dresses and blouses: Add 30
  (US size 10 = European size 40)
- Men's suits and jackets: Add 10
  (US size 40 regular = European size 50)
- Men's shirts: Multiply by 2 and add about 8
  (US size 15 collar = European size 38)
- Women's shoes: Add about 30
  (US size 8 = European size 38½)
- Men's shoes: Add 32-34
  (US size 9 = European size 41; US size 11 = European size 45)

Spain's Climate

First line, average daily temperature; second line, average daily low; third line, average days without rain. For more detailed weather statistics for destinations in this book (as well as the rest of the world), check www.worldclimate.com.

	J	F	M	A	M	J	J	A	S	O	N	D
SPAIN												
Madrid												
	47°	52°	59°	65°	70°	80°	87°	85°	77°	65°	55°	48°
	35°	36°	41°	45°	50°	58°	63°	63°	57°	49°	42°	36°
	23	21	21	21	21	25	29	28	24	23	21	21
Barcelona												
	55°	57°	60°	65°	71°	78°	82°	82°	77°	69°	62°	56°
	43°	45°	48°	52°	57°	65°	69°	69°	66°	58°	51°	46°
	26	23	23	21	23	24	27	25	23	22	24	25
Almería (Costa del Sol)												
	60°	61°	64°	68°	72°	78°	83°	84°	81°	73°	67°	62°
	46°	47°	51°	55°	59°	65°	70°	71°	68°	60°	54°	49°
	25	24	26	25	28	29	31	30	27	26	26	26
MOROCCO												
Tangier												
	61°	63°	64°	66°	72°	77°	82°	84°	81°	75°	68°	63°
	48°	48°	50°	52°	55°	61°	66°	66°	64°	61°	54°	50°
	12	19	21	21	24	27	30	29	27	22	20	19

Temperature Conversion:
Fahrenheit and Celsius

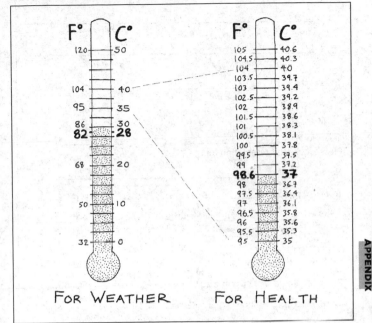

Europe takes its temperature using the Celsius scale, while we opt for Fahrenheit. For a rough conversion from Celsius to Fahrenheit, double the number and add 30. For weather, remember that 28°C is 82°F—perfect. For health, 37°C is just right.

Hotel Reservation

To: _____   _____
            hotel   email or fax

From: _____   _____
              name   email or fax

Today's date: _____ / _____ / _____
               day   month   year

Dear Hotel _____ ,

Please make this reservation for me:

Name: _____

Total # of people: _____   # of rooms: _____   # of nights: _____

Arriving: _____ / _____ / _____   My time of arrival (24-hr clock): _____
           day   month   year   (I will telephone if I will be late)

Departing: ____ / ____ / ____
            day   month   year

Room(s): Single____   Double ____   Twin ____   Triple ____   Quad____

With: Toilet ____   Shower ____   Bath ____   Sink only____

Special needs: View____   Quiet____   Cheapest ____   Ground Floor____

Please email or fax confirmation of my reservation, along with the type of room reserved and the price. Please also inform me of your cancellation policy. After I hear from you, I will quickly send my credit-card information as a deposit to hold the room. Thank you.

_____
Name

_____
Address

_____
City   **State**   **Zip Code**   **Country**

Before hoteliers can make your reservation, they want to know the information listed above. You can use this form as the basis for your email, or you can photocopy this page, fill in the information, and send it as a fax (also available online at www.ricksteves.com/reservation).

Packing Checklist

Whether you're traveling for five days or five weeks, here's what you'll need to bring. Pack light to enjoy the sweet freedom of true mobility. Happy travels!

- ❏ 5 shirts: long- and short-sleeve
- ❏ 1 sweater or lightweight fleece
- ❏ 2 pairs pants
- ❏ 1 pair shorts
- ❏ 1 swimsuit
- ❏ 5 pairs underwear and socks
- ❏ 1 pair shoes
- ❏ 1 rainproof jacket with hood
- ❏ Tie or scarf
- ❏ Money belt
- ❏ Money—your mix of:
  - ❏ Debit card (for ATM withdrawals)
  - ❏ Credit card
  - ❏ Hard cash (in easy-to-exchange $20 bills)
- ❏ Documents plus photo-copies:
  - ❏ Passport
  - ❏ Printout of airline eticket
  - ❏ Driver's license
  - ❏ Student ID and hostel card
  - ❏ Railpass/car rental voucher
  - ❏ Insurance details
- ❏ Daypack
- ❏ Electronics—your choice of:
  - ❏ Camera (and related gear)
  - ❏ Mobile phone or smart-phone
  - ❏ iPod (or other MP3 player)
  - ❏ Laptop/netbook
  - ❏ ebook reader
  - ❏ Chargers for each of the above
  - ❏ Plug adapter

- ❏ Empty water bottle
- ❏ Wristwatch and alarm clock
- ❏ Earplugs
- ❏ Toiletries kit
  - ❏ Toiletries
  - ❏ Medicines and vitamins
  - ❏ First-aid kit
  - ❏ Glasses/contacts/sunglasses (with prescriptions)
- ❏ Sealable plastic baggies
- ❏ Laundry soap
- ❏ Clothesline
- ❏ Small towel
- ❏ Sewing kit
- ❏ Travel information (guide books and maps)
- ❏ Address list (for sending postcards)
- ❏ Postcards and photos from home
- ❏ Notepad and pen
- ❏ Journal

If you plan to carry on your luggage, note that all liquids must be in 3.4-ounce or smaller containers and fit within a single quart-size sealable baggie. For details, see www.tsa.gov/travelers.

Pronunciation Guide for Place Names

For Spanish names, emphasize the bolded syllable and pronounce "*h*" as a guttural sour
The few French names (from the Basque Country) have equally stressed syllables.

Algeciras	ahl-*h*eh-**thee**-rahs
Andalucía	ahn-dah-loo-**see**-ah
Arcos de la Frontera	**ar**-kohs day lah frohn-**teh**-rah
Atapuerca	ah-tah-**pwehr**-kah
Ávila	**ah**-vee-lah
Barcelona	bar-theh-**loh**-nah
Bayonne	bai-yuhn
Biarritz	bee-ah-ritz
Bilbao	bil-**bow**
Burgos	**boor**-gohs
Cadaqués	kah-dah-**kehs**
Cantabria	kahn-**tah**-bree-ah
Catalunya	kah-tah-**loon**-yah
Ciudad Rodrigo	thee-oo-**dahd** roh-**dree**-goh
Comillas	koh-**mee**-yahs
Córdoba	**kor**-doh-bah
El Escorial	ehl ehs-kor-ee-**ahl**
Figueres	feeg-**yehr**-ehs
Frigiliana	free-*h*ee-lee-**ah**-nah
Fuenterrabía	fwehn-teh-rah-**bee**-ah
Galicia	gah-**lee**-thee-ah
Gibraltar	*h*ee-**brahl**-tar
Granada	grah-**nah**-dah
Grazalema	grah-zah-**lay**-mah
Guernica	**gehr**-nee-kah
Hendaye	**hehn**-day
Hondarribia	hohn-dah-**ree**-bee-ah
Jerez	*h*eh-**reth**
La Mancha	lah **mahn**-chah
Laguardia	lah-**gwar**-dee-ah
León	lay-**ohn**
Lequeitio	leh-**kay**-tee-oh
Logroño	loh-**grohn**-yoh
Madrid	mah-**dreed**
Marbella	mar-**bay**-yah
Montserrat	mohnt-seh-**raht**
Nerja	**nehr**-*h*ah
O Cebreiro	oh theh-**bray**-roh
Orreaga	oh-ray-**ah**-gah
Pamplona	pahm-**ploh**-nah
Picos de Europa	**pee**-kohs day yoo-**roh**-pah
Potes	**poh**-tays
Rioja	ree-**oh**-*h*ah
Roncesvalles	rohn-seh-vahl
Ronda	**rohn**-dah
Salamanca	sah-lah-**mahn**-kah
St. Jean-Pied-de-Port	san zhahn-pee-ay-duh-por
St. Jean-de-Luz	san zhahn-duh-looz
San Sebastián	sahn seh-bah-stee-**ahn**
Santiago de Compostela	sahn-tee-**ah**-goh day kohm-poh-**steh**-lah
Santillana del Mar	sahn-tee-**yah**-nah del mar
Segovia	seh-**goh**-vee-ah
Sevilla	seh-**vee**-yah
Sitges	**see**-juhz
Tangier	Tánger (**tahn**-*h*air) in Spanish, Tanja (**tahn**-zhah) in Arabic
Tarifa	tah-**ree**-fah
Toledo	toh-**lay**-doh
Vejer de la Frontera	vay-*h*ehr day lah frohn-**teh**-rah
Zahara	zah-**hah**-rah

APPENDIX

Spanish Survival Phrases

Spanish has a guttural sound similar to the J in Baja California. In the phonetics, the symbol for this clearing-your-throat sound is the italicized *h*.

Good day.	Buenos días.	bway-nohs dee-ahs
Do you speak English?	¿Habla Usted inglés?	ah-blah oo-stehd een-glays
Yes. / No.	Sí. / No.	see / noh
I (don't) understand.	(No) comprendo.	(noh) kohm-prehn-doh
Please.	Por favor.	por fah-bor
Thank you.	Gracias.	grah-thee-ahs
I'm sorry.	Lo siento.	loh see-ehn-toh
Excuse me.	Perdóneme.	pehr-doh-nay-may
(No) problem.	(No) problema.	(noh) proh-blay-mah
Good.	Bueno.	bway-noh
Goodbye.	Adiós.	ah-dee-ohs
one / two	uno / dos	oo-noh / dohs
three / four	tres / cuatro	trays / kwah-troh
five / six	cinco / seis	theen-koh / says
seven / eight	siete / ocho	see-eh-tay / oh-choh
nine / ten	nueve / diez	nway-bay / dee-ayth
How much is it?	¿Cuánto cuesta?	kwahn-toh kway-stah
Write it?	¿Me lo escribe?	may loh ay-skree-bay
Is it free?	¿Es gratis?	ays grah-tees
Is it included?	¿Está incluido?	ay-stah een-kloo-ee-doh
Where can I buy / find...?	¿Dónde puedo comprar / encontrar...?	dohn-day pway-doh kohm-prar / ayn-kohn-trar
I'd like / We'd like...	Quiero / Queremos...	kee-ehr-oh / kehr-ay-mohs
...a room.	...una habitación.	oo-nah ah-bee-tah-thee-ohn
...a ticket to ___.	...un billete para ___.	oon bee-yeh-tay pah-rah
Is it possible?	¿Es posible?	ays poh-see-blay
Where is...?	¿Dónde está...?	dohn-day ay-stah
...the train station	...la estación de trenes	lah ay-stah-thee-ohn day tray-nays
...the bus station	...la estación de autobuses	lah ay-stah-thee-ohn day ow-toh-boo-says
...the tourist information office	...la oficina de turismo	lah oh-fee-thee-nah day too-rees-moh
Where are the toilets?	¿Dónde están los servicios?	dohn-day ay-stahn lohs sehr-bee-thee-ohs
men	hombres, caballeros	ohm-brays, kah-bah-yay-rohs
women	mujeres, damas	moo-heh-rays, dah-mahs
left / right	izquierda / derecha	eeth-kee-ehr-dah / day-ray-chah
straight	derecho	day-ray-choh
When do you open / close?	¿A qué hora abren / cierran?	ah kay oh-rah ah-brehn / thee-ay-rahn
At what time?	¿A qué hora?	ah kay oh-rah
Just a moment.	Un momento.	oon moh-mehn-toh
now / soon / later	ahora / pronto / más tarde	ah-oh-rah / prohn-toh / mahs tar-day
today / tomorrow	hoy / mañana	oy / mahn-yah-nah

In a Spanish Restaurant

I'd like / We'd like...	Quiero / Queremos...	kee-**ehr**-oh / kehr-**ay**-mohs
...to reserve...	...reservar...	ray-sehr-**bar**
...a table for one / two.	...una mesa para uno / dos.	oo-nah **may**-sah **pah**-rah **oo**-noh / dohs
Non-smoking.	No fumador.	noh foo-mah-**dohr**
Is this table free?	¿Está esta mesa libre?	ay-**stah** ay-stah **may**-sah **lee**-bray
The menu (in English), please.	La carta (en inglés), por favor.	lah **kar**-tah (ayn een-**glays**) por fah-**bor**
service (not) included	servicio (no) incluido	sehr-**bee**-thee-oh (noh) een-kloo-**ee**-doh
cover charge	precio de entrada	**pray**-thee-oh day ayn-**trah**-dah
to go	para llevar	**pah**-rah yay-**bar**
with / without	con / sin	kohn / seen
and / or	y / o	ee / oh
menu (of the day)	menú (del día)	may-**noo** (dayl **dee**-ah)
specialty of the house	especialidad de la casa	ay-spay-thee-ah-lee-**dahd** day lah **kah**-sah
tourist menu	menú turístico	meh-**noo** too-**ree**-stee-koh
combination plate	plato combinado	**plah**-toh kohm-bee-**nah**-doh
bread	pan	pahn
cheese	queso	**kay**-soh
sandwich	bocadillo	boh-kah-**dee**-yoh
soup	sopa	**soh**-pah
salad	ensalada	ayn-sah-**lah**-dah
meat	carne	**kar**-nay
poultry	aves	ah-bays
fish	pescado	pay-**skah**-doh
seafood	marisco	mah-**ree**-skoh
fruit	fruta	**froo**-tah
vegetables	verduras	behr-**doo**-rahs
dessert	postres	**poh**-strays
tap water	agua del grifo	**ah**-gwah dayl **gree**-foh
mineral water	agua mineral	**ah**-gwah mee-nay-**rahl**
milk	leche	**lay**-chay
(orange) juice	zumo (de naranja)	**thoo**-moh (day nah-**rahn**-hah)
coffee	café	kah-**feh**
tea	té	tay
wine	vino	**bee**-noh
red / white	tinto / blanco	**teen**-toh / **blahn**-koh
glass / bottle	vaso / botella	**bah**-soh / boh-**tay**-yah
beer	cerveza	thehr-**bay**-thah
Cheers!	¡Salud!	sah-**lood**
More. / Another.	Más. / Otro.	mahs / **oh**-troh
The same.	El mismo.	ehl **mees**-moh
The bill, please.	La cuenta, por favor.	lah **kwayn**-tah por fah-**bor**
tip	propina	proh-**pee**-nah
Delicious!	¡Delicioso!	day-lee-thee-**oh**-soh

For hundreds more pages of survival phrases for your trip to Spain, check out *Rick Steves' Spanish Phrase Book.*

INDEX

INDEX

INDEX

MAP INDEX

MAP INDEX

Audio Europe

Join a Rick Steves tour

Enjoy Europe's warmest welcome... with the flexibility and friendship of a small group getting to know Rick's favorite places and people. It all starts with our free tour catalog and DVD.

Great guides, small groups, no grumps.

Start your trip a

Free information and great gear

▸ Plan Your Trip

Browse thousands of articles and a wealth of money-saving tips for planning your dream trip. You'll find up-to-date information on Europe's best destinations, packing smart, getting around, finding rooms, staying healthy, avoiding scams and more.

▸ Eurail Passes

Find out, step-by-step, if a railpass makes sense for your trip—and how to avoid buying more than yo need. Get free shipping on online orders

▸ Graffiti Wall & Travelers Helpline

Learn, ask, share—our online community of savvy travelers is a great resource for first-time travelers to Europe, as well as seasoned pros.

Rick Steves' Europe Through the Back Door, Inc.

www.ricksteves.com

EUROPE GUIDES

Best of Europe
Eastern Europe
Europe Through the Back Door
Mediterranean Cruise Ports

COUNTRY GUIDES

Croatia & Slovenia
England
France
Germany
Great Britain
Ireland
Italy
Portugal
Scandinavia
Spain
Switzerland

CITY & REGIONAL GUIDES

Amsterdam, Bruges & Brussels
Budapest
Florence & Tuscany
Greece: Athens & the Peloponnese
Istanbul
London
Paris
Prague & the Czech Republic
Provence & the French Riviera
Rome
Venice
Vienna, Salzburg & Tirol

SNAPSHOT GUIDES

Barcelona
Berlin
Bruges & Brussels
Copenhagen & the Best of
    Denmark
Dublin
Dubrovnik
Hill Towns of Central Italy
Italy's Cinque Terre
Krakow, Warsaw & Gdansk
Lisbon
Madrid & Toledo
Munich, Bavaria & Salzburg
Naples & the Amalfi Coast
Northern Ireland
Norway
Scotland
Sevilla, Granada & Southern Spain
Stockholm

POCKET GUIDES

London
Paris
Rome

TRAVEL CULTURE

Europe 101
European Christmas
Postcards from Europe
Travel as a Political Act

NOW AVAILABLE:
eBOOKS, APPS & BLU-RAY

eBOOKS

Most guides are available as eBooks from Amazon, Barnes & Noble, Borders, Apple, and Sony. Free apps for eBook reading are available in the Apple App Store and Android Market, and eBook readers such as Kindle, Nook, and Kobo all have free apps that work on smartphones.

RICK STEVES' EUROPE DVDs

10 New Shows 2011–2012
Austria & the Alps
Eastern Europe
England & Wales
European Christmas
European Travel Skills & Specials
France
Germany, BeNeLux & More
Greece & Turkey
Iran
Ireland & Scotland
Italy's Cities
Italy's Countryside
Scandinavia
Spain
Travel Extras

BLU-RAY

Celtic Charms
Eastern Europe Favorites
European Christmas
Italy Through the Back Door
Mediterranean Mosaic
Surprising Cities of Europe

PHRASE BOOKS & DICTIONARIES

French
French, Italian & German
German
Italian
Portuguese
Spanish

JOURNALS

Rick Steves' Pocket Travel Journal
Rick Steves' Travel Journal

APPS

Select Rick Steves guides are available as apps in the Apple App Store.

PLANNING MAPS

Britain, Ireland & London
Europe
France & Paris
Germany, Austria & Switzerland
Ireland
Italy
Spain & Portugal

Rick Steves books and DVDs are available at bookstores and through online booksellers.

Credits

Researchers
To help update this book, Rick relied on...

Amanda Buttinger

Amanda moved to Madrid in 1998, thinking she'd be there a year. Since then she's found many reasons to stay, from learning more Spanish to guiding and travel writing to the best of all—sunny city walks with her dog and her boys.

Cameron Hewitt

Cameron writes and edits guidebooks for Rick Steves. For this book, Cameron dodged Holy Week processions in Sevilla, scaled the Rock of Gibraltar, and got lost in Tangier's labyrinthine Medina. When he's not traveling, Cameron lives in Seattle with his wife, Shawna.

Contributor
Gene Openshaw

Gene is the co-author of 10 Rick Steves guidebooks. For this book he wrote material on art and history. When not traveling, Gene enjoys composing music, recovering from his 1973 trip to Europe with Rick, and living everyday life with his daughter.

Acknowledgments
Thanks to Cameron Hewitt for writing this book's original chapters on the Camino de Santiago, Santiago de Compostela, and Cantabria.

Chapter Images

The following list identifies the chapter-opening images and credits their photographers.

Barcelona: Barcelona's Montjuïc	David C. Hoerlein
Near Barcelona: Cadaqués	Rick Steves
Basque Region: Guggenheim Bilbao	Rick Steves
Camino de Santiago: Puente de la Reina	Cameron Hewitt
Santiago de Compostela: Santiago's Cathedral	Cameron Hewitt
Cantabria: Picos de Europa	Cameron Hewitt
Salamanca: Salamanca's Plaza Mayor	Rick Steves
Madrid: Madrid's Retiro Park	David C. Hoerlein
Northwest of Madrid: Segovia's Aqueduct	Rick Steves
Toledo: Toledo Overview	Rick Steves
Granada: The Alhambra	Robert Wright
Sevilla: Sevilla Skyline	Rick Steves
Córdoba: Córdoba's Mezquita	Robert Wright
Andalucía's White Hill Towns: Arcos	David C. Hoerlein
Spain's South Coast: Nerja	Rick Steves
Morocco: Moroccan Woman, Tangier	Rick Steves
Tangier: Market Vendor	Rick Steves

Rick Steves' Guidebook Series

City, Regional, and Country Guides

Rick Steves' Amsterdam, Bruges & Brussels
Rick Steves' Best of Europe
Rick Steves' Budapest
Rick Steves' Croatia & Slovenia
Rick Steves' Eastern Europe
Rick Steves' England
Rick Steves' Florence & Tuscany
Rick Steves' France
Rick Steves' Germany
Rick Steves' Great Britain
Rick Steves' Greece: Athens & the Peloponnese
Rick Steves' Ireland
Rick Steves' Istanbul
Rick Steves' Italy
Rick Steves' London
Rick Steves' Paris
Rick Steves' Portugal
Rick Steves' Prague & the Czech Republic
Rick Steves' Provence & the French Riviera
Rick Steves' Rome
Rick Steves' Scandinavia
Rick Steves' Spain
Rick Steves' Switzerland
Rick Steves' Venice
Rick Steves' Vienna, Salzburg & Tirol

Snapshot Guides

Excerpted from country guidebooks, the Snapshots Guides cover many of my favorite destinations, such as *Rick Steves' Snapshot Barcelona, Rick Steves' Snapshot Scotland,* and *Rick Steves' Snapshot Hill Towns of Central Italy.*

Pocket Guides

My new Pocket Guides are condensed, colorful guides to Europe's top cities, including Paris, London, Rome, and more. These combine the top self-guided walks and tours from my city guides with vibrant full-color photos, and are sized to slip easily into your pocket.

Rick Steves' Phrase Books

French
French/Italian/German
German
Italian
Portuguese
Spanish

More Books

Rick Steves' Europe 101: History and Art for the Traveler
Rick Steves' Europe Through the Back Door
Rick Steves' European Christmas
Rick Steves' Mediterranean Cruise Ports
Rick Steves' Postcards from Europe
Rick Steves' Travel as a Political Act

Avalon Travel
a member of the Perseus Books Group
1700 Fourth Street
Berkeley, CA 94710

Text © 2011 by Rick Steves
Maps © 2011 Europe Through the Back Door. All rights reserved.

Printed in Canada by Friesens.
First printing September 2011.

ISBN 978-1-61238-012-4
ISSN 1551-8388

For the latest on Rick's lectures, guidebooks, tours, public radio show, and public television
series, contact Europe Through the Back Door, Box 2009, Edmonds, WA 98020, 425/771-
8303, fax 425/771-0833, www.ricksteves.com, rick@ricksteves.com.

Europe Through the Back Door Reviewing Editors: Risa Laib, Jennifer Madison Davis
ETBD Editors: Suzanne Kotz, Cathy Lu, Tom Griffin, Cathy McDonald, Gretchen
Strauch, Claire Burns
Researchers: Amanda Buttinger, Cameron Hewitt, Gene Openshaw
Avalon Travel Senior Editor and Series Manager: Madhu Prasher
Avalon Travel Project Editor: Kelly Lydick
Copy Editor: Amy Scott
Proofreader: Denise Silva
Indexer: Stephen Callahan
Production and Layout: McGuire Barber Design
Cover Design: Kimberly Glyder Design
Graphic Content Director: Laura VanDeventer
Maps and Graphics: David C. Hoerlein, Lauren Mills, Twozdai Hulse, Laura
VanDeventer, Barb Geisler, Mike Morgenfeld, Brice Ticen, Kat Bennett
Front Matter Color Photos: p. i, Córdoba © Rick Steves; pxiv, Block of Discord,
Barcelona © Robyn Cronin; p. xxiv, Arcos Street © David Hoerlein
Cover Photo: Summer in Cadaqués © Xavier Arnau Serrat/Getty Images
Photography: David C. Hoerlein, Rick Steves, Cameron Hewitt, Robert Wright, Steve
Smith, Dominic Bonuccelli, Pat O'Connor, Cathy McDonald

ABOUT THE AUTHOR

RICK STEVES

 Since 1973, Rick Steves has spent 100 days every year exploring Europe. Rick produces a public television series (*Rick Steves' Europe*), a public radio show (*Travel with Rick Steves*), and an app and podcast (*Rick Steves Audio Europe*); writes a bestselling series of guidebooks and a nationally syndicated newspaper column; organizes guided tours that take over ten thousand travelers to Europe annually; and offers an information-packed website (www.ricksteves.com). With the help of his hardworking staff of 80 at Europe Through the Back Door—in Edmonds, Washington, just north of Seattle—Rick's mission is to make European travel fun, affordable, and culturally enlightening for Americans.

Foldout Color Map ▶

The foldout map on the opposite page includes:
• A map of Spain on one side
• City maps, including Madrid, Barcelona, Sevilla, Granada, Toledo, and Lisbon on the other side

Want More Spain?
Maximize the experience with Rick Steves as your guide

Planning Maps
Use the map that's in sync with your guidebook

Phrase Books
Rely on Rick's Spanish Phrase Book and Dictionary

Rick's DVDs
Preview your destinations with 8 shows on Spain

Rick's Audio Europe™ App
Hear Spain travel tips from Rick's radio shows

Small-Group Tours
Take a lively Rick Steves tour through Spain

For all the details, visit ricksteves.com

GET THE MOST
OUT OF EVERY DAY
AND EVERY DOLLAR

You can count on Rick Steves to tell you what you *really* nee
to know when traveling in Spain.

In this guide, you'll find an inviting mix of exciting cities an
cozy towns. Explore lively Madrid, Barcelona, and Sevil
and follow the Route of the White Hill Towns in Andalucí
sun-drenched countryside. Experience the works of the gre
masters—from El Greco to Picasso to Dalí—and learn how
avoid the lines at the most popular museums. Self-guided wal
lead you through the castles, cathedrals, and villages of th
ancient but modern land. End your day with a glass of Rio
wine and a plate of tapas—then join the locals at a rivetir
flamenco show.

Rick's candid, humorous advice will guide you to good-valu
hotels and restaurants. He'll help you plan where to go and wh
to see, depending on the length of your trip. You'll learn whic
sights are worth your time and money, and how to get around k
train, bus, and car. More than just reviews and directions, a Ric
Steves guidebook is a tour guide in your pocket.

Rick Steves

WATCH *RICK STEVES' EUROPE* ON PUBLIC TELEVISIO

AVALON TRAVEL
A Member of the Perseus Books Group
Distributed by Publishers Group West
www.avalontravelbooks.com

ISBN 978-1-61238-012-4   US $24.9

5 2 4 9 9

9 781612 380124